Collins

175 YEARS OF DICTIONARY PUBLISHING

French Visual

JEAN-CLAUDE CORBEIL & ARIANE ARCHAMBAULT

Dictionary

ACKNOWLEDGMENTS

Our deepest gratitude to the individuals, institutions, companies and businesses that have provided us with the latest technical documentation for use in preparing *The Mini Visual Dictionary*.

Arcand, Denys (réalisateur); Association Internationale de Signalisation Maritime; Association canadienne des paiements (Charlie Clarke); Association des banquiers canadiens (Lise Provost); Automobiles Citroën; Automobiles Peugeot; Banque du Canada (Lyse Brousseau); Banque Royale du Canada (Raymond Chouinard, Francine Morel, Carole Trottier); Barrett Xplore inc.; Bazarin, Christine;Bibliothèque du Parlement canadien (Service de renseignements); Bibliothèque nationale du Québec (Jean-François Palomino); Bluechip Kennels (Olga Gagne); Bombardier Aéronautique; Bridgestone-Firestone; Brother (Canada); Canadien National; Casavant Frères ltée; C.O.J.O. ATHENES 2004 (Bureau des Médias Internationaux); Centre Eaton de Montréal; Centre national du Costume (Recherche et de Diffusion); Cetacean Society International (William R. Rossiter); Chagnon, Daniel (architecte D.E.S. – M.E.Q.); Cohen et Rubin Architectes (Maggy Cohen); Commission Scolaire de Montréal (École St-Henri); Compagnie de la Baie d'Hudson (Nunzia Iavarone, Ron Oyama); Corporation d'hébergement du Québec (Céline Drolet); École nationale de théâtre du Canada (Bibliothèque); Élevage Le Grand Saphir (Stéphane Ayotte); Énergie atomique du Canada ltée; Eurocopter; Famous Players; Fédération bancaire française (Védi Hékiman); Fontaine, PierreHenry (biologiste); Future Shop; Garaga; Groupe Jean Coutu; Hôpital du Sacré-Cœur de Montréal; Hôtel Inter-Continental; Hydro-Québec; I.P.I.Q. (Serge Bouchard); IGA Barcelo; International Entomological Society (Dr. Michael Geisthardt); Irisbus; Jérôme, Danielle (O.D.); La Poste (Colette Gouts); Le Groupe Canam Manac inc.; Lévesque, Georges (urgentologue); Lévesque, Robert (chef machiniste); Manutan; Marriot Spring Hill suites; MATRA S.A.; Métro inc.; ministère canadien de la Défense nationale (Affaires publiques); ministère de la Défense, République Française; ministère de la Justice du Québec (Service de la gestion immobilière – Carol Sirois); ministère de l'Éducation du Québec (Direction de l'équipement scolaire- Daniel Chagnon); Muse Productions (Annick Barbery); National Aeronautics and Space Administration; National Oceanic and Atmospheric Administration; Nikon Canada inc.; Normand, Denis (consultant en télécommunications); Office de la langue française du Québec (Chantal Robinson); Paul Demers & Fils inc.; Phillips (France); Pratt & Whitney Canada inc.; Prévost Car inc.; Radio Shack Canada ltée; Réno-Dépôt inc.; Robitaille, Jean-François (Département de biologie, Université Laurentienne); Rocking T Ranch and Poultry Farm (Pete and Justine Theer); RONA inc.; Sears Canada inc.; Secrétariat d'État du Canada : Bureau de la traduction ; Service correctionnel du Canada; Société d'Entomologie Africaine (Alain Drumont); Société des musées québécois (Michel Perron); Société Radio-Canada; Sony du Canada ltée; Sûreté du Québec; Théâtre du Nouveau Monde; Transports Canada (Julie Poirier); Urgences-Santé (Éric Berry); Ville de Longueuil (Direction de la Police); Ville de Montréal (Service de la prévention des incendies); Vimont Lexus Toyota; Volvo Bus Corporation; Yamaha Motor Canada Ltd.

Collins French Visual Dictionary was created and produced by
QA International
329, rue de la Commune Ouest, 3e étage
Montréal (Québec) H2Y 2E1 Canada
T 514.499.3000 F 514.499.3010
www.qa-international.com

HarperCollins Publishers
Westerhill Road, Bishopbriggs
Glasgow, G64 2QT
Great Britain
www.collinslanguage.com

HarperCollins Publishers 2008
ISBN 978-0-00-727807-7

Printed and bound in Singapore
10 9 8 7 6 5 4 3 2 1 0
www.qa-international.com

EDITORIAL STAFF

Publisher : Jacques Fortin
Authors : Jean-Claude Corbeil and Ariane Archambault
Editorial director : François Fortin
Editor in chief : Serge D'Amico
Graphic designer : Anne Tremblay

PRODUCTION

Mac Thien Nguyen Hoang
Guylaine Houle

TERMINOLOGICAL RESEARCH

Jean Beaumont
Catherine Briand
Nathalie Guillo

ILLUSTRATIONS

Artistic director : Jocelyn Gardner
Jean-Yves Ahern
Rielle Lévesque
Alain Lemire
Mélanie Boivin
Yan Bohler
Claude Thivierge
Pascal Bilodeau
Michel Rouleau
Anouk Noël
Carl Pelletier

LAYOUT

Pascal Goyette
Janou-Ève LeGuerrier
Véronique Boisvert
Josée Gagnon
Karine Raymond
Geneviève Théroux Béliveau

DOCUMENTATION

Gilles Vézina
Kathleen Wynd
Stéphane Batigne
Sylvain Robichaud
Jessie Daigle

DATA MANAGEMENT

Programmers : Éric Gagnon, Daniel Beaulieu
Nathalie Fréchette

REVISION

Marie-Nicole Cimon

PREPRESS

Kien Tang
Karine Lévesque

CONTRIBUTIONS

QA International wishes to extend a special thank you to the following people for their contribution to *The Mini Visual Dictionary:*
Jean-Louis Martin, Marc Lalumière, Jacques Perrault, Stéphane Roy, Alice Comtois, Michel Blais, Christiane Beauregard, Mamadou Togola, Annie Maurice, Charles Campeau, Mivil Deschênes, Jonathan Jacques, Martin Lortie, Raymond Martin, Frédérick Simard, Yan Tremblay, Mathieu Blouin, Sébastien Dallaire, Hoang Khanh Le, Martin Desrosiers, Nicolas Oroc, François Escalmel, Danièle Lemay, Pierre Savoie, Benoit Bourdeau, Marie-Andrée Lemieux, Caroline Soucy, Yves Chabot, Anne-Marie Ouellette, Anne-Marie Villeneuve, Anne-Marie Brault, Nancy Lepage, Daniel Provost, François Vézina, Brad Wilson, Michael Worek, Lionel Koffler, Maraya Raduha, Dave Harvey, Mike Parkes, George Walker and Anna Simmons.

Introduction to *The Mini Visual Dictionary*

EDITORIAL POLICY

The Mini Visual Dictionary takes an inventory of the physical environment of a person who is part of today's technological age and who knows and uses a large number of specialized terms in a wide variety of fields.

Designed for the general public, it responds to the needs of anyone seeking the precise, correct terms for a wide range of personal or professional reasons: finding an unknown term, checking the meaning of a word, advertising, additional teaching material, etc.

The target user has guided the choice of contents for The Mini Visual Dictionary, which aims to bring together in one volume the technical terms required to express the contemporary world, in the specialized fields that shape our daily experience.

STRUCTURE OF THE MINI VISUAL DICTIONARY

This book has three sections: the preliminary pages, including the list of themes and table of contents; the body of the text, i.e. the detailed treatment of each theme; the index.

Information is presented moving from the most abstract to the most concrete: theme, sub-theme, title, subtitle, illustration, terminology.

The content of *The Mini Visual Dictionary* is divided into 17 THEMES, from Astronomy to Sports. More complex themes are divided into SUB-THEMES. For example, the theme Earth is divided into Geography, Geology, Meteorology and Environment.

The TITLE has a variety of functions: to name the illustration of a unique object, of which the principal parts are identified (for example, glacier, window); to bring together under one designation illustrations that belong to the same conceptual sphere, but that represent a variety of elements, each with its own designations and terminology *(e.g. configuration of the continents, household appliances)*.

At times, the chief members of a class of objects are brought together under the same SUB-TITLE, each with its own name but without a detailed terminological analysis. *(e.g. under space probe, examples of space probes)*.

The ILLUSTRATION shows realistically and precisely an object, a process or a phenomenon, and the most significant details from which they are constructed. It serves as a visual definition for each of the terms presented.

TERMINOLOGY

Each word in *The Mini Visual Dictionary* has been carefully selected following examination of high-quality documentation, at the required level of specialization.

There may be cases where different terms are used to name the same item. In such instances, the word most frequently used by the most highly regarded authors has been chosen.

The INDEX lists all words in the dictionary in alphabetical order.

METHODS OF CONSULTATION

One may gain access to the contents of *The Mini Visual Dictionary* in a variety of ways:

• From the list of THEMES on the back of the book and at the end of the preliminary pages.

• With the INDEX the user can consult *The Mini Visual Dictionary* from a word, so as to see what it corresponds to, or to verify accuracy by examining the illustration that depicts it.

• The most original aspect of *The Mini Visual Dictionary* is the fact that the illustrations enable the user to find a word even if he or she only has a vague idea of what it is. The dictionary is unique in this feature, as consultation of any other dictionary requires the user first to know the word.

COLOUR REFERENCE

On the spine and back of the book this identifies and accompanies each theme to facilitate quick access to the corresponding section in the book.

TITLE

It is highlighted in English, and the French equivalent is placed underneath in smaller characters. If the title runs over a number of pages, it is printed in grey on the pages subsequent to the first page on which it appears.

SUB-THEME

Most themes are subdivided into sub-themes. The sub-theme is given both in English and in French.

NARROW LINES

These link the word to the item indicated. Where too many lines would make reading difficult, they have been replaced by colour codes with captions or, in rare cases, by numbers.

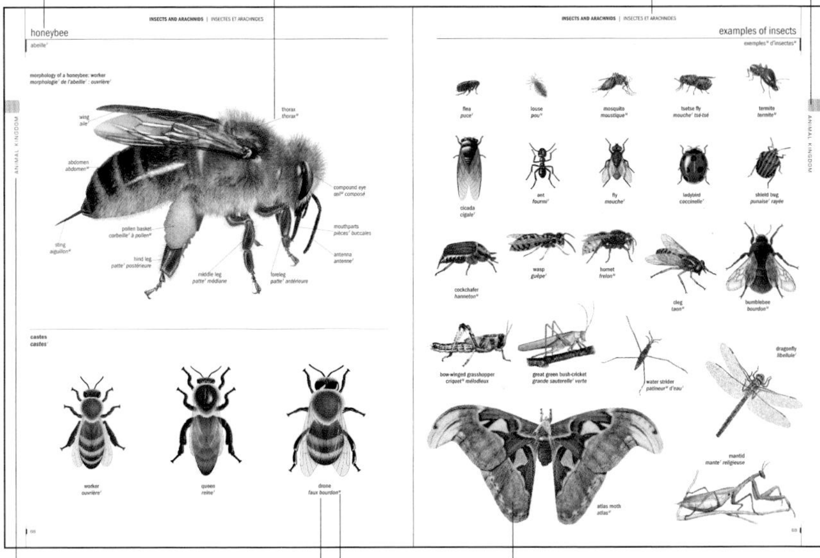

THEME

It is always unilingual, in the main language of the edition.

ILLUSTRATION

It serves as the visual definition for the terms associated with it.

GENDER INDICATION

F: feminine M: masculine

The gender of each word in a term is indicated.

The characters shown in the dictionary are men or women when the function illustrated can be fulfilled by either. In these cases, the gender assigned to the word depends on the illustration; in fact, the word is either masculine or feminine depending on the sex of the person.

TERM

Each term appears in the index with a reference to the pages on which it appears. It is given in both languages, with English as the main index entry.

Contents

ASTRONOMY 2

Celestial bodies 2
Astronomical observation 7
Astronautics 10

EARTH 14

Geography 14
Geology 26
Meteorology 37
Environment 44

PLANT KINGDOM 50

ANIMAL KINGDOM 66

Simple organisms and echinoderms 66
Insects and arachnids 67
Crustaceans 71
Molluscs 72
Fishes 74
Amphibians 75
Reptiles 76
Birds 78
Rodents and lagomorphs 82
Ungulate mammals 83
Carnivorous mammals 86
Marine mammals 90
Primate mammals 91

HUMAN BEING 92

Human body 92
Anatomy 96
Sense organs 114

FOOD AND KITCHEN 120

Food 120
Kitchen 162

HOUSE 182

Location 182
Elements of a house 185
Structure of a house 187
Heating 192
Plumbing 194
Electricity 198
House furniture 200

DO-IT-YOURSELF AND GARDENING 216

Do-it-yourself 216
Gardening 230

CLOTHING 238

PERSONAL ADORNMENT AND ARTICLES 264

Personal adornment 264
Personal articles 271

ARTS AND ARCHITECTURE 278

Architecture 278
Performing arts 290
Music 295

COMMUNICATIONS AND OFFICE AUTOMATION 312

Communications 312
Office automation 329

TRANSPORT AND MACHINERY 342

Road transport 342
Rail transport 374
Maritime transport 381
Air transport 388
Handling 396
Heavy machinery 398

ENERGY 402

Geothermy and fossil energy 402
Hydroelectricity 406
Nuclear energy 408
Solar energy 410
Wind energy 412

SCIENCE 414

Chemistry 414
Physics: electricity and magnetism 416
Physics: optics 418
Measuring devices 422
Scientific symbols 426

SOCIETY 430

City 430
Justice 440
Economy and finance 441
Education 444
Religion 446
Politics 448
Safety 454
Health 460

SPORTS AND GAMES 468

Games 468
Track and field 472
Ball sports 474
Racket sports 490
Gymnastics 496
Combat sports 498
Strength sports 500
Precision and accuracy sports 502
Winter sports 506
Aquatic and nautical sports 516
Cycling 522
Motor sports 523
Sports on wheels 526
Outdoor leisure 528

List of chapters

2 ASTRONOMY
14 EARTH
50 PLANT KINGDOM
66 ANIMAL KINGDOM
92 HUMAN BEING
120 FOOD AND KITCHEN
182 HOUSE
216 DO-IT-YOURSELF AND GARDENING
238 CLOTHING
264 PERSONAL ADORNMENT AND ARTICLES
278 ARTS AND ARCHITECTURE
312 COMMUNICATIONS AND OFFICE AUTOMATION
342 TRANSPORT AND MACHINERY
402 ENERGY
414 SCIENCE
430 SOCIETY
468 SPORTS AND GAMES
539 INDEX

solar system

système[M] solaire

outer planets
planètes[F] externes

50,000 astronomical units
50 000 unités[F] astronomiques

Saturn
Saturne

Jupiter
Jupiter

Uranus
Uranus

Neptune
Neptune

Sun
Soleil[M]

50 astronomical units
50 unités[F] astronomiques

Kuiper belt
ceinture[F] de Kuiper

Oort cloud
nuage[M] de Oort

planets and moons

planètes[F] et satellites[M]

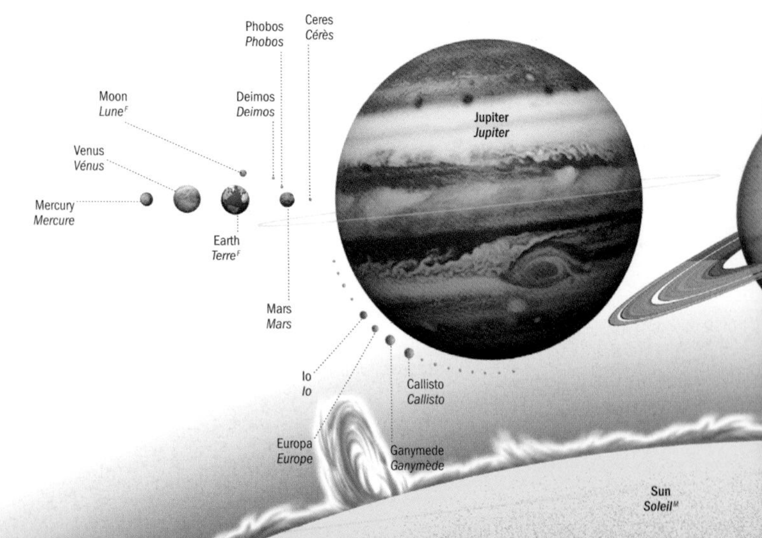

inner planets
planètes*[F] *internes

1 astronomical unit
1 unité[F] *astronomique*
Earth
Terre[F]
Mercury
Mercure
Venus
Vénus
Mars
Mars
asteroid belt
ceinture[F] *d'astéroïdes*[M]

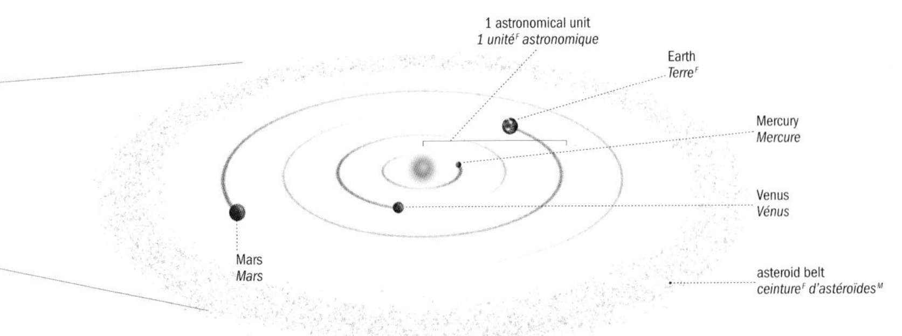

planets and moons

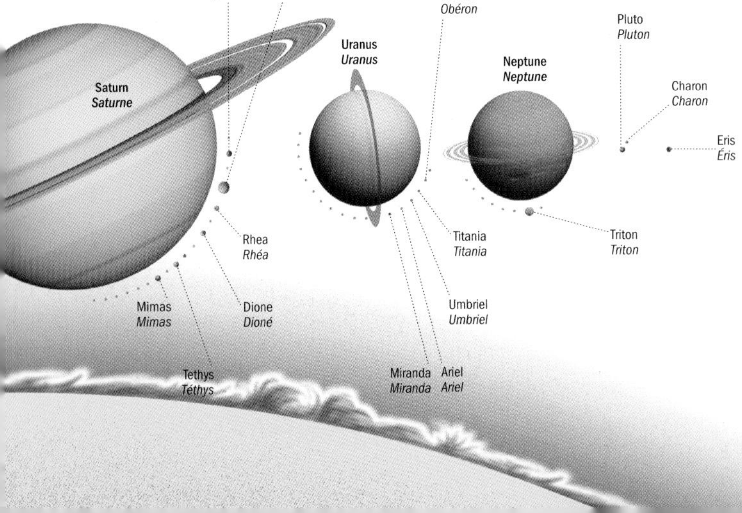

Iapetus
Japet
Titan
Titan
Oberon
Obéron
Pluto
Pluton
Uranus
Uranus
Neptune
Neptune
Saturn
Saturne
Charon
Charon
Eris
Éris
Rhea
Rhéa
Titania
Titania
Triton
Triton
Umbriel
Umbriel
Mimas
Mimas
Dione
Dioné
Tethys
Téthys
Miranda
Miranda
Ariel
Ariel

Sun

Soleil^M

structure of the Sun
structure^F du Soleil^M

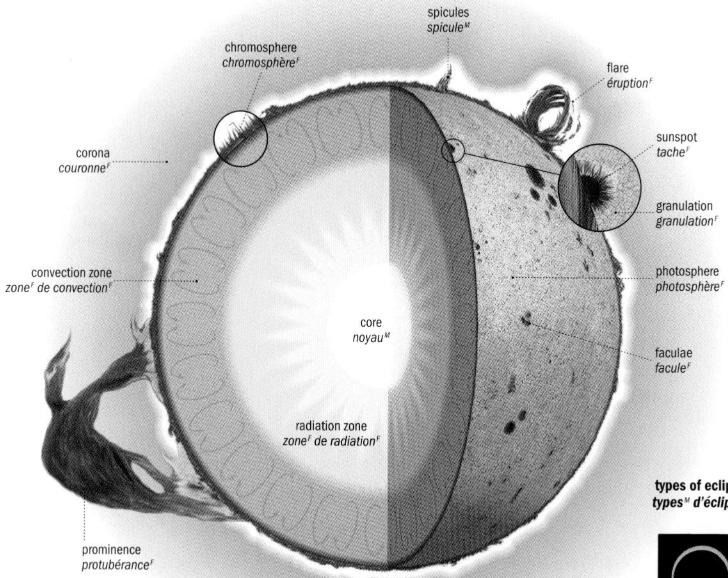

spicules
spicule^M
chromosphere
chromosphère^F
flare
éruption^F
sunspot
tache^F
corona
couronne^F
granulation
granulation^F
convection zone
zone^F de convection^F
photosphere
photosphère^F
core
noyau^M
faculae
facule^F
radiation zone
zone^F de radiation^F
prominence
protubérance^F

types of eclipses
types^M d'éclipses^F

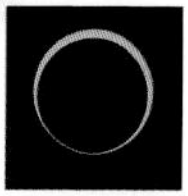

annular eclipse
éclipse^F annulaire

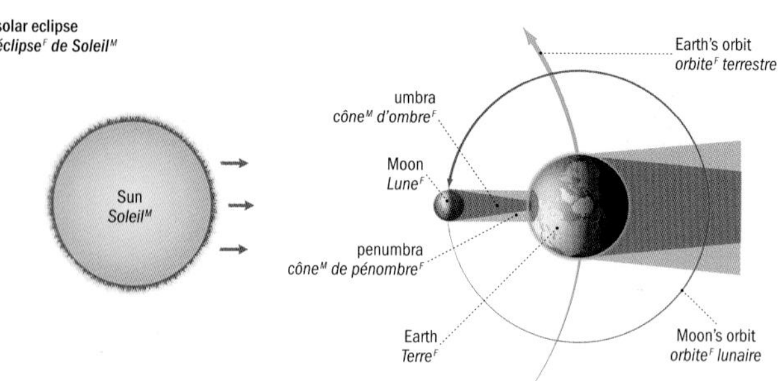

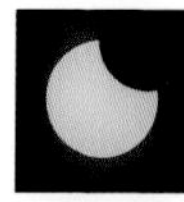

partial eclipse
éclipse^F partielle

total eclipse
éclipse^F totale

solar eclipse
éclipse^F de Soleil^M

Earth's orbit
orbite^F terrestre
umbra
cône^M d'ombre^F
Moon
Lune^F
Sun
Soleil^M
penumbra
cône^M de pénombre^F
Earth
Terre^F
Moon's orbit
orbite^F lunaire

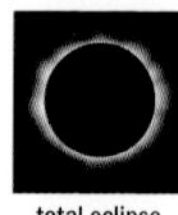

Moon

Lune[F]

types of eclipses
types[M] d'éclipses[F]

partial eclipse
éclipse[F] partielle

total eclipse
éclipse[F] totale

lunar features
relief[M] lunaire

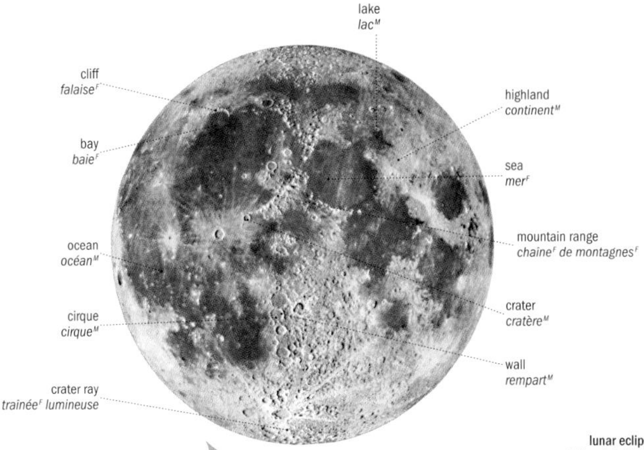

lake
lac[M]

cliff
falaise[F]

highland
continent[M]

bay
baie[F]

sea
mer[F]

mountain range
chaine[F] de montagnes[F]

ocean
océan[M]

crater
cratère[M]

cirque
cirque[M]

wall
rempart[M]

crater ray
trainée[F] lumineuse

lunar eclipse
éclipse[F] de Lune[F]

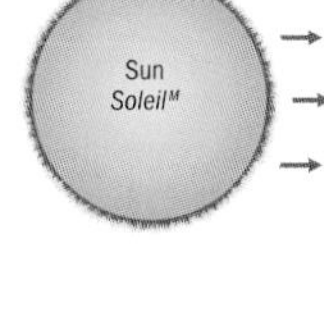

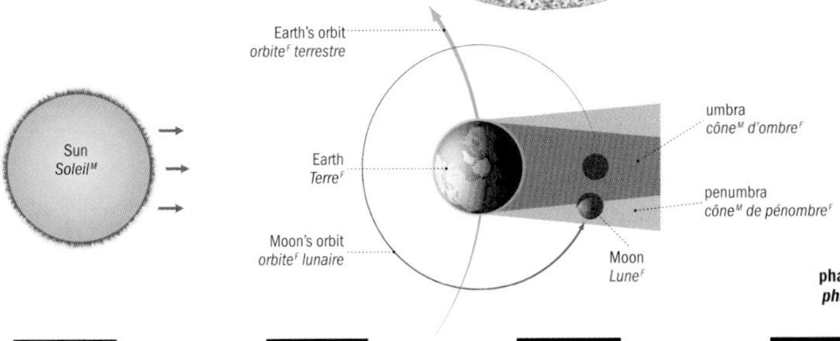

Earth's orbit
orbite[F] terrestre

umbra
cône[M] d'ombre[F]

Earth
Terre[F]

penumbra
cône[M] de pénombre[F]

Moon's orbit
orbite[F] lunaire

Moon
Lune[F]

phases of the Moon
phases[F] de la Lune[F]

new moon
nouvelle Lune[F]

new crescent
premier croissant[M]

first quarter
premier quartier[M]

waxing gibbous
gibbeuse[F] croissante

full moon
pleine Lune[F]

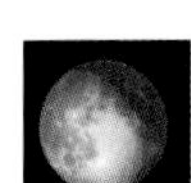

waning gibbous
gibbeuse[F] décroissante

last quarter
dernier quartier[M]

old crescent
dernier croissant[M]

galaxy

galaxie[F]

Milky Way
Voie[F] lactée

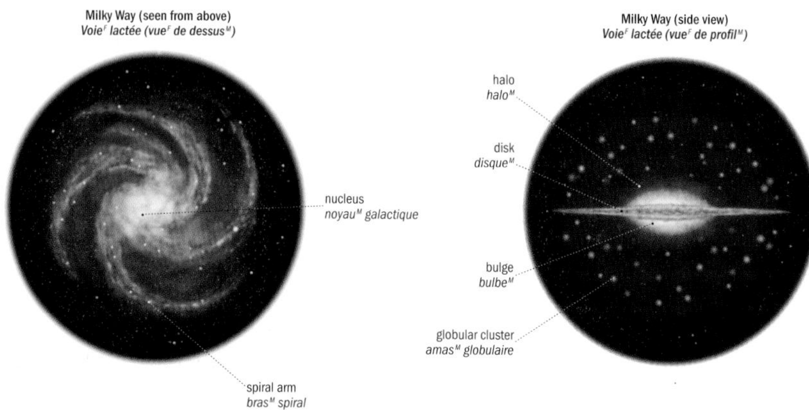

comet

comète[F]

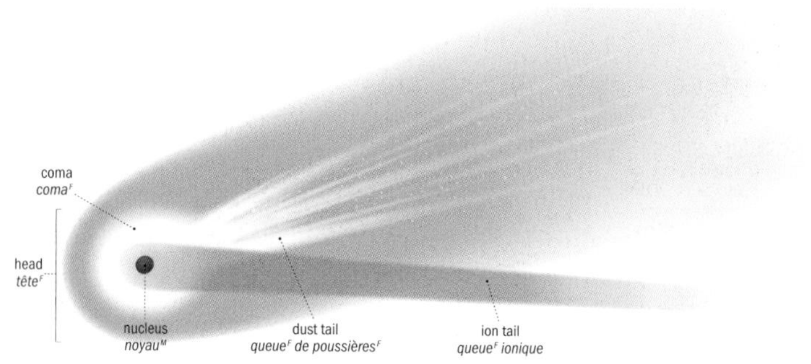

Hubble space telescope

télescope^M spatial Hubble

antenna
antenne^F
aperture door
volet^M mobile
fine guidance system
système^M de pointage^M fin
light shield
écran^M protecteur
scientific instruments
appareils^M scientifiques
secondary mirror
miroir^M secondaire
solar panel
panneau^M solaire
primary mirror
miroir^M primaire
aft shroud
bouclier^M arrière

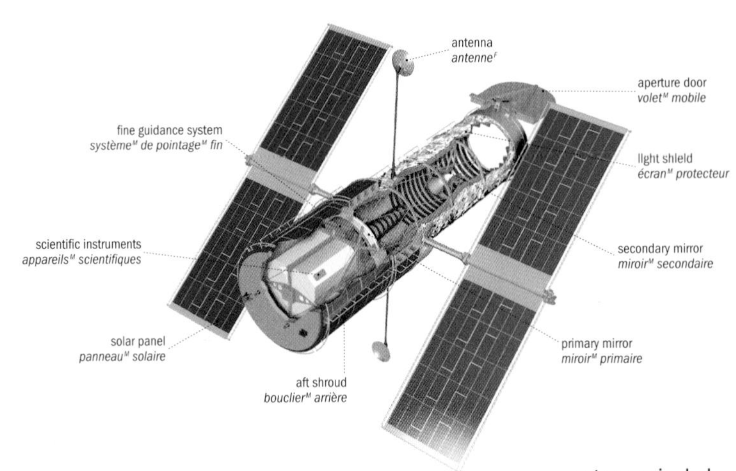

astronomical observatory

observatoire^M astronomique

cross section of an astronomical observatory
coupe^F d'un observatoire^M astronomique

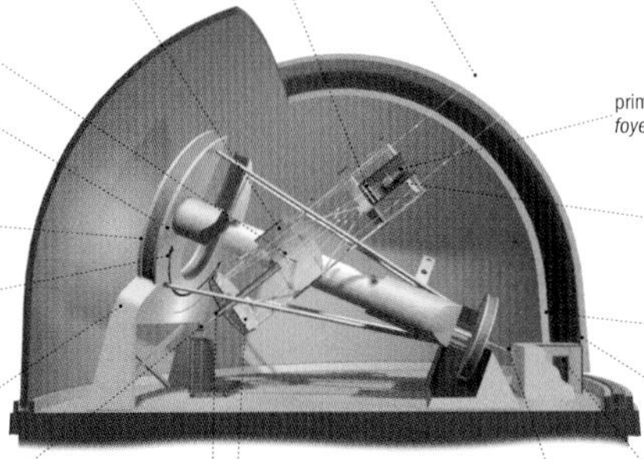

secondary mirror
miroir^M secondaire
telescope
télescope^M
light
lumière^F
flat mirror
miroir^M plan rétractable
horseshoe mount
monture^F en fer^M à cheval^M
prime focus
foyer^M primaire
hour angle gear
engrenage^M horaire
prime focus observing capsule
nacelle^F d'observation^F
polar axis
axe^M horaire
interior dome shell
enveloppe^F intérieure
telescope base
base^F
exterior dome shell
enveloppe^F extérieure
observation post
poste^M d'observation^F
Cassegrain focus
foyer^M Cassegrain
primary mirror
miroir^M primaire concave
coudé focus
foyer^M coudé
laboratory
laboratoire^M

observatory
observatoire^M

dome shutter
cimier^M mobile
rotating dome
coupole^F rotative

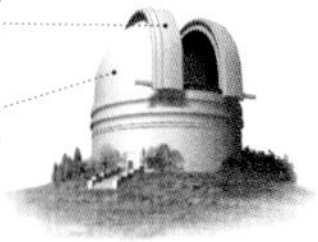

refracting telescope

lunette[F] astronomique

finderscope
chercheur[M]
cradle
bride[F] de fixation[F]
main tube
tube[M]
lens hood
pare-soleil[M]
eyepiece
oculaire[M]
eyepiece holder
tube[M] porte-oculaire[M]
star diagonal
oculaire[M] coudé
declination setting scale
cercle[M] de déclinaison[F]
azimuth clamp
vis[F] de blocage[M] (azimut[M])
focusing knob
bouton[M] de mise[F] au point[M]
altitude clamp
vis[F] de blocage[M] (latitude[F])
azimuth fine adjustment
réglage[M] micrométrique (azimut[M])
right ascension setting scale
cercle[M] d'ascension[F] droite
altitude fine adjustment
réglage[M] micrométrique (latitude[F])
counterweight
contrepoids[M]
fork
fourche[F]
tripod accessories shelf
plateau[M] pour accessoires[M]
tripod
trépied[M]

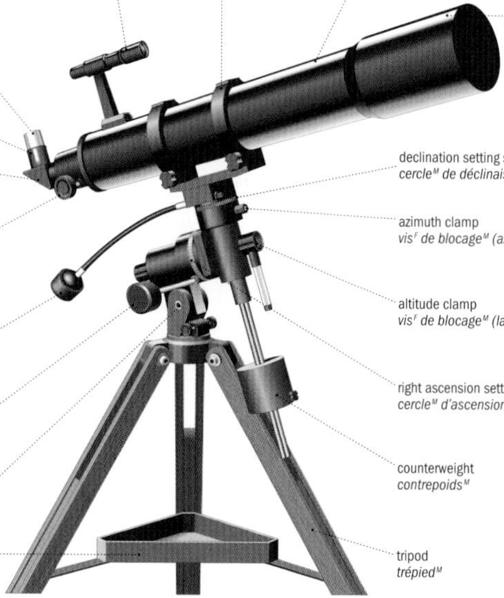

cross section of a refracting telescope
coupe[F] d'une lunette[F] astronomique

light
lumière[F]
eyepiece
oculaire[M]
objective lens
lentille[F] objectif[M]
main tube
tube[M]

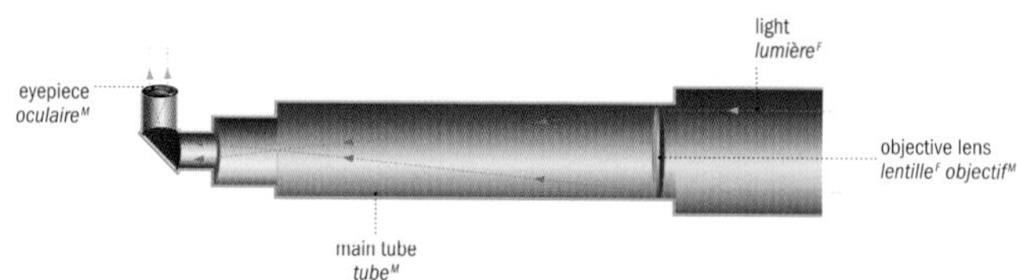

reflecting telescope

télescope^{M}

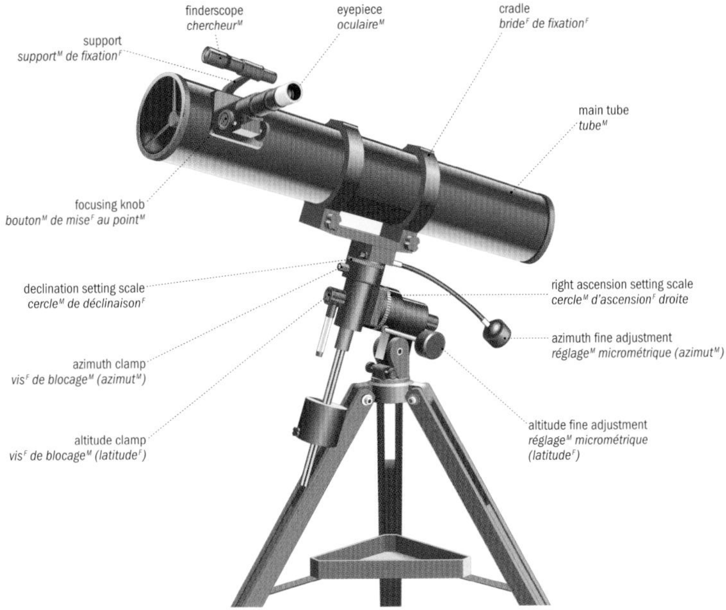

finderscope
chercheur^{M}
eyepiece
oculaire^{M}
cradle
bride^{F} de fixation^{F}
support
support^{M} de fixation^{F}
main tube
tube^{M}
focusing knob
bouton^{M} de mise^{F} au point^{M}
declination setting scale
cercle^{M} de déclinaison^{F}
right ascension setting scale
cercle^{M} d'ascension^{F} droite
azimuth fine adjustment
réglage^{M} micrométrique (azimut^{M})
azimuth clamp
vis^{F} de blocage^{M} (azimut^{M})
altitude fine adjustment
réglage^{M} micrométrique (latitude^{F})
altitude clamp
vis^{F} de blocage^{M} (latitude^{F})

cross section of a reflecting telescope
coupe^{F} d'un télescope^{M}

eyepiece
oculaire^{M}
secondary mirror
miroir^{M} secondaire
concave primary mirror
miroir^{M} primaire concave
light
lumière^{F}
main tube
tube^{M}

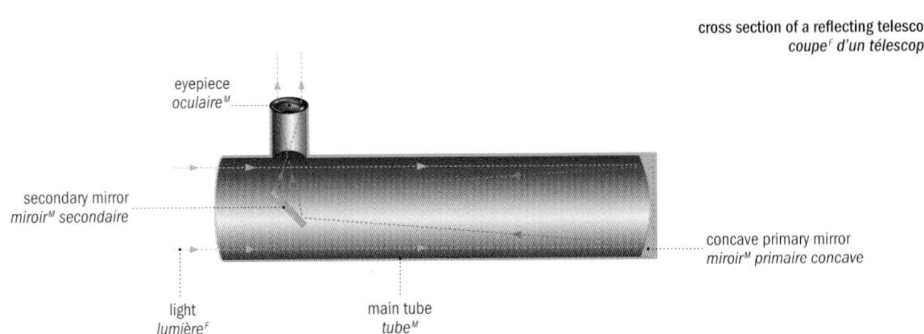

spacesuit

scaphandre^M spatial

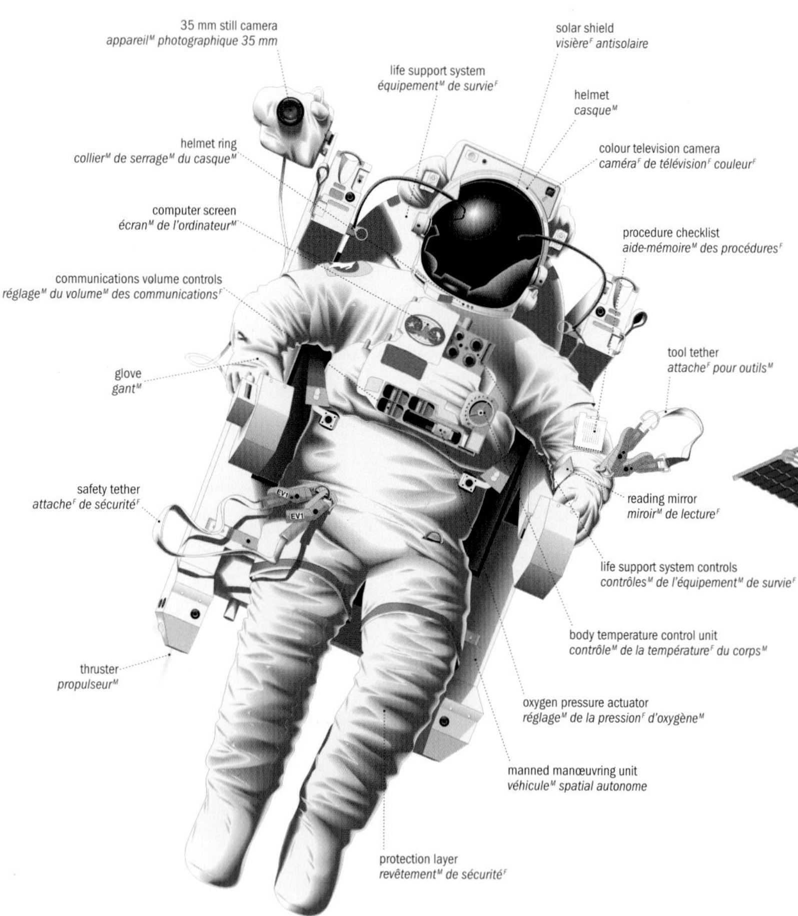

international space station

station^F spatiale internationale

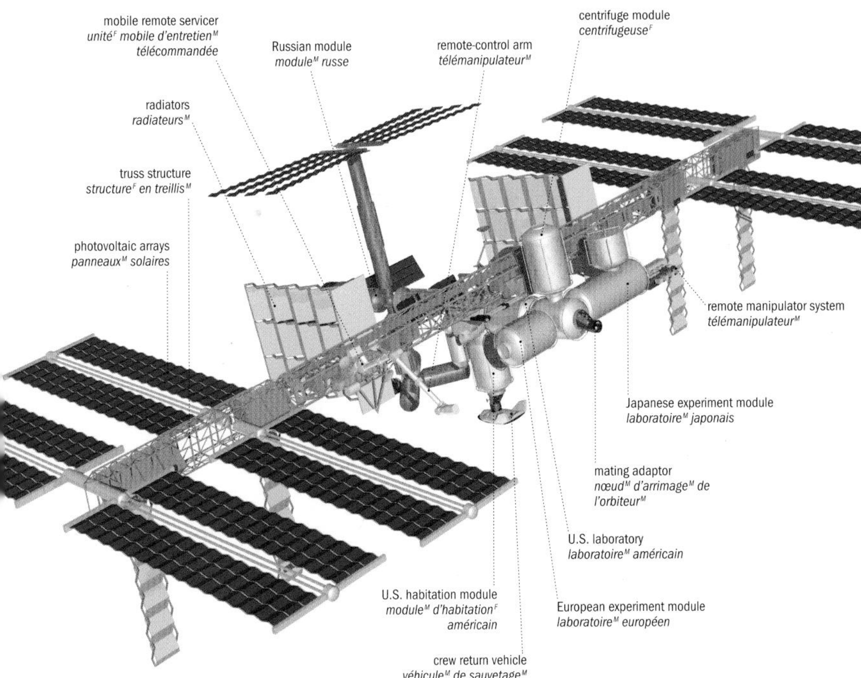

space shuttle

navette^F spatiale

space shuttle at takeoff
navette^F spatiale au décollage^M

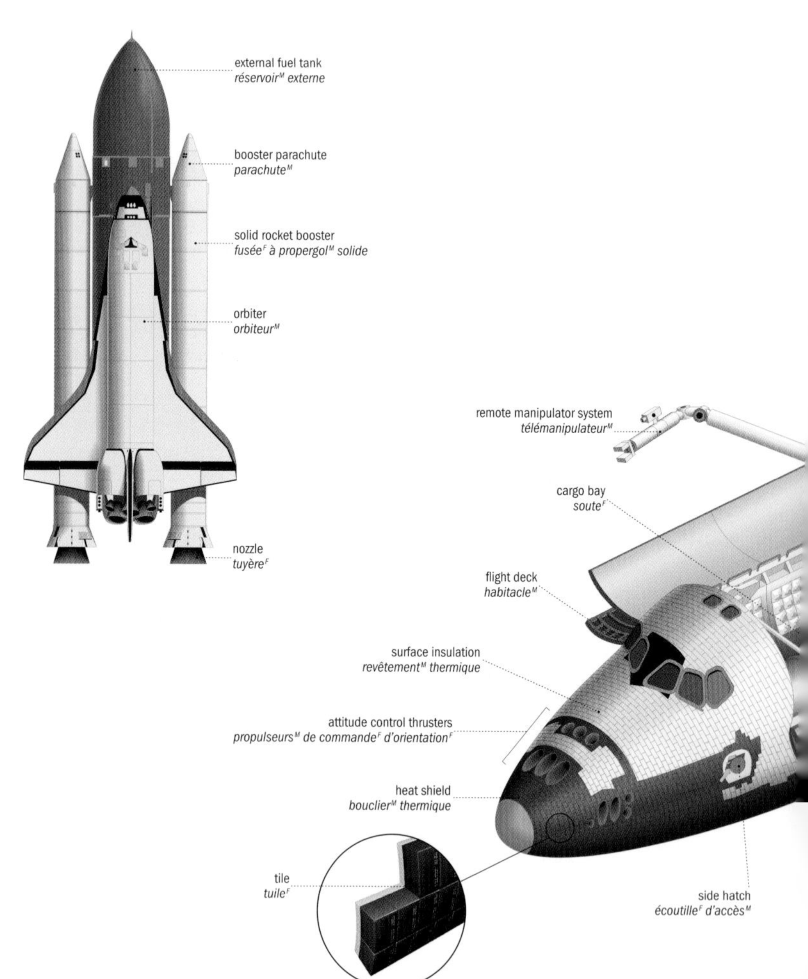

orbiter
orbiteur[M]

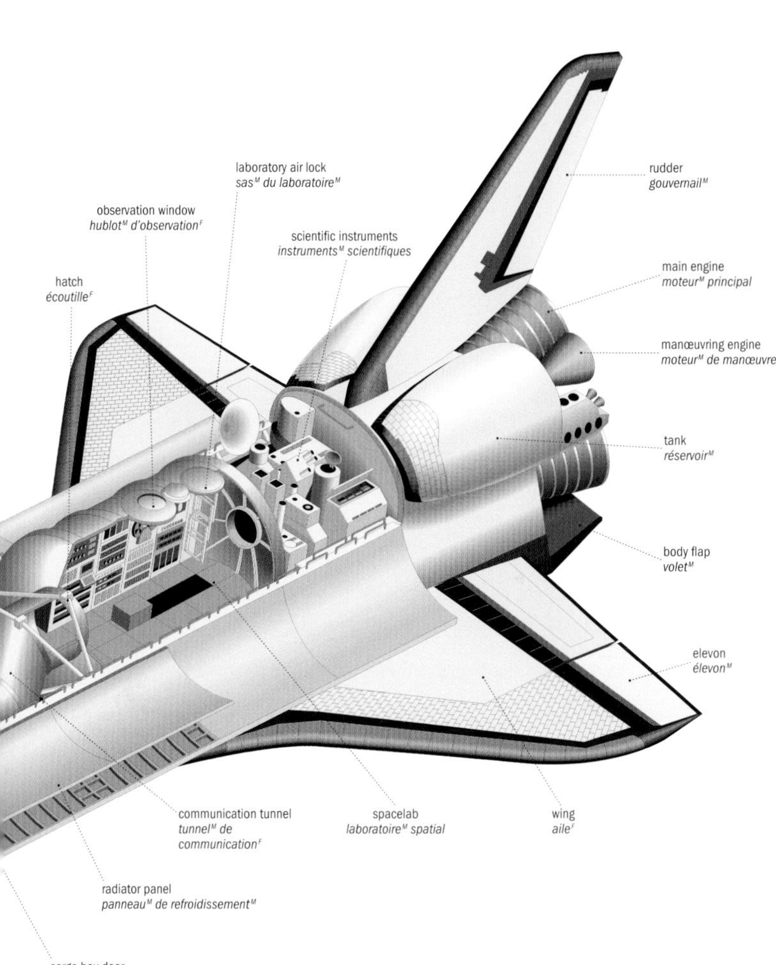

configuration of the continents

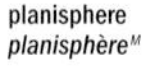

configuration[F] des continents[M]

planisphere
planisphère[M]

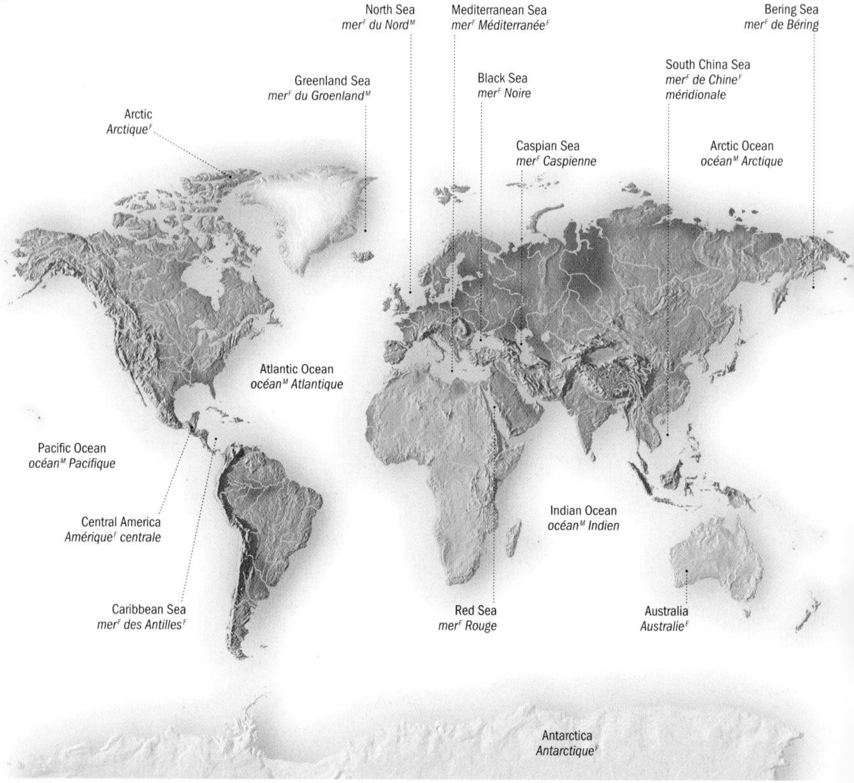

North Sea
mer[F] du Nord[M]

Mediterranean Sea
mer[F] Méditerranée[F]

Bering Sea
mer[F] de Béring

South China Sea
mer[F] de Chine[F] méridionale

Greenland Sea
mer[F] du Groenland[M]

Black Sea
mer[F] Noire

Arctic
Arctique[F]

Caspian Sea
mer[F] Caspienne

Arctic Ocean
océan[M] Arctique

Atlantic Ocean
océan[M] Atlantique

Pacific Ocean
océan[M] Pacifique

Central America
Amérique[F] centrale

Indian Ocean
océan[M] Indien

Caribbean Sea
mer[F] des Antilles[F]

Red Sea
mer[F] Rouge

Australia
Australie[F]

Antarctica
Antarctique[F]

North America
Amérique[F] du Nord[M]

Europe
Europe[F]

Eurasia
Eurasie[F]

South America
Amérique[F] du Sud[M]

Asia
Asie[F]

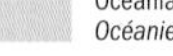

Oceania
Océanie[F]

Africa
Afrique[F]

Antarctica
*Antarctique*F

Atlantic Ocean
océanM Atlantique
Antarctic Circle
cercleM polaire antarctique
South Pole
pôleM Sud
Drake Passage
détroitM de Drake
Queen Maud Land
TerreF de la ReineF-Maud
Weddell Sea
merF de Weddell
Antarctic Peninsula
péninsuleF Antarctique
Amery Ice Shelf
banquiseF d'Amery
Filchner Ice Shelf
banquiseF de Filchner
Wilkes Land
TerreF de Wilkes
Marie Byrd Land
TerreF Marie-Byrd
Indian Ocean
océanM Indien
Pacific Ocean
océanM Pacifique
Ross Ice Shelf
banquiseF de Ross
Transantarctic Mountains
montsM Transantarctiques

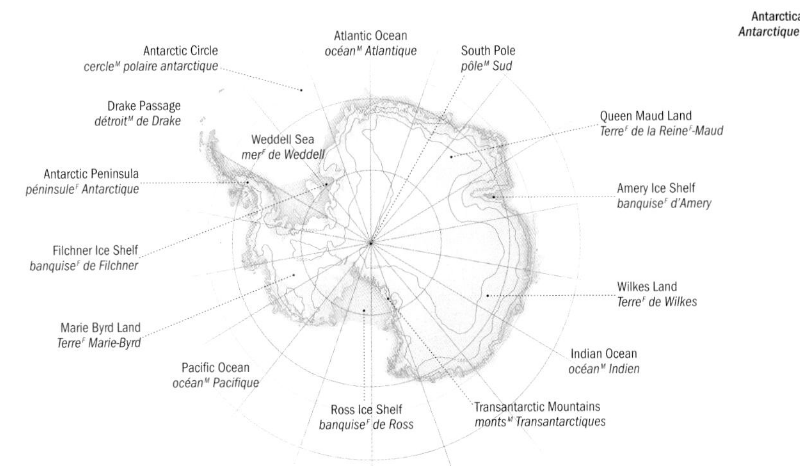

Oceania
*Océanie*F

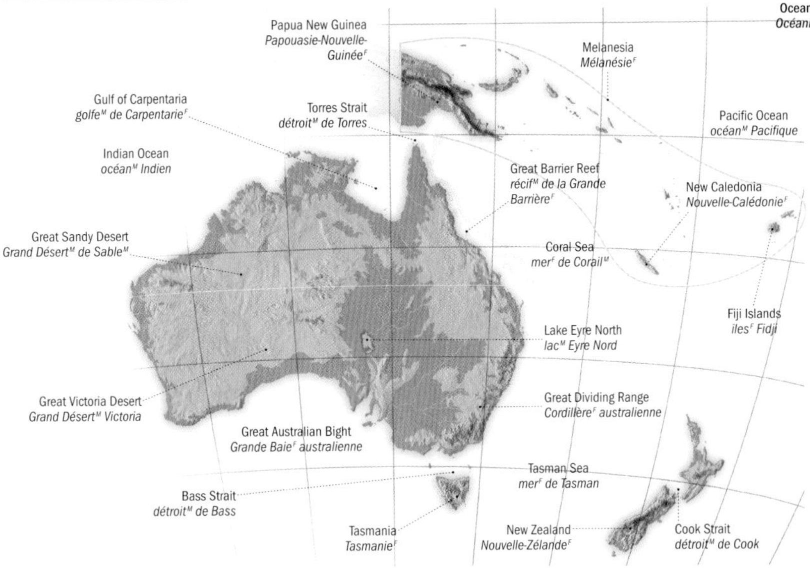

Papua New Guinea
Papouasie-Nouvelle-Guinée F
Melanesia
MélanésieF
Gulf of Carpentaria
golfeM de CarpentarieF
Torres Strait
détroitM de Torres
Pacific Ocean
océanM Pacifique
Indian Ocean
océanM Indien
Great Barrier Reef
récifM de la Grande BarrièreF
New Caledonia
Nouvelle-CalédonieF
Great Sandy Desert
Grand DésertM de SableM
Coral Sea
merF de CorailM
Fiji Islands
îlesF Fidji
Lake Eyre North
lacM Eyre Nord
Great Victoria Desert
Grand DésertM Victoria
Great Dividing Range
CordillèreF australienne
Great Australian Bight
Grande BaieF australienne
Tasman Sea
merF de Tasman
Bass Strait
détroitM de Bass
Tasmania
TasmanieF
New Zealand
Nouvelle-ZélandeF
Cook Strait
détroitM de Cook

North America
Amérique[F] *du Nord*[M]

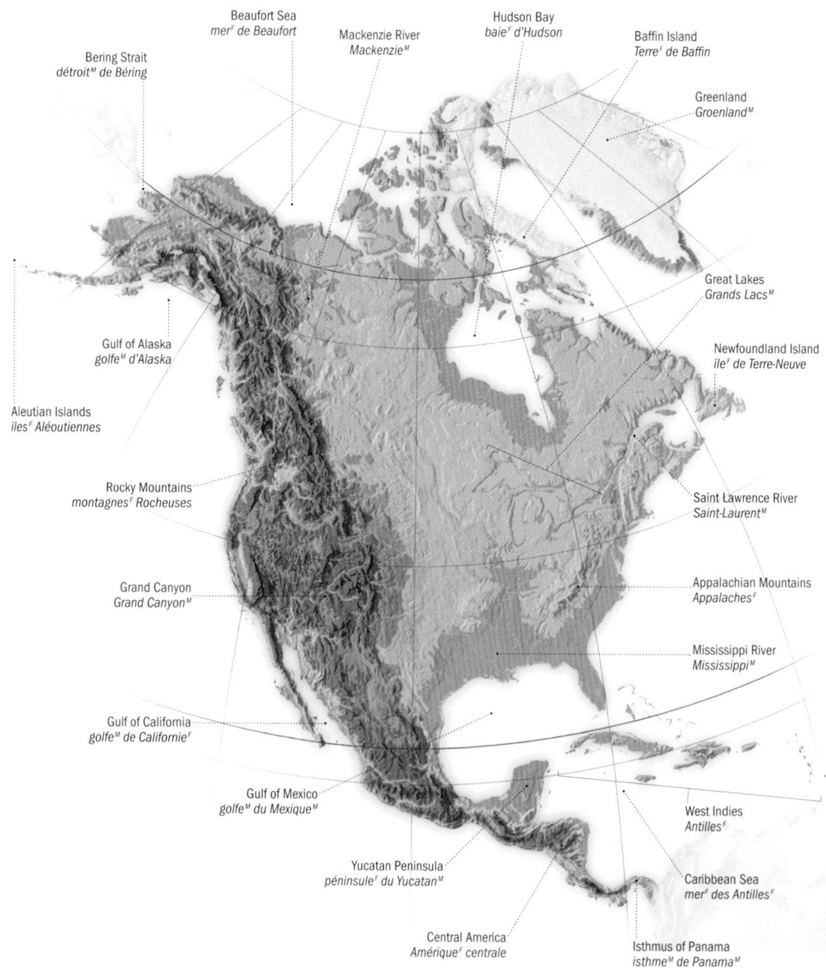

South America
Amérique^F du Sud^M

Europe
Europe[F]

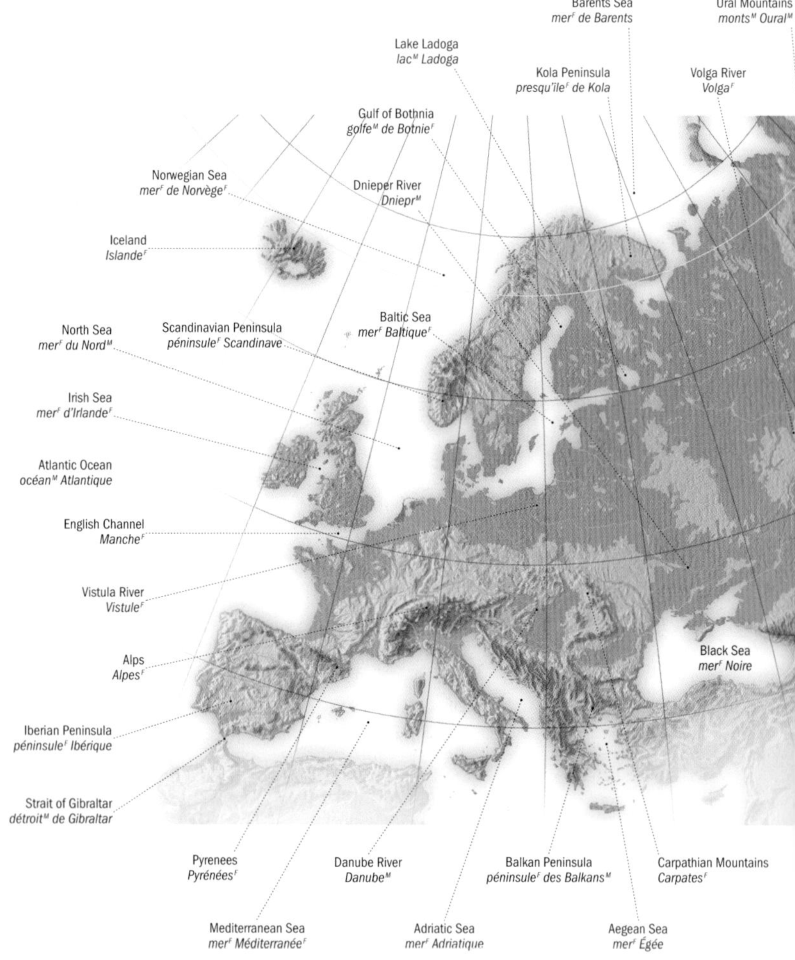

Asia
Asie^F

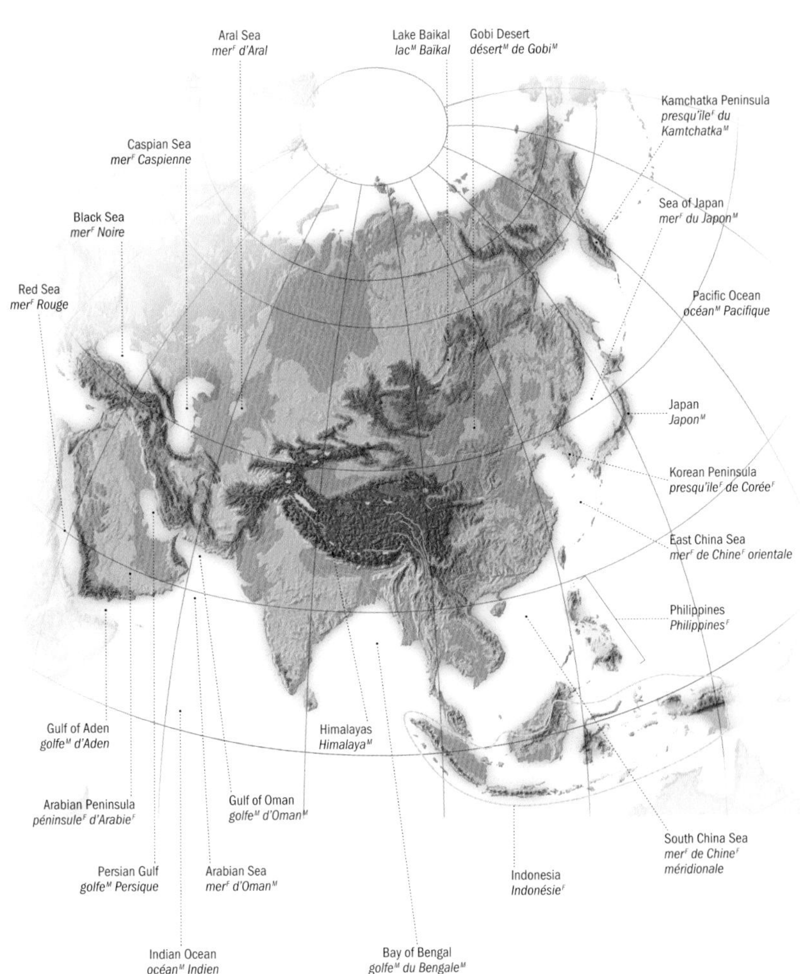
Aral Sea
mer^F d'Aral
Lake Baikal
lac^M Baïkal
Gobi Desert
désert^M de Gobi^M
Kamchatka Peninsula
presqu'île^F du Kamtchatka^M
Caspian Sea
mer^F Caspienne
Sea of Japan
mer^F du Japon^M
Black Sea
mer^F Noire
Red Sea
mer^F Rouge
Pacific Ocean
océan^M Pacifique
Japan
Japon^M
Korean Peninsula
presqu'île^F de Corée^F
East China Sea
mer^F de Chine^F orientale
Philippines
Philippines^F
Gulf of Aden
golfe^M d'Aden
Himalayas
Himalaya^M
Arabian Peninsula
péninsule^F d'Arabie^F
Gulf of Oman
golfe^M d'Oman^M
South China Sea
mer^F de Chine^F méridionale
Persian Gulf
golfe^M Persique
Arabian Sea
mer^F d'Oman^M
Indonesia
Indonésie^F
Indian Ocean
océan^M Indien
Bay of Bengal
golfe^M du Bengale^M

Africa
Afrique[F]

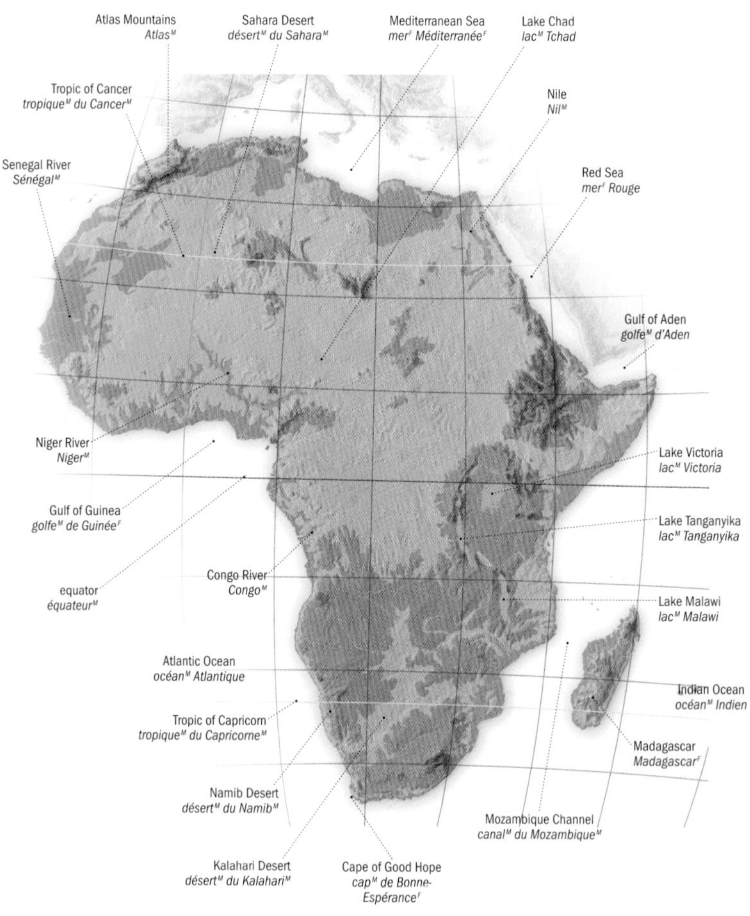

cartography

cartographie^F

Earth coordinate system
coordonnées^F terrestres

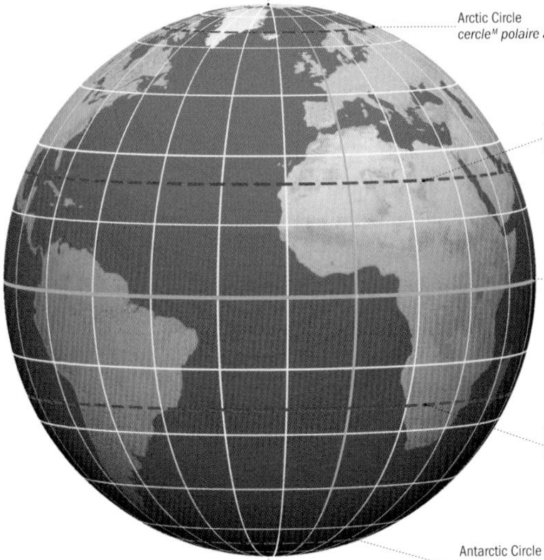

North Pole
pôle^M Nord
Arctic Circle
cercle^M polaire arctique
Northern hemisphere
hémisphère^M boréal
Tropic of Cancer
tropique^M du Cancer^M
equator
équateur^M
Southern hemisphere
hémisphère^M austral
Tropic of Capricorn
tropique^M du Capricorne^M
Antarctic Circle
cercle^M polaire antarctique
South Pole
pôle^M Sud

hemispheres
hémisphères^M

Northern hemisphere
hémisphère^M boréal
Southern hemisphere
hémisphère^M austral

Western hemisphere
hémisphère^M occidental
Eastern hemisphere
hémisphère^M oriental

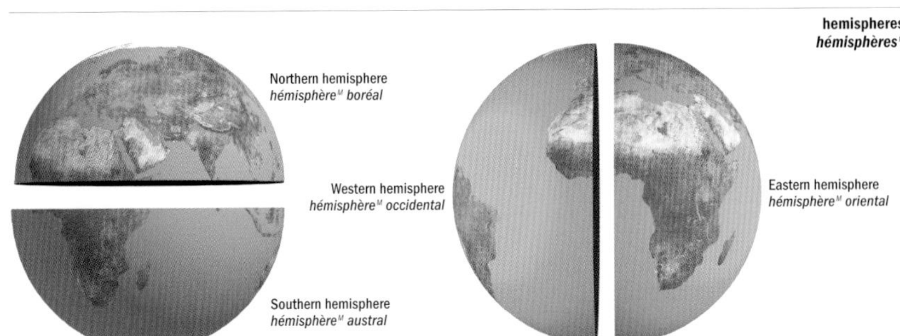

grid system
divisions^F cartographiques

lines of latitude
latitude^F

Arctic Circle
cercle^M polaire arctique

Tropic of Cancer
tropique^M du Cancer^M

Equator
équateur^M

Tropic of Capricorn
tropique^M du Capricorne^M

Antarctic Circle
cercle^M polaire antarctique

parallel
parallèle^M

lines of longitude
longitude^F

Eastern meridian
méridien^M est

prime meridian
méridien^M de Greenwich

Western meridian
méridien^M ouest

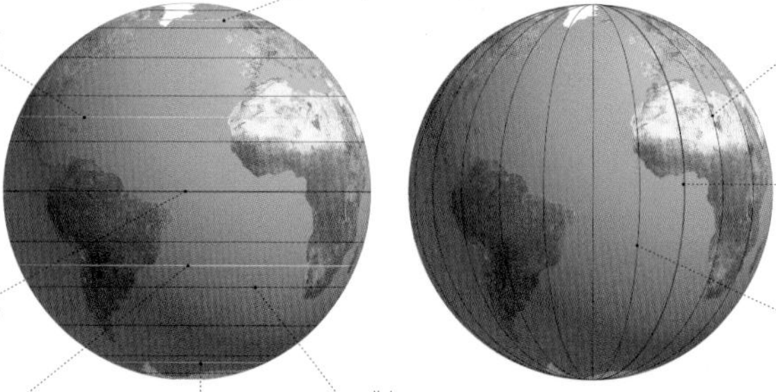

map projections
projections^F cartographiques

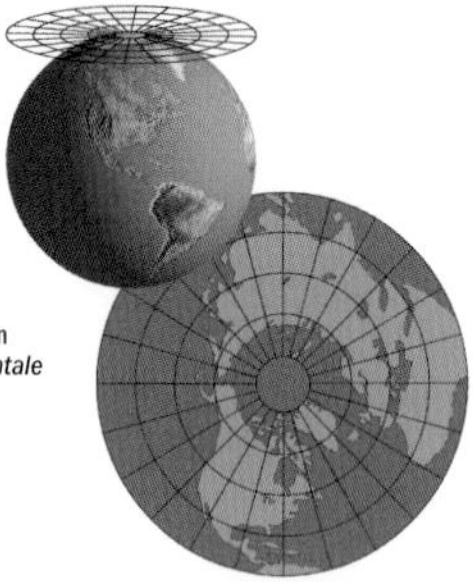

plane projection
projection^F horizontale

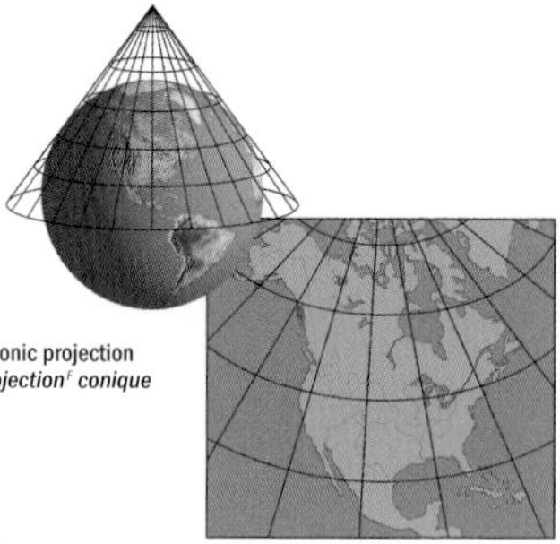

conic projection
projection^F conique

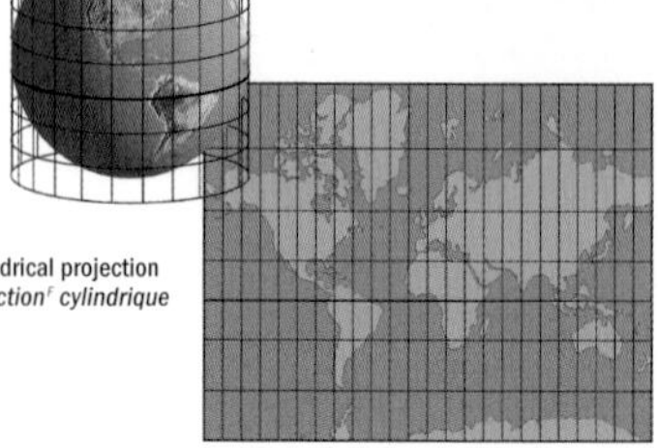

cylindrical projection
projection^F cylindrique

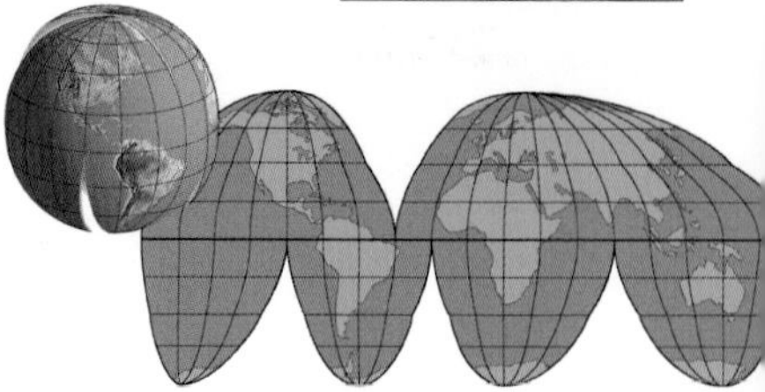

interrupted projection
projection^F interrompue

compass card
rose[F] des vents[M]

North
Nord[M]

North-Northwest
Nord[M] Nord-Ouest

North-Northeast
Nord[M] Nord-Est

Northwest
Nord[M] Ouest

Northeast
Nord[M] Est

West-Northwest
Ouest[M] Nord-Ouest

East-Northeast
Est[M] Nord-Est

West
Ouest[M]

East
Est[M]

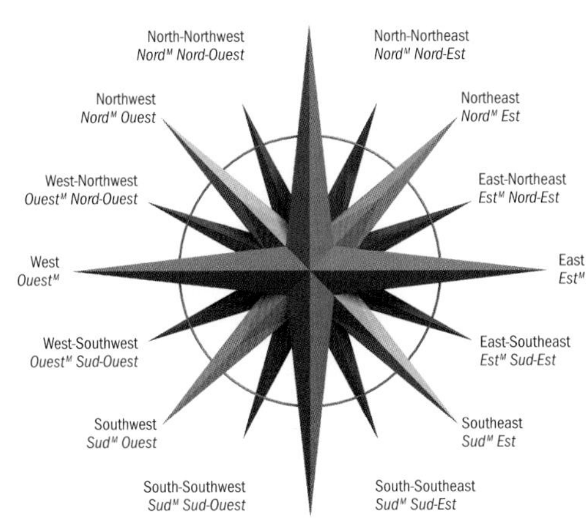

West-Southwest
Ouest[M] Sud-Ouest

East-Southeast
Est[M] Sud-Est

Southwest
Sud[M] Ouest

Southeast
Sud[M] Est

South-Southwest
Sud[M] Sud-Ouest

South-Southeast
Sud[M] Sud-Est

South
Sud[M]

political map
carte[F] politique

province
province[F]

internal boundary
division[F] territoriale

city
grande ville[F]

frontier
frontière[F]

capital
capitale[F]

state
État[M]

country
pays[M]

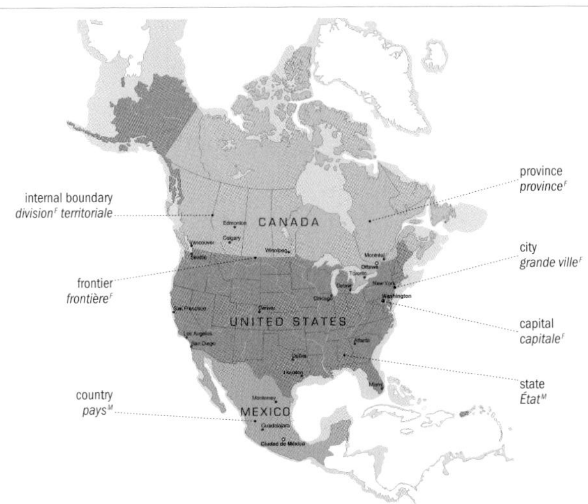

physical map
carte*[F] *physique

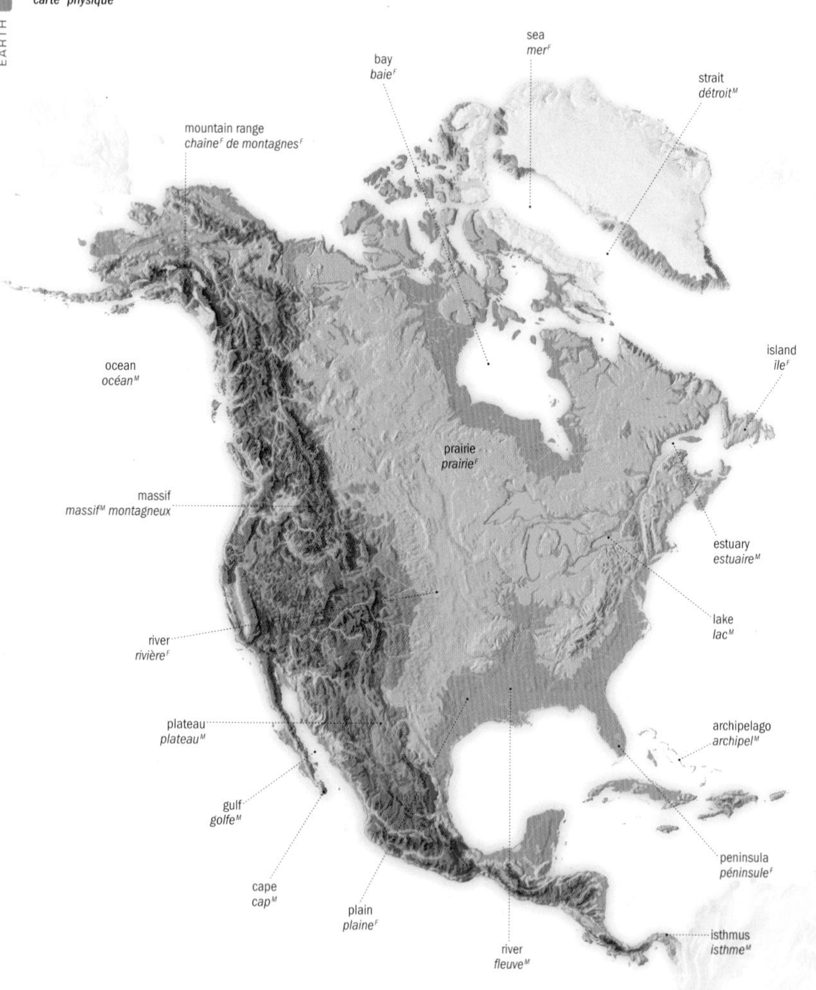

urban map
plan[M] urbain

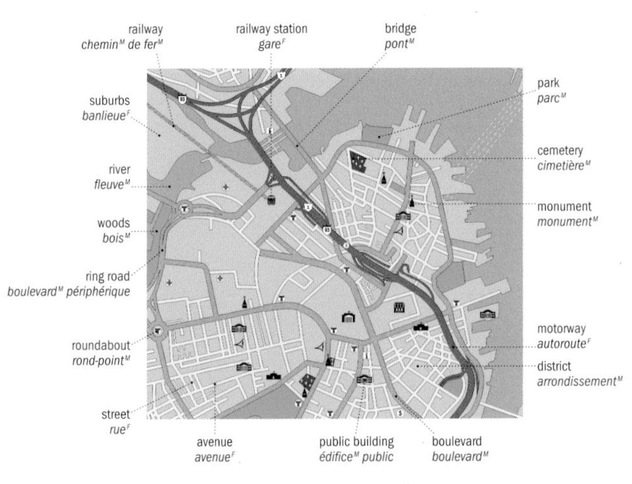

road map
carte[F] routière

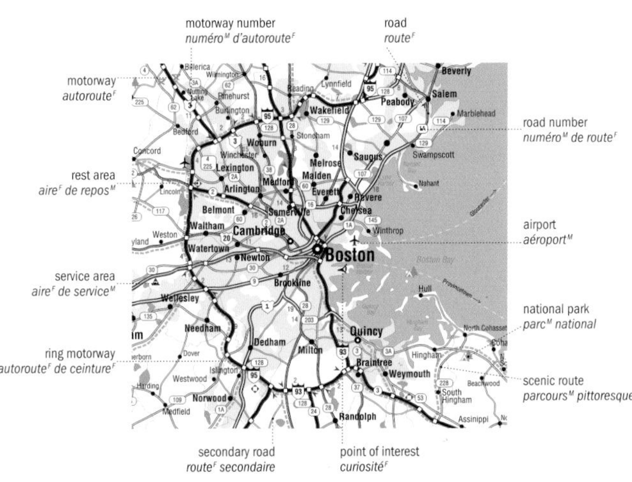

section of the Earth's crust

coupe[F] de la croûte[F] terrestre

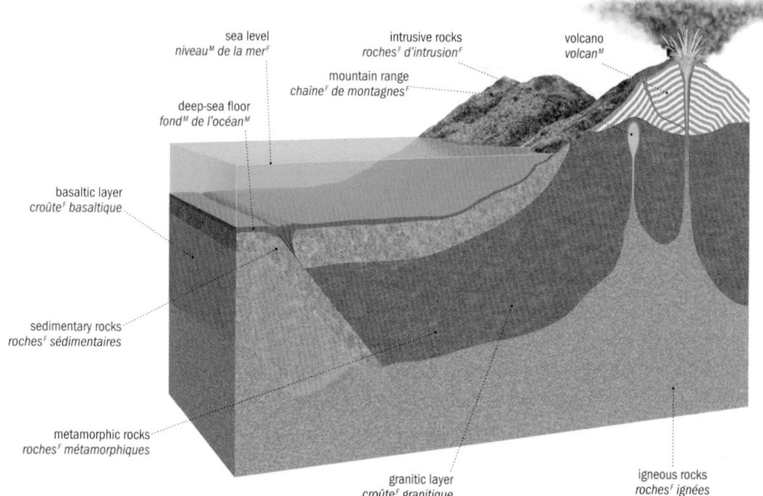

structure of the Earth

structure[F] de la Terre[F]

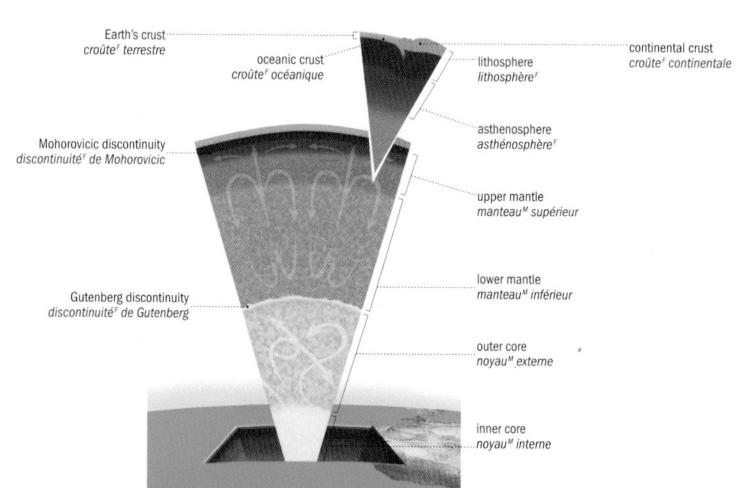

tectonic plates

plaques[F] tectoniques

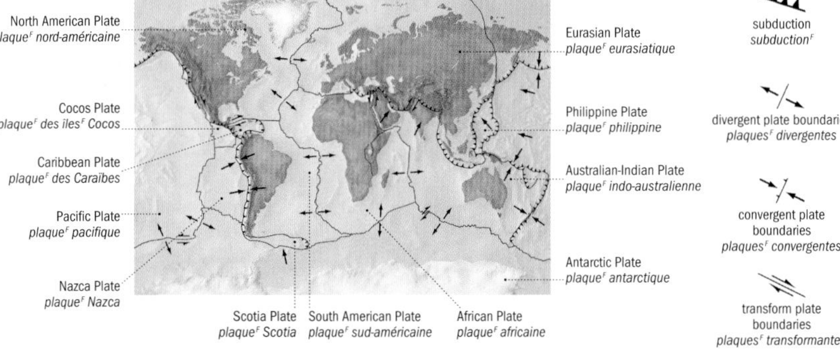

earthquake

séisme[M]

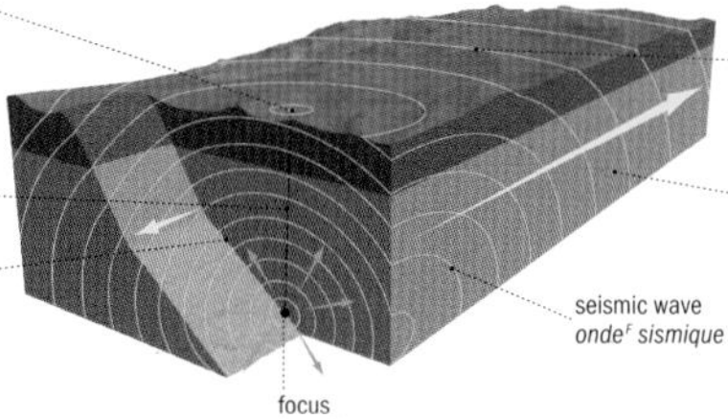

epicentre
épicentre[M]

isoseismal line
ligne[F] isosiste

depth of focus
profondeur[F] du foyer[M]

Earth's crust
croûte[F] terrestre

fault
faille[F]

seismic wave
onde[F] sismique

focus
foyer[M]

seismographs
sismographes[M]

vertical seismograph
sismographe[M] vertical

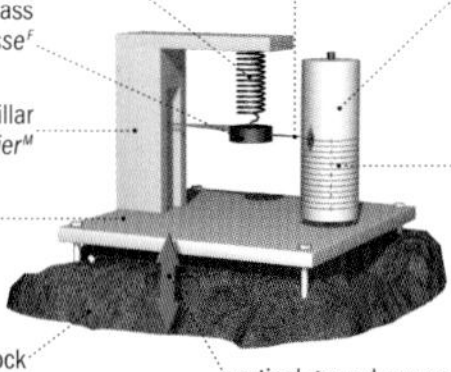

spring
ressort[M]

pen
plume[F]

rotating drum
cylindre[M] enregistreur

mass
masse[F]

pillar
pilier[M]

seismogram
sismogramme[M]

stand
socle[M]

bedrock
roc[M]

vertical ground movement
mouvement[M] vertical du sol[M]

horizontal seismograph
sismographe[M] horizontal

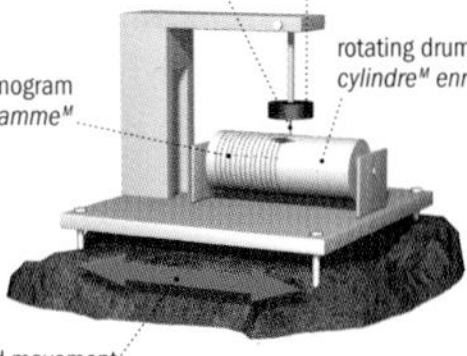

mass
masse[F]

pen
plume[F]

rotating drum
cylindre[M] enregistreur

seismogram
sismogramme[M]

horizontal ground movement
mouvement[M] horizontal du sol[M]

volcano

volcan^M

volcano during eruption
volcan^M en éruption^F

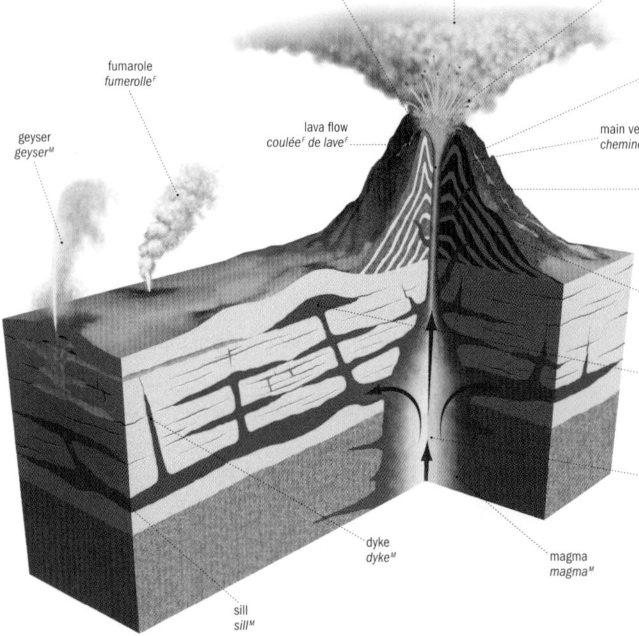

crater
cratère^M
cloud of volcanic ash
nuage^M de cendres^F
volcanic bomb
bombe^F volcanique
fumarole
fumerolle^F
lava layer
couche^F de laves^F
geyser
geyser^M
lava flow
coulée^F de lave^F
main vent
cheminée^F
side vent
cône^M adventif
ash layer
couche^F de cendres^F
laccolith
laccolite^F
magma chamber
réservoir^M magmatique
dyke
dyke^M
magma
magma^M
sill
sill^M

examples of volcanoes
exemples^M de volcans^M

explosive volcano
volcan^M explosif

effusive volcano
volcan^M effusif

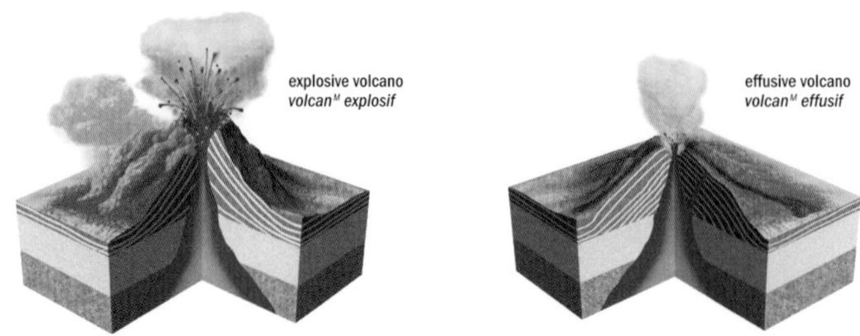

mountain

montagne[F]

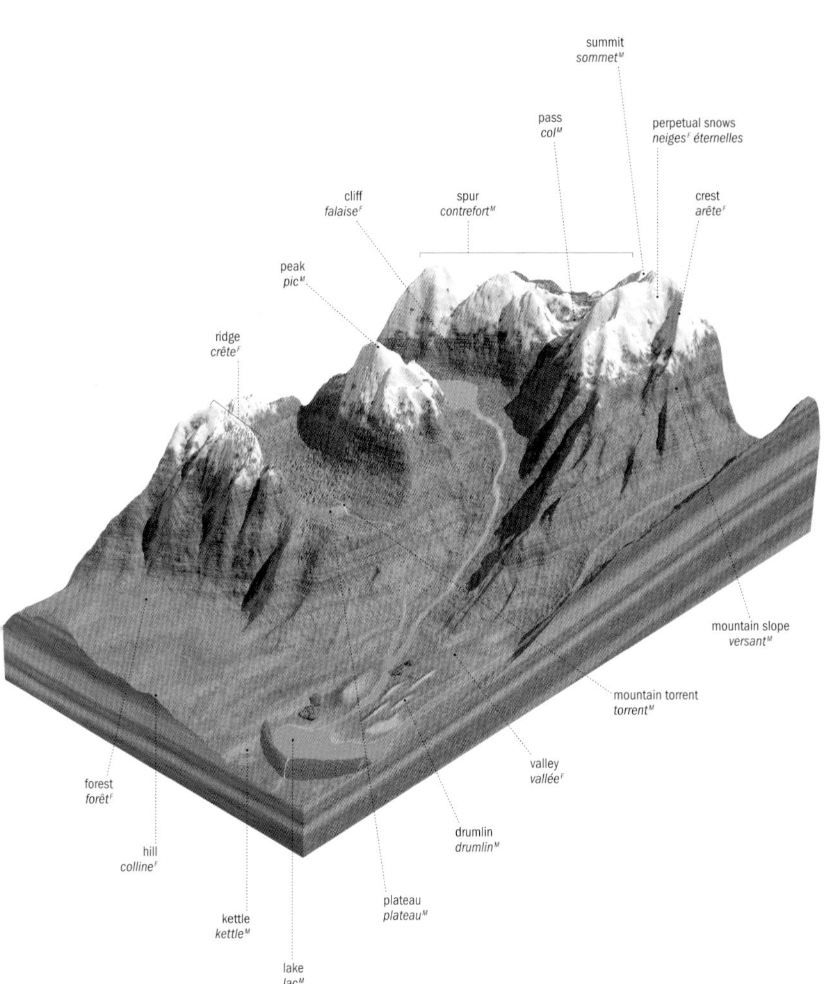

glacier

glacier[M]

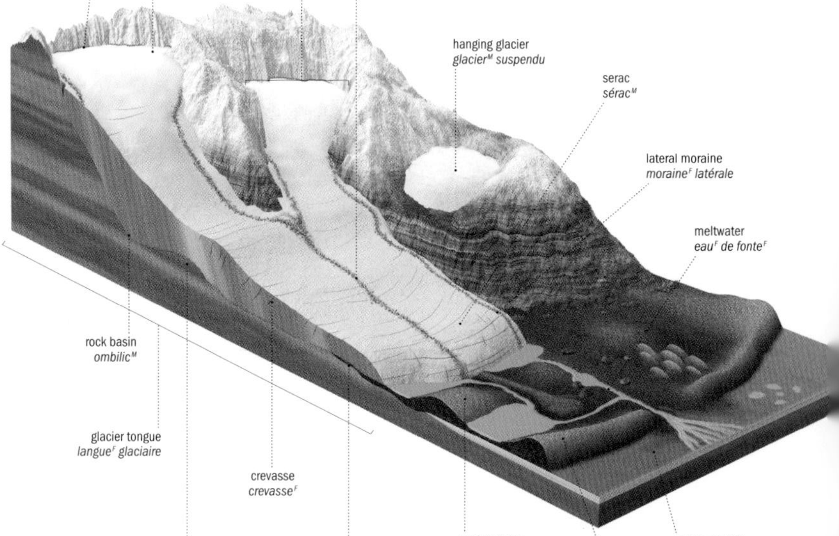

bergschrund
rimaye[F]

glacial cirque
cirque[M] glaciaire

névé
névé[M]

medial moraine
moraine[F] médiane

hanging glacier
glacier[M] suspendu

serac
sérac[M]

lateral moraine
moraine[F] latérale

meltwater
eau[F] de fonte[F]

rock basin
ombilic[M]

glacier tongue
langue[F] glaciaire

crevasse
crevasse[F]

riegel
verrou[M]

ground moraine
moraine[F] de fond[M]

end moraine
moraine[F] frontale

outwash plain
plaine[F] fluvio-glaciaire

terminal moraine
moraine[F] terminale

cave

grotte^F

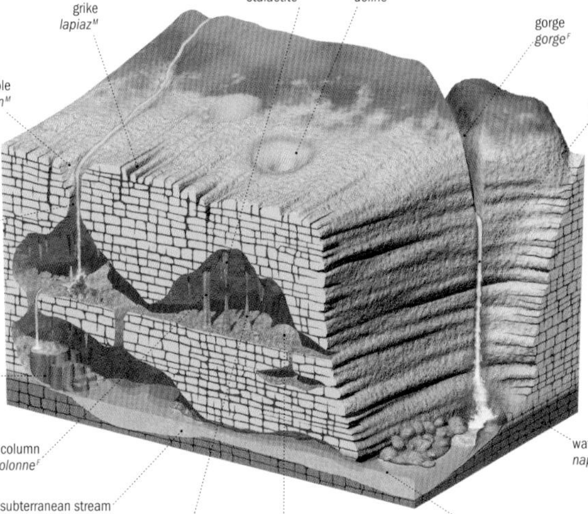

stalactite
stalactite^F
dolina
doline^F
grike
lapiaz^M
gorge
gorge^F
pothole
aven^M
waterfall
chute^F
swallow hole
gouffre^M
gour
gour^M
column
colonne^F
water table
nappe^F phréatique
subterranean stream
rivière^F souterraine
stalagmite
stalagmite^F
dry gallery
galerie^F sèche
resurgence
résurgence^F

landslides

mouvements^M de terrain^M

creep
reptation^F

rockslide
éboulement^M

mudflow
coulée^F de boue^F

earthflow
glissement^M de terrain^M

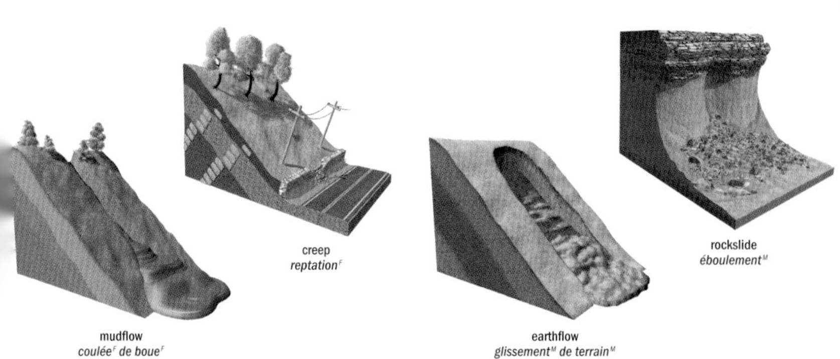

watercourse

cours[M] d'eau[F]

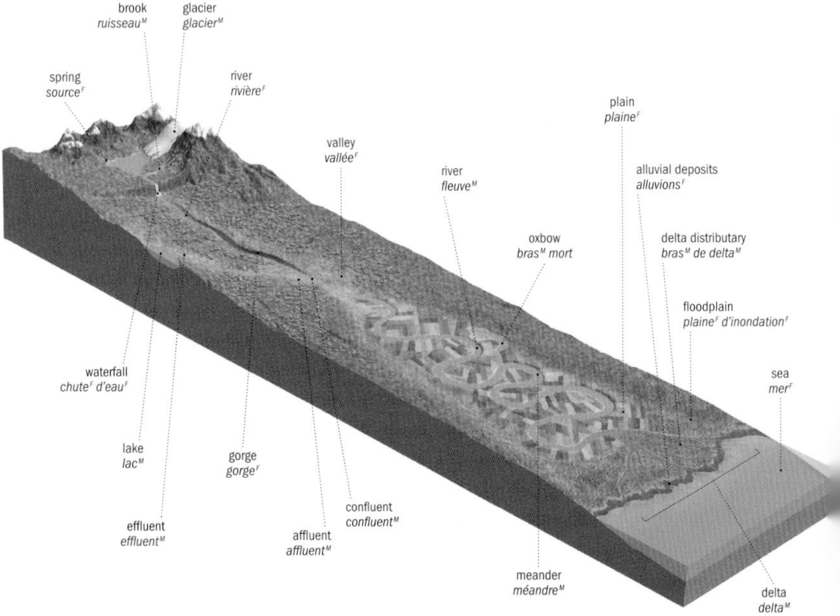

brook
ruisseau[M]

glacier
glacier[M]

spring
source[F]

river
rivière[F]

plain
plaine[F]

valley
vallée[F]

river
fleuve[M]

alluvial deposits
alluvions[F]

oxbow
bras[M] mort

delta distributary
bras[M] de delta[M]

floodplain
plaine[F] d'inondation[F]

waterfall
chute[F] d'eau[F]

sea
mer[F]

lake
lac[M]

gorge
gorge[F]

confluent
confluent[M]

effluent
effluent[M]

affluent
affluent[M]

meander
méandre[M]

delta
delta[M]

lakes

lacs[M]

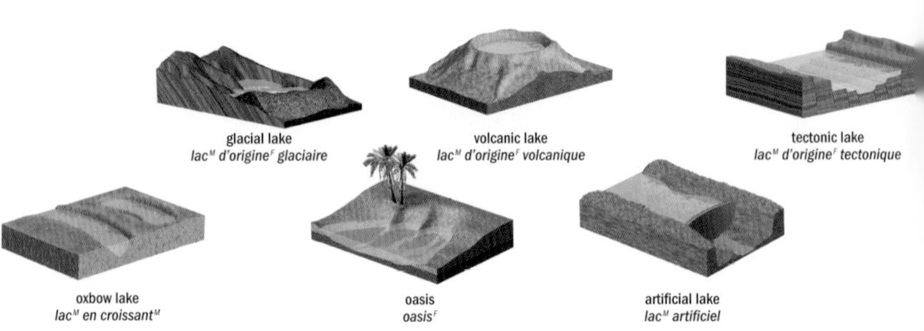

glacial lake
lac[M] d'origine[F] glaciaire

volcanic lake
lac[M] d'origine[F] volcanique

tectonic lake
lac[M] d'origine[F] tectonique

oxbow lake
lac[M] en croissant[M]

oasis
oasis[F]

artificial lake
lac[M] artificiel

wave
vague[F]

crest
crête[F]
wave length
longueur[F] de la vague[F]
breaker
vague[F] déferlante
shore
côte[F]
wave height
hauteur[F] de la vague[F]
wave base
base[F] de la vague[F]
still water level
niveau[M] d'équilibre[M]
trough
creux[M]
sandbank
banc[M] de sable[M]
foam
écume[F]

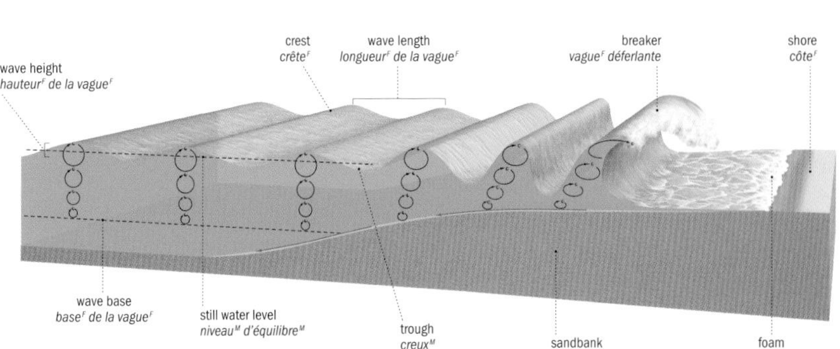

ocean floor
fond[M] de l'océan[M]

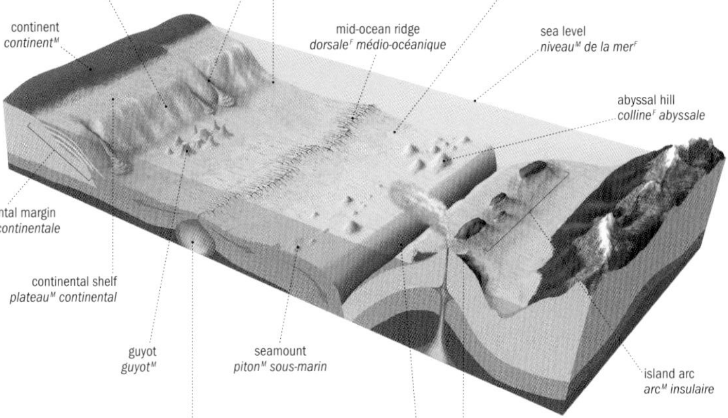

continental slope
talus[M] continental
submarine canyon
canyon[M] sous-marin
continental rise
glacis[M] précontinental
abyssal plain
plaine[F] abyssale
continent
continent[M]
mid-ocean ridge
dorsale[F] médio-océanique
sea level
niveau[M] de la mer[F]
abyssal hill
colline[F] abyssale
continental margin
marge[F] continentale
continental shelf
plateau[M] continental
guyot
guyot[M]
seamount
piton[M] sous-marin
island arc
arc[M] insulaire
magma
magma[M]
trench
fosse[F] abyssale
volcanic island
île[F] volcanique

ocean trenches and ridges

fosses^F et dorsales^F océaniques

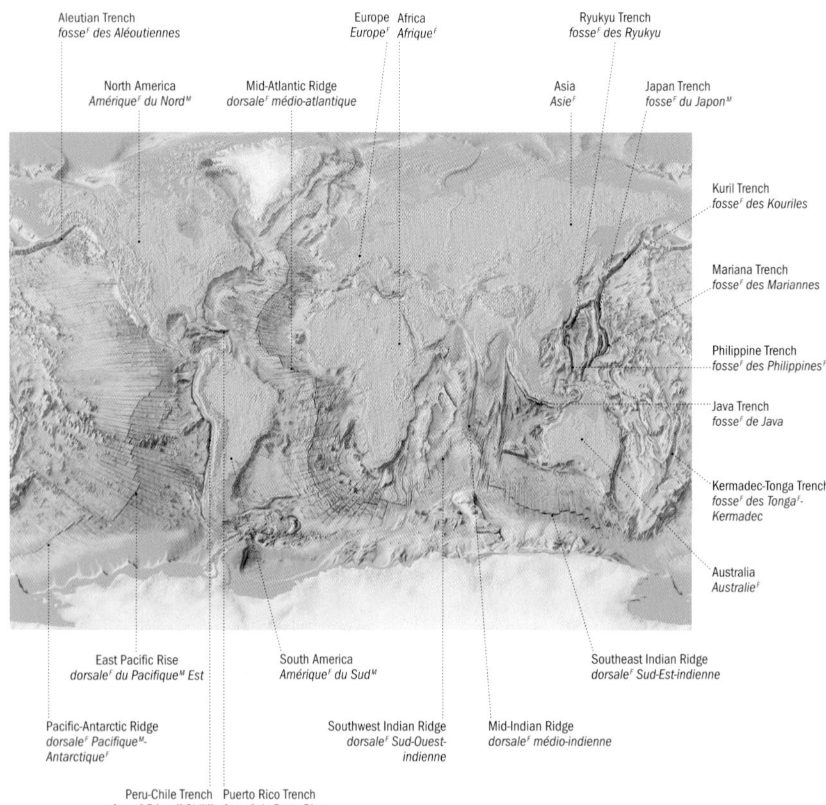

common coastal features

configuration[F] du littoral[M]

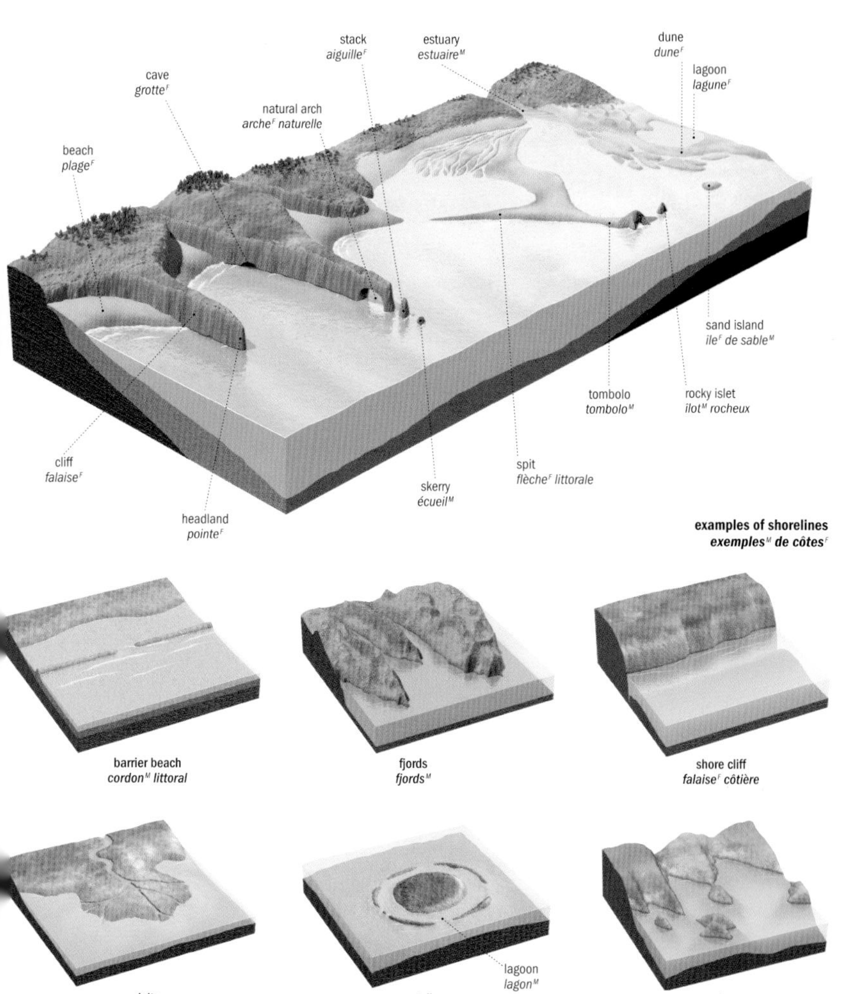

desert

désert[M]

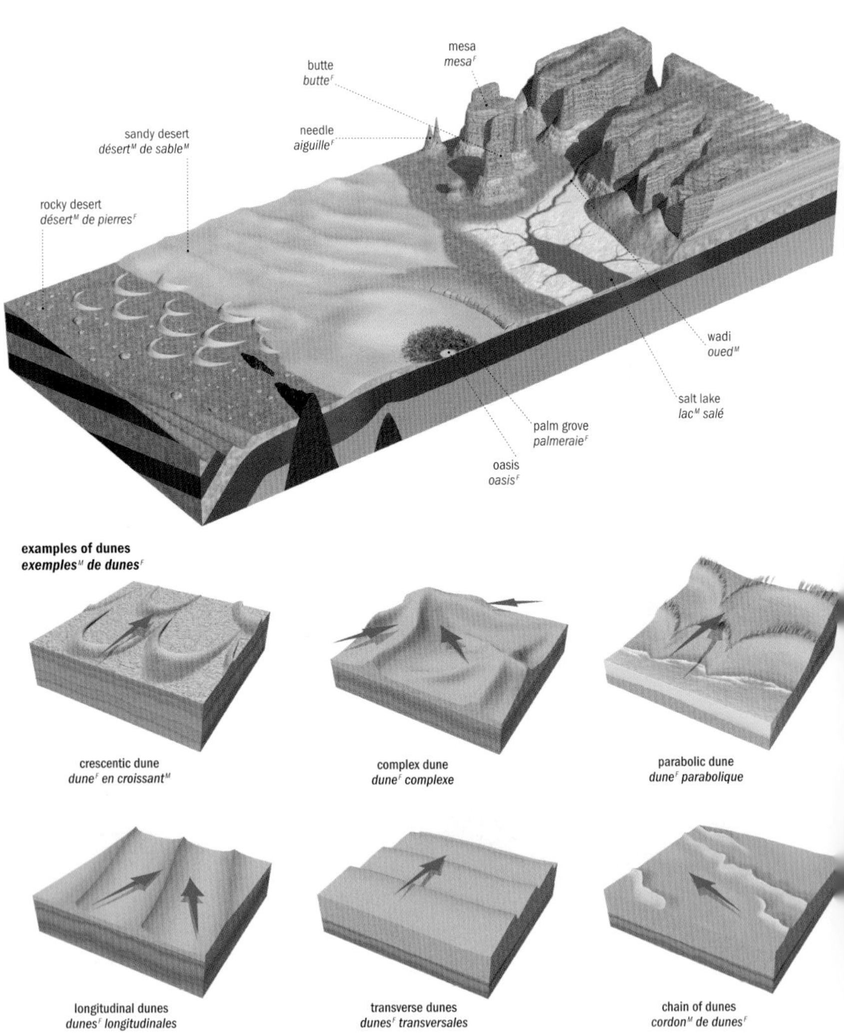

profile of the Earth's atmosphere

coupe[F] de l'atmosphère[F] terrestre

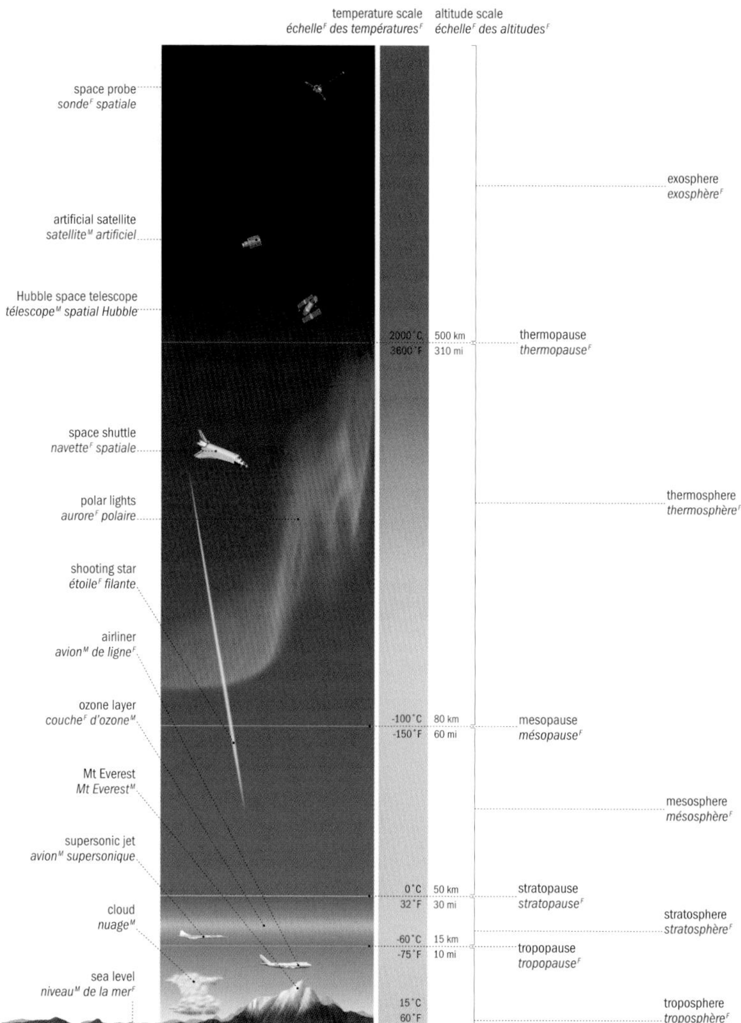

seasons of the year

cycle[M] des saisons[F]

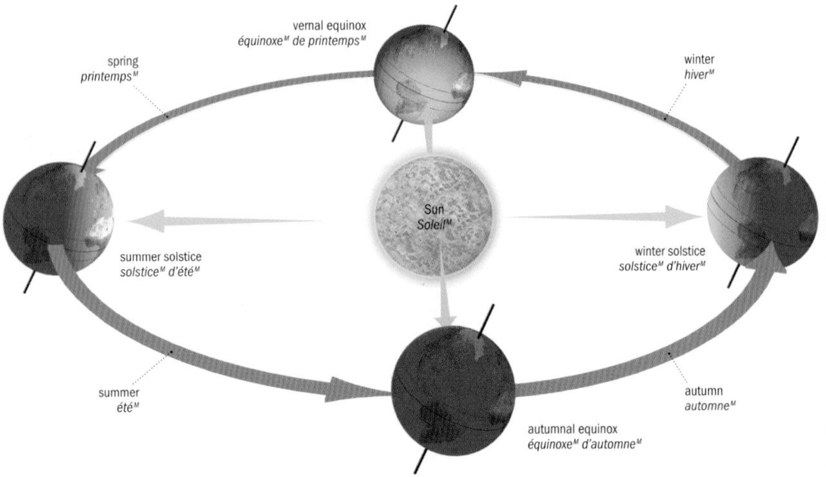

vernal equinox
équinoxe[M] de printemps[M]

spring
printemps[M]

winter
hiver[M]

Sun
Soleil[M]

summer solstice
solstice[M] d'été[M]

winter solstice
solstice[M] d'hiver[M]

summer
été[M]

autumn
automne[M]

autumnal equinox
équinoxe[M] d'automne[M]

meteorological forecast

prévision[F] météorologique

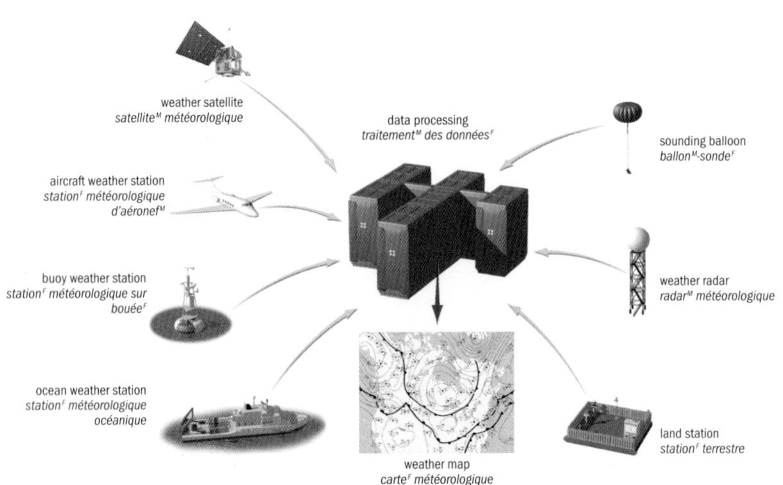

weather map

carte[F] météorologique

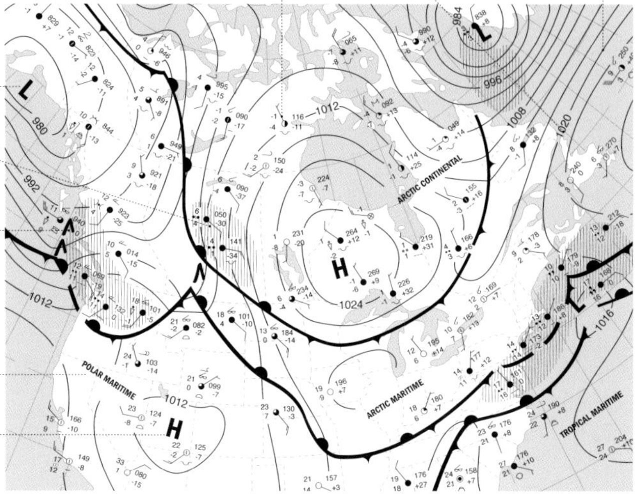

wind direction and speed
direction[F] et force[F] du vent[M]
barometric pressure
pression[F] barométrique
isobar
isobare[F]
depression
dépression[F]
precipitation area
zone[F] de précipitation[F]
trough
creux[M] barométrique
type of air mass
type[M] de la masse[F] d'air[M]
anticyclone
anticyclone[M]
L
H
980
992
1012
1024
984
996
1008
1020
1016
ARCTIC CONTINENTAL
POLAR MARITIME
ARCTIC MARITIME
TROPICAL MARITIME

station model

disposition[F] des informations[F] d'une station[F]

type of high cloud
type[M] de nuage[M] élevé
type of middle cloud
type[M] de nuage[M] moyen
wind speed
force[F] du vent[M]
station circle
cercle[M] de la station[F]
air temperature
température[F] de l'air[M]
-2
995
sea-level pressure
pression[F] au niveau[M] de la mer[F]
sky coverage
nébulosité[F]
wind direction
direction[F] du vent[M]
+16
barometric tendency
tendance[F] barométrique
present state of weather
état[M] présent du temps[M]
-6
temperature of dew point
température[F] du point[M] de rosée[F]
type of low cloud
type[M] de nuage[M] bas
pressure change
évolution[F] de la pression[F]

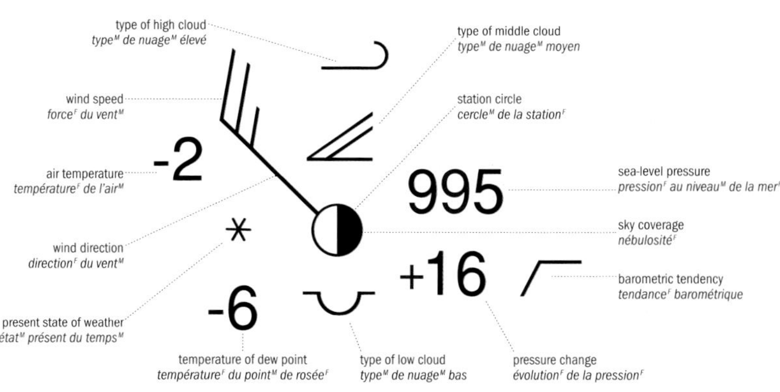

climates of the world

climats[M] du monde[M]

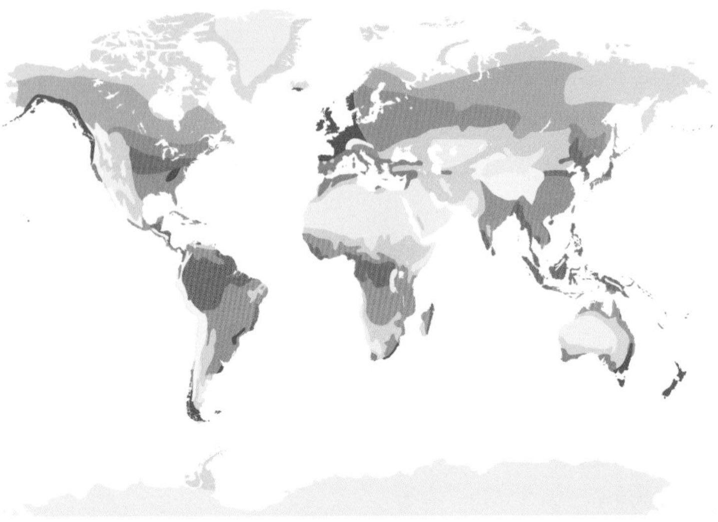

tropical climates
climats[M] tropicaux

tropical rain forest
tropical humide

tropical wet-and-dry (savanna)
tropical humide et sec (savane[F])

dry climates
climats[M] arides

steppe
steppe[F]

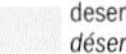
desert
désert[M]

cold temperate climates
climats[M] tempérés froids

humid continental - hot summer
continental humide, à été[M] chaud

humid continental - warm summer
continental humide, à été[M] frais

subarctic
subarctique

warm temperate climates
climats[M] tempérés chauds

humid subtropical
subtropical humide

Mediterranean subtropical
méditerranéen

marine
océanique

polar climates
climats[M] polaires

polar tundra
toundra[F]

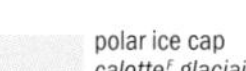
polar ice cap
calotte[F] glaciaire

highland climates
climats[M] de montagne[F]

highland
climats[M] de montagne[F]

precipitations

précipitations[F]

winter precipitations
précipitations[F] hivernales

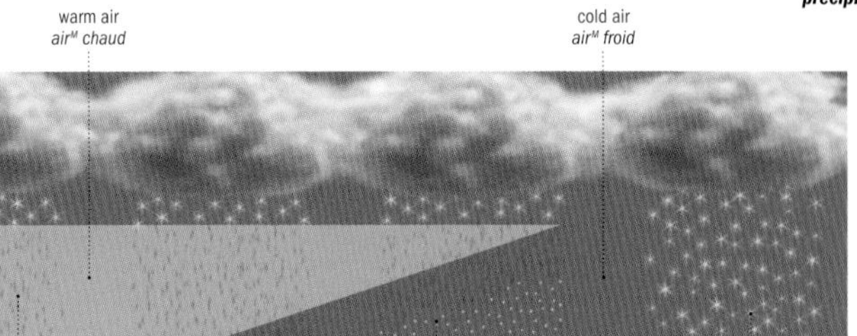

stormy sky
ciel[M] d'orage[M]

dew
rosée[F]

mist
brume[F]

fog
brouillard[M]

rime
givre[M]

glazed frost
verglas[M]

clouds

nuages[M]

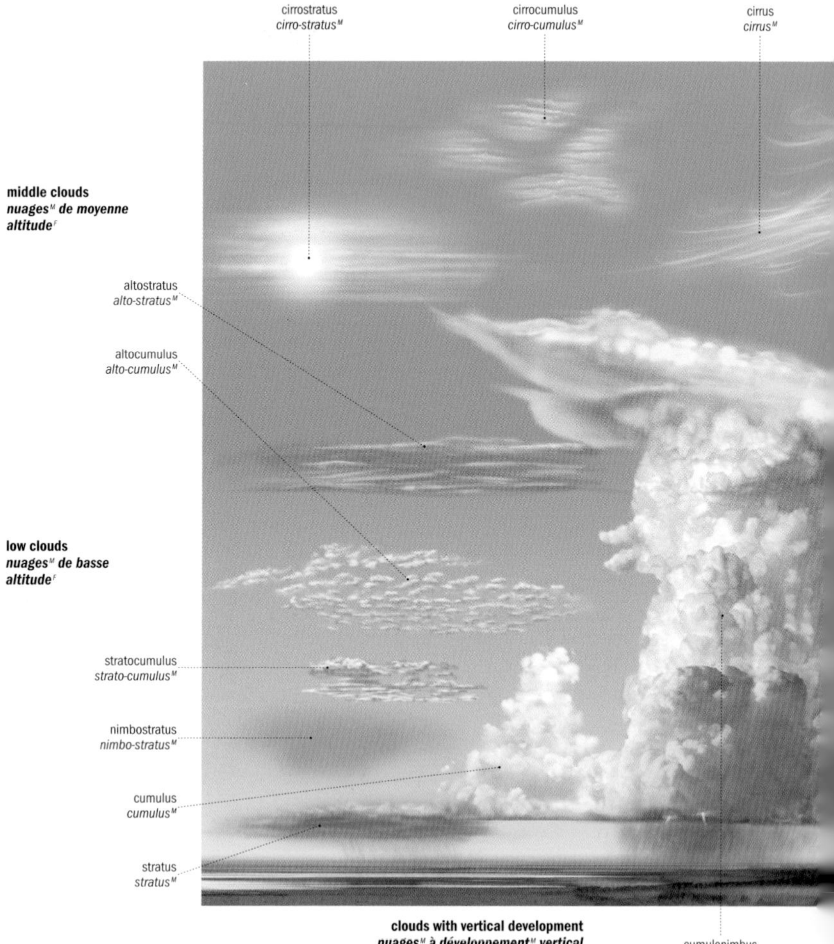

tornado and waterspout

tornade[F] et trombe[F] marine

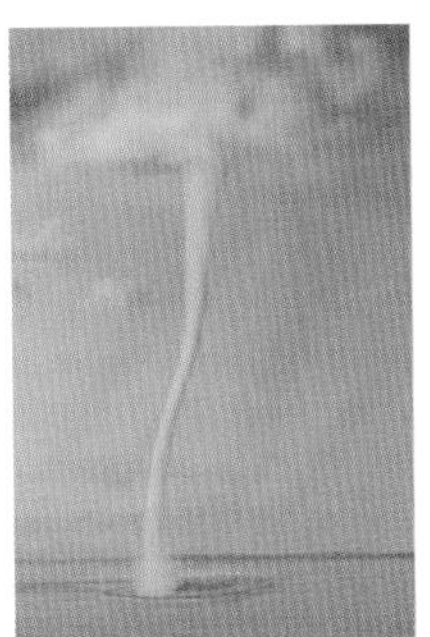

waterspout
trombe[F] marine

wall cloud
mur[M] de nuages[M]
funnel cloud
nuage[M] en entonnoir[M]
debris
buisson[M]

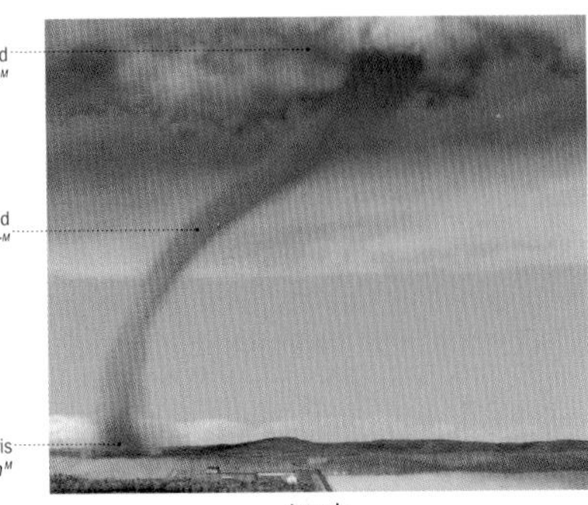

tornado
tornade[F]

tropical cyclone

cyclone[M] tropical

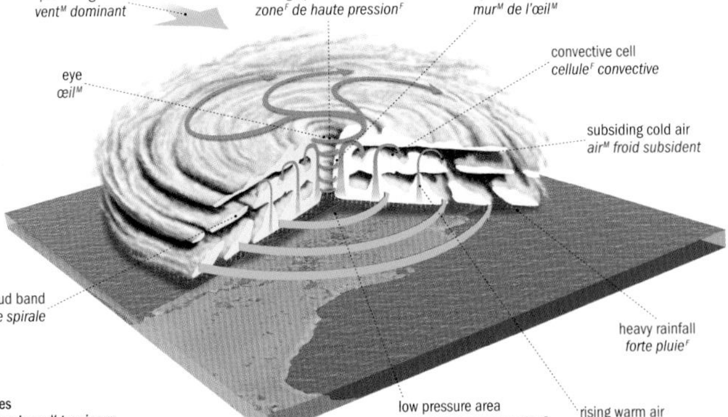

prevailing wind
vent[M] dominant
high pressure area
zone[F] de haute pression[F]
eye wall
mur[M] de l'œil[M]
convective cell
cellule[F] convective
eye
œil[M]
subsiding cold air
air[M] froid subsident
spiral cloud band
bande[F] nuageuse spirale
heavy rainfall
forte pluie[F]
low pressure area
zone[F] de basse pression[F]
rising warm air
air[M] chaud ascendant

tropical cyclone names
dénominations[F] des cyclones[M] tropicaux

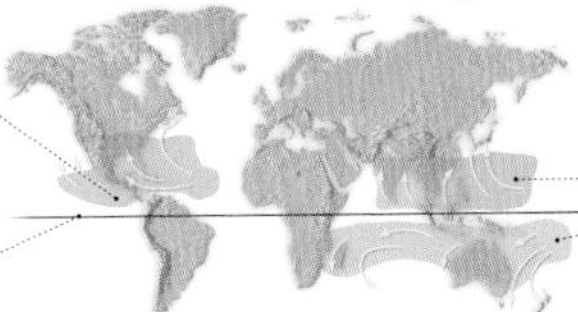

hurricane
ouragan[M]
typhoon
typhon[M]
equator
équateur[M]
cyclone
cyclone[M]

vegetation and biosphere

végétation[F] et biosphère[F]

vegetation regions
distribution[F] de la végétation[F]

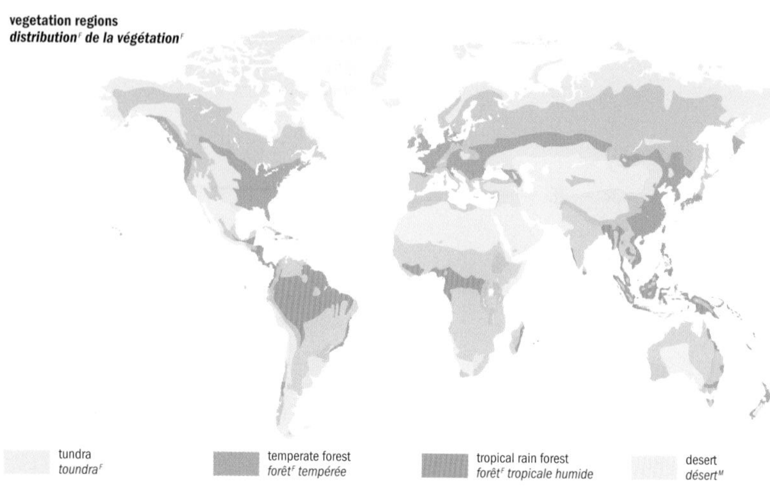

tundra
toundra[F]

temperate forest
forêt[F] tempérée

tropical rain forest
forêt[F] tropicale humide

desert
désert[M]

boreal forest
forêt[F] boréale

grassland
prairie[F] tempérée

savanna
savane[F]

maquis
maquis[M]

elevation zones and vegetation
paysage[M] végétal selon l'altitude[F]

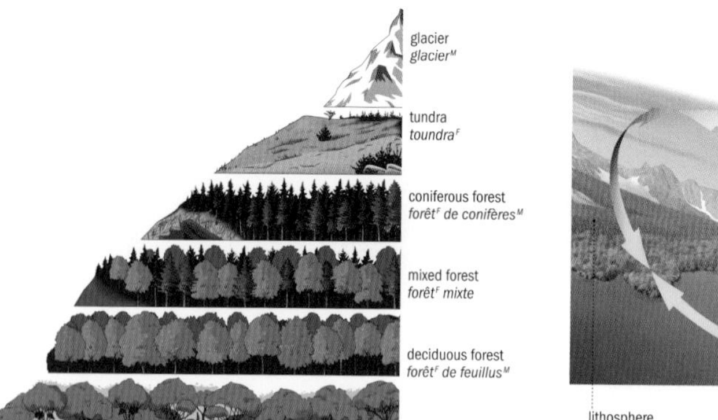

structure of the biosphere
structure[F] de la biosphère[F]

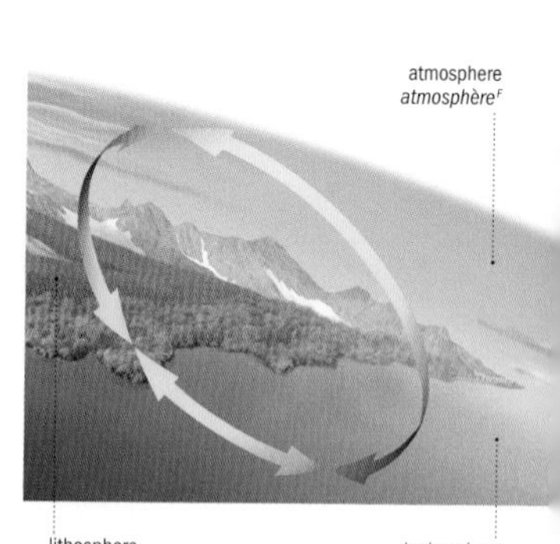

food chain

chaîne^F alimentaire

carnivores
carnivores^M
tertiary consumers
consommateurs^M tertiaires
heterotrophs
hétérotrophes^M
carnivores
carnivores^M
secondary consumers
consommateurs^M secondaires
autotrophs
autotrophes^M
herbivores
herbivores^M
primary consumers
consommateurs^M primaires
decomposers
décomposeurs^M
basic source of food
source^F alimentaire fondamentale
inorganic matter
matière^F inorganique

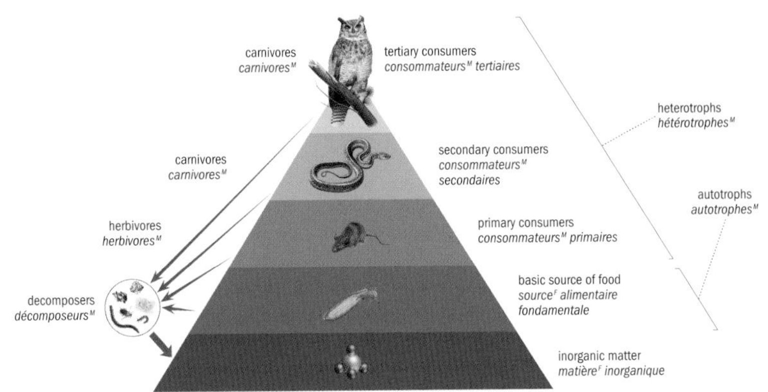

hydrologic cycle

cycle^M de l'eau^F

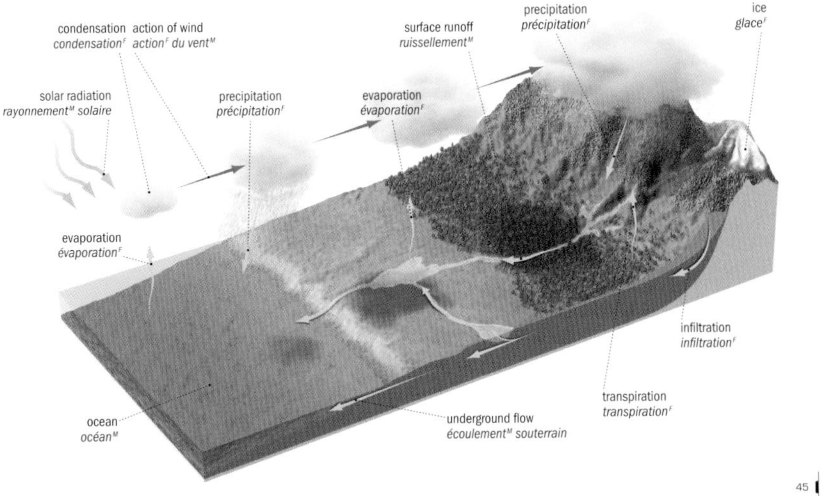

condensation
condensation^F
action of wind
action^F du vent^M
surface runoff
ruissellement^M
precipitation
précipitation^F
ice
glace^F
solar radiation
rayonnement^M solaire
precipitation
précipitation^F
evaporation
évaporation^F
evaporation
évaporation^F
infiltration
infiltration^F
transpiration
transpiration^F
ocean
océan^M
underground flow
écoulement^M souterrain

greenhouse effect

effet[M] de serre[F]

natural greenhouse effect
effet[M] de serre[F] naturel

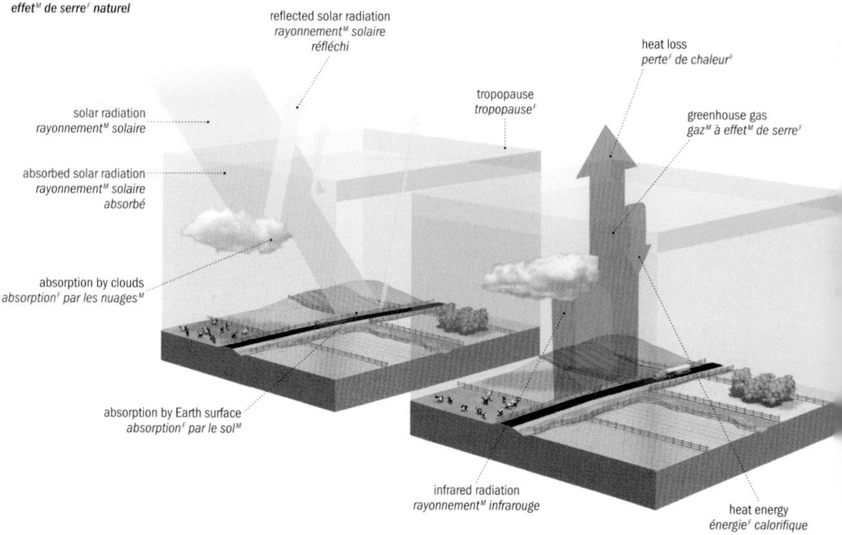

reflected solar radiation
rayonnement[M] solaire réfléchi

heat loss
perte[F] de chaleur[F]

tropopause
tropopause[F]

solar radiation
rayonnement[M] solaire

greenhouse gas
gaz[M] à effet[M] de serre[F]

absorbed solar radiation
rayonnement[M] solaire absorbé

absorption by clouds
absorption[F] par les nuages[M]

absorption by Earth surface
absorption[F] par le sol[M]

infrared radiation
rayonnement[M] infrarouge

heat energy
énergie[F] calorifique

enhanced greenhouse effect
augmentation[F] de l'effet[M] de serre[F]

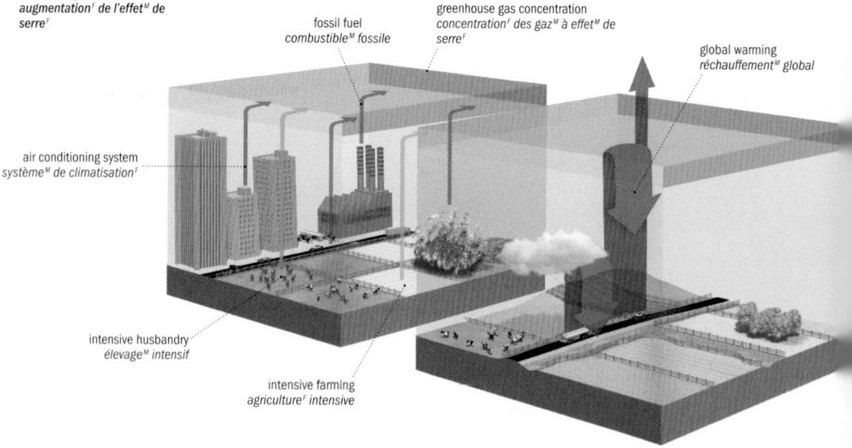

fossil fuel
combustible[M] fossile

greenhouse gas concentration
concentration[F] des gaz[M] à effet[M] de serre[F]

global warming
réchauffement[M] global

air conditioning system
système[M] de climatisation[F]

intensive husbandry
élevage[M] intensif

intensive farming
agriculture[F] intensive

air pollution

pollution[F] de l'air[M]

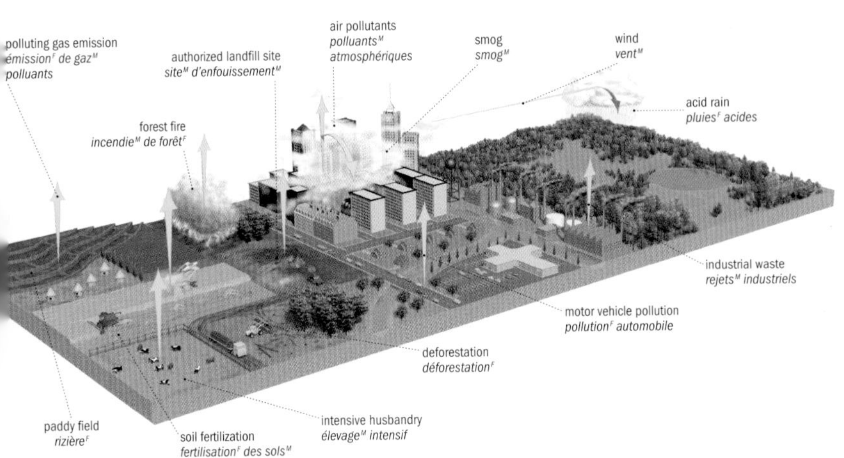

land pollution

pollution[F] du sol[M]

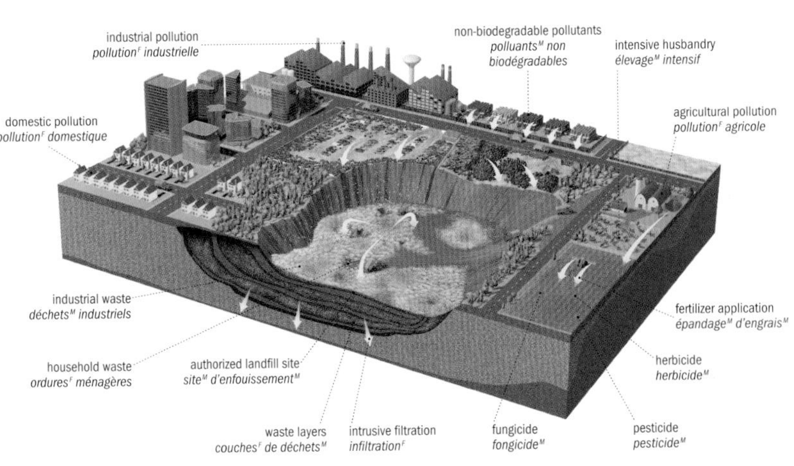

water pollution

pollution[F] de l'eau[F]

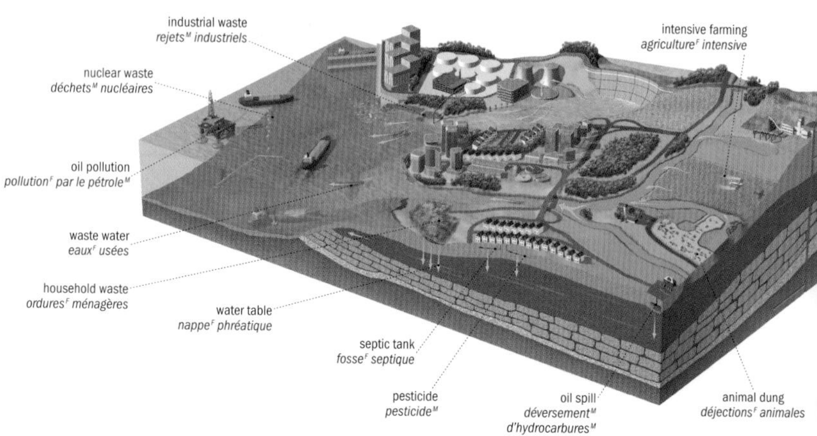

acid rain

pluies[F] acides

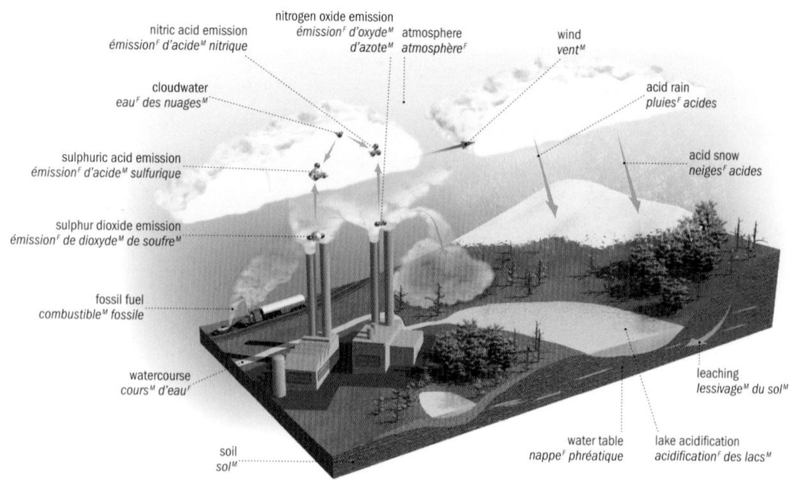

selective sorting of waste

tri[M] sélectif des déchets[M]

sorting plant
centre[M] de tri[M]

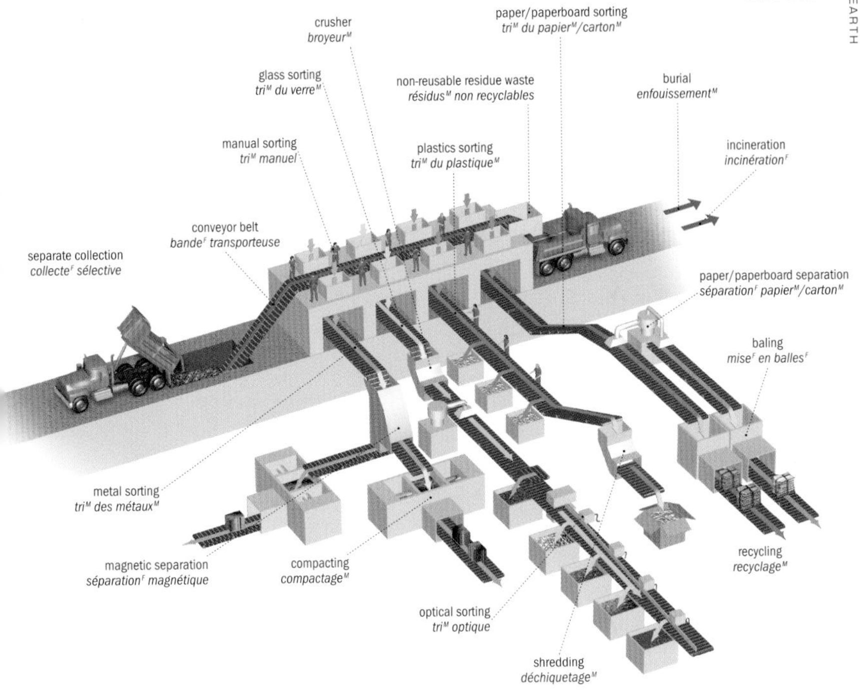

crusher
broyeur[M]

paper/paperboard sorting
tri[M] du papier[M]/carton[M]

glass sorting
tri[M] du verre[M]

non-reusable residue waste
résidus[M] non recyclables

burial
enfouissement[M]

manual sorting
tri[M] manuel

plastics sorting
tri[M] du plastique[M]

incineration
incinération[F]

conveyor belt
bande[F] transporteuse

separate collection
collecte[F] sélective

paper/paperboard separation
séparation[F] papier[M]/carton[M]

baling
mise[F] en balles[F]

metal sorting
tri[M] des métaux[M]

recycling
recyclage[M]

magnetic separation
séparation[F] magnétique

compacting
compactage[M]

optical sorting
tri[M] optique

shredding
déchiquetage[M]

recycling containers
conteneurs[M] de collecte[F] sélective

paper recycling container
conteneur[M] à papier[M]

glass recycling container
conteneur[M] à verre[M]

aluminium recycling container
conteneur[M] à boîtes[F] métalliques

paper collection unit
colonne[F] de collecte[F] du papier[M]

glass collection unit
colonne[F] de collecte[F] du verre[M]

recycling bin
bac[M] de recyclage[M]

plant cell

cellule^F végétale

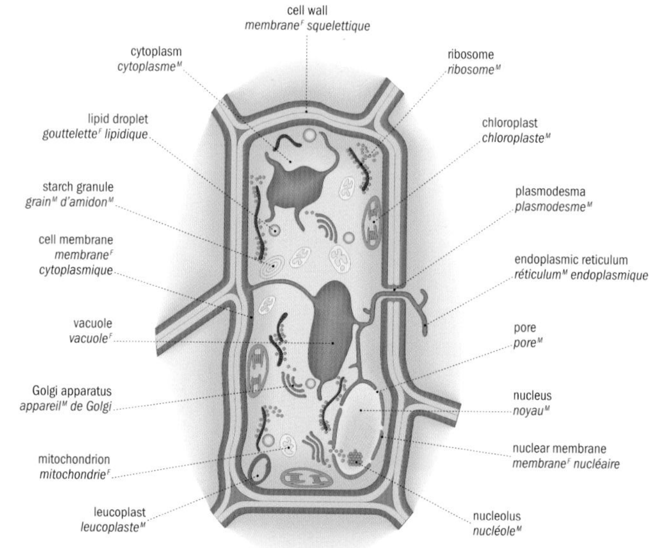

lichen

lichen^M

structure of a lichen
structure^F d'un lichen^M

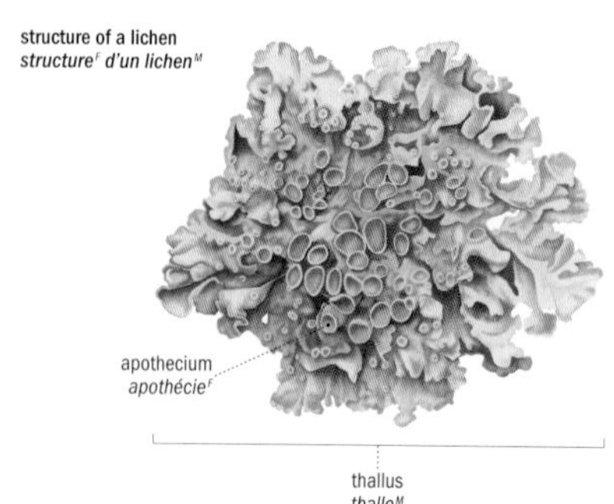

examples of lichens
exemples^M de lichens^M

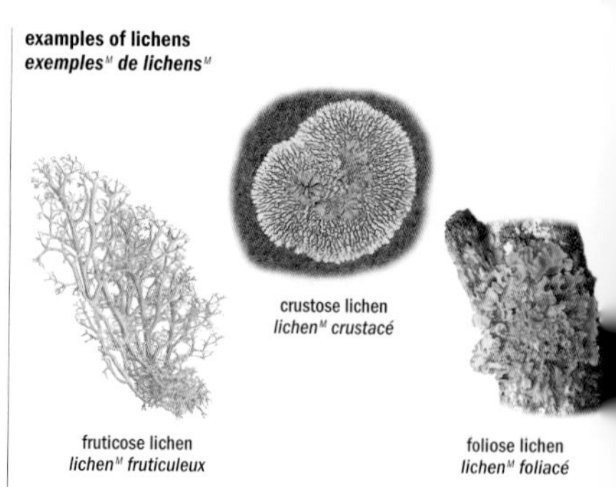

moss
mousse[F]

structure of a moss
structure[F] d'une mousse[F]

capsule
capsule[F]
stalk
pédicelle[M]
leaf
feuille[F]
stem
tige[F]
rhizoid
rhizoïde[M]

examples of mosses
exemples[M] de mousses[F]

prickly sphagnum
sphaigne[F] squarreuse

common hair cap moss
polytric[M] commun

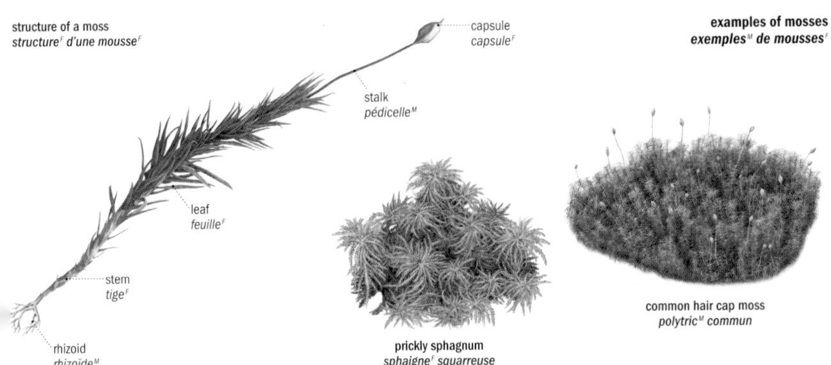

alga
algue[F]

structure of an alga
structure[F] d'une algue[F]

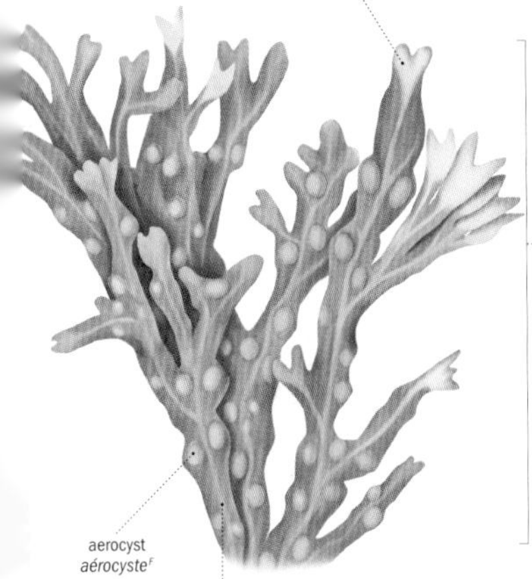

receptacle
réceptacle[M]
thallus
thalle[M]
aerocyst
aérocyste[F]
midrib
nervure[F] médiane

examples of algae
exemples[M] d'algues[F]

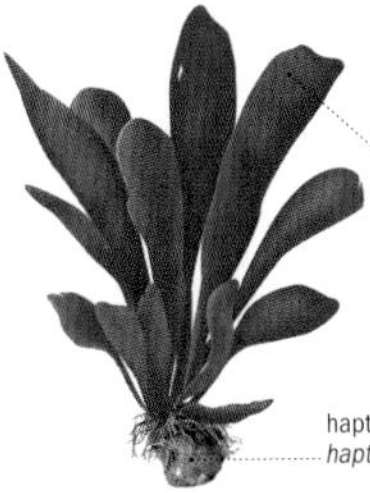

lamina
fronde[F]
hapteron
haptère[F]

red alga
algue[F] rouge

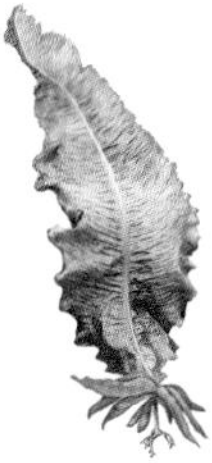

green alga
algue[F] verte

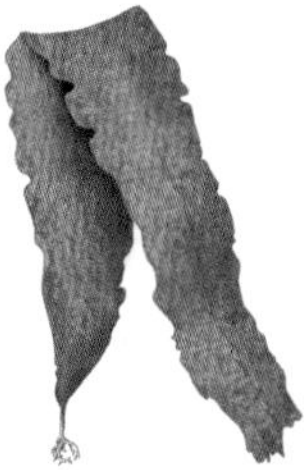

brown alga
algue[F] brune

mushroom

champignon[M]

structure of a mushroom
structure[F] d'un champignon[M]

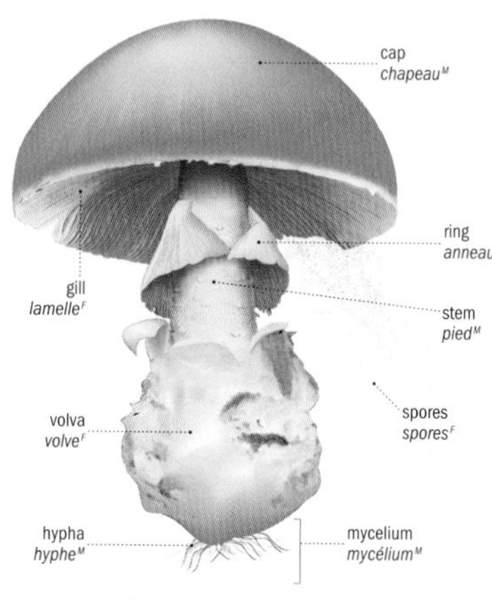

deadly poisonous mushroom
champignon[M] mortel

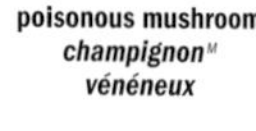

poisonous mushroom
champignon[M] vénéneux

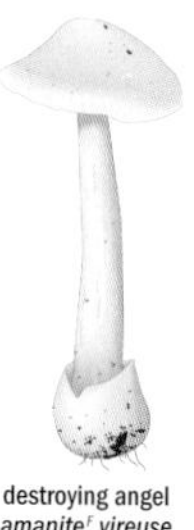

destroying angel
amanite[F] vireuse

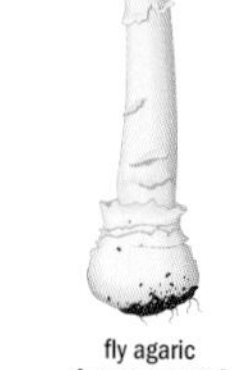

fly agaric
fausse oronge[F]

fern

fougère[F]

structure of a fern
structure[F] d'une fougère[F]

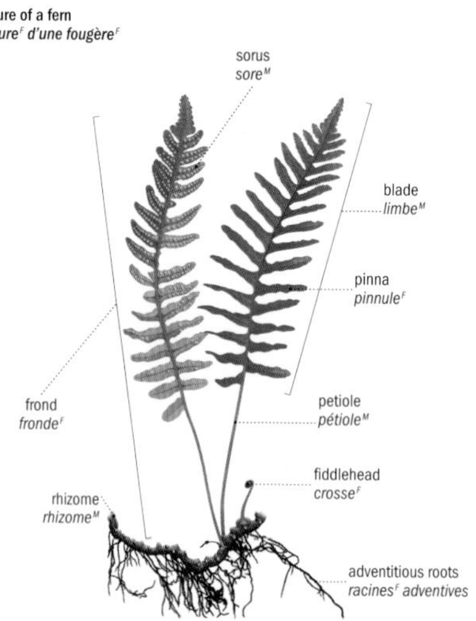

examples of ferns
exemples[M] de fougères

structure of a plant
structureF d'une planteF

germination
germinationF

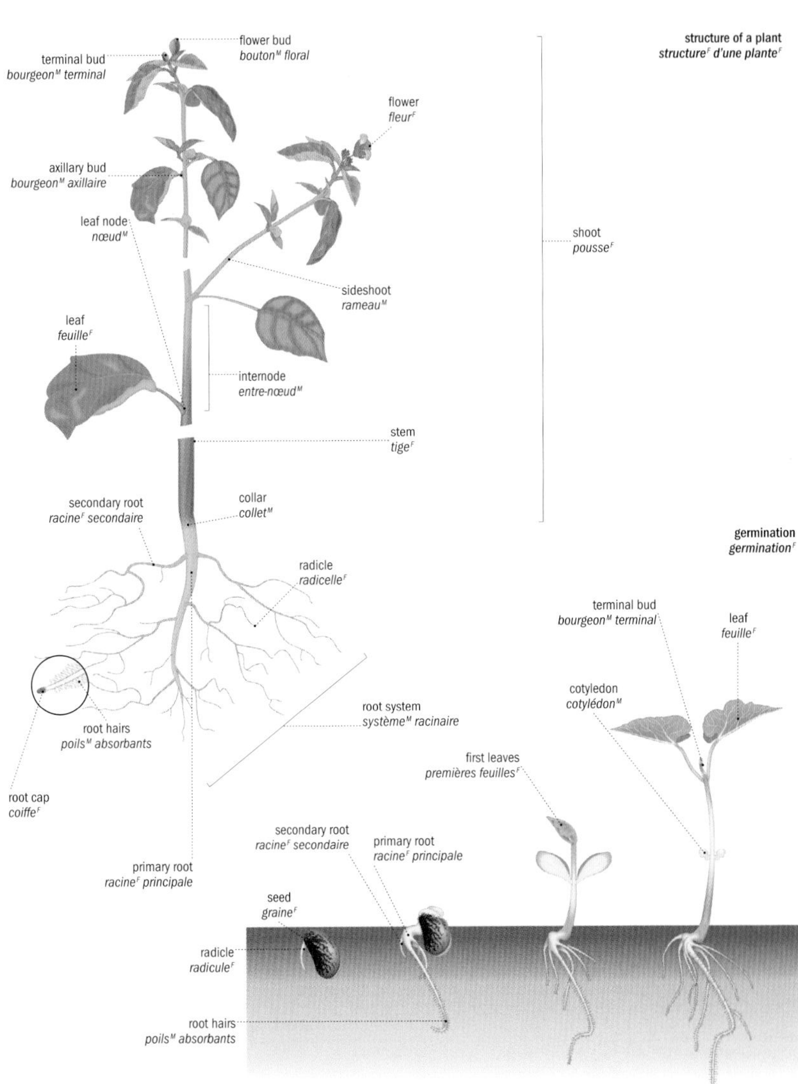

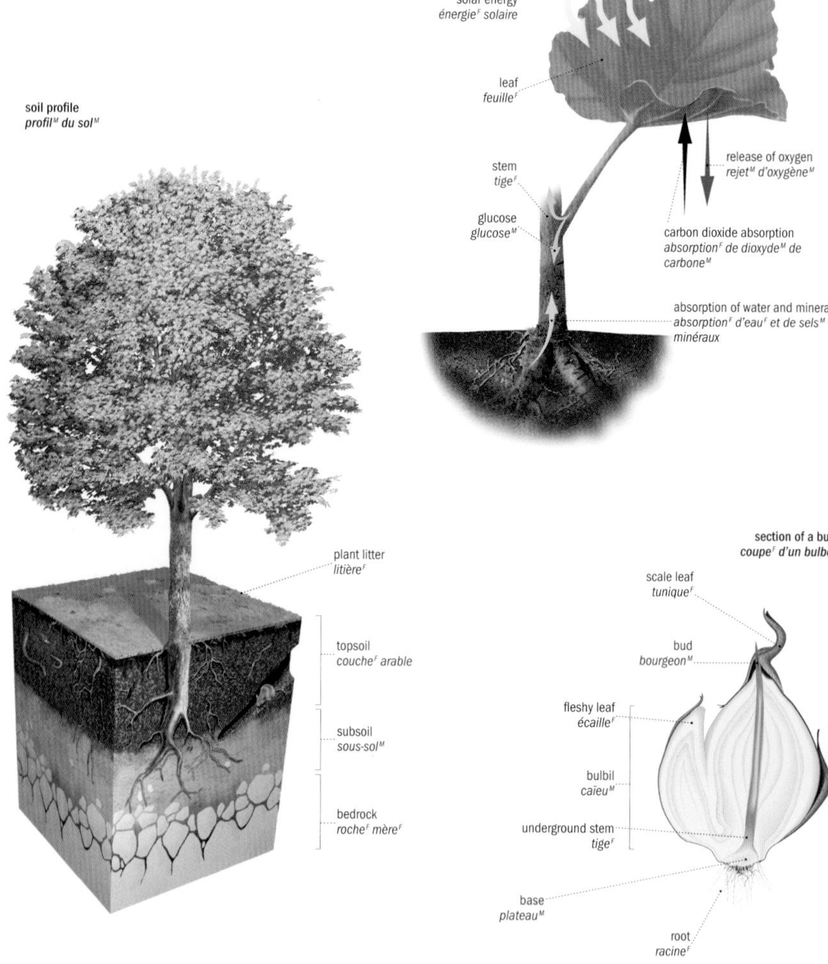
photosynthesis
photosynthèse[F]
solar energy
énergie[F] solaire
leaf
feuille[F]
release of oxygen
rejet[M] d'oxygène[M]
stem
tige[F]
glucose
glucose[M]
carbon dioxide absorption
absorption[F] de dioxyde[M] de carbone[M]
absorption of water and mineral s
absorption[F] d'eau[F] et de sels[M] minéraux
soil profile
profil[M] du sol[M]
plant litter
litière[F]
topsoil
couche[F] arable
subsoil
sous-sol[M]
bedrock
roche[F] mère[F]
section of a bulb
coupe[F] d'un bulbe
scale leaf
tunique[F]
bud
bourgeon[M]
fleshy leaf
écaille[F]
bulbil
caïeu[M]
underground stem
tige[F]
base
plateau[M]
root
racine[F]

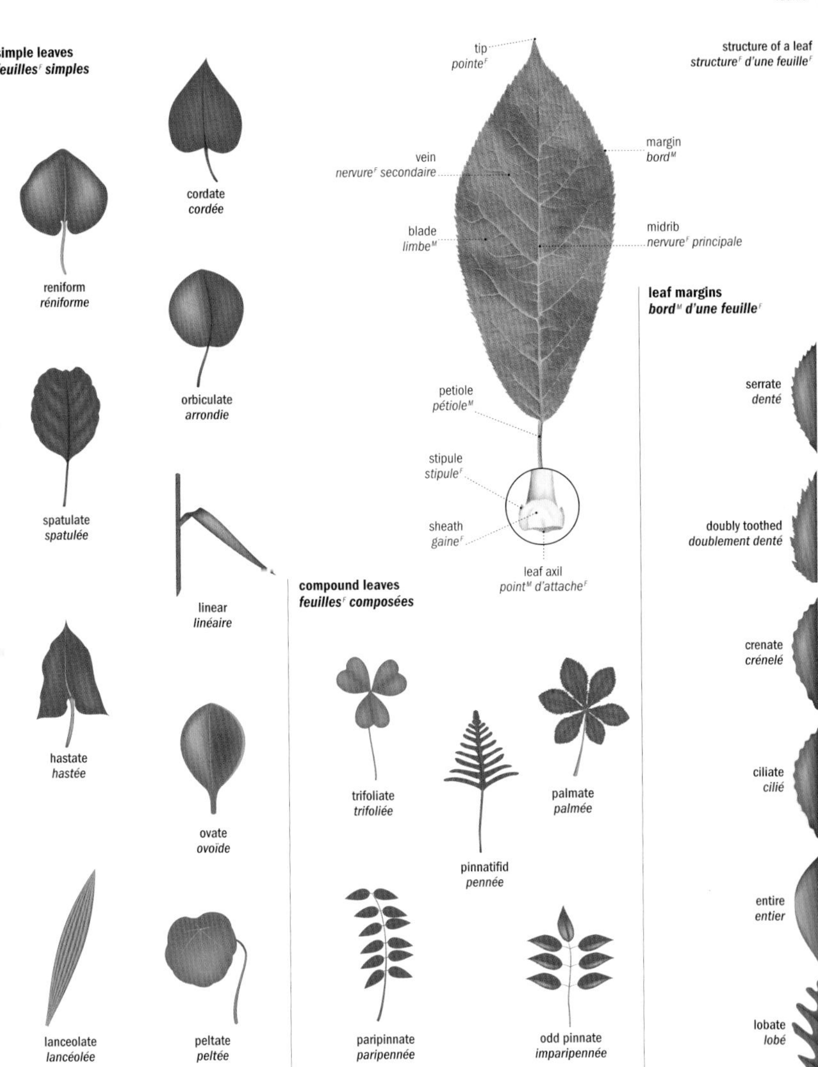
simple leaves
feuilles simples
reniform
réniforme
cordate
cordée
orbiculate
arrondie
spatulate
spatulée
linear
linéaire
hastate
hastée
ovate
ovoïde
lanceolate
lancéolée
peltate
peltée
structure of a leaf
structure d'une feuille
tip
pointe
vein
nervure secondaire
margin
bord
blade
limbe
midrib
nervure principale
petiole
pétiole
stipule
stipule
sheath
gaine
leaf axil
point d'attache
compound leaves
feuilles composées
trifoliate
trifoliée
palmate
palmée
pinnatifid
pennée
paripinnate
paripennée
odd pinnate
imparipennée
leaf margins
bord d'une feuille
serrate
denté
doubly toothed
doublement denté
crenate
crénelé
ciliate
cilié
entire
entier
lobate
lobé

flower

fleur[F]

structure of a flower
structure[F] d'une fleur[F]

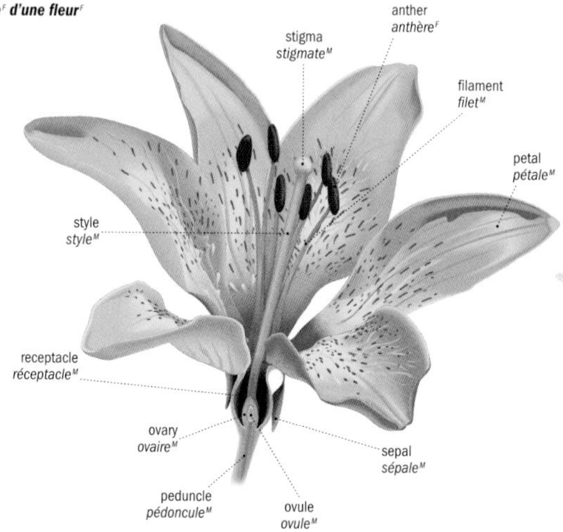

stigma
stigmate[M]

anther
anthère[F]

filament
filet[M]

petal
pétale[M]

style
style[M]

receptacle
réceptacle[M]

ovary
ovaire[M]

sepal
sépale[M]

peduncle
pédoncule[M]

ovule
ovule[M]

pistil
pistil[M]

corolla
corolle[F]

stamen
étamine[F]

calyx
calice[M]

examples of flowers
exemples[M] de fleurs[F]

orchid
orchidée[F]

daffodil
jonquille[F]

poppy
coquelicot[M]

tulip
tulipe[F]

lily of the valley
muguet[M]

carnation
œillet[M]

rose
rose[F]

begonia
bégonia[M]

lily
lis[M]

violet
violette[F]

crocus
crocus[M]

sunflower
tournesol[M]

types of inflorescence
modes[M] d'inflorescence[F]

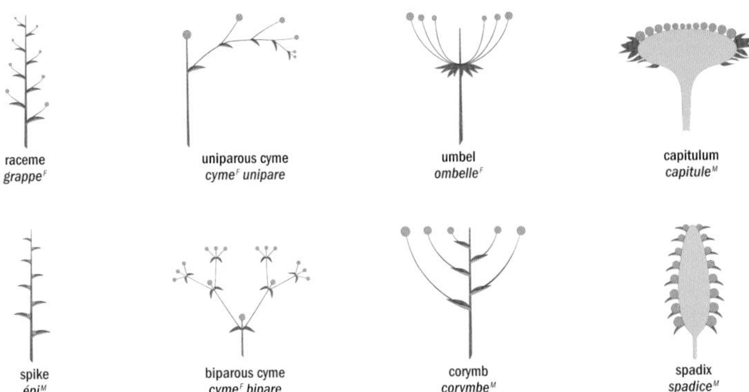

fruits

fruits[M]

fleshy stone fruit
fruit[M] charnu à noyau[M]

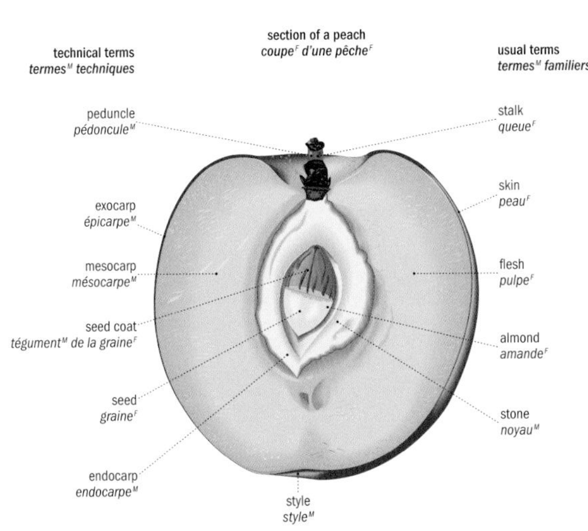

fleshy pome fruit
fruitM charnu à pépinsM

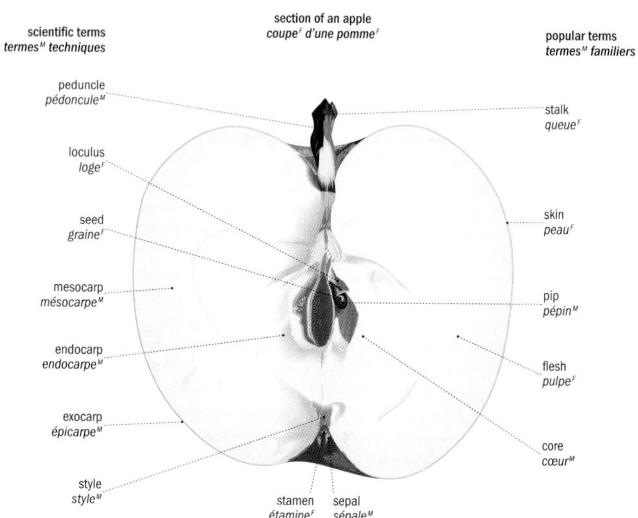

fleshy fruit: citrus fruit
fruitM charnu : agrumeM

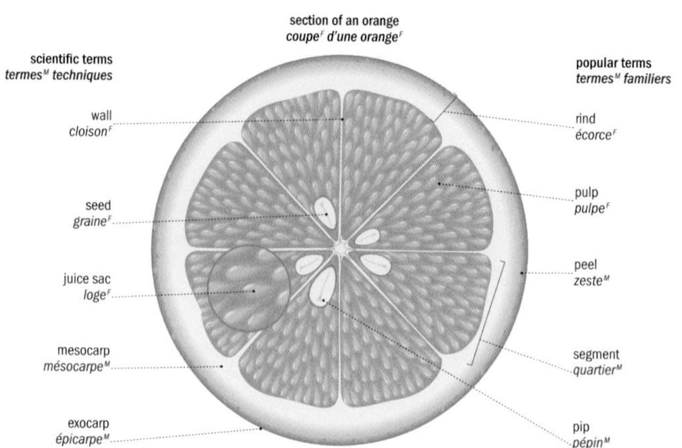

fleshy fruit: berry fruit
fruit^M charnu : baie^F

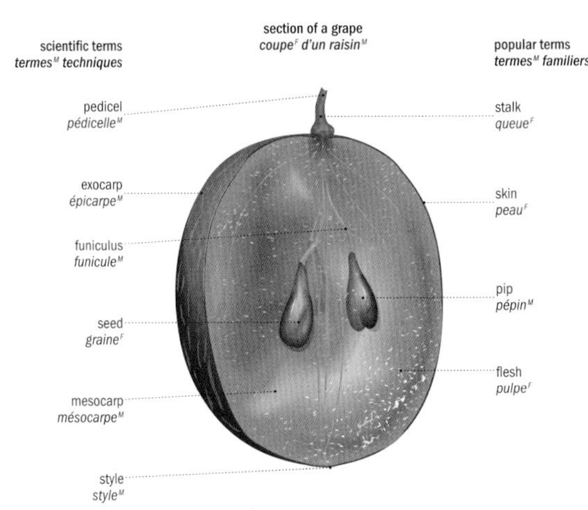

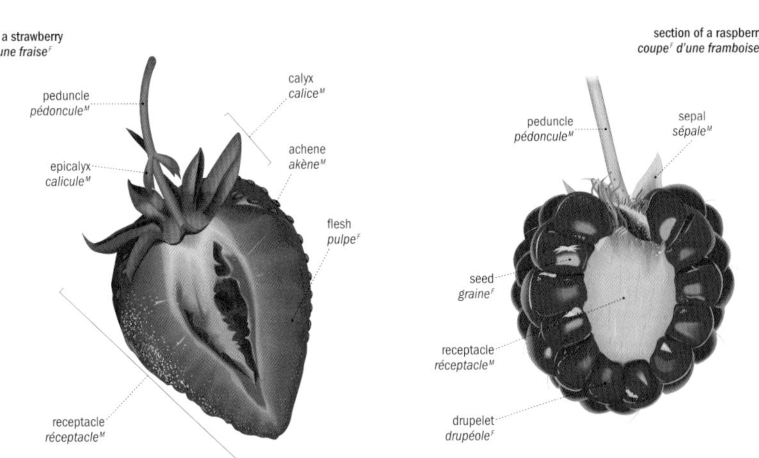

dry fruits
fruits^M secs

husk
brou^M

section of a follicle: star anise
coupe^F d'un follicule^M : anis^M étoilé

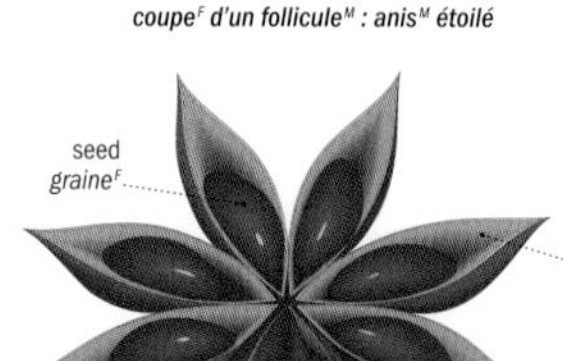

section of a silique: mustar
coupe^F d'une silique^F : moutarde

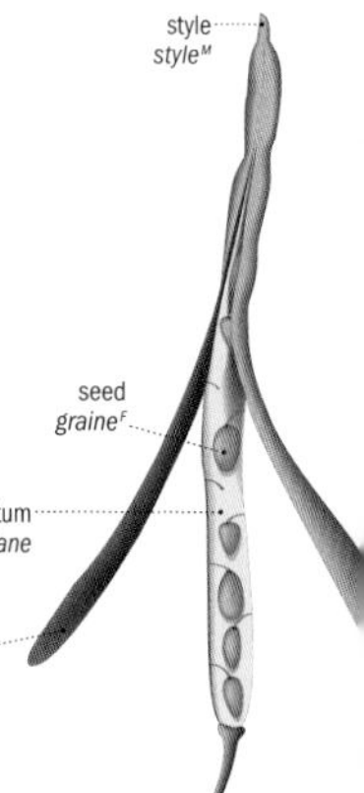

section of a hazelnut
coupe^F d'une noisette^F

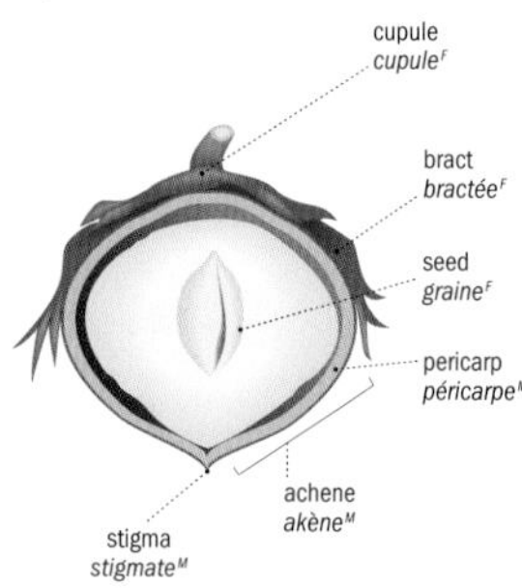

section of a legume: pea
coupe^F d'une gousse^F : pois^M

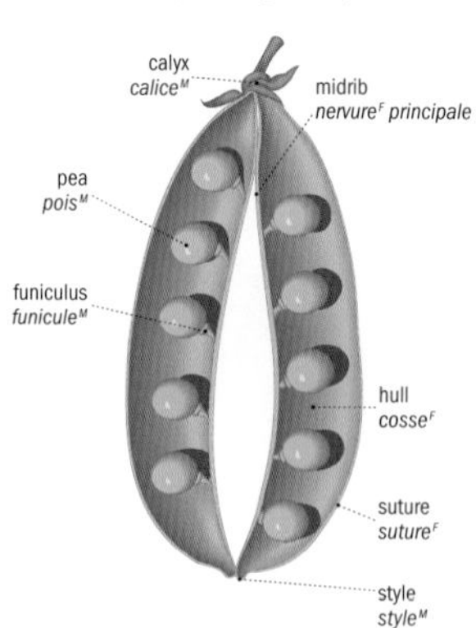

section of a walnut
coupe^F d'une noix^F

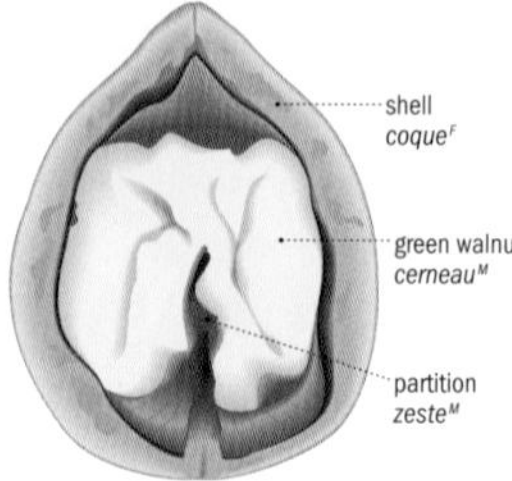

section of a capsule: po
coupe^F d'une capsule^F : pav

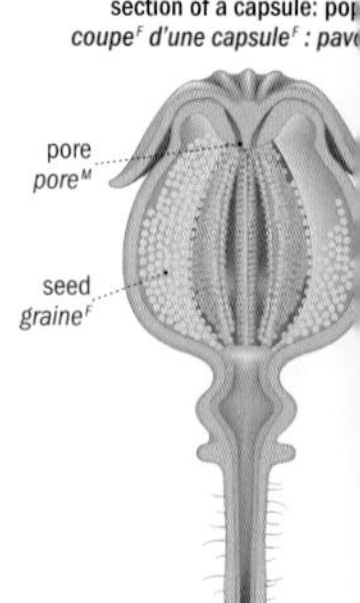

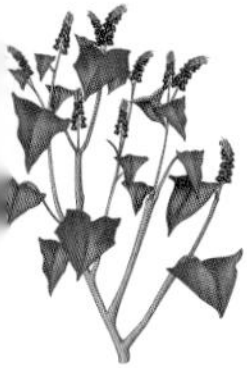

buckwheat
sarrasin[M]

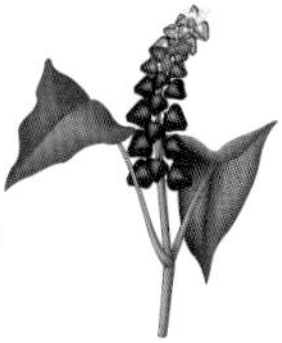

buckwheat: raceme
sarrasin[M] : grappe[F]

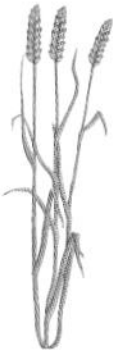

wheat
blé[M]

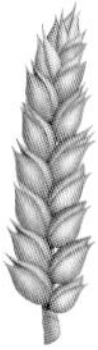

wheat: spike
blé[M] : épi[M]

section of a grain of wheat
coupe[F] d'un grain[M] de blé[M]

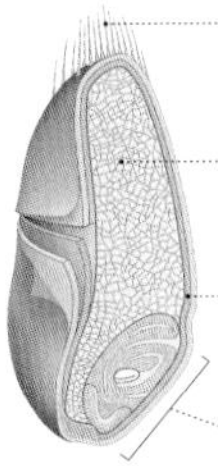

brush
brosse[F]
starch
albumen[M] farineux
seed coat
tégument[M]
germ
germe[M]

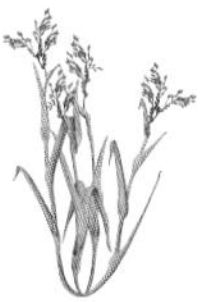

rice
riz[M]

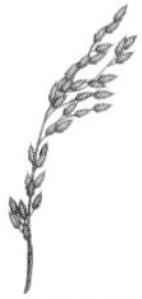

rice: panicle
riz[M] : panicule[F]

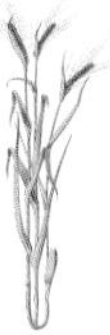

barley
orge[F]

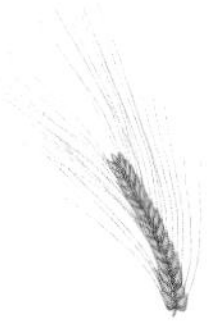

barley: spike
orge[F] : épi[M]

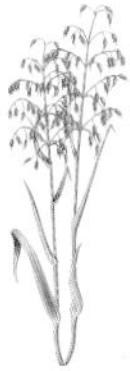

oats
avoine[F]

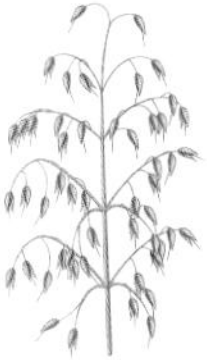

oats: panicle
avoine[F] : panicule[F]

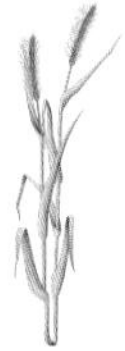

rye
seigle[M]

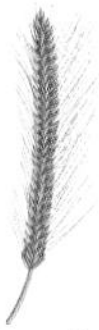

rye: spike
seigle[M] : épi[M]

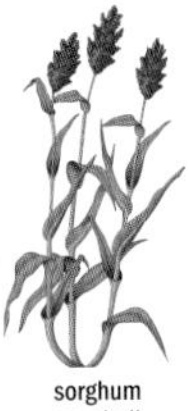

sorghum
sorgho[M]

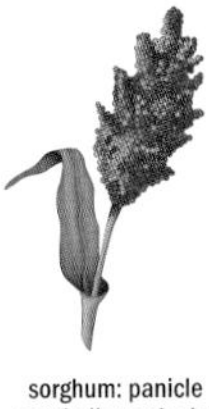

sorghum: panicle
sorgho[M] : panicule[F]

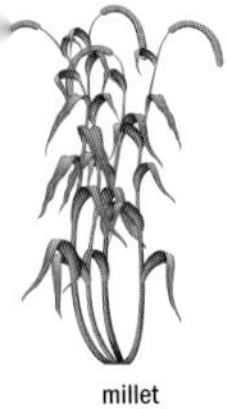

millet
millet[M]

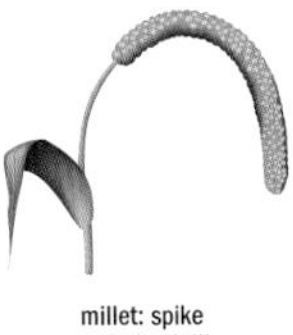

millet: spike
millet[M] : épi[M]

sweetcorn
maïs[M]

silk
barbe[F]
cob
épi[M]
husk
feuille[F]
kernel
grain[M]

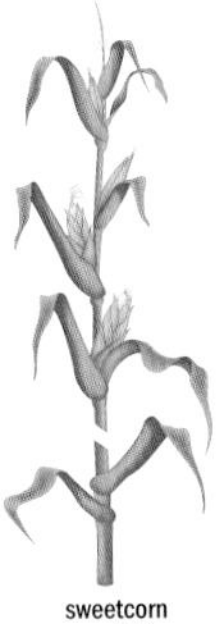

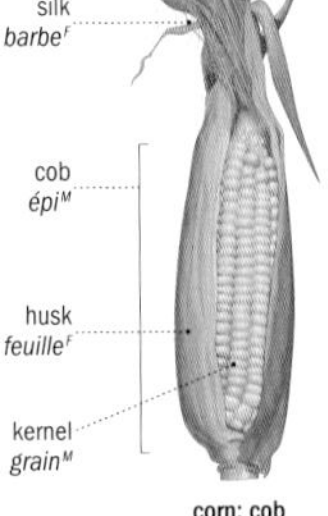

corn: cob
maïs[M] : épi[M]

grape

vigne[F]

bunch of grapes
grappe[F] de raisin[M]

branch
rameau[M]

pedicel
pédicelle[M]

tendril
vrille[F]

peduncle
pédoncule[M]

grape
raisin[M]

vine stock
cep[M] de vigne[F]

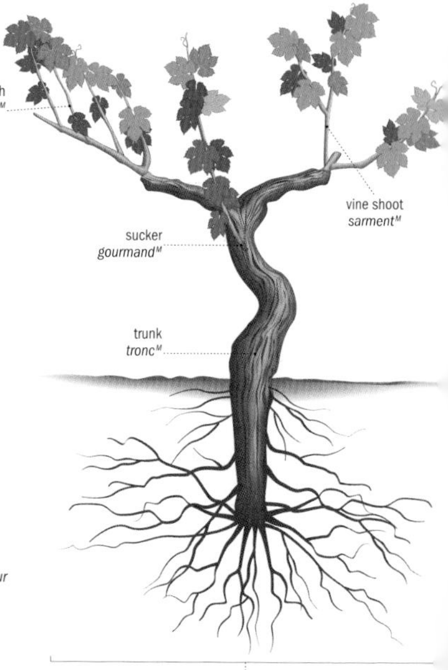

fruit branch
branche[F] à fruits[M]

vine shoot
sarment[M]

sucker
gourmand[M]

trunk
tronc[M]

root system
système[M] racinaire

vine leaf
feuille[F] de vigne[F]

upper lateral lobe
lobe[M] latéral supérieur

terminal lobe
lobe[M] terminal

upper lateral sinus
sinus[M] latéral supérieur

lower lateral lobe
lobe[M] latéral inférieur

lower lateral sinus
sinus[M] latéral inférieur

petiolar sinus
sinus[M] pétiolaire

steps to ripeness
étapes[F] de maturation[F]

flowering
floraison[F]

fruiting
nouaison[F]

ripening
véraison[F]

ripeness
maturité[F]

structure of a tree
structure^F d'un arbre^M

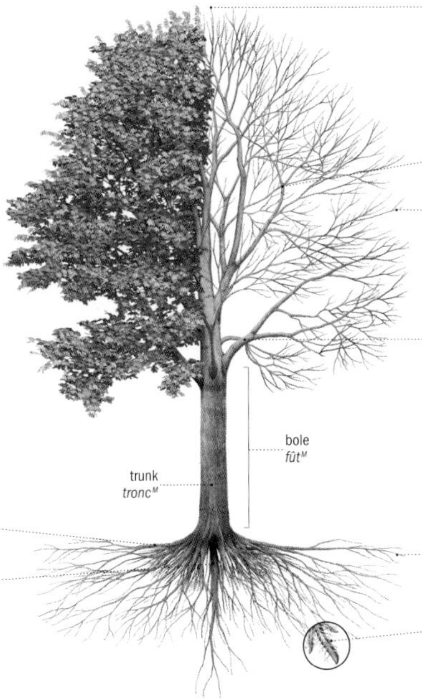

foliage
feuillage^M
branches
ramure^F
top
cime^F
branch
rameau^M
twig
ramille^F
crown
houppier^M
limb
branche^F maîtresse
bole
fût^M
trunk
tronc^M
shallow root
racine^F traçante
radicle
radicelle^F
taproot
racine^F pivotante
root-hair zone
chevelu^M

cross section of a trunk
coupe^F transversale du tronc^M

medullary ray
rayon^M médullaire
pith
moelle^F
annual ring
cerne^M annuel
heartwood
bois^M de cœur^M
cambium
cambium^M
phloem
liber^M
bark
écorce^F
sapwood
aubier^M

stump
souche^F

shoot
rejet^M

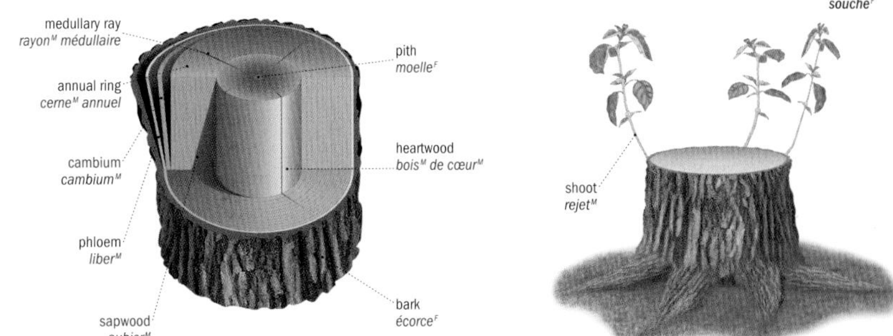

examples of broadleaved trees
exemples[M] d'arbres[M] feuillus

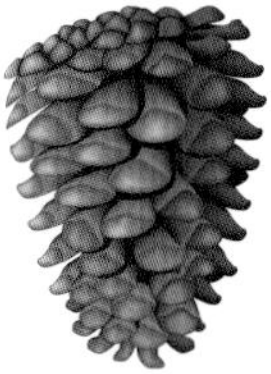

conifer

conifère[M]

cone
cône[M]

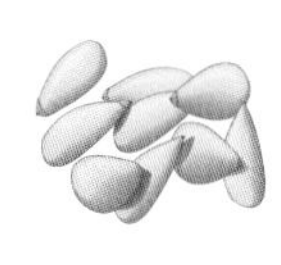

pine seed
pignon[M]

branch
rameau[M]

examples of leaves
exemples[M] de feuilles[F]

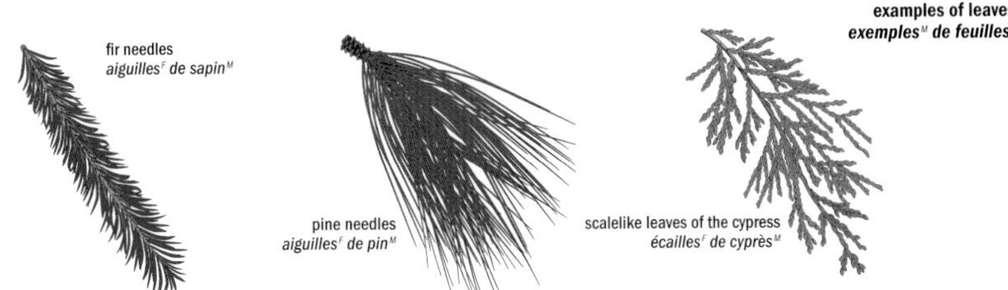

examples of conifers
exemples[M] de conifères[M]

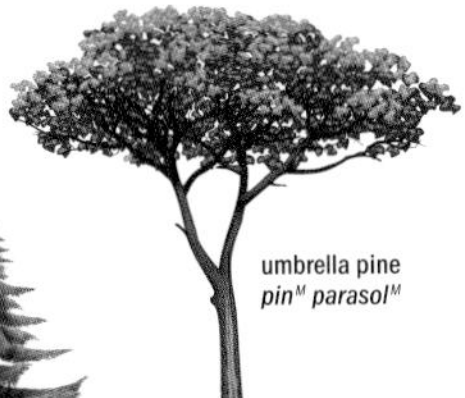

umbrella pine
pin[M] parasol[M]

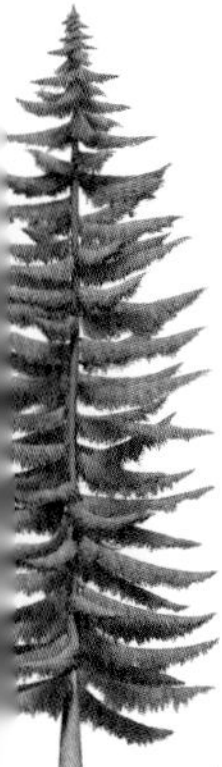

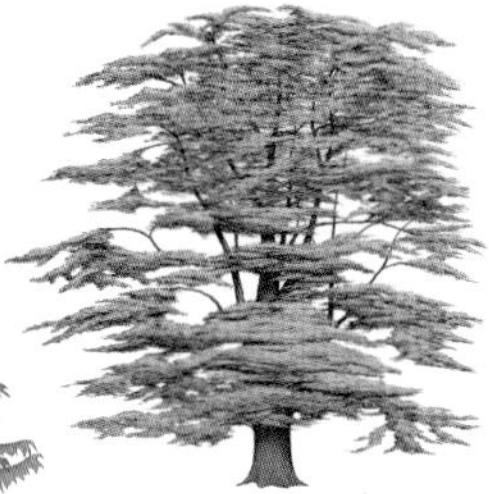

cedar of Lebanon
cèdre[M] du Liban[M]

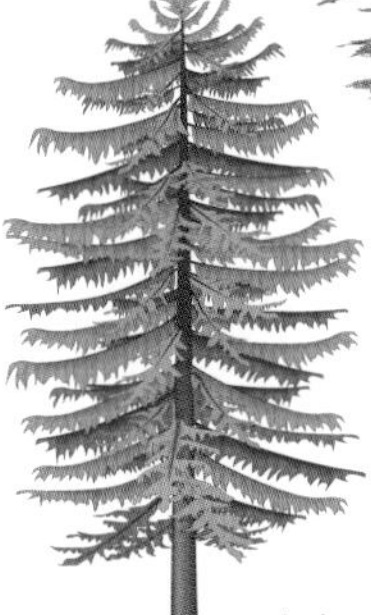

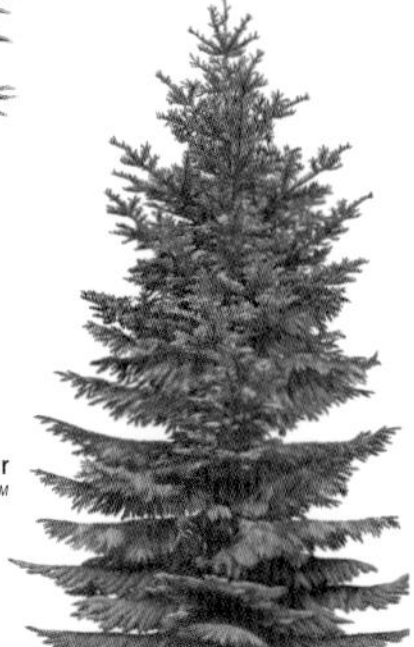

spruce
épicéa[M]

larch
mélèze[M]

fir
sapin[M]

animal cell

cellule^F animale

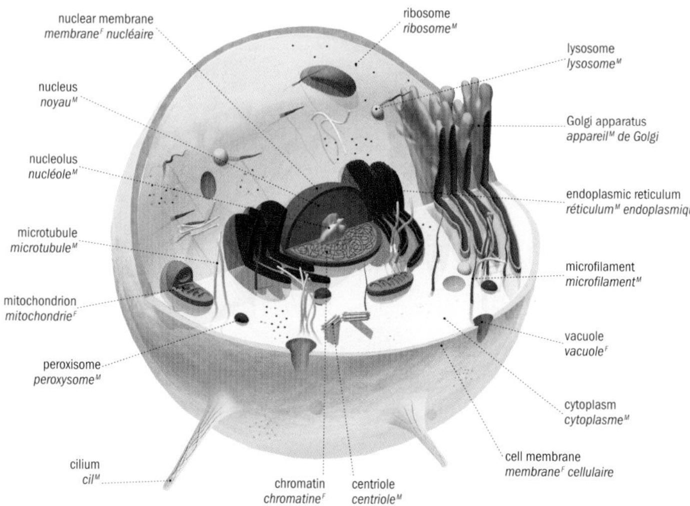

unicellulars

unicellulaires^M

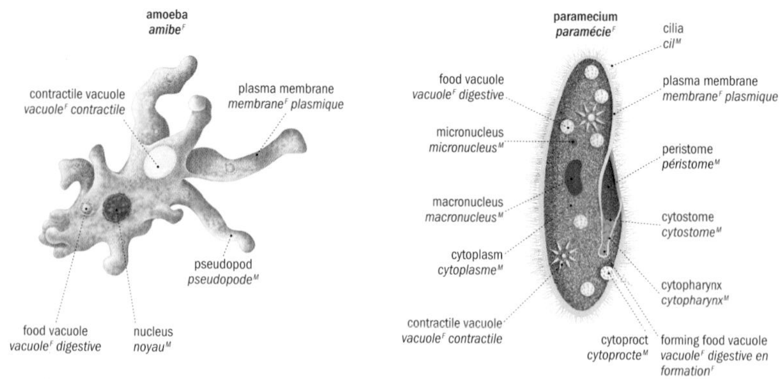

butterfly

papillon[M]

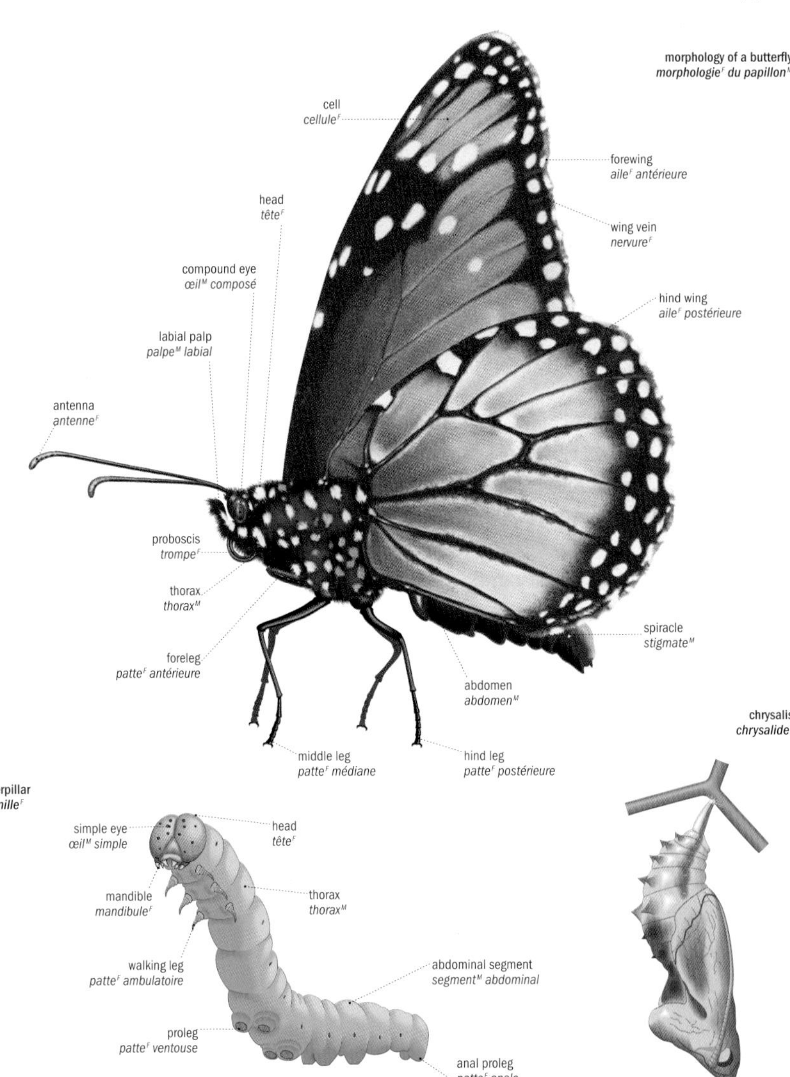

honeybee

abeille[F]

morphology of a honeybee: worker
morphologie[F] de l'abeille[F] : ouvrière[F]

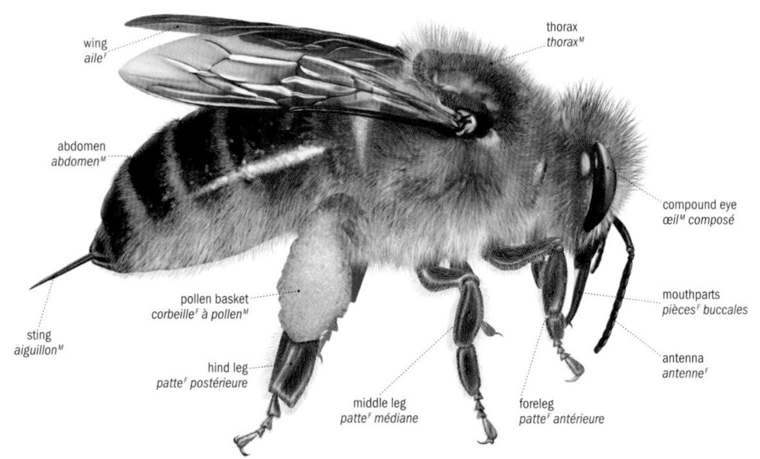

castes
castes[F]

examples of insects

exemples[M] d'insectes[M]

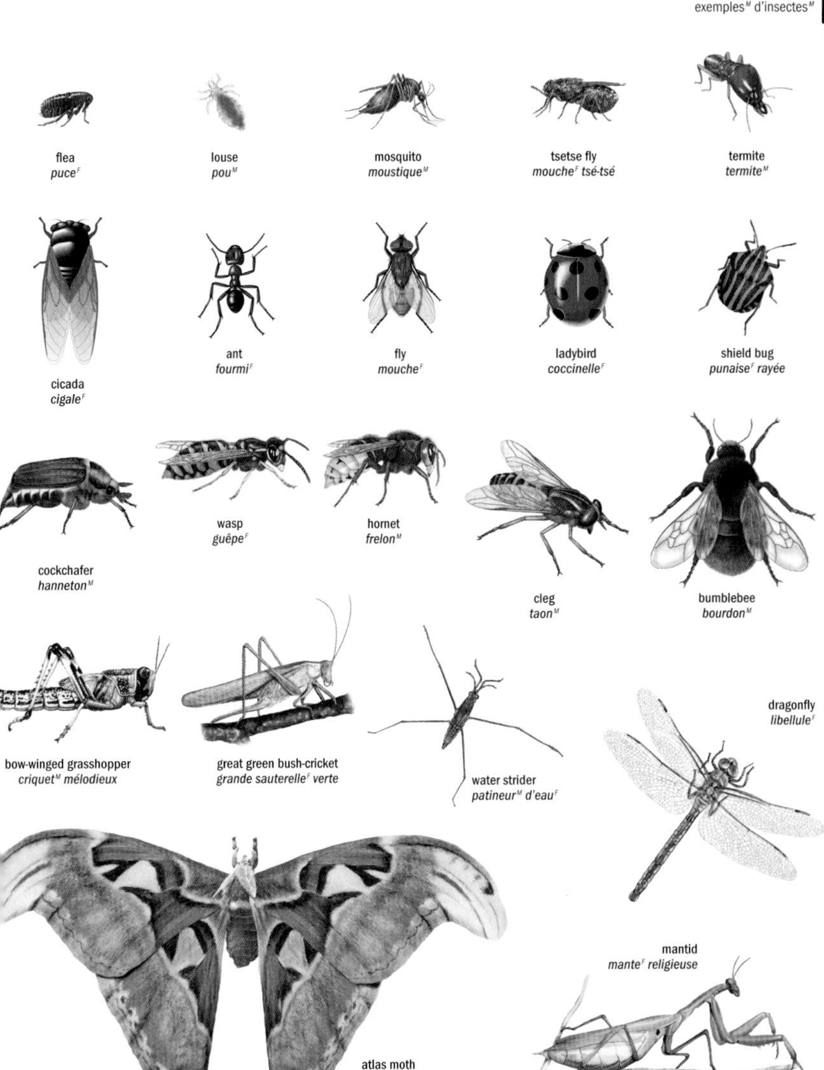

spider

araignée^F

spider web
toile^F d'araignée^F

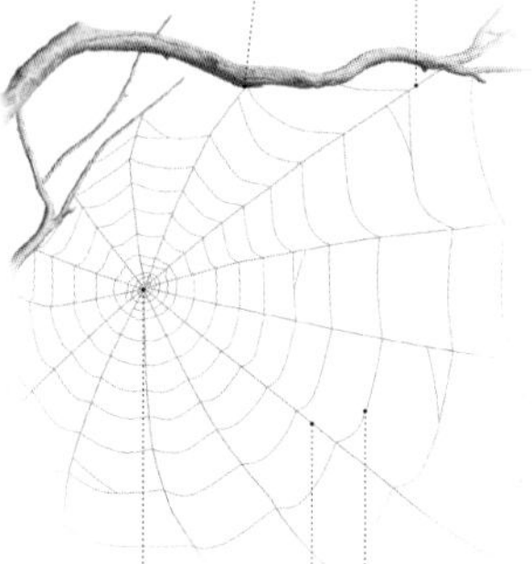

anchor point
point^M d'attache^F
support thread
fil^M d'attache^F
hub
spirale^F centrale
spiral thread
spirale^F
radial thread
rayon^M

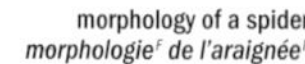

morphology of a spider
morphologie^F de l'araignée^F

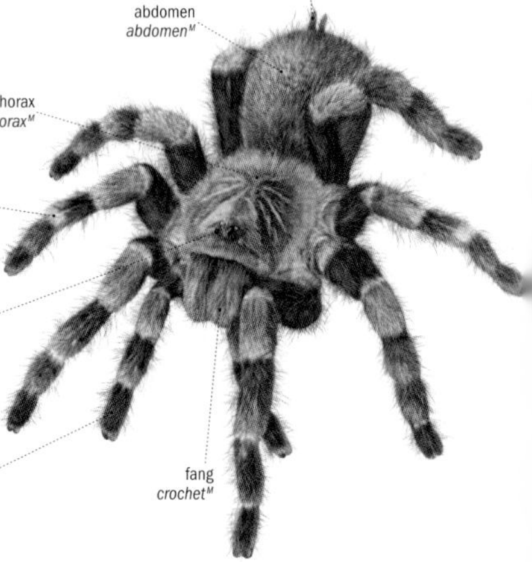

spinneret
filière^F
abdomen
abdomen^M
cephalothorax
céphalothorax^M
walking leg
patte^F locomotrice
eye
œil^M
pedipalp
pédipalpe^M
fang
crochet^M

examples of arachnids

exemples^M d'arachnides^M

tick
tique^F

crab spider
araignée^F-crabe^M

water spider
argyronète^F

garden spider
épeire^F

red-kneed tarantula
mygale^F du Mexique^M

scorpion
scorpion^M

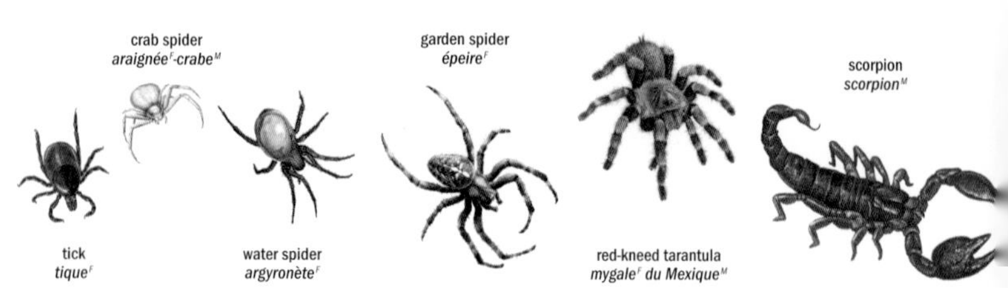

lobster

homard[M]

morphology of a lobster

morphologie[F] du homard[M]

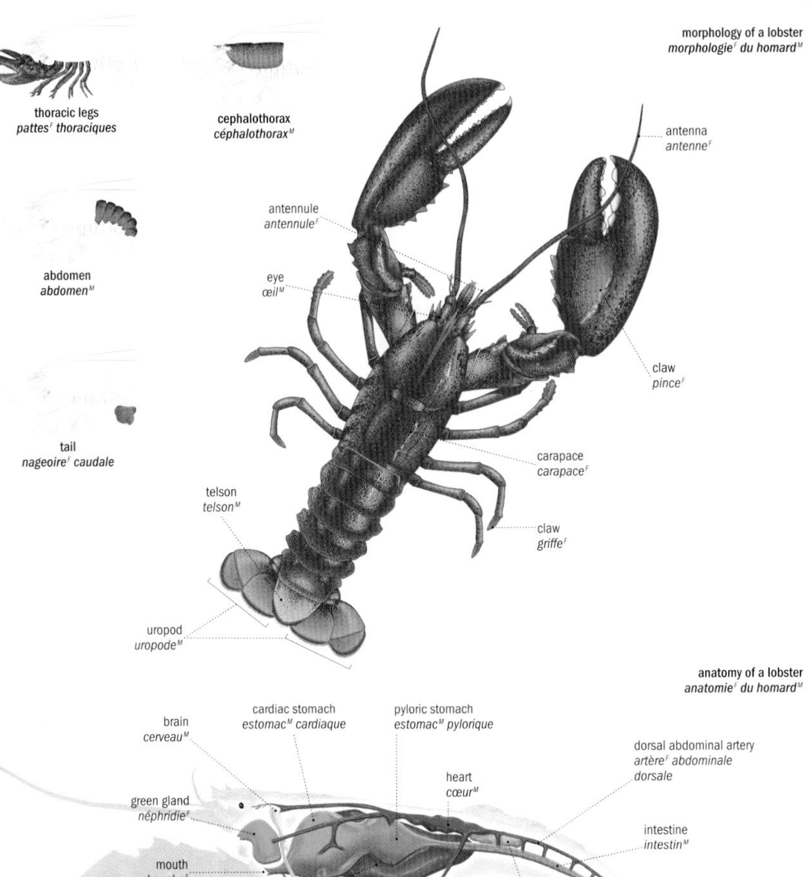

anatomy of a lobster

anatomie[F] du homard[M]

snail

escargot[M]

morphology of a snail
morphologie[F] de l'escargot[M]

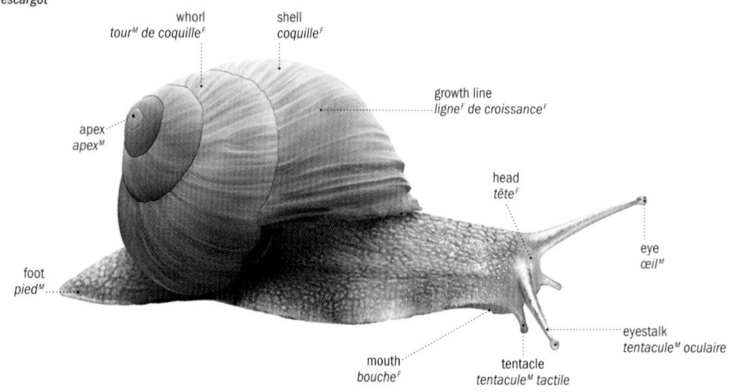

octopus

pieuvre[F]

morphology of an octopus
morphologie[F] de la pieuvre[F]

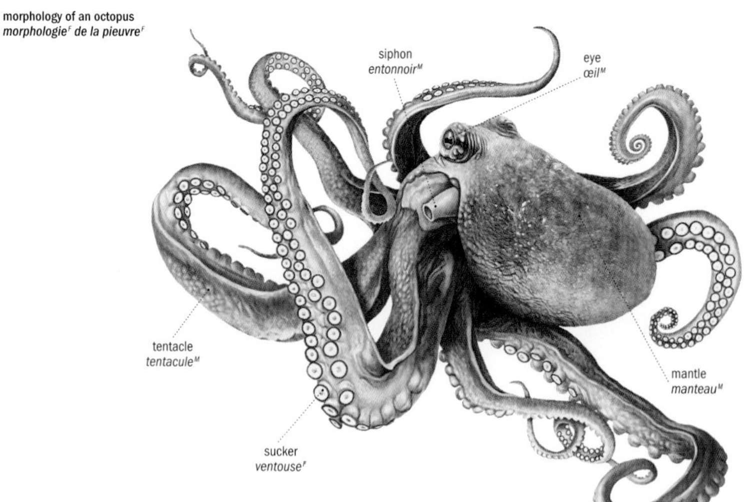

univalve shell

coquillage[M] univalve

morphology of a univalve shell
morphologie[F] du coquillage[M] univalve

apex
apex[M]
nuclear whorl
tour[M] embryonnaire
columella
columelle[F]
whorl
tour[M] de spire[F]
axial rib
côte[F] axiale
suture
ligne[F] de suture[F]
spiral rib
côte[F] spiralée
aperture
ouverture[F]
outer lip
bord[M] externe
columella fold
pli[M] de la columelle[F]
inner lip
bord[M] interne
siphonal canal
canal[M] siphonal

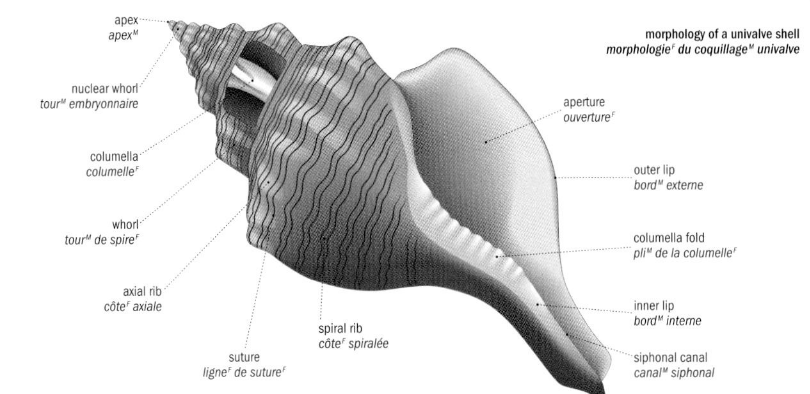

bivalve shell

coquillage[M] bivalve

anatomy of a bivalve shell
anatomie[F] du coquillage[M] bivalve

kidney
rein[M]
shell
coquille[F]
heart
cœur[M]
umbo
crochet[M]
ligament
ligament[M]
posterior adductor muscle
muscle[M] adducteur postérieur
digestive gland
glande[F] digestive
anus
anus[M]
stomach
estomac[M]
anterior adductor muscle
muscle[M] adducteur antérieur
visceral ganglion
ganglion[M] viscéral
gills
branchies[F]
palp
palpe[M]
mantle
manteau[M]
gonad
gonade[F]
mouth
bouche[F]
intestine
intestin[M]
foot
pied[M]
cerebropleural ganglion
ganglion[M] cérébropleural

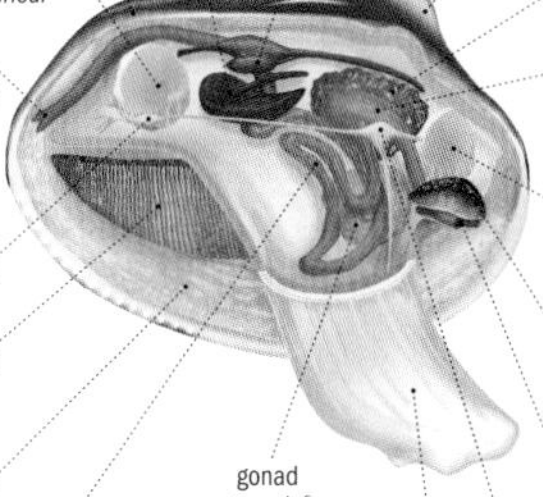

morphology of a bivalve shell
morphologie[F] du coquillage[M] bivalve

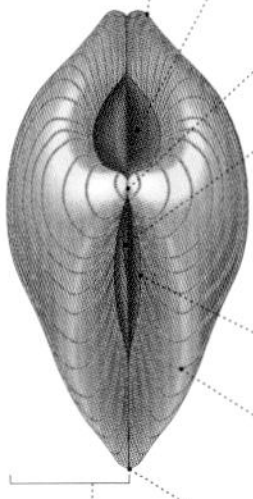

anterior end
bord[M] antérieur
lunule
lunule[F]
umbo
crochet[M]
ligament
ligament[M]
escutcheon
écusson[M]
growth line
ligne[F] de croissance[F]
valve
valve[F]
posterior end
bord[M] postérieur

ANIMAL KINGDOM

cartilaginous fish

poisson^{M} cartilagineux

morphology of a shark
morphologie^{F} du requin^{M}

first dorsal fin
première nageoire^{F} dorsale
carina
carène^{F}
second dorsal fin
seconde nageoire^{F} dorsale
caudal fin
nageoire^{F} caudale
snout
museau^{M}
nostril
narine^{F}
tooth
dent^{F}
pelvic fin
nageoire^{F} pelvienne
gill openings
fentes^{F} branchiales
pectoral fin
nageoire^{F} pectorale
anal fin
nageoire^{F} anale

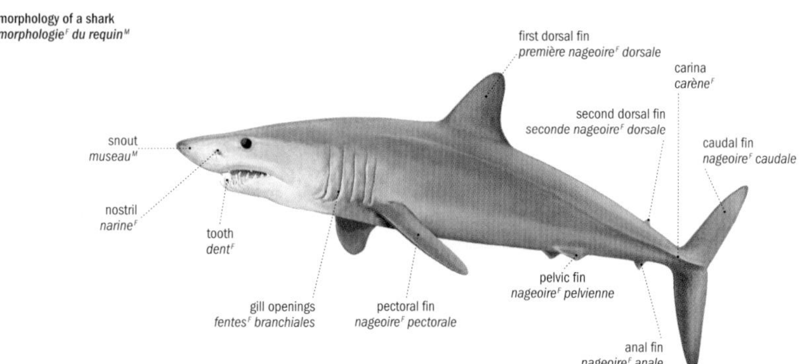

bony fish

poisson^{M} osseux

morphology of a perch
morphologie^{F} de la perche^{F}

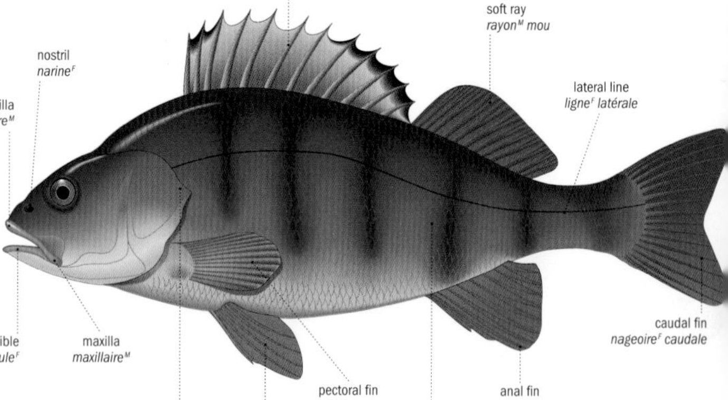

spiny ray
rayon^{M} épineux
soft ray
rayon^{M} mou
nostril
narine^{F}
lateral line
ligne^{F} latérale
premaxilla
prémaxillaire^{M}
caudal fin
nageoire^{F} caudale
mandible
mandibule^{F}
maxilla
maxillaire^{M}
pectoral fin
nageoire^{F} pectorale
anal fin
nageoire^{F} anale
operculum
opercule^{M}
pelvic fin
nageoire^{F} pelvienne
scale
écaille^{F}

ANIMAL KINGDOM

frog

grenouille[F]

morphology of a frog

morphologie[F] de la grenouille[F]

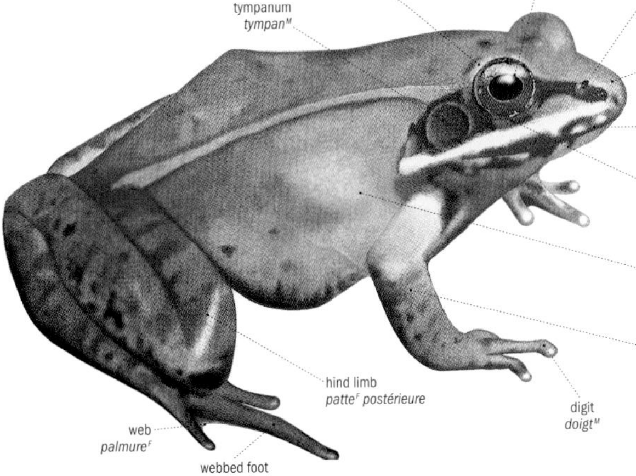

upper eyelid
paupière[F] supérieure
eyeball
globe[M] oculaire
nostril
narine[F]
tympanum
tympan[M]
snout
museau[M]
mouth
bouche[F]
lower eyelid
paupière[F] inférieure
trunk
tronc[M]
forelimb
patte[F] antérieure
hind limb
patte[F] postérieure
digit
doigt[M]
web
palmure[F]
webbed foot
doigt[M] palmé

examples of amphibians

exemples[M] d'amphibiens[M]

salamander
salamandre[F]

wood frog
grenouille[F] des bois[M]

common frog
grenouille[F] rousse

tree frog
rainette[F]

adhesive disc
ventouse[F]

newt
triton[M]

common toad
crapaud[M] commun

Northern leopard frog
grenouille[F] léopard[M]

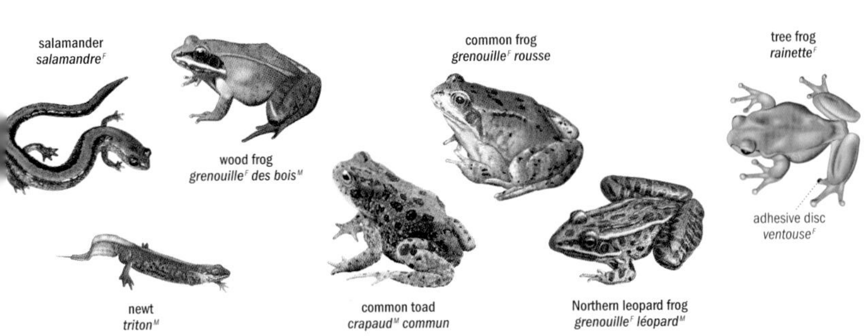

snake

serpent^M

ANIMAL KINGDOM

morphology of a venomous snake: head
morphologie^F du serpent^M venimeux : tête^F

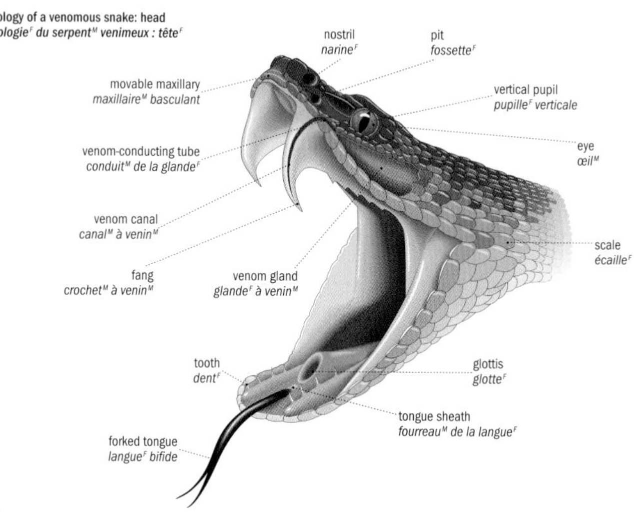

turtle

tortue^F

morphology of a turtle
morphologie^F de la tortue^F

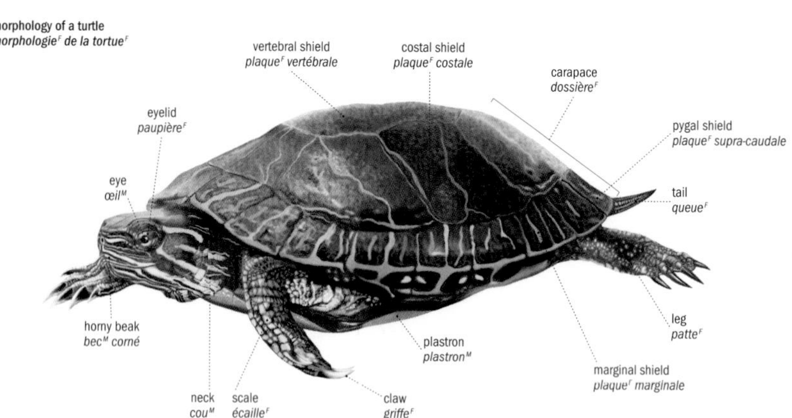

examples of reptiles

exemples^M de reptiles^M

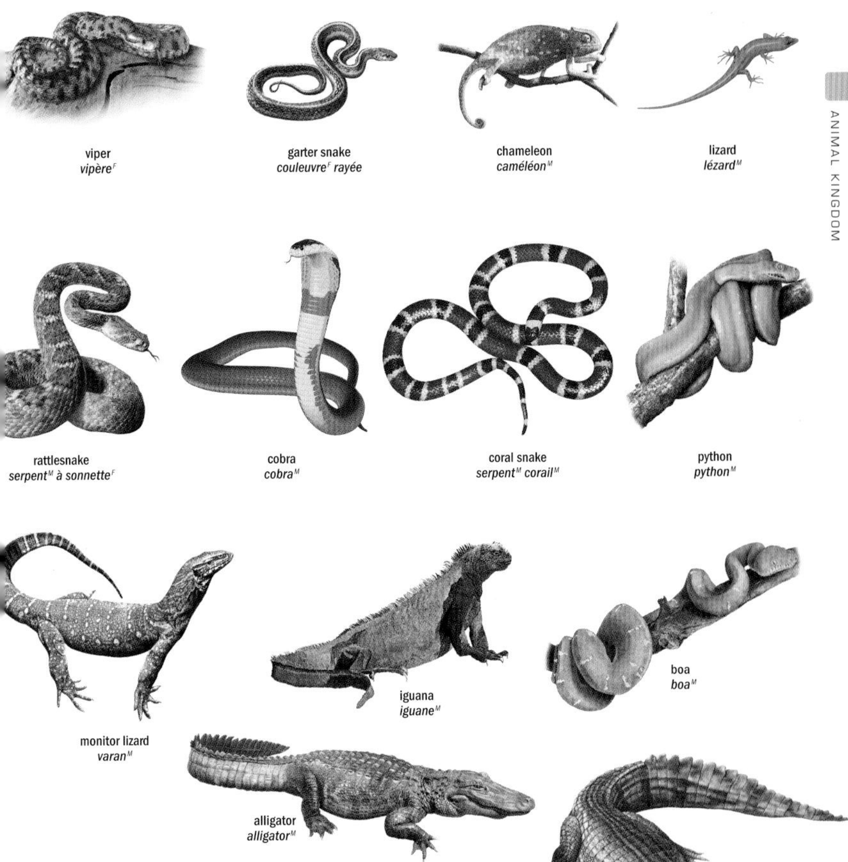

bird

oiseau[M]

morphology of a bird
morphologie[F] de l'oiseau[M]

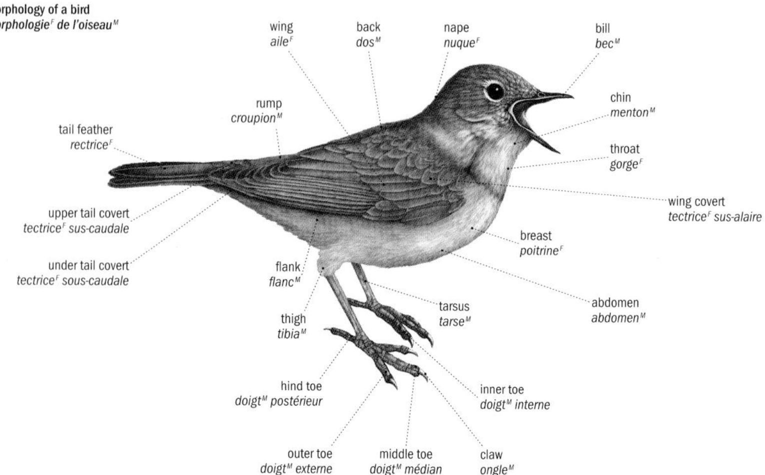

head
tête[F]

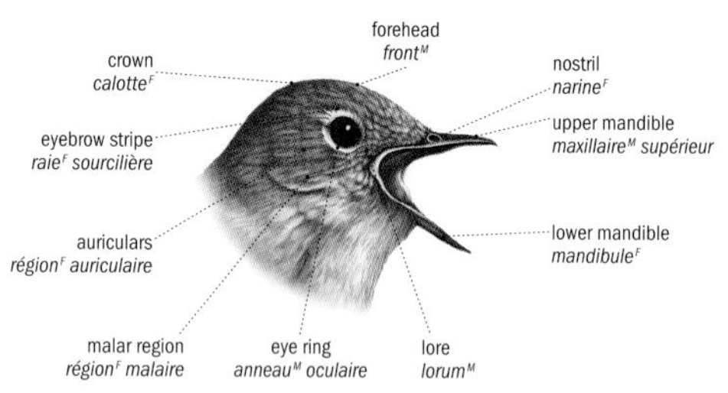

wing
aile[F]

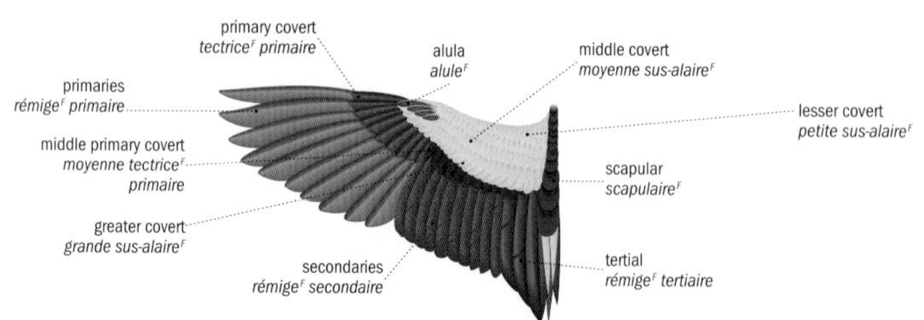

egg
œuf[M]

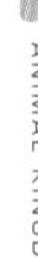

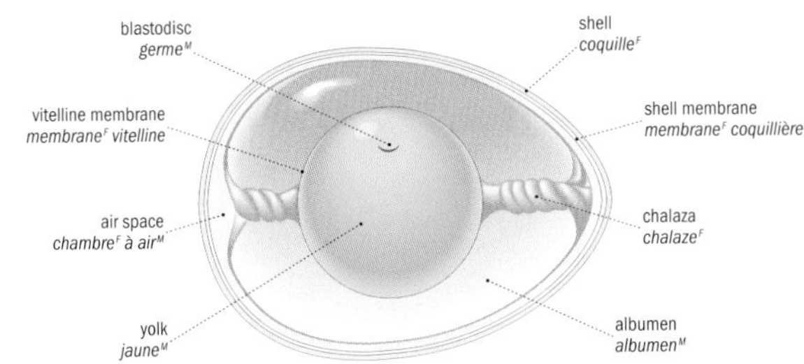

examples of bills
***exemples*[M] *de becs*[M]**

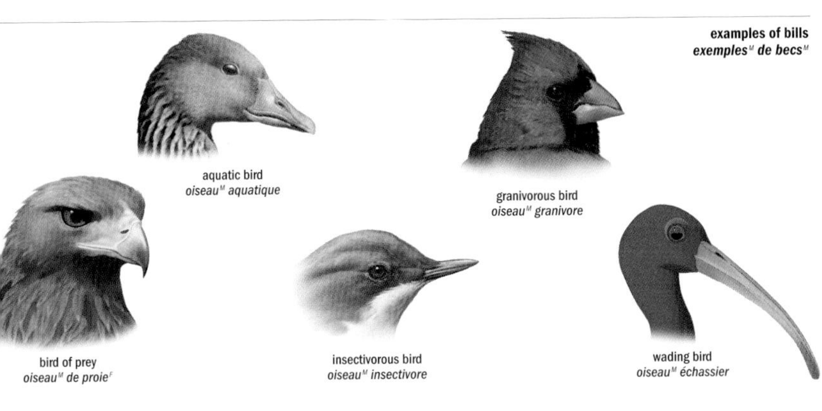

examples of feet
***exemples*[M] *de pattes*[F]**

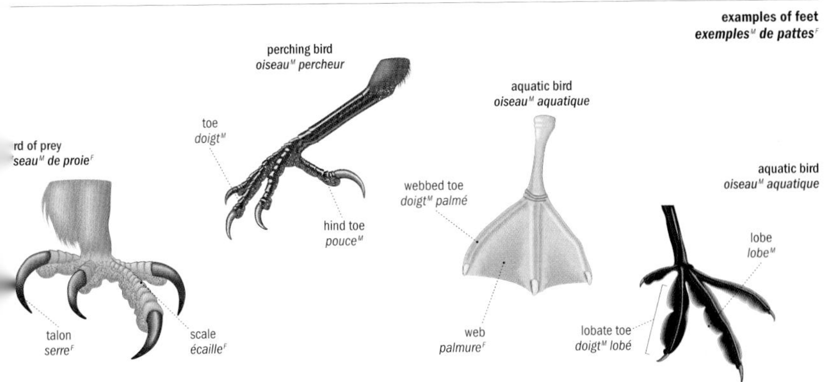

examples of birds

exemples[M] d'oiseaux[M]

pheasant
faisan[M]
great horned owl
grand duc[M] *d'Amérique*[F]
falcon
faucon[M]
quail
caille[F]
eagle
aigle[M]
duck
canard[M]
hen
poule[F]
pigeon
pigeon[M]
turkey
dindon[M]
guinea fowl
pintade[F]
goose
oie[F]
rooster
coq[M]
ostrich
autruche[F]
peacock
paon[M]
flamingo
flamant[M]

rodent

rongeur[M]

morphology of a rat
morphologie[F] du rat[M]

examples of rodents

exemples[M] de mammifères[M] rongeurs[M]

examples of lagomorphs

exemples[M] de mammifères[M] lagomorphes[M]

pika
pika[M]

rabbit
lapin[M]

hare
lièvre[M]

horse

cheval^{M}

morphology of a horse
morphologie^{F} du cheval^{M}

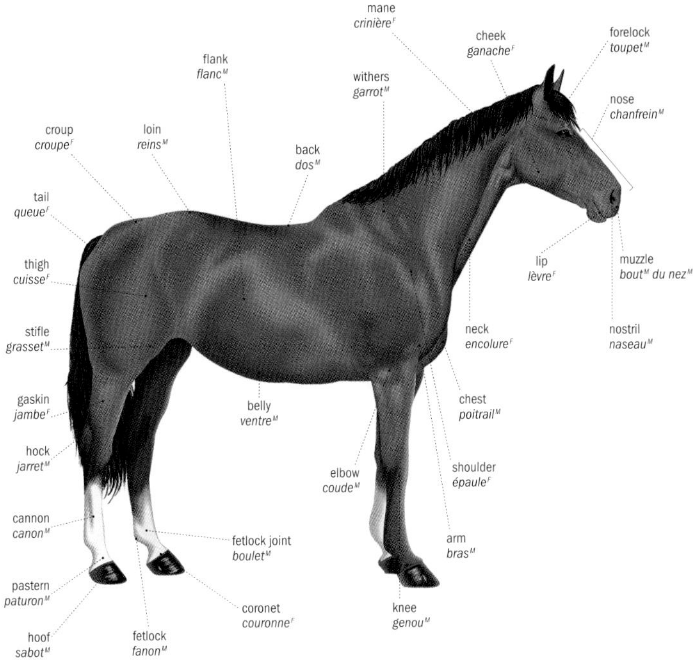

mane *crinière^{F}*

cheek *ganache^{F}*

forelock *toupet^{M}*

flank *flanc^{M}*

withers *garrot^{M}*

nose *chanfrein^{M}*

croup *croupe^{F}*

loin *reins^{M}*

back *dos^{M}*

tail *queue^{F}*

thigh *cuisse^{F}*

lip *lèvre^{F}*

muzzle *bout^{M} du nez^{M}*

stifle *grasset^{M}*

neck *encolure^{F}*

nostril *naseau^{M}*

gaskin *jambe^{F}*

belly *ventre^{M}*

chest *poitrail^{M}*

hock *jarret^{M}*

elbow *coude^{M}*

shoulder *épaule^{F}*

cannon *canon^{M}*

fetlock joint *boulet^{M}*

arm *bras^{M}*

pastern *paturon^{M}*

coronet *couronne^{F}*

knee *genou^{M}*

hoof *sabot^{M}*

fetlock *fanon^{M}*

gaits
allures^{F}

.lk
s^{M}

amble
amble^{M}

t
t^{M}

gallop
galop^{M}

examples of ungulate mammals

exemples[M] de mammifères[M] ongulés

peccary
pécari[M]

wild boar
sanglier[M]

pig
porc[M]

goat
chèvre[F]

antelope
antilope[F]

sheep
mouton[M]

calf
veau[M]

white-tailed deer
cerf[M] *de Virginie*

mouflon
mouflon[M]

reindeer
renne[M]

Canadian elk
cerf[M] *du Canada*

okapi
okapi[M]

donkey
âne[M]

mule
mulet[M]

cow
vache[F]

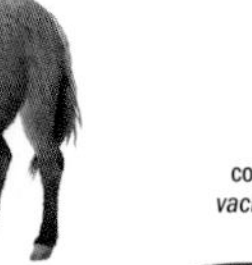

zebra
zèbre[M]

llama
lama[M]

bison
bison[M]

buffalo
buffle[M]

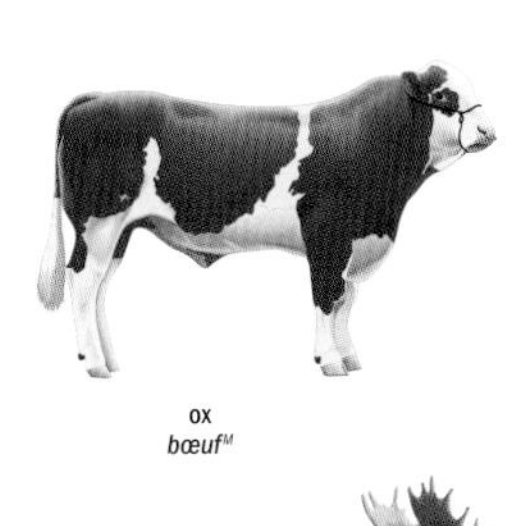
ox
bœuf[M]

yak
yack[M]

horse
cheval[M]

elk
élan[M]

camel
chameau[M]

dromedary
dromadaire[M]

rhinoceros
rhinocéros[M]

hippopotamus
hippopotame[M]

giraffe
girafe[F]

elephant
éléphant[M]

dog

chien[M]

morphology of a dog
morphologie[F] du chien[M]

stop
stop[M]
muzzle
museau[M]
cheek
joue[F]
flews
babines[F]
withers
garrot[M]
back
dos[M]
thigh
cuisse[F]
shoulder
épaule[F]
elbow
coude[M]
forearm
avant-bras[M]
knee
genou[M]
tail
queue[F]
wrist
poignet[M]
hock
jarret[M]
toe
orteil[M]

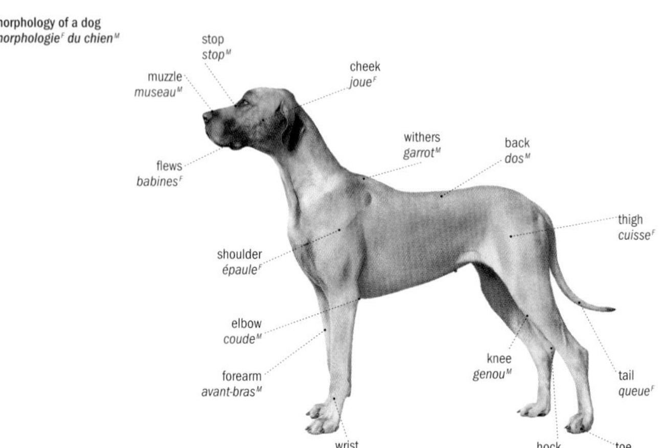

dog breeds

races[F] de chiens[M]

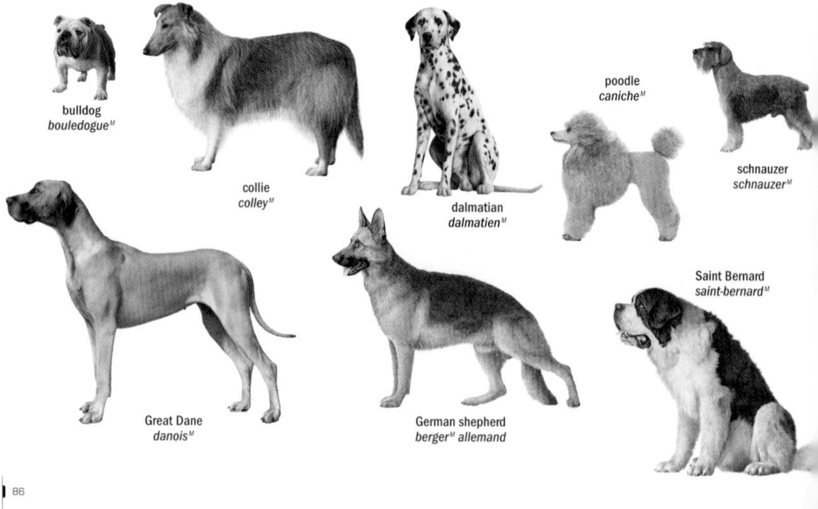
bulldog
bouledogue[M]
collie
colley[M]
dalmatian
dalmatien[M]
poodle
caniche[M]
schnauzer
schnauzer[M]
Great Dane
danois[M]
German shepherd
berger[M] allemand
Saint Bernard
saint-bernard[M]

cat
chat[M]

cat's head
tête[F]

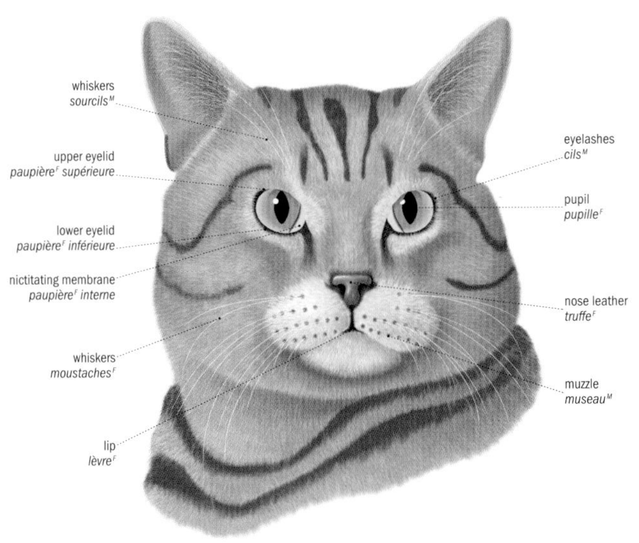

cat breeds
races[F] de chats[M]

examples of carnivorous mammals

exemples^M de mammifères^M carnivores

examples of carnivorous mammals

dolphin

dauphin[M]

morphology of a dolphin
morphologie[F] du dauphin[M]

blowhole
évent[M]
dorsal fin
nageoire[F] dorsale
mouth
bouche[F]
tail
queue[F]
eye
œil[M]
caudal fin
nageoire[F] caudale
pectoral fin
nageoire[F] pectorale

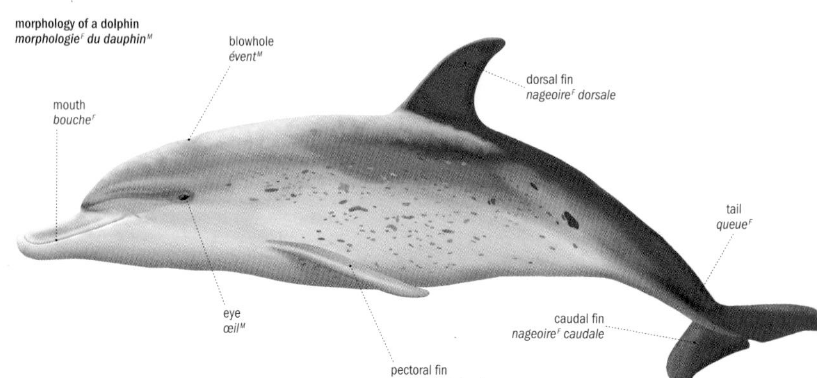

examples of marine mammals

exemples[M] de mammifères[M] marins

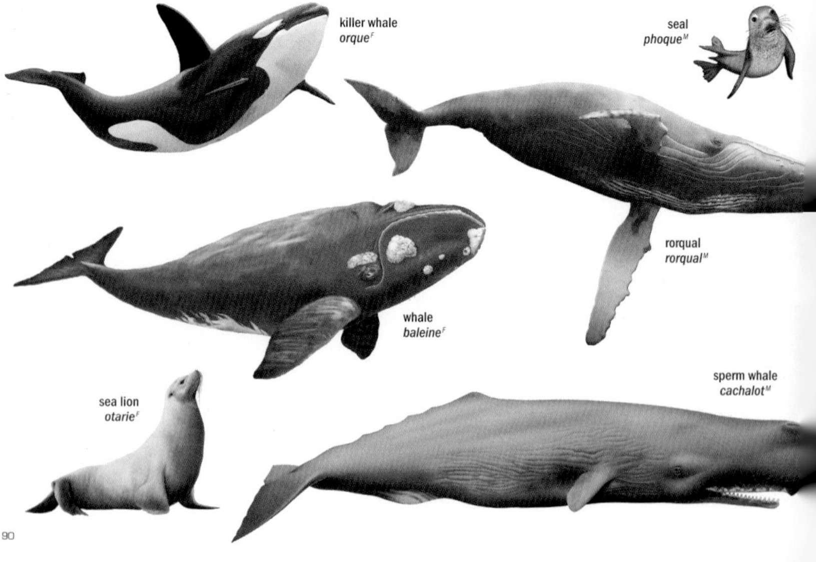

killer whale
orque[F]
seal
phoque[M]
rorqual
rorqual[M]
whale
baleine[F]
sperm whale
cachalot[M]
sea lion
otarie[F]

gorilla

gorille[M]

morphology of a gorilla
morphologie[F] du gorille[M]

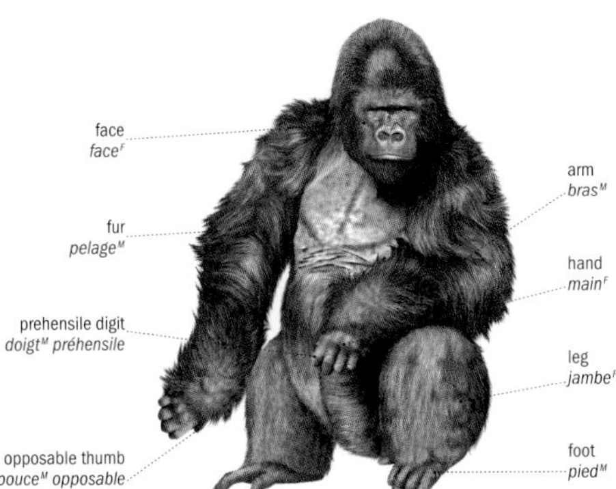

examples of primates

exemples[M] de mammifères[M] primates

tamarin
tamarin[M]

baboon
babouin[M]

macaque
macaque[M]

marmoset
ouistiti[M]

orangutan
orang-outan[M]

chimpanzee
chimpanzé[M]

lemur
lémurien[M]

gibbon
gibbon[M]

man

homme[M]

anterior view
face[F] antérieure

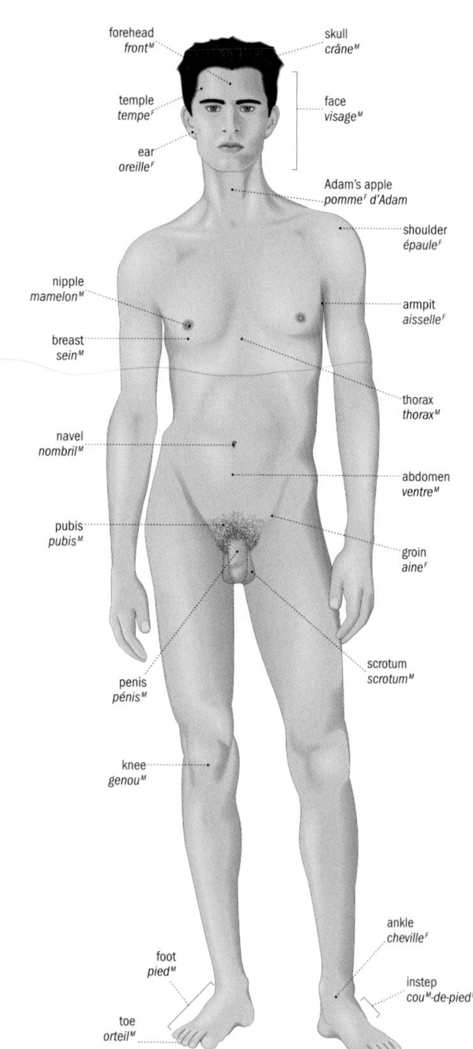

posterior view
face^F postérieure

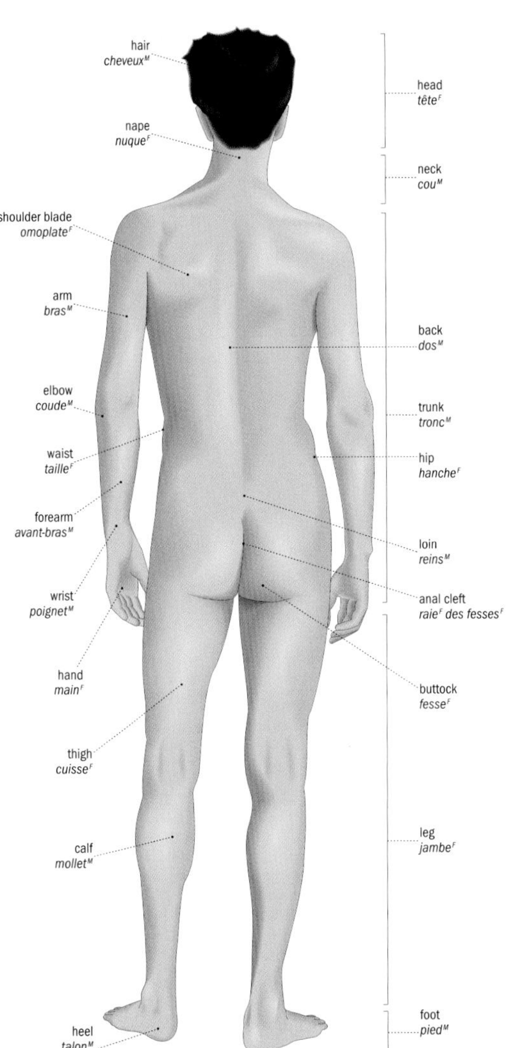

woman

femme[F]

anterior view
face[F] antérieure

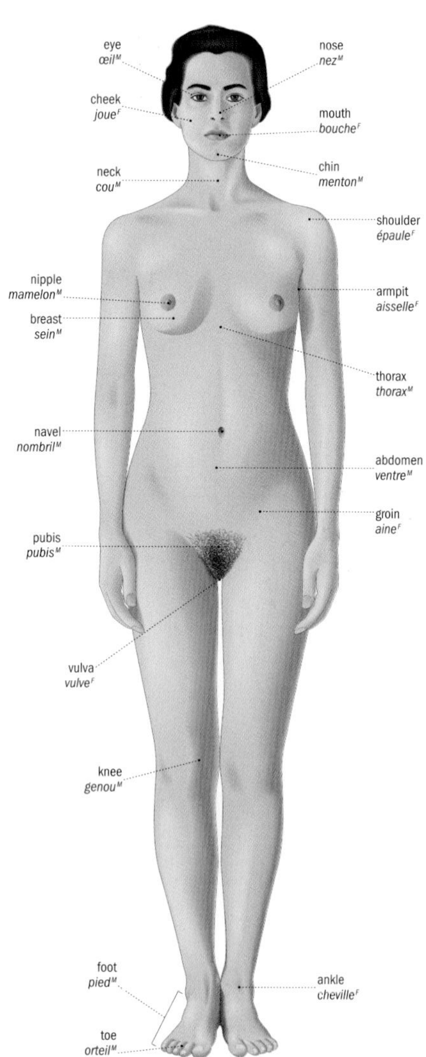

posterior view
face[F] postérieure

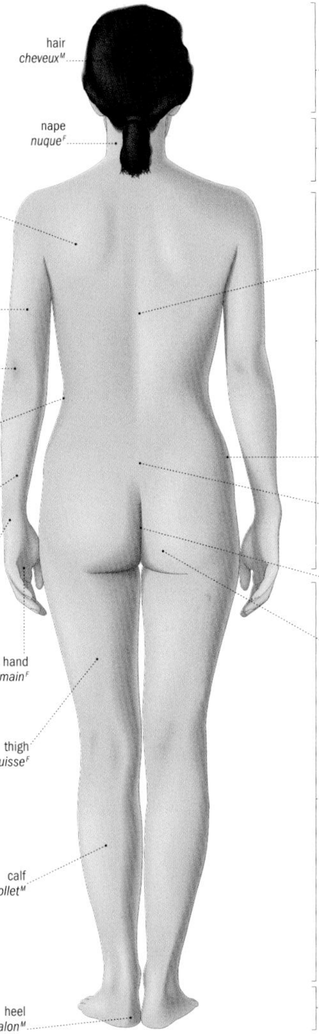

hair
cheveux[M]

head
tête[F]

nape
nuque[F]

neck
cou[M]

shoulder blade
omoplate[F]

back
dos[M]

arm
bras[M]

trunk
tronc[M]

elbow
coude[M]

waist
taille[F]

hip
hanche[F]

forearm
avant-bras[M]

loin
reins[M]

anal cleft
raie[F] des fesses[F]

wrist
poignet[M]

hand
main[F]

buttock
fesse[F]

thigh
cuisse[F]

leg
jambe[F]

calf
mollet[M]

foot
pied[M]

heel
talon[M]

muscles

muscles[M]

anterior view
face[F] antérieure

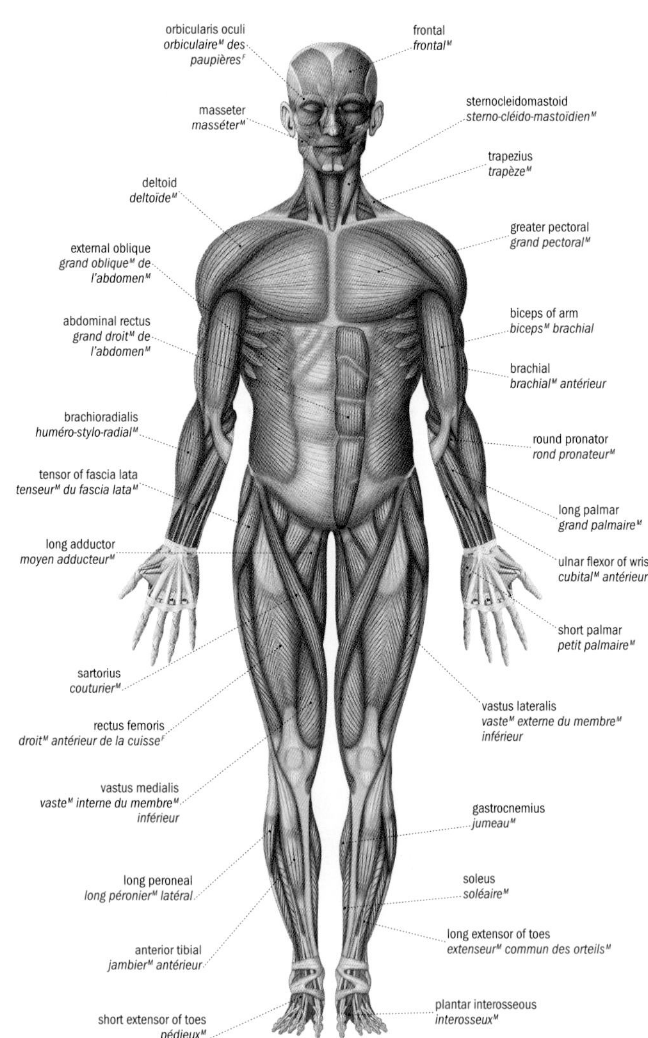

posterior view
face[F] postérieure

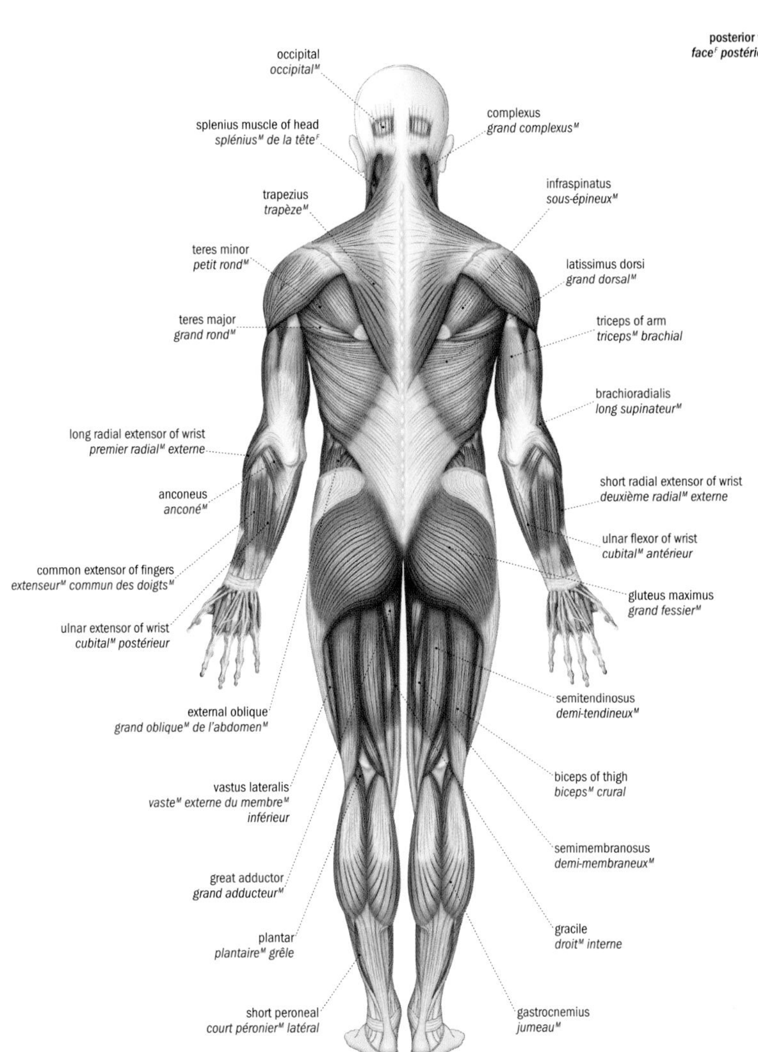

skeleton

squelette[M]

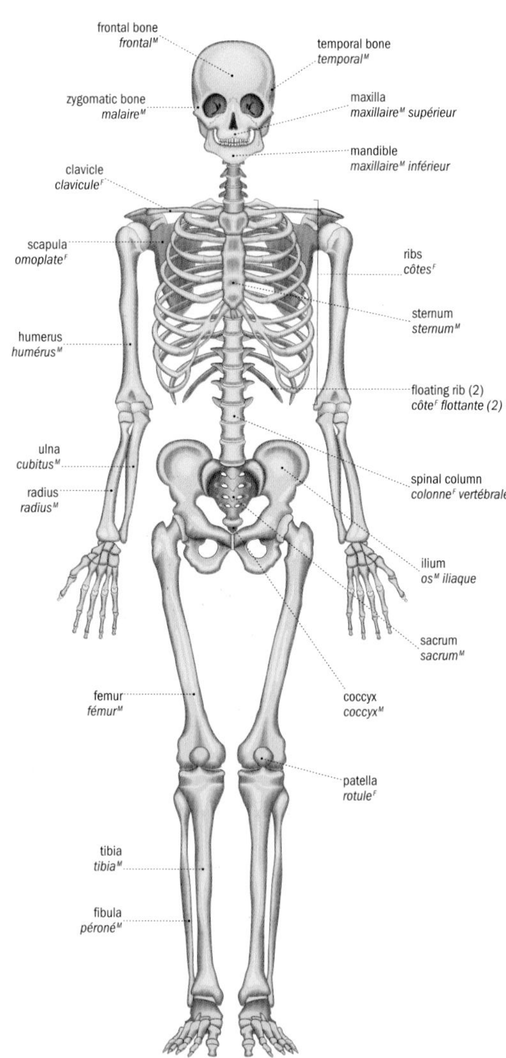

posterior view
vue[F] postérieure

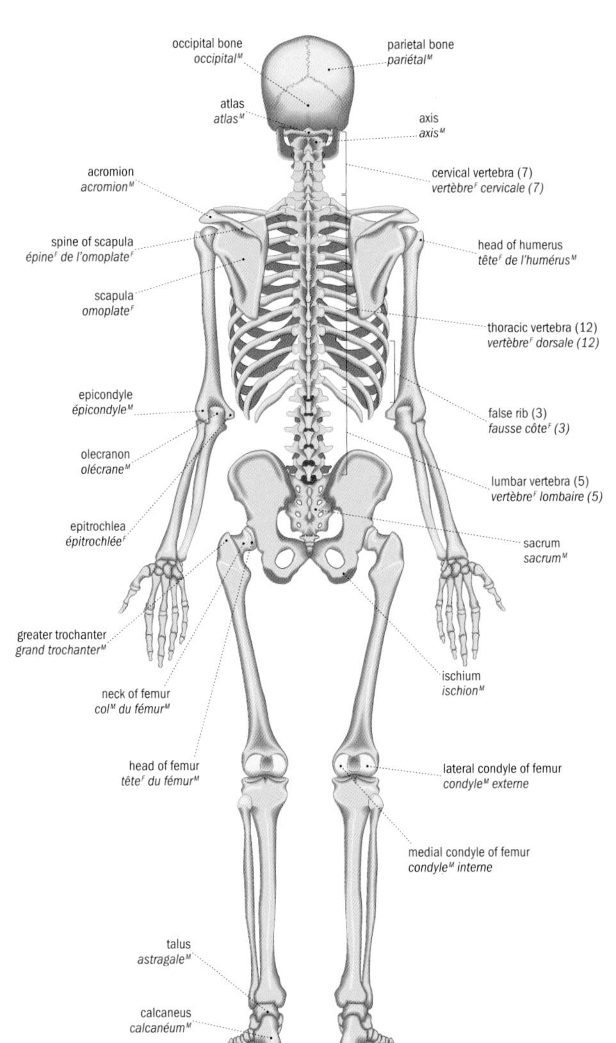

skeleton

lateral view of skull
vue[F] latérale du crâne[M]

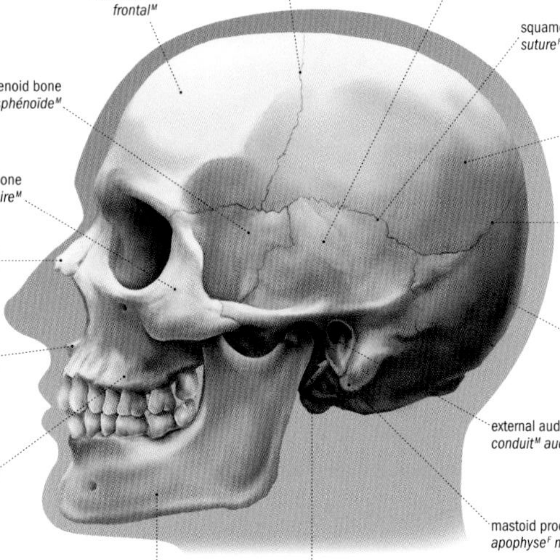

frontal bone
frontal[M]

coronal suture
suture[F] coronale

temporal bone
temporal[M]

squamous suture
suture[F] squameuse

sphenoid bone
sphénoïde[M]

parietal bone
pariétal[M]

zygomatic bone
malaire[M]

lambdoid suture
suture[F] lambdoïde

nasal bone
nasal[M]

occipital bone
occipital[M]

anterior nasal spine
épine[F] nasale antérieure

external auditory meatus
conduit[M] auditif externe

maxilla
maxillaire[M] supérieur

mastoid process
apophyse[F] mastoïde

mandible
maxillaire[M] inférieur

styloid process
apophyse[F] styloïde

child's skull
crâne[M] d'enfant[M]

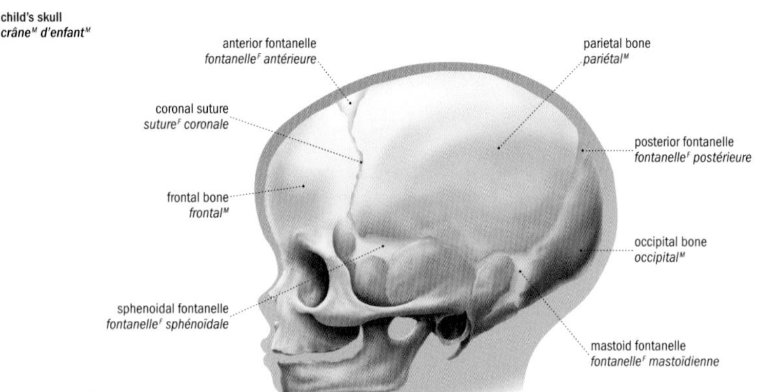

teeth

dents[F]

human denture
denture[F] humaine

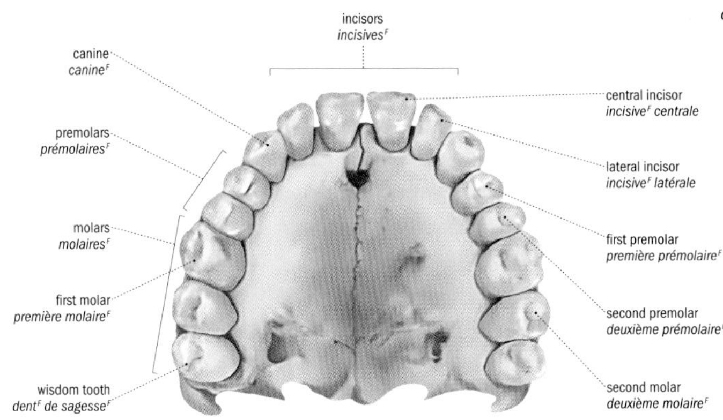

cross section of a molar
coupe[F] d'une molaire[F]

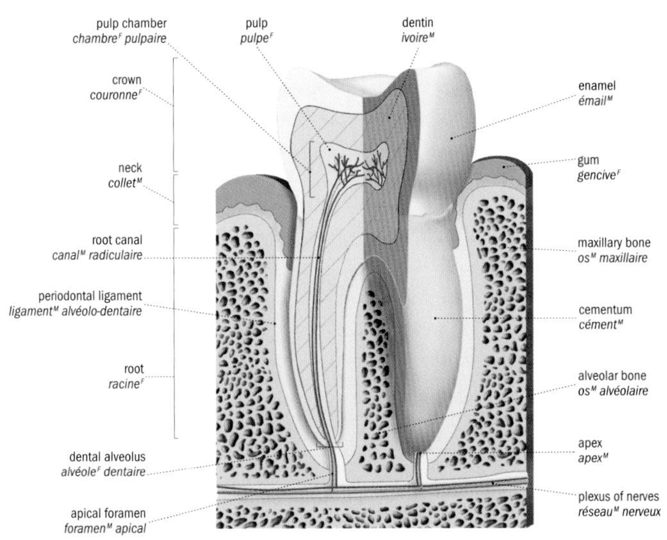

blood circulation

circulation[F] sanguine

principal veins and arteries
principales veines[F] et artères[F]

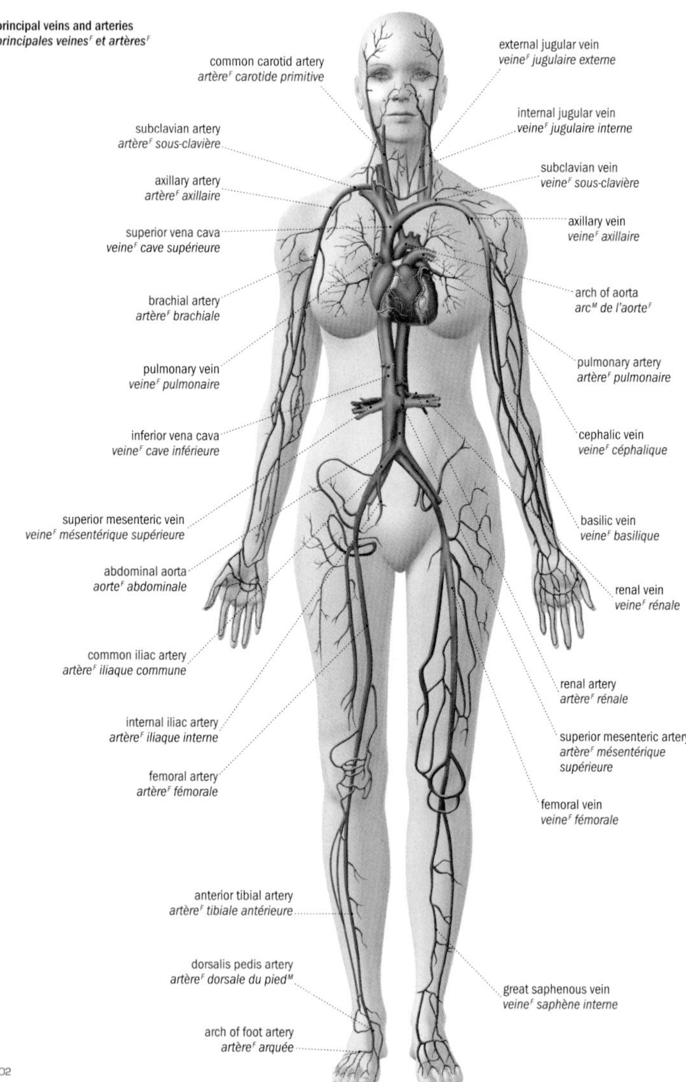

circulation diagram
***schéma*[M] *de la circulation*[F]**

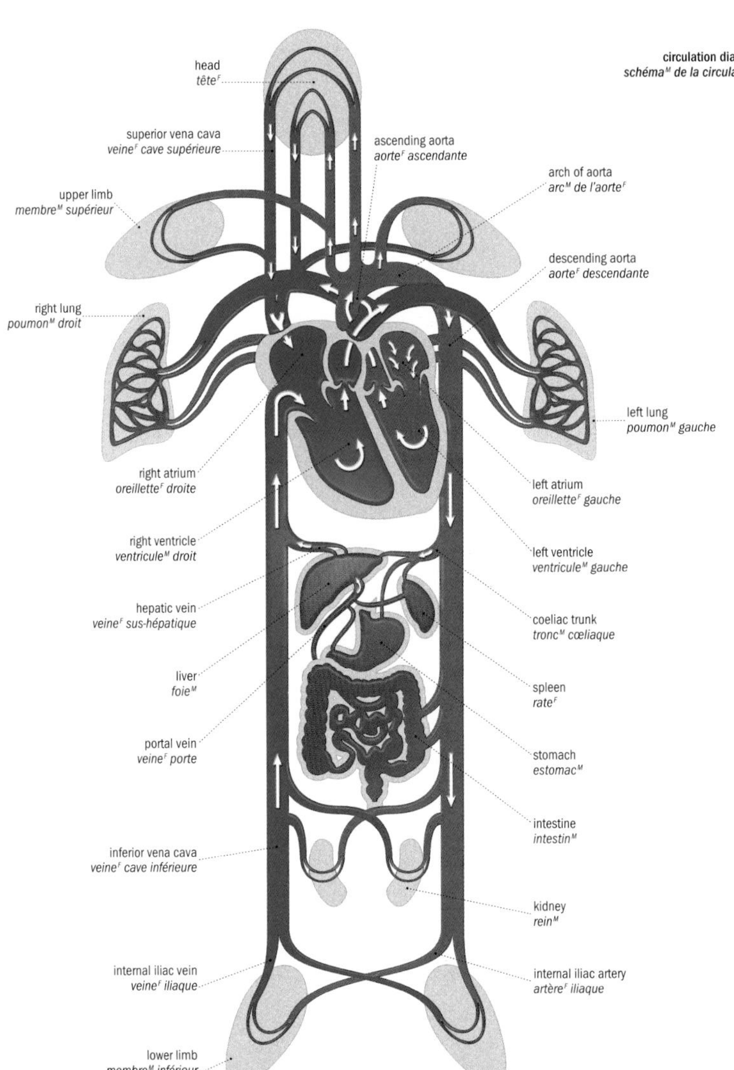

blood circulation

composition of the blood
composition^{F} du sang^{M}

white blood cell
globule^{M} blanc
blood vessel
vaisseau^{M} sanguin
red blood cell
globule^{M} rouge
platelet
plaquette^{F}
plasma
plasma^{M}

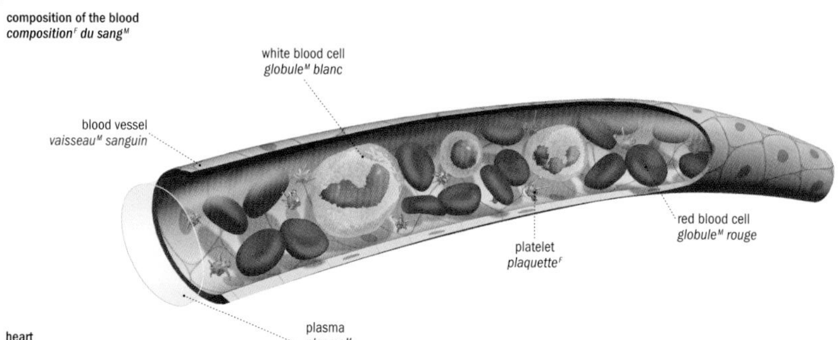

heart
cœur^{M}

oxygenated blood
sang^{M} oxygéné

deoxygenated blood
sang^{M} désoxygéné

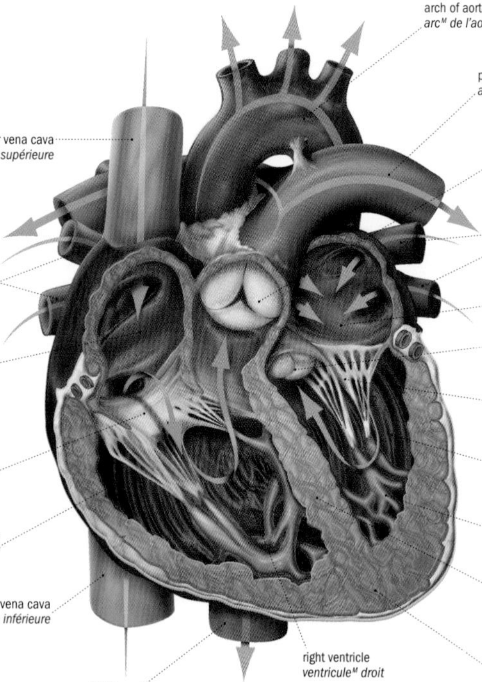

arch of aorta
arc^{M} de l'aorte^{F}
pulmonary trunk
artère^{F} pulmonaire
pulmonary valve
valvule^{F} pulmonaire
superior vena cava
veine^{F} cave supérieure
left pulmonary vein
veine^{F} pulmonaire gauc
right pulmonary vein
veine^{F} pulmonaire droite
left atrium
oreillette^{F} gauche
aortic valve
valvule^{F} aortique
right atrium
oreillette^{F} droite
mitral valve
valvule^{F} mitrale
tricuspid valve
valvule^{F} tricuspide
left ventricle
ventricule^{M} gauche
endocardium
endocarde^{M}
papillary muscle
muscle^{M} papillaire
inferior vena cava
veine^{F} cave inférieure
interventricular septum
septum^{M} interventricula
right ventricle
ventricule^{M} droit
myocardium
myocarde^{M}
aorta
aorte^{F}

respiratory system

appareil^{M} respiratoire

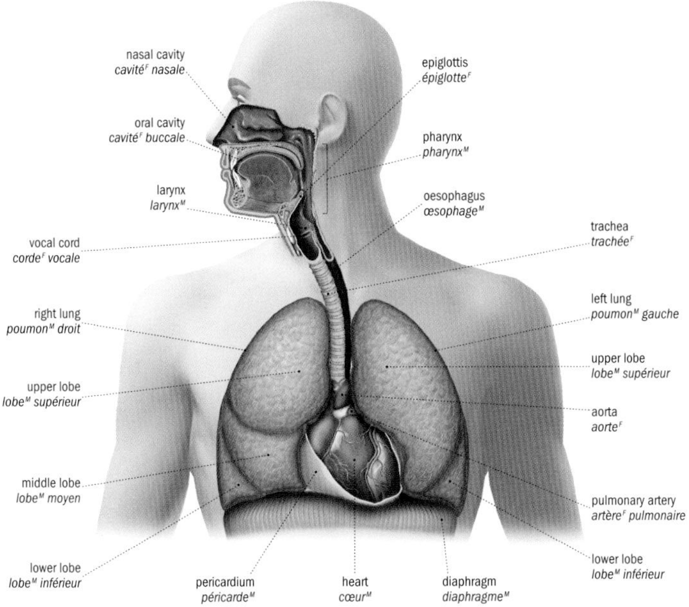

nasal cavity
cavité^{F} nasale
oral cavity
cavité^{F} buccale
larynx
larynx^{M}
vocal cord
corde^{F} vocale
right lung
poumon^{M} droit
upper lobe
lobe^{M} supérieur
middle lobe
lobe^{M} moyen
lower lobe
lobe^{M} inférieur
pericardium
péricarde^{M}
heart
cœur^{M}
diaphragm
diaphragme^{M}
epiglottis
épiglotte^{F}
pharynx
pharynx^{M}
oesophagus
œsophage^{M}
trachea
trachée^{F}
left lung
poumon^{M} gauche
upper lobe
lobe^{M} supérieur
aorta
aorte^{F}
pulmonary artery
artère^{F} pulmonaire
lower lobe
lobe^{M} inférieur

lungs
poumons^{M}

upper lobe
lobe^{M} supérieur
trachea
trachée^{F}
main bronchus
bronche^{F} principale
lobe bronchus
bronche^{F} lobaire
terminal bronchiole
bronchiole^{F} terminale
parietal pleura
plèvre^{F} pariétale
pleural cavity
cavité^{F} pleurale
visceral pleura
plèvre^{F} viscérale
oblique fissure
scissure^{F} oblique
lower lobe
lobe^{M} inférieur

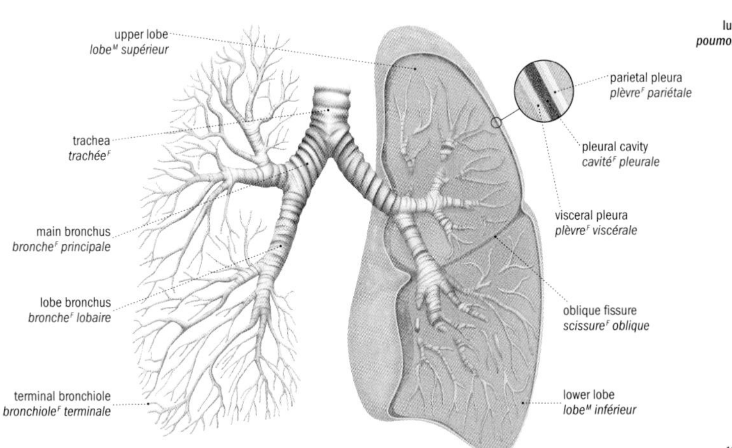

digestive system

appareil[M] digestif

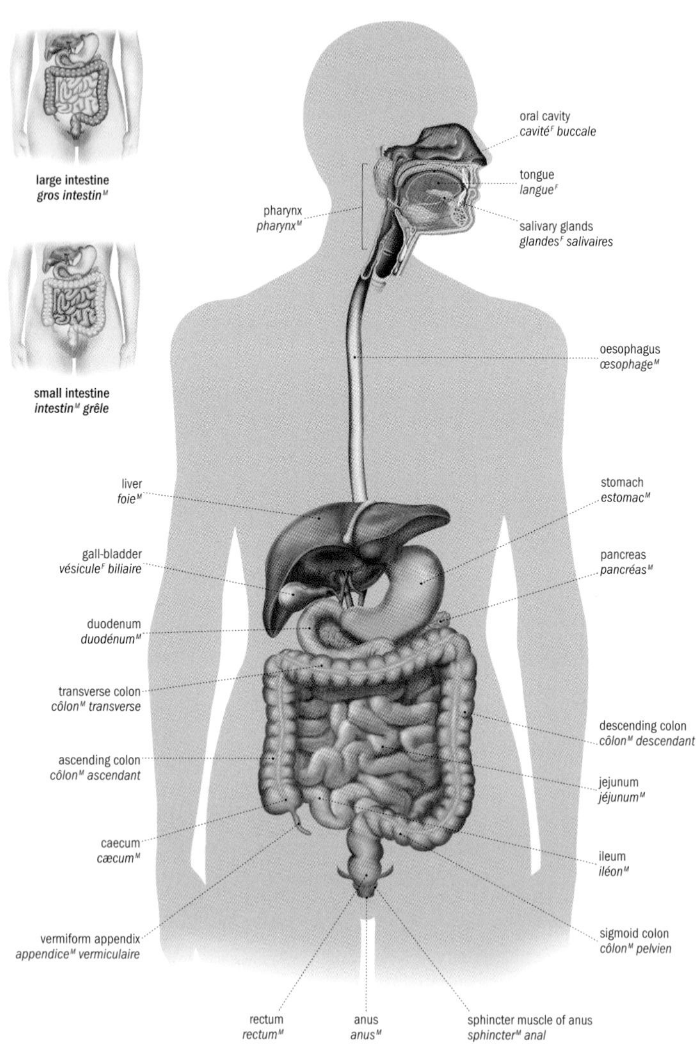

urinary system

appareil[M] urinaire

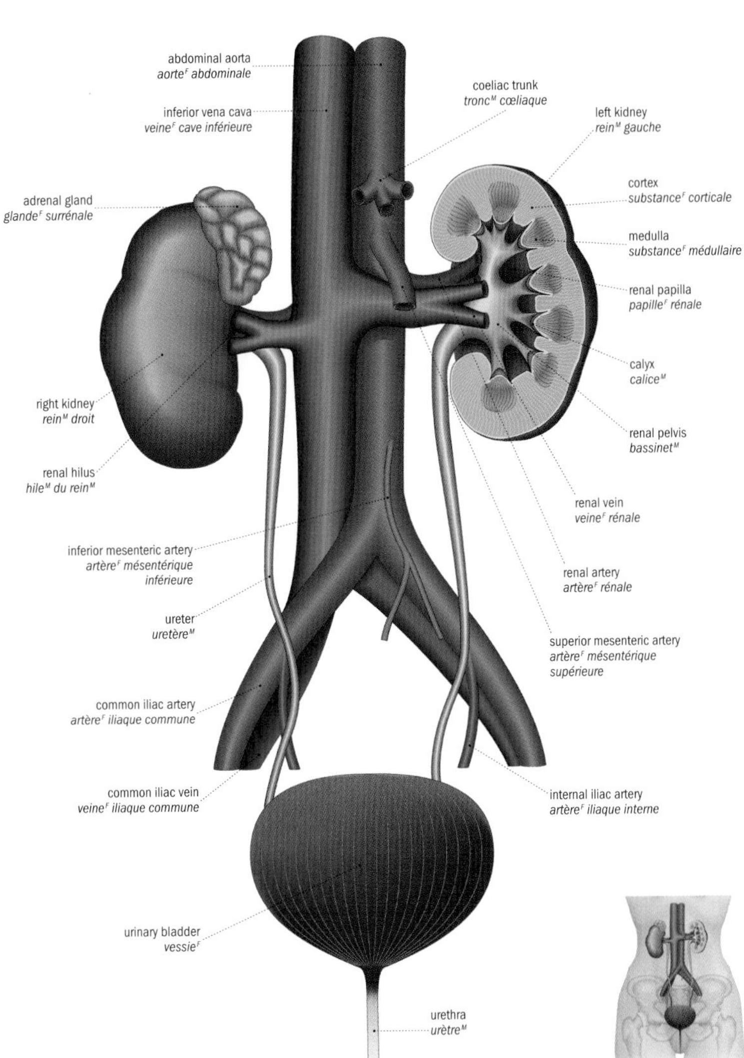

nervous system

système[M] nerveux

peripheral nervous system
système[M] nerveux périphérique

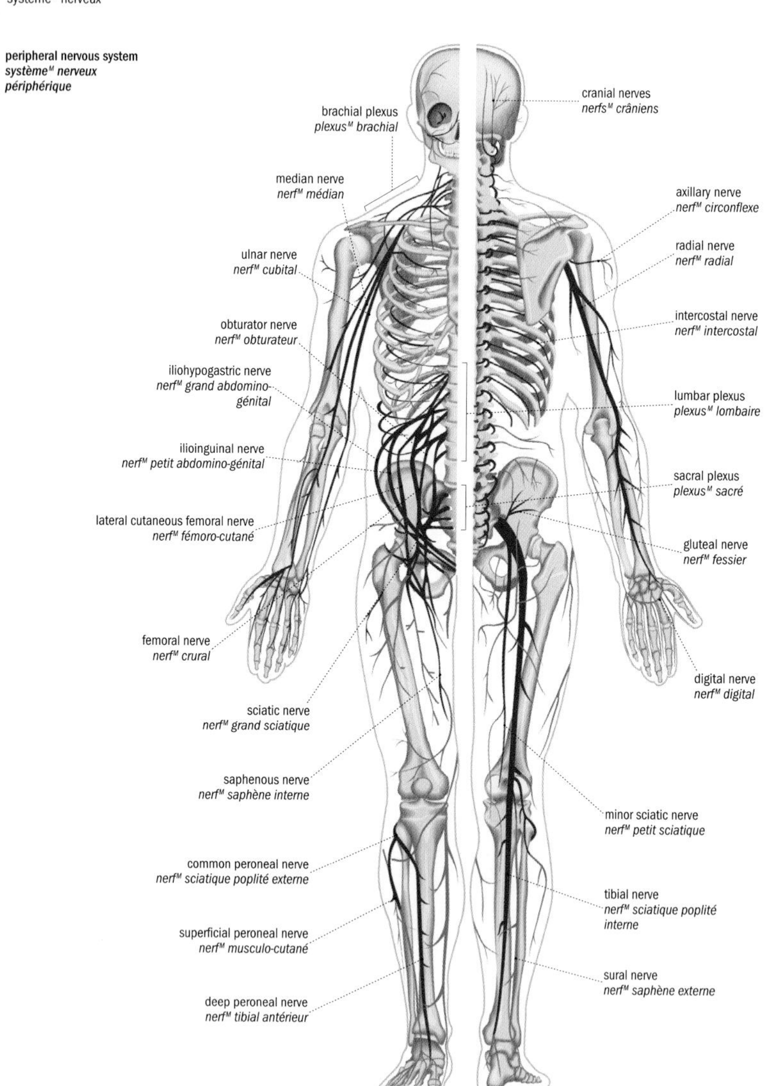

central nervous system
système[M] nerveux central

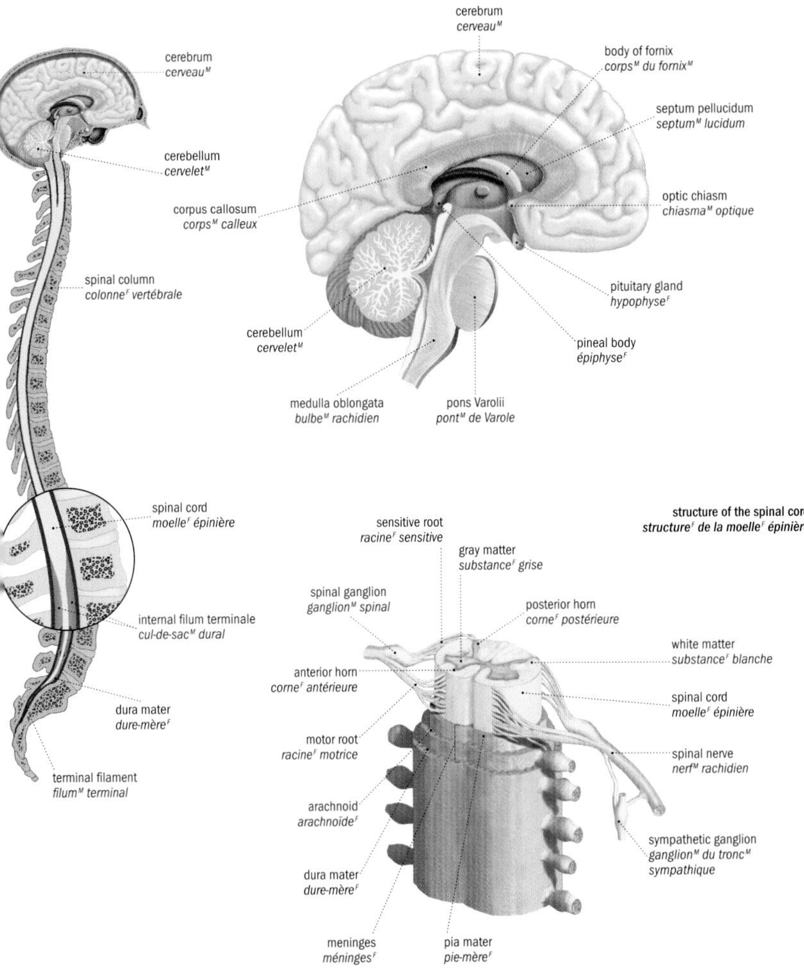

nervous system

chain of neurons
chaîne^F de neurones^M

synapse
synapse^F
collateral
collatérale^F
sheath of Schwann
gaine^F de Schwann
cell body
corps^M cellulaire
nucleus
noyau^M
dendrite
dendrite^F
node of Ranvier
nœud^M de Ranvier
axon hillock
collet^M de l'axone^M
terminal arborization
arborisation^F terminale
myelin sheath
gaine^F de myéline^F
axon
axone^M

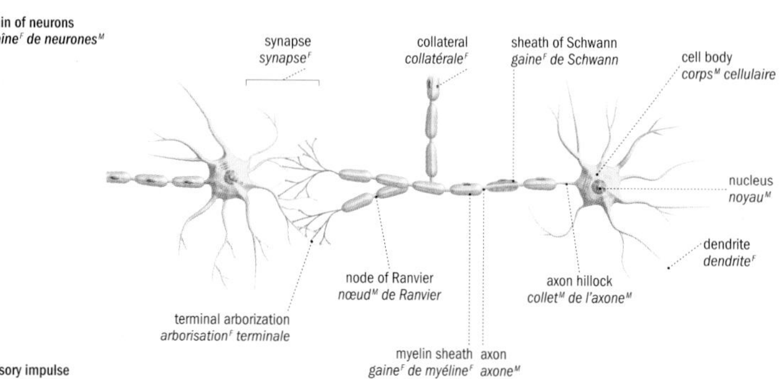

sensory impulse
influx^M nerveux

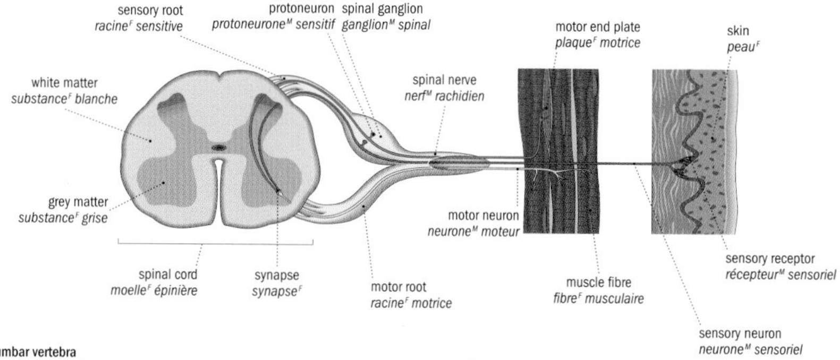

sensory root
racine^F sensitive
protoneuron
protoneurone^M sensitif
spinal ganglion
ganglion^M spinal
motor end plate
plaque^F motrice
skin
peau^F
white matter
substance^F blanche
spinal nerve
nerf^M rachidien
grey matter
substance^F grise
motor neuron
neurone^M moteur
spinal cord
moelle^F épinière
synapse
synapse^F
motor root
racine^F motrice
muscle fibre
fibre^F musculaire
sensory receptor
récepteur^M sensoriel
sensory neuron
neurone^M sensoriel

lumbar vertebra
vertèbre^F lombaire

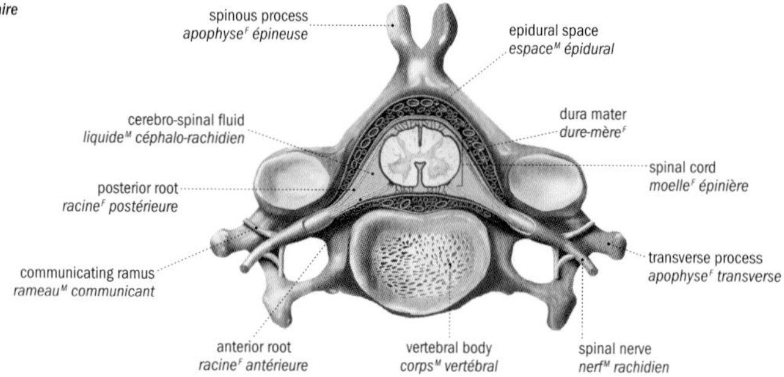

spinous process
apophyse^F épineuse
epidural space
espace^M épidural
cerebro-spinal fluid
liquide^M céphalo-rachidien
dura mater
dure-mère^F
posterior root
racine^F postérieure
spinal cord
moelle^F épinière
communicating ramus
rameau^M communicant
transverse process
apophyse^F transverse
anterior root
racine^F antérieure
vertebral body
corps^M vertébral
spinal nerve
nerf^M rachidien

male genital organs

organes[M] génitaux masculins

sagittal section
coupe[F] sagittale

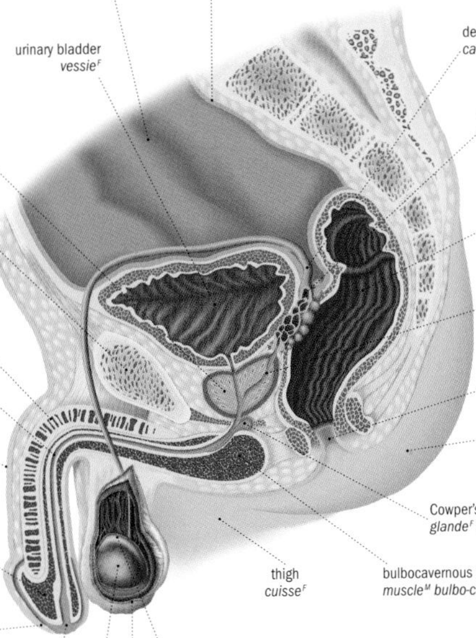

abdominal cavity
cavité[F] abdominale
peritoneum
péritoine[M]
urinary bladder
vessie[F]
deferent duct
canal[M] déférent
prostate
prostate[F]
seminal vesicle
vésicule[F] séminale
symphysis pubis
symphyse[F] pubienne
rectum
rectum[M]
corpus cavernosum
corps[M] caverneux
ejaculatory duct
canal[M] éjaculateur
male urethra
urètre[M] pénien
anus
anus[M]
penis
verge[F]
buttock
fesse[F]
Cowper's gland
glande[F] de Cowper
glans penis
gland[M]
thigh
cuisse[F]
bulbocavernous muscle
muscle[M] bulbo-caverneux
prepuce
prépuce[M]
epididymis
épididyme[M]
urinary meatus
méat[M] de l'urètre[M]
testicle
testicule[M]
scrotum
scrotum[M]

spermatozoon
spermatozoïde[M]

head
tête[F]
end piece
pièce[F] terminale
tail
queue[F]
neck
cou[M]
middle piece
pièce[F] intermédiaire

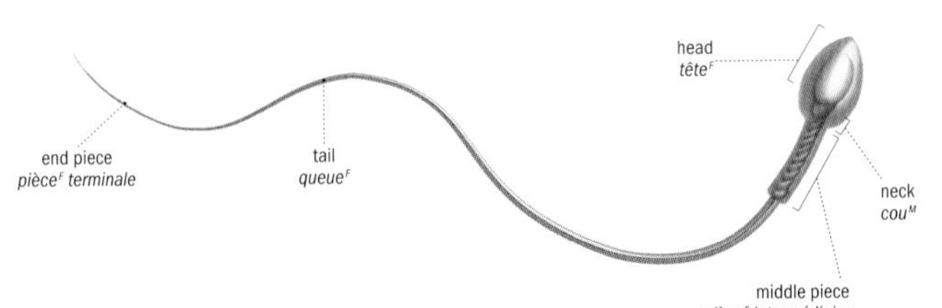

female genital organs

organes[M] génitaux féminins

sagittal section
coupe[F] sagittale

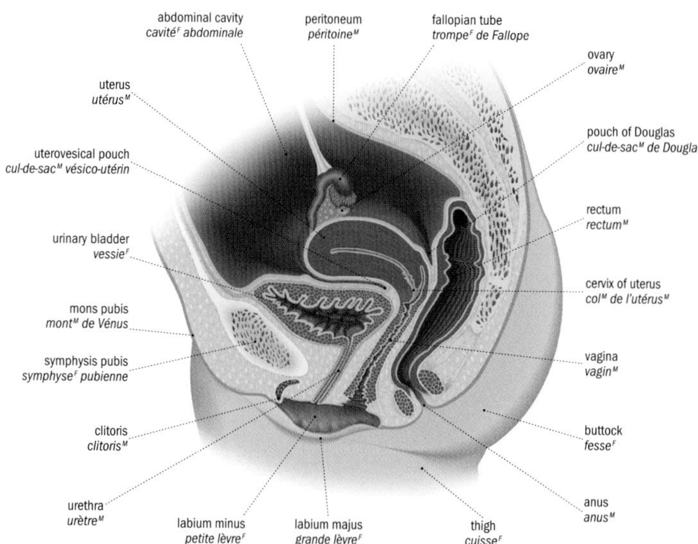

egg
ovule[M]

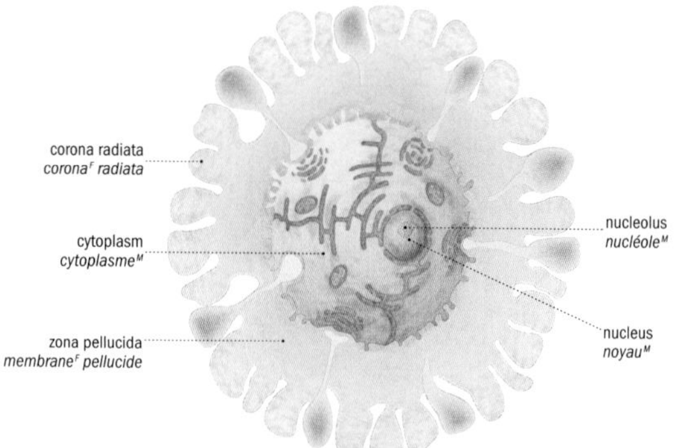

female genital organs

posterior view
vue*[F] *postérieure

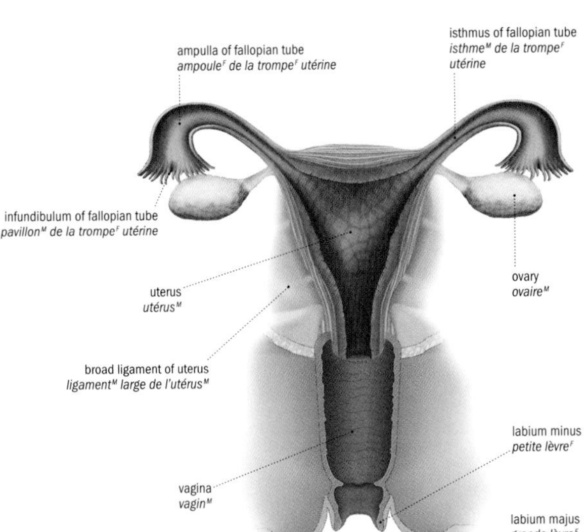

fallopian tubes
trompes*[F] *de Fallope

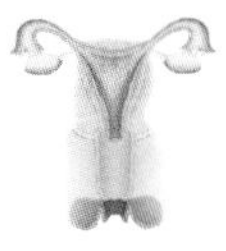

vulva
***vulve*[F]**

breast

sein[M]

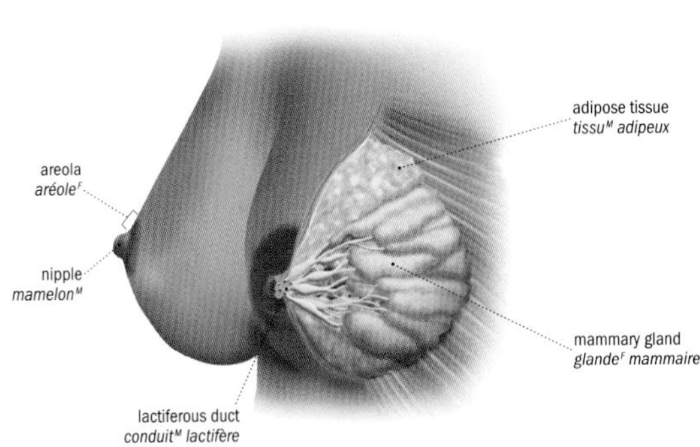

touch

toucher[M]

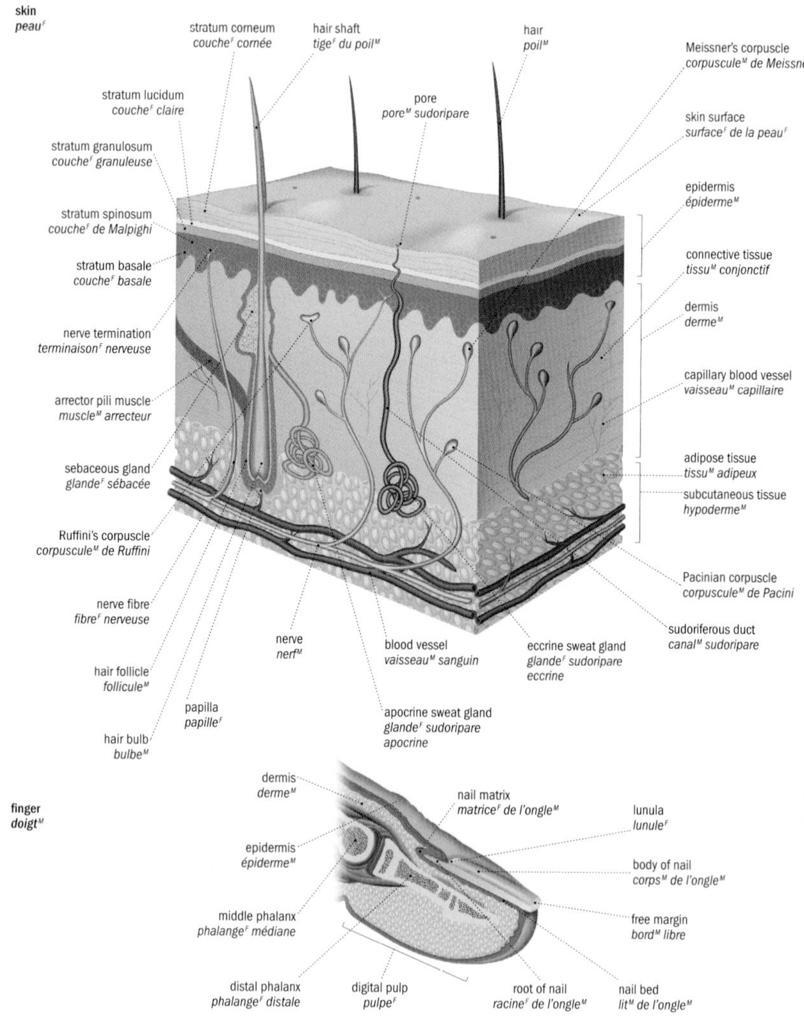

touch

hand
main[F]

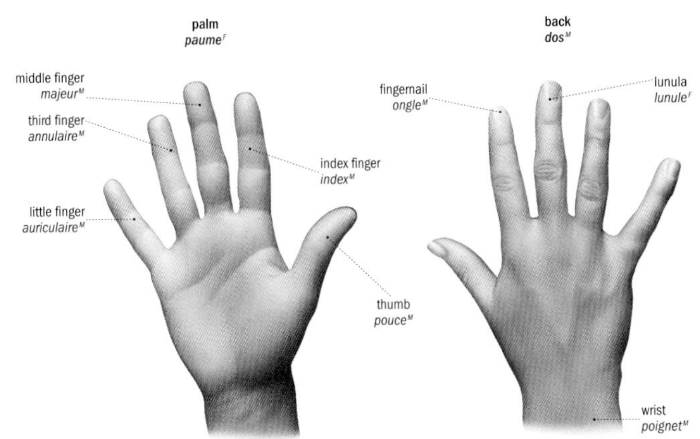

hearing

ouïe[F]

auricle
pavillon[M]

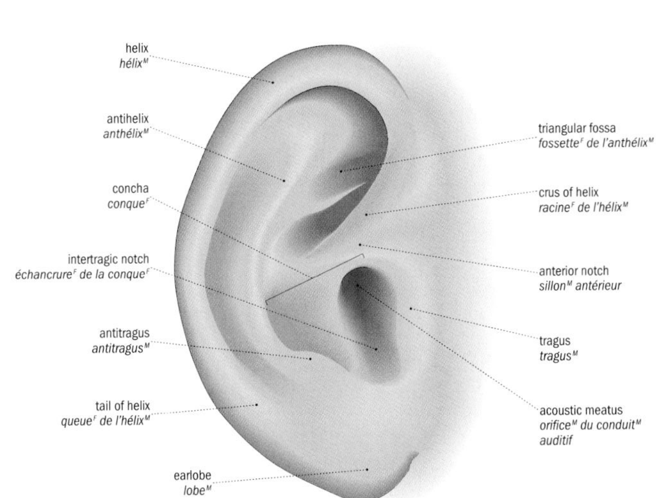

hearing

structure of the ear
structure[F] de l'oreille[F]

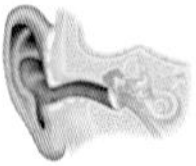

external ear
oreille[F] externe

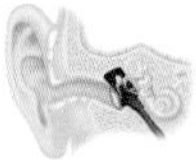

middle ear
oreille[F] moyenne

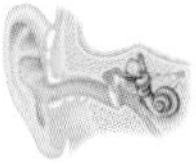

internal ear
oreille[F] interne

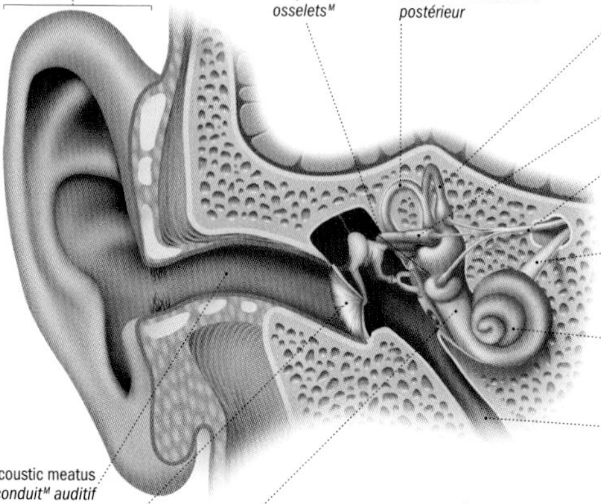

auricle
pavillon[M]
auditory ossicles
osselets[M]
posterior semicircular canal
canal[M] semi-circulaire postérieur
superior semicircular canal
canal[M] semi-circulaire antér
lateral semicircular canal
canal[M] semi-circulaire externe
vestibular nerve
nerf[M] vestibulaire
cochlear nerve
nerf[M] cochléaire
cochlea
cochlée[F]
Eustachian tube
trompe[F] d'Eustache
acoustic meatus
conduit[M] auditif
ear drum
membrane[F] du tympan[M]
vestibule
vestibule[M]

auditory oss
osse

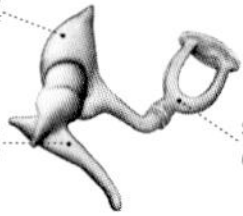

incus
enclume[F]
malleus
marteau[M]
stapes
étrier[M]

smell and taste

odorat[M] et goût[M]

mouth
bouche[F]

upper lip
lèvre[F] supérieure
gum
gencive[F]
superior dental arch
arcade[F] dentaire supérieure
hard palate
voûte[F] du palais[M]
isthmus of fauces
isthme[M] du gosier[M]
soft palate
voile[M] du palais[M]
commissure of lips of mouth
commissure[F] labiale
palatoglossal arch
pilier[M] du voile[M]
tongue
langue[F]
tonsil
amygdale[F]
uvula
luette[F]
inferior dental arch
arcade[F] dentaire inférieure
lower lip
lèvre[F] inférieure

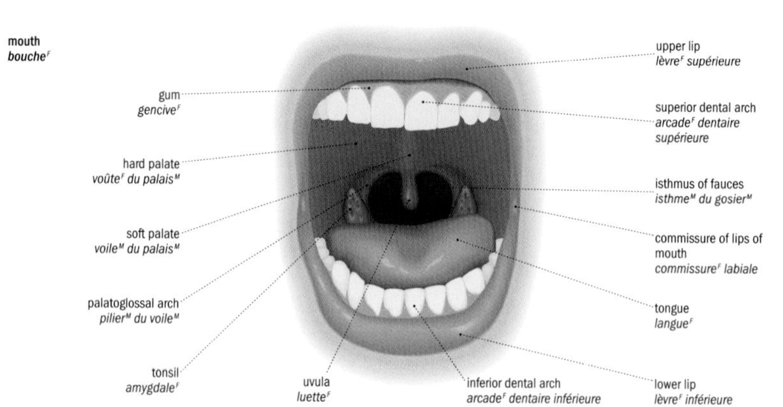

external nose
***parties*^F *externes du nez*^M**

bridge of nose
racine^F du nez^M
dorsum of nose
dos^M du nez^M
tip of nose
lobe^M du nez^M
septum
cloison^F
ala
aile^F du nez^M
naris
narine^F
philtrum
sillon^M naso-labial

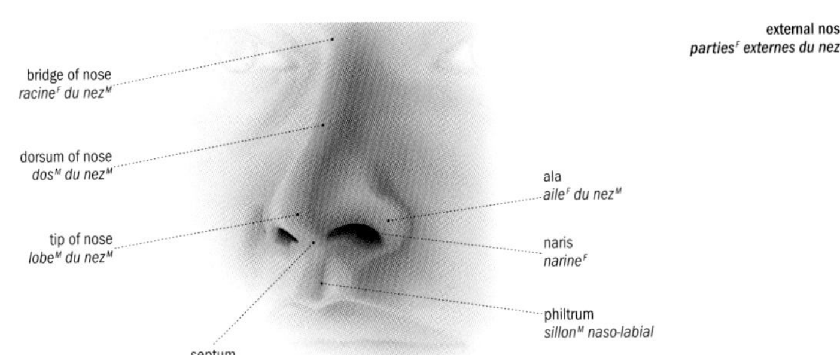

nasal fossae
fosses*^F *nasales

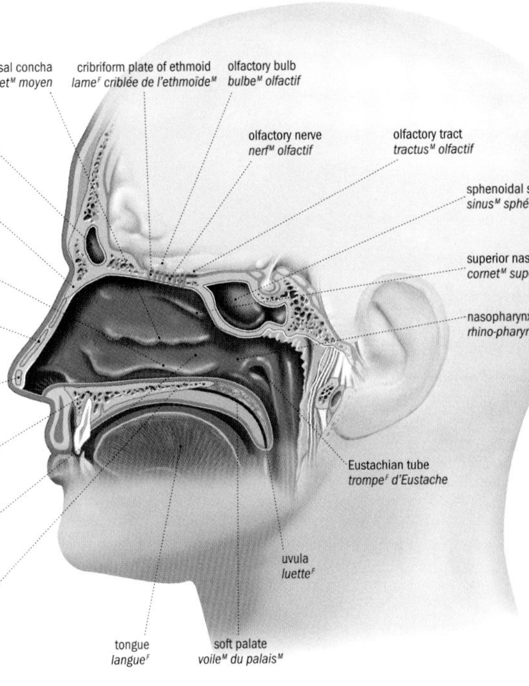

middle nasal concha
cornet^M moyen
cribriform plate of ethmoid
lame^F criblée de l'ethmoïde^M
olfactory bulb
bulbe^M olfactif
frontal sinus
sinus^M frontal
olfactory nerve
nerf^M olfactif
olfactory tract
tractus^M olfactif
nasal bone
os^M propre du nez^M
sphenoidal sinus
sinus^M sphénoïdal
inferior nasal concha
cornet^M inférieur
superior nasal concha
cornet^M supérieur
septal cartilage of nose
cartilage^M de la cloison^F
nasopharynx
rhino-pharynx^M
greater alar cartilage
cartilage^M de l'aile^F du nez^M
maxilla
maxillaire^M
Eustachian tube
trompe^F d'Eustache
olfactory mucosa
muqueuse^F olfactive
uvula
luette^F
hard palate
voûte^F du palais^M
tongue
langue^F
soft palate
voile^M du palais^M

dorsum of tongue
dos[M] de la langue[F]

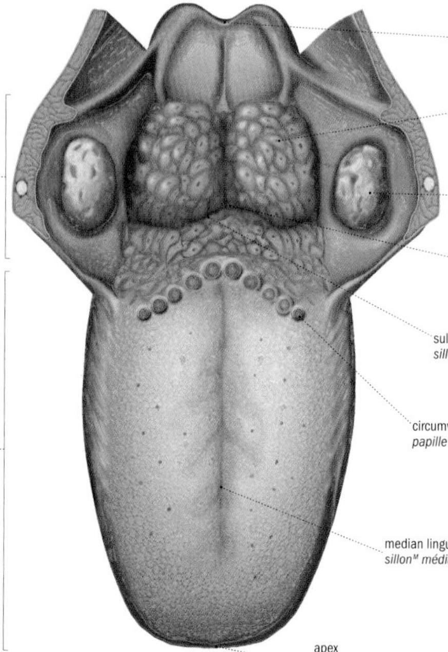

epiglottis
épiglotte[F]
lingual tonsil
amygdale[F] linguale
root
base[F]
palatine tonsil
amygdale[F] palatine
foramen caecum
foramen[M] cæcum[M]
sulcus terminalis
sillon[M] terminal
circumvallate papilla
papille[F] caliciforme
body
corps[M]
median lingual sulcus
sillon[M] médian
apex
apex[M]

taste receptors
récepteurs[M] du goût[M]

fongiform papilla
papille[F] fongiforme
filiform papilla
papille[F] filiforme
salivary gland
glande[F] salivaire
circumvallate papilla
papille[F] caliciforme
foliate papilla
papille[F] foliée
furrow
sillon[M]
taste bud
bourgeon[M] gustatif

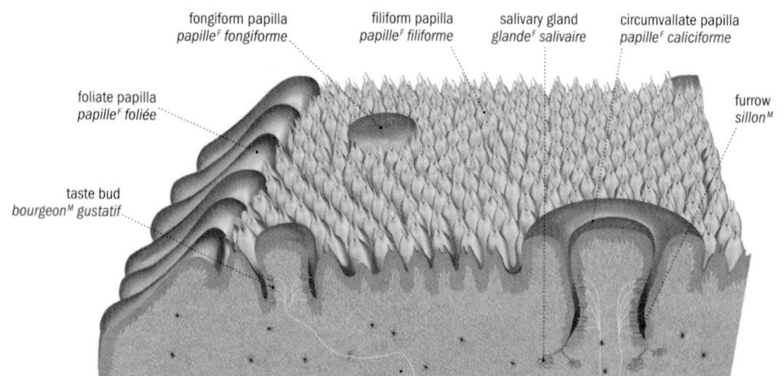

sight
vue[F]

eye
œil[M]

upper eyelid
paupière[F] supérieure
eyelash
cil[M]
lachrymal caruncle
caroncule[F] lacrymale
lachrymal canal
canal[M] lacrymal
iris
iris[M]
lower eyelid
paupière[F] inférieure
sclera
sclérotique[F]
pupil
pupille[F]
lachrymal gland
glande[F] lacrymale

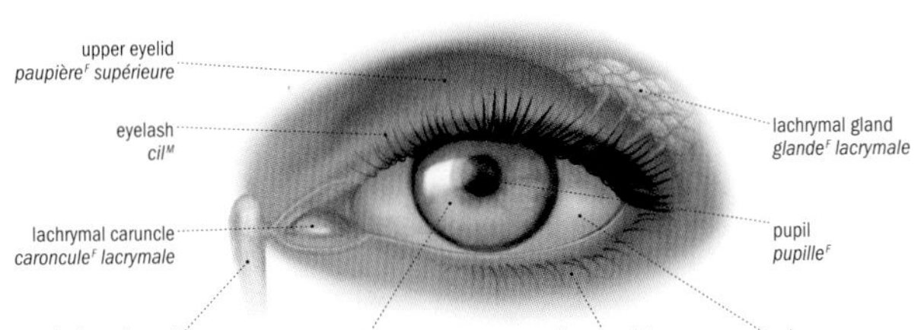

eyeball
globe[M] ***oculaire***

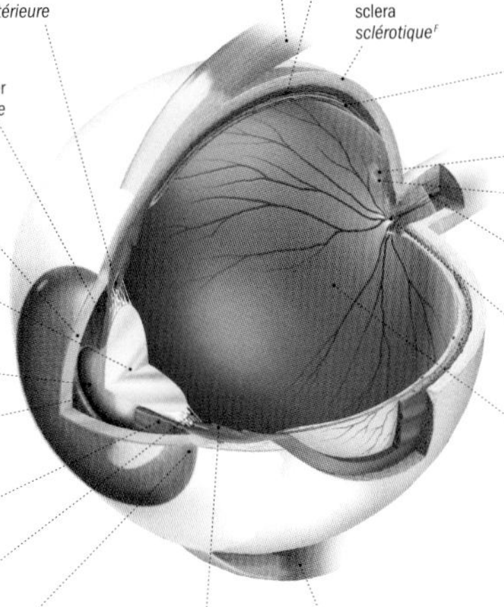

superior rectus muscle
muscle[M] droit supérieur
choroid
choroïde[F]
posterior chamber
chambre[F] postérieure
sclera
sclérotique[F]
retina
rétine[F]
anterior chamber
chambre[F] antérieure
fovea
fovéa[F]
cornea
cornée[F]
macula
tache[F] jaune
lens
cristallin[M]
optic nerve
nerf[M] optique
pupil
pupille[F]
papilla
papille[F]
aqueous humour
humeur[F] aqueuse
vitreous body
corps[M] vitré
iris
iris[M]
suspensory ligament
ligament[M] suspenseur
conjunctiva
conjonctive[F]
ciliary body
corps[M] ciliaire
inferior rectus muscle
muscle[M] droit inférieur

photoreceptors
photorécepteurs[M]

cone
cône[M]

rod
bâtonnet[M]

HUMAN BEING

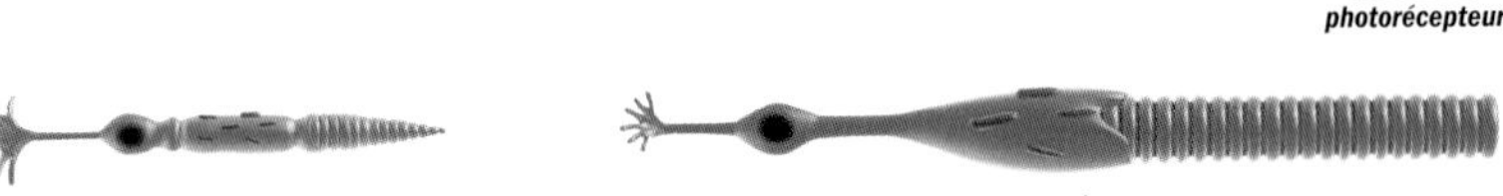

supermarket

supermarché[M]

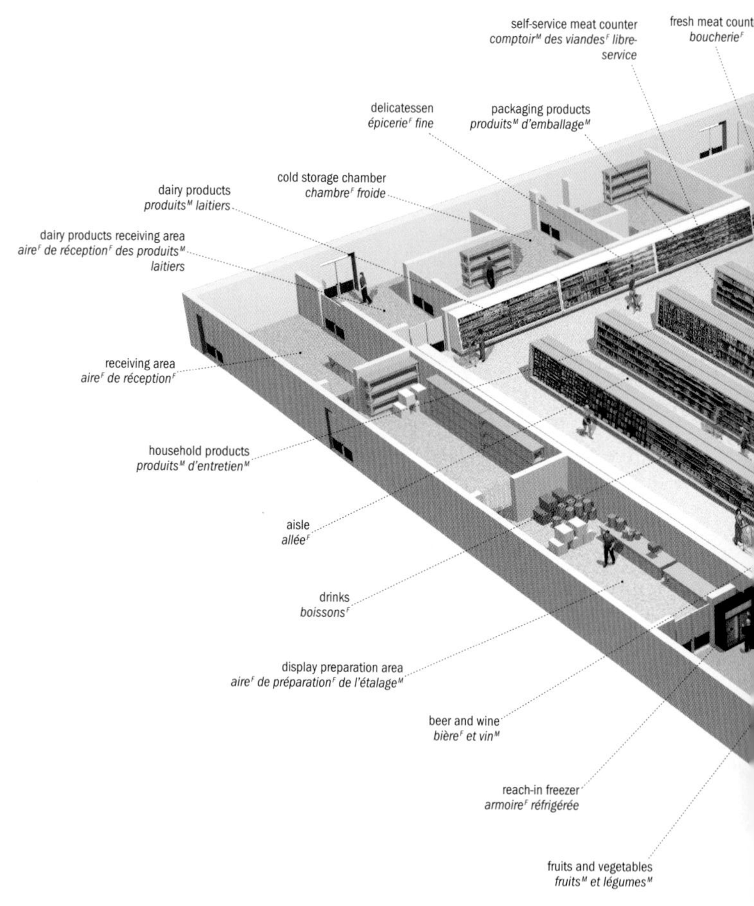

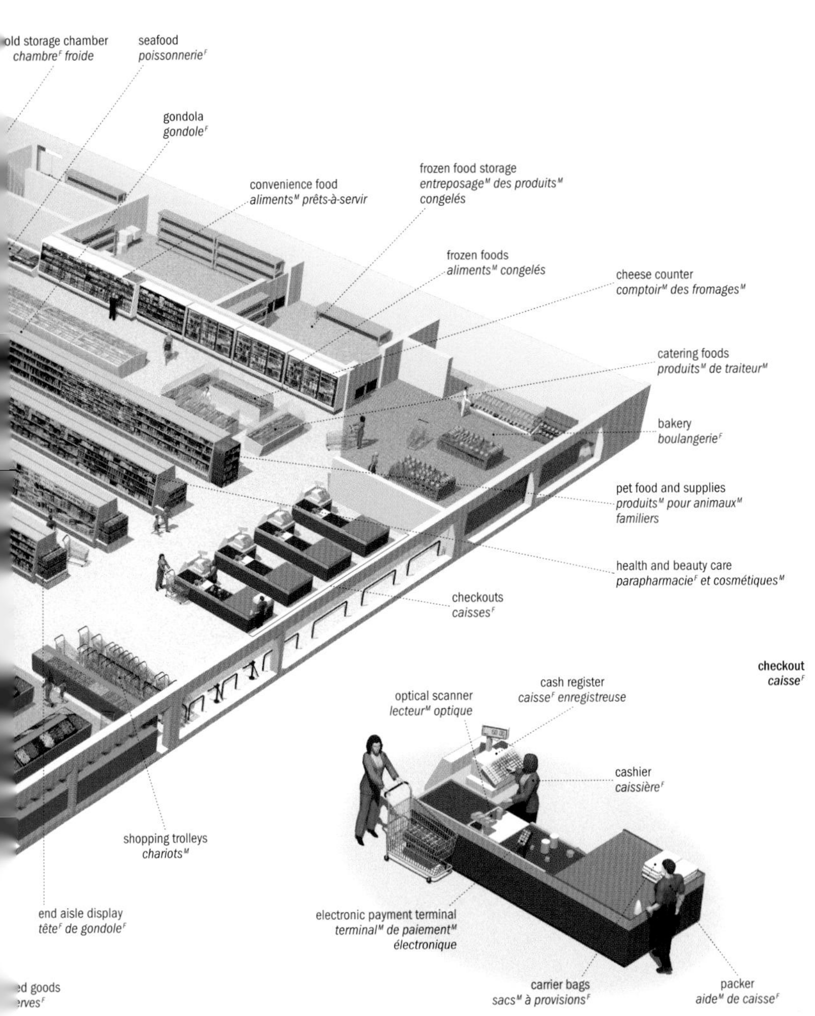

checkout
caisse

farmstead

ferme[F]

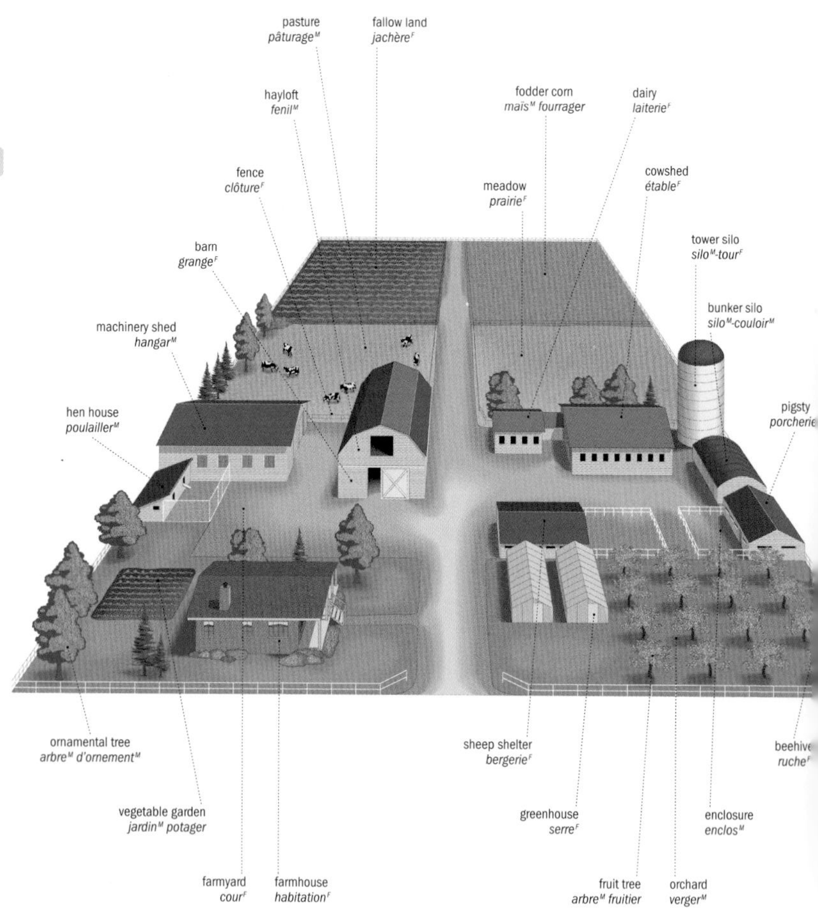

mushrooms
champignons[M]

truffle
truffe[F]

wood ear
oreille-de-Judas[F]

royal agaric
oronge[F] vraie

delicious lactarius
lactaire[M] délicieux

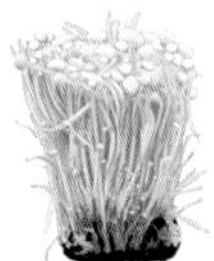
enoki mushroom
collybie[F] à pied[M] velouté

oyster mushroom
urote[M] en forme[F] d'huître[F]

cultivated mushroom
champignon[M] de couche[F]

green russula
russule[F] verdoyante

morel
morille[F]

edible boletus
cèpe[M]

shiitake
shiitake[M]

chanterelle
chanterelle[F] commune

seaweed
algues[F]

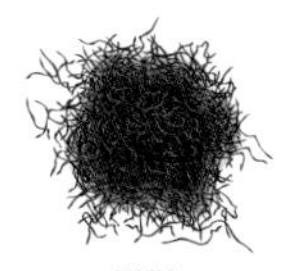
arame
aramé[M]

wakame
wakamé[M]

kombu
kombu[M]

spirulina
spiruline[F]

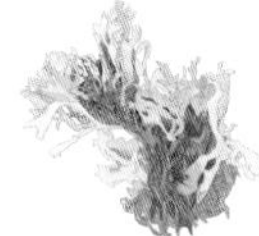
Irish moss
mousse[F] d'Irlande[F]

hijiki
hijiki[M]

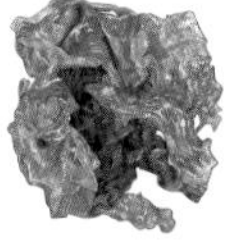
sea lettuce
laitue[F] de mer[F]

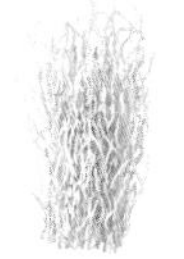
agar-agar
agar-agar[M]

nori
nori[M]

dulse
rhodyménie[M] palmé

vegetables

légumes[M]

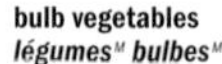

bulb vegetables
légumes[M] bulbes[M]

leek
poireau[M]

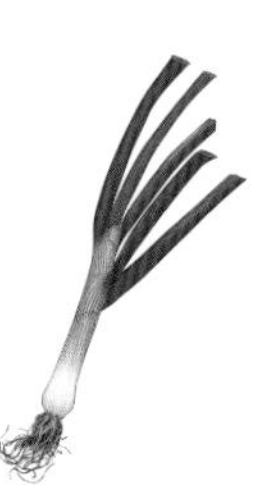

green onion
oignon[M] vert

spring onion
ciboule[F]

shallot
échalote[F]

water chestnut
châtaigne[F] d'eau[F]

garlic
ail[M]

chive
ciboulette[F]

yellow onion
oignon[M] jaune

red onion
oignon[M] rouge

white onion
oignon[M] blanc

pickling onion
oignon[M] à mariner

tuber vegetables
légumes[M] tubercules[M]

cassava
manioc[M]

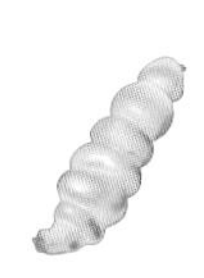

crosne
crosne[M]

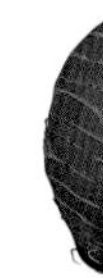

taro
taro[M]

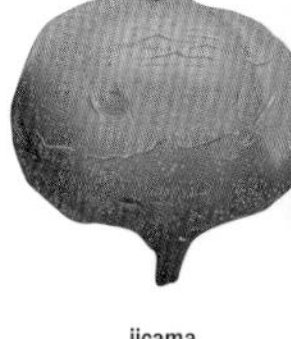

jicama
jicama[M]

sweet potato
igname[F]

Jerusalem artichoke
topinambour[M]

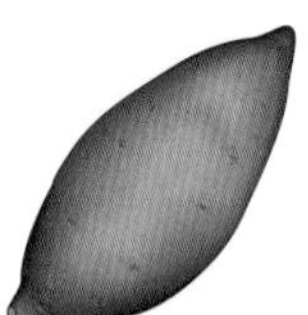

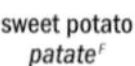

sweet potato
patate[F]

potato
pomme[F] de terre[F]

stalk vegetables
légumes[M] *tiges*[F]

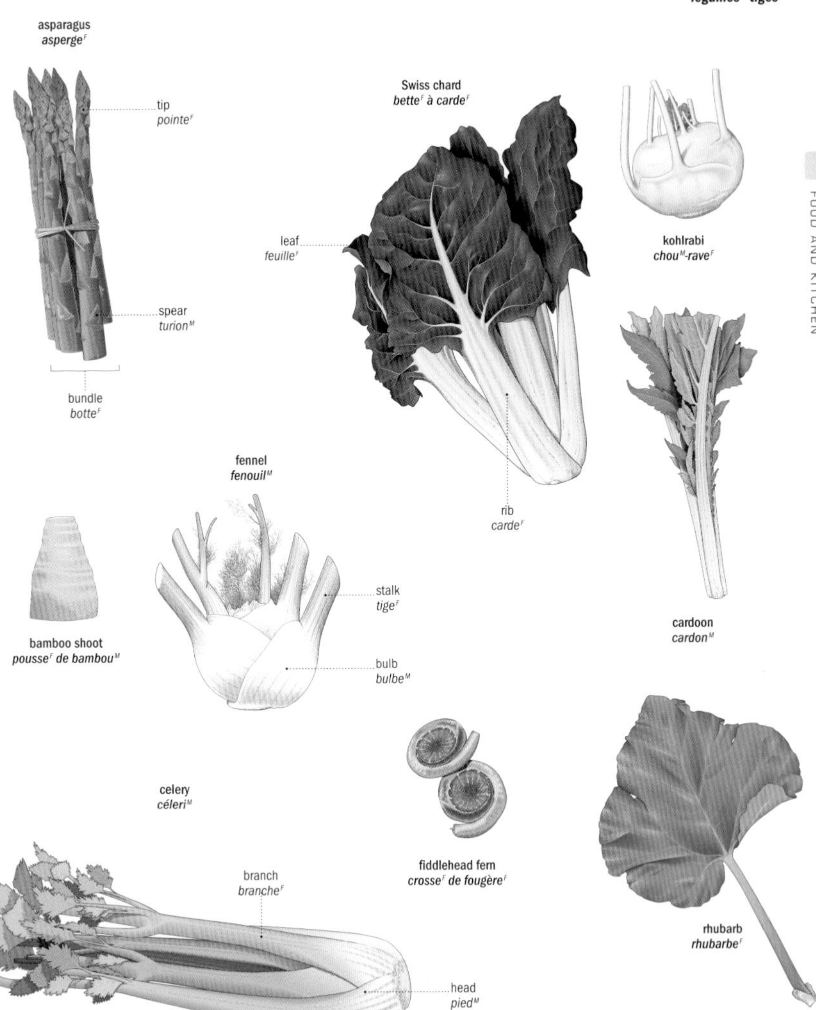

leaf vegetables
légumes[M] *feuilles*[F]

leaf lettuce
laitue[F] *frisée*

cos lettuce
romaine[F]

celtuce
laitue[F] *asperge*[F]

sea kale
chou[M] *marin*

collards
chou[M] *cavalier*[M]

escarole
scarole[F]

butterhead lettuce
laitue[F] *pommée*

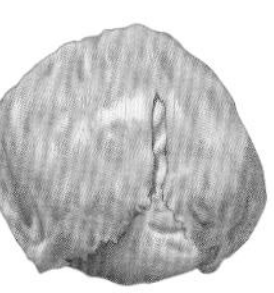
iceberg lettuce
laitue[F] *iceberg*[M]

radicchio
chicorée[F] *de Trévise*

ornamental kale
chou[M] *laitue*[F]

curly kale
chou[M] *frisé*

vine leaf
feuille[F] *de vigne*[F]

Brussels sprouts
choux[M] *de Bruxelles*

red cabbage
chou[M] *pommé rouge*

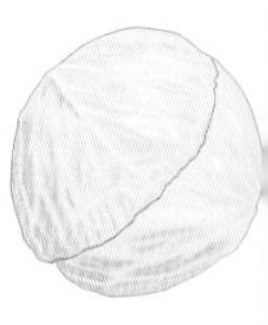
white cabbage
chou[M] *pommé blanc*

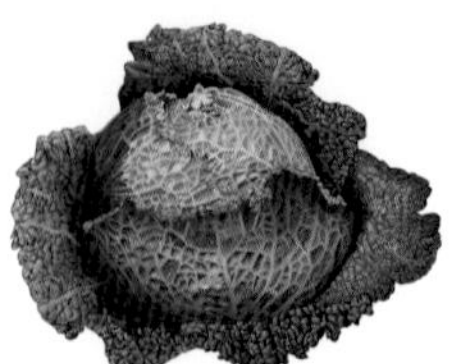
savoy cabbage
chou[M] *de Milan*

green cabbage
chou[M] *pommé vert*

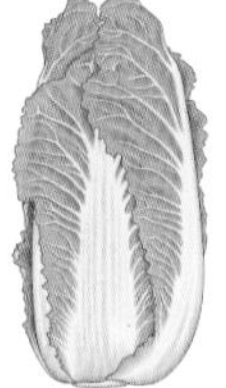
pe-tsai
pe-tsaï[M]

pak-choi
pak-choï[M]

purslane
pourpier[M]

nettle
ortie[F]

watercress
cresson[M] *de fontaine*[F]

dandelion
pissenlit[M]

corn salad
mâche[F]

rocket
roquette[F]

spinach
épinard[M]

garden cress
cresson[M] *alénois*

garden sorrel
oseille[F]

curly endive
chicorée[F] *frisée*

chicory
endive[F]

inflorescent vegetables
légumes[M] *fleurs*[F]

cauliflower
chou[M]*-fleur*[F]

broccoli
brocoli[M]

Gai-lohn
Gai lon[M]

broccoli raab
brocoli[M] *italien*

artichoke
artichaut[M]

fruit vegetables
***légumes*[M] *fruits*[M]**

avocado
avocat[M]

tomato
tomate[F]

currant tomato
tomate[F] *en grappe*[F]

tomatillo
tomatille[F]

olive
olive[F]

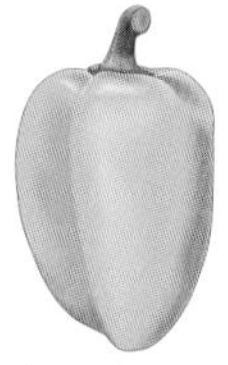
yellow sweet pepper
poivron[M] *jaune*

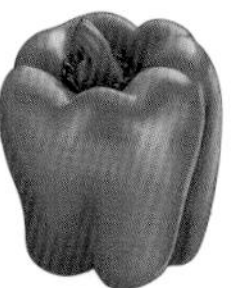
green sweet pepper
poivron[M] *vert*

red sweet pepper
poivron[M] *rouge*

chilli
piment[M]

okra
gombo[M]

gherkin
cornichon[M]

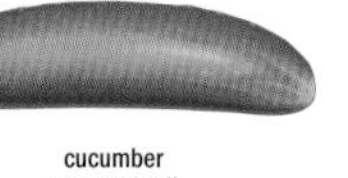
cucumber
concombre[M]

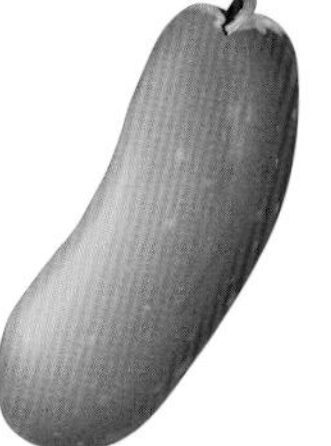
wax gourd
melon[M] *d'hiver*[M] *chinois*

aubergine
aubergine[F]

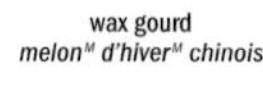
seedless cucumber
concombre[M] *sans pépins*[M]

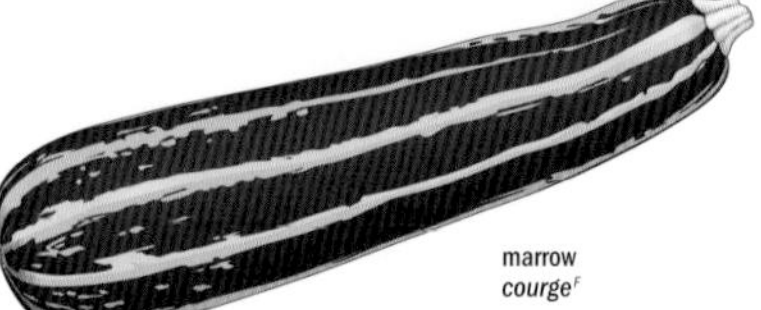
marrow
courge[F]

courgette
courgette[F]

bitter melon
margose[F]

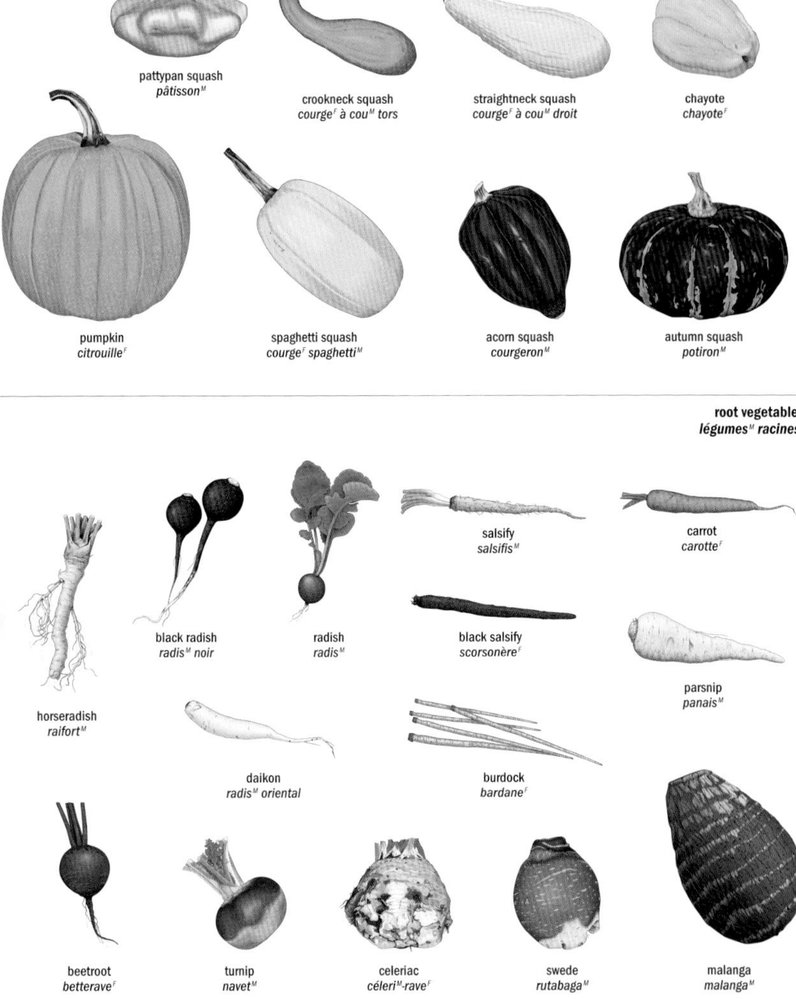
pattypan squash
pâtisson[M]
crookneck squash
courge[F] *à cou*[M] *tors*
straightneck squash
courge[F] *à cou*[M] *droit*
chayote
chayote[F]
pumpkin
citrouille[F]
spaghetti squash
courge[F] *spaghetti*[M]
acorn squash
courgeron[M]
autumn squash
potiron[M]
root vegetables
légumes[M] ***racines***[F]
horseradish
raifort[M]
black radish
radis[M] *noir*
radish
radis[M]
salsify
salsifis[M]
carrot
carotte[F]
black salsify
scorsonère[F]
parsnip
panais[M]
daikon
radis[M] *oriental*
burdock
bardane[F]
beetroot
betterave[F]
turnip
navet[M]
celeriac
céleri[M]*-rave*[F]
swede
rutabaga[M]
malanga
malanga[M]

legumes

légumineuses[F]

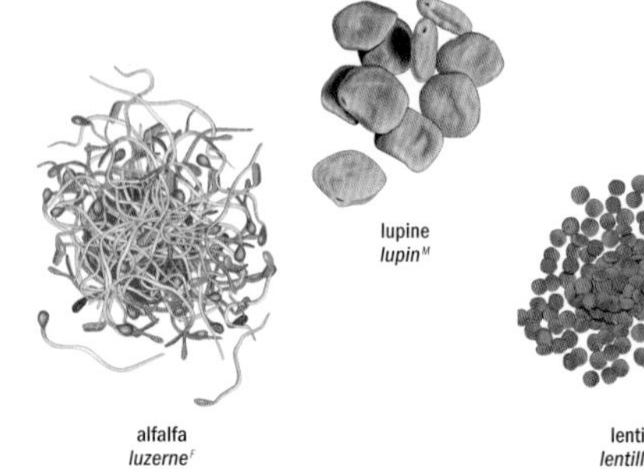

lupine
lupin[M]

alfalfa
luzerne[F]

lentils
lentilles[F]

peanut
arachide[F]

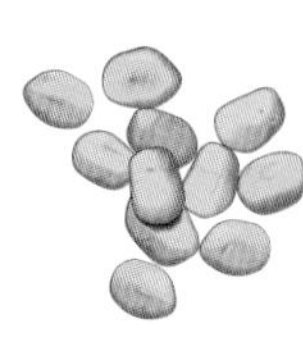

broad beans
fèves[F]

peas
pois[M]

chick peas
pois[M] chiches

split peas
pois[M] cassés

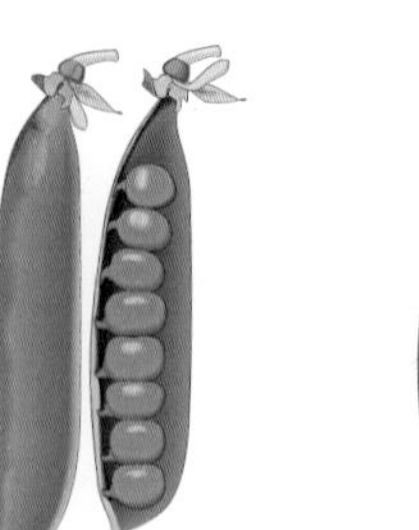

green peas
petits pois[M]

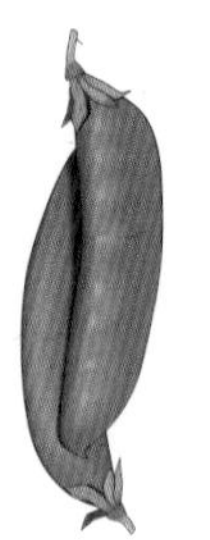

mangetout
pois[M] mange-tout[M]

dolichos beans
doliques[M]

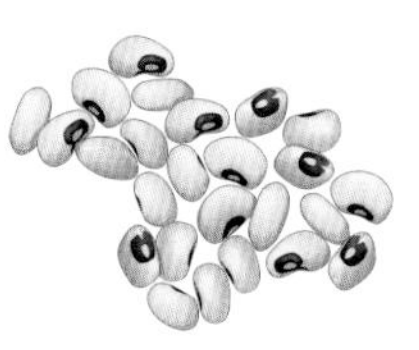

black-eyed pea
dolique[M] à œil[M] noir

lablab bean
dolique[M] d'Égypte[F]

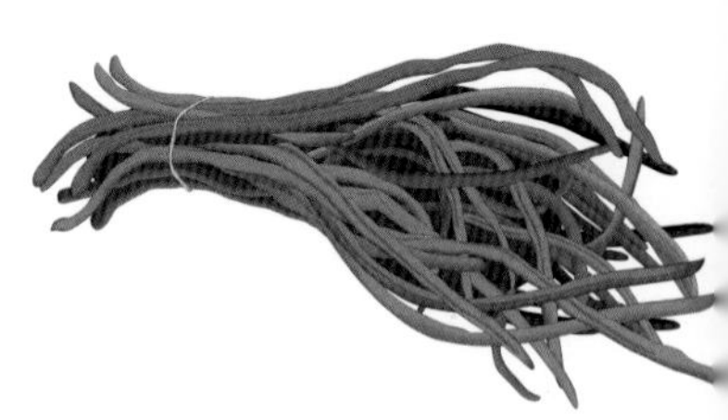

yard-long bean
dolique[M] asperge[F]

beans
***haricots*[M]**

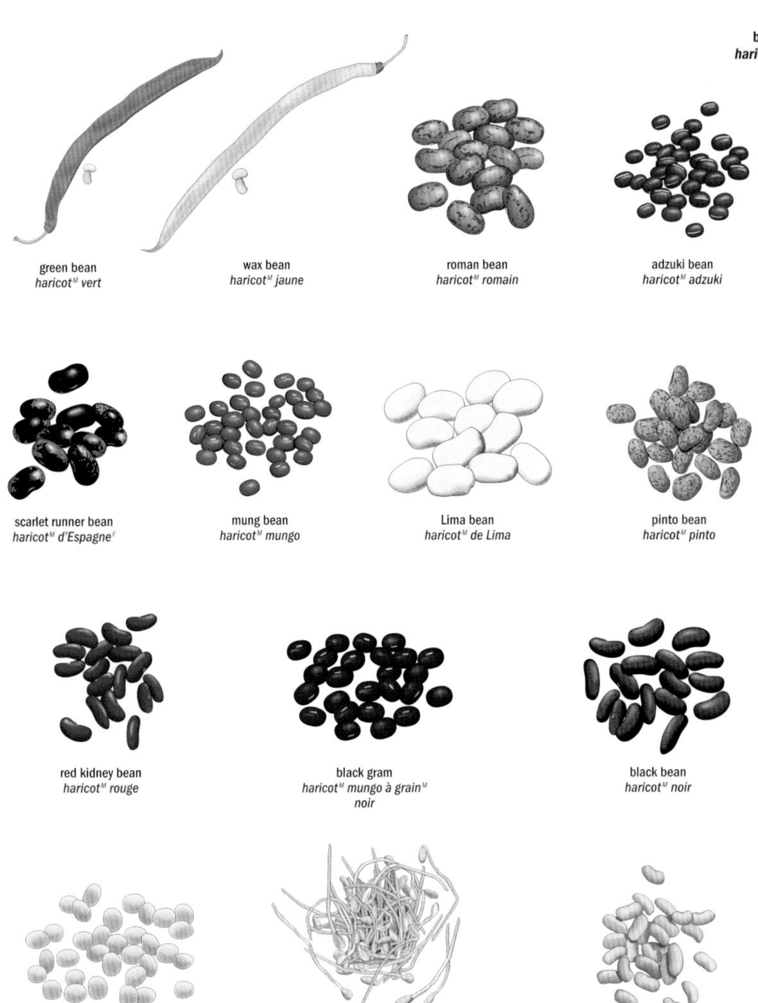

green bean
haricot[M] *vert*

wax bean
haricot[M] *jaune*

roman bean
haricot[M] *romain*

adzuki bean
haricot[M] *adzuki*

scarlet runner bean
haricot[M] *d'Espagne*[F]

mung bean
haricot[M] *mungo*

Lima bean
haricot[M] *de Lima*

pinto bean
haricot[M] *pinto*

red kidney bean
haricot[M] *rouge*

black gram
haricot[M] *mungo à grain*[M] *noir*

black bean
haricot[M] *noir*

soybeans
graine[F] *de soja*[M]

soybean sprouts
germes[M] *de soja*[M]

flageolet
flageolet[M]

fruits

fruits[M]

berries
***baies**[F]*

redcurrant
groseille[F] à grappes[F]

blackcurrant
cassis[M]

gooseberry
groseille[F] à maquereau[M]

grape
raisin[M]

blueberry
bleuet[M]

bilberry
myrtille[F]

red whortleberry
airelle[F]

alkekengi
alkékenge[M]

cranberry
canneberge[F]

raspberry
framboise[F]

blackberry
mûre[F]

strawberry
fraise[F]

stone fruits
***fruits**[M] **à noyau**[M]*

plum
prune[F]

peach
pêche[F]

nectarine
nectarine[F]

apricot
abricot[M]

cherry
cerise[F]

date
datte[F]

dry fruits
fruits^{M} secs

macadamia nut
noix^{F} de macadamia^{M}

ginkgo nut
noix^{F} de ginkgo^{M}

pistachio nut
pistache^{F}

pine nut
pignon^{M}

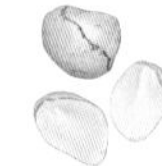

cola nut
noix^{F} de cola^{M}

pecan nut
noix^{F} de pacane^{F}

cashew
noix^{F} de cajou^{M}

almond
amande^{F}

hazelnut
noisette^{F}

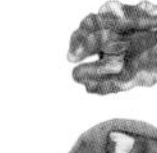

walnut
noix^{F}

coconut
noix^{F} de coco^{M}

chestnut
marron^{M}

beechnut
faîne^{F}

Brazil nut
noix^{F} du Brésil^{M}

pome fruits
fruits^{M} à pépins^{M}

pear
poire^{F}

quince
coing^{M}

apple
pomme^{F}

medlar
nèfle^{F} du Japon^{M}

citrus fruits
agrumesM

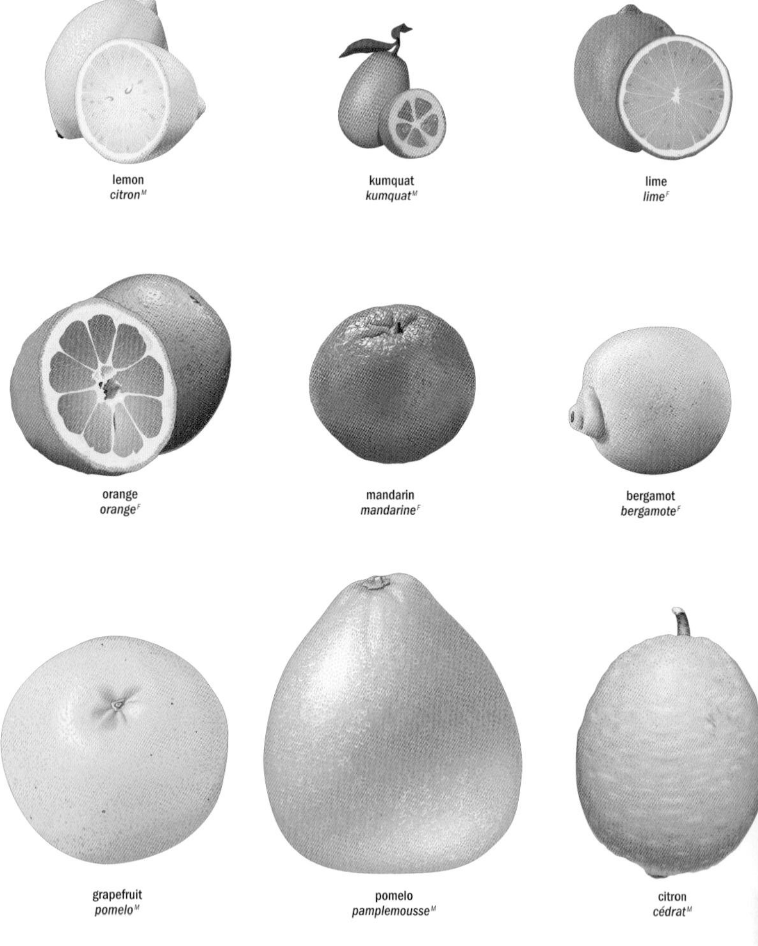

lemon
*citron*M

kumquat
*kumquat*M

lime
*lime*F

orange
*orange*F

mandarin
*mandarine*F

bergamot
*bergamote*F

grapefruit
*pomelo*M

pomelo
*pamplemousse*M

citron
*cédrat*M

melons
melons[M]

cantaloupe
cantaloup[M]

casaba melon
melon[M] *Casaba*

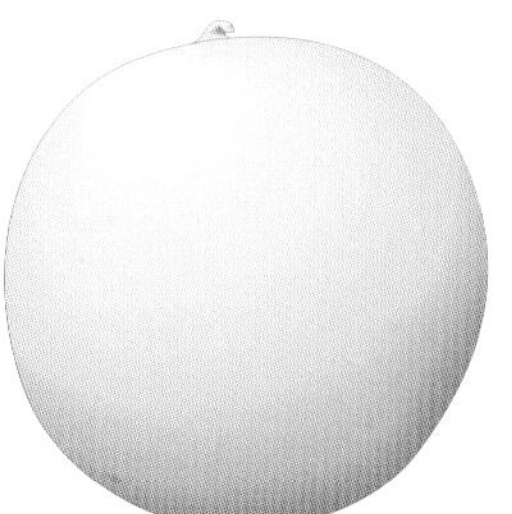

honeydew melon
melon[M] *miel*[M]

muskmelon
melon[M] *brodé*

canary melon
melon[M] *brésilien*

watermelon
pastèque[F]

Ogen melon
melon[M] *d'Ogen*

tropical fruits
fruits[M] tropicaux

jaboticaba
jaboticaba[M]

litchi; lychee
litchi[M]

fig
figue[F]

jujube
jujube[M]

sapodilla
sapotille[F]

guava
goyave[F]

rambutan
ramboutan[M]

Japanese persimmon
kaki[M]

prickly pear
figue[F] *de Barbarie*

carambola
carambole[F]

Asian pear
pomme[F] *poire*[F]

mango
mangue[F]

durian
durian[M]

papaya
papaye[F]

pepino
pepino[M]

feijoa
feijoa[M]

spices
épices[F]

juniper berry
baie[F] de genièvre[M]

clove
clou[M] de girofle[M]

allspice
piment[M] de la Jamaïque[F]

white mustard
moutarde[F] blanche

black mustard
moutarde[F] noire

black pepper
poivre[M] noir

white pepper
poivre[M] blanc

pink pepper
poivre[M] rose

green pepper
poivre[M] vert

nutmeg
noix[F] de muscade[F]

caraway
carvi[M]

cardamom
cardamome[F]

cinnamon
cannelle[F]

saffron
safran[M]

cumin
cumin[M]

curry
curry[M]

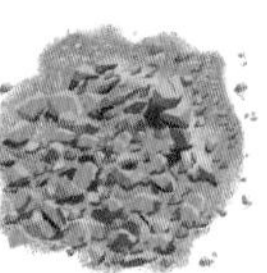
turmeric
curcuma[M]

fenugreek
fenugrec[M]

jalapeño chilli
piment[M] Jalapeño

bird's eye chilli
piment[M] oiseau[M]

crushed chillis
piments[M] broyés

dried chillis
piments[M] séchés

cayenne
piment[M] de Cayenne

paprika
paprika[M]

ajowan
ajowan[M]

asafœtida
asa-fœtida[F]

garam masala
garam masala[M]

cajun spice seasoning
mélange[M] d'épices[F] cajun

marinade spices
épices[F] à marinade[F]

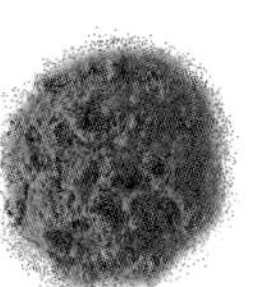
five spice powder
cinq-épices[M] chinois

chilli powder
assaisonnement[M] au chili[M]

ground pepper
poivre[M] moulu

ras el hanout
ras-el-hanout[M]

sumac
sumac[M]

poppy seeds
graines[F] de pavot[M]

ginger
gingembre[M]

condiments

condiments^M

Tabasco™ sauce
sauce^F Tabasco®

Worcestershire sauce
sauce^F Worcestershire

tamarind paste
pâte^F de tamarin^M

vanilla extract
extrait^M de vanille^F

tomato paste
concentré^M de tomate^F

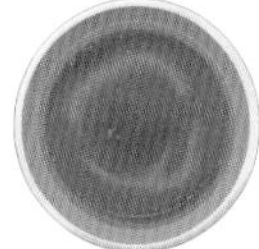

tomato coulis
coulis^M de tomate^F

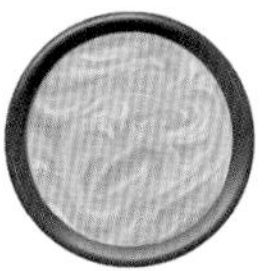

hummus
hoummos^M

tahini
tahini^M

hoisin sauce
sauce^F hoisin

soy sauce
sauce^F soja^M

powdered mustard
moutarde^F en poudre^F

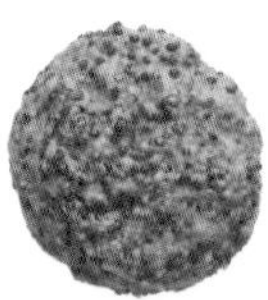

wholegrain mustard
moutarde^F à l'ancienne^F

Dijon mustard
moutarde^F de Dijon

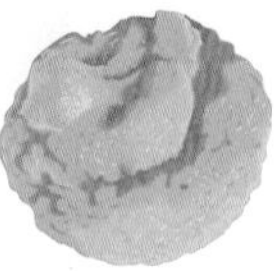

German mustard
moutarde^F allemande

English mustard
moutarde^F anglaise

American mustard
moutarde^F américaine

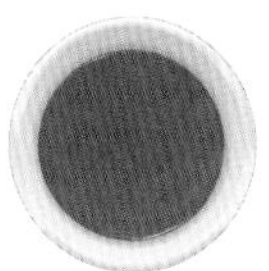
plum sauce
sauce^F aux prunes^F

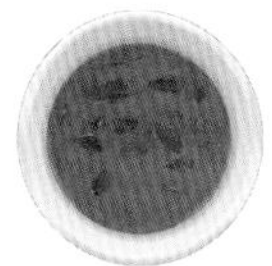
mango chutney
chutney^M à la mangue^F

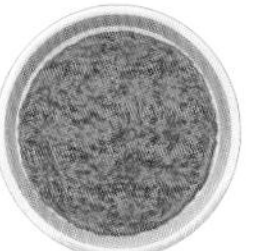
harissa
harissa^F

sambal oelek
sambal oelek^M

ketchup
ketchup^M

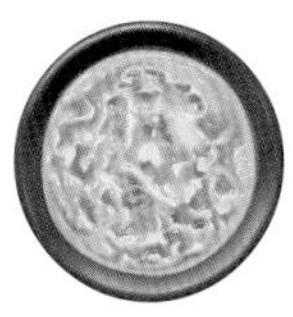
wasabi
wasabi^M

table salt
sel^M fin

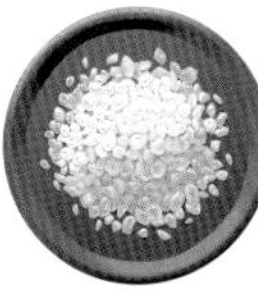
coarse salt
gros sel^M

sea salt
sel^M marin

balsamic vinegar
vinaigre^M balsamique

rice vinegar
vinaigre^M de riz^M

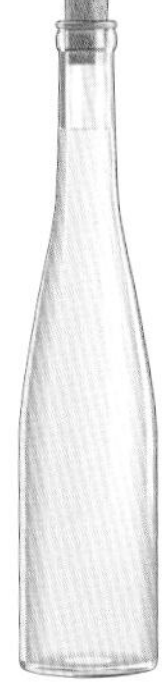
cider vinegar
vinaigre^M de cidre^M

malt vinegar
vinaigre^M de malt^M

wine vinegar
vinaigre^M de vin^M

herbs

fines herbes[F]

dill
aneth[M]

anise
anis[M]

bay
laurier[M]

oregano
origan[M]

tarragon
estragon[M]

basil
basilic[M]

sage
sauge[F]

thyme
thym[M]

mint
menthe[F]

parsley
persil[M]

chervil
cerfeuil[M]

coriander
coriandre[F]

rosemary
romarin[M]

hyssop
hysope[F]

borage
bourrache[F]

lovage
livèche[F]

savory
sarriette[F]

lemon balm
mélisse[F]

cereals

céréales[F]

rice
riz[M]

wild rice
riz[M] sauvage

spelt wheat
épeautre[M]

wheat
blé[M]

oats
avoine[F]

rye
seigle[M]

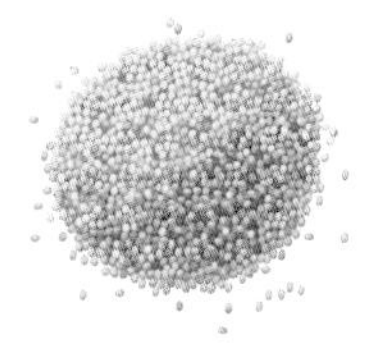

millet
millet[M]

corn
maïs[M]

barley
orge[F]

buckwheat
sarrasin[M]

quinoa
quinoa[M]

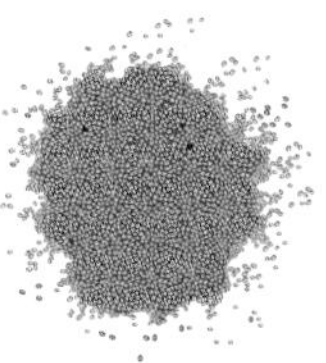

amaranth
amarante[F]

triticale
triticale[M]

cereal products

produits^M céréaliers

flour and semolina
farine^F et semoule^F

semolina
semoule^F

whole wheat flour
farine^F de blé^M complet

couscous
couscous^M

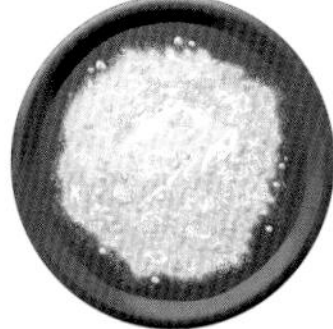

plain flour
farine^F tout usage^M

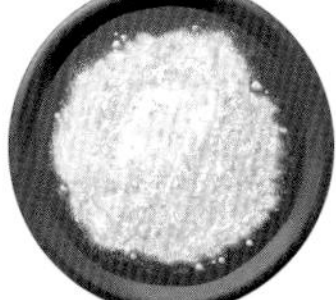

unbleached flour
farine^F non blanchie

oat flour
farine^F d'avoine^F

cornflour
farine^F de maïs^M

bread
pain^M

croissant
croissant^M

black bread
pain^M de seigle^M noir

bagel
bagel^M

Greek bread
pain^M grec

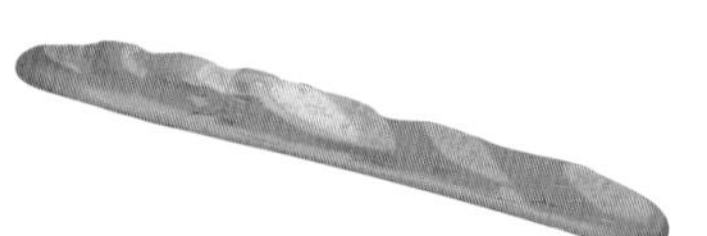

French loaf
baguette^F parisienne

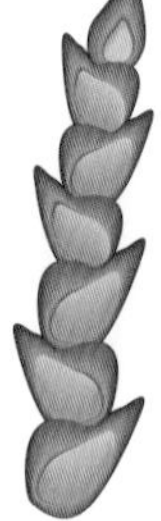

ear loaf
baguette^F épi^M

French bread
pain^M parisien

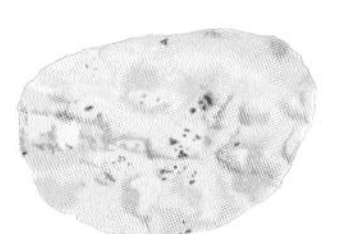

Indian chapati bread
pain[M] chapati indien

tortilla
tortilla[F]

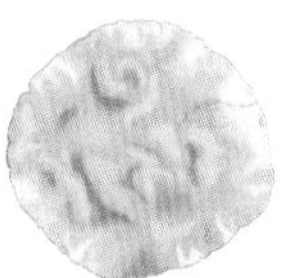

pitta bread
pain[M] pita

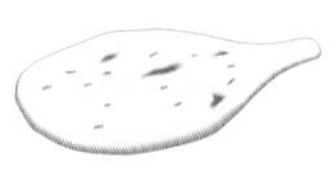

Indian naan bread
pain[M] naan indien

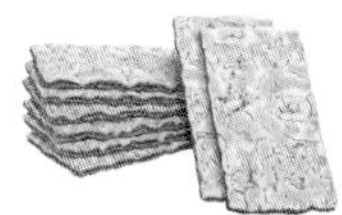

rye crispbread
cracker[M] de seigle[M]

filo dough
pâte[F] phyllo[F]

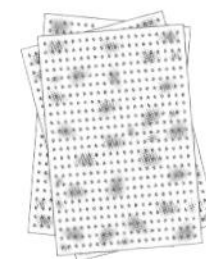

unleavened bread
pain[M] azyme

Danish rye bread
pain[M] de seigle[M] danois

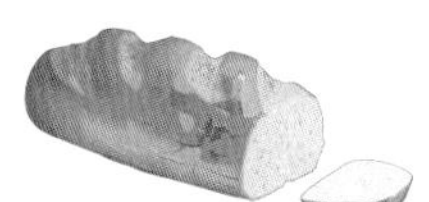

white bread
pain[M] blanc

multigrain bread
pain[M] multicéréales

Scandinavian crispbread
cracker[M] scandinave

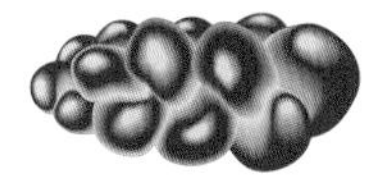

Jewish challah
pain[M] tchallah juif

American corn bread
pain[M] de maïs[M] américain

German rye bread
pain[M] de seigle[M] allemand

Russian black bread
pain[M] noir russe

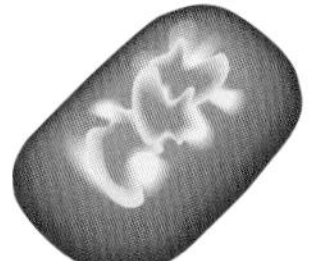

farmhouse loaf
pain[M] de campagne[F]

wholemeal bread
pain[M] complet

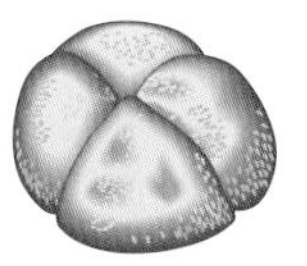

Irish soda bread
pain[M] irlandais

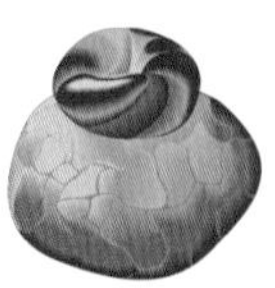

cottage loaf
pain[M] de mie[F]

pasta
pâtes[F] alimentaires

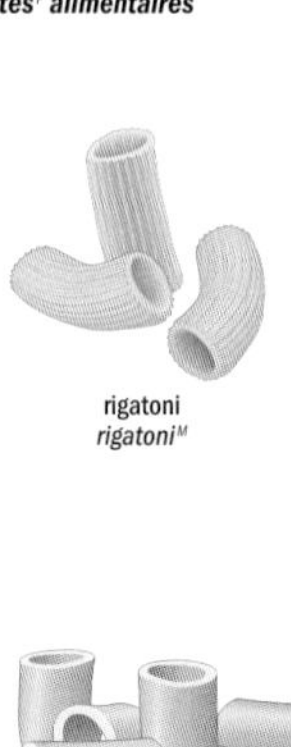

rigatoni
rigatoni[M]

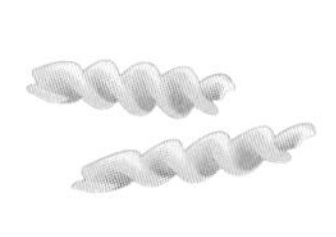

rotini
rotini[M]

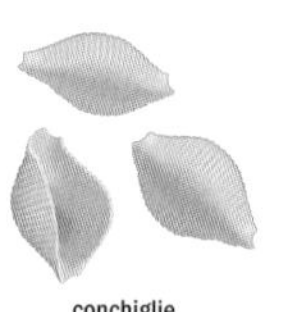

conchiglie
conchiglie[F]

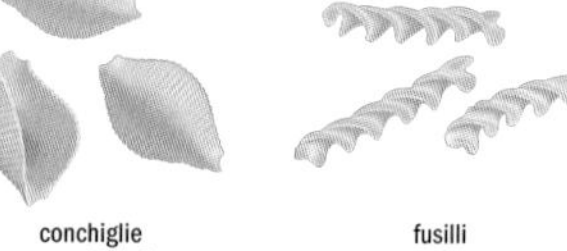

fusilli
fusilli[M]

spaghetti
spaghetti[M]

ditali
ditali[M]

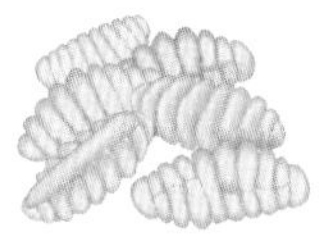

gnocchi
gnocchi[M]

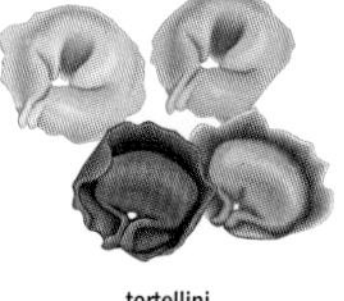

tortellini
tortellini[M]

spaghettini
spaghettini[M]

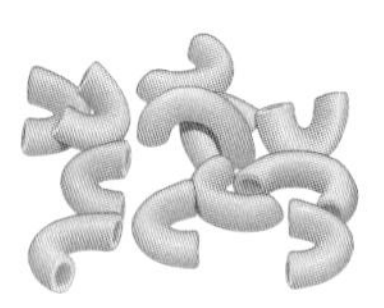

elbows
coudes[M]

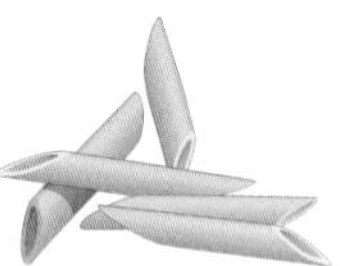

penne
penne[M]

cannelloni
cannelloni[M]

lasagne
lasagne[F]

ravioli
ravioli[M]

spinach tagliatelle
tagliatelle[M] aux épinards[M]

fettucine
fettucine[M]

Asian noodles
nouilles[F] asiatiques

soba noodles
nouilles[F] soba

somen noodles
nouilles[F] somen

udon noodles
nouilles[F] udon

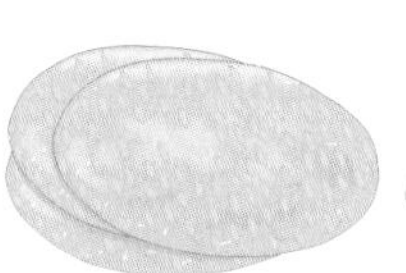

rice papers
galettes[F] de riz[M]

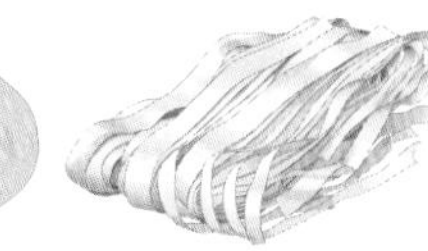

rice noodles
nouilles[F] de riz[M]

bean thread cellophane noodles
nouilles[F] de haricots[M] mungo

egg noodles
nouilles[F] aux œufs[M]

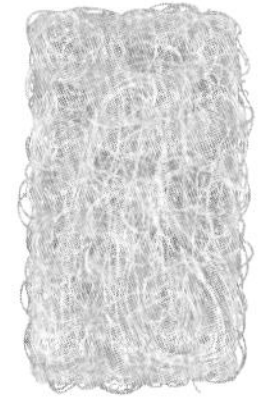

rice vermicelli
vermicelles[M] de riz[M]

won ton skins
pâtes[F] won-ton

rice
riz[M]

white rice
riz[M] blanc

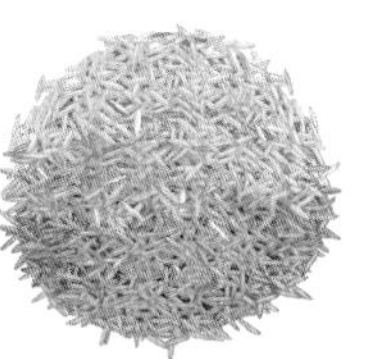

brown rice
riz[M] complet

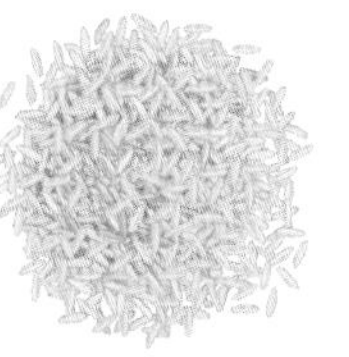

parboiled rice
riz[M] étuvé

basmati rice
riz[M] basmati

coffee and infusions

café[M] et infusions[F]

coffee
café[M]

green coffee beans
grains[M] de café[M] verts

roasted coffee beans
grains[M] de café[M] torréfiés

herbal teas
tisanes[F]

linden
tilleul[M]

chamomile
camomille[F]

verbena
verveine[F]

tea
thé[M]

green tea
thé[M] vert

black tea
thé[M] noir

oolong tea
thé[M] oolong

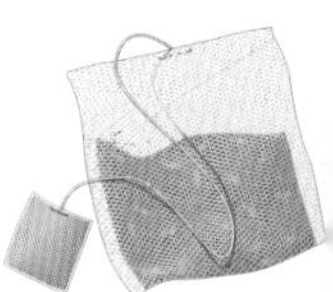

tea bag
thé[M] en sachet[M]

chocolate

chocolat[M]

dark chocolate
chocolat[M] noir

milk chocolate
chocolat[M] au lait[M]

cocoa
cacao[M]

white chocolate
chocolat[M] blanc

sugar
sucre[M]

granulated sugar
sucre[M] granulé

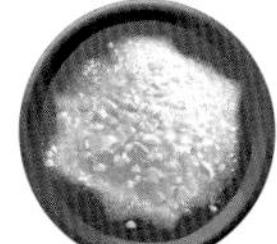
powdered sugar
sucre[M] glace[F]

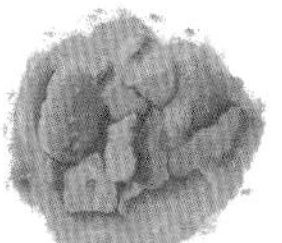
brown sugar
cassonade[F]

rock candy
sucre[M] candi

treacle
mélasse[F]

corn syrup
sirop[M] de maïs[M]

maple syrup
sirop[M] d'érable[M]

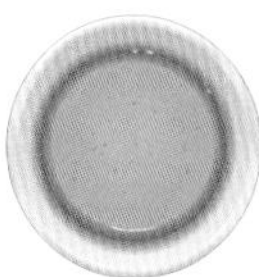
honey
miel[M]

fats and oils
huiles[F] et matières[F] grasses

corn oil
huile[F] de maïs[M]

olive oil
huile[F] d'olive[F]

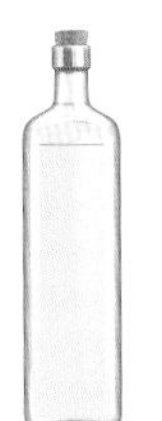
sunflower-seed oil
huile[F] de tournesol[M]

peanut oil
huile[F] d'arachide[F]

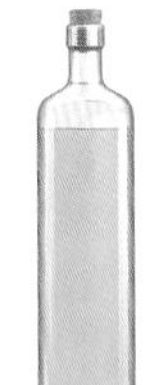
sesame oil
huile[F] de sésame[M]

shortening
saindoux[M]

lard
lard[M]

margarine
margarine[F]

dairy products

produits^M laitiers

yogurt
yaourt^M

ghee
ghee^M

butter
beurre^M

cream
crème^F

whipping cream
crème^F épaisse

sour cream
crème^F aigre

milk
lait^M

homogenized milk
lait^M homogénéisé

goat's milk
lait^M de chèvre^F

evaporated milk
lait^M concentré

buttermilk
babeurre^M

powdered milk
lait^M en poudre^F

fresh cheeses
fromages^M frais

cottage cheese
cottage^M

mozzarella
mozzarella^F

cream cheese
fromage^M à la crème^F

ricotta
ricotta^F

goat's-milk cheeses
fromages^M de chèvre^F

Chèvre cheese
chèvre^M frais

Crottin de Chavignol
crottin^M de Chavignol

pressed cheeses
fromages[M] à pâte[F] pressée

Jarlsberg
jarlsberg[M]

Emmenthal
emmenthal[M]

Raclette
raclette[F]

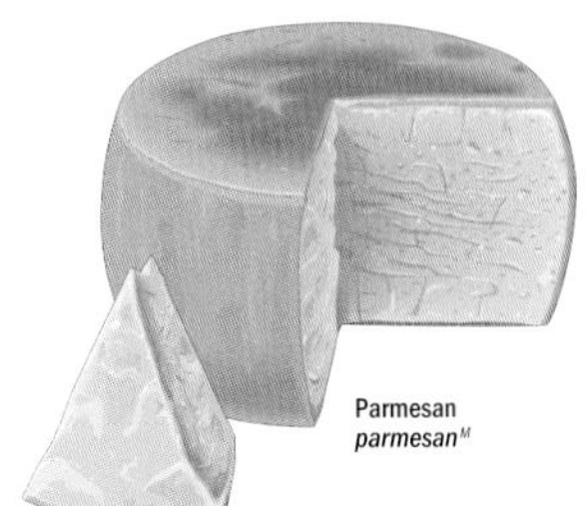

Parmesan
parmesan[M]

Gruyère
gruyère[M]

Romano
romano[M]

blue-veined cheeses
fromages[M] à pâte[F] persillée

Roquefort
roquefort[M]

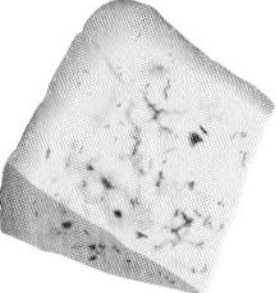

Stilton
stilton[M]

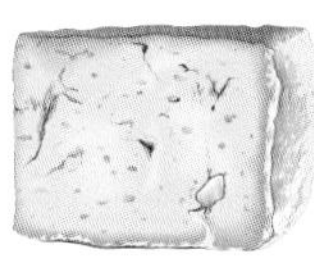

Gorgonzola
gorgonzola[M]

Danish Blue
bleu[M] danois

soft cheeses
fromages[M] à pâte[F] molle

Pont-l'Évêque
pont-l'évêque[M]

Coulommiers
coulommiers[M]

Camembert
camembert[M]

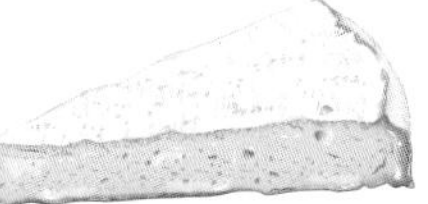

Brie
brie[M]

Munster
munster[M]

meat

viande[F]

cuts of beef
découpes[F] de bœuf[M]

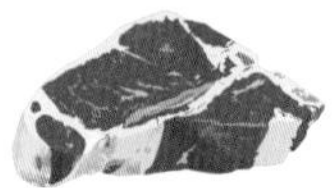

steak
bifteck[M]

diced beef
cubes[M] de bœuf[M]

minced beef
bœuf[M] haché

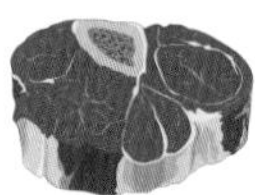

shank
jarret[M]

fillet roast
filet[M] de bœuf[M]

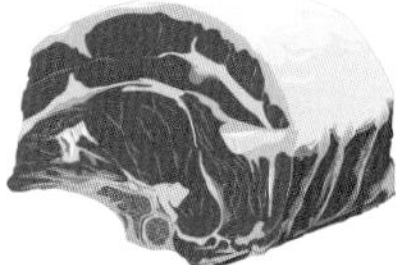

rib roast
rôti[M] de côtes[F]

back ribs
côtes[F] levées de dos[M]

cuts of veal
découpes[F] de veau[M]

diced veal
cubes[M] de veau[M]

minced veal
veau[M] haché

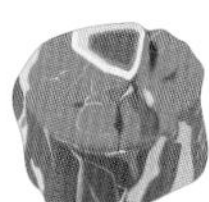

shank
jarret[M]

roast
rôti[M]

steak
bifteck[M]

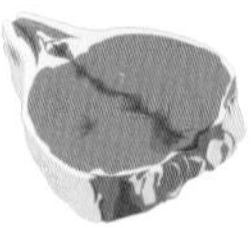

chop
côte[F]

cuts of lamb
découpes[F] d'agneau[M]

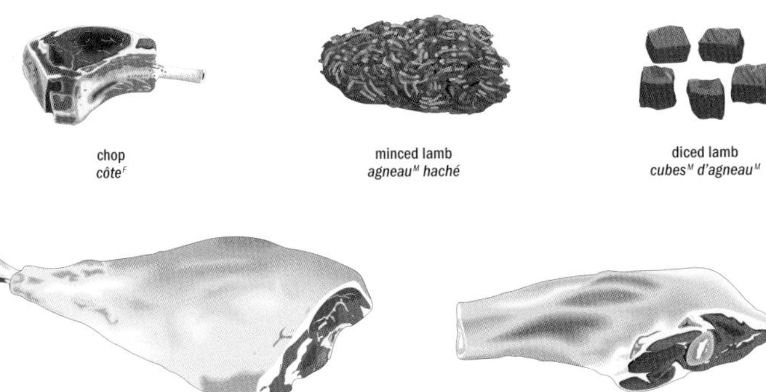

chop
côte[F]

minced lamb
agneau[M] haché

diced lamb
cubes[M] d'agneau[M]

leg of lamb
rôti[M]

shank
jarret[M]

cuts of pork
découpes[F] de porc[M]

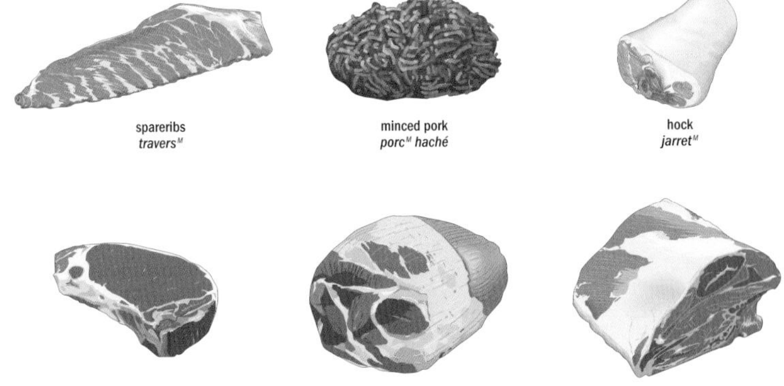

spareribs
travers[M]

minced pork
porc[M] haché

hock
jarret[M]

loin chop
côtelette[F]

smoked ham
jambon[M] fumé

roast
rôti[M]

offal

abats[M]

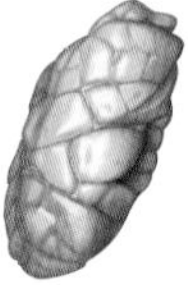

sweetbreads
ris[M]

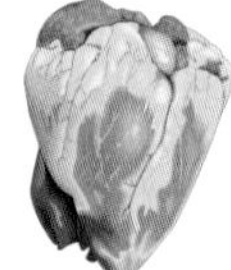

heart
cœur[M]

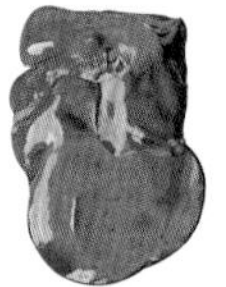

liver
foie[M]

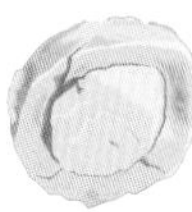

marrow
moelle[F]

tongue
langue[F]

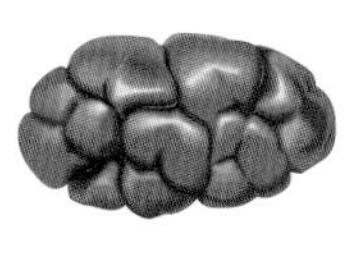

kidney
rognons[M]

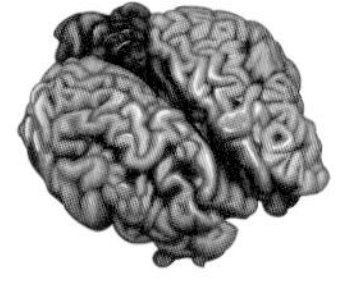

brains
cervelle[F]

tripe
tripes[F]

game

gibier[M]

quail
caille[F]

pigeon
pigeon[M]

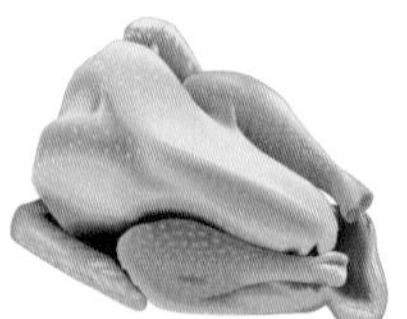

guinea fowl
pintade[F]

pheasant
faisan[M]

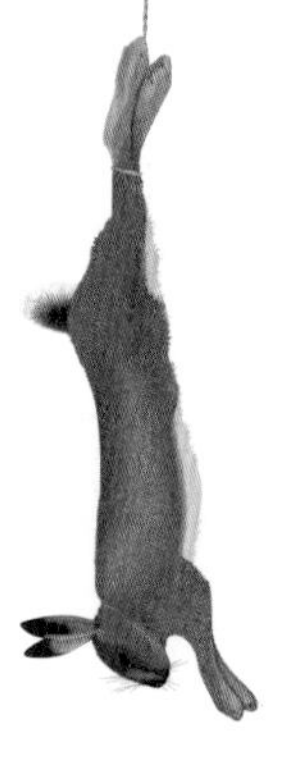

hare
lièvre[M]

rabbit
lapin[M]

poultry
volaille[F]

chicken
poulet[M]

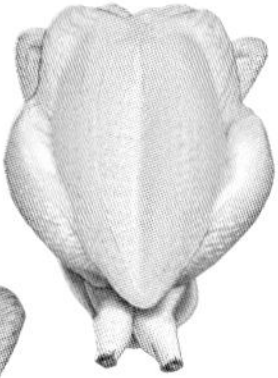

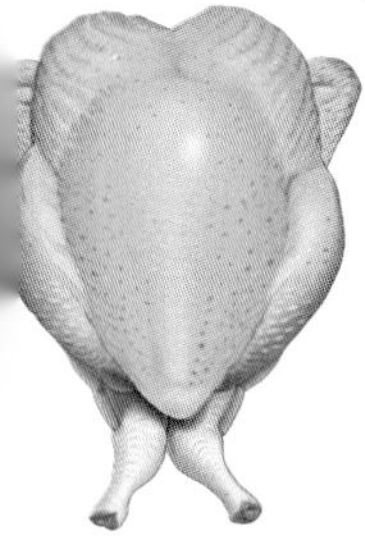

duck
canard[M]

capon
chapon[M]

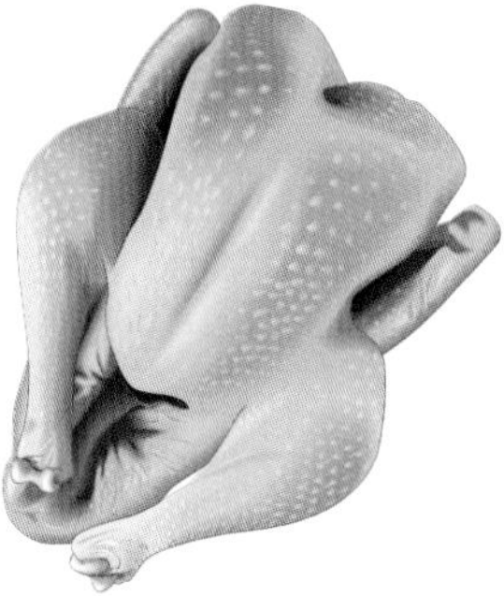

turkey
dinde[F]

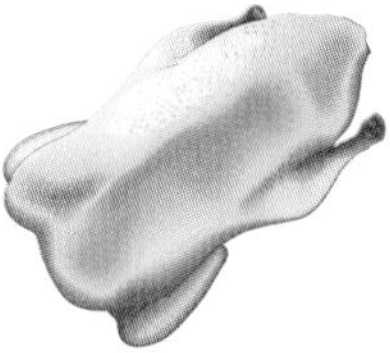

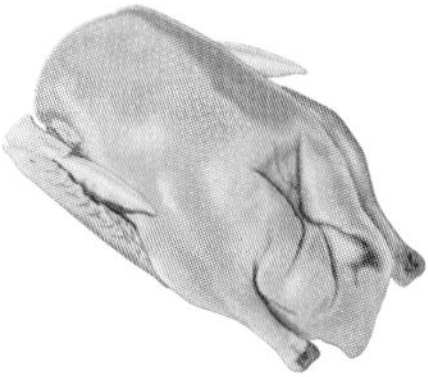

goose
oie[F]

eggs
œufs[M]

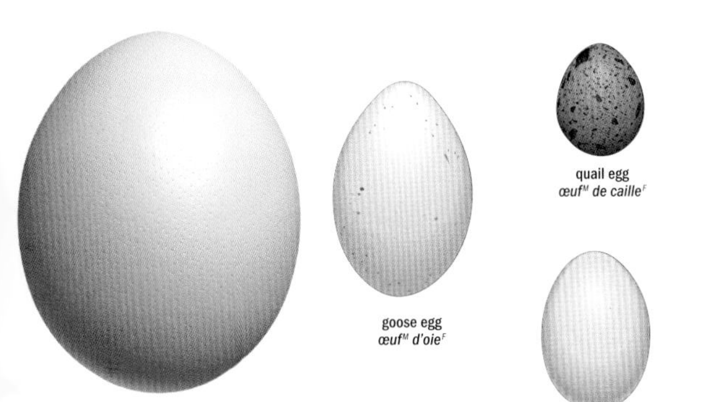

goose egg
œuf[M] d'oie[F]

ostrich egg
œuf[M] d'autruche[F]

quail egg
œuf[M] de caille[F]

pheasant egg
œuf[M] de faisane[F]

duck egg
œuf[M] de cane[F]

hen egg
œuf[M] de poule[F]

delicatessen

charcuterie[F]

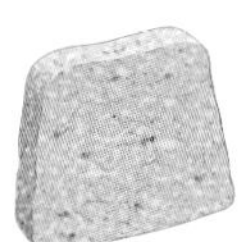
rillettes
rillettes[F]

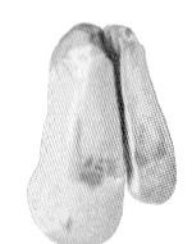
foie gras
foie[M] gras

prosciutto
prosciutto[M]

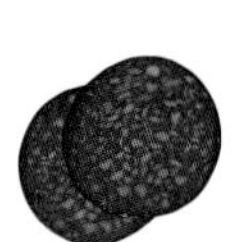
kielbasa sausage
saucisson[M] kielbasa

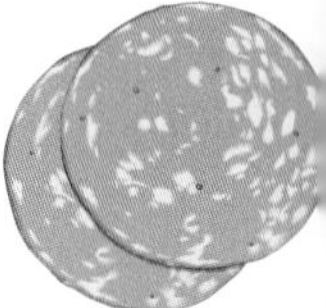
mortadella
mortadelle[F]

black pudding
boudin[M]

chorizo
chorizo[M]

pepperoni
pepperoni[M]

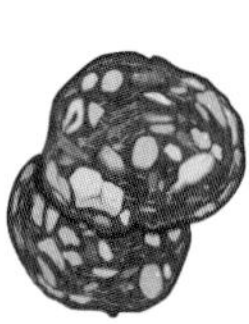
Genoa salami
salami[M] de Gênes

German salami
salami[M] allemand

Toulouse sausage
saucisse[F] de Toulouse

merguez sausage
merguez[F]

andouillette
andouillette[F]

chipolata sausage
chipolata[F]

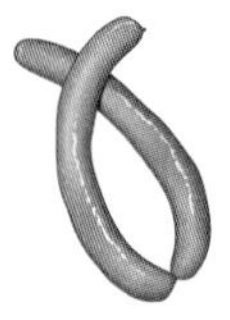
frankfurter
saucisse[F] de Francfort

pancetta
pancetta[F]

cooked ham
jambon[M] cuit

American bacon
bacon[M] américain

Canadian bacon
bacon[M] canadien

molluscs

mollusques[M]

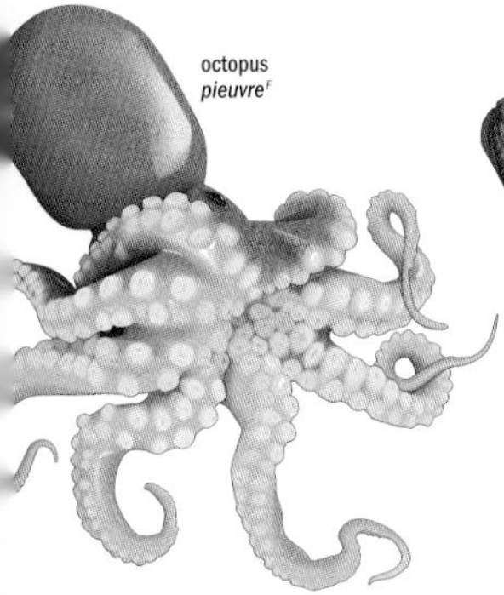

octopus
pieuvre[F]

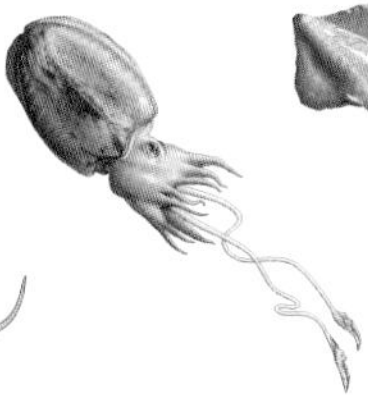

cuttlefish
seiche[F]

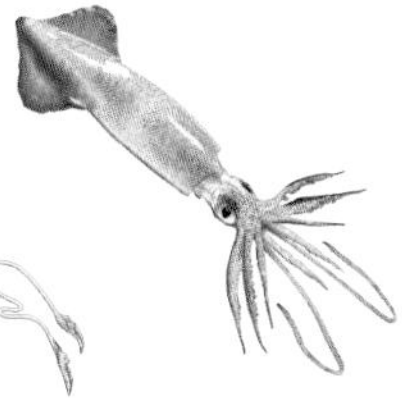

squid
calmar[M]

scallop
pétoncle[M]

hard-shell clam
palourde[F]

soft shell clam
mye[F]

abalone
ormeau[M]

great scallop
coquille[F] Saint-Jacques

snail
escargot[M]

limpet
patelle[F]

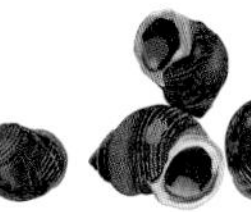

common periwinkle
bigorneau[M]

clam
praire[F]

cockle
coque[F]

razor clam
couteau[M]

oyster
huître[F] plate

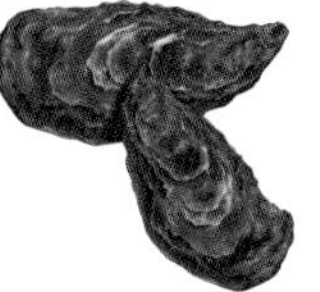

oyster
huître[F] creuse du Pacifique[M]

blue mussel
moule[F]

whelk
buccin[M]

crustaceans

crustacés[M]

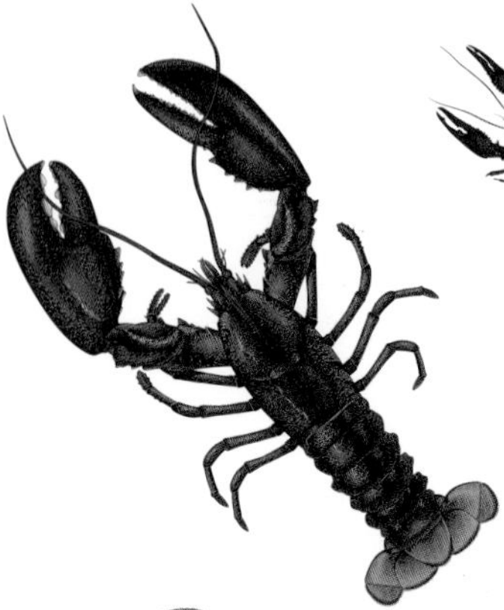

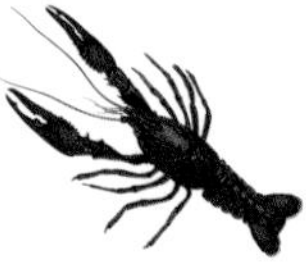

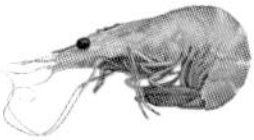

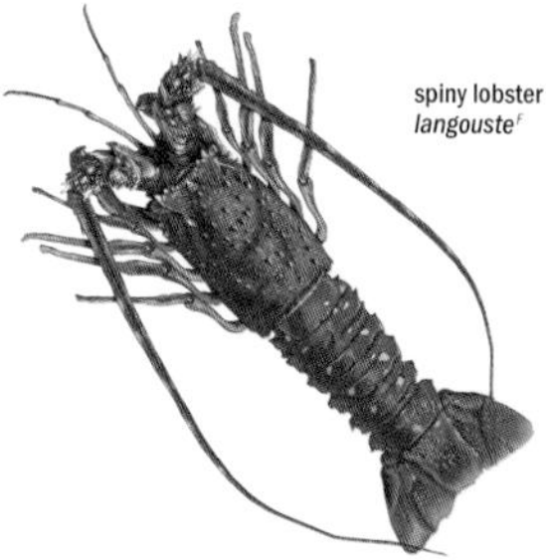

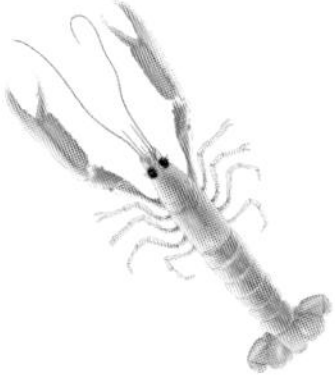

lobster
homard[M]

prawn
crevette[F]

crayfish
écrevisse[F]

spiny lobster
langouste[F]

scampi
langoustine[F]

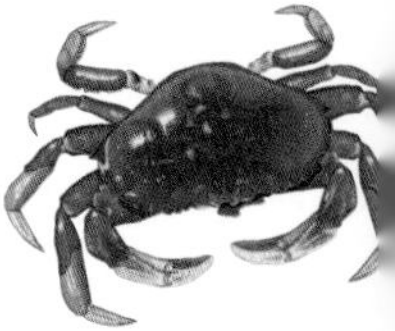

crab
crabe[M]

cartilaginous fishes

poissons[M] cartilagineux

larger spotted dogfish
grande roussette[F]

skate
raie[F]

smooth hound
émissole[F]

sturgeon
esturgeon[M]

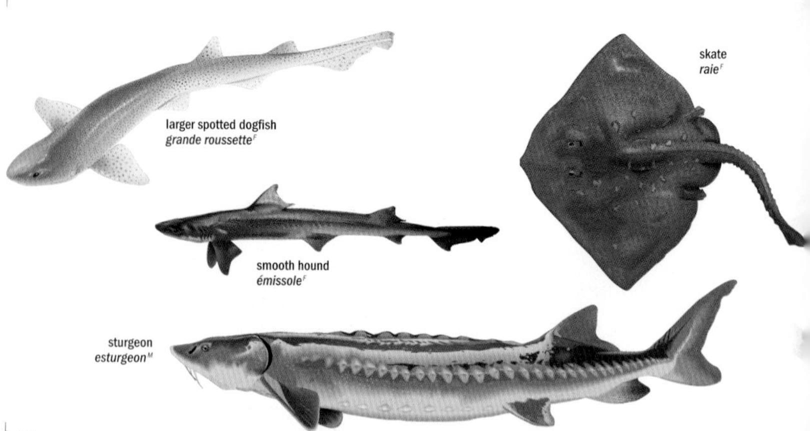

bony fishes

poissons^M osseux

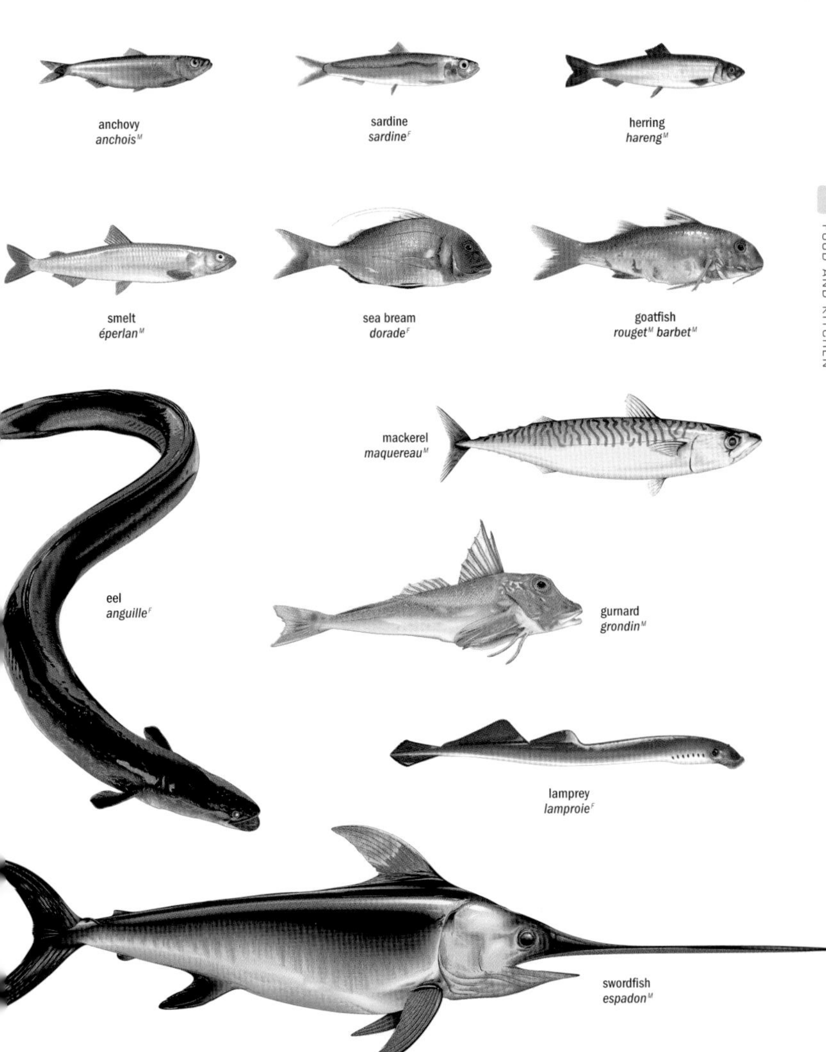

bony fishes

bass
perche^F truitée
mullet
mulet^M
carp
carpe^F
perch
perche^F
shad
alose^F
pike
brochet^M
pike perch
sandre^M
bluefish
tassergal^M
sea bass
bar^M commun
monkfish
lotte^F de mer^F
tuna
thon^M

redfish
sébaste[M]
whiting
merlan[M]
haddock
églefin[M]
black pollock
lieu[M] *noir*
Atlantic cod
morue[F] *de l'Atlantique*[M]
trout
truite[F]
Pacific salmon
saumon[M] *du Pacifique*[M]
Atlantic salmon
saumon[M] *de l'Atlantique*[M]
brook charr
omble[M] *de fontaine*[F]
John dory
saint-pierre[M]
halibut
flétan[M]
turbot
turbot[M]
common plaice
plie[F] *commune*
sole
sole[F]
FOOD AND KITCHEN

packaging

emballage[M]

pouch
sachet[M]

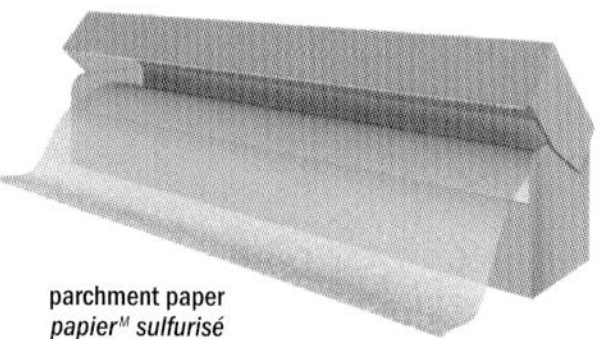

parchment paper
papier[M] sulfurisé

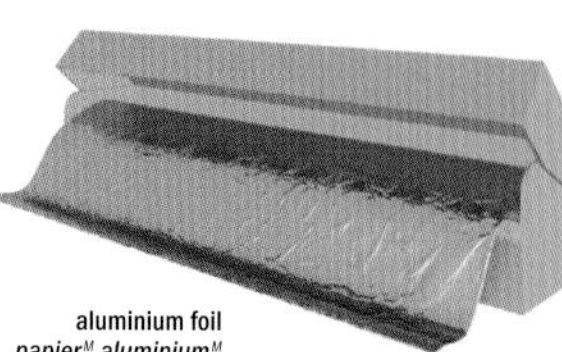

aluminium foil
papier[M] aluminium[M]

freezer bag
sac[M] de congélation[F]

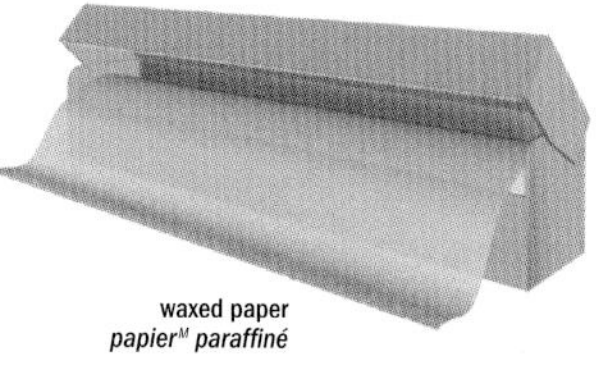

waxed paper
papier[M] paraffiné

plastic film
pellicule[F] plastique

mesh bag
sac[M]-filet[M]

canisters
boîtes[F] alimentaires

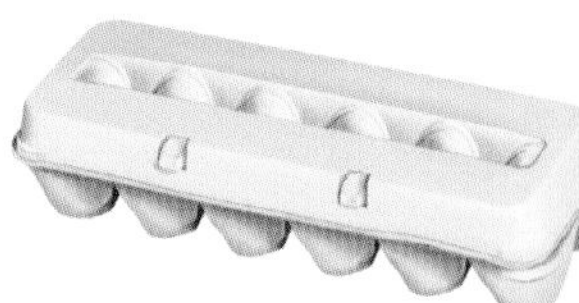

egg carton
boîte[F] à œufs[M]

food tray
barquette[F]

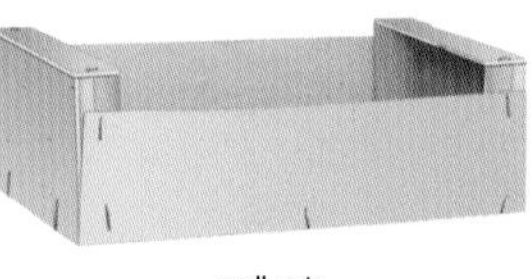

small crate
caissette[F]

small open crate
cageot[M]

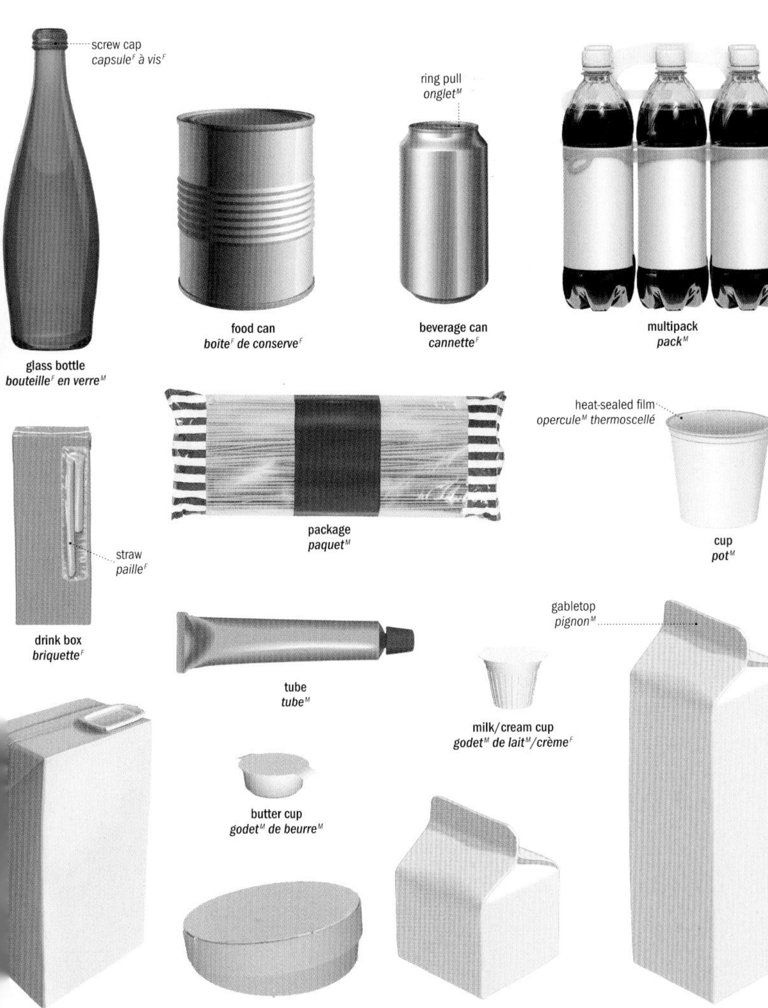
screw cap
capsule^F à vis^F
ring pull
onglet^M
food can
boîte^F de conserve^F
beverage can
cannette^F
multipack
pack^M
glass bottle
bouteille^F en verre^M
heat-sealed film
opercule^M thermoscellé
package
paquet^M
cup
pot^M
straw
paille^F
gabletop
pignon^M
drink box
briquette^F
tube
tube^M
milk/cream cup
godet^M de lait^M/crème^F
butter cup
godet^M de beurre^M
brick carton
brique^F
cheese box
boîte^F à fromage^M
small carton
berlingot^M
carton
carton^M

kitchen

cuisine[F]

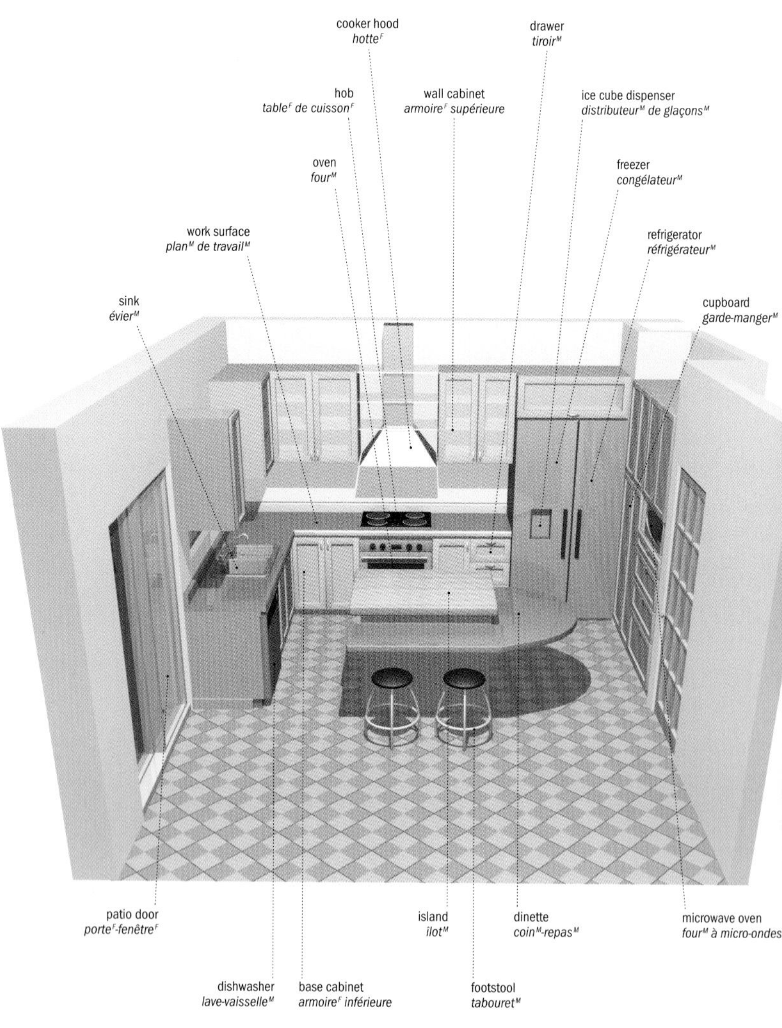

glassware

verres[M]

liqueur glass
verre[M] à liqueur[F]

port glass
verre[M] à porto[M]

champagne glass
coupe[F] à mousseux[M]

brandy glass
verre[M] à cognac[M]

hock glass
verre[M] à vin[M] d'Alsace[F]

burgundy glass
verre[M] à bourgogne[M]

bordeaux glass
verre[M] à bordeaux[M]

white wine glass
verre[M] à vin[M] blanc

water goblet
verre[M] à eau[F]

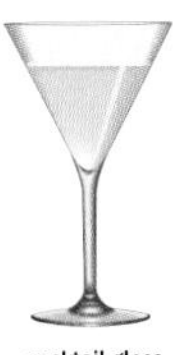

cocktail glass
verre[M] à cocktail[M]

tall tumbler
verre[M] à gin[M]

whisky tumbler
verre[M] à whisky[M]

beer glass
chope[F] à bière[F]

champagne flute
flûte[F] à champagne[M]

carafe
carafon[M]

decanter
carafe[F]

crockery

vaisselle[F]

demitasse
tasse[F] à café[M]

tea cup
tasse[F] à thé[M]

coffee mug
chope[F] à café[M]

cream jug
crémier[M]

sugar bowl
sucrier[M]

saltcellar
salière[F]

pepperpot
poivrière[F]

gravy boat
saucière[F]

butter dish
beurrier[M]

ramekin
ramequin[M]

soup bowl
bol[M]

rim soup bowl
assiette[F] creuse

dinner plate
assiette[F] plate

salad plate
assiette[F] à salade[F]

side plate
assiette[F] à dessert[M]

teapot
théière[F]

serving dish
plat[M] ovale

vegetable dish
légumier[M]

fish dish
plat[M] à poisson[M]

hors d'oeuvre dish
ravier[M]

water jug
pichet[M]

salad bowl
saladier[M]

salad dish
bol[M] à salade[F]

soup tureen
soupière[F]

cutlery
couvert^M

knife
***couteau**^M*

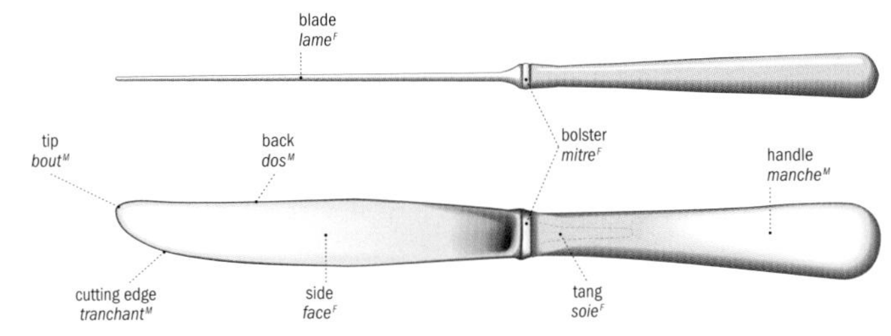

fork
***fourchette**^F*

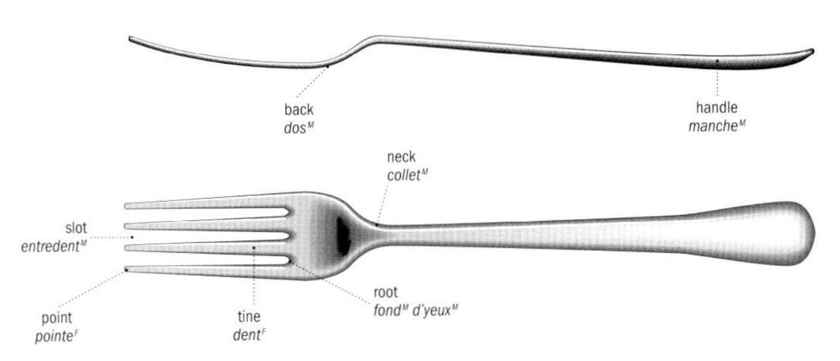

spoon
***cuiller**^F*

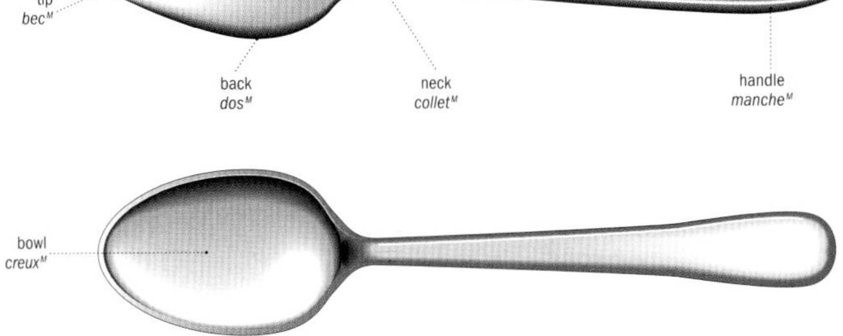

cutlery

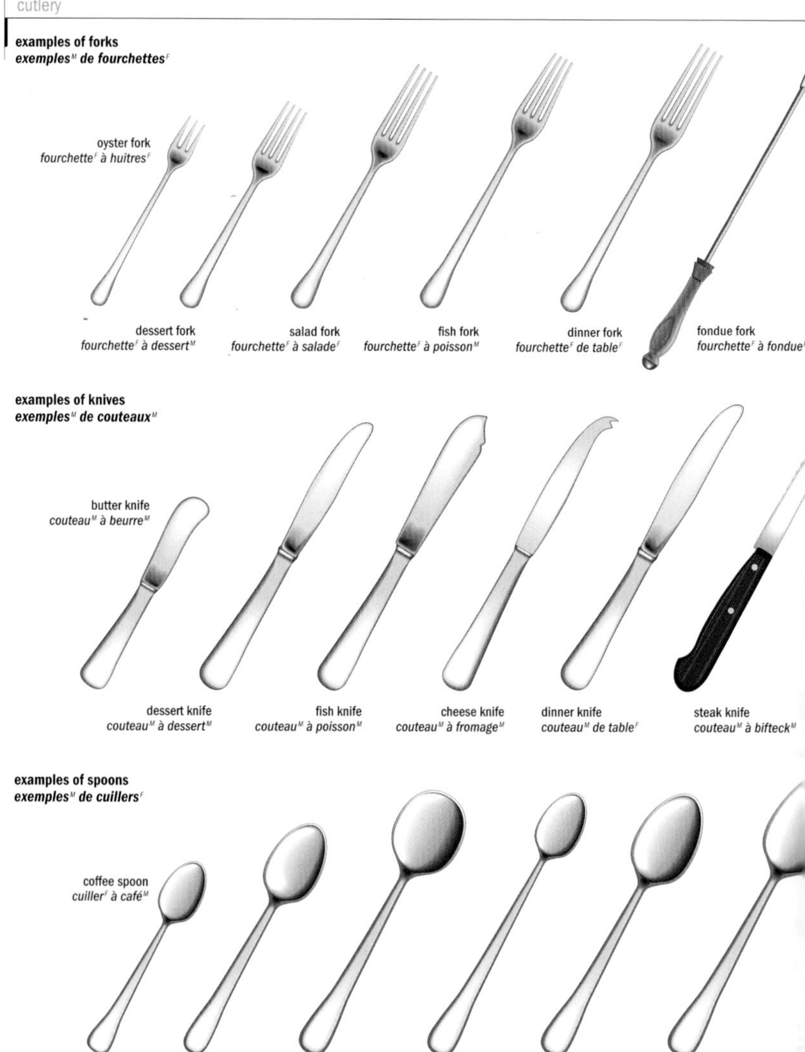
examples of forks
exemples[M] de fourchettes[F]
oyster fork
fourchette[F] à huîtres[F]
dessert fork
fourchette[F] à dessert[M]
salad fork
fourchette[F] à salade[F]
fish fork
fourchette[F] à poisson[M]
dinner fork
fourchette[F] de table[F]
fondue fork
fourchette[F] à fondue[F]
examples of knives
exemples[M] de couteaux[M]
butter knife
couteau[M] à beurre[M]
dessert knife
couteau[M] à dessert[M]
fish knife
couteau[M] à poisson[M]
cheese knife
couteau[M] à fromage[M]
dinner knife
couteau[M] de table[F]
steak knife
couteau[M] à bifteck[M]
examples of spoons
exemples[M] de cuillers[F]
coffee spoon
cuiller[F] à café[M]
teaspoon
cuiller[F] à thé[M]
soup spoon
cuiller[F] à soupe[F]
sundae spoon
cuiller[F] à soda[M]
dessert spoon
cuiller[F] à dessert[M]
tablespoon
cuiller[F] de table[F]

kitchen utensils

ustensiles[M] de cuisine[F]

kitchen knife
couteau[M] de cuisine[F]

half handle
demi-manche[M]

bolster
mitre[F]

tang
soie[F]

back
dos[M]

point
pointe[F]

heel
talon[M]

guard
épaulement[M]

blade
lame[F]

cutting edge
tranchant[M]

rivet
rivet[M]

examples of kitchen knives
exemples[M] de couteaux[M] de cuisine[F]

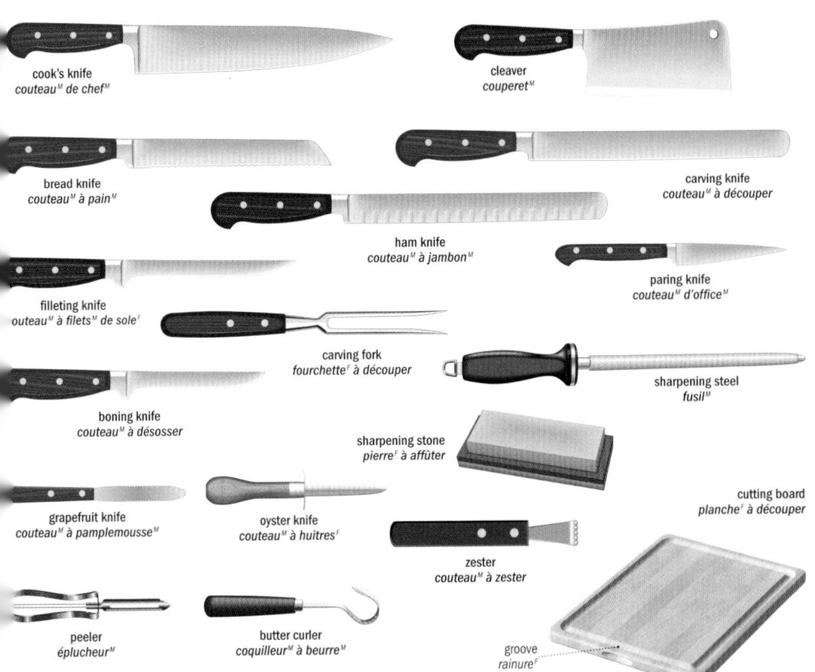

kitchen utensils

for opening
pour ouvrir

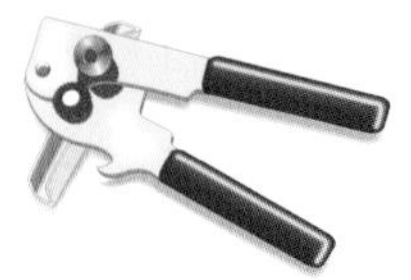
tin opener
ouvre-boîtes^{M}

bottle opener
décapsuleur^{M}

wine waiter corkscrew
tire-bouchon^{M} de sommelier^{M}

lever corkscrew
tire-bouchon^{M} à levier^{M}

for grinding and grating
pour broyer et râper

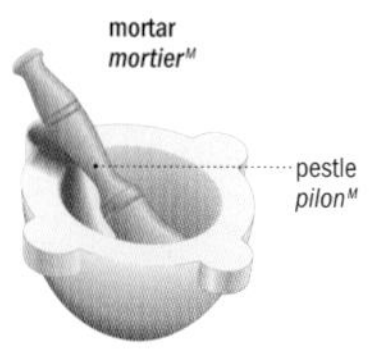
mortar
mortier^{M}

pestle
pilon^{M}

mincer
hachoir^{M}

nutcracker
casse-noix^{M}

garlic press
presse-ail^{M}

lemon squeezer
presse-agrumes^{M}

nutmeg grater
râpe^{F} à muscade^{F}

grater
râpe^{F}

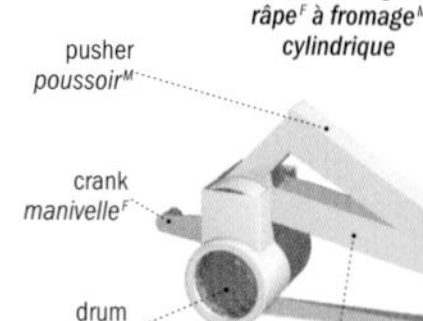
rotary cheese grater
râpe^{F} à fromage^{M} cylindrique

pusher
poussoir^{M}

crank
manivelle^{F}

drum
tambour^{M}

handle
poignée^{F}

pasta maker
machine^{F} à faire les pâtes^{F}

food mill
moulin^{M} à légumes^{M}

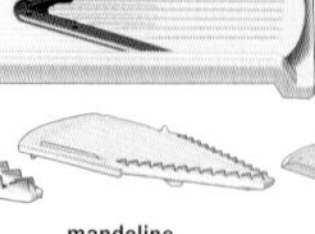
mandoline
mandoline^{F}

for measuring
pour mesurer

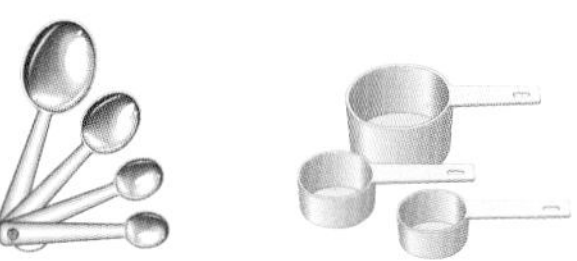

measuring spoons
cuillers[F] doseuses

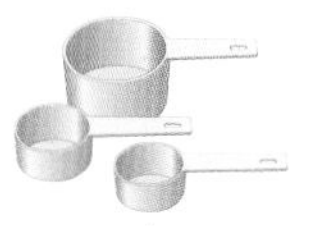

measuring cups
mesures[F]

sugar thermometer
thermomètre[M] à sucre[M]

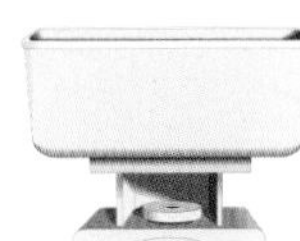

instant-read thermometer
thermomètre[M] à mesure[F] instantanée

measuring jug
tasse[F] à mesurer

meat thermometer
thermomètre[M] à viande[F]

oven thermometer
thermomètre[M] de four[M]

measuring beaker
verre[M] à mesurer

kitchen timer
minuteur[M]

egg timer
sablier[M]

kitchen scale
balance[F] de cuisine[F]

for straining and draining
pour passer et égoutter

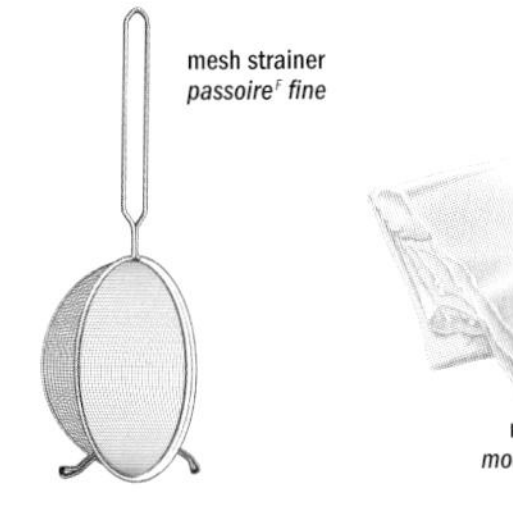

mesh strainer
passoire[F] fine

muslin
mousseline[F]

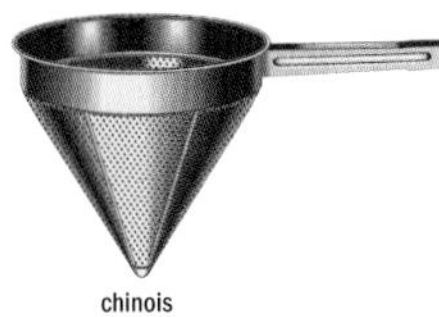

chinois
chinois[M]

funnel
entonnoir[M]

colander
passoire[F]

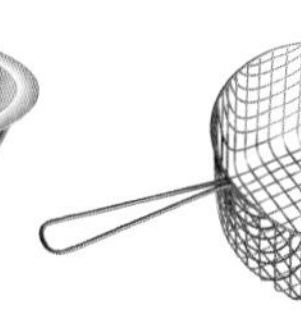

frying basket
panier[M] à friture[F]

sieve
tamis[M]

salad spinner
essoreuse[F] à salade[F]

baking utensils
***pour la pâtisserie*[F]**

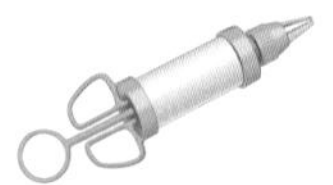

icing syringe
piston[M] *à décorer*

pastry cutting wheel
roulette[F] *de pâtissier*[M]

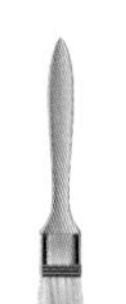

pastry brush
pinceau[M] *à pâtisserie*[F]

egg beater
batteur[M] *à œufs*[M]

whisk
fouet[M]

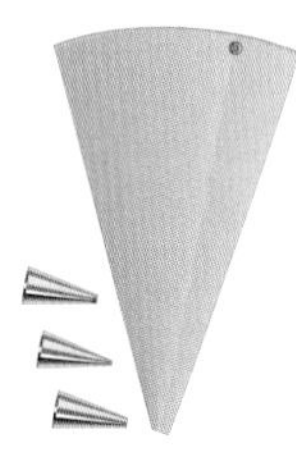

pastry bag and nozzles
poche[F] *à douilles*[F]

sifter
tamis[M] *à farine*[F]

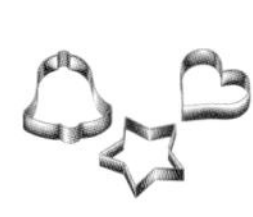

biscuit cutters
emporte-pièces[M]

dredger
saupoudreuse[F]

pastry blender
mélangeur[M] *à pâtisserie*

mixing bowls
bols[M] *à mélanger*

rolling pin
rouleau[M] *à pâtisserie*[F]

baking sheet
plaque[F] *à pâtisserie*[F]

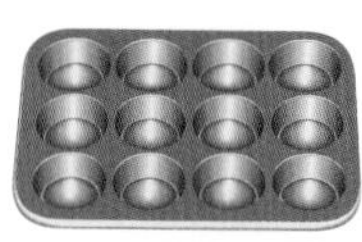

bun tin
moule[M] *à muffins*[M]

soufflé dish
moule[M] *à soufflé*[M]

charlotte mould
moule[M] *à charlotte*[F]

removable-bottomed tin
moule[M] *à fond*[M] *amovible*

pie tin
moule[M] *à tarte*[F]

quiche tin
moule[M] *à quiche*[F]

cake tin
moule[M] *à gâteau*[M]

set of utensils
jeu^M d'ustensiles^M

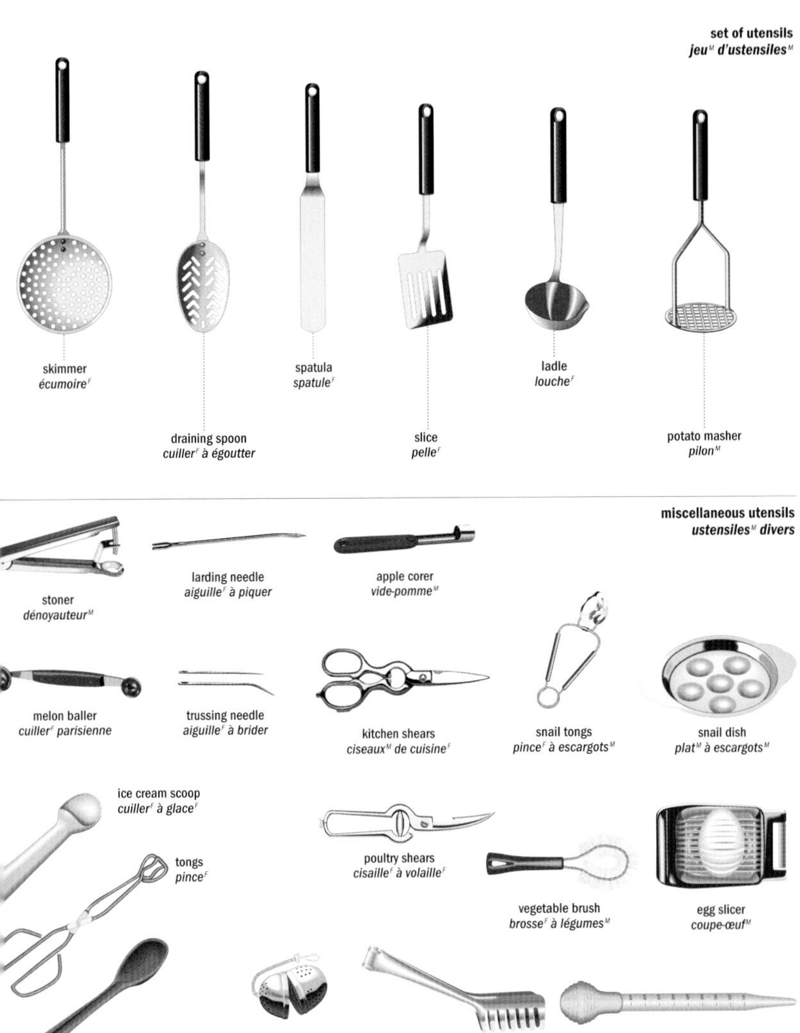

cooking utensils

batterie[F] de cuisine[F]

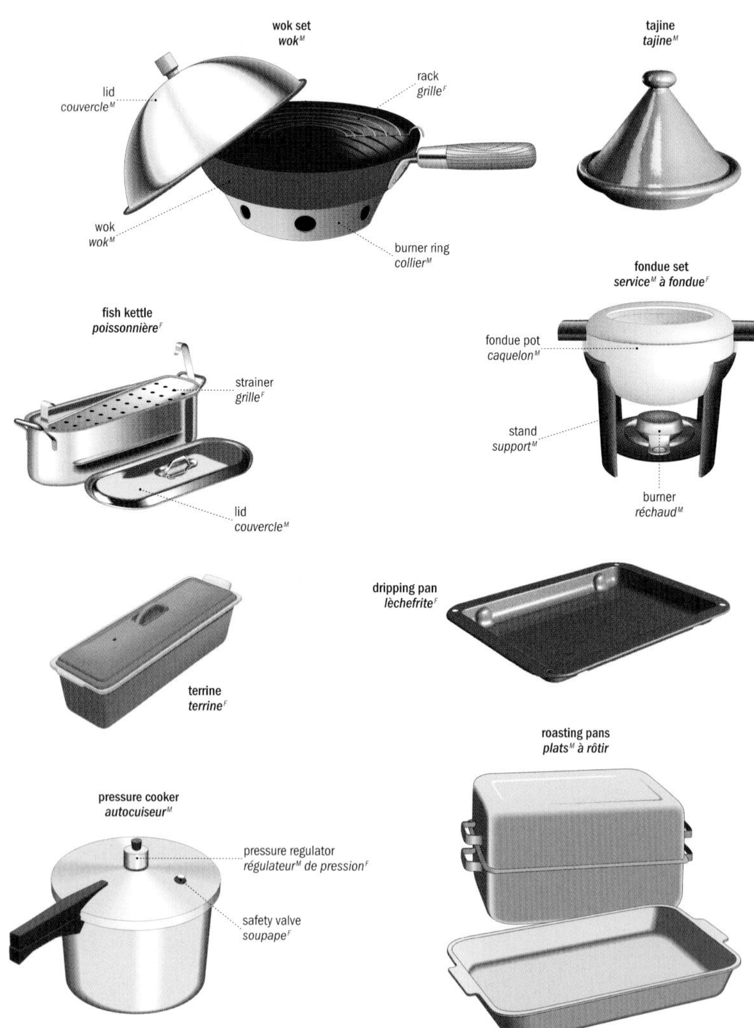

Dutch oven
faitout[M]

stock pot
marmite[F]

couscous kettle
couscoussier[M]

frying pan
poêle[F] *à frire*

steamer
cuit-vapeur[M]

egg poacher
pocheuse[F]

sauté pan
sauteuse[F]

small saucepan
poêlon[M]

diable
diable[M]

pancake pan
poêle[F] *à crêpes*[F]

steamer basket
panier[M] *cuit-vapeur*[M]

double boiler
bain-marie[M]

saucepan
casserole[F]

domestic appliances

appareils[M] électroménagers

for mixing and blending
pour mélanger et battre

blender
mélangeur[M]

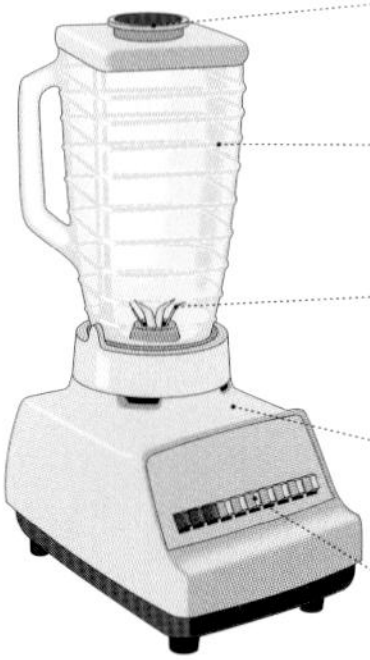

cap
bouchon[M]

container
récipient[M]

cutting blade
couteau[M]

motor unit
bloc[M]-moteur[M]

push button
bouton[M]-poussoir[M]

hand mixer
batteur[M] à main[F]

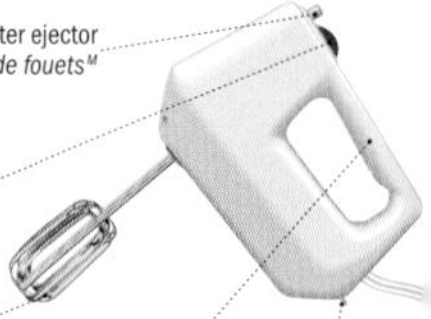

beater ejector
éjecteur[M] de fouets[M]

speed selector
sélecteur[M] de vitesse[F]

beater
fouet[M]

handle
poignée[F]

heel rest
talon[M] d'appui[M]

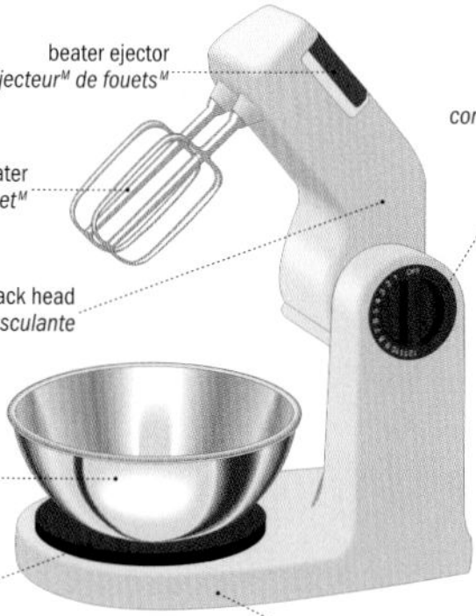

hand blender
mélangeur[M] à main[F]

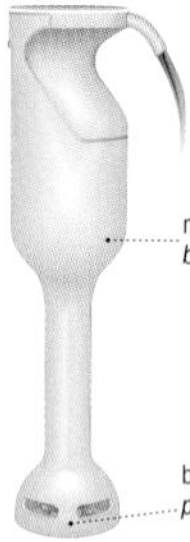

motor unit
bloc[M]-moteur[M]

blending attachment
pied[M]-mélangeur[M]

table mixer
batteur[M] sur socle[M]

beater ejector
éjecteur[M] de fouets[M]

speed control
commande[F] de vite

beater
fouet[M]

tilt-back head
tête[F] basculante

mixing bowl
bol[M]

turntable
plateau[M] tournant

stand
socle[M]

beaters
fouets[M]

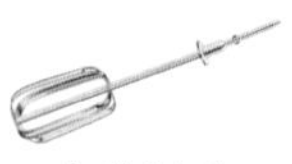

four-blade beater
fouet[M] quatre pales[F]

spiral beater
fouet[M] en spirale[F]

wire beater
fouet[M] à fil[M]

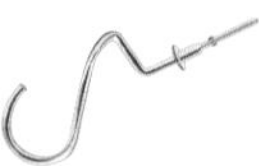

dough hook
crochet[M] pétrisseur

…processor
…t^M de cuisine^F

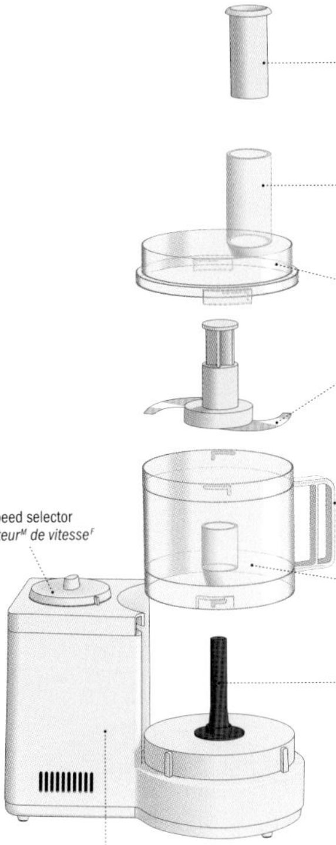

pusher
poussoir^M

feed tube
entonnoir^M

lid
couvercle^M

blade
couteau^M

handle
poignée^F

speed selector
sélecteur^M de vitesse^F

bowl
bol^M

spindle
arbre^M

motor unit
bloc^M-moteur^M

for cutting
pour couper

discs
disques^M

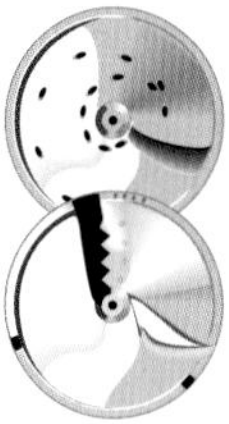

…ic knife
…eau^M électrique

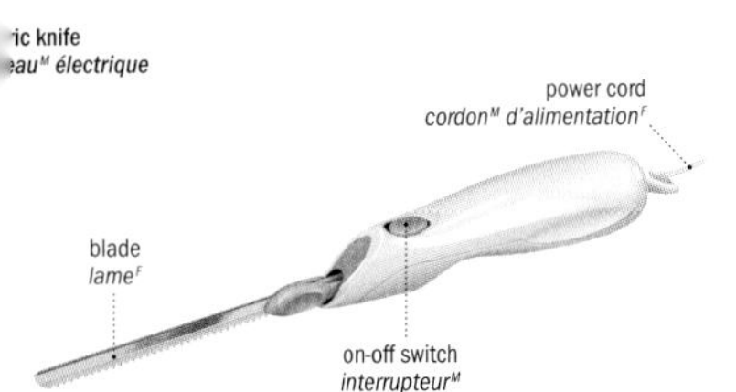

for juicing
pour presser

lemon squeezer
presse-agrumes^M

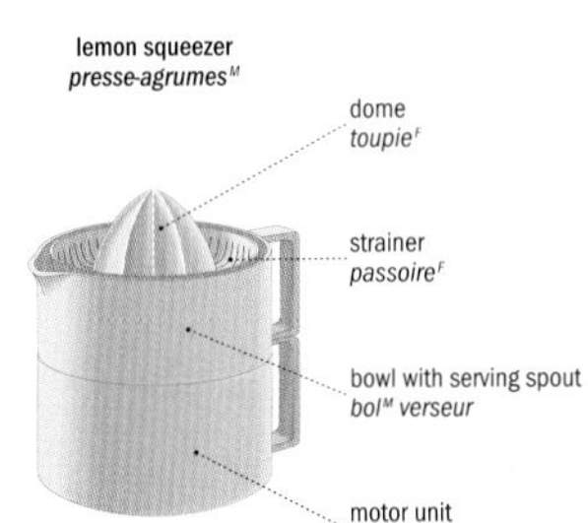

domestic appliances

for cooking
pour cuire

microwave oven
four[M] à micro-ondes[F]

door
porte[F]
sensor probe
sonde[F] thermique
probe socket
prise[F] de la sonde[F] thermique
window
hublot[M]
clock timer
horloge[F] programmatrice
latch
loquet[M]
control panel
tableau[M] de commande[F]
handle
poignée[F]

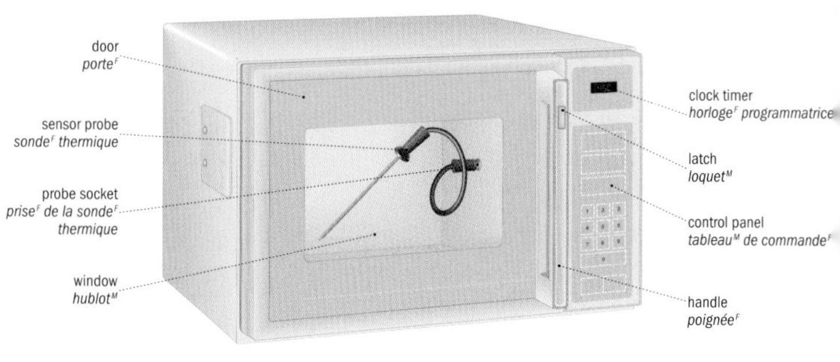

waffle iron
gaufrier[M]-gril[M]

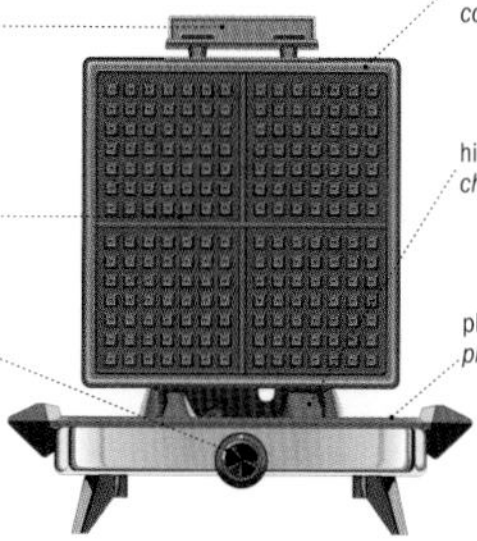

handle
poignée[F]
plate
plaque[F]
temperature selector
sélecteur[M] de température[F]
lid
couvercle[M]
hinge
charnière[F]
plate
plaque[F]

toaster
grille-pain[M]

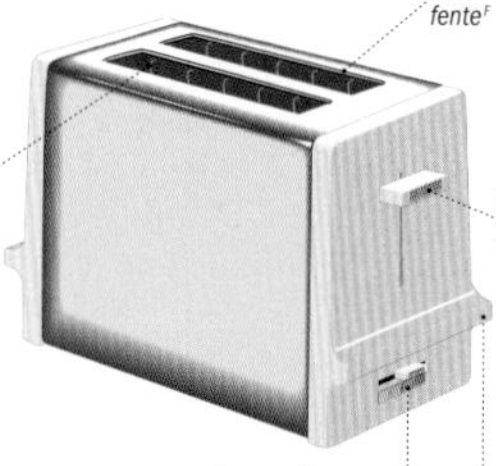

slot
fente[F]
bread guide
guide[M]
lever
manette[F]
temperature control
thermostat[M]
handle
poignée[F]

deep fryer
friteuse[F]

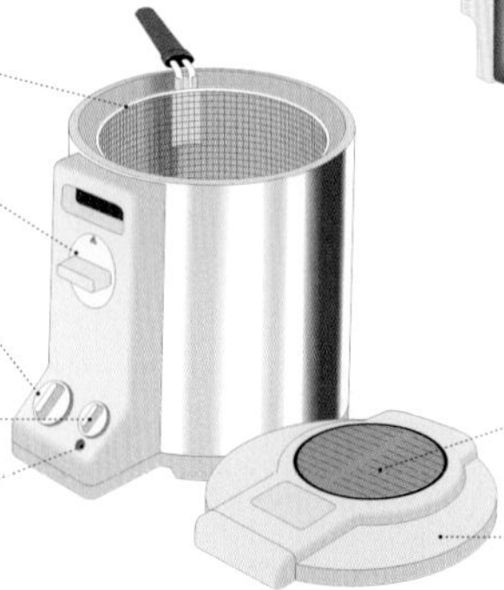

basket
panier[M]
rack
crémaillère[F]
timer
minuterie[F]
thermostat
thermostat[M]
pilot light
voyant[M] lumineux
filter
filtre[M]
lid
couvercle[M]

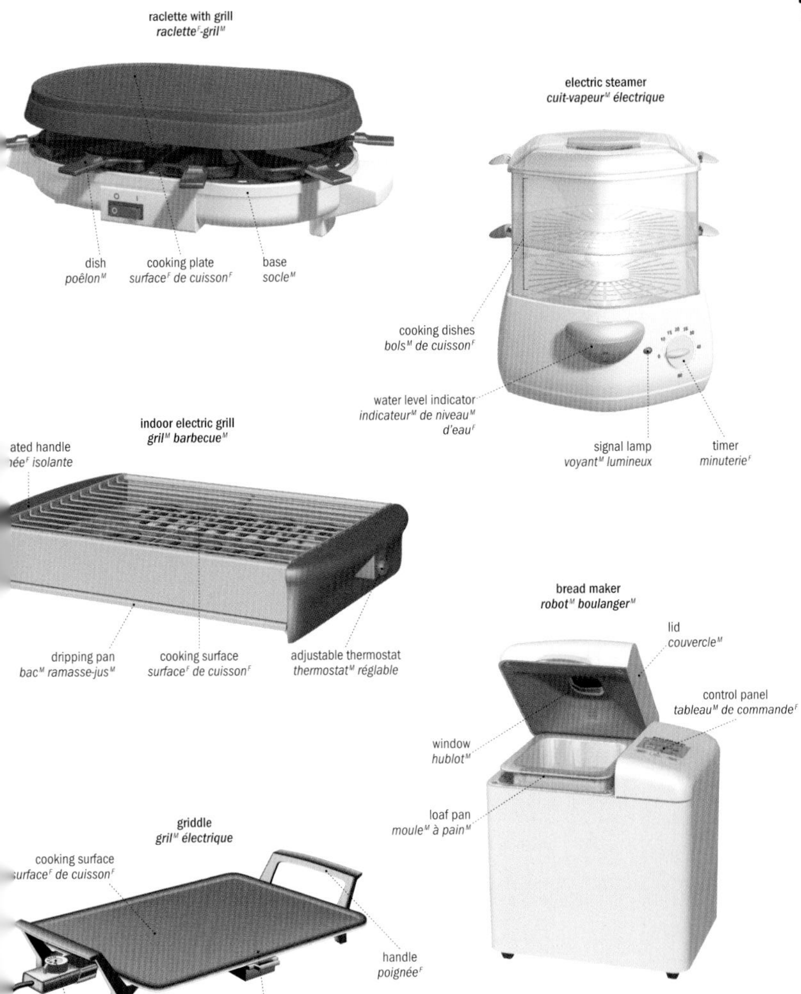
raclette with grill
raclette^F-gril^M
dish
poêlon^M
cooking plate
surface^F de cuisson^F
base
socle^M
electric steamer
cuit-vapeur^M électrique
cooking dishes
bols^M de cuisson^F
water level indicator
indicateur^M de niveau^M d'eau^F
signal lamp
voyant^M lumineux
timer
minuterie^F
indoor electric grill
gril^M barbecue^M
ated handle
née^F isolante
dripping pan
bac^M ramasse-jus^M
cooking surface
surface^F de cuisson^F
adjustable thermostat
thermostat^M réglable
bread maker
robot^M boulanger^M
lid
couvercle^M
control panel
tableau^M de commande^F
window
hublot^M
loaf pan
moule^M à pain^M
griddle
gril^M électrique
cooking surface
surface^F de cuisson^F
handle
poignée^F
detachable control
commande^F amovible
grease well
collecteur^M de graisse^F

miscellaneous domestic appliances

appareils^M électroménagers divers

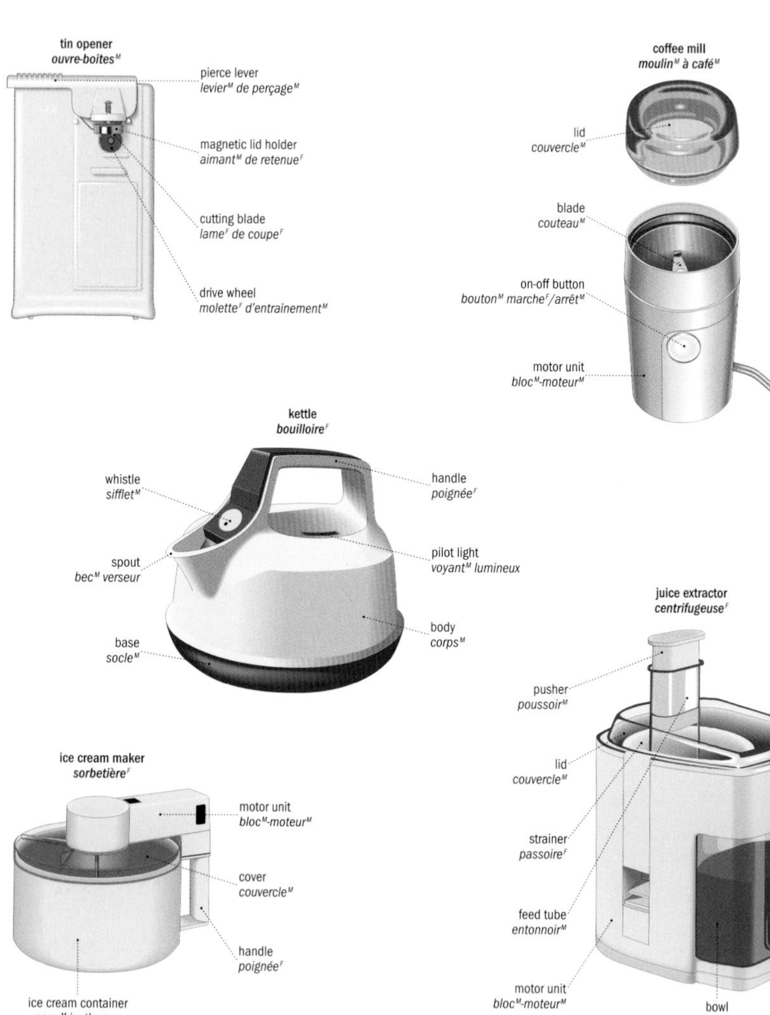

coffee makers

cafetières[F]

automatic filter coffee maker
cafetière[F] filtre[M]

lid
couvercle[M]

reservoir
réservoir[M]

filter
panier[M]

water level
niveau[M] d'eau[F]

pilot light
voyant[M] lumineux

jug
verseuse[F]

on-off switch
interrupteur[M]

warming plate
plaque[F] chauffante

Neapolitan coffee maker
cafetière[F] napolitaine

espresso machine
machine[F] à espresso[M]

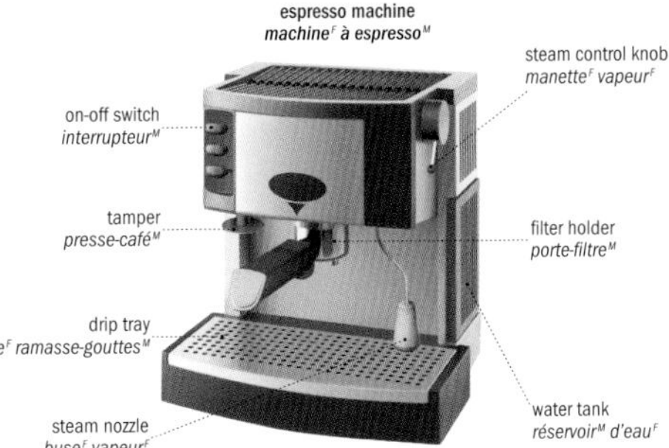

vacuum coffee maker
cafetière[F] à infusion[F]

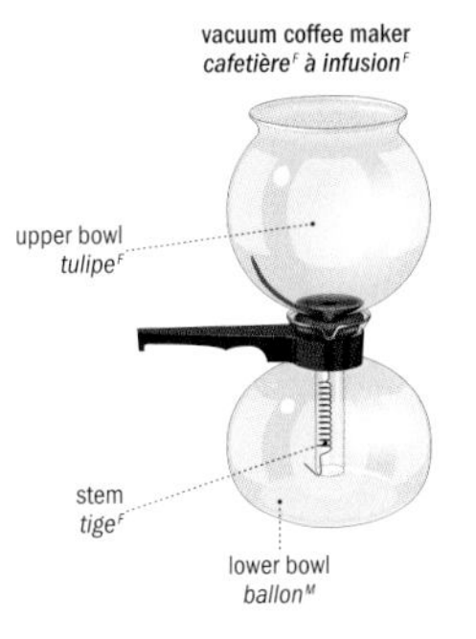

cafetière with plunger
cafetière[F] à piston[M]

espresso coffee maker
cafetière[F] espresso[M]

percolator
percolateur[M]

exterior of a house

extérieur[M] d'une maison[F]

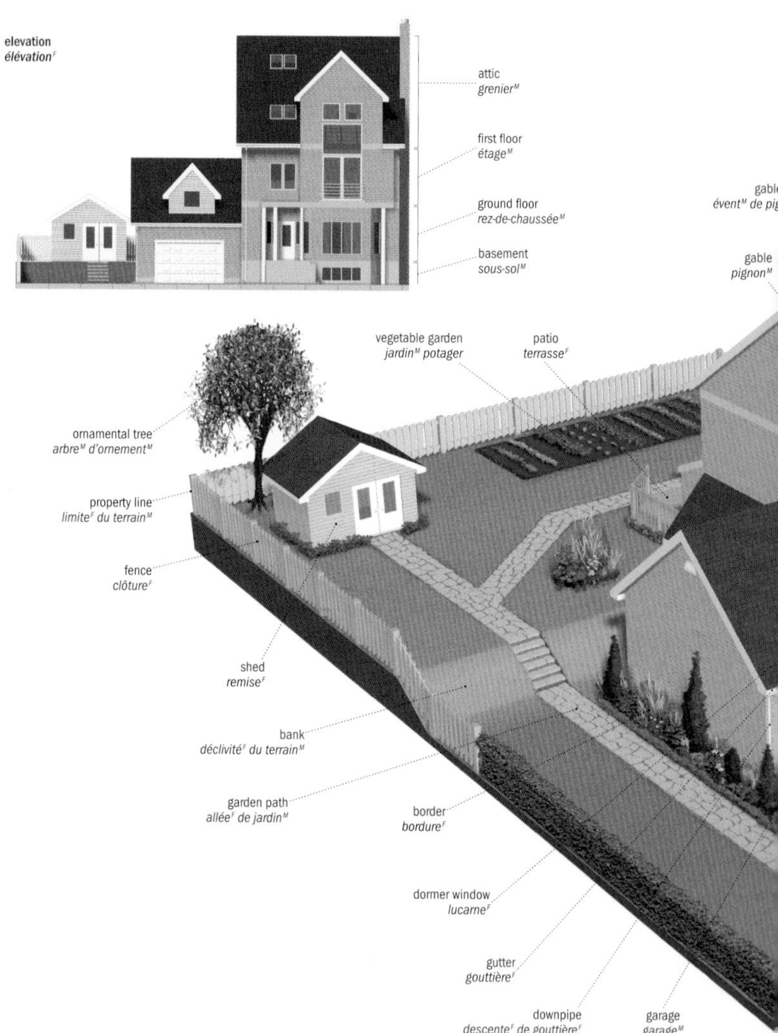

site plan
plan[M] du terrain[M]

pool

piscine[F]

above ground swimming pool
piscine[F] hors sol[M]

skimmer
skimmer[M]
filter
filtre[M]
pump
pompe[F]
upright
montant[M]
wall
mur[M]

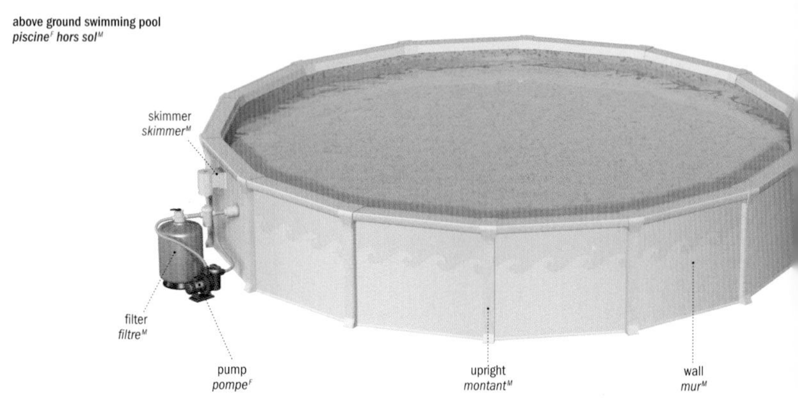

sunken swimming pool
piscine[F] enterrée

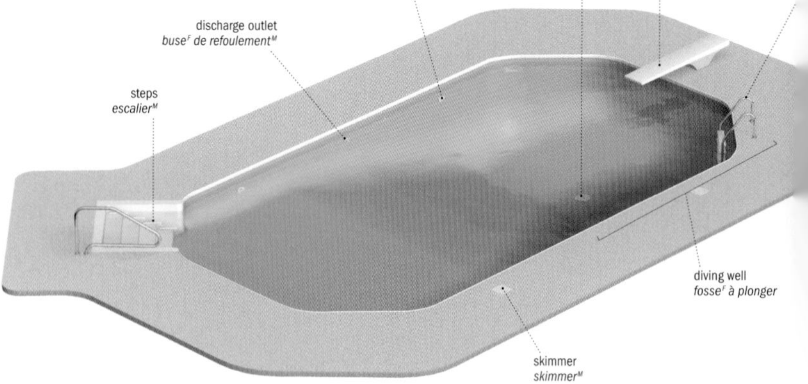

diving board
tremplin[M]
main drain
bonde[F] de fond[M]
underwater light
projecteur[M] sous-marin
ladd
échell
discharge outlet
buse[F] de refoulement[M]
steps
escalier[M]
diving well
fosse[F] à plonger
skimmer
skimmer[M]

exterior door

porte^F extérieure

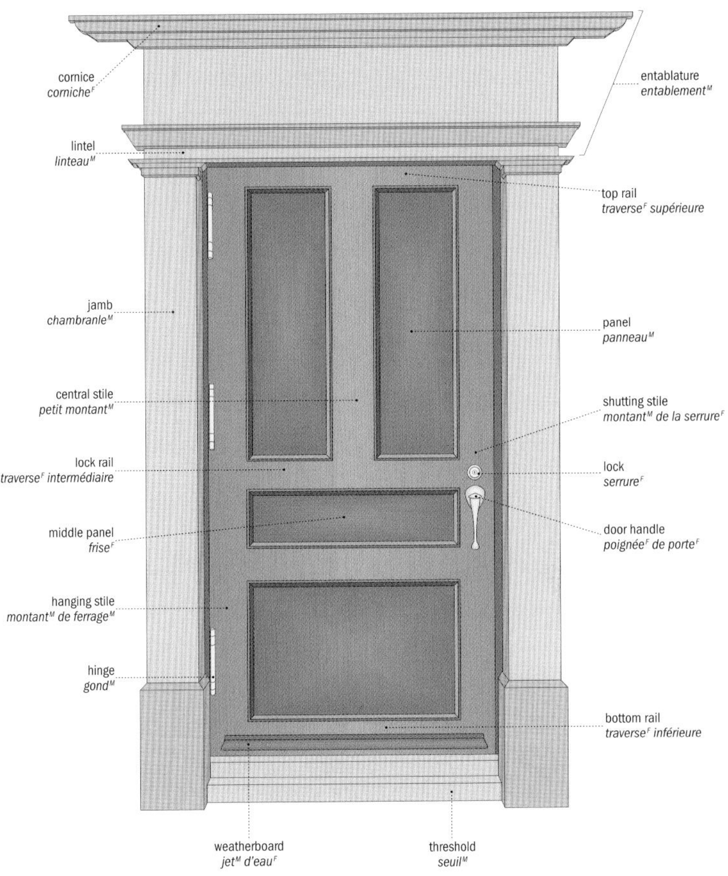

lock

serrure[F]

general view
vue[F] d'ensemble[M]

lock
serrure[F]
dead bolt
pêne[M] dormant
escutcheon
écusson[M]
rose
rosette[F]
faceplate
têtière[F]
latch bolt
pêne[M] demi-tour[M]
door handle
bec-de-cane[M]

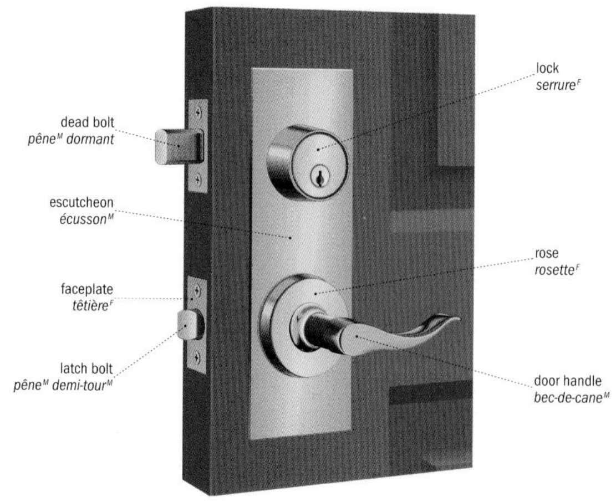

window

fenêtre[F]

structure
structure[F]

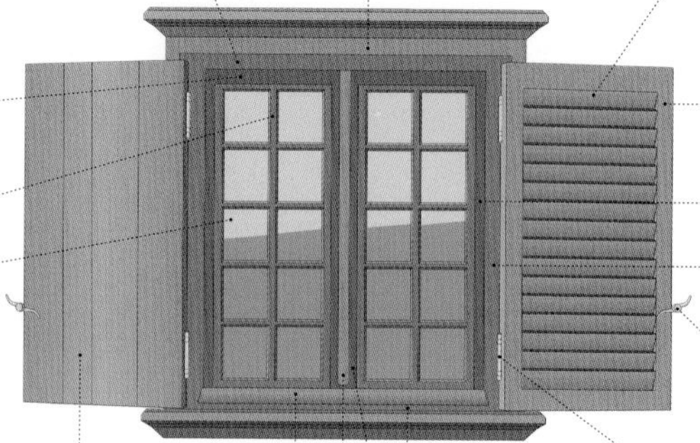

head of frame
tête[F] de dormant[M]
casing
chambranle[M]
jalousie
persienne[F]
top rail of sash
traverse[F] supérieure d'ouvrant[M]
casement
battant[M]
glazing bar
petit bois[M]
hanging stile
montant[M] de rive[F]
pane
carreau[M]
sash frame
dormant[M]
hook
crochet[M]
shutter
contrevent[M]
weatherboard
jet[M] d'eau[F]
sill of frame
base[F] de dormant[M]
hinge
paumelle[F]
stile tongue of sash
montant[M] mouton[M]
stile groove of sash
montant[M] embrevé

timber frame

charpente^F

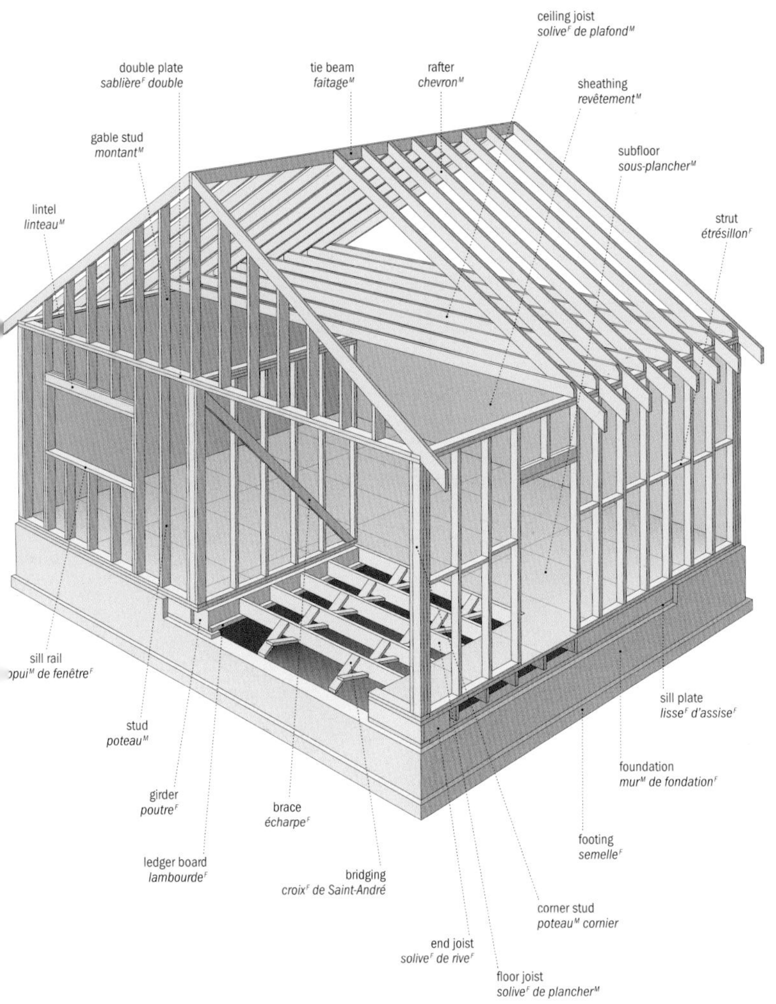

main rooms

principales pièces[F] d'une maison[F]

ground floor
rez-de-chaussée[M]

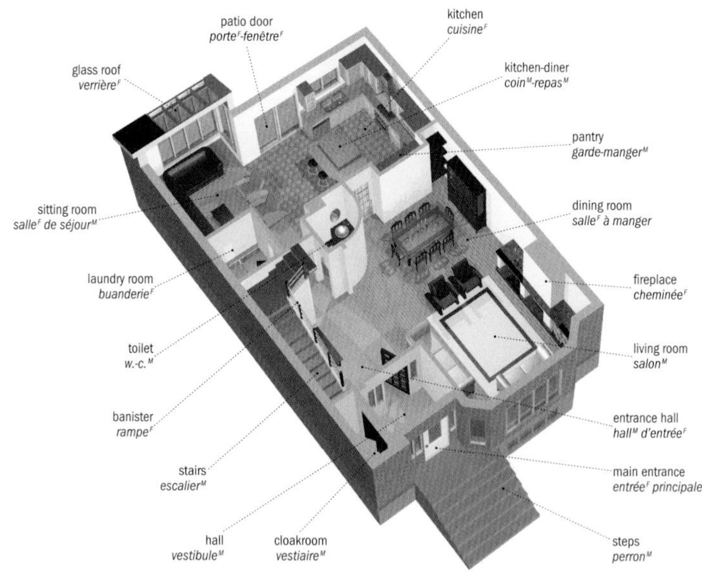

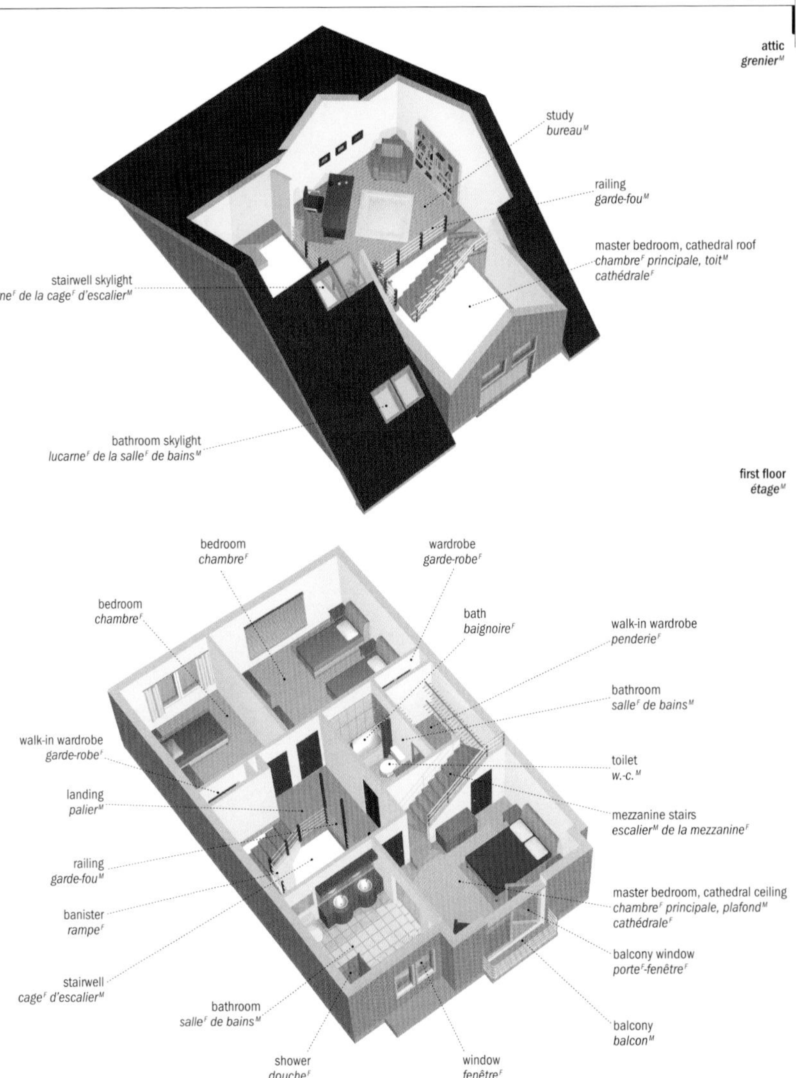
attic
grenier^M
study
bureau^M
railing
garde-fou^M
master bedroom, cathedral roof
chambre^F principale, toit^M cathédrale^F
stairwell skylight
rne^F de la cage^F d'escalier^M
bathroom skylight
lucarne^F de la salle^F de bains^M
first floor
étage^M
bedroom
chambre^F
wardrobe
garde-robe^F
bedroom
chambre^F
bath
baignoire^F
walk-in wardrobe
penderie^F
bathroom
salle^F de bains^M
walk-in wardrobe
garde-robe^F
toilet
w.-c.^M
landing
palier^M
mezzanine stairs
escalier^M de la mezzanine^F
railing
garde-fou^M
banister
rampe^F
master bedroom, cathedral ceiling
chambre^F principale, plafond^M cathédrale^F
balcony window
porte^F-fenêtre^F
stairwell
cage^F d'escalier^M
bathroom
salle^F de bains^M
balcony
balcon^M
shower
douche^F
window
fenêtre^F

wood flooring

parquet[M]

wood flooring on cement screed
parquet[M] sur chape[F] de ciment[M]

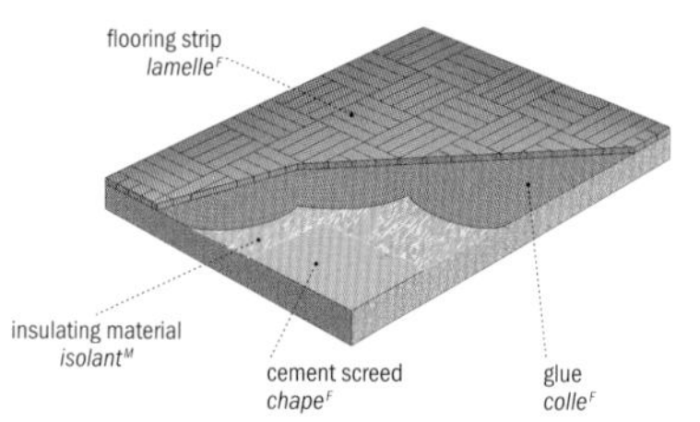

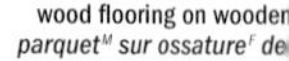
wood flooring on wooden
parquet[M] sur ossature[F] de

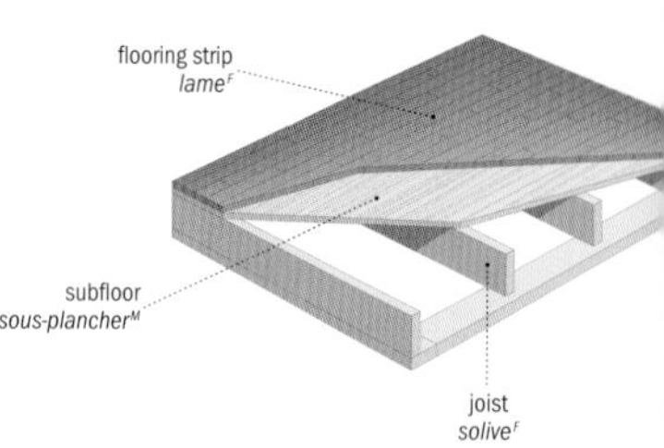

wood flooring types
arrangements[M] des parquets[M]

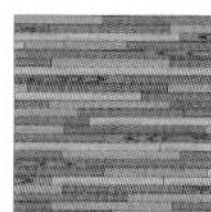

woodstrip flooring
parquet[M] à coupe[F] perdue

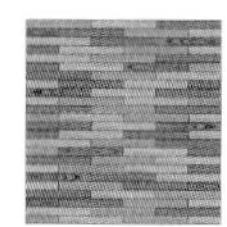

brick-bond woodstrip flooring
parquet[M] à coupe[F] de pierre[F]

herringbone parquet
parquet[M] à bâtons[M] rompus

herringbone patt
parquet[M] en chevr

inlaid parquet
parquet[M] mosaïque[F]

basket weave pattern
parquet[M] en vannerie[F]

Arenberg parquet
parquet[M] d'Arenberg

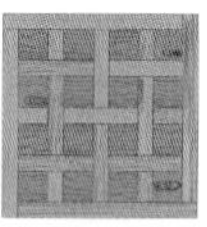

Chantilly parquet
parquet[M] Chantilly

Versailles parqu
parquet[M] Versai

textile floor coverings

revêtements[M] de sol[M] textiles

rug
tapis[M]

pile
moq

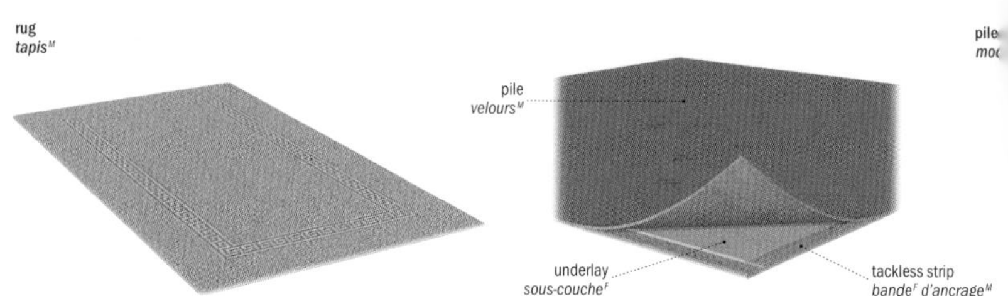

stairs
escalier[M]

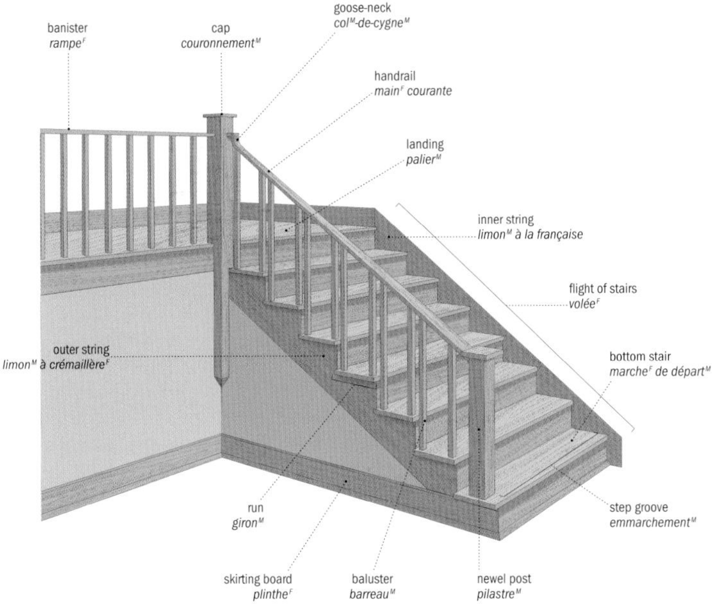

banister
rampe[F]
cap
couronnement[M]
goose-neck
col[M]-de-cygne[M]
handrail
main[F] courante
landing
palier[M]
inner string
limon[M] à la française
flight of stairs
volée[F]
outer string
limon[M] à crémaillère[F]
bottom stair
marche[F] de départ[M]
run
giron[M]
step groove
emmarchement[M]
skirting board
plinthe[F]
baluster
barreau[M]
newel post
pilastre[M]

step
marche[F]

tread
marche[F]
riser
contremarche[F]
rise
hauteur[F] de marche[F]
nosing
nez[M]-de-marche[F]

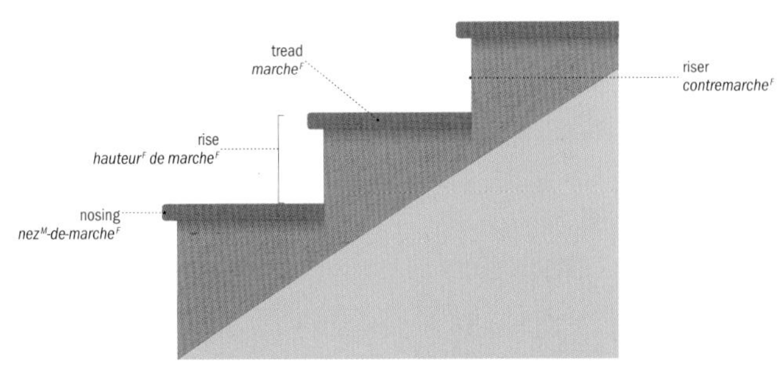

wood firing

chauffage[M] au bois[M]

fireplace
cheminée[F] à foyer[M] ouvert

hood
hotte[F]

mantlepiece
tablette[F]

corbel piece
corbeau[M]

mantle
manteau[M]

lintel
linteau[M]

jamb
jambage[M]

frame
encadrement[M]

firebrick back
cœur[M]

base
socle[M]

fireplace
âtre[M]

wood storage space
bûcher[M]

slow-burning stove
poêle[M] à combustion[F] lente

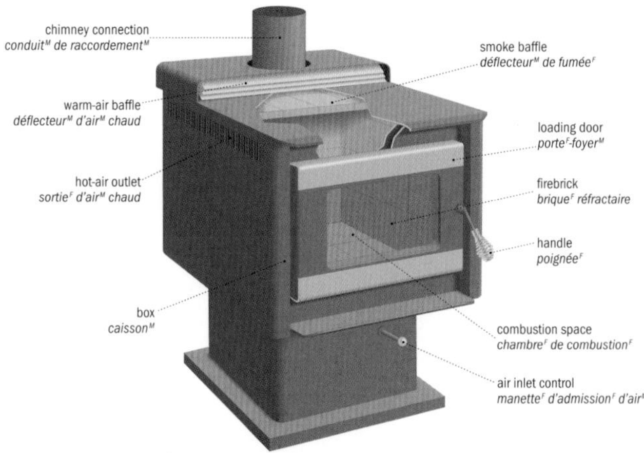

HOUSE

nney
minée[F]

rain cap
mitre[F]

roof
toit[M]

storm collar
collet[M]

flashing
solin[M]

ceiling
plafond[M]

ceiling collar
collier[M] coupe-feu[M]

pipe section
section[F] de conduit[M]

ceiling collar
collier[M] coupe-feu[M]

floor
plancher[M]

capped tee
té[M] de base[F]

fire irons
accessoires[M] de foyer[M]

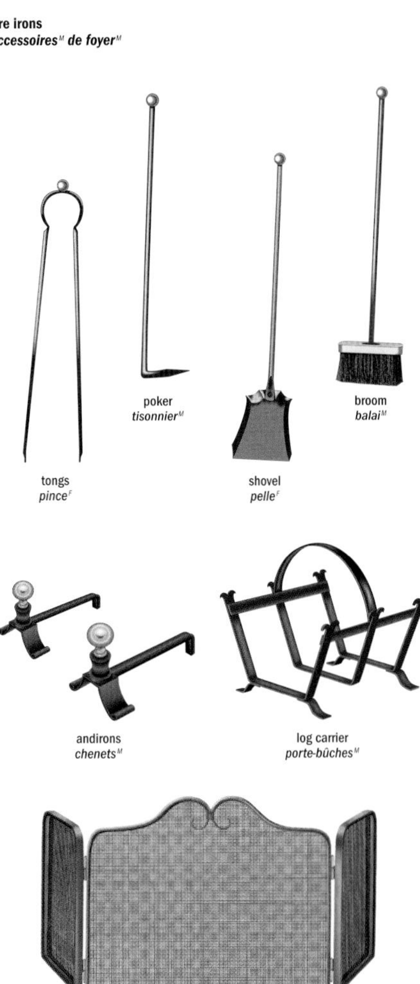

plumbing system

circuit[M] de plomberie[F]

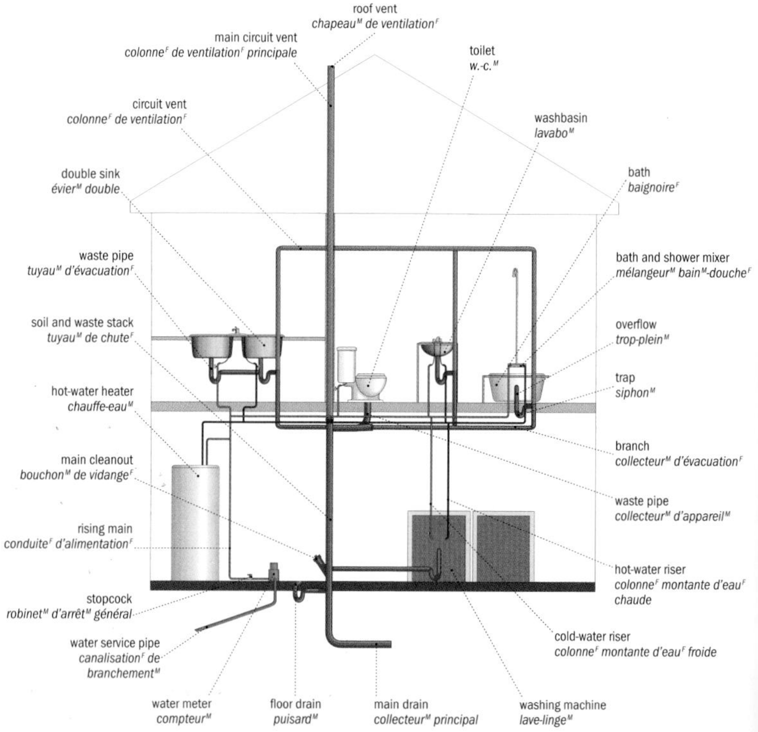

roof vent
chapeau[M] de ventilation[F]

main circuit vent
colonne[F] de ventilation[F] principale

toilet
w.-c.[M]

circuit vent
colonne[F] de ventilation[F]

washbasin
lavabo[M]

double sink
évier[M] double

bath
baignoire[F]

waste pipe
tuyau[M] d'évacuation[F]

bath and shower mixer
mélangeur[M] bain[M]-douche[F]

soil and waste stack
tuyau[M] de chute[F]

overflow
trop-plein[M]

trap
siphon[M]

hot-water heater
chauffe-eau[M]

branch
collecteur[M] d'évacuation[F]

main cleanout
bouchon[M] de vidange[F]

waste pipe
collecteur[M] d'appareil[M]

rising main
conduite[F] d'alimentation[F]

hot-water riser
colonne[F] montante d'eau[F] chaude

stopcock
robinet[M] d'arrêt[M] général

cold-water riser
colonne[F] montante d'eau[F] froide

water service pipe
canalisation[F] de branchement[M]

water meter
compteur[M]

floor drain
puisard[M]

main drain
collecteur[M] principal

washing machine
lave-linge[M]

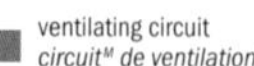
ventilating circuit
circuit[M] de ventilation[F]

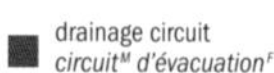
drainage circuit
circuit[M] d'évacuation[F]

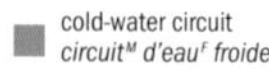
cold-water circuit
circuit[M] d'eau[F] froide

hot-water circuit
circuit[M] d'eau[F] chaude

bathroom

salle[F] de bains[M]

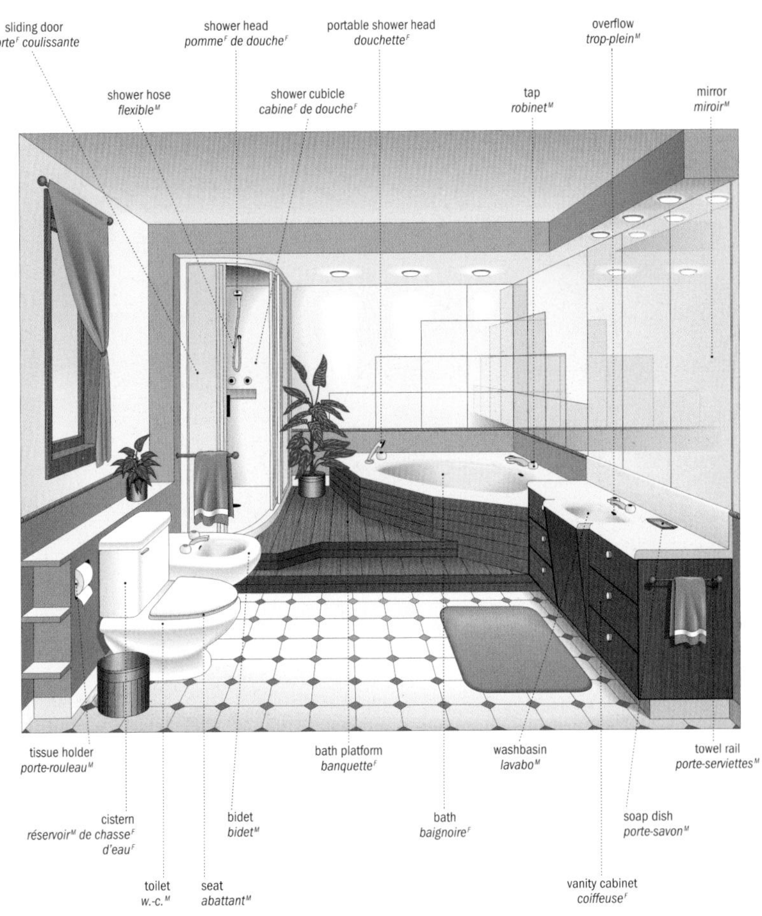

toilet

w.-c.[M]

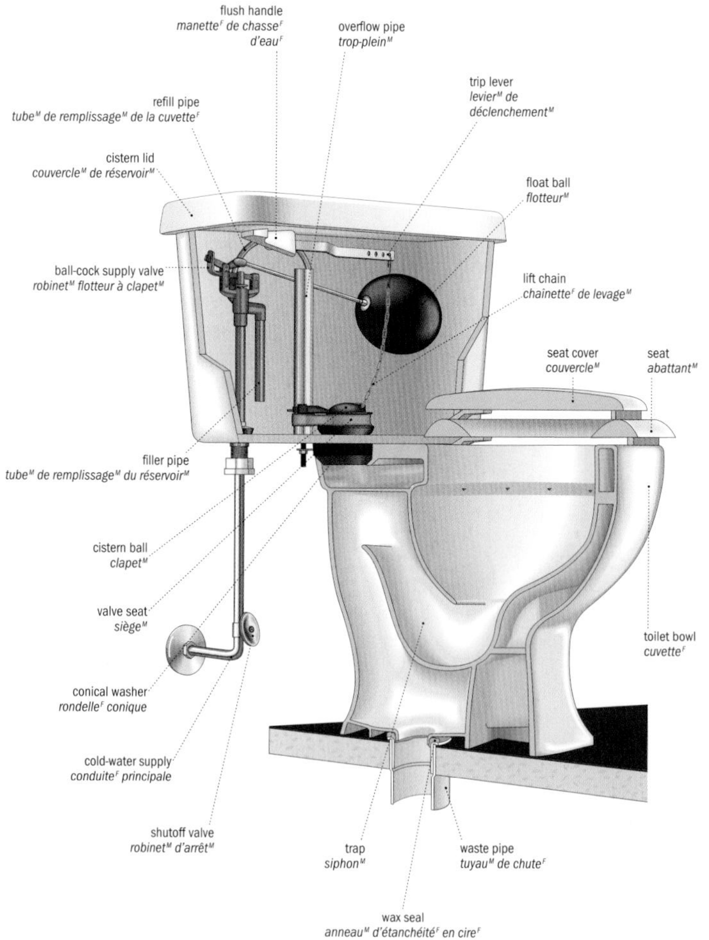
flush handle
manette[F] de chasse[F] d'eau[F]
overflow pipe
trop-plein[M]
trip lever
levier[M] de déclenchement[M]
refill pipe
tube[M] de remplissage[M] de la cuvette[F]
cistern lid
couvercle[M] de réservoir[M]
float ball
flotteur[M]
ball-cock supply valve
robinet[M] flotteur à clapet[M]
lift chain
chainette[F] de levage[M]
seat cover
couvercle[M]
seat
abattant[M]
filler pipe
tube[M] de remplissage[M] du réservoir[M]
cistern ball
clapet[M]
valve seat
siège[M]
toilet bowl
cuvette[F]
conical washer
rondelle[F] conique
cold-water supply
conduite[F] principale
shutoff valve
robinet[M] d'arrêt[M]
trap
siphon[M]
waste pipe
tuyau[M] de chute[F]
wax seal
anneau[M] d'étanchéité[F] en cire[F]

examples of branching

exemples[M] de branchement[M]

sink with waste disposal unit
évier[M]-broyeur[M]

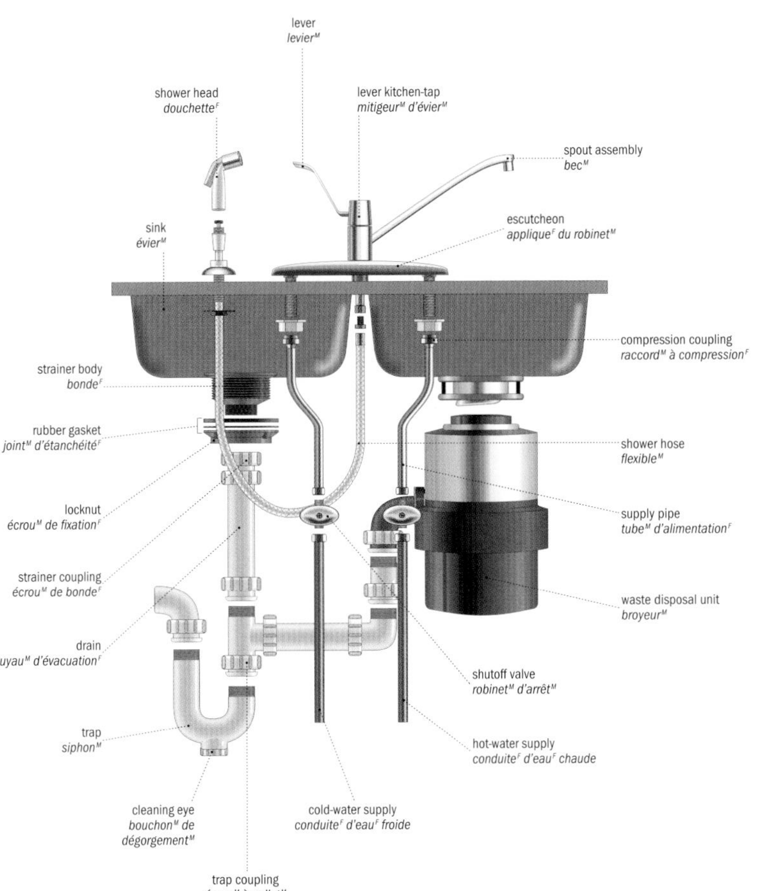

network connection

branchement[M] au réseau[M]

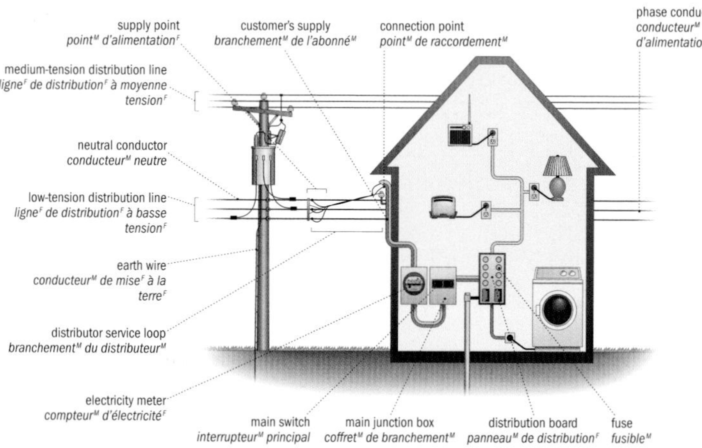

contact devices

dispositifs[M] de contact[M]

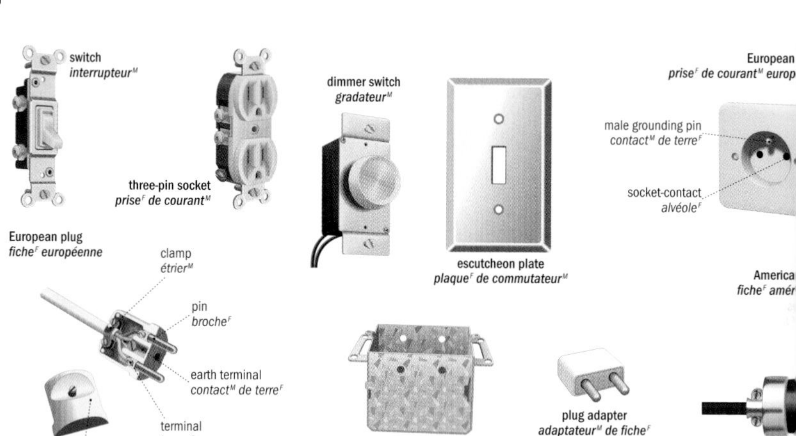

lighting
éclairage[M]

ndescent light bulb
be[F] à incandescence[F]

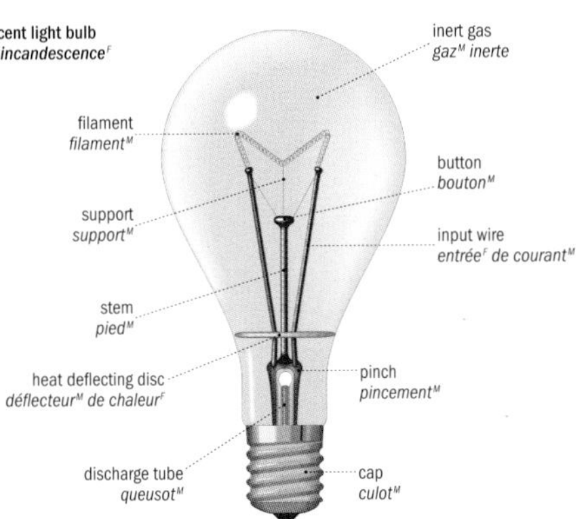

lampholder
douille[F] de lampe[F]

tube
ampoule[F]

screw cap
culot[M] à vis[F]

gy saving bulb
e[F] à économie[F] d'énergie[F]

fluorescent tube
tube[M] fluorescent

bulb
ampoule[F]

tube retention clip
attache[F] du tube[M]

mounting plate
plaque[F] de montage[M]

electronic ballast
ballast[M] électronique

housing
boîtier[M]

cap
culot[M]

bayonet cap
culot[M] à baïonnette[F]

scent tube
fluorescent

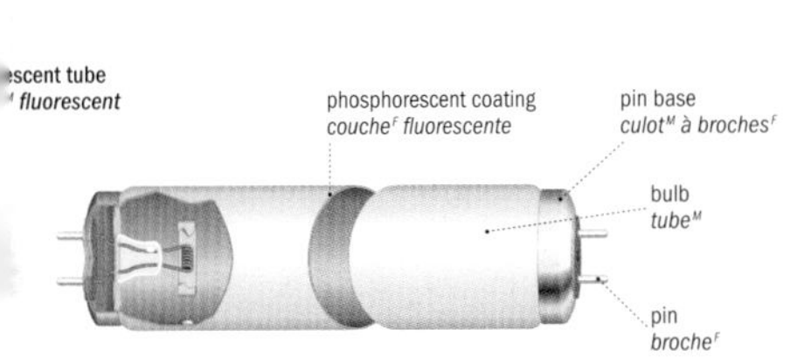

tungsten-halogen bulb
lampe[F] à halogène[M]

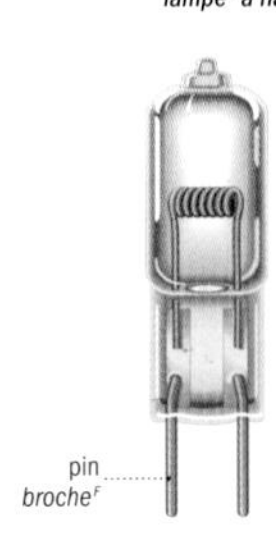

armchair

fauteuil[M]

parts
parties[F]

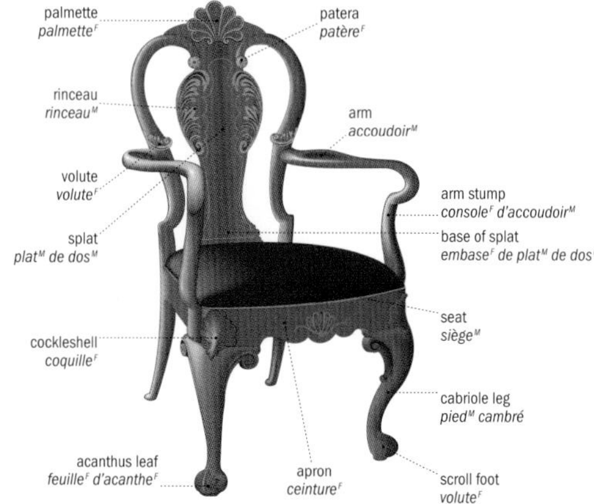

examples of armchairs
exemples[M] de fauteuils[M]

Wassily chair
fauteuil[M] Wassily

director's chair
fauteuil[M] metteur[M] en scène[F]

rocking chair
fauteuil[M] à bascule[F]

cabriole chair
cabriolet[M]

méridienne
méridienne[F]

chaise longue
récamier[M]

club chair
fauteuil[M] club[M]

bergère
bergère[F]

sofa
canapé[M]

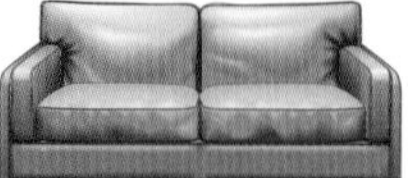

two-seater settee
causeuse[F]

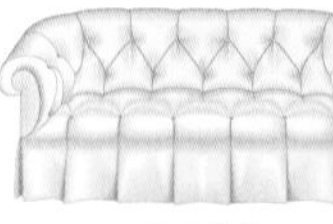

chesterfield
canapé[M] capitonné

side chair

chaise^F

parts
parties^F

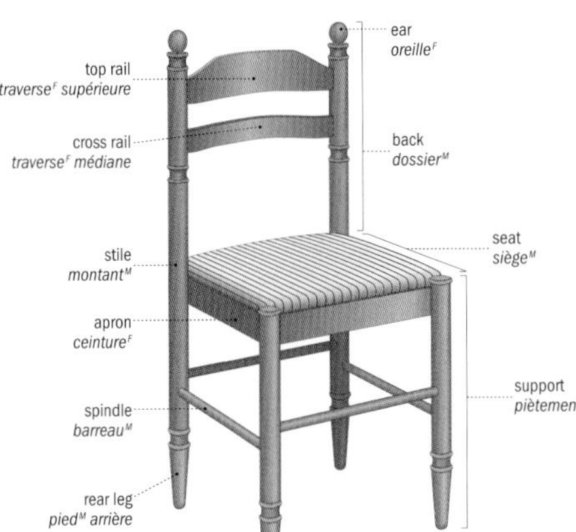

examples of chairs
exemples^M de chaises^F

rocking chair
berceuse^F

stacking chairs
chaises^F empilables

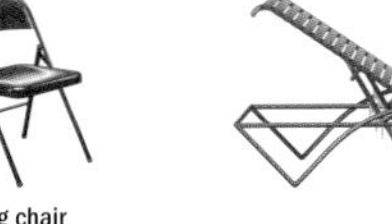

folding chair
chaise^F pliante

recliner
chaise^F longue

seats

sièges^M

bean bag chair
fauteuil^M-sac^M

ottoman
pouf^M

step chair
chaise^F-escabeau^M

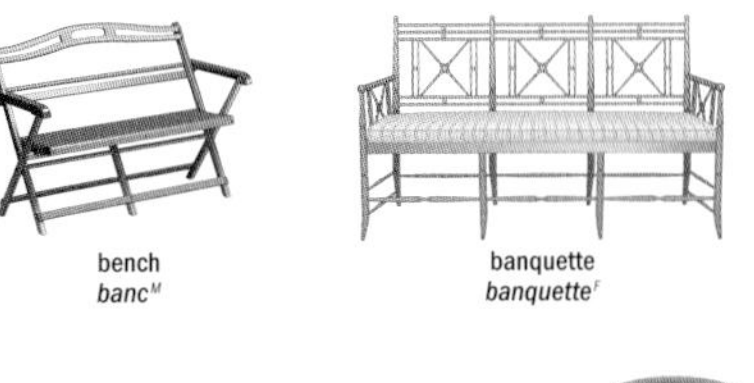

bench
banc^M

banquette
banquette^F

footstool
tabouret^M

bar stool
tabouret^M-bar^M

table

table[F]

gate-leg table
table[F] à abattants[M]

drawer
tiroir[M]
knob
bouton[M]
top
plateau[M]
drop-leaf
abattant[M]
stretcher
traverse[F]
leg
pied[M]
gate-leg
tréteau[M]
apron
ceinture[F]
crosspiece
entrejambe[M]

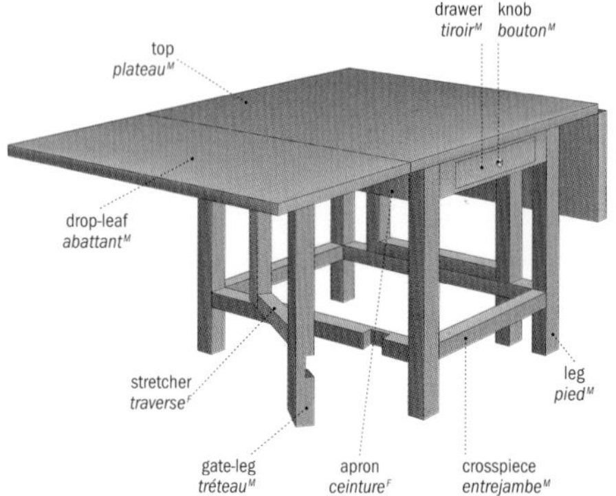

examples of tables
exemples[M] de tables[F]

extending table
table[F] à rallonges[F]

top
plateau[M]
extension
rallonge[F]

nest of tables
tables[F] gigognes

serving trolley
desserte[F]

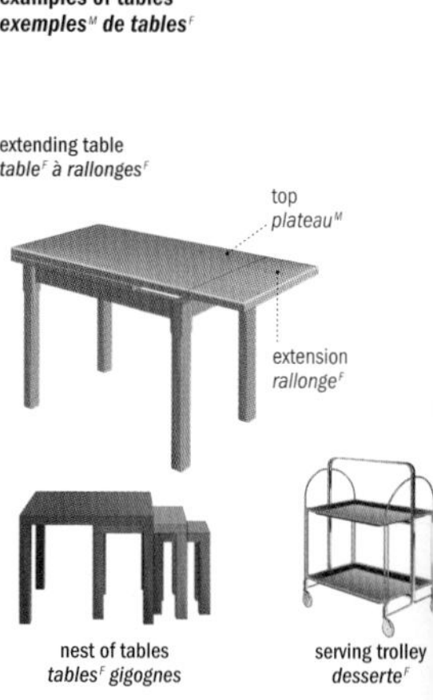

storage furniture

meubles[M] de rangement[M]

armoire
armoire[F]

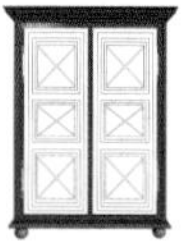

frame
bâti[M]

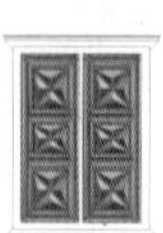

door
vantail[M]

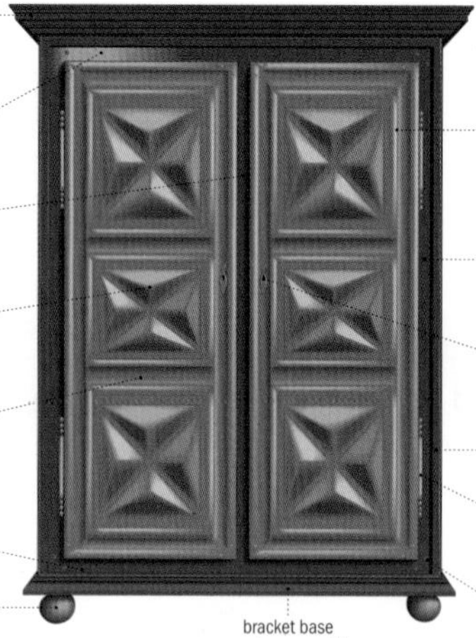

frieze
frise[F]
cornice
corniche[F]
top rail
traverse[F] supérieure
door panel
panneau[M] de vantail[M]
centre post
dormant[M]
hanging stile
montant[M] de ferrage[M]
diamond point
pointe[F] de diamant[M]
lock
serrure[F]
rail
traverse[F]
frame stile
montant[M] de bâti[M]
hinge
gond[M]
bottom rail
traverse[F] inférieure
peg
cheville[F]
foot
pied[M]
bracket base
soubassement[M]

HOUSE

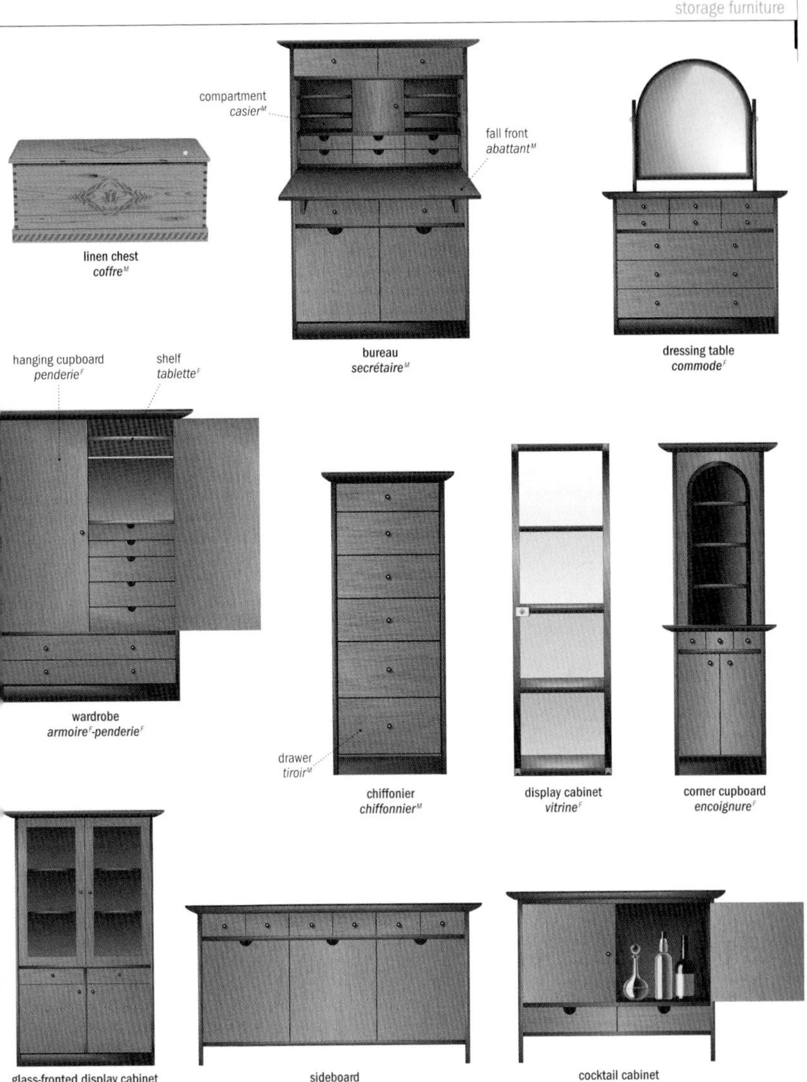

linen chest
coffre^M

bureau
secrétaire^M

dressing table
commode^F

wardrobe
armoire^F*-penderie*^F

chiffonier
chiffonnier^M

display cabinet
vitrine^F

corner cupboard
encoignure^F

glass-fronted display cabinet
buffet^M*-vaisselier*^M

sideboard
buffet^M

cocktail cabinet
bar^M

bed

lit[M]

sofa bed
canapé[M] convertible

parts
parties[F]

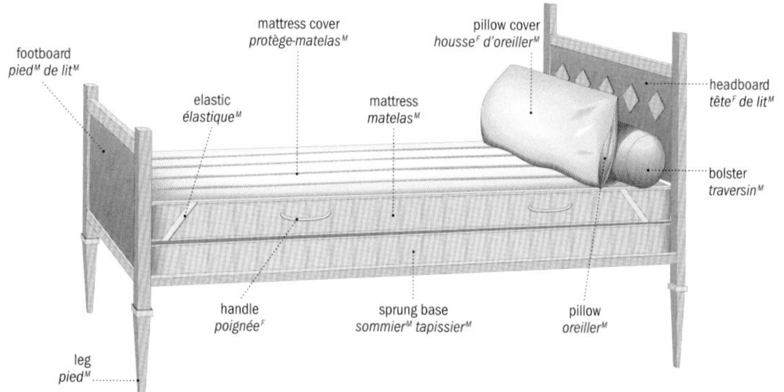

bed linen
literie[F]

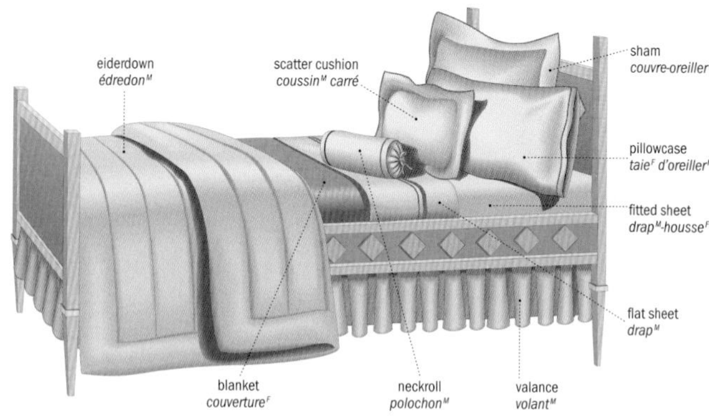

children's furniture

meubles^{M} d'enfants^{M}

cot
iant

changing table
plan^{M} à langer
top rail
bordure^{F}
mesh
filet^{M}
mattress
matelas^{M}

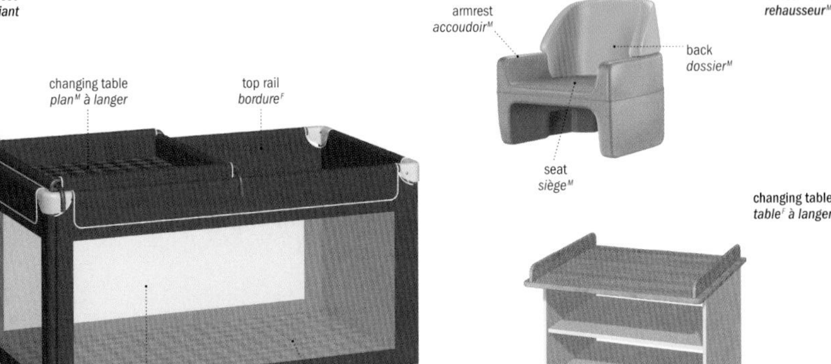

booster seat
rehausseur^{M}

armrest
accoudoir^{M}
back
dossier^{M}
seat
siège^{M}

changing table
table^{F} à langer

HOUSE

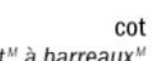

hair
e^{F} haute

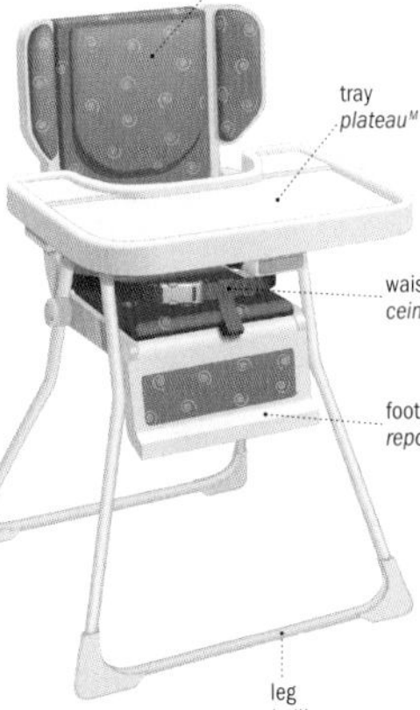

back
dossier^{M}
tray
plateau^{M}
waist belt
ceinture^{F} ventrale
footrest
repose-pieds^{M}
leg
pied^{M}

cot
lit^{M} à barreaux^{M}

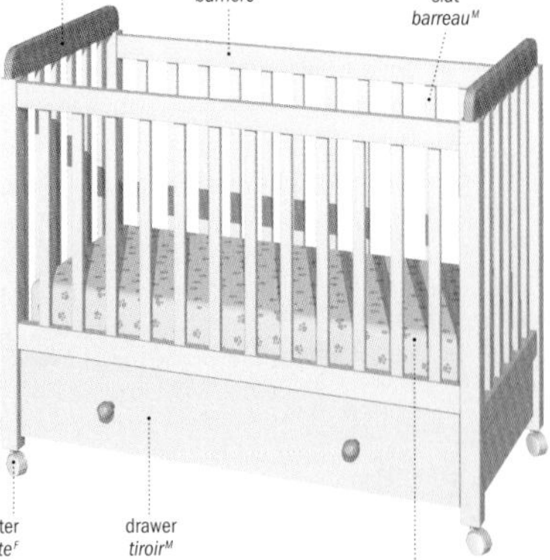

headboard
tête^{F} de lit^{M}
barrier
barrière^{F}
slat
barreau^{M}
caster
roulette^{F}
drawer
tiroir^{M}
mattress
matelas^{M}

lights

luminaires[M]

elier
sconce
coupelle^F
crystal drop
pendeloque^F
crystal button
pampille^F
column
fût^M
track lighting
rail^M d'éclairage^M
track frame
gouttière^F
transformer
transformateur^M
contact lever
manette^F de contact^M
spot
spot^M
wall lantern
lanterne^F murale
wall light
applique^F
swivel wall lamp
applique^F orientable
multiple light fitting
rampe^F d'éclairage^M
post lantern
lanterne^F de pied^M

domestic appliances

appareils^M électroménagers

steam iron
fer^M à vapeur^F

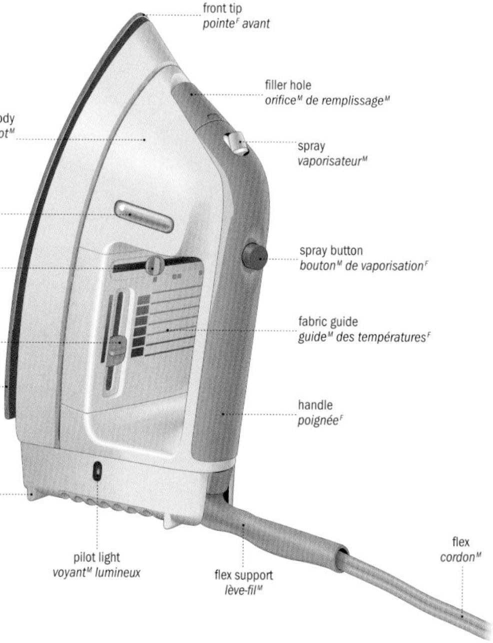

front tip
pointe^F avant
filler hole
orifice^M de remplissage^M
body
capot^M
spray
vaporisateur^M
water-level tube
repère^M de niveau^M d'eau^F
spray control
contrôle^M de la vapeur^F
spray button
bouton^M de vaporisation^F
temperature control
réglage^M des températures^F
fabric guide
guide^M des températures^F
soleplate
semelle^F
handle
poignée^F
heel rest
talon^M d'appui^M
pilot light
voyant^M lumineux
flex support
lève-fil^M
flex
cordon^M

hand vacuum cleaner
aspirateur^M à main^F

locking button
verrouillage^M
on-off switch
interrupteur^M
dust receiver
godet^M à poussière^F
recharging base
socle^M-chargeur^M
motor unit
bloc^M-moteur^M

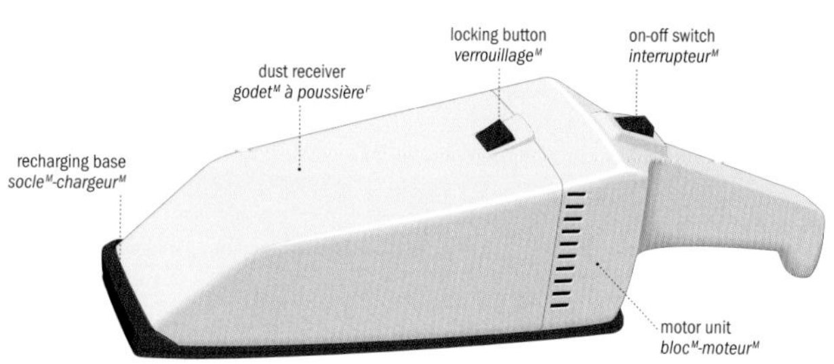

: vacuum cleaner
eur[M]-balai[M]

on/off switch
interrupteur[M]

tool storage area
compartiment[M] d'accessoires[M]

hose
tuyau[M] flexible

bag compartment
partiment[M] de sac[M]

er height adjustment knob
ecteur[M] de hauteur[F]

brush
brosse[F]

tools
accessoires[M]

cylinder vacuum cleaner
aspirateur[M]-traîneau[M]

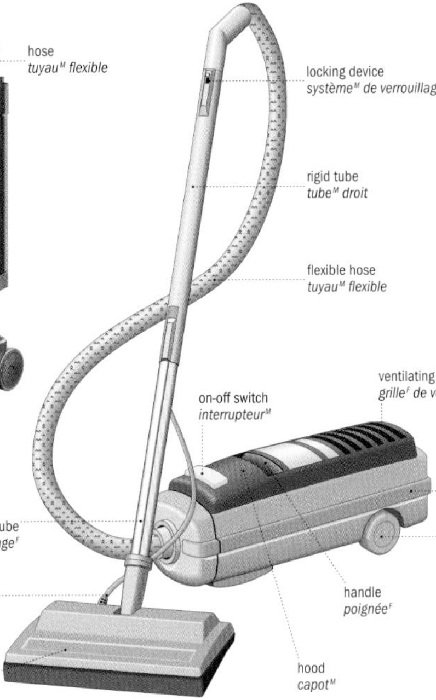

locking device
système[M] de verrouillage[M]

rigid tube
tube[M] droit

flexible hose
tuyau[M] flexible

ventilating grille
grille[F] de ventilation[F]

on-off switch
interrupteur[M]

bumper
pare-chocs[M]

extension tube
rallonge[F]

caster
roulette[F]

flex
cordon[M]

handle
poignée[F]

carpet and floor brush
suceur[M] à tapis[M] et planchers[M]

hood
capot[M]

cleaning tools
accessoires[M]

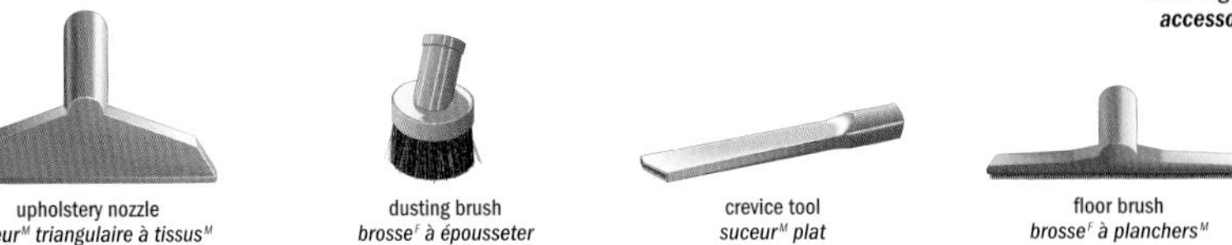

upholstery nozzle
ur[M] triangulaire à tissus[M]

dusting brush
brosse[F] à épousseter

crevice tool
suceur[M] plat

floor brush
brosse[F] à planchers[M]

domestic appliances

extractor hood
hotte[F]

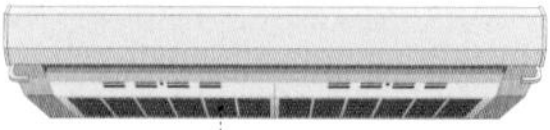

filter
filtre[M]

gas
cuisinière

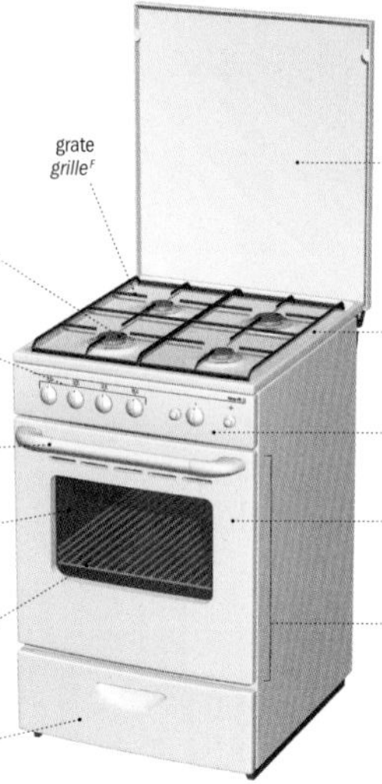

grate
grille[F]
lid
couvercle[M] de prop
burner
brûleur[M]
hob
table[F] de travail[M]
burner control knobs
robinets[M]
control panel
tableau[M] de comm
handle
poignée[F]
window
hublot[M]
door
porte[F]
rack
grille[F]
oven
four[M]
drawer
tiroir[M]

surface element
serpentin[M]

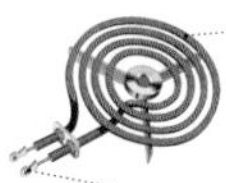

tubular element
élément[M] tubulaire
terminal
borne[F]

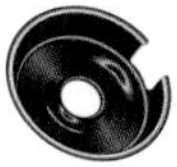

drip bowl
cuvette[F]

trim ring
anneau[M]

electric
cuisinière[F] él

oven control knob
réglage[M] du four[M]
clock timer
horloge[F] programmatrice
pilot light
voyant[M] lumineux
back panel
dosseret[M]
control knob
bouton[M] de commande[F]
timer socket
prise[F] chronométrée
control panel
tableau[M] de commande[F]
hob
surface[F] de cuisson[F]
cooker ring
serpentin[M]
hob edge
rebord[M]
shelf
grille[F]
handle
poignée[F]
oven
four[M]
window
hublot[M]
drawer
tiroir[M]

HOUSE

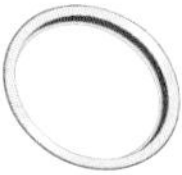

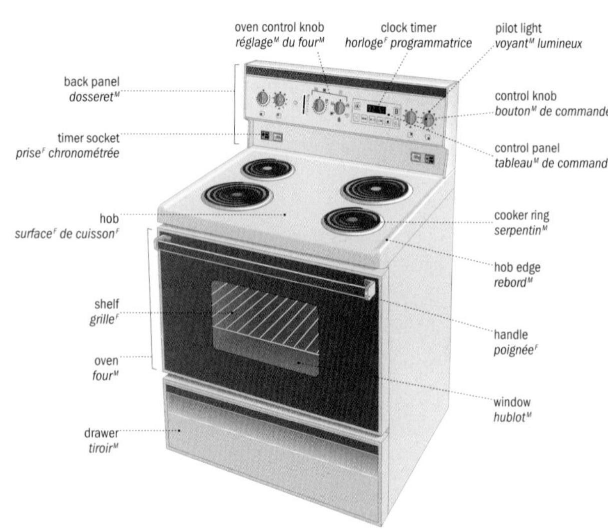

chest freezer
congélateur[M] coffre[M]

lock
serrure[F]
lid
couvercle[M]
basket
panier[M]
cabinet
cuve[F]
temperature control
thermostat[M]
defrost drain
bouchon[M] de vidange[F]

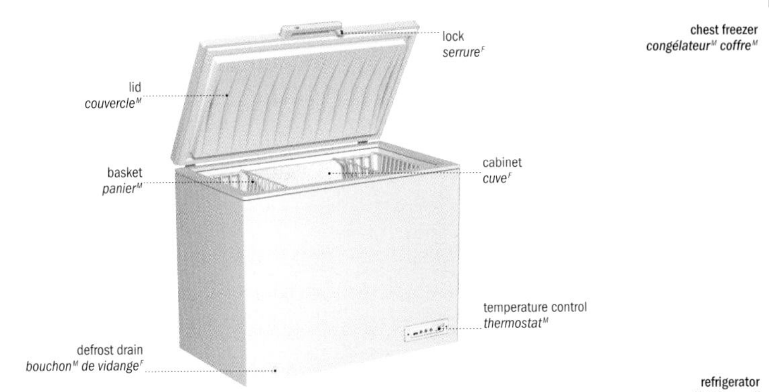

refrigerator
réfrigérateur[M]

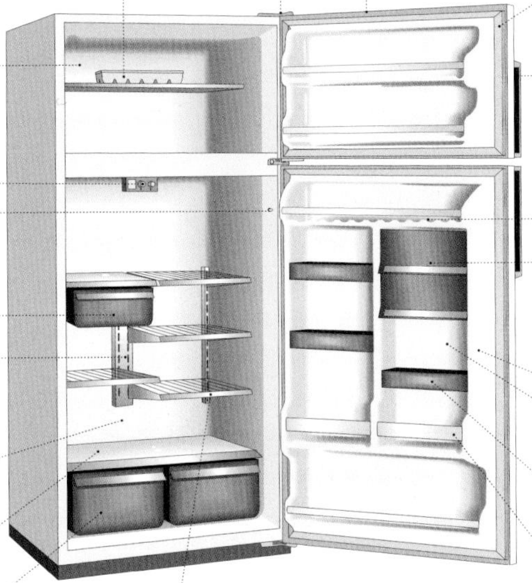

ice cube tray
bac[M] à glaçons[M]
door stop
butée[F] de porte[F]
freezer door
porte[F]
magnetic gasket
joint[M] magnétique
freezer compartment
congélateur[M]
handle
poignée[F]
thermostat control
nde[F] de température[F]
switch
interrupteur[M]
egg tray
œufrier[M]
butter compartment
casier[M] à beurre[M]
meat keeper
bac[M] à viande[F]
shelf channel
crémaillère[F]
storage door
porte[F] étagère[F]
dairy compartment
casier[M] laitier
erator compartment
réfrigérateur[M]
door shelf
balconnet[M]
glass cover
tablette[F] de verre[M]
guard rail
barre[F] de retenue[F]
salad crisper
bac[M] à légumes[M]
shelf
clayette[F]

washing machine
lave-linge^M

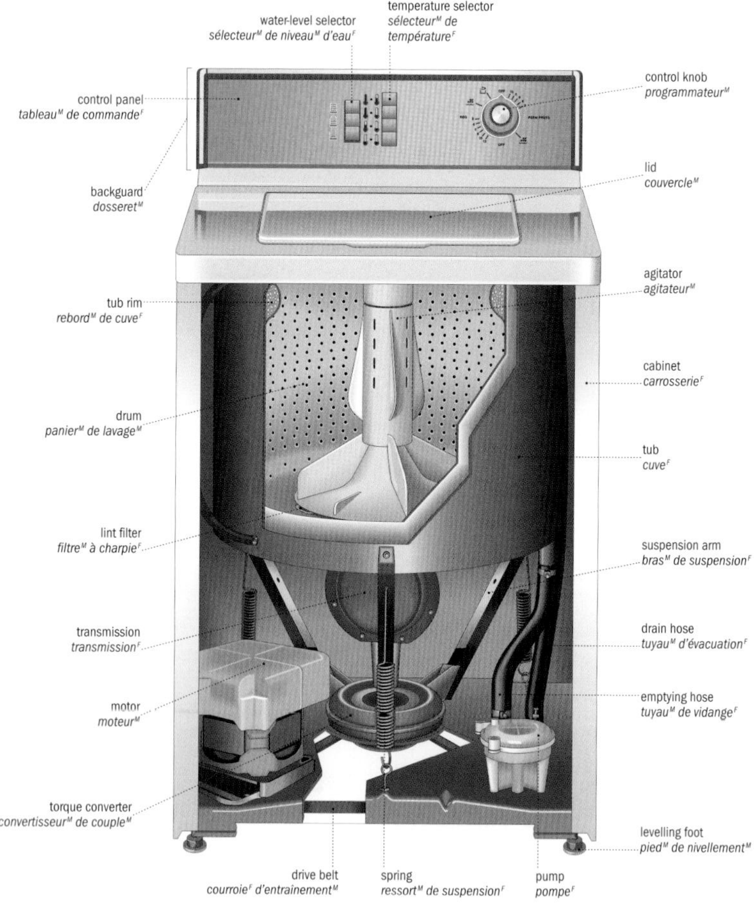

electric tumble dryer
sèche-linge[M] électrique

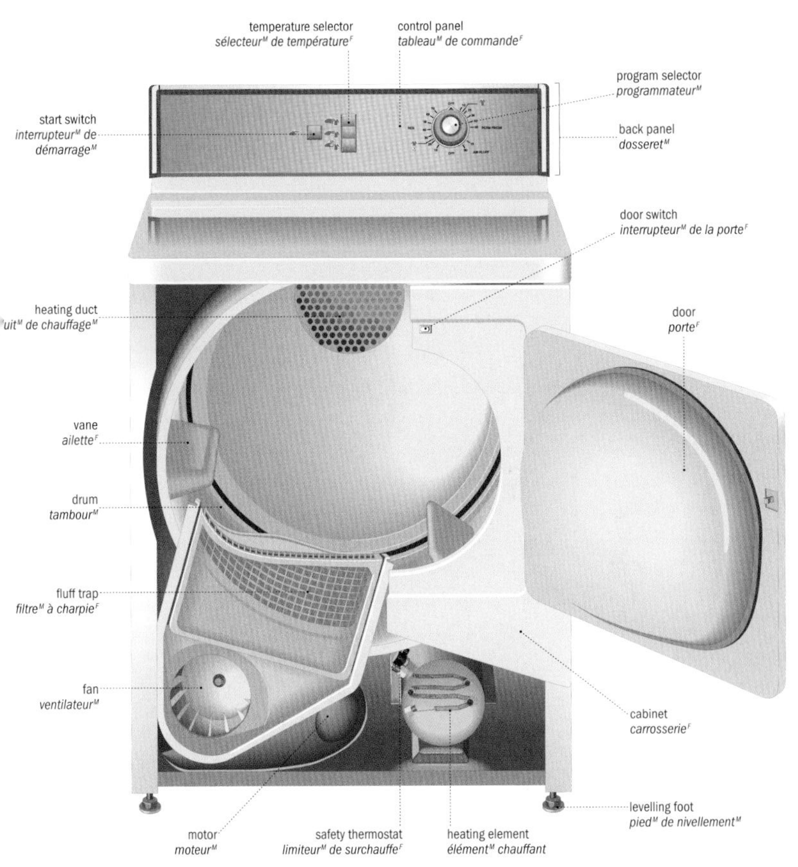

control panel
***tableau*[M] *de commande*[F]**

pilot light
voyant[M] *lumineux*
program selector
programmateur[M]
push button
bouton[M]*-poussoir*[M]
air vent
grille[F] *d'aération*[F]
latch
loquet[M]

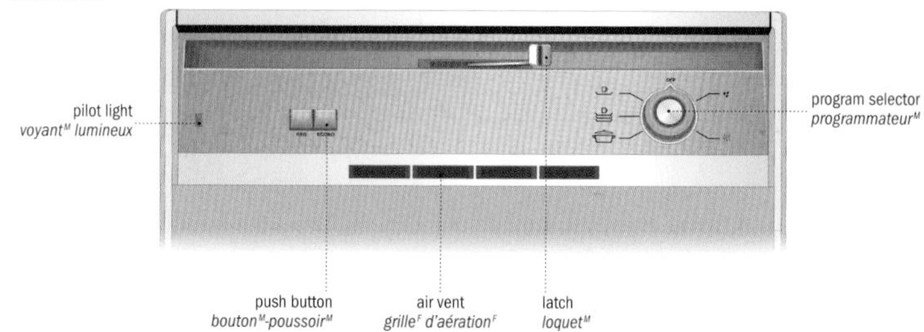

dishwasher
***lave-vaisselle*[M]**

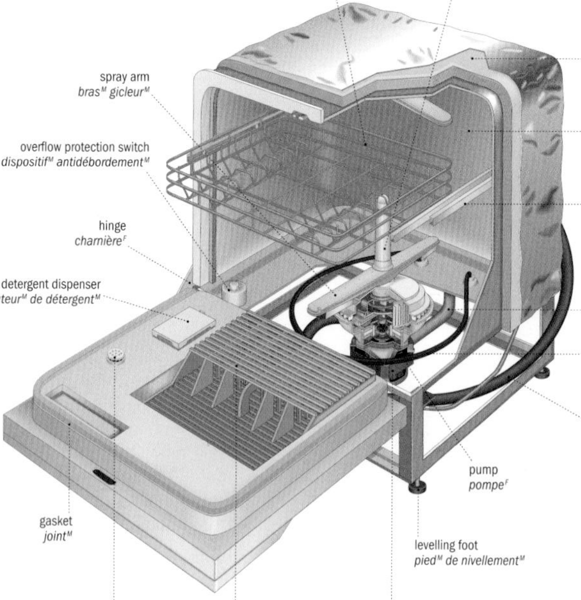

rack
panier[M]
wash tower
tourelle[F]
insulating material
isolant[M]
spray arm
bras[M] *gicleur*[M]
tub
cuve[F]
overflow protection switch
dispositif[M] *antidébordement*[M]
slide
glissière[F]
hinge
charnière[F]
detergent dispenser
distributeur[M] *de détergent*[M]
water hose
conduite[F] *d'eau*[F]
heating element
élément[M] *chauffant*
drain hose
tuyau[M] *de vidange*[F]
pump
pompe[F]
gasket
joint[M]
levelling foot
pied[M] *de nivellement*[M]
rinse-aid dispenser
distributeur[M] *de produit*[M] *de rinçage*[M]
cutlery basket
panier[M] *à couverts*[M]
motor
moteur[M]

household equipment

articles[M] ménagers

plumbing tools

plomberie^F : outils^M

plunger
ventouse^F

plumber's snake
furet^M de dégorgement^M

Teflon tape
ruban^M de Téflon^M

wrenches
clés^F

plumbing wrench
clé^F coudée à tuyau^M

pipe wrench
clé^F à tuyau^M

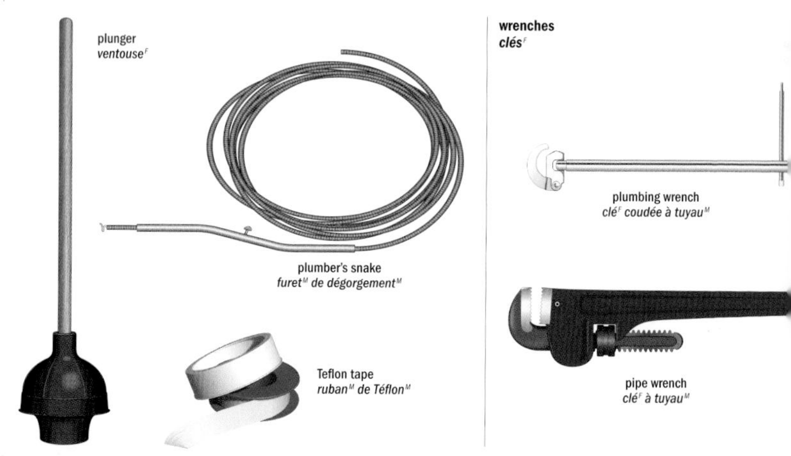

masonry tools

maçonnerie^F : outils^M

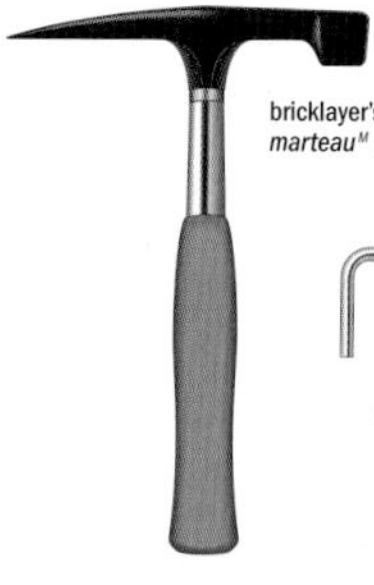

bricklayer's hammer
marteau^M de maçon^M

caul
pistolet^M à c

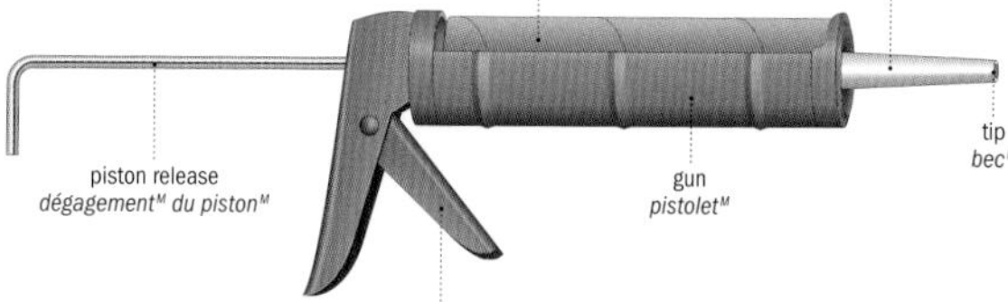

cartridge
cartouche^F
nozzle
buse^F
tip
bec^M
piston release
dégagement^M du piston^M
gun
pistolet^M
piston lever
levier^M du piston^M

masor
truelle^F de

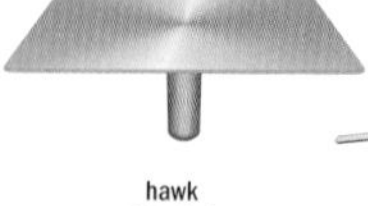

hawk
taloche^F

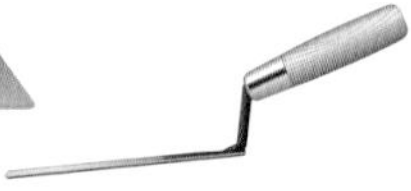

joint filler
tire-joint^M

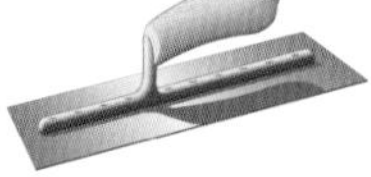

square trowel
truelle^F de plâtrier^M

blade
lame^F
tang
soie^F

m

DO-IT-YOURSELF AND GARDENING

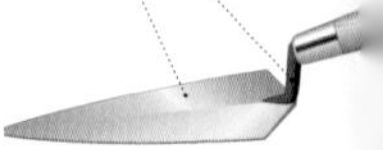

electricity tools

électricité[F] : outils[M]

on light
se[F]

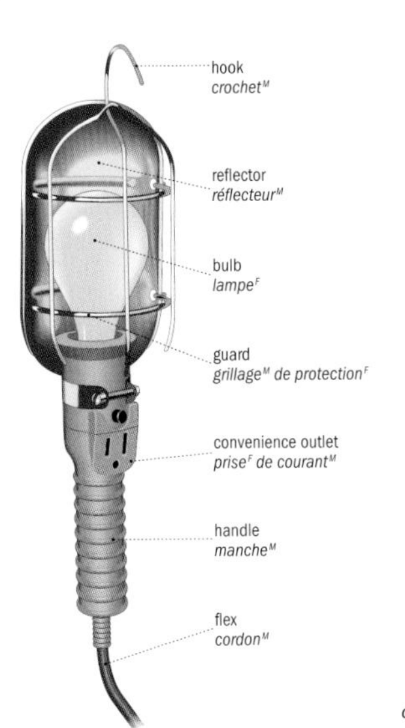

test-lamp
vérificateur[M] de circuit[M]

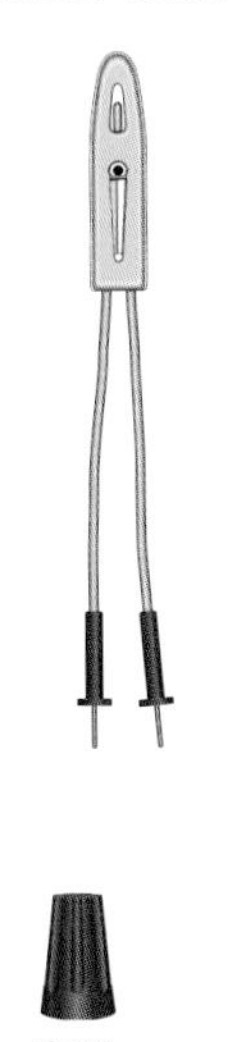

tester screwdriver
vérificateur[M] de tension[F]

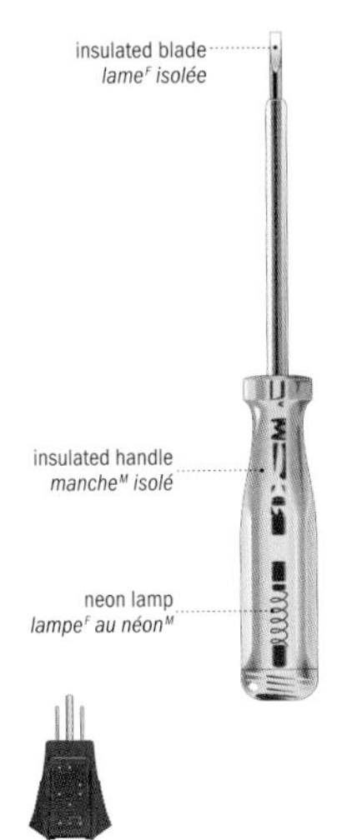

wire nut
capuchon[M] de connexion[F]

socket tester
vérificateur[M] de prise[F] de courant[M]

pose tool
niverselle

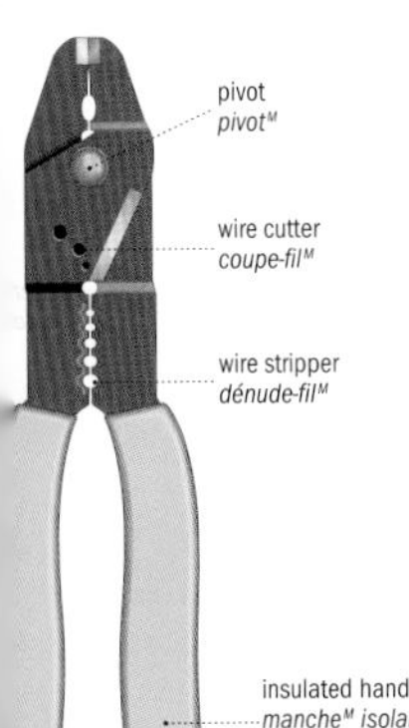

needle-nose pliers
pince[F] à long bec[M]

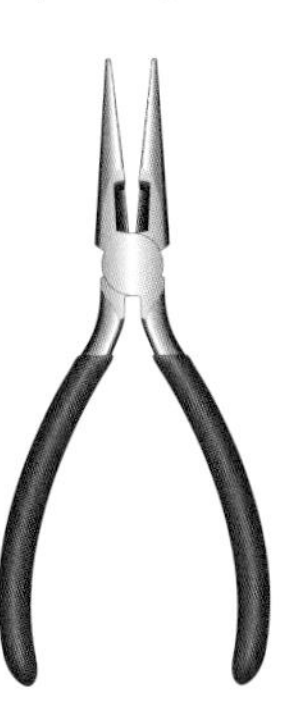

combination pliers
pince[F] d'électricien[M]

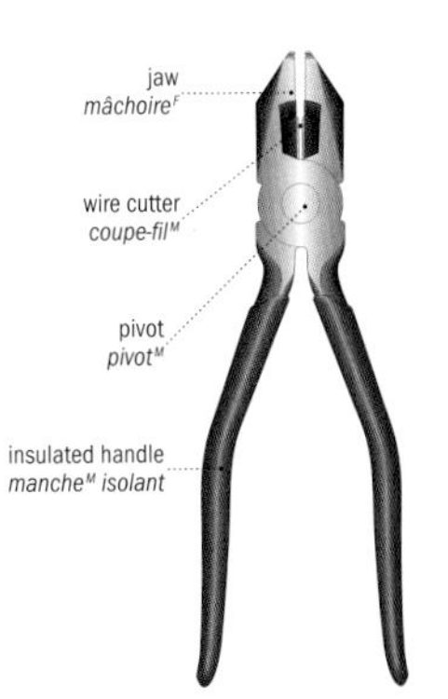

soldering and welding tools

soudage[M] : outils[M]

soldering gun
pistolet[M] à souder

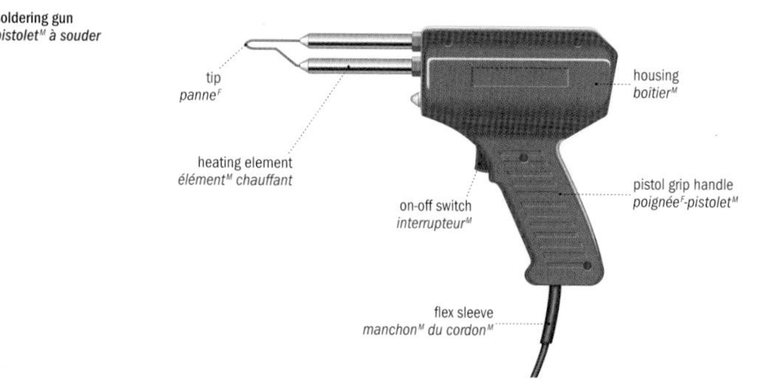

striker
briquet[M]

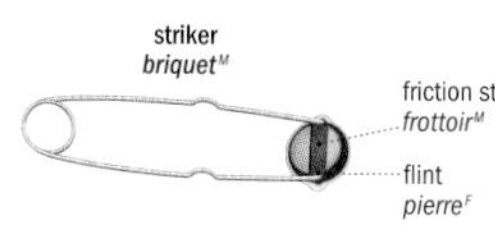

solder
soudure[F]

nozzle cleaners
aiguilles[F] de nettoyage[M]

blowtorch
lampe[F] à souder

pencil point tip
brûleur[M] flamme[F] crayon[M]

disposable gas cylinder
cartouche[F] jetable

flame spreader
brûleur[M] bec[M] plat

goggles
lunettes[F]

soldering iron
fer[M] à souder

painting upkeep

peinture[F] d'entretien[M]

paint roller
rouleau[M]

handle
poignée[F]
roller frame
armature[F]
roller sleeve
manchon[M]

tray
bac[M]

heat gun
décapeur[M] thermique

nozzle
buse[F]
switch
interrupteur[M]

paintbrush
pinceau[M]

handle
manche[M]
ferrule
virole[F]
bristles
soies[F]

scraper
grattoir[M]

knurled bolt
bouton[M] moleté
blade
lame[F]
handle
manche[M]

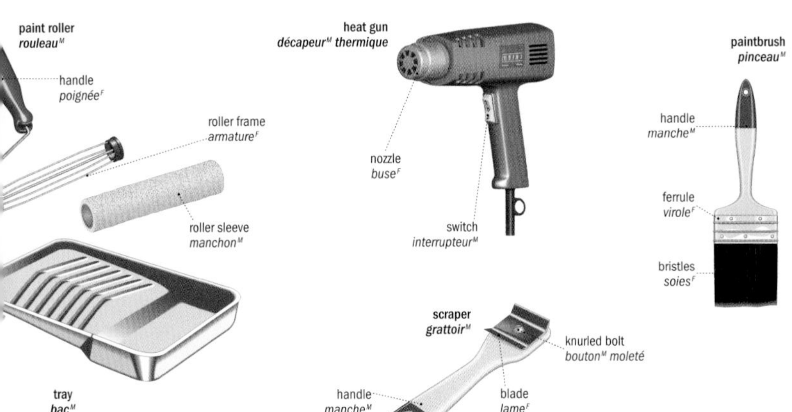

ladders and stepladders

échelles[F] et escabeaux[M]

sion ladder
e[F] coulissante

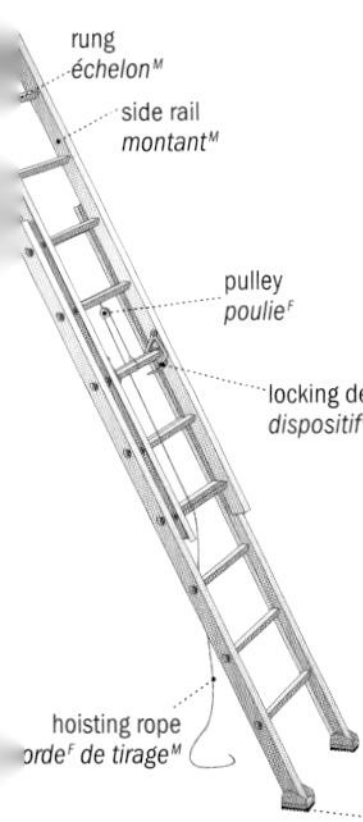

rung
échelon[M]
side rail
montant[M]
pulley
poulie[F]
locking device
dispositif[M] de blocage[M]
hoisting rope
orde[F] de tirage[M]
anti-slip foot
patin[M] antidérapant

platform ladder
marchepied[M]

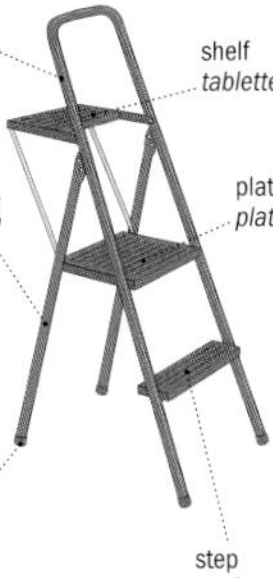

safety rail
garde-corps[M]
shelf
tablette[F]
frame
piètement[M]
platform
plate-forme[F]
rubber stopper
embout[M]
step
marche[F]

step stool
tabouret[M]-escabeau[M]

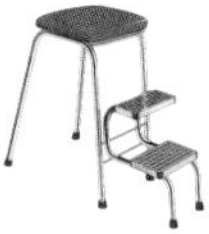

stepladder
escabeau[M]

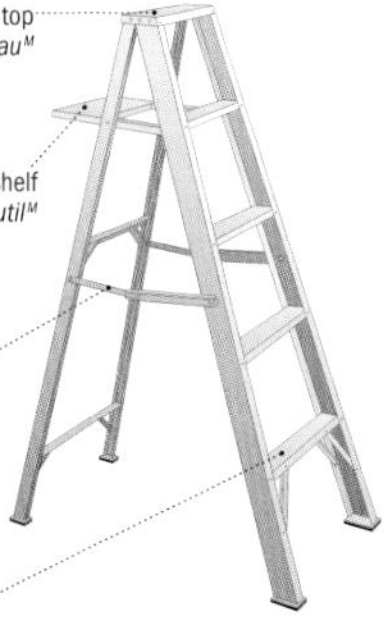

top
plateau[M]
tool shelf
tablette[F] porte-outil[M]
brace
entretoise[F]
step
marche[F]

carpentry: nailing tools

menuiserie^F : outils^M pour clouer

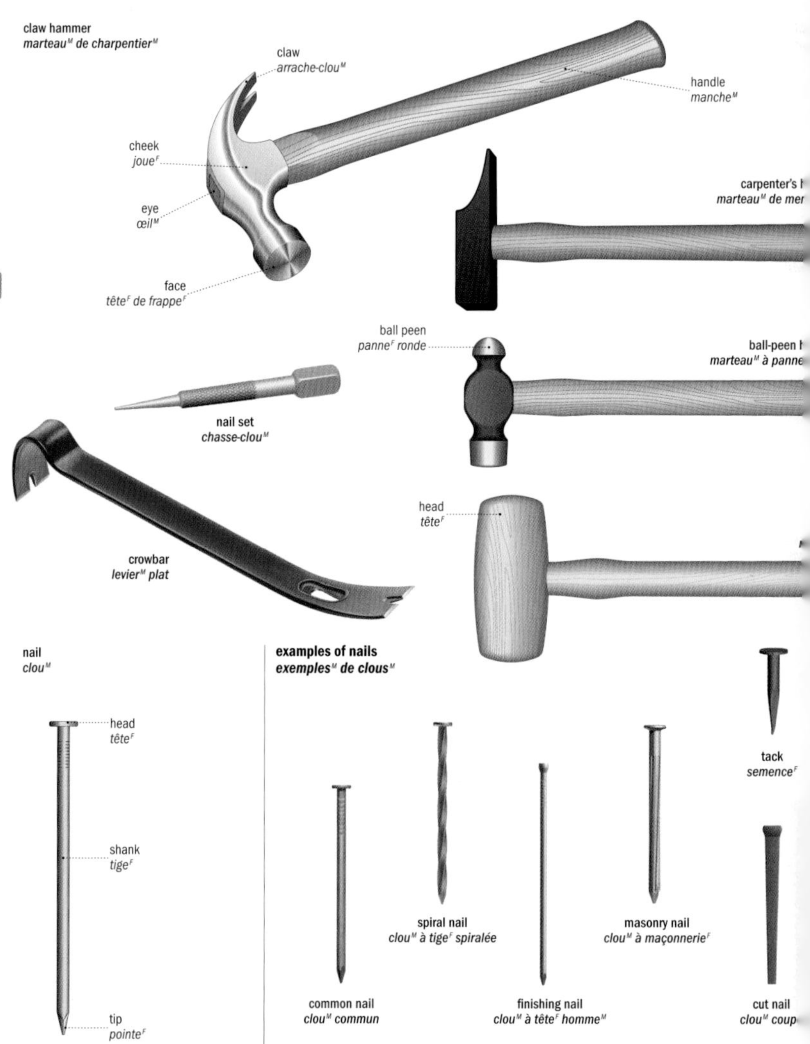

carpentry: screwing tools

menuiserie[F] : outils[M] pour visser

driver
vis[M]

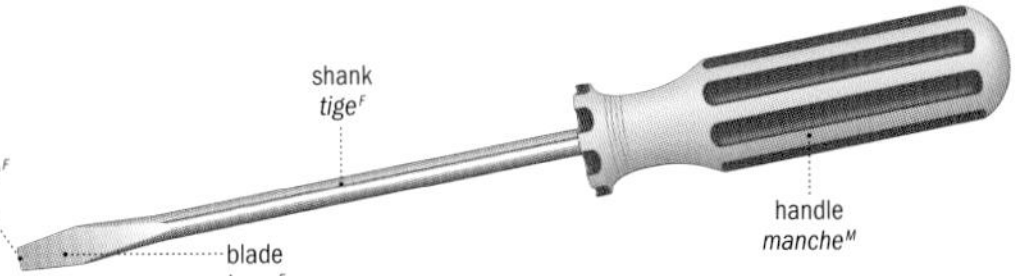

tip
pointe[F]
shank
tige[F]
blade
lame[F]
handle
manche[M]

screwdriver
vis[M] à spirale[F]

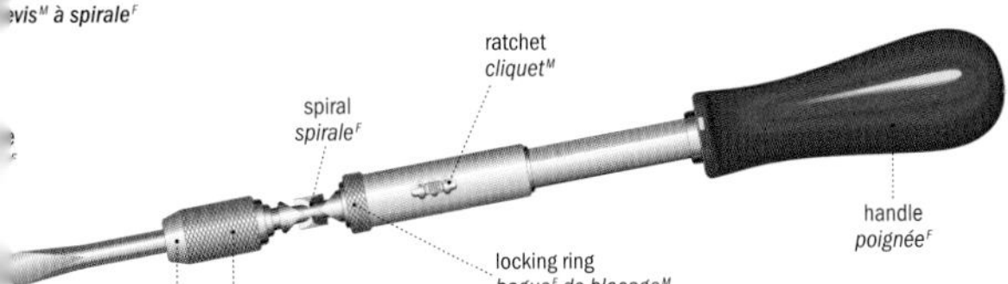

ratchet
cliquet[M]
spiral
spirale[F]
handle
poignée[F]
locking ring
bague[F] de blocage[M]
jaw
mors[M]
chuck
mandrin[M]

ss screwdriver
vis[M] sans fil[M]

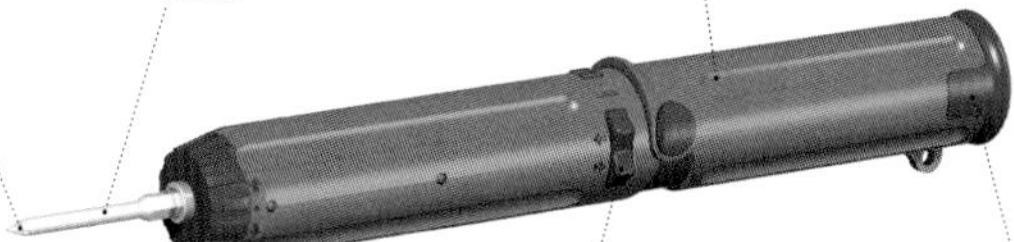

bit
embout[M]
handle
poignée[F]
tip
pointe[F]
reversing switch
inverseur[M] de marche[F]
battery
batterie[F]

examples of tips
exemples[M] de pointes[F]

square-headed tip
pointe[F] carrée

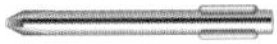

cross-headed tip
pointe[F] cruciforme

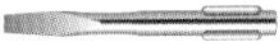

flat tip
pointe[F] plate

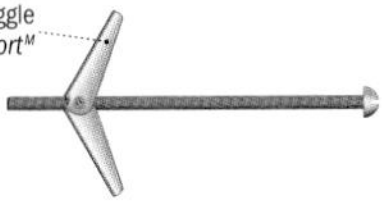

spring toggle
ailette[F] à ressort[M]

toggle bolt
boulon[M] à ailettes[F]

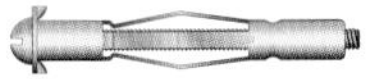

expansion bolt
boulon[M] à gaine[F] d'expansion[F]

head
tête[F]
slot
fente[F]
shank
fût[M]
thread
filet[M]

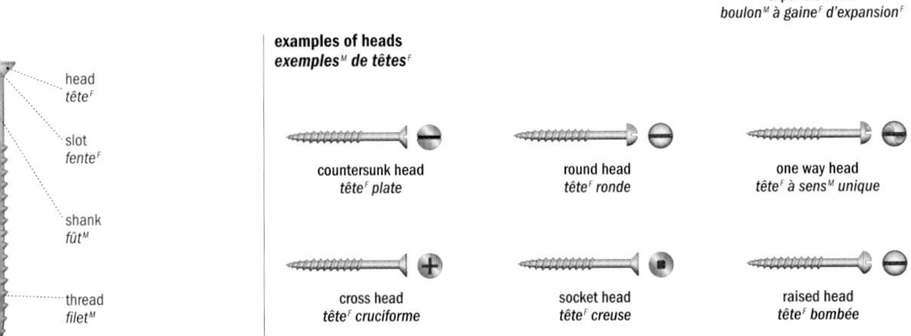

examples of heads
exemples[M] de têtes[F]

countersunk head
tête[F] plate

round head
tête[F] ronde

one way head
tête[F] à sens[M] unique

cross head
tête[F] cruciforme

socket head
tête[F] creuse

raised head
tête[F] bombée

carpentry: gripping and tightening tools

menuiserie[F] : outils[M] pour serrer

pliers
pinces[F]

slip joint pliers
pince[F] à joint[M] coulissant

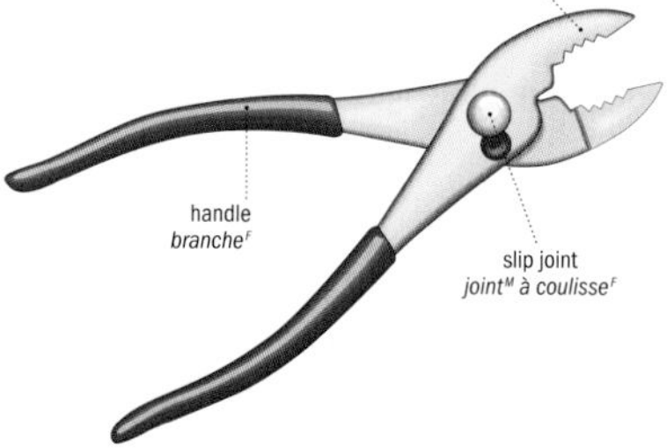

curved jaw
mâchoire[F] incurvée

handle
branche[F]

slip joint
joint[M] à coulisse[F]

water pump plie
pince[F] multipri

straight jaw
mâchoire[F] droite

bolt
boulon[M]

adjustable channel
cran[M] de réglage[M]

nut
écrou[M]

handle
branche[F]

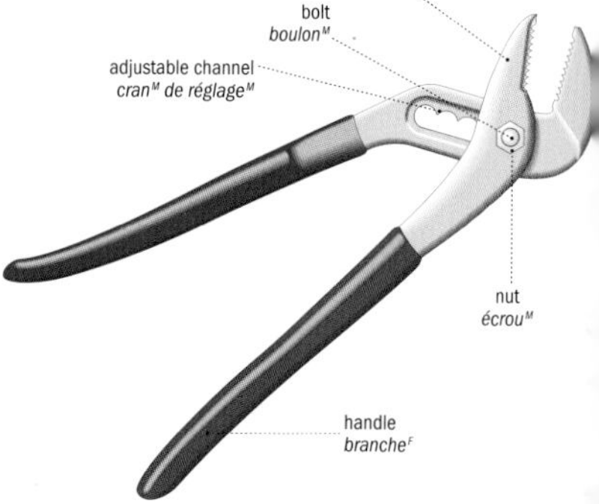

mole wrench
pince[F]-étau[M]

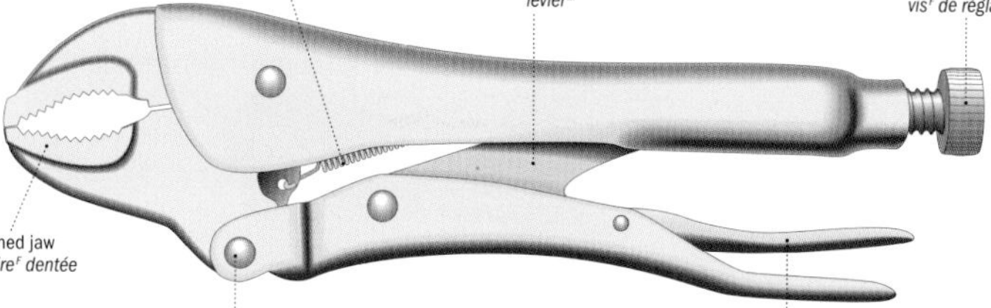

spring
ressort[M]

lever
levier[M]

adjusting screw
vis[F] de réglage[M]

toothed jaw
mâchoire[F] dentée

rivet
rivet[M]

release lever
levier[M] de dégagement[M]

washers
rondelles[F]

flat washer
rondelle[F] plate

spring washer
rondelle[F] à ressort[M]

external tooth lock washer
rondelle[F] à denture[F] extérieure

internal tooth lock washer
rondelle[F] à denture[F] intérieure

wrenches
clés^F

adjustable spanner
clé^F à molette^F

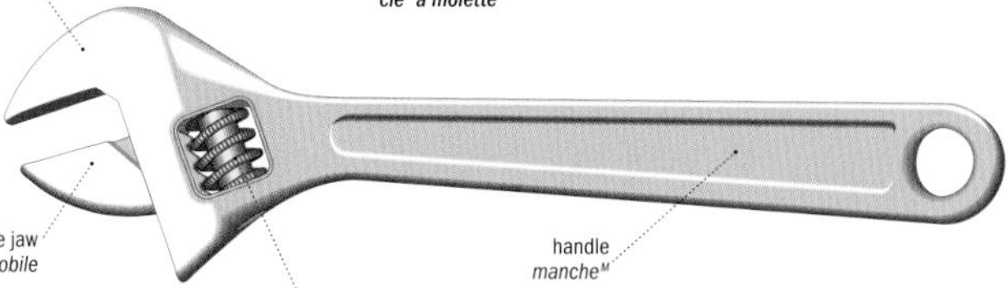

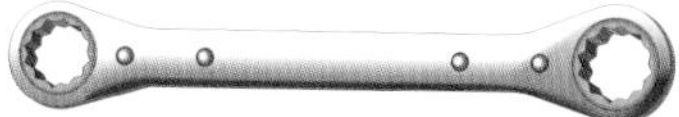

fixed jaw
mâchoire^F fixe
movable jaw
mâchoire^F mobile
thumbscrew
molette^F
handle
manche^M

ratchet ring spanner
clé^F polygonale à cliquet^M

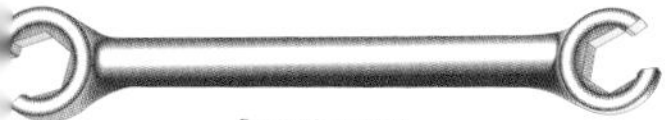

flare nut spanner
clé^F polygonale à têtes^F fendues

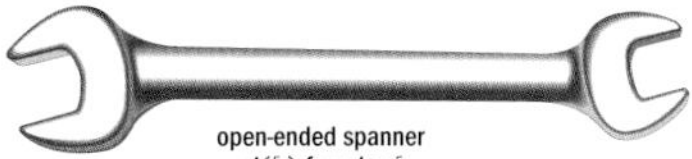

open-ended spanner
clé^F à fourches^F

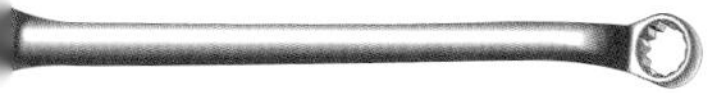

ring spanner
clé^F polygonale

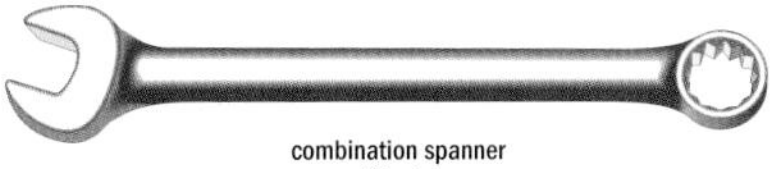

combination spanner
clé^F mixte

t socket wrench
douille^F à cliquet^M

socket set
jeu^M de douilles^F

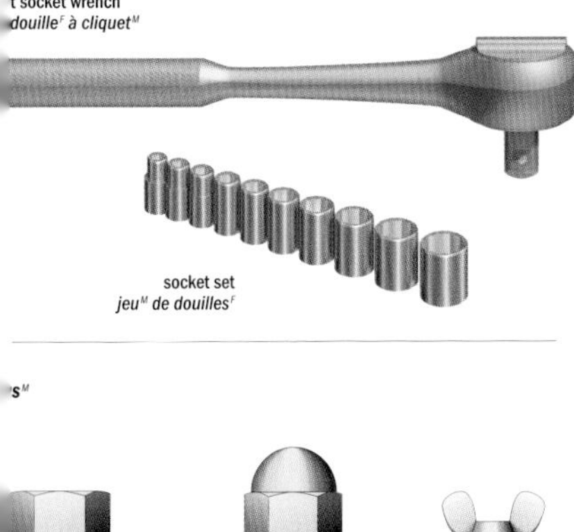

s^M

hexagon nut
rou^M hexagonal

cap nut
écrou^M borgne

wing nut
écrou^M à oreilles^F

bolts
boulons^M

bolt
boulon^M

nut
écrou^M
head
tête^F

shoulder bolt
boulon^M à épaulement^M

threaded rod
tige^F filetée
shoulder
épaulement^M

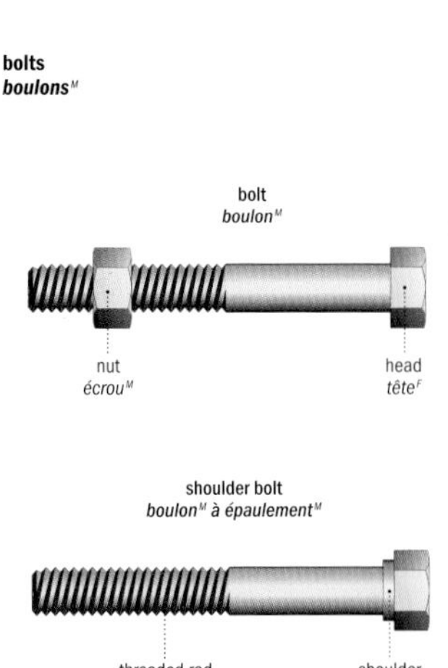

carpentry: gripping and tightening tools

G-clamp
serre-joint[M]

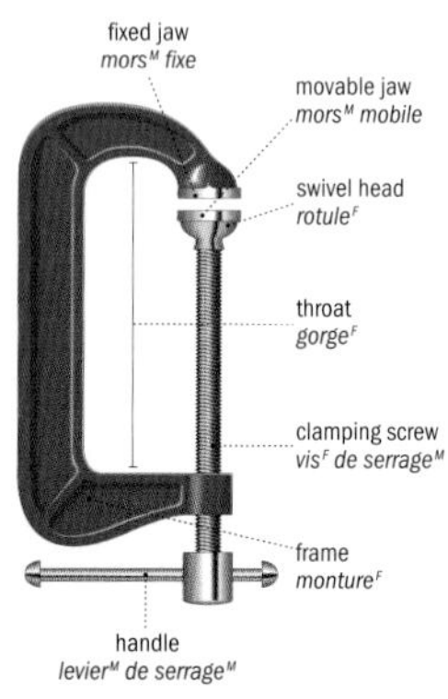

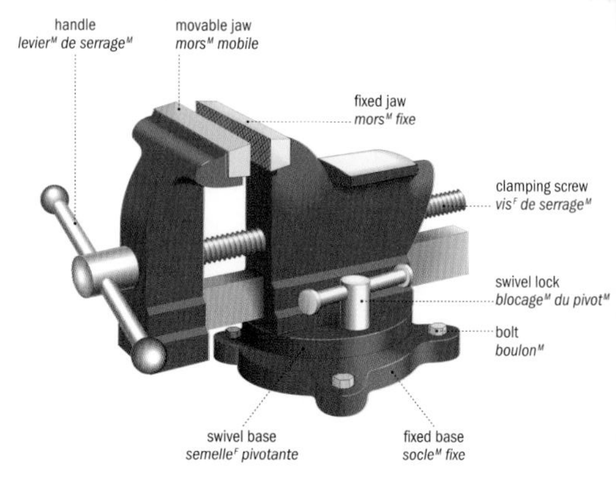

pipe clamp
serre-joint[M] à tuyau[M]

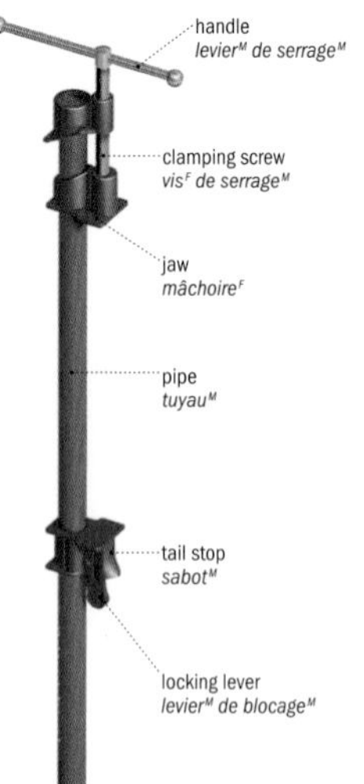

work bench a
établi

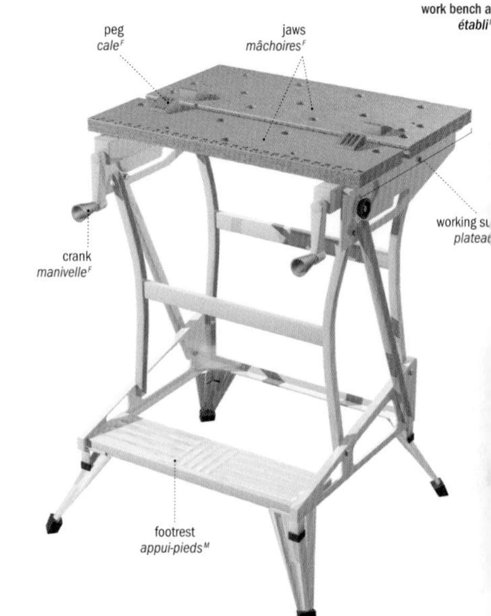

carpentry: measuring and marking tools

menuiserie^{F} : instruments^{M} de traçage^{M} et de mesure^{F}

3 4 5 6 7 8 9 10 11 12 13 14 15 16 17 18 19 20 21 22 23
1 2 3 4 5 6 7 8 9 10 11 12 13 14 15 16 17 18 19 20 21 22

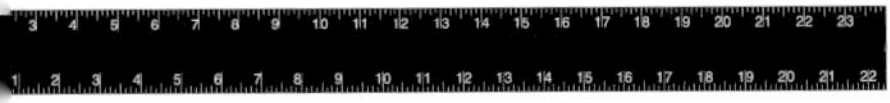

setsquare
équerre^{F}

spirit level
niveau^{M} à bulle^{F}

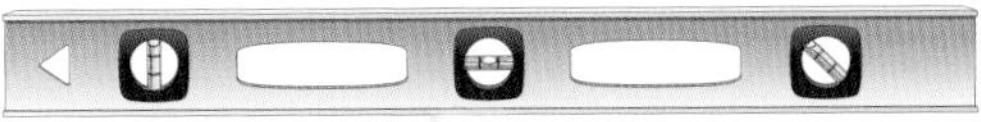

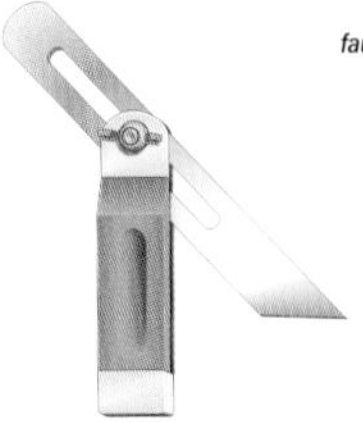

bevel square
fausse-équerre^{F}

tape measure
mètre^{M} à ruban^{M}

tape lock
bouton^{M} de blocage^{M}
scale
graduation^{F}
hook
crochet^{M}
case
boîtier^{M}
tape
ruban^{M}

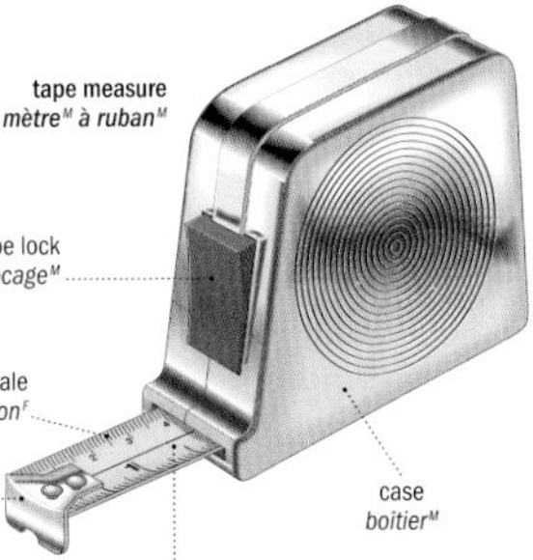

chalk line
cordeau^{M} à tracer

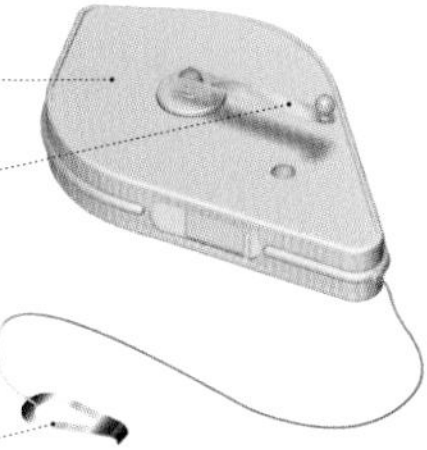

case
boîtier^{M}
crank handle
manivelle^{F} d'enroulement^{M}
line
cordeau^{M}
hook
crochet^{M}

carpentry: miscellaneous material

menuiserie^{F} : matériel^{M} divers

box
^{F} à outils^{M}

handle
poignée^{F}
lid
couvercle^{M}
tray
plateau^{M}

tool belt
ceinture^{F} porte-outils^{M}

belt
ceinture^{F}
hammer loop
porte-marteau^{M}
pocket
poche^{F}

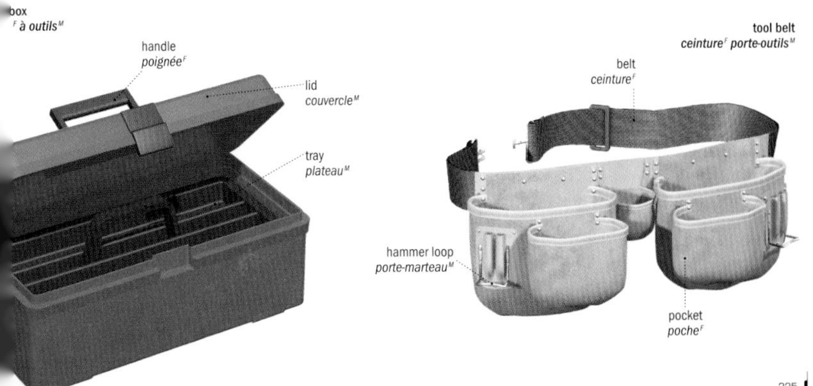

carpentry: sawing tools

menuiserie[F] : outils[M] pour scier

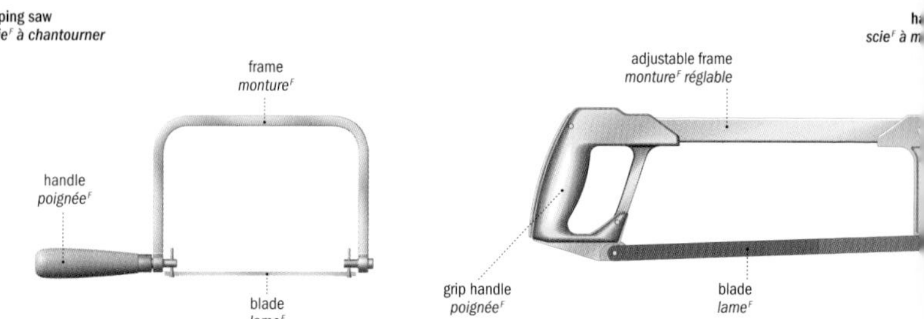

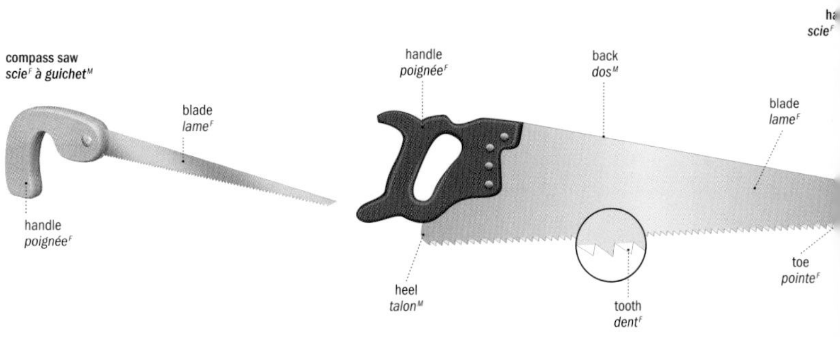

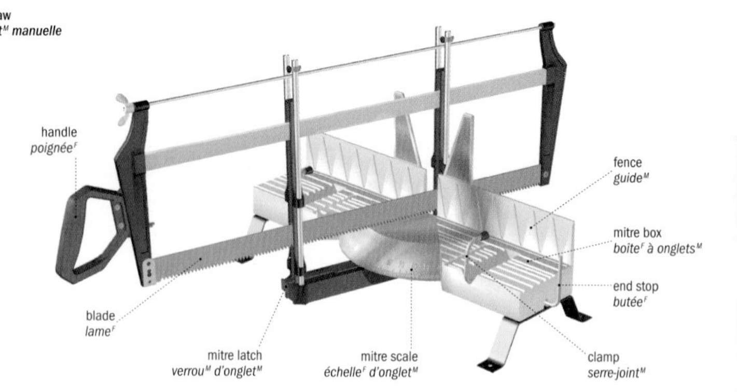

jigsaw
scie[F] sauteuse

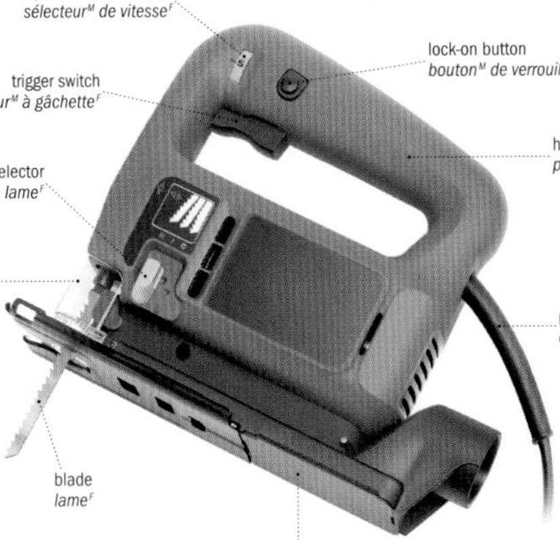

speed selector switch
sélecteur[M] de vitesse[F]
lock-on button
bouton[M] de verrouillage[M] de l'interrupteur[M]
trigger switch
interrupteur[M] à gâchette[F]
handle
poignée[F]
orbital-action selector
sélecteur[M] d'inclinaison[F] de la lame[F]
chip cover
déflecteur[M] de copeaux[M]
power cord
cordon[M] d'alimentation[F]
blade
lame[F]
base
semelle[F]

r saw blade
de scie[F] circulaire

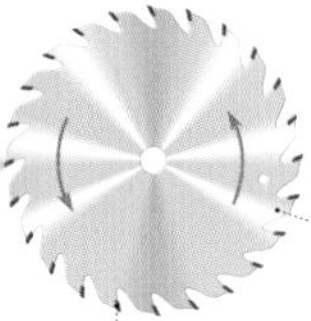

tooth
dent[F]
tip
pointe[F]

circular saw
scie[F] circulaire

handle
poignée[F]
trigger switch
interrupteur[M] à gâchette[F]
upper blade guard
protège-lame[M] supérieur
height adjustment scale
échelle[F] de profondeur[F]
blade
lame[F]
motor
moteur[M]
lower guard retracting lever
[M] du protège-lame[M] inférieur
blade tilting mechanism
inclinaison[F] de la semelle[F]
knob handle
bouton[M]-guide[M]
blade locking bolt
écrou[M] de la lame[F]
lower blade guard
protège-lame[M] inférieur
blade tilting lock
blocage[M] de l'inclinaison[F]
rip fence
guide[M] parallèle
base plate
semelle[F]

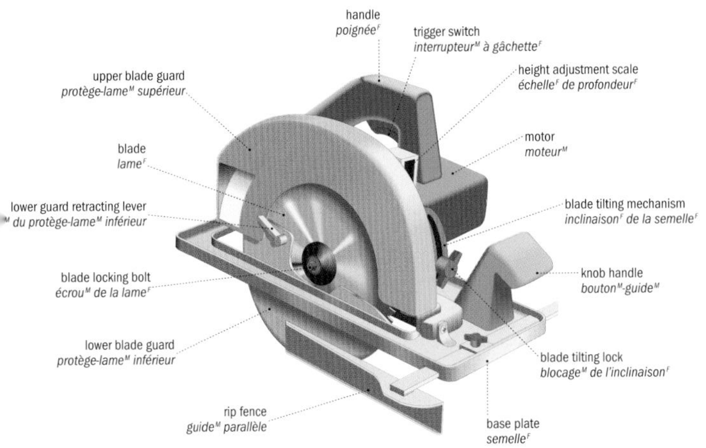

carpentry: drilling tools

menuiserie^F : outils^M pour percer

cordless drill-driver
perceuse^F-visseuse^F sans fil^M

electric drill
perceuse^F électrique

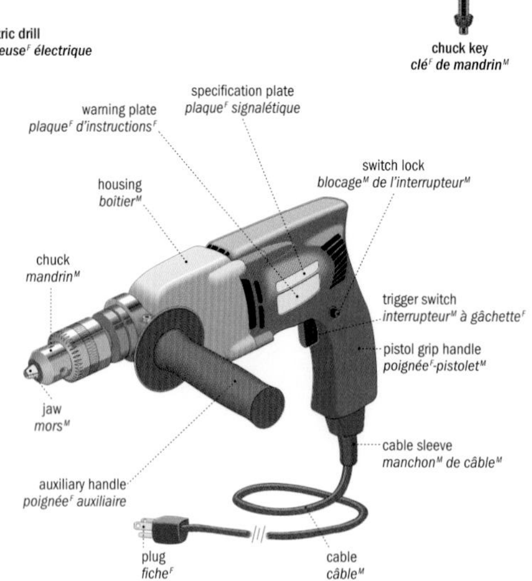

examples of bits and drills
exemples^M de mèches^F et de forets^M

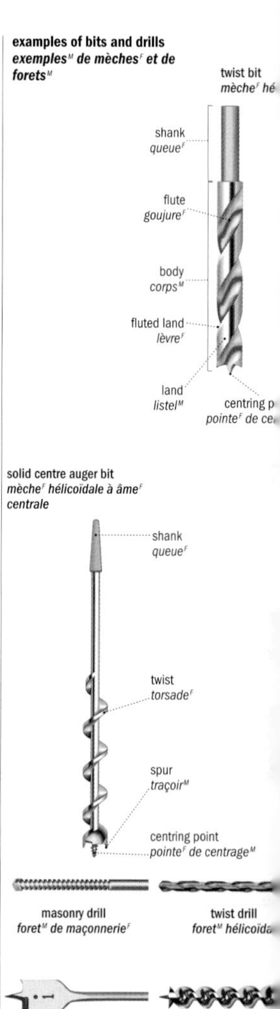

carpentry: shaping tools

menuiserie[F] : outils[M] pour façonner

plane
***rabot*[M]**

lateral-adjustment lever
levier[M] de réglage[M] latéral
wedge lever
levier[M] du bloc[M]
handle
poignée[F]
lever cap
bloc[M] d'arrêt[M]
depth-of-cut adjustment knob
molette[F] de réglage[M] de la saillie[F]
knob
pommeau[M]
heel
talon[M]
toe
nez[M]
sole
semelle[F]
frog-adjustment screw
réglage[M] de l'angle[M]
blade
fer[M]
cap iron
contre-fer[M]

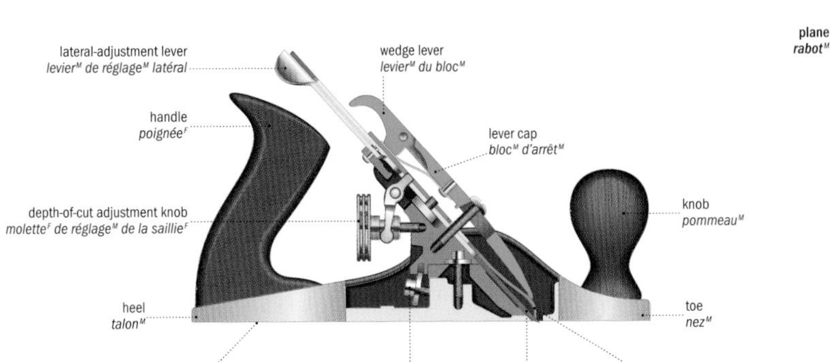

m orbit sander
use*[F] *excentrique

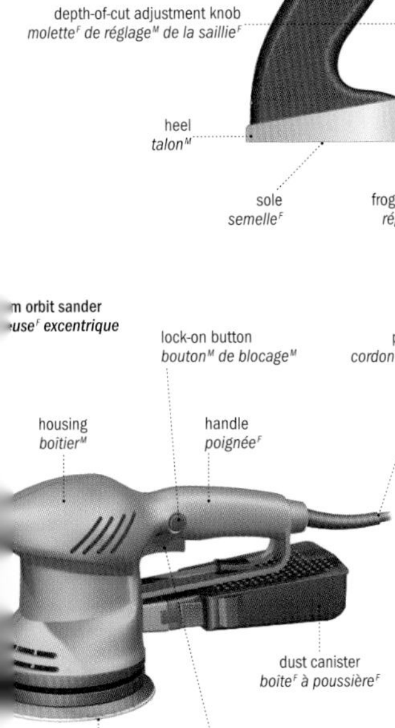

lock-on button
bouton[M] de blocage[M]
power cord
cordon[M] d'alimentation[F]
housing
boîtier[M]
handle
poignée[F]
dust canister
boîte[F] à poussière[F]
sanding disc
disque[M] abrasif
trigger switch
interrupteur[M] à gâchette[F]

router
***défonceuse*[F]**

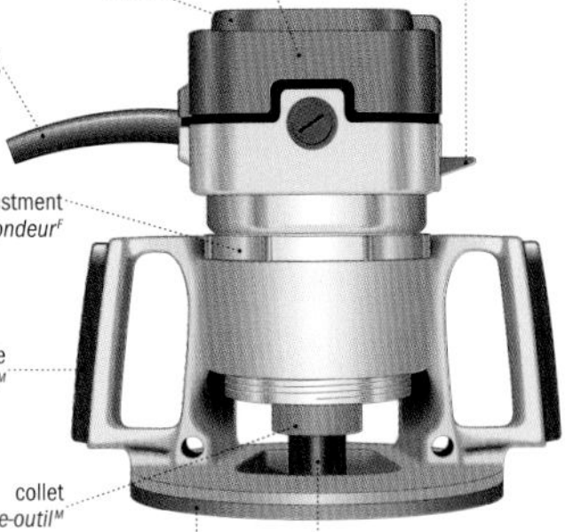

motor
moteur[M]
head
tête[F]
switch
interrupteur[M]
flex sleeve
manchon[M] du cordon[M]
depth adjustment
réglage[M] de profondeur[F]
guide handle
poignée[F] de guidage[M]
collet
écrou[M] du porte-outil[M]
base
semelle[F]
tool holder
porte-outil[M]

ding pad
teau[M] de ponçage[M]

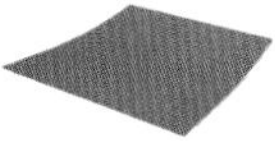

sandpaper
***papier*[M] *de verre*[M]**

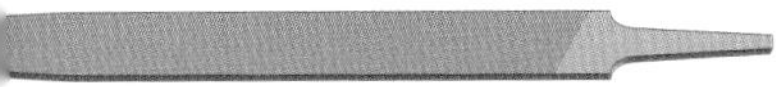

file
***lime*[F]**

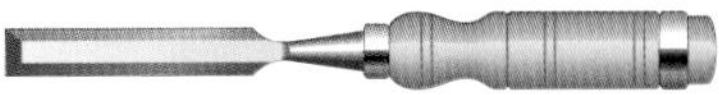

wood chisel
***ciseau*[M] *à bois*[M]**

pleasure garden

jardin[M] d'agrément[M]

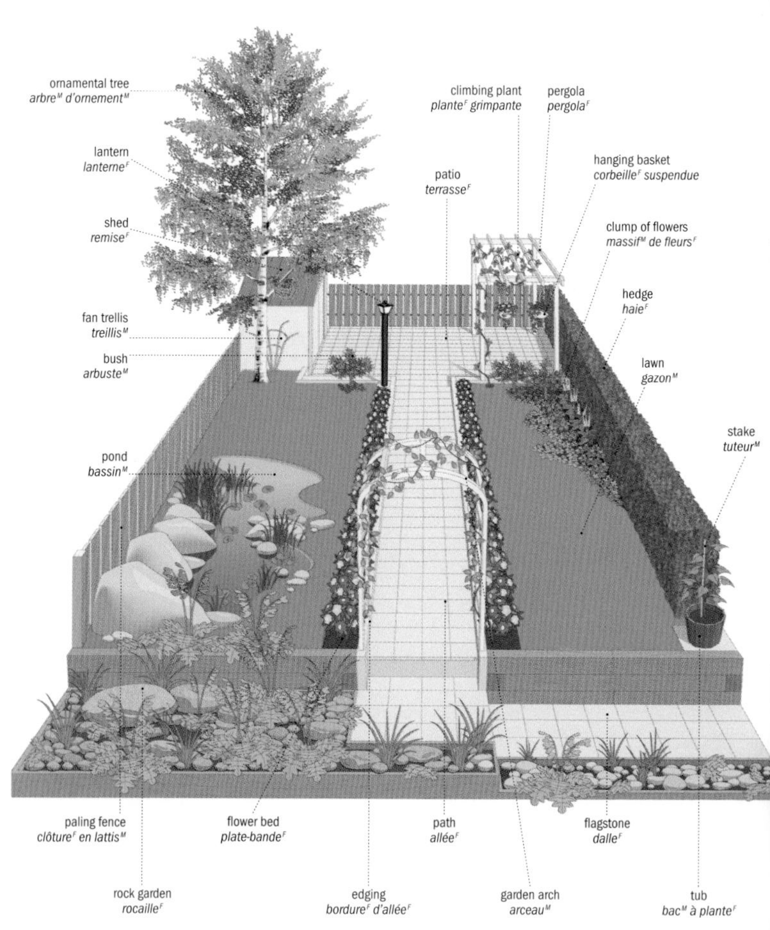

miscellaneous equipment

équipement[M] divers

ost bin
à compost[M]

wheelbarrow
brouette[F]

seeding and planting tools

outils[M] pour semer et planter

garden line
cordeau[M]

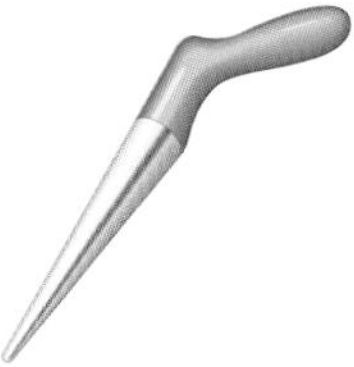

dibber
plantoir[M]

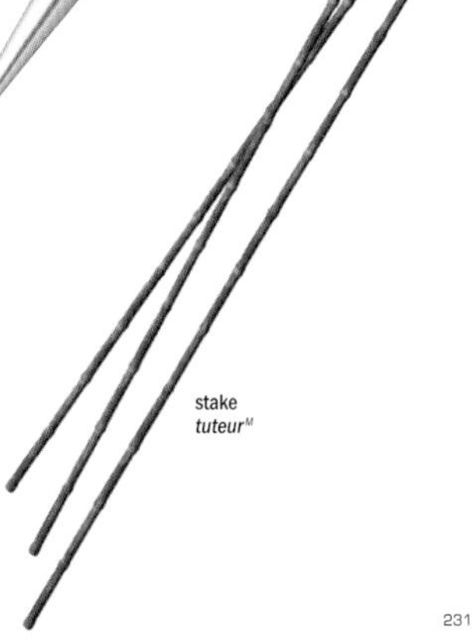

bulb dibber
plantoir[M] à bulbes[M]

seeder
semoir[M] à main[F]

stake
tuteur[M]

hand tools

jeu[M] de petits outils[M]

small hand cultivator
griffe[F] à fleurs[F]

trowel
transplantoir[M]

weeder
tire-racine[M]

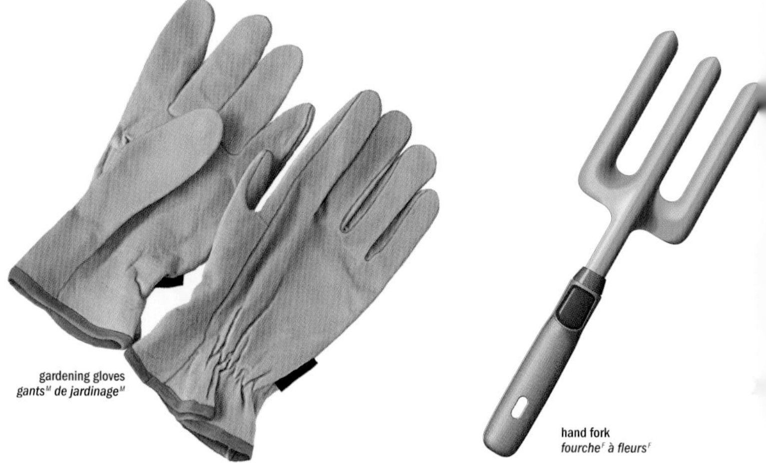

gardening gloves
gants[M] de jardinage[M]

hand fork
fourche[F] à fleurs[F]

tools for loosening the earth

outils[M] pour remuer la terre[F]

pruning and cutting tools

outils^M pour couper

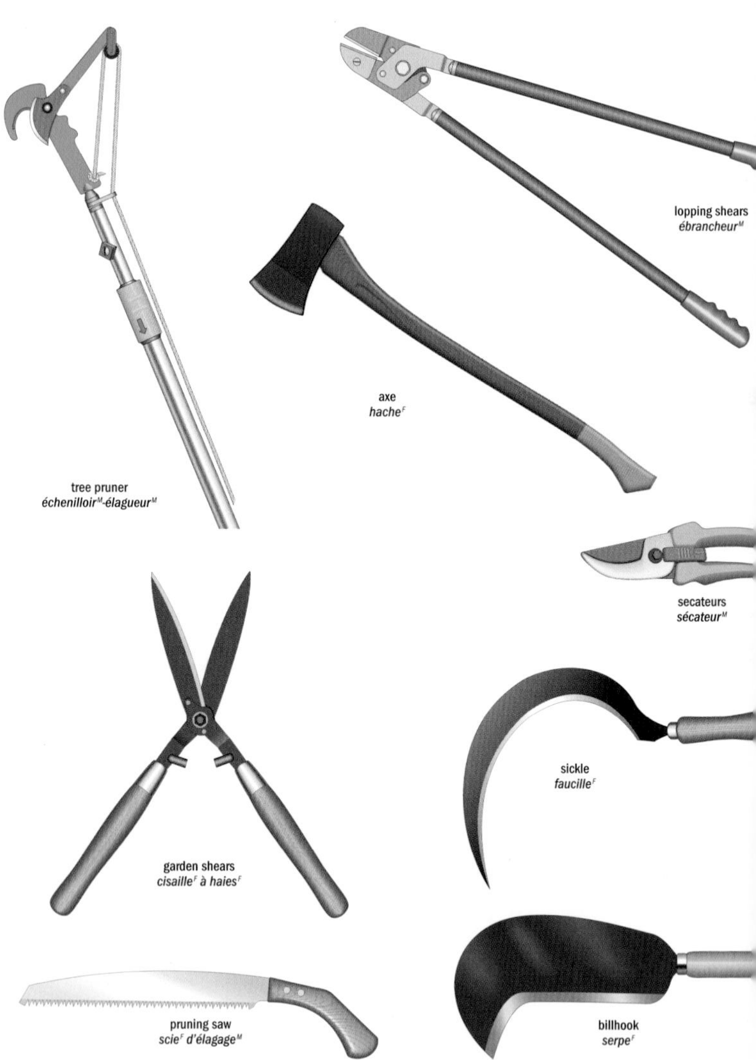

pruning and cutting tools

hedge trimmer
taille-haies[M]

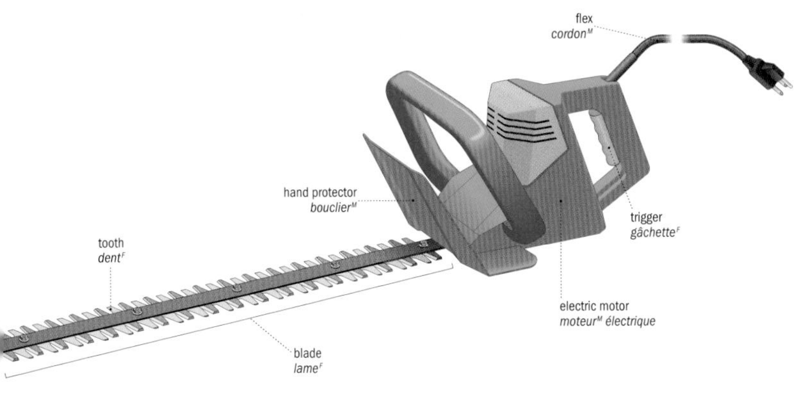

chainsaw
tronçonneuse[F]

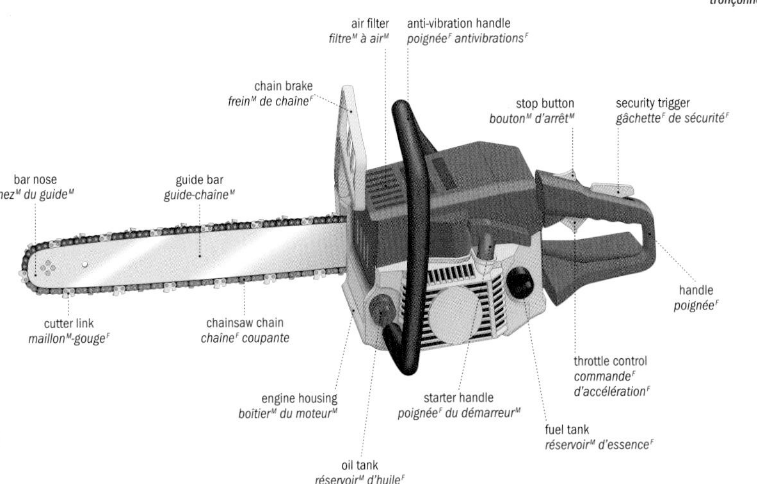

watering tools

outils[M] pour arroser

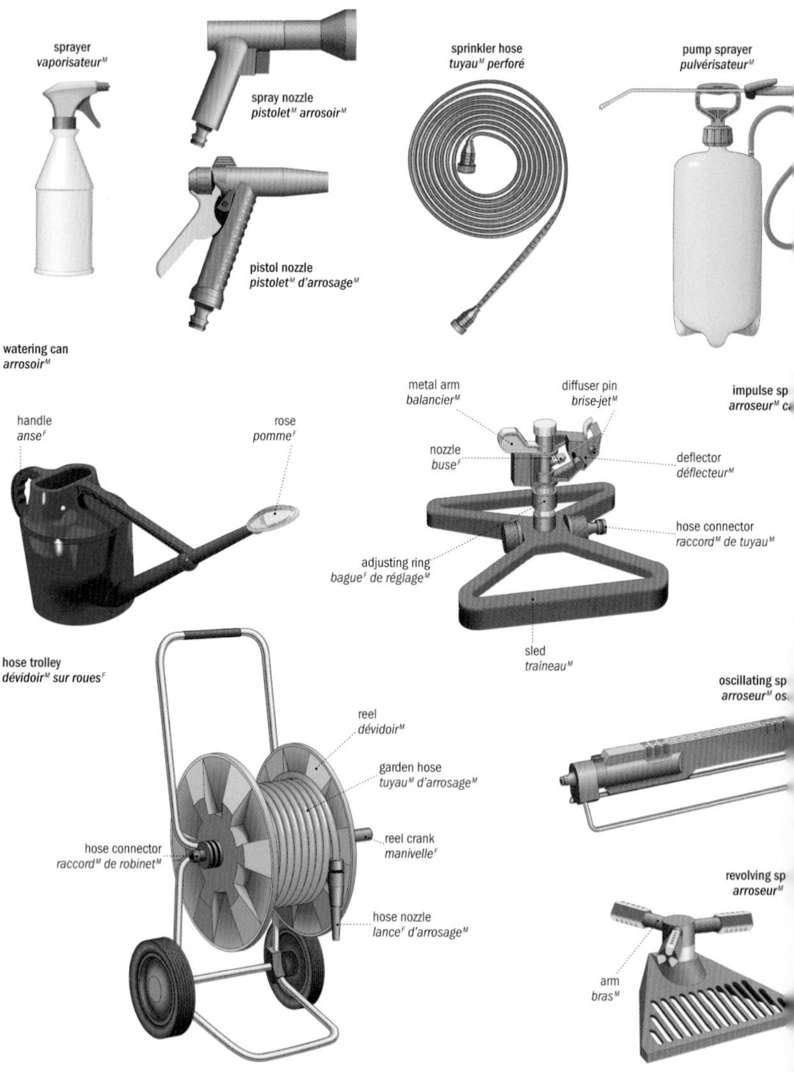

lawn care

soins^M de la pelouse^F

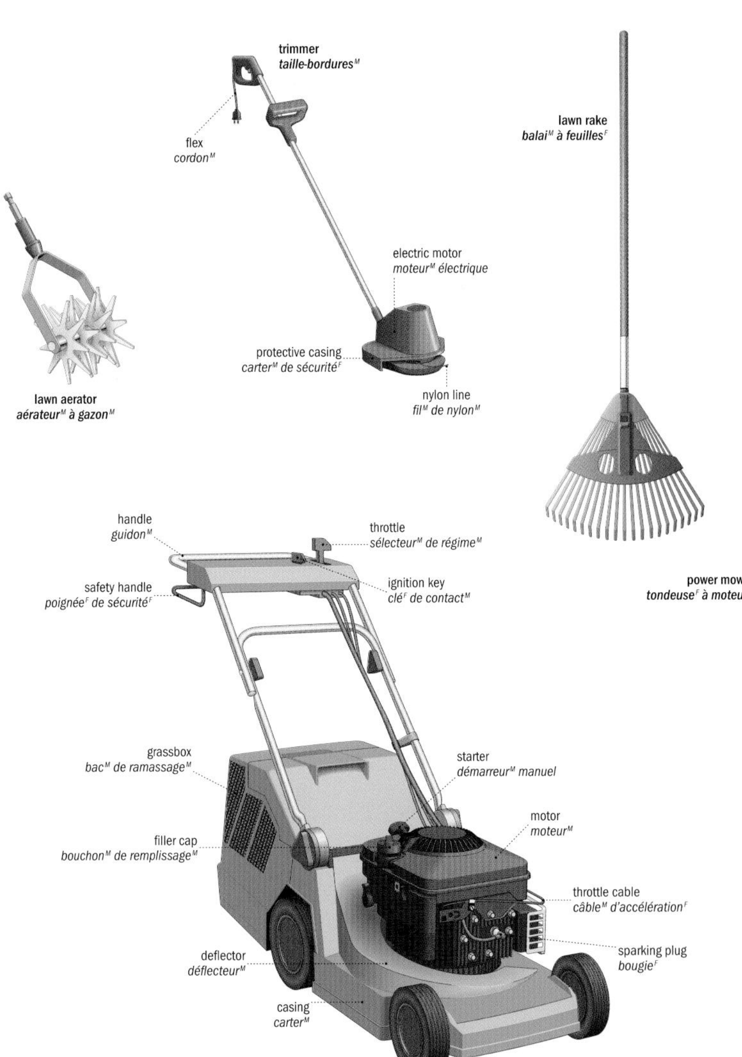

headgear

coiffure[F]

women's headgear
coiffures^F de femme^F

pillbox hat
tambourin^M

cartwheel hat
capeline^F

cloche
cloche^F

toque
toque^F

rain hat
bob^M

crown
calotte^F

brim
bord^M

turban
turban^M

sou'wester
suroît^M

unisex headgear
coiffures^F unisexes

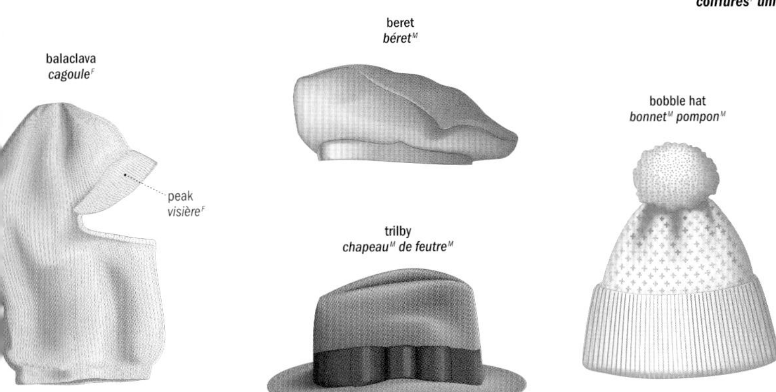

men's shoes
chaussures^F d'homme^M

women's shoes
chaussures[F] de femme[F]

unisex shoes
chaussures[F] unisexes

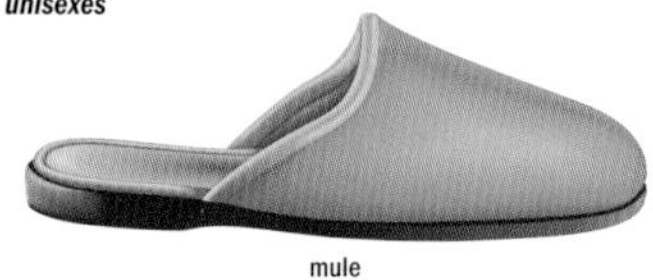

mule
mule[F]

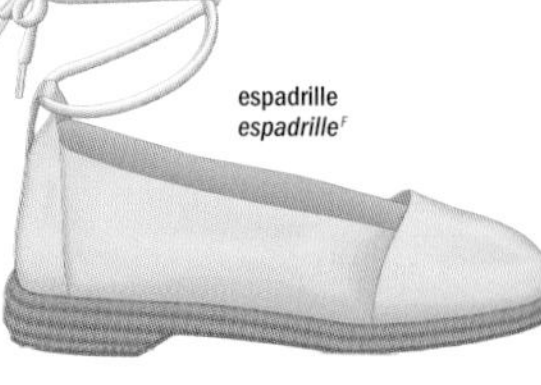

espadrille
espadrille[F]

plimsoll
tennis[M]

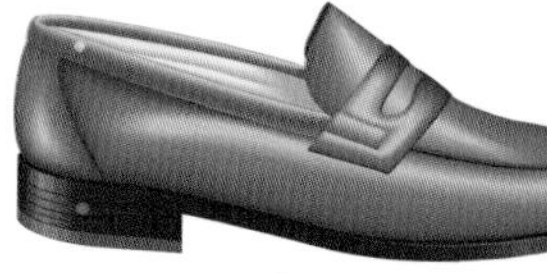

slip-on
loafer[M]

toe-strap
nu-pied[M]

moccasin
mocassin[M]

flip-flop
tong[M]

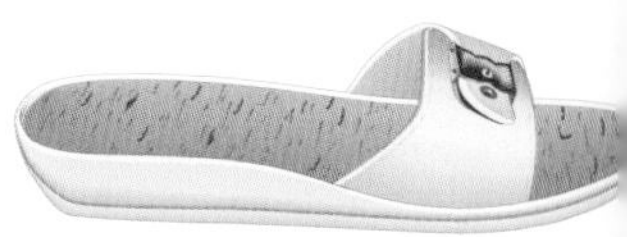

clog
socque[M]

sandal
sandalette[F]

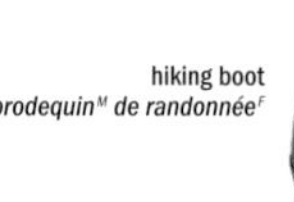

hiking boot
brodequin[M] de randonnée[F]

men's gloves
gants^M d'homme^M

back of a glove
dos^M d'un gant^M

stitching
baguette^F

palm of a glove
paume^F d'un gant^M

fourchette
fourchette^F

glove finger
doigt^M

thumb
pouce^M

palm
paume^F

seam
couture^F d'assemblage^M

snap fastener
bouton^M-pression^F

opening
fenêtre^F

perforation
perforation^F

driving glove
gant^M de conduite^F

mitten
moufle^F

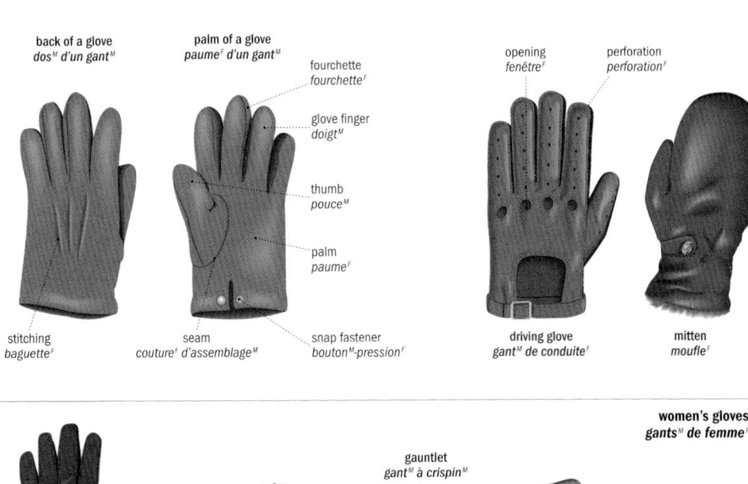

women's gloves
gants^M de femme^F

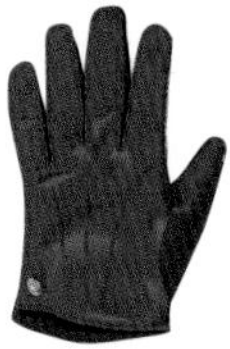

short glove
gant^M court

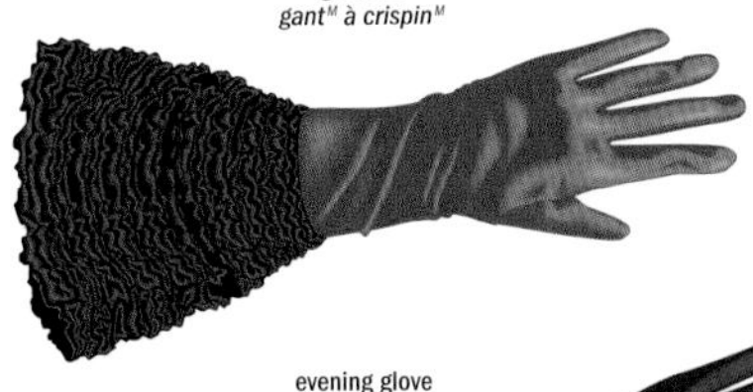

gauntlet
gant^M à crispin^M

wrist-length glove
gant^M saxe

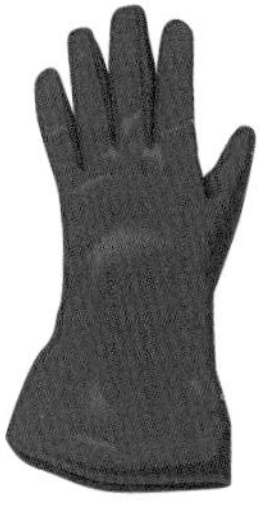

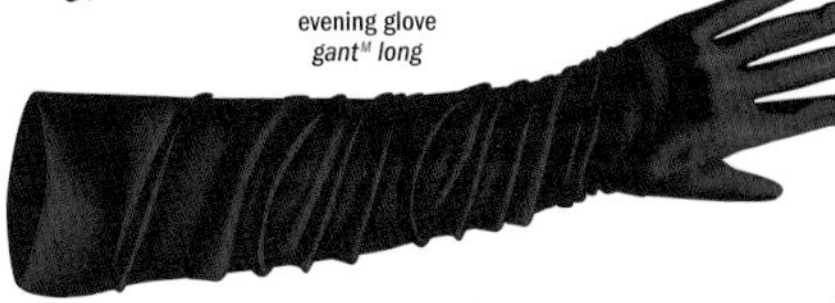

evening glove
gant^M long

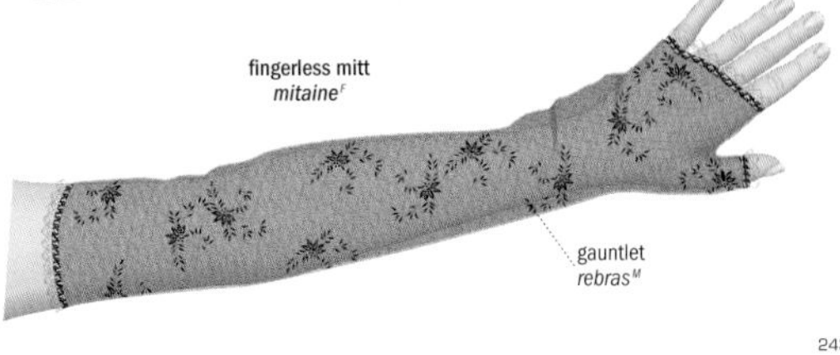

fingerless mitt
mitaine^F

gauntlet
rebras^M

jackets
vestonᴹ et vesteᶠ

shirt
chemise[F]

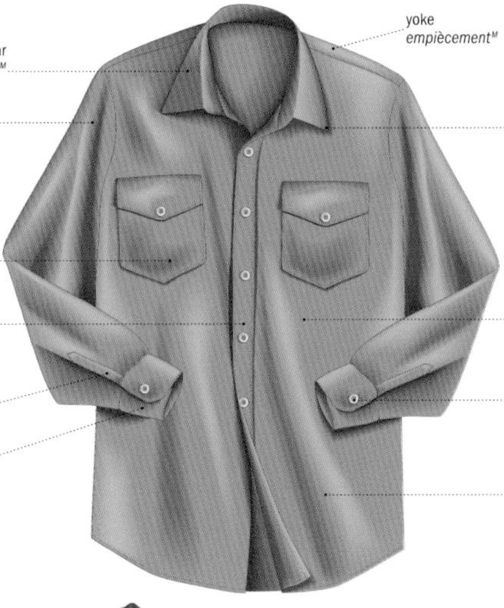

collar
col[M]
yoke
empiècement[M]
set-in sleeve
manche[F] montée
collar point
pointe[F] de col[M]
breast pocket
poche[F] poitrine[F]
button facing
patte[F] de boutonnage[M]
front
devant[M]
pointed tab end
patte[F] capucin[M]
button
bouton[M]
cuff
poignet[M]
shirttail
pan[M]

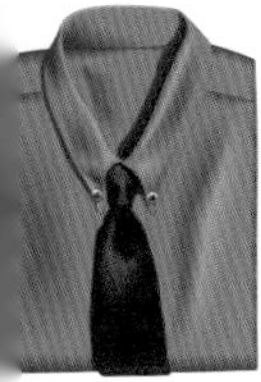

buttondown collar
l[M] pointes[F] boutonnées

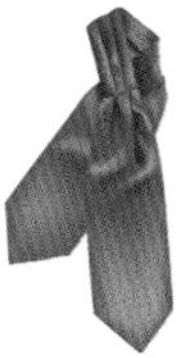

cravat
ascot[F]

bow tie
nœud[M] papillon[M]

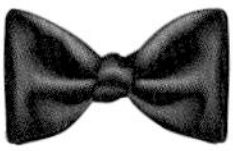

collar stiffener
baleine[F] de col[M]

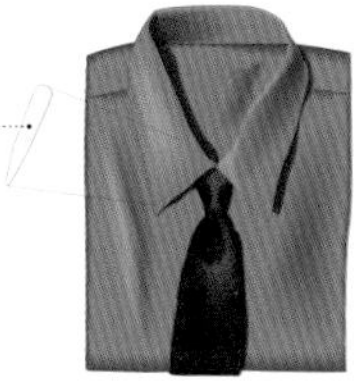

spread collar
col[M] italien

necktie
cravate[F]

front apron
pan[M] avant
neck end
tour[M] de cou[M]
rear apron
pan[M] arrière
lining
doublure[F]
loop
passant[M]
slip-stitched seam
couture[F] médiane

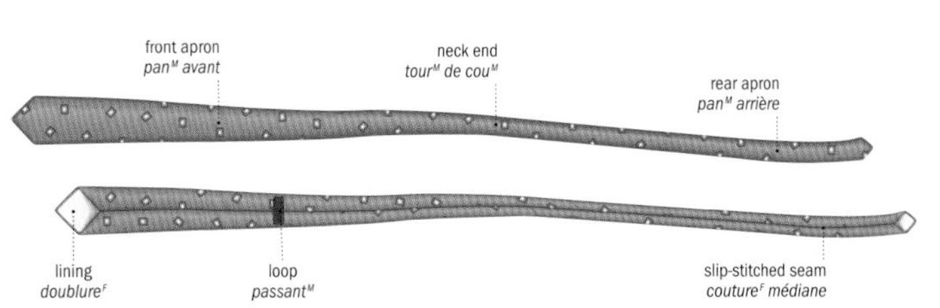

CLOTHING

trousers
pantalon[M]

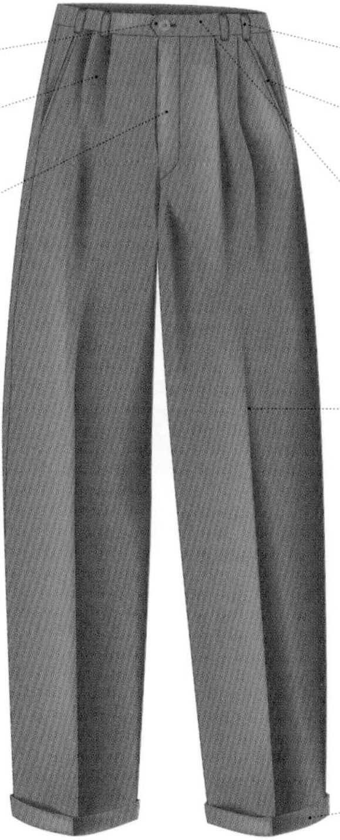

waistband extension
patte[F] boutonnée
knife pleat
pli[M] plat
fly
braguette[F]
belt loop
passant[M]
front top pocket
poche[F] cavalière
waistband
ceinture[F] montée
crease
pli[M]
turn-up
revers[M]

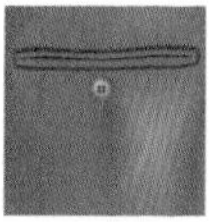

back pocket
poche[F]-revolver[M]

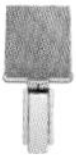

brace clip
pince[F]

braces
bretelles[F]

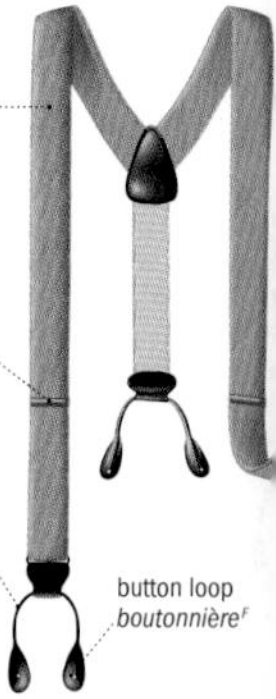

elastic webbing
bande[F] élastique
adjustment slide
coulisse[F]
leather end
patte[F]
button loop
boutonnière[F]

belt
ceinture[F]

top stitching
surpiqûre[F]
panel
croûte[F] de cuir[M]
tip
pointe[F]
punch hole
cran[M]
belt loop
passant[M]
tongue
ardillon[M]
buckle
boucle[F]

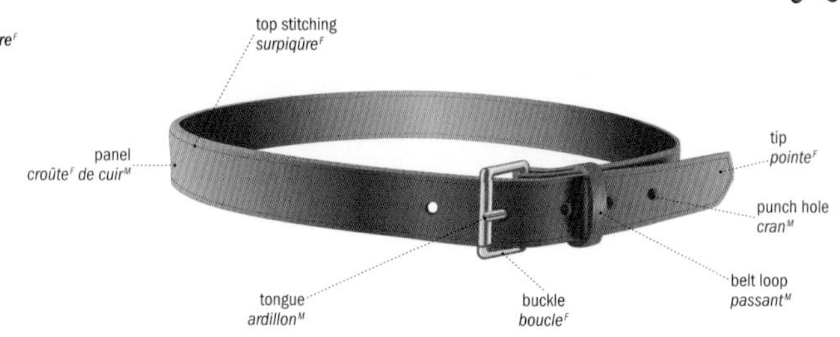

CLOTHING

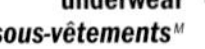

underwear
sous-vêtements[M]

vest
maillot[M] de corps[M]

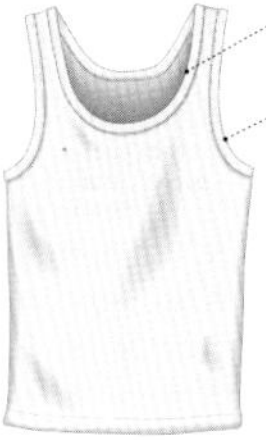

neckhole
encolure[F]

armhole
emmanchure[F]

briefs
slip[M]

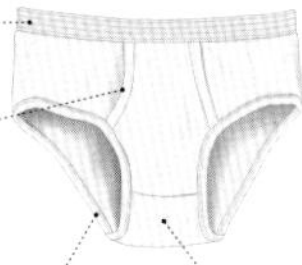

waistband
ceinture[F] élastique

fly
braguette[F]

elasticized leg opening
jambe[F] élastique

crotch
entrejambe[M]

combinations
combinaison[F]

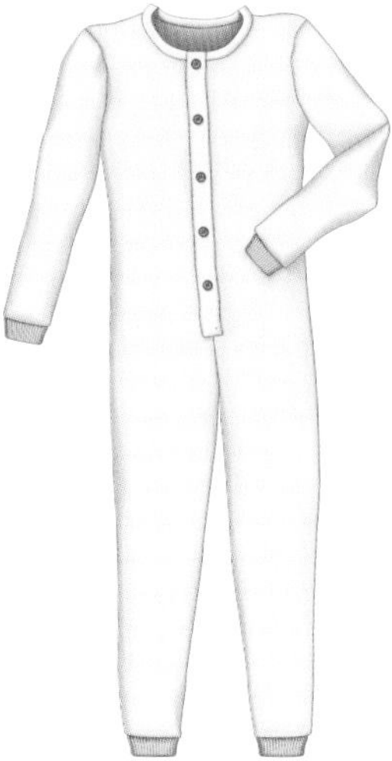

long johns
caleçon[M] long

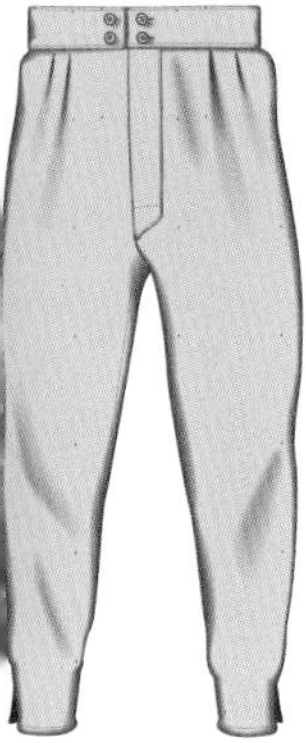

mini briefs
minislip[M]

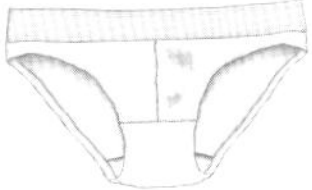

boxer shorts
caleçon[M]

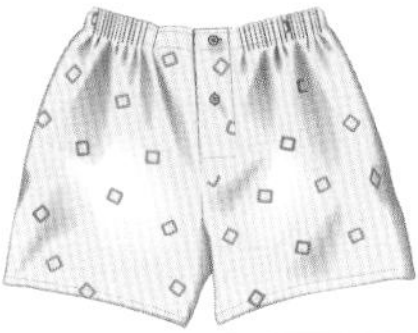

CLOTHING

socks
chaussettes[F]

straight-up ribbed top
bord[M]-côte[F]

leg
jambe[F]

heel
talon[M]

foot
pied[M]

sole
semelle[F]

toe
pointe[F]

knee-length sock
mi-bas[M]

mid-calf length sock
chaussette[F]

ankle sock
mi-chaussette[F]

coats
manteaux[M] et blousons[M]

raincoat
imperméable[M]

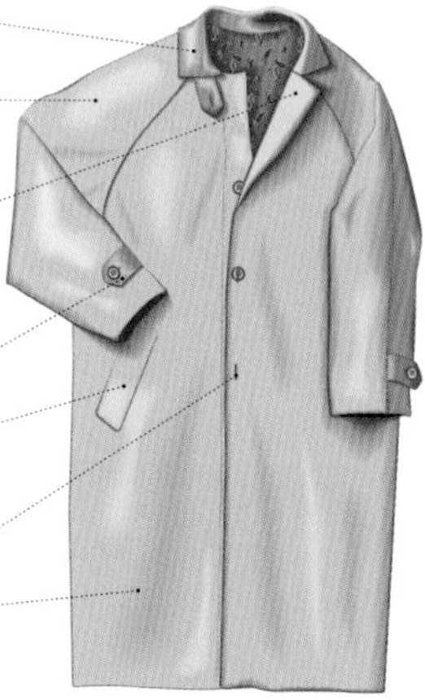

collar
col[M]
raglan sleeve
manche[F] raglan
notched lapel
revers[M] cranté
tab
patte[F]
broad welt side pocket
poche[F] raglan
buttonhole
boutonnière[F]
side panel
pan[M]

overcoat
pardessus[M]

notched lapel
revers[M] cranté
breast pocket
poche[F] poitrin
breast dart
pince[F] de taill
flap pocket
poche[F] à raba

trench coat
trench[M]

two-way collar
col[M] transformable
epaulet
patte[F] d'épaule[F]
raglan sleeve
manche[F] raglan
gun flap
bavolet[M]
sleeve strap loop
passant[M]
double-breasted buttoning
double boutonnage[M]
belt
ceinture[F]
sleeve strap
patte[F] de serrage[M]
belt loop
passant[M]
broad welt side pocket
poche[F] raglan
buckle
boucle[F] de ceinture[F]

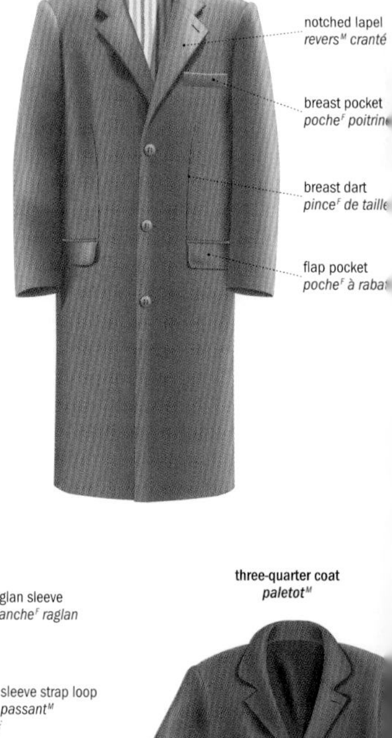

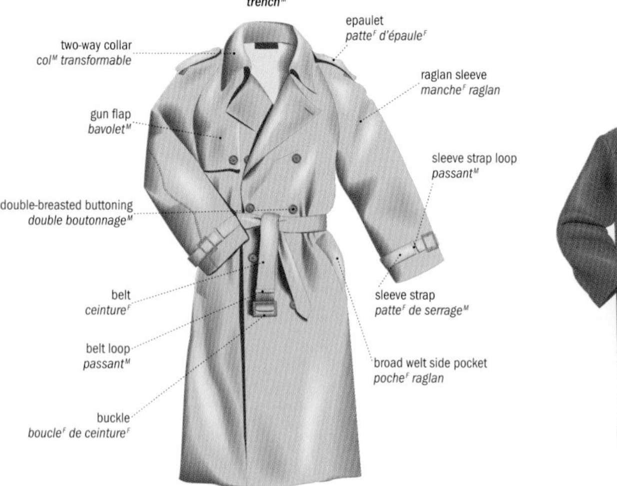

three-quarter coat
paletot[M]

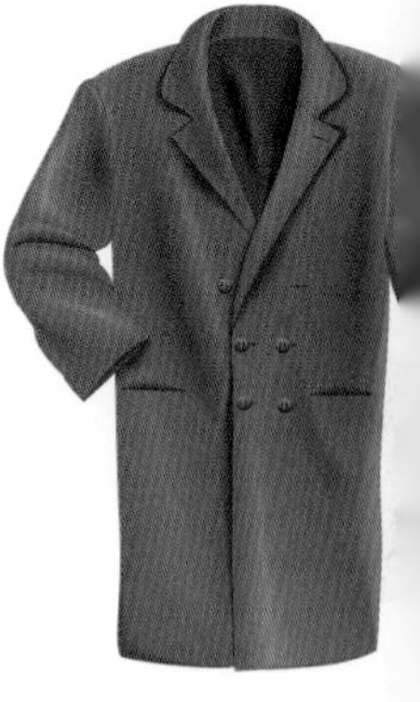

parka
***parka*[F]**

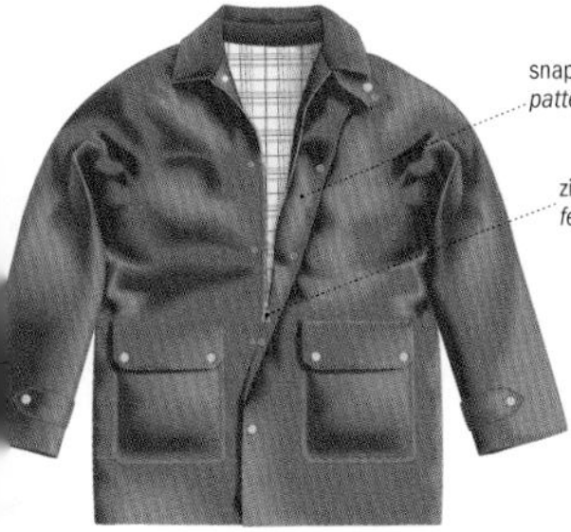

snap-fastening tab
patte[F] à boutons[M]-pression[F]
zip fastener
fermeture[F] à glissière[F]

sheepskin jacket
***canadienne*[F]**

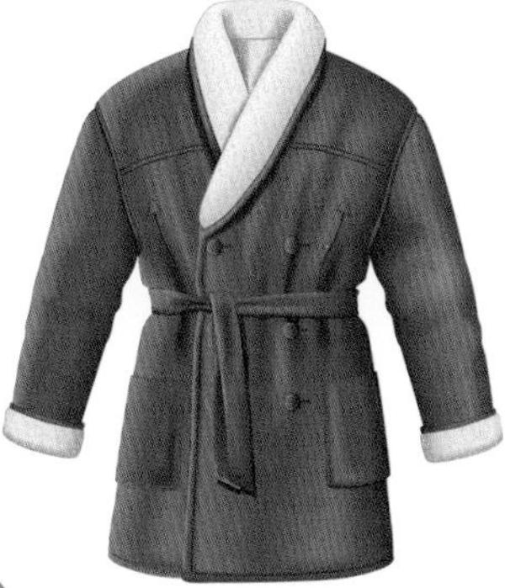

duffle coat
***duffle-coat*[M]**

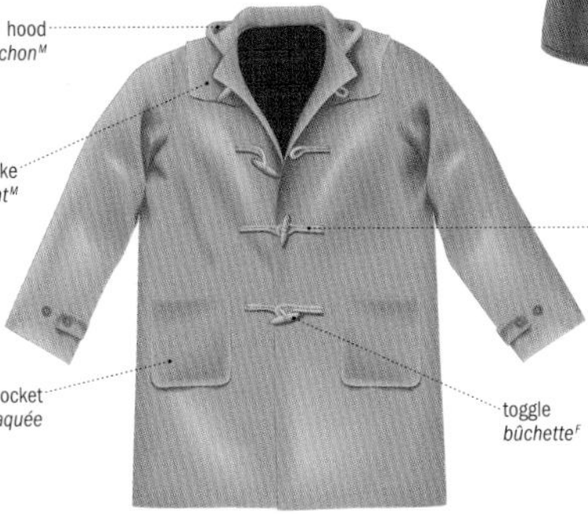

hood
capuchon[M]
yoke
empiècement[M]
frog
brandebourg[M]
patch pocket
poche[F] plaquée
toggle
bûchette[F]

windcheater
blouson*[M] *court

snap fastener
bouton[M]-pression[F]
hand-warmer pocket
poche[F] repose-bras[M]
elastic waistband
ceinture[F] élastique

windcheater
blouson*[M] *long

waistband
ceinture[F] montée
drawstring
cordon[M] coulissant

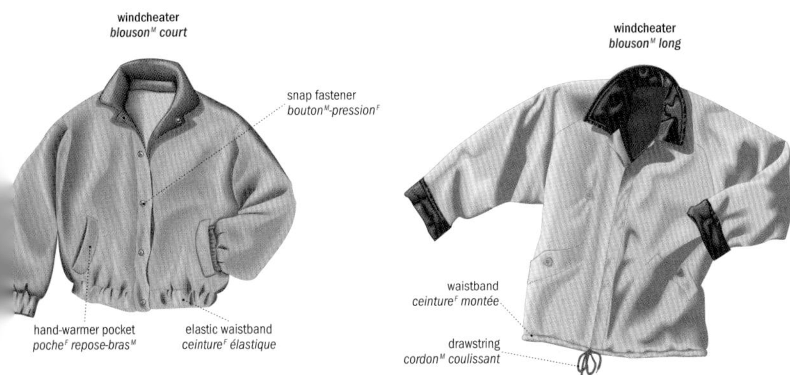

sweaters

tricots[M]

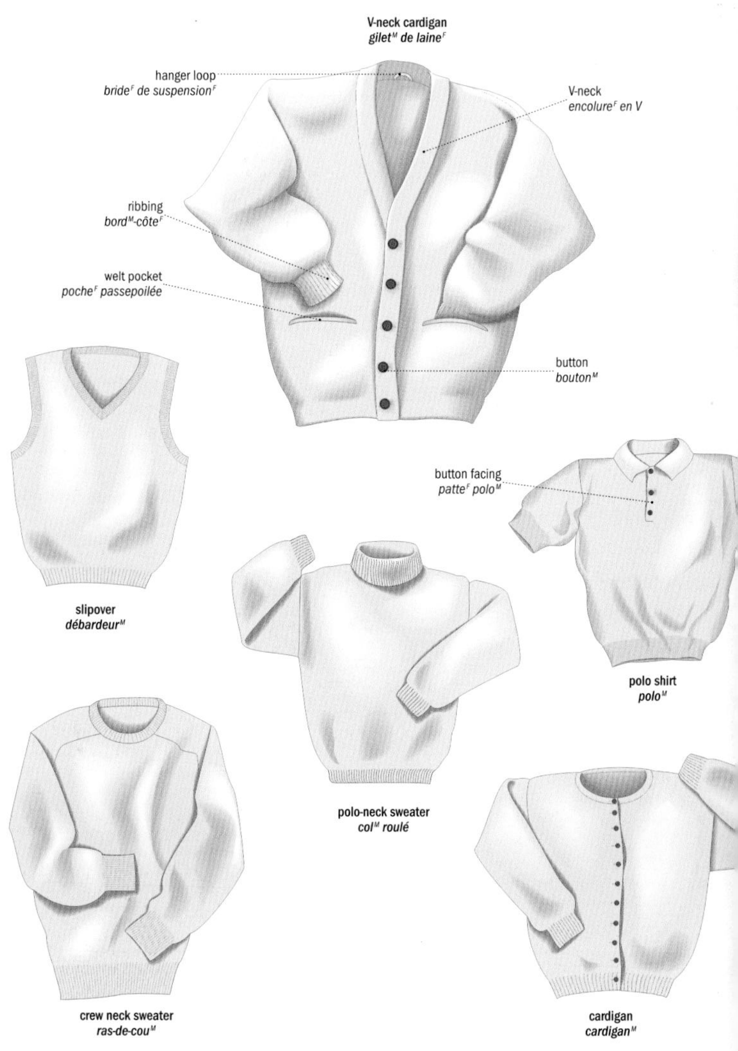

slipover
débardeur[M]

polo shirt
polo[M]

polo-neck sweater
col[M] roulé

crew neck sweater
ras-de-cou[M]

cardigan
cardigan[M]

coats
manteaux[M]

examples of dresses
exemples[M] de robes[F]

sheath dress
robe[F] fourreau[M]

princess dress
robe[F] princesse[F]

coat dress
robe[F]-manteau[M]

polo dress
robe[F]-polo[M]

house dress
robe[F] de maison[F]

shirtwaist dress
robe[F] chemisier[M]

drop waist dress
robe[F] taille[F] basse

A-line dress
robe[F] trapèze[M]

sundress
robe[F] bain[M]-de-soleil[M]

wrapover dress
robe[F] enveloppe[F]

tunic dress
robe[F] tunique[F]

pinafore
chasuble[F]

examples of skirts
exemples[M] de jupes[F]

gored skirt
jupe[F] à lés[M]

kilt
kilt[M]

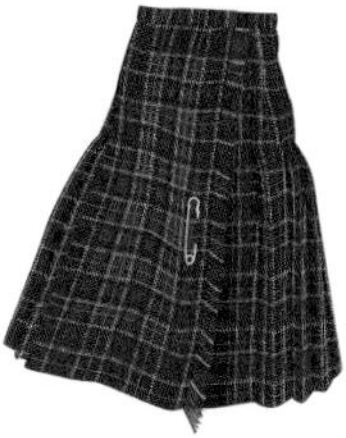

sarong
paréo[M]

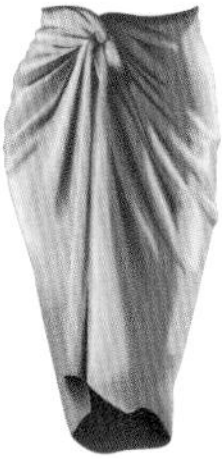

wrapover skirt
jupe[F] portefeuille[M]

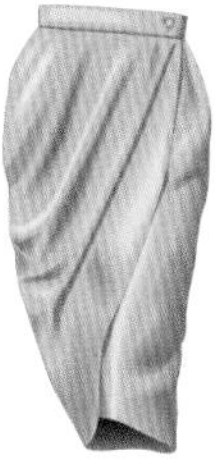

sheath skirt
jupe[F] fourreau[M]

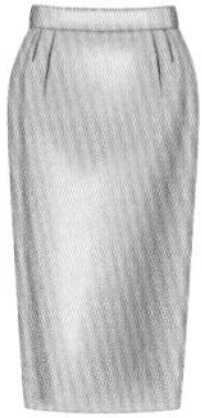

ruffled skirt
pe[F] à volants[M] étagés

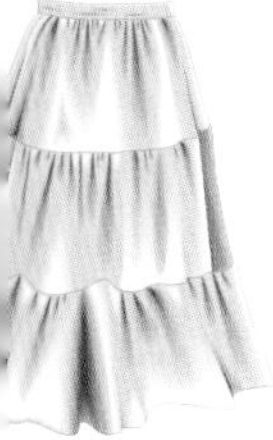

straight skirt
jupe[F] droite

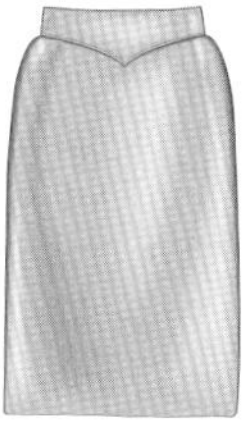

yoke skirt
jupe[F] à empiècement[M]

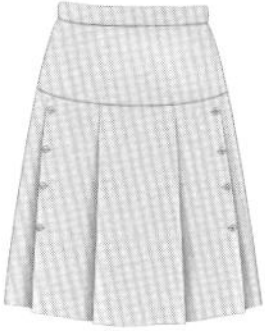

gather skirt
jupe[F] froncée

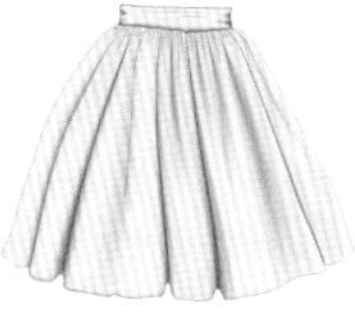

culottes
jupe[F]-culotte[F]

examples of pleats
exemples[M] de plis[M]

inverted pleat
pli[M] creux

kick pleat
pli[M] d'aisance[F]

accordion pleat
plissé[M] accordéon[M]

top stitched pleat
pli[M] surpiqué

knife pleat
pli[M] plat

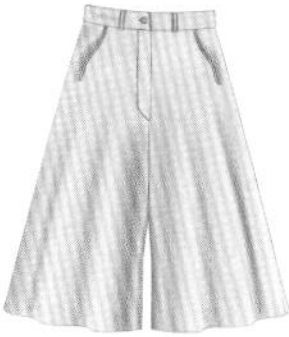

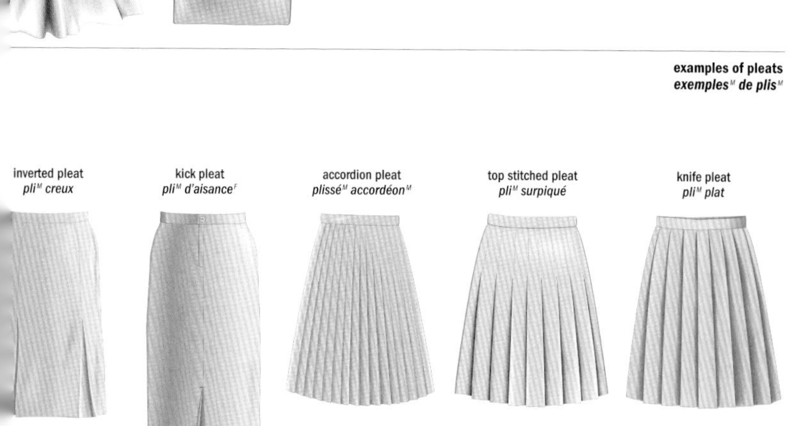

examples of trousers
exemples^M de pantalons^M

shorts
short^M

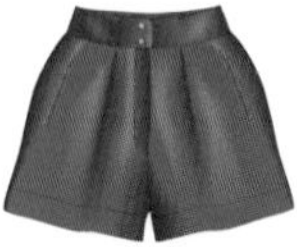

Bermuda shorts
bermuda^M

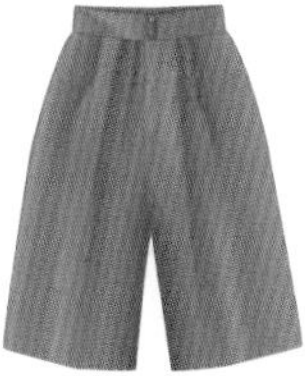

knickerbockers
knicker^M

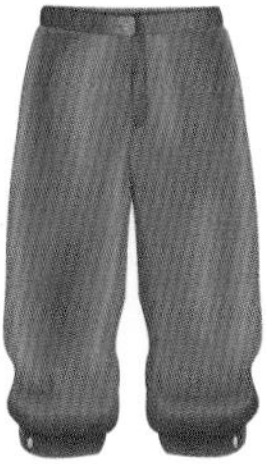

pedal pushers
corsaire^M

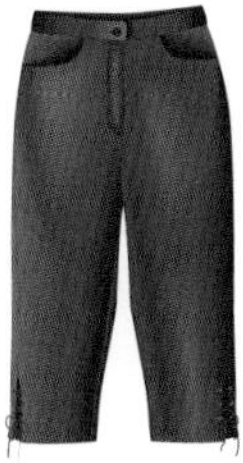

jeans
jean^M

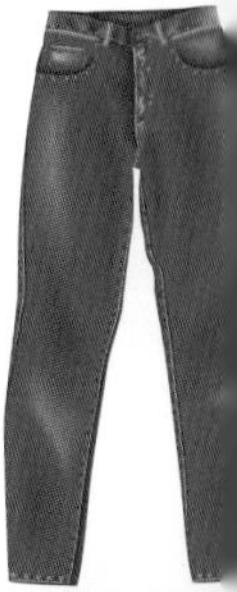

ski pants
fuseau^M

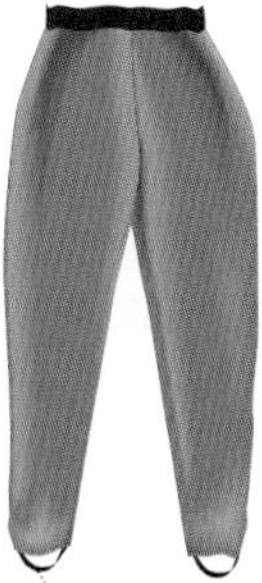

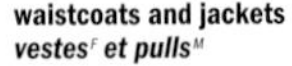

footstrap
sous-pied^M

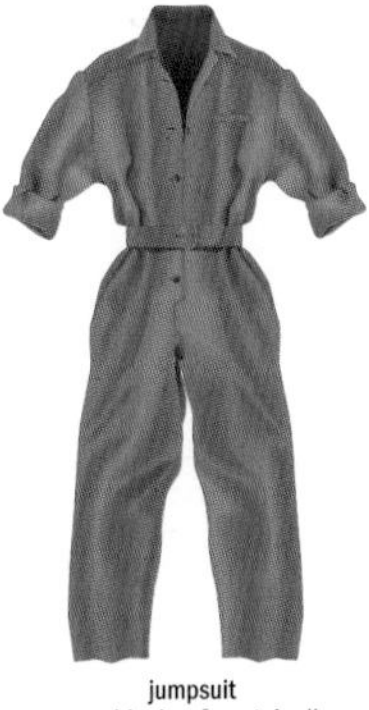

jumpsuit
combinaison^F-pantalon^M

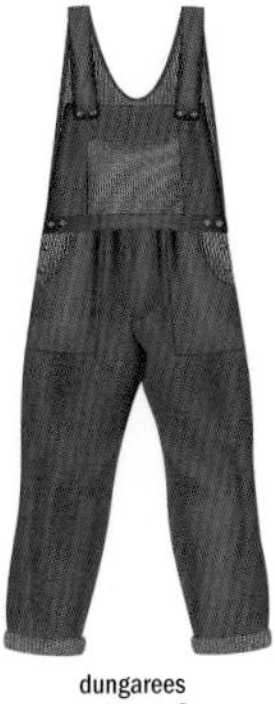

dungarees
salopette^F

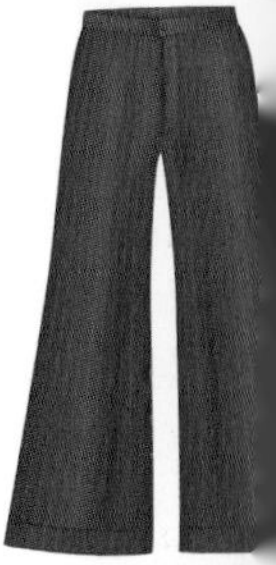

bell bottoms
pantalon^M pattes^F d'élép

waistcoats and jackets
vestes^F et pulls^M

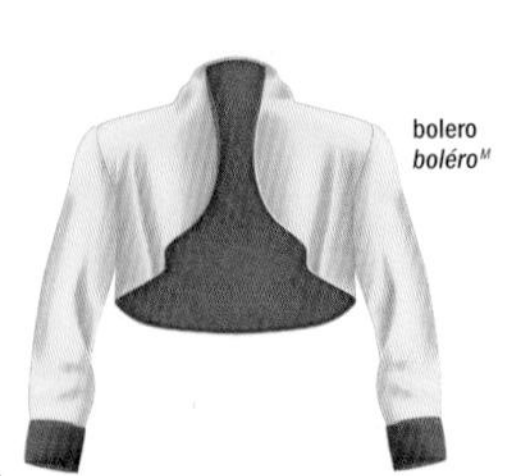

bolero
boléro^M

spencer
spencer^M

blazer
blazer^M

CLOTHING

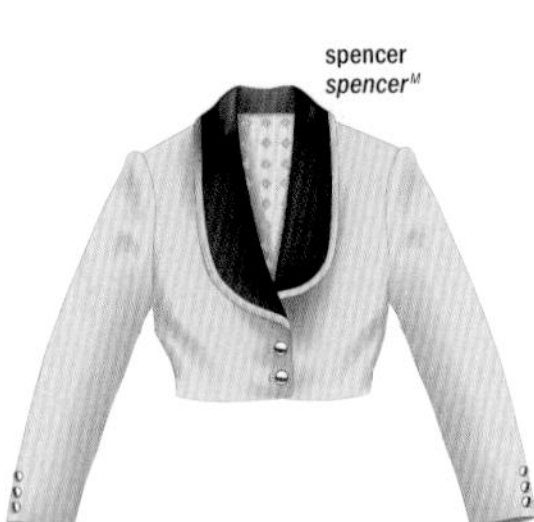

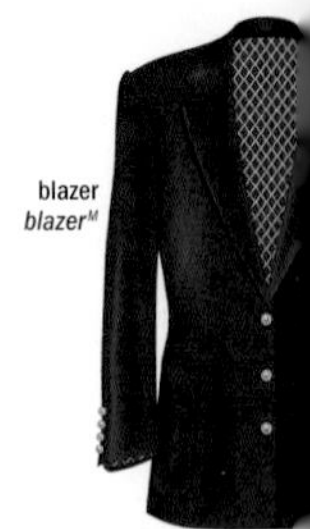

safari jacket
saharienne^F
gusset pocket
poche^F soufflet^M
waistcoat
gilet^M
twin-set
tandem^M
crew neck sweater
ras-de-cou^M
cardigan
cardigan^M
examples of blouses
exemples^M de corsages^M
body
corsage^M-culotte^F
crotch piece
patte^F d'entrejambe^M
sailor tunic
marinière^F
yoke
empiècement^M
gather
fronce^F
shirttail
pan^M
overshirt
liquette^F
classic blouse
chemisier^M classique
button-through smock
tablier^M-blouse^F
smock
tunique^F
wrapover top
cache-cœur^M
polo shirt
polo^M
tunic
casaque^F

nightwear
vêtements[M] de nuit[F]

nightgown
chemise[F] de nuit[F]

baby doll
nuisette[F]

kimono
kimono[M]

bathrobe
peignoir[M]

pyjamas
pyjama[M]

dressing gown
déshabillé[M]

hose
bas[M]

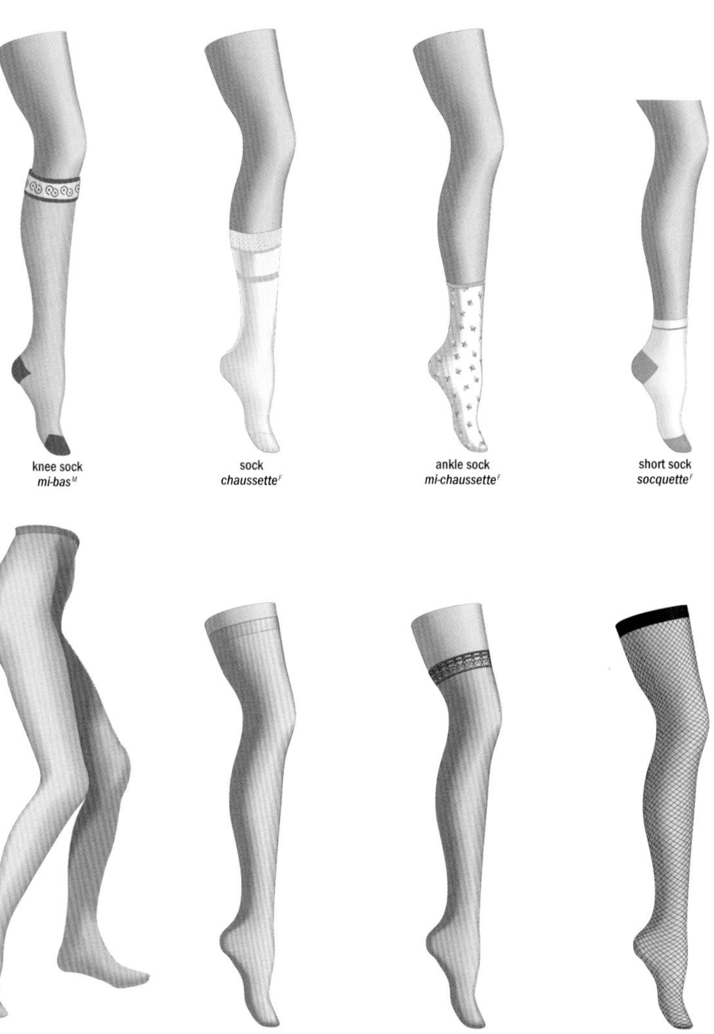

knee sock
mi-bas[M]

sock
chaussette[F]

ankle sock
mi-chaussette[F]

short sock
socquette[F]

tights
collant[M]

stocking
bas[M]

thigh stocking
bas[M]*-cuissarde*[F]

fishnet stocking
bas[M] *résille*[F]

underwear
sous-vêtements [M]

corselette
combiné [M]

camisole
caraco [M]

teddy
teddy [M]

body
body [M]

panty corselette
combiné [M]*-culotte* [F]

half-slip
jupon [M]

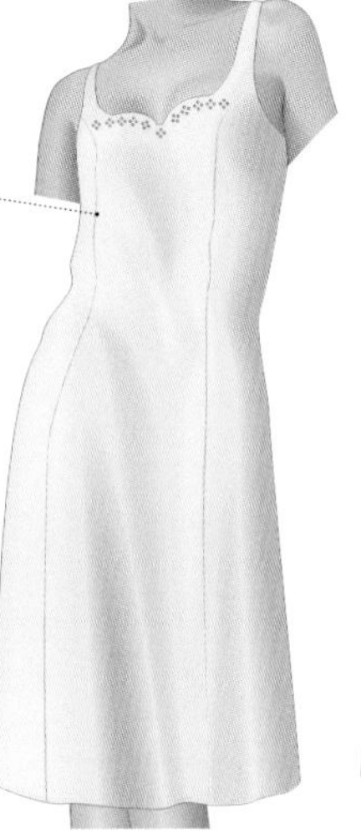

foundation slip
fond [M] *de robe* [F]

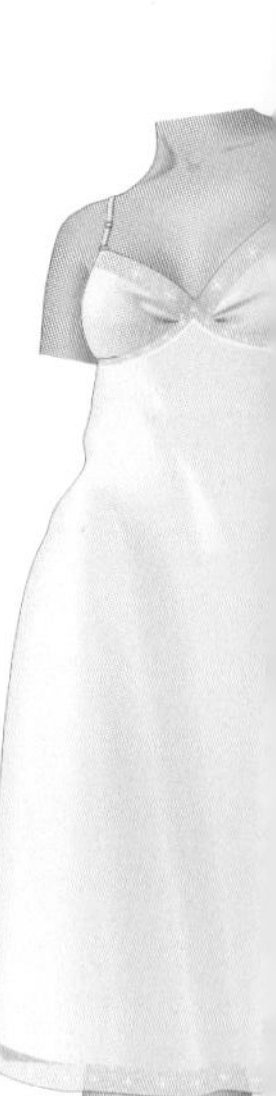

slip
combinaison [F]*-jupor*

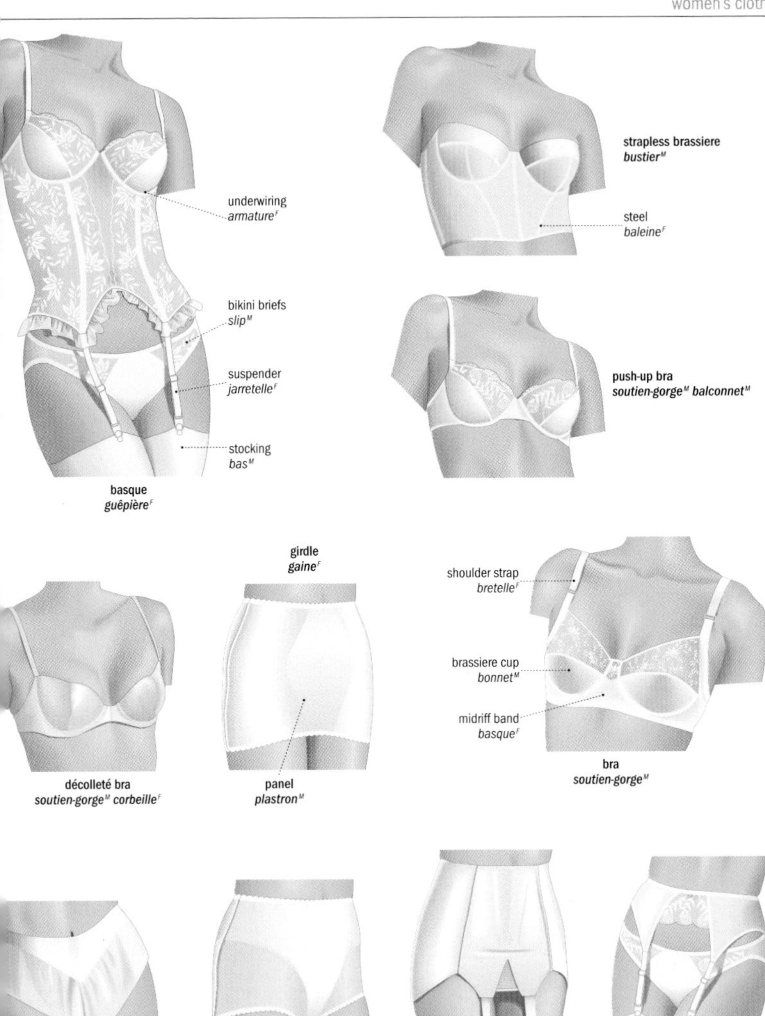

briefs
culotte

panty girdle
gaine-culotte

corset
corset

suspender belt
porte-jarretelles

newborn children's clothing

vêtements[M] de nouveau-né[M]

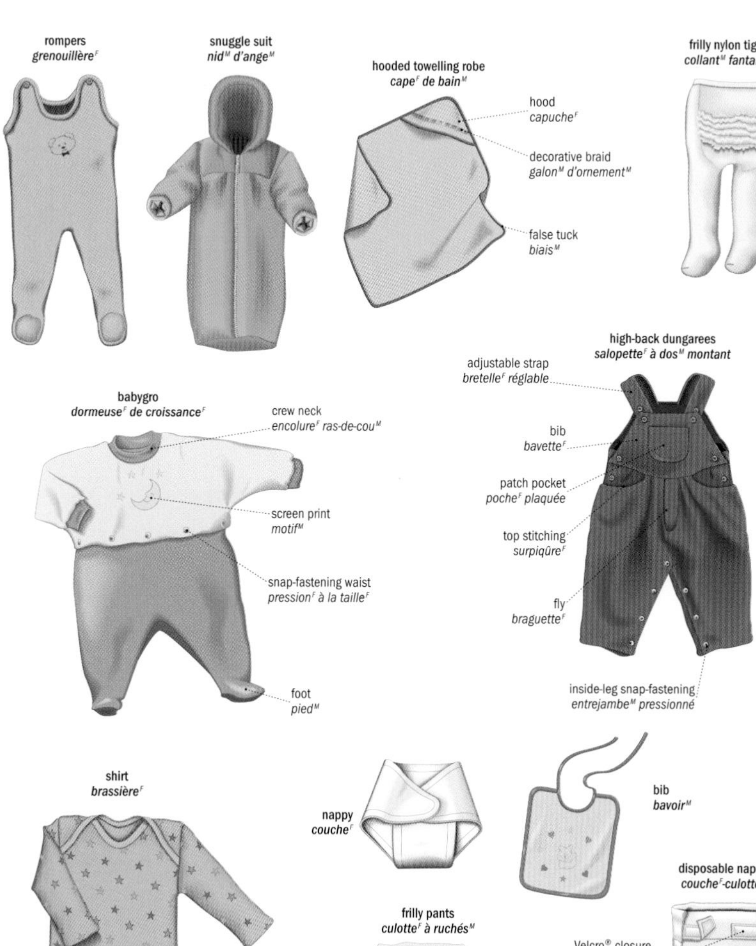

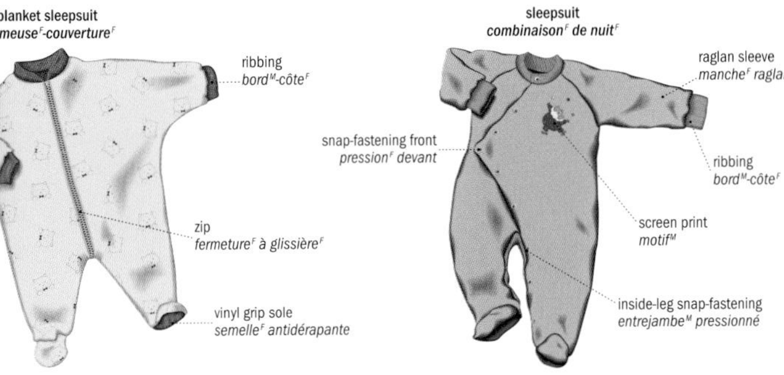

children's clothing

vêtements^{M} d'enfant^{M}

dungarees with crossover back straps
salopette^{F} à bretelles^{F} croisées

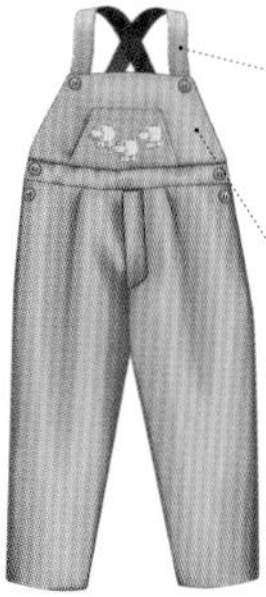

button strap
bretelle^{F} boutonnée

bib
bavette^{F}

snowsuit
esquimau^{M}

drawstring hood
capuchon^{M} coulissé

fly front closing
fermeture^{F} sous patte^{F}

slip-on pyjamas
polojama^{M}

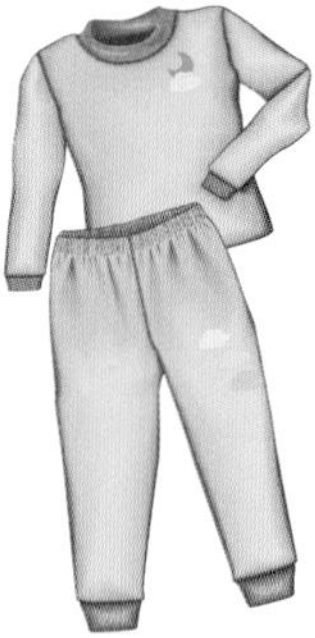

T-shirt dress
robe^{F} tee-shirt^{M}

rompers
barboteuse^{F}

training set
tenue^{F} d'exercice^{M}

vest
débardeur^{M}

shorts
short^{M}

jumpsuit
combinaison^{F}

sportswear

tenue[F] d'exercice[M]

running shoe
chaussure[F] de sport[M]

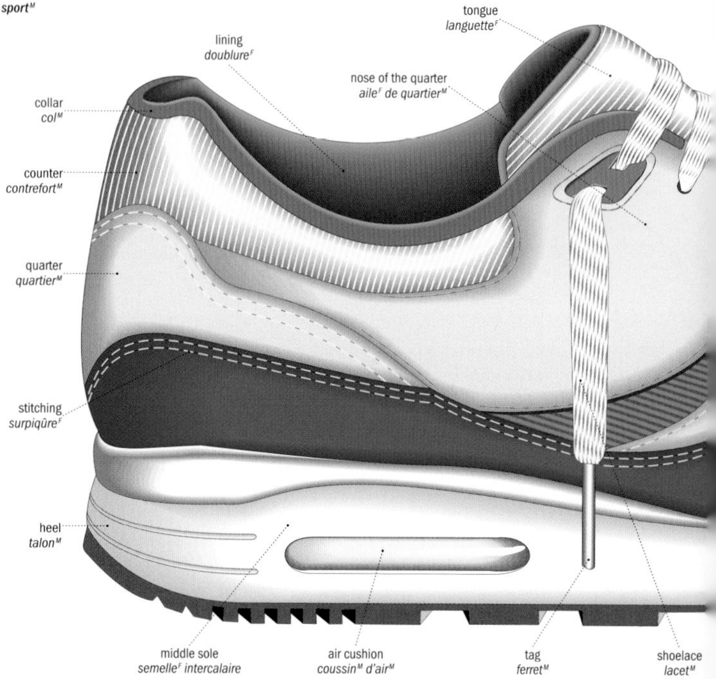

tongue
languette[F]

lining
doublure[F]

nose of the quarter
aile[F] de quartier[M]

collar
col[M]

counter
contrefort[M]

quarter
quartier[M]

stitching
surpiqûre[F]

heel
talon[M]

middle sole
semelle[F] intercalaire

air cushion
coussin[M] d'air[M]

tag
ferret[M]

shoelace
lacet[M]

training suit
survêtement[M]

jogging pants
pantalon[M] molleton[M]

hooded sweat shirt
sweat[M] à capuche[F]

sweat shirt
sweat-shirt[M]

exercise wear
vêtements[M] d'exercice[M]

swimming trunks
slip[M] de bain[M]

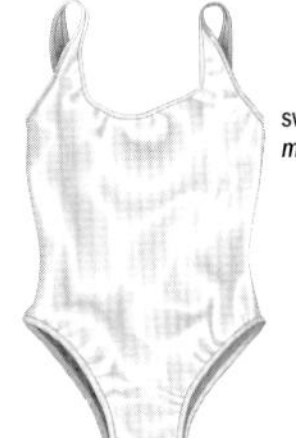
swimsuit
maillot[M] de bain[M]

leotard
justaucorps[M]

eyelet
œillet[M]

vamp
claque[F]

punch hole
perforation[F]

stud
crampon[M]

outsole
semelle[F] d'usure[F]

footless tights
collant[M] sans pieds[M]

leg-warmer
jambière[F]

trousers
pantalon[M]

anorak
anorak[M]

running shorts
short[M] boxeur[M]

vest
débardeur[M]

CLOTHING

jewellery

bijouterie[F]

earrings
boucles[F] d'oreille[F]

clip earrings
boucles[F] d'oreille[F] à pince[F]

screw earrings
boucles[F] d'oreille[F] à vis[F]

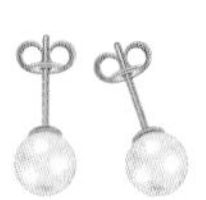
ear studs
boucles[F] d'oreille[F] à tige[F]

drop earrings
pendants[M] d'oreille[F]

hoop earrings
anneaux[M]

necklaces
colliers[M]

matinee-length necklace
collier[M] de perles[F], longueur[F] matinée[F]

velvet-band choker
collier[M]-de-chien[M]

pendant
pendentif[M]

rope
sautoir[M]

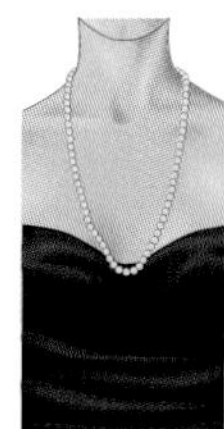
opera-length necklace
sautoir[M], longueur[F] opéra[M]

bib necklace
collier[M] de soirée[F]

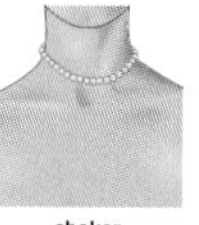
choker
ras-de-cou[M]

locket
médaillon[M]

bracelets
bracelets[M]

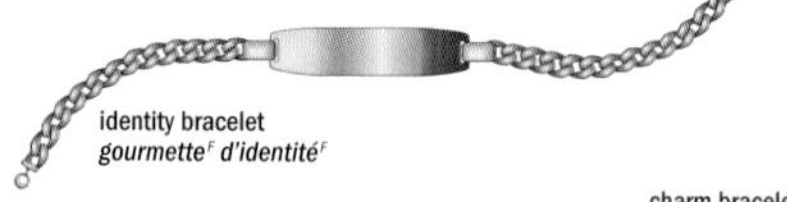
identity bracelet
gourmette[F] d'identité[F]

charm bracelet
gourmette[F]

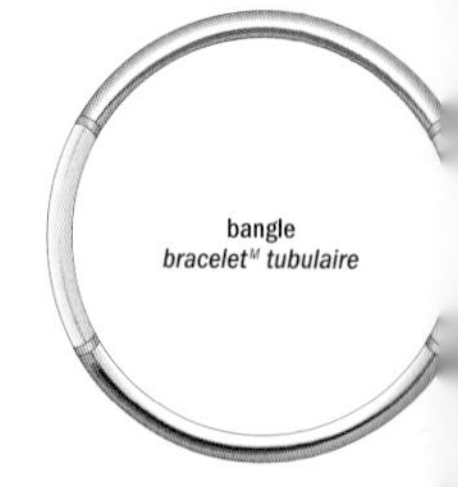
bangle
bracelet[M] tubulaire

rings
bagues[F]

band ring
jonc[M]

signet ring
chevalière[F]

solitaire ring
bague[F] solitaire[M]

engagement ring
bague[F] de fiançailles[F]

wedding ring
alliance[F]

manicure
manucure^F

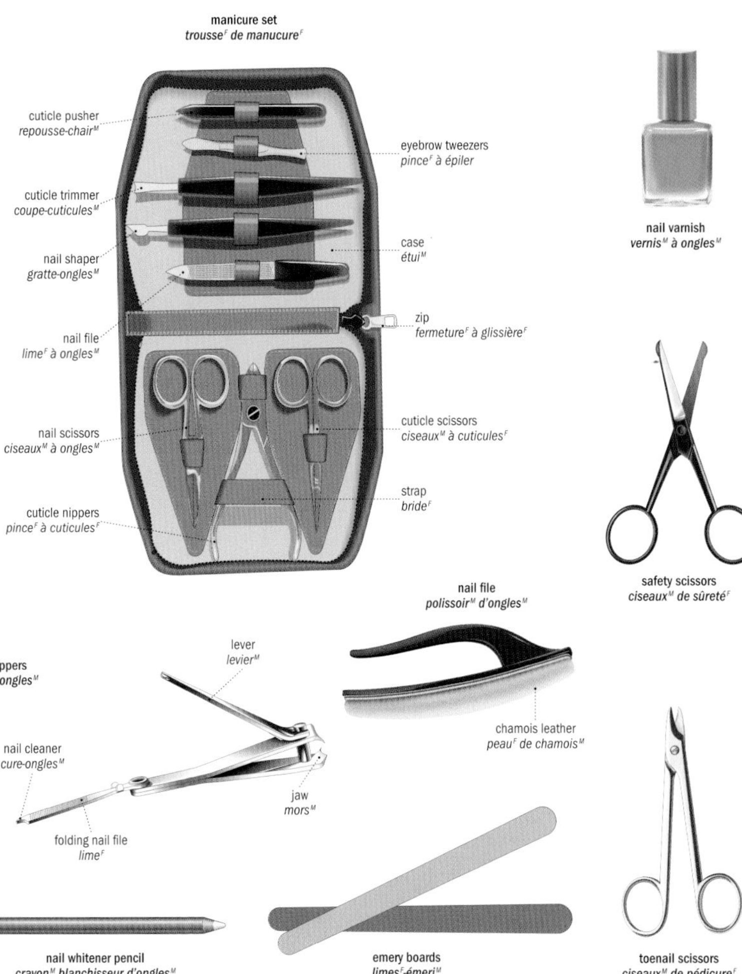

make-up

maquillage^{M}

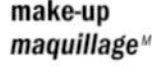

make-up
maquillage^{M}

fan brush
pinceau^{M} éventail^{M}

powder puff
houppette^{F}

synthetic sponge
éponge^{F} synthétique

blusher brush
pinceau^{M} pour fard^{M} à joues^{F}

powder blusher
fard^{M} à joues^{F} en poudre^{F}

loose powder
poudre^{F} libre

loose powder brush
pinceau^{M} pour poudre^{F} libre

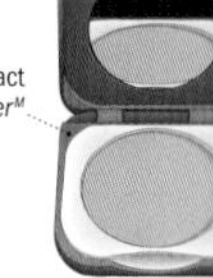

compact
poudrier^{M}

pressed powd
poudre^{F} presse

liquid foundat
fond^{M} de teint^{M} li

eye make-up
maquillage^{M} des yeux^{M}

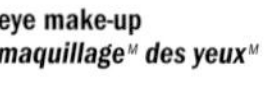

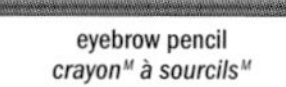

eyebrow pencil
crayon^{M} à sourcils^{M}

eyelash curler
recourbe-cils^{M}

brow brush and lash comb
brosse^{F}-peigne^{M} pour cils^{M} et sourcils^{M}

mascara brush
brosse^{F} à mascara^{M}

cake mascara
mascara^{M} en pain^{M}

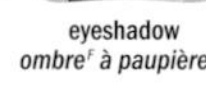

sponge-tipped applicator
applicateur^{M}-mousse^{F}

eyeshadow
ombre^{F} à paupières^{F}

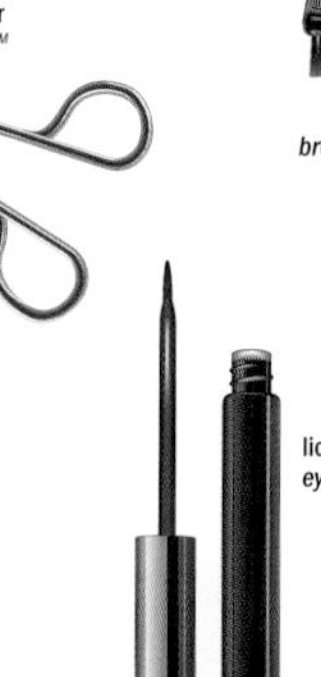

liquid eyeliner
eye-liner^{M} liquide

liquid mascara
mascara^{M} liquide

lip make-up
maquillage^{M} des lèvres^{F}

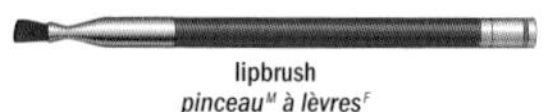

lipbrush
pinceau^{M} à lèvres^{F}

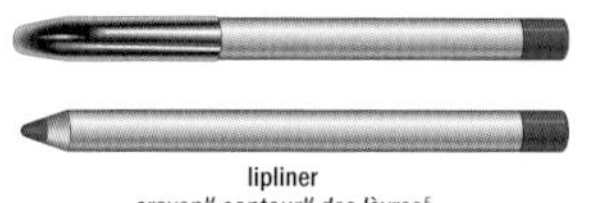

lipliner
crayon^{M} contour^{M} des lèvres^{F}

lipstick
rouge^{M} à lèvres^{F}

body care

soins[M] du corps[M]

stopper
bouchon[M]

bottle
flacon[M]

eau de parfum
eau[F] de parfum[M]

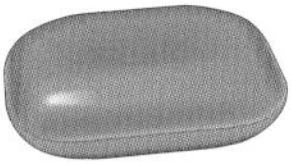

toilet soap
savon[M] de toilette[F]

hair colour
colorant[M] capillaire

hair conditioner
après-shampooing[M]

shampoo
shampooing[M]

deodorant
déodorant[M]

eau de toilette
eau[F] de toilette[F]

bubble bath
bain[M] moussant

face flannel
gant[M] de toilette[F]

face flannel
débarbouillette[F]

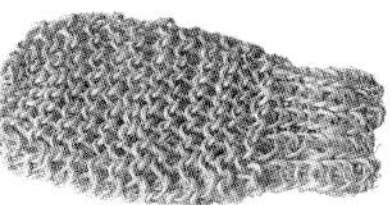

massage glove
gant[M] de crin[M]

vegetable sponge
éponge[F] végétale

bath sheet
drap[M] de bain[M]

bath towel
serviette[F] de toilette[F]

natural sponge
éponge[F] de mer[F]

back brush
brosse[F] pour le dos[M]

bath brush
brosse[F] pour le bain[M]

hairdressing

coiffure[F]

hairbrushes
brosses[F] à cheveux[M]

flat-back brush
brosse[F] pneumatique

round brush
brosse[F] ronde

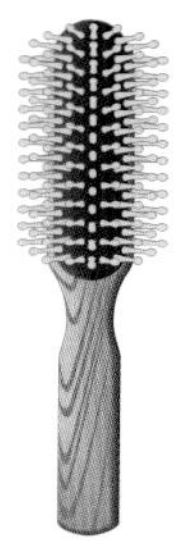
quill brush
brosse[F] anglaise

vent brush
brosse[F]-araignée[F]

combs
peignes[M]

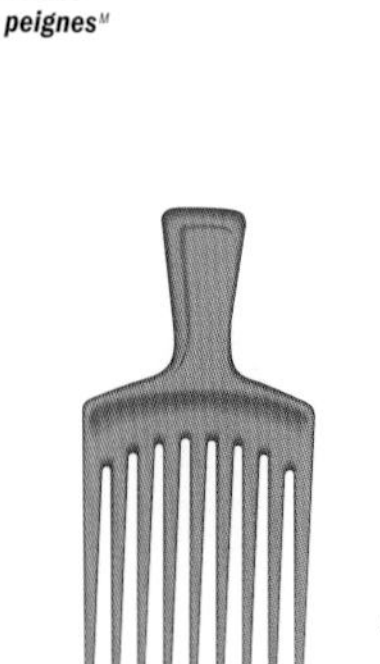
Afro pick
peigne[M] afro

teaser comb
peigne[M] à crêper

tail comb
peigne[M] à tige[F]

barber comb
peigne[M] de coiffeur[M]

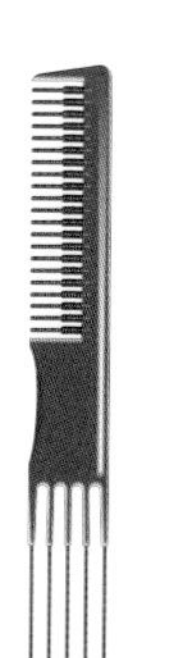
pitchfork comb
combiné[M] 2 dans 1

rake comb
démêloir[M]

hair roller
bigoudi[M]

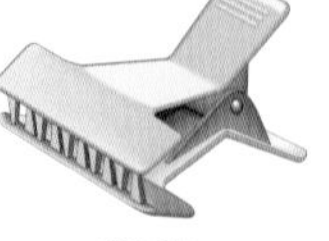
wave clip
pince[F] à boucles[F] de cheveux[M]

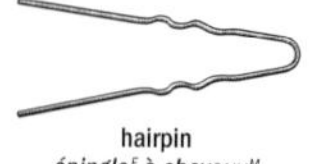
hairpin
épingle[F] à cheveux[M]

hair clip
pince[F] de mise[F] en plis[M]

hair grip
pince[F] à cheveux[M]

hair slide
barrette[F]

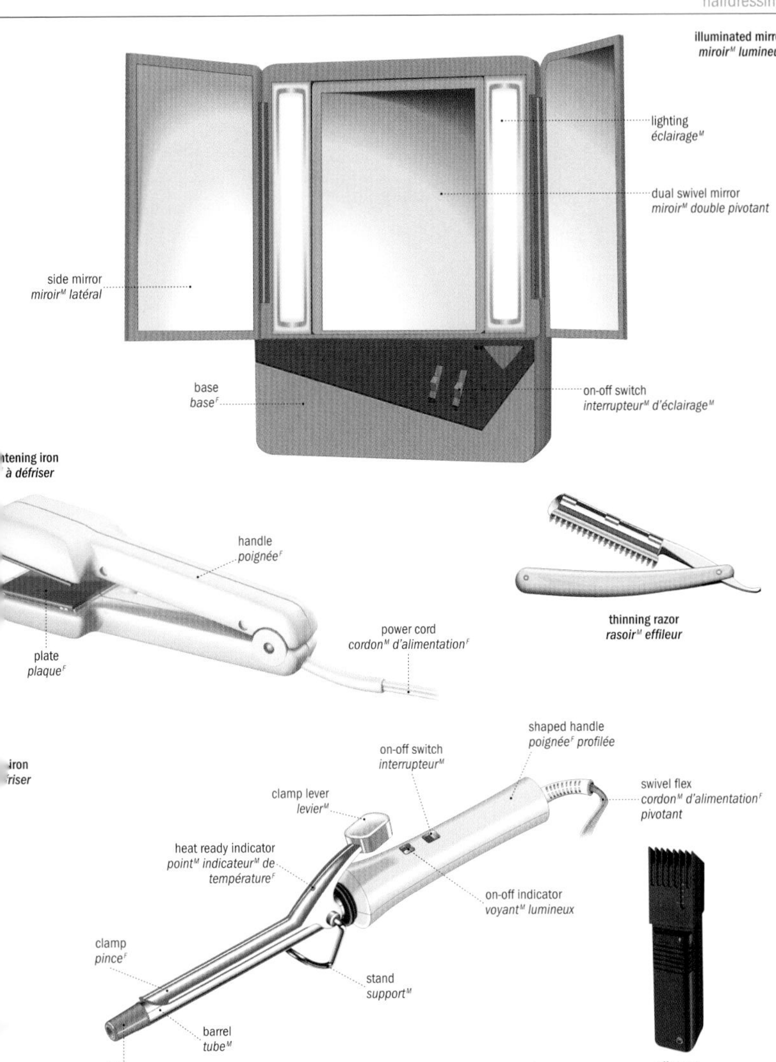
illuminated mirror
miroirM lumineux
lighting
éclairageM
dual swivel mirror
miroirM double pivotant
side mirror
miroirM latéral
base
baseF
on-off switch
interrupteurM d'éclairageM
tening iron
à défriser
handle
poignéeF
plate
plaqueF
power cord
cordonM d'alimentationF
thinning razor
rasoirM effileur
iron
friser
shaped handle
poignéeF profilée
on-off switch
interrupteurM
swivel flex
cordonM d'alimentationF pivotant
clamp lever
levierM
heat ready indicator
pointM indicateurM de températureF
on-off indicator
voyantM lumineux
clamp
pinceF
stand
supportM
barrel
tubeM
cool tip
emboutM isolant
clippers
tondeuseF

hairdressing

haircutting scissors
ciseaux[M] de coiffeur[M]

pivot
pivot[M]
ringhandle
anneau[M]
cutting edge
tranchant[M]
blade
lame[F]
blade close stop
amortisseur[M]
shank
branche[F]

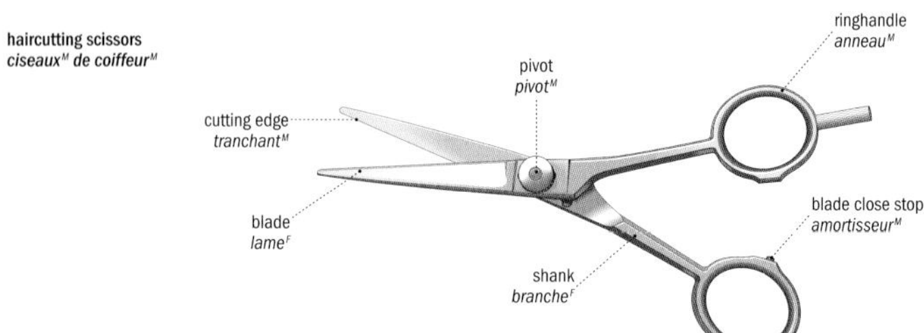

notched single-edged thinning scissors
ciseaux[M] sculpteurs

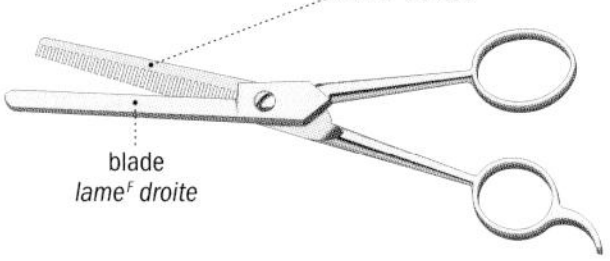

notched edge
lame[F] dentée
blade
lame[F] droite

notched double-edged t
ciseaux[M]

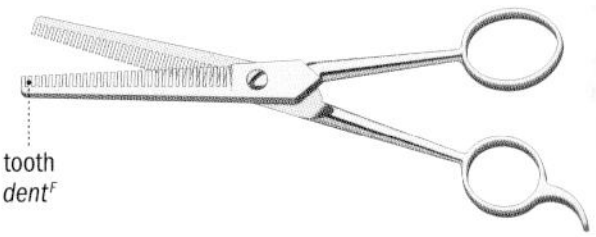

tooth
dent[F]

hair dryer
sèche-cheveux[M]

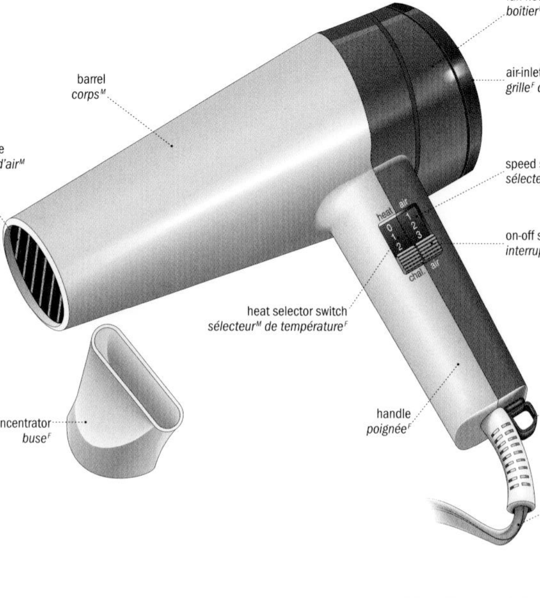

fan housing
boîtier[M] du ventilateur[M]
barrel
corps[M]
air-inlet grille
grille[F] d'aspiration[F]
air-outlet grille
grille[F] de sortie[F] d'air[M]
speed selector switch
sélecteur[M] de vitesse[F]
heat
air
0
1
2
1
2
3
chal.
air
on-off switch
interrupteur[M]
heat selector switch
sélecteur[M] de température[F]
hang-up ring
anneau[M] de susper
air concentrator
buse[F]
handle
poignée[F]
flex
cordon[M] d'alimentatio

PERSONAL ADORNMENT AND ARTICLES

shaving
rasage[M]

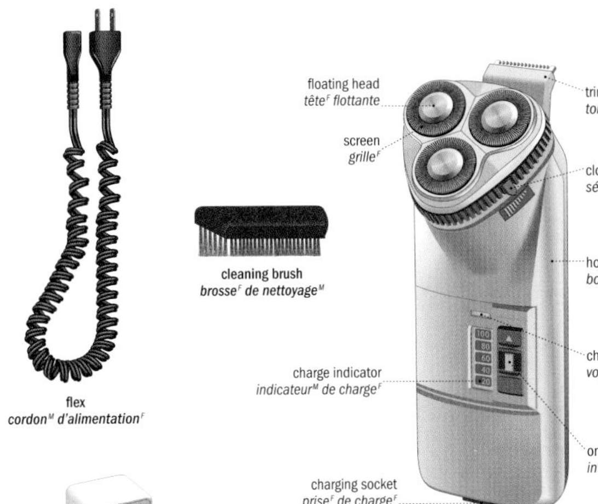

shaving foam
mousse[F] à raser

flex
cordon[M] d'alimentation[F]

cleaning brush
brosse[F] de nettoyage[M]

shaving brush
blaireau[M]

plug adapter
adaptateur[M] de fiche[F]

aftershave
après-rasage[M]

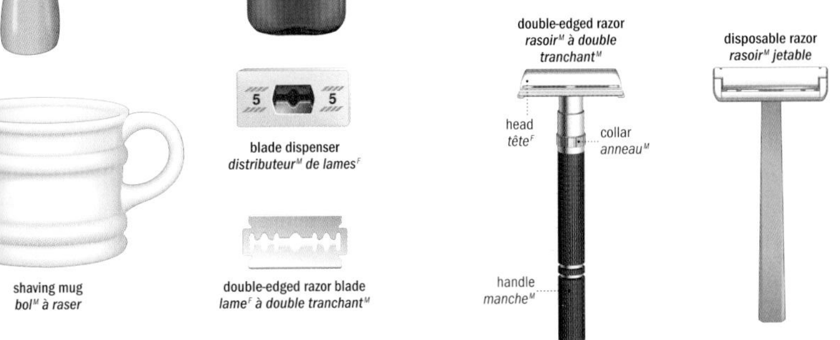

shaving mug
bol[M] à raser

blade dispenser
distributeur[M] de lames[F]

double-edged razor blade
lame[F] à double tranchant[M]

double-edged razor
rasoir[M] à double tranchant[M]

disposable razor
rasoir[M] jetable

dental care

hygiène^{F} dentaire

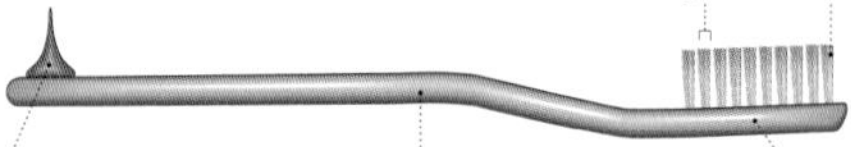

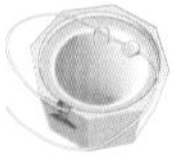

row
rang^{M}
bristle
poil^{M}
gum massager
stimulateur^{M} de gencives^{F}
handle
manche^{M}
head
tête^{F}

toothbrush
brosse^{F} à dents^{F}

dental floss
fil^{M} dentaire

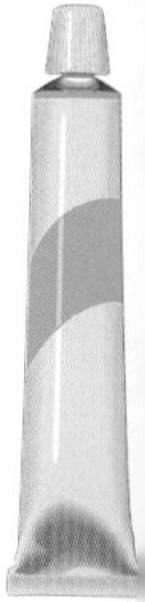

toothpaste
dentifrice^{M}

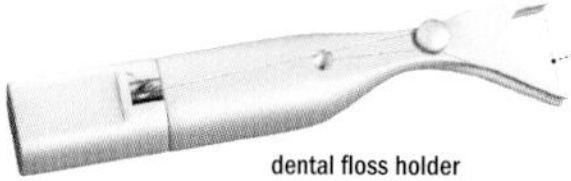

dental floss
fil^{M} dentaire

dental floss holder
porte-fil^{M} dentaire

electric toothbrush
combiné^{M} bucco-dentaire

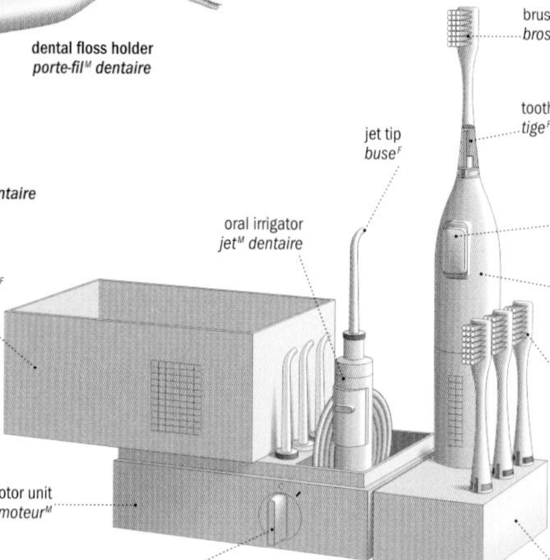

brush
brosse^{F}
toothbrush shaft
tige^{F}
jet tip
buse^{F}
on-off switch
interrupteur^{M}
oral irrigator
jet^{M} dentaire
water tank
réserve^{F} d'eau^{F}
handle
manche^{M}
toothbrush
brosse^{F} à dents^{F}
motor unit
bloc^{M}-moteur^{M}
pressure control
réglage^{M} de la pression^{F}
toothbrush well
réceptacle^{M} de brosses^{F}

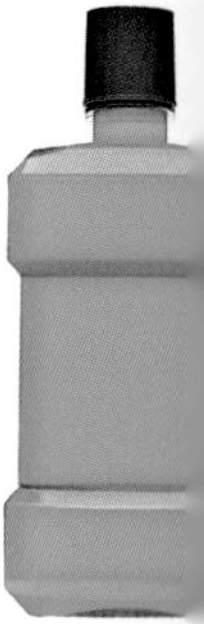

mouthwash
eau^{F} dentifric

contact lenses

lentilles^{F} de contact^{M}

multi-purpose solution
solution^{F} multifonctions

lubricant eye drops
gouttes^{F} ophtalmiques lubrifiantes

disposable contact lens
lentille^{F} jetable

soft contact lens
lentille^{F} souple

hard contact lens
lentille^{F} rigide

left side
logement^{M} gauche
right side
logement^{M} dr

lens case
étui^{M} à lentilles^{F}

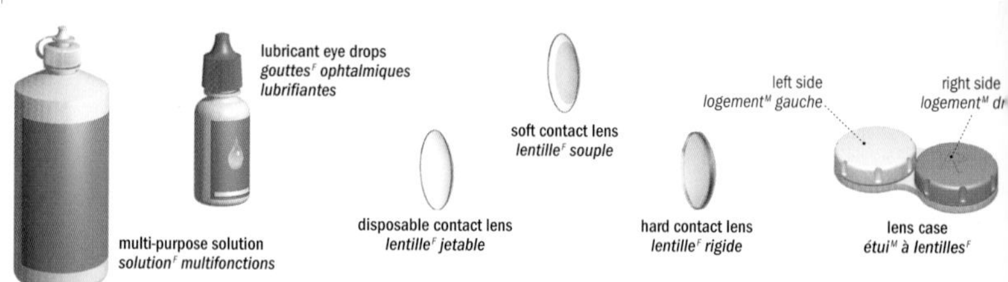

spectacles

lunettes[F]

parts of spectacles
parties[F] des lunettes[F]

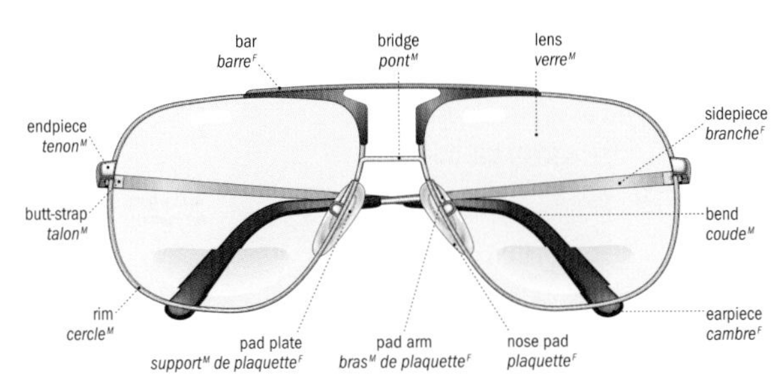

examples of spectacles
exemples[M] de lunettes[F]

opera glasses
lorgnette[F]

sunglasses
lunettes[F] de soleil[M]

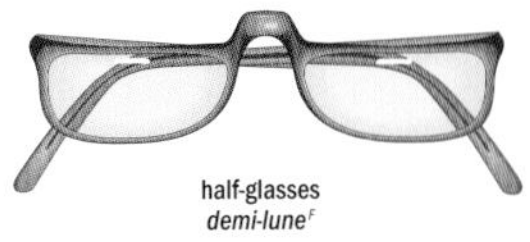

half-glasses
demi-lune[F]

umbrella and stick

parapluie[M] et canne[F]

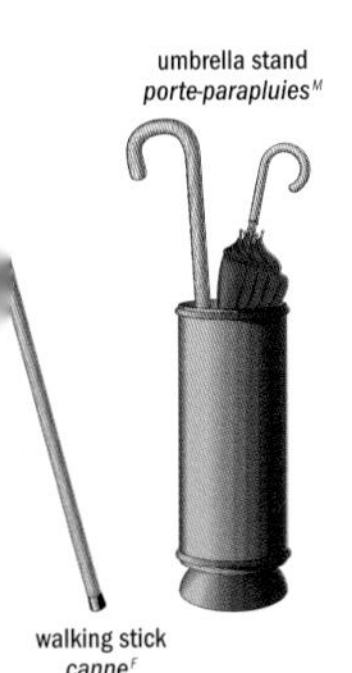

umbrella stand
porte-parapluies[M]

walking stick
canne[F]

umbrella
parapluie[M]

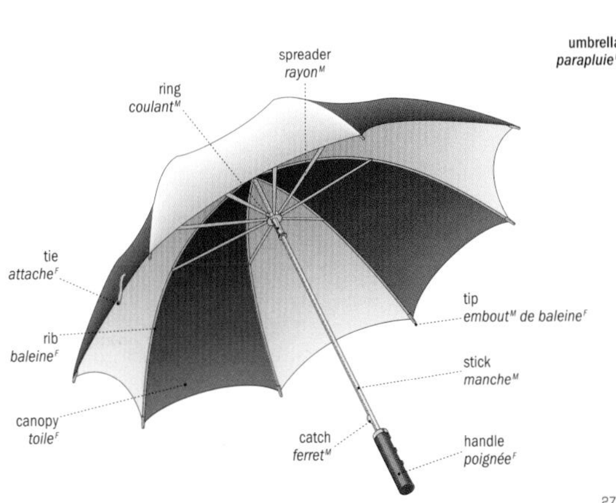

leather goods

articles^M de maroquinerie^F

attaché case
mallette^F porte-documents^M

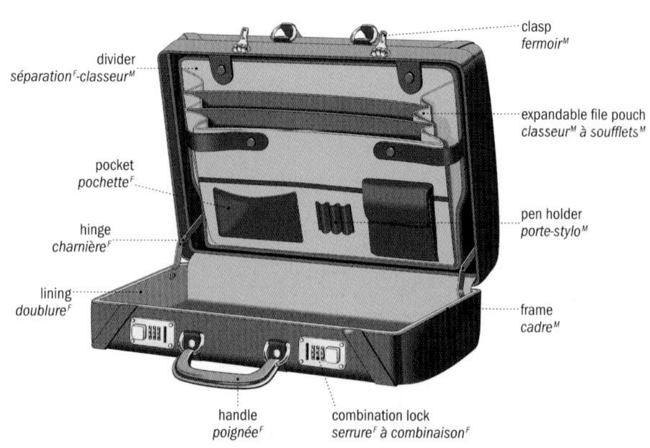

bottom-fold document case
porte-documents^M à soufflet^M

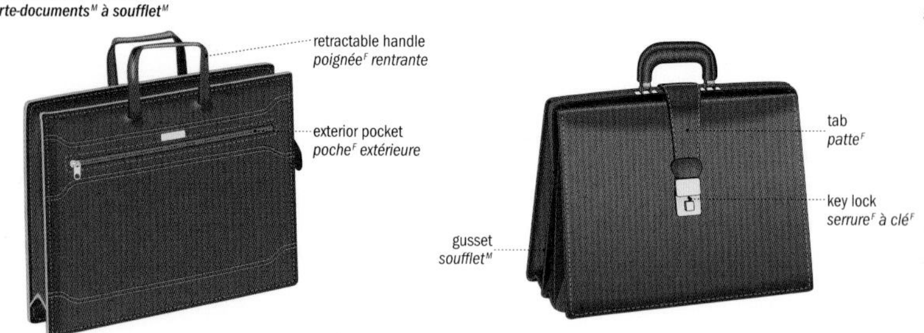

calculator/cheque book holder
portefeuille^M chéquier^M

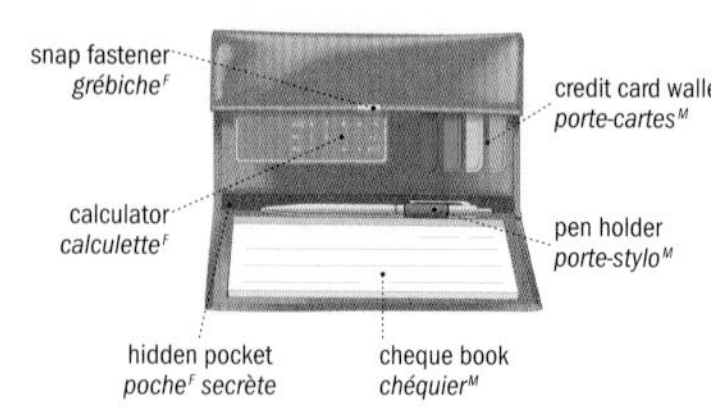

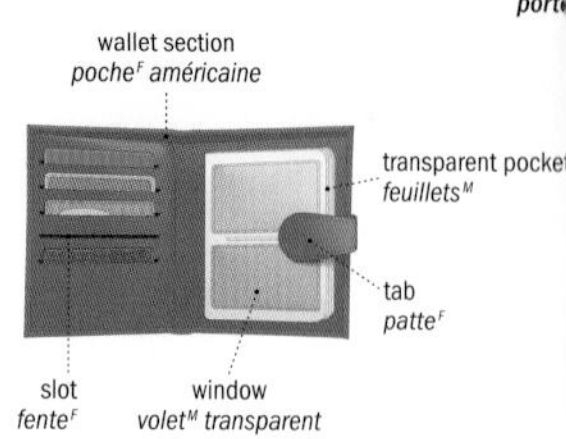

leather goods

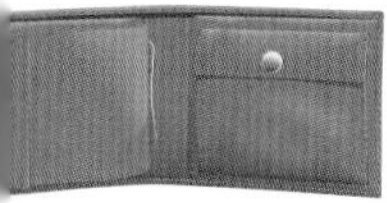

wallet
*portefeuille*ᴹ

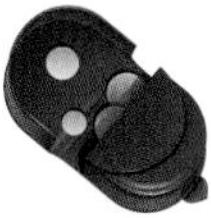

coin purse
*porte-monnaie*ᴹ

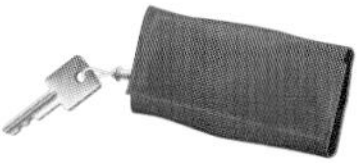

key case
*porte-clés*ᴹ

purse
*bourse*ᶠ *à monnaie*ᶠ

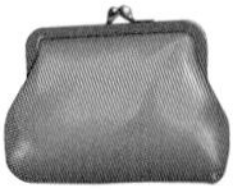

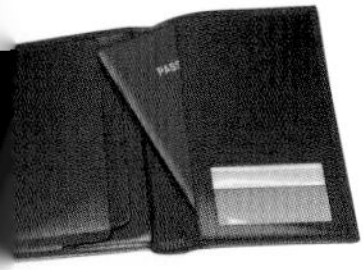

passport case
*porte-passeport*ᴹ

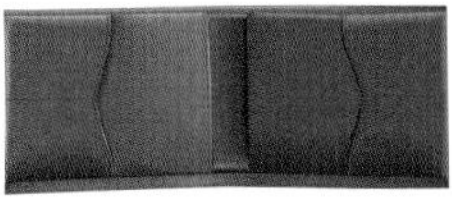

wallet
*porte-coupures*ᴹ

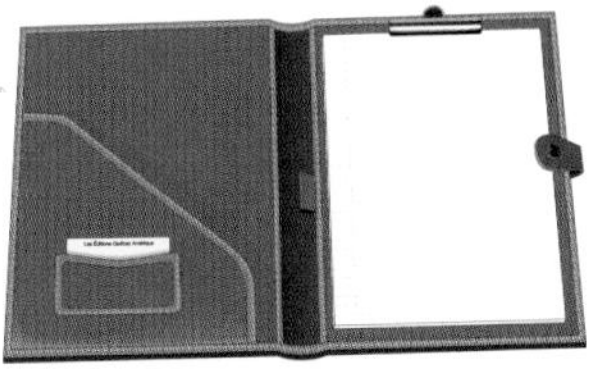

writing case
*écritoire*ᶠ

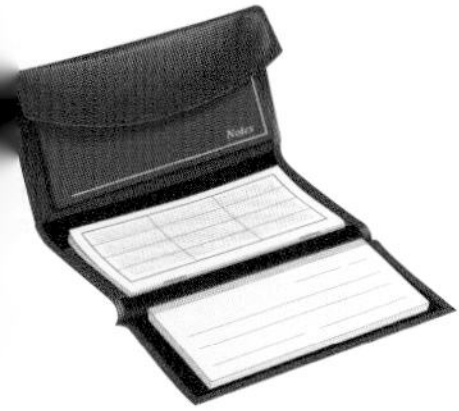

cheque book cover
*porte-chéquier*ᴹ

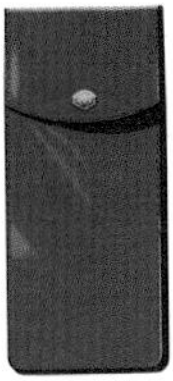

spectacles case
*étui*ᴹ *à lunettes*ᶠ

underarm briefcase
*porte-documents*ᴹ *plat*

handbags

sacsᴹ à mainᶠ

drawstring bag
*sac*ᴹ *seau*ᴹ

satchel bag
*sac*ᴹ *cartable*ᴹ

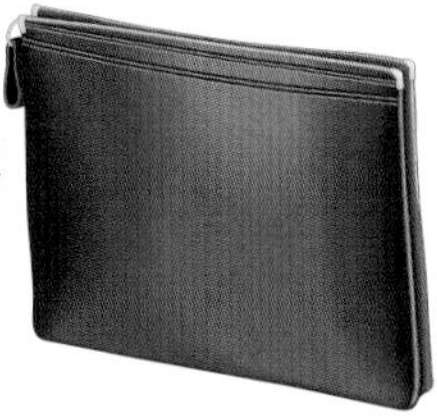

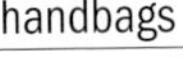

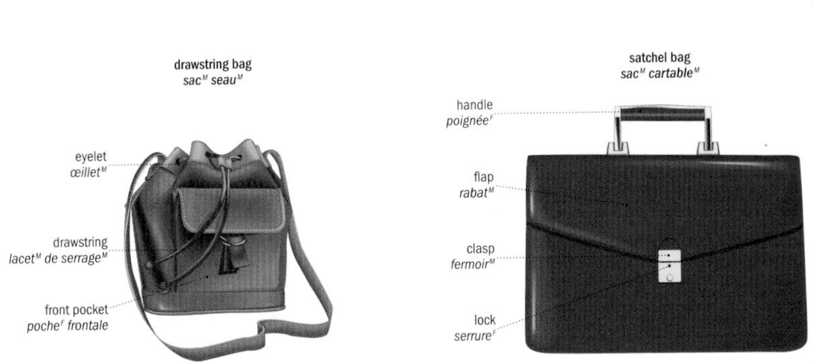

handbags

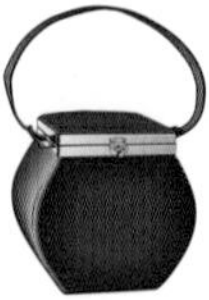

box bag
sac[M] boîte[F]

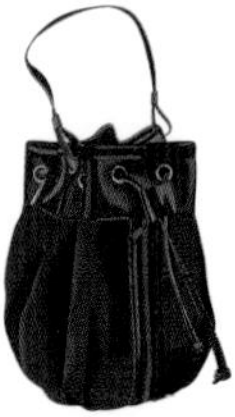

small drawstring bag
balluchon[M]

shoulder bag
sac[M] à bandoulière[F]

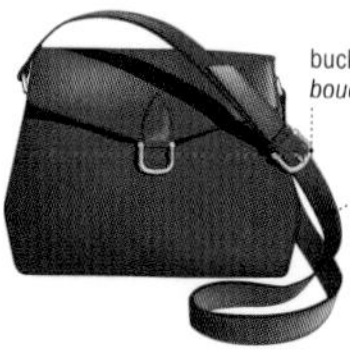

buckle
boucle[F]

shoulder strap
bandoulière[F]

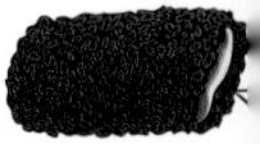

muff
manchon[M]

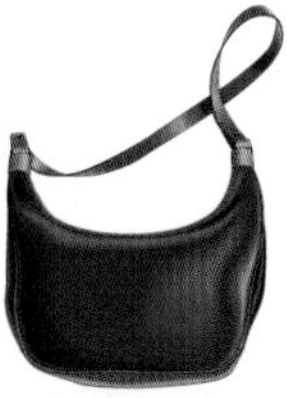

shoulder bag with zip
sac[M] besace[F]

accordion bag
sac[M] accordéon[M]

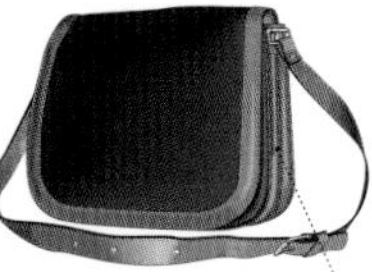

gusset
soufflet[M]

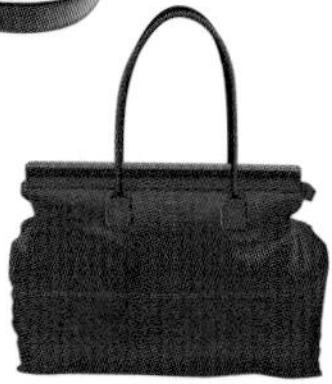

tote bag
sac[M] fourre-tout[M]

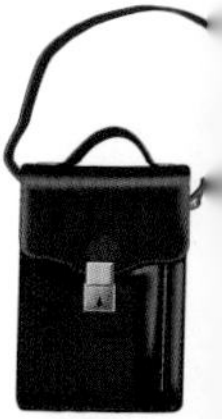

men's bag
pochette[F] d'homme

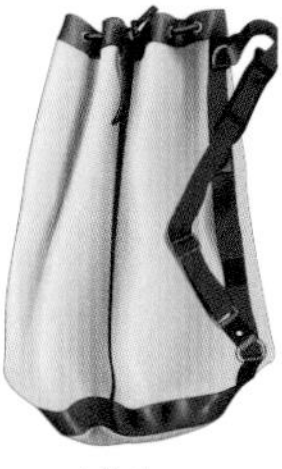

duffle bag
sac[M] marin[M]

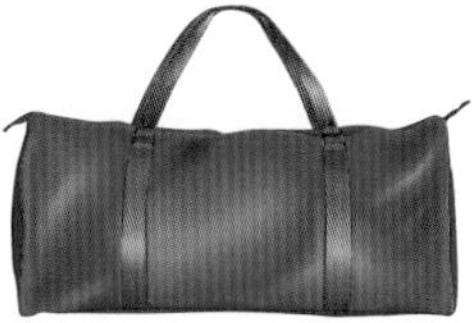

holdall
sac[M] polochon[M]

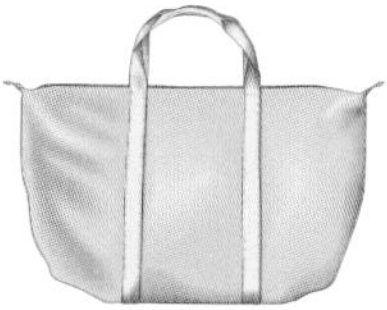

shopping bag
sac[M] à provisions[F]

shopping bag
cabas[M]

luggage

bagages[M]

toilet bag
trousse[F] de toilette[F]

travel bag
bagage[M] à main[F]

handle
poignée[F]

exterior pocket
poche[F] extérieure

shoulder strap
bandoulière[F]

flight bag
sac[M] fourre-tout[M]

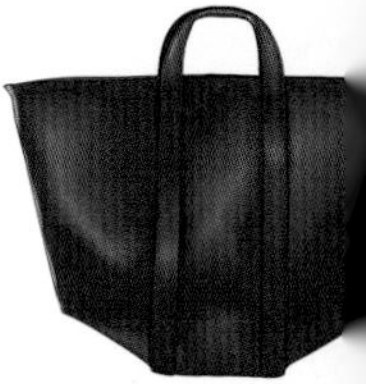

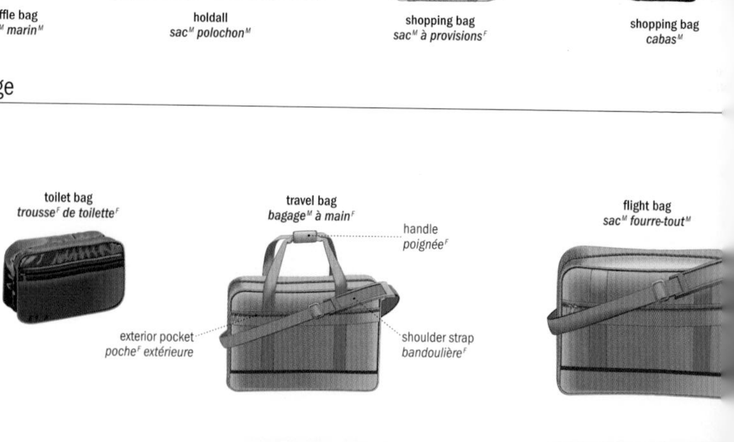

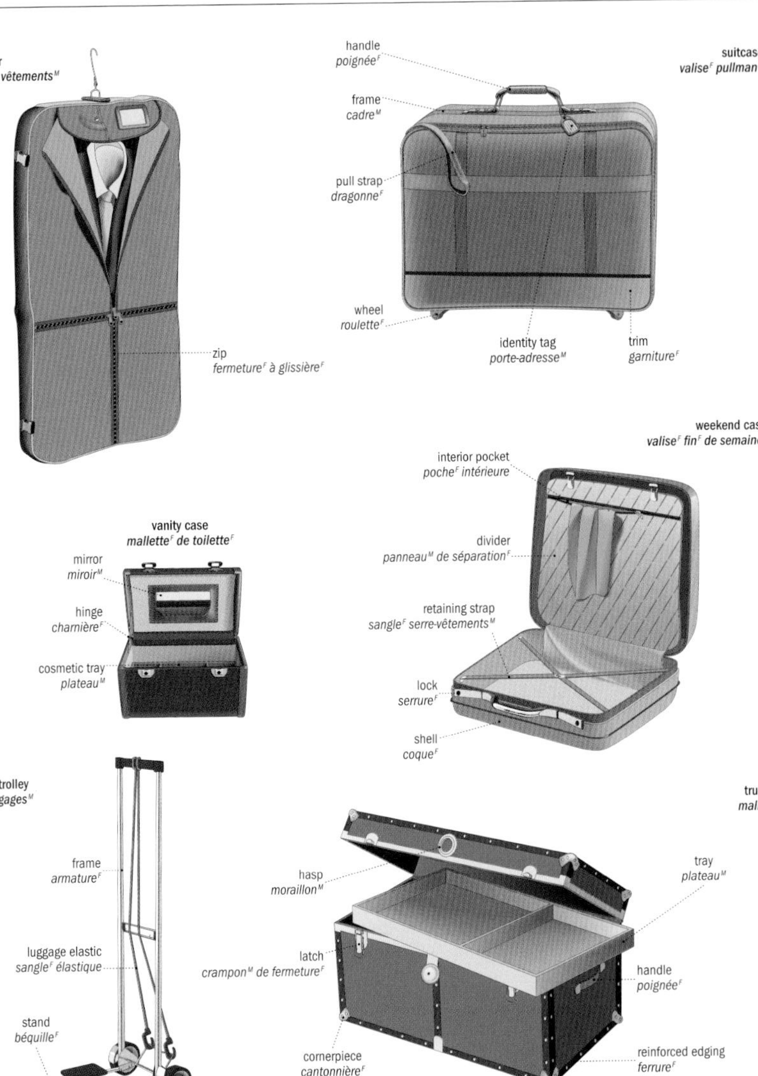
rier
F à vêtementsM
zip
fermetureF à glissièreF
handle
poignéeF
suitcase
valiseF pullmanM
frame
cadreM
pull strap
dragonneF
wheel
rouletteF
identity tag
porte-adresseM
trim
garnitureF
weekend case
valiseF finF de semaineF
interior pocket
pocheF intérieure
divider
panneauM de séparationF
retaining strap
sangleF serre-vêtementsM
lock
serrureF
shell
coqueF
vanity case
malletteF de toiletteF
mirror
miroirM
hinge
charnièreF
cosmetic tray
plateauM
e trolley
bagagesM
frame
armatureF
luggage elastic
sangleF élastique
stand
béquilleF
trunk
malleF
hasp
moraillonM
tray
plateauM
latch
cramponM de fermetureF
handle
poignéeF
cornerpiece
cantonnièreF
reinforced edging
ferrureF

pyramid

pyramide[F]

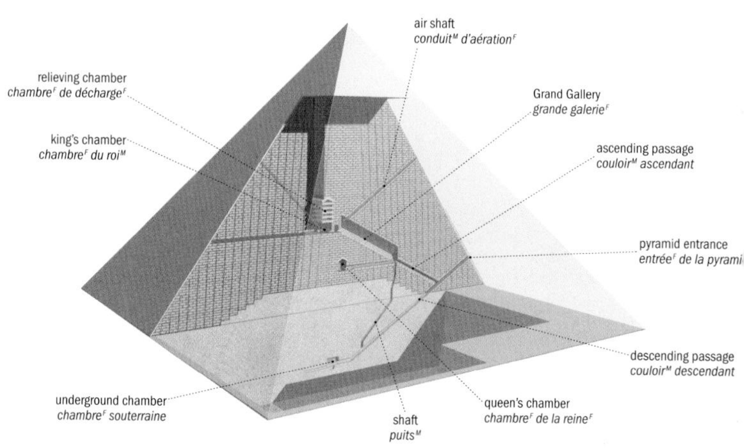

Greek theatre

théâtre[M] grec

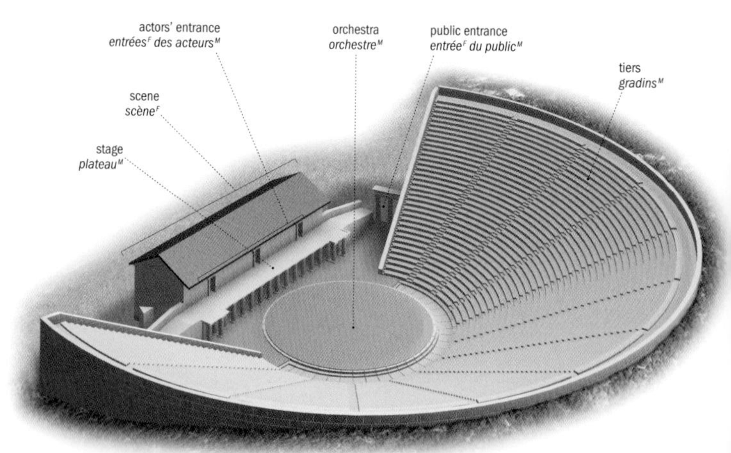

Greek temple

temple^M grec

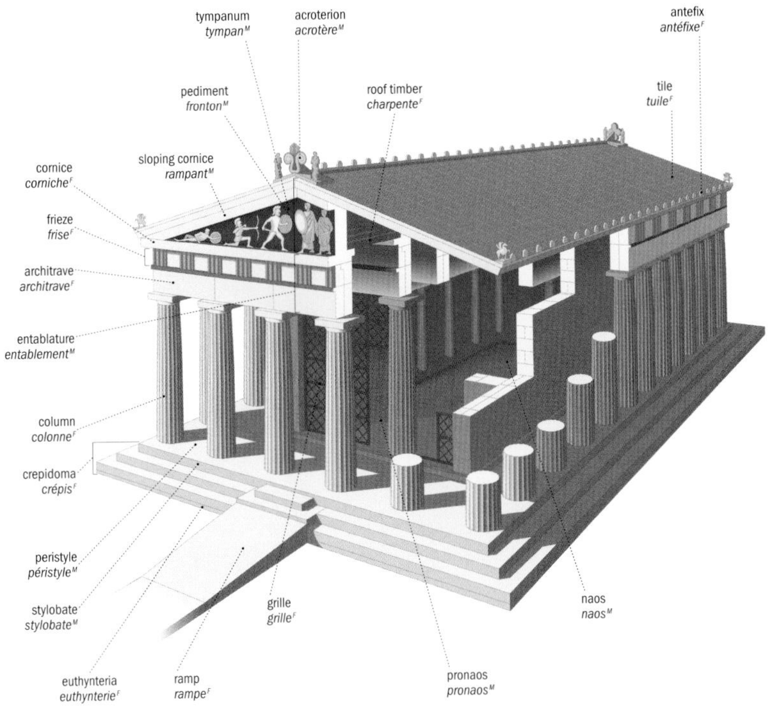

tympanum
tympan^M
acroterion
acrotère^M
antefix
antéfixe^F
pediment
fronton^M
roof timber
charpente^F
tile
tuile^F
sloping cornice
rampant^M
cornice
corniche^F
frieze
frise^F
architrave
architrave^F
entablature
entablement^M
column
colonne^F
crepidoma
crépis^F
peristyle
péristyle^M
stylobate
stylobate^M
grille
grille^F
naos
naos^M
euthynteria
euthynterie^F
ramp
rampe^F
pronaos
pronaos^M

plan
plan^M

naos
naos^M
location of the statue
emplacement^M de la statue^F
opisthodomos
opisthodome^M
pronaos
pronaos^M
peristyle
péristyle^M
crepidoma
crépis^F
column
colonne^F

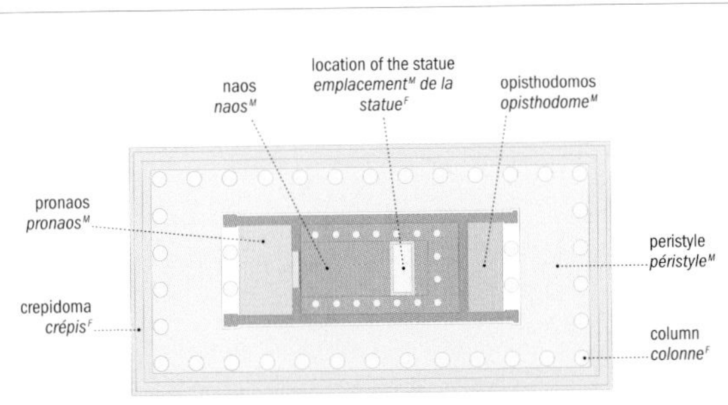

Roman house

maison^F romaine

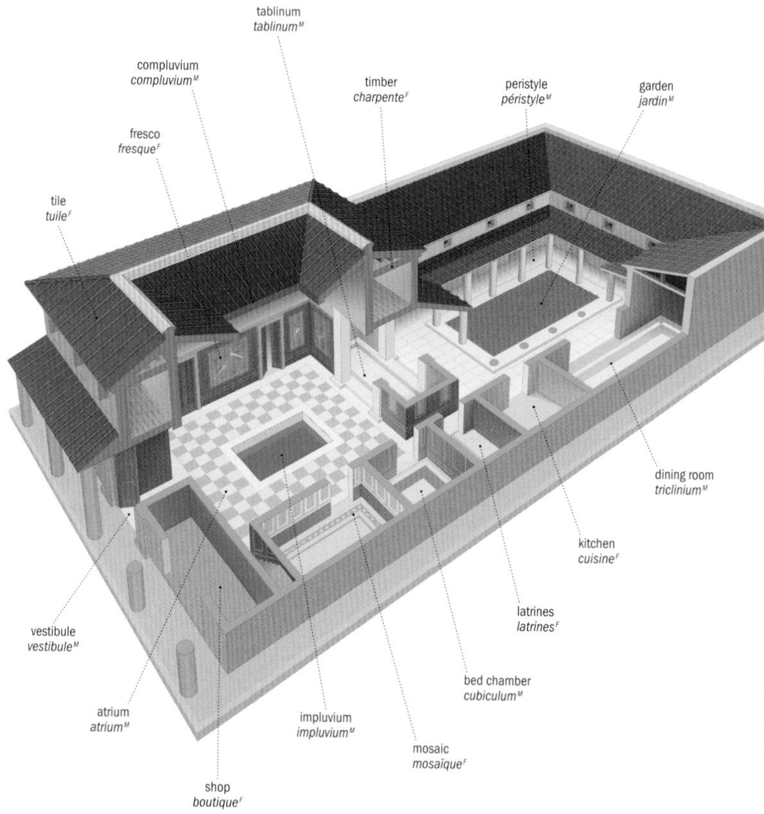

Roman amphitheatre

amphithéâtre[M] romain

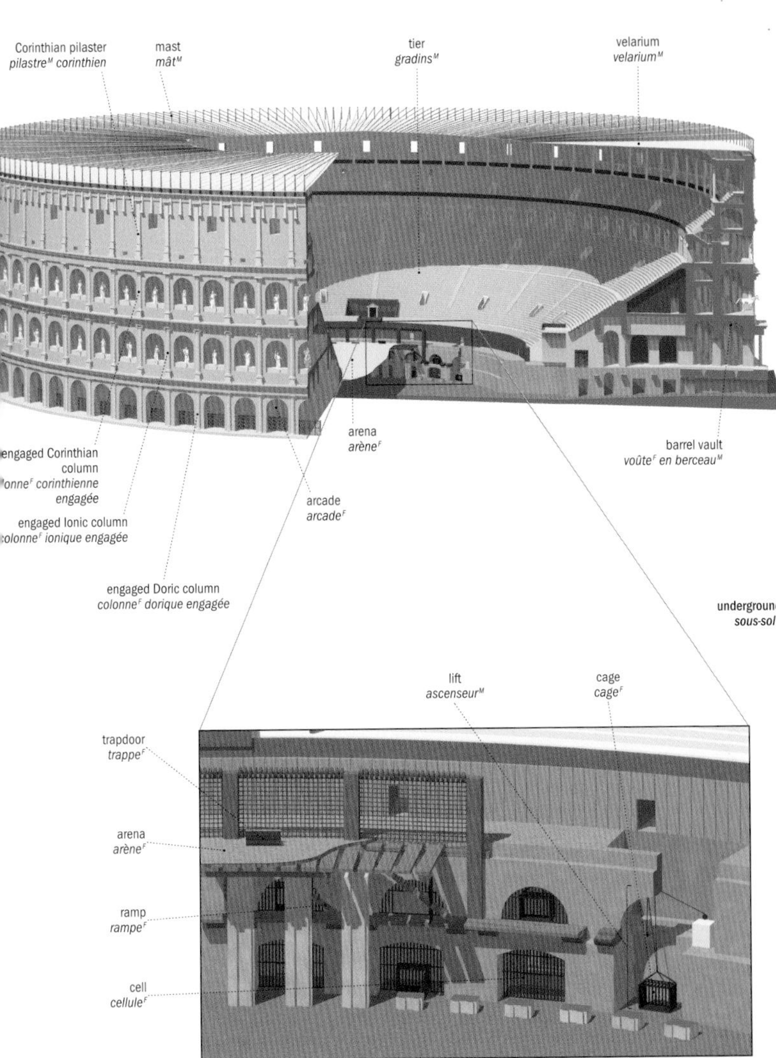

castle

château[M] fort

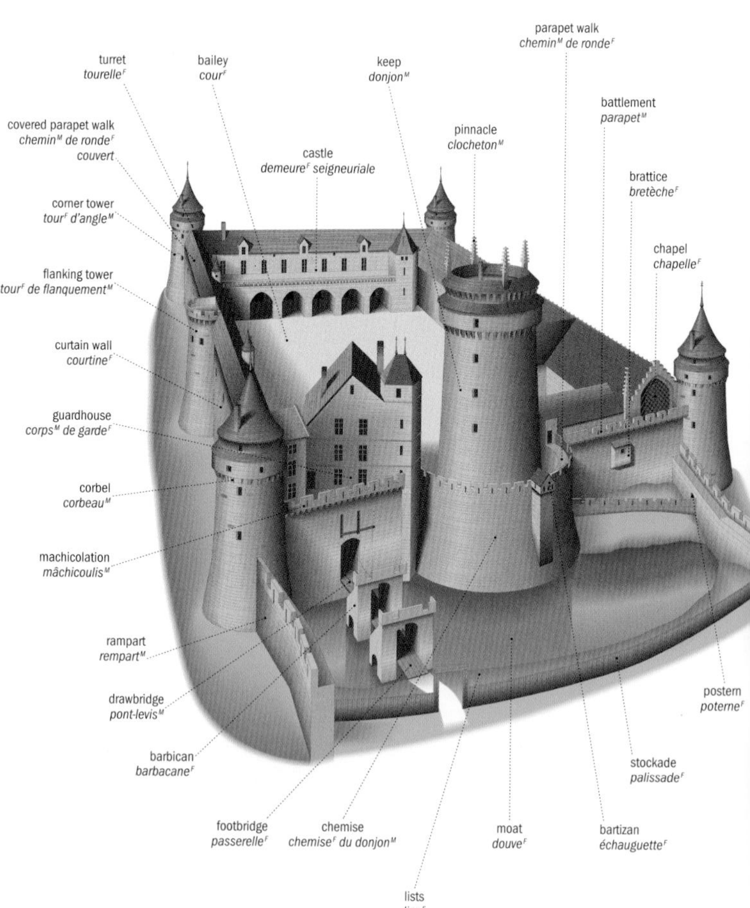

pagoda

pagode[F]

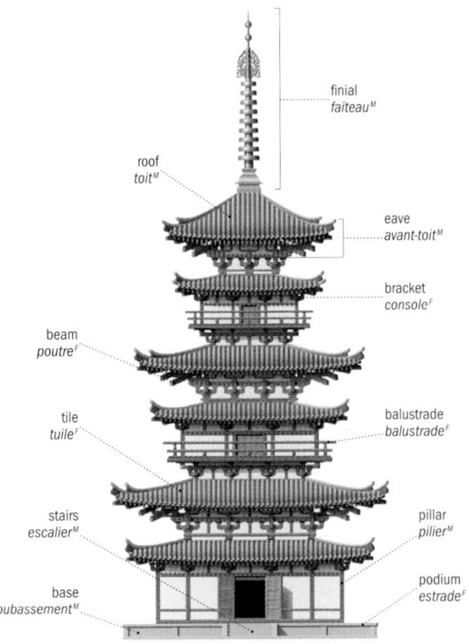

Aztec temple

temple[M] aztèque

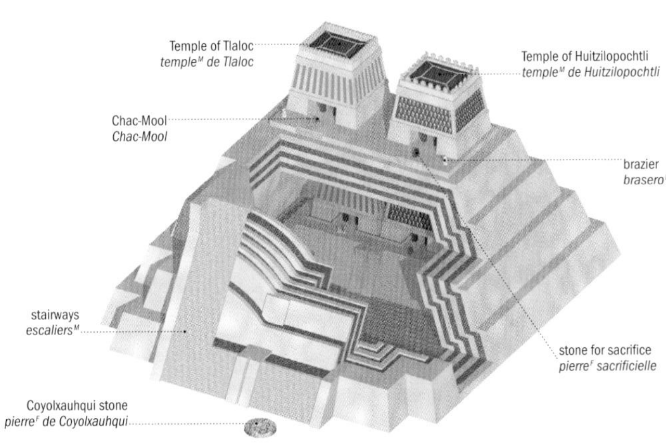

cathedral

cathédrale[F]

Gothic cathedral
cathédrale[F] gothique

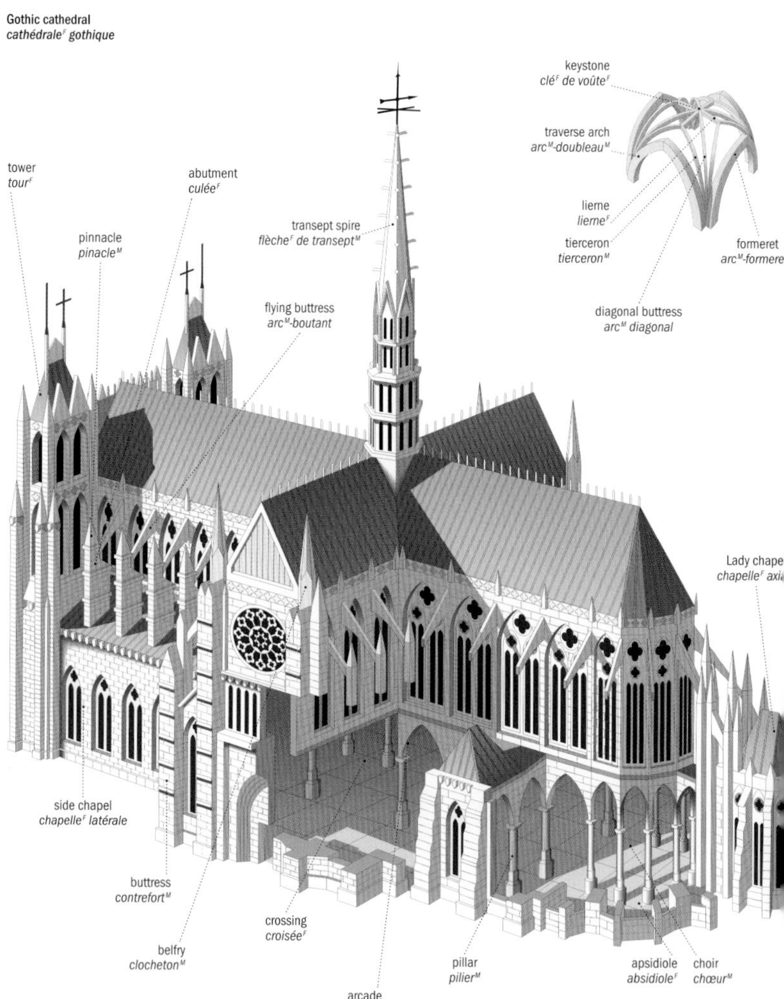

cathedral

façade
façade[F]

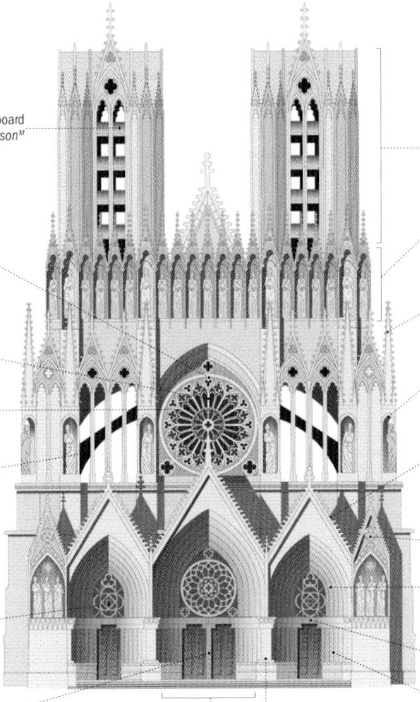

louvre-board
abat-son[M]
bell tower
clocher[M]
gallery
galerie[F]
rose window
rose[F]
spire
flèche[F]
tracery
remplage[M]
pinnacle
clocheton[M]
stained glass
vitrail[M]
gable
gâble[M]
flying buttress
arc[M]-boutant
trefoil
trèfle[M]
order
voussure[F]
tympanum
tympan[M]
lintel
linteau[M]
splay
ébrasement[M]
pier
trumeau[M]
portal
portail[M]
pier
piédroit[M]

plan
plan[M]

transept
transept[M]
ambulatory
déambulatoire[M]
apsidiole
absidiole[F]
aisle
collatéral[M]
chevet
chevet[M]
nave
nef[F]
Lady chapel
chapelle[F] axiale
porch
porche[M]
crossing
croisée[F] du transept[M]
choir
chœur[M]
apse
abside[F]

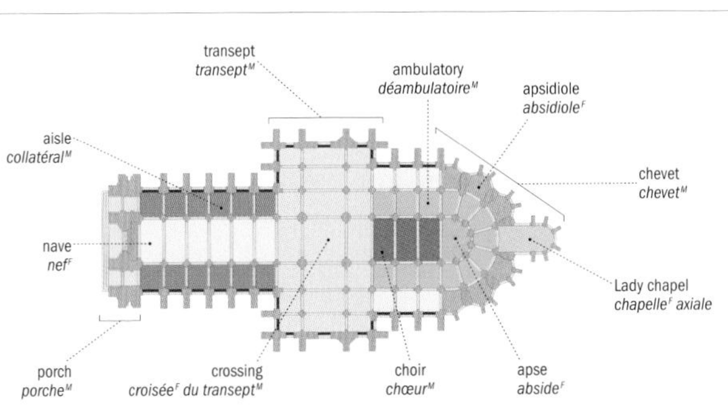

elements of architecture

éléments[M] d'architecture[F]

examples of doors
exemples[M] de portes[F]

manual revolving door
porte[F] à tambour[M] manuelle

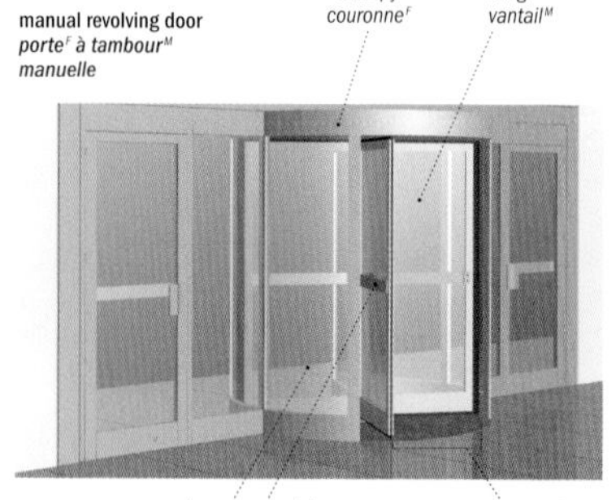

automatic slidi
porte[F] coul
auton

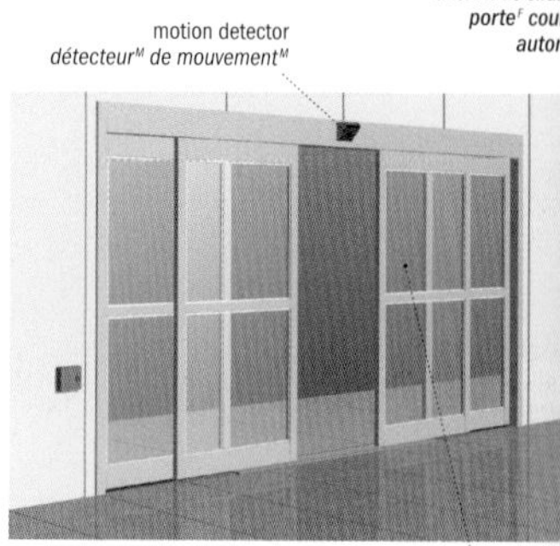

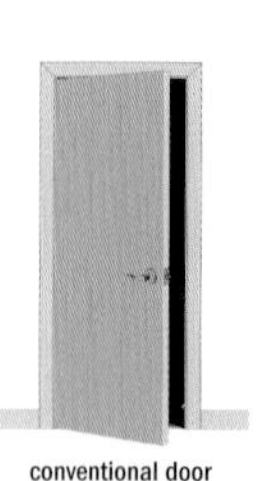

conventional door
porte[F] classique

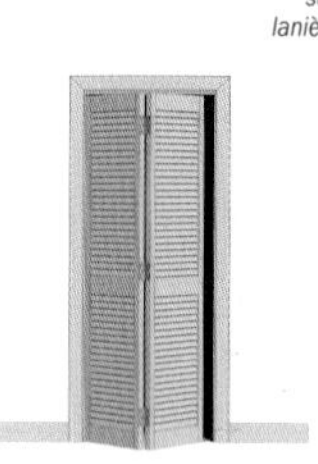

folding door
porte[F] pliante

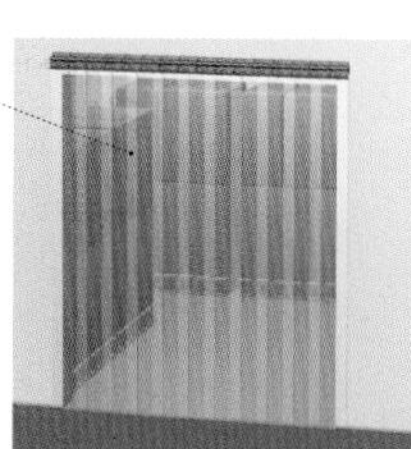

strip door
porte[F] à lanières[F]

fire door
porte[F] coupe-feu

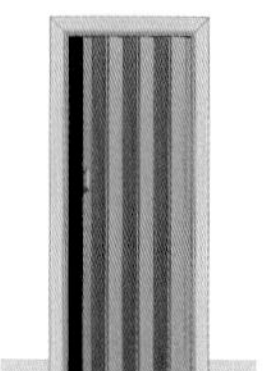

concertina-type folding door
porte[F] accordéon[M]

sliding door
porte[F] coulissante

sectional garage door
porte[F] de garage[M] sectionnelle

up-and-over garage door
porte[F] de garage[M] basculante

examples of windows
exemples^M de fenêtres^F

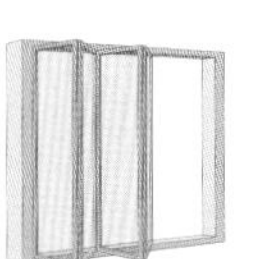
sliding folding window
fenêtre^F en accordéon^M

casement window opening inwards
fenêtre^F à la française^F

casement window
fenêtre^F à l'anglaise^F

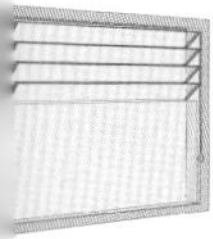

louvred window
nêtre^F à jalousies^F

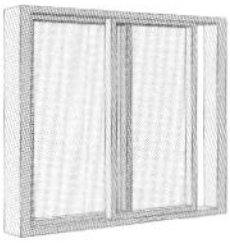

sliding window
fenêtre^F coulissante

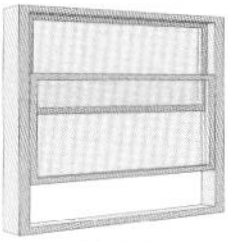

sash window
fenêtre^F à guillotine^F

horizontal pivoting window
fenêtre^F basculante

vertical pivoting window
fenêtre^F pivotante

lift
ascenseur^M

^F d'ascenseur^M

position indicator
indicateur^M de position^F

car ceiling
plafond^M de cabine^F

operating panel
tableau^M de manœuvre^F

handrail
main^F courante

car floor
plancher^M de cabine^F

door
porte^F

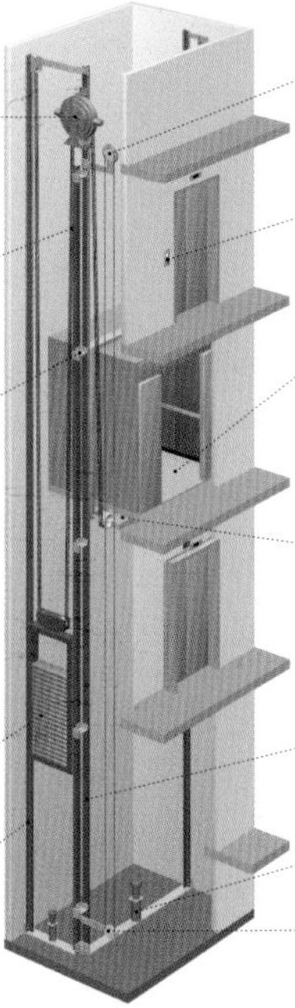

winch
treuil^M

hoisting rope
câble^M de levage^M

limit switch
interrupteur^M de fin^F de course^F

counterweight
contrepoids^M

counterweight guide rail
rail^M-guide^M de contrepoids^M

speed governor
régulateur^M de vitesse^F

call button
bouton^M d'appel^M

lift car
cabine^F d'ascenseur^M

car safety
parachute^M de cabine^F

car guide rail
rail^M-guide^M de la cabine^F

buffer
amortisseur^M

governor tension sheave
poulie^F de tension^F du régulateur^M

traditional dwellings

maisons[F] traditionnelles

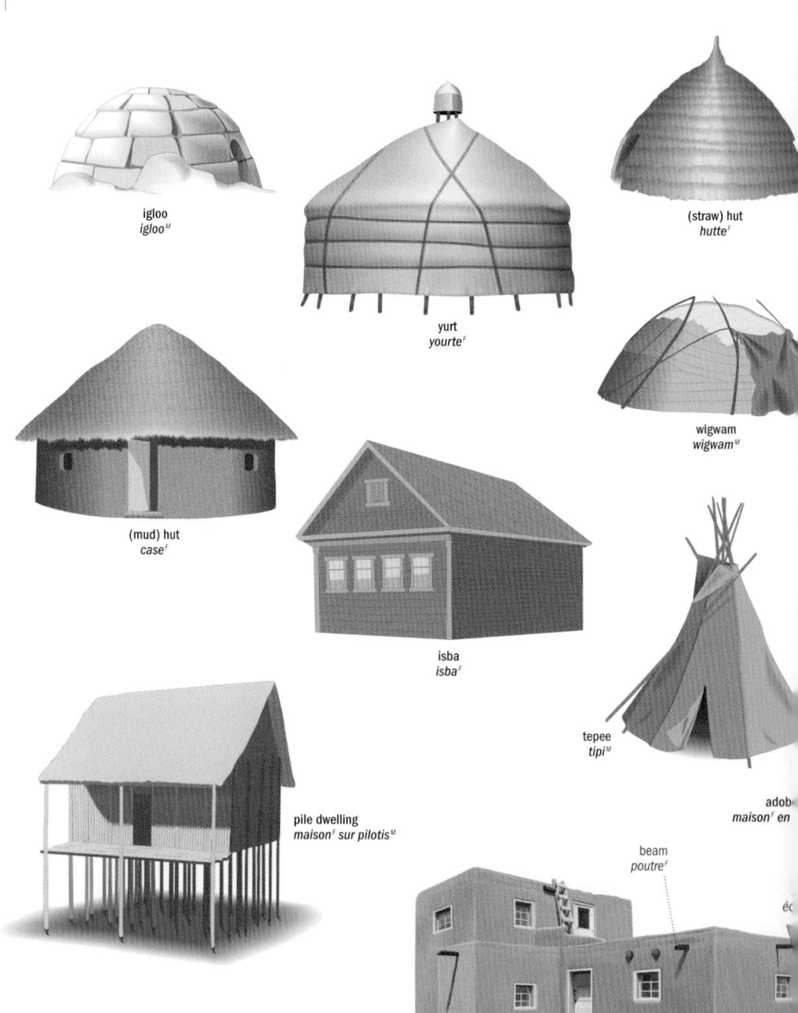

town houses

maisons^F de ville^F

two-storey house
maison^F à étage^M

one-storey-house
maison^F de plain-pied^M

semi-detached houses
maison^F jumelée

terraced houses
maisons^F en rangée^F

freehold flats
appartements^M en copropriété^F

high-rise block
tour^F d'habitation^F

shooting stage

plateau[M] de tournage[M]

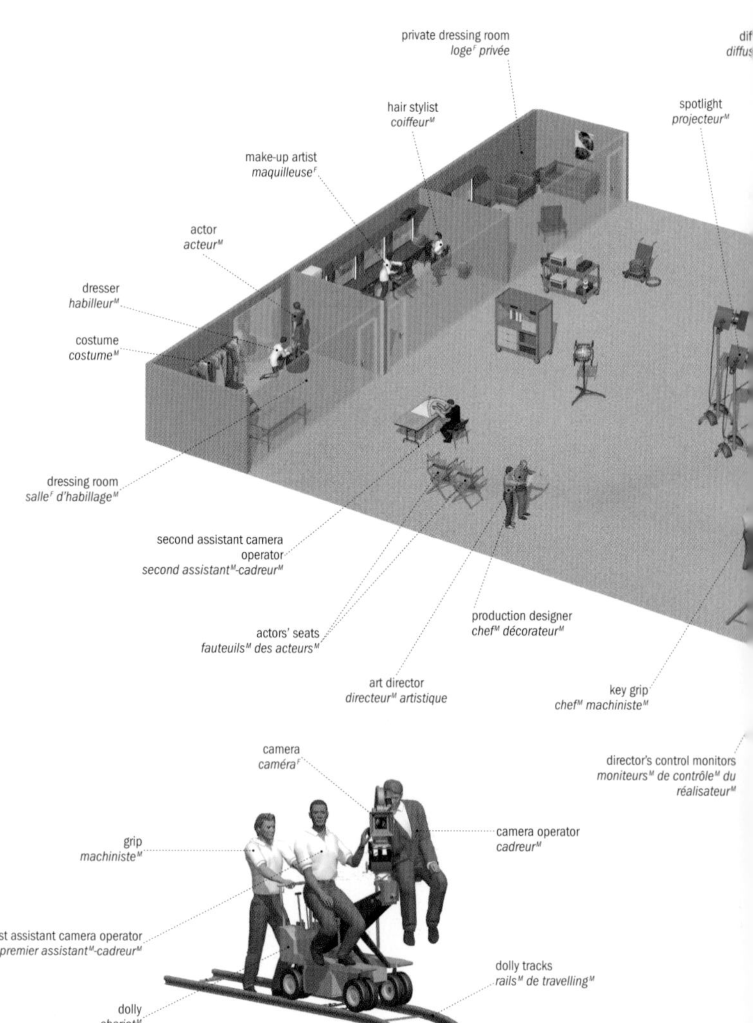

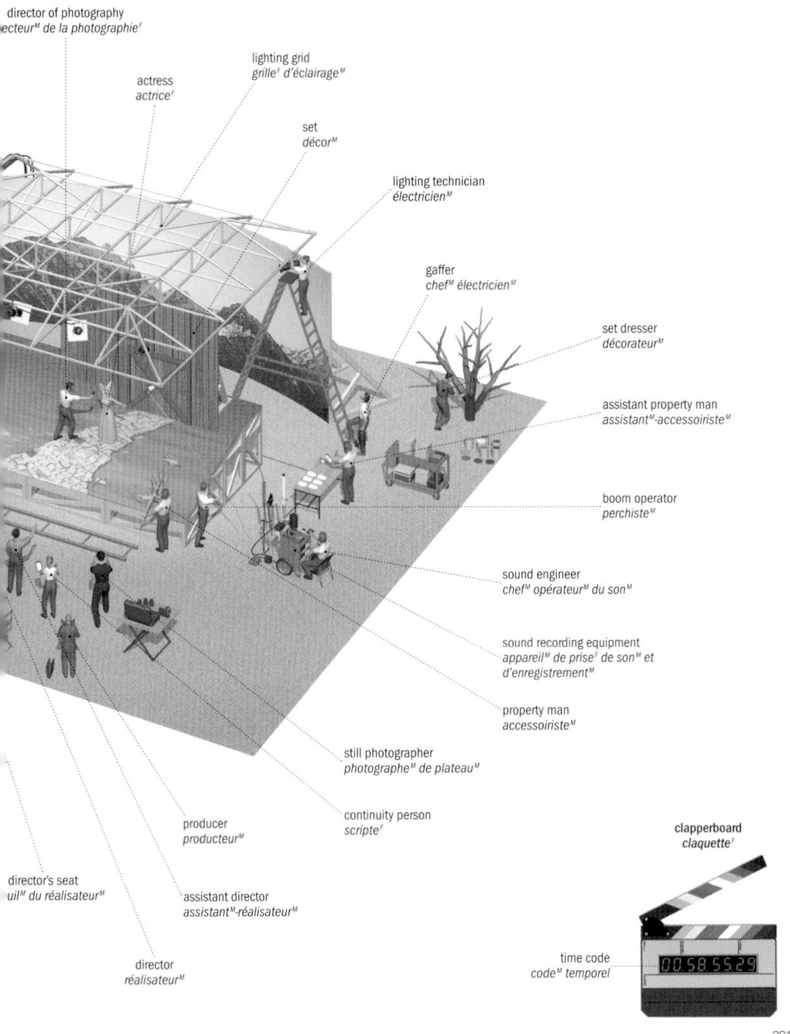
director of photography
ecteur^M de la photographie^F
lighting grid
grille^F d'éclairage^M
actress
actrice^F
set
décor^M
lighting technician
électricien^M
gaffer
chef^M électricien^M
set dresser
décorateur^M
assistant property man
assistant^M-accessoiriste^M
boom operator
perchiste^M
sound engineer
chef^M opérateur^M du son^M
sound recording equipment
appareil^M de prise^F de son^M et d'enregistrement^M
property man
accessoiriste^M
still photographer
photographe^M de plateau^M
continuity person
scripte^F
producer
producteur^M
director's seat
uil^M du réalisateur^M
assistant director
assistant^M-réalisateur^M
director
réalisateur^M
clapperboard
claquette^F
time code
code^M temporel
00 58 55 29

theatre

salle^{F} de spectacle^{M}

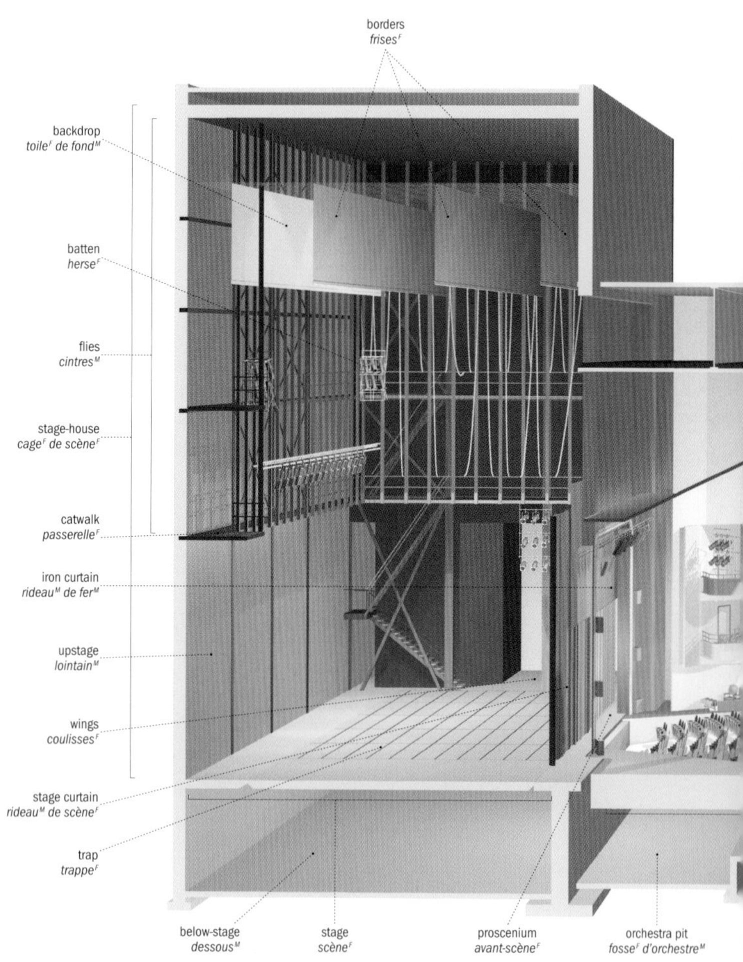

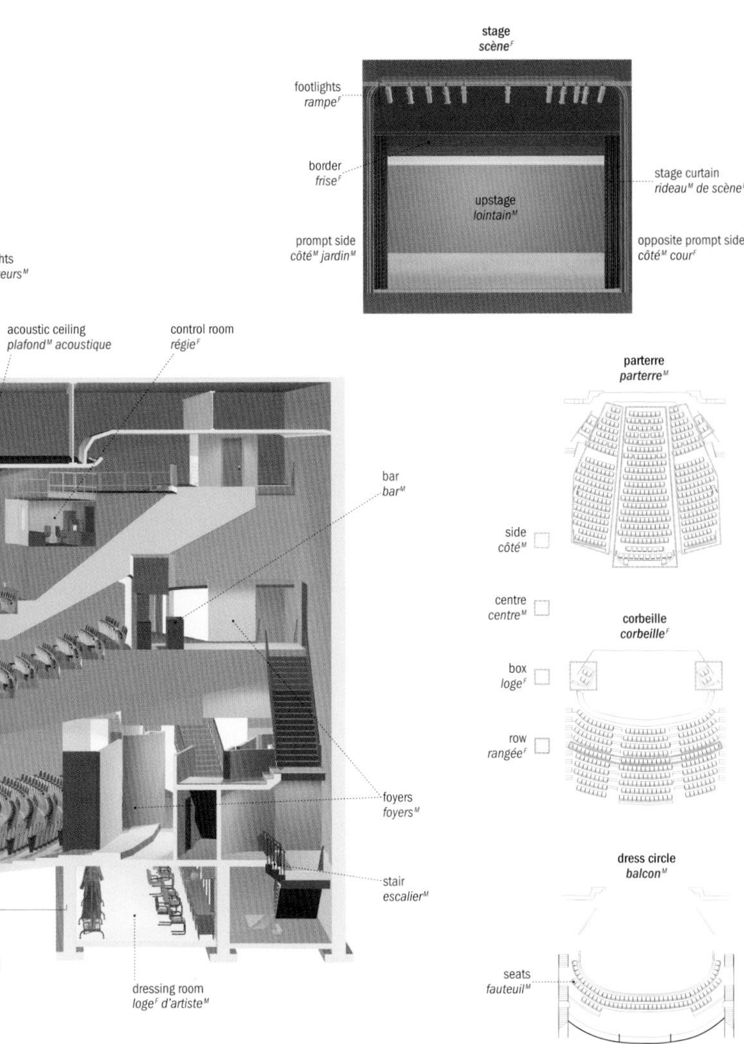

ARTS AND ARCHITECTURE

cinema

cinéma[M]

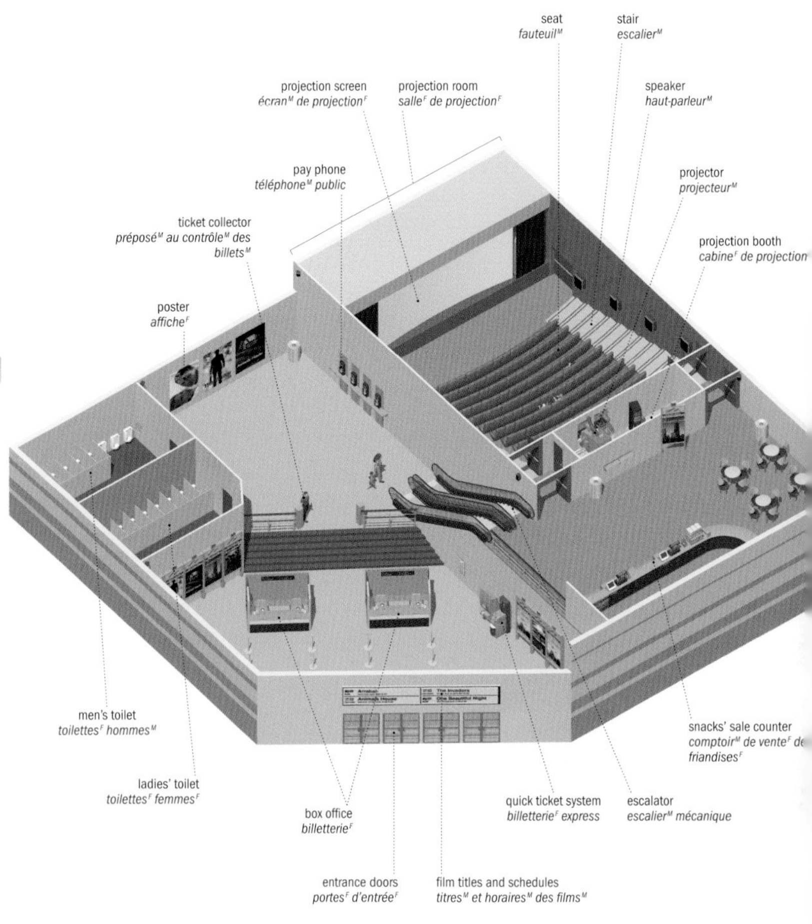

symphony orchestra

orchestre[M] symphonique

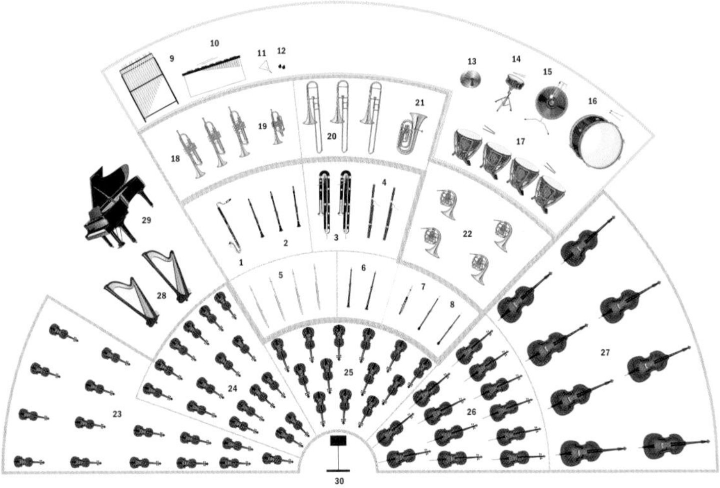

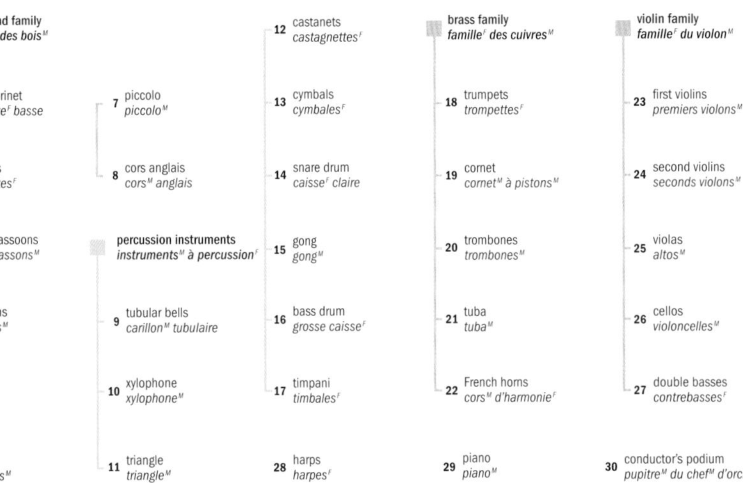

ınd family
des bois[M]

ıarinet
ɫte[F] basse

ɫs
ɫtes[F]

ıassoons
ɔassons[M]

ns
s[M]

ıs[M]

7 piccolo
piccolo[M]

8 cors anglais
cors[M] anglais

percussion instruments
instruments[M] à percussion[F]

9 tubular bells
carillon[M] tubulaire

10 xylophone
xylophone[M]

11 triangle
triangle[M]

12 castanets
castagnettes[F]

13 cymbals
cymbales[F]

14 snare drum
caisse[F] claire

15 gong
gong[M]

16 bass drum
grosse caisse[F]

17 timpani
timbales[F]

28 harps
harpes[F]

brass family
famille[F] des cuivres[M]

18 trumpets
trompettes[F]

19 cornet
cornet[M] à pistons[M]

20 trombones
trombones[M]

21 tuba
tuba[M]

22 French horns
cors[M] d'harmonie[F]

29 piano
piano[M]

violin family
famille[F] du violon[M]

23 first violins
premiers violons[M]

24 second violins
seconds violons[M]

25 violas
altos[M]

26 cellos
violoncelles[M]

27 double basses
contrebasses[F]

30 conductor's podium
pupitre[M] du chef[M] d'orchestre[M]

traditional musical instruments

instruments[M] traditionnels

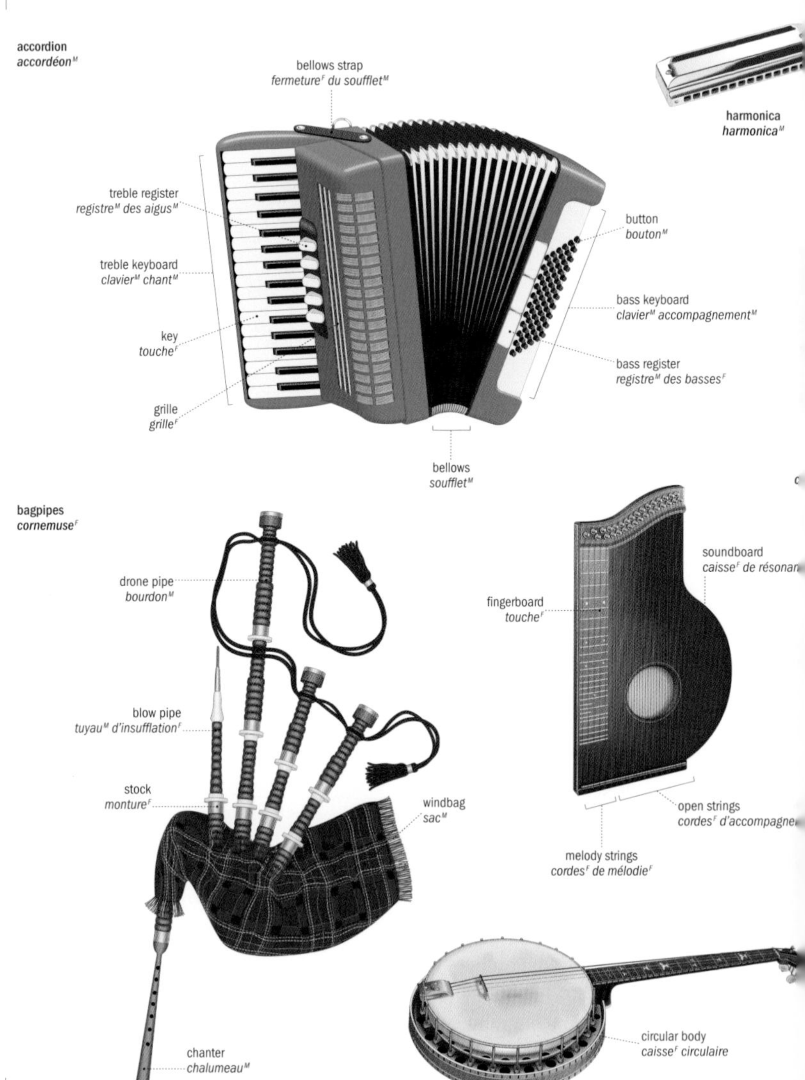

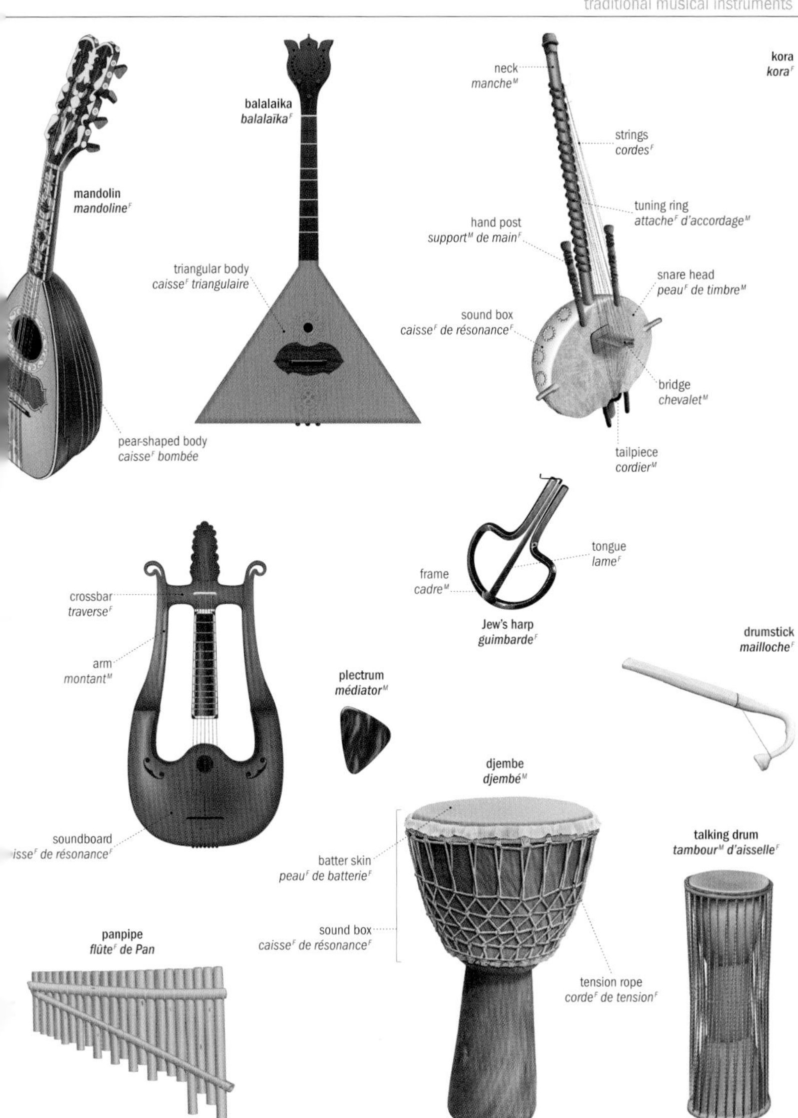
mandolin
mandolineF
pear-shaped body
caisseF bombée
balalaika
balalaïkaF
triangular body
caisseF triangulaire
kora
koraF
neck
mancheM
strings
cordesF
tuning ring
attacheF d'accordageM
hand post
supportM de mainF
snare head
peauF de timbreM
sound box
caisseF de résonanceF
bridge
chevaletM
tailpiece
cordierM
tongue
lameF
frame
cadreM
Jew's harp
guimbardeF
drumstick
mailloche F
crossbar
traverseF
arm
montantM
plectrum
médiatorM
soundboard
isseF de résonanceF
djembe
djembéM
batter skin
peauF de batterieF
sound box
caisseF de résonanceF
tension rope
cordeF de tensionF
talking drum
tambourM d'aisselleF
panpipe
flûteF de Pan

musical notation

notation[F] musicale

staff
portée[F]

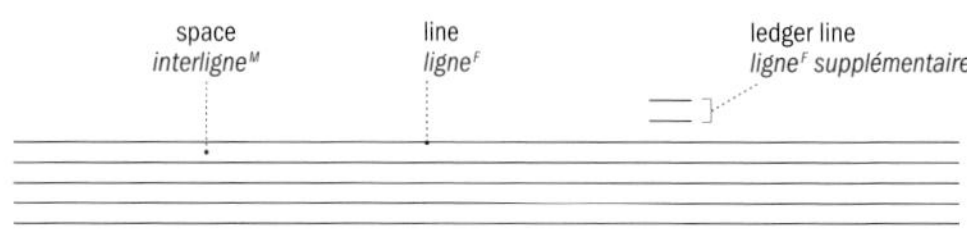

clefs
clés[F]

time signatures
mesures[F]

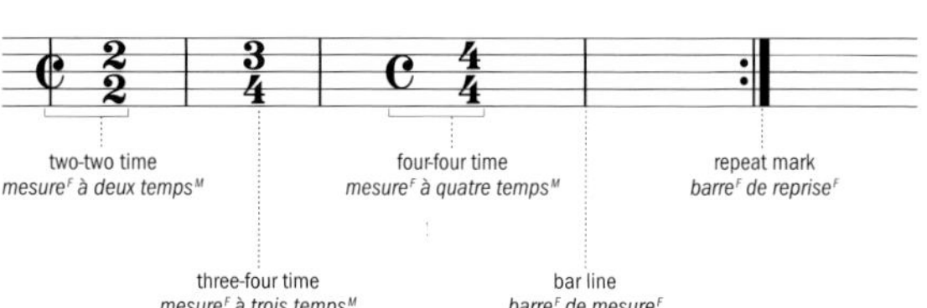

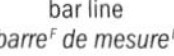

intervals
intervalles[M]

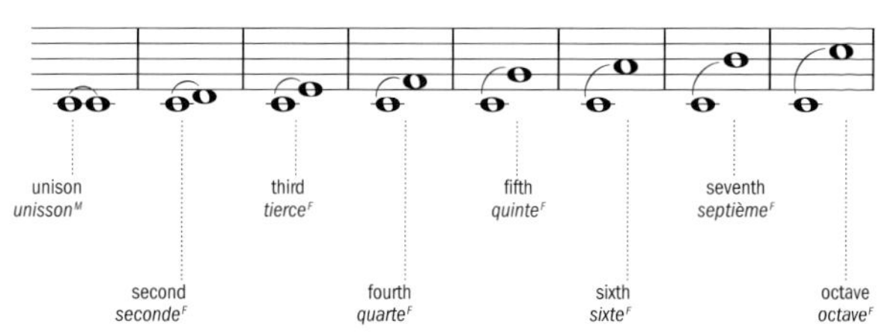

scale
gamme[F]

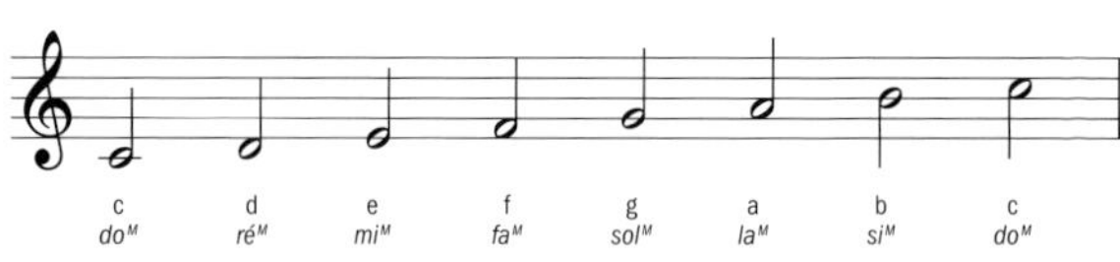

rest values
valeur[F] des silences[M]

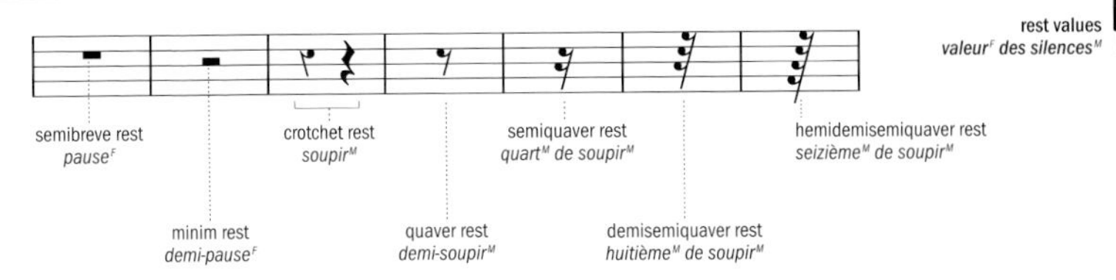

ornaments
ornements[M]

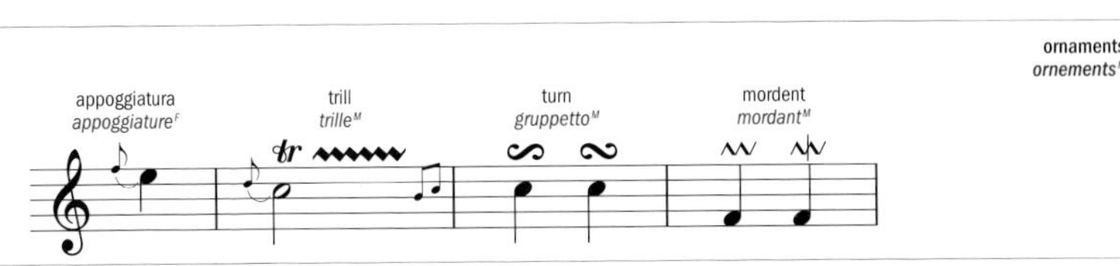

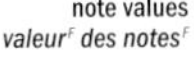
note values
valeur[F] des notes[F]

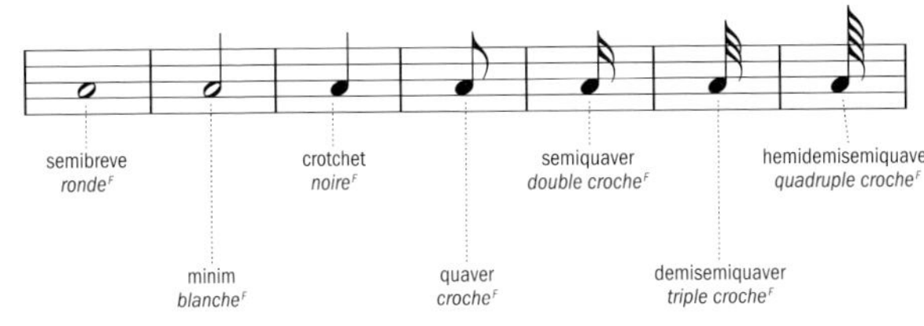

accidentals
altérations[F]

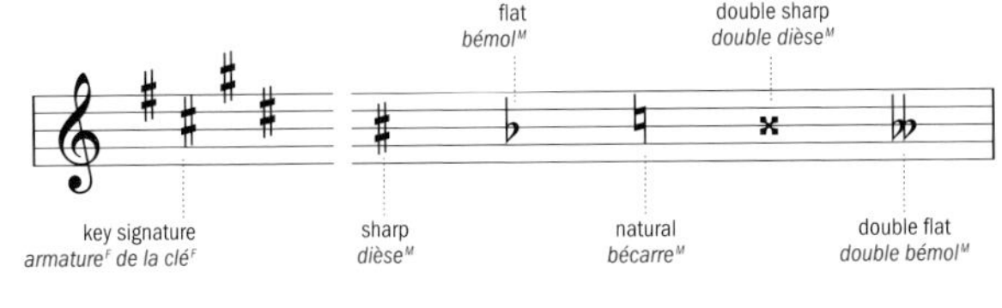

other signs
autres signes[M]

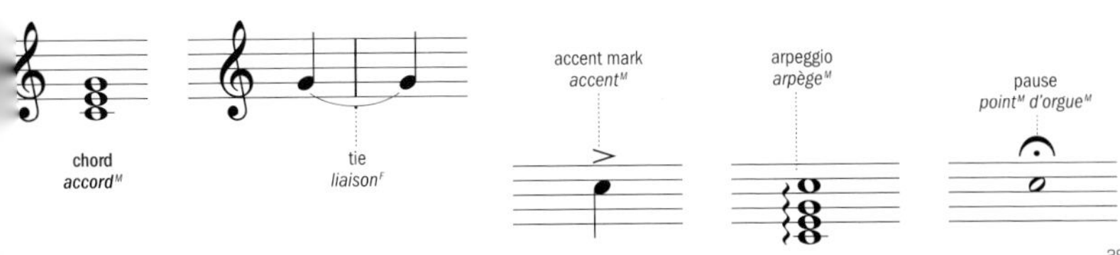

ARTS AND ARCHITECTURE

examples of instrumental groups

exemples[M] de groupes[M] instrumentaux

duo
duo[M]

trio
trio[M]

quartet
quatuor[M]

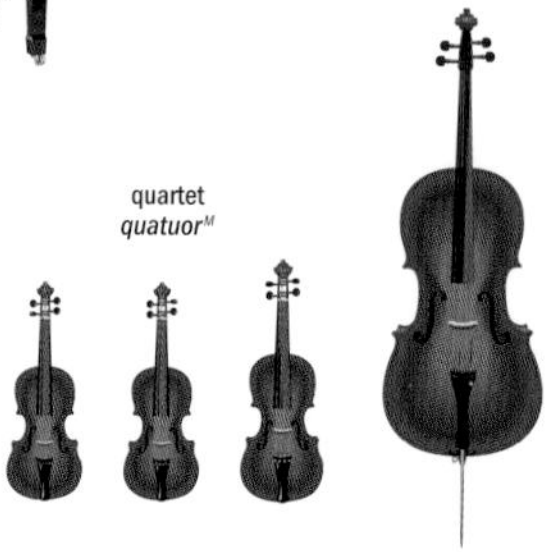

quintet
quintette[M]

sextet
sextuor[M]

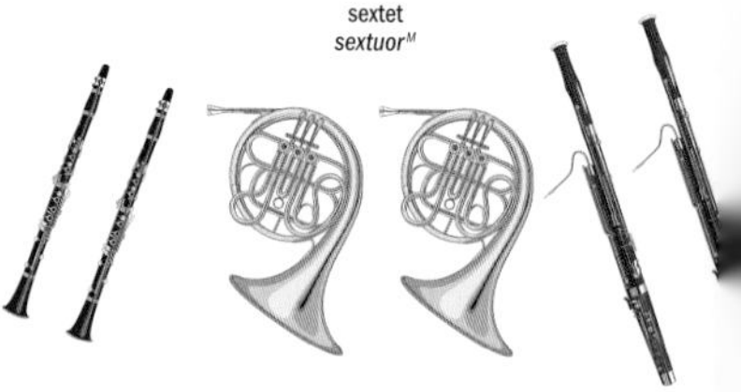

jazz band
formation[F] *de jazz*[M]

stringed instruments

instruments[M] à cordes[F]

violin
violon[M]

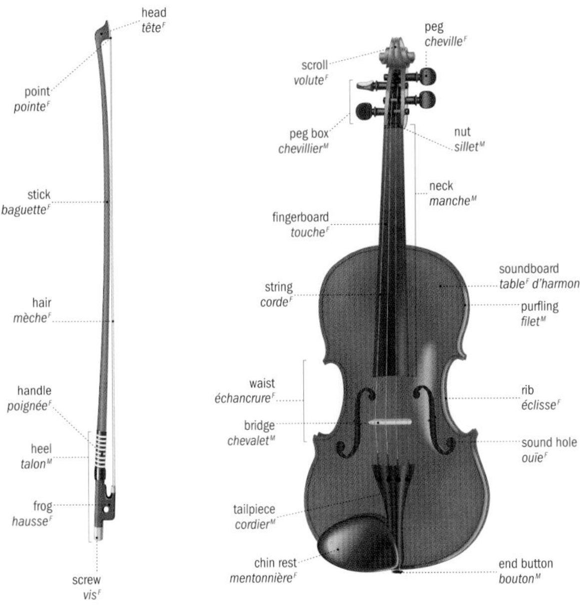

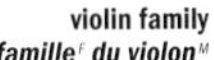

violin family
famille[F] du violon[M]

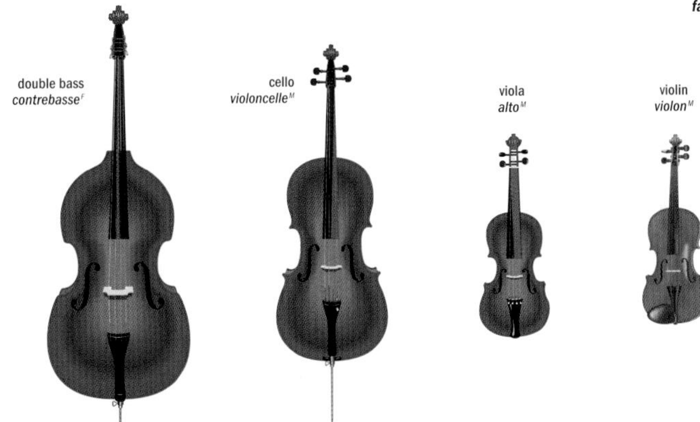

stringed instruments

harp
***harpe*^F**

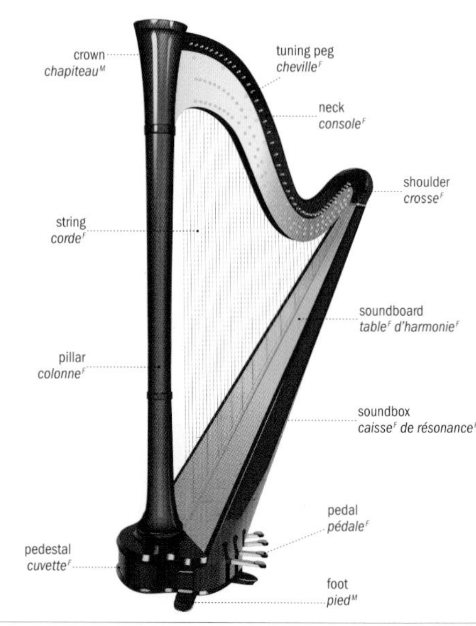

acoustic guitar
guitare*^F *acoustique

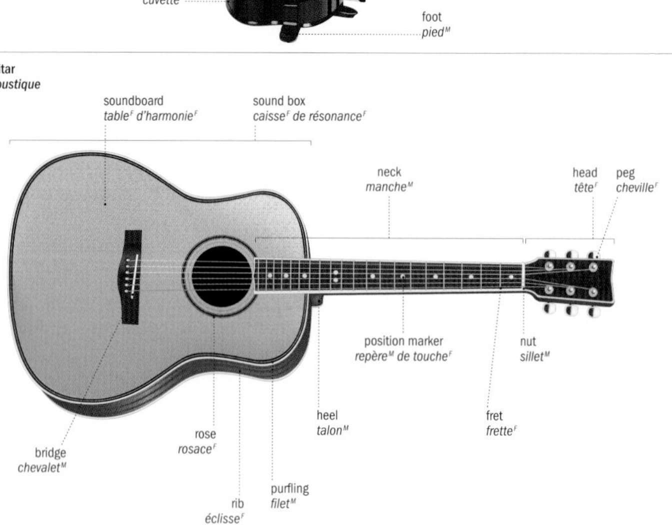

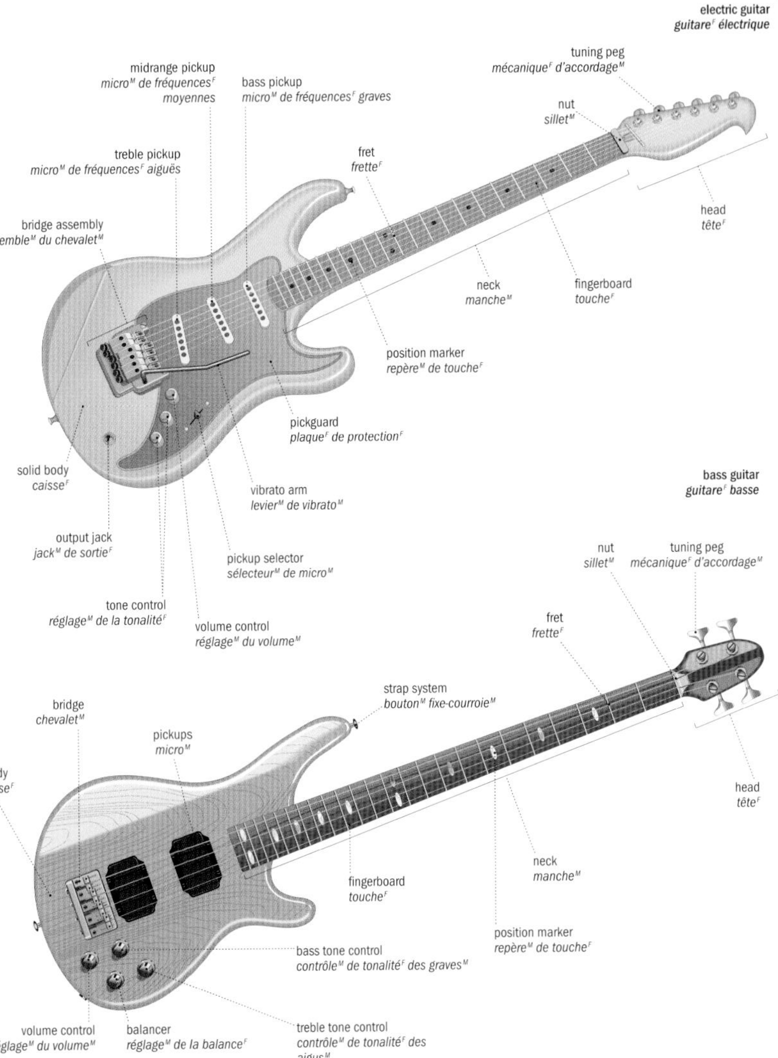
electric guitar
guitare électrique
tuning peg
mécanique d'accordage
midrange pickup
micro de fréquences moyennes
bass pickup
micro de fréquences graves
nut
sillet
treble pickup
micro de fréquences aiguës
fret
frette
head
tête
bridge assembly
semble du chevalet
neck
manche
fingerboard
touche
position marker
repère de touche
pickguard
plaque de protection
solid body
caisse
vibrato arm
levier de vibrato
output jack
jack de sortie
pickup selector
sélecteur de micro
tone control
réglage de la tonalité
volume control
réglage du volume
bass guitar
guitare basse
nut
sillet
tuning peg
mécanique d'accordage
fret
frette
strap system
bouton fixe-courroie
bridge
chevalet
pickups
micro
dy
sse
head
tête
neck
manche
fingerboard
touche
position marker
repère de touche
bass tone control
contrôle de tonalité des graves
volume control
églage du volume
balancer
réglage de la balance
treble tone control
contrôle de tonalité des aigus

keyboard instruments

instruments^M à clavier^M

upright piano
piano^M droit

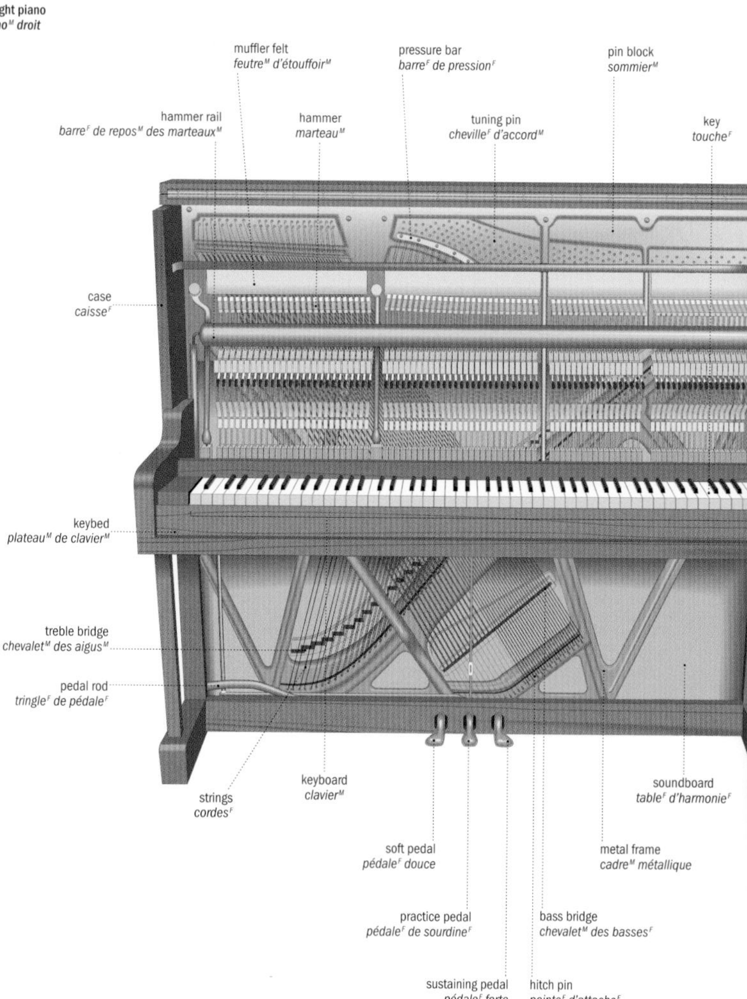

organ
orgue[M]

organ console
***console*[F] *d'orgue*[M]**

music rest
pupitre[M]

stop knob
bouton[M] *de registre*[M]

swell organ manual
clavier[M] *de récit*[M]

coupler-tilt tablet
lomino[M] *d'accouplement*[M]

choir organ manual
clavier[M] *de positif*[M]

great organ manual
clavier[M] *de grand orgue*[M]

manuals
claviers[M] *manuels*

thumb piston
outon[M] *de combinaisons*[F]

crescendo pedal
pédale[F] *crescendo*[M]

toe piston
édale[F] *de combinaisons*[F]

pedal key
touche[F] *de pédalier*[M]

swell pedals
pédales[F] *d'expression*[F]

pedal keyboard
pédalier[M]

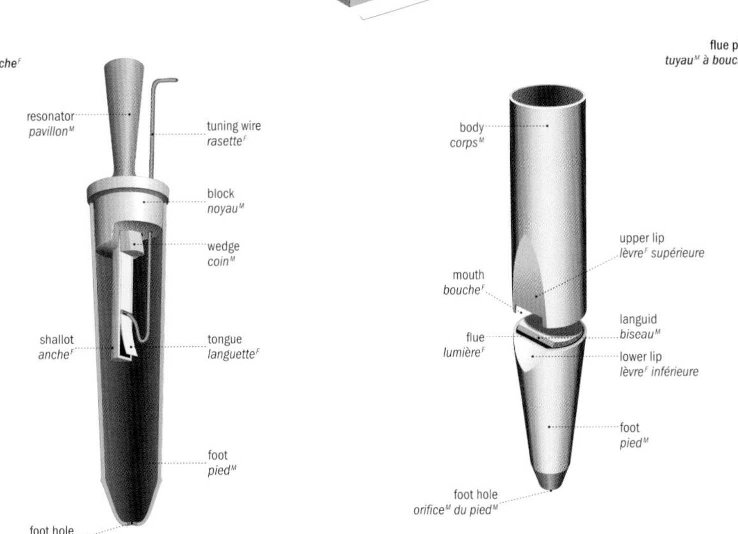

ARTS AND ARCHITECTURE

wind instruments

instruments[M] à vent[M]

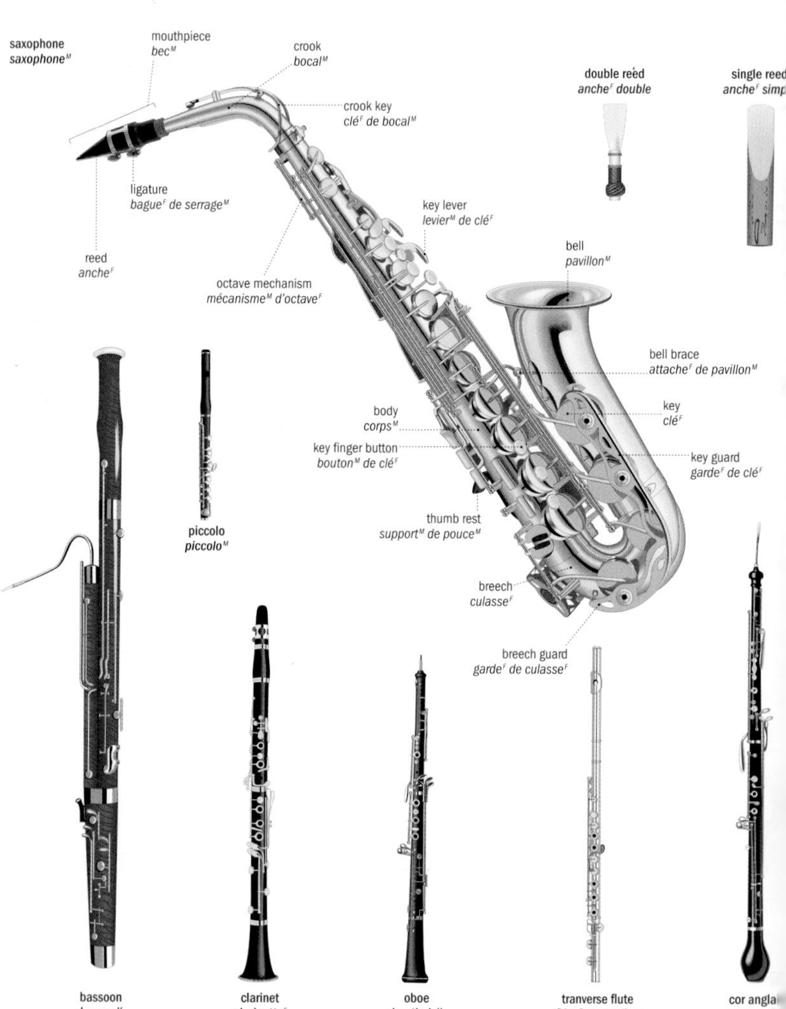

trumpet
trompette
finger button
bouton de piston
little finger hook
crochet de petit doigt
bell
pavillon
mouthpipe
branche d'embouchure
ring
bague
mouthpiece receiver
eau d'embouchure
mouthpiece
mbouchure
tuning slide
coulisse d'accord
first valve slide
coulisse du premier piston
water key
soupape d'évacuation
third valve slide
coulisse du troisième piston
thumb hook
crochet de pouce
valve
piston
valve casing
corps de piston
second valve slide
coulisse du deuxième piston
mute
sourdine
French horn
cor d'harmonie
cornet
cornet à pistons
bugle
clairon
saxhorn
saxhorn
tuba
tuba
trombone
trombone

percussion instruments

instruments[M] à percussion[F]

drums
batterie[F]

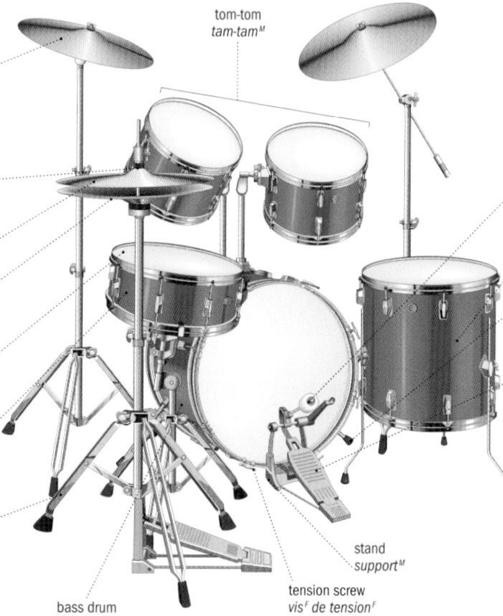

tom-tom
tam-tam[M]
cymbal
cymbale[F] suspendue
Charleston cymbal
cymbale[F] charleston
superior cymbal
cymbale[F] supérieure
inferior cymbal
cymbale[F] inférieure
drumhead
peau[F] de batterie[F]
snare drum
caisse[F] claire
tripod stand
trépied[M]
bass drum
grosse caisse[F]
tension screw
vis[F] de tension[F]
stand
support[M]
leg
pied[M]
pedal
pédale[F]
spur
éperon[M]
tenor drum
caisse[F] roulante
mallet
mailloche[F]

ke

snare drum
caisse[F] claire

lug
attache[F]
tension rod
tringle[F] de tension[F]
snare strainer
tendeur[M] de timbre[M]
snare
cordes[F] de timbre[M]
snare head
peau[F] de timbre[M]

tension screw
tirant[M]
drumhead
peau[F] de batterie[F]
metal counterhoop
cercle[M] de serrage[M]
tuning gauge
manomètre[M] d'ac
shell
fût[M]
strut
châssis[M]
tension rod
tringle[F] de tensior
crown
couronne[F]
pedal
pédale[F]
caster
roulette[F]
foot
pied[M]

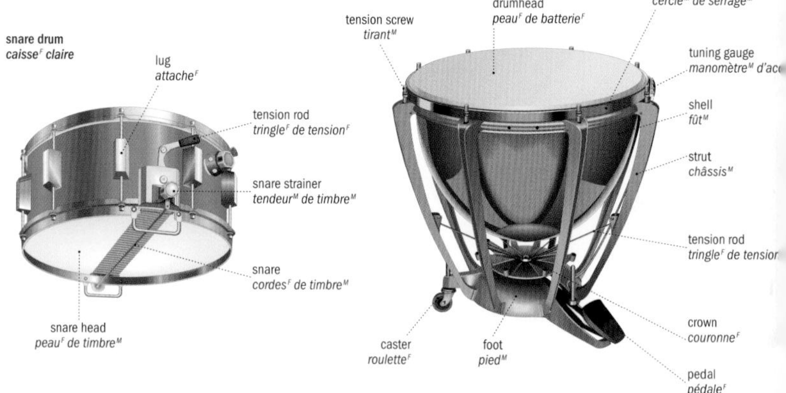

sleigh bells
grelots^M
set of bells
clochettes^F
sistrum
sistre^M
castanets
castagnettes^F
cymbals
cymbales^F
tambourine
tambour^M de basque^M
head
peau^F
jingle
cymbalette^F
triangle
triangle^M
metal rod
battant^M
bongos
bongo^M
wire brush
balai^M métallique
gong
gong^M
sticks
baguettes^F
tubular bells
carillon^M tubulaire
xylophone
xylophone^M
resonator
tube^M de résonance^F
frame
châssis^M
bar
lame^F
mallets
mailloches^F

electronic instruments

instruments[M] électroniques

sequencer
séquenceur[M]

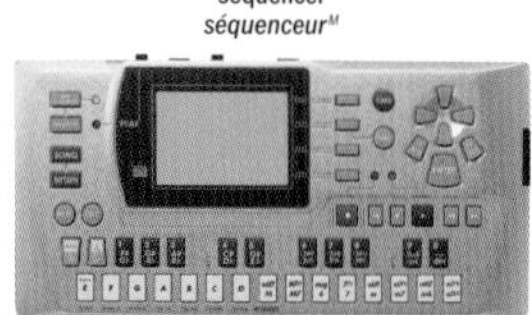

échantil

headphone jack
prise[F] casque[M]

function display
affichage[M] des fonctions[F]

disc
lecteur[M] de disque

expander
expandeur[M]

synthesizer
synthétiseur[M]

volume control
contrôle[M] du volume[M]

fine data entry control
modification[F] fine des variables[F]

disc drive
lecteur[M] de disquette[F]

system buttons
fonctions[F] système[M]

function display
affichage[M] des fonctions[F]

sequencer control
contrôle[M] du séquenceur[M]

fast data entry control
modification[F] rapide des variables[F]

program selector
sélecteur[M] de programme[M]

keyboard
clavier[M]

modulation wheel
modulation[F] du timbre[M] du son[M]

voice edit butto
programmation[F] des vo

pitch wheel
modulation[F] de la hauteur[F] du son[M]

ARTS AND ARCHITECTURE

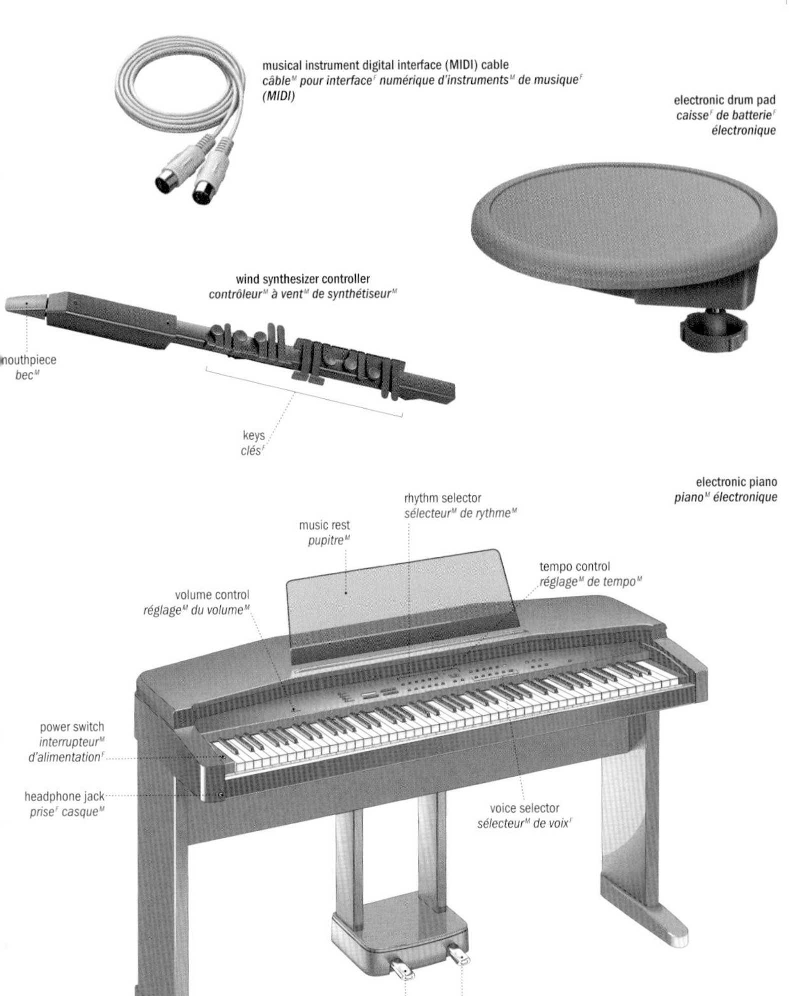
musical instrument digital interface (MIDI) cable
câble[M] pour interface[F] numérique d'instruments[M] de musique[F] (MIDI)
electronic drum pad
caisse[F] de batterie[F] électronique
wind synthesizer controller
contrôleur[M] à vent[M] de synthétiseur[M]
mouthpiece
bec[M]
keys
clés[F]
electronic piano
piano[M] électronique
rhythm selector
sélecteur[M] de rythme[M]
music rest
pupitre[M]
tempo control
réglage[M] de tempo[M]
volume control
réglage[M] du volume[M]
power switch
interrupteur[M] d'alimentation[F]
headphone jack
prise[F] casque[M]
voice selector
sélecteur[M] de voix[F]
soft pedal
pédale[F] douce
sustaining pedal
pédale[F] forte

writing instruments

instruments^M d'écriture^F

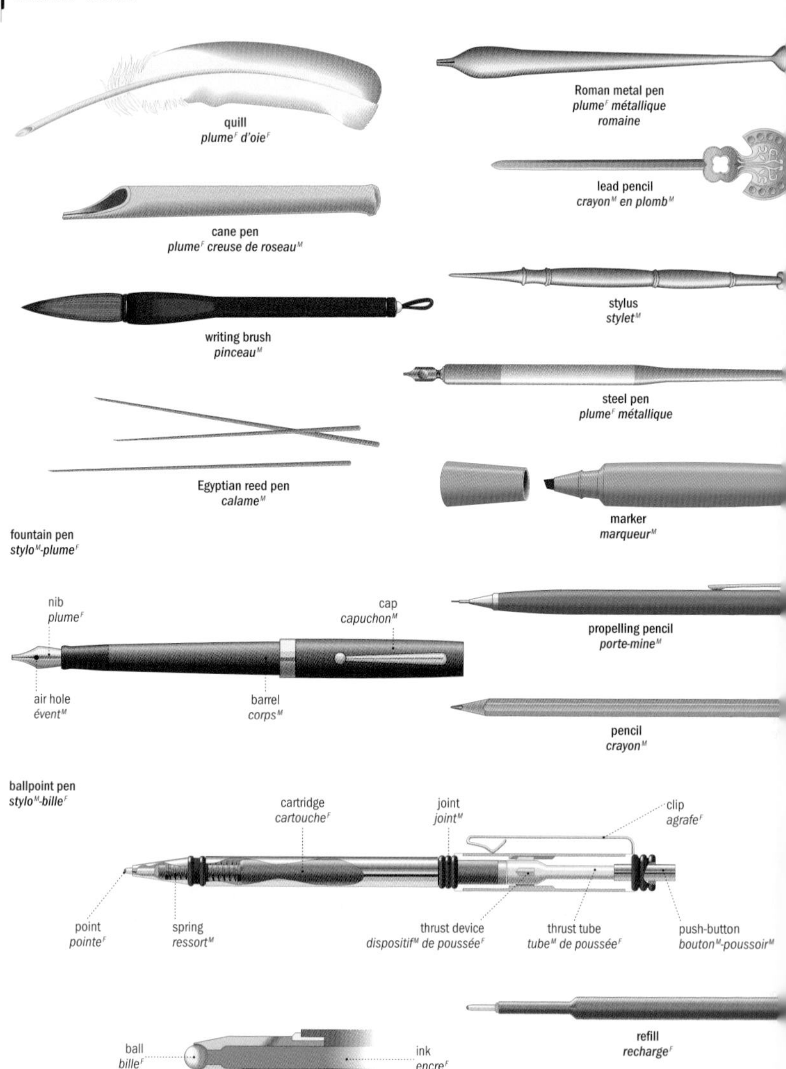

newspaper

journal[M]

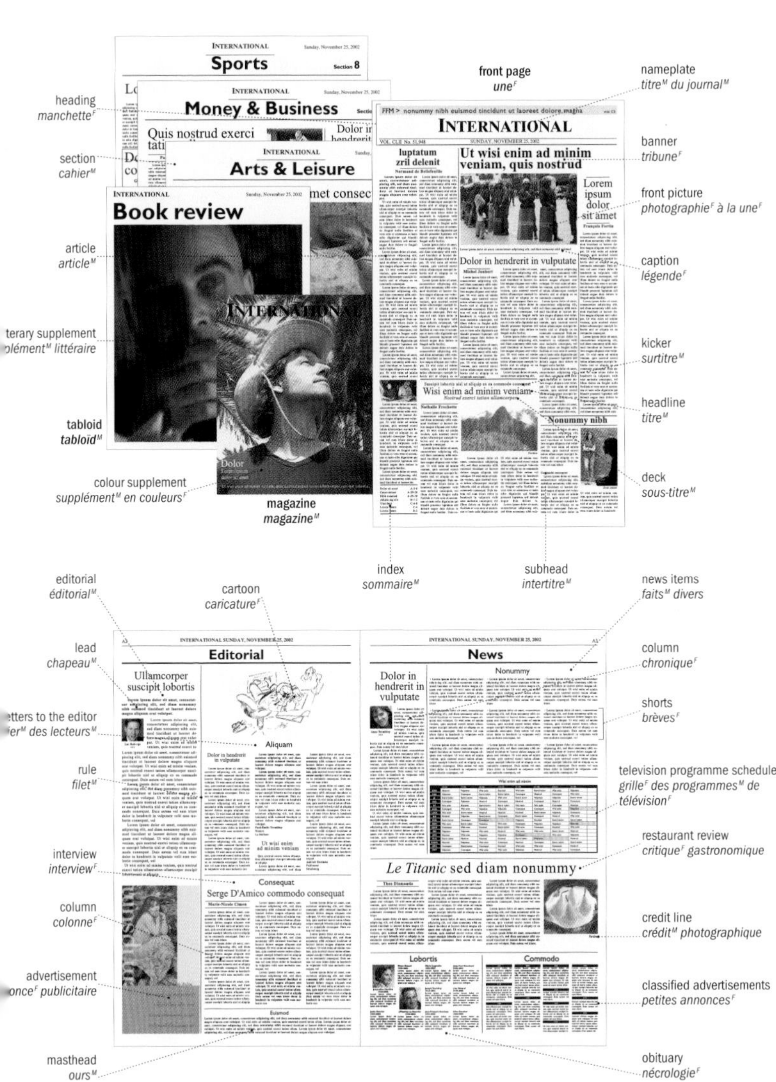

photography

photographie[F]

single-lens reflex (SLR) camera: front view
appareil[M] à visée[F] reflex mono-objectif[M] : vue avant

exposure adjustment knob
correction[F] d'exposition[F]

accessory shoe
griffe[F] porte-accessoires[M]

hot-shoe contact
contact[M] électrique

drive mode
mode[M] d'acquisition[F]

data panel
écran[M] de contrôle[M]

exposure mode
mode[M] d'exposition[F]

program selector
sélecteur[M] de fonctions[F]

multiple exposure mode
surimpression[F]

on/off switch
commutateur[M] marche[F]/arrêt[M]

sensitivity
sensibilité[F]

shutter release button
déclencheur[M]

remote control terminal
prise[F] de télécommand

self-timer indicator
témoin[M] du retardateur[M]

focus mode selector
mode[M] de mise[F] au point[M]

camera body
boîtier[M]

lens release button
déverrouillage[M] de l'objectif[M]

lens
objectif[M]

depth-of-field preview button
vérification[F] de la profondeur[F] de champ[M]

lenses
objectifs[M]

wide-angle lens
objectif[M] grand-angulaire

telephoto lens
téléobjectif[M]

zoom lens
objectif[M] zoom[M]

macro lens
objectif[M] macro

lens acc
accessoires[M] de l'

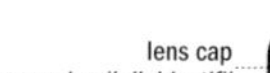

lens cap
capuchon[M] d'objectif[M]

lens hood
parasoleil[M]

polarizing filter
filtre[M] de polarisation[F]

digital reflex camera: camera back
appareil^{M} à visée^{F} reflex numérique : dos^{M}

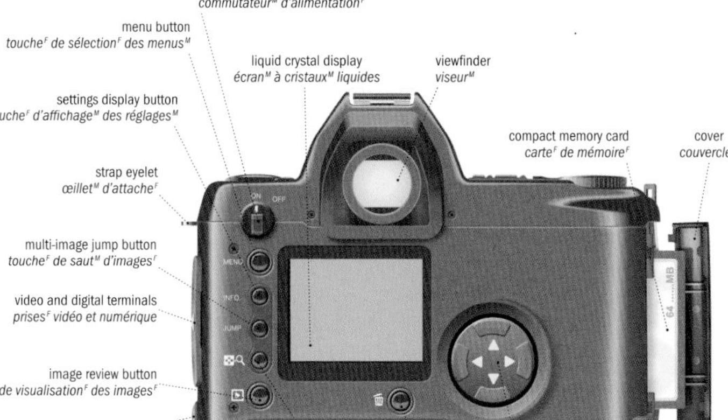

still cameras
appareils^{M} photographiques

olaroid® Land camera
Polaroid$^{®M}$

medium format SLR (6 x 6)
appareil^{M} reflex 6 X 6 mono-objectif^{M}

ultracompact camera
appareil^{M} ultracompact

compact camera
appareil^{M} compact

disposable camera
appareil^{M} jetable

view camera
chambre^{F} photographique

satellite broadcasting

télédiffusion*F* par satellite*M*

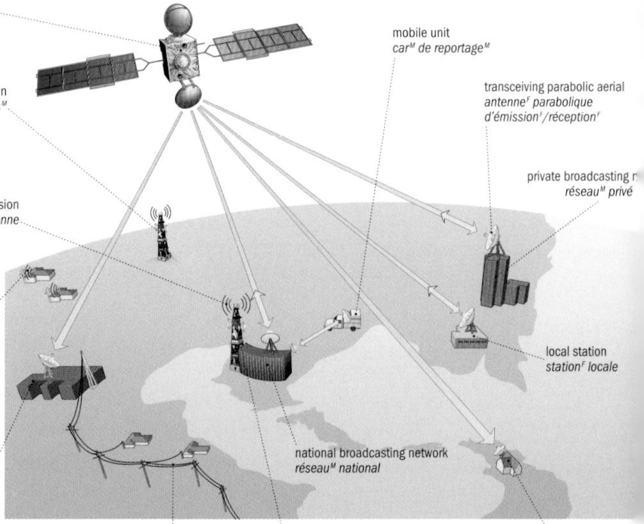

satellite
*satellite*M
mobile unit
*car*M *de reportage*M
relay station
*station*F*-relais*M
transceiving parabolic aerial
*antenne*F *parabolique d'émission*F*/réception*F
private broadcasting n
*réseau*M *privé*
Hertzian wave transmission
*transmission*F *hertzienne*
home aerial
*antenne*F *domestique*
local station
*station*F *locale*
national broadcasting network
*réseau*M *national*
cable distributor
*câblodistributeur*M
distribution by aerial cable network
*transmission*F *par câble*M *aérien*
transmitting tower
*tour*F *d'émission*F
direct home reception
*réception*F *directe*

telecommunication satellites

satellites*M* de télécommunications*F*

Eutelsat
***Eutelsat*M**
transceiving dish
*antenne*F *d'émission*F*/réception*F
solar reflectors
*réflecteurs*M *solaires*
communication module
*module*M *de communication*F
service module
*module*M *de service*M
solar array
*panneau*M *solaire*
propulsion module
*module*M *de propulsion*F
transmission dish
*antenne*F *d'émission*F

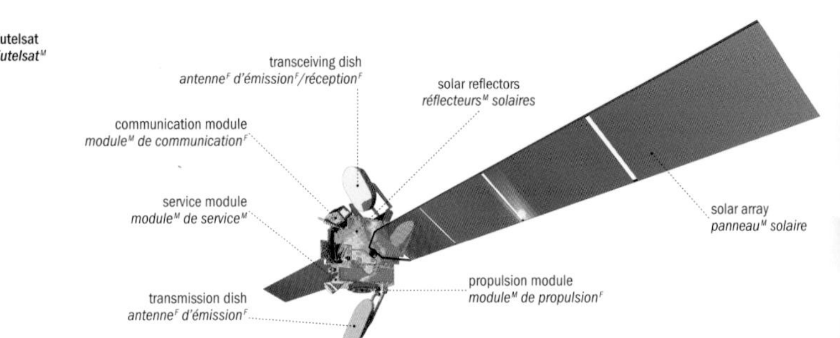

telecommunications by satellite

télécommunications*F* par satellite*M*

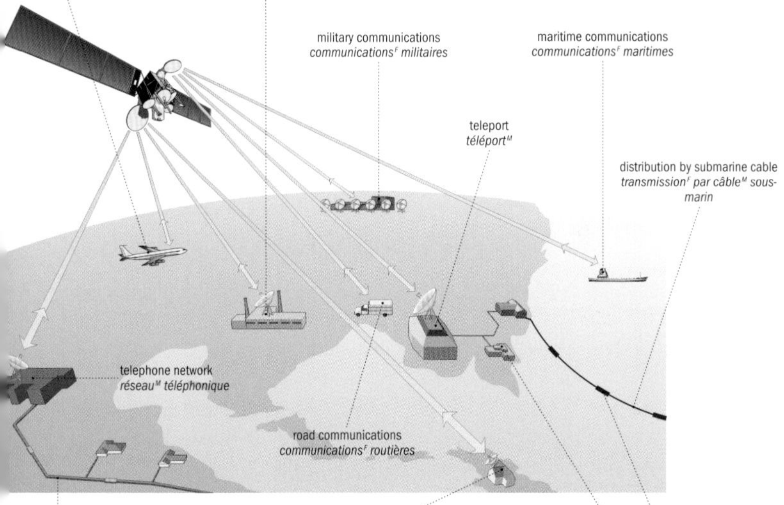

n-flight communications
mmunications*F* aériennes
industrial communications
*communications*F* industrielles*
military communications
*communications*F* militaires*
maritime communications
*communications*F* maritimes*
teleport
*téléport*M**
distribution by submarine cable
*transmission*F* par câble*M* sous-marin*
telephone network
*réseau*M* téléphonique*
road communications
*communications*F* routières*
tion by underground cable network
ısmission*F* par câble*M* souterrain
personal communications
*communications*F* individuelles*
consumer
*client*M**
repeater
*répéteur*M**

telecommunication satellites

Anik
*Anik*M**
Intelsat
*Intelsat*M**

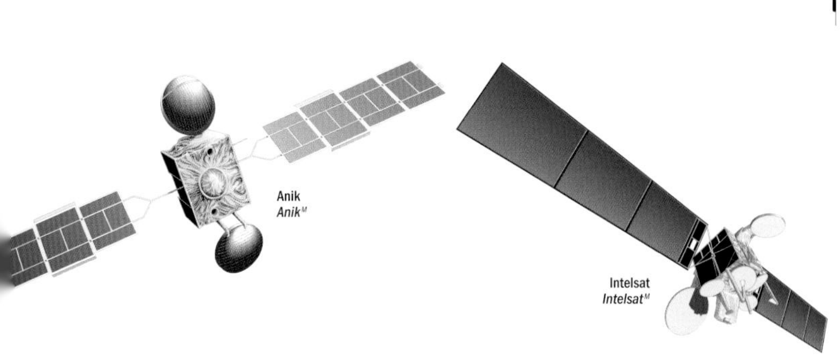

television

télévision[F]

liquid crystal display (LCD) television
téléviseur[M] à cristaux[M] liquides

plasma television
téléviseur[M] à plasma[M]

cathode ray tube (CRT) television
téléviseur[M] à écran[M] cathodique

picture tube
tube[M]-image[F]

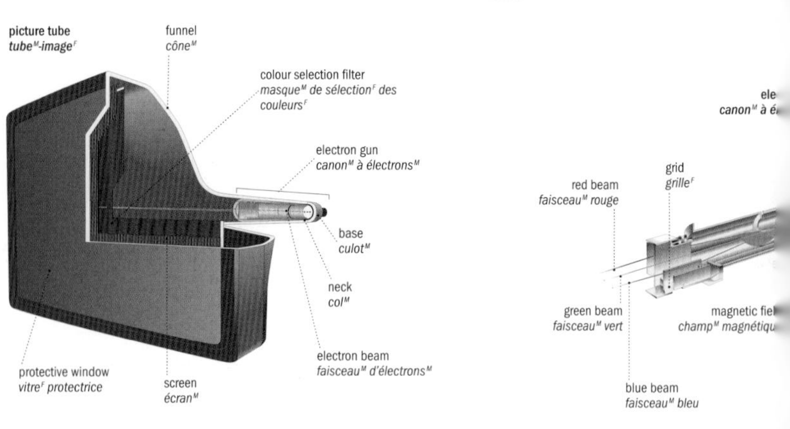

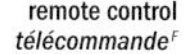

remote control
télécommande [F]

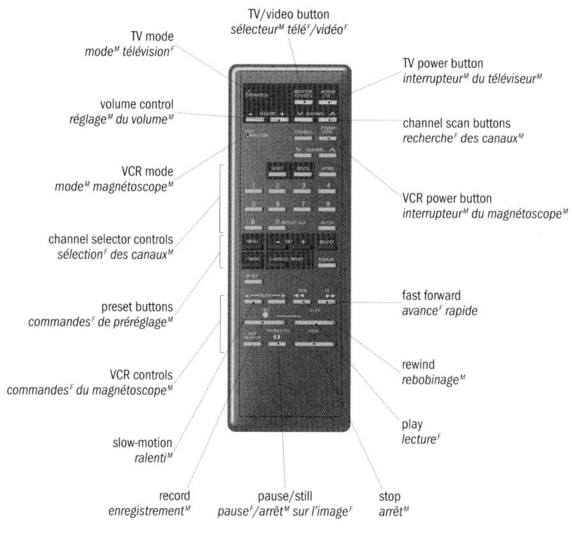

DVD recorder
enregistreur[M] de DVD[M] vidéo

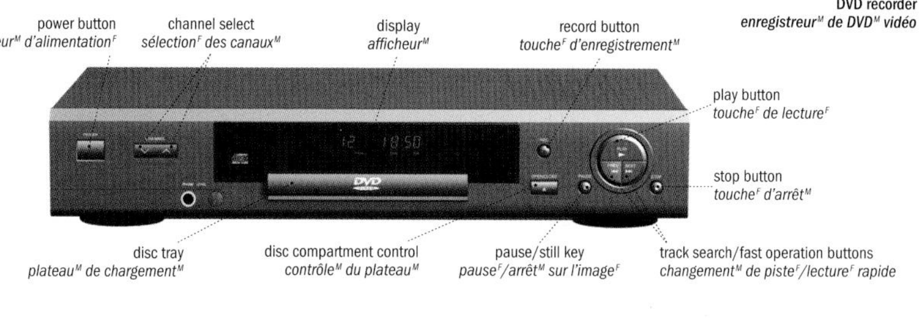

…ssette
…[F] vidéo

recording media
supports[M] d'enregistrement[M]

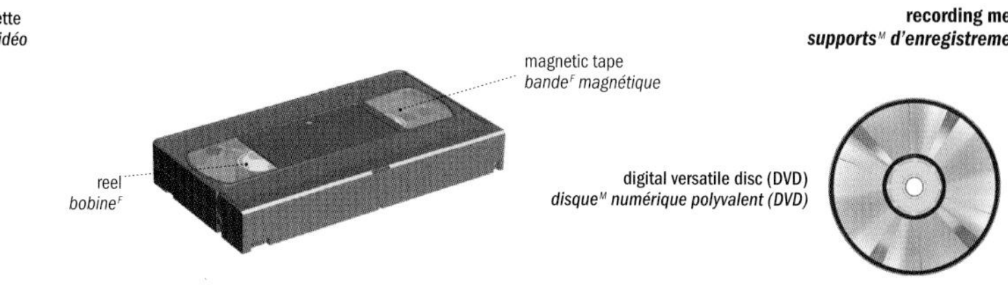

COMMUNICATIONS AND OFFICE AUTOMATION

mini-DV camcorder: front view
caméscope ^M^ ***mini-DV : vue*** ^F^ ***avant***

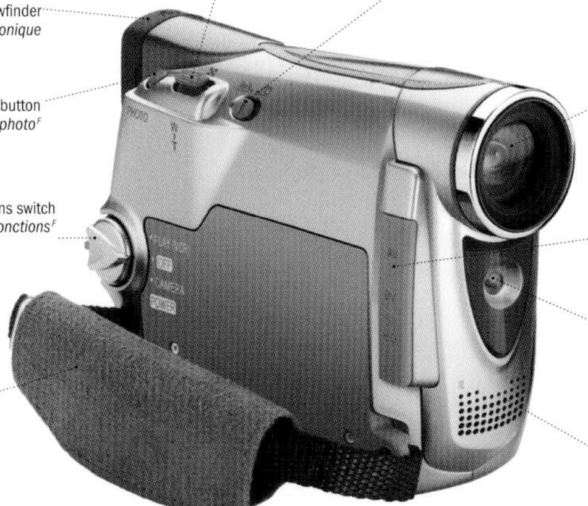

zoom button
commande^F^ *du zoom*^M^
recording mode
mode^M^ *d'enregistrement*^M^
electronic viewfinder
viseur^M^ *électronique*
zoom lens
objectif^M^ *zoom*^M^
photoshot button
touche^F^ *photo*^F^
power/functions switch
commutateur^M^ *alimentation*^F^*/fonctions*^F^
terminal cover
couvre-prises^M^
lamp
lampe^F^
hand strap
dragonne^F^
microphone
microphone^M^

mini-DV camcorder: rear view
caméscope ^M^ ***mini-DV : vue*** ^F^ ***arrière***

focus button
touche^F^ *de mise*^F^ *au point*^M^
videotape operation controls
commandes^F^ *de la bande*^F^ *vidéo*
nightshot button
touche^F^ *de prise*^F^ *de vues*^F^ *nocturne*
eyepiece
oculaire^M^
liquid crystal display
écran^M^ *à cristaux*^M^ *liquides*
recording start/stop button
touche^F^ *d'enregistrement*^M^
rechargeable battery pack
pile^F^ *rechargeable*
card slot
logement^M^ *de la carte*^F^ *mémoire*^F^
menu button
touche^F^ *de menu*^M^
speaker
haut-parleur^M^
backlighting button
touche^F^ *de rétroéclairage*^M^
widescreen/data code button
touche^F^ *écran*^M^ *large/code*^M^ *de données*^F^

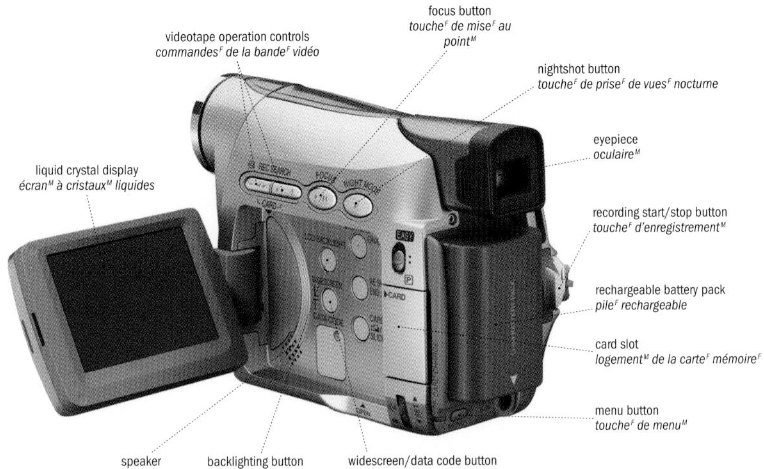

receiver
terminal[M] numérique

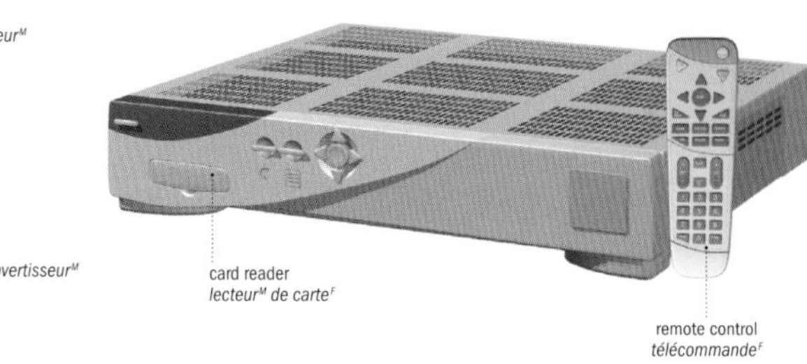

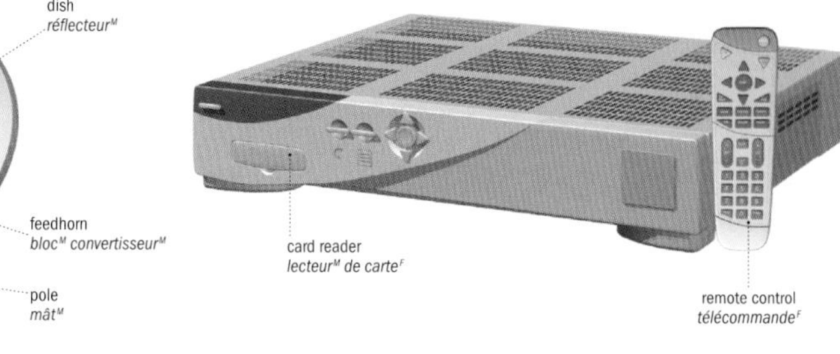

home theatre
cinéma[M] maison[F]

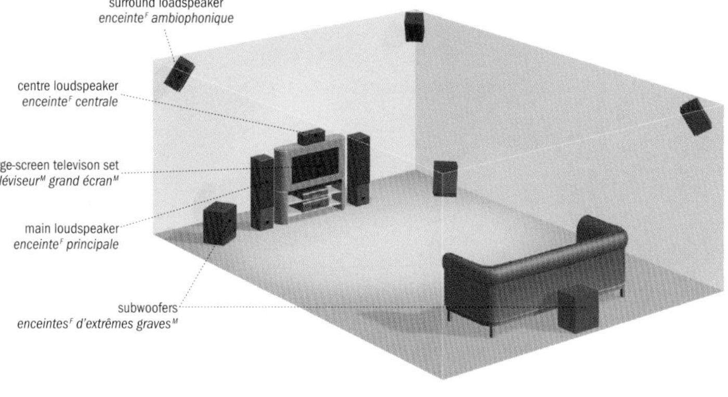

videocassette recorder
magnétoscope[M]

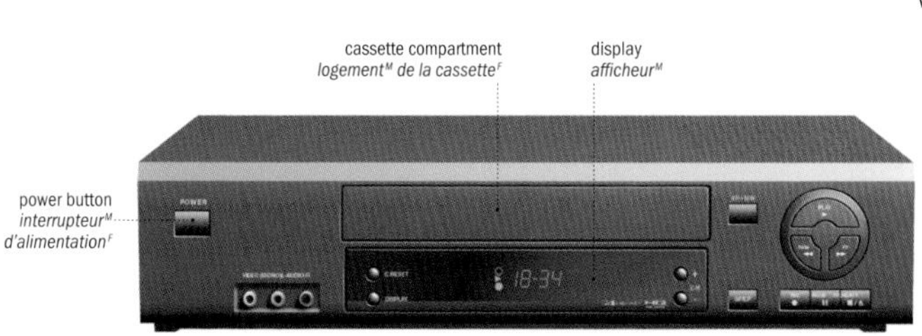

stereo sound system

chaîne^{F} stéréo

ampli-tuner: front view
ampli^{M}-syntoniseur^{M} : vue^{F} avant

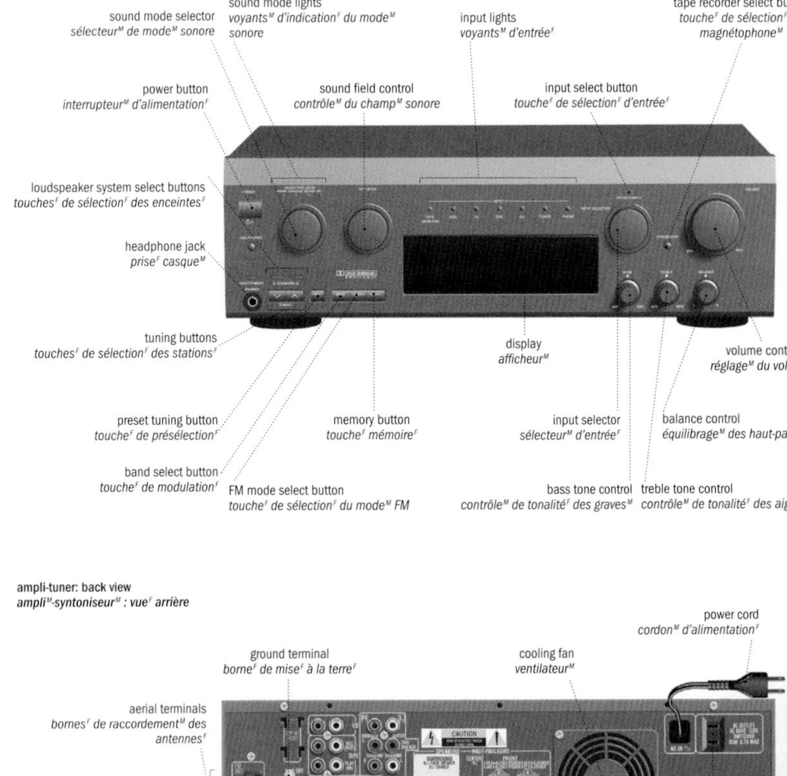

cassette tape deck
platine^{F} cassette^{F}

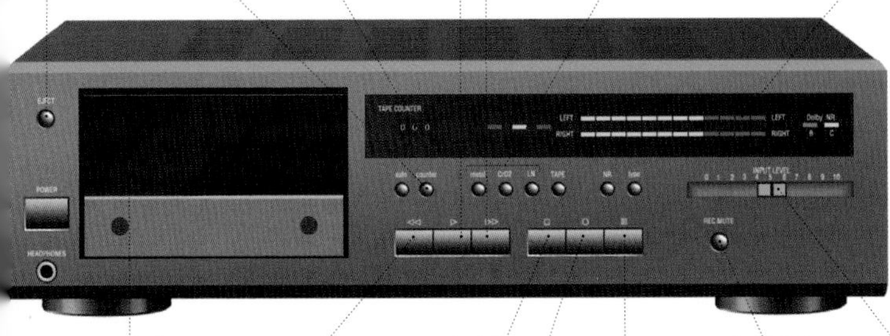

counter reset button
bouton^{M} de remise^{F} à zéro^{M}
play button
lecture^{F}
fast-forward button
avance^{F} rapide
eject button
ton^{M} d'éjection^{F}
tape counter
compteur^{M}
tape selector
sélecteur^{M} de bandes^{F}
peak level meter
indicateur^{M} de niveau^{M}
cassette holder
logement^{M} de cassette^{F}
stop button
arrêt^{M}
record muting button
interrupteur^{M} d'accord^{M}
rewind button
rebobinage^{M}
record button
enregistrement^{M}
pause button
pause^{F}
recording level control
réglage^{M} de niveau^{M} d'enregistrement^{M}

compact disc player
lecteur^{M} de disque^{M} compact

outton
pteur^{M} d'alimentation^{F}
shuffle play
lecture^{F} aléatoire
direct disc access keys
touches^{F} numériques
repeat key
touche^{F} de répétition^{F}
track search/fast operation keys
changement^{M} de piste^{F}/lecture^{F} rapide
stop key
arrêt^{M}
pause key
pause^{F}
play key
lecture^{F}
disc skip
changement^{M} de disque^{M}
eadphone jack
rise^{F} casque^{M}
disc compartment
logement^{M} du plateau^{M}
display
afficheur^{M}
disc compartment control
contrôle^{M} du plateau^{M}

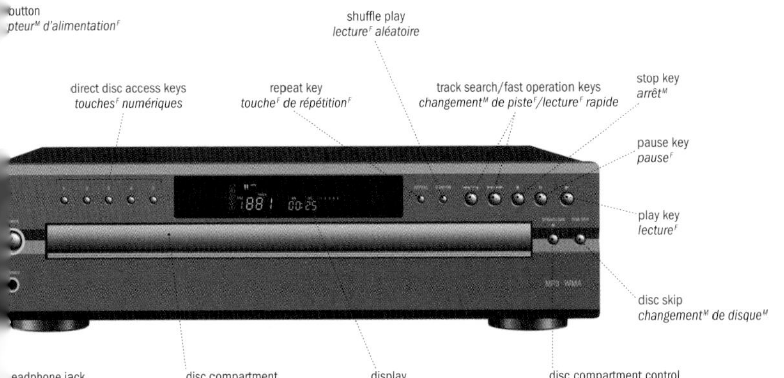

headphones
casque^M d'écoute^F

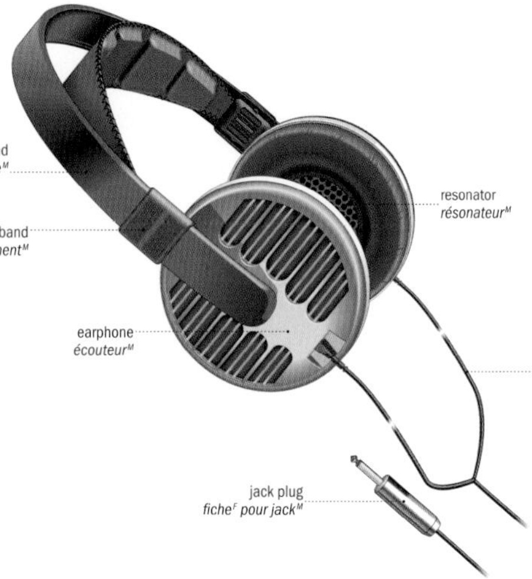

headband
serre-tête^M

adjusting band
glissière^F d'ajustement^M

earphone
écouteur^M

resonator
résonateur^M

connecting cable
câble^M de raccordeme

jack plug
fiche^F pour jack^M

loudspeaker
enceinte^F acoustique

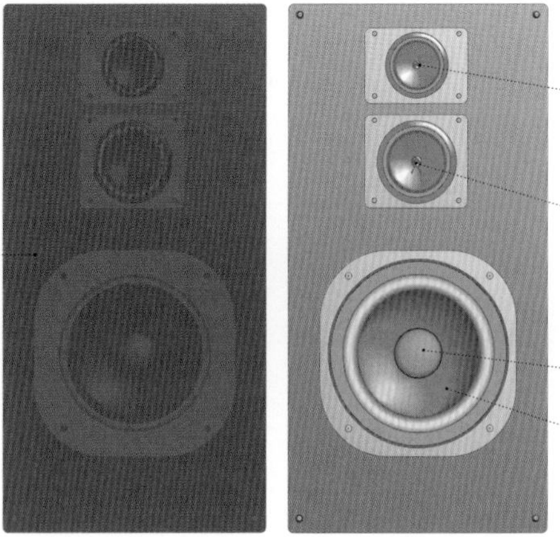

right channel
canal^M droit

left channel
canal^M gauche

speaker cover
treillis^M

tweeter
haut-parleur^M d'aigus^M

midrange speaker
haut-parleur^M de médiu

woofer
haut-parleur^M de graves

diaphragm
membrane^F

mini stereo sound system

minichaîne[F] stéréo

compact disc player
~~teur~~[M] de disque[M] compact
ampli-tuner
ampli[M]-syntoniseur[M]
loudspeaker
enceinte[F] acoustique
compact disc recorder
graveur[M] de disque[M] compact
dual cassette deck
double platine[F] cassette[F]

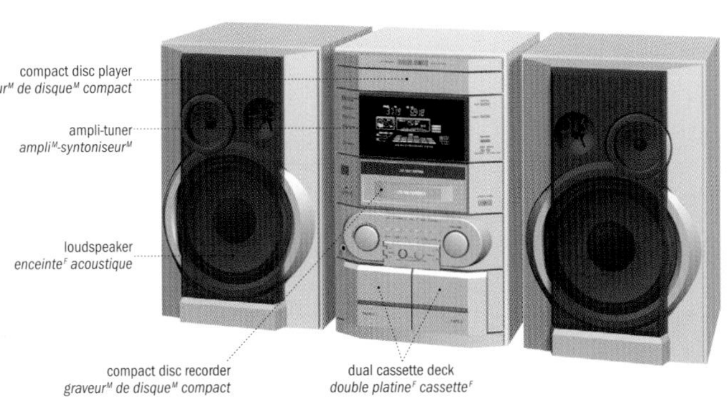

portable sound systems

appareils[M] de son[M] portatifs

ck radio
lio[F]-réveil[M]

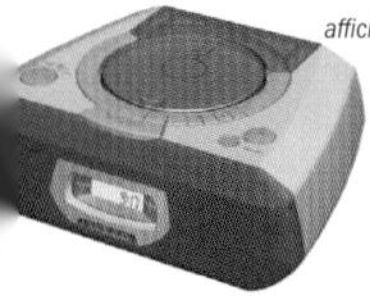

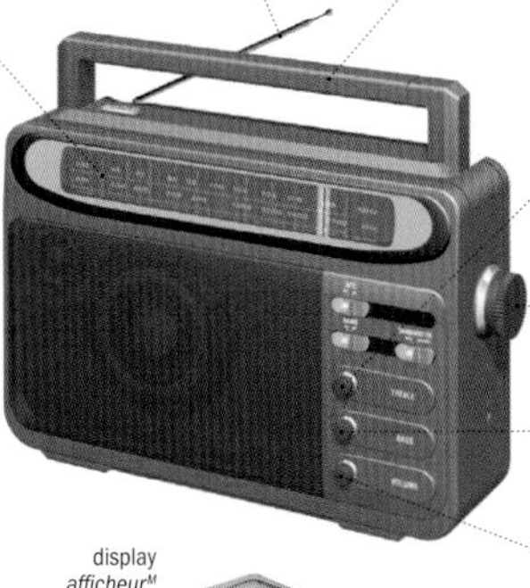

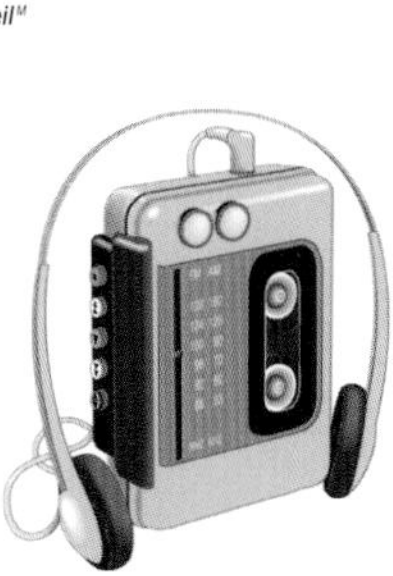

telescopic aerial
antenne[F] télescopique
handle
poignée[F]
frequency display
affichage[M] des stations[F]
treble tone control
contrôle[M] de tonalité[F] des aigus[M]
tuning control
sélecteur[M] de stations[F]
bass tone control
contrôle[M] de tonalité[F] des graves[M]
volume control
réglage[M] du volume[M]

portable radio
radio[F] portable

personal radio cassette player
baladeur[M]

display
afficheur[M]
earphones
écouteurs[M]

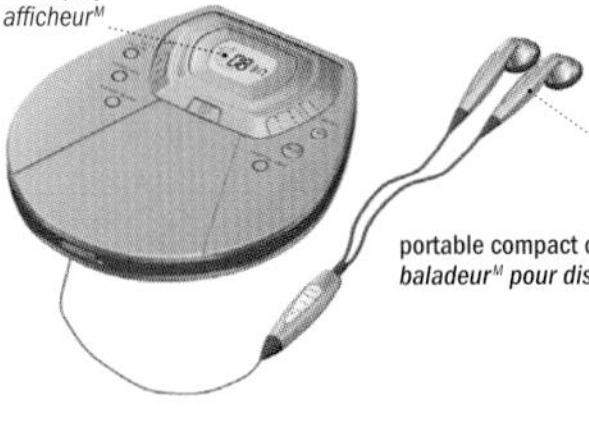

portable compact disc player
baladeur[M] pour disque[M] compact

portable sound systems

portable digital audio player
baladeur[M] numérique

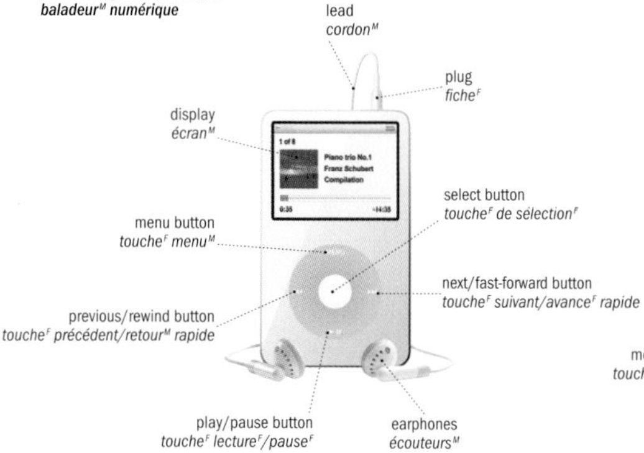
lead
cordon[M]
plug
fiche[F]
display
écran[M]
select button
touche[F] de sélection[F]
menu button
touche[F] menu[M]
next/fast-forward button
touche[F] suivant/avance[F] rapide
previous/rewind button
touche[F] précédent/retour[M] rapide
play/pause button
touche[F] lecture[F]/pause[F]
earphones
écouteurs[M]

satellite radio r
récepteur[M] de radio[F] par sa

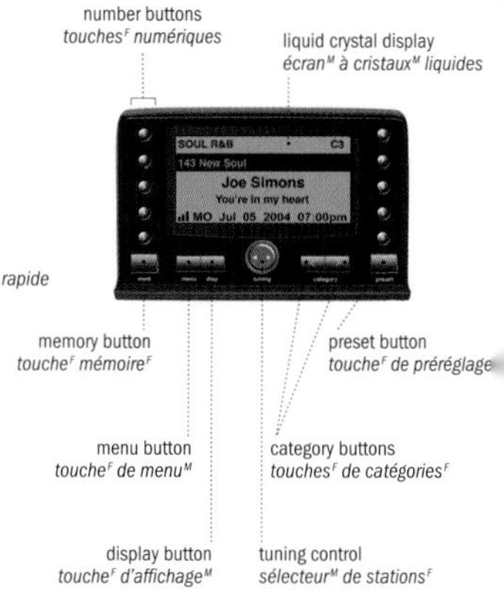
number buttons
touches[F] numériques
liquid crystal display
écran[M] à cristaux[M] liquides
SOUL R&B
C3
143 New Soul
Joe Simons
You're in my heart
MO Jul 05 2004 07:00pm
memory button
touche[F] mémoire[F]
preset button
touche[F] de préréglage
menu button
touche[F] de menu[M]
category buttons
touches[F] de catégories[F]
display button
touche[F] d'affichage[M]
tuning control
sélecteur[M] de stations[F]

portable CD radio cassette recorder
radiocassette[F] laser[M]

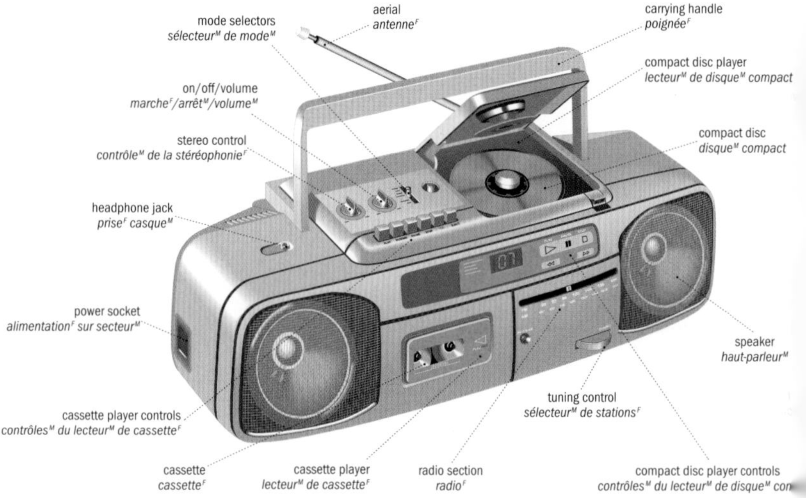
aerial
antenne[F]
mode selectors
sélecteur[M] de mode[M]
carrying handle
poignée[F]
compact disc player
lecteur[M] de disque[M] compact
on/off/volume
marche[F]/arrêt[M]/volume[M]
compact disc
disque[M] compact
stereo control
contrôle[M] de la stéréophonie[F]
headphone jack
prise[F] casque[M]
power socket
alimentation[F] sur secteur[M]
speaker
haut-parleur[M]
tuning control
sélecteur[M] de stations[F]
cassette player controls
contrôles[M] du lecteur[M] de cassette[F]
cassette
cassette[F]
cassette player
lecteur[M] de cassette[F]
radio section
radio[F]
compact disc player controls
contrôles[M] du lecteur[M] de disque[M] com

communication by telephone

communication^F par téléphone^M

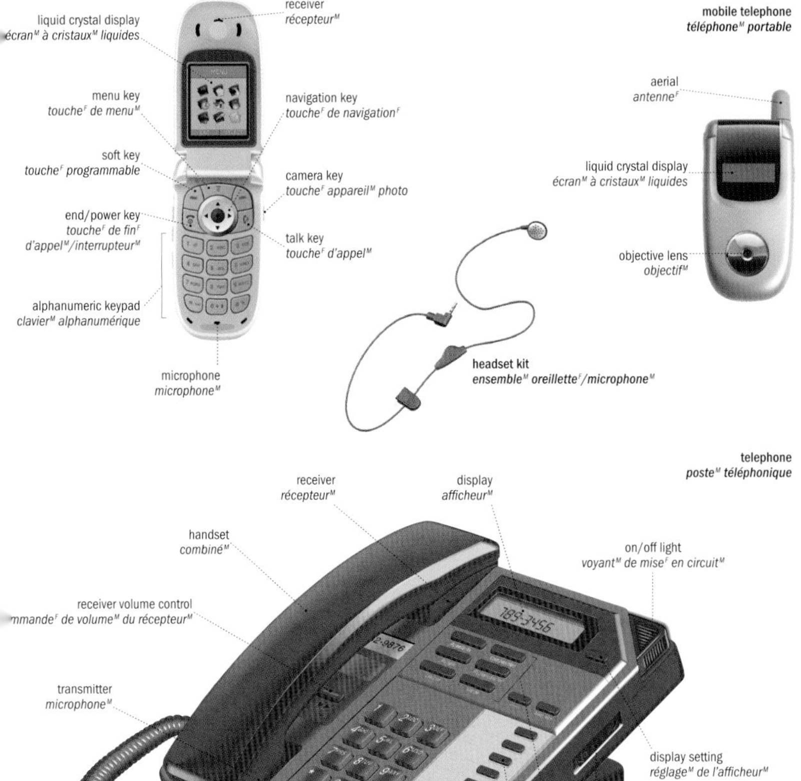

digital answering machine
répondeur*[M] *numérique

speaker
haut-parleur[M]
delete
suppression[F]
previous
message[M] *précédent*
setup
réglages[M]
power button
interrupteur[M] *d'alimentatio*
next
message[M] *suivant*
display
afficheur[M]
volume
volume[M]
play
lecture[F]
stop
arrêt[M]
microphone
microphone[M]
PLAY

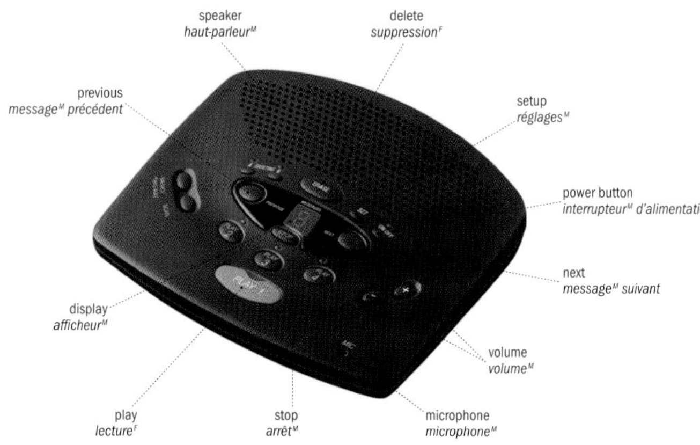

fax machine
***télécopieur*[M]**

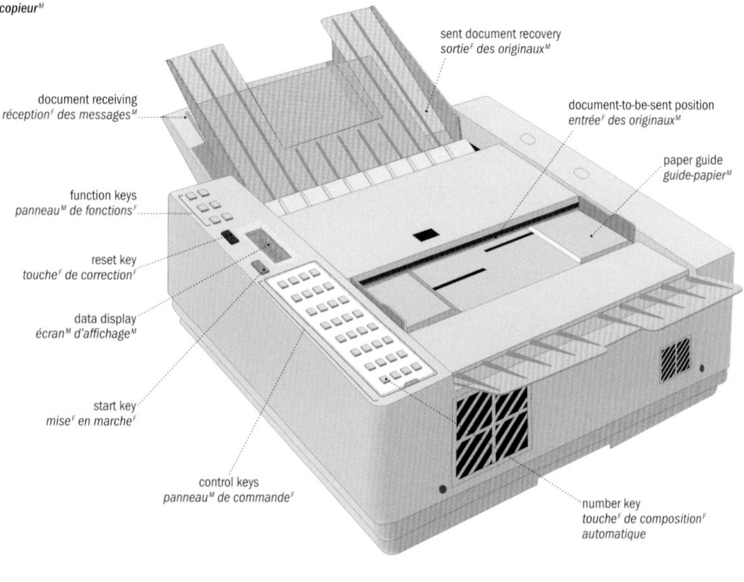

sent document recovery
sortie[F] *des originaux*[M]
document receiving
réception[F] *des messages*[M]
document-to-be-sent position
entrée[F] *des originaux*[M]
paper guide
guide-papier[M]
function keys
panneau[M] *de fonctions*[F]
reset key
touche[F] *de correction*[F]
data display
écran[M] *d'affichage*[M]
start key
mise[F] *en marche*[F]
control keys
panneau[M] *de commande*[F]
number key
touche[F] *de composition*[F] *automatique*

personal computer

micro-ordinateur^{M}

video monitor
écran^{M}

vertical control
réglage^{M} vertical
horizontal control
réglage^{M} horizontal
centring control
réglage^{M} de centrage^{M}
contrast control
réglage^{M} du contraste^{M}
power indicator
témoin^{M} d'alimentation^{F}
power switch
interrupteur^{M}
brightness control
réglage^{M} de la luminosité^{F}

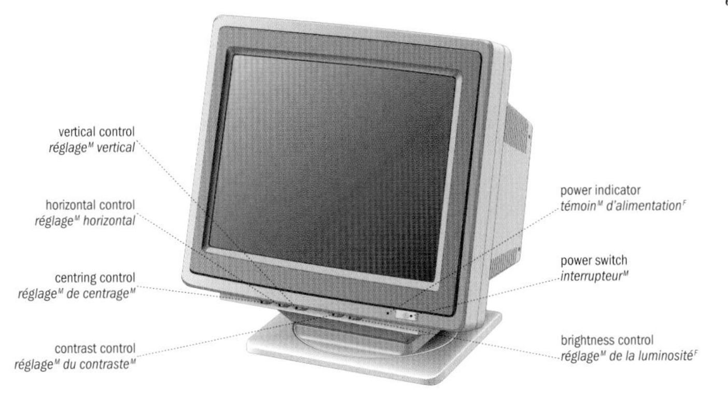

case: back view
-^{M} tour^{F} : vue^{F} arrière

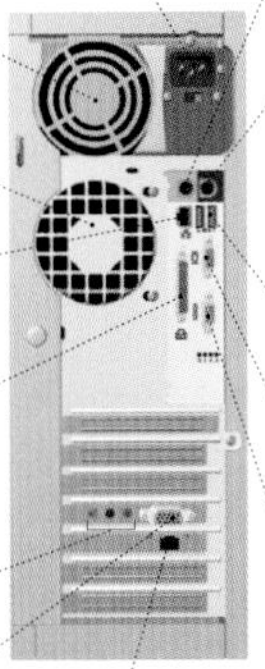

power cable plug
prise^{F} d'alimentation^{F}
mouse port
port^{M} souris^{F}
power supply fan
ventilateur^{M} du bloc^{M} d'alimentation^{F}
keyboard port
port^{M} clavier^{M}
case fan
ventilateur^{M} du boîtier^{M}
network port
port^{M} réseau^{M}
parallel port
port^{M} parallèle
USB port
port^{M} USB
video port
port^{M} vidéo
audio jack
prise^{F} audio
game/MIDI port
port^{M} jeux^{M}/MIDI
serial port
port^{M} série^{F}
internal modem port
port^{M} modem^{M} interne

tower case: front view
boîtier^{M} tour^{F} : vue^{F} avant

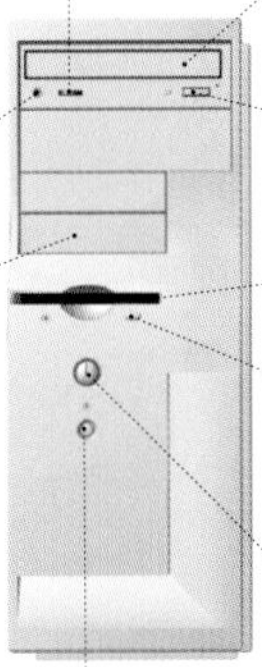

volume control
réglage^{M} du volume^{M}
CD/DVD-ROM drive
lecteur^{M} de CD/DVD-ROM^{M}
CD/DVD-ROM eject button
bouton^{M} d'éjection^{F} du CD/DVD-ROM^{M}
earphone jack
prise^{F} pour écouteurs^{M}
bay filler panel
obturateur^{M} de baie^{F}
floppy disk drive
lecteur^{M} de disquette^{F}
floppy disk eject button
bouton^{M} d'éjection^{F} de la disquette^{F}
power button
bouton^{M} de démarrage^{M}
reset button
bouton^{M} de réinitialisation^{F}

input devices

périphériques[M] d'entrée[F]

keyboard and pictograms
clavier[M] et pictogrammes[M]

function keys
touches[F] de fonction[F]

Internet keys
touches[F] Internet[M]

email key
touche[F] de courriel[M]

escape key
touche[F] d'échappement[M]

tabulation key
touche[F] de tabulation[F]

capitals lock key
touche[F] de verrouillage[M] des majuscules[F]

shift key
touche[F] majuscule

control key
touche[F] de contrôle[M]

start key
touche[F] de démarrage[M]

alternative key
touche[F] alternative

detachable palm rest
repose-poignets[M] détachable

space bar
barre[F] d'espacement[M]

alphanumeric keypad
pavé[M] alphanumérique

escape
échappement[M]

tabulation left
tabulation[F] à gauche

tabulation right
tabulation[F] à droite

capitals lock
verrouillage[M] des majuscules[F]

alternate: level 3 select
alternative : sélection[F] du niveau[M] 3

shift: level 2 select
majuscule[F] : sélection[F] du niveau[M] 2

control: group select
contrôle[M] : sélection[F] de groupe[M]

control
contrôle[M]

alternate
alternative

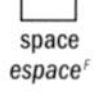

space
espace[F]

non-breaking sp
espace[F] inséca

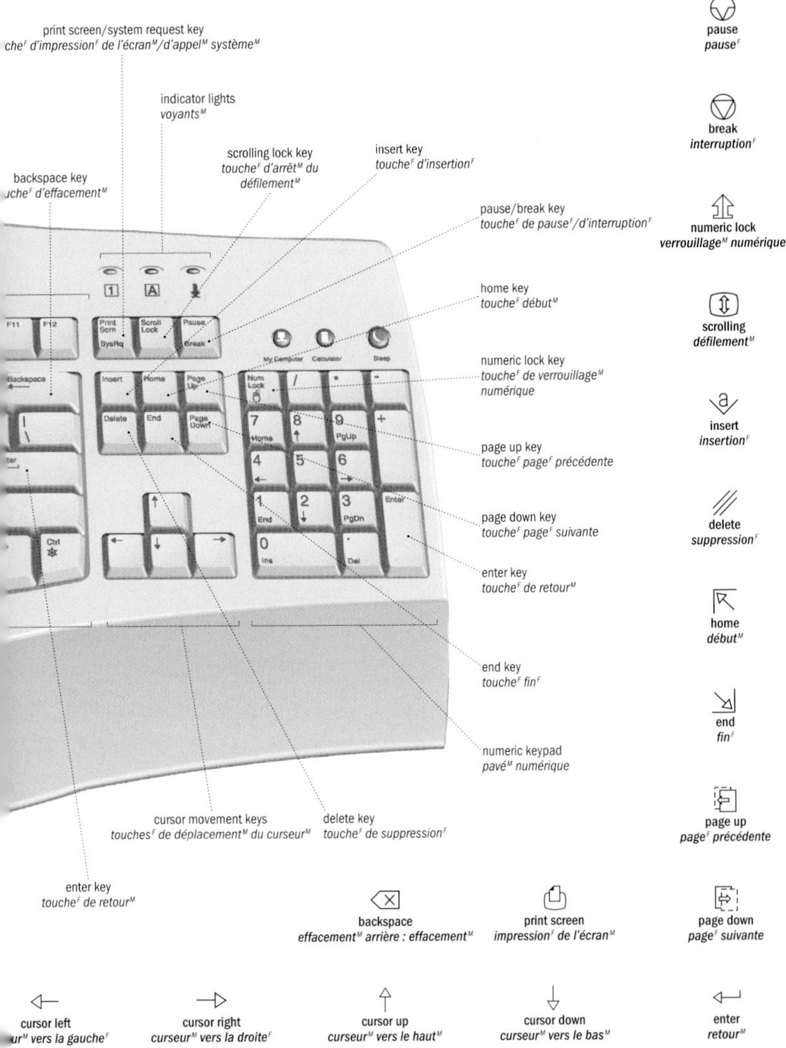

pause
pauseF

break
interruptionF

numeric lock
verrouillageM numérique

scrolling
défilementM

insert
insertionF

delete
suppressionF

home
débutM

end
finF

page up
pageF précédente

backspace
effacementM arrière : effacementM

print screen
impressionF de l'écranM

page down
pageF suivante

cursor left
urM vers la gaucheF

cursor right
curseurM vers la droiteF

cursor up
curseurM vers le hautM

cursor down
curseurM vers le basM

enter
retourM

input devices

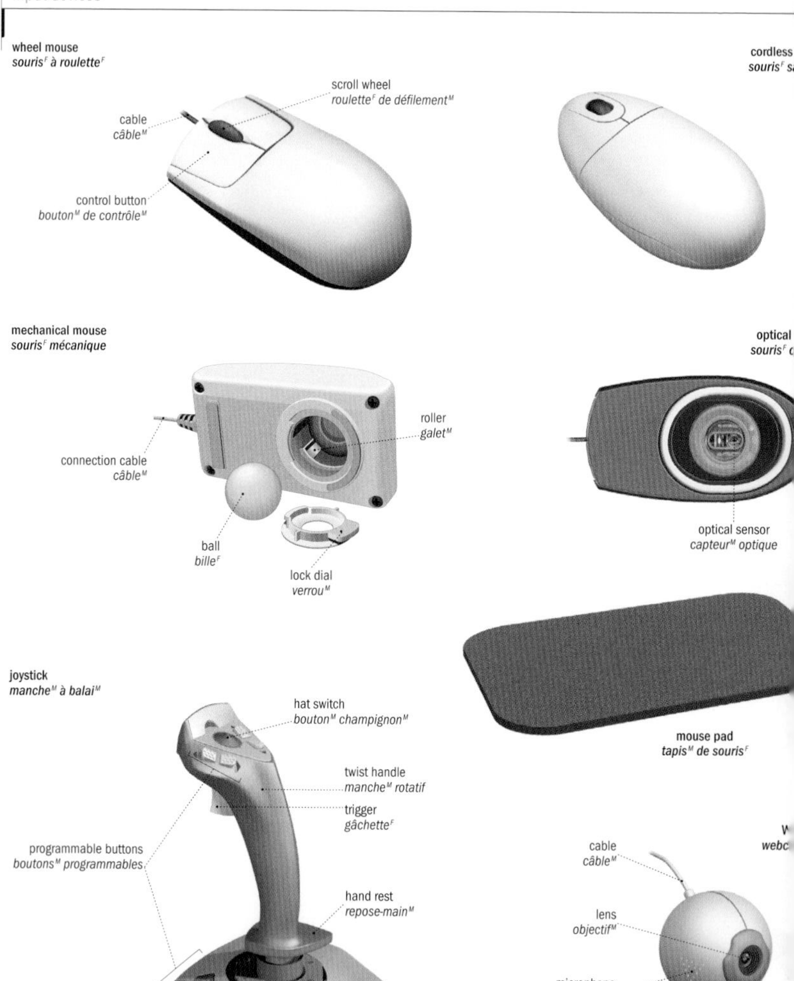

output devices

périphériques[M] de sortie[F]

inkjet printer
imprimante[F] à jet[M] d'encre[F]

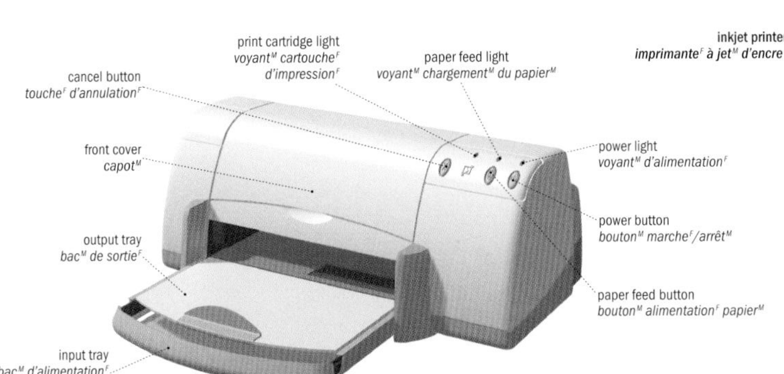

data storage devices

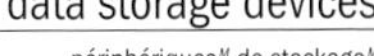

périphériques[M] de stockage[M]

removable hard disk drive
lecteur[M] de disque[M] dur amovible

removable hard disk
disque[M] dur amovible

hard disk drive
lecteur[M] de disque[M] dur

disk
disque[M]

read/write head
tête[F] de lecture[F]/écriture[F]

actuator arm
guide[M]

cassette
cassette[F]

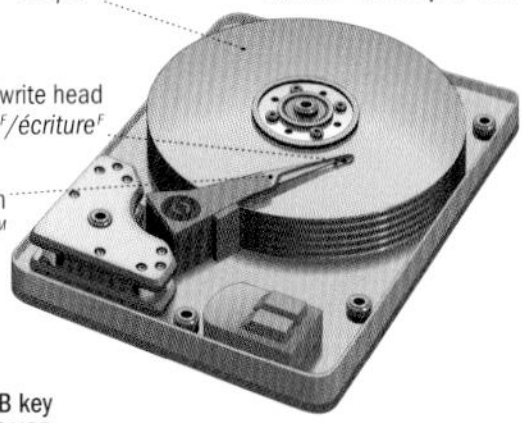

cassette drive
lecteur[M] de cassette[F]

USB key
clé[F] USB

USB connector
connecteur[M] USB

memory card reader
lecteur[M] de carte[F] mémoire[F]

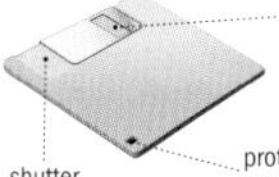

DVD burner
graveur[M] de DVD[M]

diskette, floppy disk
disquette[F]

access window
fenêtre[F] de lecture[F]

protect tab
taquet[M] de verrouillage[M]

shutter
volet[M]

external floppy disk drive
ecteur[M] de disquette[F] externe

Internet

Internet^{M}

URL (uniform resource locator)
adresse^{F} URL^{F} (localisateur^{M} universel de ressources^{F})

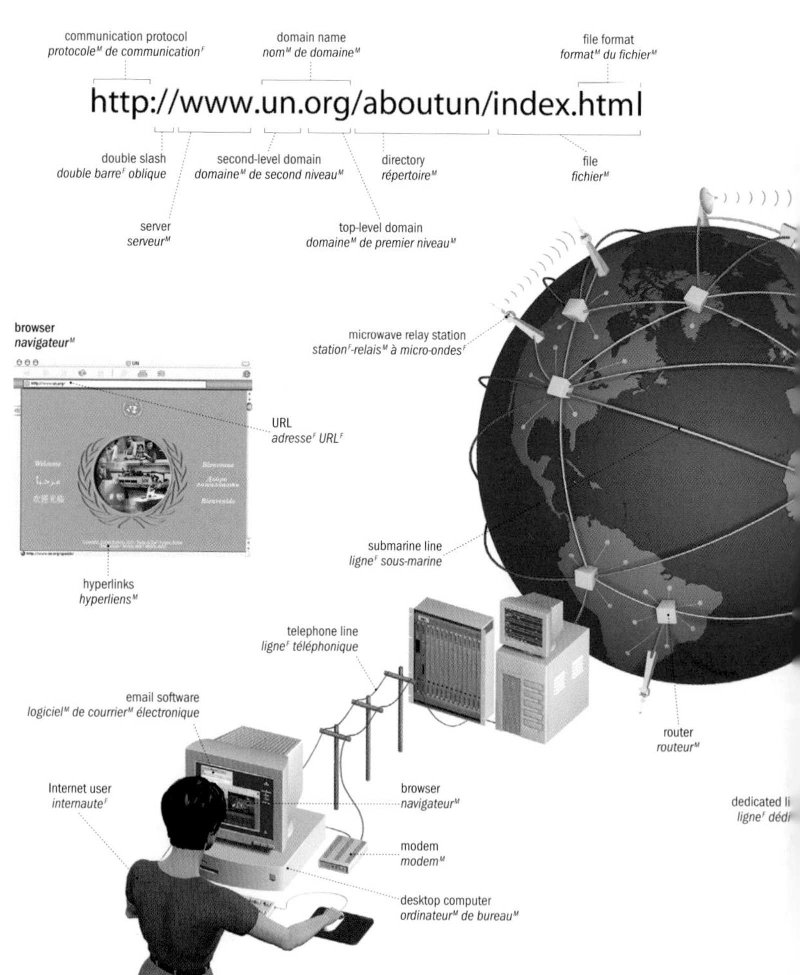

Internet uses

utilisations^F d'Internet^M

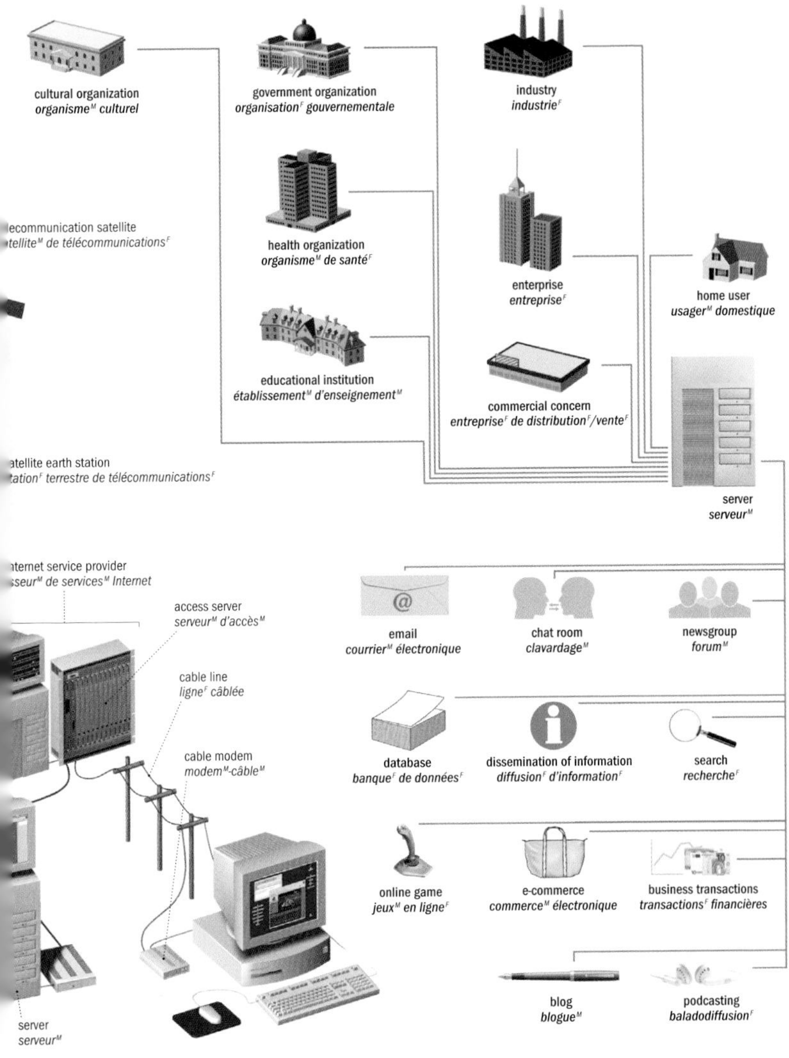

cultural organization
organisme^M culturel

government organization
organisation^F gouvernementale

industry
industrie^F

health organization
organisme^M de santé^F

enterprise
entreprise^F

home user
usager^M domestique

educational institution
établissement^M d'enseignement^M

commercial concern
entreprise^F de distribution^F/vente^F

server
serveur^M

...lecommunication satellite
...tellite^M de télécommunications^F

...atellite earth station
...tation^F terrestre de télécommunications^F

...nternet service provider
...sseur^M de services^M Internet

access server
serveur^M d'accès^M

cable line
ligne^F câblée

cable modem
modem^M-câble^M

server
serveur^M

email
courrier^M électronique

chat room
clavardage^M

newsgroup
forum^M

database
banque^F de données^F

dissemination of information
diffusion^F d'information^F

search
recherche^F

online game
jeux^M en ligne^F

e-commerce
commerce^M électronique

business transactions
transactions^F financières

blog
blogue^M

podcasting
baladodiffusion^F

laptop computer

ordinateur^{M} portable

laptop computer: front view
ordinateur^{M} portable : vue^{F} avant

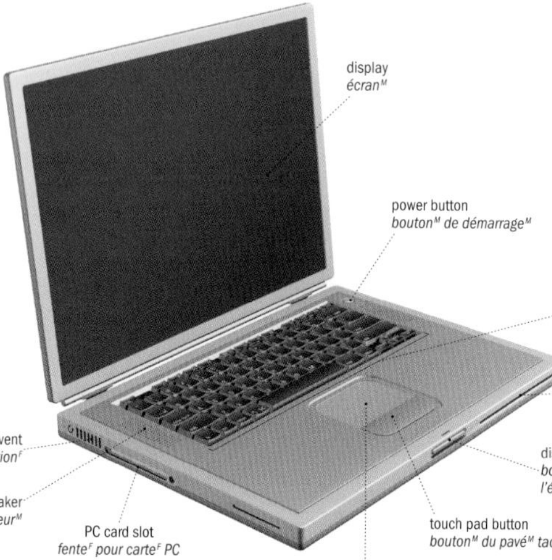

display
écran^{M}
power button
bouton^{M} de démarrage^{M}
keyboard
clavier^{M}
CD/DVD-ROM drive
lecteur^{M} de CD/DV
display release button
bouton^{M} de déverrouillage^{M} de l'écran^{M}
touch pad button
bouton^{M} du pavé^{M} tactile
touch pad
pavé^{M} tactile
PC card slot
fente^{F} pour carte^{F} PC
speaker
haut-parleur^{M}
cooling vent
fentes^{F} d'aération^{F}

laptop computer: re
ordinateur^{M} portab

power adapter
adaptateur^{M} de courant^{M}

direct-current power cord
cordon^{M} d'alimentation^{F} en courant^{M} continu
alternating-current power cord
cordon^{M} d'alimentation^{F} secteur^{M}
infrared port
port^{M} infrarouge
internal modem po
port^{M} modem^{M} inte
S-Video output
sortie^{F} S-Video
video port
port^{M} vidéo
cooling vent
fentes^{F} d'aération^{F}
power adapter port
port^{M} pour adaptateur^{M} de courant^{M}
FireWire port
port^{M} FireWire
Ethernet port
port^{M} Ethernet^{M}
USB port
port^{M} USB

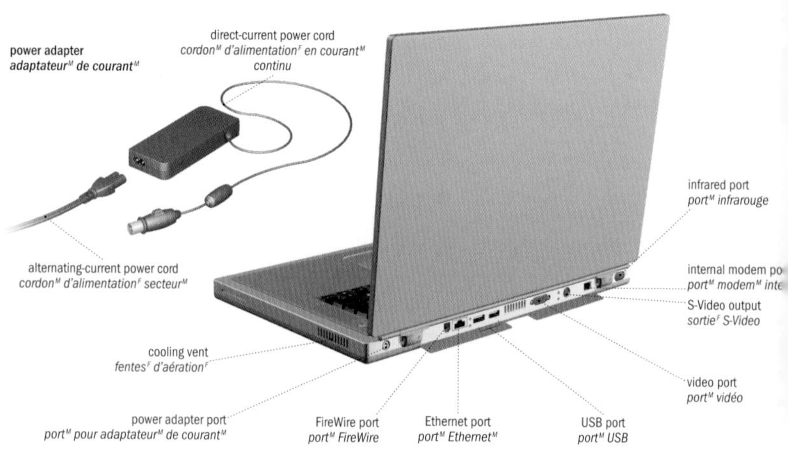

PDA

ordinateur[M] de poche[F]

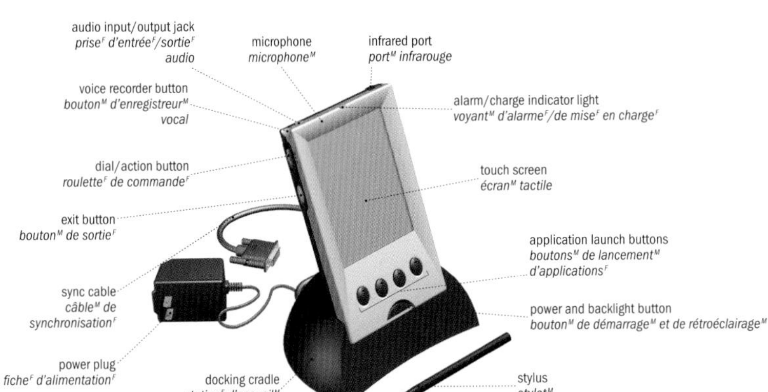

stationery

articles[M] de bureau[M]

pocket calculator
calculette[F]

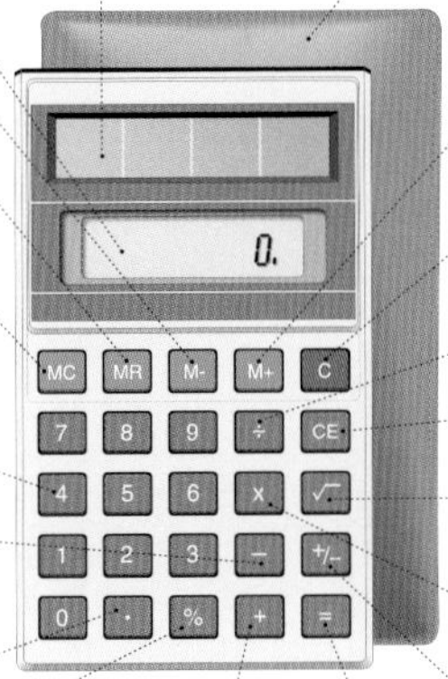

display
affichage[M]

solar cell
alimentation[F] solaire

wallet
étui[M]

ic calculator
trice[F] scientifique

subtract from memory
soustraction[F] en mémoire[F]

add in memory
addition[F] en mémoire[F]

memory recall
rappel[M] de mémoire[F]

clear key
effacement[M] total

memory cancel
effacement[M] de mémoire[F]

divide key
division[F]

clear-entry key
effacement[M] partiel

number key
touche[F] numérique

machine
trice[F] à imprimante[F]

square root key
racine[F] carrée

subtract key
soustraction[F]

multiply key
multiplication[F]

decimal key
touche[F] de décimale[F]

percent key
pourcentage[M]

add key
addition[F]

equals key
touche[F] de résultat[M]

change sign key
inverseur[M] de signe[M]

0. MC MR M- M+ C 7 8 9 ÷ CE 4 5 6 x √ 1 2 3 – +/- 0 · % + =

stationery

for time use
pour l'emploi[M] *du temps*[M]

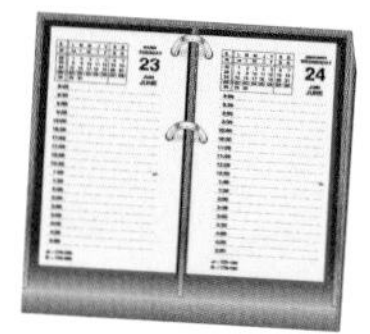

calendar pad
bloc[M]*-éphéméride*[F]

tear-off calendar
calendrier[M]*-mémorandum*[M]

personal or
orga

display
écran[M]

alphabetical keypad
pavé[M] *alphabétique*

numeric
pavé[M] *nu*

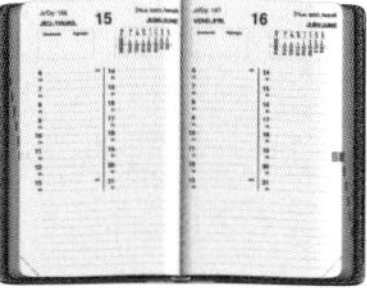

appointment book
agenda[M]

self-stick note
feuillet[M] *adhésif*

memo pad
bloc[M]*-notes*[F]

for correspondence
pour la correspondance[F]

rubber stamp
timbre[M] *caoutchouc*[M]

stamp pad
tampon[M] *encreur*

numbering stamp
numéroteur[M]

date stamp
timbre[M] *dateu*

desk tray
boîte[F] *à courrier*[M]

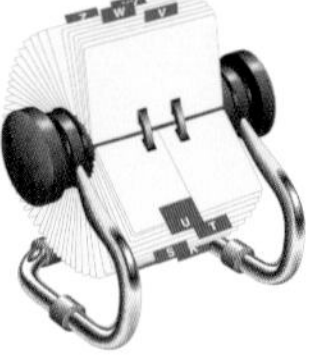

rotary file
fichier[M] *rotatif*

telephone index
répertoire[M] *téléphonique*

COMMUNICATIONS AND OFFICE AUTOMATION

for filing
pour le classement[M]

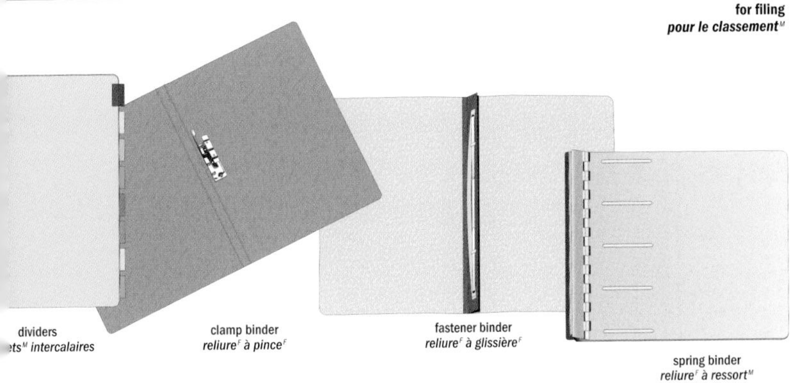

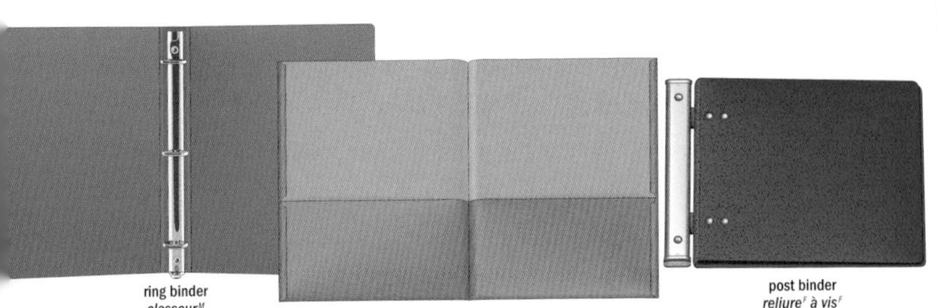

stationery

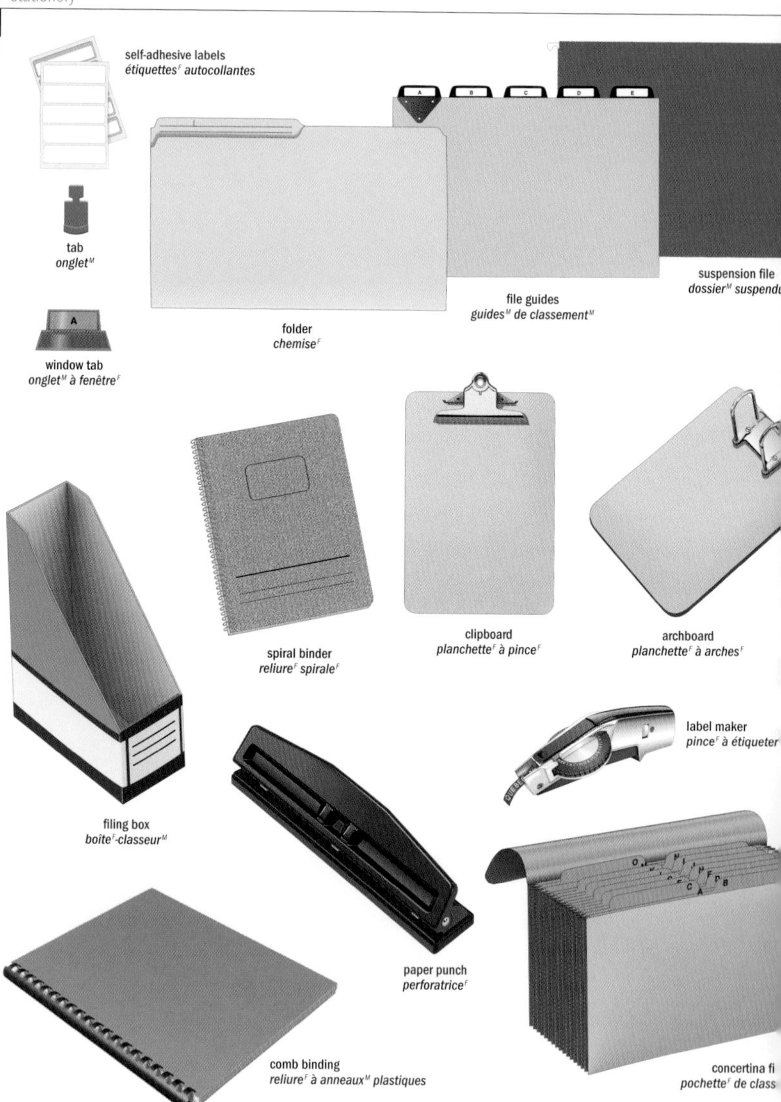
self-adhesive labels
étiquettes^F autocollantes
tab
onglet^M
window tab
onglet^M à fenêtre^F
folder
chemise^F
file guides
guides^M de classement^M
suspension file
dossier^M suspendu
spiral binder
reliure^F spirale^F
clipboard
planchette^F à pince^F
archboard
planchette^F à arches^F
label maker
pince^F à étiqueter
filing box
boîte^F-classeur^M
paper punch
perforatrice^F
comb binding
reliure^F à anneaux^M plastiques
concertina fi
pochette^F de class

miscellaneous articles
articles[M] divers

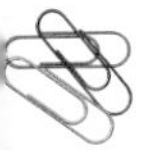

paper clips
trombones[M]

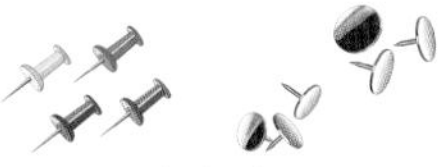

drawing pins
punaises[F]

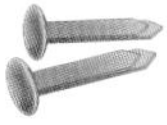

paper fasteners
attaches[F] parisiennes

parcel tape dispenser
dévidoir[M] pistolet[M]

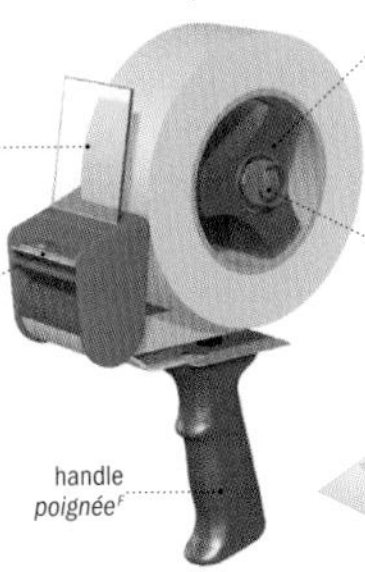

hub
moyeu[M]

tape guide
guide-bande[M]

tension adjustment screw
vis[F] de réglage[M] de tension[F]

cutting blade
lame[F]

handle
poignée[F]

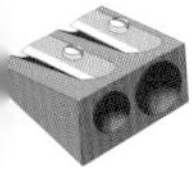

pencil sharpener
taille-crayon[M]

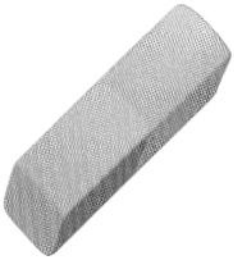

eraser
gomme[F]

spike file
pique-notes[M]

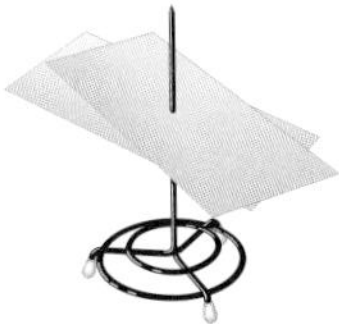

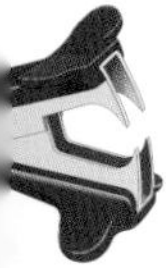

aple remover
dégrafeuse[F]

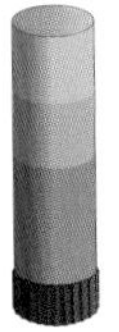

tape dispenser
dévidoir[M] de ruban[M] adhésif

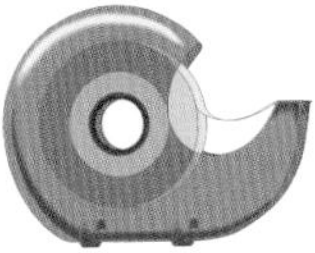

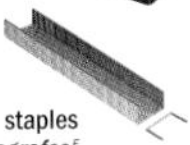

glue stick
bâtonnet[M] de colle[F]

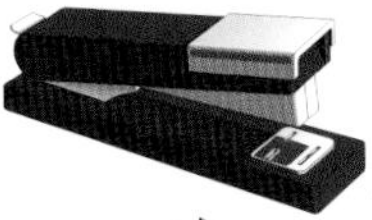

stapler
agrafeuse[F]

staples
agrafes[F]

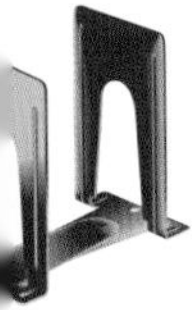

book ends
serre-livres[M]

paper-clip holder
distributeur[M] de trombones[M]

magnet
aimant[M]

pencil sharpener
taille-crayon[M]

oard
[M] d'affichage[M]

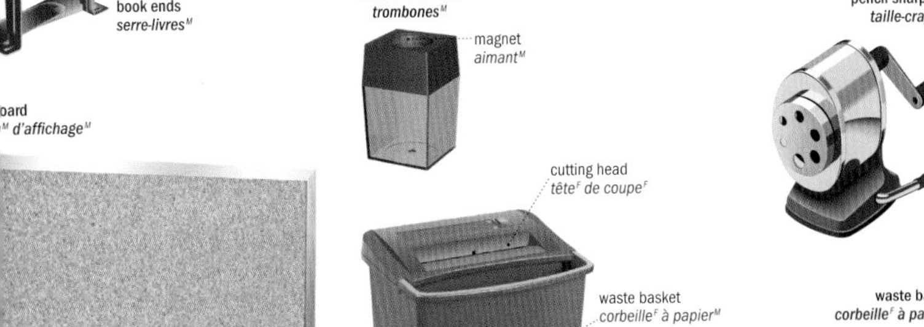

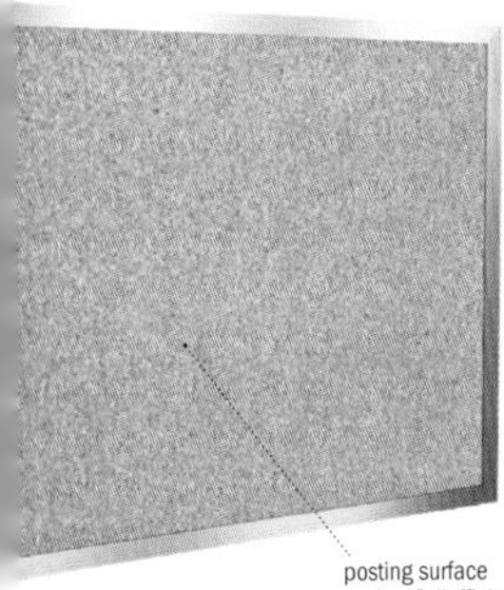

cutting head
tête[F] de coupe[F]

waste basket
corbeille[F] à papier[M]

waste basket
corbeille[F] à papier[M]

posting surface
surface[F] d'affichage[M]

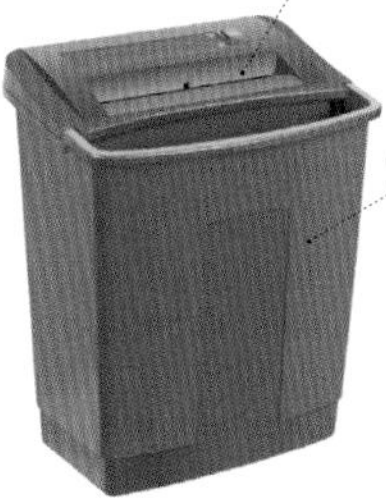

paper shredder
destructeur[M] de documents[M]

road system

système[M] routier

cross section of a road
coupe[F] d'une route[F]

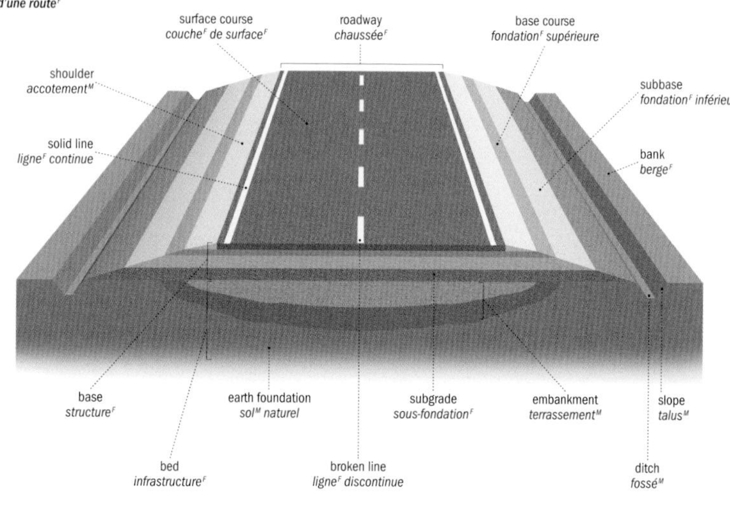

examples of interchanges
exemples[M] d'échangeurs[M]

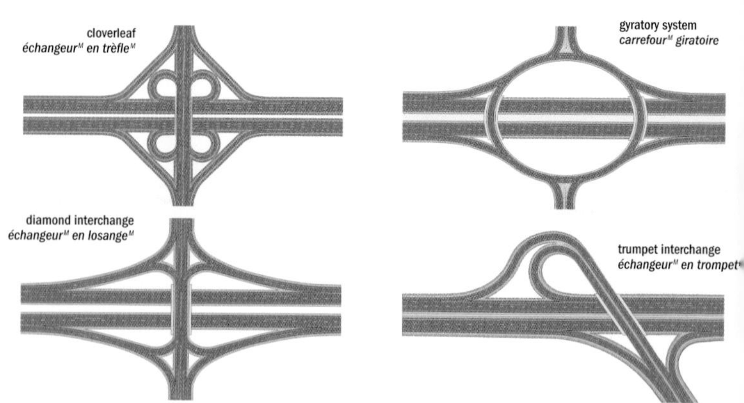

cloverleaf
échangeur[M] en trèfle[M]

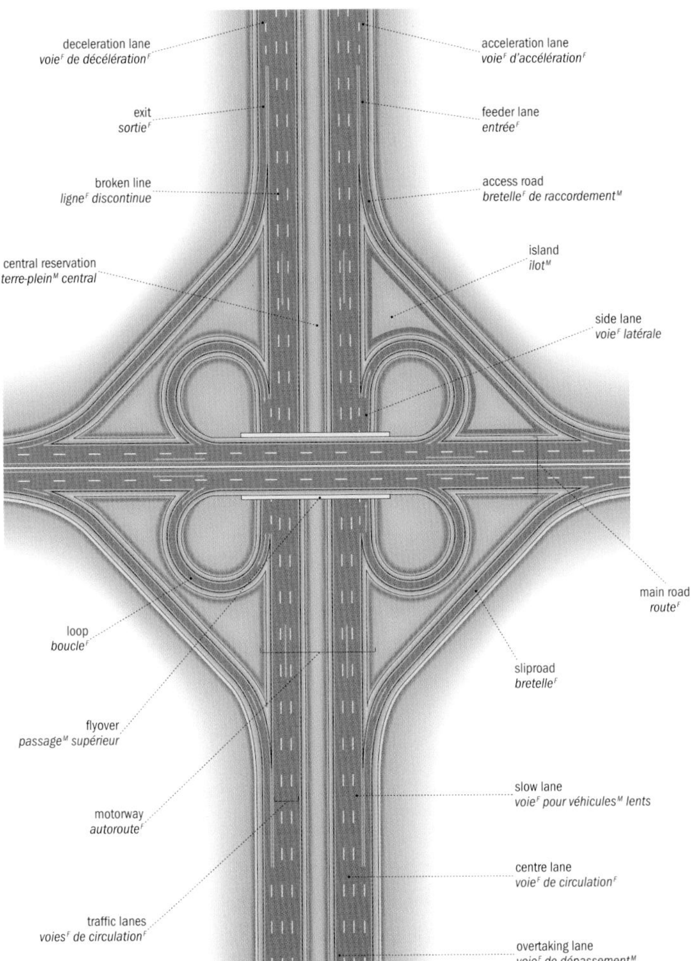

fixed bridges

ponts^M fixes

beam bridge
pont^M à poutre^F

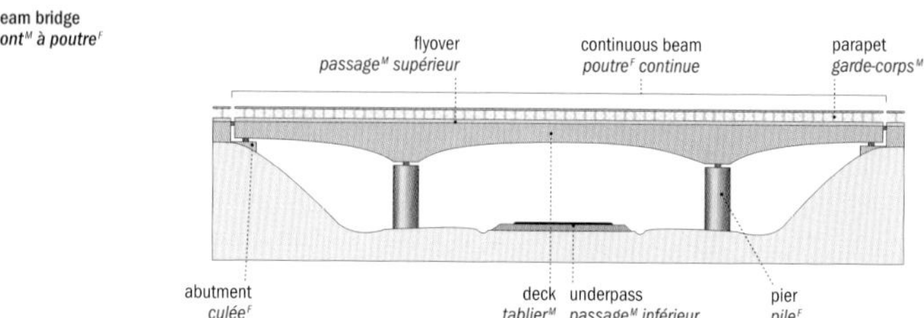

suspension bridge
pont^M suspendu à câble^M porteur

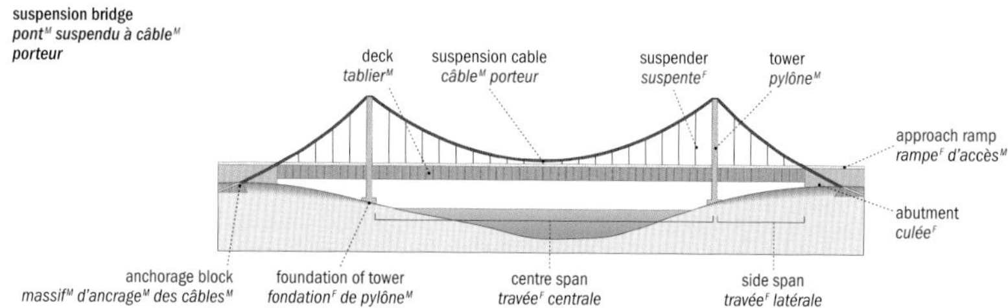

cantilever bridge
pont^M cantilever

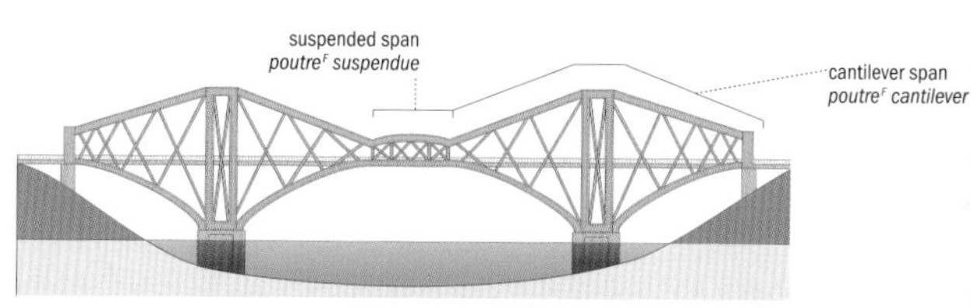

movable bridges

ponts^M mobiles

swing bridge
pont^M tournant

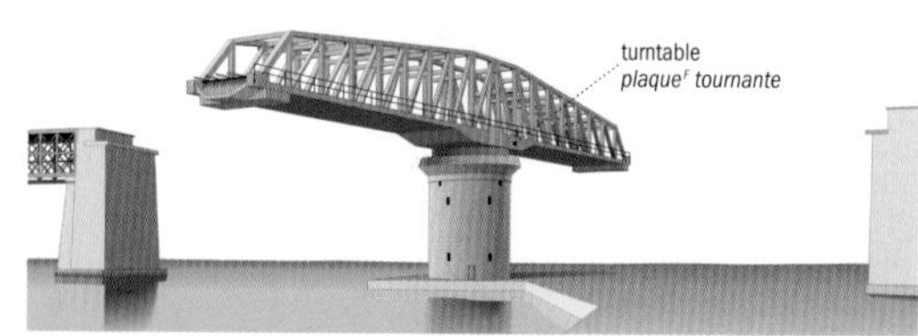

movable bridges

counterweight
contrepoids^M

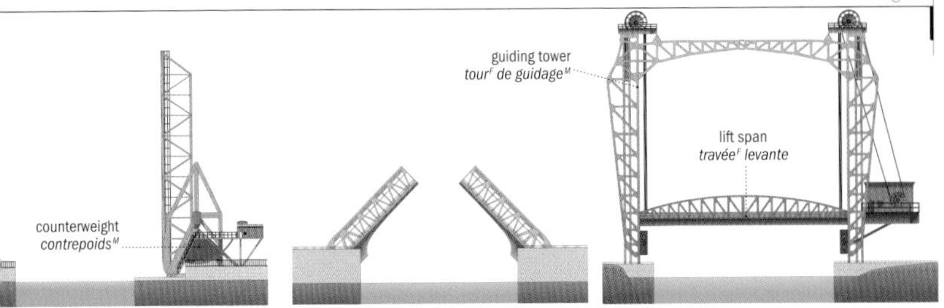

single-leaf bascule bridge
pont^M basculant à simple volée^F

double-leaf bascule bridge
pont^M basculant à double volée^F

guiding tower
tour^F de guidage^M
lift span
travée^F levante

lift bridge
pont^M levant

road tunnel

tunnel^M routier

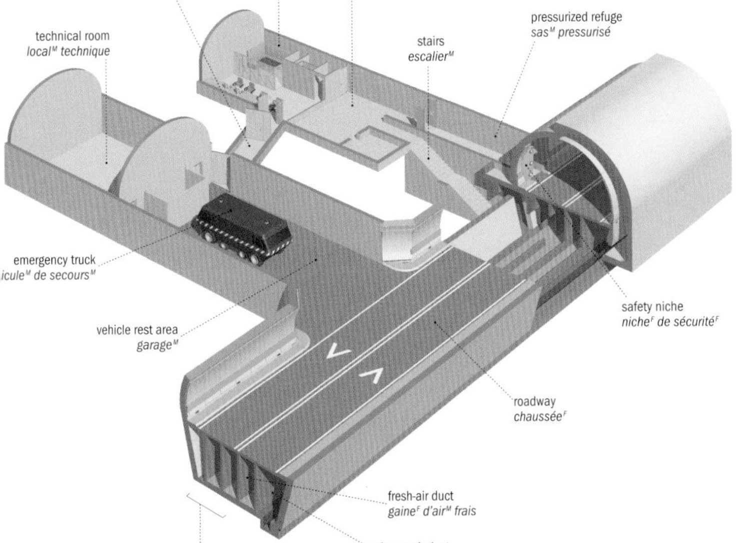

connecting gallery
galerie^F de liaison^F
emergency station
poste^M de secours^M
shelter
abri^M
technical room
local^M technique
pressurized refuge
sas^M pressurisé
stairs
escalier^M
emergency truck
icule^M de secours^M
safety niche
niche^F de sécurité^F
vehicle rest area
garage^M
roadway
chaussée^F
fresh-air duct
gaine^F d'air^M frais
exhaust air duct
gaine^F d'air^M vicié
evacuation route
chemin^M d'évacuation^F

TRANSPORT AND MACHINERY

service station

station[F]-service[M]

petrol pump
distributeur[M] d'essence[F]

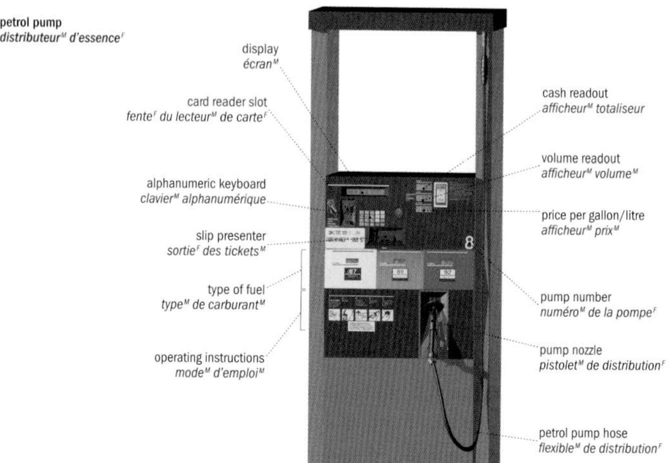

service station
station[F]-service[M]

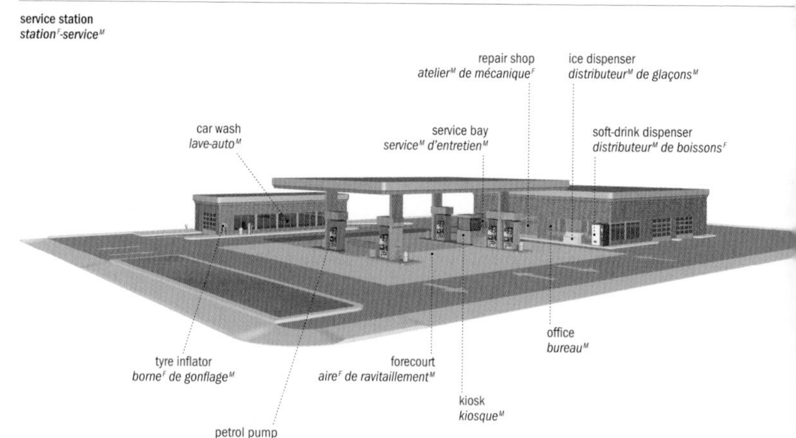

car
automobile^F

examples of bodywork
exemples^M de carrosseries^F

sports car
voiture^F sport^M

Micro Compact Car
voiture^F micro-compacte

hatchback
trois-portes^F

coupé
coupé^M

convertible
cabriolet^M

four-door saloon
berline^F

estate car
break^M

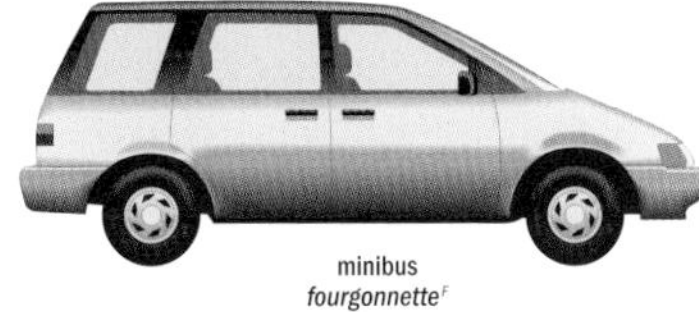
minibus
fourgonnette^F

all-terrain vehicle
véhicule^M tout-terrain^M

pickup truck
camionnette^F

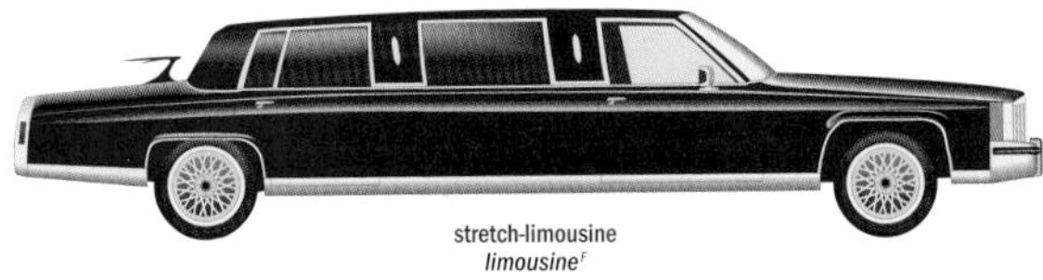
stretch-limousine
limousine^F

body
carrosserie^F

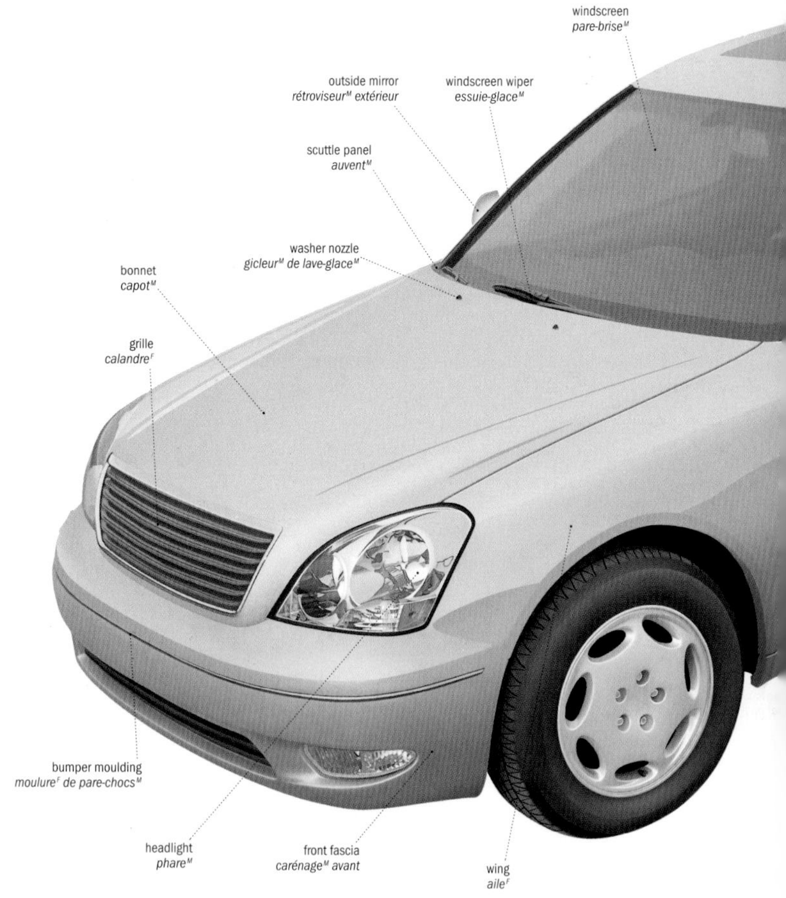

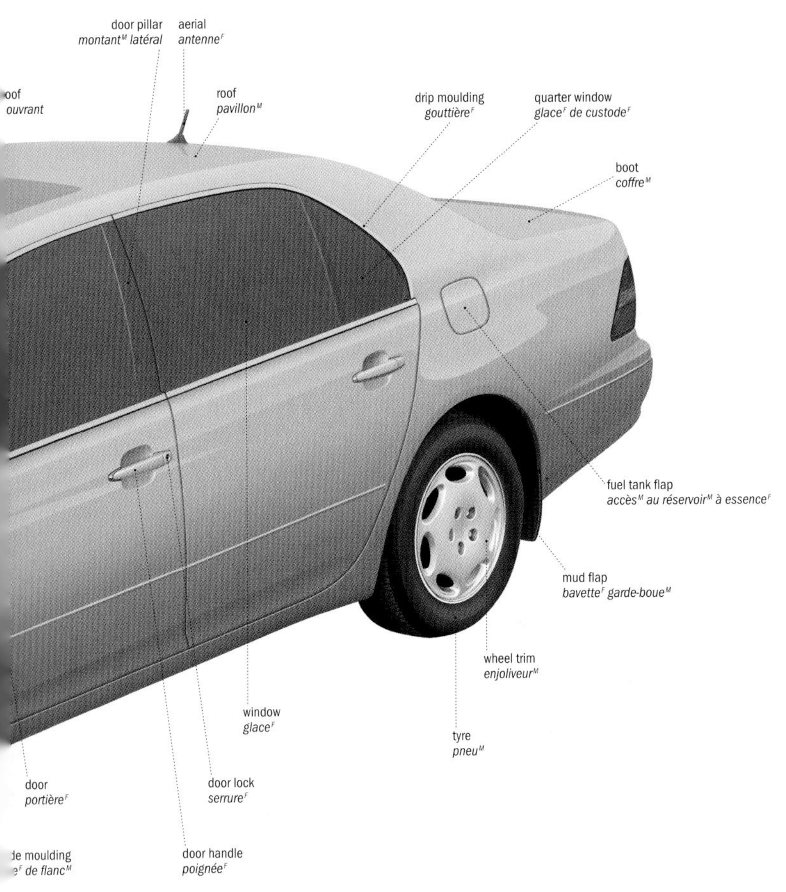
door pillar
montant^M latéral
aerial
antenne^F
oof
ouvrant
roof
pavillon^M
drip moulding
gouttière^F
quarter window
glace^F de custode^F
boot
coffre^M
fuel tank flap
accès^M au réservoir^M à essence^F
mud flap
bavette^F garde-boue^M
wheel trim
enjoliveur^M
window
glace^F
tyre
pneu^M
door
portière^F
door lock
serrure^F
de moulding
e^F de flanc^M
door handle
poignée^F

car

car systems: main parts
principaux organes[M] des systèmes[M] automobiles

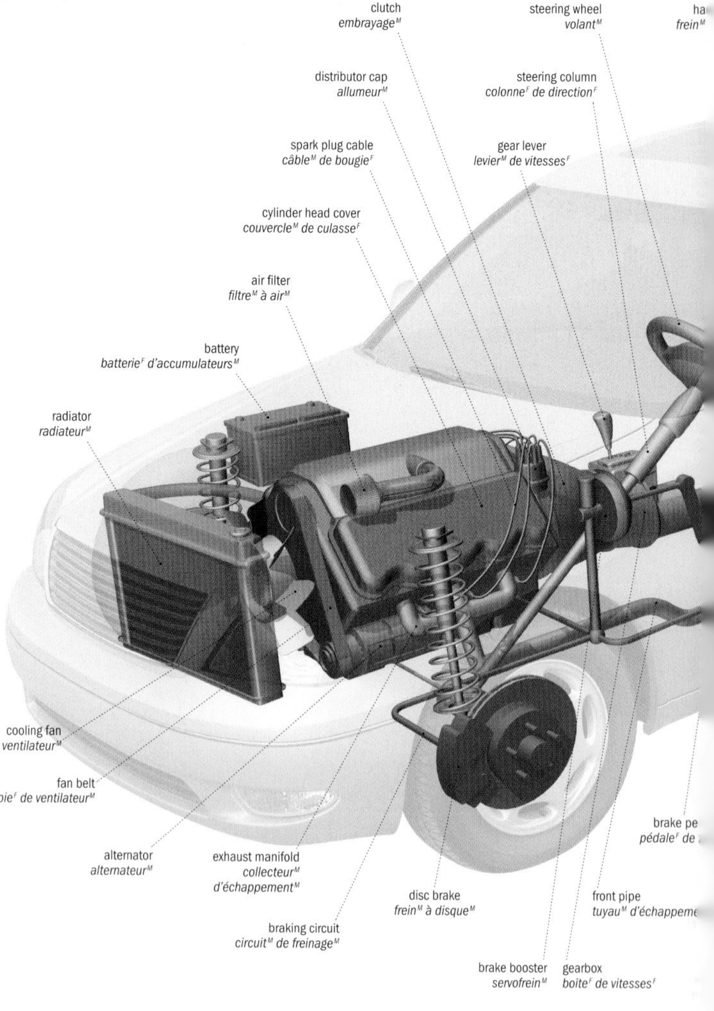

clutch
embrayage[M]

steering wheel
volant[M]

ha
frein[M]

distributor cap
allumeur[M]

steering column
colonne[F] de direction[F]

spark plug cable
câble[M] de bougie[F]

gear lever
levier[M] de vitesses[F]

cylinder head cover
couvercle[M] de culasse[F]

air filter
filtre[M] à air[M]

battery
batterie[F] d'accumulateurs[M]

radiator
radiateur[M]

cooling fan
ventilateur[M]

fan belt
courroie[F] de ventilateur[M]

brake pe
pédale[F] de

alternator
alternateur[M]

exhaust manifold
collecteur[M] d'échappement[M]

disc brake
frein[M] à disque[M]

front pipe
tuyau[M] d'échappeme

braking circuit
circuit[M] de freinage[M]

brake booster
servofrein[M]

gearbox
boite[F] de vitesses[F]

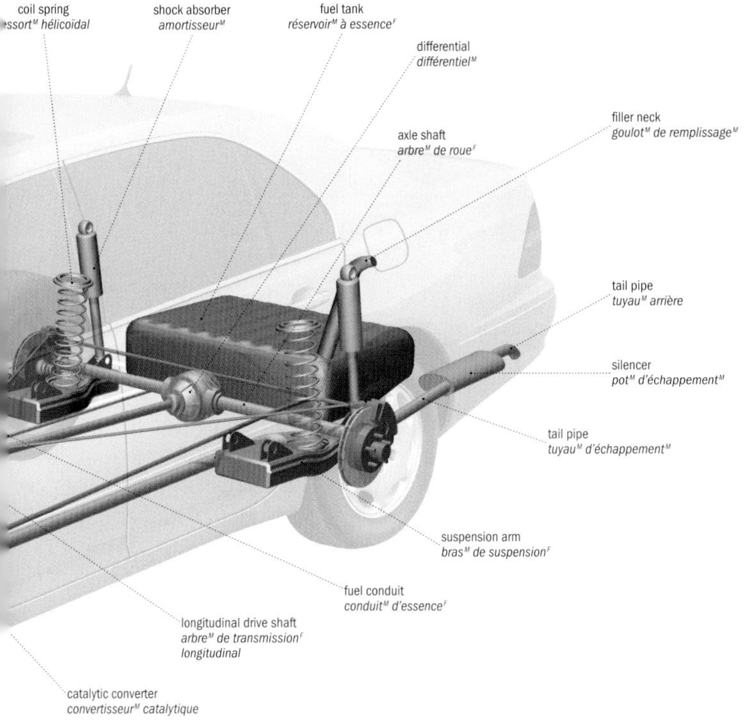

coil spring
ssort[M] hélicoïdal
shock absorber
amortisseur[M]
fuel tank
réservoir[M] à essence[F]
differential
différentiel[M]
filler neck
goulot[M] de remplissage[M]
axle shaft
arbre[M] de roue[F]
tail pipe
tuyau[M] arrière
silencer
pot[M] d'échappement[M]
tail pipe
tuyau[M] d'échappement[M]
suspension arm
bras[M] de suspension[F]
fuel conduit
conduit[M] d'essence[F]
longitudinal drive shaft
arbre[M] de transmission[F] longitudinal
catalytic converter
convertisseur[M] catalytique

car systems
systèmes[M] automobiles

suspension system
système[M] de suspension[F]

ansmission system
stème[M] de transmission[F]

fuel supply system
système[M] d'alimentation[F] en essence[F]

steering system
système[M] de direction[F]

braking system
système[M] de freinage[M]

ectrical system
stème[M] électrique

exhaust system
système[M] d'échappement[M]

petrol engine
moteur[M] à essence[F]

cooling system
système[M] de refroidissement[M]

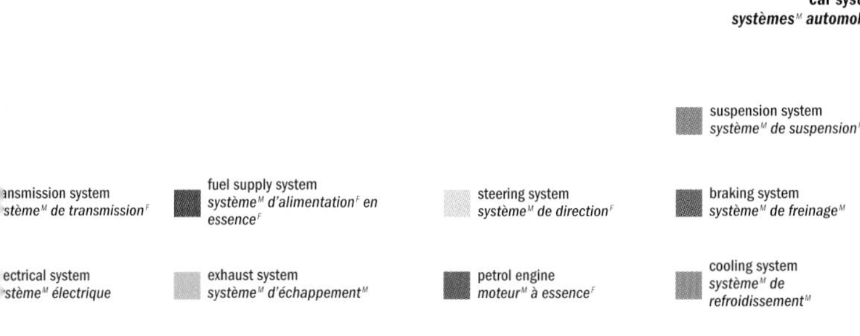

car

front lights
feux[M] avant

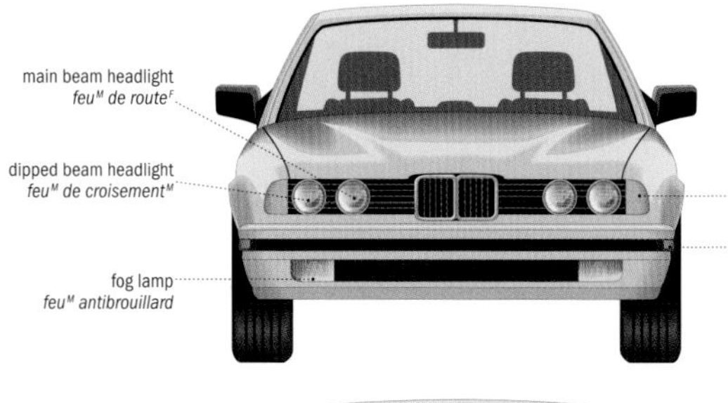

rear lights
feux[M] arrière

door
portière[F]

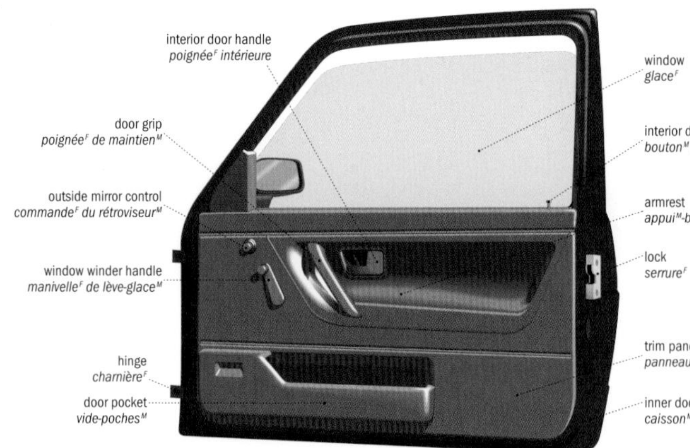

TRANSPORT AND MACHINERY

et seat: front view
^{M}-baquet^{M} : vue^{F} de face^{F}

bucket seat: side view
siège^{M}-baquet^{M} : vue^{F} de profil^{M}

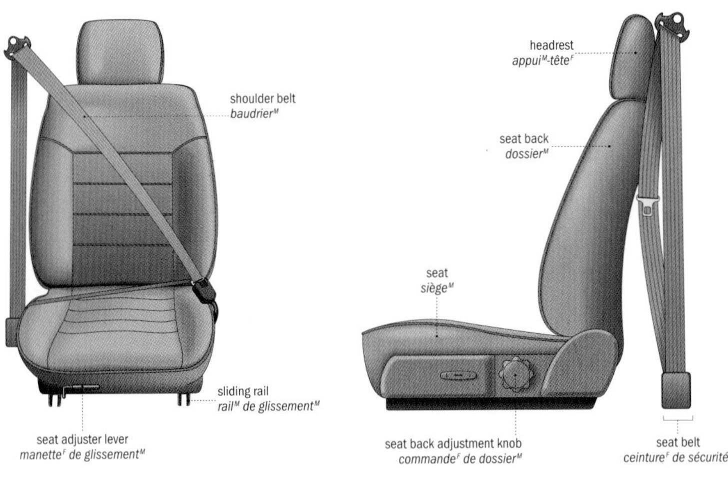

rear seat
banquette^{F} arrière

car

dashboard
***tableau**ᴹ **de bord**ᴹ*

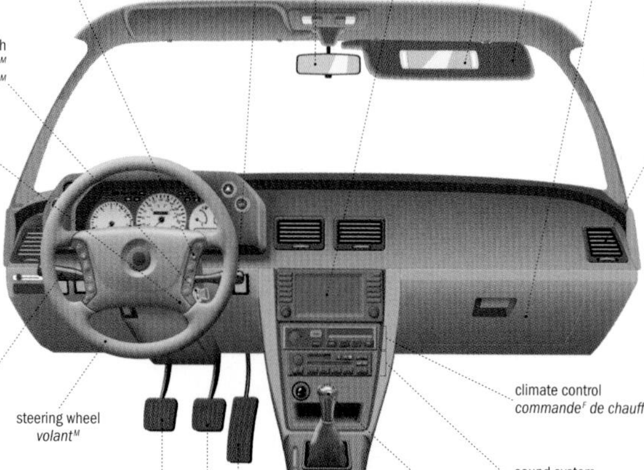

rearview mirror
*rétroviseur*ᴹ
vanity mirror
*miroir*ᴹ *de courtoisie*ᶠ
wiper control
*commande*ᶠ *d'essuie-glace*ᴹ
on-board computer
*ordinateur*ᴹ *de bord*ᴹ
sun visor
*pare-soleil*ᴹ
cruise control
*régulateur*ᴹ *de vitesse*ᶠ
glove compartment
*boite*ᶠ *à gants*ᴹ
ignition switch
*commutateur*ᴹ *d'allumage*ᴹ
vent
*bouche*ᶠ *d'air*ᴹ
horn
*avertisseur*ᴹ
climate control
*commande*ᶠ *de chauffage*ᴹ
steering wheel
*volant*ᴹ
sound system
*système*ᴹ *audio*
clutch pedal
*pédale*ᶠ *de débrayage*ᴹ
gear lever
*levier*ᴹ *de vitesse*ᶠ
dipping/indicator stalk
*éclairage*ᴹ*/clignotant*ᴹ
handbrake lever
*levier*ᴹ *de frein*ᴹ *à main*ᶠ
centre console
*console*ᶠ *centrale*
brake pedal
*pédale*ᶠ *de frein*ᴹ
accelerator pedal
*pédale*ᶠ *d'accélérateur*ᴹ

air bag restraint system
système**ᴹ **de retenue**ᶠ **à sacs**ᴹ **gonflables

air bag
*sac*ᴹ *gonflable*
safing sensor
*détecteur*ᴹ *de sécurité*ᶠ
primary crash sensor
*détecteur*ᴹ *d'impact*ᴹ *primaire*
electrical cable
*câble*ᴹ *électrique*

TRANSPORT AND MACHINERY

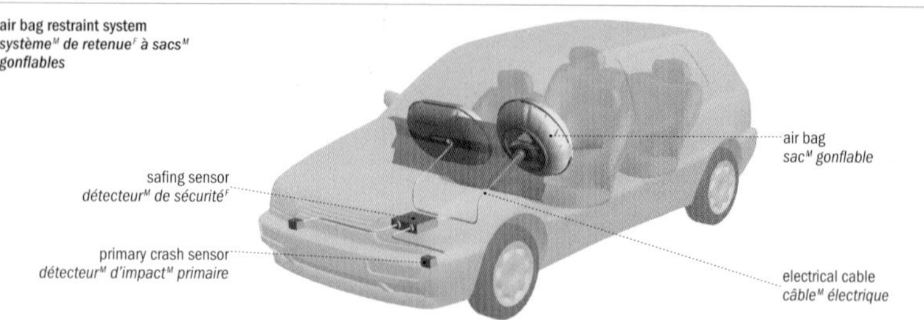

instrument panel
instruments[M] de bord[M]

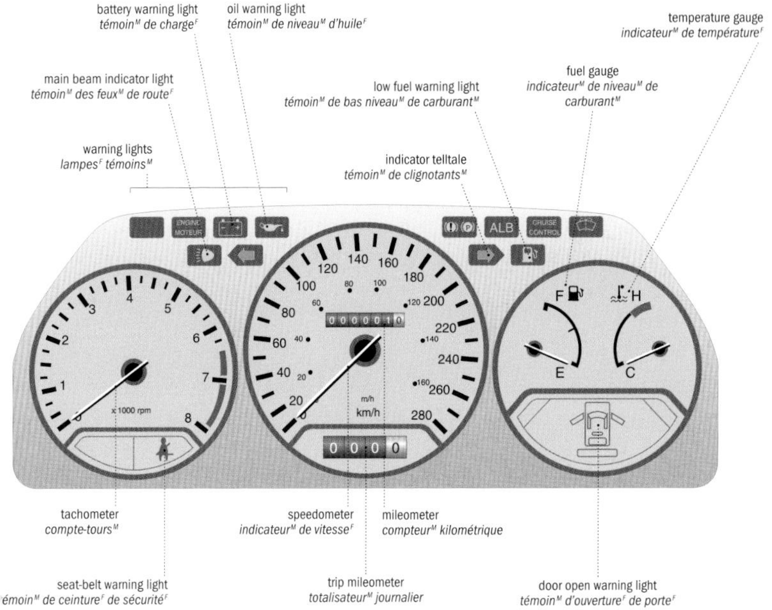

battery warning light
témoin[M] de charge[F]

oil warning light
témoin[M] de niveau[M] d'huile[F]

temperature gauge
indicateur[M] de température[F]

main beam indicator light
témoin[M] des feux[M] de route[F]

low fuel warning light
témoin[M] de bas niveau[M] de carburant[M]

fuel gauge
indicateur[M] de niveau[M] de carburant[M]

warning lights
lampes[F] témoins[M]

indicator telltale
témoin[M] de clignotants[M]

ENGINE MOTEUR ALB CRUISE CONTROL F H E C 0 1 2 3 4 5 6 7 8 x 1000 rpm 20 40 60 80 100 120 140 160 180 200 220 240 260 280 m/h km/h 0000010 0000

tachometer
compte-tours[M]

speedometer
indicateur[M] de vitesse[F]

mileometer
compteur[M] kilométrique

seat-belt warning light
témoin[M] de ceinture[F] de sécurité[F]

trip mileometer
totalisateur[M] journalier

door open warning light
témoin[M] d'ouverture[F] de porte[F]

windscreen wiper
essuie-glace[M]

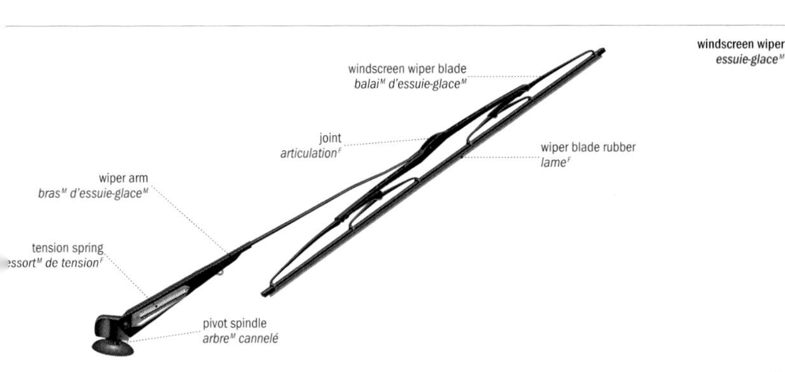

accessories
accessoires[M]

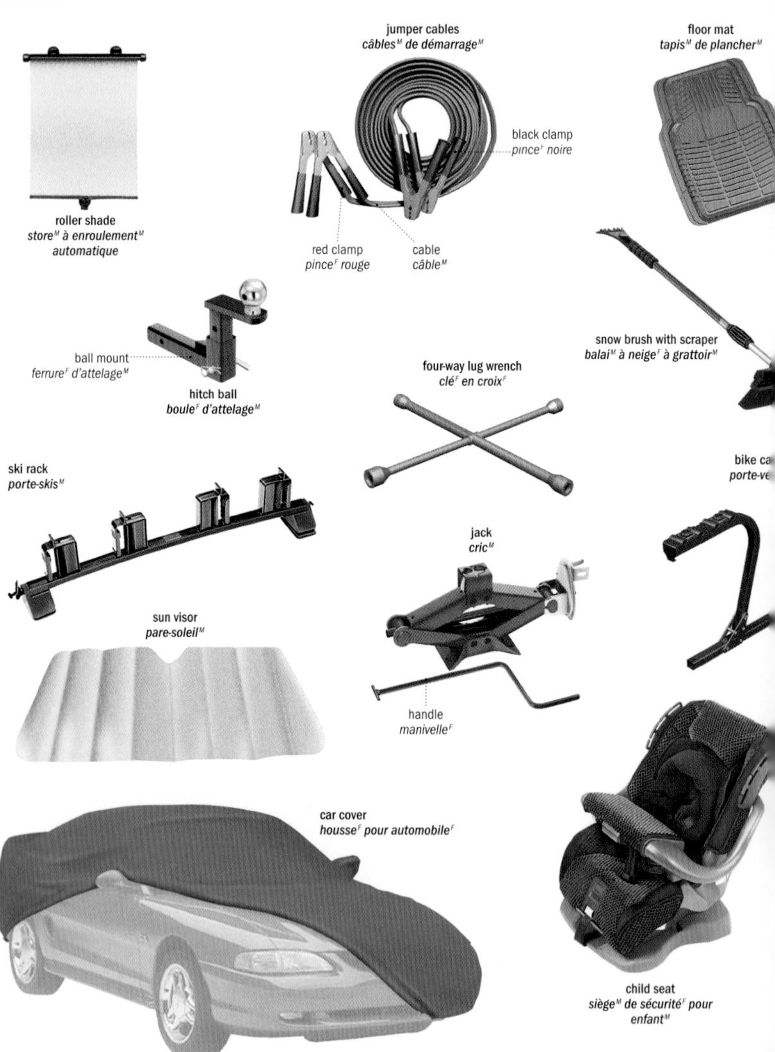

brakes
freins[M]

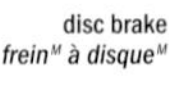

disc brake
frein[M] à disque[M]

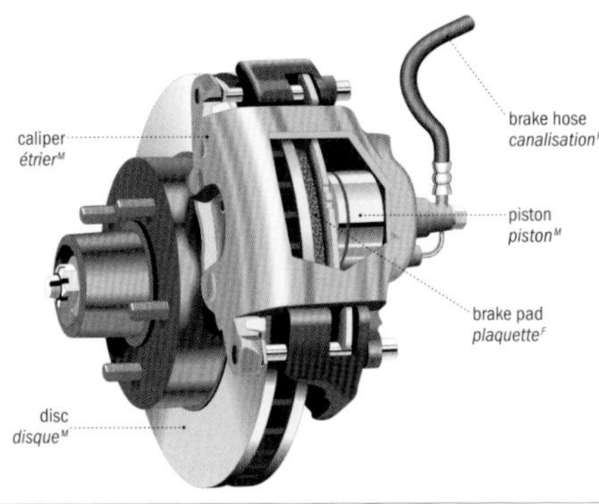

drum brake
frein[M] à tambour[M]

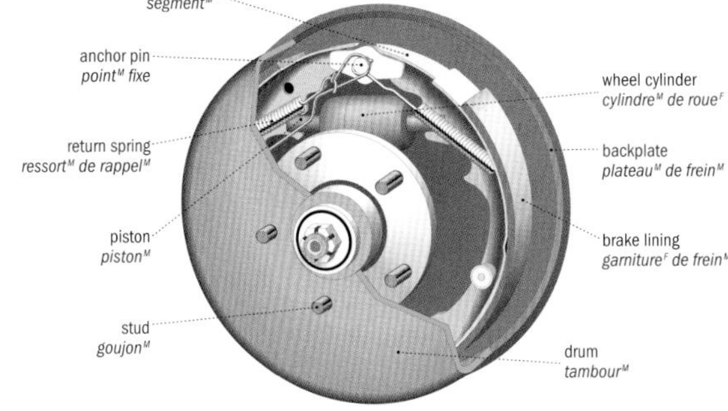

antilock braking system (ABS)
système[M] de freinage[M] antiblocage

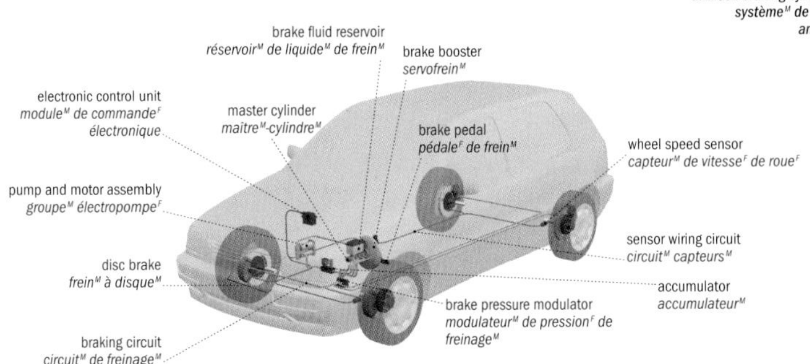

tyre

pneu[M]

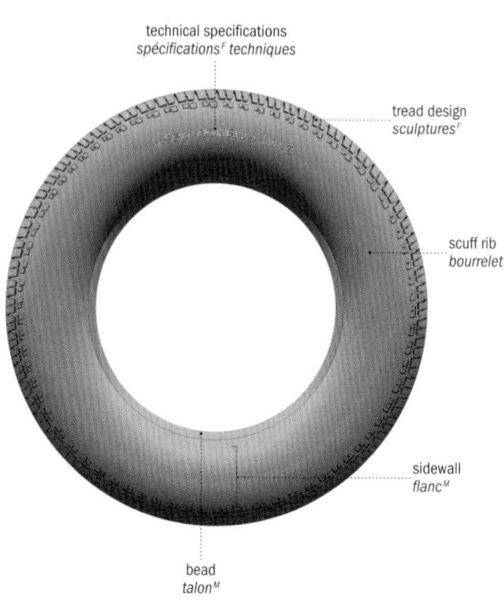

examples of tyres
exemples[M] de pneus[M]

performance tyre
pneu[M] de performance[F]

all-season tyre
pneu[M] toutes saisc

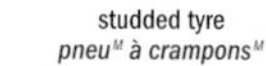

studded tyre
pneu[M] à crampons[M]

winter tyre
pneu[M] d'hiver[M]

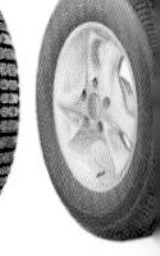

touring ty
pneu[M] autorc

radiator

radiateur[M]

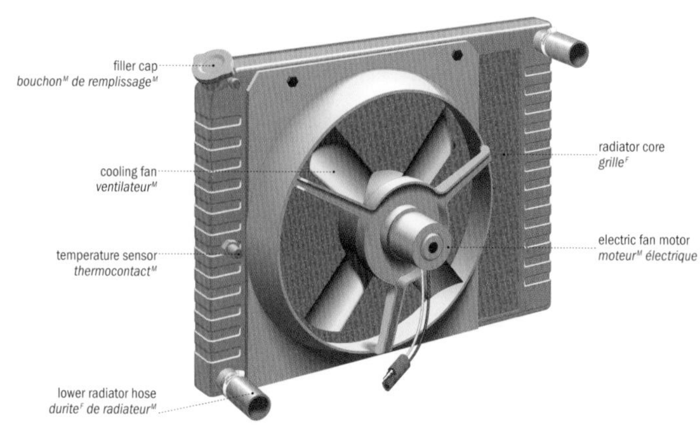

spark plug

bougie^F d'allumage^M

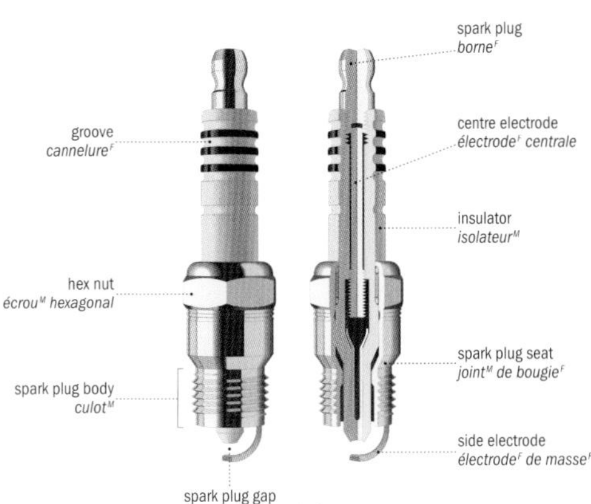

battery

batterie^F d'accumulateurs^M

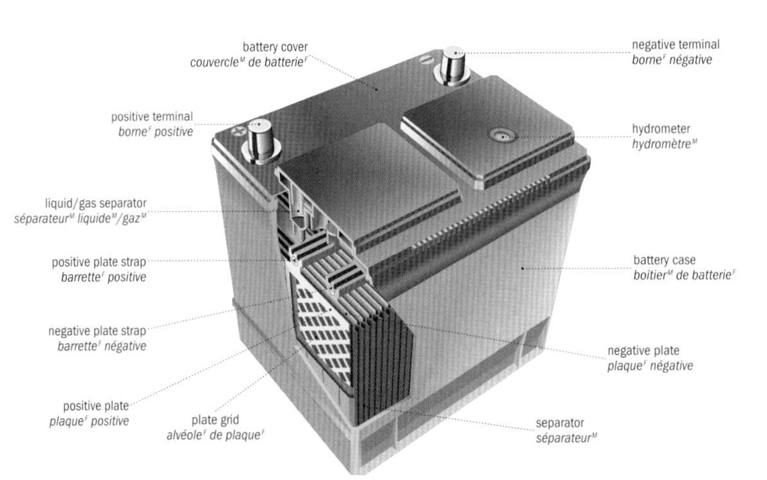

petrol engine

moteur[M] à essence[F]

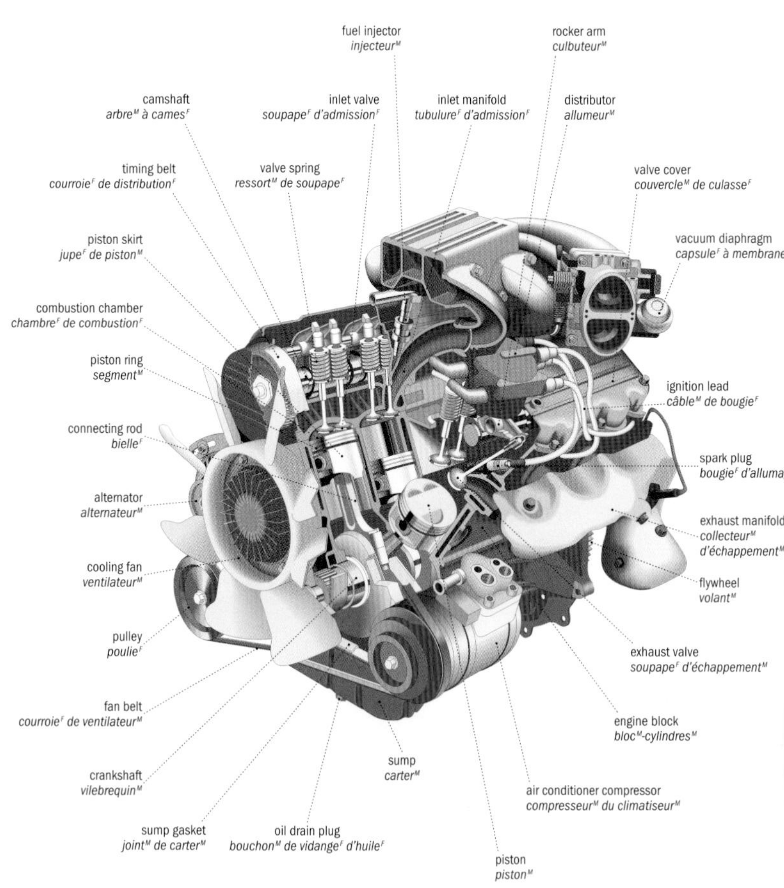

TRANSPORT AND MACHINERY

caravan

caravane[F]

trailer caravan
caravane[F] tractée

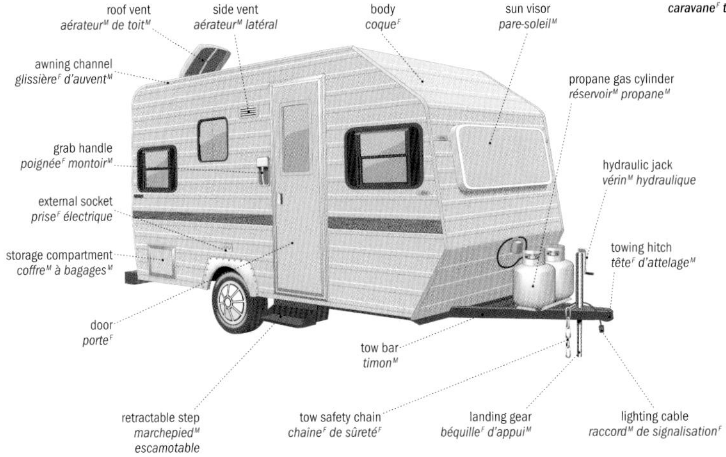

roof vent
aérateur[M] de toit[M]
side vent
aérateur[M] latéral
body
coque[F]
sun visor
pare-soleil[M]
awning channel
glissière[F] d'auvent[M]
propane gas cylinder
réservoir[M] propane[M]
grab handle
poignée[F] montoir[M]
hydraulic jack
vérin[M] hydraulique
external socket
prise[F] électrique
towing hitch
tête[F] d'attelage[M]
storage compartment
coffre[M] à bagages[M]
door
porte[F]
tow bar
timon[M]
retractable step
marchepied[M] escamotable
tow safety chain
chaîne[F] de sûreté[F]
landing gear
béquille[F] d'appui[M]
lighting cable
raccord[M] de signalisation[F]

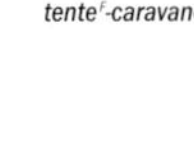

trailer tent
tente[F]-caravane[F]

roof
toit[M]
canopy
auvent[M]
window
fenêtre[F]
bunk
lit[M]
spare tyre
roue[F] de secours[M]
body
coque[F]
stabilizer jack
béquille[F] d'appoint[M]
screen door
porte[F] moustiquaire[F]

camper
auto[F]-caravane[F]

air conditioner
climatiseur[M]
luggage rack
porte-bagages[M]
ladder
échelle[F]

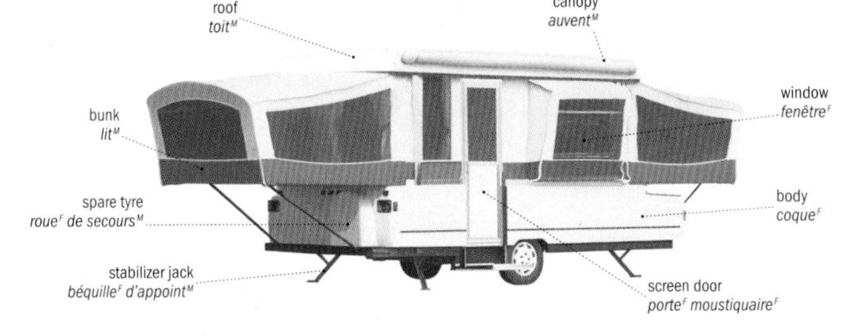

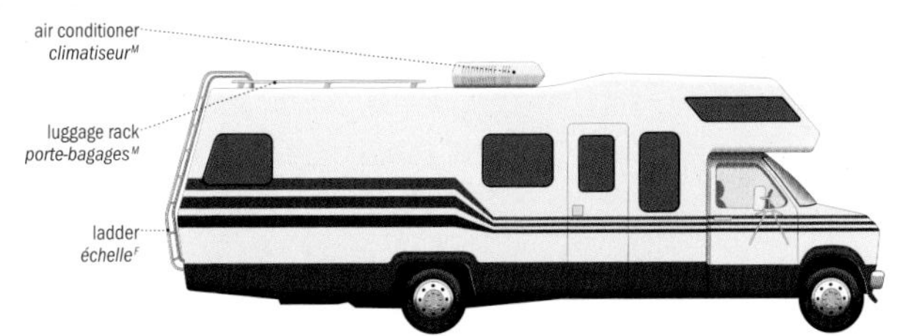

bus

autobus[M]

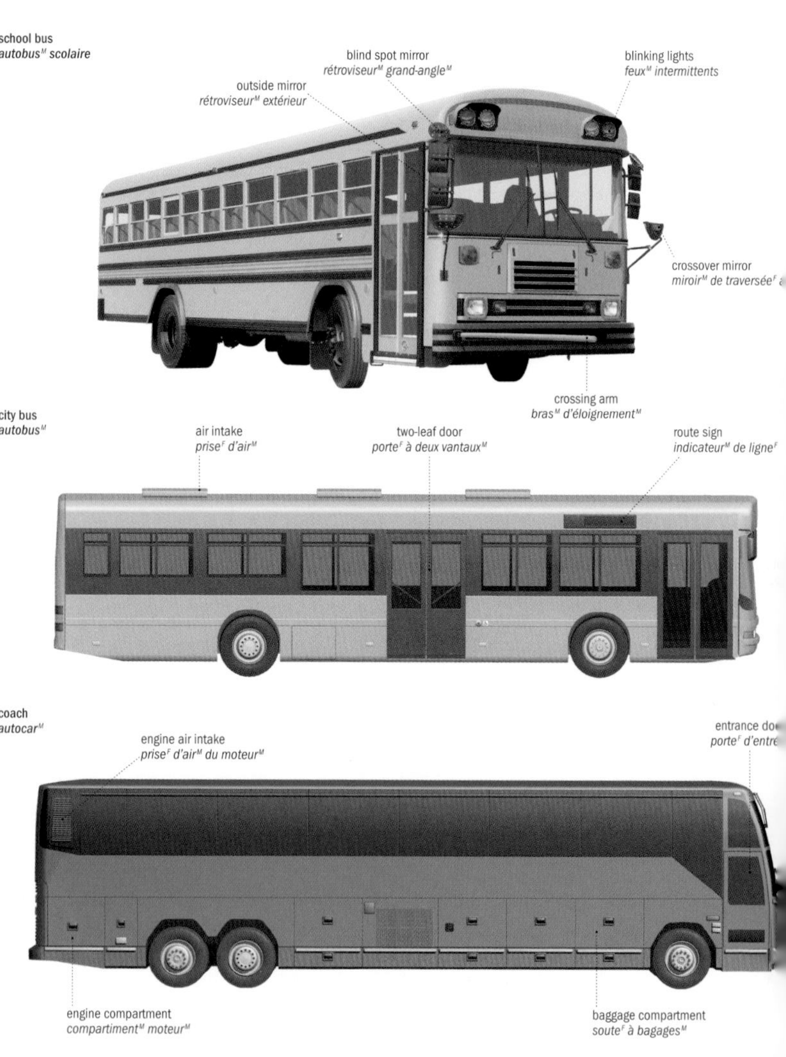

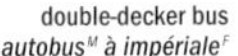

double-decker bus
autobus[M] *à impériale*[F]

minibus
minibus[M]

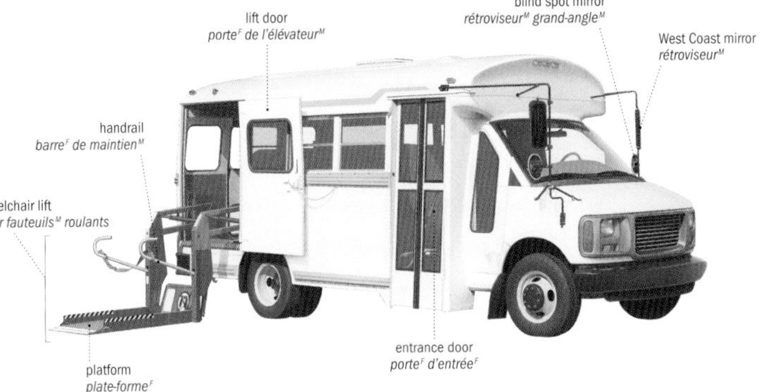

articulated bus
autobus[M] *articulé*

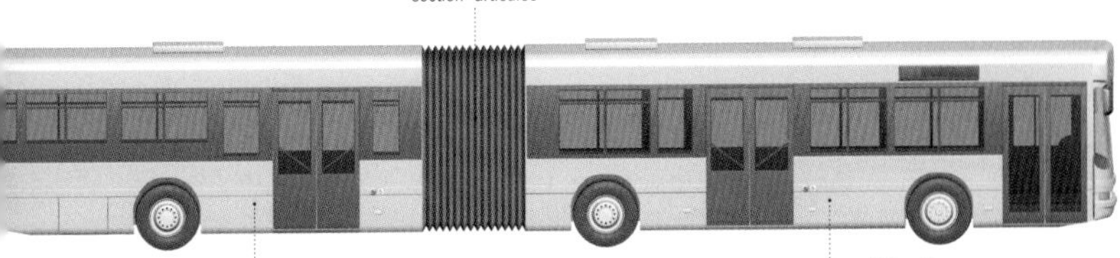

trucking

camionnage[M]

tractor unit
tracteur[M] routier

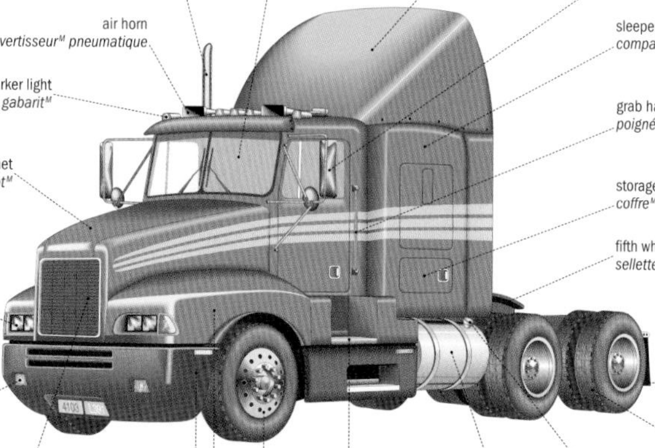

exhaust stack
cheminée[F] d'échappement[M]
windscreen
pare-brise[M]
wind deflector
déflecteur[M]
trail-view mirror
rétroviseur[M]
air horn
avertisseur[M] pneumatique
sleeper-cab
compartiment[M]-couchette[F]
side marker light
feu[M] de gabarit[M]
grab handle
poignée[F] montoir[M]
bonnet
capot[M]
storage compartment
coffre[M] de rangement[M]
fifth wheel
sellette[F] d'attelage[M]
headlight
phare[M]
mud flap
bavette[F] garde-bou
tyre
pneu[M]
fog light
feu[M] antibrouillard
bumper
pare-chocs[M]
step
marchepied[M]
filler cap
bouchon[M] du réservoir[M]
radiator grille
calandre[F]
wing
aile[F]
wheel
roue[F]
fuel tank
réservoir[M] à carburant[M]

examples of trucks
exemples[M] de camions[M]

tanker body
citerne[F]

tanker
camion[M]-citerne[F]

collection truck
benne[F] à ordures[F]

loading hopper
trémie[F] de chargement[M]
packer body
benne[F] tasseuse

boom
poutre[F] de levage[M]
cable
câble[M]
hook
crochet[M]
towing device
dispositif[M] de remorquage[M]
winch controls
commandes[F] du treuil[M]
elevating cylinder
vérin[M]
winch
treuil[M]

to
dépan

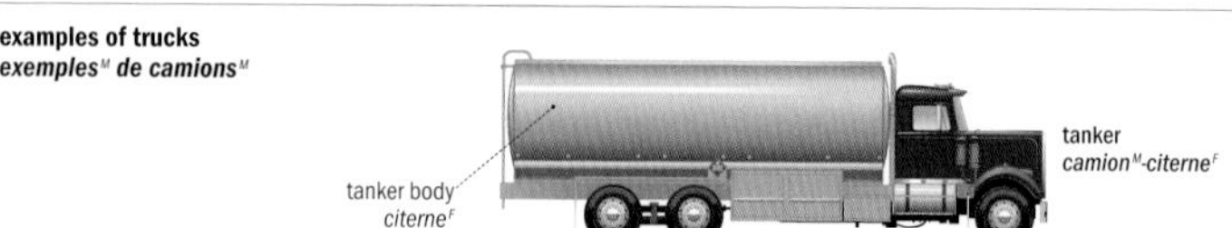

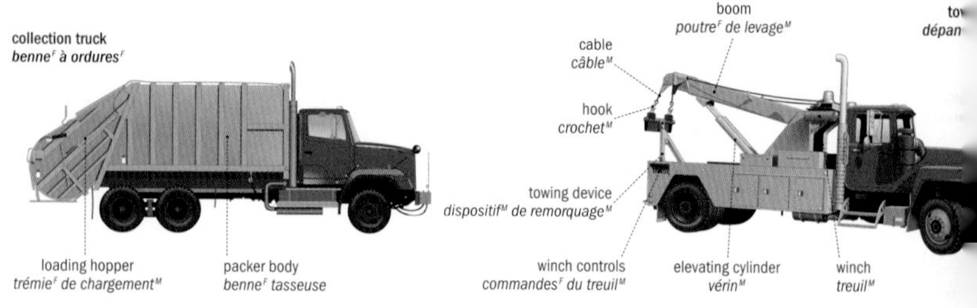

refrigerated semitrailer
semi-remorque[F] frigorifique

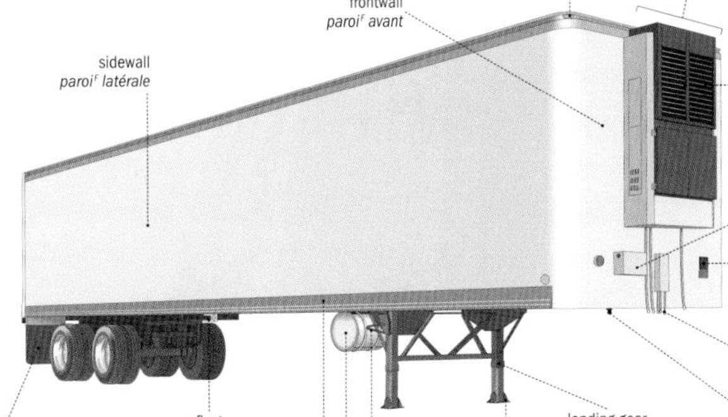

side marker light
feu[M] de gabarit[M]
refrigeration unit
groupe[M] frigorifique
frontwall
paroi[F] avant
sidewall
paroi[F] latérale
vent door
volet[M] d'air[M]
battery box
boitier[M] de batterie[F]
partlow chart
disque[M] de papier[M]-diagramme[M]
electrical connection
accouplement[M] électrique
reflector
réflecteur[M]
landing gear
béquille[F]
kingpin
pivot[M] d'attelage[M]
lap
te[F] garde-boue[M]
side rail
longeron[M]
sand shoe
sabot[M]
auxiliary tank
réservoir[M] auxiliaire
landing gear crank
manivelle[F]

van
camion[M] porteur[M] fourgon[M]

concrete mixer truck
camion[M]-toupie[F]

street sweeper
balayeuse[F]

collection body
réceptacle[M] à déchets[M]
central brush
brosse[F] centrale
lateral brush
brosse[F] latérale
watering tube
canalisation[F] d'arrosage[M]

lower
e-neige[M] à soufflerie[F]

projection device
canal[M] de projection[F]
worm
vis[F] sans fin[F]

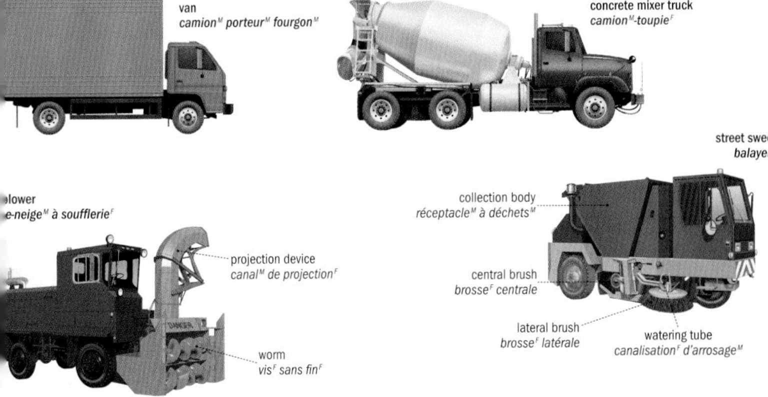

motorcycle

moto^F

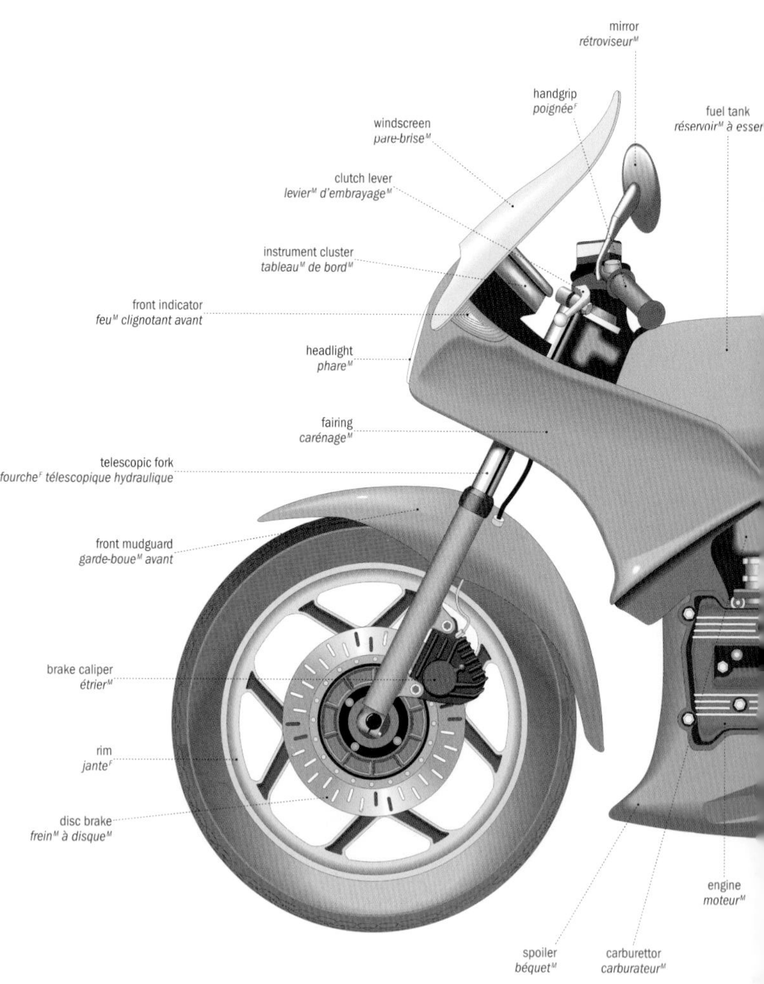

TRANSPORT AND MACHINERY

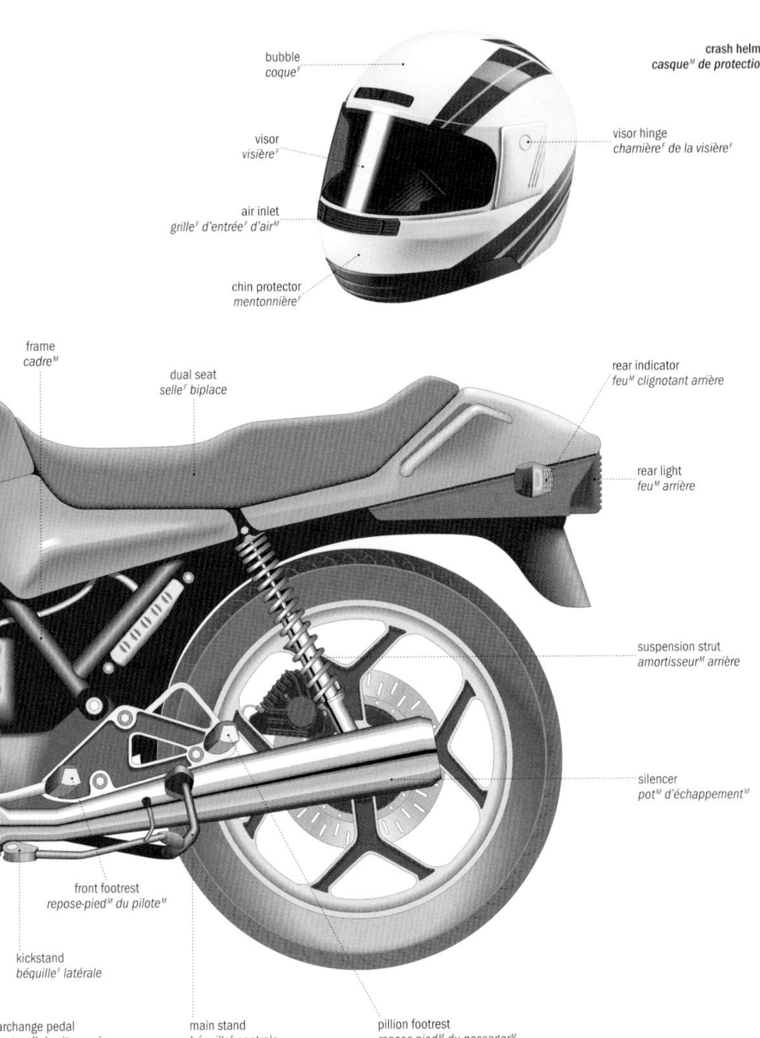
crash helmet
casque^M de protection^F
bubble
coque^F
visor
visière^F
visor hinge
charnière^F de la visière^F
air inlet
grille^F d'entrée^F d'air^M
chin protector
mentonnière^F
frame
cadre^M
dual seat
selle^F biplace
rear indicator
feu^M clignotant arrière
rear light
feu^M arrière
suspension strut
amortisseur^M arrière
silencer
pot^M d'échappement^M
front footrest
repose-pied^M du pilote^M
kickstand
béquille^F latérale
earchange pedal
électeur^M de vitesses^F
main stand
béquille^F centrale
pillion footrest
repose-pied^M du passager^M

motorcycle

instrument cluster
tableau[M] de bord[M]

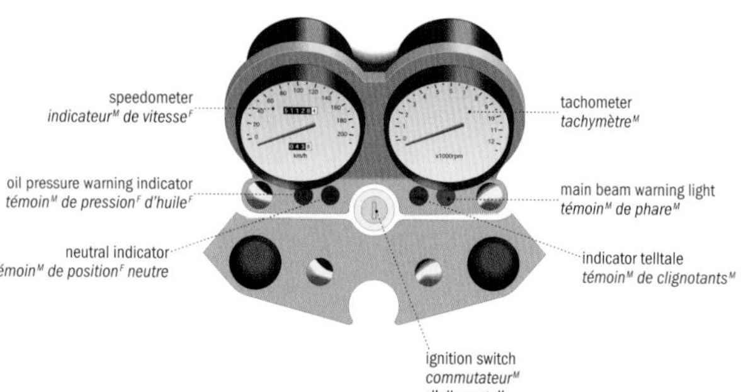

motorcycle: view from above
moto[F] : vue[F] en plongée[F]

headlight
phare[M]

front indicator
feu[M] clignotant avant

mirror
rétroviseur[M]

front brake lever
levier[M] de frein[M] avant

clutch lever
levier[M] d'embrayage[M]

twist grip throttle
poignée[F] des gaz[M]

dip switch
inverseur[M] route[F]-croisement[M]

emergency switch
coupe-circuit[M] d'urgence[F]

horn
avertisseur[M]

starter button
bouton[M] de démarreur[M]

petrol tank cap
bouchon[M] du réservoir[M]

clutch housing
carter[M] d'embrayage[M]

gearchange pedal
sélecteur[M] de vitesses[F]

rear brake pedal
pédale[F] de frein[M] arrière

front footrest
repose-pied[M] du pilote[M]

pillion footrest
repose-pied[M] du passager[M]

silencer
pot[M] d'échappement[M]

rear indicator
feu[M] clignotant arrière

rear light
feu[M] arrière

motorcycle

examples of motorcycles
exemples[M] de motos[F]

' scooter
er[M]

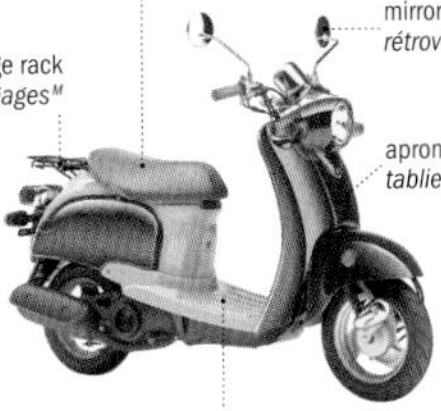
seat
selle[F]
mirror
rétroviseur[M]
luggage rack
porte-bagages[M]
apron
tablier[M]
floorboard
plancher[M]

off-road motorcycle
moto[F] tout-terrain

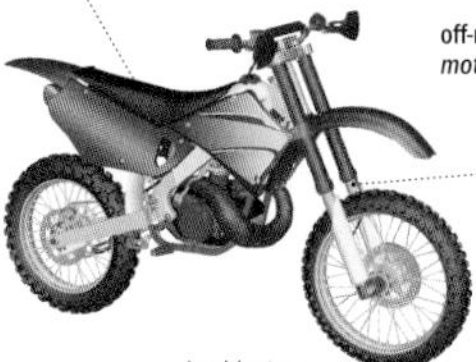
seat
selle[F]
telescopic front fork
fourche[F] télescopique
knobby tyre
pneu[M] à crampons[M]

d
noteur[M]

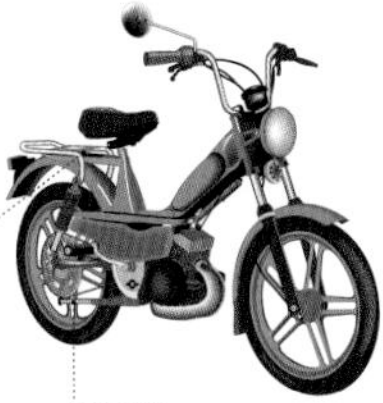
carrier
rte-bagages[M]
kickstand
béquille[F] latérale

touring motorcycle
moto[F] de tourisme[M]

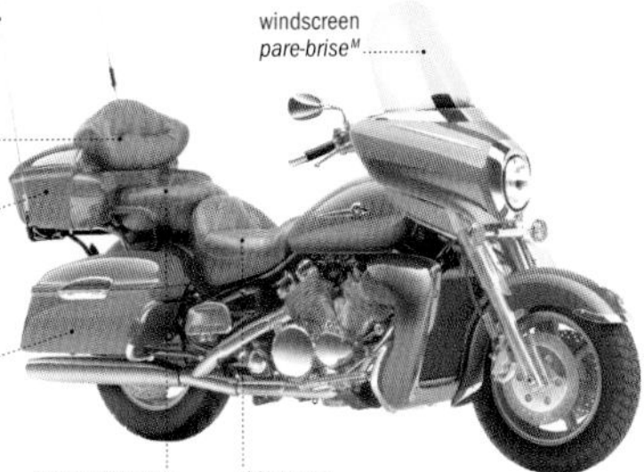
antenna
antenne[F]
windscreen
pare-brise[M]
backrest
dossier[M]
top box
coffre[M]
saddlebag
sacoche[F]
passenger seat
selle[F] passager[M]
driver seat
selle[F] conducteur[M]

quad bike

quad[M]

rear cargo rack
porte-bagages[M] arrière
seat
selle[F]
fuel tank
réservoir[M] à essence[F]
handgrip
poignée[F]
rear bumper
garde-boue[M] arrière
bumper
pare-chocs[M]
silencer
pot[M] d'échappement[M]
front shock absorber
amortisseur[M] avant
gear lever
sélecteur[M] de vitesses[F]

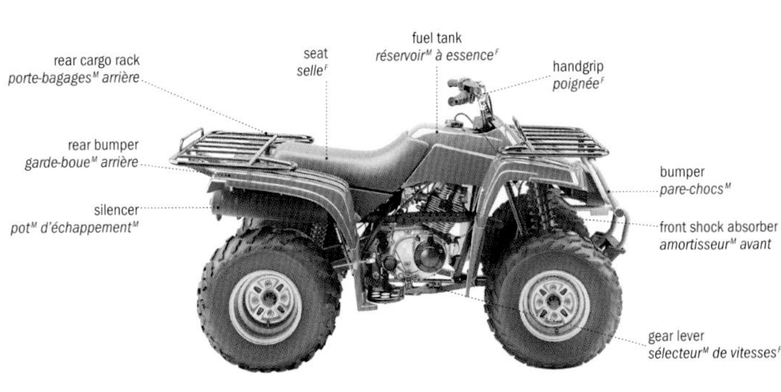

bicycle

bicyclette[F]

parts of a bicycle
parties[F] d'une bicyclette[F]

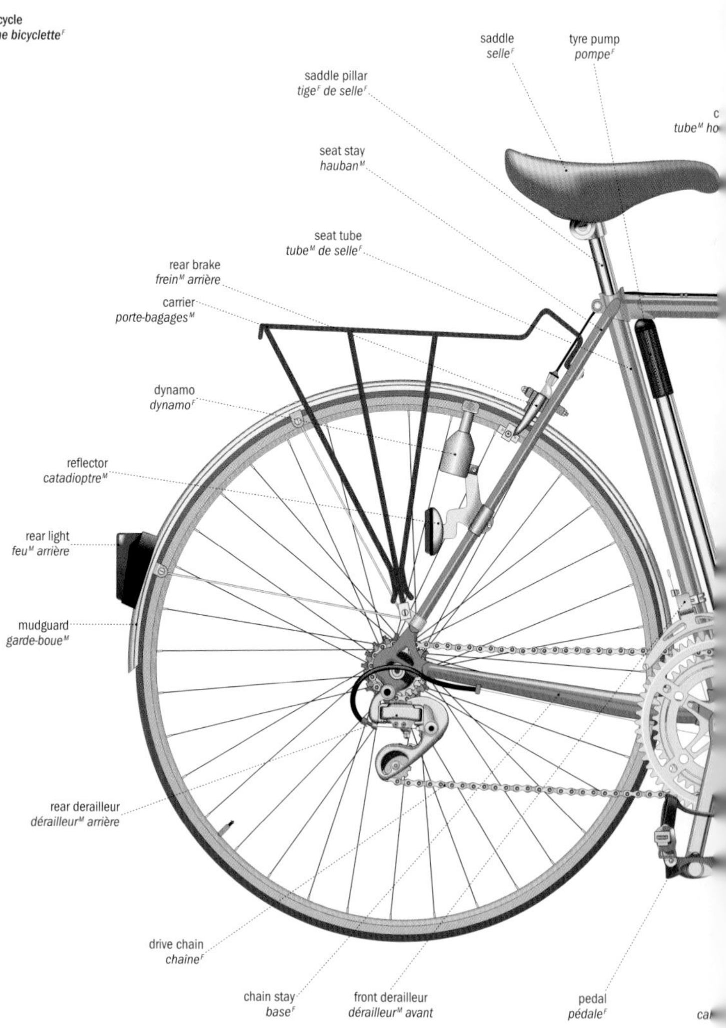

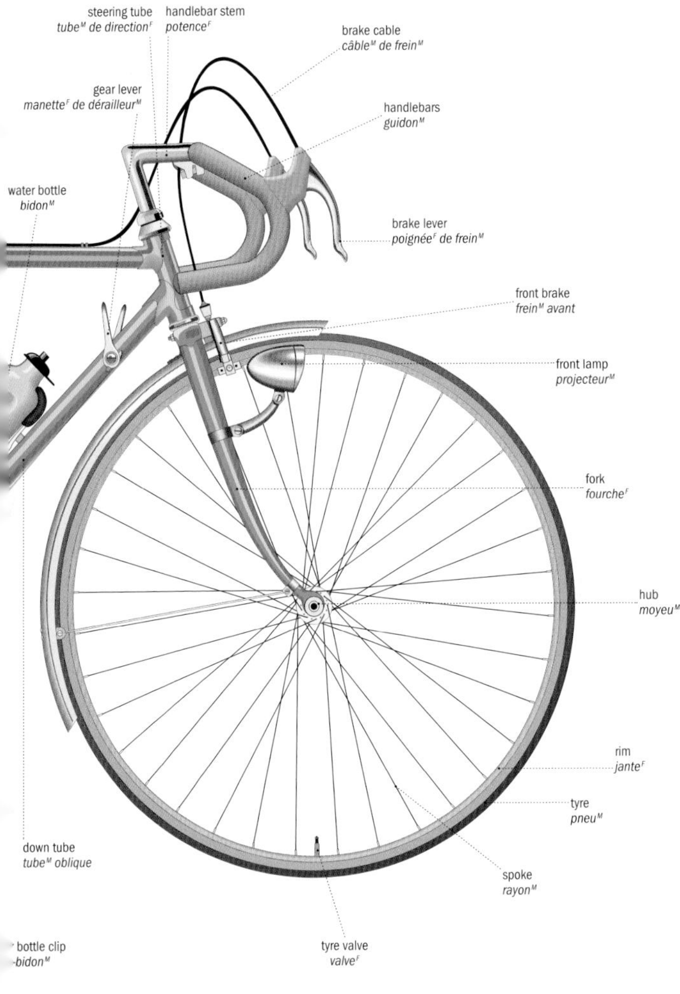
steering tube
tube^M de direction^F
handlebar stem
potence^F
brake cable
câble^M de frein^M
gear lever
manette^F de dérailleur^M
handlebars
guidon^M
water bottle
bidon^M
brake lever
poignée^F de frein^M
front brake
frein^M avant
front lamp
projecteur^M
fork
fourche^F
hub
moyeu^M
rim
jante^F
tyre
pneu^M
down tube
tube^M oblique
spoke
rayon^M
bottle clip
-bidon^M
tyre valve
valve^F

bicycle

power train
mécanisme[M] de propulsion[F]

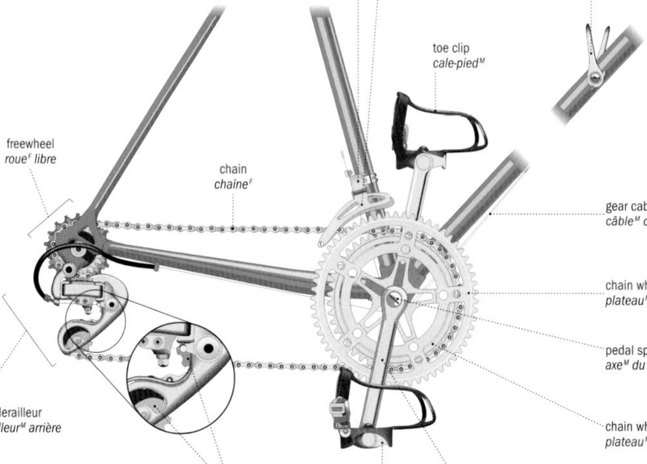

front derailleur
dérailleur[M] avant

chain guide
guide-chaîne[M]

gear lever
manette[F] de dérailleur[M]

toe clip
cale-pied[M]

freewheel
roue[F] libre

chain
chaîne[F]

gear cable
câble[M] de commande[F]

chain wheel A
plateau[M] A

pedal spindle
axe[M] du pédalier[M]

rear derailleur
dérailleur[M] arrière

chain wheel B
plateau[M] B

jockey rollers
galets[M] tendeurs

pedal
pédale[F]

crank
manivelle[F]

accessories
accessoires[M]

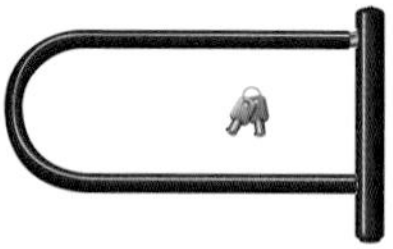

cycle lock
cadenas[M]

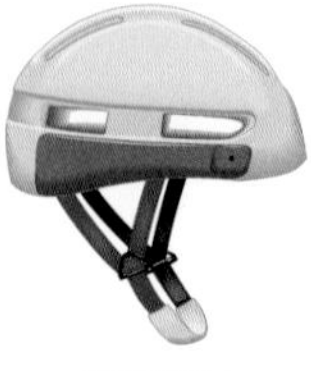

cycling helmet
casque[M] de protection[F]

tool kit
trousse[F] de dépannage[M]

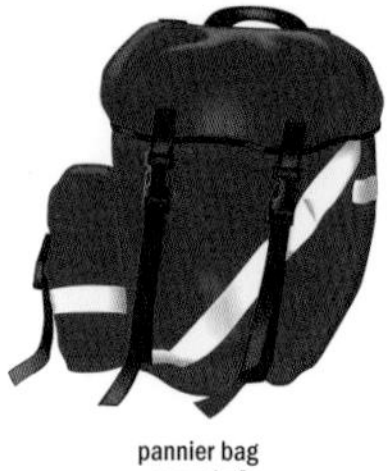

pannier bag
sacoche[F]

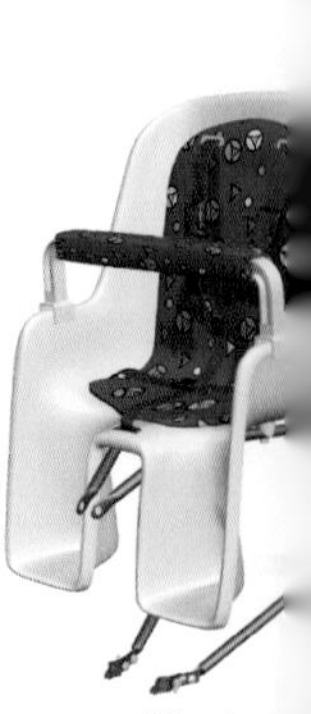

child carrier
siège[M] de vélo[M] pour en

examples of bicycles
exemples[M] de bicyclettes[F]

passenger station

gare^F de voyageurs^M

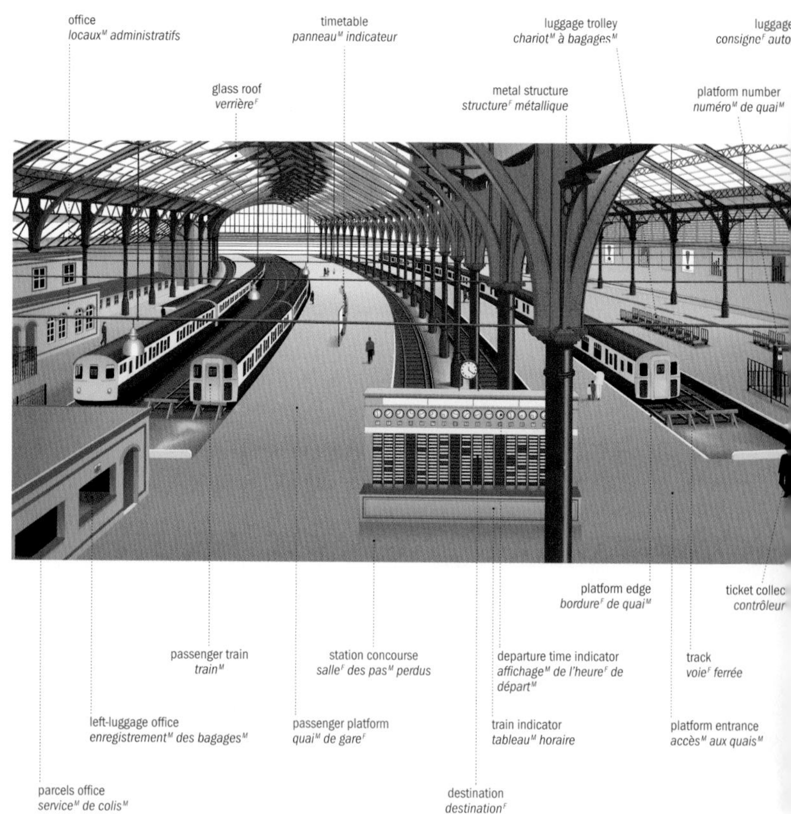

railway station

gare^{F}

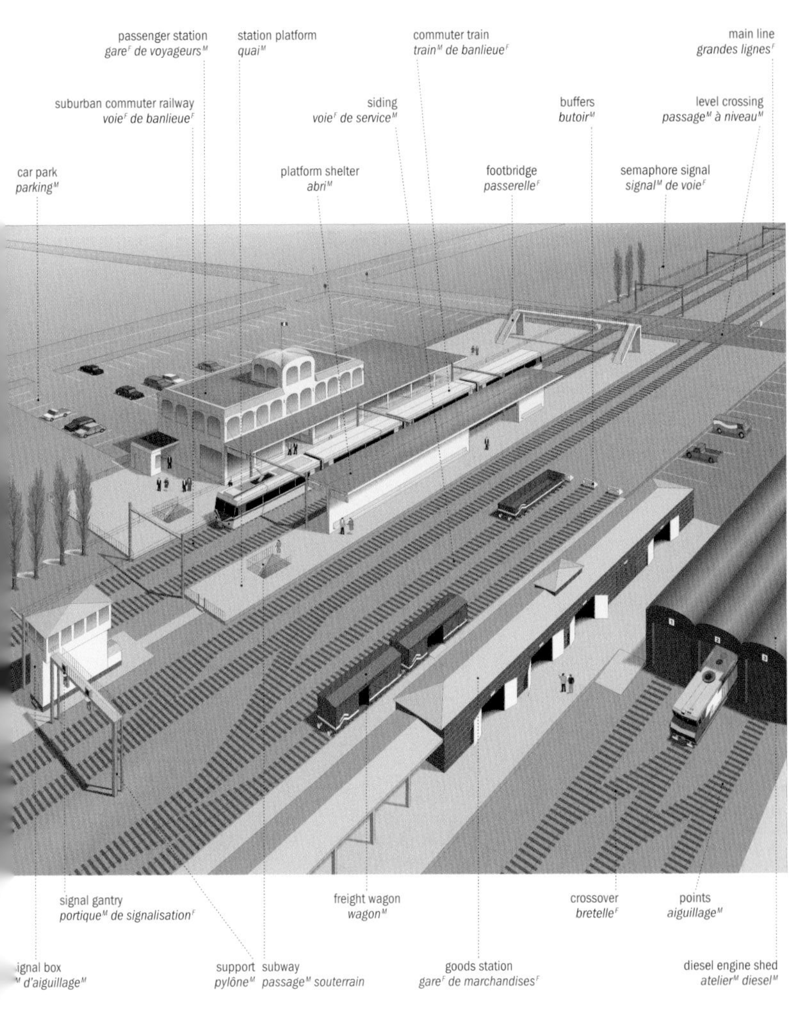

high-speed train

train[M] à grande vitesse[F] (T.G.V.)

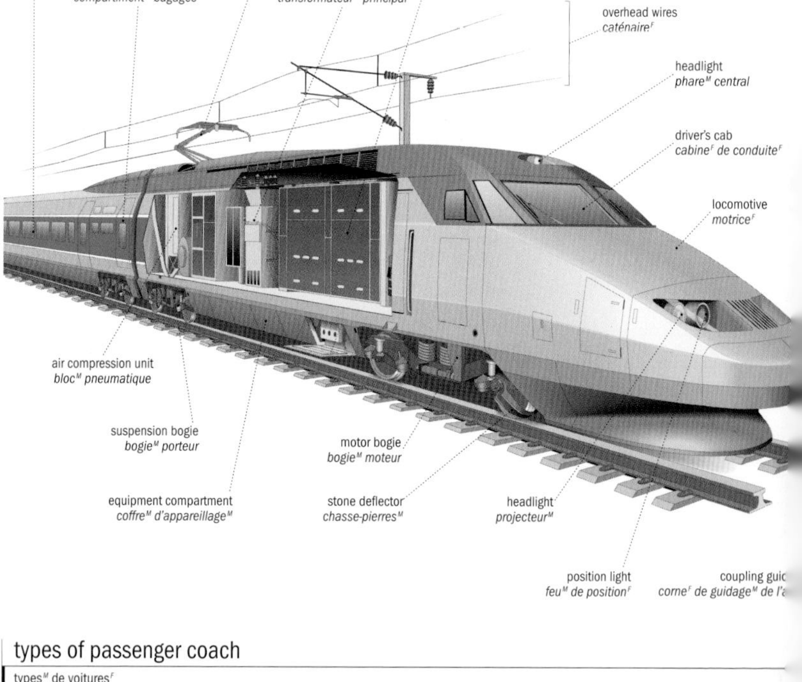

passenger car
compartiment[M] voyageurs[M]

pantograph
pantographe[M]

luggage compartment
compartiment[M] bagages[M]

main transformer
transformateur[M] principal

motor unit
bloc[M]-moteur[M]

overhead wires
caténaire[F]

headlight
phare[M] central

driver's cab
cabine[F] de conduite[F]

locomotive
motrice[F]

air compression unit
bloc[M] pneumatique

suspension bogie
bogie[M] porteur

motor bogie
bogie[M] moteur

equipment compartment
coffre[M] d'appareillage[M]

stone deflector
chasse-pierres[M]

headlight
projecteur[M]

position light
feu[M] de position[F]

coupling guic
corne[F] de guidage[M] de l'a

types of passenger coach

types[M] de voitures[F]

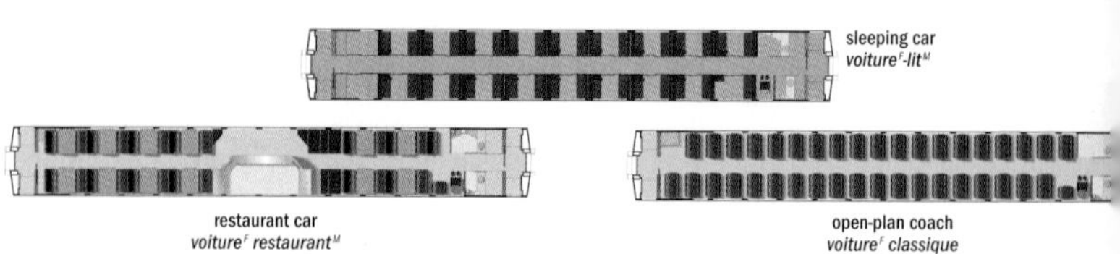

diesel-electric locomotive

locomotive[F] diesel-électrique

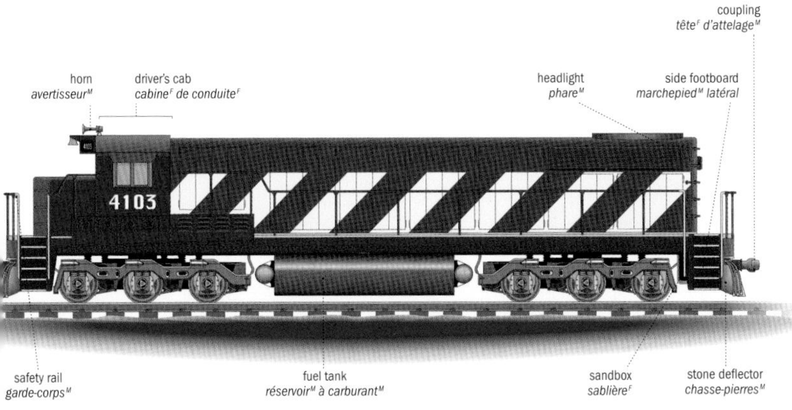

examples of freight wagons

exemples[M] de wagons[M]

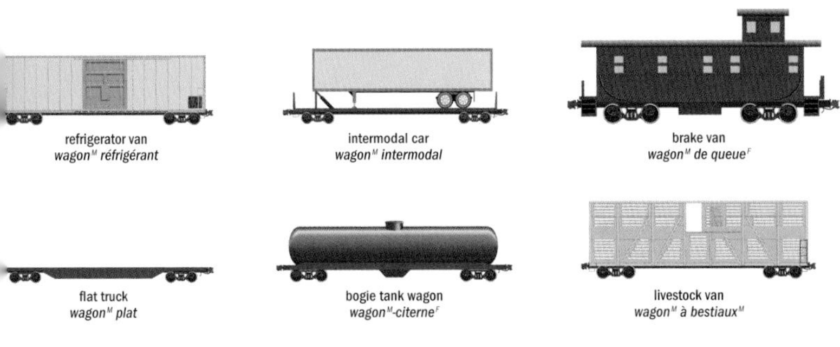

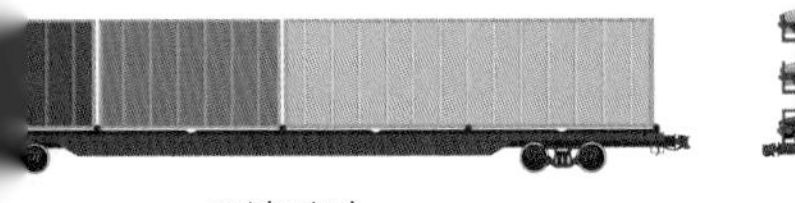

container truck
wagon[M] porte-conteneurs[M]

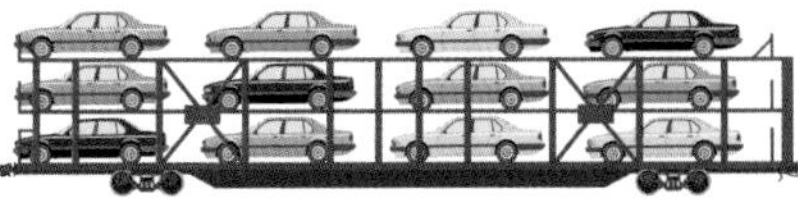

three-tier car carrier
wagon[M] porte-automobiles[M]

underground railway

chemin^M de fer^M métropolitain

underground station
station^F de métro^M

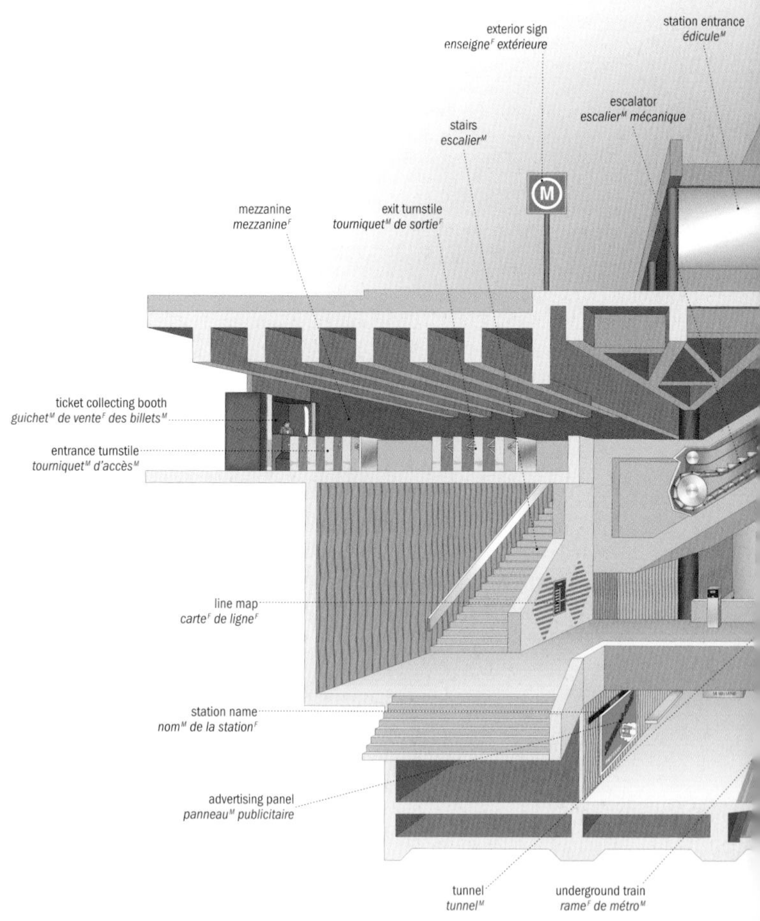

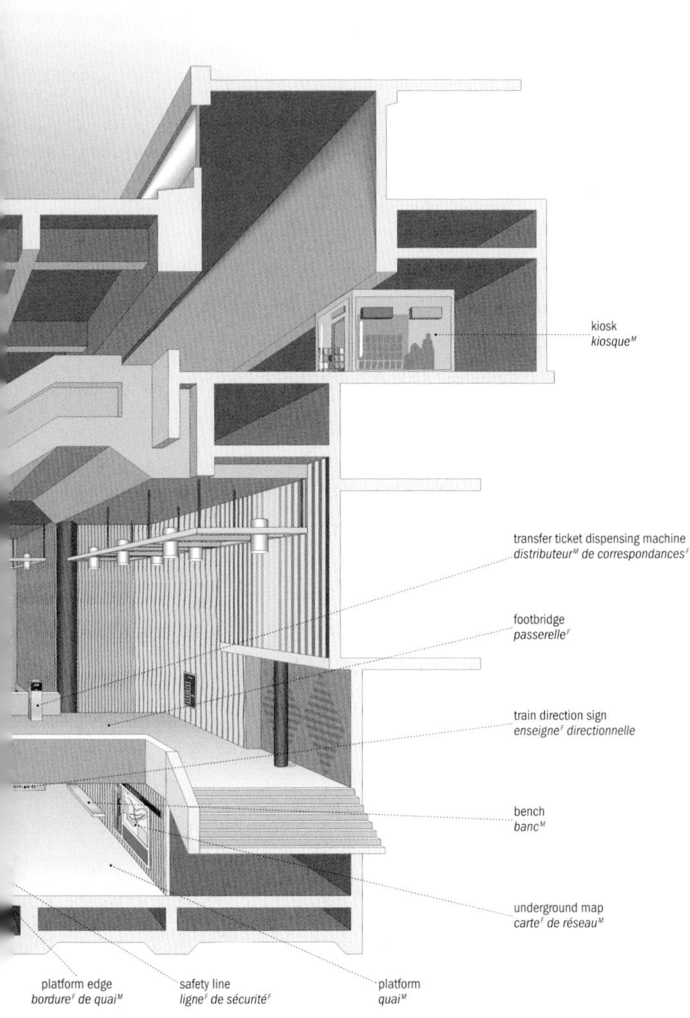
kiosk
kiosque[M]
transfer ticket dispensing machine
distributeur[M] de correspondances[F]
footbridge
passerelle[F]
train direction sign
enseigne[F] directionnelle
bench
banc[M]
underground map
carte[F] de réseau[M]
platform edge
bordure[F] de quai[M]
safety line
ligne[F] de sécurité[F]
platform
quai[M]

underground railway

passenger car
***voiture*[F]**

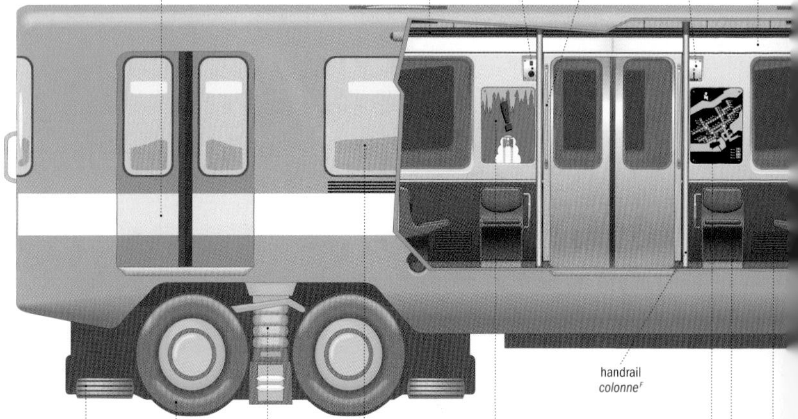

communication set
poste[M] de communication[F]

emergency brake
frein[M] d'urgence[F]

side door
porte[F] latérale

ventilator
grille[F] d'aération[F]

side handrail
poignée[F]

light
éclairage[M]

handrail
colonne[F]

inflated guiding tyre
pneumatique[M] de guidage[M]

window
fenêtre[F]

underground map
carte[F] de réseau[M]

suspension
suspension[F]

advertising poster
affiche[F] publicitaire

single seat
siège[M] simple

inflated carrying tyre
pneumatique[M] porteur

heating grille
grille[F] de chauffage[M]

doub
siège[M]

underground train
***rame*[F] *de métro*[M]**

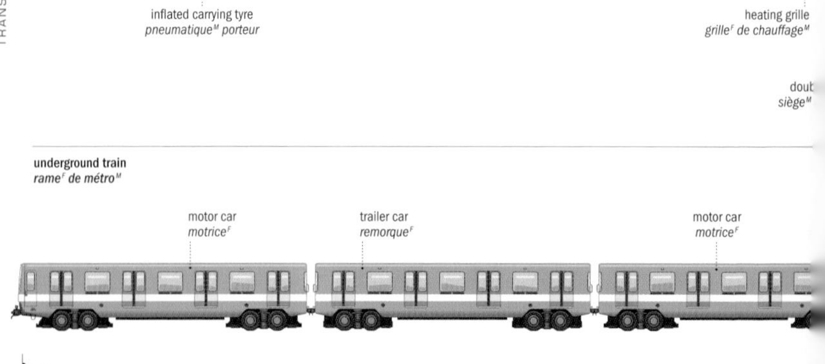

motor car
motrice[F]

trailer car
remorque[F]

motor car
motrice[F]

harbour

port^M maritime

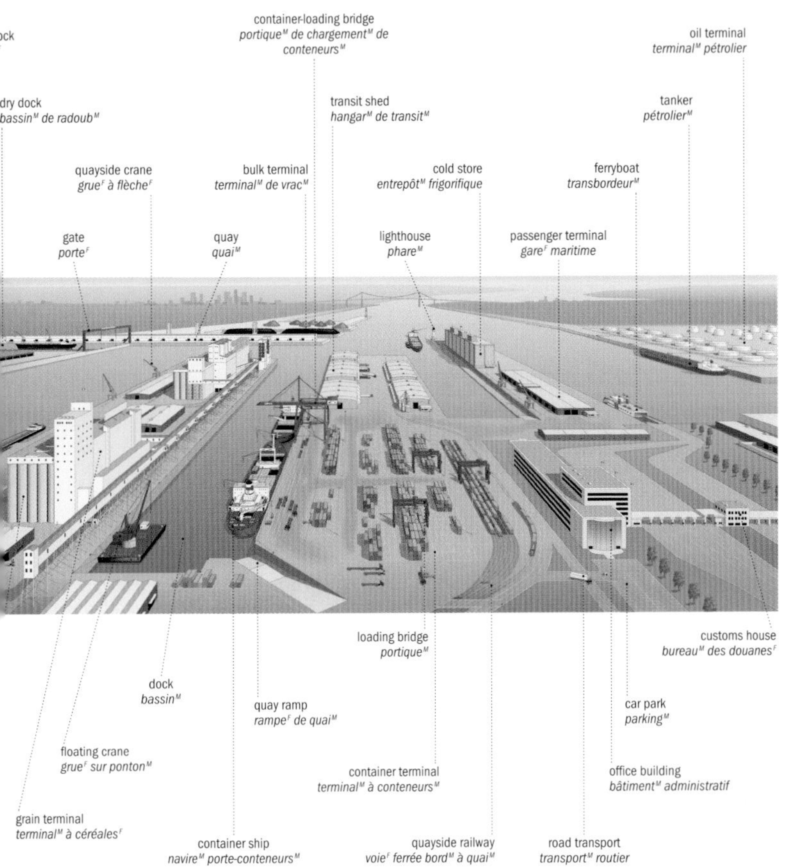

examples of boats and ships

exemples^M de bateaux^M et d'embarcations^F

drill ship
navire^M de forage^M

derrick
tour^F de forage^M

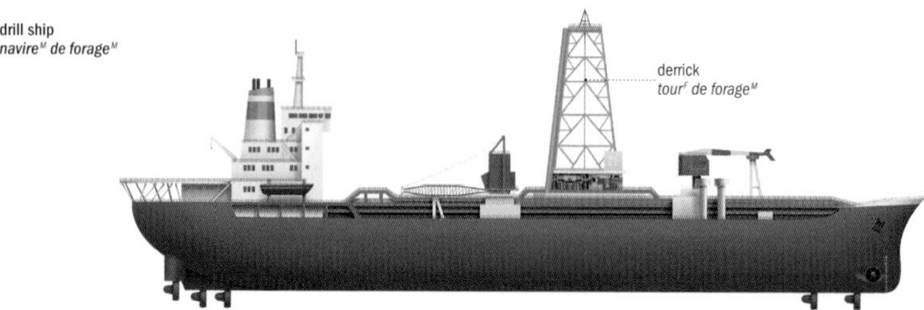

bulk carrier
vraquier^M

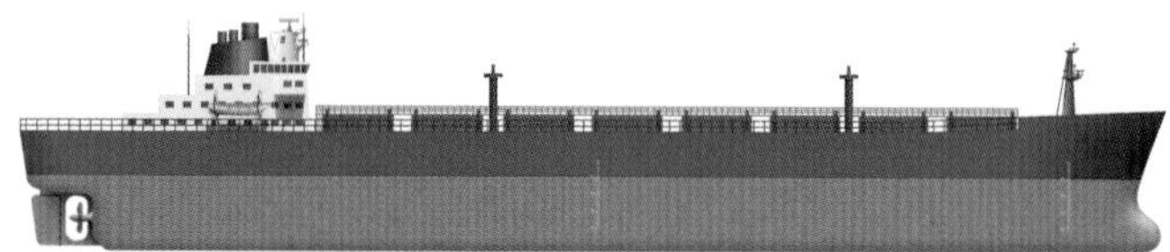

container ship
navire^M porte-conteneurs^M

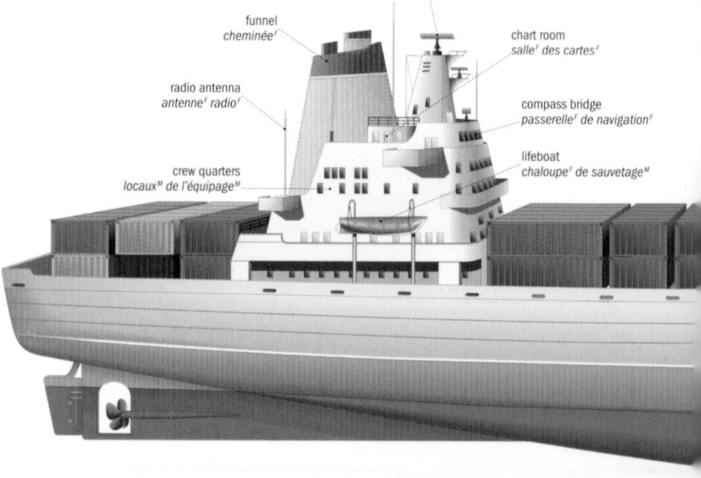
radar
radar^M
funnel
cheminée^F
chart room
salle^F des cartes^F
radio antenna
antenne^F radio^F
compass bridge
passerelle^F de navigation^F
lifeboat
chaloupe^F de sauvetage^M
crew quarters
locaux^M de l'équipage^M

hovercraft
aéroglisseur M

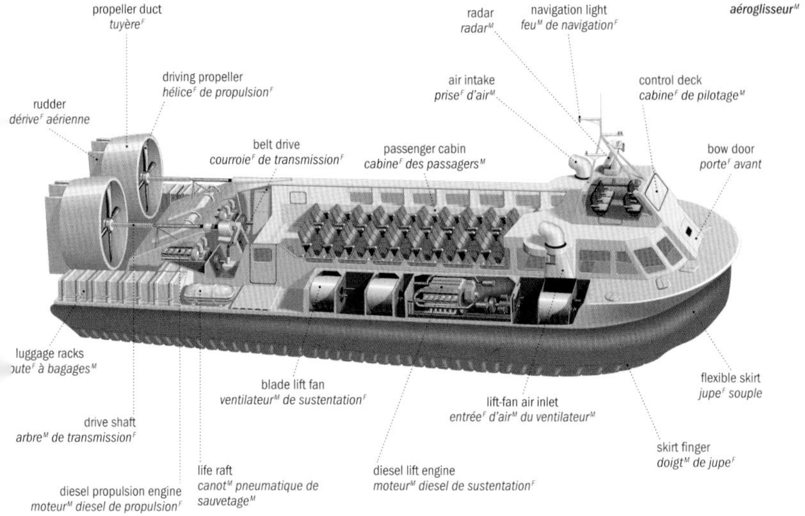

propeller duct
tuyère F
radar
radar M
navigation light
feu M de navigation F
driving propeller
hélice F de propulsion F
air intake
prise F d'air M
control deck
cabine F de pilotage M
rudder
dérive F aérienne
belt drive
courroie F de transmission F
passenger cabin
cabine F des passagers M
bow door
porte F avant
luggage racks
soute F à bagages M
blade lift fan
ventilateur M de sustentation F
flexible skirt
jupe F souple
lift-fan air inlet
entrée F d'air M du ventilateur M
drive shaft
arbre M de transmission F
skirt finger
doigt M de jupe F
life raft
canot M pneumatique de sauvetage M
diesel lift engine
moteur M diesel de sustentation F
diesel propulsion engine
moteur M diesel de propulsion F

masthead light
feu M de tête F de mât M
container
conteneur M
container hold
cale F à conteneurs M
forecastle
plage F avant
hawse pipe
écubier M

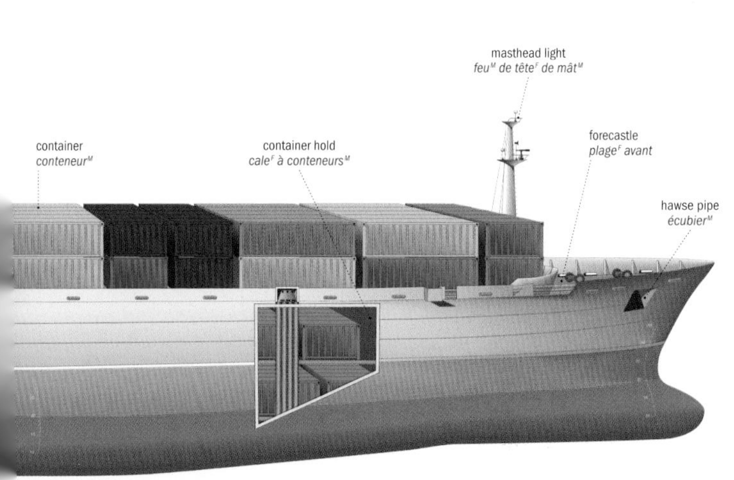

examples of boats and ships

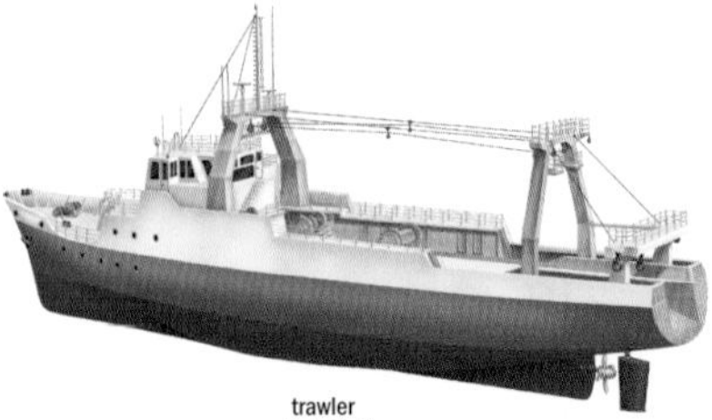

trawler
chalutier[M]

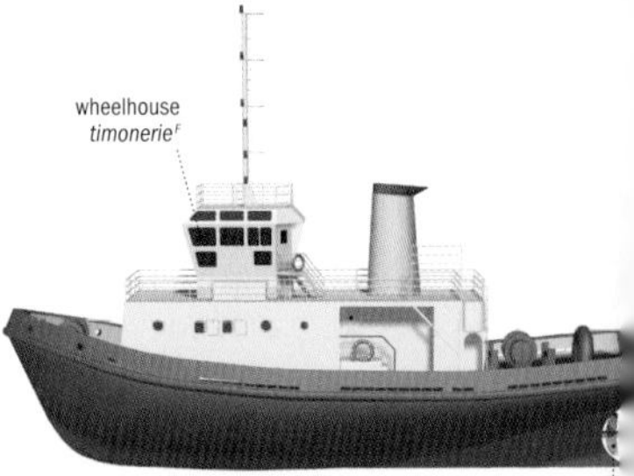

wheelhouse
timonerie[F]

tug
remorqueur[M]

propeller
hélice[F]

rudder bl
saf

stem
étrave[F]

stem propeller
hélice[F] d'étrave[F]

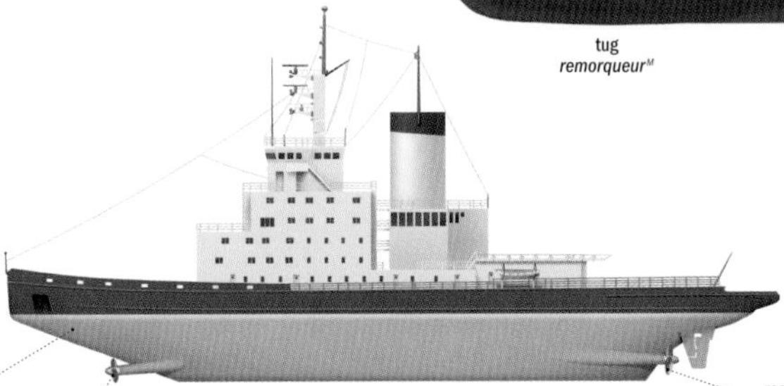

ice-breaker
brise-glace[M]

rear propeller
hélice[F] arrière

tanker
pétrolier[M]

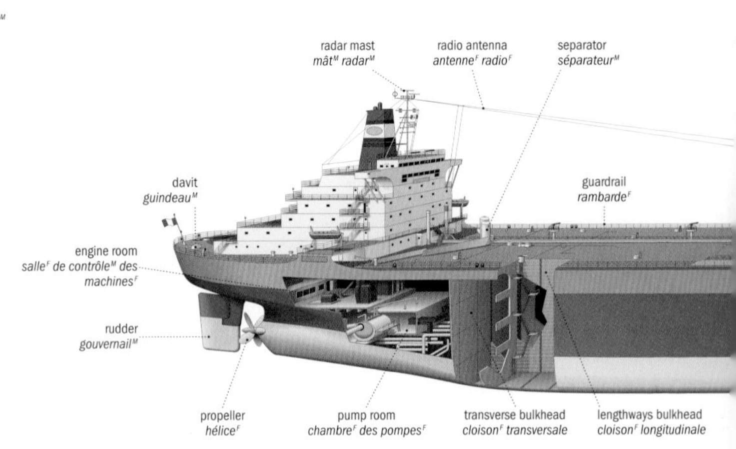

pilot house
cabine^F de pilotage^M

fore-and-aft passage
passavant^M

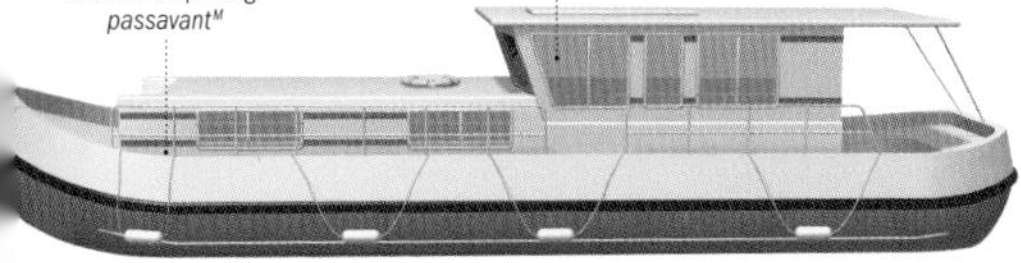

houseboat
caravane^F flottante

steering wheel
volant^M

windscreen
pare-brise^M

outboard engine
moteur^M hors-bord

handrail
main^F courante

runabout
hors-bord^M

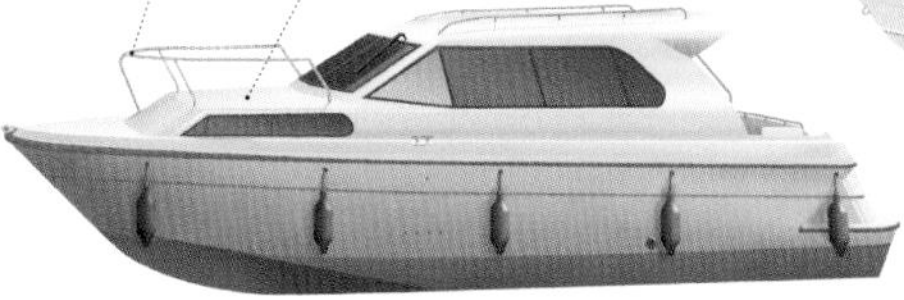

handrail
main^F courante

sun deck
solarium^M

motor yacht
yacht^M à moteur^M

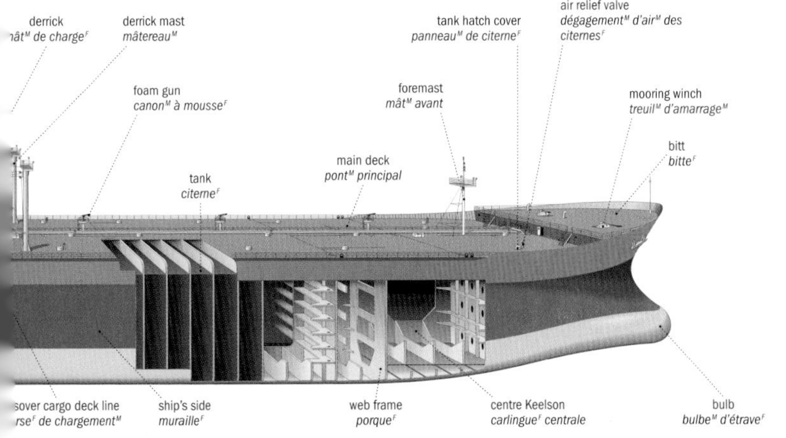

examples of boats and ships

ferry boat
transbordeurM

telecommunication antenna
antenneF de télécommunicationF
passenger cabin
cabineF des passagersM
radar
radarM
radio antenna
antenneF radioF
compass bridge
passerelleF de navigati
heating/air conditioning equipment
conditionnementM d'airM
bow loading door
porteF avant
restaurant
restaurantM
folding ramp
rampeF d'accèsM
car deck
compartimentM des voituresF

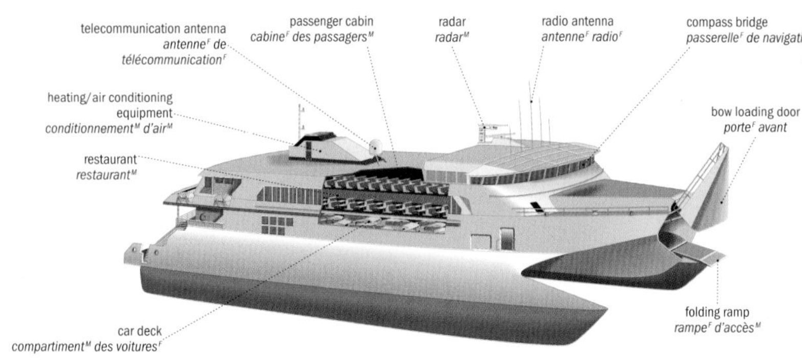

cruiseliner
paquebotM

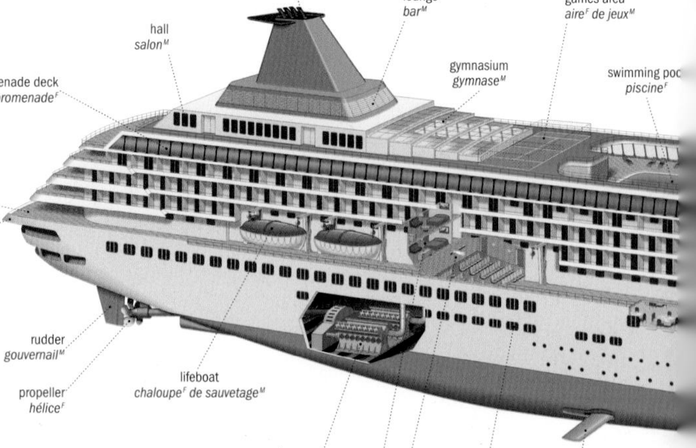

funnel
cheminéeF antisuie
lounge
barM
games area
aireF de jeuxM
hall
salonM
gymnasium
gymnaseM
swimming poo
piscineF
promenade deck
pontM-promenadeF
quarter-deck
plageF arrière
stern
poupeF
rudder
gouvernailM
propeller
héliceF
lifeboat
chaloupeF de sauvetageM
engine room
salleF des machinesF
porthole
hublotM
dinin
salleF à
cabin
cabineF
cinema
cinémaM
stabilizer fin
stabilisateurM de rou

hydrofoil boat
hydroptère[M]

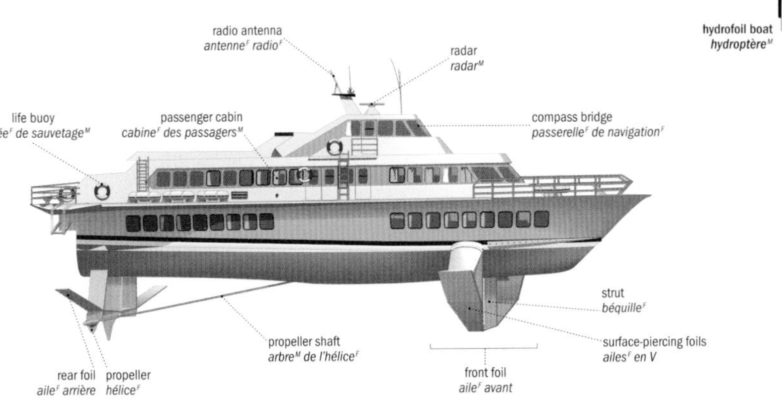

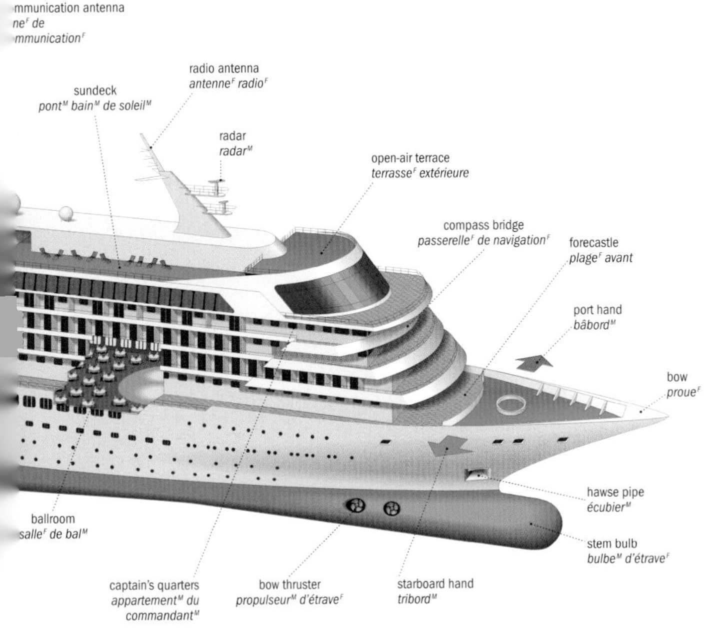

mmunication antenna
ne[F] de
mmunication[F]

radio antenna
antenne[F] radio[F]

sundeck
pont[M] bain[M] de soleil[M]

radar
radar[M]

open-air terrace
terrasse[F] extérieure

compass bridge
passerelle[F] de navigation[F]

forecastle
plage[F] avant

port hand
bâbord[M]

bow
proue[F]

hawse pipe
écubier[M]

ballroom
salle[F] de bal[M]

stem bulb
bulbe[M] d'étrave[F]

captain's quarters
appartement[M] du commandant[M]

bow thruster
propulseur[M] d'étrave[F]

starboard hand
tribord[M]

TRANSPORT AND MACHINERY

airport

aéroport[M]

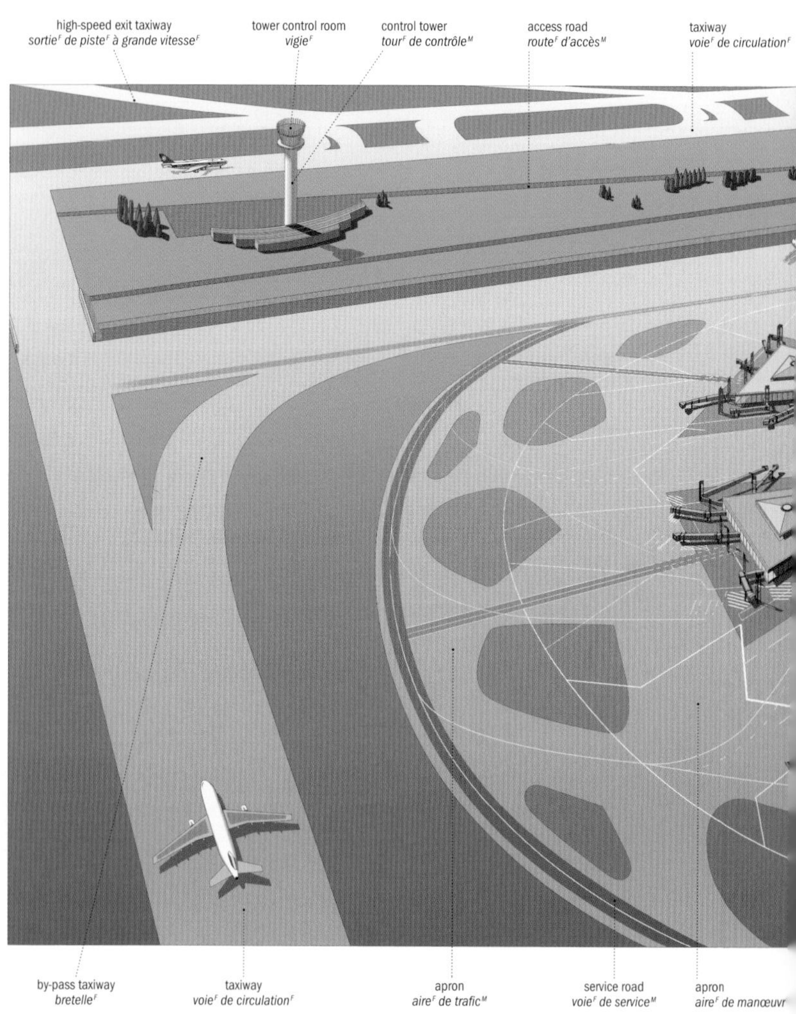

passenger terminal
rogare^F de passagers^M
maintenance hangar
hangar^M
parking area
aire^F de stationnement^M
telescopic corridor
serelle^F télescopique
service area
aire^F de service^M
boarding walkway
quai^M d'embarquement^M
taxiway line
marques^F de circulation^F
satellite terminal
aérogare^F satellite^M

airport

passenger terminal
aérogare^F

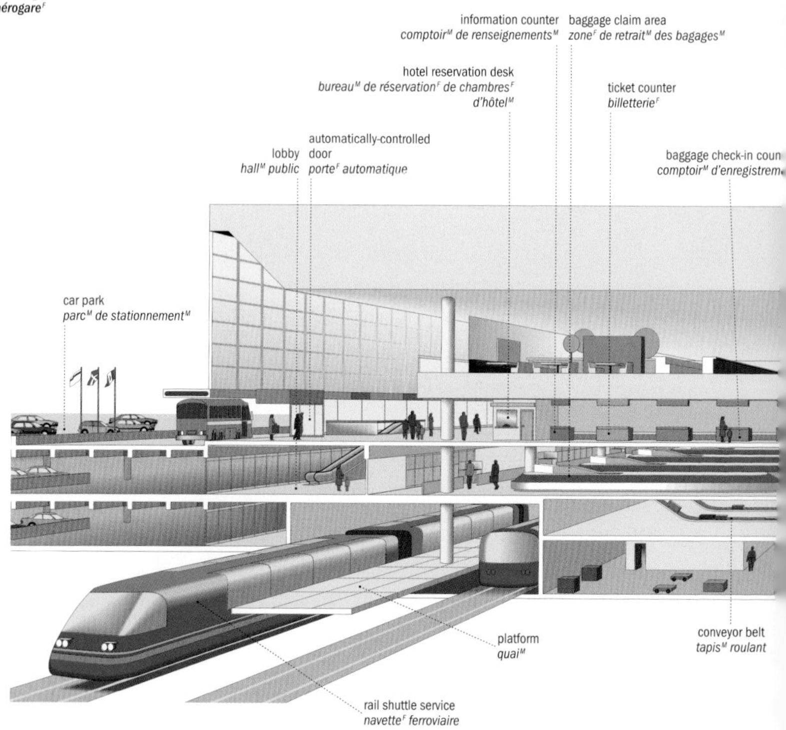

information counter
comptoir^M de renseignements^M
baggage claim area
zone^F de retrait^M des bagages^M
hotel reservation desk
bureau^M de réservation^F de chambres^F d'hôtel^M
ticket counter
billetterie^F
automatically-controlled door
porte^F automatique
lobby
hall^M public
baggage check-in coun
comptoir^M d'enregistrem
car park
parc^M de stationnement^M
platform
quai^M
conveyor belt
tapis^M roulant
rail shuttle service
navette^F ferroviaire

runway
piste^F

holding area marking
marque^F de point^M d'attente^F
runway designation marking
marques^F d'identification^F
runway centre line markings
marque^F d'axe^M de piste^F
runway side stripe markings
marques^F latérales de piste^F

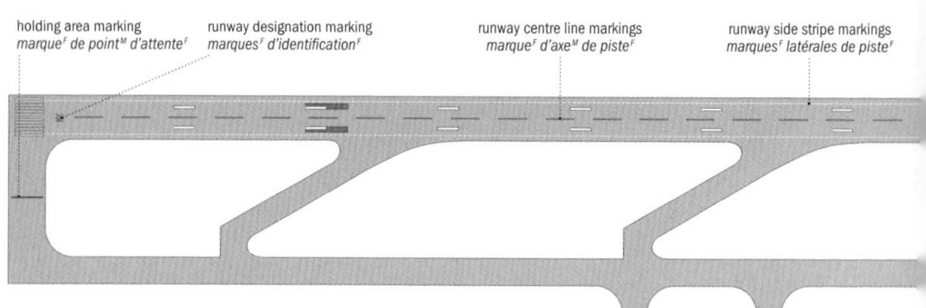

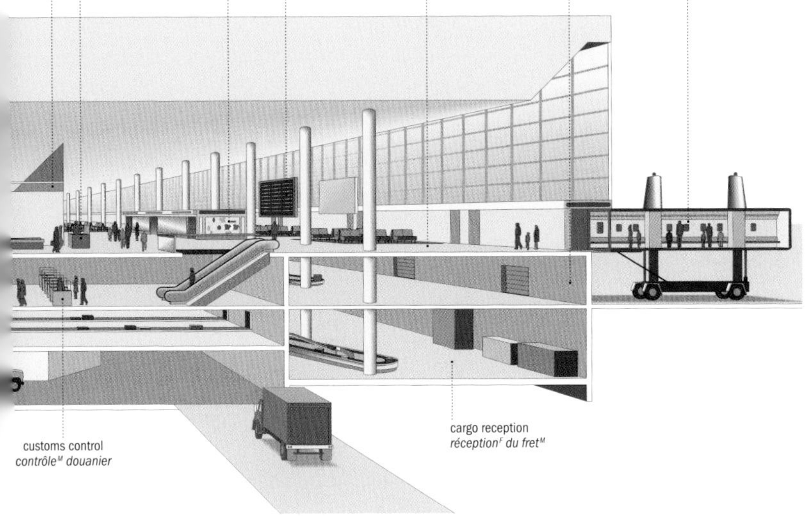

rity check
rôle^M de sécurité^F
duty-free shop
boutique^F hors taxe^F
observation deck
terrasse^F
flight information board
tableau^M d'affichage^M des vols^M
cargo dispatch
expédition^F du fret^M
passport control
contrôle^M des passeports^M
departure lounge
salle^F d'embarquement^M
passenger transfer vehicle
transbordeur^M
cargo reception
réception^F du fret^M
customs control
contrôle^M douanier

exit taxiway
sortie^F de piste^F
runway touchdown zone marking
marque^F d'aire^F de prise^F de contact^M
runway threshold markings
marques^F de seuil^M de piste^F
fixed distance marking
marque^F de distance^F
constante

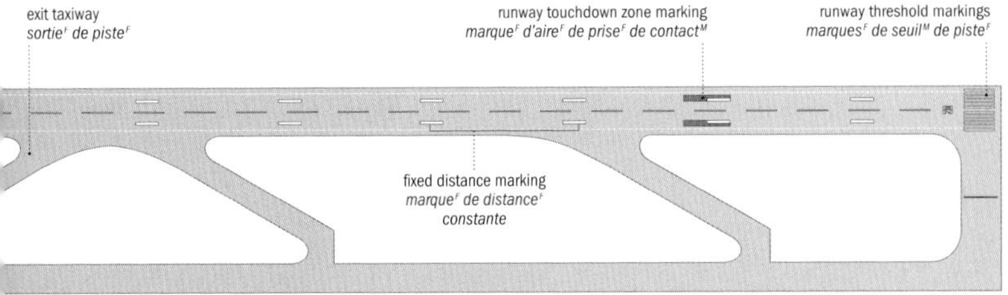

long-range jet airliner

avion[M] long-courrier[M]

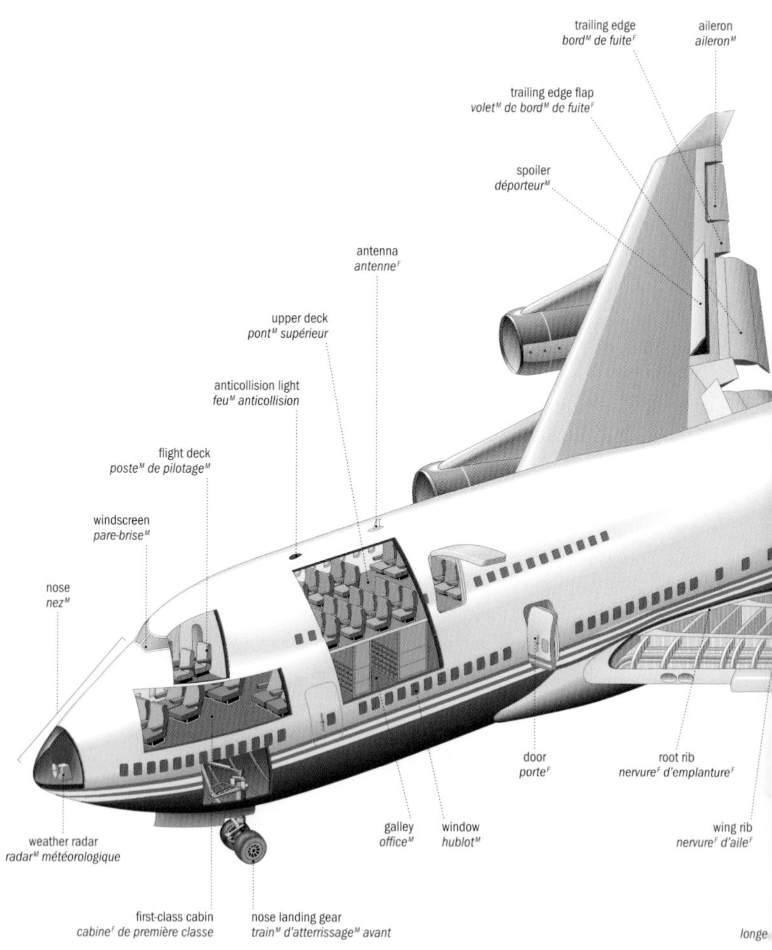

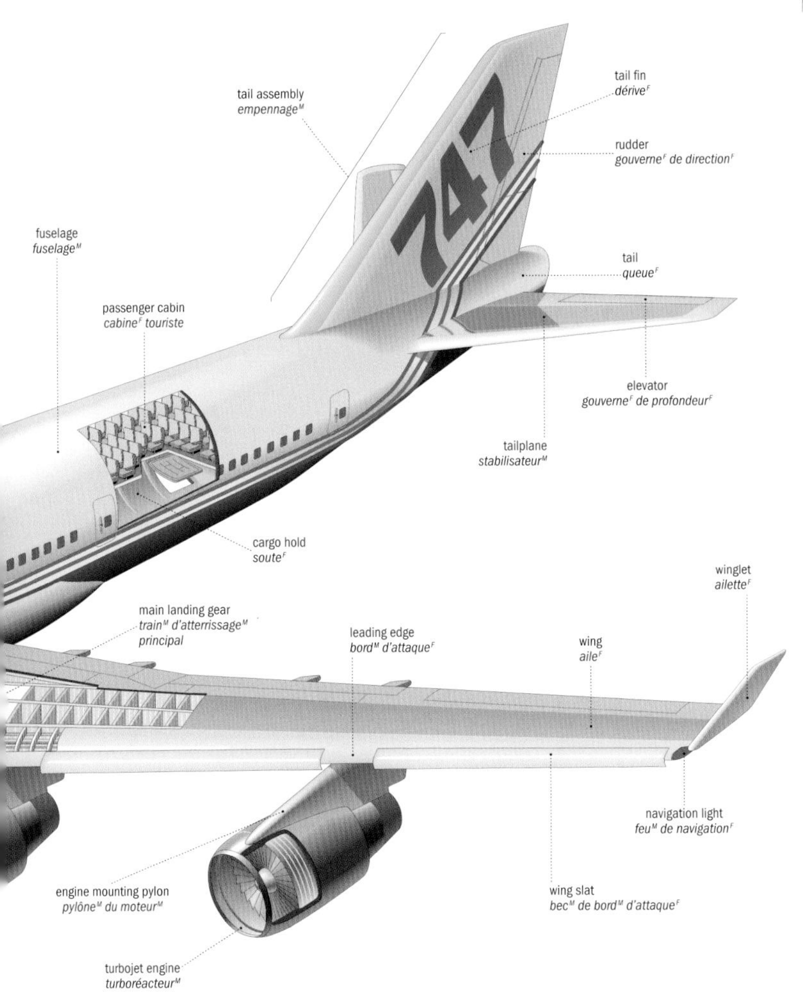
tail assembly
*empennage*M
tail fin
*dérive*F
rudder
*gouverne*F *de direction*F
fuselage
*fuselage*M
tail
*queue*F
passenger cabin
*cabine*F *touriste*
elevator
*gouverne*F *de profondeur*F
tailplane
*stabilisateur*M
cargo hold
*soute*F
winglet
*ailette*F
main landing gear
*train*M *d'atterrissage*M *principal*
leading edge
*bord*M *d'attaque*F
wing
*aile*F
navigation light
*feu*M *de navigation*F
engine mounting pylon
*pylône*M *du moteur*M
wing slat
*bec*M *de bord*M *d'attaque*F
turbojet engine
*turboréacteur*M

examples of aircraft

exemples[M] d'avions[M]

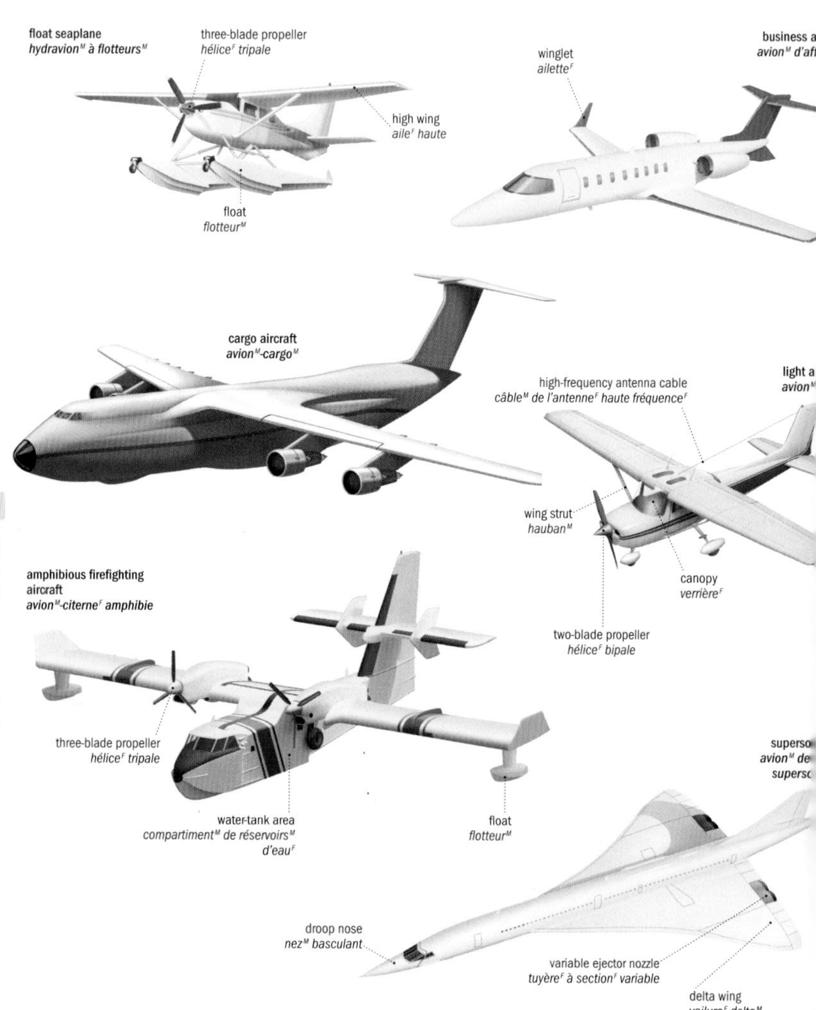

movements of an aircraft

mouvements[M] de l'avion[M]

pitch
tangage[M]

yaw
lacet[M]

roll
roulis[M]

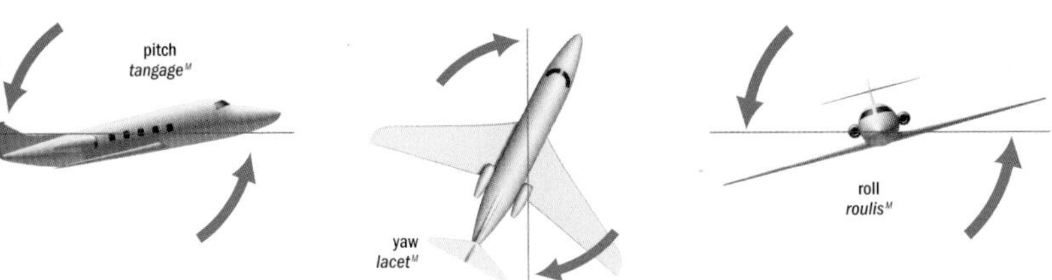

helicopter

hélicoptère[M]

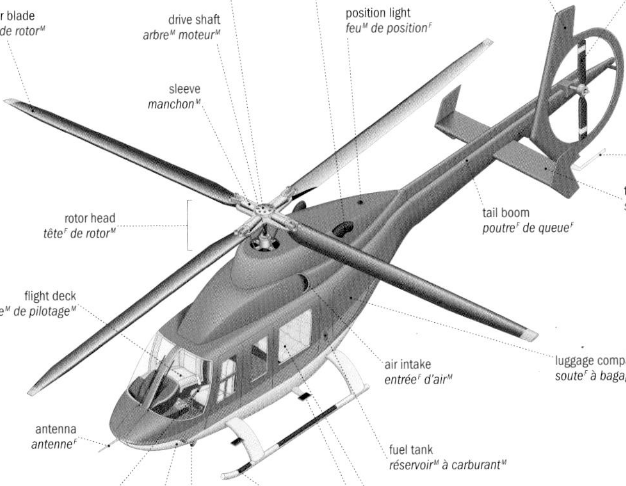

rotor hub
moyeu[M] rotor[M]
exhaust pipe
tuyère[F]
tail fin
dérive[F]
anti-torque tail rotor
rotor[M] anticouple
rotor blade
pale[F] de rotor[M]
drive shaft
arbre[M] moteur[M]
position light
feu[M] de position[F]
sleeve
manchon[M]
tail skid
béquille[F]
tailplane
stabilisateur[M]
rotor head
tête[F] de rotor[M]
tail boom
poutre[F] de queue[F]
flight deck
poste[M] de pilotage[M]
air intake
entrée[F] d'air[M]
luggage compartment
soute[F] à bagages[M]
antenna
antenne[F]
fuel tank
réservoir[M] à carburant[M]
skid
patin[M]
control stick
manche[M] à balai[M]
cabin
cabine[F]
landing window
hublot[M] d'atterrissage[M]
landing light
phare[M] d'atterrissage[M]
boarding step
marchepied[M]

TRANSPORT AND MACHINERY

material handling

manutention[F]

forklift truck
chariot[M] élévateur

mast
mât[M]

crosshead
tête[F] du vérin[M] de levage[M]

lifting chain
chaîne[F] de levage[M]

hydraulic system
système[M] hydraulique

carriage
tablier[M]

fork arm
bras[M] de fourche[F]

fork
fourches[F]

overhead guard
toit[M] de protection[F]

mast operating lever
levier[M] de manœuvre[F] d

engine compartment
moteur[M]

frame
châssis[M]

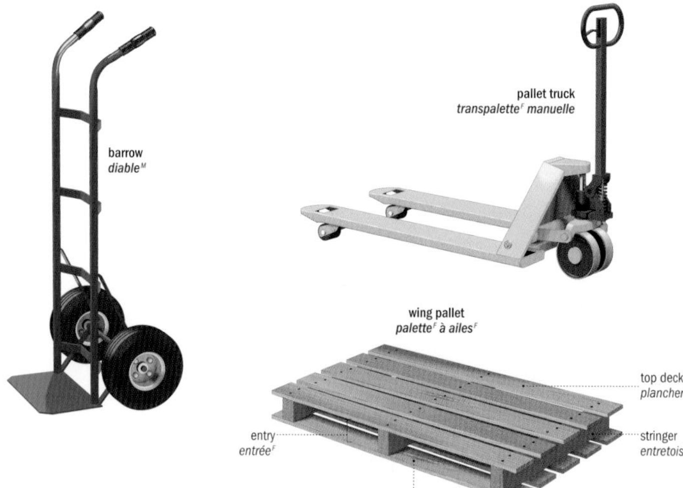

cranes

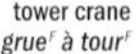

grues[F] et portique[M]

tower crane
grue[F] à tour[F]

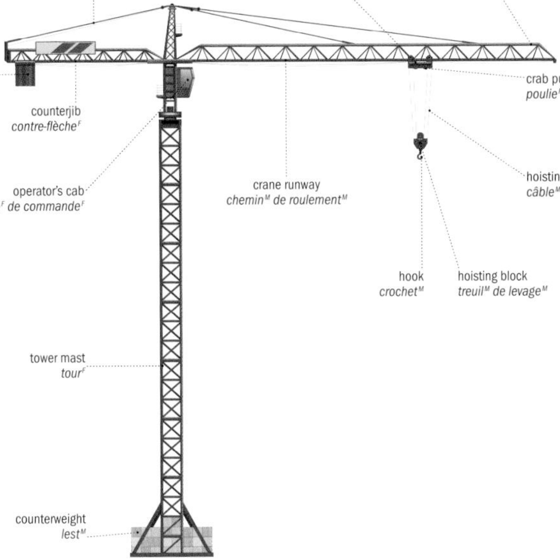

jib tie
tirant[M]

travelling crab
chariot[M]

jib
flèche[F]

counterjib ballast
contrepoids[M]

crab pulley
poulie[F] de chariot[M]

counterjib
contre-flèche[F]

operator's cab
cabine[F] de commande[F]

crane runway
chemin[M] de roulement[M]

hoisting rope
câble[M] de levage[M]

hook
crochet[M]

hoisting block
treuil[M] de levage[M]

tower mast
tour[F]

counterweight
lest[M]

truck crane
grue[F] sur porteur[M]

telescopic boom
flèche[F] télescopique

elevating cylinder
vérin[M] de dressage[M]

operator's cab
cabine[F] de commande[F]

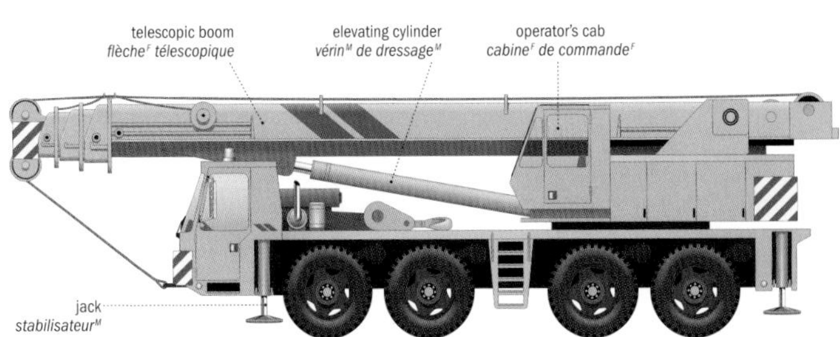

jack
stabilisateur[M]

bulldozer

bulldozer[M]

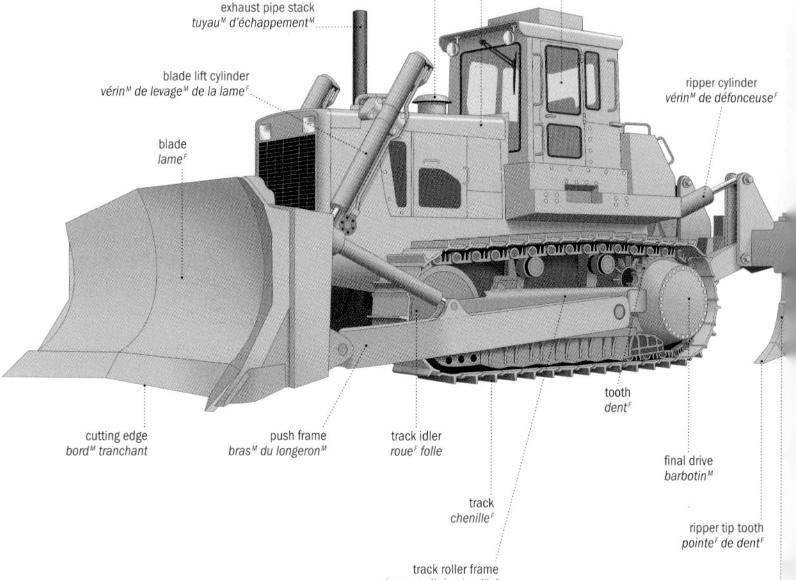

air pre-cleaner filter
filtre[M] à air[M]

diesel motor compartment
moteur[M] diesel

cab
cabine[F]

exhaust pipe stack
tuyau[M] d'échappement[M]

blade lift cylinder
vérin[M] de levage[M] de la lame[F]

ripper cylinder
vérin[M] de défonceuse[F]

blade
lame[F]

tooth
dent[F]

cutting edge
bord[M] tranchant

push frame
bras[M] du longeron[M]

track idler
roue[F] folle

final drive
barbotin[M]

track
chenille[F]

ripper tip tooth
pointe[F] de dent[F]

track roller frame
longeron[M] de chenille[F]

shank protecto
sabot[M] de protection

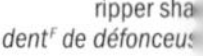

ripper sha
dent[F] de défonceus

tracklaying tractor
tracteur[M] à chenilles[F]

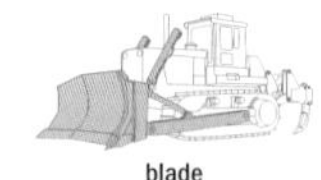

blade
lame[F]

ripper
défonceuse[F]

backhoe loader

chargeuse[F]-pelleteuse[F]

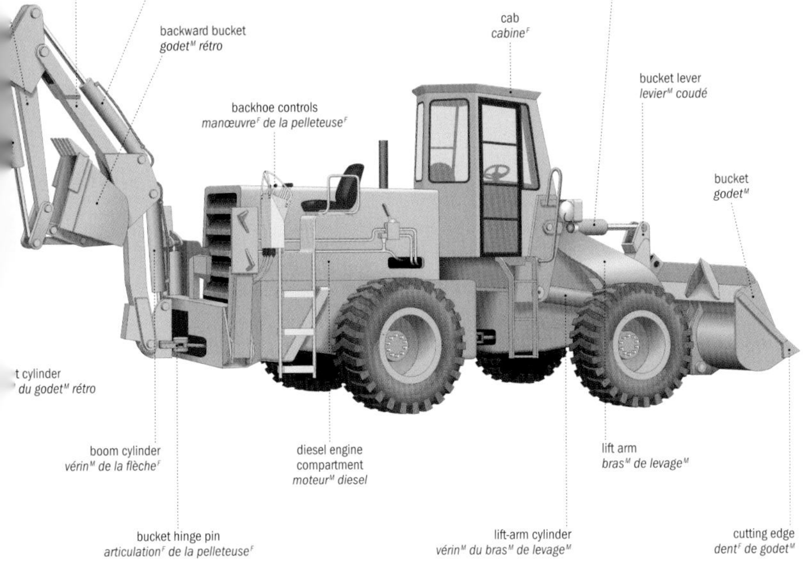

per arm
s[M]

dipper arm cylinder
vérin[M] du bras[M]

boom
flèche[F]

backward bucket
godet[M] rétro

backhoe controls
manœuvre[F] de la pelleteuse[F]

cab
cabine[F]

bucket cylinder
vérin[M] du godet[M]

bucket lever
levier[M] coudé

bucket
godet[M]

t cylinder
du godet[M] rétro

boom cylinder
vérin[M] de la flèche[F]

diesel engine compartment
moteur[M] diesel

lift arm
bras[M] de levage[M]

bucket hinge pin
articulation[F] de la pelleteuse[F]

lift-arm cylinder
vérin[M] du bras[M] de levage[M]

cutting edge
dent[F] de godet[M]

front-end loader
chargeuse[F] frontale

wheel tractor
tracteur[M]

backhoe
pelleteuse[F]

scraper

décapeuse^F

gooseneck
col^M-de-cygne^M
steering cylinder
vérin^M de direction^F
tractor engine compartment
tracteur^M-remorqueur^M
elevator
élévateur^M
draught tube
palonnier^M
skip
benne^F
cutting edge
lame^F racleuse
draught arm
brancard^M

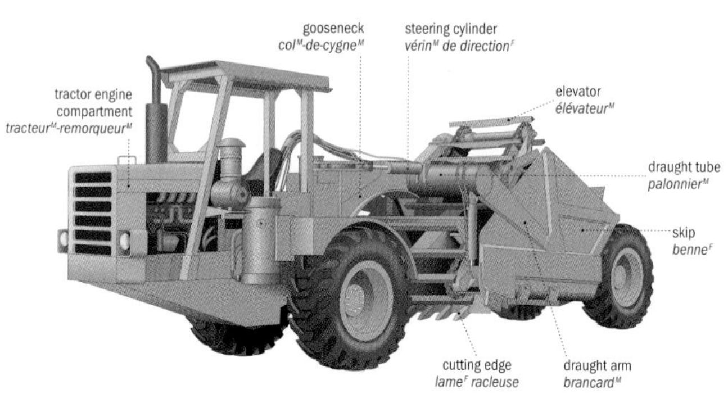

hydraulic shovel

pelle^F hydraulique

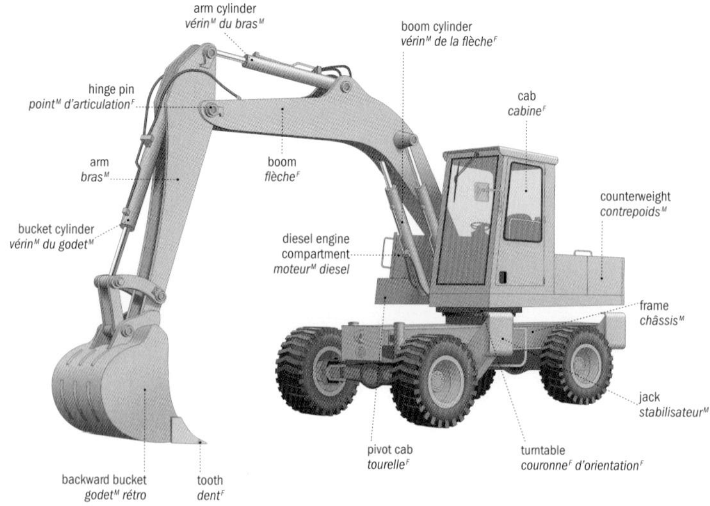
arm cylinder
vérin^M du bras^M
boom cylinder
vérin^M de la flèche^F
hinge pin
point^M d'articulation^F
cab
cabine^F
arm
bras^M
boom
flèche^F
counterweight
contrepoids^M
bucket cylinder
vérin^M du godet^M
diesel engine compartment
moteur^M diesel
frame
châssis^M
jack
stabilisateur^M
pivot cab
tourelle^F
turntable
couronne^F d'orientation^F
backward bucket
godet^M rétro
tooth
dent^F

grader

niveleuse[F]

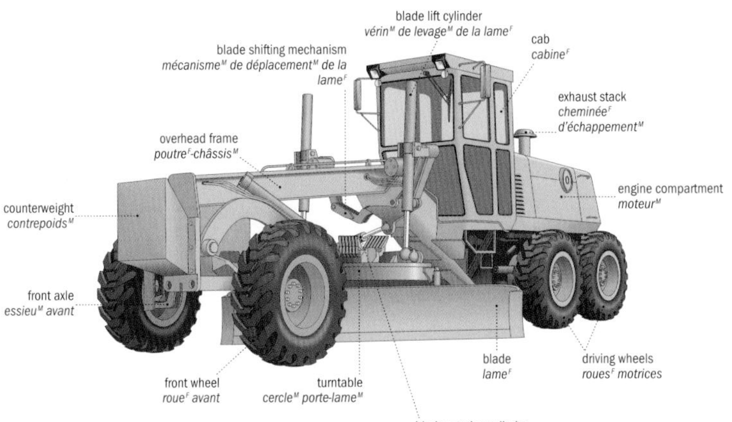

tipper truck

camion[M]-benne[F]

production of electricity from geothermal energy

productionF d'électricitéF par énergieF géothermique

turbine
turbineF
generator
alternateurM
condenser
condenseurM
steam
vapeurF
high-tension electricity transmiss
transportM de l'électricitéF à hau
tensionF
separator
séparateurM
voltage increase
élévationF de la tensionF
water-steam mix
mélangeM eauF-vapeurF
cooling tower
tourF de refroidissementM
upper confining bed
toitM imperméable
water
eauF
geothermal field
champM géothermique
lower confining bed
substratumM imperméable
production well
puitsM de productionF
confined aquifer
aquifèreM captif
injection well
puitsM d'injectionF
magma chamber
réservoirM magmatique

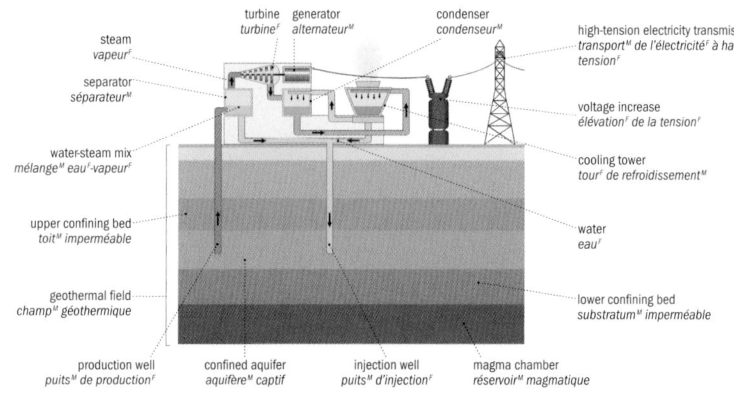

thermal energy

énergieF thermique

production of electricity from thermal energy
productionF d'électricitéF par énergieF thermique

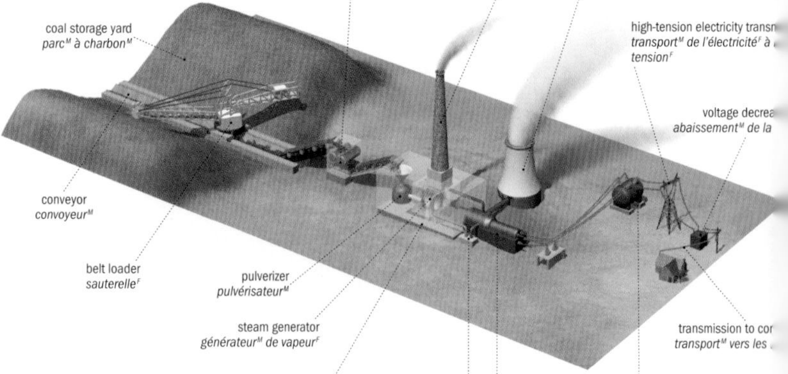

crusher
broyeurM
stack
cheminéeF
cooling tower
tourF de refroidissementM
coal storage yard
parcM à charbonM
high-tension electricity transm
transportM de l'électricitéF à
tensionF
voltage decrea
abaissementM de la
conveyor
convoyeurM
belt loader
sauterelleF
pulverizer
pulvérisateurM
steam generator
générateurM de vapeurF
transmission to cor
transportM vers les
coal-fired thermal power station
centraleF thermique au charbonM
condenser
condenseurM
turbo-alternator unit
groupeM turbo-alternateurM
voltage increase
élévationF de la tensionF

oil

pétrole[M]

surface prospecting
prospection[F] terrestre

seismographic recording
enregistrement[M] sismographique

shock wave
onde[F] de choc[M]

petroleum trap
gisement[M] de pétrole[M]

drilling rig
appareil[M] de forage[M]

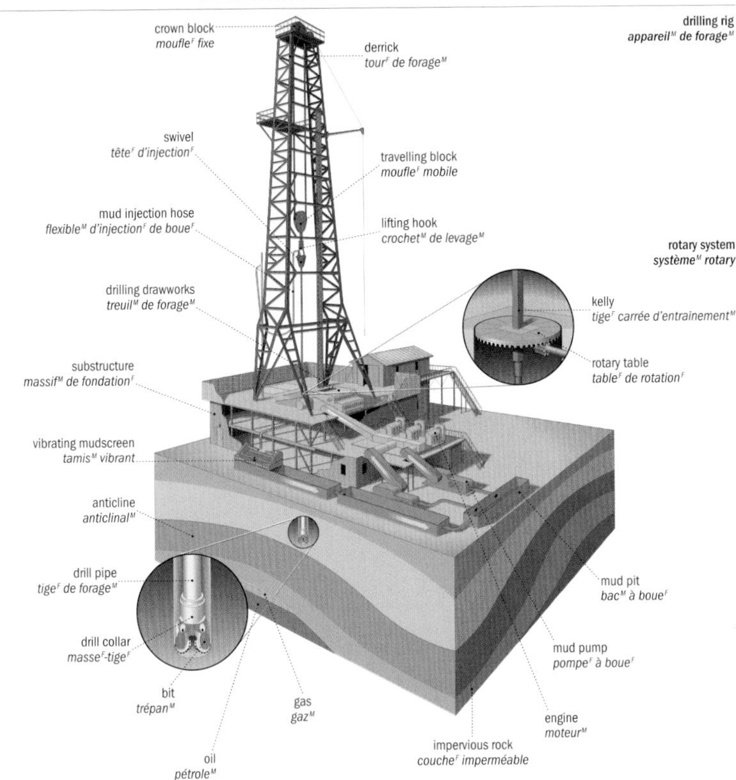

floating-roof tank
réservoir[M] à toit[M] flottant

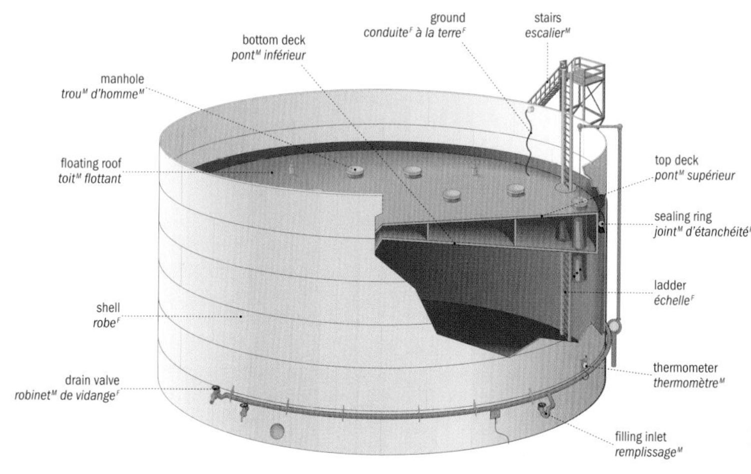

crude-oil pipeline
réseau[M] d'oléoducs[M]

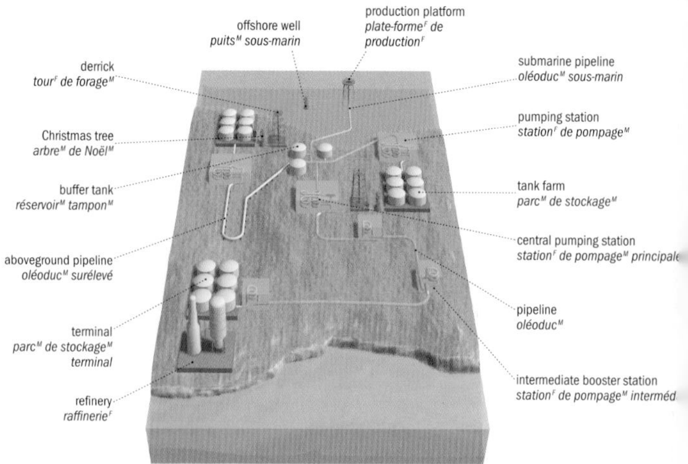

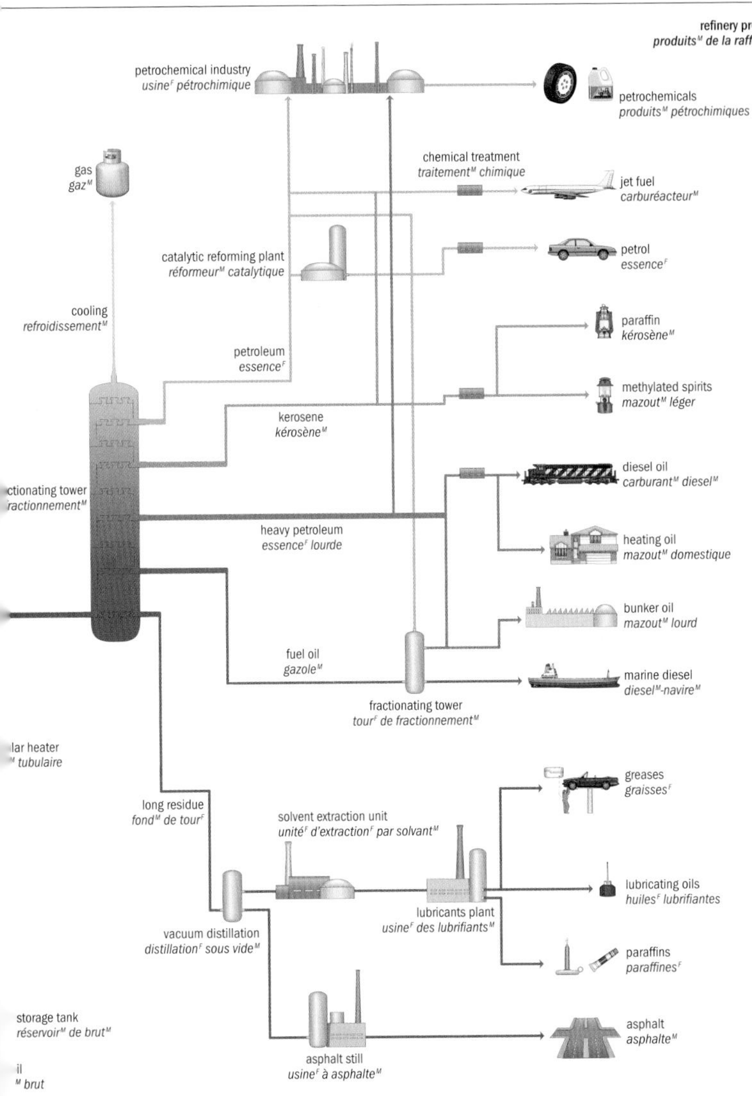
refinery products
produits[M] de la raffinerie[F]
petrochemical industry
usine[F] pétrochimique
petrochemicals
produits[M] pétrochimiques
gas
gaz[M]
chemical treatment
traitement[M] chimique
jet fuel
carburéacteur[M]
catalytic reforming plant
réformeur[M] catalytique
petrol
essence[F]
cooling
refroidissement[M]
paraffin
kérosène[M]
petroleum
essence[F]
methylated spirits
mazout[M] léger
kerosene
kérosène[M]
diesel oil
carburant[M] diesel[M]
ctionating tower
ractionnement[M]
heavy petroleum
essence[F] lourde
heating oil
mazout[M] domestique
bunker oil
mazout[M] lourd
fuel oil
gazole[M]
marine diesel
diesel[M]-navire[M]
fractionating tower
tour[F] de fractionnement[M]
lar heater
[M] tubulaire
greases
graisses[F]
long residue
fond[M] de tour[F]
solvent extraction unit
unité[F] d'extraction[F] par solvant[M]
lubricating oils
huiles[F] lubrifiantes
lubricants plant
usine[F] des lubrifiants[M]
vacuum distillation
distillation[F] sous vide[M]
paraffins
paraffines[F]
storage tank
réservoir[M] de brut[M]
asphalt
asphalte[M]
asphalt still
usine[F] à asphalte[M]
il
[M] brut

hydroelectric complex

complexe^M hydroélectrique

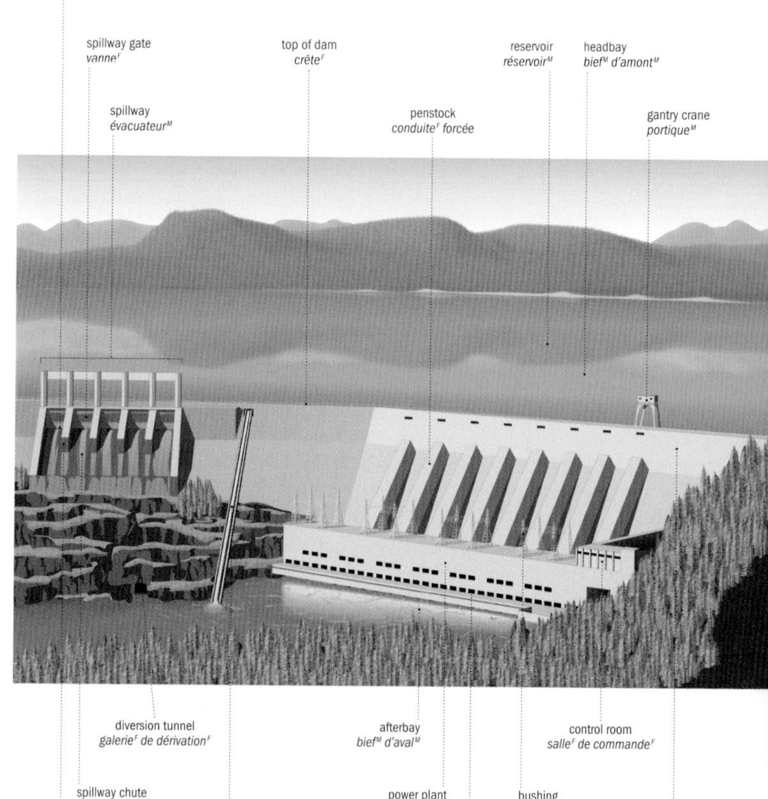

cross section of a hydroelectric power plant
coupe*^F *d'une centrale*^F *hydroélectrique

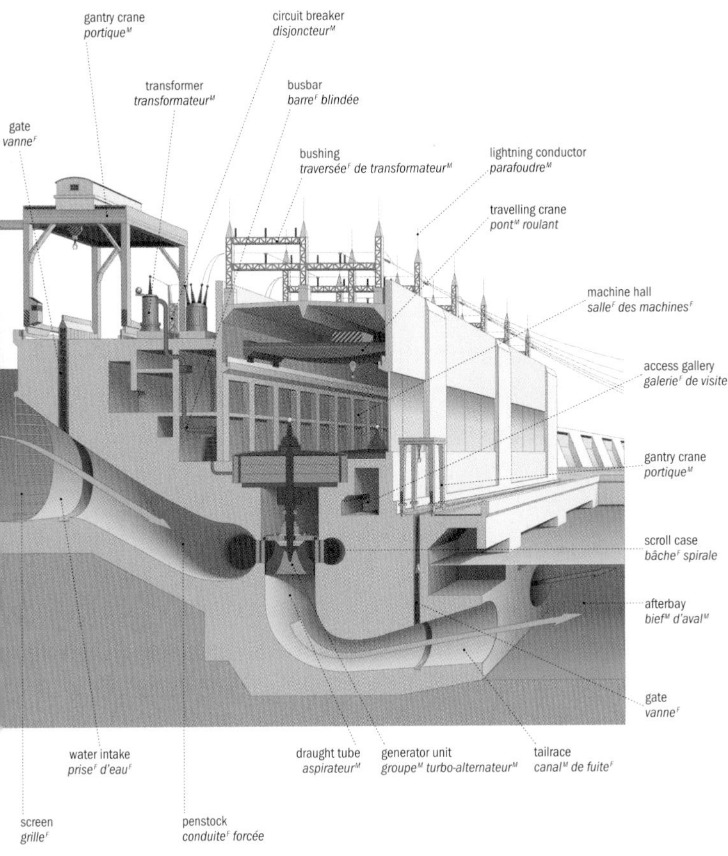

ir
ir^M

production of electricity from nuclear energy

production^F d'électricité^F par énergie^F nucléaire

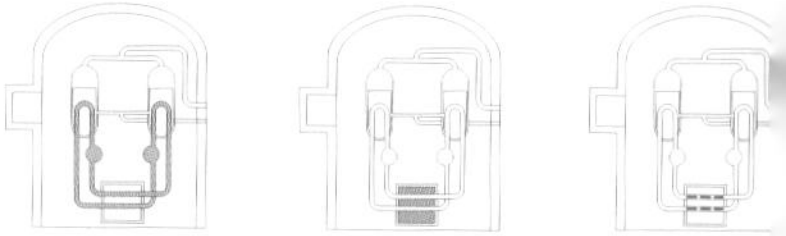

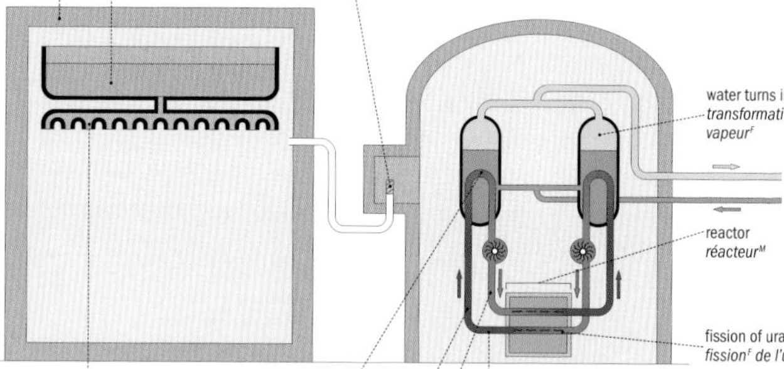

coolant
caloporteur^M
moderator
modérateur^M
fuel
combustible^M

dousing water tank
réservoir^M d'arrosage^M
containment building
enceinte^F de confinement^M
safety valve
soupape^F de sûreté^F
water turns into steam
transformation^F de l'eau^F vapeur^F
reactor
réacteur^M
fission of uranium fuel
fission^F de l'uranium^M
sprinklers
gicleurs^M
transfer of heat to water
transmission^F de la chaleur^F à l'eau^F
heat production
production^F de chaleur^F
hot coolant
caloporteur^M chaud
cold coolant
caloporteur^M refroidi

steam pressure drives turbine
entraînement^M de la turbine^F par la vapeur^F
turbine shaft turns generator
entraînement^M du rotor^M de l'alternateur^M
production of electricity by generator
production^F d'électricité^F par l'alternateur^M
voltage increase
water is pumped back into steam generator
retour^M de l'eau^F au générateur^M de vapeur^F
condensation of steam into water
condensation^F de la vapeur^F
water cools used steam
refroidissement^M de la vapeur^F par l'eau^F

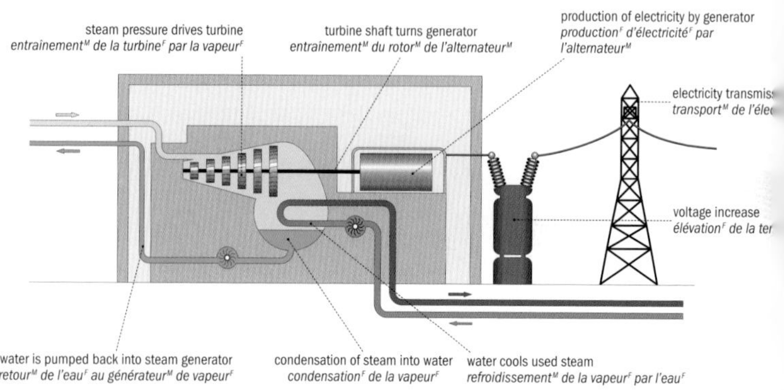

fuel bundle

grappe^F de combustible^M

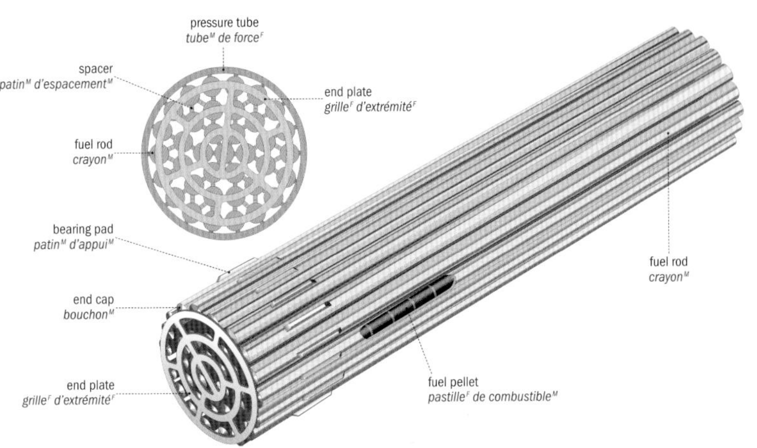

nuclear reactor

réacteur^M nucléaire

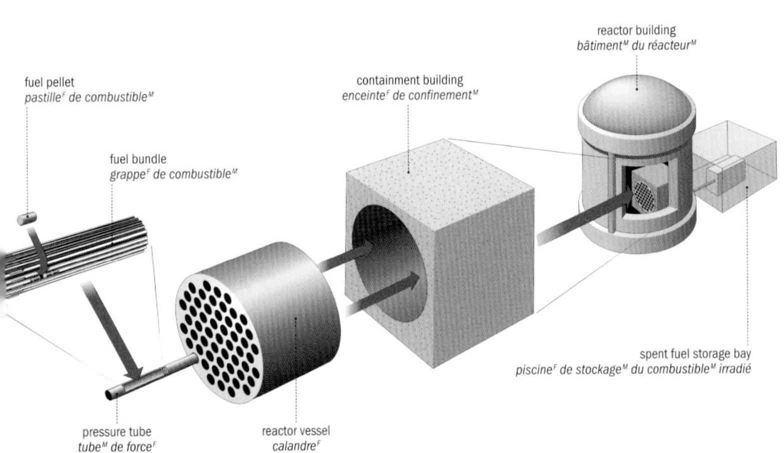

solar cell

photopile[F]

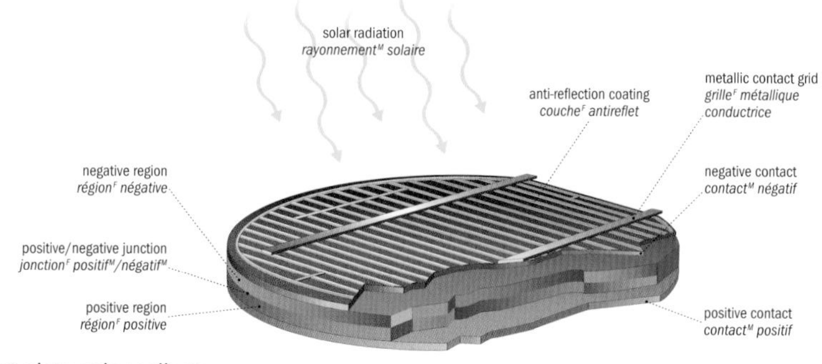

flat-plate solar collector

capteur[M] solaire plan

solar radiation
rayonnement[M] solaire

coolant outlet
sortie[F] du caloporteur[M]

glass
vitrage[M]

frame
coffre[M]

flow tube
tube[M] de circulation[F]

absorbing plate
plaque[F] absorbante

coolant inlet
entrée[F] du caloporteur[M]

insulation
isolant[M]

solar-cell system

circuit[M] de photopiles[F]

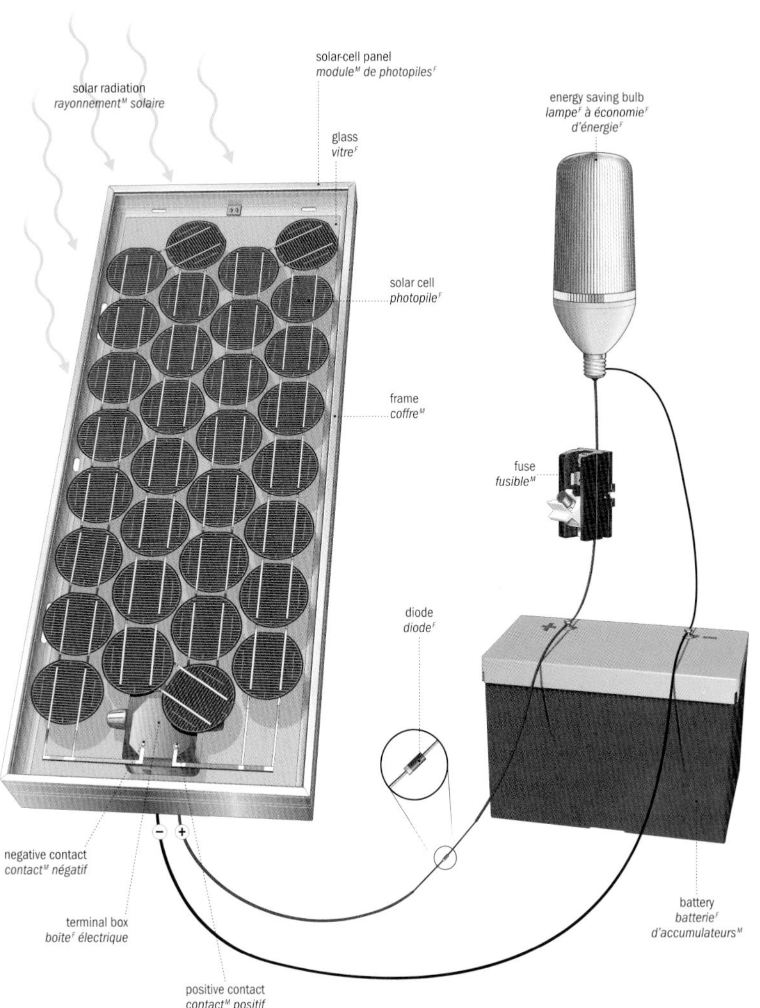

windmill

moulin^M à vent^M

tower mill
moulin^M tour^F

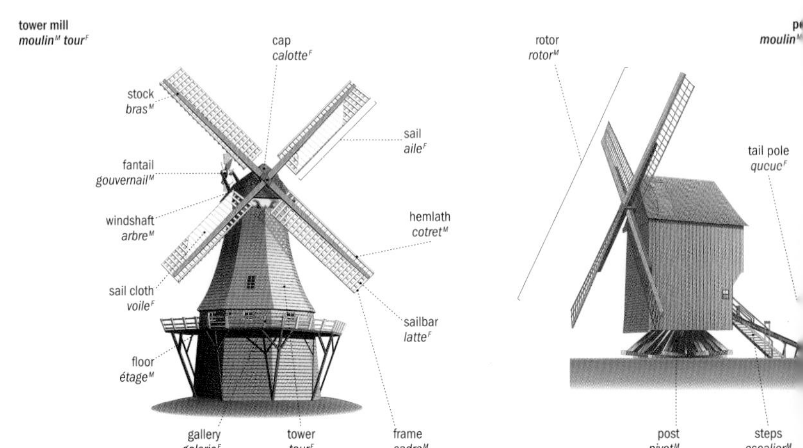

wind turbines and electricity production

éoliennes^F et production^F d'électricité^F

vertical-axis wind turbine
éolienne^F à axe^M vertical

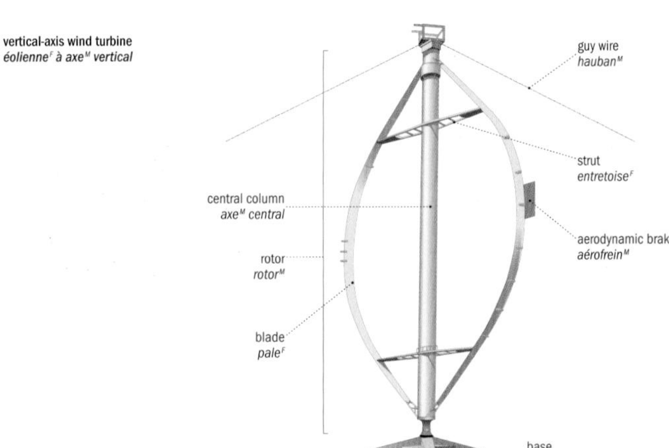

ENERGY

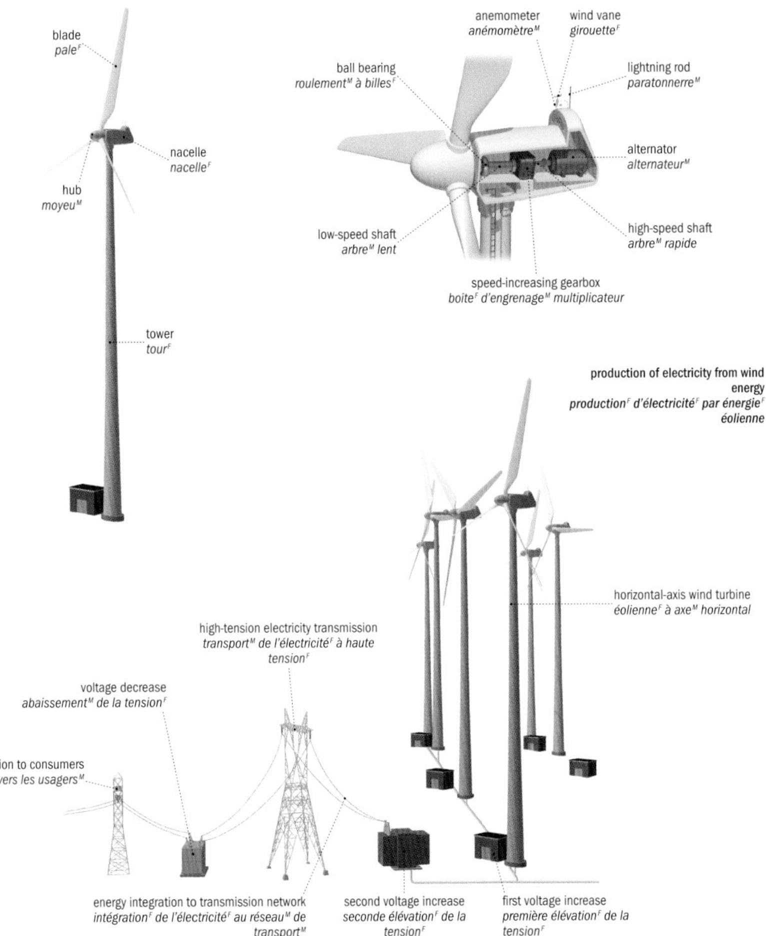
ntal-axis wind turbine
ne^F à axe^M horizontal
blade
pale^F
nacelle
nacelle^F
hub
moyeu^M
tower
tour^F
nacelle cross-section
coupe^F de la nacelle^F
anemometer
anémomètre^M
wind vane
girouette^F
ball bearing
roulement^M à billes^F
lightning rod
paratonnerre^M
alternator
alternateur^M
low-speed shaft
arbre^M lent
high-speed shaft
arbre^M rapide
speed-increasing gearbox
boîte^F d'engrenage^M multiplicateur
production of electricity from wind energy
production^F d'électricité^F par énergie^F éolienne
horizontal-axis wind turbine
éolienne^F à axe^M horizontal
high-tension electricity transmission
transport^M de l'électricité^F à haute tension^F
voltage decrease
abaissement^M de la tension^F
ssion to consumers
^M vers les usagers^M
energy integration to transmission network
intégration^F de l'électricité^F au réseau^M de transport^M
second voltage increase
seconde élévation^F de la tension^F
first voltage increase
première élévation^F de la tension^F

matter

matière^F

atom
atome^M

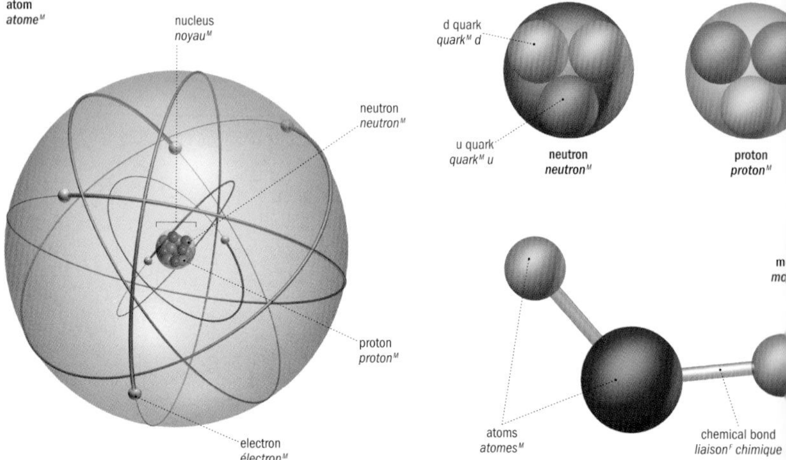

states of matter
états^M de la matière^F

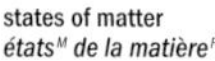

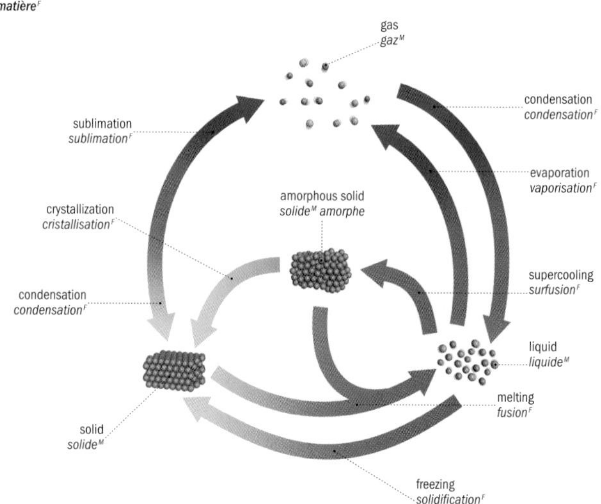

nuclear fission
fission^F nucléaire

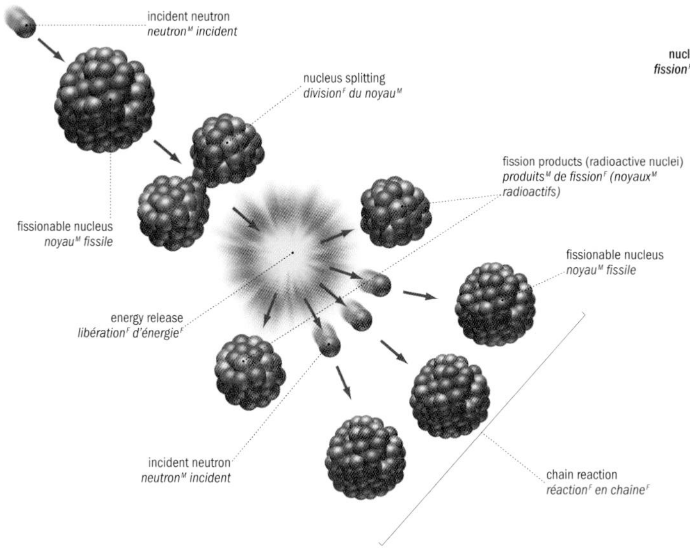

incident neutron
neutron^M incident
nucleus splitting
division^F du noyau^M
fission products (radioactive nuclei)
produits^M de fission^F (noyaux^M radioactifs)
fissionable nucleus
noyau^M fissile
fissionable nucleus
noyau^M fissile
energy release
libération^F d'énergie^F
incident neutron
neutron^M incident
chain reaction
réaction^F en chaîne^F

heat transfer
transfert^M de la chaleur^F

convection
convection^F
vapour
vapeur^F
liquid
liquide^M
radiation
rayonnement^M
convection current
courant^M de convection^F
solid
solide^M
conduction
conduction^F
flame
flamme^F

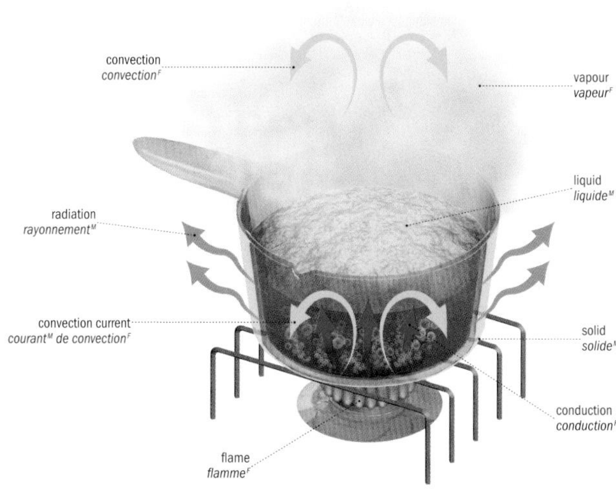

SCIENCE

magnetism

magnétisme[M]

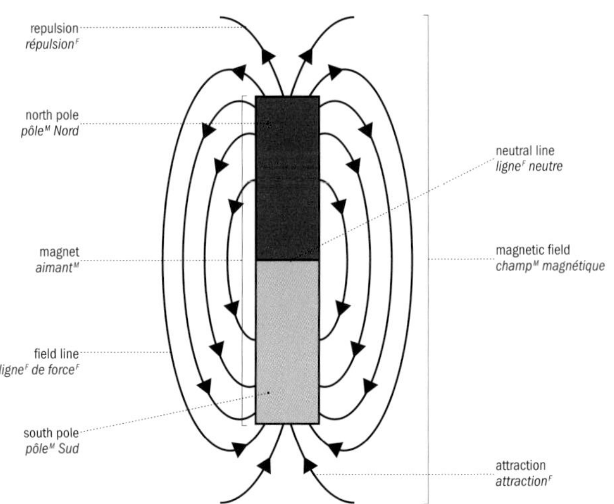

parallel electrical circuit

circuit[M] électrique en parallèle[F]

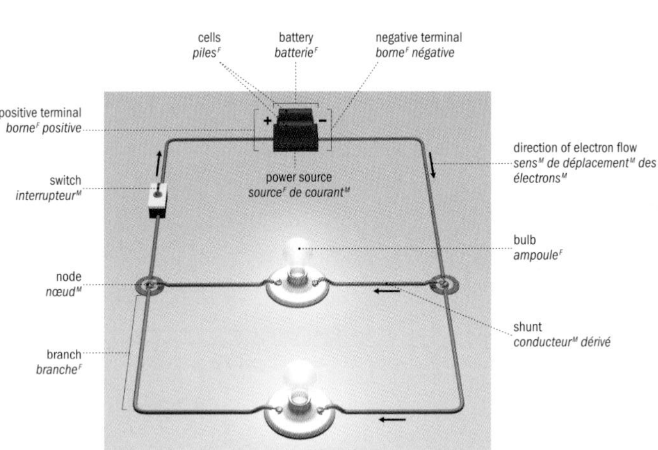

SCIENCE

dry cells

piles[F] sèches

›n-zinc cell
carbone[M]-zinc[M]

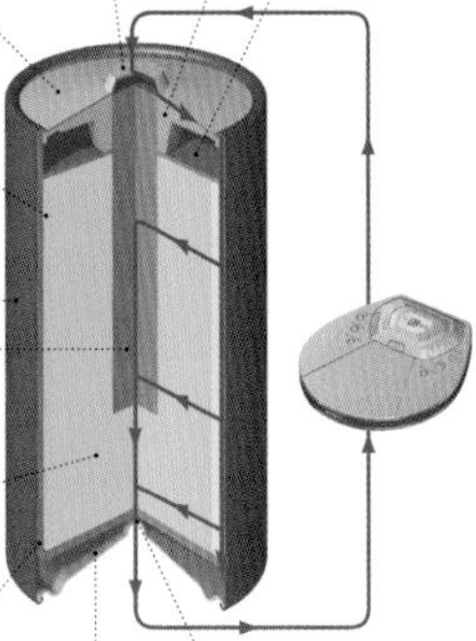

sealing plug
bouchon[M] de scellement[M]
positive terminal
borne[F] positive
washer
rondelle[F]
top cap
couvercle[M] supérieur
electrolytic separator
rateur[M] électrolytique
jacket
gaine[F]
carbon rod (cathode)
carbone[M] (cathode[F])
depolarizing mix
élange[M] dépolarisant
zinc can (anode)
e[F] en zinc[M] (anode[F])
bottom cap
couvercle[M] inférieur
negative terminal
borne[F] négative

alkaline manganese-zinc cell
pile[F] alcaline manganèse[M]-zinc[M]

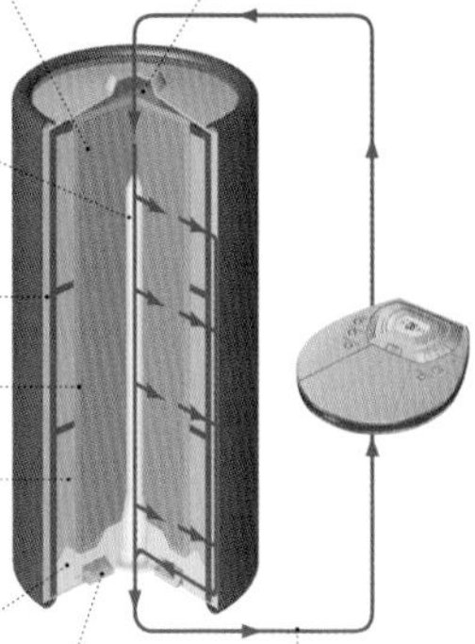

zinc-electrolyte mix (anode)
mélange[M] de zinc[M] et d'électrolyte[M] (anode[F])
sealing material
matériau[M] de scellement[M]
electron collector
collecteur[M] d'électrons[M]
steel casing
chemise[F] en acier[M]
separator
séparateur[M]
manganese mix (cathode)
mélange[M] au manganèse[M] (cathode[F])
sealing plug
bouchon[M] de scellement[M]
bottom cap
couvercle[M] inférieur
direction of electron flow
sens[M] de déplacement[M] des électrons[M]

electronics

électronique[F]

› circuit board
de circuit[M] imprimé

ceramic capacitor
condensateur[M] céramique
electrolytic capacitors
condensateurs[M] électrolytiques
plastic film capacitor
condensateur[M] à film[M] plastique
›ed integrated circuit
[M] intégré en boîtier[M]
resistors
résistances[F]
printed circuit
circuit[M] imprimé

packaged integrated circuit
circuit[M] intégré en boîtier[M]

integrated circuit
circuit[M] intégré
lid
capot[M]
wire
fil[M]
dual-in-line package
boîtier[M] à double rangée[F] de connexions[F]
connection pin
broche[F] de connexion[F]

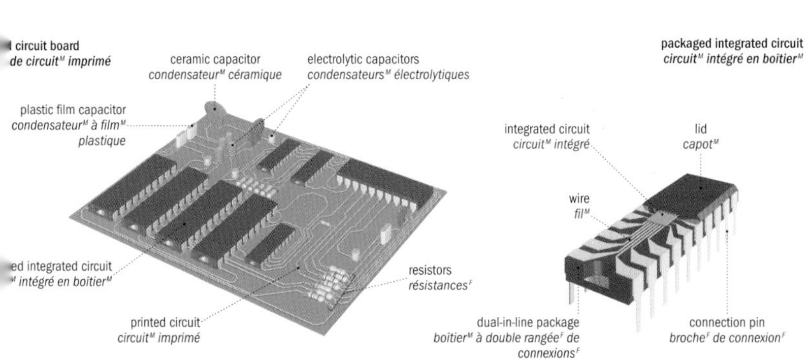

SCIENCE

electromagnetic spectrum

spectre[M] électromagnétique

ultraviolet radiation
rayonnement[M] ultraviolet

microwaves
micro-ondes[F]

infrared radiation
rayonnement[M] infrarouge

radio waves
ondes[F] radio

X-rays
rayons[M] X

gamma rays
rayons[M] gamma

visible light
lumière[F] visible

wave

onde[F]

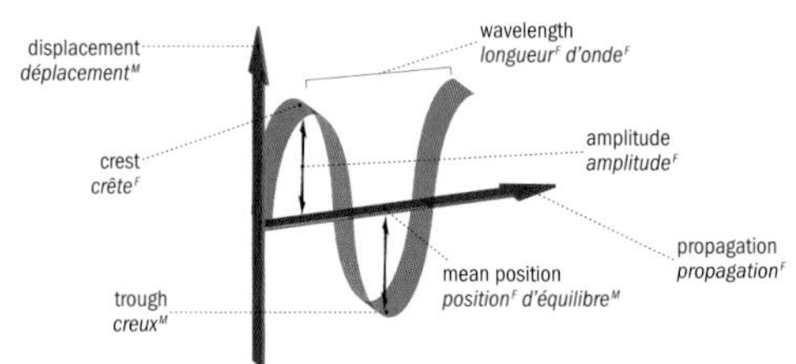

colour synthesis

synthèse[F] des couleurs[F]

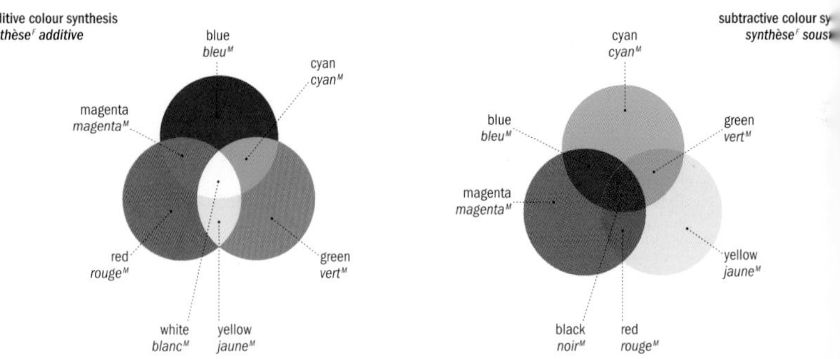

vision
vision[F]

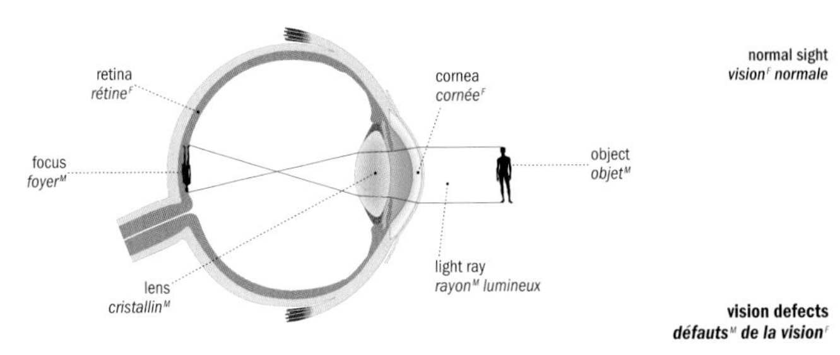

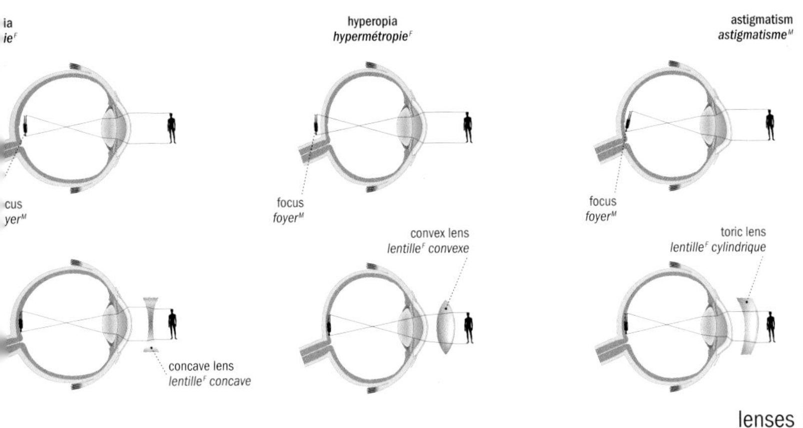

lenses
lentilles[F]

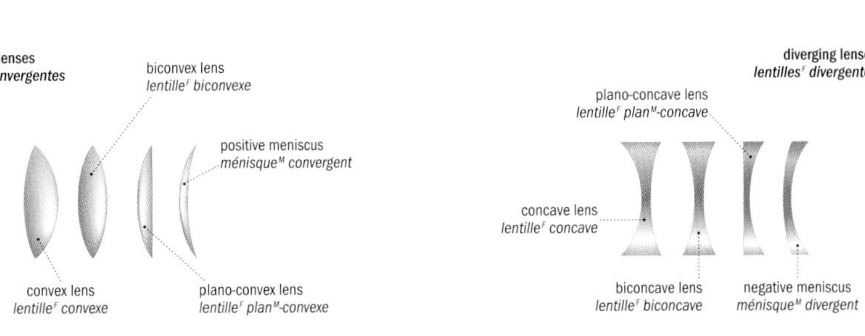

SCIENCE

pulsed ruby laser

laser[M] à rubis[M] pulsé

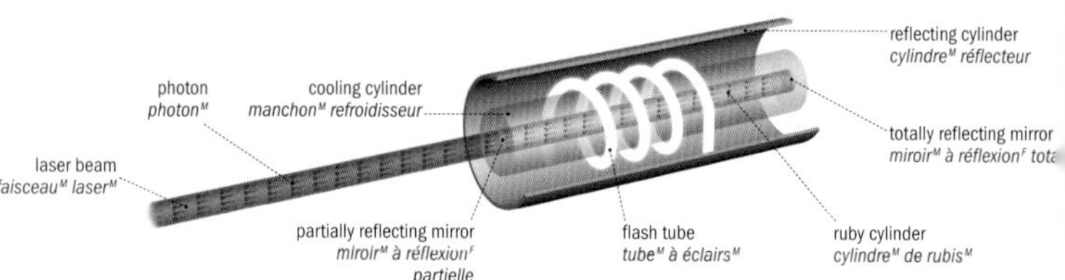

prism binoculars

jumelles[F] à prismes[M]

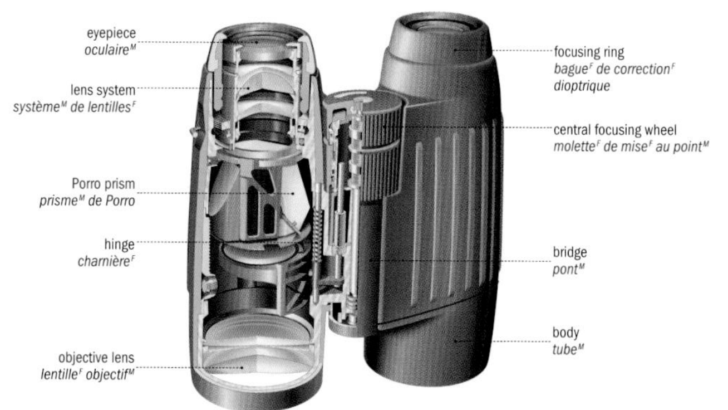

telescopic sight

lunette[F] de visée[F]

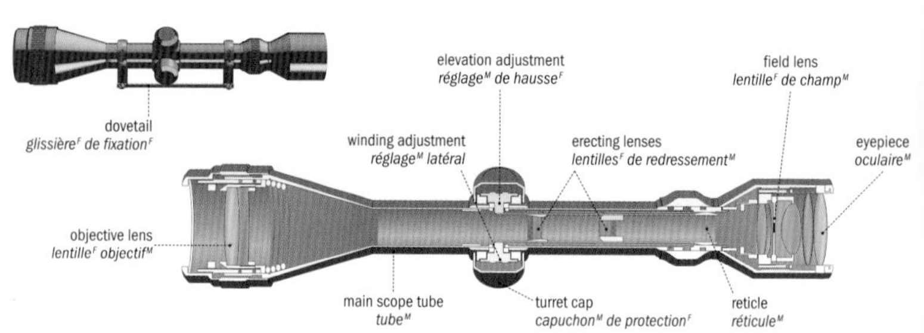

SCIENCE

magnifying glass and microscopes

loupe^F et microscopes^M

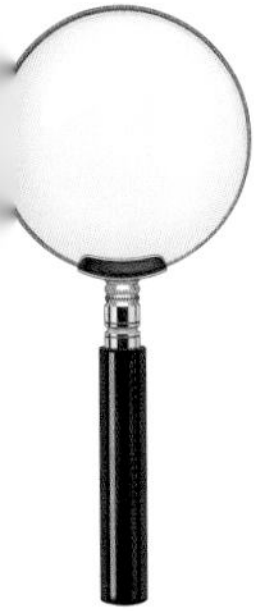

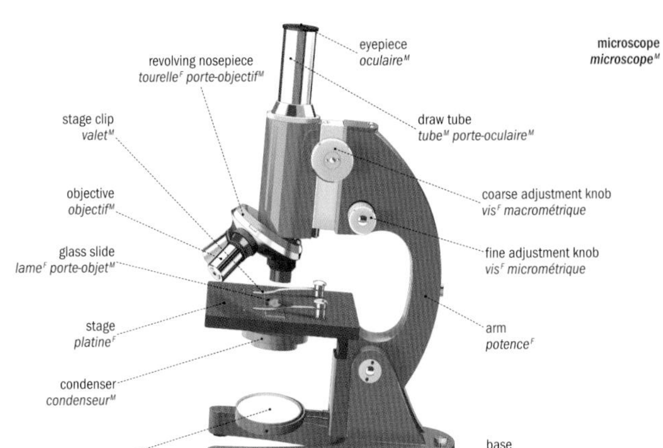

magnifying glass
loupe^F

microscope
microscope^M

eyepiece
oculaire^M
revolving nosepiece
tourelle^F porte-objectif^M
stage clip
valet^M
draw tube
tube^M porte-oculaire^M
objective
objectif^M
coarse adjustment knob
vis^F macrométrique
glass slide
lame^F porte-objet^M
fine adjustment knob
vis^F micrométrique
stage
platine^F
arm
potence^F
condenser
condenseur^M
base
pied^M
mirror
miroir^M

binocular microscope
microscope^M binoculaire

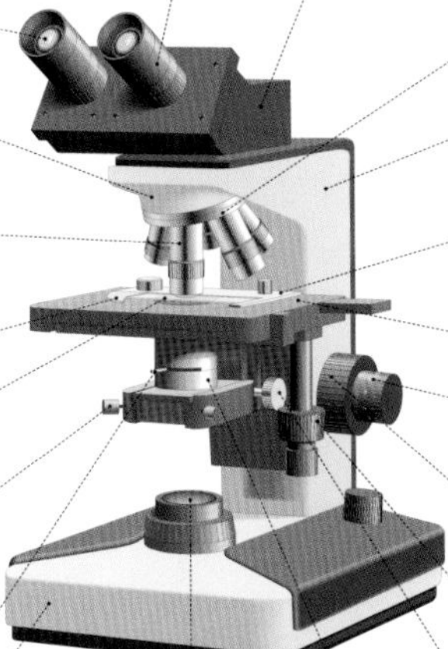

draw tube
tube^M porte-oculaire^M
body tube
corps^M
eyepiece
oculaire^M
revolving nosepiece
tourelle^F porte-objectif^M
limb top
porte-tube^M
arm
potence^F
objective
objectif^M
mechanical stage
chariot^M
stage clip
valet^M
stage
platine^F
glass slide
lame^F porte-objet^M
fine adjustment knob
vis^F micrométrique
condenser adjustment knob
vis^F de réglage^M du condenseur^M
coarse adjustment knob
vis^F macrométrique
mechanical stage control
commande^F du chariot^M
field lens adjustment
réglage^M du diaphragme^M
base
pied^M
lamp
lampe^F
condenser
condenseur^M
condenser height adjustment
réglage^M en hauteur^F du condenseur^M

SCIENCE

measurement of weight

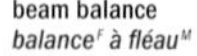

mesure^F de la masse^F

beam balance
balance^F à fléau^M

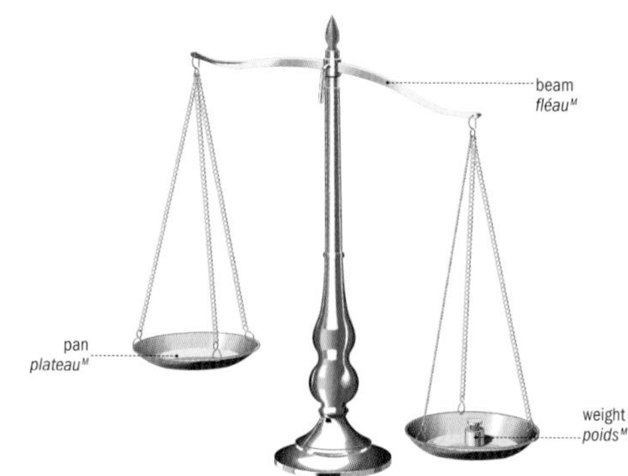

steelyard
balance^F romaine

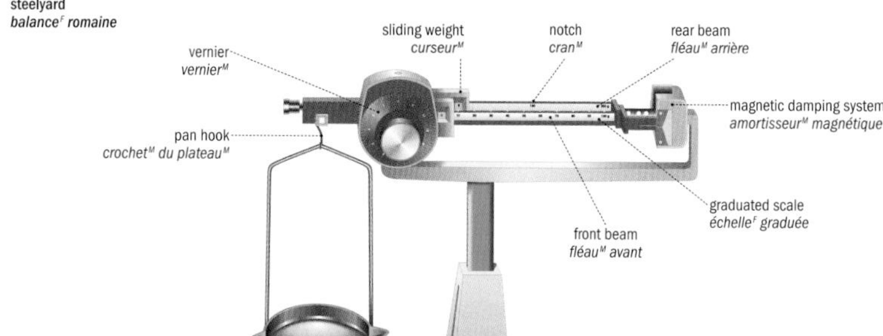

Roberval's balance
balance^F de Roberval

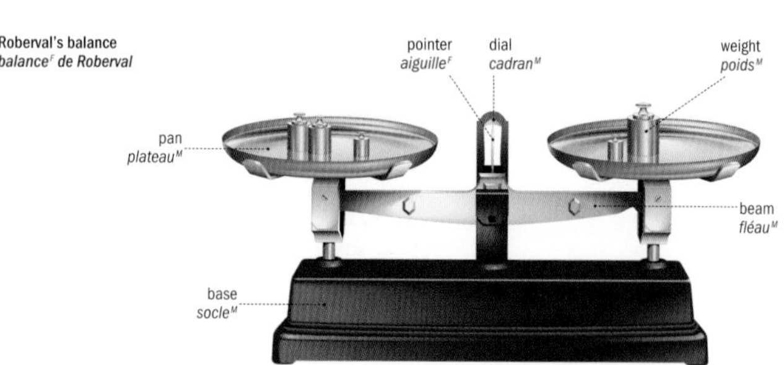

measurement of weight

g balance
n[M]

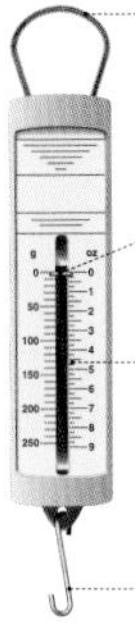

ring
anneau[M]

pointer
index[M]

graduated scale
échelle[F] *graduée*

hook
crochet[M]

electronic scales
balance*[F] *électronique

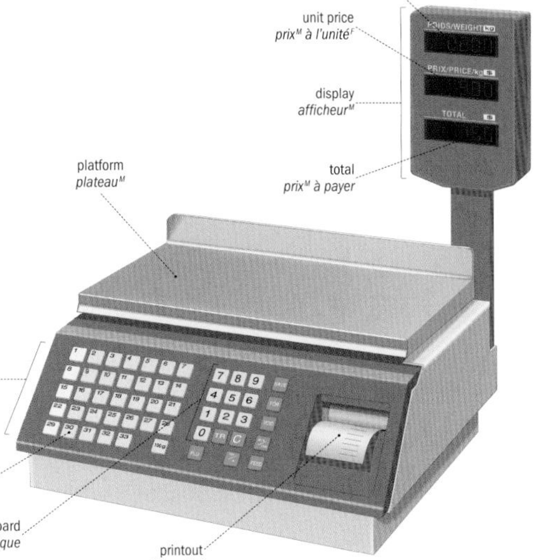

weight
poids[M]

unit price
prix[M] *à l'unité*[F]

display
afficheur[M]

total
prix[M] *à payer*

platform
plateau[M]

function keys
touches[F] *de fonctions*[F]

product code
code[M] *des produits*[M]

numeric keyboard
clavier[M] *numérique*

printout
étiquette[F]

ɔom scales
ɔersonne[M]

analytical balance
***balance*[F] *de précision*[F]**

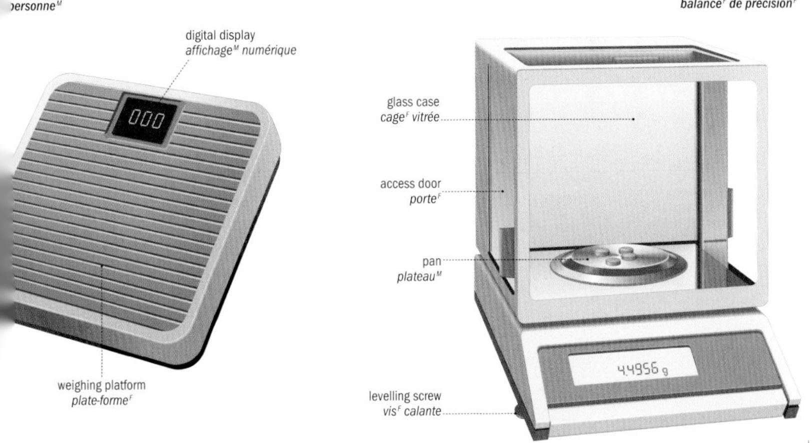

SCIENCE

measurement of temperature

mesure^{F} de la température^{F}

thermometer
thermomètre^{M}

Fahrenheit scale
échelle^{F} Fahrenheit
Celsius scale
échelle^{F} Celsius
degrees Fahrenheit
°F
degrees Celsius
°C
alcohol column
colonne^{F} d'alcool^{M}
alcohol bulb
réservoir^{M} d'alcool^{M}

clinical thermo
thermomètre^{M} me

capillary tube
tube^{M} capillaire
expansion chamber
chambre^{F} d'expansion^{F}
scale
graduation^{F}
column of mercury
colonne^{F} de mercure^{M}
stem
tige^{F}
mercury bulb
réservoir^{M} de mercure^{M}
constriction
étranglement^{M}

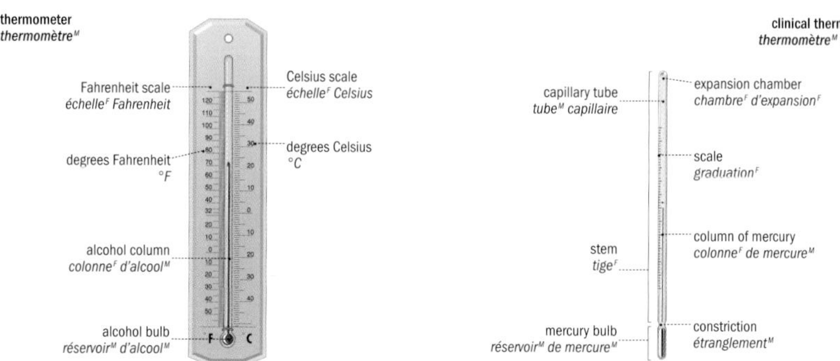

measurement of time

mesure^{F} du temps^{M}

stopwatch
chronomètre^{M}

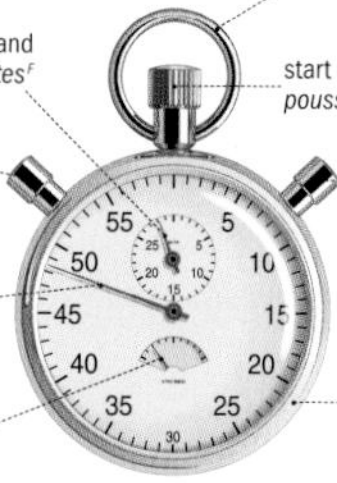

ring
anneau^{M}
minute hand
aiguille^{F} des minutes^{F}
start button
poussoir^{M} de mise^{F} en marche^{F}
reset button
poussoir^{M} de remise^{F} à zéro^{M}
stop button
poussoir^{M} d'arrêt^{M}
second hand
trotteuse^{F}
1/10 second hand
aiguille^{F} des dixièmes^{M} de seconde^{F}
case
boîtier^{M}

analogue
montre^{F} à affic
anal

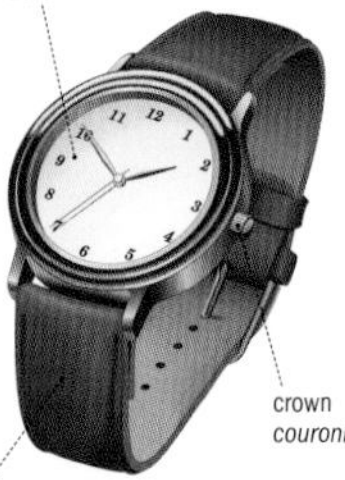

dial
cadran^{M}
crown
couronne^{F}
strap
bracelet^{M}

digital watch
montre^{F} à affichage^{M} numérique

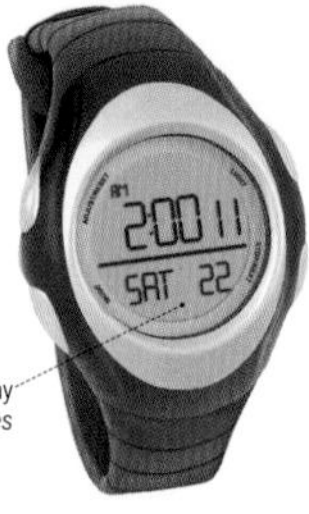

2:00 11
SAT 22
liquid crystal display
cristaux^{M} liquides

cadran^{M}

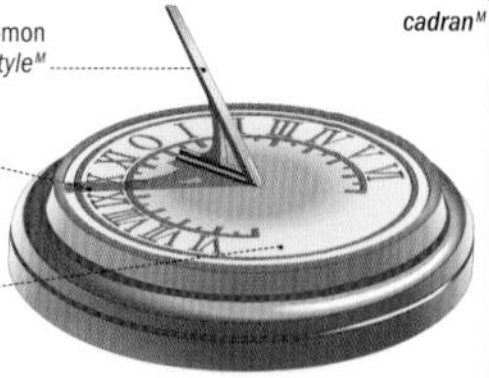

gnomon
style^{M}
shadow
ombre^{F}
dial
cadran^{M}

SCIENCE

measurement of length

mesure^F de la longueur^F

ruler
règle^F graduée

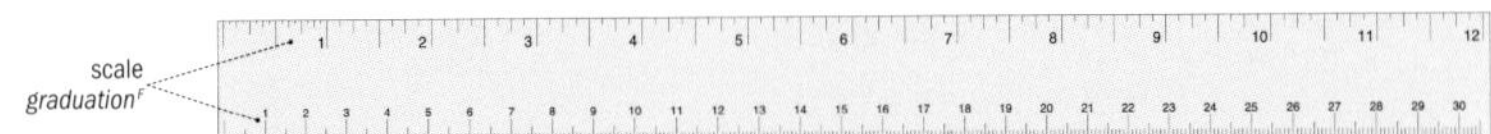

measurement of thickness

mesure^F de l'épaisseur^F

vernier caliper
pied^M à coulisse^F à vernier^M

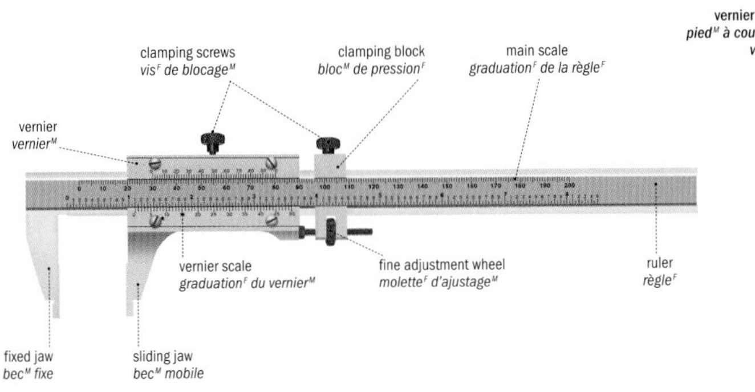

micrometer caliper
micromètre^M palmer^M

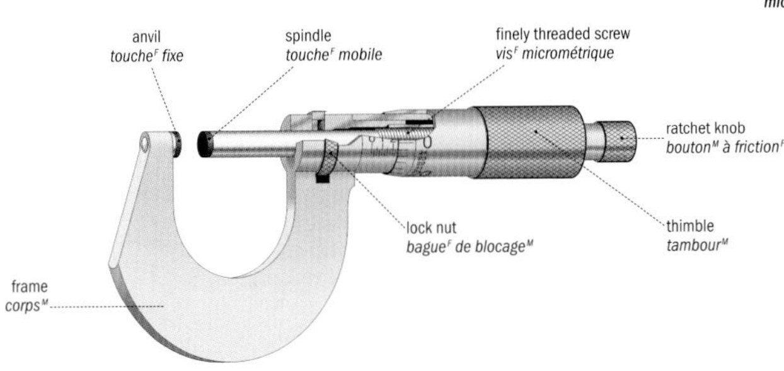

international system of units

systèmeᴹ international d'unités

measurement of frequency
mesure[F] de la fréquence[F]

Hz
hertz
hertz[M]

measurement of electric potential difference
mesure[F] de la différence[F] de potentiel[M] électrique

V
volt
volt[M]

measurement of electric charge
mesure[F] de la charge[F] électrique

C
coulomb
coulomb[M]

measurement
mesure[F] de l'

J
joule
joule[M]

measurement of power
mesure[F] de la puissance[F]

W
watt
watt[M]

measurement of force
mesure[F] de la force[F]

N
newton
newton[M]

measurement of electric resistance
mesure[F] de la résistance[F] électrique

Ω
ohm
ohm[M]

measurement of electri
mesure[F] du courant[M] é

A
ampere
ampère[M]

measurement of length
mesure[F] de la longueur[F]

m
metre
mètre[M]

measurement of mass
mesure[F] de la masse[F]

kg
kilogram
kilogramme[M]

measurement of Celsius temperature
mesure[F] de la température[F] Celsius

°C
degree Celsius
degré[M] Celsius

measurement of thermodyna temperature
mesure[F] de la températur thermodynamique

K
kelvin
kelvin[M]

measurement of amount of substance
mesure[F] de la quantité[F] de matière[F]

mol
mole
mole[F]

measurement of radioactivity
mesure[F] de la radioactivité[F]

Bq
becquerel
becquerel[M]

measurement of pressure
mesure[F] de la pression[F]

Pa
pascal
pascal[M]

measurement of luminous
mesure[F] de l'intensité[F] lu

cd
candela
candela[F]

biology

biologie[F]

female
femelle[F]

Rh-
blood factor negative
facteur[M] rhésus négatif

*
born
naissance[F]

♂
male
mâle[M]

Rh+
blood factor positive
facteur[M] rhésus positif

died
mort[F]

SCIENCE

mathematics

mathématiques[F]

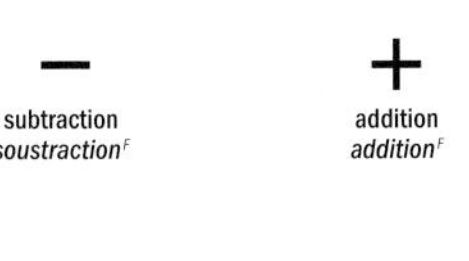

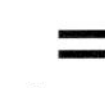
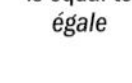

subtraction
soustraction[F]

addition
addition[F]

multiplication
multiplication[F]

division
division[F]

is equal to
égale

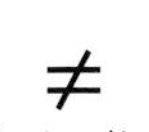
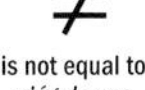

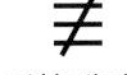

is not equal to
n'égale pas

is approximately equal to
égale à peu près

is equivalent to
équivaut à

is identical with
est identique à

is not identical with
n'est pas identique à

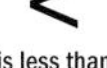

plus or minus
plus ou moins

is equal to or less than
égal ou plus petit que

is greater than
plus grand que

is equal to or greater than
égal ou plus grand que

is less than
plus petit que

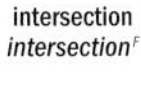
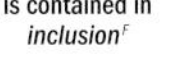

empty set
ensemble[M] vide

union
réunion[F]

intersection
intersection[F]

is contained in
inclusion[F]

percent
pourcentage[M]

belongs to
appartenance[F]

does not belong to
non-appartenance[F]

sum
sommation[F]

square root of
racine[F] carrée de

fraction
fraction[F]

infinity
infini[M]

integral
intégrale[F]

factorial
factorielle[F]

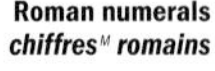

Roman numerals
chiffres[M] romains

one
un[M]

five
cinq[M]

ten
dix[M]

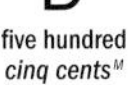

fifty
cinquante[M]

one hundred
cent[M]

five hundred
cinq cents[M]

one thousand
mille[M]

geometry

géométrie[F]

°	′	″	π	⊥
degree *degré[M]*	minute *minute[F]*	second *seconde[F]*	pi *pi[M]*	perpendicular *perpendiculaire[F]*

∥	∦	∟		∠
is parallel to *parallèle*	is not parallel to *non parallèle*	right angle *angle[M] droit*	obtuse angle *angle[M] obtus*	acute angle *angle[M] aigu*

geometrical shapes

formes[F] géométriques

examples of angles
exemples[M] d'angles[M]

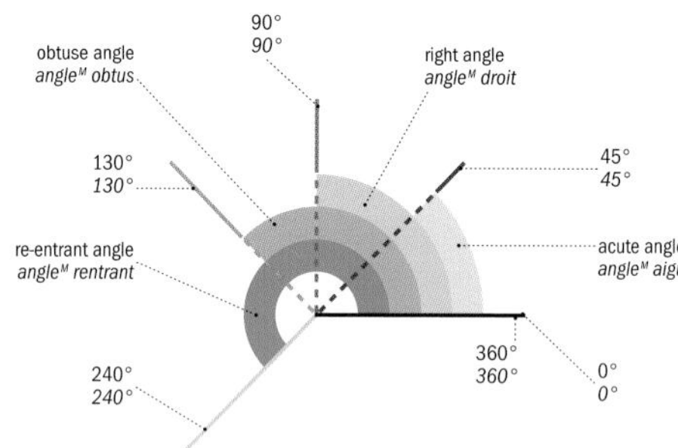

plane surfaces
surfaces[F]

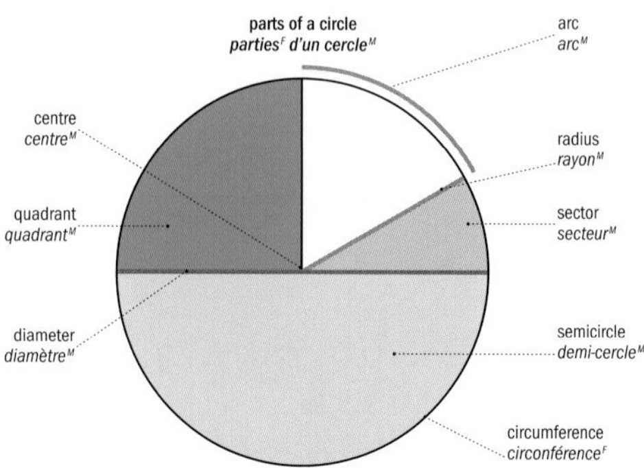

polygons
polygones[M]

triangle
triangle[M]

square
carré[M]

rectangle
rectangle[M]

rhombus
losange[M]

trapezoid
trapèze[M]

parallelogram
parallélogramme[M]

quadrilateral
quadrilatère[M]

regular pentagon
pentagone[M] *régulier*

regular hexagon
hexagone[M] *régulier*

regular heptagon
heptagone[M] *régulier*

regular octagon
octogone[M] *régulier*

regular nonagon
ennéagone[M] *régulier*

regular decagon
décagone[M] *régulier*

regular hendecagon
hendécagone[M] *régulier*

regular dodecagon
dodécagone[M] *régulier*

solids
volumes[M]

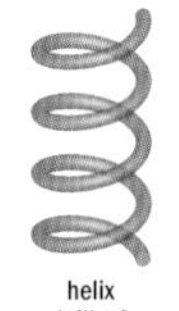
helix
hélice[F]

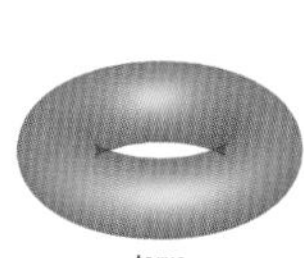
torus
tore[M]

hemisphere
hémisphère[M]

sphere
sphère[F]

cube
cube[M]

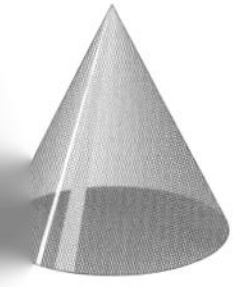
cone
cône[M]

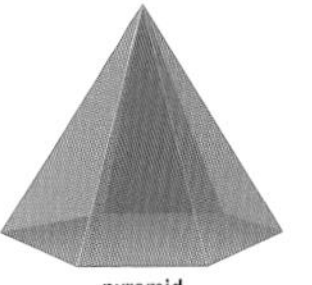
pyramid
pyramide[F]

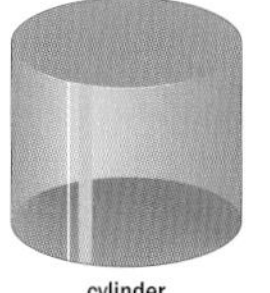
cylinder
cylindre[M]

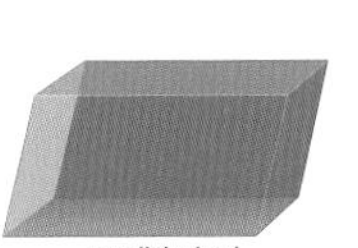
parallelepiped
parallélépipède[M]

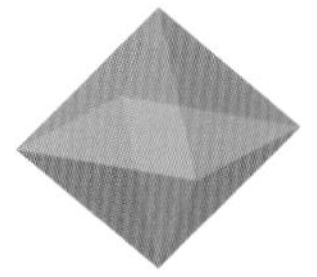
regular octahedron
octaèdre[M] *régulier*

conurbation

agglomération^F

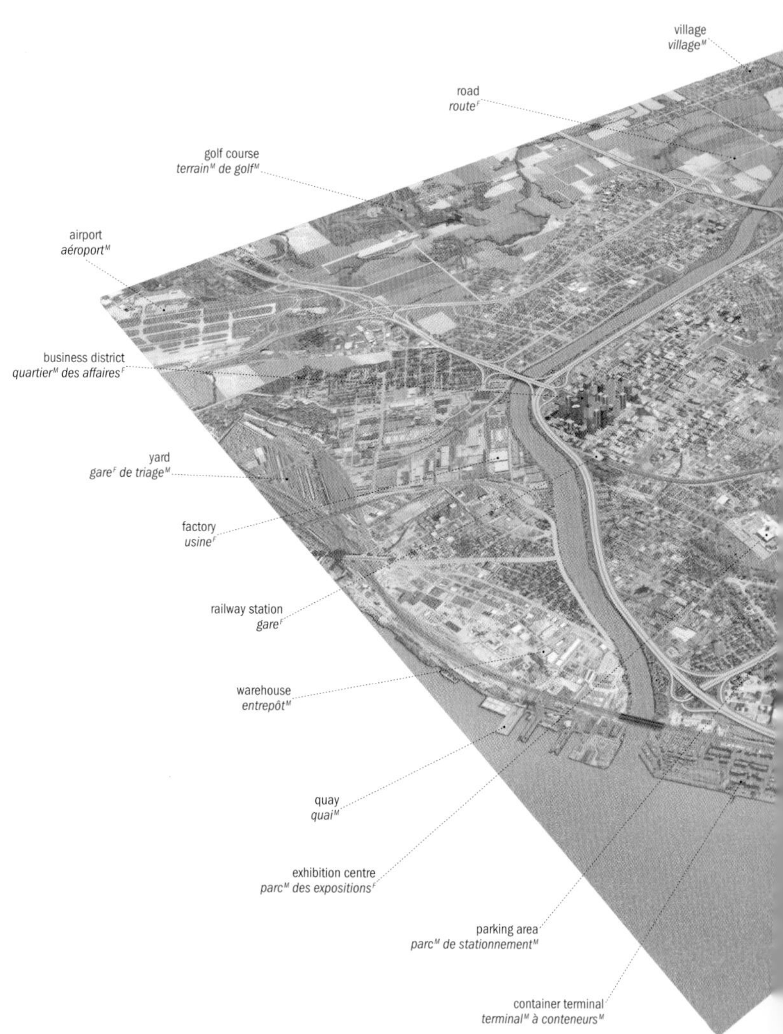

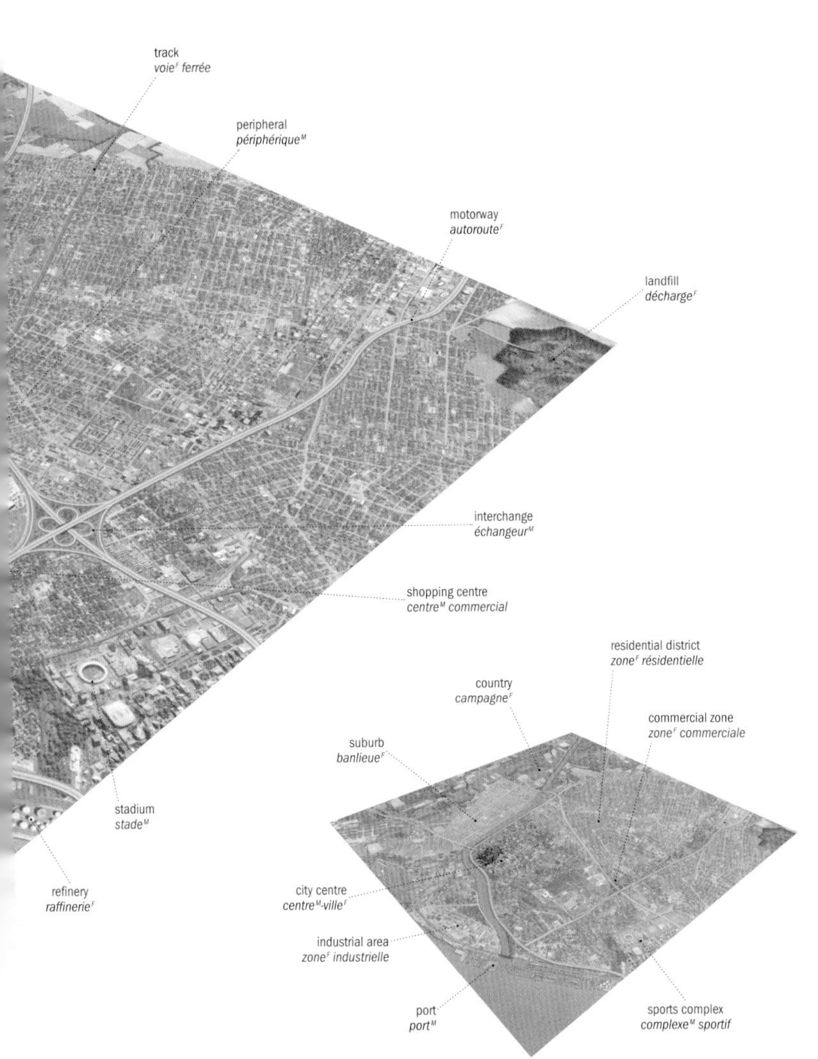
track
voie^F ferrée
peripheral
périphérique^M
motorway
autoroute^F
landfill
décharge^F
interchange
échangeur^M
shopping centre
centre^M commercial
residential district
zone^F résidentielle
country
campagne^F
commercial zone
zone^F commerciale
suburb
banlieue^F
stadium
stade^M
refinery
raffinerie^F
city centre
centre^M-ville^F
industrial area
zone^F industrielle
port
port^M
sports complex
complexe^M sportif

city centre

centre[M]-ville[F]

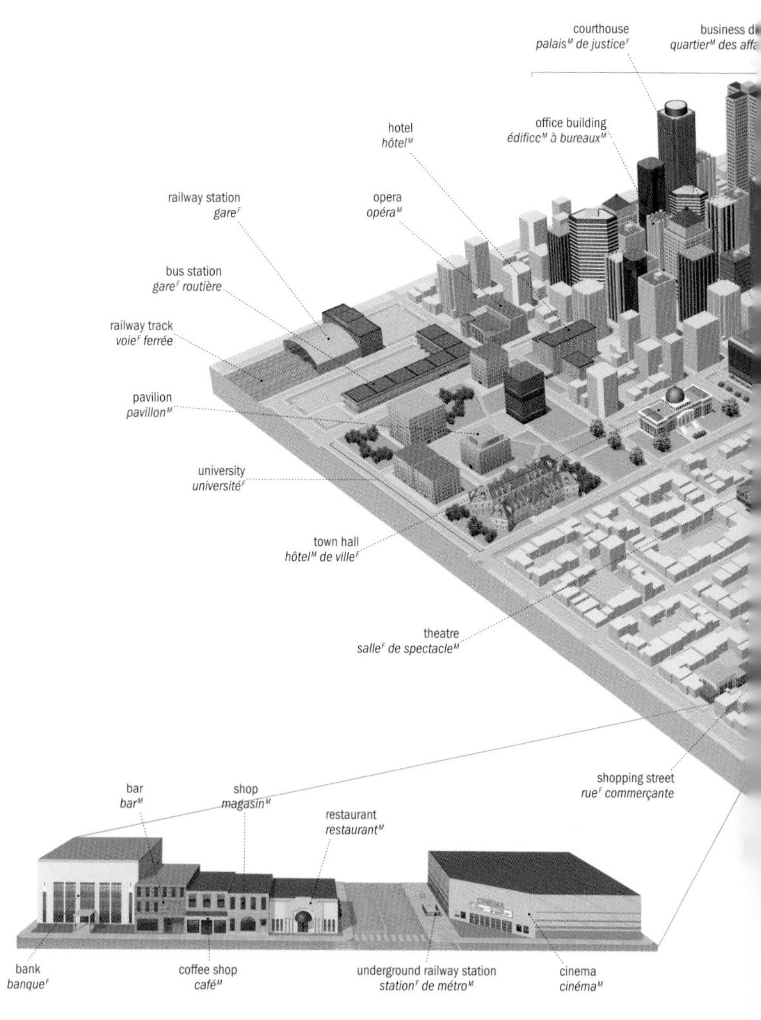

SOCIETY

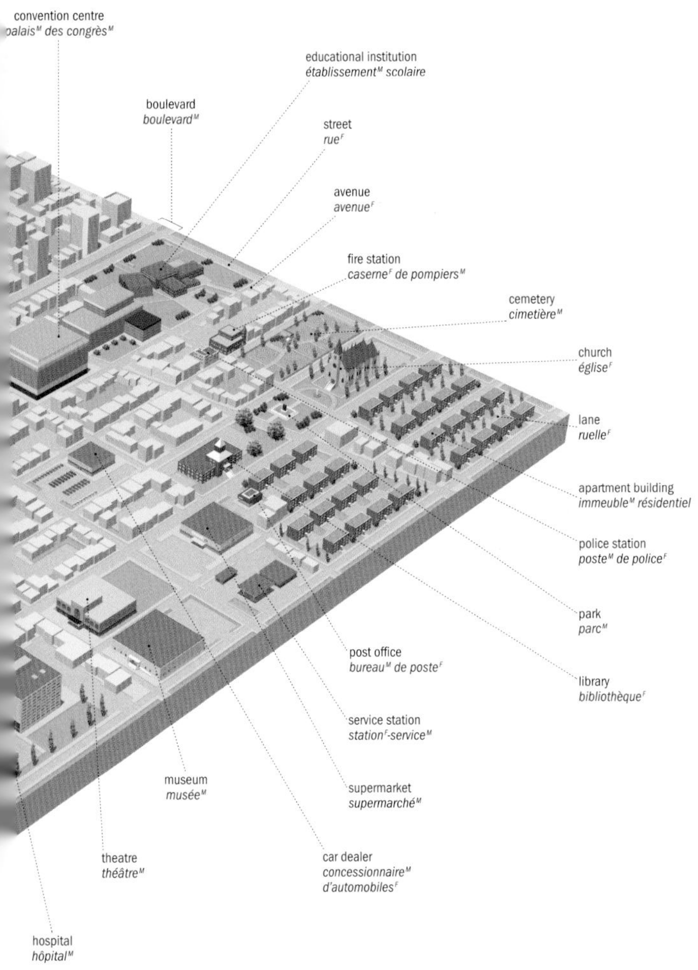
convention centre
palais[M] des congrès[M]
educational institution
établissement[M] scolaire
boulevard
boulevard[M]
street
rue[F]
avenue
avenue[F]
fire station
caserne[F] de pompiers[M]
cemetery
cimetière[M]
church
église[F]
lane
ruelle[F]
apartment building
immeuble[M] résidentiel
police station
poste[M] de police[F]
park
parc[M]
post office
bureau[M] de poste[F]
library
bibliothèque[F]
service station
station[F]-service[M]
museum
musée[M]
supermarket
supermarché[M]
theatre
théâtre[M]
car dealer
concessionnaire[M]
d'automobiles[F]
hospital
hôpital[M]

cross section of a street

coupe[F] d'une rue[F]

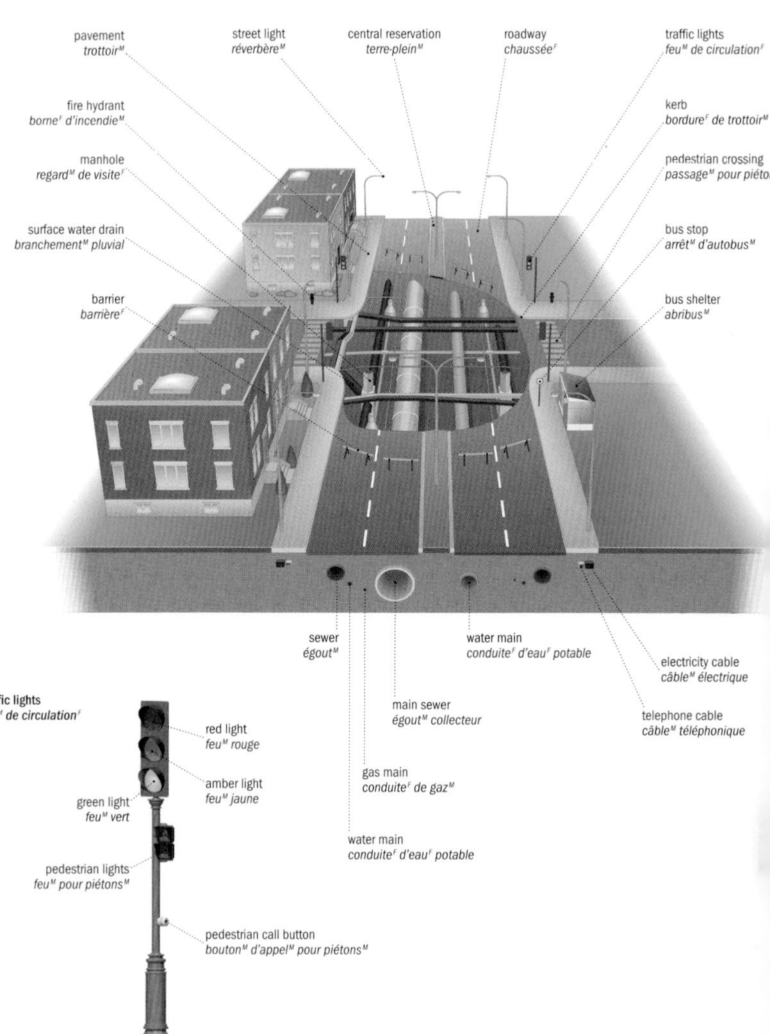

office building

édifice^M à bureaux^M

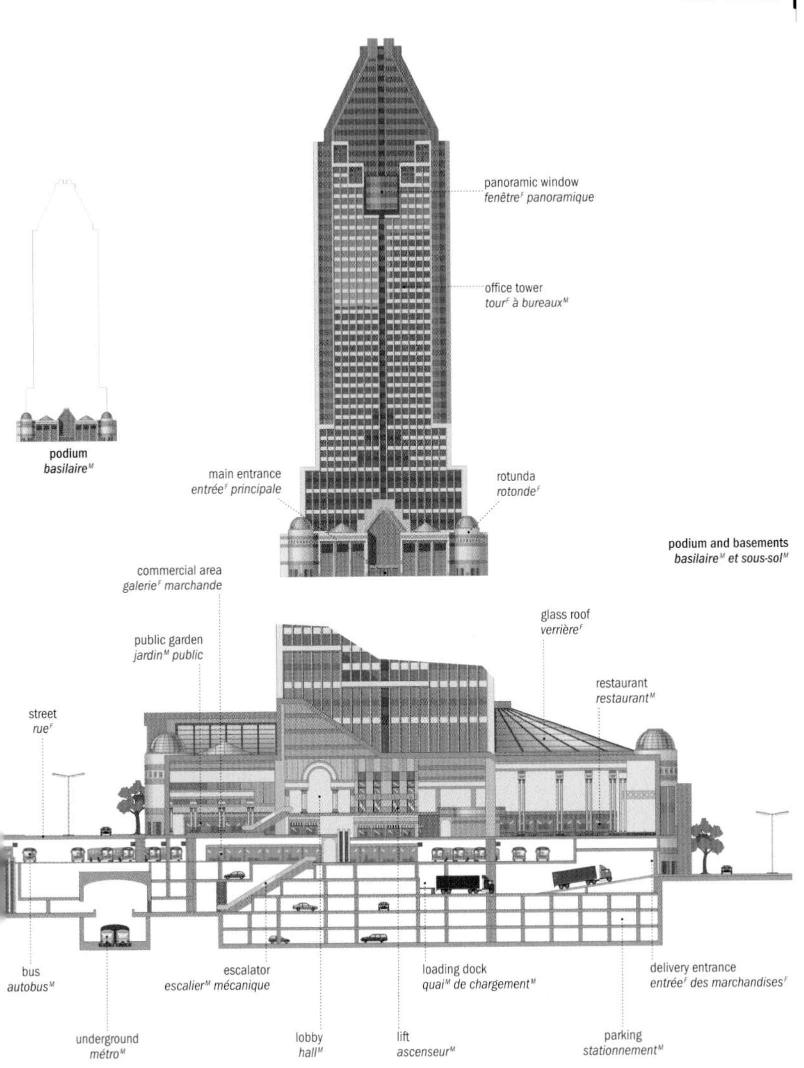

shopping centre

centre[M] commercial

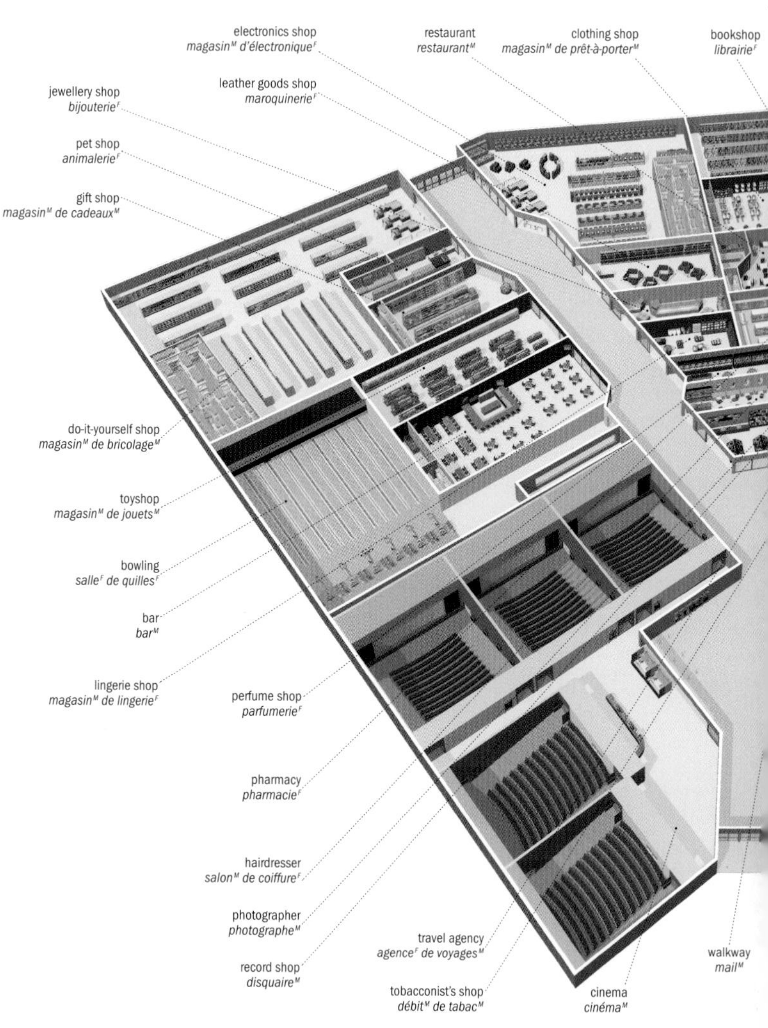

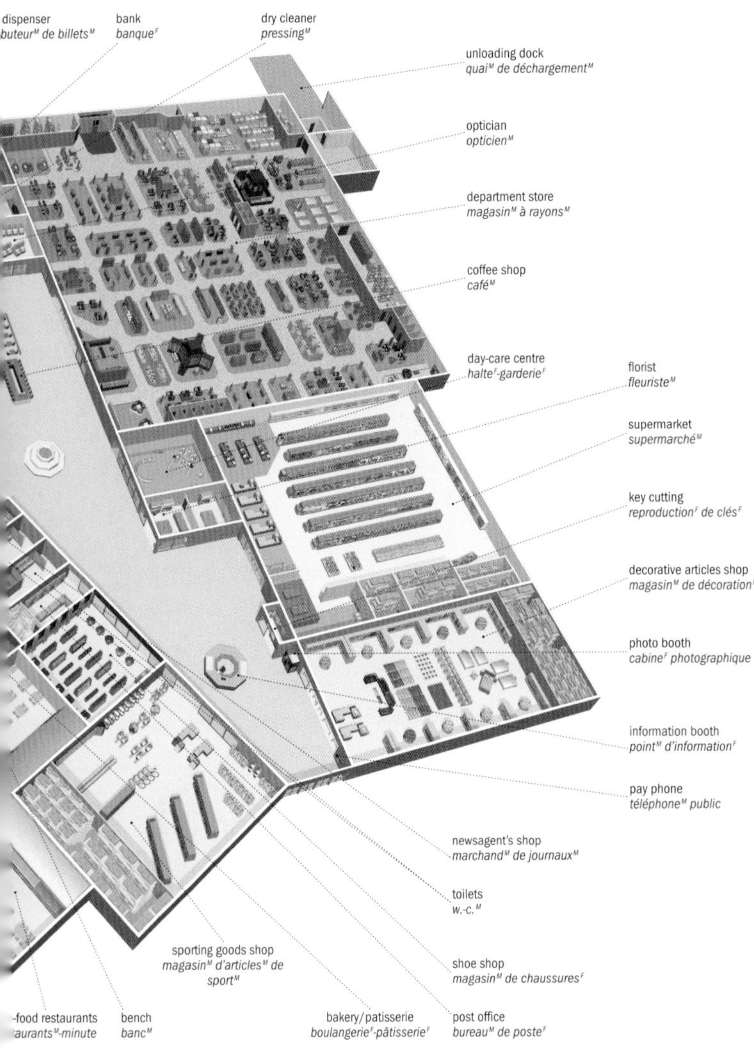
dispenser
buteur^M de billets^M
bank
banque^F
dry cleaner
pressing^M
unloading dock
quai^M de déchargement^M
optician
opticien^M
department store
magasin^M à rayons^M
coffee shop
café^M
day-care centre
halte^F-garderie^F
florist
fleuriste^M
supermarket
supermarché^M
key cutting
reproduction^F de clés^F
decorative articles shop
magasin^M de décoration^F
photo booth
cabine^F photographique
information booth
point^M d'information^F
pay phone
téléphone^M public
newsagent's shop
marchand^M de journaux^M
toilets
w.-c.^M
shoe shop
magasin^M de chaussures^F
post office
bureau^M de poste^F
bakery/patisserie
boulangerie^F-pâtisserie^F
sporting goods shop
magasin^M d'articles^M de sport^M
bench
banc^M
-food restaurants
aurants^M-minute

SOCIETY

restaurant

restaurant^M

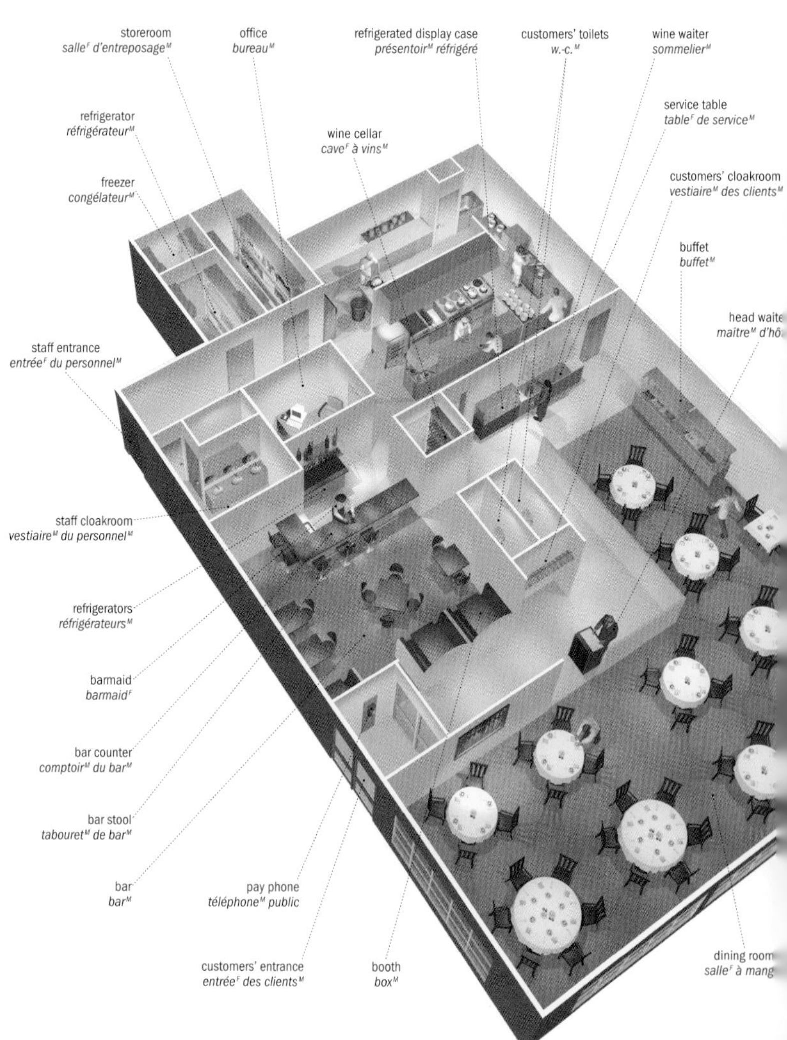

SOCIETY

hotel

hôtel[M]

reception level
niveau[M] de la réception[F]

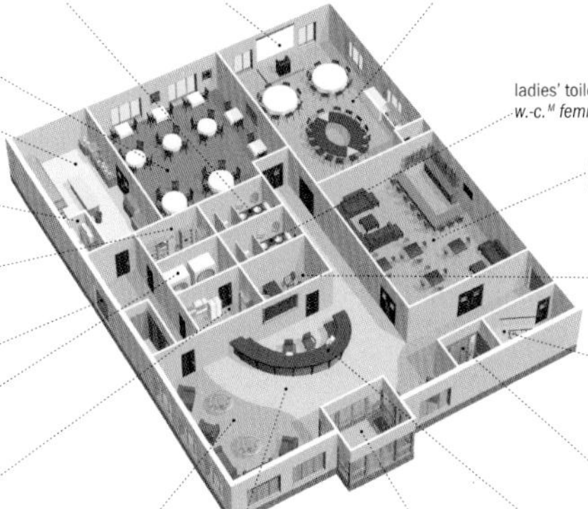

hotel room
chambres[F] d'hôtel[M]

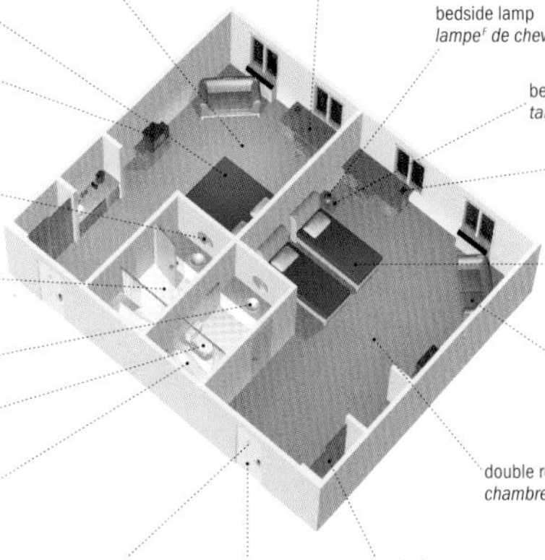

court

tribunal[M]

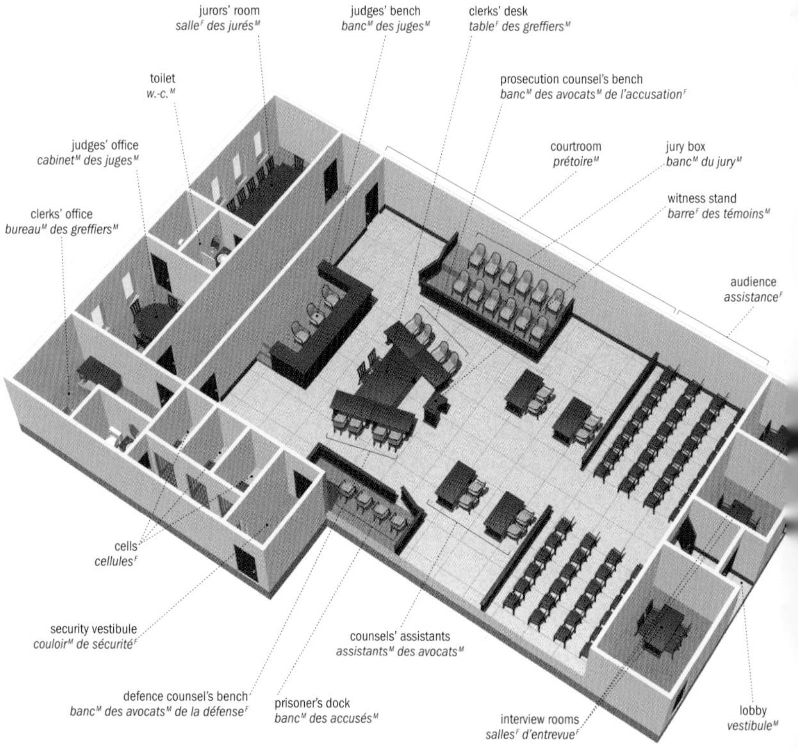

jurors' room
salle[F] des jurés[M]

judges' bench
banc[M] des juges[M]

clerks' desk
table[F] des greffiers[M]

toilet
w.-c.[M]

prosecution counsel's bench
banc[M] des avocats[M] de l'accusation[F]

judges' office
cabinet[M] des juges[M]

courtroom
prétoire[M]

jury box
banc[M] du jury[M]

clerks' office
bureau[M] des greffiers[M]

witness stand
barre[F] des témoins[M]

audience
assistance[F]

cells
cellules[F]

security vestibule
couloir[M] de sécurité[F]

counsels' assistants
assistants[M] des avocats[M]

defence counsel's bench
banc[M] des avocats[M] de la défense[F]

prisoner's dock
banc[M] des accusés[M]

interview rooms
salles[F] d'entrevue[F]

lobby
vestibule[M]

examples of currency abbreviations

exemples[M] d'unités[F] monétaires

dollar
dollar[M]

cent
cent[M]

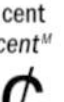

rupee
roupie[F]

euro
euro[M]

new shekel
nouveau shekel[M]

peso
peso[M]

yen
yen[M]

pound
livre[F]

SOCIETY

money and modes of payment

monnaie[F] et modes[M] de paiement[M]

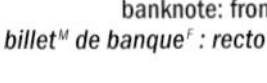

obverse
F : avers[M]

date
millésime[M]

edge
tranche[F]

banknote: front
billet[M] de banque[F] : recto[M]

initials of issuing bank
initiales[F] de la banque[F] émettrice

security thread
fil[M] de sécurité[F]

hologram foil strip
bande[F] métallisée holographique

watermark
filigrane[M]

official signature
signature[F] officielle

colour shifting ink
encre[F] à couleur[F] changeante

portrait
effigie[F]

serial number
numéro[M] de série[F]

reverse
F : revers[M]

outer ring
couronne[F]

denomination
valeur[F]

banknote: back
billet[M] de banque[F] : verso[M]

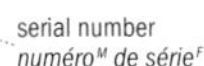

European Union flag
drapeau[M] de l'Union[F] européenne

serial number
numéro[M] de série[F]

motto
devise[F]

denomination
valeur[F]

currency name
nom[M] de la monnaie[F]

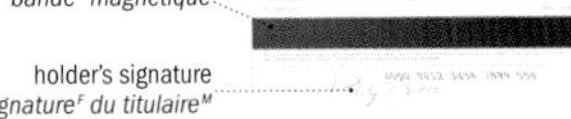

magnetic strip
bande[F] magnétique

credit card
carte[F] de crédit[M]

holder's signature
signature[F] du titulaire[M]

cheques
chèques[M]

card number
numéro[M] de carte[F]

holder's name
nom[M] du titulaire[M]

expiry date
date[F] d'expiration[F]

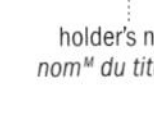

traveller's cheque
chèque[M] de voyage[M]

bank

banque[F]

cash dispenser
distributeur[M] de billets[M]

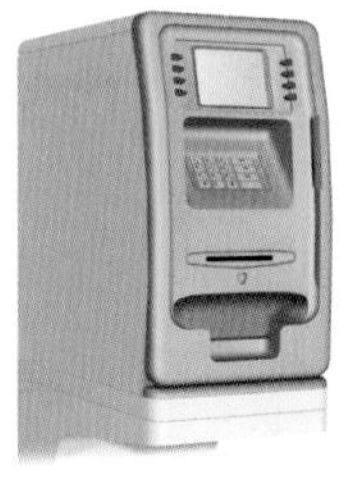

professional training o
bureau[M] de forma
professionn

waiting area
aire[F] d'attente[F]

insurance services
services[M] d'assurance[F]

brochure rack
présentoir[M] de brochures[F]

reprography
reprographie[F]

financial services
services[M] financiers

information desk
comptoir[M] de renseignements[M]

conference room
salle[F] de conférences[F]

reception desk
accueil[M]

loan services
services[M] de crédit[M]

meeting room
salle[F] de réunion[F]

security grille
grille[F] de sécurité[F]

ve

automatic teller machine
guichet[M] automatique bancaire

operation keys
touches[F] d'opérations[F]

deposit slot
fente[F] de dépôt[M]

display
écran[M]

card reader slot
fente[F] du lecteur[M] de carte[F]

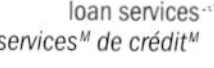

transaction record slot
fente[F] de relevé[M] d'opération[F]

alphanumeric keyboard
clavier[M] alphanumérique

note presenter
sortie[F] des billets[M]

passbook update slot
fente[F] de mise[F] à jour[M] du livret[M] bancaire

SOCIETY

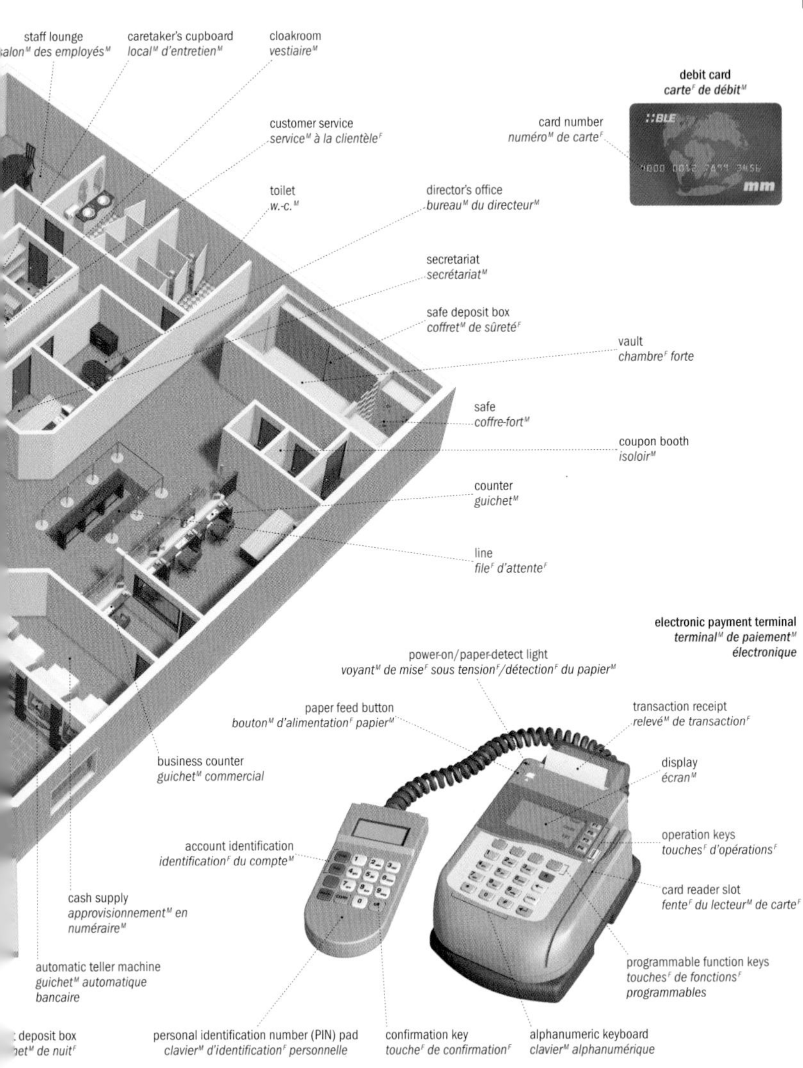
staff lounge
salon des employés
caretaker's cupboard
local d'entretien
cloakroom
vestiaire
customer service
service à la clientèle
toilet
w.-c.
director's office
bureau du directeur
secretariat
secrétariat
safe deposit box
coffret de sûreté
vault
chambre forte
safe
coffre-fort
coupon booth
isoloir
counter
guichet
line
file d'attente
business counter
guichet commercial
cash supply
approvisionnement en numéraire
automatic teller machine
guichet automatique bancaire
deposit box
het de nuit
debit card
carte de débit
card number
numéro de carte
electronic payment terminal
terminal de paiement électronique
power-on/paper-detect light
voyant de mise sous tension/détection du papier
paper feed button
bouton d'alimentation papier
transaction receipt
relevé de transaction
display
écran
operation keys
touches d'opérations
card reader slot
fente du lecteur de carte
account identification
identification du compte
programmable function keys
touches de fonctions programmables
personal identification number (PIN) pad
clavier d'identification personnelle
confirmation key
touche de confirmation
alphanumeric keyboard
clavier alphanumérique

SOCIETY

school

écoleF

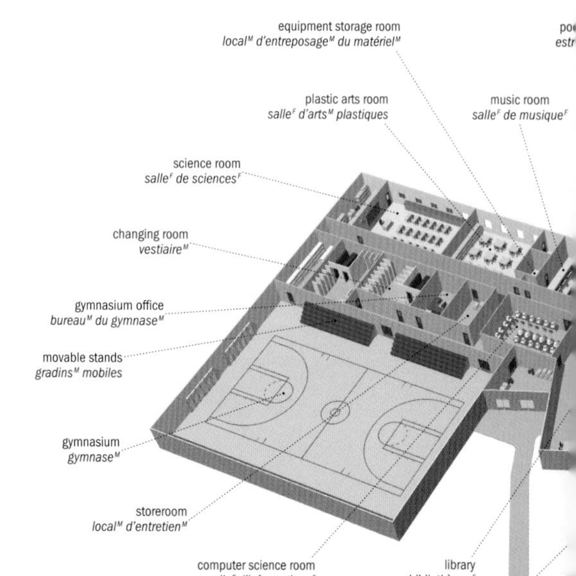

classroom
salleF de classeF

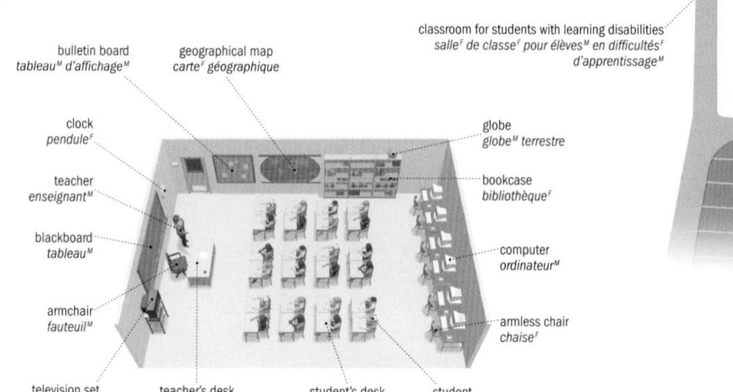

SOCIETY

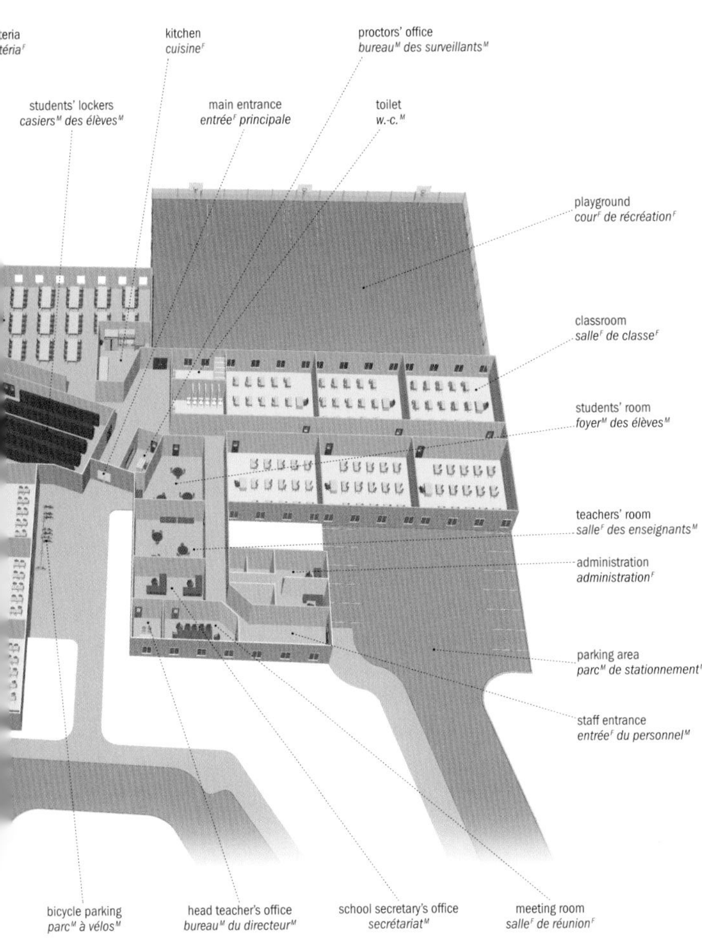

eria
téria^F
kitchen
cuisine^F
proctors' office
bureau^M des surveillants^M
students' lockers
casiers^M des élèves^M
main entrance
entrée^F principale
toilet
w.-c.^M
playground
cour^F de récréation^F
classroom
salle^F de classe^F
students' room
foyer^M des élèves^M
teachers' room
salle^F des enseignants^M
administration
administration^F
parking area
parc^M de stationnement^M
staff entrance
entrée^F du personnel^M
bicycle parking
parc^M à vélos^M
head teacher's office
bureau^M du directeur^M
school secretary's office
secrétariat^M
meeting room
salle^F de réunion^F

church

église^F

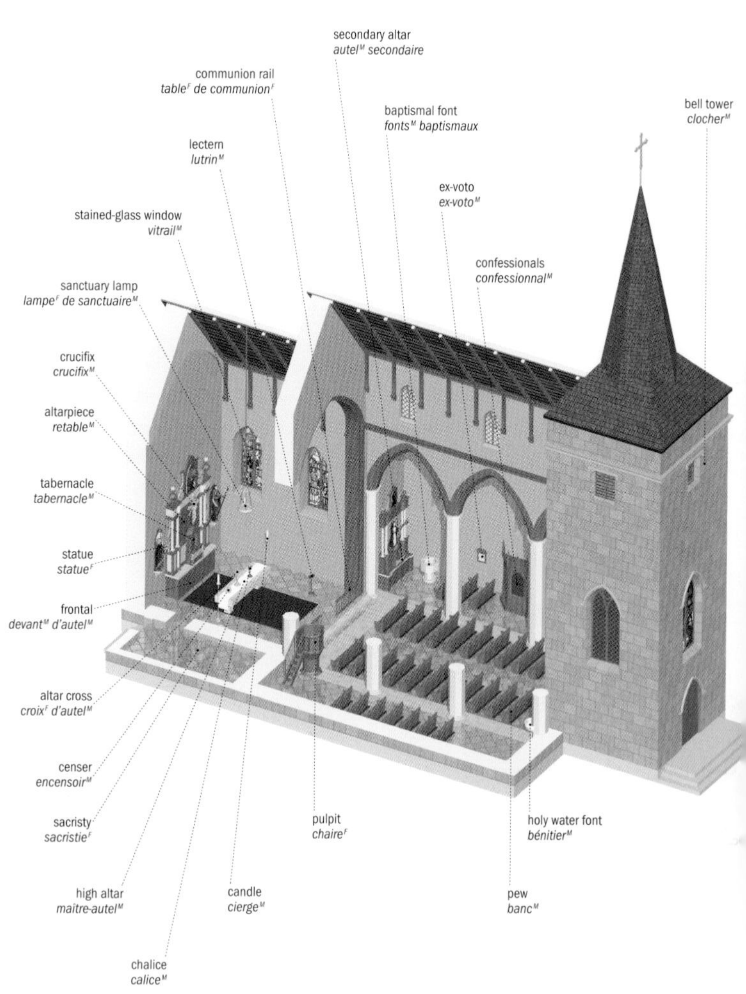

synagogue

synagogue^F

menorah
menora^F
balcony
balcon^M
memorial board
tableau^M du souvenir^M
pulpit
table^F de lecture^F
bimah
bimah^F
eternal light
lumière^F perpétuelle
Torah scrolls
rouleaux^M de la Torah^F
star of David
étoile^F de David
ten commandments
les dix commandements^M
ark
arche^F
rabbi's seat
siège^M du rabbin^M

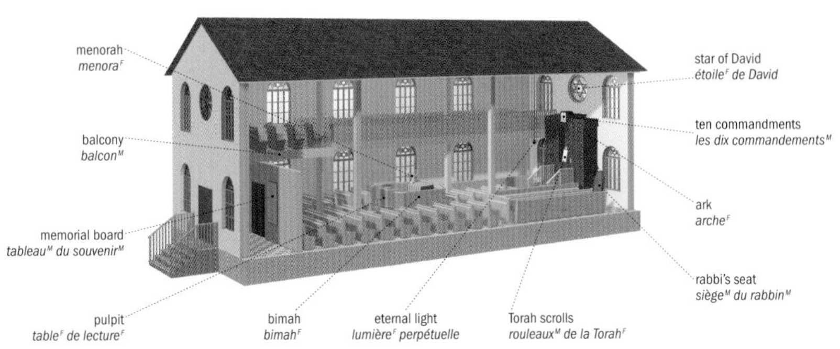

mosque

mosquée^F

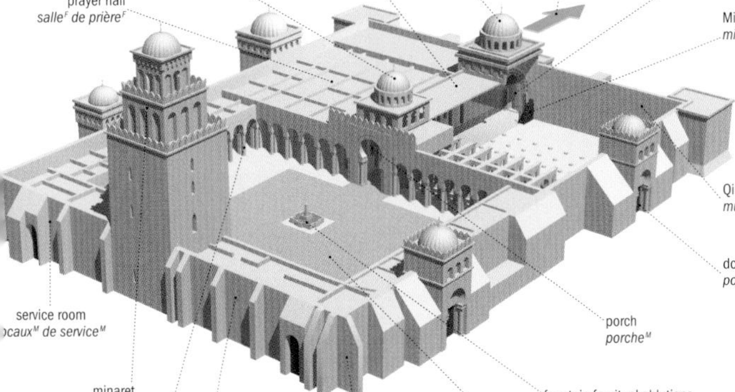

porch dome
coupole^F du porche^M
central nave
nef^F centrale
Mihrab dome
coupole^F du mihrab^M
direction of Mecca
direction^F de La Mecque^F
Mihrab
mihrab^M
prayer hall
salle^F de prière^F
Minbar
minbar^M
Qibla wall
mur^M de la qibla^F
door
porte^F
service room
ocaux^M de service^M
porch
porche^M
minaret
minaret^M
fountain for ritual ablutions
fontaine^F des ablutions^F
arcades
portique^M
reception hall
salle^F de réception^F
fortified wall
mur^M fortifié
courtyard
cour^F

flags

drapeaux[M]

Americas
***Amériques**[F]*

1 
Canada
Canada[M]

2 
United States of America
États-Unis[M] d'Amérique[F]

3 
Mexico
Mexique[M]

4 
Honduras
Honduras[M]

5 
Guatemala
Guatemala[M]

6 
Belize
Belize[M]

7 
El Salvador
El Salvador[M]

8 
Nicaragua
Nicaragua[M]

9 
Costa Rica
Costa Rica[M]

10 
Panama
Panama[M]

11 
Colombia
Colombie[F]

12 
Venezuela
Venezuela[M]

13 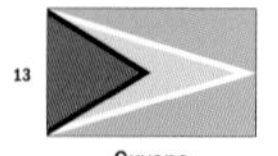
Guyana
Guyana[F]

14 
Suriname
Suriname[M]

15 
Ecuador
Équateur[M]

16 
Peru
Pérou[M]

17 
Brazil
Brésil[M]

18 
Bolivia
Bolivie[F]

19 
Paraguay
Paraguay[M]

20 
Chile
Chili[M]

21 
Argentina
Argentine[F]

22 
Uruguay
Uruguay[M]

Caribbean Islands
***Antilles**[F]*

23 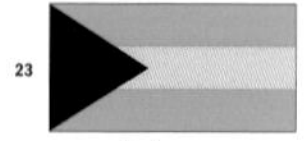
Bahamas
Bahamas[F]

24 
Cuba
Cuba[F]

25 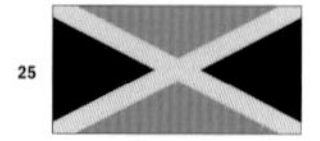
Jamaica
Jamaïque[F]

26 
Haiti
Haïti[M]

SOCIETY

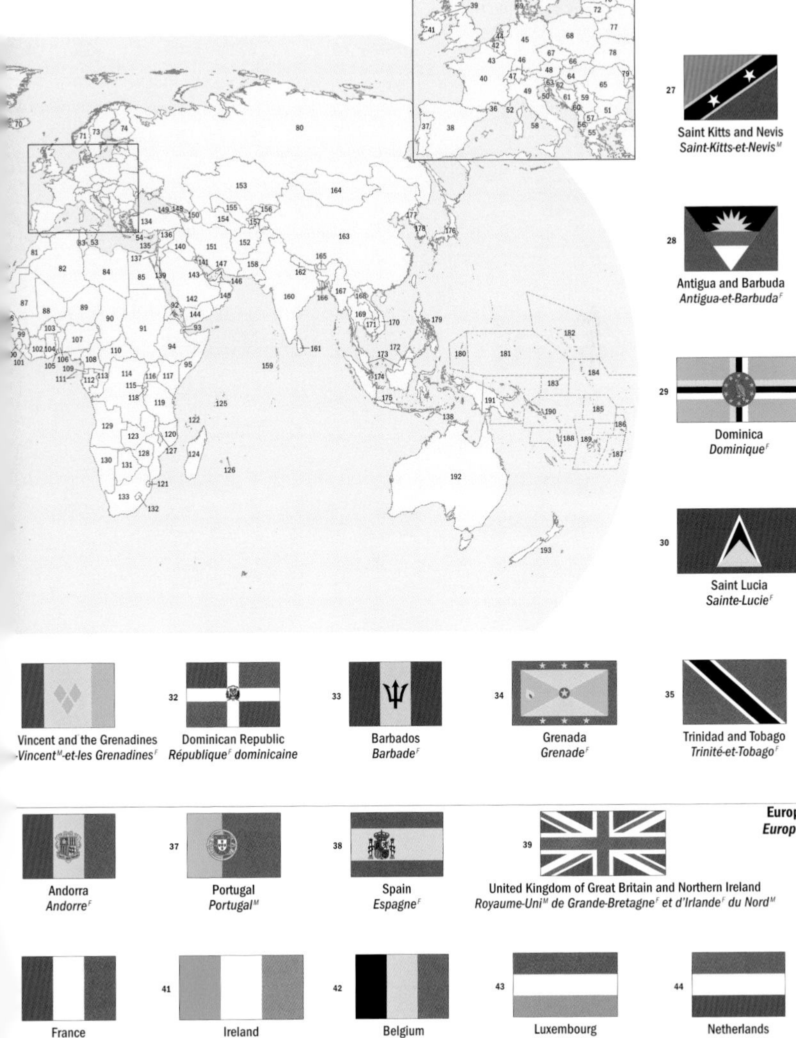

27 Saint Kitts and Nevis
Saint-Kitts-et-Nevis[M]

28 Antigua and Barbuda
Antigua-et-Barbuda[F]

29 Dominica
Dominique[F]

30 Saint Lucia
Sainte-Lucie[F]

Vincent and the Grenadines
-Vincent[M]*-et-les Grenadines*[F]

32 Dominican Republic
République[F] *dominicaine*

33 Barbados
Barbade[F]

34 Grenada
Grenade[F]

35 Trinidad and Tobago
Trinité-et-Tobago[F]

Europe
Europe[F]

Andorra
Andorre[F]

37 Portugal
Portugal[M]

38 Spain
Espagne[F]

39 United Kingdom of Great Britain and Northern Ireland
Royaume-Uni[M] *de Grande-Bretagne*[F] *et d'Irlande*[F] *du Nord*[M]

France
France[F]

41 Ireland
Irlande[F]

42 Belgium
Belgique[F]

43 Luxembourg
Luxembourg[M]

44 Netherlands
Pays-Bas[M]

SOCIETY

flags

45 Germany
*Allemagne*F

46 Liechtenstein
*Liechtenstein*M

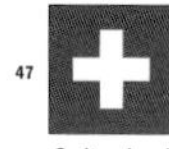

47 Switzerland
*Suisse*F

48 Austria
*Autriche*F

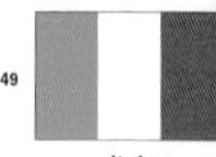

49 Italy
*Italie*F

50 San Marino
*Saint-Marin*M

51 Bulgaria
*Bulgarie*F

52 Monaco
*Monaco*M

53 Malta
*Malte*F

54 Cyprus
*Chypre*F

55 Greece
*Grèce*F

56 Albania
*Albanie*F

57 The Former Yugoslav Republic of Macedonia
*Ex-République*F *yougoslave de Macédoine*F

58 Vatican City State
*État*M *de la cité*F *du Vatican*M

59 Serbia
*Serbie*F

60 Montenegro
*Monténégro*M

61 Bosnia-Herzegovina
*Bosnie-Herzégovine*F

62 Croatia
*Croatie*F

63 Slovenia
*Slovénie*F

64 Hungary
*Hongrie*F

65 Romania
*Roumanie*F

66 Slovakia
*Slovaquie*F

67 Czech Republic
*République*F *tchèque*

68 Poland
*Pologne*F

69 Denmark
*Danemark*M

70 Iceland
*Islande*F

71 Norway
*Norvège*F

72 Lithuania
*Lituanie*F

73 Sweden
*Suède*F

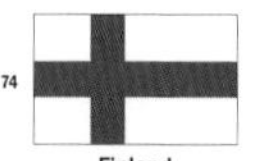

74 Finland
*Finlande*F

75 Estonia
*Estonie*F

76 Latvia
*Lettonie*F

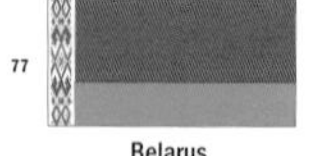

77 Belarus
*Bélarus*M

78 Ukraine
*Ukraine*F

79 Moldova
*République*F *de Moldova*F

80 Russian Federati
*Fédération*F *de Ru*

SOCIETY

Africa
Afrique[F]

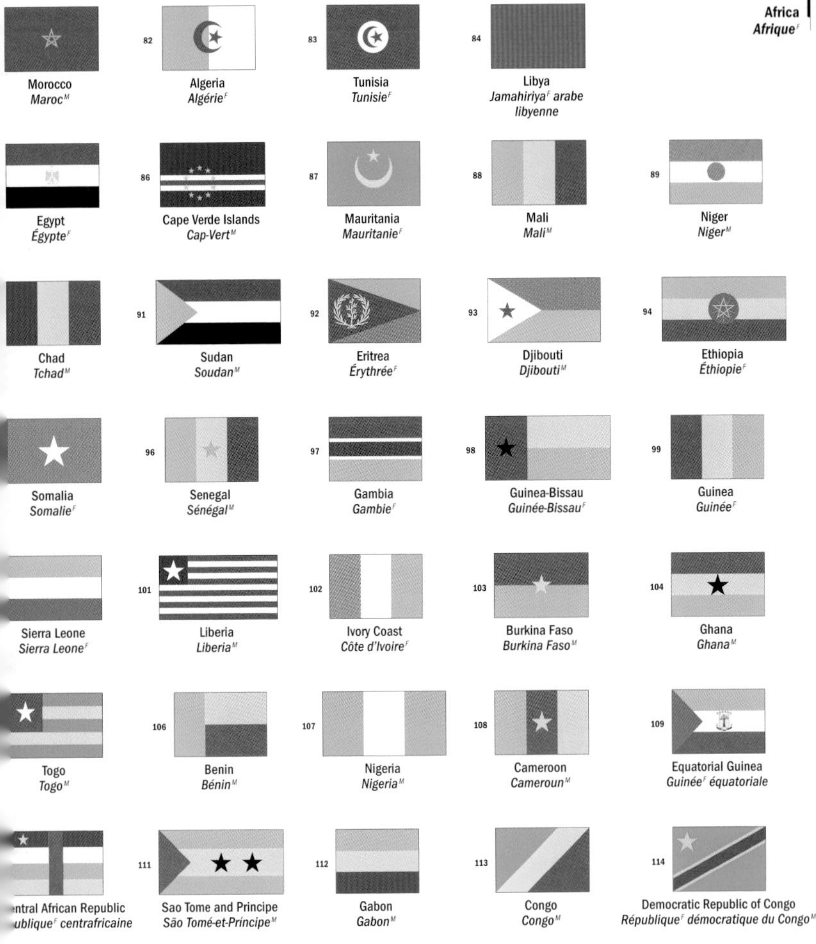

Morocco *Maroc*[M]

82 Algeria *Algérie*[F]

83 Tunisia *Tunisie*[F]

84 Libya *Jamahiriya*[F] *arabe libyenne*

Egypt *Égypte*[F]

86 Cape Verde Islands *Cap-Vert*[M]

87 Mauritania *Mauritanie*[F]

88 Mali *Mali*[M]

89 Niger *Niger*[M]

Chad *Tchad*[M]

91 Sudan *Soudan*[M]

92 Eritrea *Érythrée*[F]

93 Djibouti *Djibouti*[M]

94 Ethiopia *Éthiopie*[F]

Somalia *Somalie*[F]

96 Senegal *Sénégal*[M]

97 Gambia *Gambie*[F]

98 Guinea-Bissau *Guinée-Bissau*[F]

99 Guinea *Guinée*[F]

Sierra Leone *Sierra Leone*[F]

101 Liberia *Liberia*[M]

102 Ivory Coast *Côte d'Ivoire*[F]

103 Burkina Faso *Burkina Faso*[M]

104 Ghana *Ghana*[M]

Togo *Togo*[M]

106 Benin *Bénin*[M]

107 Nigeria *Nigeria*[M]

108 Cameroon *Cameroun*[M]

109 Equatorial Guinea *Guinée*[F] *équatoriale*

ntral African Republic *ublique*[F] *centrafricaine*

111 Sao Tome and Principe *São Tomé-et-Príncipe*[M]

112 Gabon *Gabon*[M]

113 Congo *Congo*[M]

114 Democratic Republic of Congo *République*[F] *démocratique du Congo*[M]

Rwanda *Rwanda*[M]

116 Uganda *Ouganda*[M]

117 Kenya *Kenya*[M]

118 Burundi *Burundi*[M]

119 Tanzania *République*[F]*-Unie de Tanzanie*[F]

SOCIETY

flags

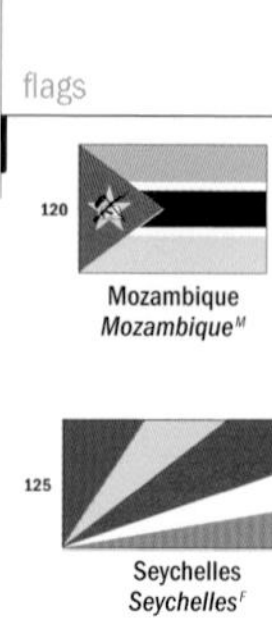

120 Mozambique
Mozambique[M]

121 Swaziland
Swaziland[M]

122 Comoros
Comores[F]

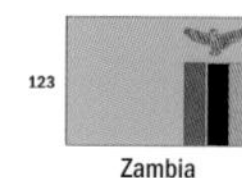

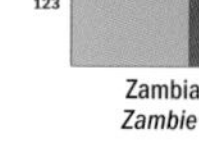

123 Zambia
Zambie[F]

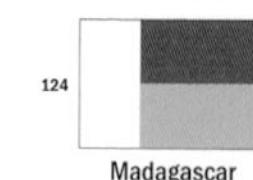

124 Madagascar
Madagascar[F]

125 Seychelles
Seychelles[F]

126 Mauritius
Maurice[F]

127 Malawi
Malawi[M]

128 Zimbabwe
Zimbabwe[M]

129 Angola
Angola[M]

130 Namibia
Namibie[F]

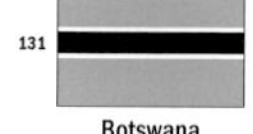

131 Botswana
Botswana[M]

132 Lesotho
Lesotho[M]

133 South Africa
Afrique[F] du Sud[M]

Asia
Asie[F]

134 Turkey
Turquie[F]

135 Lebanon
Liban[M]

136 Syria
République[F] arabe syrienne

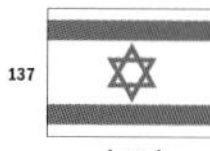

137 Israel
Israël[M]

138 East Timor
Timor[M] oriental

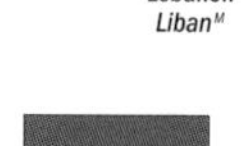

139 Jordan
Jordanie[F]

140 Iraq
Iraq[M]

141 Kuwait
Koweït[M]

142 Saudi Arabia
Arabie[F] saoudite

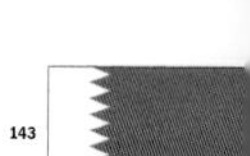

143 Bahrain
Bahreïn[M]

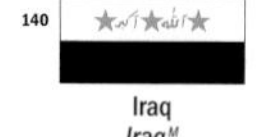

144 Yemen
Yémen[M]

145 Oman
Oman[M]

146 United Arab Emirates
Émirats[M] arabes unis

147 Qatar
Qatar[M]

148 Georgia
Géorgie[F]

149 Armenia
Arménie[F]

150 Azerbaijan
Azerbaïdjan[M]

151 Iran
Iran[M]

152 Afghanistan
Afghanistan[M]

153 Kazakhstan
Kazakhstan[M]

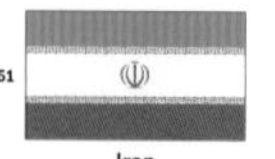

154 Turkmenistan
Turkménistan[M]

155 Uzbekistan
Ouzbékistan[M]

156 Kyrgyzstan
Kirghizistan[M]

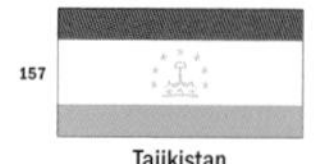

157 Tajikistan
Tadjikistan[M]

158 Pakistan
Pakistan[M]

SOCIETY

9 
Maldives
Maldives[F]

160 
India
Inde[F]

161 
Sri Lanka
Sri Lanka[M]

162 
Nepal
Népal[M]

163 
China
Chine[F]

Mongolia
Mongolie[F]

165 
Bhutan
Bhoutan[M]

166 
Bangladesh
Bangladesh[M]

167 
Myanmar
Myanmar[M]

168 
Laos
République[F] *démocratique populaire lao*

Thailand
Thaïlande[F]

170 
Vietnam
Viet Nam[M]

171 
Cambodia
Cambodge[M]

172 
Brunei Darussalam
Brunéi Darussalam[M]

173 
Malaysia
Malaisie[F]

Singapore
Singapour[F]

175 
Indonesia
Indonésie[F]

176 
Japan
Japon[M]

177 
Democratic People's Republic of Korea
République[F] *populaire démocratique de Corée*[F]

178 
Republic of Korea
République[F] *de Corée*[F]

Oceania and Polynesia
Océanie[F] *et Polynésie*[F]

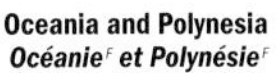

Philippines
Philippines[F]

180 
Palau
Palaos[M]

181 

Micronesia
Micronésie[F]

Marshall Islands
Îles[F] *Marshall*

183 
Nauru
Nauru[F]

184
Kiribati
Kiribati[F]

185 
Tuvalu
Tuvalu[M]

Samoa
Samoa[F]

187 
Tonga
Tonga[F]

188 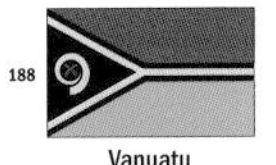
Vanuatu
Vanuatu[M]

189 
Fiji
Fidji[F]

Solomon Islands
Îles[F] *Salomon*

191 
Papua New Guinea
Papouasie-Nouvelle-Guinée[F]

192 
Australia
Australie[F]

193 
New Zealand
Nouvelle-Zélande[F]

SOCIETY

fire prevention

prévention^F des incendies^M

fire-fighting material
matériel^M de lutte^F contre les incendies^M

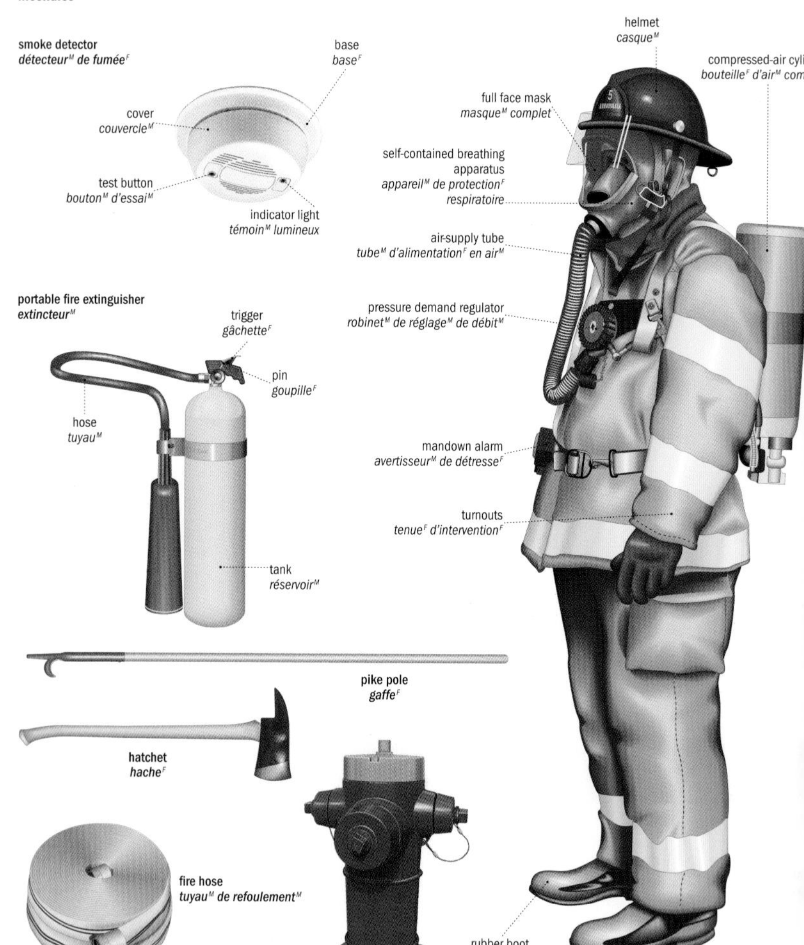

SOCIETY

fire engines
camions[M] d'incendie[M]

pumper
fourgon[M]-pompe[F]

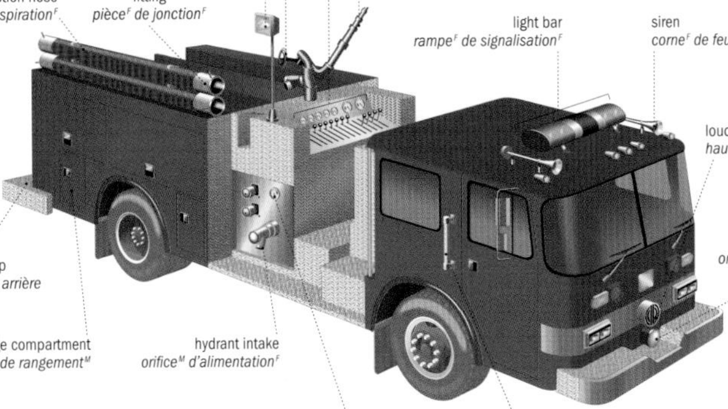

control wheel
volant[M] de manœuvre[F]

control panel
panneau[M] de commande[F]

spotlight
projecteur[M] orientable

water cannon
lance[F]-canon[M]

suction hose
tuyau[M] d'aspiration[F]

fitting
pièce[F] de jonction[F]

light bar
rampe[F] de signalisation[F]

siren
corne[F] de feu[M]

loudspeaker
haut-parleur[M]

hydrant intake
orifice[M] d'alimentation[F]

rear step
marchepied[M] arrière

storage compartment
coffre[M] de rangement[M]

hydrant intake
orifice[M] d'alimentation[F]

water pressure gauge
manomètre[M]

grab handle
poignée[F] montoir[M]

aerial ladder truck
grande échelle[F]

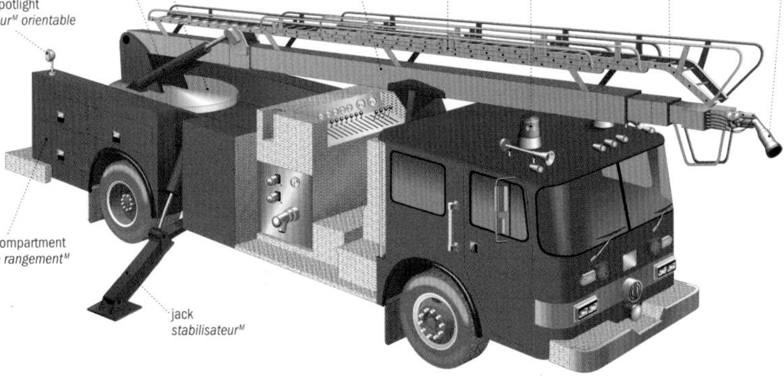

telescopic boom
flèche[F] télescopique

rotating light
gyrophare[M]

ladder pipe nozzle
lance[F] à eau[F]

elevating cylinder
vérin[M] de dressage[M]

turntable mounting
tourelle[F]

tower ladder
parc[M] à échelles[F]

top ladder
échelle[F] de tête[F]

spotlight
projecteur[M] orientable

storage compartment
coffre[M] de rangement[M]

jack
stabilisateur[M]

crime prevention

prévention^F de la criminalité^F

police officer
agent^M de police^F

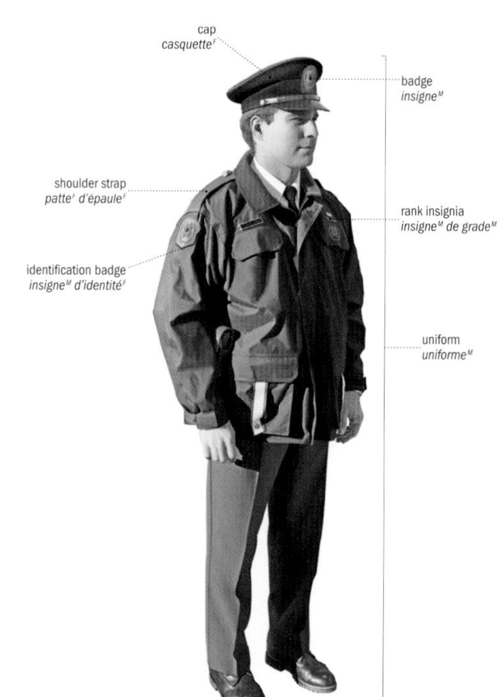

duty belt
ceinturon^M de service^M

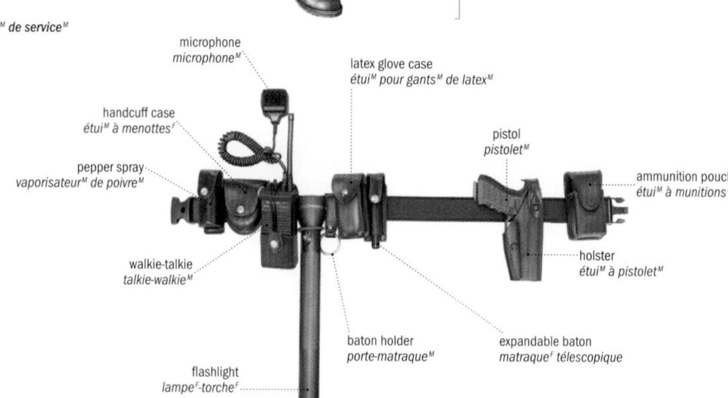

dashboard equipment
équipement^{M} du tableau^{M} de bord^{M}

lightbar controller
système^{M} de contrôle^{M} de la rampe^{F} de signalisation^{F}
radar transceiver
émetteur^{M}-récepteur^{M} radar^{M}
reading light
lampe^{F} de lecture^{F}
microphones
microphones^{M}
dashboard computer
ordinateur^{M} de bord^{M}
computer programs
programmes^{M} informatiques
radar display
affichage^{M} radar^{M}
radio
radio^{F}

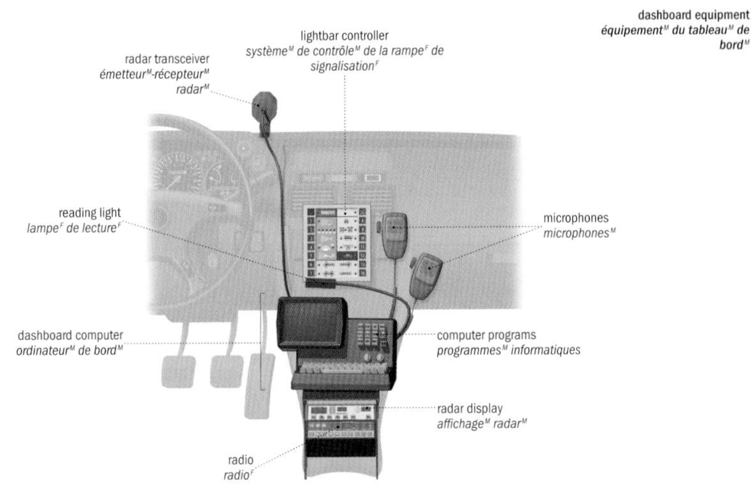

police car
voiture^{F} de police^{F}

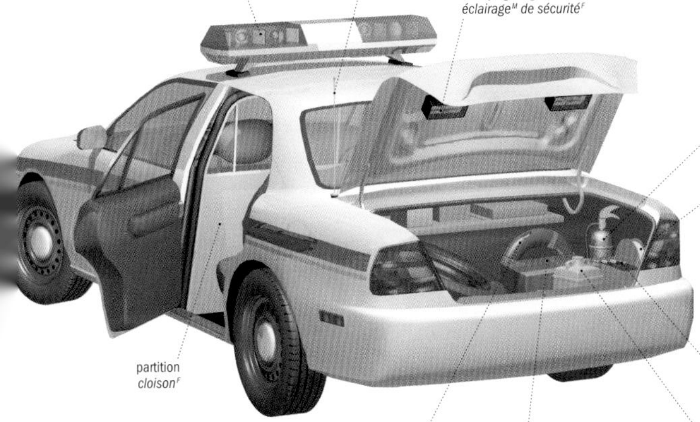

lightbar
rampe^{F} de signalisation^{F}
antenna
antenne^{F}
safety lighting
éclairage^{M} de sécurité^{F}
fire extinguisher
extincteur^{M}
barrier barricade tape
ruban^{M} de bouclage^{M}
road flare
fusée^{F} éclairante
partition
cloison^{F}
lifebuoy
bouée^{F} de sauvetage^{M}
first aid kit
trousse^{F} de secours^{M}
used syringe box
boîte^{F} pour seringues^{F} usagées

ear protection

protection[F] de l'ouïe[F]

safety earmuffs
serre-tête[M] antibruit

earp
protège-tymp

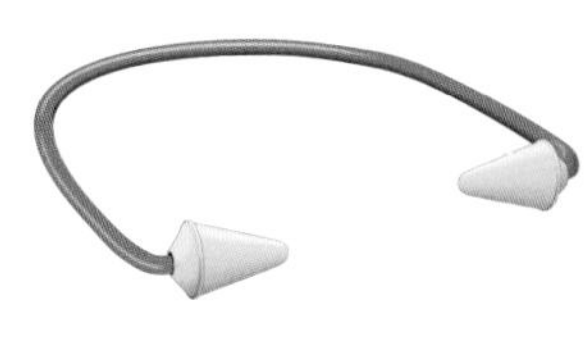

eye protection

protection[F] des yeux[M]

safety glasses
lunettes[F] de sécurité[F]

safety go
lunettes[F] de protec

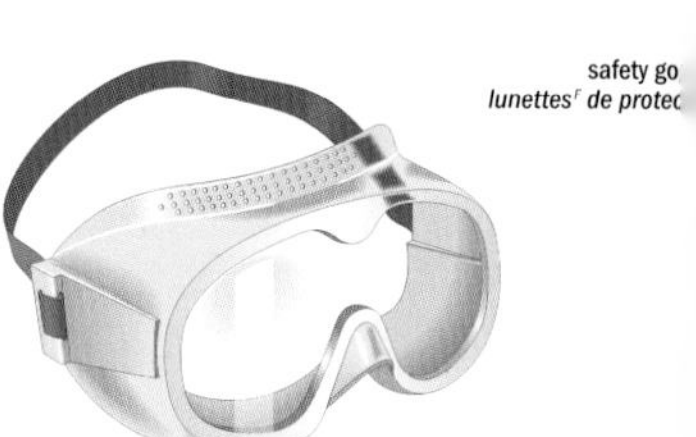

head protection

protection[F] de la tête[F]

hard hat
casque[M] de sécurité[F]

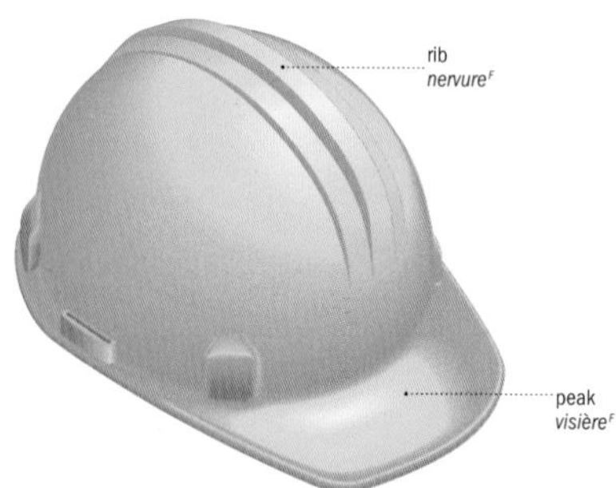

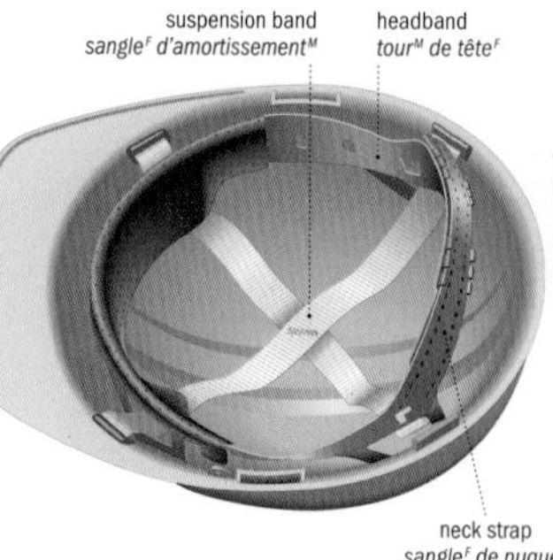

SOCIETY

respiratory system protection

protection[F] des voies[F] respiratoires

respirator
masque[M] respiratoire

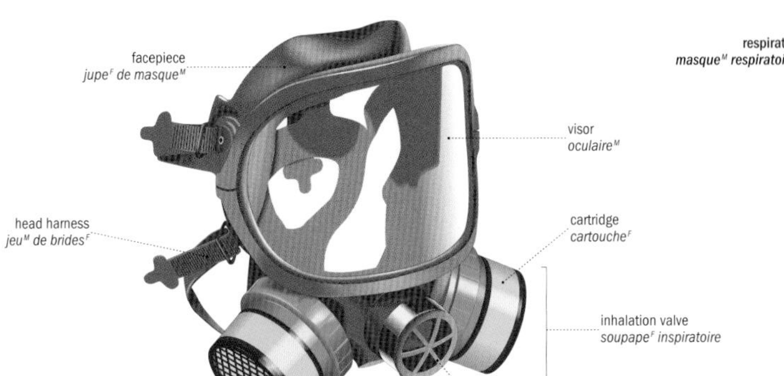

half-mask respirator
masque[M] bucco-nasal

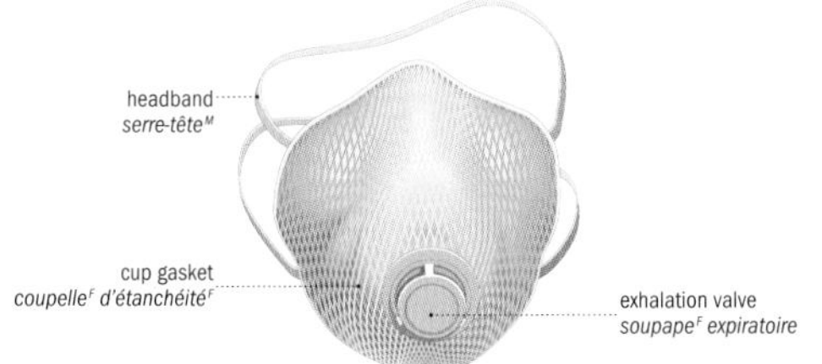

foot protection

protection[F] des pieds[M]

ty boot
equin[M] de sécurité[F]

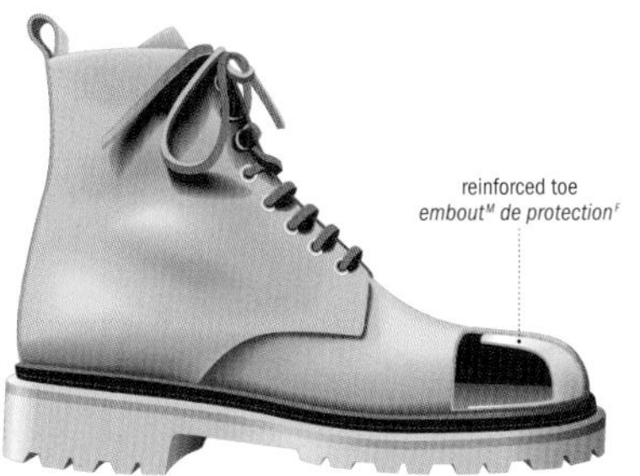

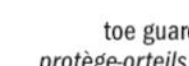

first aid equipment

matériel[M] de secours[M]

stethoscope
stéthoscope[M]

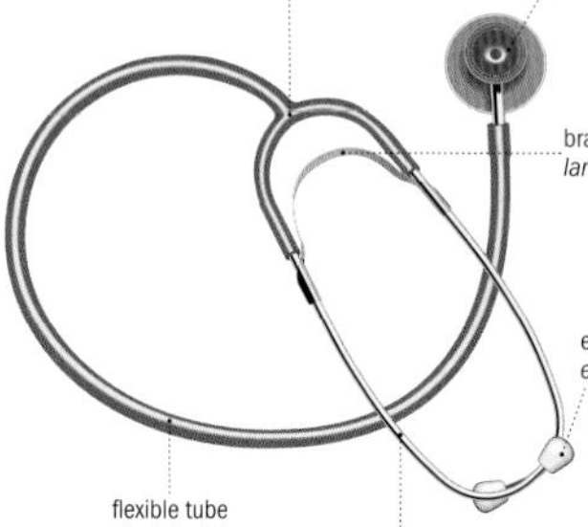

Y-tube
tube[M] en Y[M]
sound receiver
récepteur[M] de son[M]
branch clip
lame[F]-ressort[M]
earpiece
embout[M] auriculaire
flexible tube
tube[M] flexible
branch
branche[F]

syri
sering

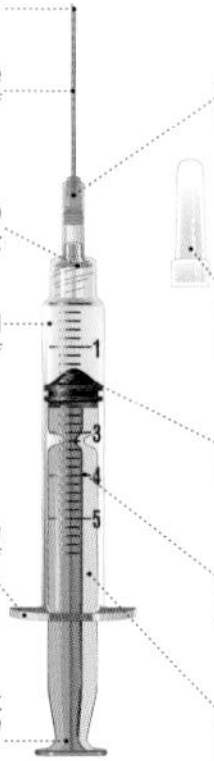

bevel
biseau[M]
needle
aiguille[F]
needle hub
pavillon[M]
Luer-Lock tip
embout[M] Luer Lock
hollow barrel
corps[M] de pompe[F]
tip protector
protecteur[M] d'embout
rubber bulb
bouchon[M]
finger flange
anneau[M] de retenue[F]
scale
graduation[F]
thumb rest
poussoir[M]
plunger
piston[M]

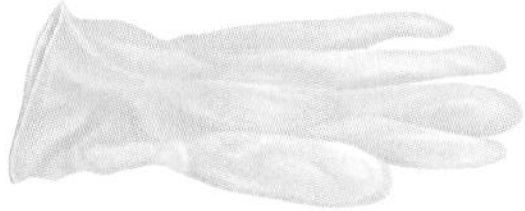

latex glove
gant[M] en latex[M]

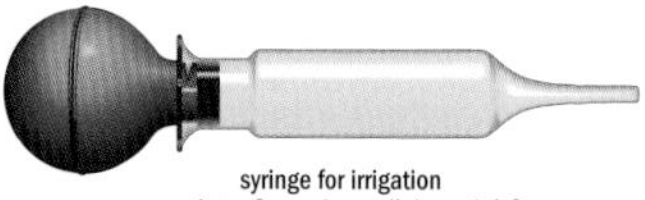

syringe for irrigation
seringue[F] pour lavage[M] de cavités[F]

hospital trolley
civière[F]

reclining back
dossier[M] inclinable
mattress
matelas[M]
frame
cadre[M]
telescopic leg
pied[M] télescopique
pulling ring
anneau[M] de traction[F]
hook
crochet[M]

stre
branc

SOCIETY

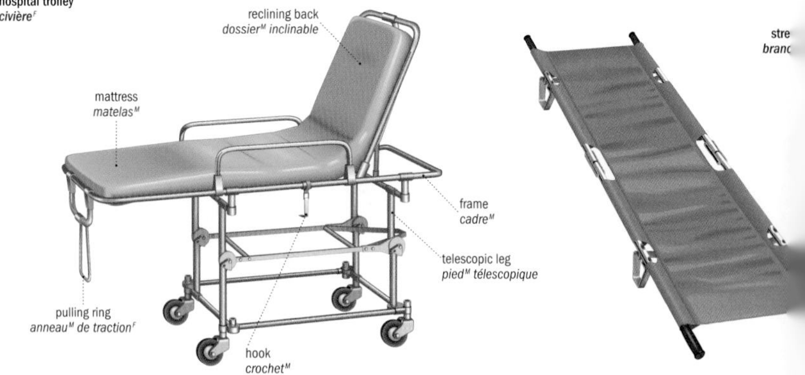

first aid kit

trousse[F] de secours[M]

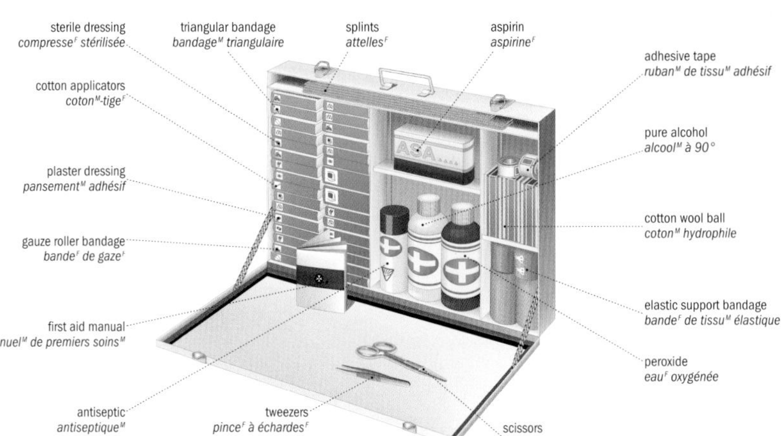

clinical thermometers

thermomètres[M] médicaux

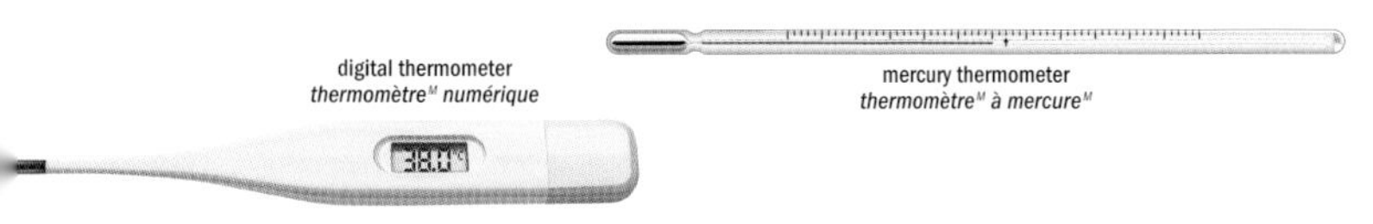

SOCIETY

blood pressure monitor

tensiomètre[M]

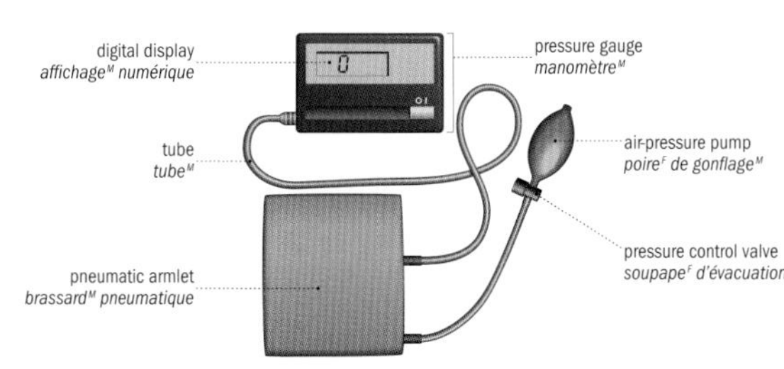

hospital

hôpital[M]

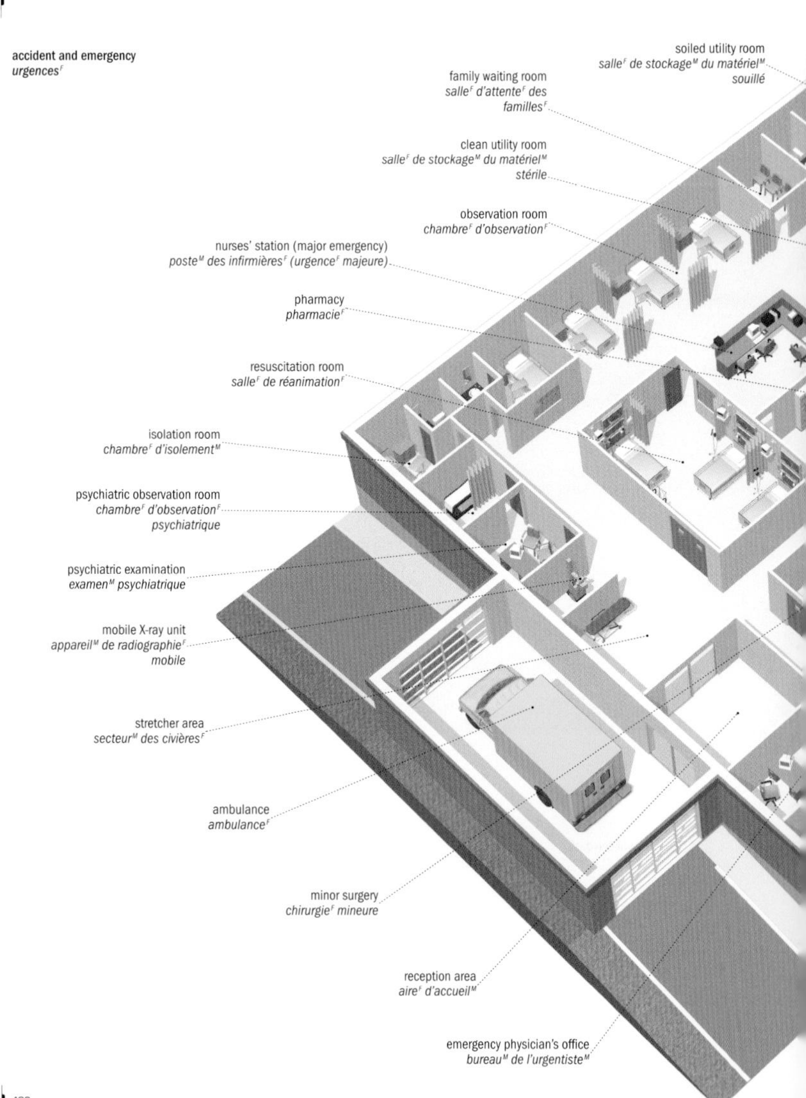

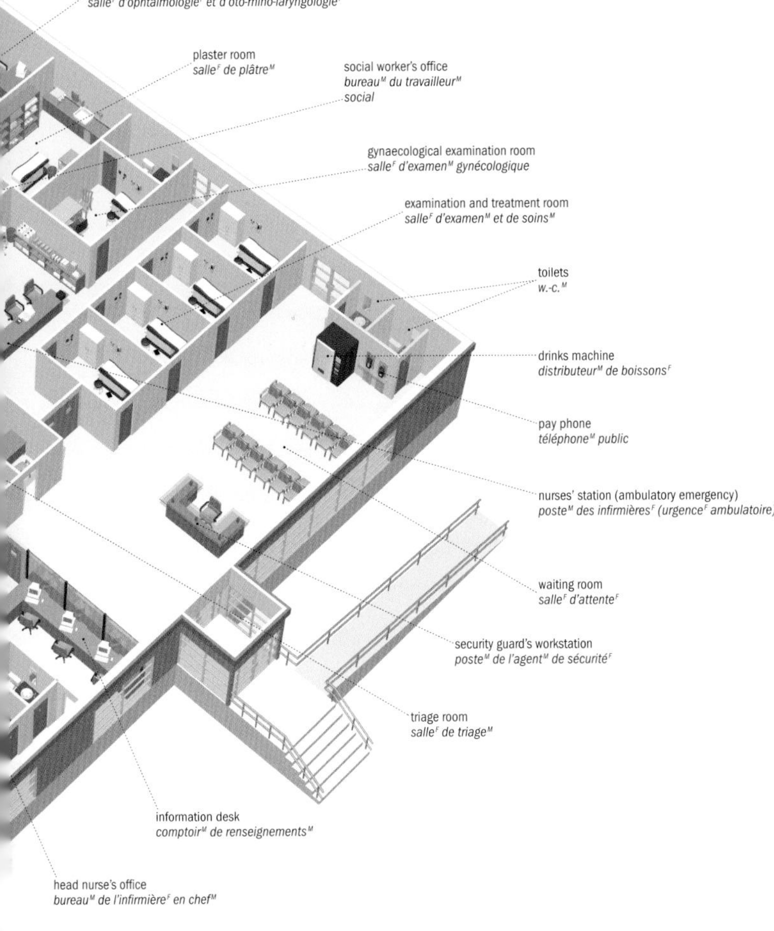
ophthalmology and ENT room
salle^F d'ophtalmologie^F et d'oto-rhino-laryngologie^F
plaster room
salle^F de plâtre^M
social worker's office
bureau^M du travailleur^M social
gynaecological examination room
salle^F d'examen^M gynécologique
examination and treatment room
salle^F d'examen^M et de soins^M
toilets
w.-c.^M
drinks machine
distributeur^M de boissons^F
pay phone
téléphone^M public
nurses' station (ambulatory emergency)
poste^M des infirmières^F (urgence^F ambulatoire)
waiting room
salle^F d'attente^F
security guard's workstation
poste^M de l'agent^M de sécurité^F
triage room
salle^F de triage^M
information desk
comptoir^M de renseignements^M
head nurse's office
bureau^M de l'infirmière^F en chef^M
staff lounge
salon^M du personnel^M

patient room
chambre [F] ***d'hôpital*** [M]

bedside lamp
lampe^F de chevet^M
junior doctor
résidente^F
intravenous stand
pied^M à perfusion^F
physician
médecin^M
oxygen outlet
prise^F d'oxygène^M
patient
patient^M
shower
douche^F
overbed table
table^F de lit^M
bedside table
table^F de chevet^M
privacy curtain
rideau^M séparateur
toilet
w.-c.^M
patient's chair
fauteuil^M de repos^M
bathroom
salle^F de bains^M
hospital bed
lit^M d'hôpital^M
nurse
infirmière^F

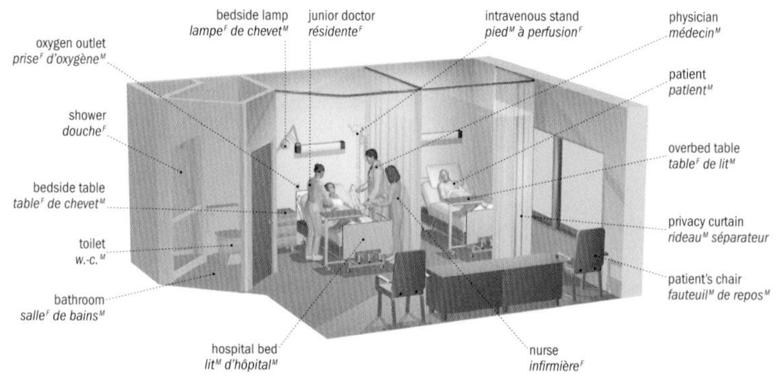

operating suite
bloc [M] ***opératoire***

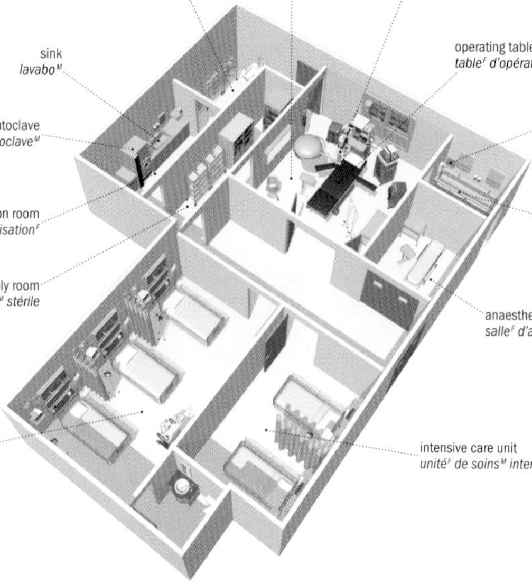

soiled utility room
salle^F de stockage^M du matériel^M souillé
operating theatre
salle^F d'opération^F
medical gas cylinder
bouteille^F à gaz^M médical
sink
lavabo^M
operating table
table^F d'opération^F
glove storage
rangement^M pour les gants^M
autoclave
autoclave^M
scrub room
salle^F de préparation^F chirurgicale
sterilization room
salle^F de stérilisation^F
supply room
arsenal^M stérile
anaesthesia room
salle^F d'anesthésie^F
recovery room
salle^F de réveil^M
intensive care unit
unité^F de soins^M intensifs

outpatients' department
unité[F] de soins[M] ambulatoires

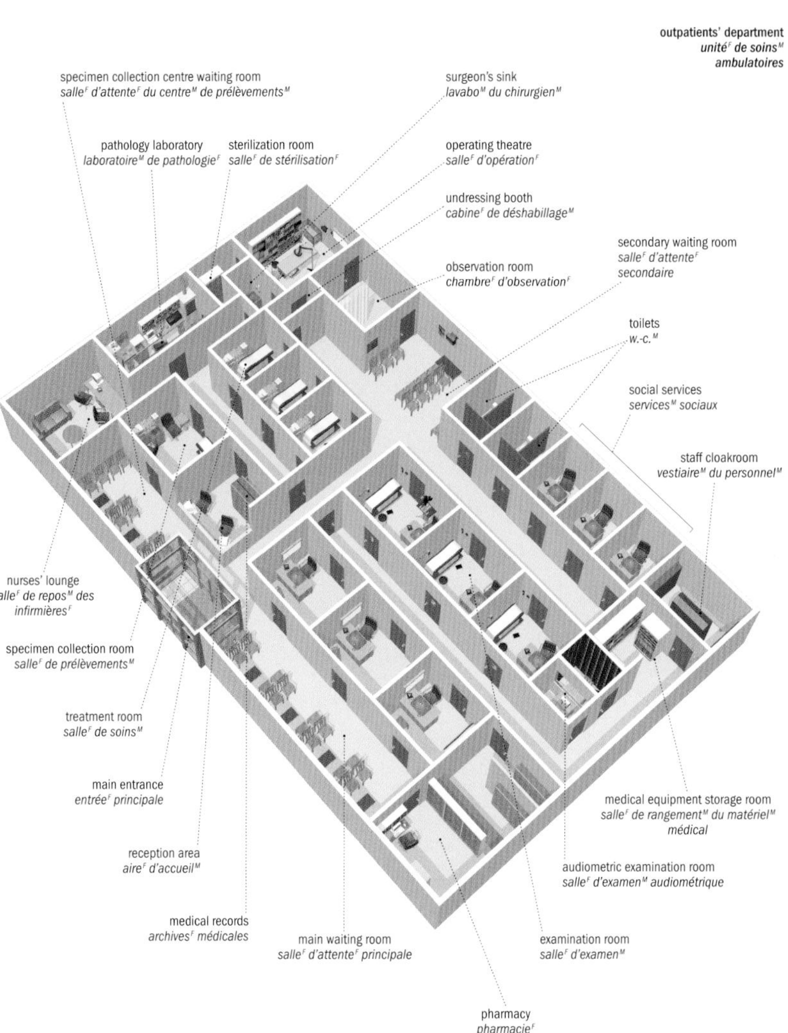

walking aids

aides[F] à la marche[F]

forearm crutch
béquille[F] d'avant-bras[M]

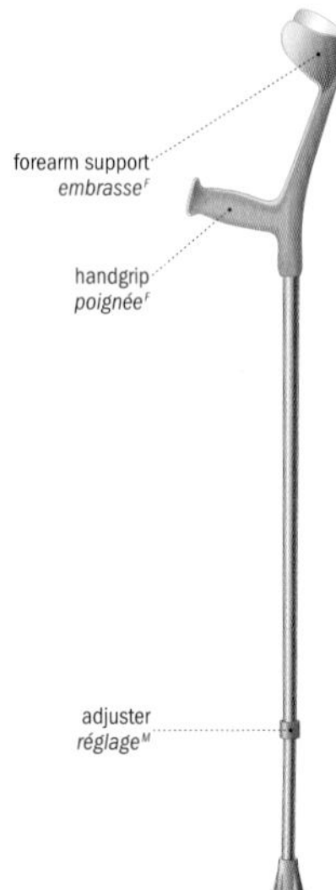

underarm cr
béquille[F] comm

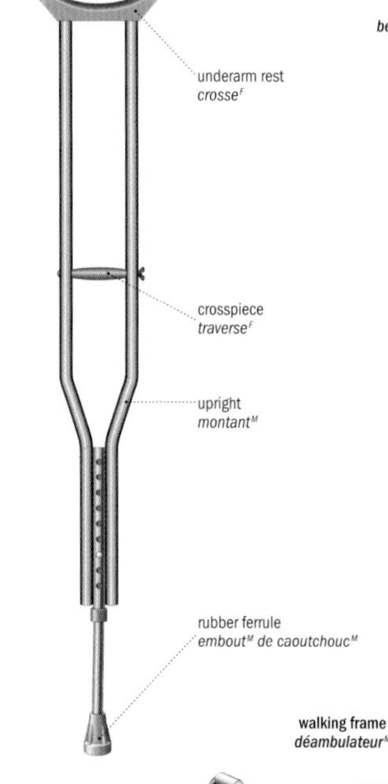

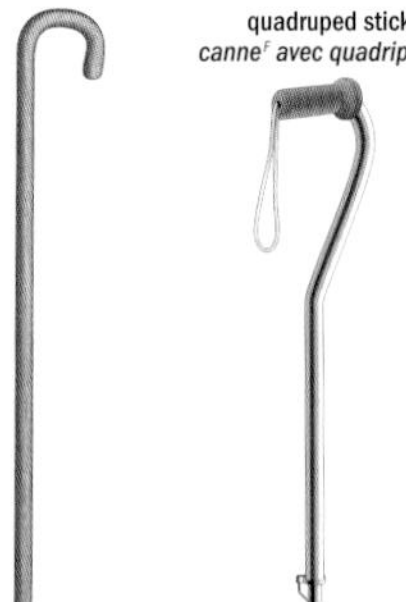

walking stick
canne[F] en C[M]

quadruped stick
canne[F] avec quadripode[M]

English stick
canne[F] en T[M]

ortho-stick
canne[F] avec poignée[F] orthopédique

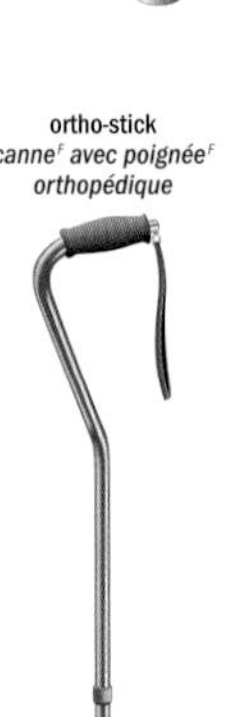

walking frame
déambulateur[M]

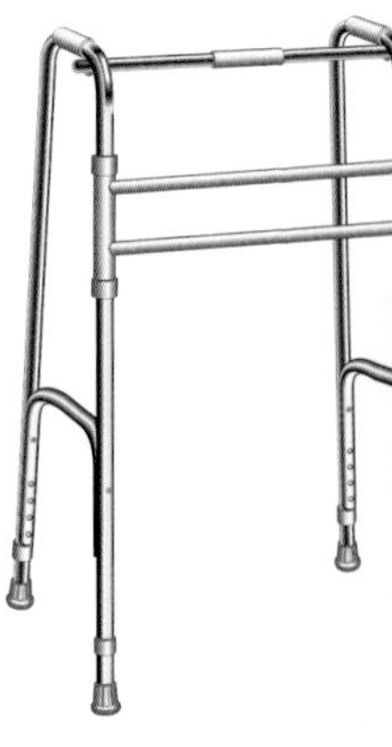

wheelchair

fauteuil[M] roulant

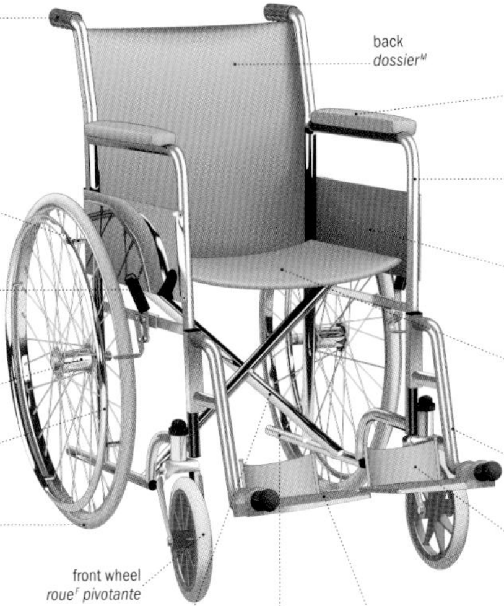

handle
poignée[F] de conduite[F]
back
dossier[M]
armrest
accoudoir[M]
spacer
barre[F] d'espacement[M]
arm
bras[M]
brake
poignée[F] de frein[M]
clothing guard
panneau[M] de protection[F] latéral
seat
siège[M]
hub
moyeu[M]
push rim
main[F] courante
hanger bracket
potence[F]
large wheel
roue[F]
heel loop
butée[F] talonnière[F]
front wheel
roue[F] pivotante
cross brace
croisillon[M]
stabilizer
dispositif[M] anti-bascule
footrest
repose-pied[M]

pharmaceutical forms of medication

formes[F] pharmaceutiques des médicaments[M]

100 ml

cough syrup
sirop[M] antitussif

mouthpiece
embout[M] buccal
cap
capuchon[M]

metered dose inhaler
inhalateur[M] doseur[M]

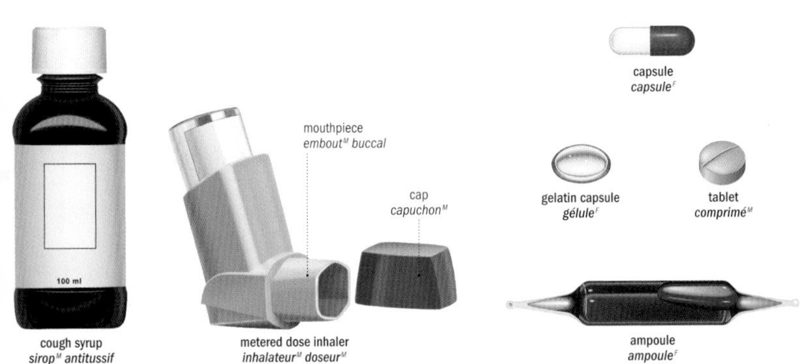

capsule
capsule[F]

gelatin capsule
gélule[F]

tablet
comprimé[M]

ampoule
ampoule[F]

SOCIETY

dice and dominoes

dés[M] et dominos[M]

ordinary die
dé[M] régulier

poker die
dé[M] à poker[M]

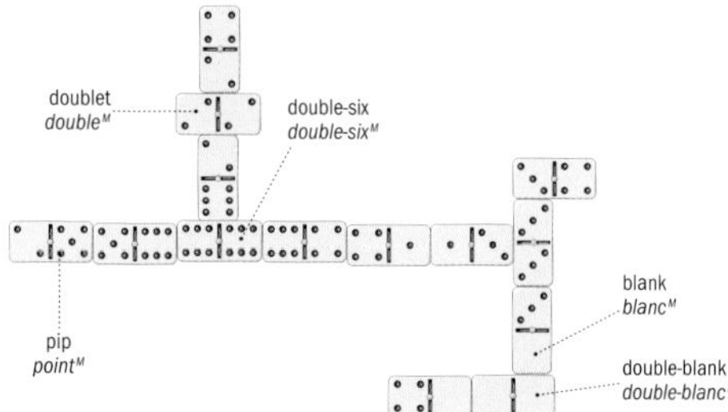

card games

cartes[F]

symbols
symboles[M]

heart
cœur[M]

diamond
carreau[M]

club
trèfle[M]

spade
pique[M]

Joker
Joker[M]

Ace
As[M]

King
Roi[M]

Queen
Dame[F]

Jack
Valet[M]

standard poker hands
combinaisons[F] au poker[M]

high card
carte[F] isolée

one pair
paire[F]

two pairs
double paire[F]

three-of-a-kind
brelan[M]

straight
séquence[F]

flush
couleur[F]

full house
main[F] pleine

four-of-a-kind
carré[M]

straight flush
quinte[F]

royal flush
quinte[F] roya

board game
jeux[M] de plateau[M]

backgammon
jacquet[M]

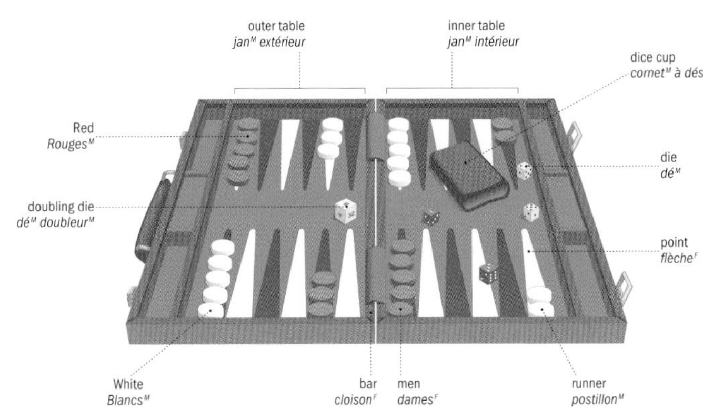

snakes and ladders
serpents[M] et échelles[F]

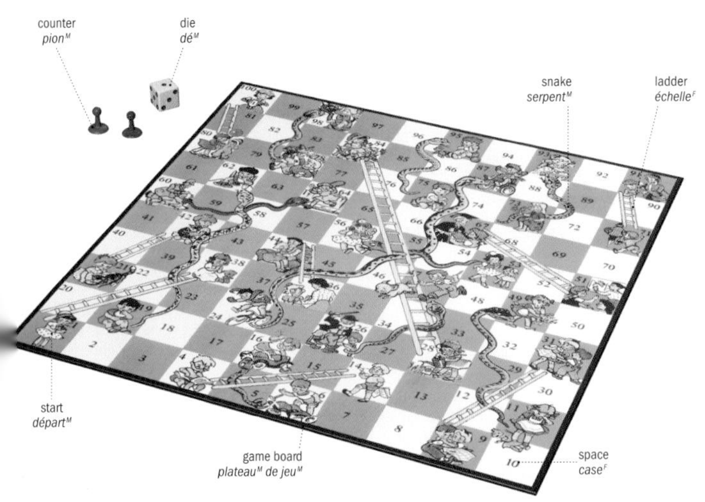

board game

chess
échecs[M]

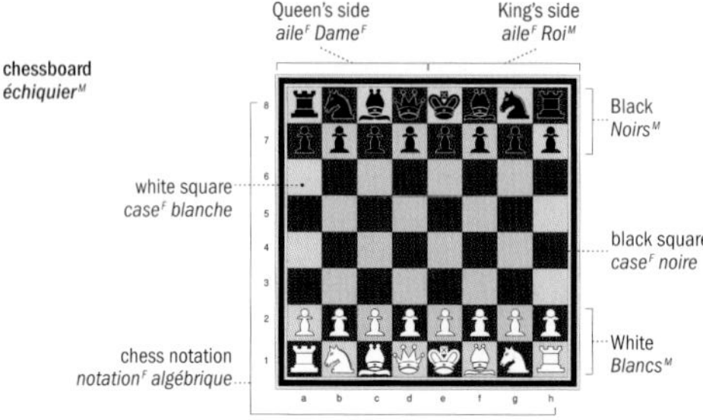

pi

Pawn
Pion[M]

Castle
Tour[F]

Bishop
Fou[M]

Knight
Cavalier[M]

types of move
types[M] *de déplacements*[M]

diagonal move
déplacement[M] *diagonal*

vertical move
déplacement[M] *vertical*

square move
déplacement[M] *en équerre*[F]

horizontal move
déplacement[M] *horizontal*

King
Roi[M]

Queen
Dame[F]

go
go[M]

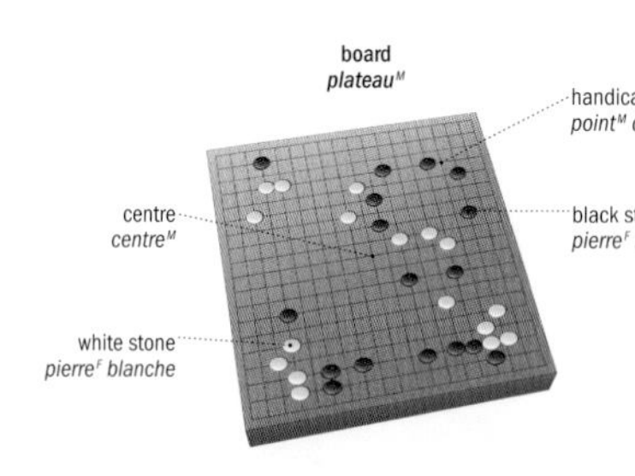

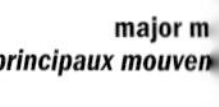

connection
connexion[F]

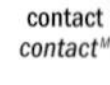

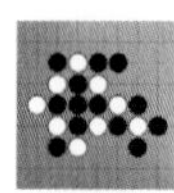

capture
capture[F]

SPORTS AND GAMES

draughts
jeu[M] *de dames*[F]

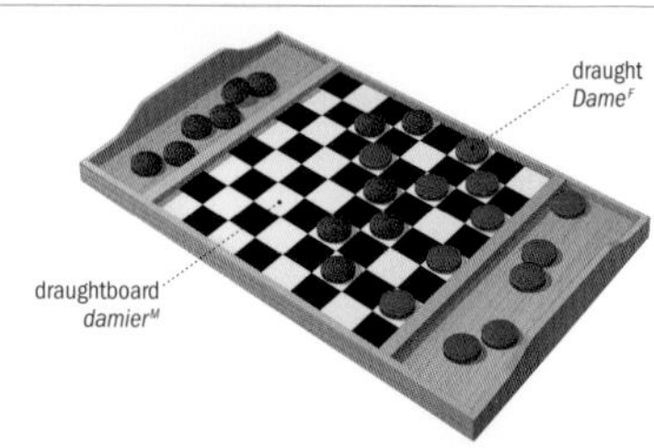

video entertainment system

système^{M} de jeux^{M} vidéo

game console
console^{F} de jeu^{M}
visual display
écran^{M}
memory card slots
ports^{M} pour carte^{F} mémoire^{F}
CD/DVD player
lecteur^{M} CD^{M}/DVD^{M}
controller ports
ports^{M} pour manette^{F}
action buttons
touches^{F} d'action^{F}
reset button
bouton^{M} de réinitialisation^{F}
directional buttons
touches^{F} directionnelles
eject button
touche^{F} d'éjection^{F}
controller
manette^{F} de jeu^{M}
joysticks
manches^{M} à balai^{M}

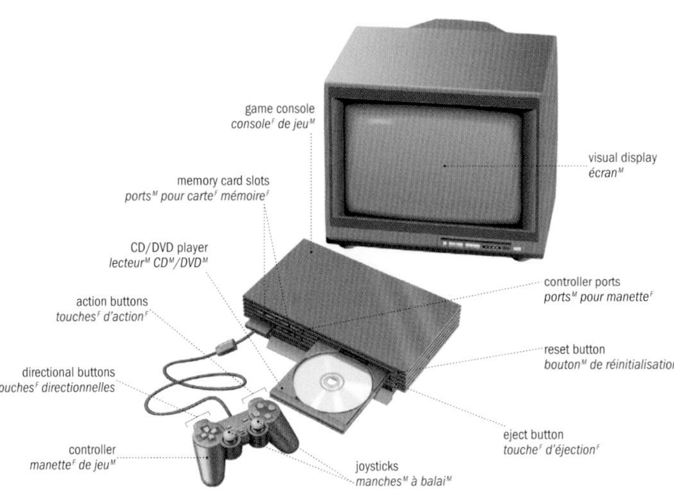

game of darts

jeu^{M} de fléchettes^{F}

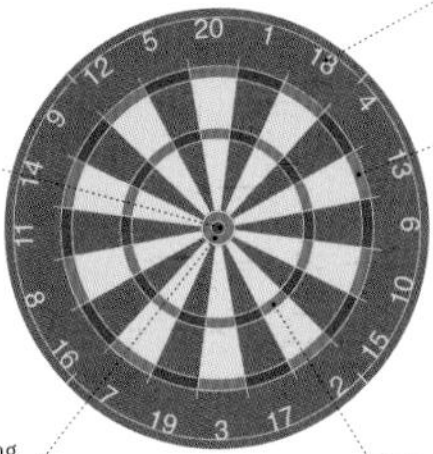

segment score number
valeur^{F} des segments^{M}
20
1
18
4
13
6
10
15
2
17
3
19
7
16
8
11
14
9
12
5
double ring
score^{M} doublé
bull's-eye
50 points^{M}
25 ring
25 points^{M}
treble ring
score^{M} triplé

shaft
fût^{M}
flight
empennage^{M}
barrel
corps^{M}
point
pointe^{F}

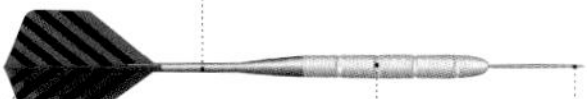

playing area
aire^{F} de jeu^{M}

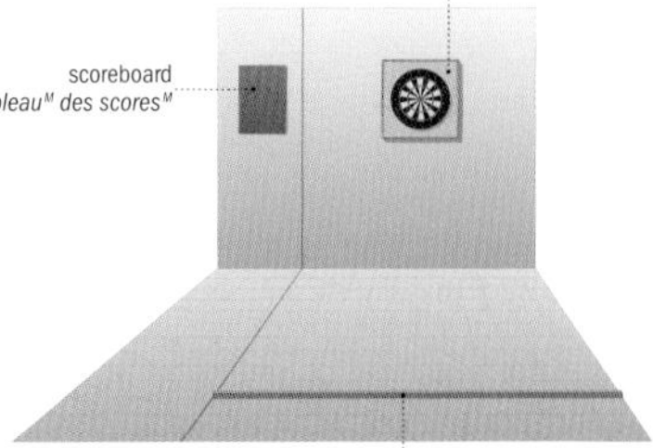

protective surround
fond^{M} de protection^{F}
scoreboard
tableau^{M} des scores^{M}
oche
ligne^{F} de jeu^{M}

SPORTS AND GAMES

arena

stade[M]

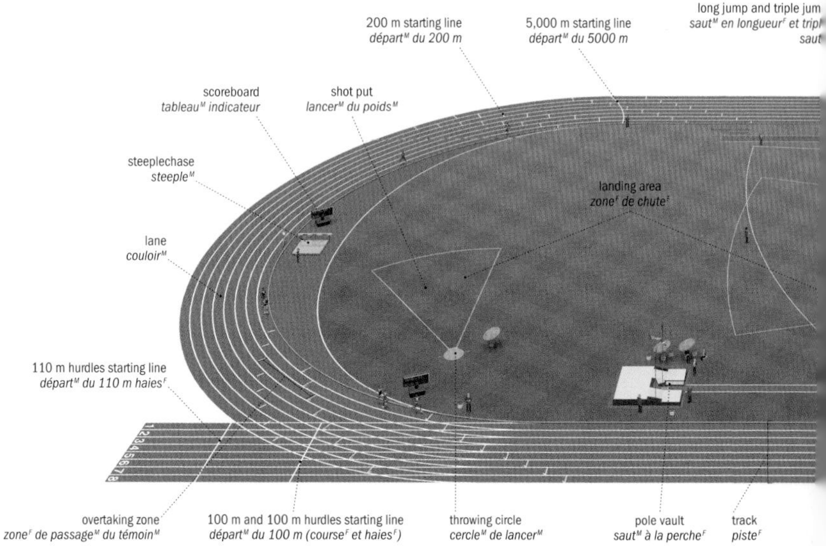

200 m starting line
départ[M] du 200 m
5,000 m starting line
départ[M] du 5000 m
long jump and triple jum
saut[M] en longueur[F] et tripl
saut
scoreboard
tableau[M] indicateur
shot put
lancer[M] du poids[M]
steeplechase
steeple[M]
landing area
zone[F] de chute[F]
lane
couloir[M]
110 m hurdles starting line
départ[M] du 110 m haies[F]
1 2 3 4 5 6 7 8
overtaking zone
zone[F] de passage[M] du témoin[M]
100 m and 100 m hurdles starting line
départ[M] du 100 m (course[F] et haies[F])
throwing circle
cercle[M] de lancer[M]
pole vault
saut[M] à la perche[F]
track
piste[F]

equipment
***équipement*[M]**

starting pistol
pistolet[M] de départ[M]

shot
poids[M]

baton
témoin[M]

discus
disque[M]

hammer
marteau[M]

javelin
javelot[M]

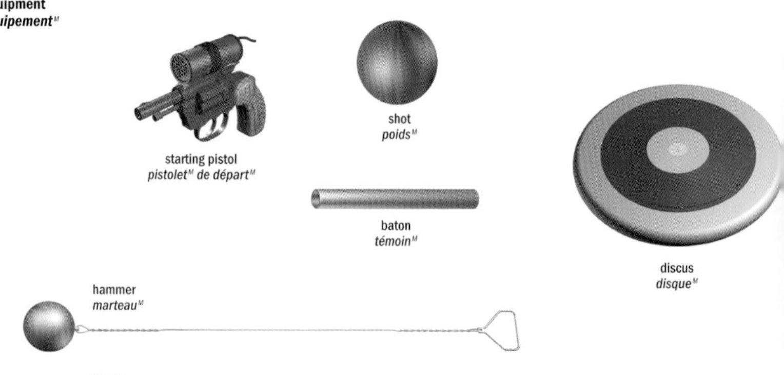

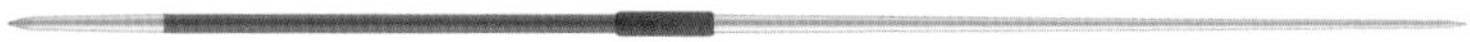

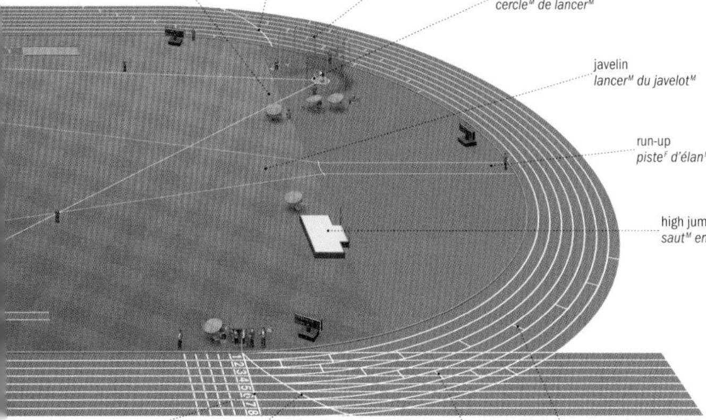

discus and hammer
lancer[M] disque[M] et marteau[M]
1,500 m starting line
départ[M] du 1500 m
safety cage
cage[F]
throwing circle
cercle[M] de lancer[M]
javelin
lancer[M] du javelot[M]
run-up
piste[F] d'élan[M]
high jump
saut[M] en hauteur[F]
12345678
finish line
[F] d'arrivée[F]
10,000 m and 4 x 400 m relay starting line
départ[M] du 10 000 m et du relais[M] 4 x 400 m
800 m starting line
départ[M] du 800 m
400 m, 400 m hurdles, 4 x 100 m relay starting line
départ[M] des 400 m (course[F], haies[F], relais[M])

athlete: starting block
athlète[F] : bloc[M] de départ[M]

shirt
maillot[M]
number
dossard[M]
shorts
short[M]
pedal
sabot[M]
running shoe
chaussure[F] de piste[F]
notch
cran[M]
start line
ligne[F] de départ[M]
anchor
fixation[F]
lane line
ligne[F] de couloir[M]
rack
crémaillère[F]
spike
pointe[F]
block
bloc[M]
base
embase[F]

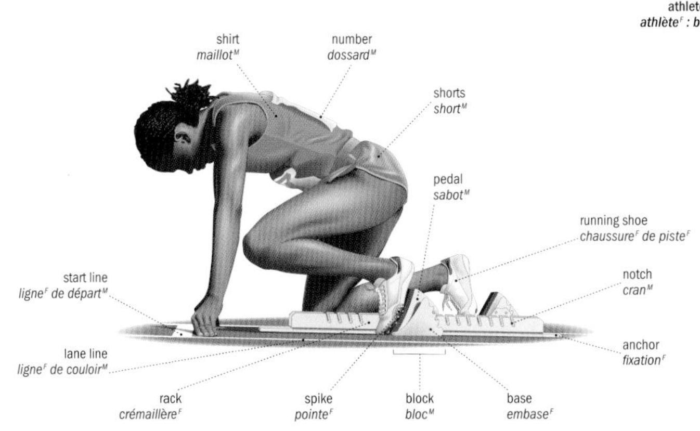

baseball

baseball^M

player positions
position^F des joueurs^M

left fielder
voltigeur^M gauche
centre fielder
voltigeur^M de centre^M
shortstop
arrêt-court^M
right fielder
voltigeur^M droit
third baseman
troisième-but^M
second baseman
deuxième-but^M
catcher
receveur^M
pitcher
lanceur^M
first baseman
premier-but^M

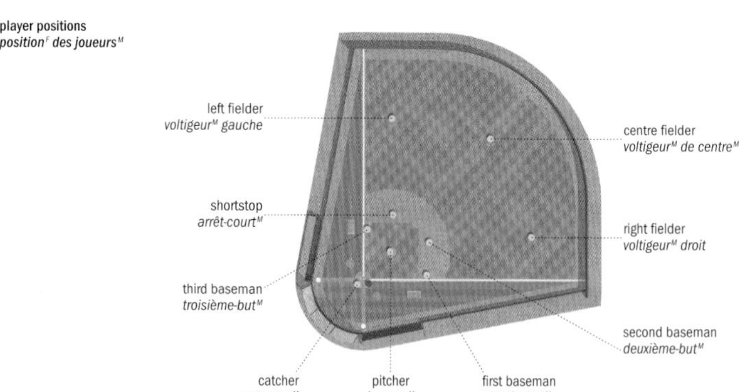

field
terrain^M

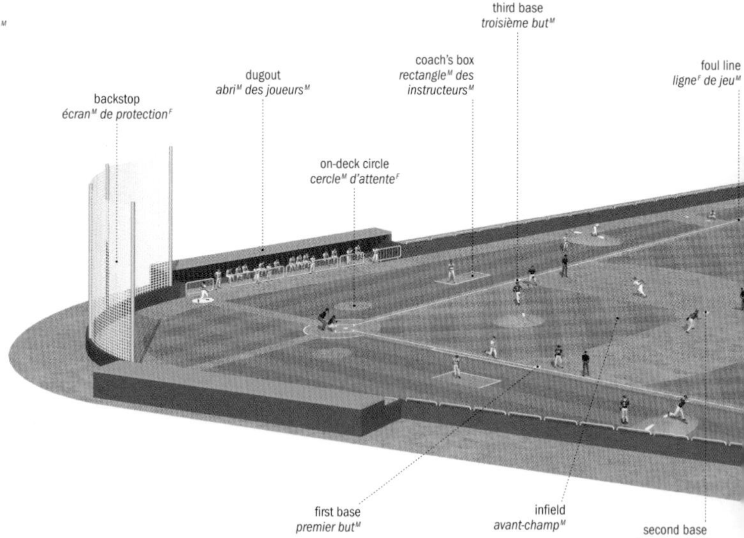

third base
troisième but^M
coach's box
rectangle^M des instructeurs^M
foul line
ligne^F de jeu^M
dugout
abri^M des joueurs^M
backstop
écran^M de protection^F
on-deck circle
cercle^M d'attente^F
first base
premier but^M
infield
avant-champ^M
second base
deuxième but^M

SPORTS AND GAMES

pitch
lancer[M]

home-plate umpire
arbitre[M] en chef[M]
batter
frappeur[M]
pitcher
lanceur[M]
catcher
receveur[M]
home plate
marbre[M]
pitcher's mound
monticule[M]
pitcher's plate
plaque[F] du lanceur[M]

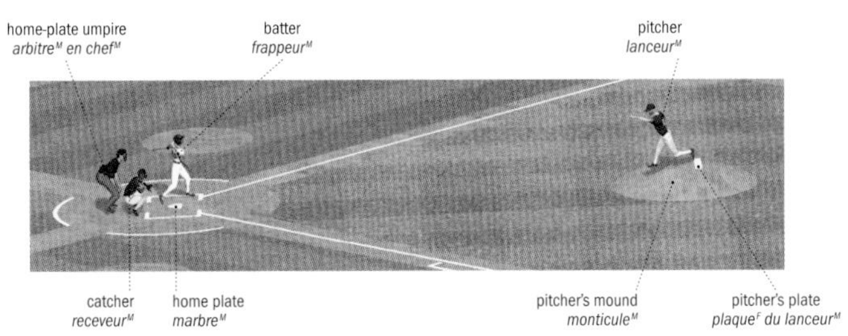

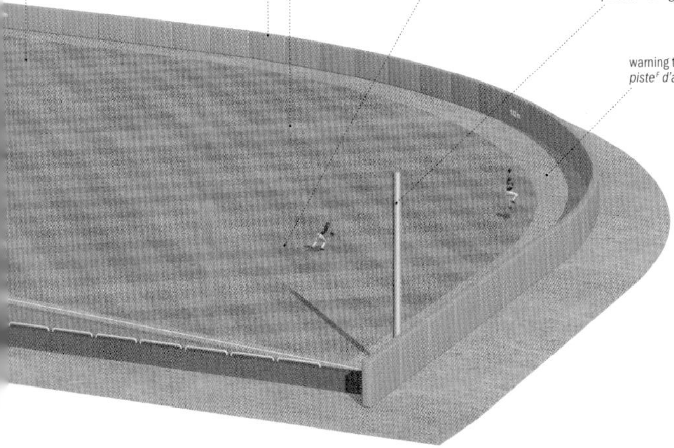

outfield fence
clôture[F] du champ[M] extérieur
left field
champ[M] gauche
centre field
champ[M] centre[M]
right field
champ[M] droit
foul line post
poteau[M] de ligne[F] de jeu[M]
warning track
piste[F] d'avertissement[M]

baseball

baseball
balle^F de baseball^M
bat
bâton^M
batter's helmet
casque^M de frappeur^M
catcher
receveur^M
throat protector
protège-gorge^M
mask
masque^M
frame
grille^F
chest protector
plastron^M
catcher's glove
gant^M de receveur^M
team shirt
maillot^M d'équipe^F
undershirt
maillot^M de corps^M
batting glove
gant^M de frappeur^M
trousers
pantalon^M
stirrup sock
chaussette^F-étrier^M
spiked shoe
chaussure^F à crampons^M
toe guard
protège-orteils^M
leg guard
jambière^F
knee pad
genouillère^F
ankle guard
protège-cheville^M

baseball

bat
bâton[M]

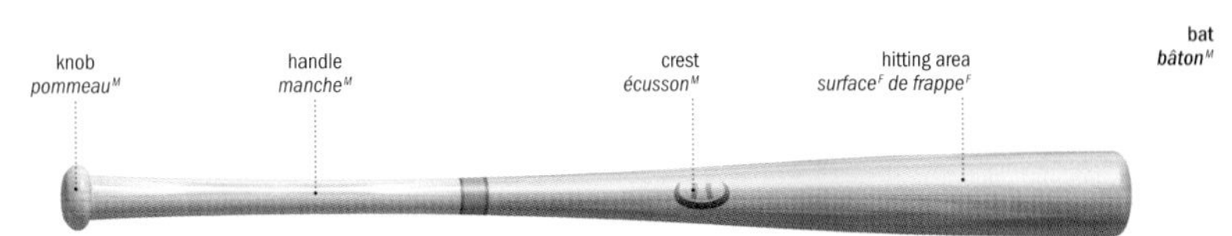

fielder's glove
gant[M]

s section of a baseball
oe[F] de la balle[F]

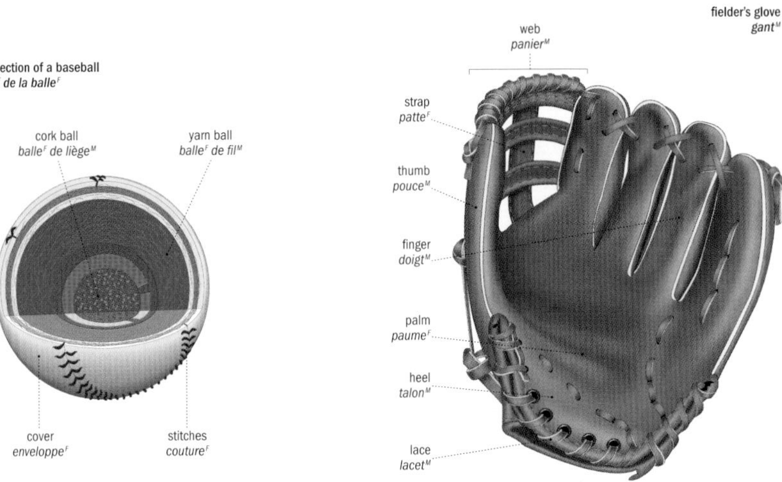

softball

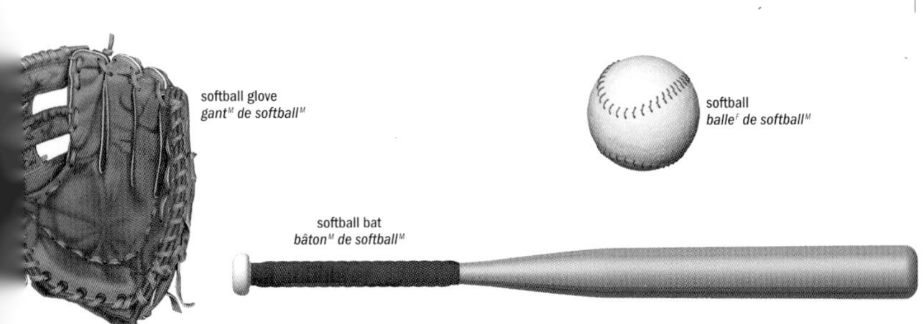

cricket

cricket[M]

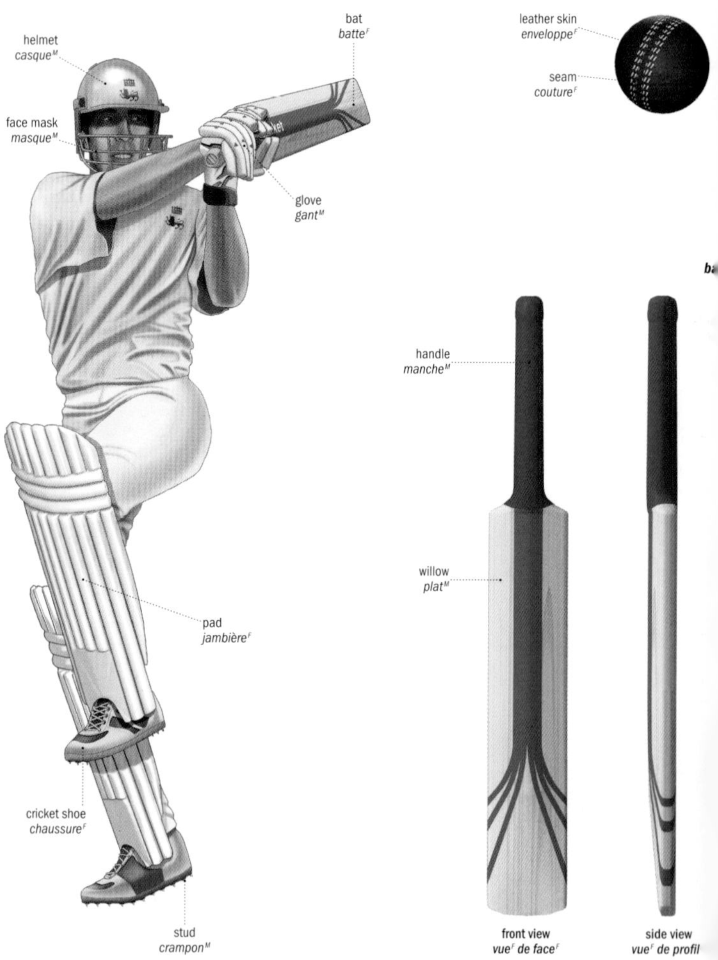

field
***terrain**[M]*

pitch
livrée[F]
wicketkeeper
gardien[M] de guichet[M]
screen
écran[M]
bowler
lanceur[M]
fielders
équipe[F] au champ[M]
umpire
arbitre[M]
umpire
arbitre[M]

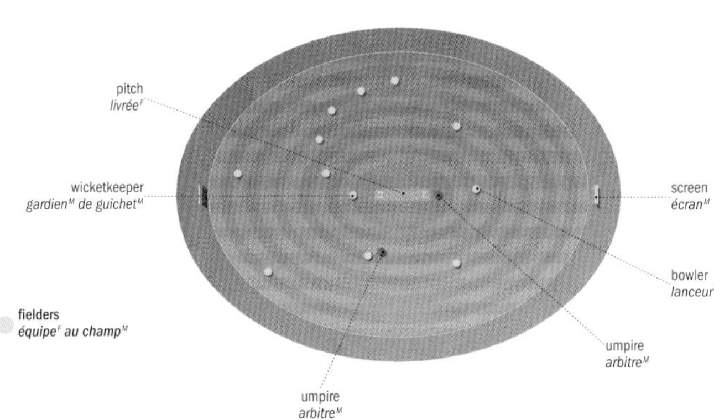

ket
***het**[M]*

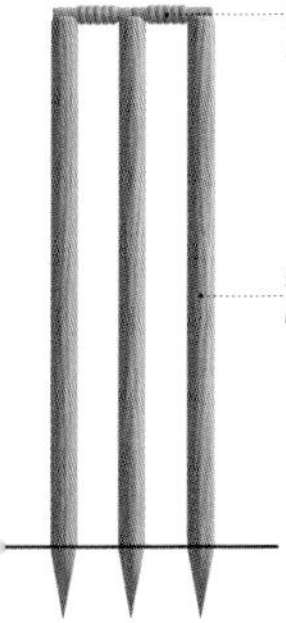

bail
barreau[M]
stump
piquet[M]

pitch
***livrée**[F]*

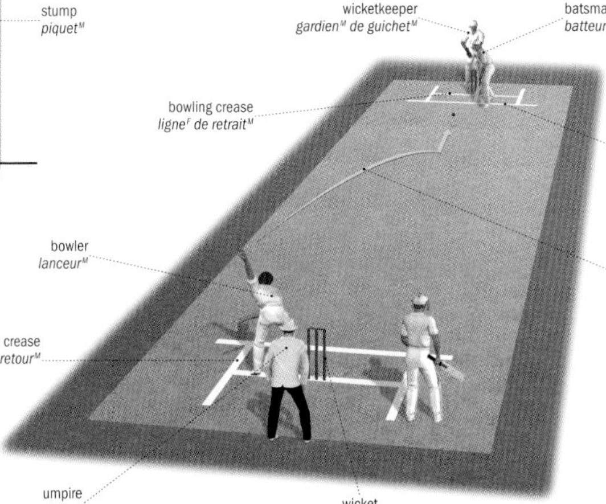

wicketkeeper
gardien[M] de guichet[M]
batsman
batteur[M]
bowling crease
ligne[F] de retrait[M]
popping crease
limite[F] du batteur[M]
bowler
lanceur[M]
delivery
lancer[M]
return crease
limite[F] de retour[M]
umpire
arbitre[M]
wicket
guichet[M]

association football

football[M]

playing field
terrain[M]

centre flag
drapeau[M] de centr

penalty spot
point[M] de réparation[F]

goal area
surface[F] de but[M]

goal
but[M]

penalty area
surface[F] de réparation[F]

penalty area marking
ligne[F] de surface[F] de réparation[F]

penalty arc
arc[M] de cercle[M]

SPORTS AND GAMES

player positions
***position*[F] *des joueurs*[M]**

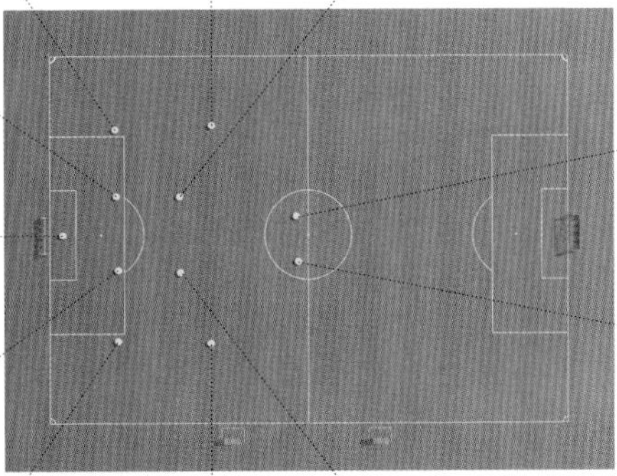

left back
arrière[M] *gauche*
left midfielder
milieu[M] *offensif gauche*
central midfielder
milieu[M] *défensif*
centre half
libero[M]
striker
attaquant[M] *de soutien*[M]
goalkeeper
gardien[M] *de but*[M]
striker
attaquant[M] *de pointe*[F]
centre half
stoppeur[M]
right back
arrière[M] *droit*
right midfielder
milieu[M] *offensif droit*
central midfielder
milieu[M] *défensif*

feree
bitre[M]
corner flag
drapeau[M] *de coin*[M]
centre spot
centre[M]
corner arc
surface[F] *de coin*[M]
linesman
juge[M] *de touche*[F]
touchline
ligne[F] *de touche*[F]
centre circle
cercle[M] *central*
halfway line
ligne[F] *médiane*
substitutes' bench
banc[M] *des remplaçants*[M]

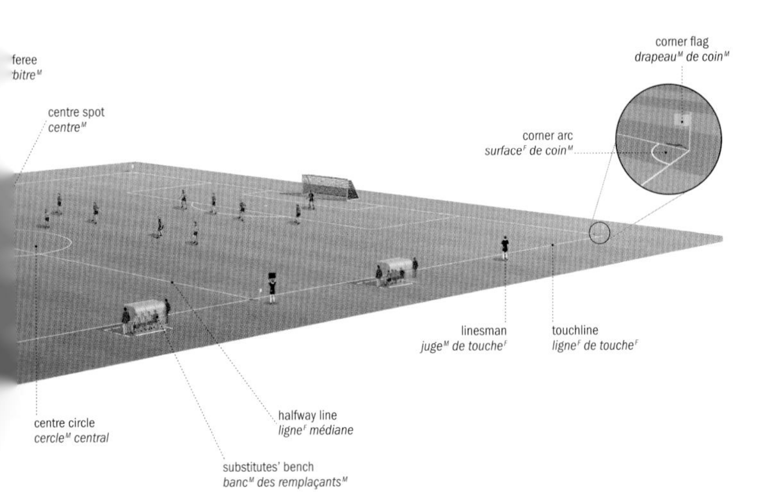

rugby

rugby^{M}

player positions
position^{F} des joueurs^{M}

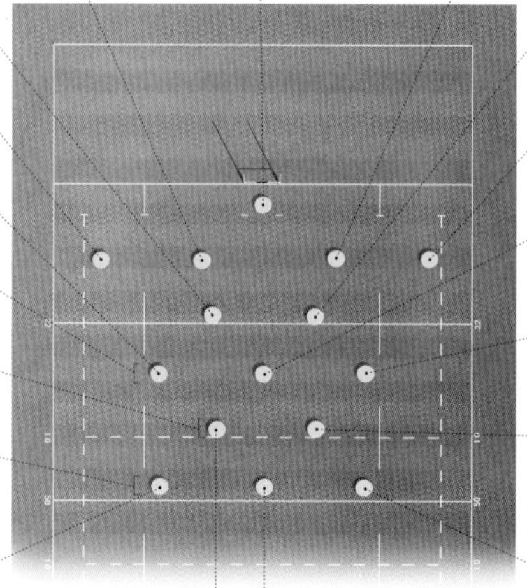

right centre
centre^{M} droit
full back
arrière^{M}
left centre
centre^{M} gauche
fly half
demi^{M} d'ouverture^{F}
scrum half
demi^{M} de mêlée^{F}
right wing
ailier^{M} droit
left wing
ailier^{M} gauche
flank forward
aile^{F} droite
no. 8 forward
centre^{M}
third row
troisième ligne^{F}
flank forward
aile^{F} gauche
second row
deuxième ligne^{F}
lock forward
avant^{M} gauche
first row
première ligne^{F}
tight head prop
pilier^{M} droit
loose head prop
pilier^{M} gauche
lock forward
avant^{M} droit
hooker
talonneur^{M}

field
terrain^{M}

10 m
ligne^{F} des
flag
drapeau^{M}
goal line
ligne^{F} de but^{M}
goal
but^{M}
dead ball line
ligne^{F} de ballon^{M} mort
22 m
ligne^{F} des 2

SPORTS AND GAMES

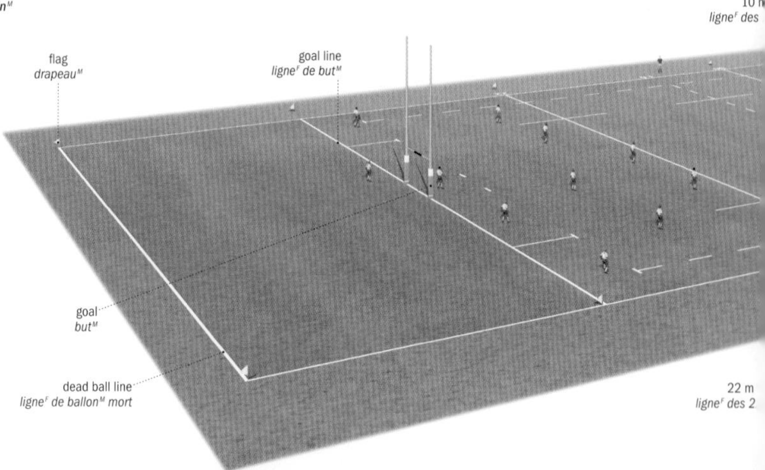

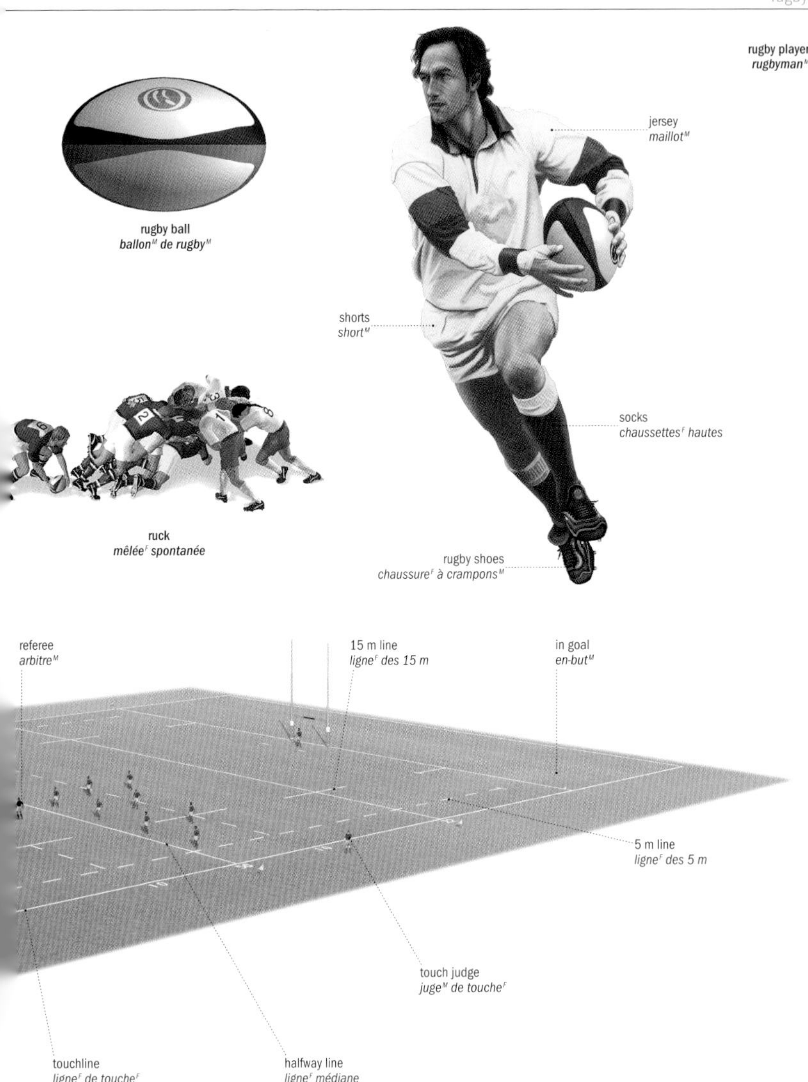
rugby player
rugbyman[M]
jersey
maillot[M]
rugby ball
ballon[M] de rugby[M]
shorts
short[M]
socks
chaussettes[F] hautes
ruck
mêlée[F] spontanée
rugby shoes
chaussure[F] à crampons[M]
referee
arbitre[M]
15 m line
ligne[F] des 15 m
in goal
en-but[M]
5 m line
ligne[F] des 5 m
touch judge
juge[M] de touche[F]
touchline
ligne[F] de touche[F]
halfway line
ligne[F] médiane

American football

football[M] américain

scrimmage: defence
mêlée[F] : défense[F]

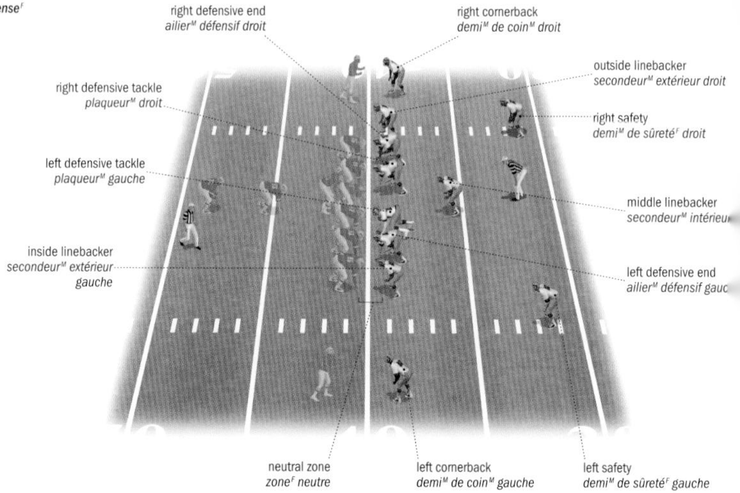

right defensive end
ailier[M] défensif droit
right cornerback
demi[M] de coin[M] droit
outside linebacker
secondeur[M] extérieur droit
right defensive tackle
plaqueur[M] droit
right safety
demi[M] de sûreté[F] droit
left defensive tackle
plaqueur[M] gauche
middle linebacker
secondeur[M] intérieu
inside linebacker
secondeur[M] extérieur gauche
left defensive end
ailier[M] défensif gauc
neutral zone
zone[F] neutre
left cornerback
demi[M] de coin[M] gauche
left safety
demi[M] de sûreté[F] gauche

playing field for American football
terrain[M] de football[M] américain

inbound line
trait[M] de mise[F] au jeu[M]
goal line
ligne[F] de but[M]
centre line
ligne[F] de centre[M]
end zone
zone[F] de but[M]
end line
ligne[F] de fond[M]
yard line
ligne[F] des verges[F]
sideline
ligne[F] de touche[F]

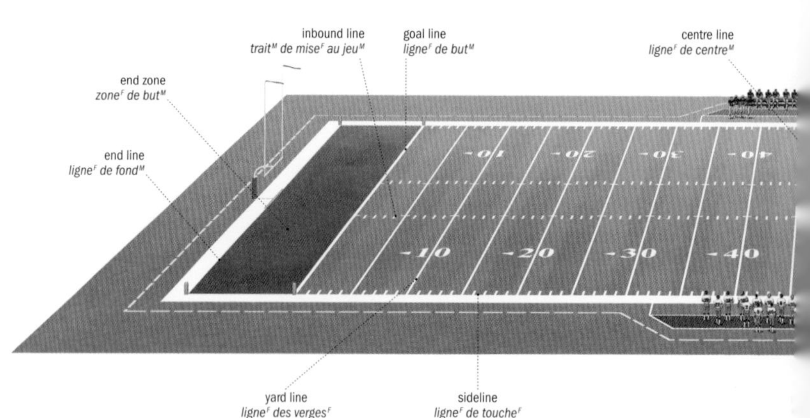

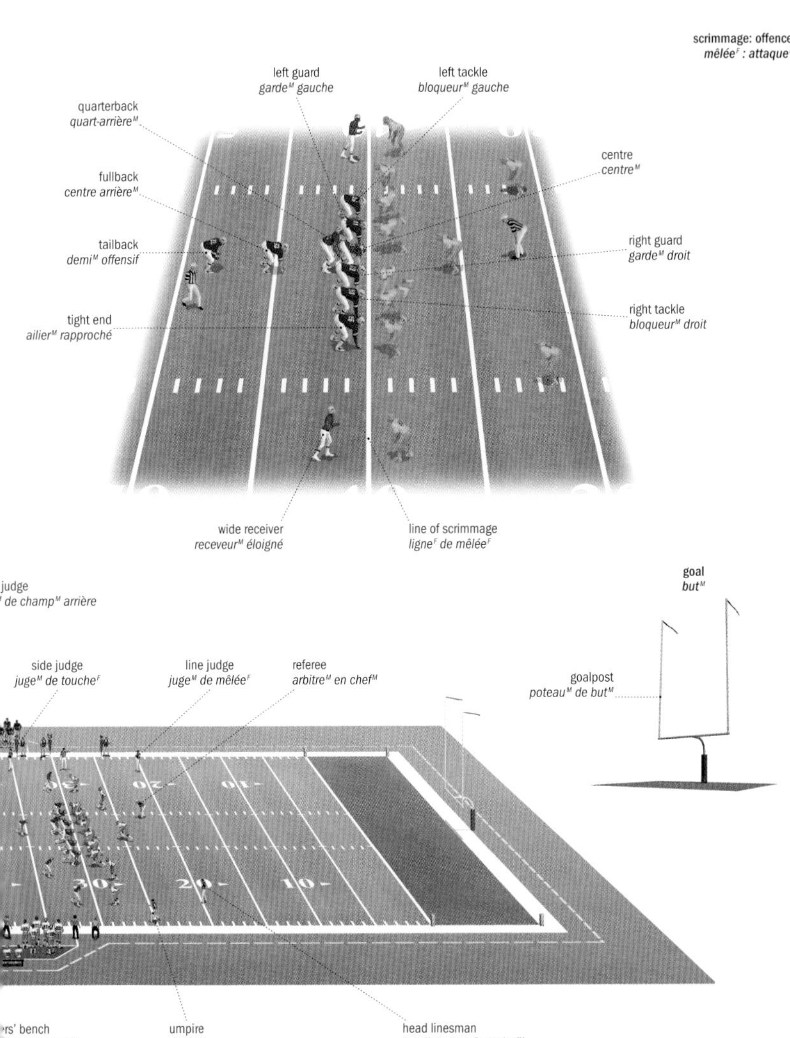

SPORTS AND GAMES

American football

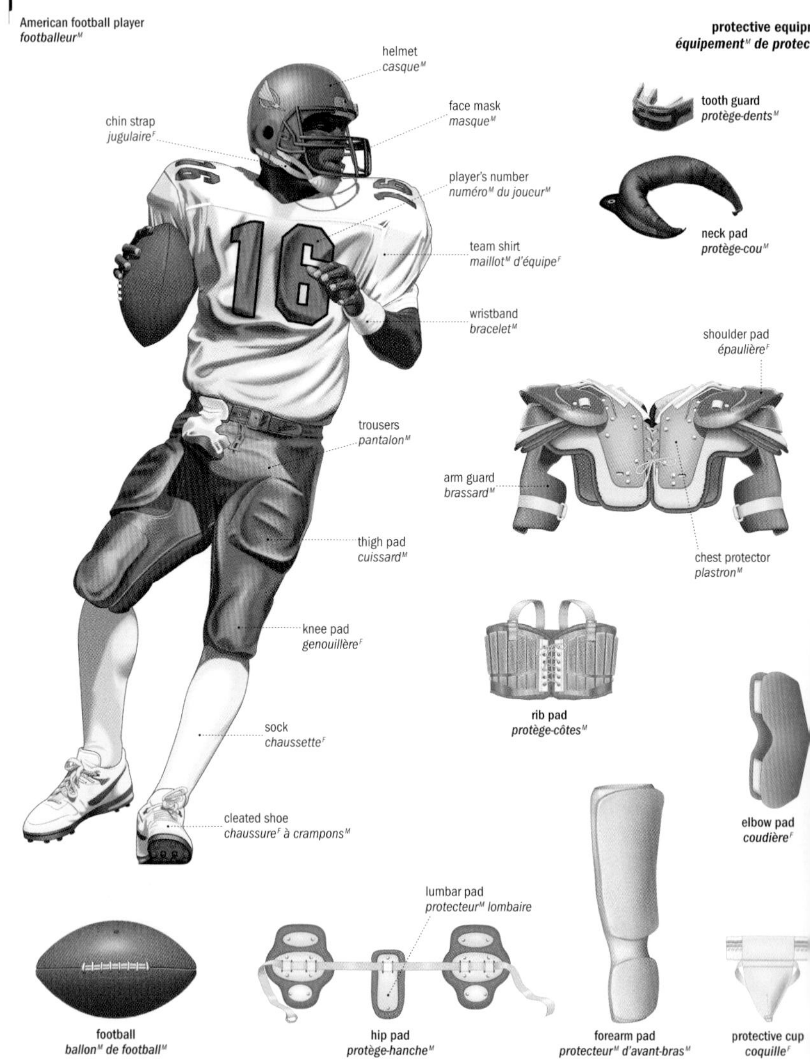

volleyball

volleyball[M]

court
terrain[M]

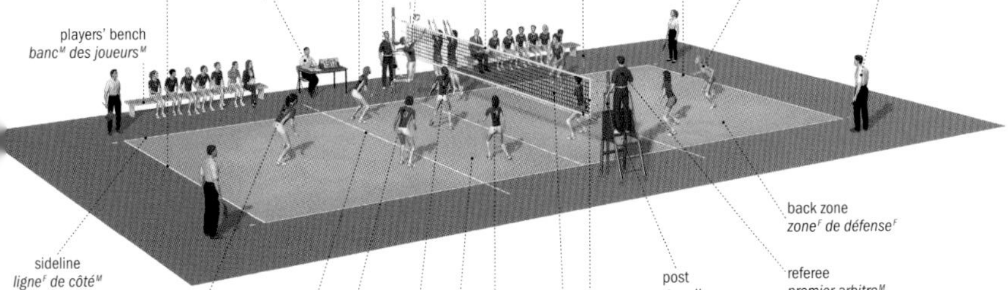

umpire
second arbitre[M]

left attacker
attaquant[M] gauche

end line
ligne[F] de fond[M]

left back
arrière[M] gauche

white tape
bande[F] blanche

libero
libero[M]

clear space
zone[F] libre

scorer
marqueur[M]

antenna
antenne[F]

linesman
juge[M] de ligne[F]

players' bench
banc[M] des joueurs[M]

back zone
zone[F] de défense[F]

sideline
ligne[F] de côté[M]

post
poteau[M]

referee
premier arbitre[M]

middle back
arrière[M] centre

vertical side band
bande[F] verticale de côté[M]

attack line
ligne[F] d'attaque[F]

net
filet[M]

right back
arrière[M] droit

right attacker
attaquant[M] droit

middle attacker
attaquant[M] central

attack zone
zone[F] d'attaque[F]

volleyball
ballon[M] de volleyball[M]

techniques
techniques[F]

tip
touche[F]

bump
manchette[F]

serve
service[M]

basketball

basketball[M]

basketball player
joueur[M] de basketball[M]

court
terrain[M]

player positions
position^{F} des joueurs^{M}

point guard
meneur^{M} de jeu^{M}
centre
pivot^{M}
guard
arrière^{M}
left forward
ailier^{M} gauche
right forward
ailier^{M} droit

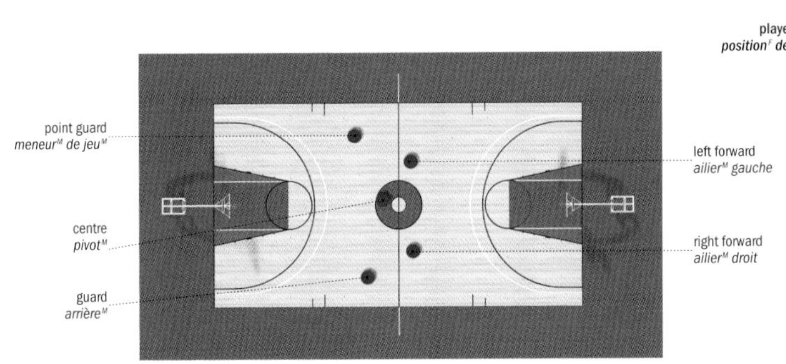

backstop
but^{M}

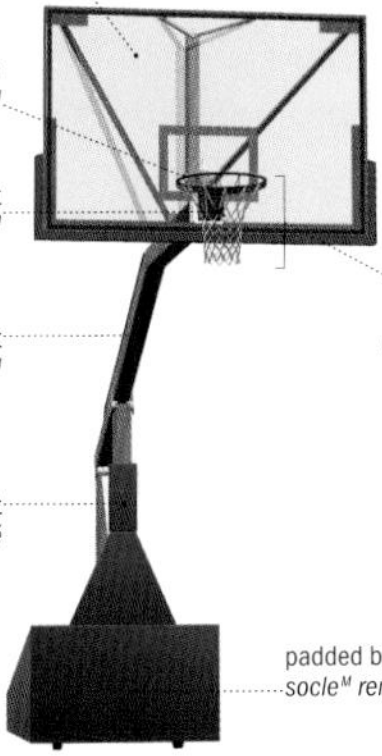

backboard
panneau^{M}
rim
anneau^{M}
net
filet^{M}
basket
panier^{M}
backboard support
support^{M} de panneau^{M}
padded upright
montant^{M} rembourré
padded base
socle^{M} rembourré

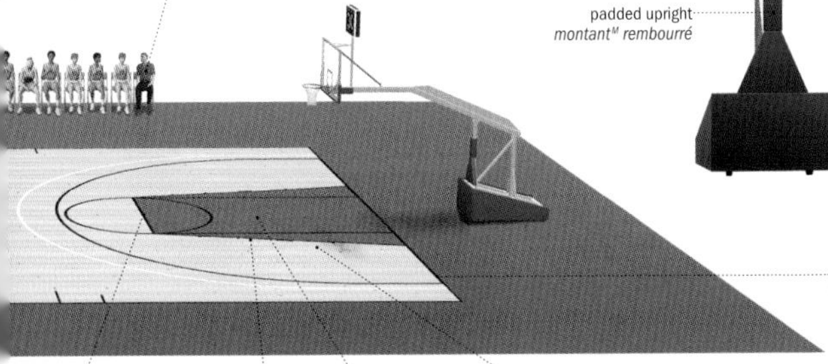

ch
aineur^{M}
stant coach
aineur^{M} adjoint
trainer
soigneur^{M}
end line
ligne^{F} de fond^{M}
free throw line
ne^{F} de lancer^{M} franc
second space
deuxième espace^{M}
restricted area
zone^{F} réservée
first space
premier espace^{M}

tennis

tennis[M]

court
court[M]

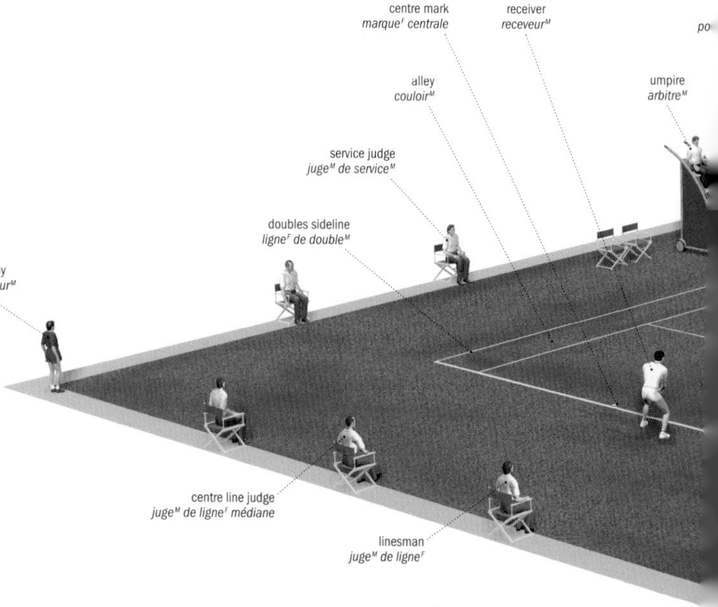

centre mark
marque[F] *centrale*

receiver
receveur[M]

po

alley
couloir[M]

umpire
arbitre[M]

service judge
juge[M] *de service*[M]

doubles sideline
ligne[F] *de double*[M]

ball boy
ramasseur[M]

centre line judge
juge[M] *de ligne*[F] *médiane*

linesman
juge[M] *de ligne*[F]

strokes
coups[M]

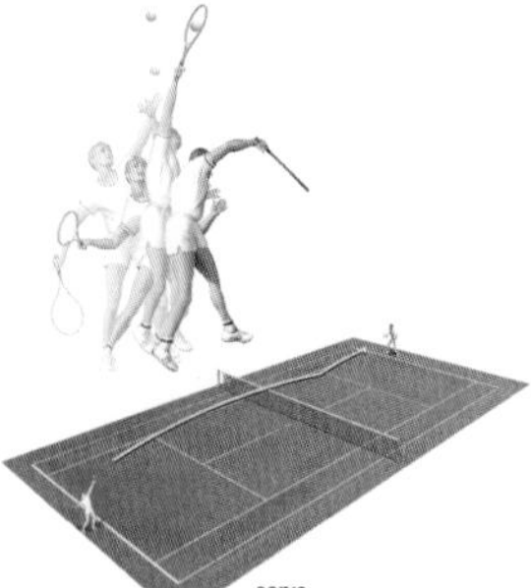

serve
service[M]

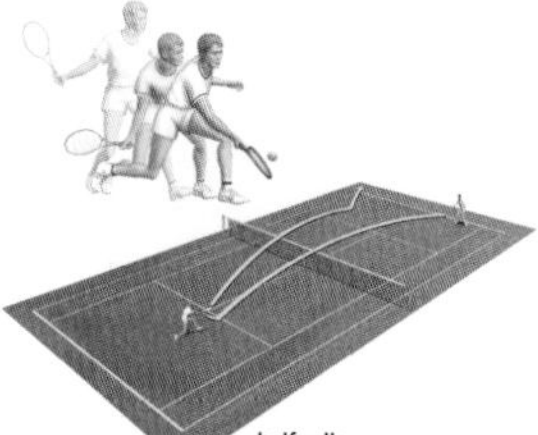

half-volley
demi-volée[F]

volley
volée[F]

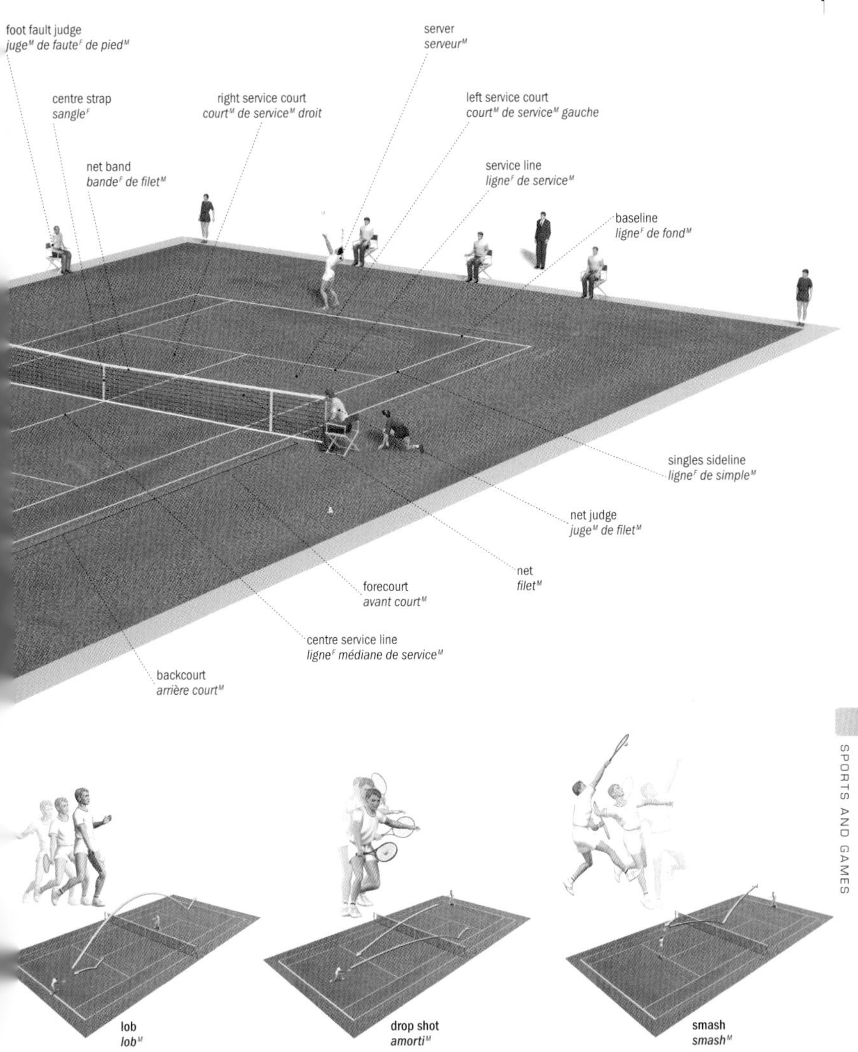
foot fault judge
jugeᴹ de fauteᶠ de piedᴹ
server
serveurᴹ
centre strap
sangleᶠ
right service court
courtᴹ de serviceᴹ droit
left service court
courtᴹ de serviceᴹ gauche
net band
bandeᶠ de filetᴹ
service line
ligneᶠ de serviceᴹ
baseline
ligneᶠ de fondᴹ
singles sideline
ligneᶠ de simpleᴹ
net judge
jugeᴹ de filetᴹ
net
filetᴹ
forecourt
avant courtᴹ
centre service line
ligneᶠ médiane de serviceᴹ
backcourt
arrière courtᴹ
lob
lobᴹ
drop shot
amortiᴹ
smash
smashᴹ

tennis

tennis racket
raquette[F] de tennis[M]

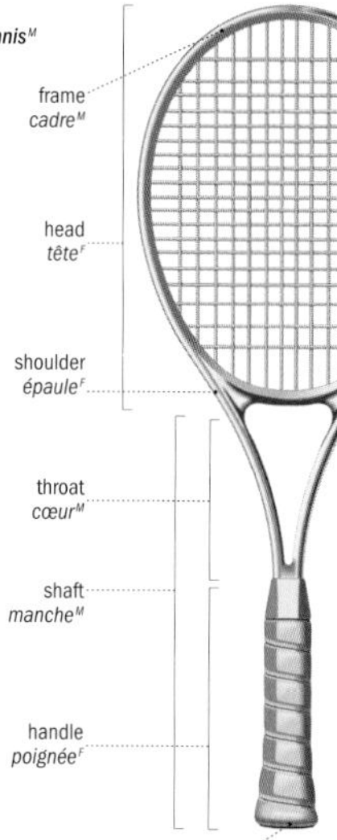

frame
cadre[M]
head
tête[F]
shoulder
épaule[F]
throat
cœur[M]
shaft
manche[M]
handle
poignée[F]
butt
talon[M]
stringing
tamis[M]

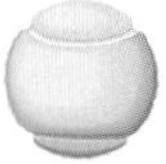

tennis ball
balle[F] de tennis[M]

tennis pla
joueuse[F] de tenni

polo shirt
polo[M]
skirt
jupette[F]
wristband
serre-poignet[M]
sock
chaussette[F]
tennis shoe
chaussure[F] de tennis[M]

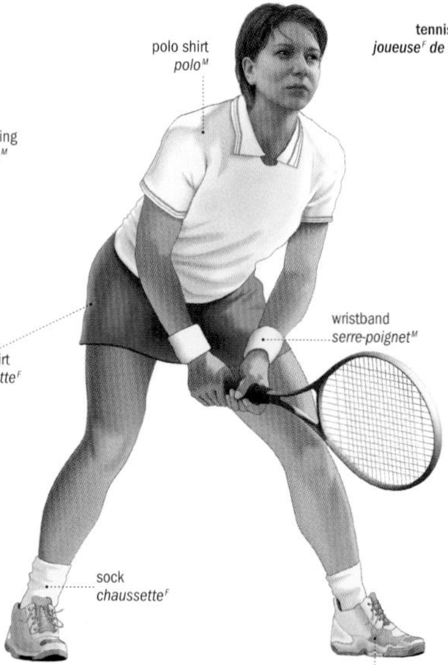

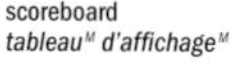

scoreboard
tableau[M] d'affichage[M]

set
manche[F]
previous sets
manches[F] précédentes
points
points[M]
players
joueurs[M]
game
jeu[M]

playing surfaces
surfaces[F] de jeu[M]

grass
gazon[M]

clay
terre[F] battue

hard surface (cement)
surface[F] dure (ciment[M])

synthetic surface
revêtement[M] synthétique

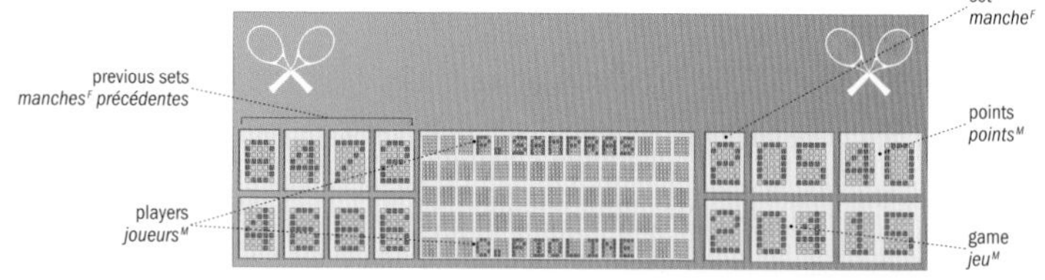

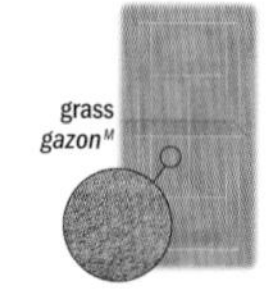

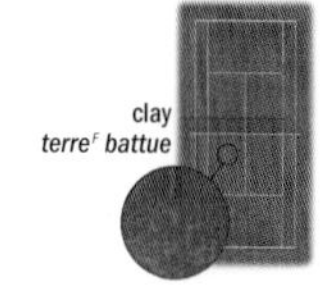

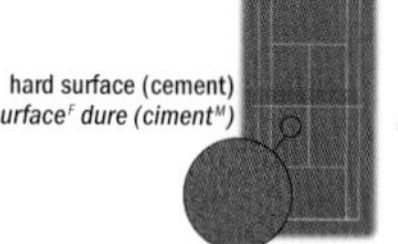

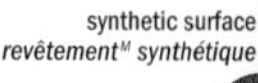

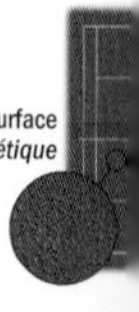

table tennis

tennis[M] de table[F]

table
table[F]

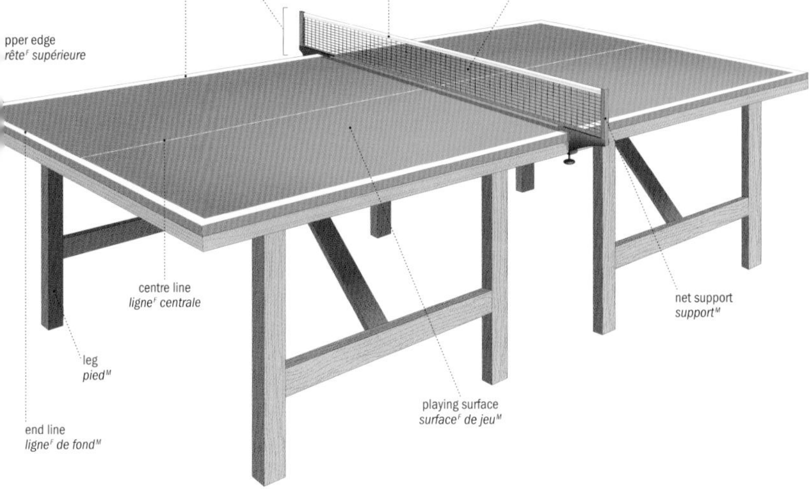

white tape
ruban[M] blanc
mesh
maille[F]
side line
ligne[F] latérale
net
filet[M]
pper edge
rête[F] supérieure
centre line
ligne[F] centrale
net support
support[M]
leg
pied[M]
playing surface
surface[F] de jeu[M]
end line
ligne[F] de fond[M]

e tennis bat
uette[F] de tennis[M] de table[F]

handle
manche[M]
face
face[F]
blade
palette[F]
covering
revêtement[M]

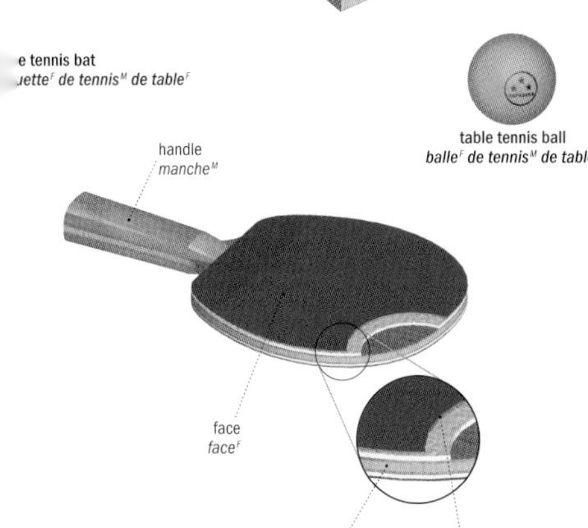

table tennis ball
balle[F] de tennis[M] de table[F]

types of grip
types[M] de prises[F]

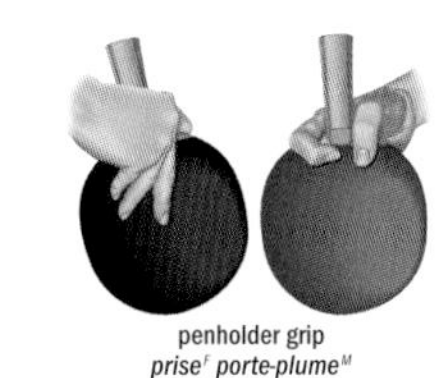

penholder grip
prise[F] porte-plume[M]

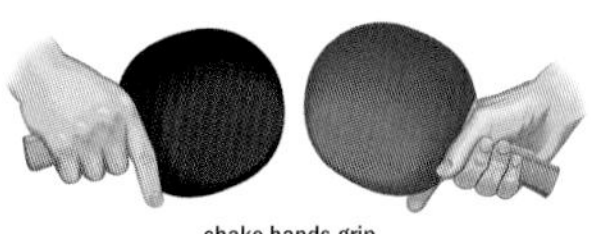

shake-hands grip
prise[F] classique

badminton

badminton[M]

court
terrain[M]

service judge
juge[M] de service[M]

centre line
ligne[F] médiane

linesman
juge[M] de ligne[F]

back boundary line
ligne[F] de fond[M]

long service line
ligne[F] de service[M] long

server
serveur[M]

badminton racket
raquette[F] de badminton[M]

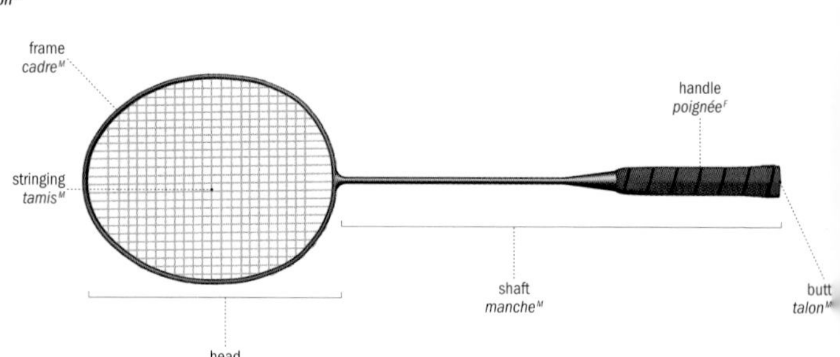

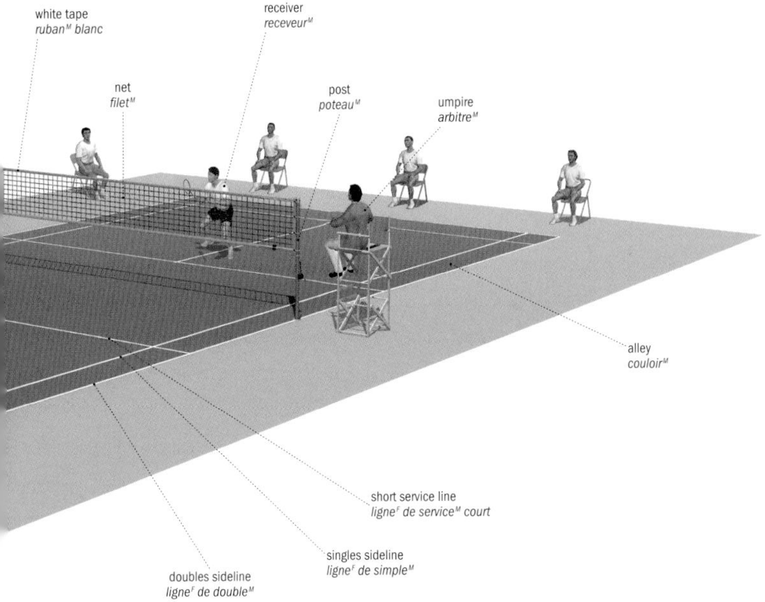

white tape
ruban^M blanc
receiver
receveur^M
net
filet^M
post
poteau^M
umpire
arbitre^M
alley
couloir^M
short service line
ligne^F de service^M court
singles sideline
ligne^F de simple^M
doubles sideline
ligne^F de double^M

service zones
zones^F de service^M

doubles service court
demi-court^M de service^M en double^M
singles service court
demi-court^M de service^M en simple^M

synthetic shuttlecock
volant^M synthétique

feathered shuttlecock
volant^M de plumes^F

feather crown
empennage^M
cork tip
tête^F en liège^M

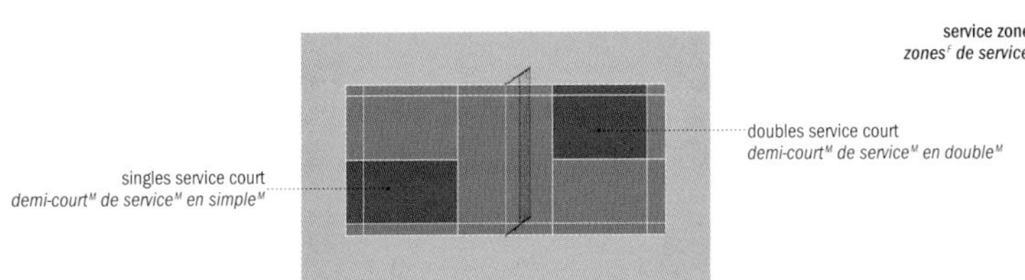

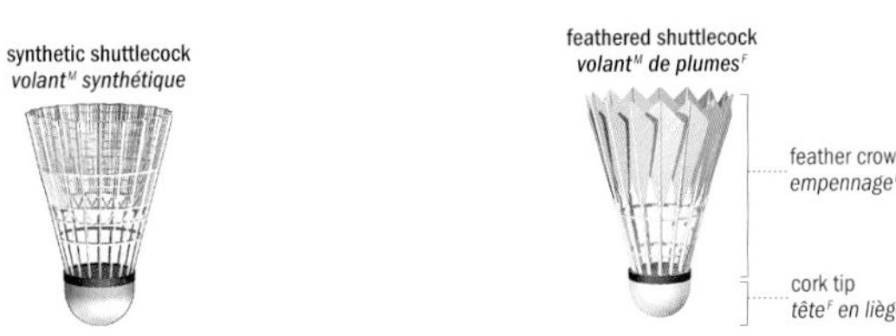

gymnastics

gymnastique[F]

event platform
podium[M] des épreuves[F]

overall standings scoreboard
tableau[M] de classement[M] général

balance beam
poutre[F]

floor exercise a
praticable[M] pour exercices

asymmetrical bars
barres[F] asymétriques

pommel horse
cheval[M] d'arçons[M]

line judge
juge[M] de ligne[F]

judges
juges[M]

floor mats
tapis[M] de réception[F]

horizontal bar
barre[F] fixe

vaulting horse
cheval[M] sautoir[M]

approach runs
pistes[F] d'élan[M]

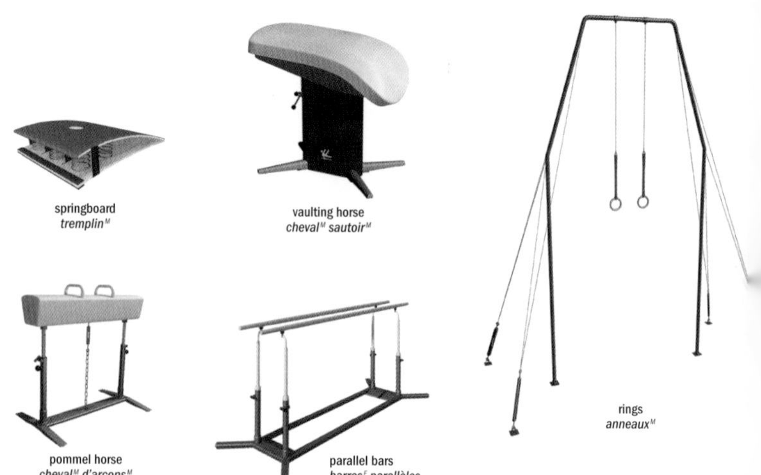

gymnastics

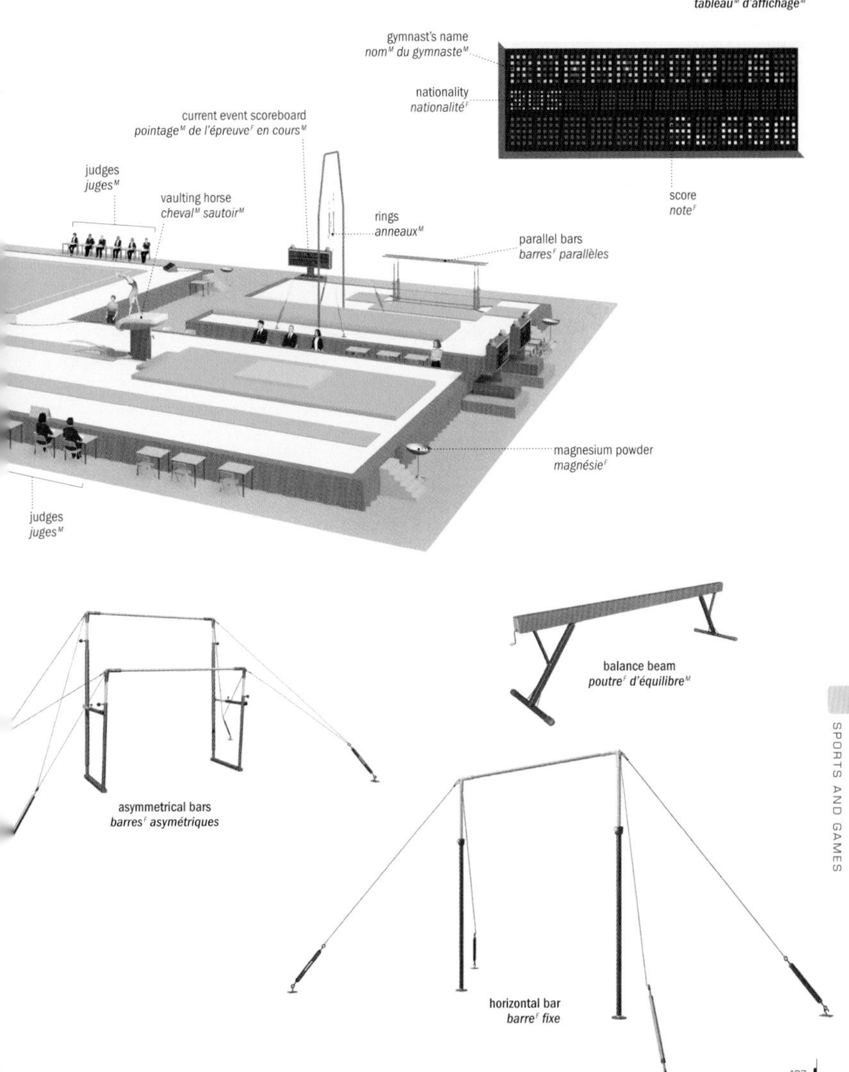
scoreboard
tableau d'affichage
gymnast's name
nom du gymnaste
nationality
nationalité
current event scoreboard
pointage de l'épreuve en cours
judges
juges
vaulting horse
cheval sautoir
rings
anneaux
parallel bars
barres parallèles
score
note
magnesium powder
magnésie
judges
juges
balance beam
poutre d'équilibre
asymmetrical bars
barres asymétriques
horizontal bar
barre fixe

boxing

boxe[F]

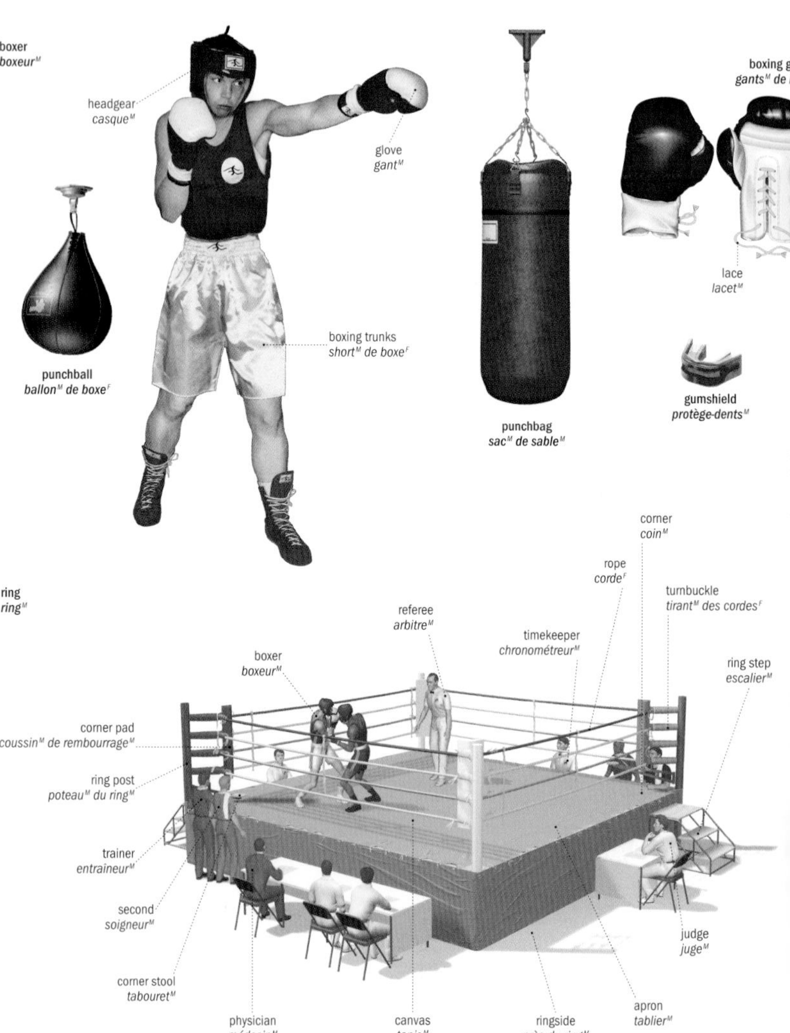

judo
judo[M]

scorers and timekeepers
marqueurs[M] et chronométreurs[M]
mat
tapis[M]
medical team
équipe[F] médicale
contestant
combattant[M]
safety area
surface[F] de sécurité[F]
danger area
zone[F] de danger[M]
scoreboard
tableau[M] d'affichage[M]
contest area
surface[F] de combat[M]
referee
arbitre[M]
judge
juge[M]
examples of holds
exemples[M] de prises[F]
gi
gi[M]
jacket
veste[F]
holding
immobilisation[F]
stomach throw
projection[F] en cercle[M]
sweeping hip throw
hanche[F] ailée
major outer reaping throw
grand fauchage[M] extérieur
major inner reaping throw
grand fauchage[M] intérieur
naked strangle
étranglement[M]
trousers
pantalon[M]
belt
ceinture[F]
arm lock
clé[F] de bras[M]
one-arm shoulder throw
projection[F] d'épaule[F] par un côté[M]

weightlifting

haltérophilie[F]

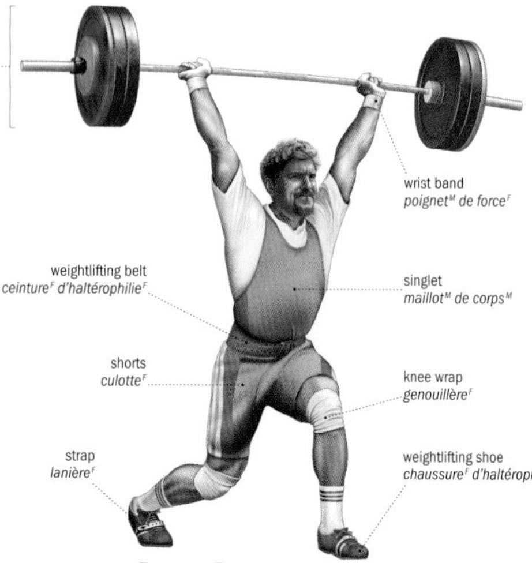

barbell
haltère[M] long
wrist band
poignet[M] de force[F]
weightlifting belt
ceinture[F] d'haltérophilie[F]
singlet
maillot[M] de corps[M]
shorts
culotte[F]
knee wrap
genouillère[F]
strap
lanière[F]
weightlifting shoe
chaussure[F] d'haltérophilie[F]

clean and jerk
épaulé[M]-jeté[M]

s
arr

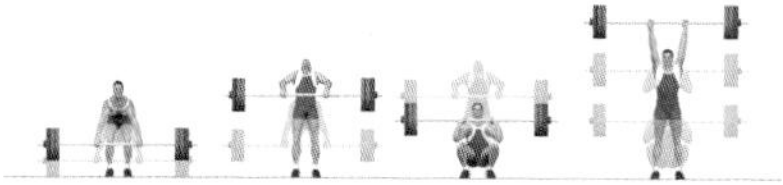

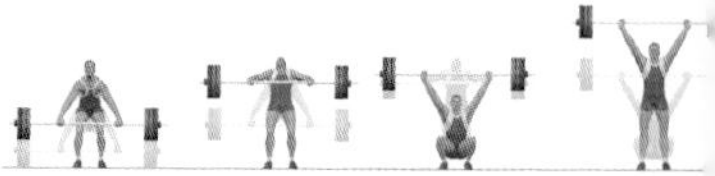

fitness equipment

appareils[M] de conditionnement[M] physique

dumbbell
haltère[M] court

bar
barre[F]
weight
poids[M]

handgrips
poignées[F] à ressort[M]

ankle/wrist weight
bracelet[M] lesté

skipping-rope
corde[F] à sauter

twist bar
ressort[M] athlétique

tension spring
ressort[M] de tension[F]
grip
poignée[F]

chest expander
extenseur[M]

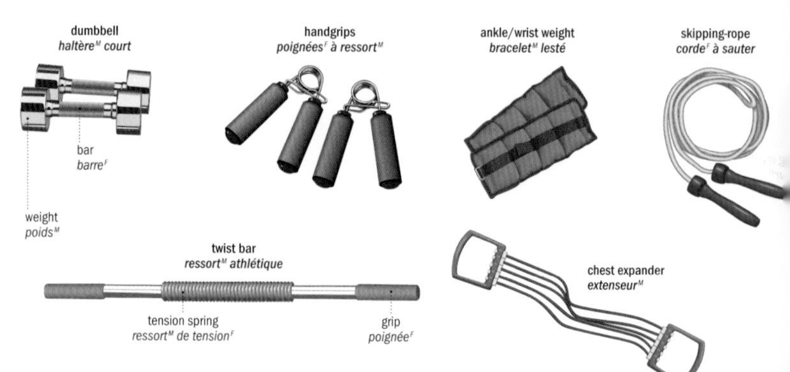

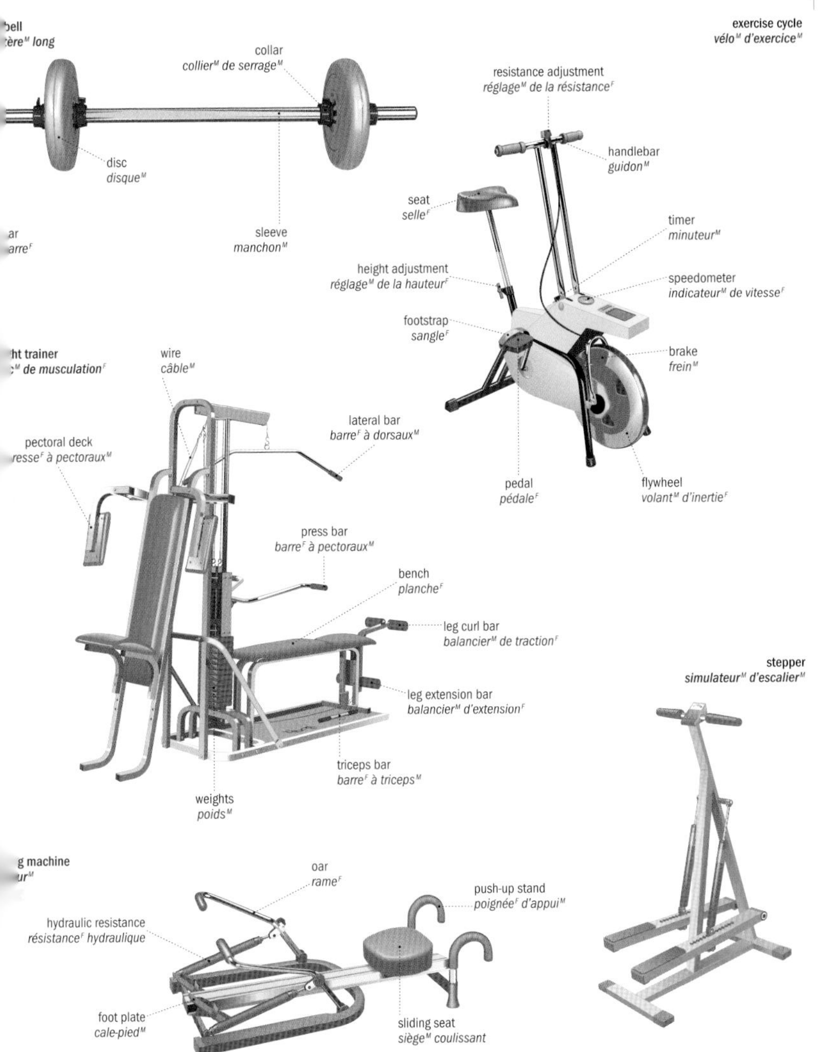
bell
ère[M] long
collar
collier[M] de serrage[M]
disc
disque[M]
ar
arre[F]
sleeve
manchon[M]
exercise cycle
vélo[M] d'exercice[M]
resistance adjustment
réglage[M] de la résistance[F]
handlebar
guidon[M]
seat
selle[F]
timer
minuteur[M]
height adjustment
réglage[M] de la hauteur[F]
speedometer
indicateur[M] de vitesse[F]
footstrap
sangle[F]
brake
frein[M]
pedal
pédale[F]
flywheel
volant[M] d'inertie[F]
ht trainer
[M] de musculation[F]
wire
câble[M]
pectoral deck
resse[F] à pectoraux[M]
lateral bar
barre[F] à dorsaux[M]
press bar
barre[F] à pectoraux[M]
bench
planche[F]
leg curl bar
balancier[M] de traction[F]
leg extension bar
balancier[M] d'extension[F]
triceps bar
barre[F] à triceps[M]
weights
poids[M]
stepper
simulateur[M] d'escalier[M]
g machine
ur[M]
oar
rame[F]
push-up stand
poignée[F] d'appui[M]
hydraulic resistance
résistance[F] hydraulique
foot plate
cale-pied[M]
sliding seat
siège[M] coulissant

billiards

billard^{M}

carom billiards
billard^{M} français

cue ball
bille^{F} de choc^{M}

red ball
bille^{F} rouge

white spot ball
bille^{F} de visée^{F} blanche

billard^{M}

object balls
billes^{F} numérotées

pocket
poche^{F}

cue ball
bille^{F} de choc^{M}

table
table^{F}

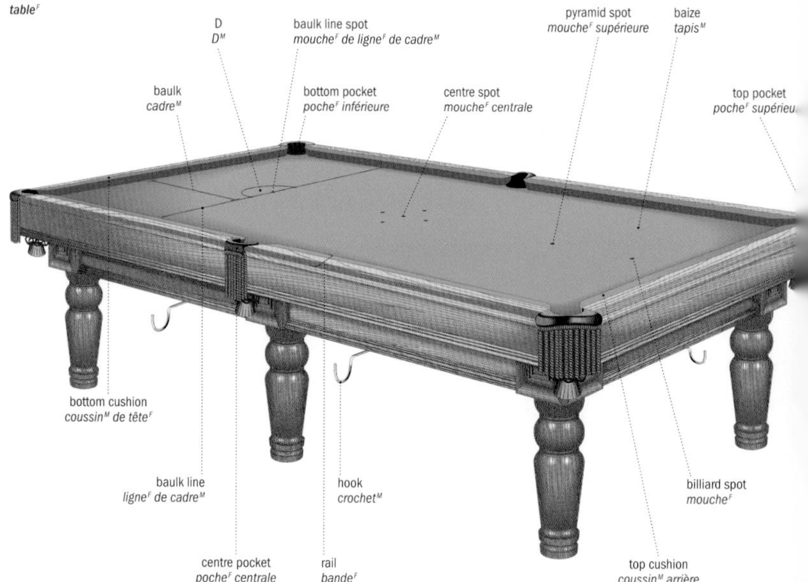

SPORTS AND GAMES

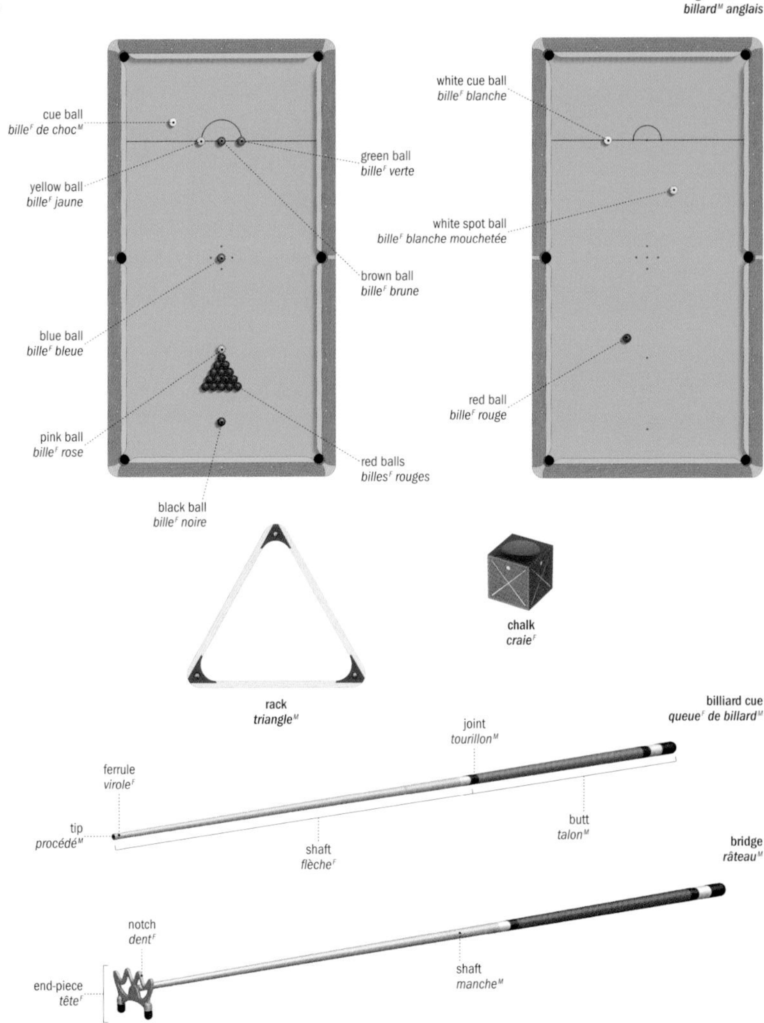
ɔoker
ɔoker
English billiards
billard anglais
cue ball
bille de choc
yellow ball
bille jaune
green ball
bille verte
brown ball
bille brune
blue ball
bille bleue
pink ball
bille rose
red balls
billes rouges
black ball
bille noire
white cue ball
bille blanche
white spot ball
bille blanche mouchetée
red ball
bille rouge
chalk
craie
rack
triangle
billiard cue
queue de billard
joint
tourillon
ferrule
virole
tip
procédé
shaft
flèche
butt
talon
bridge
râteau
notch
dent
end-piece
tête
shaft
manche

golf

golf[M]

course
parcours[M]

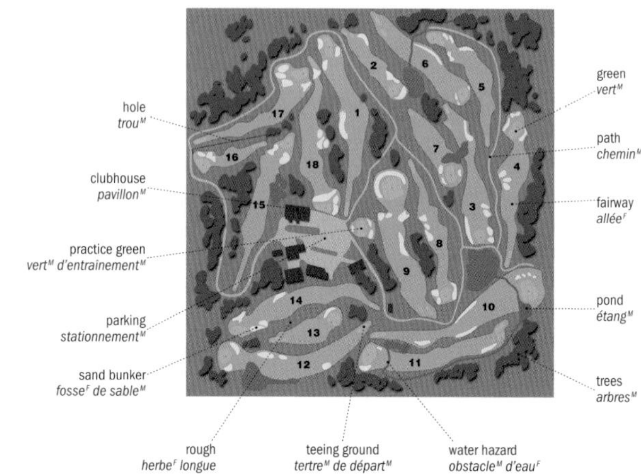

par 5 hole
trou[M] de normale[F] 5

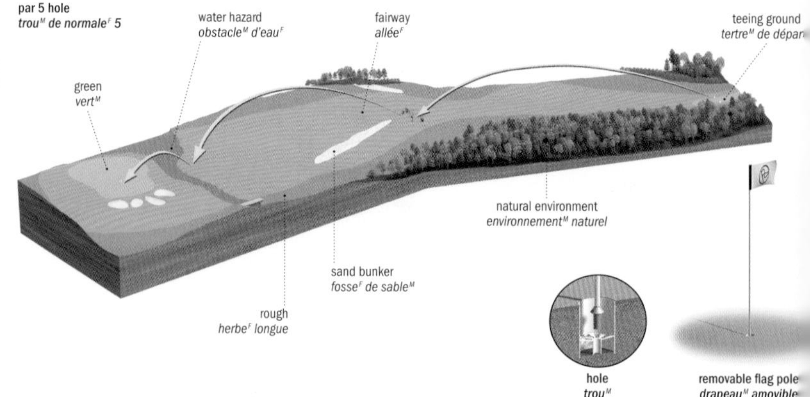

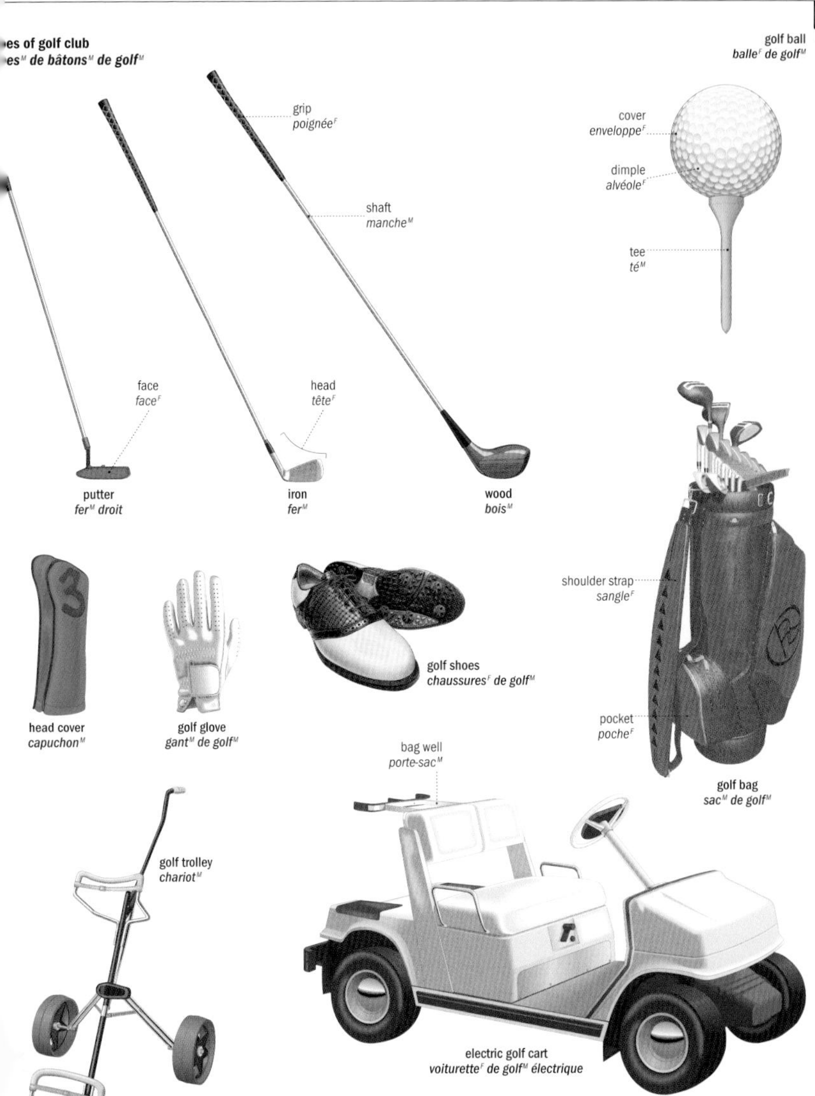

SPORTS AND GAMES

ice hockey

hockey[M] sur glace[F]

ice hockey player
hockeyeur[M]

helmet
casque[M]
visor
visière[F]
player's number
numéro[M] du joueur[M]
team's emblem
emblème[M] d'équipe[F]
glove
gant[M]
trousers
culotte[F]
stocking
bas[M]
skate
patin[M]
blade
lame[F]

player's s
crosse[F] de jou

butt end
embout[M]
shaft
manche[M]
heel
talon[M]
blade
lame[F]

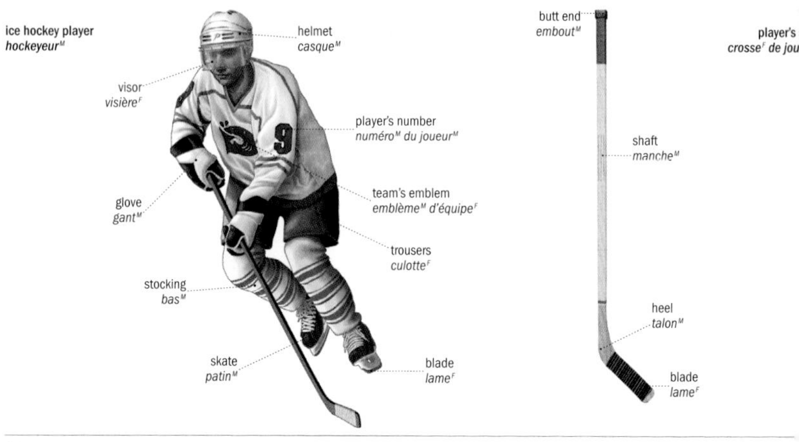

rink
patinoire[F]

face-off spot
point[M] de mise[F] au jeu[M]
right defence
défenseur[M] droit
left defence
défenseur[M] gauche
goal line
ligne[F] de but[M]
glass protector
vitre[F] de protection[F]
players' bench
banc[M] des joueurs[M]
rink corner
coin[M] de patinoire[F]
goal judge
juge[M] de but[M]
goalkeeper
gardien[M] de but[M]
boards
bande[F]
face-off circle
cercle[M] de mise[F] au jeu[M]

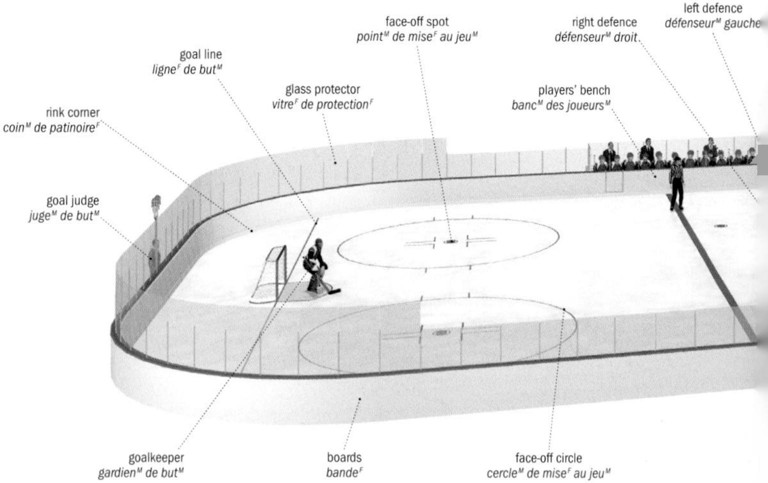

oalkeeper
ardien^{M} de but^{M}

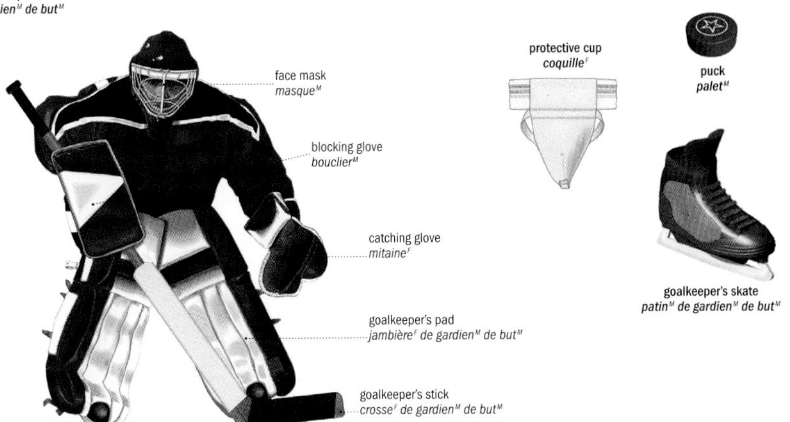

ving
-^{M} gauche

coach
entraîneur^{M}

assistant coach
entraîneur^{M} adjoint

goal crease
zone^{F} de but^{M}

blue line
ligne^{F} bleue

referee
arbitre^{M}

goal
but^{M}

neutral zone
zone^{F} neutre

linesman
juge^{M} de ligne^{F}

goal lights
lumières^{F} de but^{M}

penalty bench official
préposé^{M} au banc^{M} des pénalités^{F}

penalty bench
banc^{M} des pénalités^{F}

centre line
ligne^{F} centrale

centre face-off circle
cercle^{M} central

tre
tre^{M}

right wing
ailier^{M} droit

officials' bench
banc^{M} des officiels^{M}

speed skating

patinage[M] de vitesse[F]

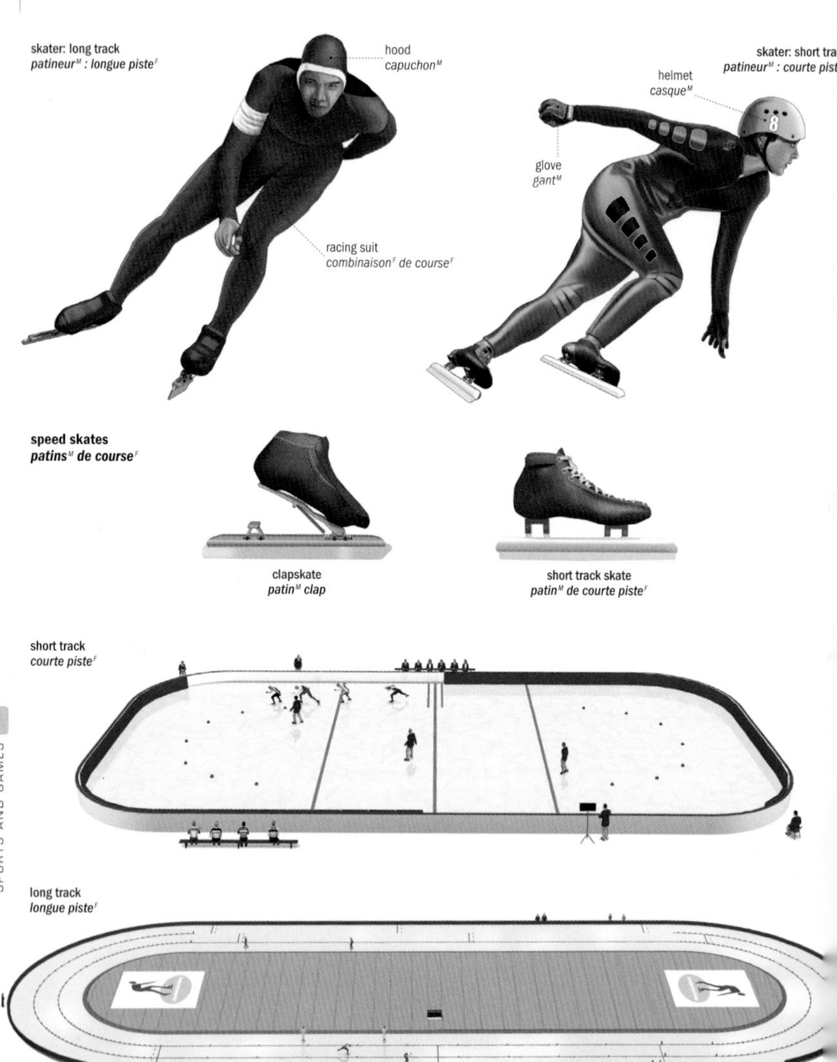

figure skating

patinage[M] artistique

figure skate
patin[M] de figure[F]

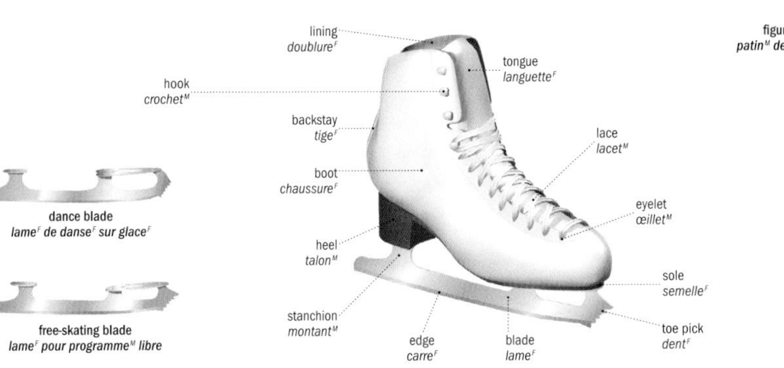

examples of jumps
exemples[M] de sauts[M]

rink
patinoire[F]

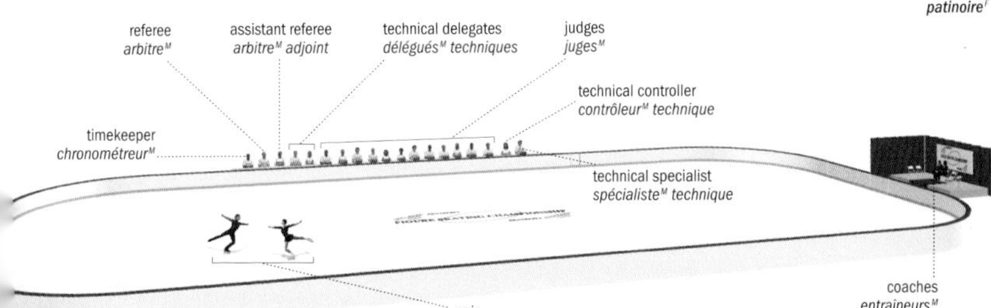

SPORTS AND GAMES

alpine skiing

ski[M] alpin

alpine skier
skieur[M] alpin

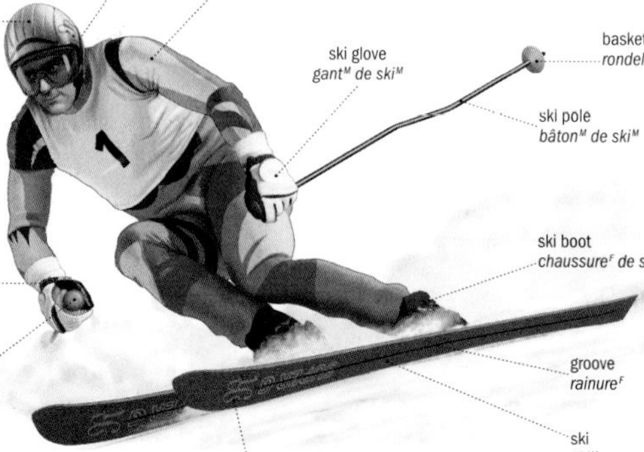

ski goggles
lunettes[F] de ski[M]

ski suit
combinaison[F] de ski[M]

helmet
casque[M]

basket
rondelle[F]

ski glove
gant[M] de ski[M]

ski pole
bâton[M] de ski[M]

ski boot
chaussure[F] de ski[M]

wrist strap
dragonne[F]

handle
poignée[F]

groove
rainure[F]

ski
ski[M]

bottom face
semelle[F]

safety binding
fixation[F] de sécurité[F]

tip
pointe[F]

t
talo

shovel
spatule[F]

edge
carre[F]

ski
ski[M]

examples of skis
exemples[M] de skis[M]

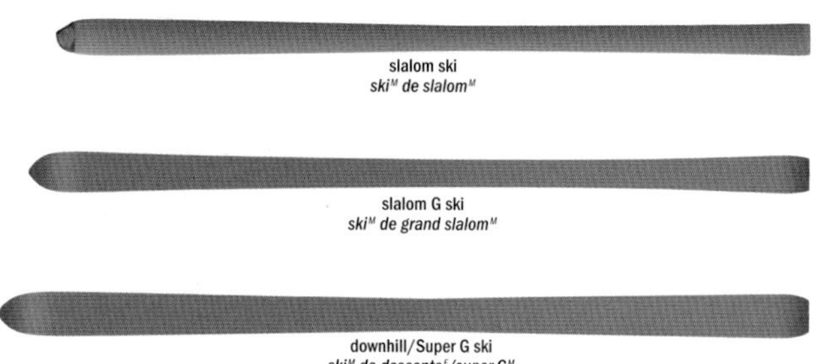

slalom ski
ski[M] de slalom[M]

slalom G ski
ski[M] de grand slalom[M]

downhill/Super G ski
ski[M] de descente[F]/super-G[M]

technical events
*épreuves*ᶠ

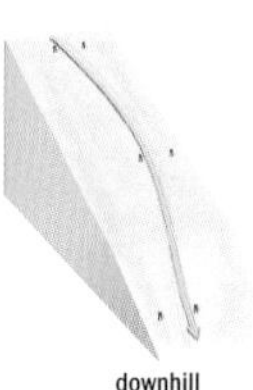

downhill
*descente*ᶠ

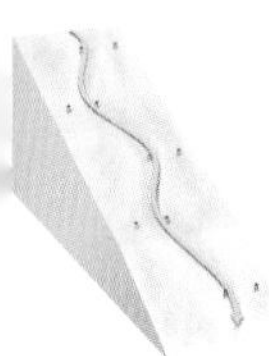

super giant slalom
*super-géant*ᴹ

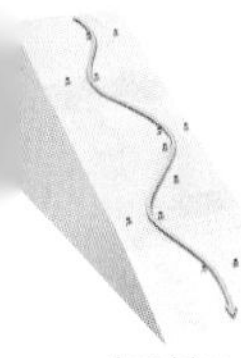

giant slalom
*slalom*ᴹ *géant*

special slalom
*slalom*ᴹ *spécial*

ski boot
*chaussure*ᶠ *de ski*ᴹ

safety binding
*fixation*ᶠ *de sécurité*ᶠ

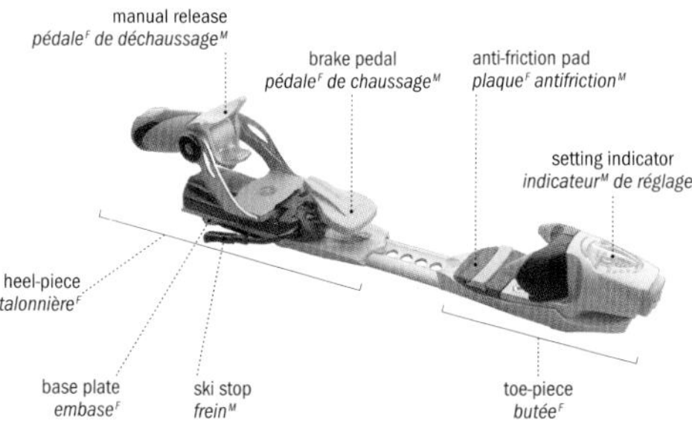

ski resort

station^F de ski^M

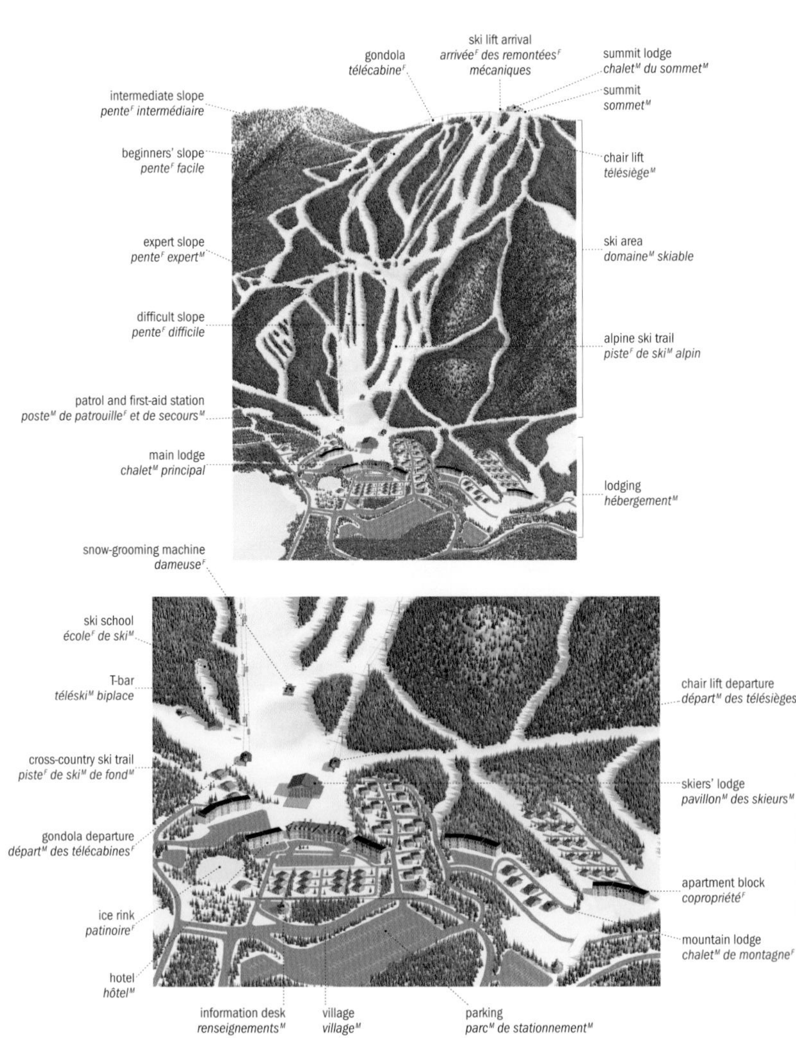

snowboarding

surf[M] des neiges[F]

snowboarder
surfeur[M]

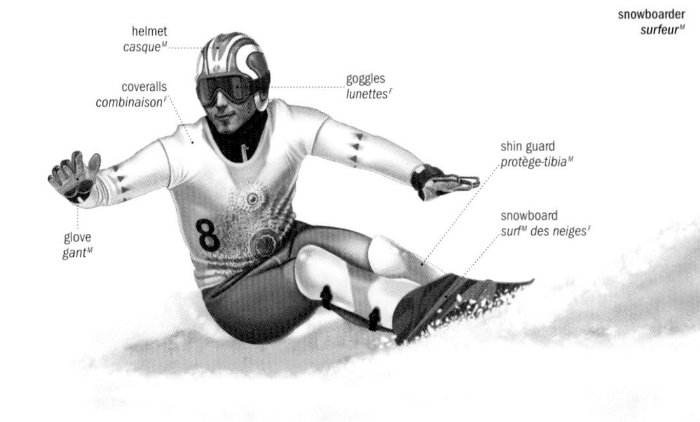

hard boot
botte[F] rigide

flexible boot
botte[F] souple

eestyle snowboard
urf[M] acrobatique

alpine snowboard
surf[M] alpin

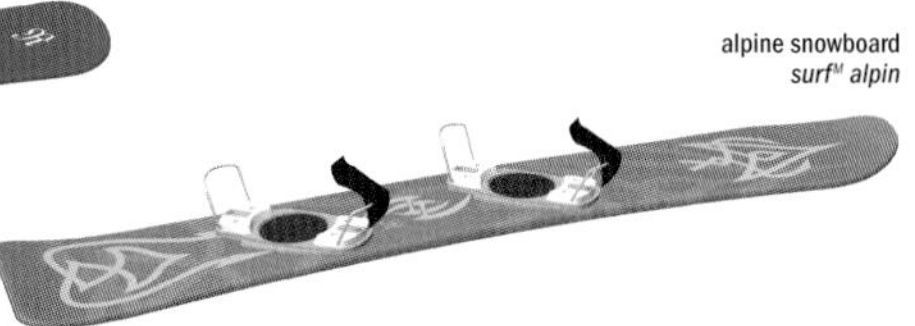

ski jumping

saut[M] à ski[M]

ski jumper
sauteur[M]

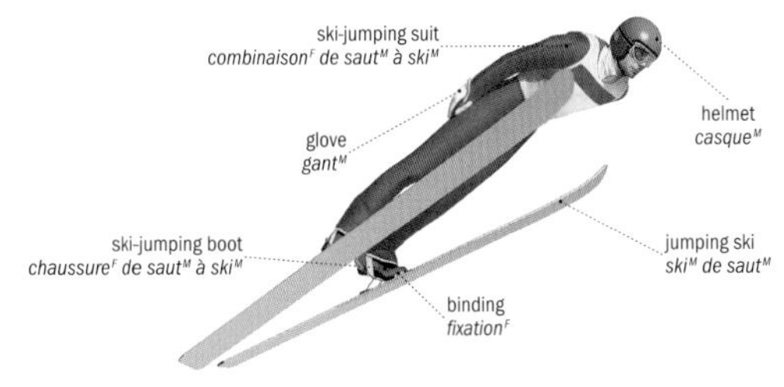

cross-country skiing

ski^M de fond^M

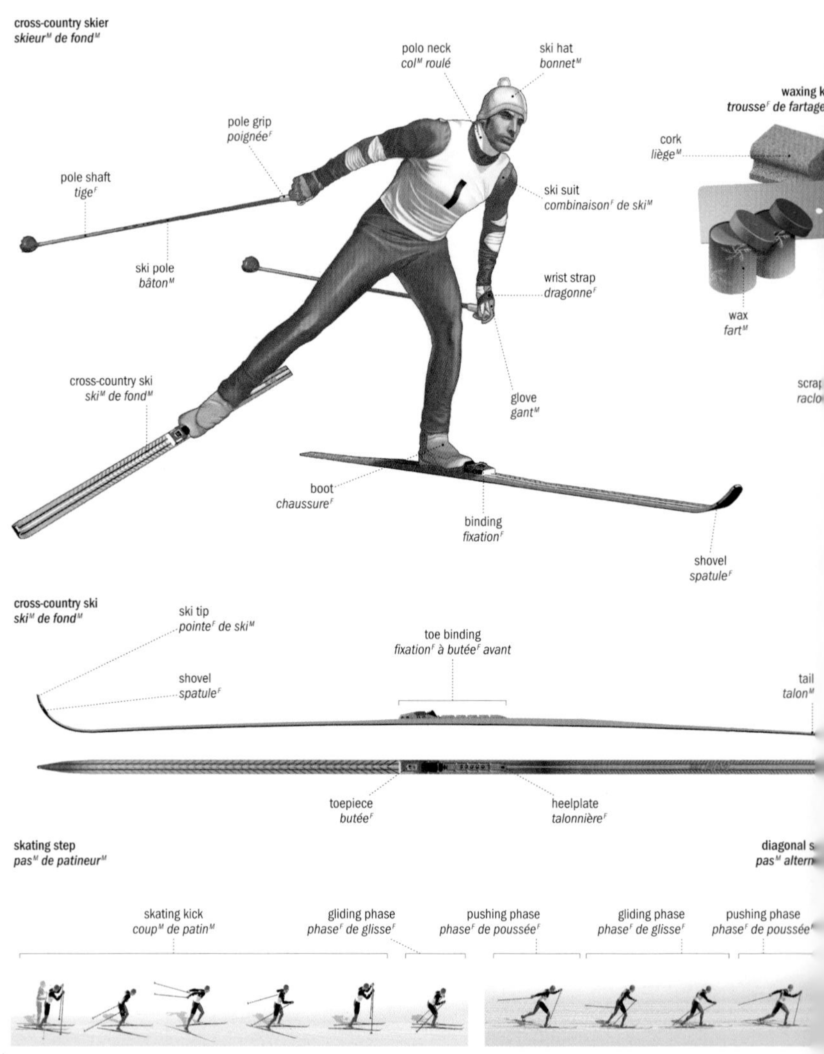

curling

curling[M]

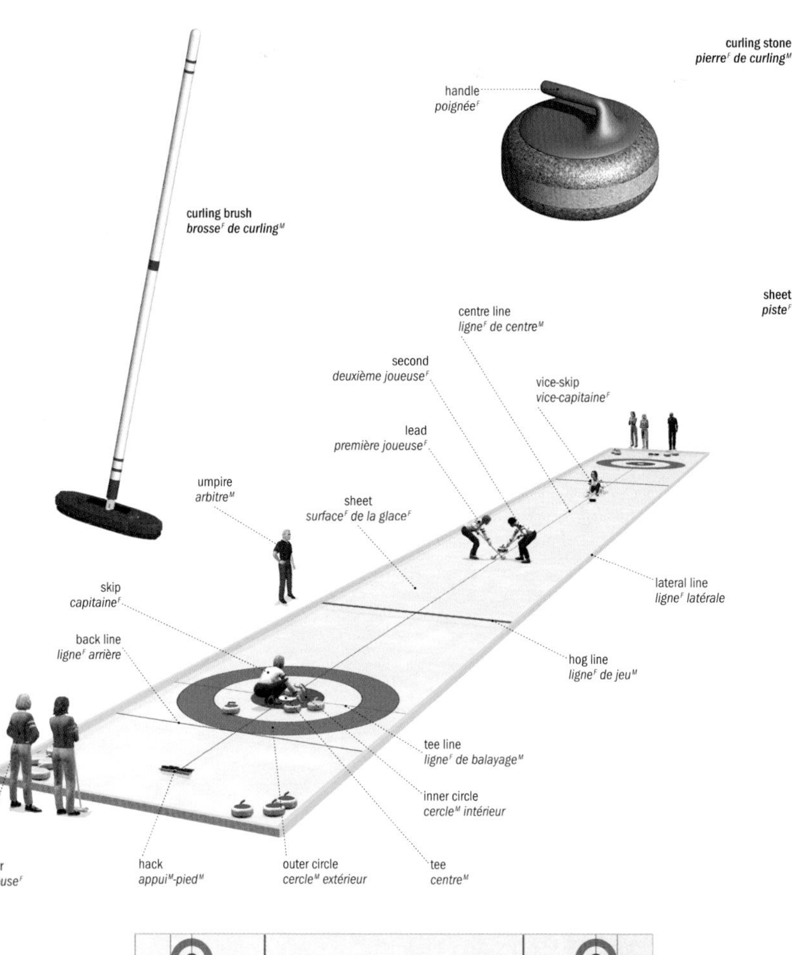

swimming

natation[F]

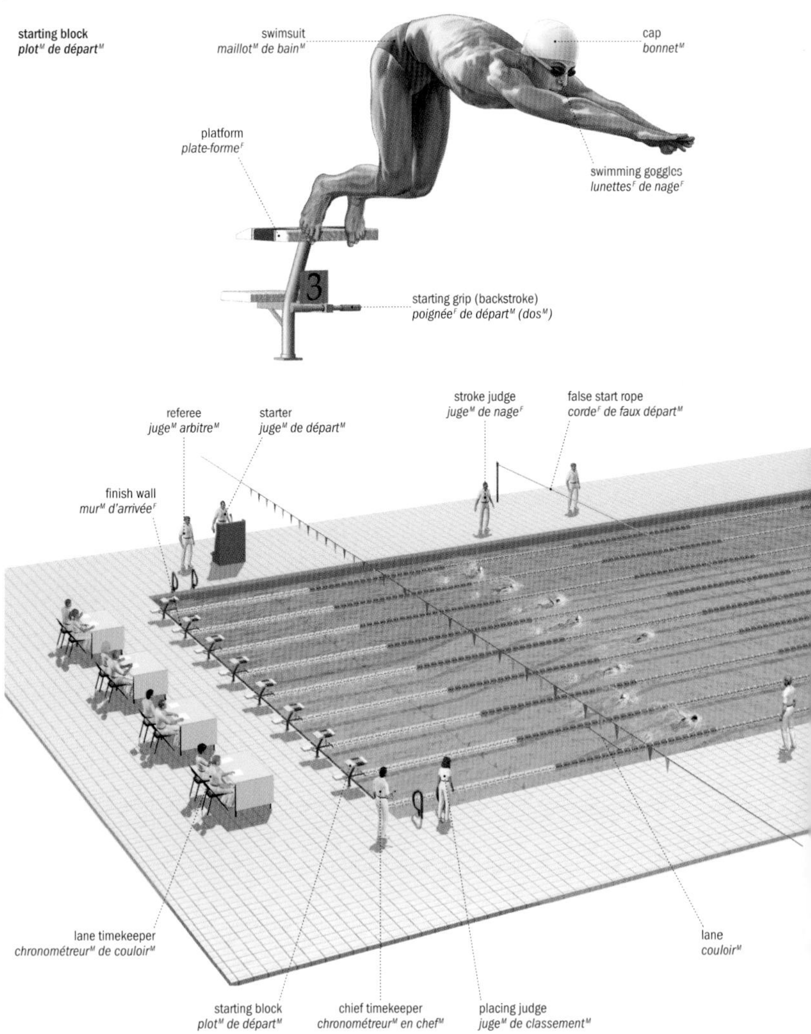

types of stroke
***types*[M] *de nages*[F]**

rawl stroke
rawl[M]

butterfly stroke
papillon[M]

eastsstroke
asse[F]

backstroke
nage[F] *sur le dos*[M]

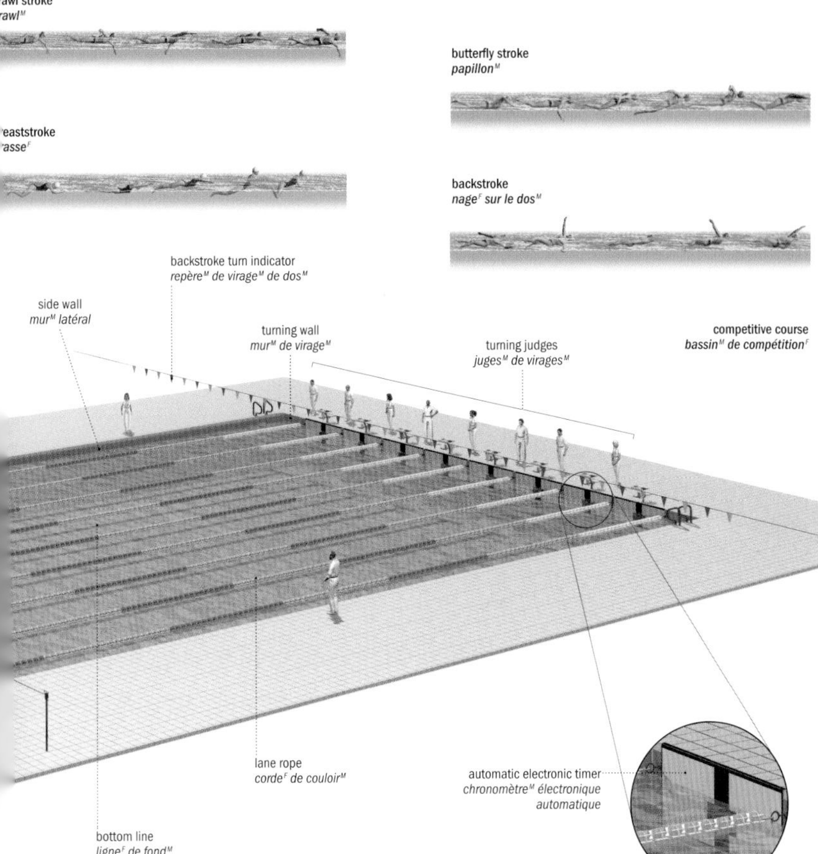

mming pool
ssin[M]

diving

plongeon[M]

starting positions
positions[F] de départ[M]

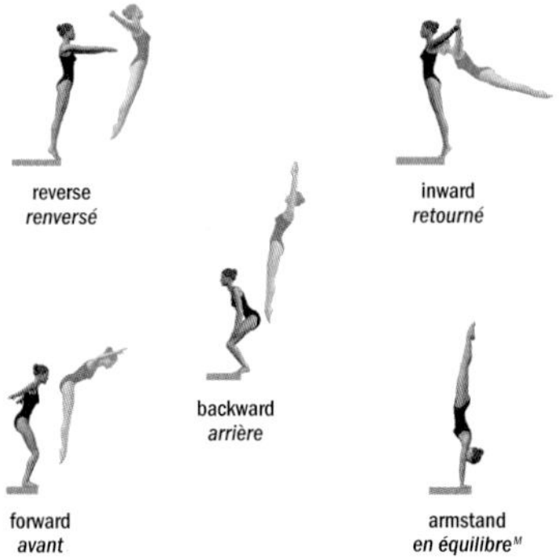

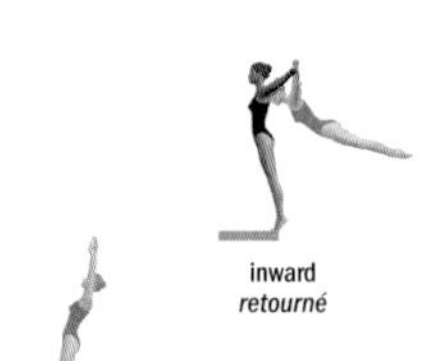

reverse
renversé
inward
retourné
backward
arrière
forward
avant
armstand
en équilibre[M]

flights
vols[M]

tuck position
position[F] groupée
straight position
position[F] droite
pike position
position[F] carpée

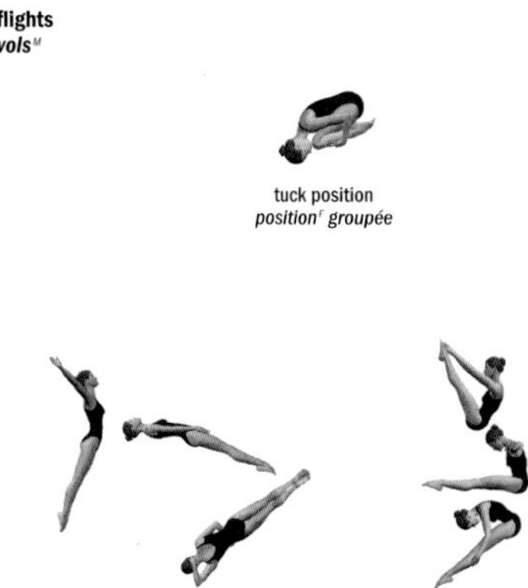

diving apparatus
plongeoir[M]

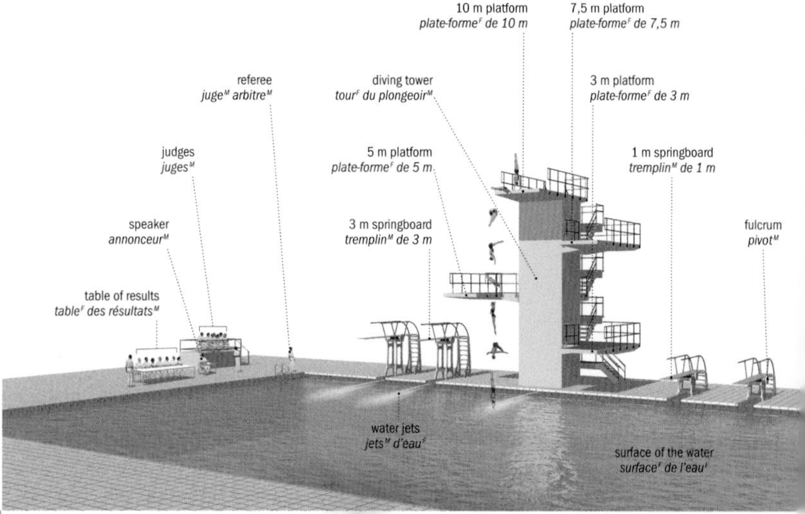

10 m platform
plate-forme[F] de 10 m
7,5 m platform
plate-forme[F] de 7,5 m
referee
juge[M] arbitre[M]
diving tower
tour[F] du plongeoir[M]
3 m platform
plate-forme[F] de 3 m
judges
juges[M]
5 m platform
plate-forme[F] de 5 m
1 m springboard
tremplin[M] de 1 m
speaker
annonceur[M]
3 m springboard
tremplin[M] de 3 m
fulcrum
pivot[M]
table of results
table[F] des résultats[M]
water jets
jets[M] d'eau[F]
surface of the water
surface[F] de l'eau[F]

sailboard

planche[F] à voile[F]

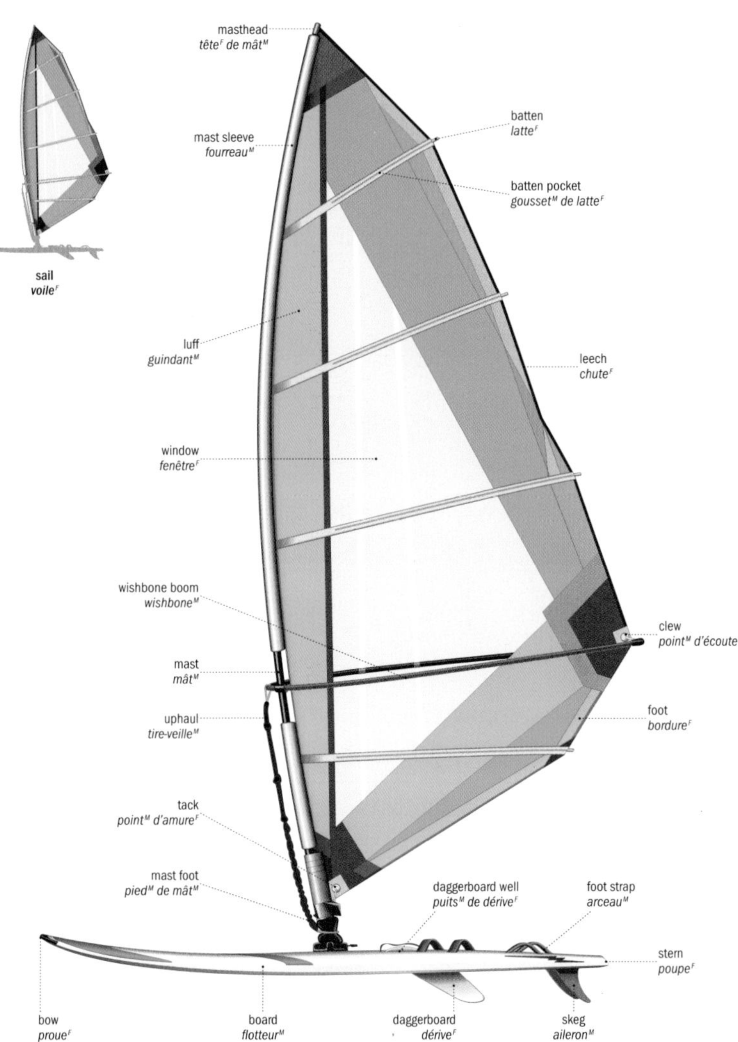

sailing

voile[F]

sailing boat
dériveur[M]

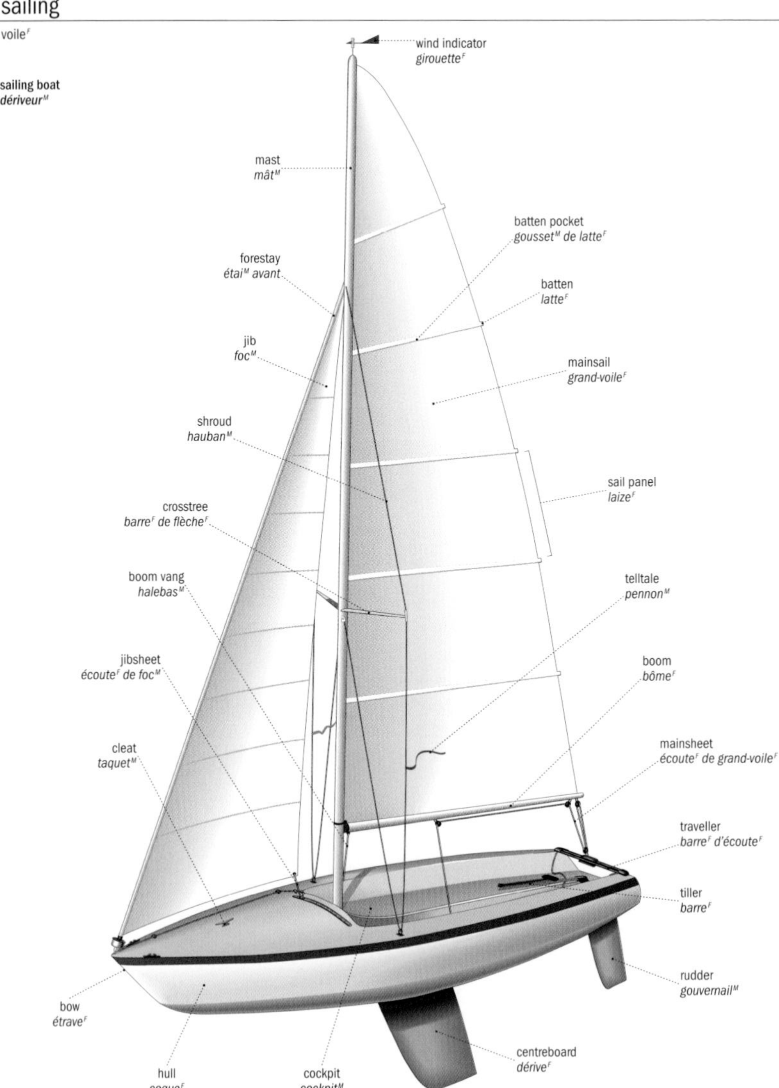

ulti-hulls
ulticoques^{M}

trimaran
trimaran^{M}

catamaran
catamaran^{M}

mono-hulls
monocoques^{M}

centreboard boat
dériveur^{M}

keel boat
quillard^{M}

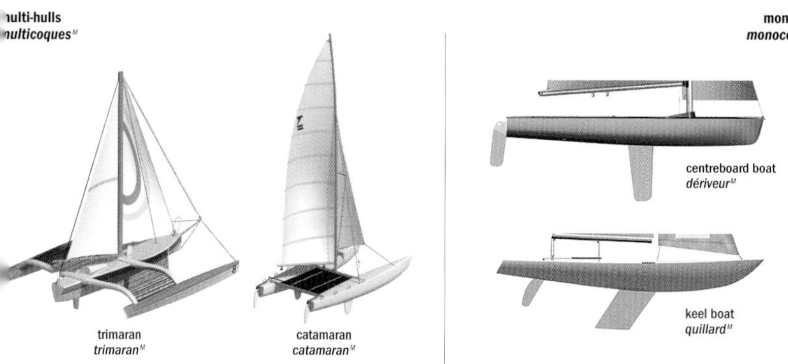

upperworks
accastillage^{M}

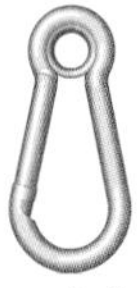

snap shackle
mousqueton^{M} *à ressort*^{M}

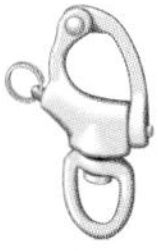

hank
mousqueton^{M}

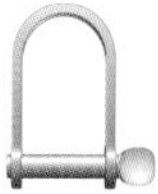

shackle
manille^{F}

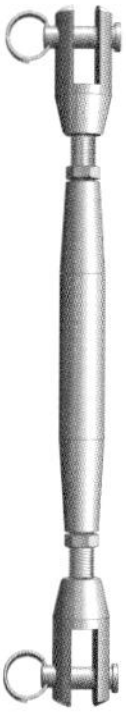

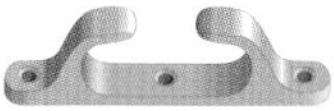

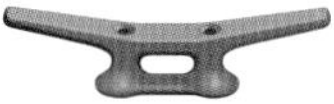

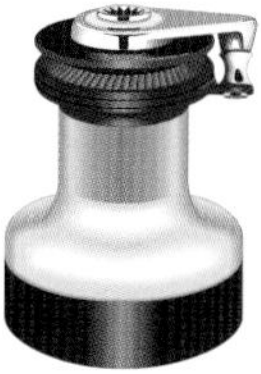

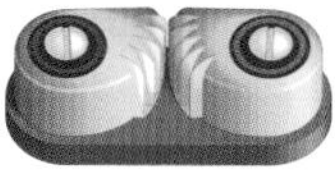

turnbuckle
ridoir^{M}

fairlead
chaumard^{M}

cleat
taquet^{M}

winch
winch^{M}

clam cleat
taquet^{M} *coinceur*

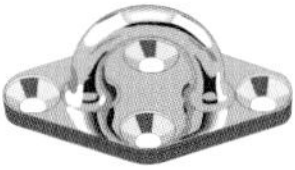

sheet lead
filoir^{M} *d'écoute*^{F}

traveller
barre^{F} *d'écoute*^{F}

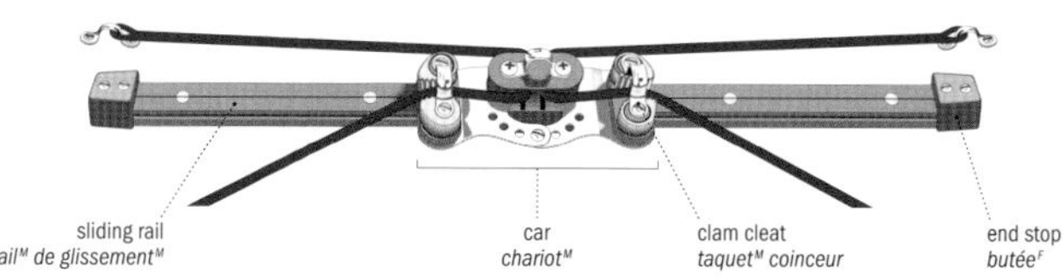

road racing

cyclisme^{M} sur route^{F}

road-racing bicycle and cyclist
vélo^{M} de course^{F} et cycliste^{M}

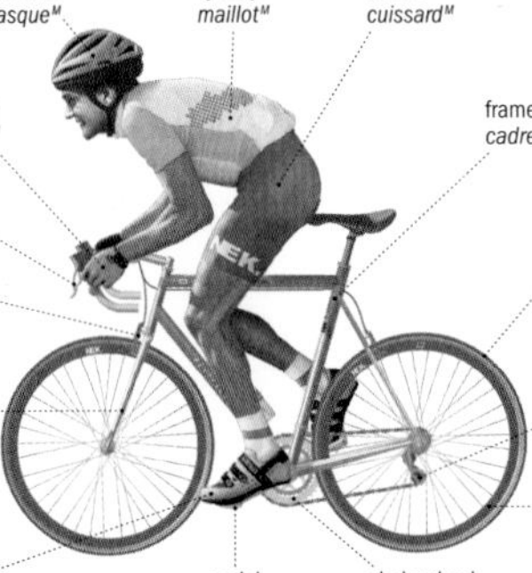

helmet
casque^{M}
jersey
maillot^{M}
shorts
cuissard^{M}
glove
gant^{M}
frame
cadre^{M}
brake lever and shifter
poignée^{F} de frein^{M} et manette^{F} de dérailleur^{M}
tyre
pneu^{M}
brake
frein^{M}
derailleur
dérailleur^{M}
fork
fourche^{F}
wheel
roue^{F}
shoe
chaussure^{F}
pedal
pédale^{F}
chain wheel
plateau^{M}

road cycling competition
compétition^{F} de cyclisme^{M} sur route^{F}

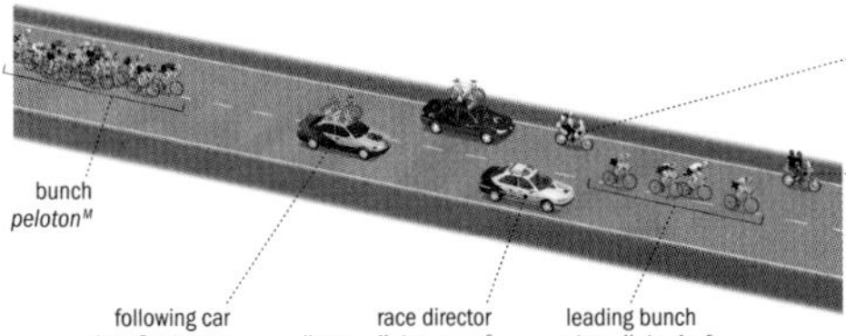

motorcycle-mounted camera
moto^{F}-caméra^{F}
leading motorcycle
moto^{F} de tête^{F}
bunch
peloton^{M}
following car
voiture^{F} suiveuse
race director
directeur^{M} de course^{F}
leading bunch
peloton^{M} de tête^{F}

mountain biking

vélo^{M} de montagne^{F}

cross-country bicycle and cyclist
vélo^{M} de cross-country^{M} et cycliste^{M}

goggles
lunettes^{F}
back suspension
suspension^{F} arrière
front fork
fourche^{F} avant
clipless pedal
pédale^{F} automatique

downhill bicycle and c
vélo^{M} de descen
cyc

protective goggles
lunettes^{F} de protection^{F}
chin strap
mentonnière^{F}
raised handlebar
guidon^{M} surélevé
pedal with wide platform
pédale^{F} avec cale^{F} élargie
hydraulic disc brake
frein^{M} hydraulique à d

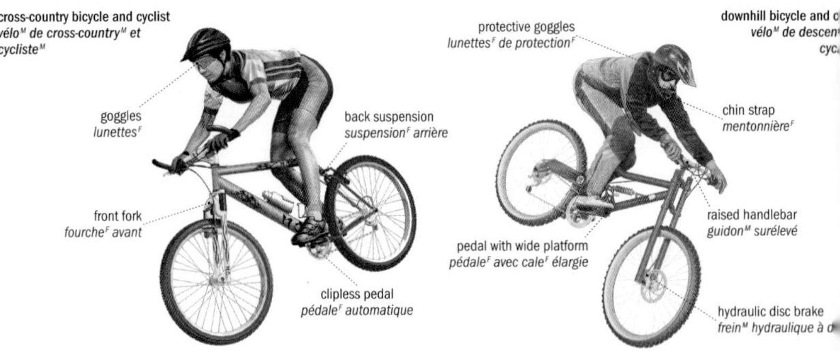

personal watercraft

scooter[M] de mer[F]

handlebar
guidon[M]
mirror
rétroviseur[M]
seat
selle[F]
sponson
stabilisateur[M]
hull
coque[F]

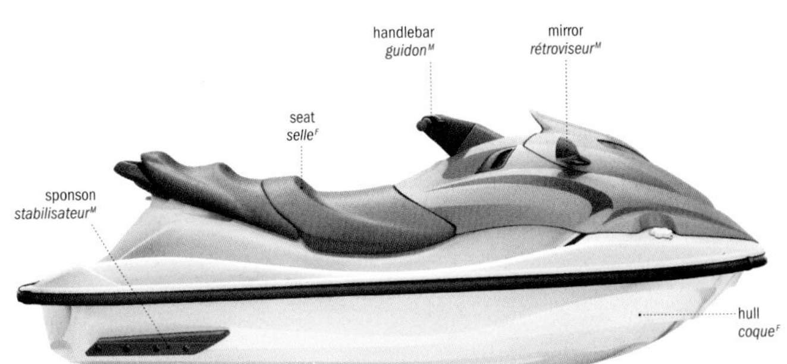

snowmobile

motoneige[F]

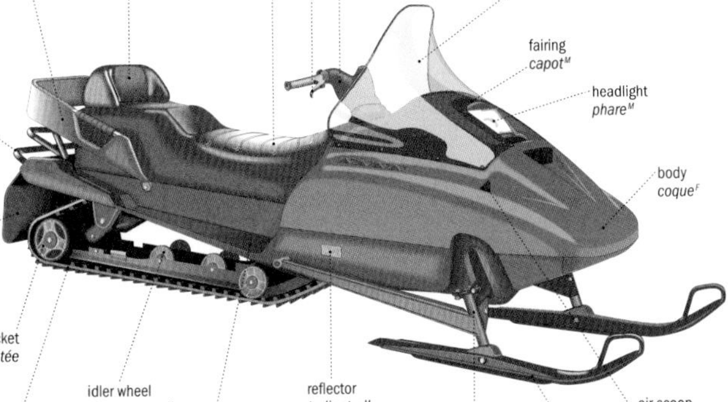

seat
selle[F]
brake handle
manette[F] du frein[M]
luggage rack
support[M] à bagages[M]
backrest
dossier[M]
handlebars
guidon[M]
windscreen
pare-brise[M]
rear bumper
pare-chocs[M] arrière
fairing
capot[M]
headlight
phare[M]
body
coque[F]
snow guard
bavette[F] garde-neige[M]
sprocket
roue[F] dentée
idler wheel
roue[F] de support[M]
reflector
catadioptre[M]
air scoop
prise[F] d'air[M]
track
chenille[F]
footboard
marchepied[M]
shock absorber
amortisseur[M]
ski
ski[M]

motor racing

course[F] automobile

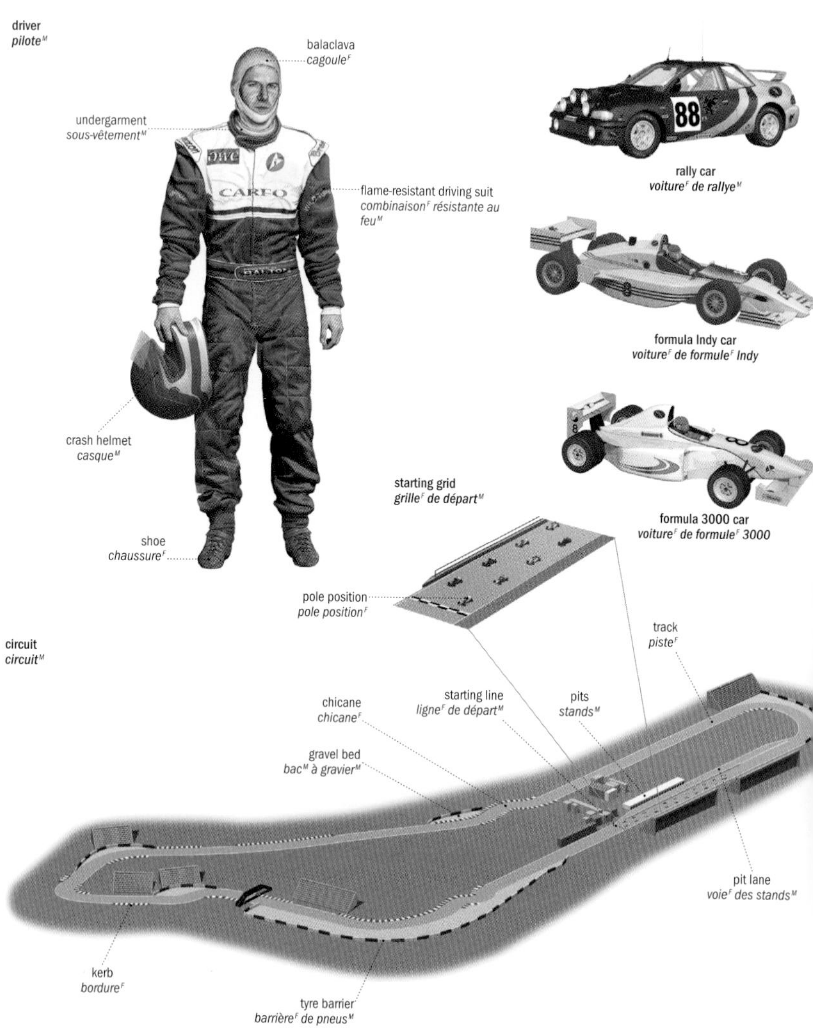

formula 1 car
voiture[F] de formule[F] 1

wing
aileron[M]
camera
caméra[F]
cockpit
habitacle[M]
radio antenna
antenne[F] radio[F]
Pitot tube
tube[M] de Pitot
side fairings
ponton[M]
roll structure
structure[F] antitonneau
steering wheel
volant[M]

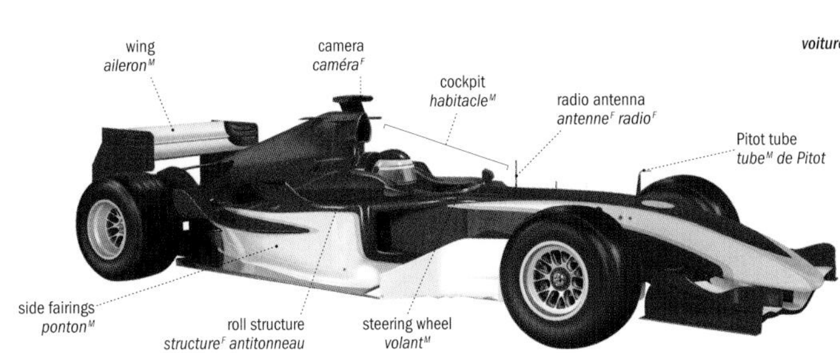

motorcycling

motocyclisme[M]

motocross and supercross motorcycle
moto[F] de motocross[M] et supercross[M]

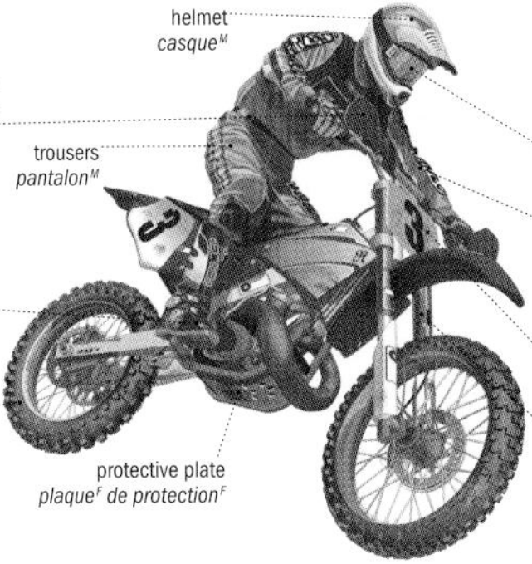

helmet
casque[M]
hand protector
protège-main[M]
trousers
pantalon[M]
boot
botte[F]
nubby tyre
pneu[M] à crampons[M]
protective plate
plaque[F] de protection[F]
protective goggles
lunettes[F] de protection[F]
protective suit
combinaison[F] de protection[F]
number plate
plaque[F]-numéro[M]
fork
fourche[F]

speed grand prix motorcycle and rider
moto[F] de Grand Prix[M] et pilote[M]

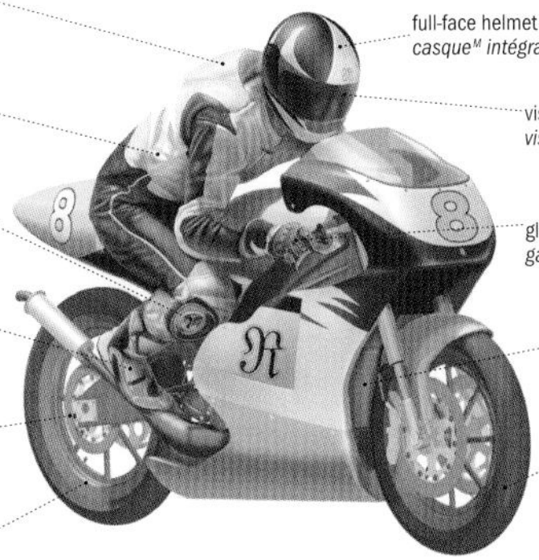

neck support
renfort[M] de nuque[F]
racing suit
combinaison[F]
rub protection
protection[F] d'usure[F]
boot
botte[F]
disc brake
frein[M] à disque[M]
wheel
roue[F]
full-face helmet
casque[M] intégral
visor
visière[F]
glove
gant[M]
air intake for engine cooling
prise[F] d'air[M] de refroidissement[M] du moteur[M]
tyre
pneu[M]

skateboarding

planche^F à roulettes^F

skateboard
planche^F à roulettes^F

tail
queue^F
truck
bloc^M-essieu^M
nose
nez^M

grip tape
bande^F antidérapante
wheel
roulette^F

skateboarde
planchiste

knee pad
genouillère^F
elbow pad
protège-coude^M
helmet
casque^M
coping
arête^F

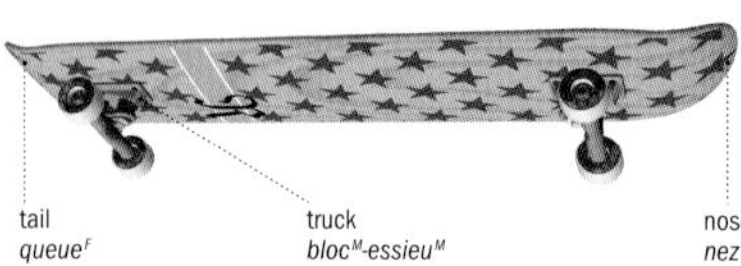

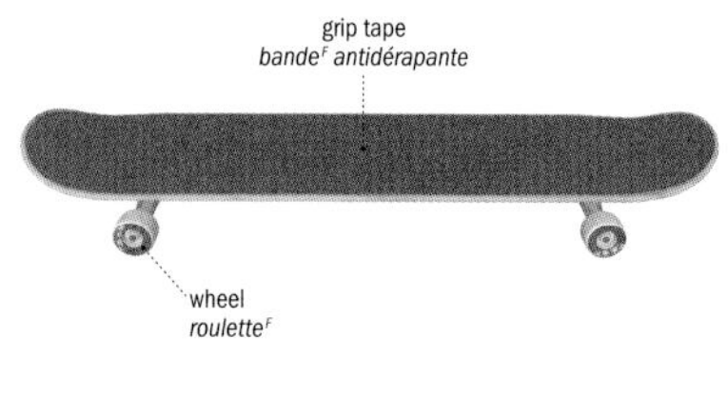

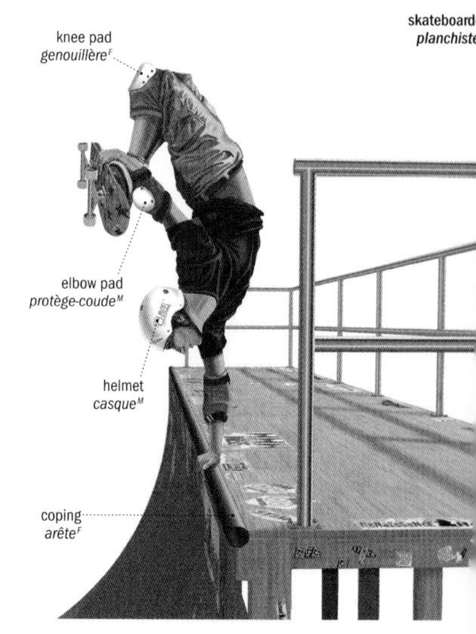

ramp
rampe^F

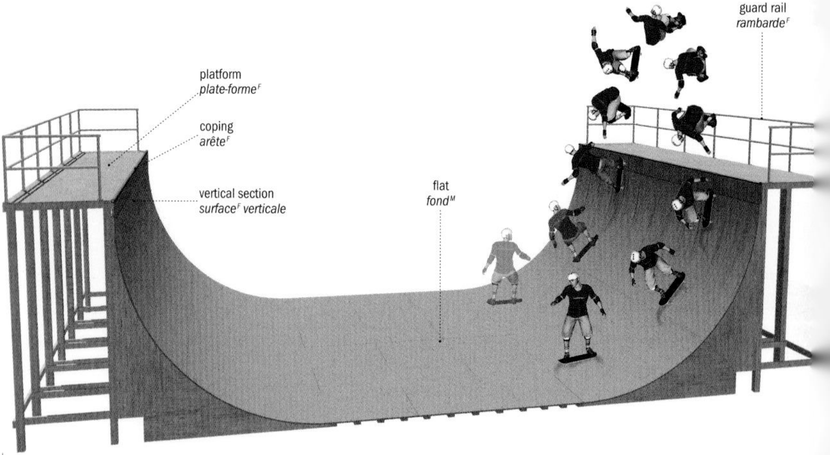

guard rail
rambarde^F
platform
plate-forme^F
coping
arête^F
vertical section
surface^F verticale
flat
fond^M

inline skating

patin[M] à roues[F] alignées

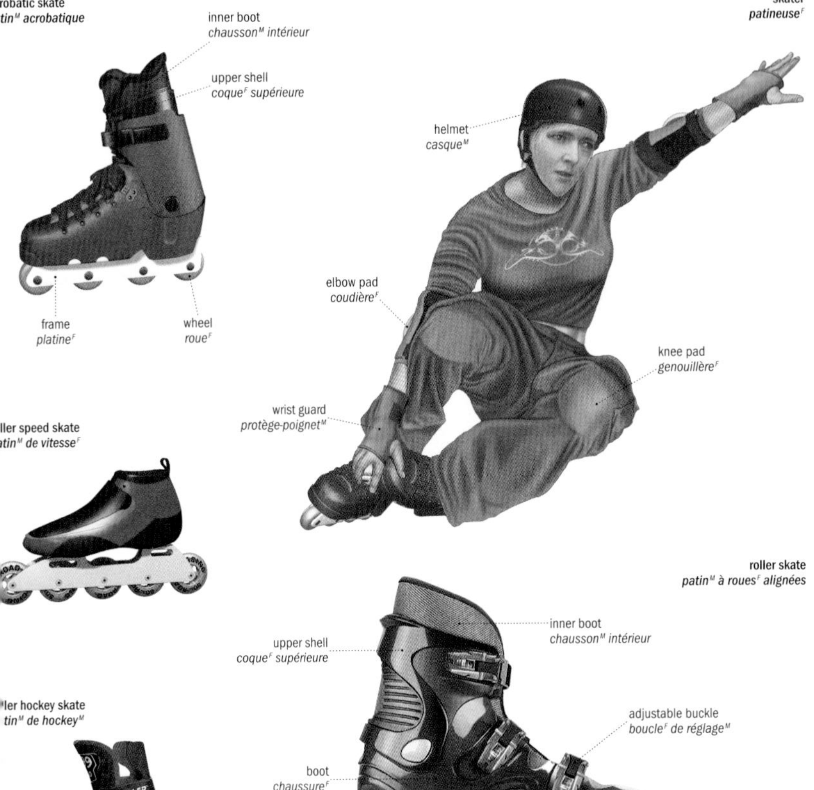

camping

camping^{M}

examples of tents
exemples^{M} de tentes^{F}

two-person te
tente^{F} deux place

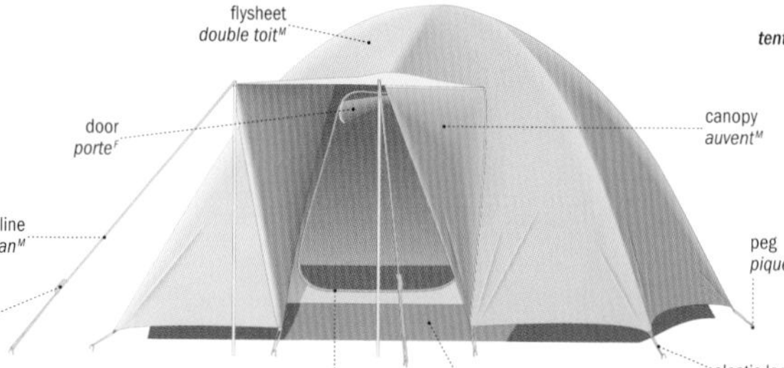

flysheet
double toit^{M}

door
porte^{F}

canopy
auvent^{M}

guy line
hauban^{M}

peg
piquet^{M}

tension adjuster
tendeur^{M}

elastic loop
Sandow$^{®M}$

zip
fermeture^{F} à glissière^{F}

inner tent
tente^{F} intérieure

family tent
tente^{F} familiale

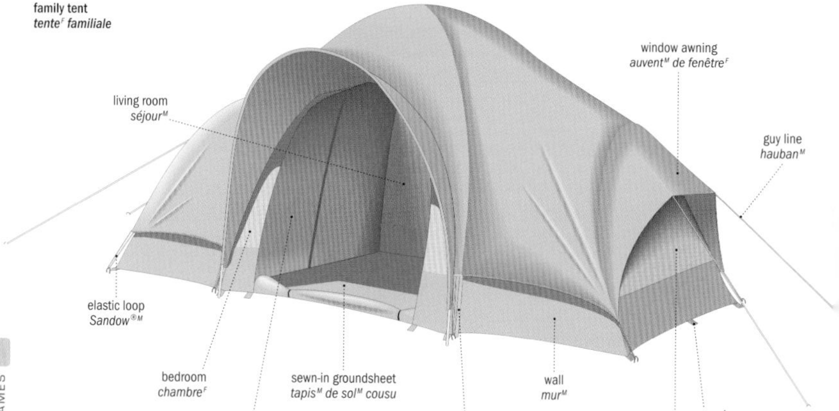

window awning
auvent^{M} de fenêtre^{F}

living room
séjour^{M}

guy line
hauban^{M}

elastic loop
Sandow$^{®M}$

bedroom
chambre^{F}

sewn-in groundsheet
tapis^{M} de sol^{M} cousu

wall
mur^{M}

peg loop
boucle^{F} de piquet^{M}

canvas divider
cloison^{F}

frame
armature^{F}

screen window
fenêtre^{F} moustiquaire^{F}

wagon tent
tente^{F} grange^{F}

wall t
tente^{F} rectangula

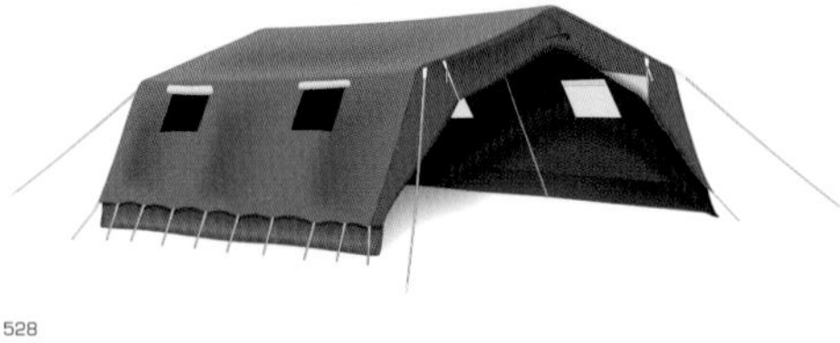

SPORTS AND GAMES

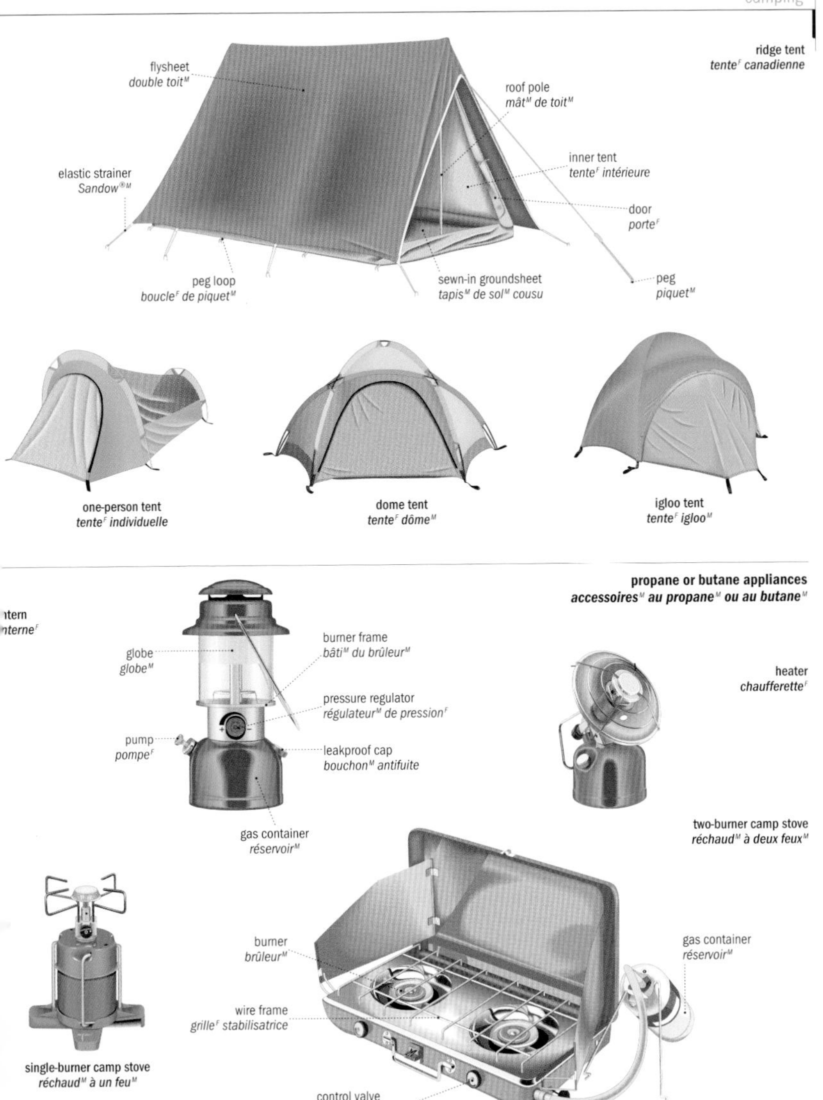
ridge tent
tente[F] canadienne
flysheet
double toit[M]
roof pole
mât[M] de toit[M]
inner tent
tente[F] intérieure
elastic strainer
Sandow®[M]
door
porte[F]
peg loop
boucle[F] de piquet[M]
sewn-in groundsheet
tapis[M] de sol[M] cousu
peg
piquet[M]
one-person tent
tente[F] individuelle
dome tent
tente[F] dôme[M]
igloo tent
tente[F] igloo[M]
propane or butane appliances
accessoires[M] au propane[M] ou au butane[M]
ntern
nterne[F]
globe
globe[M]
burner frame
bâti[M] du brûleur[M]
pressure regulator
régulateur[M] de pression[F]
pump
pompe[F]
leakproof cap
bouchon[M] antifuite
gas container
réservoir[M]
heater
chaufferette[F]
two-burner camp stove
réchaud[M] à deux feux[M]
burner
brûleur[M]
gas container
réservoir[M]
wire frame
grille[F] stabilisatrice
single-burner camp stove
réchaud[M] à un feu[M]
control valve
robinet[M] relais[M]

examples of sleeping bags
exemples[M] de sacs[M] de couchage[M]

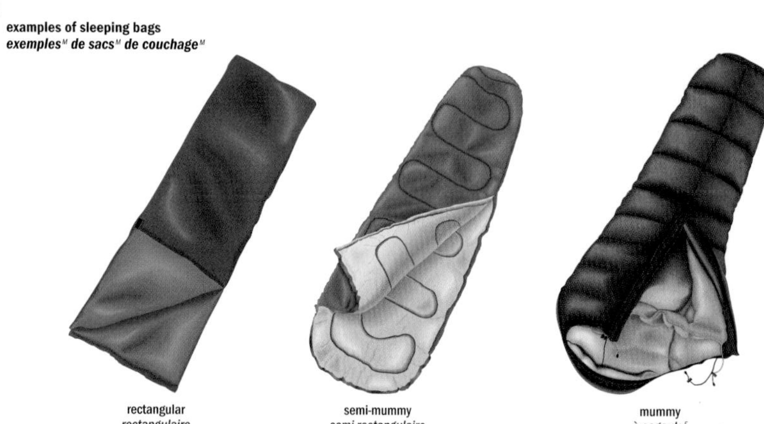

rectangular
rectangulaire

semi-mummy
semi-rectangulaire

mummy
à cagoule[F]

bed and mattress
lit[M] et matelas[M]

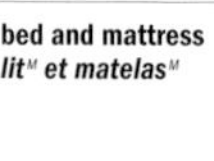

camp bed
lit[M] de camp[M] pliant

air mattress
matelas[M] pneumatique

self-inflating mattress
matelas[M] autogonflant

foam pad
matelas[M] mousse[F]

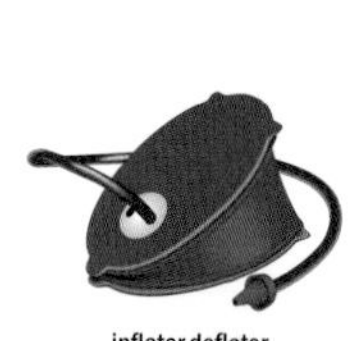

inflator-deflator
gonfleur[M]-dégonfleur[M]

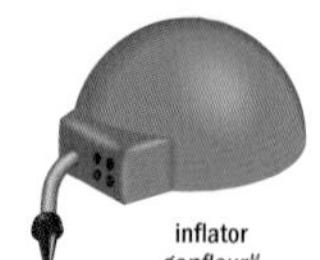

inflator
gonfleur[M]

ry set
nsiles[M] de campeur[M]

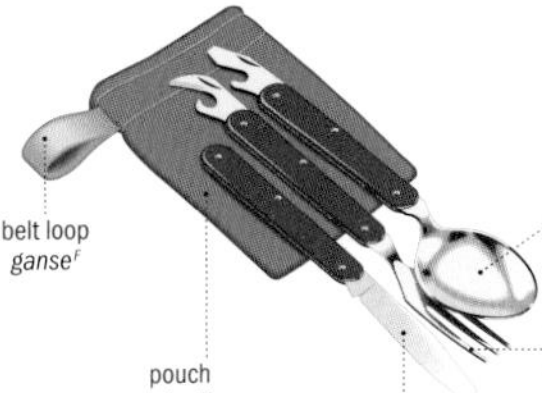

belt loop
ganse[F]

spoon
cuiller[F]

pouch
étui[M]

fork
fourchette[F]

knife
couteau[M]

cooking set
popote[F]

plate
assiette[F] plate

saucepan
faitout[M]

handle
queue[F]

frying pan
poêle[F] à frire

coffee pot
cafetière[F]

cup
tasse[F]

camping equipment
matériel[M] de camping[M]

Swiss army knife
couteau[M] suisse

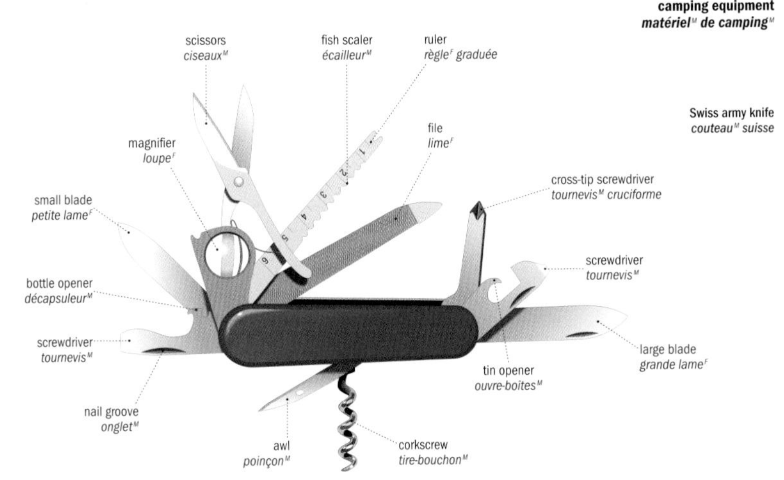

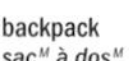

camping

backpack
sac[M] à dos[M]

shoulder strap
bretelle[F]

side compression strap
sangle[F] de compression[F]

waist belt
ceinture[F]

top flap
rabat[M]

tightening buckle
boucle[F] de réglage[M]

front compression strap
sangle[F] de fermeture[F]

strap loop
passe-sangle[M]

folding shovel
pelle[F]-pioche[F] pliante

hurricane lamp
lampe[F]-tempête[F]

vacuum flask
bouteille[F] isolante

bottle
bouteille[F]

stopper
bouchon[M]

cup
tasse[F]

canteen
gourde[F]

cool box
glacière[F]

water carrier
cruche[F]

SPORTS AND GAMES

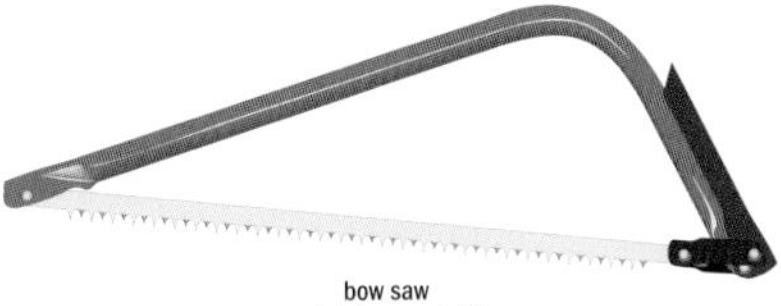

bow saw
scie[F] de camping[M]

knife
couteau[M]

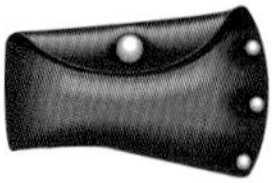

leather sheath
étui[M] de cuir[M]

sheath
gaine[F]

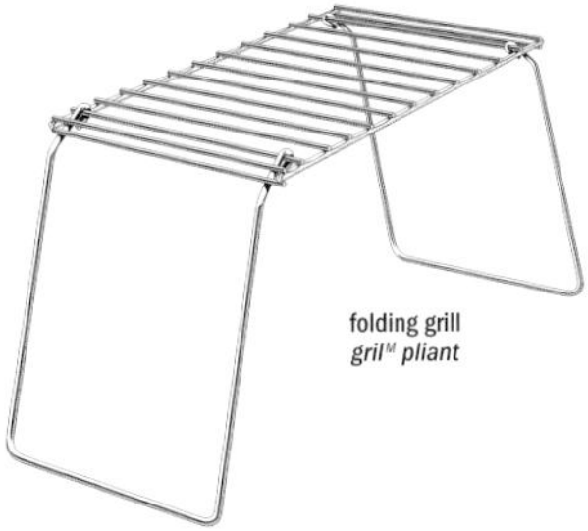

folding grill
gril[M] pliant

hatchet
hachette[F]

magnetic compass
boussole[F] magnétique

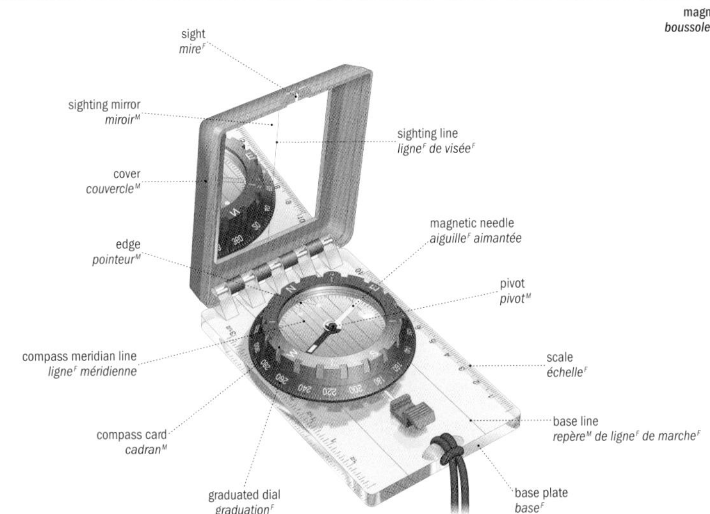

hunting

chasse[F]

rifle (rifled bore)
carabine[F] (canon[M] rayé)

breechblock
bloc[M] de culasse[F]

pistol grip
poignée[F]

hammer
chien[M]

telescopic sight
lunette[F] de visée[F]

rear sight
hausse[F]

butt plate
plaque[F] de couche[F]

trigger guard
pontet[M]

barrel
canon[M]

lever
levier[M]

trigger
détente[F]

stock
crosse[F]

shotgun (smooth-bore)
fusil[M] (canon[M] lisse)

hammer
chien[M]

ventilated rib
bande[F] ventilée

pistol grip
poignée[F]

butt plate
plaque[F] de couche[F]

breechblock
bloc[M] de culasse[F]

forearm
fût[M]

barrel
canon[M]

trigger guard
pontet[M]

trigger
détente[F]

stock
crosse[F]

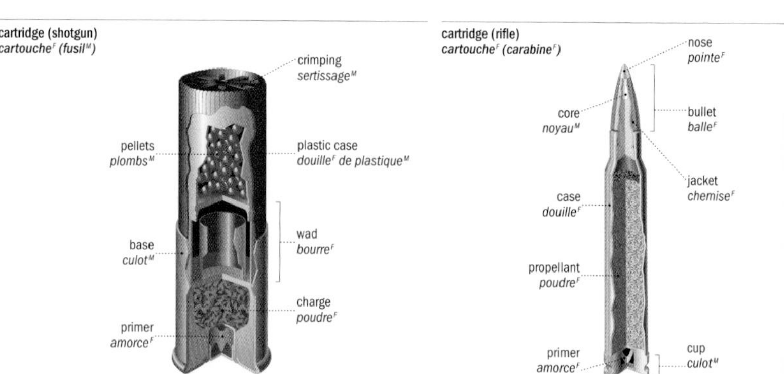

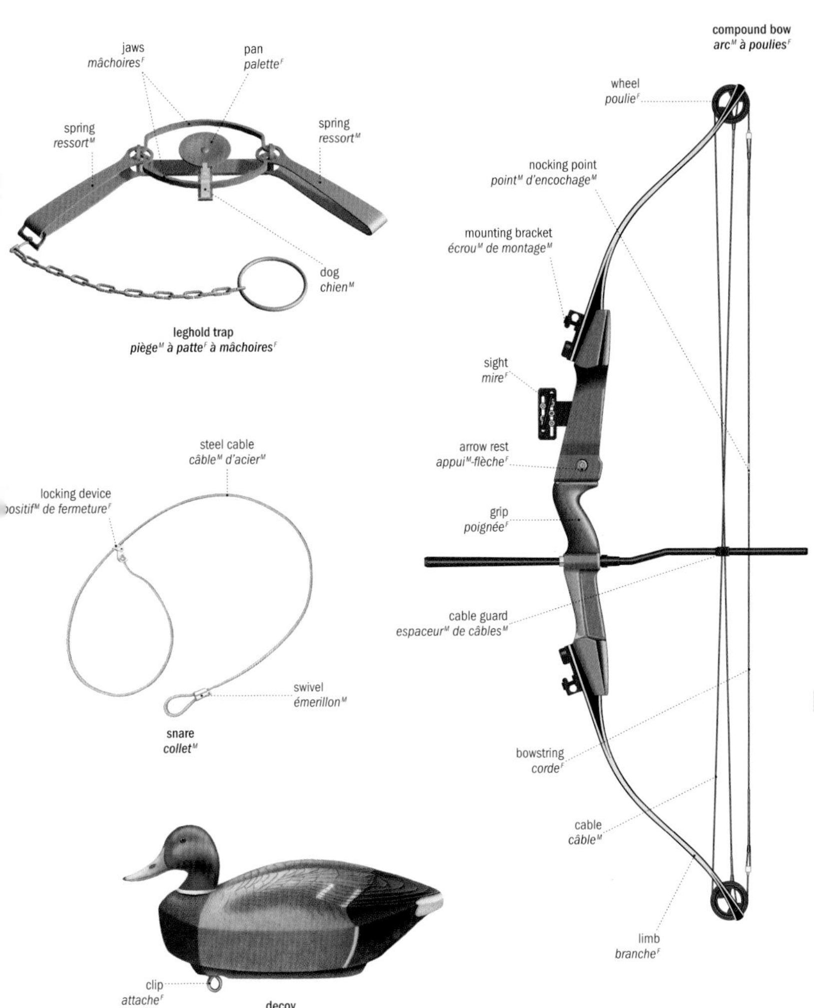
jaws
mâchoires[F]
pan
palette[F]
spring
ressort[M]
spring
ressort[M]
dog
chien[M]
leghold trap
***piège**[M] **à patte**[F] **à mâchoires**[F]*
steel cable
câble[M] *d'acier*[M]
locking device
ositif[M] *de fermeture*[F]
swivel
émerillon[M]
snare
collet[M]
clip
attache[F]
decoy
appeau[M]
compound bow
***arc**[M] **à poulies**[F]*
wheel
poulie[F]
nocking point
point[M] *d'encochage*[M]
mounting bracket
écrou[M] *de montage*[M]
sight
mire[F]
arrow rest
appui[M]*-flèche*[F]
grip
poignée[F]
cable guard
espaceur[M] *de câbles*[M]
bowstring
corde[F]
cable
câble[M]
limb
branche[F]

fishing

pêche[F]

flyfishing
pêche[F] à la mouche[F]

fly reel
moulinet[M] à mouche[F]

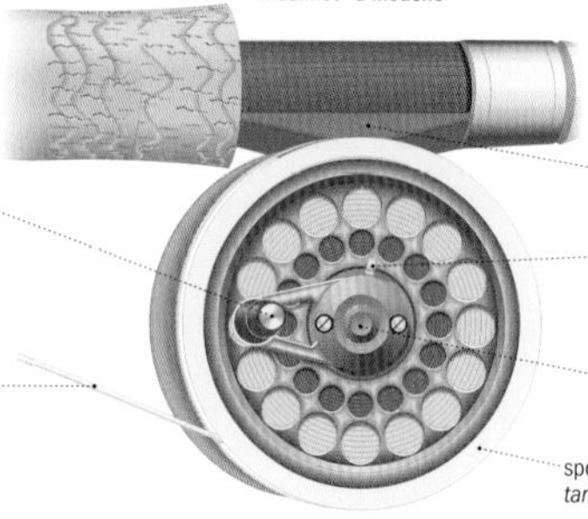

handle
poignée[F]
fly line
soie[F]
foot
pied[M]
catch
cran[M]
drag
frein[M]
spool
tambour[M]

fly rod
canne[F] à mouche[F]

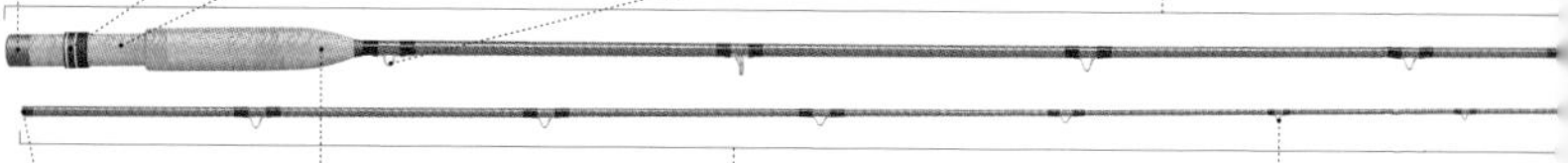

screw locking nut
écrou[M] de blocage[M]
butt cap
embout[M]
reel seat
porte-moulinet[M]
keeper ring
accroche-mouche[M]
butt section
talon[M]
male fe
virole[F]
female ferrule
virole[F] femelle
hand grip
poignée[F]
tip section
scion[M]
guide ring
anneau[M]
tête[F] de

artificial fly
mouche[F] artificielle

wing
aile[F]
topping
coiffe[F]
ribbing
côte[F]
veil
voile[M]
cheek
joue[F]
tail
cerques[M]
joint
articulation[F]
tip
bout[M]
head
tête[F]
butt
talon[M]
shoulder
épaule[F]
fishhook
hameçon[M]
body
corps[M]
hackle
hackle[M]

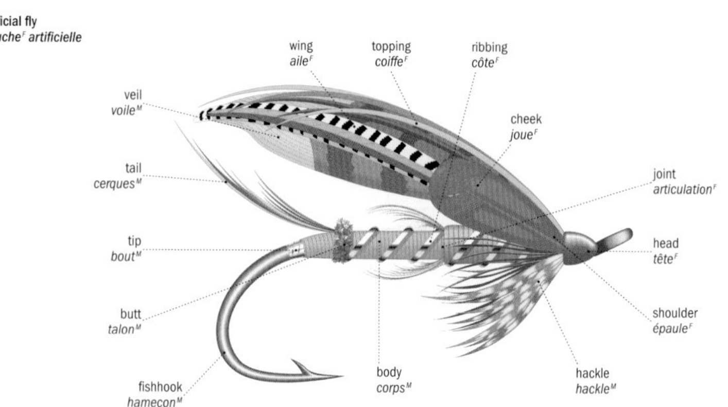

casting
pêche[F] au lancer[M]

nning rod
ne[F] à lancer[M]

screw locking nut
écrou[M] de blocage[M]
reel seat
porte-moulinet[M]
male ferrule
virole[F] mâle
emale ferrule
role[F] femelle
butt grip
poignée[F] arrière
butt guide
anneau[M] de départ[M]
tip-ring
anneau[M] de tête[F]

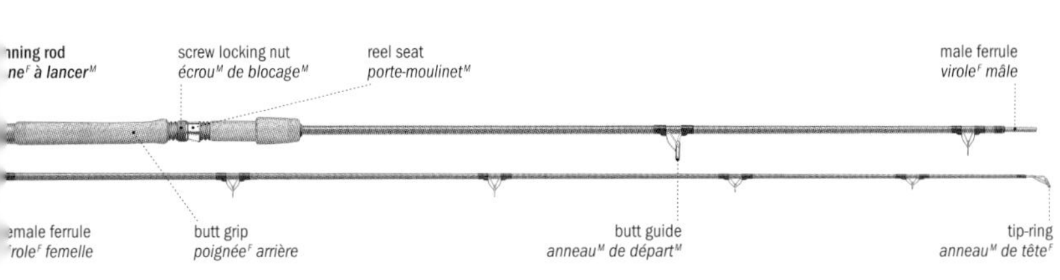

-face spinning reel
linet[M] à tambour[M] fixe

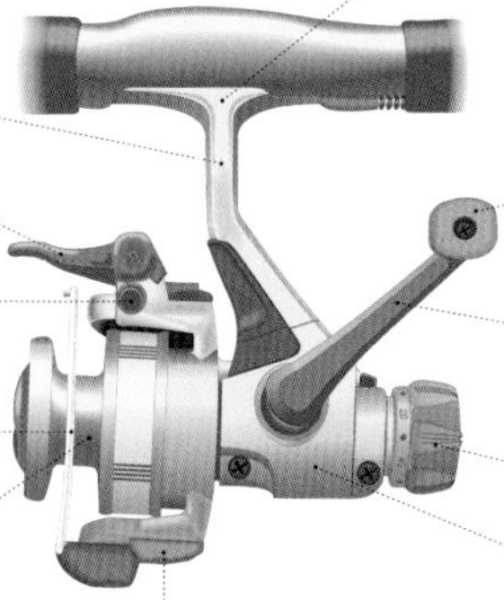

foot
talon[M]
leg
pied[M]
bail arm opening mechanism
mécanisme[M] d'ouverture[F] de l'anse[F]
handle
poignée[F]
line guide
guide-ligne[M]
crank
manivelle[F]
bail arm
anse[F]
tension adjustment
réglage[M] de la tension[F]
spool
tambour[M]
gear housing
carter[M]
rotor
rotor[M]

sting reel
net[M] à tambour[M] tournant

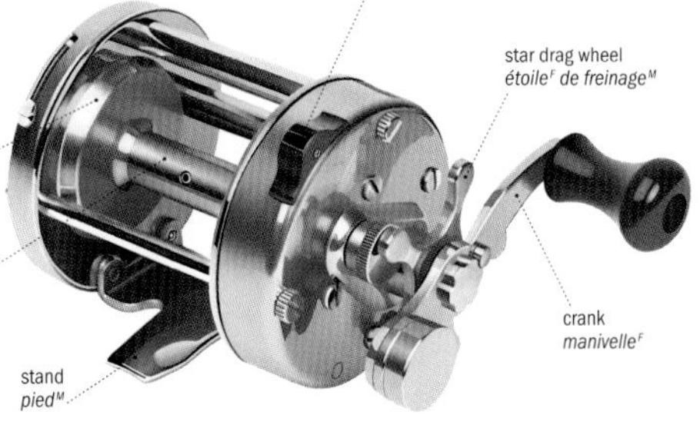

spool-release mechanism
mécanisme[M] de débrayage[M] du tambour[M]
star drag wheel
étoile[F] de freinage[M]
spool
tambour[M]
spool axle
axe[M] de tambour[M]
crank
manivelle[F]
stand
pied[M]

fishing

fishhook
***hameçon*[M]**

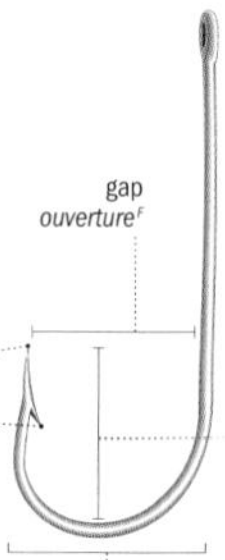

eye
œillet[M]

gap
ouverture[F]

shank
hampe[F]

point
pointe[F]

barb
ardillon[M]

throat
gorge[F]

bend
courbure[F]

terminal ta
bas*[M] *de

float
flotteur[M]

swivel
émerillon[M]

leader
avançon[M]

sinker
plomb[M]

snap
mousqueton[M]

snelled fishhook
hameçon[M] *monté*

spinner
***cuiller*[F]**

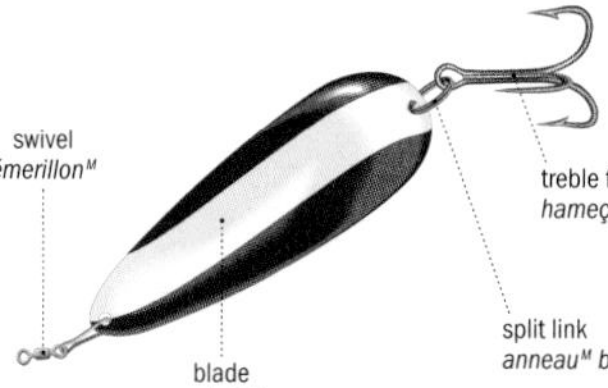

swivel
émerillon[M]

treble fishhook
hameçon[M] *triple*

split link
anneau[M] *brisé*

blade
palette[F]

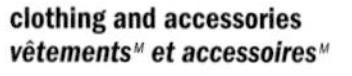

clothing and accessories
***vêtements*[M] *et accessoires*[M]**

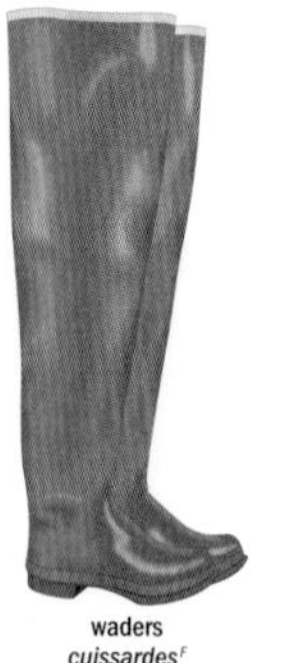

waders
cuissardes[F]

tackle box
boîte[F] *à leurres*[M]

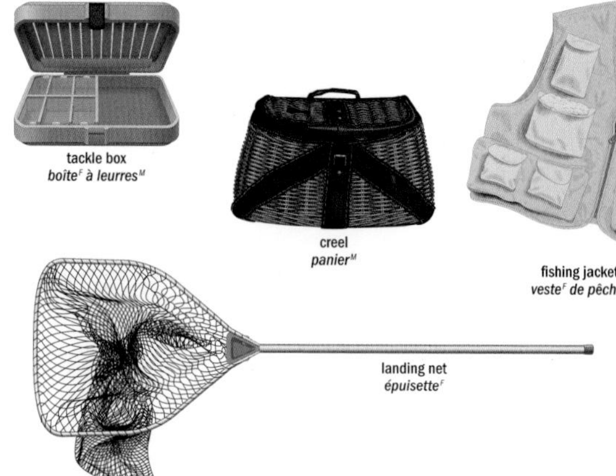

creel
panier[M]

fishing jacket
veste[F] *de pêche*[F]

landing net
épuisette[F]

SPORTS AND GAMES

English Index

A

3
dress 252
ne 157
men 67, 68, 70, 71, 78, 92, 94
minal aorta 102, 107
minal cavity 111, 112
minal rectus 96
minal segment 67
ground swimming pool 184
ground pipeline 404
bed solar radiation 46
ber, shock 351
bing plate 410
otion by clouds 46
otion by Earth surface 46
otion of water and mineral salts

otion, carbon dioxide 54
ent 284, 344
al hill 33
al plain 33
nian 87
nus leaf 200
ration lane 343
rator pedal 354
mark 299
door 423
gallery 407
road 343, 388
server 335
window 333
ories 356, 372
ories, clothing and 538
ory shoe 314
nt and emergency 462
ntals 299
on 296
on bag 276
ion pleat 253
t identification 443
lator 357
8
59, 60
n 47, 48
ow 48
ation, lake 48
quash 129
ceiling 293
guitar 302
meatus 115, 116
c skate 527
n 99
on 279
uttons 471
f wind 45
actor 290
actors' entrance 278
actors' seats 290
actress 291
actuator arm 333
acute angle 428
Adam's apple 92
adapter, plug 271
adapter, power 336
adaptor, mating 11
add in memory 337
add key 337
adding machine 337
addition 427
additive colour synthesis 418
adductor muscle, anterior 73
adductor muscle, posterior 73
Aden, Gulf of 19, 20
adhesive disc 75
adhesive tape 461
adipose tissue 113, 114
adjustable buckle 527
adjustable catch 511
adjustable channel 222
adjustable clamp 206
adjustable frame 226
adjustable lamp 206
adjustable spanner 223
adjustable strap 260
adjustable thermostat 179
adjustable waist tab 244
adjuster 466
adjusting band 324
adjusting ring 236
adjusting screw 222
adjustment slide 246
administration 445
adobe house 288
adrenal gland 107
Adriatic Sea 18
adventitious roots 52
advertisement 313
advertisements, classified 313
advertising panel 378
advertising poster 380
adzuki bean 131
Aegean Sea 18
aerial 326, 327, 349
aerial ladder truck 455
aerial terminals 322
aerial, dish 321
aerial, home 316
aerial, telescopic 325
aerial, transceiving parabolic 316
aerocyst 51
aerodynamic brake 412
affluent 32
Afghanistan 452
Africa 14, 20, 34, 451
African Plate 27
Afro pick 268
aft shroud 7
afterbay 406, 407
aftershave 271
agar-agar 123
agency, travel 436
agitator 212
agricultural pollution 47
aileron 392
air bag 354
air bag restraint system 354
air bubbles 339
air compression unit 376
air concentrator 270
air conditioner 361
air conditioner compressor 360
air conditioning system 46
air cushion 262
air filter 235, 350
air hole 312
air horn 364
air inlet 367
air inlet control 192
air intake 362, 383, 395
air intake for engine cooling 525
air intake, engine 362
air mattress 530
air pollutants 47
air pollution 47
air pre-cleaner filter 398
air relief valve 385
air scoop 523
air shaft 278
air space 79
air temperature 39
air transport 388
air vent 214
air, cold 41
air, rising warm 43
air, subsiding cold 43
air, warm 41
air-inlet grille 270
air-outlet grille 270
air-pressure pump 461
air-supply tube 454
aircraft weather station 38
aircraft, business 394
aircraft, cargo 394
aircraft, examples of 394
aircraft, light 394
aircraft, movements of 395
airliner 37
airport 25, 388, 430
aisle 120, 285
ajowan 139
ala 117
alarm/charge indicator light 337
Alaska, Gulf of 16
Albania 450
albatross 80
albumen 79
alcohol bulb 424
alcohol column 424
Aleutian Islands 16
Aleutian Trench 34
alfalfa 130
alga 51
alga, brown 51
alga, green 51
alga, red 51
alga, structure of 51
algae, examples of 51
Algeria 451
alkaline manganese-zinc cell 417
alkekengi 132
all-season tyre 358
all-terrain bicycle 373
all-terrain vehicle 347
alley 490, 495
alligator 77
allspice 138
alluvial deposits 32
almond 57, 133
alphabetical keypad 338
alphanumeric keyboard 346, 442, 443
alphanumeric keypad 327, 330
alpine ski trail 512
alpine skier 510
alpine skiing 510
alpine snowboard 513
Alps 18
altar cross 446
altar, high 446
altar, secondary 446
altarpiece 446
alternate 330
alternate: level 3 select 330
alternating-current power cord 336
alternative key 330
alternator 350, 360, 413
altitude clamp 8, 9
altitude fine adjustment 8, 9
altitude scale 37
alto clef 298
altocumulus 42
altostratus 42
alula 78
aluminium foil 162
aluminium recycling container 49
alveolar bone 101
amaranth 143
Amazon River 17
amber light 434
amble 83
ambulance 460, 462
ambulatory 285
America, Central 16
America, North 16, 34
America, South 17, 34
American bacon 156
American corn bread 145
American football 484
American football player 486
American mustard 140
American plug 198
Americas 448
Amery Ice Shelf 15
ammunition pouch 456
amoeba 66
amorphous solid 414
amount of substance, measurement of 426
ampere 426
amphibians 75
amphibians, examples of 75
amphibious firefighting aircraft 394
amphitheatre, Roman 281
ampli-tuner 325
ampli-tuner: back view 322
ampli-tuner: front view 322
amplitude 418
ampoule 467
ampulla of fallopian tube 113
anaesthesia room 464
anal cleft 93, 95
anal fin 74
anal proleg 67
analogue watch 424
analytical balance 423
anatomy 96
anatomy of a bivalve shell 73
anatomy of a lobster 71
anchor 473
anchor pin 357
anchor point 70
anchorage block 344
anchovy 159
anconeus 97
Andes Cordillera 17
andirons 193
Andorra 449
andouillette 156
anemometer 413
angle, acute 428
angle, obtuse 428
angle, re-entrant 428
angle, right 428

angles, examples of 428
Angola 452
Anik 317
animal cell 66
animal dung 48
animal kingdom 66
anise 142
ankle 92, 94
ankle boot 241
ankle guard 476
ankle sock 247, 257
ankle-strap 241
ankle/wrist weight 500
annual ring 63
annular eclipse 4
anorak 263
ant 69
Antarctic Circle 15, 21, 22
Antarctic Peninsula 15
Antarctic Plate 27
Antarctica 14, 15
antefix 279
antelope 84
antenna 7, 67, 68, 71, 369, 392, 395, 457, 487
antenna cable, high-frequency 394
antenna, radio 525
antennule 71
anterior adductor muscle 73
anterior chamber 119
anterior end 73
anterior fontanelle 100
anterior horn 109
anterior nasal spine 100
anterior notch 115
anterior root 110
anterior tibial 96
anterior tibial artery 102
anterior view 92, 94, 96, 98
anther 56
anti-friction pad 511
anti-reflection coating 410
anti-slip foot 219
anti-torque tail rotor 395
anti-vibration handle 235
anticline 403
anticollision light 392
anticyclone 39
Antigua and Barbuda 449
antihelix 115
antilock braking system (ABS) 357
antiseptic 461
antitragus 115
anus 71, 73, 106, 111, 112
anvil 425
aorta 104, 105
aortic valve 104
apartment block 512
apartment building 433
aperture 73
aperture door 7
apex 72, 73, 101, 118
apical foramen 101
apocrine sweat gland 114
apothecium 50
Appalachian Mountains 16
apple 133
apple corer 173
apple, section of 58
application launch buttons 337
application, fertilizer 47
appoggiatura 299
appointment book 338
approach ramp 344
approach runs 496
apricot 132
apron 200, 201, 202, 369, 388, 498
apse 285
apsidiole 284, 285
aquatic bird 79
aquatic sports 516
aqueous humour 119
aquifer, confined 402
Arabian Peninsula 19
Arabian Sea 19
arachnids, examples of 70
arachnids, insects and 67
arachnoid 109
Aral Sea 19
arame 123
arc 428
arc, island 33
arcade 281, 284
arcades 447
arch of aorta 102, 103, 104
arch of foot artery 102
archboard 340
archipelago 24
architecture 278
architecture, elements of 286
architrave 279
Arctic 14
Arctic Circle 21, 22
Arctic Ocean 14
area, floor exercise 496
area, high pressure 43
area, industrial 431
area, low pressure 43
area, parking 430, 445
area, receiving 120
area, reception 462, 465
area, ski 512
area, stretcher 462
area, waiting 442
area, water-tank 394
arena 281, 472
Arenberg parquet 190
areola 113
Argentina 448
Ariel 3
ark 447
arm 83, 91, 93, 95, 200, 206, 236, 297, 400, 421, 467
arm cylinder 400
arm guard 486
arm lock 499
arm slit 251
arm stump 200
arm, crossing 362
arm, remote-control 11
arm, suspension 351
armchair 200, 444
armchairs, examples of 200
Armenia 452
armhole 247
armless chair 444
armoire 202
armpit 92, 94
armrest 205, 352, 353, 467
armstand 518
arpeggio 299
arrays, photovoltaic 11
arrector pili muscle 114
arrival, ski lift 512
arrow rest 535
art director 290
arteries 102
artery, dorsal abdominal 71
artery, sternal 71
artery, ventral 71
artichoke 127
article 313
articles, miscellaneous 341
articulated bus 363
articulated joint 363
artificial fly 536
artificial lake 32
artificial satellite 37
artist, make-up 290
arts and architecture 278
arts, performing 294
asafœtida 139
ascending aorta 103
ascending colon 106
ascending passage 278
ash layer 28
Asia 14, 19, 34, 452
Asian noodles 147
Asian pear 137
asparagus 125
asphalt 405
asphalt still 405
aspirin 461
assistant camera operator, first 290
assistant camera operator, second 290
assistant coach 489, 507
assistant director 291
assistant property man 291
assistant referee 509
assistants, counsels' 440
association football 480
asteroid belt 3
asthenosphere 26
astigmatism 419
astrakhan cap 238
astronautics 10
astronomical observation 7
astronomical observatory 7
astronomical observatory, cross section of an 7
astronomical unit 3
astronomical units 2
astronomy 2
asymmetrical bars 496, 497
Atacama Desert 17
athlete: starting block 473
Atlantic cod 161
Atlantic Ocean 14, 15, 18, 20
Atlantic salmon 161
atlas 99
atlas moth 69
Atlas Mountains 20
atmosphere 44, 48
atoll 35
atom 414
atoms 414
atrium 280
attaché case 274
attack line 487
attack zone 487
attacker, left 487
attacker, middle 487
attacker, right 487
attic 182, 189
attitude control thrusters 12
attraction 416
aubergine 128
audience 440
audio input/output jack 337
audio jack 329
audiometric examination room 465
auditory ossicles 116
auricle 116
auricle, ear 115
auriculars 78
Australia 14, 34, 453
Australian-Indian Plate 27
Austria 450
authorized landfill site 47
autoclave 464
automatic dialling index 327
automatic electronic timer 517
automatic filter coffee maker 181
automatic sliding door 286
automatic teller machine 442, 443
automatically-controlled door 390
autotrophs 45
autumn 38
autumn squash 129
autumnal equinox 38
auxiliary handle 228
auxiliary tank 365
avenue 25, 433
avocado 128
awl 531
awning channel 361
axe 234
Axel 509
axial rib 73
axillary artery 102
axillary bud 53
axillary nerve 108
axillary vein 102
axis 99
axle 527
axle shaft 351
axle, spool 537
axon 110
axon hillock 110
Azerbaijan 452
azimuth clamp 8, 9
azimuth fine adjustment 8, 9
Aztec temple 283

B

b 298
baboon 91
baby doll 256
babygro 260
back 78, 83, 86, 93, 95, 115, 167, 169, 201, 205, 226, 244, 467
back boundary line 494
back brush 267
back judge 485
back line 515
back of a glove 243
back panel 210, 213
back pocket 246
back ribs 152
back suspension 522
back zone 487
back, middle 487
back, right 481, 487
backboard 489
backboard support 489
backcourt 491
backdrop 292
backgammon 469
backguard 212
backhoe 399
backhoe controls 399
backhoe loader 399
backlighting button 320
backpack 532
backplate 357
backrest 369, 523
backspace 331
backspace key 331
backstay 509
backstop 474, 489
backstroke 517
backstroke turn indicator 517
backward 518
backward bucket 399, 400
bacon, American 156
bacon, Canadian 156
badge 456
badge, identification 456
badger 88
badminton 494
badminton racket 494
Baffin Island 16
bag compartment 209
bag well 505
bag, air 354
bag, freezer 162
bag, mesh 162
bag, tea 148
bagel 144
baggage check-in counter 390
baggage claim area 390
baggage compartment 362
bagpipes 296
bags, carrier 121
Bahamas 448
Bahrain 452
Baikal, Lake 19
bail 479
bail arm 537
bail arm opening mechanism 537
bailey 282
baitcasting reel 537
baize 502
bakery 121
bakery/patisserie 437
baking sheet 172
baking utensils 172
balaclava 239, 524
balalaika 297
balance beam 496, 497
balance control 322
balancer 303
balcony 189, 447
balcony window 189
baling 49
Balkan Peninsula 18
ball 312, 332
ball bearing 413
ball boy 490
ball mount 356
ball peen 220
ball sports 474
ball, hitch 356
ball-cock supply valve 196
ball-peen hammer 220
baller, melon 173
balloon, sounding 38
ballpoint pen 312
ballroom 387
balm, lemon 142
balsamic vinegar 141
Baltic Sea 18
baluster 191
balustrade 283
bamboo shoot 125
banana 136
band ring 264
band select button 322
band, spiral cloud 43
band, wrist 500
Bangladesh 453
bangle 264
banister 188, 189, 191
banjo 296
bank 182, 342, 432, 437, 442
banknote: back 441
banknote: front 441
banner 313
banquette 201
baptismal font 446
bar 273, 293, 309, 432, 436, 4
469, 500, 501
bar counter 438
bar line 298
bar nose 235
bar stool 201, 438
bar, glazing 186
bar, horizontal 496
bar, push 286
barb 538
Barbados 449
barbell 500, 501
barber comb 268
barbican 282
Barents Sea 18
bark 63
barley 61, 143
barley: spike 61
barmaid 438
barn 122
barometric pressure 39
barometric tendency 39
barrel 269, 270, 312, 471, 53
barrel vault 281
barrier 205, 434
barrier barricade tape 457
barrier beach 35
barrier, tyre 524
barrow 396
bars, asymmetrical 496
bars, parallel 497
bartizan 282
basaltic layer 26
base 54, 179, 180, 192, 206,
229, 269, 283, 318, 332,
412, 421, 422, 454, 473,
base cabinet 164
base course 342
base line 533
base of splat 200
base plate 227, 511, 533
base, padded 489
baseball 474, 476
baseball, cross section of 477
baseline 491
basement 182
basement window 183
basic source of food 45
basil 142
basilic vein 102
basket 178, 211, 489, 510
basket weave pattern 190
basket, frying 171
basket, steamer 175
basket, waste 341
basketball 488
basketball player 488
basmati rice 147
basque 259
bass 160
bass bridge 304

ss clarinet 295
ss clef 298
ss drum 295, 308
ss guitar 303
ss keyboard 296
ss pickup 303
ss register 296
ss Strait 15
ss tone control 303, 322, 325
ss, sea 160
ssoon 306
ssoons 295
ter 173
476, 477, 478
softball 477
n 189, 194, 195
n and shower 439
n and shower mixer 194
n brush 267
n platform 195
n sheet 267
n towel 267
, bubble 267
hrobe 256
hroom 189, 195, 439, 464
hroom scales 423
hroom skylight 189
on 472
on holder 456
on, expandable 456
man 479
en 292, 519, 520
en pocket 519, 520
er 475, 476
er skin 297
er's helmet 476
ery 221, 350, 359, 411, 416
ery box 365
ery case 359
ery cover 359
ery pack 228
ery pack, rechargeable 320
ery warning light 355
ng glove 476
ement 282
k 502
k line 502
k line spot 502
5, 24, 142
iller panel 329
of Bengal 19
cargo 12
Hudson 16
net cap 199
h 35
n, barrier 35
358
er, measuring 171
283, 288, 422
balance 422
bridge 344
, balance 496
, laser 420
bag chair 201
thread cellophane noodles 147
adzuki 131
black 131
lablab 130
Lima 131
mung 131
pinto 131
roman 131
scarlet runner 131
wax 131
yard-long 130
131
, dolichos 130
, green coffee 148
black 89
polar 89
g pad 409
176
ejector 176
s 176
ort Sea 16
82
erel 426
33, 204, 342
ed mattress 530

bed chamber 280
bed lamp 206
bed linen 204
bed, double 439
bed, gravel 524
bed, hospital 464
bed, single 439
bed, sofa 204
bedrock 27, 54
bedroom 189, 528
bedside lamp 439, 464
bedside table 439, 464
beech 64
beechnut 133
beef, cuts of 152
beef, diced 152
beef, minced 152
beehive 122
beer and wine 120
beer glass 165
beetroot 129
beginners' slope 512
begonia 56
Belarus 450
belfry 284
Belgium 449
Belize 448
bell 306, 307
bell bottoms 254
bell brace 306
bell tower 285, 446
bellows 296
bellows strap 296
belly 83
belongs to 427
below-stage 292
belt 225, 246, 248, 499
belt drive 383
belt loader 402
belt loop 246, 248, 531
belt, conveyor 49
belt, duty 456
belt, fan 350
belt, Kuiper 2
belt, tool 225
belt, waist 205, 532
bench 201, 379, 437, 501
bench seat 353
bench, defence counsel's 440
bench, judges' 440
bench, prosecution counsel's 440
bench, substitutes' 481
bend 273, 538
Bengal, Bay of 19
Benin 451
beret 239
bergamot 134
bergère 200
bergschrund 30
Bering Sea 14
Bering Strait 16
Bermuda shorts 254
Bernard, Saint 86
berries 132
berry, juniper 138
bevel 460
bevel square 225
beverage can 163
Bhutan 453
bib 260, 261
bib necklace 264
biceps of arm 96
biceps of thigh 97
biconcave lens 419
biconvex lens 419
bicycle 370
bicycle parking 445
bicycle, accessories 372
bicycle, all-terrain 373
bicycle, city 373
bicycle, Dutch 373
bicycle, parts of a 370
bicycle, road 373
bicycle, touring 373
bicycles, examples of 373
bidet 195
Bight, Great Australian 15
bike carrier 356
bike, BMX 373

bike, quad 369
biking, mountain 522
bikini briefs 259
bilberry 132
bill 78
billhook 234
billiard cue 503
billiard spot 502
billiards 502
bills, examples of 79
bimah 447
bin, compost 231
bin, recycling 49
binding 238, 513, 514
binding, comb 340
binding, safety 510
binocular microscope 421
biology 426
biosphere, structure of 44
biparous cyme 57
birch 64
bird 78
bird of prey 79
bird's eye chilli 139
bird's nest fern 52
bird, morphology of 78
birds 78
birds, examples of 80
biscuit cutters 172
Bishop 470
bison 84
bit 221, 403
bit, screwdriver 228
bit, spade 228
bit, twist 228
bits and drills, examples of 228
bitt 385
bitter melon 128
bivalve shell 73
bivalve shell, anatomy of 73
bivalve shell, morphology of 73
Black 470
black 418
black ball 503
black bean 131
black bear 89
black bread 144
black clamp 356
black gram 131
black mustard 138
black pepper 138
black pollock 161
black pudding 156
black radish 129
black salsify 129
Black Sea 14, 18, 19
black square 470
black stone 470
black tea 148
black-eyed pea 130
blackberry 132
blackboard 444
blackcurrant 132
blade 52, 55, 167, 169, 177, 180, 216, 219, 221, 226, 227, 229, 235, 270, 271, 398, 401, 412, 413, 493, 506, 509, 538
blade close stop 270
blade dispenser 271
blade lift cylinder 398, 401
blade lift fan 383
blade locking bolt 227
blade rotation cylinder 401
blade shifting mechanism 401
blade tilting lock 227
blade tilting mechanism 227
blade, cutting 341
blade, dance 509
blade, free-skating 509
blade, rudder 384
blank 468
blanket 204
blanket sleepsuit 261
blastodisc 79
blazer 254
blender 176
blender, pastry 172
blending attachment 176
blind spot mirror 362, 363

blinking lights 362
block 215, 305, 473
block, apartment 512
block, clamping 425
blocking glove 507
blog 335
blood circulation 102
blood factor negative 426
blood factor positive 426
blood pressure monitor 461
blood vessel 104, 114
blood, composition of 104
blood, deoxygenated 104
blood, oxygenated 104
blouses, examples of 255
blow pipe 296
blowhole 90
blowtorch 218
blue 418
blue ball 503
blue beam 318
blue line 507
blue mussel 157
Blue, Danish 151
blue-veined cheeses 151
blueberry 132
bluefish 160
blusher brush 266
BMX bike 373
boa 77
boar, wild 84
board 470, 519
board game 469
board, bulletin 444
board, cutting 169
board, diving 184
board, game 469
board, memorial 447
boarding step 395
boarding walkway 389
boards 506
boat, centreboard 521
boat, keel 521
boater 238
boats and ships, examples of 382
bobble hat 239
bodies, celestial 2
body 118, 180, 208, 228, 255, 258, 303, 305, 306, 348, 361, 420, 523, 536
body care 267
body flap 13
body of fornix 109
body of nail 114
body side moulding 349
body temperature control unit 10
body tube 421
body, collection 365
body, packer 364
body, tanker 364
bodywork, examples of 347
bogie tank wagon 377
bole 63
bolero 254
boletus, edible 123
Bolivia 448
bolster 167, 169, 204
bolt 222, 223, 224
bolts 223
bomb, volcanic 28
bond, chemical 414
bone, frontal 100
bone, nasal 100
bone, occipital 100
bone, parietal 100
bone, sphenoid 100
bone, temporal 100
bone, zygomatic 100
bongos 309
boning knife 169
bonnet 348, 364
bony fish 74
bony fishes 159
book ends 341
bookcase 444
bookshop 436
boom 364, 399, 400, 520
boom cylinder 399, 400
boom operator 291

boom vang 520
booster parachute 12
booster seat 205
booster, brake 350, 357
booster, solid rocket 12
boot 241, 349, 509, 514, 525, 527
boot, flexible 513
boot, football 480
boot, hard 513
boot, hiking 242
boot, inner 527
boot, ski-jumping 513
bootee 240
booth 438
booth, coupon 443
booth, information 437
booth, photo 437
booth, projection 294
booth, ticket collecting 378
booth, undressing 465
borage 142
bordeaux glass 165
border 182, 293
borders 292
boreal forest 44
born 426
Bosnia-Herzegovina 450
Bothnia, Gulf of 18
Botswana 452
bottle 267, 532
bottle opener 170, 531
bottle, glass 163
bottom cap 417
bottom cushion 502
bottom deck 404
bottom deckboard 396
bottom face 510
bottom line 517
bottom pocket 502
bottom rail 185, 202
bottom stair 191
bottom-fold document case 274
boulevard 25, 433
bow 238, 301, 387, 519, 520
bow door 383
bow loading door 386
bow saw 533
bow thruster 387
bow tie 245
bow, compound 535
bow-winged grasshopper 69
bowl 167, 177, 180
bowl with serving spout 177
bowler 238, 479
bowling 436
bowling crease 479
bowstring 535
box 192, 293
box bag 276
box office 294
box, cheese 163
box, drink 163
box, jury 440
box, mitre 226
box, night deposit 443
box, safe deposit 443
box, sound 297
box, tool 225
box, top 369
boxer 498
boxer shorts 247
boxing 498
boxing gloves 498
boxing trunks 498
bra 259
brace 187, 219
brace clip 246
bracelets 264
braces 246
brachial 96
brachial artery 102
brachial plexus 108
brachioradialis 96, 97
bracket 283
bracket base 202
bracket, mounting 535
bract 60
brain 71
brains 154

brake 467, 501, 522
brake booster 350, 357
brake cable 371
brake caliper 366
brake fluid reservoir 357
brake handle 523
brake hose 357
brake lever 371
brake lever and shifter 522
brake light 352
brake lining 357
brake pad 357
brake pedal 350, 354, 357, 511
brake pressure modulator 357
brake shoe 357
brake van 377
brake, disc 350, 357, 525
brakes 357
braking circuit 350, 357
braking system 351
branch 62, 63, 65, 125, 194, 416, 460
branch clip 460
branches 63
branching, examples of 197
brandy glass 165
brass family 295
brassiere cup 259
brattice 282
brazier 283
Brazil 448
Brazil nut 133
bread 144
bread guide 178
bread knife 169
bread maker 179
bread, multigrain 145
bread, white 145
break 331
breaker 33
bream, sea 159
breast 78, 92, 94, 113
breast dart 248
breast pocket 245, 248
breast welt pocket 244
breaststroke 517
breech 306
breech guard 306
breechblock 534
breeds, dog 86
brick carton 163
brick-bond woodstrip flooring 190
bricklayer's hammer 216
bridge 25, 273, 297, 301, 302, 303, 420, 503
bridge assembly 303
bridge of nose 117
bridging 187
Brie 151
briefcase 274
briefs 247, 259
brightness control 329
brim 238, 239
bristle 271, 272
bristles 219
broad beans 130
broad ligament of uterus 113
broad welt side pocket 248, 251
broadleaved trees, examples of 64
broccoli 127
broccoli raab 127
brochure rack 442
broken line 342, 343
bronchus, lobe 105
bronchus, main 105
brook 32
brook charr 161
broom 193, 215
brow brush and lash comb 266
brown alga 51
brown ball 503
brown rice 147
brown sugar 149
browser 334
Brunei Darussalam 453
brush 61, 209, 215, 272
brush, back 267
brush, bath 267
brush, central 365
brush, curling 515
brush, lateral 365
Brussels sprouts 126
bubble 367
bubble bath 267
bubbles, air 339
bucket 215, 399
bucket cylinder 399, 400
bucket hinge pin 399
bucket lever 399
bucket seat: front view 353
bucket seat: side view 353
buckle 246, 248, 276, 353, 511
buckle, tightening 532
buckwheat 61, 143
buckwheat: raceme 61
bud 54
bud, flower 53
bud, taste 118
bud, terminal 53
buffalo 84
buffer 287
buffer tank 404
buffers 375
buffet 438
bug, shield 69
bugle 307
building, apartment 433
building, office 432
bulb 125, 199, 217, 385, 416
bulb dibber 231
bulb vegetables 124
bulb, section of 54
bulbil 54
bulbocavernous muscle 111
Bulgaria 450
bulge 6
bulk carrier 382
bulk terminal 381
bull's-eye 471
bulldog 86
bulldozer 398
bullet 534
bulletin board 444
bumblebee 69
bump 487
bumper 209, 364, 369
bumper moulding 348
bumper, rear 369
bun tin 172
bunch 522
bunch of grapes 62
bunch, leading 522
bundle 125
bunk 361
bunker oil 405
bunker silo 122
bunker, sand 504
buoy weather station 38
burdock 129
bureau 203
burgundy glass 165
burial 49
Burkina Faso 451
burner 174, 210, 529
burner control knobs 210
burner frame 529
burner ring 174
Burundi 451
bus 362, 435
bus shelter 434
bus station 432
bus stop 434
bus, articulated 363
bus, city 362
bus, double-decker 363
bus, school 362
busbar 407
bush 230
bushing 406, 407
business aircraft 394
business counter 443
business district 430, 432
business transactions 335
butt 492, 494, 503, 536
butt cap 536
butt end 506
butt grip 537
butt guide 537
butt plate 534
butt section 536
butt-strap 273
butte 36
butter 150
butter compartment 211
butter cup 163
butter curler 169
butter dish 166
butter knife 168
butterfly 67
butterfly stroke 517
butterfly, morphology of 67
butterhead lettuce 126
buttermilk 150
buttock 93, 95, 111, 112
button 199, 245, 250, 296
button facing 245, 250
button loop 246
button strap 261
button, band select 322
button, call 287
button, cancel 333
button, CD/DVD-ROM eject 329
button, control 332
button, dial/action 337
button, display release 336
button, eject 315, 471
button, erase 315
button, exit 337
button, floppy disk eject 329
button, focus 320
button, image review 315
button, index/enlarge 315
button, input select 322
button, lock-on 227, 229
button, memory 322
button, menu 315
button, multi-image jump 315
button, nightshot 320
button, paper feed 333, 443
button, power 319, 329, 333, 336
button, power and backlight 337
button, preset tuning 322
button, reset 329, 471
button, settings display 315
button, test 454
button, touch pad 336
button, voice recorder 337
button-through smock 255
buttondown collar 245
buttonhole 248
buttons, action 471
buttons, application launch 337
buttons, directional 471
buttons, programmable 332
buttons, tuning 322
buttress 284
by-pass taxiway 388

C

c 298
cab 398, 399, 400, 401
cabbage, red 126
cabbage, savoy 126
cabin 386, 395
cabinet 211, 212, 213, 318
cabinet, base 164
cabinet, wall 164
cable 228, 332, 356, 364, 535
cable distributor 316
cable guard 535
cable line 335
cable modem 335
cable sleeve 228
cable, electrical 354
cable, spark plug 350
cable, steel 535
cable, sync 337
cables, jumper 356
cabriole chair 200
cabriole leg 200
caecum 106
cafeteria 445
cafetière with plunger 181
cage 281
caiman 77
cajun spice seasoning 139
cake mascara 266
cake tin 172
calcaneus 99
calculator 274
calculator, scientific 337
calculator/cheque book holder 274
calendar pad 338
calf 84, 93, 95
California, Gulf of 16
caliper 357
caliper, vernier 425
call button 287
call button, pedestrian 434
Callisto 2
calyx 56, 59, 60, 107
cambium 63
Cambodia 453
camel 85
Camembert 151
camera 290, 525
camera body 314
camera key 327
camera operator 290
camera, motorcycle-mounted 522
Cameroon 451
camisole 258
camp bed 530
camper 361
camping 528
camping equipment 531
camshaft 360
can, beverage 163
can, food 163
Canada 448
Canadian bacon 156
Canadian elk 84
canal lock 381
canary melon 135
cancel button 333
Cancer, Tropic of 20
candela 426
candle 446
candy, rock 149
cane pen 312
canine 101
canister, dust 229
canisters 162
canned goods 121
cannelloni 146
cannon 83
canopy 273, 286, 361, 394, 401, 528
cantaloupe 135
canteen 532
cantilever bridge 344
cantilever span 344
canvas 498
canvas divider 528
Canyon, Grand 16
cap 52, 176, 191, 199, 238, 312, 412, 456, 467, 516
cap iron 229
cap nut 223
cap, bottom 417
cap, distributor 350
cap, lever 229
cap, screw 163
cap, top 417
capacitor, ceramic 417
capacitor, plastic film 417
capacitors, electrolytic 417
cape 24, 251
Cape Horn 17
Cape of Good Hope 20
Cape Verde Islands 451
capillary blood vessel 114
capillary tube 424
capital 23
capitals lock 330
capitals lock key 330
capitulum 57
capon 155
capped tee 193
Capricorn, Tropic of 20
capsule 51, 467
captain's quarters 387
caption 313
capture 470
car 347, 521
car ceiling 287
car coat 251
car cover 356
car dealer 433
car deck 386
car floor 287
car guide rail 287
car park 375, 381, 390
car safety 287
car systems 351
car systems: main parts 350
car wash 346
car, following 522
car, formula 1 525
car, formula 3000 524
car, formula Indy 524
car, lift 287
car, Micro Compact 347
car, police 457
car, rally 524
car, trailer 380
carafe 165
carambola 137
carapace 71, 76
caravan 361
caraway 138
carbon dioxide absorption 54
carbon rod (cathode) 417
carbon-zinc cell 417
carburettor 366
card games 468
card number 441, 443
card reader 321
card reader slot 346, 442, 443
card slot 320
card, compass 23
card, credit 441
card, debit 443
cardamom 138
cardiac stomach 71
cardigan 250, 255
cardinal 80
cardoon 125
care, body 267
care, health and beauty 121
care, lawn 237
caretaker's cupboard 443
cargo aircraft 394
cargo bay 12
cargo bay door 13
cargo dispatch 391
cargo hold 393
cargo rack, rear 369
cargo reception 391
Caribbean Islands 448
Caribbean Plate 27
Caribbean Sea 14, 16
carina 74
carnation 56
carnivores 45
carnivorous mammals 86
carnivorous mammals, example 88
carom billiards 502
carp 160
Carpathian Mountains 18
Carpentaria, Gulf of 15
carpenter's hammer 220
carpentry: drilling tools 228
carpentry: gripping and tightenir tools 222
carpentry: measuring and marki tools 225
carpentry: miscellaneous materi
carpentry: nailing tools 220
carpentry: sawing tools 226
carpentry: screwing tools 221
carpentry: shaping tools 229
carpet and floor brush 209
carpet, pile 190
carriage 396
carrier 369, 370
carrier bags 121
carrier, bike 356
carrier, bulk 382
carrier, child 372
carrot 129
carrying handle 326
cartilaginous fish 74

ENGLISH INDEX

artilaginous fishes 158
artography 21
arton 163
arton, brick 163
arton, egg 162
arton, small 163
artoon 313
artridge 216, 312, 459
artridge (rifle) 534
artridge (shotgun) 534
artwheel hat 239
arving fork 169
arving knife 169
asaba melon 135
ise 225, 265, 304, 424, 534
ise fan 329
se, handcuff 456
se, lens 272
sement 186
sement window 287
sement window opening inwards 287
sh dispenser 437, 442
sh readout 346
sh register 121
sh supply 443
shew 133
shier 121
sing 186, 237
sing, steel 417
spian Sea 14, 19
sava 124
ssegrain focus 7
sette 326, 333
sette compartment 320, 321
sette drive 333
sette holder 323
sette player 326
sette player controls 326
sette tape deck 323
sette, video 319
tanets 295, 309
ter 205, 209, 308
es 68
ing 537
tle 470
le 282
ual shoe 241
87
breeds 87
s head 87
lytic converter 351
lytic reforming plant 405
maran 521
h 273, 536
her 474, 475, 476
her's glove 476
hing glove 507
gory buttons 326
ing foods 121
pillar 67
edral 284
edral, plan 285
ode ray tube television 318
alk 292
al fin 74, 90
flower 127
king gun 216
31, 35
nne 139
DVD player 471
DVD-ROM drive 329, 336
DVD-ROM eject button 329
of Lebanon 65
g 193
g collar 193
g fitting 206
g joist 187
g, acoustic 293
g, car 287
ac 129
125
ial bodies 2
7, 281
ody 110
embrane 50, 66
all 50
lkaline manganese-zinc 417
arbon-zinc 417
cell, convective 43
cell, red blood 104
cell, white blood 104
cellar, wine 438
cello 301
cellos 295
cells 416, 440
cells, dry 417
Celsius scale 424
Celsius temperature, measurement of 426
Celsius, degree 426
celtuce 126
cement screed 190
cementum 101
cemetery 25, 433
censer 446
cent 440
Central African Republic 451
Central America 14, 16
central brush 365
central column 412
central focusing wheel 420
central incisor 101
central midfielder 481
central nave 447
central nervous system 109
central pumping station 404
central reservation 343, 434
central stile 185
centre 293, 428, 470, 485, 489, 507
centre back vent 244
centre circle 481, 488
centre console 354
centre electrode 359
centre face-off circle 507
centre field 475
centre fielder 474
centre flag 480
centre half 481
centre Keelson 385
centre lane 343
centre line 484, 488, 493, 494, 507, 515
centre line judge 490
centre loudspeaker 321
centre mark 490
centre pocket 502
centre post 202
centre service line 491
centre span 344
centre spot 481, 502
centre strap 491
centre, city 431, 432
centre, convention 433
centre, day-care 437
centre, exhibition 430
centre, shopping 431, 436
centreboard 520
centreboard boat 521
centrifuge module 11
centring control 329
centring point 228
centriole 66
cephalic vein 102
cephalothorax 70, 71
ceramic capacitor 417
cereal products 144
cereals 61, 143
cerebellum 109
cerebro-spinal fluid 110
cerebropleural ganglion 73
cerebrum 109
Ceres 2
cervical vertebra 99
cervix of uterus 112
Chac-Mool 283
Chad 451
Chad, Lake 20
chain 372
chain brake 235
chain guide 372
chain of dunes 36
chain of neurons 110
chain reaction 415
chain stay 370
chain wheel 522
chain wheel A 372
chain wheel B 372
chain, food 45
chainsaw 235
chainsaw chain 235
chair lift 512
chair lift departure 512
chair, armless 444
chair, high 205
chair, patient's 464
chairs, examples of 201
chaise longue 200
chalaza 79
chalice 446
chalk 503
chalk line 225
chamber, cold storage 120, 121
chamber, king's 278
chamber, magma 402
chamber, queen's 278
chamber, relieving 278
chamber, underground 278
chameleon 77
chamois leather 265
chamomile 148
champagne flute 165
champagne glass 165
chandelier 207
change sign key 337
changing room 444
changing table 205
channel scan buttons 319
channel select 319
channel selector controls 319
Channel, English 18
Channel, Mozambique 20
chanter 296
chanterelle 123
Chantilly parquet 190
chapel 282
charge 534
charge indicator 271
charger 228
charging light 271
charging socket 271
Charleston cymbal 308
charlotte mould 172
charm bracelet 264
Charon 3
charr, brook 161
chart room 382
chat room 335
chayote 129
checkout 121
checkouts 121
cheek 83, 86, 94, 220, 536
cheese box 163
cheese counter 121
cheese knife 168
cheese, Chèvre 150
cheese, cottage 150
cheese, cream 150
cheeses, blue-veined 151
cheeses, fresh 150
cheeses, goat's-milk 150
cheeses, pressed 151
cheeses, soft 151
cheetah 89
chemical bond 414
chemical treatment 405
chemise 282
chemistry 414
cheque book 274
cheque book cover 275
cheque, traveller's 441
cheques 441
cherimoya 136
cherry 132
chervil 142
chess 470
chess notation 470
chessboard 470
chest 83
chest expander 500
chest freezer 211
chest protector 476, 486
chesterfield 200
chestnut 133
chestnut, water 124
chevet 285
Chèvre cheese 150
chicane 524
chick peas 130
chicken 155
chicory 127
chief timekeeper 516
chiffonier 203
child carrier 372
child seat 356
child's skull 100
child's tricycle 373
children's clothing 261
children's furniture 205
Chile 448
chilli 128
chilli powder 139
chilli, bird's eye 139
chilli, jalapeño 139
chillis, crushed 139
chillis, dried 139
chimney 183, 193
chimney connection 192
chimney pot 183
chimpanzee 91
chin 78, 94
chin protector 367
chin rest 301
chin strap 486, 522
China 453
chinois 171
chip cover 227
chipmunk 82
chipolata sausage 156
chive 124
chloroplast 50
chocolate 148
chocolate, dark 148
chocolate, milk 148
chocolate, white 148
choir 284, 285
choir organ manual 305
choker 264
chop 152, 153
chop, loin 153
chord 299
chorizo 156
choroid 119
Christmas tree 404
chromatin 66
chromosphere 4
chrysalis 67
chuck 221, 228
chuck key 228
chuck, keyless 228
chukka 240
church 433, 446
chutney, mango 141
cicada 69
cider vinegar 141
cilia 66
ciliary body 119
ciliate 55
cilium 66
cinema 294, 386, 432, 436
cinnamon 138
Circle, Antarctic 15, 22
circle, parts of 428
circuit 524
circuit board, printed 417
circuit breaker 407
circuit vent 194
circuit, braking 350, 357
circuit, integrated 417
circuit, printed 417
circular body 296
circular saw 227
circular saw blade 227
circulation diagram 103
circumference 428
circumvallate papilla 118
cirque 5
cirrocumulus 42
cirrostratus 42
cirrus 42
cistern 195
cistern ball 196
cistern lid 196
citron 134
citrus fruits 134
city 23, 430
city bicycle 373
city bus 362
city centre 431, 432
clam 157
clam cleat 521
clam, hard-shell 157
clamp 198, 226, 269
clamp binder 339
clamp lever 269
clamp spotlight 206
clamp, black 356
clamp, pipe 224
clamp, red 356
clamping block 425
clamping screw 224
clamping screws 425
clapperboard 291
clapskate 508
clarinet 306
clarinets 295
clasp 274, 275
classic blouse 255
classified advertisements 313
classroom 444, 445
classroom for students with learning disabilities 444
clavicle 98
claw 71, 76, 78, 82, 220
claw hammer 220
clay 492
clean and jerk 500
clean utility room 462
cleaner height adjustment knob 209
cleaner's cupboard 439
cleaner, dry 437
cleaning brush 271
cleaning eye 197
cleaning tools 209
clear key 337
clear space 487
clear-entry key 337
cleat 520, 521
cleated shoe 486
cleaver 169
clefs 298
cleg 69
clerks' desk 440
clerks' office 440
clew 519
cliff 5, 29, 35
cliff, shore 35
climate control 354
climates of the world 40
climates, cold temperate 40
climates, dry 40
climates, warm temperate 40
climbing plant 230
clinical thermometer 424
clinical thermometers 461
clip 312, 535
clip earrings 264
clipboard 340
clipless pedal 522
clippers 269
clitoris 112
cloakroom 188, 443
cloakroom, customers' 438
cloakroom, staff 438, 465
cloche 239
clock 444
clock operator 488
clock radio 325
clock timer 178, 210
clog 242
closeness setting 271
clothing 238
clothing and accessories 538
clothing guard 467
clothing shop 436
clothing, children's 261
clothing, newborn children's 260
cloud 37, 41
cloud of volcanic ash 28
cloud, funnel 43
cloud, Oort 2
cloud, wall 43
clouds 42
clouds with vertical development 42
cloudwater 48

ENGLISH INDEX

clove 138
cloverleaf 342, 343
club 468
club chair 200
clubhouse 504
clump of flowers 230
cluster, globular 6
clutch 350
clutch housing 368
clutch lever 366, 368
clutch pedal 354
coach 362, 489, 507
coach's box 474
coach, assistant 489, 507
coaches 509
coal storage yard 402
coal-fired thermal power station 402
coarse adjustment knob 421
coarse salt 141
coastal features 35
coat dress 252
coats 248, 251
cob 61
cobra 77
coccyx 98
cochlea 116
cochlear nerve 116
cockchafer 69
cockle 157
cockleshell 200
cockpit 520, 525
cocktail cabinet 203
cocktail glass 165
cocktail lounge 439
cocoa 148
coconut 133
Cocos Plate 27
cod, Atlantic 161
code, time 291
coeliac trunk 103, 107
coffee 148
coffee and infusions 148
coffee beans, roasted 148
coffee makers 181
coffee mill 180
coffee mug 166
coffee pot 531
coffee shop 432, 437
coffee spoon 168
coil spring 351
coin purse 275
coin: obverse 441
coin: reverse 441
cola nut 133
colander 171
cold air 41
cold coolant 408
cold storage chamber 120, 121
cold store 381
cold temperate climates 40
cold-water circuit 194
cold-water riser 194
cold-water supply 196, 197
collar 53, 244, 245, 248, 262, 271, 501
collar point 245
collar stiffener 245
collar, torque adjustment 228
collards 126
collateral 110
collection body 365
collection truck 364
collection, separate 49
collector, electron 417
collet 229
collie 86
Colombia 448
colour selection filter 318
colour shifting ink 441
colour supplement 313
colour synthesis 418
colour synthesis, additive 418
colour synthesis, subtractive 418
colour television camera 10
colour, hair 267
columella 73
columella fold 73
column 31, 207, 279, 313
column of mercury 424
column, steering 350
coma 6
comb binding 340
combat sports 498
combination lock 274
combination pliers 217
combination spanner 223
combinations 247
combs 268
combustion chamber 360
combustion space 192
comet 6
commandments, ten 447
commercial area 435
commercial concern 335
commercial zone 431
commissure of lips of mouth 116
common carotid artery 102
common coastal features 35
common extensor of fingers 97
common frog 75
common hair cap moss 51
common iliac artery 102, 107
common iliac vein 107
common nail 220
common periwinkle 157
common peroneal nerve 108
common plaice 161
common polypody 52
common toad 75
communicating ramus 110
communication by telephone 327
communication module 316
communication protocol 334
communication set 380
communication tunnel 13
communications 312
communications and office automation 312
communications volume controls 10
communion rail 446
commuter train 375
Comoros 452
comouter, on-board 354
compact 266
compact camera 315
compact disc 326
compact disc player 323, 325, 326
compact disc player controls 326
compact disc player, portable 325
compact disc recorder 325
compact memory card 315
compact video cassette adapter 320
compacting 49
compartment 203, 286
compartment, bag 209
compartment, baggage 362
compartment, cassette 320
compartment, engine 362
compartment, glove 354
compass bridge 382, 386, 387
compass card 23, 533
compass meridian line 533
compass saw 226
competition, road cycling 522
competitive course 517
complex dune 36
complex, sports 431
complexus 97
compluvium 280
composition of the blood 104
compost bin 231
compound bow 535
compound eye 67, 68
compound leaves 55
compressed-air cylinder 454
compression coupling 197
compression strap, front 532
compression strap, side 532
computer 444
computer programs 457
computer science room 444
computer screen 10
computer, dashboard 457
computer, desktop 334
computer, laptop 336
concave lens 419
concave primary mirror 9
concern, commercial 335
concertina file 340
concertina-type folding door 286
concha 115
conchiglie 146
concrete mixer truck 365
condensation 45, 414
condensation of steam into water 408
condenser 402, 421
condenser adjustment knob 421
condenser height adjustment 421
condiments 140
conditioner, hair 267
condor 80
conduction 415
conductor's podium 295
conduit, fuel 351
cone 65, 119, 429
conference room 442
confessionals 446
configuration of the continents 14
confined aquifer 402
confining bed, lower 402
confining bed, upper 402
confirmation key 443
confluent 32
Congo 451
Congo River 20
conic projection 22
conical washer 196
conifer 65
coniferous forest 44
conifers, examples of 65
conjunctiva 119
connecting cable 324
connecting gallery 345
connecting rod 360
connection 470
connection cable 332
connection pin 417
connection point 198
connection, network 198
connective tissue 114
console, game 471
constriction 424
consumer 317
contact 470
contact devices 198
contact lens, disposable 272
contact lens, hard 272
contact lens, soft 272
contact lenses 272
contact lever 207
container 176, 231, 383
container hold 383
container ship 381, 382
container terminal 381, 430
container truck 377
container, aluminium recycling 49
container, glass recycling 49
container, paper recycling 49
container, refuse 215
container-loading bridge 381
containers, recycling 49
containment building 408, 409
contest area 499
contestant 499
continent 33
continental crust 26
continental margin 33
continental rise 33
continental shelf 33
continental slope 33
continents, configuration 14
continuity person 291
continuous beam 344
contrabassoons 295
contractile vacuole 66
contrast control 329
control 330
control button 332
control deck 383
control key 330
control keys 328
control knob 210, 212
control knobs, burner 210
control monitors, director's 290
control panel 178, 179, 210, 212, 213, 214, 455
control room 293, 406
control stick 395
control tower 388
control unit, electronic 357
control valve 529
control wheel 455
control, bass tone 325
control, cruise 354
control, remote 321
control, sound field 322
control, temperature 211
control, treble tone 325
control, tuning 325
control, volume 303, 325, 329
control: group select 330
controller 471
controller ports 471
controller, lightbar 457
controls, videotape operation 320
controls, winch 364
conurbation 430
convection 415
convection current 415
convection zone 4
convective cell 43
convenience food 121
convenience outlet 217
convention centre 433
conventional door 286
convergent plate boundaries 27
converging lenses 419
convertible 347
convex lens 419
conveyor 402
conveyor belt 49, 390
Cook Strait 15
cook's knife 169
cooked ham 156
cooker hood 164
cooker ring 210
cooker, gas 210
cooking dishes 179
cooking plate 179
cooking set 531
cooking surface 179
cooking utensils 174
cool box 532
cool tip 269
coolant 408
coolant inlet 410
coolant outlet 410
coolant, cold 408
coolant, hot 408
cooling 405
cooling cylinder 420
cooling fan 322, 350, 358, 360
cooling system 351
cooling tower 402
cooling vent 336
Coon, Maine 87
coping 526
coping saw 226
cor anglais 306
Coral Sea 15
coral snake 77
corbeille 293
corbel 282
corbel piece 192
cord, power 177, 227, 229, 269, 322
cord, spinal 109
cord, ventral nerve 71
cordate 55
Cordillera, Andes 17
cordless drill-driver 228
cordless mouse 332
cordless screwdriver 221
core 4, 58, 534
corer, apple 173
coriander 142
Corinthian column, engaged 281
Corinthian pilaster 281
cork 514
cork ball 477
cork tip 495
corkscrew 531
corn 143
corn oil 149
corn salad 127
corn syrup 149
corn: cob 61
cornea 119, 419
corner 498
corner arc 481
corner cupboard 203
corner flag 481
corner pad 498
corner stool 498
corner stud 187
corner tower 282
cornerpiece 277
cornet 295, 307
cornflour 144
cornice 183, 185, 202, 279
corolla 56
corona 4
corona radiata 112
coronal suture 100
coronet 83
corpus callosum 109
corpus cavernosum 111
cors anglais 295
corselette 258
corset 259
cortex 107
corymb 57
cos lettuce 126
cosmetic tray 277
Costa Rica 448
costal shield 76
costume 290
cot 205
cottage cheese 150
cottage loaf 145
cotton applicators 461
cotton wool ball 461
cotyledon 53
coudé focus 7
cougar 88
cough syrup 467
coulis, tomato 140
coulomb 426
Coulommiers 151
counsels' assistants 440
counter 262, 443, 469
counter reset button 323
counter, bar 438
counter, business 443
counter, cheese 121
counter, fresh meat 120
counterjib 397
counterjib ballast 397
countersunk head 221
counterweight 8, 287, 345, 397, 401
counterweight guide rail 287
country 23, 431
coupé 347
coupler-tilt tablet 305
coupling 377
coupling guide device 376
coupon booth 443
courgette 128
course 504
course, golf 430
court 241, 440, 487, 488, 490,
courthouse 432
courtroom 440
courtyard 447
couscous 144
couscous kettle 175
cover 180, 198, 315, 454, 477, 533
cover, car 356
cover, chip 227
cover, cylinder head 350
cover, front 333
coverage, sky 39
coveralls 513
covered parapet walk 282
covering 493
cow 84
Cowper's gland 111
cowshed 122
Coyolxauhqui stone 283
crab 158
crab pulley 397
crab spider 70
cradle 8, 9
cradle, docking 337

ranberry 132
rane runway 397
ranes 397
ranial nerves 108
rank 170, 224, 372, 537
rank handle 225
rank, landing gear 365
rankshaft 360
rash helmet 367, 524
rash sensor, primary 354
ate, small 162
ate, small open 162
rater 5, 28
ater ray 5
avat 245
awl stroke 517
ayfish 158
eam 150
eam cheese 150
eam jug 166
eam, sour 150
eam, whipping 150
ease 246
edit card 441
edit card wallet 274
edit line 313
eel 538
eep 31
enate 55
epidoma 279
escendo pedal 305
escentic dune 36
ess, garden 127
est 29, 33, 418, 477
est of spillway 406
evasse 30
evice tool 209
ew neck 260
w neck sweater 250, 255
w quarters 382
w return vehicle 11
briform plate of ethmoid 117
ket 478
ket ball 478
ket player: batsman 478
ket shoe 478
ne prevention 456
nping 534
atia 450
ckery 166
codile 77
cus 56
issant 144
ok 306
ok key 306
okneck squash 129
sne 124
ss brace 467
ss head 221
ss rail 201
ss section of a baseball 477
s section of a hydroelectric power
lant 407
ss section of a molar 101
s section of a reflecting telescope
s section of a refracting telescope
s section of a road 342
s section of a street 434
s section of an astronomical
bservatory 7
s, altar 446
s-country bicycle and cyclist 522
s-country ski 514
s-country ski trail 512
s-country skier 514
s-country skiing 514
s-headed tip 221
s-tip screwdriver 531
sbar 297, 370
shead 396
sing 284, 285
sing arm 362
sover 375
sover cargo deck line 385
over mirror 362
piece 202, 466
tree 520
crotch 247
crotch piece 255
crotchet 299
crotchet rest 299
Crottin de Chavignol 150
croup 83
crowbar 220
crown 63, 78, 101, 238, 239, 302, 308, 424
crown block 403
CRT television 318
crucifix 446
crude oil 405
crude-oil pipeline 404
cruise control 354
cruiseliner 386
crus of helix 115
crushed chillis 139
crusher 49, 402
crust, continental 26
crust, oceanic 26
crustaceans 71, 158
crustose lichen 50
crystal button 207
crystal drop 207
crystallization 414
Cuba 448
cube 429
cucumber 128
cucumber, seedless 128
cue ball 502, 503
cuff 240, 245
culottes 253
cultivated mushroom 123
cultural organization 335
cumin 138
cumulonimbus 42
cumulus 42
cup 163, 531, 532, 534
cup gasket 459
cup, butter 163
cup, milk/cream 163
cupboard 164
cupboard, caretaker's 443
cupule 60
curler 515
curling 515
curling brush 515
curling iron 269
curling stone 515
curly endive 127
curly kale 126
currant tomato 128
currency name 441
current event scoreboard 497
current, convection 415
curry 138
cursor down 331
cursor left 331
cursor movement keys 331
cursor right 331
cursor up 331
curtain wall 282
curtain, iron 292
curtain, privacy 464
curtain, stage 292
curved jaw 222
customer service 443
customer's supply 198
customers' cloakroom 438
customers' entrance 438
customers' toilets 438
customs control 391
customs house 381
cut nail 220
cut-throat razor 271
cuticle nippers 265
cuticle pusher 265
cuticle scissors 265
cuticle trimmer 265
cutlery 167
cutlery basket 214
cutlery set 531
cuts of beef 152
cuts of lamb 153
cuts of pork 153
cuts of veal 152
cutter link 235
cutting blade 176, 180, 341
cutting board 169
cutting edge 167, 169, 270, 398, 399, 400
cutting head 341
cutting, key 437
cuttlefish 157
cyan 418
cycle lock 372
cycle, hydrologic 45
cycling 522
cycling helmet 372
cyclone 43
cyclone, tropical 43
cylinder 429
cylinder head cover 350
cylinder vacuum cleaner 209
cylinder, cooling 420
cylinder, elevating 364
cylinder, master 357
cylinder, reflecting 420
cylinder, ruby 420
cylindrical projection 22
cymbal 308
cymbals 295, 309
Cyprus 450
cytopharynx 66
cytoplasm 50, 66, 112
cytoproct 66
cytostome 66
Czech Republic 450

D

d 298
d quark 414
daffodil 56
daggerboard 519
daggerboard well 519
daikon 129
dairy 122
dairy compartment 211
dairy products 120, 150
dairy products receiving area 120
dalmatian 86
dam 406
dance blade 509
dandelion 127
Dane, Great 86
danger area 499
Danish Blue 151
Danish rye bread 145
Danube River 18
dark chocolate 148
dart 471
dartboard 471
dashboard 354
dashboard computer 457
dashboard equipment 457
data display 328
data panel 314
data processing 38
data storage devices 333
database 335
date 132, 441
date stamp 338
date, expiry 441
David, star of 447
davit 384
day-care centre 437
dead ball line 482
dead bolt 186
deadly poisonous mushroom 52
dealer, car 433
debit card 443
debris 43
decagon, regular 429
decanter 165
deceleration lane 343
deciduous forest 44
decimal key 337
deck 313, 344
deck, dual cassette 325
deck, sun 385
deck, upper 363
declination setting scale 8, 9
décolleté bra 259
decomposers 45
decorative articles shop 437
decorative braid 260
decoy 535
decrease, voltage 402
dedicated line 334
deep fryer 178
deep peroneal nerve 108
deep-sea floor 26
defects, vision 419
defence counsel's bench 440
deferent duct 111
deflector 236, 237
deforestation 47
defrost drain 211
degree 428
degree Celsius 426
degrees Celsius 424
degrees Fahrenheit 424
Deimos 2
delegates, technical 509
delete 328, 331
delete key 331
delicatessen 120, 156
delicious lactarius 123
delivery 479
delivery entrance 435
delta 32, 35
delta distributary 32
delta wing 394
deltoid 96
demisemiquaver 299
demisemiquaver rest 299
demitasse 166
Democratic People's Republic of Korea 453
Democratic Republic of Congo 451
dendrite 110
Denmark 450
denomination 441
dental alveolus 101
dental care 272
dental floss 272
dental floss holder 272
dentin 101
deodorant 267
deoxygenated blood 104
department store 437
departure lounge 391
departure time indicator 374
departure, chair lift 512
departure, gondola 512
depolarizing mix 417
deposit slot 442
deposits, alluvial 32
depression 39
depth adjustment 229
depth of focus 27
depth-of-cut adjustment knob 229
depth-of-field preview button 314
derailleur 522
dermis 114
derrick 382, 385, 403, 404
derrick mast 385
descending aorta 103
descending colon 106
descending passage 278
desert 36, 40, 44
Desert, Atacama 17
Desert, Gobi 19
Desert, Great Sandy 15
Desert, Great Victoria 15
Desert, Kalahari 20
Desert, Namib 20
Desert, Sahara 20
designer, production 290
desk 439
desk lamp 206
desk lamp, halogen 206
desk tray 338
desk, clerks' 440
desk, front 439
desk, information 442, 463, 512
desk, reception 442
desk, student's 444
desk, teacher's 444
desktop computer 334
dessert fork 168
dessert knife 168
dessert spoon 168
destination 374
destroying angel 52
detachable control 179
detachable palm rest 330
detector, motion 286
detector, smoke 454
detergent dispenser 214
device, locking 535
device, projection 365
device, towing 364
devices, contact 198
dew 41
diable 175
diagonal buttress 284
diagonal move 470
diagonal step 514
dial 422, 424
dial/action button 337
diameter 428
diamond 468
diamond interchange 342
diamond point 202
diaphragm 105, 324
dibber 231
dice and dominoes 468
dice cup 469
diced beef 152
diced lamb 153
diced veal 152
die 469
died 426
diesel engine compartment 399, 400, 401
diesel engine shed 375
diesel lift engine 383
diesel motor compartment 398
diesel oil 405
diesel propulsion engine 383
diesel-electric locomotive 377
differential 351
difficult slope 512
diffuser 290
diffuser pin 236
digestive gland 71, 73
digestive system 106
digging fork 233
digit 75, 82
digit, prehensile 91
digital answering machine 328
digital audio player, portable 326
digital display 423, 461
digital nerve 108
digital pulp 114
digital reflex camera: camera back 315
digital thermometer 461
digital versatile disc (DVD) 319
digital watch 424
Dijon mustard 140
dill 142
dimmer switch 198
dimple 505
dinette 164
dining room 188, 280, 386, 438, 439
dinner fork 168
dinner knife 168
dinner plate 166
diode 411
Dione 3
dip switch 368
dipped beam headlight 352
dipper arm 399
dipper arm cylinder 399
dipping/indicator stalk 354
direct disc access keys 323
direct home reception 316
direct-current power cord 336
direction of electron flow 416, 417
direction of Mecca 447
directional buttons 471
director 291
director of photography 291
director's chair 200
director's control monitors 290
director's office 443
director's seat 291
director, art 290
director, assistant 291
director, race 522
directory 334
disc 357, 501

disc brake 350, 357, 366, 525
disc brake, hydraulic 522
disc compartment 323
disc compartment control 319, 323
disc drive 310
disc skip 323
disc tray 319
disc, sanding 229
discharge outlet 184
discharge tube 199
discs 177
discus 472
discus and hammer 473
dish 179, 321
dish aerial 321
dish, soufflé 172
dishes, cooking 179
dishwasher 164, 214
disk 6, 333
diskette, floppy disk 333
dispenser, cash 437, 442
dispenser, ice cube 164
displacement 418
display 319, 321, 322, 323, 325, 326, 327, 328, 336, 337, 338, 346, 423, 442, 443
display button 326
display cabinet 203
display case, refrigerated 438
display preparation area 120
display release button 336
display setting 327
display, end aisle 121
display, frequency 325
display, liquid crystal 315, 320
display, radar 457
disposable camera 315
disposable contact lens 272
disposable gas cylinder 218
disposable nappy 260
disposable razor 271
dissemination of information 335
distal phalanx 114
distributary, delta 32
distribution board 198
distribution by aerial cable network 316
distribution by submarine cable 317
distribution by underground cable network 317
distributor 360
distributor cap 350
distributor service loop 198
district 25
district, business 430, 432
district, residential 431
ditali 146
ditch 342
divergent plate boundaries 27
diverging lenses 419
diversion tunnel 406
divide key 337
divider 274, 277
dividers 339
diving 518
diving apparatus 518
diving board 184
diving tower 518
diving well 184
division 427
djembe 297
Djibouti 451
Dnieper River 18
do-it-yourself 216
do-it-yourself and gardening 216
do-it-yourself shop 436
dock 381
dock, prisoner's 440
dock, unloading 437, 439
docking cradle 337
doctor, junior 464
document folder 339
document receiving 328
document-to-be-sent position 328
dodecagon, regular 429
does not belong to 427
dog 86, 535
dog breeds 86
dog, morphology of 86
dogfish, larger spotted 158
dolichos beans 130
dolina 31
dollar 440
dolly 290
dolly tracks 290
dolphin 90
dolphin, morphology of 90
domain name 334
domain, second-level 334
domain, top-level 334
dome 177
dome shutter 7
dome tent 529
domestic appliances 176, 208
domestic appliances, miscellaneous 180
domestic pollution 47
Dominica 449
Dominican Republic 449
dominoes, dice and 468
dominos 468
donkey 84
door 178, 202, 210, 213, 287, 349, 352, 361, 392, 439, 447, 528, 529
door grip 352
door handle 185, 186, 349
door lock 349
door open warning light 355
door panel 202
door pillar 349
door pocket 352
door shelf 211
door stop 211
door switch 213
door, cargo bay 13
door, entrance 362, 363
door, fire 286
door, lift 363
door, patio 164
door, screen 361
door, strip 286
door, two-leaf 362
doors, entrance 294
doors, examples of 286
Doric column, engaged 281
dormer window 182
dorsal abdominal artery 71
dorsal fin 90
dorsalis pedis artery 102
dorsum of nose 117
dorsum of tongue 118
double bass 301
double basses 295
double bed 439
double boiler 175
double flat 299
double plate 187
double reed 306
double ring 471
double room 439
double seat 380
double sharp 299
double sink 194
double slash 334
double-blank 468
double-breasted buttoning 248
double-breasted jacket 244
double-decker bus 363
double-edged razor 271
double-edged razor blade 271
double-leaf bascule bridge 345
double-six 468
double-twist auger bit 228
doubles service court 495
doubles sideline 490, 495
doublet 468
doubling die 469
doubly toothed 55
dough hook 176
dough, filo 145
dousing water tank 408
dovetail 420
down tube 371
downhill 511
downhill bicycle and cyclist 522
downhill/Super G ski 510
downpipe 182
drag 536
drag wheel, star 537
dragonfly 69
drain 197
drain hose 212, 214
drain valve 404
drain, defrost 211
drain, main 184
drainage circuit 194
draining spoon 173
Drake Passage 15, 17
draught 470
draught arm 400
draught tube 400, 407
draughtboard 470
draughts 470
draw hoe 233
draw tube 421
drawbridge 282
drawer 164, 202, 203, 205, 210
drawing pins 341
drawstring 249, 275
drawstring bag 275
drawstring hood 261
dredger 172
dress circle 293
dress, A-line 252
dresser 290
dresser, set 291
dresses, examples of 252
dressing gown 256
dressing room 290, 293
dressing room, private 290
dressing table 203
dried chillis 139
drill collar 403
drill pipe 403
drill ship 382
drill, masonry 228
drill, twist 228
drill-driver, cordless 228
drilling drawworks 403
drilling rig 403
drink box 163
drinks 120
drinks machine 463
drip bowl 210
drip moulding 349
drip tray 181
dripping pan 174, 179
drive belt 212
drive chain 370
drive mode 314
drive shaft 383, 395
drive shaft, longitudinal 351
drive wheel 180
drive, CD/DVD-ROM 329, 336
drive, floppy disk 329
driver 524
driver seat 369
driver's cab 376, 377
driveway 183
driving glove 243
driving propeller 383
driving wheels 401
dromedary 85
drone 68
drone pipe 296
droop nose 394
drop earrings 264
drop shot 491
drop waist dress 252
drop-leaf 202
drum 170, 212, 213, 357
drum brake 357
drum, rotating 27
drum, talking 297
drumhead 308
drumlin 29
drums 308
drumstick 297
drupelet 59
dry cells 417
dry cleaner 437
dry climates 40
dry dock 381
dry fruits 60, 133
dry gallery 31
dual cassette deck 325
dual seat 367
dual swivel mirror 269
dual-in-line package 417
duck 81, 155
duck egg 155
duct, exhaust air 345
duct, fresh-air 345
duffle bag 276
duffle coat 249
dugout 474
dulse 123
dumbbell 500
dune 35
dunes, examples of 36
dung, animal 48
dungarees 254
dungarees with crossover back straps 261
duo 300
duodenum 106
dura mater 109, 110
durian 137
dust canister 229
dust receiver 208
dust tail 6
dusting brush 209
dustpan 215
Dutch bicycle 373
Dutch oven 175
duty belt 456
duty-free shop 391
DVD burner 333
DVD recorder 319
dyke 28
dynamo 370

E

e 298
e-commerce 335
eagle 81
ear 92, 201
ear drum 116
ear flap 238
ear loaf 144
ear protection 458
ear studs 264
ear, auricle 115
ear, structure of 116
ear, wood 123
earlobe 115
earphone 324
earphone jack 329
earphones 325, 326
earpiece 273, 460
earplugs 458
earrings 264
Earth 2, 3, 4, 5, 14
Earth coordinate system 21
earth foundation 342
earth station, satellite 335
earth terminal 198
earth wire 198
Earth's atmosphere, profile 37
Earth's crust 26, 27
Earth's crust, section 26
Earth's orbit 4, 5
Earth, structure 26
earthflow 31
earthing pin 198
earthquake 27
East 23
East China Sea 19
East Pacific Rise 34
East Timor 452
East-Northeast 23
East-Southeast 23
Eastern hemisphere 21
Eastern meridian 22
eau de parfum 267
eau de toilette 267
eave 283
eccrine sweat gland 114
eclipses, types 4, 5
economy and finance 441
Ecuador 448
edge 441, 509, 510, 533
edging 230
edible boletus 123
editorial 313
education 444
educational institution 335, 433
eel 159
effect, greenhouse 46
effluent 32
effusive volcano 28
egg 79, 112
egg beater 172
egg carton 162
egg noodles 147
egg poacher 175
egg slicer 173
egg timer 171
egg tray 211
egg, duck 155
egg, goose 155
egg, hen 155
egg, ostrich 155
egg, pheasant 155
egg, quail 155
eggs 155
Egypt 451
Egyptian reed pen 312
eiderdown 204
ejaculatory duct 111
eject button 315, 323, 471
ejector nozzle, variable 394
El Salvador 448
elastic 204
elastic loop 528
elastic strainer 529
elastic support bandage 461
elastic waistband 249
elastic webbing 246
elasticized leg opening 247
elbow 83, 86, 93, 95
elbow pad 486, 526, 527
elbows 146
electric charge, measurement of 4
electric cooker 210
electric current, measurement of 4
electric drill 228
electric fan motor 358
electric golf cart 505
electric guitar 303
electric knife 177
electric motor 235, 237
electric potential difference, measurement of 426
electric razor 271
electric resistance, measurement
426
electric steamer 179
electric toothbrush 272
electric tumble dryer 213
electrical box 198
electrical cable 354
electrical circuit, parallel 416
electrical connection 365
electrical system 351
electricity 198
electricity cable 434
electricity meter 198
electricity tools 217
electricity transmission 408
electrolytic capacitors 417
electrolytic separator 417
electromagnetic spectrum 418
electron 414
electron beam 318
electron collector 417
electron flow, direction of 416, 4
electron gun 318
electronic ballast 199
electronic control unit 357
electronic drum pad 311
electronic instruments 310
electronic payment terminal 121,
electronic piano 311
electronic scales 423
electronic timer, automatic 517
electronic viewfinder 320
electronics 417
electronics shop 436
element, surface 210
elements of a house 185
elements of architecture 286
elephant 85

ENGLISH INDEX

evating cylinder 364, 397, 455
evation 182
evation adjustment 420
evation zones and vegetation 44
evator 393, 400
evon 13
x 85
nail 335
nail key 330
nail software 334
bankment 342
blem, team's 506
ergency brake 380
ergency physician's office 462
ergency station 345
ergency switch 368
ergency truck 345
ery boards 265
ission, nitric acid 48
ission, nitrogen oxide 48
ission, polluting gas 47
ission, sulphur dioxide 48
ission, sulphuric acid 48
menthal 151
pty set 427
ptying hose 212
mel 101
losure 122, 286
331
aisle display 121
button 301
cap 409
joist 187
key 331
line 484, 487, 489, 493
moraine 30
piece 111
plate 409
stop 226, 521
zone 484
piece 503
power key 327
ocardium 104
ocarp 57, 58
oplasmic reticulum 50, 66
piece 273
gy 402
gy integration to transmission
etwork 413
gy release 415
gy saving bulb 199, 411
gy, heat 46
gy, measurement of 426
gy, solar 54
gy, thermal 402
ged Corinthian column 281
ged Doric column 281
ged Ionic column 281
gement ring 264
e 366, 403
ne air intake 362
ne block 360
ne compartment 362, 396, 401
ne housing 235
e mounting pylon 393
e room 384, 386
e, main 13
e, outboard 385
e, petrol 351
eer, sound 291
es, fire 455
h billiards 503
h Channel 18
h Index 539
sh mustard 140
h stick 466
aced greenhouse effect 46
mushroom 123
ature 185, 279
331
key 331
rise 335
55
ce door 362, 363
ce doors 294
ce hall 188
ce turnstile 378
ce, actors' 278
ce, customers' 438
entrance, main 445, 465
entrance, public 278
entrance, pyramid 278
entrance, staff 438, 445
entry 396
envelope, padded 339
environment 44
environment, natural 504
epaulet 248
epicalyx 59
epicentre 27
epicondyle 99
epidermis 114
epididymis 111
epidural space 110
epiglottis 105, 118
epitrochlea 99
equals key 337
Equator 22
equator 17, 20, 21, 43
Equatorial Guinea 451
equipment 472
equipment compartment 376
equipment storage room 444
equipment, dashboard 457
equipment, household 215
equipment, miscellaneous 231
equipment, sound recording 291
erase button 315
eraser 341
erecting lenses 420
Eris 3
Eritrea 451
escalator 294, 378, 435
escape 330
escape key 330
escarole 126
escutcheon 73, 186, 197
escutcheon plate 198
espadrille 242
espresso coffee maker 181
espresso machine 181
estate car 347
Estonia 450
estuary 24, 35
eternal light 447
Ethernet port 336
Ethiopia 451
Eurasia 14
Eurasian Plate 27
euro 440
Europa 2
Europe 14, 18, 34, 449
European experiment module 11
European outlet 198
European plug 198
European robin 80
European Union flag 441
Eustachian tube 116, 117
Eutelsat 316
euthynteria 279
evacuation route 345
evaporated milk 150
evaporation 45, 414
evening glove 243
event platform 496
events, technical 511
ex-voto 446
examination and treatment room 463
examination room 465
examination, psychiatric 462
examples of aircraft 394
examples of algae 51
examples of amphibians 75
examples of angles 428
examples of arachnids 70
examples of armchairs 200
examples of bicycles 373
examples of bills 79
examples of birds 80
examples of bits and drills 228
examples of blouses 255
examples of boats and ships 382
examples of bodywork 347
examples of branching 197
examples of broadleaved trees 64
examples of carnivorous mammals 88
examples of chairs 201
examples of conifers 65
examples of currency abbreviations 440
examples of doors 286
examples of dresses 252
examples of dunes 36
examples of feet 79
examples of ferns 52
examples of flowers 56
examples of forks 168
examples of freight wagons 377
examples of heads 221
examples of holds 499
examples of insects 69
examples of instrumental groups 300
examples of interchanges 342
examples of jumps 509
examples of kitchen knives 169
examples of knives 168
examples of lagomorphs 82
examples of leaves 65
examples of lichens 50
examples of marine mammals 90
examples of mosses 51
examples of motorcycles 369
examples of nails 220
examples of pleats 253
examples of primates 91
examples of reptiles 77
examples of rodents 82
examples of shorelines 35
examples of skirts 253
examples of skis 510
examples of sleeping bags 530
examples of spectacles 273
examples of spoons 168
examples of tables 202
examples of tents 528
examples of tips 221
examples of trousers 254
examples of trucks 364
examples of tyres 358
examples of ungulate mammals 84
examples of volcanoes 28
examples of windows 287
exercise cycle 501
exercise wear 263
exhalation valve 459
exhaust air duct 345
exhaust manifold 350, 360
exhaust pipe 395
exhaust pipe stack 398
exhaust stack 364, 401
exhaust system 351
exhaust valve 360
exhibition centre 430
exit 343
exit button 337
exit taxiway 391
exit turnstile 378
exocarp 57, 58, 59
exosphere 37
expandable baton 456
expandable file pouch 274
expander 310
expansion bolt 221
expansion chamber 424
expert slope 512
expiry date 441
explosive volcano 28
exposure adjustment knob 314
exposure mode 314
extending table 202
extension 202
extension ladder 219
extension tube 209
exterior dome shell 7
exterior door 185
exterior of a house 182
exterior pocket 274, 276
exterior sign 378
external auditory meatus 100
external ear 116
external floppy disk drive 333
external fuel tank 12
external jugular vein 102
external nose 117
external oblique 96, 97
external socket 361
external tooth lock washer 222
extinguisher, fire 457
extractor hood 210
eye 43, 70, 71, 72, 76, 90, 94, 119, 220, 538
eye drops, lubricant 272
eye make-up 266
eye protection 458
eye ring 78
eye wall 43
eyeball 75, 119
eyebrow pencil 266
eyebrow stripe 78
eyebrow tweezers 265
eyelash 119
eyelash curler 266
eyelashes 87
eyelet 240, 263, 275, 509
eyelet tab 240
eyelet, strap 315
eyelid 76
eyepiece 8, 9, 320, 420, 421
eyepiece holder 8
eyeshadow 266
eyestalk 72

F

f 298
fabric guide 208
façade 285
face 91, 92, 220, 493, 505
face flannel 267
face mask 478, 486, 507
face-off circle 506
face-off spot 506
facepiece 459
faceplate 186
factorial 427
factory 430
faculae 4
Fahrenheit scale 424
fairing 366, 523
fairings, side 525
fairlead 521
fairway 504
falcon 81
Falkland Islands 17
fall front 203
fallopian tube 112
fallopian tubes 113
fallow land 122
false rib 99
false start rope 516
false tuck 260
family tent 528
family waiting room 462
fan 213
fan belt 350, 360
fan brush 266
fan housing 270
fan trellis 230
fan, case 329
fan, cooling 322, 350
fan, power supply 329
fang 70, 76
fantail 412
farmhouse 122
farmhouse loaf 145
farming, intensive 46, 48
farmstead 122
farmyard 122
fascia, front 348
fast data entry control 310
fast forward 319
fast-food restaurants 437
fast-forward button 323
fastener binder 339
fats and oils 149
fault 27
fax machine 328
feather crown 495
feathered shuttlecock 495
feed tube 177, 180
feeder lane 343
feedhorn 321
feet, examples of 79
feijoa 137
female 426
female cone 65
female ferrule 536, 537
female genital organs 112
femoral artery 102
femoral nerve 108
femoral vein 102
femur 98
fence 122, 182, 226
fence, outfield 475
fennec 88
fennel 125
fenugreek 138
fern 52
fern, bird's nest 52
fern, fiddlehead 125
fern, structure of 52
fern, tree 52
ferns, examples of 52
ferrule 219, 503
ferrule, female 537
ferrule, male 537
ferry boat 386
ferryboat 381
fertilization, soil 47
fertilizer application 47
fetlock 83
fetlock joint 83
fettucine 146
fibres 215
fibula 98
fiddlehead 52
fiddlehead fern 125
field 474, 479, 482
field lens 420
field lens adjustment 421
field line 416
field magnetic 416
field mouse 82
field, geothermal 402
field, paddy 47
field, track and 472
fielder's glove 477
fielders 479
fifth 298
fifth wheel 364
fifty 427
fig 137
figure skate 509
figure skating 509
Fiji 453
Fiji Islands 15
filament 56, 199
Filchner Ice Shelf 15
file 229, 334, 531
file format 334
file guides 340
file, nail 265
filiform papilla 118
filing box 340
filler cap 237, 358, 364
filler hole 208
filler neck 351
filler pipe 196
fillet roast 152
filleting knife 169
filling inlet 404
film titles and schedules 294
film, heat-sealed 163
film, plastic 162
filo dough 145
filter 178, 181, 184, 210
filter cover 459
filter holder 181
filter, air 350
filtration, intrusive 47
fin, anal 74
fin, caudal 74, 90
fin, dorsal 90
fin, first dorsal 74
fin, pectoral 74, 90
fin, pelvic 74
fin, second dorsal 74
final drive 398
finance, economy and 441
financial services 442
finch 80
finderscope 8, 9
fine adjustment knob 421
fine adjustment wheel 425
fine data entry control 310

fine guidance system 7
finely threaded screw 425
finger 114, 477
finger button 307
finger flange 460
finger tip 339
fingerboard 296, 301, 303
fingerless mitt 243
fingernail 115
finial 283
finish line 473
finish wall 516
finishing nail 220
Finland 450
fir 65
fir needles 65
fire door 286
fire engines 455
fire extinguisher 457
fire hose 454
fire hydrant 434, 454
fire irons 193
fire prevention 454
fire station 433
fire, forest 47
fire-fighting material 454
firebrick 192
firebrick back 192
firefighter 454
firefighting aircraft, amphibious 394
fireplace 188, 192
fireplace screen 193
FireWire port 336
firing, wood 192
first aid equipment 460
first aid kit 457, 461
first aid manual 461
first assistant camera operator 290
first base 474
first baseman 474
first dorsal fin 74
first floor 182, 189
first leaves 53
first molar 101
first premolar 101
first quarter 5
first row 482
first space 489
first valve slide 307
first violins 295
first voltage increase 413
first-class cabin 392
fish dish 166
fish fork 168
fish kettle 174
fish knife 168
fish scaler 531
fish, bony 74
fish, cartilaginous 74
fishes 74
fishes, bony 159
fishes, cartilaginous 158
fishhook 536, 538
fishing 536
fishing jacket 538
fishnet stocking 257
fission of uranium fuel 408
fission products (radioactive nuclei) 415
fission, nuclear 415
fissionable nucleus 415
fissure, oblique 105
fitness equipment 500
fitted sheet 204
fitting 455
five 427
five hundred 427
five spice powder 139
fixed base 224
fixed bridges 344
fixed distance marking 391
fixed jaw 223, 224, 425
fjords 35
flag 482
flag pole, removable 504
flag, European Union 441
flageolet 131
flags 448
flagstone 230
flame 415
flame spreader 218
flame-resistant driving suit 524
flamingo 81
flank 78, 83
flank forward 482
flanking tower 282
flannel, face 267
flap 244, 275
flap pocket 244, 248
flap, fuel tank 349
flap, self-sealing 339
flap, top 532
flare 4
flare nut spanner 223
flare, road 457
flash tube 420
flashing 193
flashlight 456
flask, vacuum 532
flat 299, 526
flat mirror 7
flat sheet 204
flat tip 221
flat truck 377
flat washer 222
flat-back brush 268
flat-plate solar collector 410
flea 69
flesh 57, 58, 59
fleshy fruit: berry fruit 59
fleshy fruit: citrus fruit 58
fleshy leaf 54
fleshy pome fruit 58
fleshy stone fruit 57
flews 86
flex 208, 209, 217, 235, 237, 270, 271
flex sleeve 218, 229
flex support 208
flexible boot 513
flexible hose 209
flexible skirt 383
flexible tube 460
flies 292
flight 471
flight bag 276
flight deck 12, 392, 395
flight information board 391
flight of stairs 191
flights 518
flint 218
flip 509
flip-flop 242
float 394, 538
float ball 196
float seaplane 394
floating crane 381
floating head 271
floating rib 98
floating roof 404
floating-roof tank 404
floodplain 32
floor 193, 412
floor brush 209
floor coverings, textile 190
floor drain 194
floor exercise area 496
floor joist 187
floor mat 356
floor mats 496
floor, car 287
floor, ocean 33
floorboard 369
flooring strip 190
floppy disk drive 329
floppy disk drive, external 333
floppy disk eject button 329
florist 437
floss, dental 272
flour and semolina 144
flour, oat 144
flour, plain 144
flour, unbleached 144
flour, whole wheat 144
flow tube 410
flower 53, 56
flower bed 230
flower bud 53
flower, structure 56
flowering 62
flowers, examples of 56
flue 305
flue pipe 305
fluff trap 213
fluid, cerebro-spinal 110
fluorescent tube 199
flush 468
flush handle 196
flute 228
fluted land 228
flutes 295
fly 69, 246, 247, 260
fly agaric 52
fly front closing 251, 261
fly half 482
fly line 536
fly reel 536
fly rod 536
fly, tsetse 69
flyfishing 536
flying buttress 284, 285
flyover 343, 344
flysheet 528, 529
flywheel 360, 501
FM mode select button 322
foam 33
foam cushion 458
foam gun 385
foam pad 530
foam, shaving 271
focus 27, 419
focus button 320
focus mode selector 314
focus, Cassegrain 7
focus, coudé 7
focusing knob 8, 9
focusing ring 420
fodder corn 122
fog 41
fog lamp 352
fog light 364
foie gras 156
foil stip, hologram 441
foil, aluminium 162
folder 340
folding chair 201
folding door 286
folding grill 533
folding nail file 265
folding ramp 386
folding shovel 532
foliage 63
foliate papilla 118
foliose lichen 50
follicle 60
following car 522
fondue fork 168
fondue pot 174
fondue set 174
fongiform papilla 118
font, baptismal 446
font, holy water 446
fontanelle, anterior 100
fontanelle, mastoid 100
fontanelle, posterior 100
fontanelle, sphenoidal 100
food 120
food and kitchen 120
food can 163
food chain 45
food mill 170
food processor 177
food store 439
food tray 162
food vacuole 66
food, convenience 121
foods, catering 121
foods, frozen 121
foot 72, 73, 91, 92, 93, 94, 95, 202, 247, 260, 302, 305, 308, 519, 536, 537
foot fault judge 491
foot hole 305
foot plate 501
foot protection 459
foot strap 519
football 480, 486
football boot 480
football, American 484
footballer 480
footboard 204, 523
footbridge 282, 375, 379
footing 187
footless tights 263
footlights 293
footrest 205, 224, 467
footstool 164, 201
footstrap 254, 501
for cooking 178
for correspondence 338
for cutting 177
for filing 339
for juicing 177
for measuring 171
for mixing and blending 176
for opening 170
for time use 338
foramen caecum 118
force, measurement of 426
fore-and-aft passage 385
forearm 86, 93, 95, 534
forearm crutch 466
forearm pad 486
forearm support 466
forecast, meteorological 38
forecastle 383, 387
forecourt 346, 491
forehead 78, 92
foreleg 67, 68
forelimb 75
forelock 83
foremast 385
forest 29
forest fire 47
forest, boreal 44
forest, coniferous 44
forest, deciduous 44
forest, mixed 44
forest, temporal 44
forest, tropical 44
forest, tropical rain 44
forestay 520
forewing 67
fork 8, 167, 371, 396, 522, 525, 531
fork arm 396
fork, front 522
forked tongue 76
forklift truck 396
forks, examples of 168
format, file 334
Former Yugoslav Republic of Macedonia 450
formeret 284
forming food vacuole 66
formula 1 car 525
formula 3000 car 524
formula Indy car 524
fortified wall 447
forward 518
fossil energy, geothermy and 402
fossil fuel 46, 48
foul line 474
foul line post 475
foundation 187
foundation of tower 344
foundation slip 258
fountain for ritual ablutions 447
fountain pen 312
four-blade beater 176
four-door saloon 347
four-four time 298
four-of-a-kind 468
four-way lug wrench 356
four-way selector 315
fourchette 243
fourth 298
fovea 119
fowl, guinea 81, 154
fox 88
foyers 293
fraction 427
fractionating tower 405
frame 192, 202, 204, 219, 224, 2
274, 277, 297, 309, 367, 396, 400, 401, 410, 411, 412, 425, 460, 476, 492, 494, 522, 527, 528
frame stile 202
France 449
frankfurter 156
franking machine 339
free guard zone 515
free margin 114
free throw line 489
free-skating blade 509
freehold flats 289
freestyle snowboard 513
freewheel 372
freezer 164, 438
freezer bag 162
freezer compartment 211
freezer door 211
freezer, chest 211
freezer, reach-in 120
freezing 414
freezing rain 41
freight wagon 375
freight wagons, examples of 377
French bread 144
French horn 307
French horns 295
French loaf 144
frequency display 325
frequency, measurement of 426
fresco 280
fresh cheeses 150
fresh meat counter 120
fresh-air duct 345
fret 302, 303
friction strip 218
frieze 202, 279
frilly nylon tights 260
frilly pants 260
frog 75, 249, 301
frog, common 75
frog, morphology of 75
frog, Northern leopard 75
frog, wood 75
frog-adjustment screw 229
frond 52
front 244, 245
front apron 245
front axle 401
front beam 422
front brake 371
front brake lever 368
front compression strap 532
front cover 333
front derailleur 370, 372
front desk 439
front fascia 348
front foil 387
front footrest 367, 368
front fork 522
front fork, telescopic 369
front indicator 366, 368
front lamp 371
front leg 201
front lights 352
front mudguard 366
front page 313
front picture 313
front pipe 350
front pocket 275
front rigid section 363
front shock absorber 369
front sight 534
front tip 208
front top pocket 246
front view 478
front wheel 401, 467
front-end loader 399
frontal 96, 446
frontal bone 98, 100
frontal sinus 117
frontier 23
frontwall 365
frozen food storage 121
frozen foods 121
fruit branch 62
fruit tree 122

uit vegetables 128
uit, fleshy pome 58
uit, fleshy stone 57
uit, fleshy: berry fruit 59
uit, fleshy: citrus fruit 58
uit, passion 136
uiting 62
uits 57, 132
uits and vegetables 120
its, citrus 134
its, dry 60, 133
its, pome 133
its, stone 132
ticose lichen 50
ing basket 171
ing pan 175, 531
el 408
el bundle 409
el conduit 351
el gauge 355
el injector 360
el oil 405
el pellet 409
el rod 409
l supply system 351
l tank 235, 351, 364, 366, 369, 377, 395
l tank flap 349
, fossil 46, 48
rum 518
back 482
face mask 454
house 468
moon 5
face helmet 525
back 485
narole 28
ction display 310
ction keys 328, 330, 423
ction keys, programmable 443
ction selectors 327
gicide 47
culus 59, 60
nel 171, 318, 382, 386
nel cloud 43
32, 91
iture, children's 205
iture, house 200
ow 118
198, 411
lage 393
li 146
n 204

G

8
amp 224
e 182, 285
e stud 187
e vent 182
etop 163
on 451
r 291
ohn 127
horse 83
y 6
ladder 106
ry 285, 412
ry, connecting 345
ry, Grand 278
y 392
o 83
h 240
bia 451
154, 492
board 469
console 471
of darts 471
, board 469
, online 335
/MIDI port 329
s 468
s area 386
s, sports and 468
a rays 418
on, cerebropleural 73
on, spiral 109
on, visceral 73
gantry crane 406, 407
Ganymede 2
gap 538
garage 182
garage door, sectional 286
garage door, up-and-over 286
garam masala 139
garden 280
garden arch 230
garden cress 127
garden hose 236
garden line 231
garden path 182
garden shears 234
garden sorrel 127
garden spider 70
gardening 230
gardening gloves 232
garlic 124
garlic press 170
garter snake 77
gas 403, 405, 414
gas container 529
gas cooker 210
gas cylinder, medical 464
gas main 434
gas, greenhouse 46
gasket 214
gaskin 83
gastrocnemius 96, 97
gate 381, 407
gate-leg 202
gate-leg table 202
gather 255
gather skirt 253
gauntlet 243
gauze roller bandage 461
gear cable 372
gear housing 537
gear lever 350, 354, 369, 371, 372
gear, landing 361, 365
gearbox 350
gearchange pedal 367, 368
gelatin capsule 467
general view 186
generator 402
generator unit 407
generator, steam 402
Genoa salami 156
geographical map 444
geography 14
geology 26
geometrical shapes 428
geometry 428
Georgia 452
geothermal field 402
geothermy and fossil energy 402
germ 61
German mustard 140
German rye bread 145
German salami 156
German shepherd 86
Germany 450
germination 53
geyser 28
Ghana 451
ghee 150
gherkin 128
giant slalom 511
gibbon 91
Gibraltar, Strait of 18
gift shop 436
gill 52
gill openings 74
gills 73
ginger 139
ginkgo nut 133
giraffe 85
girder 187
girdle 259
glacial cirque 30
glacial lake 32
glacier 30, 32, 44
glacier tongue 30
gland, digestive 71, 73
gland, green 71
gland, salivary 118
glans penis 111
glass 410, 411
glass bottle 163
glass case 423
glass collection unit 49
glass cover 211
glass protector 506
glass recycling container 49
glass roof 188, 374, 435
glass slide 421
glass sorting 49
glass, magnifying 421
glass-fronted display cabinet 203
glassware 165
glazed frost 41
glazing bar 186
gliding phase 514
global warming 46
globe 444, 529
globular cluster 6
glottis 76
glove 10, 478, 498, 506, 508, 513, 514, 522, 525
glove compartment 354
glove finger 243
glove storage 464
glove, back of 243
glove, blocking 507
glove, catching 507
glove, latex 460
glove, massage 267
glove, palm of 243
glove, softball 477
gloves 243
gloves, gardening 232
gloves, goalkeeper's 480
gloves, men's 243
gloves, women's 243
glucose 54
glue 190
glue stick 341
gluteal nerve 108
gluteus maximus 97
gnocchi 146
gnomon 424
go 470
goal 480, 482, 485, 507
goal area 480
goal crease 507
goal judge 506
goal lights 507
goal line 482, 484, 506
goalkeeper 481, 506, 507
goalkeeper's gloves 480
goalkeeper's pad 507
goalkeeper's skate 507
goalkeeper's stick 507
goalpost 485
goat 84
goat's milk 150
goat's-milk cheeses 150
goatfish 159
Gobi Desert 19
goggles 218, 513, 522
goggles, protective 522, 525
goggles, swimming 516
golf 504
golf bag 505
golf ball 505
golf course 430
golf glove 505
golf shoes 505
golf trolley 505
Golgi apparatus 50, 66
gonad 73
gondola 121, 512
gondola departure 512
gong 295, 309
Good Hope, Cape of 20
goods station 375
goods, canned 121
goose 81, 155
goose egg 155
goose-neck 191
gooseberry 132
gooseneck 400
gored skirt 253
gorge 31, 32
Gorgonzola 151
gorilla 91
gorilla, morphology of 91
Gothic cathedral 284
gour 31
gourd, wax 128
government organization 335
governor tension sheave 287
governor, speed 287
grab handle 361, 364, 455
gracile 97
grader 401
graduated dial 533
graduated scale 422, 423
grain of wheat, section 61
grain terminal 381
gram, black 131
Grand Canyon 16
Grand Gallery 278
granitic layer 26
granivorous bird 79
granulated sugar 149
granulation 4
grape 62, 132
grape, section of 59
grapefruit 134
grapefruit knife 169
grass 492
grassbox 237
grasshopper, bow-winged 69
grassland 44
grate 210
grater 170
grater, nutmeg 170
grater, rotary cheese 170
grating, utensils for 170
gravel bed 524
gravy boat 166
gray matter 109
grease well 179
greases 405
great adductor 97
Great Australian Bight 15
Great Barrier Reef 15
Great Dane 86
Great Dividing Range 15
great green bush-cricket 69
great horned owl 81
Great Lakes 16
great organ manual 305
Great Sandy Desert 15
great saphenous vein 102
great scallop 157
Great Victoria Desert 15
greater alar cartilage 117
greater covert 78
greater pectoral 96
greater trochanter 99
Greece 450
Greek bread 144
Greek temple 279
Greek temple, plan 279
Greek theatre 278
green 418, 504
green alga 51
green ball 503
green beam 318
green bean 131
green cabbage 126
green coffee beans 148
green gland 71
green light 434
green onion 124
green peas 130
green pepper 138
green russula 123
green sweet pepper 128
green tea 148
green walnut 60
greenhouse 122
greenhouse effect 46
greenhouse effect, enhanced 46
greenhouse effect, natural 46
greenhouse gas 46
greenhouse gas concentration 46
Greenland 16
Greenland Sea 14
Grenada 449
grey matter 110
grid 318
grid system 22
grid, lighting 291
grid, starting 524
griddle 179
grike 31
grill, indoor electric 179
grille 279, 296, 348
grille, security 442
grinding, utensils for 170
grip 290, 500, 505, 535
grip handle 226
grip tape 526
grip, key 290
groin 92, 94
groove 169, 359, 510
ground 404
ground floor 182, 188
ground moraine 30
ground pepper 139
ground terminal 322
ground, teeing 504
groundhog 82
growth line 72, 73
Gruyère 151
guard 169, 217, 489
guard rail 211, 526
guard, ankle 476
guard, cable 535
guard, leg 476
guard, point 489
guard, shin 513
guard, tooth 486
guard, wrist 527
guardhouse 282
guardrail 384
Guatemala 448
guava 137
guide bar 235
guide handle 229
guide rail, car 287
guide rail, counterweight 287
guide ring 536
guide, tape 341
guiding tower 345
Guinea 451
guinea fowl 81, 154
guinea pig 82
Guinea, Gulf of 20
Guinea-Bissau 451
guitar, bass 303
gulf 24
Gulf of Aden 19, 20
Gulf of Alaska 16
Gulf of Bothnia 18
Gulf of California 16
Gulf of Carpentaria 15
Gulf of Guinea 20
Gulf of Mexico 16
Gulf of Oman 19
Gulf of Panama 17
Gulf, Persian 19
gum 101, 116
gum massager 272
gumshield 498
gun 216
gun flap 248
gun, heat 219
gurnard 159
gusset 274, 276
gusset pocket 255
Gutenberg discontinuity 26
gutter 182
guy line 528
guy wire 412
Guyana 448
guyot 33
gymnasium 386, 444
gymnasium office 444
gymnast's name 497
gymnastics 496
gynaecological examination room 463
gyratory system 342

H

hack 515
hackle 536
hacksaw 226
haddock 161
hair 93, 95, 114, 301
hair bulb 114
hair clip 268
hair colour 267
hair conditioner 267
hair dryer 270
hair follicle 114
hair grip 268
hair roller 268
hair roller pin 268
hair shaft 114
hair slide 268
hair stylist 290
hairbrushes 268
haircutting scissors 270
hairdresser 436
hairdressing 268
hairpin 268
hairs, root 53
Haiti 448
half handle 169
half-glasses 273
half-mask respirator 459
half-slip 258
half-volley 490
halfway line 481, 483
halibut 161
hall 188, 386, 439
hall, entrance 188
hall, town 432
halo 6
halogen desk lamp 206
ham knife 169
ham, cooked 156
ham, smoked 153
hammer 304, 472, 534
hammer loop 225
hammer rail 304
hamster 82
hand 91, 93, 95, 115
hand blender 176
hand fork 232
hand grip 536
hand mitre saw 226
hand mixer 176
hand post 297
hand protector 235, 525
hand rest 332
hand strap 320
hand tools 232
hand vacuum cleaner 208
hand warmer pocket 251
hand, 1/10 second 424
hand-warmer pocket 249
handbags 275
handbrake 350
handbrake lever 354
handcuff case 456
handgrip 366, 369, 466
handgrips 500
handicap spot 470
handle 167, 170, 176, 177, 178, 179, 180, 192, 204, 208, 209, 210, 211, 215, 216, 217, 219, 220, 221, 222, 223, 224, 225, 226, 227, 229, 231, 235, 236, 237, 269, 270, 271, 272, 273, 274, 275, 276, 277, 301, 325, 341, 356, 467, 477, 478, 492, 493, 494, 510, 515, 531, 536, 537
handle, crank 225
handle, insulated 179
handle, twist 332
handlebar 501, 523
handlebar stem 371
handlebar, raised 522
handlebars 371, 523
handling 396
handrail 191, 287, 363, 380, 385
handsaw 226
handset 327
handset flex 327
hang-up ring 270
hanger bracket 467
hanger loop 250
hanging basket 230
hanging cupboard 203
hanging glacier 30
hanging pendant 206
hanging stile 185, 186, 202
hank 521
hapteron 51
harbour 381
hard boot 513
hard contact lens 272
hard disk drive 333
hard disk drive, removable 333
hard disk, removable 333
hard hat 458
hard palate 116, 117
hard surface (cement) 492
hard-shell clam 157
hare 82, 154
harissa 141
harmonica 296
harp 302
harps 295
hasp 277
hastate 55
hat switch 332
hatband 238
hatch 13
hatch, side 12
hatchback 347
hatchet 454, 533
hawk 216
hawse pipe 383, 387
hayloft 122
hazard, water 504
hazelnut 133
hazelnut, section 60
head 6, 67, 72, 78, 93, 95, 103, 111, 125, 220, 221, 223, 229, 271, 272, 301, 302, 303, 309, 492, 494, 505, 536
head cover 505
head harness 459
head linesman 485
head nurse's office 463
head of femur 99
head of frame 186
head of humerus 99
head protection 458
head teacher's office 445
head waiter 438
head, bird 78
head, cutting 341
head, snare 297
headband 324, 458, 459
headbay 406
headboard 204, 205
headgear 238, 498
headgear, men's 238
headgear, unisex 239
headgear, women's 239
heading 313
headland 35
headlight 348, 364, 366, 368, 376, 377, 523
headline 313
headphone jack 310, 311, 322, 323, 326
headphones 324
headrest 353
heads, examples of 221
headset kit 327
health 460
health and beauty care 121
health organization 335
hearing 115
heart 71, 73, 104, 105, 154, 468
heartwood 63
heat deflecting disc 199
heat energy 46
heat gun 219
heat loss 46
heat production 408
heat ready indicator 269
heat selector switch 270
heat shield 12
heat transfer 415
heat-sealed film 163
heater 529
heating 192
heating duct 213
heating element 213, 214, 218
heating grille 380
heating oil 405
heating/air conditioning equipment 386
heavy machinery 398
heavy petroleum 405
heavy rainfall 43
heavy-duty boot 240
hedge 183, 230
hedge trimmer 235
heel 93, 95, 169, 226, 229, 240, 247, 262, 301, 302, 477, 506, 509
heel grip 240
heel loop 467
heel rest 176, 208
heel stop 527
heel-piece 511
heelplate 514
height adjustment 501
height adjustment scale 227
helicopter 395
helix 115, 429
helmet 10, 454, 478, 486, 506, 508, 510, 513, 522, 525, 526, 527
helmet ring 10
helmet, crash 524
helmet, full-face 525
hemidemisemiquaver 299
hemidemisemiquaver rest 299
hemisphere 429
hemispheres 21
hemlath 412
hen 81
hen egg 155
hen house 122
hendecagon, regular 429
hepatic vein 103
heptagon, regular 429
herbal teas 148
herbicide 47
herbivores 45
herbs 142
heron 80
herring 159
herringbone parquet 190
herringbone pattern 190
hertz 426
Hertzian wave transmission 316
heterotrophs 45
hex nut 359
hexagon nut 223
hexagon, regular 429
hidden pocket 274
high altar 446
high card 468
high chair 205
high clouds 42
high jump 473
high pressure area 43
high wing 394
high-back dungarees 260
high-frequency antenna cable 394
high-rise block 289
high-speed exit taxiway 388
high-speed shaft 413
high-speed train 376
high-tension electricity transmission 402, 413
highland 5, 40
highland climates 40
hijiki 123
hiking boot 242
hill 29
Himalayas 19
hind leg 67, 68
hind limb 75
hind toe 78, 79
hind wing 67
hinge 178, 185, 186, 202, 214, 274, 277, 352, 420, 511
hinge pin 400
hip 93, 95
hip pad 486
hippopotamus 85
hitch ball 356
hitch pin 304
hitting area 477
hob 164, 210
hob edge 210
hock 83, 86, 153
hock glass 165
hoe 233
hoe-fork 233
hog line 515
hoisin sauce 140
hoisting block 397
hoisting rope 219, 287, 397
holdall 276
holder's name 441
holder's signature 441
holder, baton 456
holder, dental floss 272
holder, filter 181
holder, paper-clip 341
holding 499
holding area marking 390
hole 504
hollow barrel 460
hologram foil strip 441
holster 456
holy water font 446
home 331
home aerial 316
home key 331
home plate 475
home theatre 321
home user 335
home-plate umpire 475
homogenized milk 150
Honduras 448
honey 149
honeybee 68
honeydew melon 135
hood 192, 209, 249, 260, 508
hood, cooker 164
hooded sweat shirt 262
hooded towelling robe 260
hoof 83
hook 186, 217, 225, 364, 397, 423, 460, 502, 509
hooker 482
hoop earrings 264
hopper, loading 364
horizontal bar 496, 497
horizontal control 329
horizontal ground movement 27
horizontal move 470
horizontal pivoting window 287
horizontal seismograph 27
horizontal-axis wind turbine 413
horn 354, 368, 377
horn, anterior 109
Horn, Cape 17
horn, posterior 109
horned melon 136
hornet 69
horny beak 76
hors d'oeuvre dish 166
horse 83, 85
horse, gaits 83
horse, morphology of 83
horse, pommel 496
horse, vaulting 496, 497
horseradish 129
horseshoe mount 7
hose 209, 257, 454
hose connector 236
hose nozzle 236
hose trolley 236
hospital 433, 462
hospital bed 464
hospital trolley 460
hot coolant 408
hot-air outlet 192
hot-shoe contact 314
hot-water circuit 194
hot-water heater 194
hot-water riser 194
hot-water supply 197
hotel 432, 439, 512
hotel reservation desk 390
hotel room 439
hound, smooth 158
hour angle gear 7
house 182, 293, 515
house dress 252
house furniture 200
house, adobe 288
house, elements of 185
house, exterior 182
house, one-storey 289
house, pilot 385
house, structure 188
house, two-storey 289
houseboat 385
household equipment 215
household products 120
household waste 47, 48
housing 199, 218, 228, 229, 271
hovercraft 383
hub 70, 341, 371, 413, 467
Hubble space telescope 7, 37
Hudson Bay 16
Huitzilopochtli, Temple of 283
hull 60, 520, 523
human being 92
human body 92
human denture 101
humerus 98
humid continental - hot summer 4
humid continental - warm summer
humid subtropical 40
hummingbird 80
hummus 140
Hungary 450
hunting 534
hunting cap 238
hurricane 43
hurricane lamp 532
husbandry, intensive 46, 47
husk 60, 61
hydrant intake 455
hydrant, fire 454
hydraulic disc brake 522
hydraulic jack 361
hydraulic resistance 501
hydraulic shovel 400
hydraulic system 396
hydroelectric complex 406
hydroelectricity 406
hydrofoil boat 387
hydrologic cycle 45
hydrometer 359
hydrosphere 44
hyena 88
hyperlinks 334
hyperopia 419
hypha 52
hyssop 142

I

Iapetus 3
Iberian Peninsula 18
ice 45
ice cream container 180
ice cream maker 180
ice cream scoop 173
ice cube dispenser 164
ice cube tray 211
ice dispenser 346
ice hockey 506
ice hockey player 506
ice rink 512
Ice Shelf, Amery 15
Ice Shelf, Filchner 15
Ice Shelf, Ross 15
ice-breaker 384
iceberg lettuce 126
Iceland 18, 450
icing syringe 172
identification badge 456
identification, account 443
identity bracelet 264
identity tag 277
idler wheel 523
igloo 288
igloo tent 529
igneous rocks 26
ignition key 237
ignition lead 360

gnition switch 354, 368
guana 77
eum 106
ohypogastric nerve 108
oinguinal nerve 108
um 98
uminated mirror 269
nage review button 315
npervious rock 403
npluvium 280
npulse sprinkler 236
goal 483
flight communications 317
oound line 484
candescent light bulb 199
cident neutron 415
cineration 49
cisors 101
crease, voltage 402
cus 116
dex 539
dex 313
dex finger 115
dex/enlarge button 315
dia 453
ian chapati bread 145
dian naan bread 145
dian Ocean 14, 15, 19, 20
icator 352
dicator light 454
icator lights 331
icator telltale 355, 368
icator, position 287
icator, water level 179
icators 318
onesia 19, 453
oor electric grill 179
ustrial area 431
ustrial communications 317
ustrial pollution 47
ustrial waste 47, 48
ustry 335
t gas 199
rior cymbal 308
rior dental arch 116
rior mesenteric artery 107
rior nasal concha 117
rior rectus muscle 119
rior vena cava 102, 103, 104,
07
ld 474
ration 45
ity 427
ted carrying tyre 380
ted guiding tyre 380
tor 530
tor-deflator 530
rescent vegetables 127
mation booth 437
mation counter 390
mation desk 442, 463, 512
mation, dissemination of 335
red port 336, 337
ed radiation 46, 418
spinatus 97
dibulum of fallopian tube 113
ions, coffee and 148
ation valve 459
er, metered dose 467
ls of issuing bank 441
ion well 402
12
olour shifting 441
printer 333
parquet 190
manifold 360
valve 360
skating 527
boot 511, 527
circle 515
core 26
door shell 352
lip 73
planets 3
string 191
table 469
tent 528, 529

inner toe 78
inorganic matter 45
input devices 330
input lights 322
input select button 322
input selector 322
input tray 333
input wire 199
input/output video jacks 322
insectivorous bird 79
insects and arachnids 67
insects, examples of 69
insert 331
insert key 331
inside linebacker 484
inside-leg snap-fastening 260, 261
insignia, rank 456
inspection light 217
instant-read thermometer 171
instep 92
institution, educational 335, 433
instructions, operating 346
instrument cluster 366, 368
instrument panel 355
insulated blade 217
insulated handle 179, 217
insulating material 190, 214
insulation 410
insulator 359
insurance services 442
intake, air 362
integral 427
integrated circuit 417
integrated circuit, packaged 417
Intelsat 317
intensive care unit 464
intensive farming 46
intensive farming 48
intensive husbandry 46, 47
interchange 431
interchanges, examples of 342
intercostal nerve 108
interior dome shell 7
interior door handle 352
interior door lock button 352
interior pocket 277
intermediate booster station 404
intermediate slope 512
intermodal car 377
internal boundary 23
internal ear 116
internal filum terminale 109
internal iliac artery 102, 103, 107
internal iliac vein 103
internal jugular vein 102
internal modem port 329, 336
internal tooth lock washer 222
international space station 11
international system of units 426
Internet 334
Internet keys 330
Internet service provider 335
Internet user 334
Internet uses 335
internode 53
interrupted projection 22
intersection 427
intertragic notch 115
intervals 298
interventricular septum 104
interview 313
interview rooms 440
intestine 71, 73, 103
intravenous stand 464
intrusive filtration 47
intrusive rocks 26
inverted pleat 253
inward 518
Io 2
ion tail 6
Ionic column, engaged 281
Iran 452
Iraq 452
Ireland 449
iris 119
Irish moss 123
Irish Sea 18

Irish soda bread 145
iron 505
iron curtain 292
iron, straightening 269
is approximately equal to 427
is contained in 427
is equal to 427
is equal to or greater than 427
is equal to or less than 427
is equivalent to 427
is greater than 427
is identical with 427
is less than 427
is not equal to 427
is not identical with 427
is not parallel to 428
is parallel to 428
isba 288
ischium 99
island 24, 164, 343
island arc 33
Island, Baffin 16
Island, Newfoundland 16
Islands, Aleutian 16
Islands, Falkland 17
Islands, Fiji 15
islet, rocky 35
isobar 39
isolation room 462
isoseismal line 27
Israel 452
isthmus 24
isthmus of fallopian tube 113
isthmus of fauces 116
Isthmus of Panama 16
Italy 450
items, news 313
Ivory Coast 451

J

jaboticaba 137
Jack 468
jack 356, 397, 400, 455
jack plug 324
jack, audio 329
jack, audio input/output 337
jack, earphone 329
jack, stabilizer 361
jacket 251, 417, 499, 534
jackets 244
jackfruit 136
jaguar 89
jalapeño chilli 139
jalousie 186
Jamaica 448
jamb 185, 192
Japan 19, 453
Japan Trench 34
Japan, Sea of 19
Japanese experiment module 11
Japanese persimmon 137
Jarlsberg 151
Java Trench 34
javelin 472, 473
jaw 217, 221, 224, 228, 265
jaw, fixed 425
jaw, sliding 425
jaws 224, 535
jay 80
jazz band 300
jeans 254
jejunum 106
jerboa 82
jerk, clean and 500
jersey 483, 522
Jerusalem artichoke 124
jet fuel 405
jet tip 272
jet, supersonic 37, 394
jets, water 518
Jew's harp 297
jewellery 264
jewellery shop 436
Jewish challah 145
jib 397, 520
jib tie 397

jibsheet 520
jicama 124
jigsaw 227
jingle 309
jockey rollers 372
jogging pants 262
John dory 161
joint 312, 355, 503, 536
joint filler 216
joint, articulated 363
joist 190
Joker 468
Jordan 452
joule 426
joystick 332
joysticks 471
judge 498, 499
judge, centre line 490
judge, line 496
judge, side 485
judges 496, 497, 509, 518
judges' bench 440
judges' office 440
judges, turning 517
judo 499
judogi 499
jug 181
jug, measuring 171
juice extractor 180
juice sac 58
jujube 137
jumper cables 356
jumper, ski 513
jumping ski 513
jumping, ski 513
jumps, examples of 509
jumpsuit 254, 261
junior doctor 464
juniper berry 138
Jupiter 2
jurors' room 440
jury box 440
justice 440

K

Kalahari Desert 20
kale, ornamental 126
kale, sea 126
Kamchatka Peninsula 19
Kazakhstan 452
keel boat 521
keep 282
keeper ring 536
kelly 403
kelvin 426
Kenya 451
kerb 434, 524
Kermadec-Tonga Trench 34
kernel 61
kerosene 405
ketchup 141
kettle 29, 180
kettledrum 308
key 296, 304, 306
key case 275
key cutting 437
key finger button 306
key grip 290
key guard 306
key lever 306
key lock 274
key signature 299
key, alternative 330
key, backspace 331
key, capitals lock 330
key, confirmation 443
key, delete 331
key, email 330
key, end 331
key, enter 331
key, escape 330
key, home 331
key, insert 331
key, numeric lock 331
key, page down 331
key, page up 331

key, pause/break 331
key, print screen/system request 331
key, scrolling lock 331
key, start 330
key, tabulation 330
key, talk 327
keybed 304
keyboard 304, 310, 336
keyboard and pictograms 330
keyboard instruments 304
keyboard port 329
keyboard, alphanumeric 346, 442, 443
keyless chuck 228
keypad, alphabetical 338
keypad, alphanumeric 327, 330
keypad, numeric 338
keys 311
keys, function 330
keys, Internet 330
keys, operation 442, 443
keystone 284
kick pleat 253
kick, skating 514
kicker 313
kickstand 367, 369
kidney 73, 103, 154
kidney bean, red 131
kielbasa sausage 156
killer whale 90
kilogram 426
kilt 253
kimono 256
King 468, 470
king's chamber 278
King's side 470
kingfisher 80
kingpin 365
kiosk 346, 379
Kiribati 453
kit, first aid 457
kit, headset 327
kit, tool 372
kit, waxing 514
kitchen 162, 164, 188, 280, 439, 445
kitchen knife 169
kitchen knives, examples of 169
kitchen scale 171
kitchen shears 173
kitchen timer 171
kitchen towel 215
kitchen utensils 169
kitchen, food and 120
kitchen-diner 188
kiwi 136
knee 83, 86, 92, 94
knee pad 476, 486, 526, 527
knee sock 257
knee wrap 500
knee-length sock 247
knickerbockers 254
knife 167, 531, 533
knife pleat 246, 253
knife, electric 177
Knight 470
knives, examples of 168
knob 202, 229, 477
knob handle 227
knob, coarse adjustment 421
knob, fine adjustment 421
knob, steam control 181
knobby tyre 369
knurled bolt 219
kohlrabi 125
Kola Peninsula 18
kombu 123
kora 297
Korean Peninsula 19
Kuiper belt 2
kumquat 134
Kuril Trench 34
Kuwait 452
Kyrgyzstan 452

L

label maker 340
labial palp 67
labium majus 112, 113
labium minus 112, 113
lablab bean 130
laboratory 7
laboratory air lock 13
laboratory, pathology 465
laboratory, U.S. 11
laccolith 28
lace 477, 498, 509
lace-up 240
lachrymal canal 119
lachrymal caruncle 119
lachrymal gland 119
lactiferous duct 113
ladder 184, 288, 361, 401, 404, 469
ladder pipe nozzle 455
ladders 219
ladies' toilet 294, 439
ladle 173
Ladoga, Lake 18
Lady chapel 284, 285
ladybird 69
lagomorphs, examples of 82
lagomorphs, rodents and 82
lagoon 35
lake 5, 24, 29, 32
lake acidification 48
Lake Baikal 19
Lake Chad 20
Lake Eyre North 15
Lake Ladoga 18
Lake Malawi 20
Lake Tanganyika 20
Lake Titicaca 17
Lake Victoria 20
lake, artificial 32
lake, glacial 32
lake, oxbow 32
lake, tectonic 32
lake, volcanic 32
lakes 32
Lakes, Great 16
lamb, cuts of 153
lamb, diced 153
lamb, leg 153
lamb, minced 153
lambdoid suture 100
lamina 51
lamp 320, 421
lamp, bedside 439, 464
lamp, sanctuary 446
lamp, signal 179
lampholder 199
lamprey 159
lanceolate 55
land 228
land pollution 47
land station 38
landfill 431
landfill site, authorized 47
landing 189, 191
landing area 472
landing gear 361, 365
landing gear crank 365
landing light 395
landing net 538
landing window 395
landslides 31
lane 433, 472, 516
lane line 473
lane rope 517
lane timekeeper 516
lane, pit 524
languid 305
lantern 230, 529
Laos 453
lap belt 353
lapel 244
laptop computer 336
laptop computer: front view 336
laptop computer: rear view 336
larch 65
lard 149
larding needle 173
large blade 531
large intestine 106
large wheel 467
large-screen television set 321
larger spotted dogfish 158
larynx 105
lasagne 146
laser beam 420
laser, pulsed ruby 420
last quarter 5
latch 178, 214, 277
latch bolt 186
latch, mitre 226
lateral bar 501
lateral brush 365
lateral condyle of femur 99
lateral cutaneous femoral nerve 108
lateral incisor 101
lateral line 74, 515
lateral moraine 30
lateral semicircular canal 116
lateral view of skull 100
lateral-adjustment lever 229
latex glove 460
latex glove case 456
latissimus dorsi 97
latrines 280
Latvia 450
laundry 439
laundry room 188
lava flow 28
lava layer 28
lawn 183, 230
lawn aerator 237
lawn care 237
lawn edger 233
lawn rake 237
layer, ozone 37
layers, waste 47
leaching 48
lead 313, 326, 515
lead pencil 312
leader 538
leading bunch 522
leading edge 393
leading motorcycle 522
leaf 51, 53, 54, 55, 125
leaf axil 55
leaf lettuce 126
leaf margins 55
leaf node 53
leaf vegetables 126
leaf, fleshy 54
leaf, scale 54
leaf, structure of 55
leakproof cap 529
leather end 246
leather goods 274
leather goods shop 436
leather sheath 533
leather skin 478
leather, chamois 265
leaves, examples of 65
leaves, first 53
Lebanon 452
Lebanon, cedar of 65
lectern 446
ledger board 187
ledger line 298
leech 519
leek 124
left atrium 103, 104
left attacker 487
left back 481, 487
left centre 482
left channel 324
left cornerback 484
left defence 506
left defensive end 484
left defensive tackle 484
left field 475
left fielder 474
left forward 489
left guard 485
left kidney 107
left lung 103, 105
left midfielder 481
left pulmonary vein 104
left safety 484
left service court 491
left side 272
left tackle 485
left ventricle 103, 104
left wing 482, 507
left-luggage office 374
leg 76, 91, 93, 95, 202, 204, 205, 231, 247, 308, 493, 537
leg curl bar 501
leg extension bar 501
leg guard 476
leg of lamb 153
leg, walking 70
leg-warmer 263
leghold trap 535
legumes 130
leisure, outdoor 528
lemon 134
lemon balm 142
lemon squeezer 170, 177
lemur 91
length, measurement of 426
lengthways bulkhead 384
lens 119, 273, 314, 332, 419
lens accessories 314
lens cap 314
lens case 272
lens hood 8, 314
lens release button 314
lens system 420
lens, concave 419
lens, convex 419
lens, macro 314
lens, toric 419
lens, zoom 320
lenses 314, 419
lenses, contact 272
lentils 130
leopard 89
leotard 263
Lesotho 452
lesser covert 78
letter opener 339
letter scale 339
letters to editor 313
lettuce, butterhead 126
lettuce, iceberg 126
lettuce, leaf 126
lettuce, sea 123
leucoplast 50
level crossing 375
level, reception 439
level, sea 37
levelling foot 212, 213, 214
levelling screw 423
lever 178, 197, 222, 265, 534
lever cap 229
lever corkscrew 170
lever kitchen-tap 197
lever, gear 350, 369
lever, locking 224
Liberia 451
libero 487
library 433, 444
Libya 451
lichen 50
lichen, crustose 50
lichen, foliose 50
lichen, fruticose 50
lichen, structure of 50
lichens, examples of 50
lid 174, 177, 178, 179, 180, 181, 210, 211, 212, 215, 225, 417
Liechtenstein 450
lierne 284
life buoy 387
life raft 383
life support system 10
life support system controls 10
lifeboat 382, 386
lifebuoy 457
lift 281, 287, 435, 439
lift arm 399
lift bridge 345
lift car 287
lift chain 196
lift door 363
lift span 345
lift, chair 512
lift, wheelchair 363
lift-arm cylinder 399
lift-fan air inlet 383
lifting chain 396
lifting hook 403
ligament 73
ligature 306
light 7, 8, 9, 380
light aircraft 394
light bar 455
light ray 419
light shield 7
light, amber 434
light, eternal 447
light, green 434
light, indicator 454
light, paper feed 333
light, power 333
light, print cartridge 333
light, reading 457
light, red 434
light, underwater 184
light, visible 418
lightbar 457
lightbar controller 457
lighthouse 381
lighting 199, 269
lighting cable 361
lighting grid 291
lighting technician 291
lighting, safety 457
lightning 41
lightning conductor 183, 407
lightning rod 413
lights 206
lights, blinking 362
lights, goal 507
lights, indicator 331
lights, input 322
lights, pedestrian 434
lights, sound mode 322
lights, traffic 434
lily 56
lily of the valley 56
Lima bean 131
limb 63, 535
limb top 421
lime 134
limit switch 287
limpet 157
linden 148
line 225, 298, 443
line guide 537
line judge 485, 496
line map 378
line of scrimmage 485
line, 10 m 482
line, 15 m 483
line, 23 m 482
line, 5 m 483
line, back 515
line, broken 342, 343
line, cable 335
line, chalk 225
line, credit 313
line, dedicated 334
line, field 416
line, hog 515
line, neutral 416
line, solid 342
line, starting 524
line, submarine 334
line, tee 515
line, telephone 334
linear 55
linen chest 203
linen room 439
lines of latitude 22
lines of longitude 22
linesman 481, 487, 490, 494, 507
lingerie shop 436
lingual tonsil 118
lining 240, 244, 245, 262, 274, 50
lint filter 212
lintel 185, 187, 192, 285
lion 89
lip 83, 87
lip make-up 266
lipbrush 266
lipid droplet 50
lipliner 266
lipstick 266
liqueur glass 165
liquid 414, 415
liquid crystal display 315, 320, 326, 327, 424
liquid crystal display (LCD) televisio 318
liquid eyeliner 266
liquid foundation 266
liquid mascara 266
liquid/gas separator 359
lists 282
litchi; lychee 137
literary supplement 313
lithosphere 26, 44
Lithuania 450
litter, plant 54
little finger 115
little finger hook 307
liver 103, 106, 154
livestock van 377
living room 188, 528
lizard 77
lizard, monitor 77
llama 84
loader, belt 402
loading bridge 381
loading dock 435
loading door 192
loading hopper 364
loaf pan 179
loan services 442
lob 491
lobate 55
lobate toe 79
lobby 390, 435, 439, 440, 442
lobe 79
lobe bronchus 105
lobe, lower 105
lobe, upper 105
lobster 71, 158
lobster, anatomy of 71
lobster, morphology of 71
local station 316
location 182
location of the statue 279
lock 185, 186, 202, 211, 275, 2 352
lock dial 332
lock forward 482
lock nut 425
lock rail 185
lock, capitals 330
lock, numeric 331
lock-on button 227, 229
lockers, students' 445
locket 264
locking button 208
locking device 209, 219, 535
locking lever 224
locking ring 221
locknut 197
locomotive 376
loculus 58
lodge, main 512
lodge, mountain 512
lodge, skiers' 512
lodge, summit 512
lodging 512
log carrier 193
log chute 406
loin 83, 93, 95
loin chop 153
long adductor 96
long extensor of toes 96
long johns 247

ong jump and triple jump 472
ong palmar 96
ong peroneal 96
ong radial extensor of wrist 97
ng residue 405
ng service line 494
ng track 508
ng-range jet airliner 392
ngan 136
ngitudinal drive shaft 351
ngitudinal dunes 36
op 245, 343
op, hammer 225
op, strap 532
op, toe 509
ose head prop 482
ose powder 266
ose powder brush 266
pping shears 234
re 78
ss, heat 46
udspeaker 324, 325, 455
udspeaker system select buttons 322
udspeaker terminals 322
idspeaker, centre 321
idspeaker, main 321
idspeaker, surround 321
inge 386, 439
inge, cocktail 439
inge, nurses' 465
inge, staff 443, 463
ise 69
vre-board 285
vred window 287
age 142
clouds 42
fuel warning light 355
pressure area 43
-speed shaft 413
-tension distribution line 198
er blade guard 227
er bowl 181
er confining bed 402
er eyelid 75, 87, 119
er guard retracting lever 227
er lateral lobe 62
er lateral sinus 62
er limb 103
er lip 116, 305
er lobe 105
er mandible 78
er mantle 26
er radiator hose 358
er shell 511
icant eye drops 272
icants plant 405
icating oils 405
-Lock tip 460
519
308
age 276
age compartment 376, 395
age elastic 277
age lockers 374
age rack 361, 369, 523
age racks 383
age trolley 277, 374
bar pad 486
bar plexus 108
bar vertebra 99, 110
nous intensity, measurement of 426
r eclipse 5
features 5
105
a 114, 115
e 73
e 130
509
mbourg 449
88
297
ome 66

M

macadamia nut 133
macaque 91
macaw 80
machicolation 282
machine hall 406, 407
machine, automatic teller 442, 443
machine, espresso 181
machine, franking 339
machine, snow-grooming 512
machinery shed 122
machinery, transport and 342
Mackenzie River 16
mackerel 159
macro lens 314
macronucleus 66
macula 119
Madagascar 20, 452
magazine 313
magenta 418
magma 28, 33
magma chamber 28, 402
magnesium powder 497
magnet 341, 416
magnetic compass 533
magnetic damping system 422
magnetic field 318, 416
magnetic gasket 211
magnetic lid holder 180
magnetic needle 533
magnetic separation 49
magnetic strip 441
magnetic tape 319
magnetism 416
magnifier 531
magnifying glass 421
magnifying glass and microscopes 421
main beam headlight 352
main beam indicator light 355
main beam warning light 368
main bronchus 105
main circuit vent 194
main cleanout 194
main deck 385
main drain 184, 194
main engine 13
main entrance 188, 435, 445, 465
main junction box 198
main landing gear 393
main line 375
main lodge 512
main loudspeaker 321
main road 343
main rooms 188
main scale 425
main scope tube 420
main sewer 434
main stand 367
main switch 198
main transformer 376
main tube 8, 9
main vent 28
main waiting room 465
Maine Coon 87
mainsail 520
mainsheet 520
maintenance hangar 389
major inner reaping throw 499
major motions 470
major outer reaping throw 499
make-up 266
make-up artist 290
maker, bread 179
malanga 129
malar region 78
Malawi 452
Malawi, Lake 20
Malaysia 453
Maldives 453
male 426
male cone 65
male ferrule 536, 537
male genital organs 111
male grounding pin 198
male urethra 111
Mali 451
mallet 220, 308
mallets 309
malleus 116
malt vinegar 141
Malta 450
mammals, carnivorous 86
mammals, marine 90
mammals, primate 91
mammals, ungulate 83
mammary gland 113
man 92
man, property 291
mandarin 134
mandible 67, 74, 98, 100
mandolin 297
mandoline 170
mandown alarm 454
mane 83
manganese mix (cathode) 417
mangetout 130
mango 137
mango chutney 141
mangosteen 136
manhole 404, 434
manicure 265
manicure set 265
manned manœuvring unit 10
manœuvring engine 13
mantid 69
mantle 72, 73, 192
mantlepiece 192
manual release 511
manual revolving door 286
manual sorting 49
manuals 305
Manx 87
map projections 22
map, geographical 444
map, weather 38
maple 64
maple syrup 149
maquis 44
margarine 149
margin 55
marginal shield 76
Mariana Trench 34
Marie Byrd Land 15
marinade spices 139
marine 40
marine diesel 405
marine mammals 90
marine mammals, examples of 90
maritime communications 317
maritime transport 381
marker 312
marker, position 303
marmoset 91
marrow 128, 154
Mars 2, 3
Marshall Islands 453
marten 88
marten, stone 88
mascara brush 266
mask 476
mask, face 478
mason's trowel 216
masonry drill 228
masonry nail 220
masonry tools 216
mass 27
mass, measurement of 426
massage glove 267
masseter 96
massif 24
mast 281, 396, 519, 520
mast foot 519
mast operating lever 396
mast sleeve 519
master bedroom, cathedral ceiling 189
master bedroom, cathedral roof 189
master cylinder 357
masthead 313, 519
masthead light 383
mastoid fontanelle 100
mastoid process 100
mat 499
mat, floor 356
mater, dura 109
mater, pia 109
material handling 396
material, fire-fighting 454
material, sealing 417
mathematics 427
matinee-length necklace 264
mating adaptor 11
mats, floor 496
matter 414
matter, grey 109
matter, inorganic 45
matter, states of 414
matter, white 109
mattress 204, 205, 460
mattress cover 204
Mauritania 451
Mauritius 452
maxilla 74, 98, 100, 117
maxillary bone 101
meadow 122
mean position 418
meander 32
measurement of amount of substance 426
measurement of Celsius temperature 426
measurement of electric charge 426
measurement of electric current 426
measurement of electric potential difference 426
measurement of electric resistance 426
measurement of energy 426
measurement of force 426
measurement of frequency 426
measurement of length 425, 426
measurement of luminous intensity 426
measurement of mass 426
measurement of power 426
measurement of pressure 426
measurement of radioactivity 426
measurement of temperature 424
measurement of thermodynamic temperature 426
measurement of thickness 425
measurement of time 424
measurement of weight 422
measuring beaker 171
measuring cups 171
measuring devices 424
measuring jug 171
measuring spoons 171
measuring, utensils 171
meat 152
meat counter, self-service 120
meat keeper 211
meat thermometer 171
meatus, external auditory 100
mechanical mouse 332
mechanical stage 421
mechanical stage control 421
mechanism, spool-release 537
medial condyle of femur 99
medial moraine 30
median lingual sulcus 118
median nerve 108
medical equipment storage room 465
medical gas cylinder 464
medical records 465
medical team 499
Mediterranean Sea 14, 18, 20
Mediterranean subtropical 40
medium format SLR (6 x 6) 315
medium-tension distribution line 198
medlar 133
medulla 107
medulla oblongata 109
medullary ray 63
meeting room 439, 442, 445
Meissner's corpuscle 114
Melanesia 15
melody strings 296
melon baller 173
melon, bitter 128
melon, canary 135
melon, casaba 135
melon, honeydew 135
melon, horned 136
melon, Ogen 135
melons 135
melting 414
meltwater 30
membrane, plasma 66
memo pad 338
memorial board 447
memory button 322, 326, 327
memory cancel 337
memory card reader 333
memory card slots 471
memory card, compact 315
memory recall 337
men 469, 470
men's bag 276
men's clothing 244
men's gloves 243
men's headgear 238
men's shoes 240
men's toilet 294, 439
meninges 109
menorah 447
menu button 315, 320, 326
menu key 327
Mercury 2, 3
mercury bulb 424
mercury thermometer 461
merguez sausage 156
méridienne 200
mesa 36
mesh 205, 493
mesh bag 162
mesh strainer 171
mesocarp 57, 58, 59
mesopause 37
mesosphere 37
metal arm 236
metal counterhoop 308
metal frame 304
metal rod 309
metal sorting 49
metal structure 374
metallic contact grid 410
metamorphic rocks 26
meteorological forecast 38
meteorology 37
meteorology, station model 39
metered dose inhaler 467
methylated spirits 405
metre 426
Mexico 448
Mexico, Gulf of 16
mezzanine 378
mezzanine stairs 189
Micro Compact Car 347
microfilament 66
micrometer caliper 425
Micronesia 453
micronucleus 66
microphone 320, 327, 328, 332, 337, 456
microphones 457
microscope 421
microscopes, magnifying glass and 421
microtubule 66
microwave oven 164, 178
microwave relay station 334
microwaves 418
Mid-Atlantic Ridge 34
mid-calf length sock 247
Mid-Indian Ridge 34
mid-ocean ridge 33
middle attacker 487
middle back 487
middle clouds 42
middle covert 78
middle ear 116
middle finger 115
middle leg 67, 68
middle linebacker 484
middle lobe 105
middle nasal concha 117
middle panel 185
middle phalanx 114
middle piece 111
middle primary covert 78
middle sole 262
middle toe 78
midfielder, central 481
midfielder, left 481
midfielder, right 481
midrange pickup 303
midrange speaker 324
midrib 51, 55, 60
midriff band 259
Mihrab 447
Mihrab dome 447

mileometer 355
military communications 317
milk 150
milk chocolate 148
milk, evaporated 150
milk, goat's 150
milk, homogenized 150
milk, powdered 150
milk/cream cup 163
Milky Way 6
Milky Way (seen from above) 6
Milky Way (side view) 6
mill, food 170
millet 61, 143
millet: spike 61
Mimas 3
minaret 447
Minbar 447
minced beef 152
minced lamb 153
minced pork 153
minced veal 152
mincer 170
mini briefs 247
mini stereo sound system 325
mini-DV camcorder: front view 320
mini-DV camcorder: rear view 320
minibus 347, 363
minim 299
minim rest 299
mink 88
minor sciatic nerve 108
minor surgery 462
mint 142
minute 428
minute hand 424
Miranda 3
mirror 195, 277, 366, 368, 369, 421, 439, 523
mirror, blind spot 362, 363
mirror, concave primary 9
mirror, crossover 362
mirror, outside 362
mirror, partially reflecting 420
mirror, secondary 7, 9
mirror, totally reflecting 420
mirror, West Coast 363
miscellaneous articles 341
miscellaneous domestic appliances 180
miscellaneous equipment 231
miscellaneous utensils 173
Mississippi River 16
mist 41
mitochondrion 50, 66
mitral valve 104
mitre box 226
mitre latch 226
mitre scale 226
mitten 243
mix, depolarizing 417
mix, water-steam 402
mixed forest 44
mixing bowl 176
mixing bowls 172
moat 282
mobile remote servicer 11
mobile telephone 327
mobile unit 316
mobile X-ray unit 462
moccasin 242
mock pocket 251
mode selectors 326
modem 334
modem, cable 335
moderator 408
modulation wheel 310
module, centrifuge 11
module, European experiment 11
module, Japanese experiment 11
module, Russian 11
module, U.S. habitation 11
Mohorovicic discontinuity 26
moistener 339
molar, cross section 101
molars 101
Moldova 450
mole 426
mole wrench 222
molecule 414
molluscs 72, 157
Monaco 450
money and modes of payment 441
Mongolia 453
mongoose 88
monitor lizard 77
monkfish 160
mono-hulls 521
mons pubis 112
Montenegro 450
monument 25
Moon 2, 4, 5
Moon's orbit 4, 5
Moon, phases 5
moons 2
mooring winch 385
mop 215
moped 369
moraine, end 30
moraine, terminal 30
mordent 299
morel 123
Morocco 451
morphology of a bird 78
morphology of a bivalve shell 73
morphology of a butterfly 67
morphology of a dog 86
morphology of a dolphin 90
morphology of a frog 75
morphology of a gorilla 91
morphology of a honeybee: worker 68
morphology of a horse 83
morphology of a lobster 71
morphology of a perch 74
morphology of a rat 82
morphology of a shark 74
morphology of a snail 72
morphology of a spider 70
morphology of a turtle 76
morphology of a univalve shell 73
morphology of a venomous snake: head 76
morphology of an octopus 72
mortadella 156
mortar 170
mosaic 280
mosque 447
mosquito 69
moss 51
moss, common hair cap 51
moss, Irish 123
moss, structure of 51
mosses, examples of 51
moth, atlas 69
motion detector 286
motocross and supercross motorcycle 525
motor 212, 213, 214, 227, 229, 237
motor bogie 376
motor car 380
motor end plate 110
motor neuron 110
motor racing 524
motor root 109, 110
motor scooter 369
motor sports 524
motor unit 176, 177, 180, 208, 272, 376
motor vehicle pollution 47
motor yacht 385
motorcycle 366
motorcycle, leading 522
motorcycle, off-road 369
motorcycle, touring 369
motorcycle-mounted camera 522
motorcycle: view from above 368
motorcycles, examples of 369
motorcycling 525
motorway 25, 343, 431
motorway number 25
motto 441
mouflon 84
mould, charlotte 172
moulding, bumper 348
mount, ball 356
mountain 29
mountain biking 522
mountain lodge 512
mountain range 5, 24, 26
mountain slope 29
mountain torrent 29
Mountains, Appalachian 16
Mountains, Atlas 20
Mountains, Carpathian 18
Mountains, Rocky 16
Mountains, Transantarctic 15
Mountains, Ural 18
mounting bracket 535
mounting plate 199
mouse pad 332
mouse port 329
mouse, cordless 332
mouse, field 82
mouse, mechanical 332
mouse, optical 332
mouse, wheel 332
mouth 71, 72, 73, 75, 90, 94, 116, 305
mouthparts 68
mouthpiece 306, 307, 311, 467
mouthpiece receiver 307
mouthpipe 307
mouthwash 272
movable bridges 344
movable jaw 223, 224
movable maxillary 76
movable stands 444
movement, horizontal ground 27
movement, vertical ground 27
movements of aircraft 395
Mozambique 452
Mozambique Channel 20
mozzarella 150
Mt Everest 37
mud flap 349, 364, 365
mud hut 288
mud injection hose 403
mud pit 403
mud pump 403
mudflow 31
mudguard 370
muff 276
muffler felt 304
mule 84, 242
mullet 160
multi-hulls 521
multi-image jump button 315
multi-purpose solution 272
multigrain bread 145
multipack 163
multiple exposure mode 314
multiple light fitting 207
multiplication 427
multiply key 337
multipurpose tool 217
mummy 530
mung bean 131
Munster 151
muscle fibre 110
muscles 96
museum 433
mushroom 52
mushroom, enoki 123
mushroom, structure 52
mushrooms 123
music 296
music rest 305, 311
music room 444
musical instrument digital interface (MIDI) cable 311
musical notation 298
muskmelon 135
muslin 171
mustard, American 140
mustard, black 138
mustard, Dijon 140
mustard, English 140
mustard, German 140
mustard, powdered 140
mustard, white 138
mustard, wholegrain 140
mute 307
muzzle 83, 86, 87, 534
Myanmar 453
mycelium 52
myelin sheath 110
myocardium 104
myopia 419

N

nacelle 413
nacelle cross-section 413
nail 220
nail bed 114
nail cleaner 265
nail clippers 265
nail file 265
nail groove 531
nail matrix 114
nail scissors 265
nail set 220
nail shaper 265
nail varnish 265
nail whitener pencil 265
nail, common 220
nail, cut 220
nail, finishing 220
nail, masonry 220
nail, spiral 220
nails, examples of 220
naked strangle 499
name, currency 441
name, domain 334
name, gymnast's 497
name, holder's 441
nameplate 313
names, tropical cyclone 43
Namib Desert 20
Namibia 452
naos 279
nape 78, 93, 95
nappy 260
nappy, disposable 260
naris 117
nasal bone 100, 117
nasal cavity 105
nasal fossae 117
nasopharynx 117
national broadcasting network 316
national park 25
nationality 497
natural 299
natural arch 35
natural environment 504
natural greenhouse effect 46
natural sponge 267
Nauru 453
nautical sports 516
nave 285
navel 92, 94
navigation key 327
navigation light 383, 393
Nazca Plate 27
Neapolitan coffee maker 181
neck 76, 83, 93, 94, 95, 101, 111, 167, 297, 301, 302, 303, 318
neck end 245
neck of femur 99
neck pad 486
neck strap 458
neck support 525
neck, filler 351
neckhole 247
necklaces 264
neckroll 204
necktie 245
nectarine 132
needle 36, 460
needle hub 460
needle, larding 173
needle, trussing 173
needle-nose pliers 217
negative contact 410, 411
negative meniscus 419
negative plate 359
negative plate strap 359
negative region 410
negative terminal 359, 416, 417
neon lamp 217
Nepal 453
Neptune 2, 3
nerve 114
nerve fibre 114
nerve termination 114
nerve, olfactory 117
nerve, spinal 109
nervous system 108
nest of tables 202
net 487, 489, 491, 493, 495
net band 491
net judge 491
net support 493
Netherlands 449
nettle 127
network connection 198
network port 329
neurons 110
neutral conductor 198
neutral indicator 368
neutral line 416
neutral zone 484, 507
neutron 414
neutron, incident 415
névé 30
New Caledonia 15
new crescent 5
new moon 5
new shekel 440
New Zealand 15, 453
newborn children's clothing 260
newel post 191
Newfoundland Island 16
news items 313
newsagent's shop 437
newsgroup 335
newspaper 313
newt 75
newton 426
next 328
next/fast-forward button 326
nib 312
Nicaragua 448
niche, safety 345
nictitating membrane 87
Niger 451
Niger River 20
Nigeria 451
night deposit box 443
nightgown 256
nightingale 80
nightshot button 320
nightwear 256
Nile 20
nimbostratus 42
nipple 92, 94, 113
nitric acid emission 48
nitrogen oxide emission 48
no. 8 forward 482
nocking point 535
node 416
node of Ranvier 110
non-biodegradable pollutants 47
non-breaking space 330
non-reusable residue waste 49
nonagon, regular 429
noodles, Asian 147
noodles, bean thread cellophane
noodles, egg 147
noodles, rice 147
noodles, soba 147
noodles, somen 147
noodles, udon 147
nori 123
normal sight 419
North 23
North America 14, 16, 34
North American Plate 27
North Pole 21
north pole 416
North Sea 14, 18
North-Northeast 23
North-Northwest 23
Northeast 23
Northern hemisphere 21
Northern leopard frog 75
Northwest 23
Norway 450
Norwegian Sea 18
nose 82, 83, 94, 117, 392, 526
nose landing gear 392
nose leather 87
nose of the quarter 240, 262
nose pad 273
nose, droop 394
nosepiece, revolving 421
nosing 191

nostril 74, 75, 76, 78, 83
notch 244, 422, 473, 503
notched double-edged thinning scissors 270
notched edge 270
notched lapel 248
notched single-edged thinning scissors 270
note presenter 442
note values 299
noticeboard 341
nozzle 12, 216, 219, 236
nozzle cleaners 218
nozzle, steam 181
nubby tyre 525
nuclear energy 408
nuclear fission 415
nuclear membrane 50, 66
nuclear reactor 409
nuclear waste 48
nuclear whorl 73
ucleolus 50, 66, 112
ucleus 6, 50, 66, 110, 112, 414
ucleus splitting 415
ucleus, fissionable 415
umber 473
umber buttons 326
umber key 328, 337
umber plate 525
umber plate light 352
umber, card 441, 443
umber, player's 488, 506
umber, pump 346
umber, room 439
umber, serial 441
umbering stamp 338
umerals, Roman 427
umeric keyboard 423
umeric keypad 331, 338
umeric lock 331
umeric lock key 331
rse 464
rses' lounge 465
rses' station (ambulatory emergency) 463
rses' station (major emergency) 462
t 222, 223, 301, 302, 303
t, cola 133
t, ginkgo 133
t, hexagon 223
t, macadamia 133
cracker 170
tmeg 138
tmeg grater 170
s 223
on line 237

O

k 64
501
sis 32, 36
flour 144
s 61, 143
s: panicle 61
eron 3
uary 313
ect 419
ect balls 502
ective 421
ective lens 8, 327, 420
que fissure 105
e 306
es 295
ervation deck 391
ervation post 7
ervation room 462, 465
ervation window 13
ervation, astronomical 7
ervatory 7
rator nerve 108
se angle 428
pital 97
pital bone 99, 100
n 5, 24, 45
n floor 33
n trenches and ridges 34
n weather station 38
Ocean, Atlantic 15, 18, 20
Ocean, Indian 15, 19, 20
Ocean, Pacific 14, 15, 19
Oceania 14, 15
Oceania and Polynesia 453
oceanic crust 26
oche 471
octagon, regular 429
octahedron, regular 429
octave 298
octave mechanism 306
octopus 72, 157
octopus, morphology of 72
odd pinnate 55
oesophagus 105, 106
off-road motorcycle 369
offal 154
office 346, 374, 438, 439
office automation 329
office building 381, 432, 435
office tower 435
office, clerks' 440
office, emergency physician's 462
office, gymnasium 444
office, head nurse's 463
office, head teacher's 445
office, judges' 440
office, post 433, 437
office, proctors' 445
office, professional training 442
office, school secretary's 445
office, social worker's 463
officer, director's 443
officer, police 456
official signature 441
official, penalty bench 507
officials' bench 507
offshore well 404
Ogen melon 135
ohm 426
oil 403
oil drain plug 360
oil pollution 48
oil pressure warning indicator 368
oil spill 48
oil tank 235
oil terminal 381
oil warning light 355
oil, corn 149
oil, olive 149
oil, peanut 149
oil, sesame 149
oil, sunflower-seed 149
oils, fats and 149
okapi 84
okra 128
old crescent 5
olecranon 99
olfactory bulb 117
olfactory mucosa 117
olfactory nerve 117
olfactory tract 117
olive 128
olive oil 149
Oman 452
Oman, Gulf of 19
on-board computer 354
on-deck circle 474
on-off button 180
on-off indicator 269
on-off switch 177, 181, 206, 208, 209, 218, 269, 270, 271, 272
on/off light 327
on/off switch 209, 314
on/off/volume 326
one 427
one hundred 427
one pair 468
one thousand 427
one way head 221
one-arm shoulder throw 499
one-bar shoe 241
one-person tent 529
one-storey house 289
onion, green 124
onion, red 124
onion, white 124
online game 335
oolong tea 148
Oort cloud 2
open strings 296
open-air terrace 387
open-ended spanner 223
open-face spinning reel 537
open-plan coach 376
opening 243
opening, utensils 170
openings, gill 74
opera 432
opera glasses 273
opera-length necklace 264
operating instructions 346
operating panel 287
operating suite 464
operating table 464
operating theatre 464, 465
operation keys 442, 443
operator's cab 397
operator's cab 397
operator, boom 291
operator, camera 290
operculum 74
ophthalmology and ENT room 463
opisthodomos 279
opposable thumb 91
opposite prompt side 293
optic chiasm 109
optic nerve 119
optical mouse 332
optical scanner 121
optical sensor 332
optical sorting 49
optician 437
oral cavity 105, 106
oral irrigator 272
orange 134
orange, section of 58
orangutan 91
orbicularis oculi 96
orbiculate 55
orbit, Earth's 4, 5
orbital-action selector 227
orbiter 12, 13
orchard 122
orchestra 278
orchestra pit 292
orchid 56
order 285
ordinary die 468
oregano 142
organ 305
organ console 305
organization, cultural 335
organization, government 335
organization, health 335
organizer, personal 338
organs, sense 114
Orinoco River 17
ornamental kale 126
ornamental tree 122, 182, 230
ornaments 299
ortho-stick 466
oscillating sprinkler 236
ostrich 81
ostrich egg 155
other signs 299
otter, river 88
ottoman 201
outboard engine 385
outdoor leisure 528
outer circle 515
outer core 26
outer lip 73
outer planets 2
outer ring 441
outer string 191
outer table 469
outer toe 78
outfield fence 475
outlet, discharge 184
outlet, European 198
outlet, oxygen 464
outlet, switched 322
outpatients' department 465
output devices 333
output jack 303
output tray 333
output, S-Video 336
outside counter 240
outside linebacker 484
outside mirror 348, 362
outside mirror control 352
outside ticket pocket 244
outsole 240, 263
outwash plain 30
ovary 56, 112, 113
ovate 55
oven 164, 210
oven control knob 210
oven thermometer 171
oven, microwave 164
overall standings scoreboard 496
overbed table 464
overcoat 248, 251
overflow 194, 195
overflow pipe 196
overflow protection switch 214
overhead frame 401
overhead guard 396
overhead wires 376
overshirt 255
overtaking lane 343
overtaking zone 472
ovule 56
owl, great horned 81
ox 85
oxbow 32
oxbow lake 32
oxford shoe 240
oxygen outlet 464
oxygen pressure actuator 10
oxygen, release of 54
oxygenated blood 104
oyster 157
oyster fork 168
oyster knife 169
oyster mushroom 123
ozone layer 37

P

Pacific Ocean 14, 15, 19
Pacific Plate 27
Pacific salmon 161
Pacific-Antarctic Ridge 34
Pacinian corpuscle 114
pack, battery 228
package 163
package, dual-in-line 417
packaged integrated circuit 417
packaging 162
packaging products 120
packer 121
packer body 364
pad 478
pad arm 273
pad plate 273
pad, elbow 526, 527
pad, forearm 486
pad, knee 526, 527
pad, mouse 332
pad, neck 486
pad, sanding 229
pad, scouring 215
pad, touch 336
padded base 489
padded envelope 339
padded upright 489
paddy field 47
page down 331
page down key 331
page up 331
page up key 331
page, front 313
pagoda 283
paint roller 219
paintbrush 219
painting upkeep 219
pair 509
pak-choi 126
Pakistan 452
palatine tonsil 118
palatoglossal arch 116
Palau 453
paling fence 230
pallet truck 396
palm 115, 243, 477
palm grove 36
palm of a glove 243
palm rest, detachable 330
palm tree 64
palmate 55
palmette 200
palp 73
pan 422, 423, 535
pan hook 422
pan, dripping 174, 179
pan, loaf 179
Panama 448
panama 238
Panama, Gulf of 17
Panama, Isthmus of 16
pancake pan 175
pancetta 156
pancreas 106
pane 186
panel 185, 246, 259
panel, bay filler 329
panel, control 179, 210
panel, operating 287
pannier bag 372
panoramic window 435
panpipe 297
pantograph 376
pantry 188
panty corselette 258
panty girdle 259
papaya 137
paper clips 341
paper collection unit 49
paper fasteners 341
paper feed button 333, 443
paper feed light 333
paper guide 328
paper punch 340
paper recycling container 49
paper shredder 341
paper, parchment 162
paper, waxed 162
paper-clip holder 341
paper/paperboard separation 49
paper/paperboard sorting 49
papers, rice 147
papilla 114, 119
papilla, circumvallate 118
papilla, filiform 118
papilla, foliate 118
papilla, fongiform 118
papillary muscle 104
paprika 139
Papua New Guinea 15, 453
par 5 hole 504
parabolic dune 36
paraffin 405
paraffins 405
Paraguay 448
parallel 22
parallel bars 496, 497
parallel electrical circuit 416
parallel port 329
parallelepiped 429
parallelogram 429
paramecium 66
Paraná River 17
parapet 344
parapet walk 282
parboiled rice 147
parcel tape dispenser 341
parcels office 374
parchment paper 162
parfum, eau de 267
parietal bone 99, 100
parietal pleura 105
paring knife 169
paripinnate 55
park 25, 433
parka 249
parking 435, 504, 512
parking area 389, 430, 445
parking, bicycle 445
Parmesan 151
parsley 142
parsnip 129
parterre 293
partial eclipse 4, 5
partially reflecting mirror 420

partition 60, 457
partlow chart 365
partridge 80
parts 200, 201, 204
parts of a bicycle 370
parts of a circle 428
parts of a shoe 240
parts of spectacles 273
pascal 426
pass 29
passage, ascending 278
passage, descending 278
Passage, Drake 15, 17
passage, fore-and-aft 385
passbook update slot 442
passenger cabin 383, 386, 387, 393
passenger car 376, 380
passenger platform 374
passenger seat 369
passenger station 374, 375
passenger terminal 381, 389, 390
passenger train 374
passenger transfer vehicle 391
passion fruit 136
passport case 275
passport control 391
pasta 146
pasta maker 170
paste, tomato 140
pastern 83
pastry bag and nozzles 172
pastry blender 172
pastry brush 172
pastry cutting wheel 172
pasture 122
Patagonia 17
patch pocket 244, 249, 260
patella 98
patera 200
path 230, 504
path, garden 182
pathology laboratory 465
patient 464
patient room 464
patient's chair 464
patio 182, 230
patio door 164, 188
patisserie/bakery 437
patrol and first-aid station 512
pattypan squash 129
pause 299, 331
pause button 323
pause key 323
pause/break key 331
pause/still 319
pause/still key 319
pavement 183, 434
pavilion 432
Pawn 470
pay phone 294, 437, 438, 463
payment terminal, electronic 443
PC card slot 336
PDA 337
pe-tsai 126
pea 60
pea jacket 251
pea, black-eyed 130
peach 132
peach, section of 57
peacock 81
peak 29, 238, 239, 458
peak level meter 323
peaked lapel 244
peanut 130
peanut oil 149
pear 133
pear, Asian 137
pear, prickly 137
pear-shaped body 297
peas 130
peas, split 130
pecan nut 133
peccary 84
pectoral deck 501
pectoral fin 74, 90
pedal 302, 308, 370, 372, 473, 501, 522
pedal key 305
pedal keyboard 305
pedal pushers 254
pedal rod 304
pedal spindle 372
pedal with wide platform 522
pedal, brake 350, 357
pedal, clipless 522
pedestal 302
pedestrian call button 434
pedestrian crossing 434
pedestrian lights 434
pedicel 59, 62
pediment 279
pedipalp 70
peduncle 56, 57, 58, 59, 62
peel 58
peeler 169
peg 202, 224, 301, 302, 528, 529
peg box 301
peg loop 528, 529
peg, tuning 303
pelerine 251
pelican 80
pellets 534
peltate 55
pelvic fin 74
pen 27
pen holder 274
penalty arc 480
penalty area 480
penalty area marking 480
penalty bench 507
penalty bench official 507
penalty spot 480
pencil 312
pencil point tip 218
pencil sharpener 341
pendant 264
penguin 80
penholder grip 493
peninsula 24
Peninsula, Antarctic 15
Peninsula, Arabian 19
Peninsula, Balkan 18
Peninsula, Iberian 18
Peninsula, Kamchatka 19
Peninsula, Kola 18
Peninsula, Korean 19
Peninsula, Scandinavian 18
Peninsula, Yucatan 16
penis 92, 111
penne 146
penstock 406, 407
pentagon, regular 429
penumbra 4, 5
pepino 137
pepper spray 456
pepper, black 138
pepper, green 138
pepper, ground 139
pepper, pink 138
pepper, white 138
pepperoni 156
pepperpot 166
percent 427
percent key 337
perch 160
perch, morphology of 74
perch, pike 160
perching bird 79
percolator 181
percussion instruments 295, 308
perforated toe cap 240
perforation 243
performance tyre 358
performing arts 294
perfume shop 436
pergola 230
pericardium 105
pericarp 60
periodontal ligament 101
peripheral 431
peripheral nervous system 108
peristome 66
peristyle 279, 280
peritoneum 111, 112
peroxide 461
peroxisome 66
perpendicular 428
perpetual snows 29
Persian 87
Persian Gulf 19
person, continuity 291
personal adornment 264
personal adornment and articles 264
personal articles 271
personal communications 317
personal computer 329
personal identification number (PIN) pad 443
personal organizer 338
personal radio cassette player 325
personal watercraft 523
Peru 448
Peru-Chile Trench 34
peso 440
pesticide 47, 48
pestle 170
pet food and supplies 121
pet shop 436
petal 56
petiolar sinus 62
petiole 52, 55
petrochemical industry 405
petrochemicals 405
petrol 405
petrol engine 351, 360
petrol pump 346
petrol pump hose 346
petrol tank cap 368
petroleum 405
petroleum trap 403
pew 446
pharmaceutical forms of medication 467
pharmacy 436, 462, 465
pharynx 105, 106
phase conductor 198
phase, gliding 514
phase, pushing 514
phases of the Moon 5
pheasant 81, 154
pheasant egg 155
Philippine Plate 27
Philippine Trench 34
Philippines 19, 453
philtrum 117
phloem 63
Phobos 2
phone, pay 437, 438, 463
phosphorescent coating 199
photo booth 437
photographer 436
photographer, still 291
photography 314
photography, director of 291
photon 420
photoreceptors 119
photoshot button 320
photosphere 4
photosynthesis 54
photovoltaic arrays 11
physical map 24
physician 464, 498
physics: electricity and magnetism 416
physics: optics 418
pi 428
pia mater 109
piano 295
piccolo 295, 306
pick 233
pickguard 303
pickling onion 124
pickup selector 303
pickup truck 347
pickups 303
picture tube 318
picture, front 313
pie tin 172
pier 285, 344
pierce lever 180
pig 84
pig, guinea 82
pigeon 81, 154
pigsty 122
pika 82
pike 160
pike perch 160
pike pole 454
pike position 518
pilaster, Corinthian 281
pile 190
pile carpet 190
pile dwelling 288
pillar 27, 283, 284, 302
pillbox hat 239
pillion footrest 367, 368
pillow 204
pillow cover 204
pillowcase 204
pilot house 385
pilot light 178, 180, 181, 208, 210, 214
pin 198, 199, 454
pin base 199
pin block 304
pin, connection 417
pin, male grounding 198
pinafore 252
pinch 199
pine needles 65
pine nut 133
pine seed 65
pineal body 109
pineapple 136
pink ball 503
pink pepper 138
pinna 52, 82
pinnacle 282, 284, 285
pinnatifid 55
pinto bean 131
pip 58, 59, 468
pipe 224
pipe clamp 224
pipe section 193
pipe wrench 216
pipeline 404
pistachio nut 133
pistil 56
pistol 456
pistol grip 534
pistol grip handle 218, 228
pistol nozzle 236
pistol, starting 472
piston 357, 360
piston lever 216
piston release 216
piston ring 360
piston skirt 360
pit 76
pit lane 524
pit, orchestra 292
pitch 395, 475, 479
pitch wheel 310
pitcher 474, 475
pitcher's mound 475
pitcher's plate 475
pitchfork comb 268
pith 63
Pitot tube 525
pits 524
pitta bread 145
pituitary gland 109
pivot 217, 270, 271, 533
pivot cab 400
pivot spindle 355
placing judge 516
plaice, common 161
plain 24, 32
plain flour 144
plan 279, 285
plan reading, elevation 182
plane 229
plane projection 22
plane surfaces 428
planets 2
planets, inner 3
planets, outer 2
planisphere 14
plano-concave lens 419
plano-convex lens 419
plant 53
plant cell 50
plant kingdom 50
plant litter 54
plant, sorting 49
plant, structure 53
plantain 136
plantar 97
plantar interosseous 96
plasma 104
plasma membrane 66
plasma television 318
plasmodesma 50
plaster dressing 461
plaster room 463
plastic arts room 444
plastic case 534
plastic film 162
plastic film capacitor 417
plastics sorting 49
plastron 76
plate 178, 269, 531
plate boundaries, convergent 27
plate boundaries, divergent 27
plate boundaries, transform 27
plate grid 359
Plate, African 27
Plate, Antarctic 27
Plate, Australian-Indian 27
Plate, Caribbean 27
Plate, Cocos 27
plate, cooking 179
Plate, Eurasian 27
Plate, Nazca 27
Plate, North American 27
plate, number 525
Plate, Pacific 27
Plate, Philippine 27
plate, protective 525
Plate, Scotia 27
Plate, South American 27
plateau 24, 29
platelet 104
plates, tectonic 27
platform 219, 363, 379, 390, 423, 516, 526
platform edge 374, 379
platform entrance 374
platform ladder 219
platform number 374
platform shelter 375
platform, 10 m 518
platform, 3 m 518
platform, 5 m 518
platform, 7,5 m 518
platform, event 496
play 319, 328
play button 319, 323
play key 323
play/pause button 326
player positions 474, 481, 482, 4
player's number 486, 488, 506
player's stick 506
player, basketball 488
player, CD/DVD 471
player, compact disc 325
player, rugby 483
players 492
players' bench 485, 487, 506
players' position 482
playground 445
playing area 471
playing field 480
playing field for American football
playing surface 493
playing surfaces 492
pleasure garden 230
pleats, examples of 253
plectrum 297
pleura, parietal 105
pleura, visceral 105
pleural cavity 105
plexus of nerves 101
pliers 222
plimsoll 242
plug 228, 326
plug adapter 198, 271
plug, power 337
plug, power cable 329
plug, sealing 417
plum 132
plum sauce 141
plumber's snake 216
plumbing 194
plumbing system 194

plumbing tools 216
plumbing wrench 216
plunger 216, 460
plus or minus 427
Pluto 3
pneumatic armlet 461
pocket 225, 274, 502, 505
pocket calculator 337
pocket handkerchief 244
podcasting 335
podium 283, 435, 444
podium and basements 435
point 167, 169, 301, 312, 469, 471, 538
point guard 489
oint of interest 25
oint, anchor 70
oint, nocking 535
ointed tab end 245
ointer 422, 423
oints 375, 492
oisonous mushroom 52
oker 193
oker die 468
oland 450
olar axis 7
olar bear 89
olar climates 40
olar ice cap 40
olar lights 37
olar tundra 40
olarizing filter 314
olaroid® Land camera 315
ole 321, 490
ole grip 514
ole position 524
ole shaft 514
ole vault 472
le, North 21
le, north 416
le, South 15, 21
le, south 416
lice car 457
lice officer 456
lice station 433
litical map 23
litics 448
llen basket 68
'lock, black 161
lutants, air 47
lutants, non-biodegradable 47
luting gas emission 47
llution, agricultural 47
lution, air 47
lution, domestic 47
lution, industrial 47
lution, land 47
'ution, motor vehicle 47
ution, oil 48
lution, water 48
o dress 252
o neck 514
o shirt 250, 255, 492
o-neck sweater 250
gons 429
pody, common 52
e fruits 133
negranate 136
nelo 134
nmel horse 496
cho 251
d 230, 504
s Varolii 109
-l'Évêque 151
dle 86
184, 502
ar 64
oing crease 479
oy 56
oy seeds 139
ular terms 58, 59
h 183, 285, 447
n dome 447
upine 82
50, 60, 114
cuts of 153
minced 153
prism 420

port 431
port glass 165
port hand 387
port, Ethernet 336
port, FireWire 336
port, game/MIDI 329
port, infrared 336, 337
port, internal modem 329, 336
port, keyboard 329
port, mouse 329
port, network 329
port, parallel 329
port, power adapter 336
port, serial 329
port, USB 329, 336
port, video 329, 336
portable CD radio cassette recorder 326
portable compact disc player 325
portable digital audio player 326
portable fire extinguisher 454
portable radio 325
portable shower head 195
portable sound systems 325
portal 285
portal vein 103
porthole 386
portrait 441
ports, controller 471
Portugal 449
position indicator 287
position light 376, 395
position marker 302, 303
position, mean 418
position, pole 524
positions, player 474, 481, 489
positive contact 410, 411
positive meniscus 419
positive plate 359
positive plate strap 359
positive region 410
positive terminal 359, 416, 417
positive/negative junction 410
post 412, 487, 495
post binder 339
post lantern 207
post mill 412
post office 433, 437
post, foul line 475
post, hand 297
post, observation 7
poster 294
posterior adductor muscle 73
posterior chamber 119
posterior end 73
posterior fontanelle 100
posterior horn 109
posterior root 110
posterior semicircular canal 116
posterior view 93, 95, 97, 99, 113
postern 282
posting surface 341
potato 124
potato masher 173
potato, sweet 124
pothole 31
pouch 162, 531
pouch of Douglas 112
pouch, ammunition 456
poultry 155
poultry shears 173
pound 440
pouring spout 215
powder blusher 266
powder puff 266
powder, chilli 139
powder, five spice 139
powder, magnesium 497
powdered milk 150
powdered mustard 140
powdered sugar 149
power adapter 336
power adapter port 336
power and backlight button 337
power button 318, 319, 321, 322, 323, 328, 329, 333, 336
power cable plug 329
power cord 177, 227, 229, 269, 322

power cord, alternating-current 336
power cord, direct-current 336
power indicator 329
power light 333
power mower 237
power plant 406
power plug 337
power socket 326
power source 416
power supply fan 329
power switch 311, 315, 329
power train 372
power, measurement of 426
power-on/paper-detect light 443
power/functions switch 320
practice green 504
practice pedal 304
prairie 24
prawn 158
prayer hall 447
precipitation 45
precipitation area 39
precipitations 41
precipitations, winter 41
precision and accuracy sports 502
prehensile digit 91
premaxilla 74
premolars 101
prepuce 111
present state of weather 39
presenter, note 442
presenter, slip 346
preset button 326
preset buttons 319
preset tuning button 322
press bar 501
pressed cheeses 151
pressed powder 266
pressure bar 304
pressure change 39
pressure control 272
pressure control valve 461
pressure cooker 174
pressure demand regulator 454
pressure gauge 461
pressure modulator, brake 357
pressure regulator 174, 529
pressure tube 409
pressure, measurement of 426
pressurized refuge 345
prevailing wind 43
prevention, crime 456
previous 328
previous sets 492
previous/rewind button 326
price per gallon/litre 346
prickly pear 137
prickly sphagnum 51
primaries 78
primary consumers 45
primary covert 78
primary crash sensor 354
primary mirror 7
primary root 53
primate mammals 91
primates, examples of 91
prime focus 7
prime focus observing capsule 7
prime meridian 22
primer 534
princess dress 252
princess seaming 258
print cartridge light 333
print screen 331
print screen/system request key 331
printed circuit 417
printed circuit board 417
printer, inkjet 333
printout 423
prism binoculars 420
prisoner's dock 440
privacy curtain 464
private broadcasting network 316
private dressing room 290
probe socket 178
proboscis 67
procedure checklist 10
process, mastoid 100

process, styloid 100
processing, data 38
proctors' office 445
producer 291
product code 423
production designer 290
production of electricity by generator 408
production of electricity from geothermal energy 402
production of electricity from nuclear energy 408
production of electricity from thermal energy 402
production of electricity from wind energy 413
production platform 404
production well 402
products, cereal 144
products, dairy 120, 150
products, household 120
products, packaging 120
professional training office 442
profile of the Earth's atmosphere 37
profile, soil 54
program selector 213, 214, 310, 314
programmable buttons 332
programmable function keys 443
programs, computer 457
projection booth 294
projection device 365
projection room 294
projection screen 294
projector 294
proleg 67
promenade deck 386
prominence 4
prompt side 293
pronaos 279
propagation 418
propane gas cylinder 361
propane or butane appliances 529
propellant 534
propeller 384, 386, 387
propeller duct 383
propeller shaft 387
propeller, rear 384
propeller, stem 384
propeller, three-blade 394
propeller, two-blade 394
propelling pencil 312
property line 182
property man 291
property man, assistant 291
propulsion module 316
proscenium 292
prosciutto 156
prosecution counsel's bench 440
prospecting, surface 403
prostate 111
protect tab 333
protection layer 10
protection, rub 525
protective casing 237
protective cup 486, 507
protective equipment 486
protective goggles 522, 525
protective plate 525
protective suit 525
protective surround 471
protective window 318
protector, glass 506
protector, hand 525
protocol, communication 334
proton 414
protoneuron 110
province 23
pruning and cutting tools 234
pruning saw 234
pseudopod 66
psychiatric examination 462
psychiatric observation room 462
pubis 92, 94
public building 25
public entrance 278
public garden 435
puck 507
pudding, black 156

Puerto Rico Trench 34
pull strap 277
pull, ring 163
pulley 219, 360
pulling ring 460
pulmonary artery 102, 105
pulmonary trunk 104
pulmonary valve 104
pulmonary vein 102
pulp 58, 101
pulp chamber 101
pulpit 446, 447
pulsed ruby laser 420
pulverizer 402
pump 184, 212, 214, 241, 529
pump and motor assembly 357
pump nozzle 346
pump number 346
pump room 384
pump sprayer 236
pumper 455
pumping station 404
pumpkin 129
punch hole 240, 246, 263
punchbag 498
punchball 498
pupil 87, 119
pure alcohol 461
purfling 301, 302
purse 275
purslane 127
push bar 286
push button 176, 214
push buttons 327
push frame 398
push rim 467
push-button 312
push-up bra 259
push-up stand 501
pusher 170, 177, 180
pushing phase 514
putter 505
pygal shield 76
pyjamas 256
pyloric stomach 71
pyramid 278, 429
pyramid entrance 278
pyramid spot 502
Pyrenees 18
python 77

Q

Qatar 452
Qibla wall 447
quad bike 369
quadrant 428
quadrilateral 429
quadruped stick 466
quail 81, 154
quail egg 155
quarter 240, 262
quarter window 349
quarter-deck 386
quarterback 485
quartet 300
quaver 299
quaver rest 299
quay 381, 430
quay ramp 381
quayside crane 381
quayside railway 381
Queen 468, 470
queen 68
Queen Maud Land 15
queen's chamber 278
Queen's side 470
queen, honeybee 68
quiche tin 172
quick ticket system 294
quill 312
quill brush 268
quince 133
quinoa 143
quintet 300

R

raab, broccoli 127
rabbi's seat 447
rabbit 82, 154
raccoon 88
race director 522
raceme 57
racing suit 508, 525
racing, motor 524
racing, road 522
rack 174, 178, 210, 214, 473, 503
rack, brochure 442
rack, luggage 369
rack, ski 356
racket sports 493
Raclette 151
raclette with grill 179
radar 382, 383, 386, 387
radar display 457
radar mast 384
radar transceiver 457
radar, weather 38
radial nerve 108
radial thread 70
radiation 415
radiation zone 4
radiation, absorbed solar 46
radiation, infrared 46, 418
radiation, reflected solar 46
radiation, solar 45, 46, 410
radiation, ultraviolet 418
radiator 350, 358
radiator core 358
radiator grille 364
radiator panel 13
radiators 11
radicchio 126
radicle 53, 63
radio 457
radio antenna 382, 384, 386, 387, 525
radio section 326
radio waves 418
radio, clock 325
radio, portable 325
radioactivity, measurement of 426
radish 129
radish, black 129
radius 98, 428
rafter 187
raglan 251
raglan sleeve 248, 251, 261
rail 202, 502
rail shuttle service 390
rail transport 374
rail, communion 446
rail, guard 526
rail, top 205
railing 189
railway 25
railway station 25, 375, 430, 432
railway track 432
rain 41
rain cap 193
rain hat 239
rain, acid 47, 48
rain, freezing 41
rainbow 41
raincoat 248
rainfall, heavy 43
raining, utensils for 171
raised handlebar 522
raised head 221
rake 233
rake comb 268
rally car 524
rambutan 137
ramekin 166
ramp 279, 281, 526
rampart 282
random orbit sander 229
Range, Great Dividing 15
rank insignia 456
ras el hanout 139
raspberry 132
raspberry, section 59
rat 82
rat, morphology of 82
ratchet 221
ratchet knob 425
ratchet ring spanner 223
ratchet socket wrench 223
rattlesnake 77
raven 80
ravioli 146
ray, crater 5
ray, light 419
rays, gamma 418
razor clam 157
re-entrant angle 428
reach-in freezer 120
reaction, chain 415
reactor 408
reactor building 409
reactor vessel 409
read/write head 333
reader, card 321
reading light 457
reading mirror 10
rear apron 245
rear beam 422
rear brake 370
rear brake pedal 368
rear bumper 369, 523
rear cargo rack 369
rear derailleur 370, 372
rear foil 387
rear indicator 367, 368
rear leg 201
rear light 352, 367, 368, 370
rear lights 352
rear propeller 384
rear rigid section 363
rear seat 353
rear sight 534
rear step 455
rearview mirror 354
receipt, transaction 443
receiver 321, 327, 490, 495
receiver volume control 327
receiver, wide 485
receiving area 120
receptacle 51, 56, 59
reception area 462, 465
reception desk 442
reception hall 447
reception level 439
receptors, taste 118
rechargeable battery pack 320
recharging base 208
recliner 201
reclining back 460
record 319
record button 319, 323
record muting button 323
record shop 436
recorder, DVD 319
recording level control 323
recording media 319
recording mode 320
recording start/stop button 320
recording, seismographic 403
records, medical 465
recovery room 464
rectangle 429
rectangular 530
rectum 106, 111, 112
rectus femoris 96
recycling 49
recycling bin 49
recycling containers 49
Red 469
red 418
red alga 51
red ball 502, 503
red balls 503
red beam 318
red blood cell 104
red cabbage 126
red clamp 356
red kidney bean 131
red light 434
red onion 124
Red Sea 14, 19, 20
red sweet pepper 128
red whortleberry 132
red-kneed tarantula 70
redcurrant 132
redfish 161
reed 306
reed pipe 305
Reef, Great Barrier 15
reel 236, 319
reel crank 236
reel seat 536, 537
reel, baitcasting 537
referee 481, 483, 485, 487, 488, 498, 499, 507, 509, 516, 518
referee, assistant 509
refill 312
refill pipe 196
refinery 404, 431
refinery products 405
reflected solar radiation 46
reflecting cylinder 420
reflecting telescope 9
reflecting telescope, cross section 9
reflector 217, 365, 370, 523
refracting telescope 8
refracting telescope, cross section 8
refrigerated display case 438
refrigerated semitrailer 365
refrigeration unit 365
refrigerator 164, 211, 438
refrigerator compartment 211
refrigerator van 377
refrigerators 438
refuge, pressurized 345
refuse container 215
regions, vegetation 44
register, cash 121
regular decagon 429
regular dodecagon 429
regular hendecagon 429
regular heptagon 429
regular hexagon 429
regular nonagon 429
regular octagon 429
regular octahedron 429
regular pentagon 429
reindeer 84
reinforced edging 277
reinforced toe 459
relay station 316
relay station, microwave 334
release lever 222
release of oxygen 54
release, energy 415
relieving chamber 278
religion 446
remote control 319, 321
remote control sensor 318
remote control terminal 314, 315
remote manipulator system 11, 12
remote-control arm 11
removable flag pole 504
removable hard disk 333
removable hard disk drive 333
removable-bottomed tin 172
renal artery 102, 107
renal hilus 107
renal papilla 107
renal pelvis 107
renal vein 102, 107
reniform 55
repair shop 346
repeat key 323
repeat mark 298
repeater 317
reprography 442
reptiles 76
reptiles, examples of 77
Republic of Korea 453
repulsion 416
reservoir 181, 406, 407
reservoir, brake fluid 357
reset button 329, 424, 471
reset key 328
residential district 431
resistance adjustment 501
resistors 417
resonator 305, 309, 324
resort, ski 512
respirator 459
respiratory system 105
respiratory system protection 459
rest area 25
rest area, vehicle 345
rest values 299
rest, arrow 535
rest, hand 332
restaurant 386, 432, 435, 436, 438
restaurant car 376
restaurant review 313
restaurants, fast-food 437
restricted area 489
restricting circle 488
results, table of 518
resurgence 31
resuscitation room 462
retaining strap 277
reticle 420
retina 119, 419
retractable handle 274
retractable step 361
return crease 479
return spring 357
reverse 518
reversing light 352
reversing switch 221, 228
review, restaurant 313
revolving door, manual 286
revolving nosepiece 421
revolving sprinkler 236
rewind 319
rewind button 323
Rhea 3
rhinoceros 85
rhizoid 51
rhizome 52
rhombus 429
rhubarb 125
rhythm selector 311
rias 35
rib 125, 273, 301, 302, 401, 458
rib pad 486
rib roast 152
ribbing 250, 261, 536
ribosome 50, 66
ribs 98
ribs, back 152
rice 61, 143, 147
rice noodles 147
rice papers 147
rice vermicelli 147
rice vinegar 141
rice, basmati 147
rice, brown 147
rice, parboiled 147
rice, white 147
rice, wild 143
rice: panicle 61
ricotta 150
ridge 29
ridge tent 529
Ridge, Mid-Atlantic 34
Ridge, Mid-Indian 34
Ridge, Pacific-Antarctic 34
Ridge, Southeast Indian 34
Ridge, Southwest Indian 34
riding coat 251
riegel 30
rifle (rifled bore) 534
rigatoni 146
right angle 428
right ascension setting scale 8, 9
right atrium 103, 104
right attacker 487
right back 481, 487
right centre 482
right channel 324
right cornerback 484
right defence 506
right defensive end 484
right defensive tackle 484
right field 475
right fielder 474
right forward 489
right guard 485
right kidney 107
right lung 103, 105
right midfielder 481
right pulmonary vein 104
right safety 484
right service court 491
right side 272
right tackle 485
right ventricle 103, 104
right wing 482, 507
rigid section, front 363
rigid section, rear 363
rigid tube 209
rillettes 156
rim 273, 366, 371, 489
rim soup bowl 166
rime 41
rinceau 200
rind 58
ring 52, 273, 307, 423, 424, 498
ring binder 339
ring motorway 25
ring post 498
ring pull 163
ring road 25
ring spanner 223
ring step 498
ring, 25 471
ring, outer 441
ring, tuning 297
ringhandle 270
ringing volume control 327
rings 264, 496, 497
ringside 498
rink 506, 509
rink corner 506
rink, ice 512
rinse-aid dispenser 214
rip fence 227
ripeness 62
ripening 62
ripper 398
ripper cylinder 398
ripper shank 398
ripper tip tooth 398
rise 191
Rise, East Pacific 34
riser 191
rising main 194
rising warm air 43
river 24, 25, 32
river otter 88
River, Amazon 17
River, Congo 20
River, Danube 18
River, Dnieper 18
River, Mackenzie 16
River, Mississippi 16
River, Niger 20
River, Orinoco 17
River, Paraná 17
River, Saint Lawrence 16
River, Senegal 20
River, Vistula 18
River, Volga 18
rivet 169, 222
road 25, 430
road bicycle 373
road communications 317
road cycling competition 522
road flare 457
road map 25
road number 25
road racing 522
road system 342
road transport 342, 381
road tunnel 345
road, cross section 342
road-racing bicycle and cyclist 52
roadway 342, 345, 434
roast 152, 153
roast, fillet 152
roast, rib 152
roasted coffee beans 148
roasting pans 174
Roberval's balance 422
robin, European 80
rock basin 30
rock candy 149
rock garden 230

ocker arm 360
ocket 127
ocking chair 200, 201
ockslide 31
ocky desert 36
ocky islet 35
Rocky Mountains 16
od 119
odent 82
odents and lagomorphs 82
odents, examples of 82
oll 395
oll structure 525
oller 268, 332
oller frame 219
oller hockey skate 527
oller shade 356
oller skate 527
oller sleeve 219
oller speed skate 527
olling pin 172
oman amphitheatre 281
oman bean 131
oman house 280
oman metal pen 312
oman numerals 427
omania 450
omano 151
mpers 260, 261
of 183, 193, 283, 349, 361
of pole 529
of timber 279
of vent 194, 361
om number 439
om, anaethesia 464
om, audiometric examination 465
om, changing 444
om, clean utility 462
om, computer science 444
om, conference 442
om, control 293
om, dining 438, 439
om, double 439
om, equipment storage 444
om, examination 465
om, examination and treatment 463
om, gynaecological examination 463
m, hotel 439
m, isolation 462
m, jurors' 440
m, linen 439
m, meeting 439, 442, 445
m, music 444
m, observation 462, 465
m, ophthalmology and ENT 463
m, patient 464
m, plaster 463
m, plastic arts 444
m, projection 294
m, psychiatric observation 462
n, recovery 464
m, resuscitation 462
n, science 444
n, scrub 464
n, single 439
n, soiled utility 462, 464
n, specimen collection 465
n, sterilization 464, 465
n, students' 445
n, supply 464
n, teachers' 445
n, technical 345
n, treatment 465
n, triage 463
n, waiting 463
ns, interview 440
ns, main 188
ter 81
54, 101, 118, 167
canal 101
cap 53
hairs 53
of nail 114
ib 392
system 53, 62
vegetables 129
motor 109
root, primary 53
root, secondary 53
root, sensitive 109
root-hair zone 63
roots, adventitious 52
rope 264, 498
rope, false start 516
rope, tension 297
Roquefort 151
rorqual 90
rose 56, 186, 236, 302
rose window 285
rosemary 142
Ross Ice Shelf 15
rotary cheese grater 170
rotary file 338
rotary system 403
rotary table 403
rotating dome 7
rotating drum 27
rotating light 455
rotini 146
rotor 412, 537
rotor blade 395
rotor head 395
rotor hub 395
rotunda 435
rough 504
round brush 268
round head 221
round pronator 96
roundabout 25
route sign 362, 363
route, evacuation 345
router 229, 334
row 272, 293
row, first 482
row, second 482
row, third 482
rowing machine 501
royal agaric 123
royal flush 468
rub protection 525
rubber boot 454
rubber bulb 460
rubber ferrule 466
rubber gasket 197
rubber stamp 338
rubber stopper 219
ruby cylinder 420
ruching 260
ruck 483
rudder 13, 383, 384, 386, 393, 520
rudder blade 384
Ruffini's corpuscle 114
ruffled skirt 253
rug 190
rugby 482
rugby ball 483
rugby player 483
rugby shoes 483
rule 313
ruler 425, 531
rump 78
run 191
run-up 473
runabout 385
rung 219
runner 469
running shoe 262, 473
running shorts 263
runs, approach 496
runway 390
runway centre line markings 390
runway designation marking 390
runway side stripe markings 390
runway threshold markings 391
runway touchdown zone marking 391
rupee 440
Russian black bread 145
Russian Federation 450
Russian module 11
Rwanda 451
rye 61, 143
rye crispbread 145
rye: spike 61
Ryukyu Trench 34

S

S-Video output 336
sacral plexus 108
sacristy 446
sacrum 98, 99
saddle 370
saddle pillar 370
saddlebag 369
safari jacket 255
safe 443
safe deposit box 443
safety 454
safety area 499
safety binding 510, 511
safety boot 459
safety cage 473
safety earmuffs 458
safety glasses 458
safety goggles 458
safety handle 237
safety lighting 457
safety line 379
safety niche 345
safety rail 219, 377
safety scissors 265
safety tether 10
safety thermostat 213
safety valve 174, 408
saffron 138
safing sensor 354
sage 142
sagittal section 111, 112
Sahara Desert 20
sail 412, 519
sail cloth 412
sail panel 520
sailbar 412
sailboard 519
sailing 520
sailing boat 520
sailor tunic 255
Saint Bernard 86
Saint Kitts and Nevis 449
Saint Lawrence River 16
Saint Lucia 449
Saint Vincent and the Grenadines 449
salad bowl 166
salad crisper 211
salad dish 166
salad fork 168
salad plate 166
salad spinner 171
salamander 75
salami, Genoa 156
salami, German 156
Salchow 509
salivary gland 118
salivary glands 106
salmon, Atlantic 161
salmon, Pacific 161
salsify 129
salt lake 36
salt, coarse 141
salt, sea 141
salt, table 141
saltcellar 166
sambal oelek 141
Samoa 453
sampler 310
San Marino 450
sanctuary lamp 446
sand bunker 504
sand island 35
sand shoe 365
sandal 242
sandbank 33
sandbox 377
sander, random orbit 229
sanding disc 229
sanding pad 229
sandpaper 229
sandy desert 36
Sao Tome and Principe 451
saphenous nerve 108
sapodilla 137
sapwood 63
sardine 159
sarong 253
sartorius 96
sash frame 186
sash window 287
satchel bag 275
satellite 316
satellite broadcasting 316
satellite earth station 335
satellite radio receiver 326
satellite terminal 389
satellite, telecommunication 335
satellite, weather 38
Saturn 2, 3
sauce, hoisin 140
sauce, plum 141
sauce, soy 140
sauce, Tabasco 140
sauce, Worcestershire 140
saucepan 175, 531
saucepan, small 175
Saudi Arabia 452
sausage, chipolata 156
sausage, kielbasa 156
sausage, merguez 156
sausage, Toulouse 156
sauté pan 175
savanna 44
savory 142
savoy cabbage 126
saw, compass 226
saw, coping 226
saw, hand mitre 226
saxhorn 307
saxophone 306
scale 74, 76, 79, 225, 298, 424, 425, 460, 533
scale leaf 54
scale, main 425
scale, mitre 226
scale, vernier 425
scalelike leaves of the cypress 65
scallop 157
scampi 158
Scandinavian crispbread 145
Scandinavian Peninsula 18
scanner, optical 121
scapula 98, 99
scapular 78
scarlet runner bean 131
scatter cushion 204
scene 278
scenic route 25
schedule, television programme 313
schnauzer 86
school 444
school bus 362
school secretary's office 445
school, ski 512
sciatic nerve 108
science 414
science room 444
scientific calculator 337
scientific instruments 7, 13
scientific symbols 426
scientific terms 58, 59
scissors 461, 531
sclera 119
sconce 207
scooter, motor 369
score 497
scoreboard 471, 472, 492, 497, 499
scoreboard, current event 497
scoreboard, overall standings 496
scorer 487, 488
scorers and timekeepers 499
scorpion 70
Scotia Plate 27
scouring pad 215
scraper 219, 400, 514
screen 271, 318, 407, 439, 479
screen door 361
screen print 260, 261
screen window 528
screen, fireplace 193
screen, print 331
screen, projection 294
screen, touch 337
screw 221, 301
screw cap 163, 199
screw earrings 264
screw locking nut 536, 537
screw, clamping 224
screw, lock 332
screw, tension adjustment 341
screw-in studs 480
screwdriver 221, 531
screwdriver bit 228
screwdriver, cordless 221
screws, clamping 425
scrimmage: defence 484
scrimmage: offence 485
scroll 301
scroll case 407
scroll foot 200
scroll wheel 332
scrolling 331
scrolling lock key 331
scrolls, Torah 447
scrotum 92, 111
scrub room 464
scrum half 482
scuff rib 358
scuffle hoe 233
scuttle panel 348
sea 5, 24, 32
sea bass 160
sea bream 159
sea kale 126
sea lettuce 123
sea level 26, 33, 37
sea lion 90
Sea of Japan 19
sea salt 141
Sea, Adriatic 18
Sea, Aegean 18
Sea, Arabian 19
Sea, Aral 19
Sea, Baltic 18
Sea, Barents 18
Sea, Beaufort 16
Sea, Black 18, 19
Sea, Caribbean 16
Sea, Caspian 19
Sea, Coral 15
Sea, East China 19
Sea, Irish 18
Sea, Mediterranean 18, 20
Sea, North 18
Sea, Norwegian 18
Sea, Red 19, 20
Sea, South China 19
Sea, Tasman 15
Sea, Weddell 15
sea-level pressure 39
seafood 121
seal 90
sealing material 417
sealing plug 417
sealing ring 404
seam 243, 478
seam pocket 251
seaming 244
seamount 33
seaplane, float 394
search 335
seasoning, cajun spice 139
seasons of the year 38
seat 195, 196, 200, 201, 205, 294, 353, 369, 467, 501, 523
seat adjuster lever 353
seat back 353
seat back adjustment knob 353
seat belt 353
seat cover 196
seat stay 370
seat tube 370
seat, booster 205
seat, child 356
seat, director's 291
seat, driver 369
seat, passenger 369
seat, rabbi's 447
seat-belt warning light 355
seats 201, 293
seats, actors' 290
seaweed 123
sebaceous gland 114
secateurs 234
second 298, 428, 498, 515

second assistant camera operator 290
second base 474
second baseman 474
second dorsal fin 74
second hand 424
second molar 101
second premolar 101
second row 482
second space 489
second valve slide 307
second violins 295
second voltage increase 413
second-level domain 334
secondaries 78
secondary altar 446
secondary consumers 45
secondary mirror 7, 9
secondary road 25
secondary root 53
secondary waiting room 465
secretariat 443
section 313
section of a bulb 54
section of a capsule: poppy 60
section of a follicle: star anise 60
section of a grape 59
section of a hazelnut 60
section of a legume: pea 60
section of a peach 57
section of a raspberry 59
section of a silique: mustard 60
section of a strawberry 59
section of a walnut 60
section of an apple 58
section of an orange 58
section of the Earth's crust 26
section, vertical 526
sectional garage door 286
sector 428
security check 391
security grille 442
security guard's workstation 463
security thread 441
security trigger 235
security vestibule 440
sedimentary rocks 26
seed 53, 57, 58, 59, 60
seed coat 57, 61
seeder 231
seeding and planting tools 231
seedless cucumber 128
seeds, poppy 139
segment 58
segment score number 471
seismic wave 27
seismogram 27
seismograph, vertical 27
seismographic recording 403
seismographs 27
select button 326
selective sorting of waste 49
selector, four-way 315
selector, orbital-action 227
selector, sound mode 322
selector, speed 176
self-adhesive labels 340
self-contained breathing apparatus 454
self-inflating mattress 530
self-sealing flap 339
self-service meat counter 120
self-stick note 338
self-timer indicator 314
semaphore signal 375
semi-circle 488
semi-detached houses 289
semi-mummy 530
semibreve 299
semibreve rest 299
semicircle 428
semimembranosus 97
seminal vesicle 111
semiquaver 299
semiquaver rest 299
semitendinosus 97
semolina 144
semolina, flour and 144
Senegal 451
Senegal River 20
sense organs 114
sensitive root 109
sensitivity 314
sensor probe 178
sensor wiring circuit 357
sensor, optical 332
sensor, safing 354
sensor, wheel speed 357
sensory impulse 110
sensory neuron 110
sensory receptor 110
sensory root 110
sent document recovery 328
sepal 56, 58, 59
separate collection 49
separation, magnetic 49
separation, paper/paperboard 49
separator 359, 384, 402, 417
separator, electrolytic 417
septal cartilage of nose 117
septic tank 48
septum 60, 117
septum pellucidum 109
sequencer 310
sequencer control 310
serac 30
Serbia 450
serial number 441
serial port 329
serrate 55
serve 487, 490
server 334, 335, 491, 494
server, access 335
service area 25, 389
service bay 346
service judge 490, 494
service line 491
service module 316
service provider, Internet 335
service road 388
service room 447
service station 346, 433
service table 438
service zones 495
service, customer 443
servicer, mobile remote 11
services, financial 442
services, insurance 442
services, loan 442
services, social 465
serving dish 166
serving trolley 202
sesame oil 149
set 291, 492
set dresser 291
set of bells 309
set of utensils 173
set, nail 220
set, socket 223
set, television 439, 444
set-in sleeve 245
sets, previous 492
setsquare 225
setting indicator 511
settings display button 315
setup 328
seventh 298
sewer 434
sewn-in groundsheet 528, 529
sextet 300
Seychelles 452
shackle 521
shad 160
shade 206
shade, roller 356
shadow 424
shaft 278, 471, 492, 494, 503, 505, 506
shaft, air 278
shaft, axle 351
shake-hands grip 493
shallot 124, 305
shallow root 63
sham 204
shampoo 267
shank 152, 153, 220, 221, 228, 270, 538
shank protector 398
shaped handle 269
shapes, geometrical 428
shapka 238
shark, morphology of 74
sharp 299
sharpening steel 169
sharpening stone 169
shaving 271
shaving brush 271
shaving foam 271
shaving mug 271
shears, kitchen 173
sheath 55, 533
sheath dress 252
sheath of Schwann 110
sheath skirt 253
sheathing 187
shed 182, 230
sheep 84
sheep shelter 122
sheepskin jacket 249
sheet 515
sheet lead 521
sheet, baking 172
sheet, bath 267
shekel, new 440
shelf 203, 210, 211, 219
shelf channel 211
shell 60, 72, 73, 79, 277, 308, 404
shell membrane 79
shell, bivalve 73
shell, univalve 73
shell, upper 527
shelter 345
shepherd, German 86
shield bug 69
shift key 330
shift: level 2 select 330
shiitake 123
shin guard 480, 513
ship's side 385
shirt 245, 260, 473, 488
shirt, polo 250
shirt, team 486
shirttail 245, 255
shirtwaist dress 252
shock absorber 351, 523
shock absorber, front 369
shock wave 403
shoe 488, 522, 524
shoe shop 437
shoe, parts 240
shoelace 240, 262
shoes 240
shoes, golf 505
shoes, men's 240
shoes, rugby 483
shoes, unisex 242
shoes, women's 241
shoot 53, 63
shoot, bamboo 125
shooting stage 290
shooting star 37
shop 280, 432
shop, clothing 436
shop, coffee 432, 437
shop, decorative articles 437
shop, do-it-yourself 436
shop, electronics 436
shop, gift 436
shop, jewellery 436
shop, leather goods 436
shop, lingerie 436
shop, newsagent's 437
shop, perfume 436
shop, pet 436
shop, record 436
shop, shoe 437
shop, sporting goods 437
shop, tobacconist's 436
shopping bag 276
shopping centre 431, 436
shopping street 432
shopping trolleys 121
shore 33
shore cliff 35
shorelines, examples of 35
short extensor of toes 96
short glove 243
short palmar 96
short peroneal 97
short radial extensor of wrist 97
short service line 495
short sock 257
short track 508
short track skate 508
shortening 149
shorts 254, 261, 313, 473, 480, 483, 488, 500, 522
shorts, running 263
shortstop 474
shot 472
shot put 472
shot, drop 491
shotgun (smooth bore) 534
shoulder 83, 86, 92, 94, 223, 302, 342, 492, 536
shoulder bag 276
shoulder bag with zip 276
shoulder belt 353
shoulder blade 93, 95
shoulder bolt 223
shoulder pad 486
shoulder strap 259, 276, 456, 505, 532
shovel 193, 233, 510, 514
shower 189, 464
shower cubicle 195
shower head 195, 197
shower hose 195, 197
shower, bath and 439
shredder, paper 341
shredding 49
shroud 520
shuffle play 323
shunt 416
shutoff valve 196, 197
shutter 186, 333
shutter release button 314
shutting stile 185
shuttlecock, feathered 495
shuttlecock, synthetic 495
Siamese 87
sickle 234
side 167, 293
side back vent 244
side chair 201
side chapel 284
side compression strap 532
side door 380
side electrode 359
side fairings 525
side footboard 377
side handrail 380
side hatch 12
side judge 485
side lane 343
side line 493
side marker light 352, 364, 365
side mirror 269
side panel 248
side plate 166
side rail 219, 365
side span 344
side vent 28, 361
side view 478
side wall 517
side, left 272
side, right 272
sideboard 203
sideline 484, 487, 488
sidepiece 273
sideshoot 53
sidewall 358, 365
siding 375
Sierra Leone 451
sieve 171
sifter 172
sight 119, 533, 535
sight, normal 419
sighting line 533
sighting mirror 533
sigmoid colon 106
sign, route 362, 363
signal box 375
signal gantry 375
signal lamp 179
signature, holder's 441
signature, official 441
signet ring 264
silencer 351, 367, 368, 369
silk 61
sill 28
sill of frame 186
sill plate 187
sill rail 187
silos 381
simple eye 67
simple leaves 55
simple organisms and echinoderms 66
Singapore 453
single bed 439
single reed 306
single room 439
single seat 380
single-breasted jacket 244
single-burner camp stove 529
single-leaf bascule bridge 345
single-lens reflex (SLR) camera: front view 314
singles service court 495
singles sideline 491, 495
singlet 500
sink 164, 197, 439, 464
sink with waste disposal unit 197
sink, surgeon's 465
sinker 538
siphon 72
siphonal canal 73
siren 455
sistrum 309
site plan 183
sitting room 188
sixth 298
skate 158, 506
skate, acrobatic 527
skate, goalkeeper's 507
skate, roller hockey 527
skate, roller speed 527
skate, short track 508
skateboard 526
skateboarder 526
skateboarding 526
skater 527
skater: long track 508
skater: short track 508
skates, speed 508
skating kick 514
skating step 514
skating, figure 509
skating, inline 527
skating, speed 508
skeg 519
skeleton 98
skerry 35
ski 510, 523
ski area 512
ski boot 510, 511
ski glove 510
ski goggles 510
ski hat 514
ski jumper 513
ski jumping 513
ski lift arrival 512
ski pants 254
ski pole 510, 514
ski rack 356
ski resort 512
ski school 512
ski stop 511
ski suit 510, 514
ski tip 514
ski trail, alpine 512
ski trail, cross-country 512
ski, downhill/Super G 510
ski, jumping 513
ski, slalom 510
ski, slalom G 510
ski-jumping boot 513
ski-jumping suit 513
skid 395
skiers' lodge 512
skimmer 173, 184
skin 57, 58, 59, 110, 114
skin surface 114
skins, won ton 147

kip 400, 515
kipping-rope 500
kirt 251, 492
kirt finger 383
kirting board 191
kirts, examples of 253
kis, examples of 510
kull 92
kull, child's 100
kull, lateral view of 100
kullcap 238
kunk 88
ky coverage 39
kylight 183
kylight, bathroom 189
kylight, stairwell 189
alom G ski 510
alom ski 510
alom, giant 511
alom, special 511
alom, super giant 511
ash, double 334
at 205
ed 236
eeper-cab 364
eeping bags, examples of 530
eeping car 376
eepsuit 261
eet 41
eeve 244, 395, 501
eeve strap 248
eeve strap loop 248
eigh bells 309
ce 173
de 214
de, glass 421
ding door 195, 286
ding door, automatic 286
ding folding window 287
ding jaw 425
ding rail 353, 521
ding seat 501
ding weight 422
ding window 287
ngback shoe 241
258
joint 222
joint pliers 222
presenter 346
, stage 421
-on 242
-on pyjamas 261
-stitched seam 245
over 250
road 343
pe 342
pe, beginners' 512
pe, difficult 512
pe, expert 512
e, intermediate 512
ing cornice 279
167, 178, 221, 274
card reader 346, 442, 443
deposit 442
passbook update 442
PC card 336
transaction record 442
s, memory card 471
akia 450
enia 450
lane 343
-burning stove 192
-motion 319
l blade 531
l carton 163
l crate 162
l drawstring bag 276
l hand cultivator 232
l intestine 106
l open crate 162
saucepan 175
h 491
and taste 116
t 159
k 255
g 47
e baffle 192
e detector 454
ed ham 153
smooth hound 158
snacks' sale counter 294
snail 72, 157
snail dish 173
snail tongs 173
snail, morphology of 72
snake 76, 469
snake, coral 77
snake, garter 77
snakes and ladders 469
snap 538
snap fastener 243, 249, 274
snap shackle 521
snap-fastening front 261
snap-fastening tab 249
snap-fastening waist 260
snare 308, 535
snare drum 295, 308
snare head 297, 308
snare strainer 308
snatch 500
snelled fishhook 538
snooker 503
snout 74, 75
snow 41
snow brush with scraper 356
snow guard 523
snow, acid 48
snow-grooming machine 512
snowblower 365
snowboard 513
snowboard, alpine 513
snowboard, freestyle 513
snowboarder 513
snowboarding 513
snowmobile 523
snowsuit 261
snuggle suit 260
soap dish 195
soap, toilet 267
soba noodles 147
social services 465
social worker's office 463
society 430
sock 257, 480, 486, 492
socket head 221
socket set 223
socket tester 217
socket-contact 198
socks 247, 483
sofa 200
sofa bed 204
soft cheeses 151
soft contact lens 272
soft key 327
soft palate 116, 117
soft pedal 304, 311
soft ray 74
soft shell clam 157
soft-drink dispenser 346
softball 477
softball bat 477
softball glove 477
software, email 334
soil 48
soil and waste stack 194
soil fertilization 47
soil profile 54
soiled utility room 462, 464
solar array 316
solar cell 337, 410, 411
solar eclipse 4
solar energy 54, 410
solar panel 7
solar radiation 45, 46, 410, 411
solar reflectors 316
solar shield 10
solar system 2
solar-cell panel 411
solar-cell system 411
solder 218
soldering and welding tools 218
soldering gun 218
soldering iron 218
sole 161, 229, 247, 509, 511
soleplate 208
soleus 96
solid 414, 415
solid body 303
solid centre auger bit 228
solid line 342
solid rocket booster 12
solid, amorphous 414
solids 429
solitaire ring 264
Solomon Islands 453
solution, multi-purpose 272
solvent extraction unit 405
Somalia 451
somen noodles 147
sorghum 61
sorghum: panicle 61
sorting plant 49
sorting, glass 49
sorting, manual 49
sorting, metal 49
sorting, optical 49
sorting, paper/paperboard 49
sorting, plastics 49
sorus 52
sou'wester 239
soufflé dish 172
sound box 297, 302
sound engineer 291
sound field control 322
sound hole 301
sound mode lights 322
sound mode selector 322
sound receiver 460
sound recording equipment 291
sound system 354
soundboard 296, 297, 301, 302, 304
soundbox 302
sounding balloon 38
soup bowl 166
soup spoon 168
soup tureen 166
sour cream 150
source, power 416
South 23
South Africa 452
South America 14, 17, 34
South American Plate 27
South China Sea 14, 19
South Pole 15, 21
south pole 416
South-Southeast 23
South-Southwest 23
Southeast 23
Southeast Indian Ridge 34
Southern hemisphere 21
Southwest 23
Southwest Indian Ridge 34
soy sauce 140
soybean sprouts 131
soybeans 131
space 298, 330, 469
space bar 330
space probe 37
space shuttle 12, 37
space shuttle at takeoff 12
space, epidural 110
space, non-breaking 330
spacelab 13
spacer 409, 467
spacesuit 10
spade 233, 468
spade bit 228
spadix 57
spaghetti 146
spaghetti squash 129
spaghetti tongs 173
spaghettini 146
Spain 449
spar 392
spare tyre 361
spareribs 153
spark plug 359, 360
spark plug body 359
spark plug cable 350
spark plug gap 359
spark plug seat 359
sparking plug 237
sparrow 80
spatula 173
spatulate 55
speaker 294, 320, 326, 328, 336, 518
speaker cover 324
spear 125
special slalom 511
specification plate 228
specimen collection centre waiting room 465
specimen collection room 465
spectacles 273
spectacles case 275
spectacles, examples of 273
spectrum, electromagnetic 418
speed control 176
speed governor 287
speed grand prix motorcycle and rider 525
speed selector 176, 177
speed selector switch 227, 228, 270
speed skates 508
speed skating 508
speed-increasing gearbox 413
speedometer 355, 368, 501
spelt wheat 143
spencer 254
spent fuel storage bay 409
sperm whale 90
spermatozoon 111
sphagnum, prickly 51
sphenoid bone 100
sphenoidal fontanelle 100
sphenoidal sinus 117
sphere 429
sphincter muscle of anus 106
spices 138
spices, marinade 139
spicules 4
spider 70
spider web 70
spider, crab 70
spider, garden 70
spider, morphology of 70
spider, water 70
spike 57, 473
spike file 341
spiked shoe 476
spill, oil 48
spillway 406
spillway chute 406
spillway gate 406
spinach 127
spinach tagliatelle 146
spinal column 98, 109
spinal cord 109, 110
spinal cord, structure of 109
spinal ganglion 109, 110
spinal nerve 109, 110
spindle 177, 201, 425
spine of scapula 99
spine, anterior nasal 100
spinner 538
spinneret 70
spinning rod 537
spinous process 110
spiny lobster 158
spiny ray 74
spiracle 67
spiral 221
spiral arm 6
spiral beater 176
spiral binder 340
spiral cloud band 43
spiral nail 220
spiral rib 73
spiral screwdriver 221
spiral thread 70
spire 285
spirit level 225
spirulina 123
spit 35
splat 200
splay 285
spleen 103
splenius muscle of head 97
splints 461
split link 538
split peas 130
splitting, nucleus 415
spoiler 366, 392
spoke 371
sponge-tipped applicator 266
sponson 523
spool 536, 537
spool axle 537
spool-release mechanism 537
spoon 167, 531
spoon, tasting 173
spoons, examples of 168
spores 52
sporting goods shop 437
sports and games 468
sports car 347
sports complex 431
sports on wheels 526
sports, ball 474
sports, motor 524
sports, precision and accuracy 502
sports, racket 493
sports, strength 500
sportswear 262
spot 207
spotlight 290, 455
spotlights 293
spout 180, 181
spout assembly 197
spout, pouring 215
spray 208
spray arm 214
spray button 208
spray control 208
spray nozzle 236
spray, pepper 456
sprayer 236
spread collar 245
spreader 273
spring 27, 32, 38, 206, 212, 222, 312, 535
spring balance 423
spring binder 339
spring onion 124
spring toggle 221
spring washer 222
spring, coil 351
springboard 496
springboard, 1 m 518
springboard, 3 m 518
sprinkler hose 236
sprinklers 408
sprocket 523
sprouts, soybean 131
spruce 65
sprung base 204
spur 29, 228, 308
squamous suture 100
square 429
square move 470
square root key 337
square root of 427
square trowel 216
square-headed tip 221
squash, acorn 129
squash, crookneck 129
squash, pattypan 129
squash, spaghetti 129
squash, straightneck 129
squid 157
squirrel 82
Sri Lanka 453
stabilizer 467
stabilizer fin 386
stabilizer jack 361
stack 35, 402
stacking chairs 201
stadium 431
staff 298
staff cloakroom 438, 465
staff entrance 438, 445
staff lounge 443, 463
stage 278, 292, 293, 421
stage clip 421
stage curtain 292, 293
stage, shooting 290
stage-house 292
stained glass 285
stained-glass window 446
stair 293, 294
stairs 188, 191, 283, 345, 378, 404, 439
stairways 283
stairwell 189

ENGLISH INDEX

stairwell skylight 189
stake 230, 231
stalactite 31
stalagmite 31
stalk 51, 57, 58, 59, 125
stalk vegetables 125
stamen 56, 58
stamp pad 338
stanchion 509
stand 27, 174, 176, 206, 269, 277, 308, 537
stand, intravenous 464
stand, witness 440
standard lamp 206
standard poker hands 468
stands, movable 444
stapes 116
staple remover 341
stapler 341
staples 341
star diagonal 8
star drag wheel 537
star of David 447
starboard hand 387
starch 61
starch granule 50
starling 80
start 469
start button 424
start key 328, 330
start line 473
start switch 213
starter 237, 516
starter button 368
starter handle 235
starting block 516
starting grid 524
starting grip (backstroke) 516
starting line 524
starting line, 1,500 m 473
starting line, 10,000 m and 4 x 400 m relay 473
starting line, 100 m and 100 m hurdles 472
starting line, 110 m hurdles 472
starting line, 200 m 472
starting line, 400 m, 400 m hurdles, 4 x 100 m relay 473
starting line, 5,000 m 472
starting line, 800 m 473
starting pistol 472
starting positions 518
state 23
states of matter 414
station circle 39
station concourse 374
station entrance 378
station model 39
station name 378
station platform 375
station, bus 432
station, emergency 345
station, fire 433
station, international space 11
station, land 38
station, police 433
station, railway 430, 432
station, relay 316
station, service 433
station, underground railway 432
stationery 337
statue 446
steak 152
steak knife 168
steam 402
steam control knob 181
steam generator 402
steam iron 208
steam nozzle 181
steam pressure drives turbine 408
steamer 175
steamer basket 175
steamer, electric 179
steel 259
steel cable 535
steel casing 417
steel pen 312
steelyard 422
steeplechase 472
steering column 350
steering cylinder 400
steering system 351
steering tube 371
steering wheel 350, 354, 385, 525
stem 51, 52, 53, 54, 181, 199, 384, 424
stem bulb 387
stem propeller 384
stem, underground 54
step 191, 219, 364
step chair 201
step groove 191
step stool 219
step, diagonal 514
step, skating 514
stepladder 219
stepladders 219
steppe 40
stepper 501
steps 184, 188, 412
steps to ripeness 62
stereo control 326
stereo sound system 322
stereo sound system, mini 325
sterile dressing 461
sterilization room 464, 465
stern 386, 519
sternal artery 71
sternocleidomastoid 96
sternum 98
stethoscope 460
stick 273, 301
sticks 309
stifle 83
stigma 56, 60
stile 201
stile groove of sash 186
stile tongue of sash 186
still camera, 35 mm 10
still cameras 315
still photographer 291
still water level 33
Stilton 151
sting 68
stipule 55
stirrup sock 476
stitch 240
stitches 477
stitching 243, 262
stock 296, 412, 534
stock pot 175
stockade 282
stocking 257, 259, 506
stomach 73, 103, 106
stomach throw 499
stomach, cardiac 71
stomach, pyloric 71
stone 57
stone deflector 376, 377
stone for sacrifice 283
stone fruits 132
stone marten 88
stone steps 183
stone, Coyolxauhqui 283
stone, sharpening 169
stoner 173
stool, bar 438
stop 86, 319, 328
stop button 235, 319, 323, 424
stop key 323
stop knob 305
stop, end 226
stop, tail 224
stopcock 194
stopper 267, 532
stopwatch 424
storage compartment 361, 364, 455
storage door 211
storage furniture 202
storage room, medical equipment 465
storage tank 405
storage, frozen food 121
storage, glove 464
store, department 437
store, food 439
storeroom 438, 444
stork 80
storm collar 193
stormy sky 41
straight 468
straight flush 468
straight jaw 222
straight position 518
straight skirt 253
straight-up ribbed top 247
straightening iron 269
straightneck squash 129
strainer 174, 177, 180
strainer body 197
strainer coupling 197
strainer, mesh 171
straining, utensils for 171
strait 24
Strait of Gibraltar 18
Strait, Bass 15
Strait, Bering 16
Strait, Cook 15
Strait, Torres 15
strap 265, 424, 477, 500
strap eyelet 315
strap loop 532
strap system 303
strap, chin 522
strap, shoulder 456, 532
strapless brassiere 259
stratocumulus 42
stratopause 37
stratosphere 37
stratum basale 114
stratum corneum 114
stratum granulosum 114
stratum lucidum 114
stratum spinosum 114
stratus 42
straw 163
straw hut 288
strawberry 132
strawberry, section 59
street 25, 433, 435
street light 434
street sweeper 365
street, shopping 432
strength sports 500
stretch-limousine 347
stretcher 202, 460
stretcher area 462
strider, water 69
striker 218, 481
string 301, 302
stringed instruments 301
stringer 396
stringing 492, 494
strings 297, 304
strip 286
strip door 286
strip, magnetic 441
strip, tackless 190
stroke judge 516
strokes 490
structure 186
structure of a fern 52
structure of a flower 56
structure of a house 188
structure of a leaf 55
structure of a lichen 50
structure of a moss 51
structure of a mushroom 52
structure of a plant 53
structure of a tree 63
structure of an alga 51
structure of the biosphere 44
structure of the ear 116
structure of the Earth 26
structure of the spinal cord 109
structure of the Sun 4
structure, roll 525
structure, truss 11
strut 187, 308, 387, 412
strut, wing 394
stud 187, 263, 357, 478
studded tyre 358
student 444
student's desk 444
students' lockers 445
students' room 445
study 189
stump 63, 479
sturgeon 158
style 56, 57, 58, 59, 60
stylist, hair 290
stylobate 279
styloid process 100
stylus 312, 337
subarctic 40
subbase 342
subclavian artery 102
subclavian vein 102
subcutaneous tissue 114
subduction 27
subfloor 187, 190
subgrade 342
subhead 313
sublimation 414
submarine canyon 33
submarine line 334
submarine pipeline 404
subsiding cold air 43
subsoil 54
substitutes' bench 481
substructure 403
subterranean stream 31
subtract from memory 337
subtract key 337
subtraction 427
subtractive colour synthesis 418
suburb 431
suburban commuter railway 375
suburbs 25
subway 375
subwoofers 321
sucker 62, 72
suction hose 455
Sudan 451
sudoriferous duct 114
sugar 149
sugar bowl 166
sugar thermometer 171
sugar, brown 149
sugar, granulated 149
sugar, powdered 149
suit 251
suit carrier 277
suit, protective 525
suit, racing 508, 525
suit, ski-jumping 513
suitcase 277
suite, operating 464
sulcus terminalis 118
sulphur dioxide emission 48
sulphuric acid emission 48
sum 427
sumac 139
summer 38
summer solstice 38
summit 29, 512
summit lodge 512
sump 360
sump gasket 360
Sun 2, 4, 5, 38
sun deck 385
sun roof 349
sun visor 354, 356, 361
Sun, structure 4
sundae spoon 168
sundeck 387
sundial 424
sundress 252
sunflower 56
sunflower-seed oil 149
sunglasses 273
sunken swimming pool 184
sunspot 4
super giant slalom 511
supercooling 414
superficial peroneal nerve 108
superior cymbal 308
superior dental arch 116
superior mesenteric artery 102, 107
superior mesenteric vein 102
superior nasal concha 117
superior rectus muscle 119
superior semicircular canal 116
superior vena cava 102, 103, 104
supermarket 120, 433, 437
supersonic jet 37, 394
supplement, colour 313
supplement, literary 313
supply pipe 197
supply point 198
supply room 464
supply, cash 443
support 9, 199, 201, 375
support thread 70
support, backboard 489
support, neck 525
sural nerve 108
surface course 342
surface element 210
surface insulation 12
surface of the water 518
surface prospecting 403
surface runoff 45
surface water drain 434
surface, cooking 179
surface, hard (cement) 492
surface, posting 341
surface, synthetic 492
surface, working 224
surface-piercing foils 387
surfaces, plane 428
surfaces, playing 492
surgeon's sink 465
surgery, minor 462
Suriname 448
surround loudspeaker 321
suspended span 344
suspender 259, 344
suspender belt 259
suspension 380
suspension arm 212, 351
suspension band 458
suspension bogie 376
suspension bridge 344
suspension cable 344
suspension file 340
suspension strut 367
suspension system 351
suspension, back 522
suspensory ligament 119
sustaining pedal 304, 311
suture 60, 73
suture, coronal 100
suture, lambdoid 100
suture, squamous 100
swallow 80
swallow hole 31
Swaziland 452
sweat shirt 262
sweater, crew neck 255
sweaters 250, 254
swede 129
Sweden 450
sweeper, street 365
sweeping hip throw 499
sweet pepper, green 128
sweet pepper, red 128
sweet pepper, yellow 128
sweet potato 124
sweetbreads 154
sweetcorn 61
swell organ manual 305
swell pedals 305
swift 80
swimming 516
swimming goggles 516
swimming pool 386, 517
swimming pool, above ground 18
swimming pool, sunken 184
swimming trunks 263
swimsuit 263, 516
swing bridge 344
Swiss army knife 531
Swiss chard 125
switch 198, 211, 219, 229, 416
switch lock 228
switch, hat 332
switch, limit 287
switch, on-off 177, 181
switch, on/off 209
switch, power 315
switch, power/functions 320
switch, reversing 221, 228
switch, speed selector 227, 228
switch, trigger 227, 228, 229
switched outlet 322

vitzerland 450
ivel 403, 535, 538
ivel base 224
ivel flex 269
ivel head 224
ivel lock 224
ivel wall lamp 207
ordfish 159
nbols 468
nbols, scientific 426
npathetic ganglion 109
nphony orchestra 295
nphysis pubis 111, 112
agogue 447
apse 110
c cable 337
thesis, colour 418
thesizer 310
thetic shuttlecock 495
thetic sponge 266
thetic surface 492
a 452
nge 460
nge for irrigation 460
p, corn 149
p, cough 467
p, maple 149
tem buttons 310
tem of units, international 426
em, air conditioning 46
em, braking 351
em, cooling 351
em, electrical 351
em, fuel supply 351
em, remote manipulator 11, 12
em, solar 2
em, steering 351
em, strap 303
em, suspension 351
em, transmission 351
ems, car 351

T

512
t dress 261
p shoe 241
48, 274, 340
sco™ sauce 140
nacle 446
202, 493, 502
lamp 206
mixer 176
of results 518
salt 141
tennis 493
tennis ball 493
tennis bat 493
bedside 439, 464
changing 205
operating 464
overhead 464
service 438
water 48
, examples of 202
poon 168
467
um 280
d 313
tion key 330
tion left 330
tion right 330
neter 355, 368
20, 519
box 538
ss strip 190
0, 262
elle, spinach 146
140
76, 82, 83, 86, 90, 111, 393,
, 514, 526, 536
embly 393
om 395
nb 268
ther 78
393, 395
elix 115
e 351
e 351
tail pole 412
tail skid 395
tail stop 224
tail, ion 6
tailback 485
tailored collar 251
tailpiece 297, 301
tailplane 393, 395
tailrace 407
Tajikistan 452
tajine 174
talk key 327
talking drum 297
tall tumbler 165
talon 79
talus 99
tamarillo 136
tamarin 91
tamarind paste 140
tambourine 309
tamper 181
tandem 373
tang 167, 169, 216
Tanganyika, Lake 20
tank 13, 385, 454
tank farm 404
tank hatch cover 385
tank, fuel 351, 366, 369
tank, septic 48
tank, water 181
tanker 364, 381, 384
tanker body 364
Tanzania 451
tap 195
tape 225
tape counter 323
tape dispenser 341
tape guide 341
tape lock 225
tape measure 225
tape recorder select button 322
tape selector 323
tape, grip 526
tape, magnetic 319
tape, Teflon 216
tape, white 487
taproot 63
tarantula, red-kneed 70
taro 124
tarragon 142
tarsus 78
Tasman Sea 15
Tasmania 15
taste bud 118
taste receptors 118
tasting spoon 173
taxiway 388
taxiway line 389
tea 148
tea bag 148
tea cup 166
tea infuser 173
tea, black 148
tea, green 148
tea, oolong 148
teacher 444
teacher's desk 444
teachers' room 445
team shirt 476, 480, 486
team's emblem 506
team, medical 499
teapot 166
tear-off calendar 338
teas, herbal 148
teaser comb 268
teaspoon 168
technical controller 509
technical delegates 509
technical events 511
technical room 345
technical specialist 509
technical specifications 358
technical terms 57
technician, lighting 291
techniques 487
tectonic lake 32
tectonic plates 27
teddy 258
tee 505, 515
tee line 515
teeing ground 504
teeth 101
Teflon tape 216
telecommunication antenna 386, 387
telecommunication satellite 335
telecommunication satellites 316
telecommunications by satellite 317
telephone 327, 439
telephone cable 434
telephone index 338
telephone line 334
telephone list 327
telephone network 317
telephone, communication 327
telephoto lens 314
teleport 317
telescope 7
telescope base 7
telescope, Hubble space 37
telescopic aerial 325
telescopic boom 397, 455
telescopic corridor 389
telescopic fork 366
telescopic front fork 369
telescopic leg 460
telescopic sight 420, 534
television 318
television programme schedule 313
television set 439, 444
television set, large-screen 321
telltale 520
telson 71
temperate forest 44
temperature control 178, 208, 211
temperature gauge 355
temperature of dew point 39
temperature scale 37
temperature selector 178, 212, 213
temperature sensor 358
temple 92
Temple of Huitzilopochtli 283
Temple of Tlaloc 283
temple, Aztec 283
tempo control 311
temporal bone 98, 100
ten 427
ten commandments 447
tendril 62
tennis 490
tennis ball 492
tennis player 492
tennis racket 492
tennis shoe 492
tenor drum 308
tension adjuster 528
tension adjustment 537
tension adjustment screw 341
tension rod 308
tension rope 297
tension screw 308
tension spring 355, 500
tensor of fascia lata 96
tent, trailer 361
tentacle 72
tents, examples of 528
tepee 288
teres major 97
teres minor 97
terminal 198, 210, 404
terminal arborization 110
terminal box 411
terminal bronchiole 105
terminal bud 53
terminal cover 320
terminal filament 109
terminal lobe 62
terminal moraine 30
terminal tackles 538
terminal, container 430
terminal, electronic payment 121
terminal, ground 322
terminal, negative 416, 417
terminal, positive 416, 417
terminal, remote control 315
terminals, aerial 322
terminals, loudspeaker 322
terminals, video and digital 315
termite 69
terraced houses 289
terrine 174
tertial 78
tertiary consumers 45
test button 454
test-lamp 217
tester screwdriver 217
testicle 111
testis 71
Tethys 3
textile floor coverings 190
Thailand 453
thallus 50, 51
theatre 292, 432, 433
theatre, Greek 278
theatre, home 321
theatre, operating 464, 465
thermal energy 402
thermodynamic temperature, measurement of 426
thermometer 404, 424
thermometer, instant-read 171
thermometer, oven 171
thermometer, sugar 171
thermopause 37
thermosphere 37
thermostat 178
thermostat control 211
thermostat, adjustable 179
thigh 78, 83, 86, 93, 95, 111, 112
thigh pad 486
thigh stocking 257
thigh-boot 241
thimble 425
thinning razor 269
third 298
third base 474
third baseman 474
third finger 115
third row 482
third valve slide 307
thoracic legs 71
thoracic vertebra (12) 99
thorax 67, 68, 92, 94
thread 221
thread, radial 70
thread, security 441
thread, spiral 70
thread, support 70
threaded rod 223
three-blade propeller 394
three-four time 298
three-of-a-kind 468
three-pin socket 198
three-quarter coat 248
three-tier car carrier 377
threshold 185
throat 78, 224, 492, 538
throat protector 476
throttle 237
throttle cable 237
throttle control 235, 332
throwing circle 472, 473
thrust device 312
thrust tube 312
thruster 10
thrusters, attitude control 12
thumb 115, 243, 477
thumb hook 307
thumb piston 305
thumb rest 306, 460
thumb, opposable 91
thumbscrew 223
thyme 142
tibia 98
tibial nerve 108
tick 70
ticket collecting booth 378
ticket collector 294, 374
ticket counter 390
tie 273, 299
tie beam 187
tier 281
tierceron 284
Tierra del Fuego 17
tiers 278
tiger 89
tight end 485
tight head prop 482
tightening buckle 532
tights 257
tile 12, 279, 280, 283
tiller 520
tilt-back head 176
timber 280
timber frame 187
time code 291
time signatures 298
timekeeper 488, 498, 509
timekeepers, scorers and 499
timer 178, 179, 501
timer socket 210
timetable 374
timing belt 360
timpani 295
tin opener 170, 180, 531
tine 167
tip 55, 125, 167, 216, 218, 220, 221, 227, 246, 273, 487, 503, 510, 536
tip of nose 117
tip protector 460
tip section 536
tip, finger 339
tip-ring 536, 537
tipper body 401
tipper truck 401
tips, examples of 221
tissue holder 195
Titan 3
Titania 3
Titicaca, Lake 17
Tlaloc, Temple of 283
toad, common 75
toaster 178
tobacconist's shop 436
toe 79, 86, 92, 94, 226, 229, 247
toe binding 514
toe clip 370, 372
toe guard 459, 476
toe loop 509
toe pick 509
toe piston 305
toe-piece 511
toe-strap 242
toenail scissors 265
toepiece 514
toggle 249
toggle bolt 221
Togo 451
toilet 188, 189, 194, 195, 196, 439, 440, 443, 445, 464
toilet bag 276
toilet bowl 196
toilet soap 267
toilet, ladies' 294, 439
toilet, men's 294, 439
toilets 437, 463, 465
toilets, customers' 438
toilette, eau de 267
tom-tom 308
tomatillo 128
tomato 128
tomato coulis 140
tomato paste 140
tomato, currant 128
tombolo 35
tone control 303
tone control, bass 303
tone control, treble 303
Tonga 453
tongs 173, 193
tongue 106, 116, 117, 154, 240, 246, 262, 297, 305, 509, 511
tongue sheath 76
tongue, dorsum 118
tonsil 116
tool belt 225
tool box 225
tool holder 229
tool kit 372
tool shelf 219
tool storage area 209
tool tether 10
tools 209
tools for loosening earth 233
tools, electricity 217
tools, hand 232

tools, masonry 216
tools, plumbing 216
tools, pruning and cutting 234
tools, seeding and planting 231
tools, soldering and welding 218
tools, watering 236
tooth 74, 76, 226, 227, 235, 270, 398, 400
tooth guard 486
toothbrush 272
toothbrush shaft 272
toothbrush well 272
toothed jaw 222
toothpaste 272
top 63, 202, 219
top box 369
top cap 417
top cushion 502
top deck 404
top deckboard 396
top flap 532
top hat 238
top ladder 455
top lift 240
top of dam 406
top pocket 502
top rail 185, 201, 202, 205
top rail of sash 186
top stitched pleat 253
top stitching 246, 260
top-level domain 334
topping 536
topsoil 54
toque 239
Torah scrolls 447
toric lens 419
tornado 43
tornado and waterspout 43
torque adjustment collar 228
torque converter 212
Torres Strait 15
tortellini 146
tortilla 145
torus 429
total 423
total eclipse 4, 5
totally reflecting mirror 420
tote bag 276
toucan 80
touch 114
touch judge 483
touch pad 336
touch pad button 336
touch screen 337
touchline 481, 483
Toulouse sausage 156
touring bicycle 373
touring motorcycle 369
touring tyre 358
tow bar 361
tow safety chain 361
tow truck 364
towel rail 195
towel, bath 267
towel, kitchen 215
tower 284, 344, 412, 413
tower case: back view 329
tower case: front view 329
tower control room 388
tower crane 397
tower ladder 455
tower mast 397
tower mill 412
tower silo 122
tower, bell 446
tower, cooling 402
tower, transmitting 316
towing device 364
towing hitch 361
town hall 432
town houses 289
toyshop 436
tracery 285
trachea 105
track 374, 378, 398, 431, 472, 523, 524
track and field 472
track frame 207
track idler 398
track lighting 207
track roller frame 398
track search/fast operation buttons 319
track search/fast operation keys 323
track, long 508
track, railway 432
track, short 508
tracklaying tractor 398
tracks, dolly 290
tractor engine compartment 400
tractor unit 364
traditional dwellings 288
traditional musical instruments 296
traffic lanes 343
traffic lights 434
tragus 115
trail-view mirror 364
trailer car 380
trailer caravan 361
trailer tent 361
trailing edge 392
trailing edge flap 392
train direction sign 379
train indicator 374
trainer 489, 498
training set 261
training suit 262
training wall 406
transaction receipt 443
transaction record slot 442
transactions, business 335
Transantarctic Mountains 15
transceiver, radar 457
transceiving dish 316
transceiving parabolic aerial 316
transept 285
transept spire 284
transfer of heat to water 408
transfer ticket dispensing machine 379
transfer, heat 415
transform plate boundaries 27
transformer 207, 407
transit shed 381
transmission 212
transmission dish 316
transmission system 351
transmission to consumers 402, 413
transmitter 327
transmitting tower 316
transparent pockets 274
transpiration 45
transport and machinery 342
transverse bulkhead 384
transverse colon 106
transverse dunes 36
transverse process 110
tranverse flute 306
trap 194, 196, 197, 292
trap coupling 197
trap, leghold 535
trap, petroleum 403
trapdoor 281
trapezius 96, 97
trapezoid 429
travel agency 436
travel bag 276
travel cot 205
traveller 520, 521
traveller's cheque 441
travelling block 403
travelling crab 397
travelling crane 407
traverse arch 284
trawler 384
tray 205, 219, 225, 277
tray, disc 319
tray, drip 181
tray, food 162
tray, input 333
tray, output 333
treacle 149
tread 191
tread design 358
treatment room 465
treble bridge 304
treble clef 298
treble fishhook 538
treble keyboard 296
treble pickup 303
treble register 296
treble ring 471
treble tone control 303, 322, 325
tree 63
tree fern 52
tree frog 75
tree pruner 234
tree, ornamental 182
tree, palm 64
tree, structure 63
tree, trunk 63
trees 504
trefoil 285
trench 33
trench coat 248
Trench, Aleutian 34
Trench, Japan 34
Trench, Java 34
Trench, Kermadec-Tonga 34
Trench, Kuril 34
Trench, Mariana 34
Trench, Peru-Chile 34
Trench, Philippine 34
Trench, Puerto Rico 34
Trench, Ryukyu 34
triage room 463
triangle 295, 309, 429
triangular bandage 461
triangular body 297
triangular fossa 115
triceps bar 501
triceps of arm 97
tricuspid valve 104
tricycle, child's 373
trifoliate 55
trigger 235, 332, 454, 534
trigger guard 534
trigger switch 227, 228, 229
trilby 238, 239
trill 299
trim 277
trim panel 352
trim ring 210
trimaran 521
trimmer 237, 271
Trinidad and Tobago 449
trio 300
trip lever 196
trip mileometer 355
tripe 154
tripod 8
tripod accessories shelf 8
tripod stand 308
triticale 143
Triton 3
trolleys, shopping 121
trombone 307
trombones 295
Tropic of Cancer 20, 21, 22
Tropic of Capricorn 20, 21, 22
tropical climates 40
tropical cyclone 43
tropical cyclone names 43
tropical forest 44
tropical fruits 136
tropical rain forest 40, 44
tropical wet-and-dry (savanna) 40
tropopause 37, 46
troposphere 37
trot 83
trough 33, 39, 418
trousers 246, 263, 476, 486, 499, 506, 525
trousers, examples of 254
trout 161
trowel 232
truck 526, 527
truck crane 397
truck, collection 364
truck, concrete mixer 365
truck, emergency 345
truck, tow 364
trucking 364
trucks, examples of 364
truffle 123
trumpet 307
trumpet interchange 342
trumpets 295
trunk 52, 62, 63, 75, 93, 95, 277
trunk, cross section 63
trunks, boxing 498
truss structure 11
trussing needle 173
tsetse fly 69
tub 212, 214, 230
tub rim 212
tuba 295, 307
tube 163, 199, 461
tube retention clip 199
tube, draw 421
tube, flash 420
tube, Pitot 525
tube, watering 365
tuber vegetables 124
tubular bells 295, 309
tubular element 210
tubular heater 405
tuck position 518
tug 384
tulip 56
tuna 160
tundra 44
tungsten-halogen bulb 199
tunic 255
tunic dress 252
tuning buttons 322
tuning control 325, 326
tuning controls 318
tuning gauge 308
tuning peg 302, 303
tuning pin 304
tuning ring 297
tuning slide 307
tuning wire 305
Tunisia 451
tunnel 378
tunnel, road 345
turban 239
turbine 402
turbine shaft turns generator 408
turbo-alternator unit 402
turbojet engine 393
turbot 161
Turkey 452
turkey 81, 155
Turkmenistan 452
turmeric 138
turn 299
turn-up 246
turnbuckle 498, 521
turning judges 517
turning wall 517
turnip 129
turnouts 454
turntable 176, 344, 400, 401
turntable mounting 455
turret 282
turret cap 420
turtle 76
turtle, morphology of 76
Tuvalu 453
TV mode 319
TV power button 319
TV/video button 319
tweeter 324
tweezers 461
twig 63
twin-set 255
twist 228
twist bar 500
twist bit 228
twist drill 228
twist grip throttle 368
twist handle 332
two pairs 468
two-blade propeller 394
two-burner camp stove 529
two-leaf door 362
two-person tent 528
two-seater settee 200, 439
two-storey house 289
two-two time 298
two-way collar 248
tympanum 75, 279, 285
type of air mass 39
type of fuel 346
type of high cloud 39
type of low cloud 39
type of middle cloud 39
types of eclipses 4, 5
types of golf club 505
types of grip 493
types of inflorescence 57
types of move 470
types of passenger coach 376
types of stroke 517
typhoon 43
tyre 349, 358, 364, 371, 522, 52
tyre barrier 524
tyre inflator 346
tyre pump 370
tyre valve 371
tyre, all-season 358
tyre, knobby 369
tyre, nubby 525
tyre, performance 358
tyre, spare 361
tyre, studded 358
tyre, touring 358
tyre, winter 358
tyres, examples of 358

U

u quark 414
U.S. habitation module 11
U.S. laboratory 11
udon noodles 147
Uganda 451
Ukraine 450
ulna 98
ulnar extensor of wrist 97
ulnar flexor of wrist 96, 97
ulnar nerve 108
ultracompact camera 315
ultraviolet radiation 418
umbel 57
umbo 73
umbra 4, 5
umbrella 273
umbrella pine 65
umbrella stand 273
Umbriel 3
umpire 479, 485, 487, 490, 49 515
unbleached flour 144
under tail covert 78
underarm briefcase 275
underarm crutch 466
underarm rest 466
undergarment 524
underground 281, 435
underground chamber 278
underground flow 45
underground map 379, 380
underground railway 378
underground railway station 43
underground station 378
underground stem 54
underground train 378, 380
underlay 190
underpass 344
undershirt 476
underwater light 184
underwear 247, 258
underwiring 259
undressing booth 465
ungulate mammals 83
ungulate mammals, examples
unicellulars 66
uniform 456
union 427
uniparous cyme 57
unisex headgear 239
unisex shoes 242
unison 298
unit price 423
unit, glass collection 49
unit, intensive care 464
unit, paper collection 49
unit, turbo-alternator 402
United Arab Emirates 452
United Kingdom of Great Brita Northern Ireland 449
United States of America 448

ivalve shell 73
ivalve shell, morphology of 73
iversity 432
leavened bread 145
loading dock 437, 439
and-over garage door 286
haul 519
holstery nozzle 209
keep, painting 219
per 511
per blade guard 227
per bowl 181
per confining bed 402
per cuff 511
per deck 363, 392
per edge 493
per eyelid 75, 87, 119
per lateral lobe 62
per lateral sinus 62
er limb 103
per lip 116, 305
er lobe 105
er mandible 78
er mantle 26
er shell 511, 527
er strap 511
er tail covert 78
erworks 521
ght 184, 466
ght piano 304
ght vacuum cleaner 209
ght, padded 489
age 292, 293
Mountains 18
us 2, 3
n map 25
er 107
ra 107, 112
ary bladder 107, 111, 112
ary meatus 111
ry system 107
334
(uniform resource locator) 334
od 71
uay 448
connector 333
key 333
port 329, 336
syringe box 457
home 335
Internet 334
Internet 335
terms 57
ils, set 173
vesical pouch 112
s 112, 113
116, 117
kistan 452

V

k 244, 250
k cardigan 250
le 50, 66
le, contractile 66
le, food 66
le, forming food 66
m cleaner, upright 209
m coffee maker 181
m diaphragm 360
m distillation 405
m flask 532
112, 113
e 204
29, 32
50, 73, 307
casing 307
cover 360
seat 196
spring 360
240, 263
65
13
extract 140
cabinet 195
case 277
mirror 354
u 453
415
variable ejector nozzle 394
varnish, nail 265
vastus lateralis 96, 97
vastus medialis 96
Vatican City State 450
vault 284, 443
vault, barrel 281
vaulting horse 496, 497
VCR controls 319
VCR mode 319
VCR power button 319
veal, cuts of 152
veal, diced 152
veal, minced 152
vegetable brush 173
vegetable dish 166
vegetable garden 122, 182
vegetable sponge 267
vegetables 124
vegetables, fruits and 120
vegetation and biosphere 44
vegetation regions 44
vehicle rest area 345
vehicle, crew return 11
veil 536
vein 55
veins 102
velarium 281
Velcro® closure 260
velvet-band choker 264
Venezuela 448
venom canal 76
venom gland 76
venom-conducting tube 76
vent 354
vent brush 268
vent door 365
vent, cooling 336
ventilated rib 534
ventilating circuit 194
ventilating grille 209
ventilator 380
ventral artery 71
ventral nerve cord 71
Venus 2, 3
verbena 148
vermicelli, rice 147
vermiform appendix 106
vernal equinox 38
vernier 422, 425
vernier caliper 425
vernier scale 425
Versailles parquet 190
vertebra, cervical 99
vertebra, lumbar 99
vertebral body 110
vertebral shield 76
vertical control 329
vertical ground movement 27
vertical move 470
vertical pivoting window 287
vertical pupil 76
vertical section 526
vertical seismograph 27
vertical side band 487
vertical-axis wind turbine 412
vessel, blood 104
vest 247, 261, 263
vestibular nerve 116
vestibule 116, 280
vestibule, security 440
vibrating mudscreen 403
vibrato arm 303
vibrissa 82
vice 224
vice-skip 515
Victoria, Lake 20
video and digital terminals 315
video cassette 319
video entertainment system 471
video monitor 329
video port 329, 336
videocassette recorder 321
videotape operation controls 320
Vietnam 453
view camera 315
view, anterior 92, 94
view, front 478
view, posterior 93, 95
view, side 478
viewfinder 315
viewfinder, electronic 320
village 430, 512
vine leaf 62, 126
vine shoot 62
vine stock 62
vinegar, balsamic 141
vinegar, cider 141
vinegar, malt 141
vinegar, rice 141
vinegar, wine 141
vinyl grip sole 261
viola 301
violas 295
violet 56
violin 301
violin family 295, 301
viper 77
visceral ganglion 73
visceral pleura 105
visible light 418
vision 419
vision defects 419
visor 367, 459, 506, 525
visor hinge 367
visor, sun 356
Vistula River 18
visual display 471
vitelline membrane 79
vitreous body 119
vocal cord 105
voice edit buttons 310
voice recorder button 337
voice selector 311
volcanic bomb 28
volcanic island 33
volcanic lake 32
volcano 26, 28
volcano during eruption 28
volcano, effusive 28
volcano, explosive 28
volcanoes, examples of 28
Volga River 18
volley 490
volleyball 487
volt 426
voltage decrease 402, 413
voltage increase 402, 408
volume 328
volume control 303, 310, 311, 319, 322, 325, 329
volume readout 346
volute 200
volva 52
vulture 80
vulva 94, 113

W

wad 534
waders 538
wadi 36
wading bird 79
waffle iron 178
wagon tent 528
waist 93, 95, 240, 301
waist belt 205, 532
waistband 246, 247, 249
waistband extension 246
waistcoat 244, 255
waistcoats and jackets 254
waiter, wine 438
waiting area 442
waiting room 463
waiting room, family 462
waiting room, main 465
waiting room, secondary 465
wakame 123
walk 83
walk-in wardrobe 189
walkie-talkie 456
walking aids 466
walking frame 466
walking leg 67, 70
walking stick 273, 466
walkway 436
wall 5, 58, 184, 528
wall cabinet 164
wall cloud 43
wall lantern 207
wall light 207
wall tent 528
wall, eye 43
wall, finish 516
wallet 275, 337
wallet section 274
walnut 64, 133
walnut, section 60
waning gibbous 5
wardrobe 189, 203, 439
wardrobe, walk-in 189
warehouse 430
warm air 41
warm temperate climates 40
warm-air baffle 192
warming plate 181
warming, global 46
warning lights 355
warning plate 228
warning track 475
wasabi 141
wash tower 214
washbasin 194, 195
washer 417
washer nozzle 348
washers 222
washing machine 194, 212
wasp 69
Wassily chair 200
waste basket 341
waste disposal unit 197
waste layers 47
waste pipe 194, 196
waste water 48
waste, household 47, 48
waste, industrial 47, 48
waste, non-reusable residue 49
waste, nuclear 48
waste, selective sorting of 49
water 402
water and mineral salts, absorption of 54
water bottle 371
water bottle clip 371
water cannon 455
water carrier 532
water chestnut 124
water cools used steam 408
water goblet 165
water hazard 504
water hose 214
water intake 407
water is pumped back into steam generator 408
water jets 518
water jug 166
water key 307
water level 181
water level indicator 179
water main 434
water meter 194
water pollution 48
water pressure gauge 455
water pump pliers 222
water service pipe 194
water spider 70
water strider 69
water table 31, 48
water tank 181, 272
water turns into steam 408
water, waste 48
water-level selector 212
water-level tube 208
water-steam mix 402
water-tank area 394
watercourse 32, 48
watercraft, personal 523
watercress 127
waterfall 31, 32
watering can 236
watering tools 236
watering tube 365
watermark 441
watermelon 135
waterproof pants 260
waterspout 43
watt 426
wave 33, 418
wave base 33
wave clip 268
wave height 33
wave length 33
wave, shock 403
wavelength 418
waves, radio 418
wax 514
wax bean 131
wax gourd 128
wax seal 196
waxed paper 162
waxing gibbous 5
waxing kit 514
Way, Milky 6
Way, Milky (seen from above) 6
Way, Milky (side view) 6
weasel 88
weather map 38, 39
weather radar 38, 392
weather satellite 38
weather station, aircraft 38
weather station, buoy 38
weather station, ocean 38
weatherboard 185, 186
web 75, 79, 477
web frame 385
web, spider 70
webbed foot 75
webbed toe 79
Webcam 332
Weddell Sea 15
wedding ring 264
wedge 305
wedge lever 229
weeder 232
weeding hoe 233
weekend case 277
weeping willow 64
weighing platform 423
weight 422, 423, 500
weight trainer 501
weightlifting 500
weightlifting belt 500
weightlifting shoe 500
weights 501
well, diving 184
well, injection 402
well, production 402
welt 240, 244
welt pocket 244, 250
West 23
West Coast mirror 363
West Indies 16
West-Northwest 23
West-Southwest 23
Western hemisphere 21
Western meridian 22
whale 90
whale, killer 90
whale, sperm 90
wheat 61, 143
wheat, grain 61
wheat, spelt 143
wheat: spike 61
wheel 231, 277, 364, 522, 525, 526, 527, 535
wheel cylinder 357
wheel mouse 332
wheel speed sensor 357
wheel tractor 399
wheel trim 349
wheel, chain 522
wheel, fine adjustment 425
wheel, scroll 332
wheel, steering 350, 385, 525
wheelbarrow 231
wheelchair 467
wheelchair lift 363
wheelhouse 384
wheels, sports on 526
whelk 157
whipping cream 150
whisk 172
whiskers 87
whisky tumbler 165
whistle 180
White 469, 470

white 418
white blood cell 104
white bread 145
white cabbage 126
white chocolate 148
white cue ball 503
white matter 109, 110
white mustard 138
white onion 124
white pepper 138
white rice 147
white spot ball 502, 503
white square 470
white stone 470
white tape 487, 493, 495
white wine glass 165
white-tailed deer 84
whiting 161
whole wheat flour 144
wholegrain mustard 140
wholemeal bread 145
whorl 72, 73
whortleberry, red 132
wicket 479
wicketkeeper 479
wide receiver 485
wide-angle lens 314
widescreen/data code button 320
wigwam 288
wild boar 84
wild rice 143
Wilkes Land 15
willow 478
willow, weeping 64
winch 287, 364, 521
winch controls 364
wind 47, 48
wind deflector 364
wind direction 39
wind direction and speed 39
wind energy 412
wind indicator 520
wind instruments 306
wind speed 39
wind synthesizer controller 311
wind turbines and electricity production 412
wind vane 413
wind, prevailing 43
windbag 296
windcheater 249
winding adjustment 420
windmill 412
window 178, 179, 186, 189, 210, 274, 349, 352, 361, 380, 392, 519
window awning 528
window tab 340
window winder handle 352
window, balcony 189
window, dormer 182
window, stained-glass 446
windows, examples of 287
windscreeen 385
windscreen 348, 364, 366, 369, 392, 523
windscreen wiper 348, 355
windscreen wiper blade 355
windshaft 412
wine cellar 438
wine vinegar 141
wine waiter 438
wine waiter corkscrew 170
wine, beer and 120
wing 13, 68, 78, 286, 348, 364, 393, 525, 536
wing covert 78
wing nut 223
wing pallet 396
wing rib 392
wing slat 393
wing strut 394
wing vein 67
wing, bird 78
wing, high 394
winglet 393, 394
wings 292
winter 38
winter precipitations 41
winter solstice 38
winter sports 515
winter tyre 358
wiper arm 355
wiper blade rubber 355
wiper control 354
wire 417, 501
wire beater 176
wire brush 309
wire cutter 217
wire frame 529
wire nut 217
wire stripper 217
wiring circuit, sensor 357
wisdom tooth 101
wishbone boom 519
withers 83, 86
witness stand 440
wok 174
wok set 174
wolf 88
woman 94
women's clothing 251
women's gloves 243
women's headgear 239
women's shoes 241
won ton skins 147
wood 505
wood chisel 229
wood ear 123
wood firing 192
wood flooring 190
wood flooring on cement screed 190
wood flooring on wooden base 190
wood flooring types 190
wood frog 75
wood storage space 192
woodpecker 80
woods 25
woodstrip flooring 190
woodwind family 295
woofer 324
Worcestershire sauce 140
work bench and vice 224
work surface 164
worker 68
worker, honeybee 68
working surface 224
workstation, security guard's 463
worm 365
wrap, knee 500
wrapover dress 252
wrapover skirt 253
wrapover top 255
wrench, four-way lug 356
wrench, ratchet socket 223
wrenches 216, 223
wrist 86, 93, 95, 115
wrist band 500
wrist guard 527
wrist strap 510, 514
wrist-length glove 243
wristband 486, 492
writing brush 312
writing case 275
writing instruments 312

X

X-ray unit, mobile 462
X-rays 418
xylophone 295, 309

Y

Y-tube 460
yacht, motor 385
yak 85
yard 430
yard line 484
yard, coal storage 402
yard-long bean 130
yarn ball 477
yaw 395
yellow 418
yellow ball 503
yellow onion 124
yellow sweet pepper 128
Yemen 452
yen 440
yogurt 150
yoke 245, 249, 255
yoke skirt 253
yolk 79
Yucatan Peninsula 16
yurt 288

Z

Zambia 452
zebra 84
zester 169
Zimbabwe 452
zinc can (anode) 417
zinc-electrolyte mix (anode) 417
zip 261, 265, 277, 528
zip fastener 249
zither 296
zona pellucida 112
zone, commercial 431
zone, free guard 515
zone, overtaking 472
zones, service 495
zoom button 320
zoom lens 314, 320
zygomatic bone 98, 100

Index français

oints 471
oints 471
nités astronomiques 2
00 unités astronomiques 2

A

issement de la tension 402, 413
-jour 206
-son 285
s 154
tant 195, 196, 202, 203
omen 67, 68, 70, 71, 78
lle 68
lle : ouvrière, morphologie 68
345, 375
des joueurs 474
ous 434
ot 132
de 285
diole 284, 285
rption d'eau 54
rption de dioxyde de carbone 54
rption de sels minéraux 54
rption par le sol 46
rption par les nuages 46
sin 87
stillage 521
nt 299
s au réservoir à essence 349
s aux quais 374
ssoires 209, 356, 372
ssoires au butane 529
ssoires au propane 529
ssoires de foyer 193
ssoires de l'objectif 314
ssoires, automobile 356
ssoires, pêche 538
ssoiriste 291
d 299
déon 296
ement 342
doir 200, 205, 467
plement électrique 365
che-mouche 536
il 442
ulateur 357
cation des lacs 48
ion 99
re 279
290
du vent 45
291
teur de cassette vidéo
pacte 320
teur de courant 336
teur de fiche 198, 271
n 337, 427
addition en mémoire 337
administration 445
adresse URL 334
adresse URL (localisateur universel de ressources) 334
aérateur à gazon 237
aérateur de toit 361
aérateur latéral 361
aérocyste 51
aérofrein 412
aérogare 390
aérogare de passagers 389
aérogare satellite 389
aéroglisseur 383
aéroport 25, 388, 430
affichage 337
affichage de l'heure de départ 374
affichage des fonctions 310
affichage des stations 325
affichage numérique 423, 461
affichage radar 457
affiche 294
affiche publicitaire 380
afficheur 319, 321, 322, 323, 325, 327, 328, 423
afficheur prix 346
afficheur totaliseur 346
afficheur volume 346
affluent 32
Afghanistan 452
Afrique 14, 20, 34, 451
Afrique du Sud 452
agar-agar 123
agence de voyages 436
agenda 338
agent de police 456
agglomération 430
agitateur 212
agneau haché 153
agrafe 312
agrafes 341
agrafeuse 341
agriculture intensive 46, 48
agrumes 134
aide de caisse 121
aide-arbitre 488
aide-mémoire des procédures 10
aides à la marche 466
aigle 81
aiguillage 375
aiguille 35, 36, 422, 460
aiguille à brider 173
aiguille à piquer 173
aiguille aimantée 533
aiguille des dixièmes de seconde 424
aiguille des minutes 424
aiguilles de nettoyage 218
aiguilles de pin 65
aiguilles de sapin 65
aiguillon 68
ail 124
aile 13, 68, 78, 348, 364, 393, 412, 536
aile antérieure 67
aile arrière 387
aile avant 387
aile Dame 470
aile de quartier 240, 262
aile droite 482
aile du nez 117
aile gauche 482
aile haute 394
aile postérieure 67
aile Roi 470
aile, oiseau 78
aileron 392, 519, 525
ailes en V 387
ailette 213, 393, 394
ailette à ressort 221
ailier défensif droit 484
ailier défensif gauche 484
ailier droit 482, 489, 507
ailier gauche 482, 489, 507
ailier rapproché 485
aimant 341, 416
aimant de retenue 180
aine 92, 94
air chaud 41
air chaud ascendant 43
air froid 41
air froid subsident 43
aire d'accueil 462, 465
aire d'attente 442
aire de jeu 471
aire de jeux 386
aire de manœuvre 388
aire de préparation de l'étalage 120
aire de ravitaillement 346
aire de réception 120
aire de réception des produits laitiers 120
aire de repos 25
aire de service 25, 389
aire de stationnement 389
aire de trafic 388
airelle 132
aisselle 92, 94
ajowan 139
akène 59, 60
Albanie 450
albatros 80
albumen 79
albumen farineux 61
alcool à 90° 461
Algérie 451
algue 51
algue brune 51
algue rouge 51
algue verte 51
algue, structure 51
algues 123
alimentation 120
alimentation solaire 337
alimentation sur secteur 326
aliments congelés 121
aliments prêts-à-servir 121
alkékenge 132
allée 120, 230, 504
allée de jardin 182
Allemagne 450
alliance 264
alligator 77
allumeur 350, 360
allures, cheval 83
alluvions 32
alose 160
Alpes 18
altérations 299
alternateur 350, 360, 402, 413
alternative 330
alternative : sélection du niveau 3 330
alto 301
alto-cumulus 42
alto-stratus 42
altos 295
alule 78
alvéole 198, 505
alvéole de plaque 359
alvéole dentaire 101
amande 57, 133
amanite vireuse 52
amarante 143
amas globulaire 6
Amazone 17
amble 83
ambulance 460, 462
Amérique centrale 14, 16
Amérique du Nord 14, 16, 34
Amérique du Sud 14, 17, 34
Amériques 448
ameublement de la maison 200
amibe 66
amidon, grain 50
amorce 534
amorti 491
amortisseur 270, 287, 351, 523
amortisseur arrière 367
amortisseur avant 369
amortisseur magnétique 422
ampère 426
amphibiens 75
amphithéâtre romain 281
ampli-syntoniseur 325
ampli-syntoniseur : vue arrière 322
ampli-syntoniseur : vue avant 322
amplitude 418
ampoule 199, 416, 467
ampoule de la trompe utérine 113
amygdale 116
amygdale linguale 118
amygdale palatine 118
ananas 136
anatomie 96
anatomie du coquillage bivalve 73
anatomie du homard 71
anche 305, 306
anche double 306
anche simple 306
anchois 159
anconé 97
Andorre 449
andouillette 156
âne 84
anémomètre 413
aneth 142
angle aigu 428
angle droit 428
angle obtus 428
angle rentrant 428
Angola 452
anguille 159
Anik 317
animalerie 436
anis 142
anneau 52, 210, 270, 271, 423, 424, 489, 536
anneau brisé 538
anneau d'étanchéité en cire 196
anneau de départ 537
anneau de retenue 460
anneau de suspension 270
anneau de tête 537
anneau de traction 460
anneau oculaire 78
anneaux 264, 496, 497
annonce publicitaire 313
annonceur 518
annulaire 115
anode 417
anorak 263
anse 215, 236, 537
Antarctique 14, 15
antéfixe 279
antenne 7, 67, 68, 71, 326, 327, 349, 369, 392, 395, 457, 487
antenne d'émission 316
antenne d'émission/réception 316
antenne de télécommunication 386, 387
antenne domestique 316
antenne parabolique 321

antenne parabolique d'émission/réception 316
antenne radio 382, 384, 386, 387, 525
antenne télescopique 325
antennule 71
anthélix 115
anthère 56
anticlinal 403
anticyclone 39
Antigua-et-Barbuda 449
Antilles 16, 448
antilope 84
antiseptique 461
antitragus 115
anus 71, 73, 106, 111, 112
aorte 104, 105
aorte abdominale 102, 107
aorte ascendante 103
aorte descendante 103
apex 72, 73, 101, 118
apophyse épineuse 110
apophyse mastoïde 100
apophyse styloïde 100
apophyse transverse 110
apothécie 50
Appalaches 16
appareil à visée reflex mono-objectif : vue avant 314
appareil à visée reflex numérique : dos 315
appareil compact 315
appareil de forage 403
appareil de Golgi 50, 66
appareil de prise de son et d'enregistrement 291
appareil de protection respiratoire 454
appareil de radiographie mobile 462
appareil digestif 106
appareil jetable 315
appareil photographique 35 mm 10
appareil reflex 6 X 6 mono-objectif 315
appareil respiratoire 105
appareil ultracompact 315
appareil urinaire 107
appareils de conditionnement physique 500
appareils de mesure 424
appareils de son portatifs 325
appareils électroménagers 176, 208
appareils électroménagers divers 180
appareils photographiques 315
appareils scientifiques 7
appartement du commandant 387
appartements en copropriété 289
appartenance 427
appeau 535
appendice vermiculaire 106
applicateur-mousse 266
applique 207
applique du robinet 197
applique orientable 207
appoggiature 299
approvisionnement en numéraire 443
appui de fenêtre 187
appui-bras 352, 353
appui-flèche 535
appui-pied 515
appui-pieds 224
appui-tête 353
après-rasage 271
après-shampooing 267
aquifère captif 402
ara 80
Arabie saoudite 452
arachide 130
arachnides 67
arachnoïde 109
araignée 70
araignée, morphologie 70
araignée-crabe 70
aramé 123
arbitre 479, 481, 483, 485, 488, 490, 495, 498, 499, 507, 509, 515
arbitre adjoint 509
arbitre en chef 475, 485
arborisation terminale 110
arbre 63, 177, 412
arbre à cames 360
arbre cannelé 355
arbre d'ornement 122, 230
arbre d'ornement 182
arbre de l'hélice 387
arbre de Noël 404
arbre de roue 351
arbre de transmission 383
arbre de transmission longitudinal 351
arbre fruitier 122
arbre lent 413
arbre moteur 395
arbre rapide 413
arbre, structure 63
arbres 504
arbres feuillus, exemples 64
arbuste 230
arc 428
arc à poulies 535
arc de cercle 480
arc de l'aorte 102, 103, 104
arc diagonal 284
arc insulaire 33
arc-boutant 284, 285
arc-doubleau 284
arc-en-ciel 41
arc-formeret 284
arcade 281, 284
arcade dentaire inférieure 116
arcade dentaire supérieure 116
arceau 230, 519
arche 447
arche naturelle 35
archet 301
archipel 24
architecture 278
architrave 279
archives médicales 465
Arctique 14
ardillon 246, 538
arène 281
aréole 113
arête 29, 526
arête supérieure 493
Argentine 448
argyronète 70
Ariel 3
armature 219, 259, 277, 528
armature de la clé 299
Arménie 452
armoire 202
armoire inférieure 164
armoire réfrigérée 120
armoire supérieure 164
armoire-penderie 203
arpège 299
arraché 500
arrache-clou 220
arrangements des parquets 190
arrêt 319, 323, 328
arrêt d'autobus 434
arrêt-court 474
arrière 482, 489, 518
arrière centre 487
arrière court 491
arrière droit 481, 487
arrière gauche 481, 487
arrivée des remontées mécaniques 512
arrondie 55
arrondissement 25
arroseur canon 236
arroseur oscillant 236
arroseur rotatif 236
arrosoir 236
arsenal stérile 464
artère abdominale dorsale 71
artère arquée 102
artère axillaire 102
artère brachiale 102
artère carotide primitive 102
artère dorsale du pied 102
artère fémorale 102
artère iliaque 103
artère iliaque commune 102, 107
artère iliaque interne 102, 107
artère mésentérique inférieure 107
artère mésentérique supérieure 102, 107
artère pulmonaire 102, 104, 105
artère rénale 102, 107
artère sous-clavière 102
artère sternale 71
artère tibiale antérieure 102
artère ventrale 71
artères 102
artichaut 127
article 313
articles de bureau 337
articles de maroquinerie 274
articles divers, bureau 341
articles ménagers 215
articulation 355, 536
articulation de la pelleteuse 399
arts 278
arts de la scène 294
As 468
asa-fœtida 139
ascenseur 281, 287, 435, 439
ascot 245
Asie 14, 19, 34, 452
asperge 125
asphalte 405
aspirateur 407
aspirateur à main 208
aspirateur-balai 209
aspirateur-traîneau 209
aspirine 461
assaisonnement au chili 139
assiette à dessert 166
assiette à salade 166
assiette creuse 166
assiette plate 166, 531
assistance 440
assistant-accessoiriste 291
assistant-réalisateur 291
assistants des avocats 440
astéroïdes, ceinture 3
asthénosphère 26
astigmatisme 419
astragale 99
astronautique 10
astronomie 2
atelier de mécanique 346
atelier diesel 375
athlète : bloc de départ 473
athlétisme 472
Atlas 20
atlas 69, 99
atmosphère 44, 48
atmosphère terrestre, coupe 37
atoll 35
atome 414
atomes 414
âtre 192
atrium 280
attache 273, 308, 535
attache d'accordage 297
attache de pavillon 306
attache de sécurité 10
attache du tube 199
attache pour outils 10
attaches parisiennes 341
attaquant central 487
attaquant de pointe 481
attaquant de soutien 481
attaquant droit 487
attaquant gauche 487
attaque 485
attelles 461
attraction 416
aubergine 128
aubier 63
augmentation de l'effet de serre 46
auriculaire 115
aurore polaire 37
Australie 14, 34, 453
autel secondaire 446
auto-caravane 361
autobus 362, 435
autobus à impériale 363
autobus articulé 363
autobus scolaire 362
autocar 362
autoclave 464
autocuiseur 174
automne 38
automobile 347
automobile, organes des systèmes 350
autoroute 25, 343, 431
autoroute de ceinture 25
autotrophes 45
autres signes 299
Autriche 450
autruche 81
auvent 348, 361, 401, 528
auvent de fenêtre 528
avance rapide 319, 323
avançon 538
avant 518
avant court 491
avant droit 482
avant gauche 482
avant-bras 86, 93, 95
avant-champ 474
avant-scène 292
avant-toit 283
aven 31
avenue 25, 433
avertisseur 354, 368, 377
avertisseur de détresse 454
avertisseur pneumatique 364
avion d'affaires 394
avion de ligne 37
avion de ligne supersonique 394
avion léger 394
avion long-courrier 392
avion supersonique 37
avion, mouvements 395
avion-cargo 394
avion-citerne amphibie 394
avions, exemples 394
avocat 128
avoine 61, 143
avoine : panicule 61
axe central 412
axe de tambour 537
axe du pédalier 372
axe horaire 7
axel 509
axis 99
axone 110
Azerbaïdjan 452
azimut 9

B

babeurre 150
babines 86
bâbord 387
babouin 91
bac 219
bac à boue 403
bac à compost 231
bac à glaçons 211
bac à gravier 524
bac à légumes 211
bac à plante 230
bac à viande 211
bac d'alimentation 333
bac de ramassage 237
bac de recyclage 49
bac de sortie 333
bac ramasse-jus 179
bâche spirale 407
bacon américain 156
bacon canadien 156
badminton 494
bagage à main 276
bagages 276
bagel 144
bague 307
bague de blocage 221, 425
bague de correction dioptrique 420
bague de fiançailles 264
bague de réglage 236
bague de réglage du couple de serrage 228
bague de serrage 306
bague solitaire 264
bagues 264
baguette 243, 301
baguette de flanc 349
baguette épi 144
baguette parisienne 144
baguettes 309
Bahamas 448
Bahreïn 452
baie 5, 24, 59
baie d'Hudson 16
baie de genièvre 138
baies 132
baignoire 189, 194, 195, 439
bain moussant 267
bain-marie 175
baladeur 325
baladeur numérique 326
baladeur pour disque compact 325
baladeuse 217
baladodiffusion 335
balai 193, 215
balai à feuilles 237
balai à franges 215
balai à neige à grattoir 356
balai d'essuie-glace 355
balai métallique 309
balalaïka 297
balance à fléau 422
balance de cuisine 171
balance de précision 423
balance de Roberval 422
balance électronique 423
balance romaine 422
balancier 236
balancier d'extension 501
balancier de traction 501
balayeuse 365
balcon 189, 293, 447
balconnet 211
baleine 90, 259, 273
baleine de col 245
ballast électronique 199
balle 534
balle de baseball 476
balle de baseball, coupe 477
balle de cricket 478
balle de fil 477
balle de golf 505
balle de liège 477
balle de softball 477
balle de tennis 492
balle de tennis de table 493
ballerine 241
ballon 181
ballon de basket 488
ballon de boxe 498
ballon de football 480, 486
ballon de rugby 483
ballon de volleyball 487
ballon-sonde 38
balluchon 276
balustrade 283
banane 136
banane plantain 136
banc 201, 379, 437, 446
banc de musculation 501
banc de sable 33
banc des accusés 440
banc des avocats de l'accusatio
banc des avocats de la défense
banc des joueurs 485, 487, 50
banc des juges 440
banc des officiels 507
banc des pénalités 507
banc des remplaçants 481
banc du jury 440
bandage triangulaire 461
bande 502, 506
bande antidérapante 526
bande blanche 487
bande d'ancrage 190
bande de filet 491
bande de gaze 461
bande de tissu élastique 461
bande élastique 246
bande magnétique 319, 441
bande métallisée holographiqu
bande nuageuse spirale 43
bande transporteuse 49
bande ventilée 534
bande verticale de côté 487
bandoulière 276
Bangladesh 453

INDEX FRANÇAIS

njo 296
nlieue 25, 431
nque 432, 437, 442
nque de données 335
nquette 195, 201, 353
nquette arrière 353
nquise d'Amery 15
nquise de Filchner 15
nquise de Ross 15
203, 293, 386, 432, 436, 438
commun 160
salon 439
bacane 282
bade 449
be 61
boteuse 261
botin 398
dane 129
naid 438
quette 162
age 406
e 273, 500, 501, 520
e à dorsaux 501
e à pectoraux 501
e à triceps 501
e blindée 407
e d'écoute 520, 521
e d'espacement 330, 467
e de flèche 520
e de maintien 363
e de mesure 298
e de poussée 286
e de pression 304
e de repos des marteaux 304
e de reprise 298
e de retenue 211
e des témoins 440
e fixe 496, 497
eau 191, 201, 205, 479
es asymétriques 496, 497
es parallèles 496, 497
tte 268
tte négative 359
te positive 359
ere 205, 434
ere de pneus 524
57, 259, 506
e ligne 538
ésille 257
uissarde 257
7, 118, 269, 370, 454, 533
de dormant 186
de la vague 33
ball 474
ball, lancer 475
ball, position des joueurs 474
ire 435
142
tball 488
e 259
230, 381, 517
de compétition 517
de radoub 381
et 107
306
s 295
x et embarcations, exemples
02
brûleur 529
ent administratif 381
nt du réacteur 409
476, 477, 514
de ski 510
de softball 477
et 119
et de colle 341
de golf, types 505
186, 309
78
221, 228, 308, 416
d'accumulateurs 359, 411
d'accumulateurs 350
de cuisine 174
478, 479
à main 176
à œufs 172
sur socle 176
r 353

bavette 260, 261
bavette garde-boue 349, 364, 365
bavette garde-neige 523
bavoir 260
bavolet 248
bec 78, 167, 197, 216, 306, 311
bec corné 76
bec de bord d'attaque 393
bec fixe 425
bec mobile 425
bec verseur 180, 181, 215
bec-de-cane 186
bécarre 299
bêche 233
becquerel 426
becs, exemples 79
bégonia 56
Bélarus 450
belette 88
Belgique 449
Belize 448
bémol 299
Bénin 451
bénitier 446
benne 400
benne à ordures 364
benne basculante 401
benne tasseuse 364
béquet 366
béquille 277, 365, 387, 395
béquille centrale 367
béquille commune 466
béquille d'appoint 361
béquille d'appui 361
béquille d'avant-bras 466
béquille latérale 367, 369
berceuse 201
béret 239
bergamote 134
berge 342
berger allemand 86
bergère 200
bergerie 122
berline 347
berlingot 163
bermuda 254
bette à carde 125
betterave 129
beurre 150
beurrier 166
Bhoutan 453
biais 260
bibliothèque 433, 444
biceps brachial 96
biceps crural 97
bicyclette 370
bicyclette de course 373
bicyclette de tourisme 373
bicyclette de ville 373
bicyclette hollandaise 373
bicyclette tout-terrain 373
bicyclette, accessoires 372
bicyclettes, exemples 373
bidet 195
bidon 371
bief d'amont 406
bief d'aval 406, 407
bielle 360
bière 120
bifteck 152
bigorneau 157
bigoudi 268
bijouterie 264, 436
billard 502
billard anglais 503
billard français 502
billard pool 502
bille 312, 332
bille blanche 503
bille blanche mouchetée 503
bille bleue 503
bille brune 503
bille de choc 502, 503
bille de visée blanche 502
bille jaune 503
bille noire 503
bille rose 503
bille rouge 502, 503
bille verte 503

billes numérotées 502
billes rouges 503
billet de banque 441
billetterie 294, 390
billetterie express 294
bimah 447
binette 233
biologie 426
biosphère 44
biosphère, structure 44
biseau 305, 460
bison 84
bitte 385
blaireau 88, 271
blanc 418, 468
blanche 299
Blancs 469, 470
blazer 254
blé 61, 143
blé : épi 61
bleu 418
bleu danois 151
bleuet 132
bloc 473
bloc convertisseur 321
bloc d'arrêt 229
bloc de culasse 534
bloc de départ 473
bloc de pression 425
bloc opératoire 464
bloc pneumatique 376
bloc-cylindres 360
bloc-éphéméride 338
bloc-essieu 526, 527
bloc-moteur 176, 177, 180, 208, 272, 376
bloc-notes 338
blocage de l'inclinaison 227
blocage de l'interrupteur 228
blocage du pivot 224
blogue 335
bloqueur droit 485
bloqueur gauche 485
blouson court 249
blouson long 249
blousons 248
boa 77
bob 239
bobine 319
bocal 306
body 258
bogie moteur 376
bogie porteur 376
bois 25, 505
bois de cœur 63
bois, famille 295
boisseau d'embouchure 307
boissons 120
boîte à courrier 338
boîte à fromage 163
boîte à gants 354
boîte à leurres 538
boîte à onglets 226
boîte à outils 225
boîte à œufs 162
boîte à poussière 229
boîte d'encastrement 198
boîte d'engrenage multiplicateur 413
boîte de conserve 163
boîte de vitesses 350
boîte électrique 411
boîte en zinc (anode) 417
boîte pour seringues usagées 457
boîte-classeur 340
boîtes alimentaires 162
boîtier 199, 218, 225, 228, 229, 271, 314, 424
boîtier à double rangée de connexions 417
boîtier de batterie 359, 365
boîtier du moteur 235
boîtier du ventilateur 270
boîtier tour : vue arrière 329
boîtier tour : vue avant 329
bol 166, 176, 177
bol à raser 271
bol à salade 166
bol verseur 177
boléro 254

Bolivie 448
bols à mélanger 172
bols de cuisson 179
bombe volcanique 28
bôme 520
bonbout 240
bonde 197
bonde de fond 184
bongo 309
bonnet 259, 514, 516
bonnet pompon 239
bord 55, 238, 239
bord antérieur 73
bord d'attaque 393
bord d'une feuille 55
bord de fuite 392
bord externe 73
bord interne 73
bord libre 114
bord postérieur 73
bord tranchant 398
bord-côte 247, 250, 261
bordure 182, 205, 519, 524
bordure d'allée 230
bordure de quai 374, 379
bordure de trottoir 434
borne 198, 210, 359
borne d'incendie 434
borne d'incendie 454
borne de gonflage 346
borne de mise à la terre 322
borne négative 359, 416, 417
borne positive 359, 416, 417
bornes de raccordement des antennes 322
bornes de raccordement des enceintes 322
Bosnie-Herzégovine 450
Botswana 452
botte 125, 241, 525
botte de caoutchouc 454
botte rigide 513
botte souple 513
bottillon 240
bottine 241
bouche 71, 72, 73, 75, 90, 94, 116, 305, 534
bouche d'air 354
boucherie 120
bouchon 176, 267, 409, 460, 532
bouchon antifuite 529
bouchon de dégorgement 197
bouchon de remplissage 237, 358
bouchon de scellement 417
bouchon de vidange 194, 211
bouchon de vidange d'huile 360
bouchon du réservoir 364, 368
boucle 246, 276, 343, 353, 511
boucle de ceinture 248
boucle de piquet 528, 529
boucle de réglage 527, 532
boucle piquée 509
boucles d'oreille 264
boucles d'oreille à pince 264
boucles d'oreille à tige 264
boucles d'oreille à vis 264
bouclier 235, 507
bouclier arrière 7
bouclier thermique 12
boudin 156
bouée de sauvetage 387, 457
bougie 237
bougie d'allumage 359, 360
bouilloire 180
boulangerie 121
boulangerie-pâtisserie 437
boule à thé 173
boule d'attelage 356
bouleau 64
bouledogue 86
boulet 83
boulevard 25, 433
boulevard périphérique 25
boulon 222, 223, 224
boulon à ailettes 221
boulon à épaulement 223
boulon à gaine d'expansion 221
boulons 223
bourdalou 238

bourdon 69, 296
bourgeon 54
bourgeon axillaire 53
bourgeon gustatif 118
bourgeon terminal 53
bourrache 142
bourre 534
bourrelet 358
bourse à monnaie 275
boussole magnétique 533
bout 167, 536
bout du nez 83
bout fleuri 240
bouteille 532
bouteille à gaz médical 464
bouteille d'air comprimé 454
bouteille en verre 163
bouteille isolante 532
boutique 280
boutique hors taxe 391
bouton 199, 202, 245, 250, 296, 301
bouton à friction 425
bouton alimentation papier 333
bouton champignon 332
bouton d'alimentation papier 443
bouton d'appel 287
bouton d'appel pour piétons 434
bouton d'arrêt 235
bouton d'éjection 323
bouton d'éjection 315
bouton d'éjection de la disquette 329
bouton d'éjection du CD/DVD-ROM 329
bouton d'enregistreur vocal 337
bouton d'essai 454
bouton de blocage 225, 229
bouton de clé 306
bouton de combinaisons 305
bouton de commande 210
bouton de contrôle 332
bouton de démarrage 329, 336
bouton de démarrage et de rétroéclairage 337
bouton de démarreur 368
bouton de déverrouillage de l'écran 336
bouton de mise au point 8, 9
bouton de piston 307
bouton de registre 305
bouton de réinitialisation 329, 471
bouton de remise à zéro 323
bouton de sortie 337
bouton de vaporisation 208
bouton de verrouillage 352
bouton de verrouillage de l'interrupteur 227
bouton du pavé tactile 336
bouton fixe-courroie 303
bouton floral 53
bouton marche/arrêt 180, 333
bouton moleté 219
bouton-guide 227
bouton-poussoir 176, 214, 312
bouton-pression 243, 249
boutonnage sous patte 251
boutonnière 246, 248
boutons de lancement d'applications 337
boutons de réglage 318
boutons programmables 332
box 438
boxe 498
boxeur 498
bœuf 85
bœuf haché 152
bracelet 424, 486
bracelet lesté 500
bracelet tubulaire 264
bracelets 264
brachial antérieur 96
bractée 60
braguette 246, 247, 260
brancard 231, 400, 460
branche 125, 222, 270, 273, 416, 460, 535
branche à fruits 62
branche d'embouchure 307
branche maîtresse 63

C

nture 200, 201, 202, 225, 246, 248, 499, 532
nture d'astéroïdes 3
nture d'haltérophilie 500
nture de Kuiper 2
nture de sécurité 353
nture élastique 247, 249
nture montée 246, 249
nture porte-outils 225
nture ventrale 205
nturon de service 456
ri 125
ri-rave 129
ule 67, 281
ule animale 66
ule convective 43
ule végétale 50
ules 440
ent 101
427, 440
rale 406
rale hydroélectrique, coupe 407
rale thermique au charbon 402
re 293, 428, 470, 481, 482, 85, 507, 515
e arrière 485
e commercial 431, 436
e de tri 49
e droit 482
e gauche 482
e-ville 431, 432
fugeuse 11, 180
ole 66
e vigne 62
123
alothorax 70, 71
e 273
e central 481, 488, 507
e d'ascension droite 8, 9
e d'attente 474
e de déclinaison 8, 9
e de la station 39
e de lancer 472, 473
e de mise au jeu 506
de serrage 308
extérieur 515
intérieur 515
polaire antarctique 15, 21, 22
polaire arctique 21, 22
porte-lame 401
restrictif 488
es 61, 143
2
Virginie 84
Canada 84
l 142
132
annuel 63
u 60
s 536
u 71, 109
t 109
e 154
ool 283
370, 372
alimentaire 45
coupante 235
de levage 396
de montagnes 5, 24, 26
de neurones 110
de sûreté 361
nerveuse ventrale 71
stéréo 322
e de levage 196
46
201, 444
haute 205
longue 201
pliante 201
escabeau 201
empilables 201
exemples 201
79
e montagne 512
u sommet 512
rincipal 512
e de sauvetage 382, 386
au 296
384

chambranle 185, 186
chambre 189, 528
chambre à air 79
chambre antérieure 119
chambre d'expansion 424
chambre d'hôpital 464
chambre d'isolement 462
chambre d'observation 462, 465
chambre d'observation psychiatrique 462
chambre de combustion 192, 360
chambre de décharge 278
chambre de la reine 278
chambre des pompes 384
chambre double 439
chambre du roi 278
chambre forte 443
chambre froide 120, 121
chambre photographique 315
chambre postérieure 119
chambre principale, plafond cathédrale 189
chambre principale, toit cathédrale 189
chambre pulpaire 101
chambre simple 439
chambre souterraine 278
chambres d'hôtel 439
chameau 85
champ centre 475
champ droit 475
champ gauche 475
champ géothermique 402
champ magnétique 318, 416
champignon 52
champignon de couche 123
champignon mortel 52
champignon vénéneux 52
champignon, structure 52
champignons 123
chanfrein 83
changement de disque 323
changement de piste/lecture rapide 319, 323
chanterelle commune 123
chape 190
chapeau 52, 313
chapeau de feutre 238, 239
chapeau de ventilation 194
chapelle 282
chapelle axiale 284, 285
chapelle latérale 284
chapiteau 302
chapon 155
chapska 238
charcuterie 156
charge électrique, mesure 426
chargeur 228
chargeuse frontale 399
chargeuse-pelleteuse 399
chariot 290, 397, 421, 505, 521
chariot à bagages 374
chariot élévateur 396
chariots 121
Charles IX 241
charnière 178, 214, 274, 277, 352, 420, 511
charnière de la visière 367
Charon 3
charpente 187, 279, 280
chasse 534
chasse-clou 220
chasse-neige à soufflerie 365
chasse-pierres 376, 377
châssis 308, 309, 396, 400, 401
chasuble 252
chat 87
chat de l'île de Man 87
chat, tête 87
châtaigne d'eau 124
château fort 282
chats, races 87
chauffage 192
chauffage au bois 192
chauffe-eau 194
chaufferette 529
chaumard 521
chaussée 342, 345, 434
chaussette 247, 257, 480, 486, 492

chaussette-étrier 476
chaussettes 247
chaussettes hautes 483
chausson intérieur 511, 527
chaussure 478, 488, 509, 514, 522, 524, 527
chaussure à crampons 476, 483, 486
chaussure d'haltérophilie 500
chaussure de football 480
chaussure de piste 473
chaussure de saut à ski 513
chaussure de ski 510, 511
chaussure de sport 262
chaussure de tennis 492
chaussure, parties 240
chaussures 240
chaussures d'homme 240
chaussures de femme 241
chaussures de golf 505
chaussures unisexes 242
chayote 129
chef décorateur 290
chef électricien 291
chef machiniste 290
chef opérateur du son 291
chemin 504
chemin d'évacuation 345
chemin de fer 25
chemin de fer métropolitain 378
chemin de ronde 282
chemin de ronde couvert 282
chemin de roulement 397
cheminée 28, 183, 188, 193, 382, 402
cheminée à foyer ouvert 192
cheminée antisuie 386
cheminée d'échappement 364, 401
chemise 245, 340, 534
chemise de nuit 256
chemise du donjon 282
chemise en acier 417
chemisier classique 255
chêne 64
chenets 193
chenille 67, 398, 523
chèque de voyage 441
chèques 441
chéquier 274
chercheur 8, 9
chérimole 136
cheval 83, 85
cheval d'arçons 496
cheval d'arçons 496
cheval sautoir 496, 497
cheval, morphologie 83
chevalet 297, 301, 302, 303
chevalet des aigus 304
chevalet des basses 304
chevalière 264
chevelu 63
chevet 285
cheveux 93, 95
cheville 92, 94, 202, 301, 302
cheville d'accord 304
chevillier 301
chèvre 84
chèvre frais 150
chevron 187
chiasma optique 109
chicane 524
chicorée de Trévise 126
chicorée frisée 127
chien 86, 534, 535
chien, morphologie 86
chiens, races 86
chiffonnier 203
chiffres romains 427
Chili 448
chimie 414
chimpanzé 91
Chine 453
chinois 171
chipolata 156
chirurgie mineure 462
chloroplaste 50
chocolat 148
chocolat au lait 148
chocolat blanc 148
chocolat noir 148

chope à bière 165
chope à café 166
chorizo 156
choroïde 119
chou cavalier 126
chou de Milan 126
chou frisé 126
chou laitue 126
chou marin 126
chou pommé blanc 126
chou pommé rouge 126
chou pommé vert 126
chou-fleur 127
chou-rave 125
choux de Bruxelles 126
chœur 284, 285
chromatine 66
chromosphère 4
chronique 313
chronomètre 424
chronomètre électronique automatique 517
chronométreur 488, 498, 509
chronométreur de couloir 516
chronométreur des trente secondes 488
chronométreur en chef 516
chronométreurs 499
chrysalide 67
chukka 240
chute 31, 519
chute d'eau 32
chutney à la mangue 141
Chypre 450
cible 471
ciboule 124
ciboulette 124
ciel d'orage 41
cierge 446
cigale 69
cigogne 80
cil 66, 119
cilié 55
cils 87
cime 63
cimetière 25, 433
cimier mobile 7
cinéma 294, 386, 432, 436
cinéma maison 321
cinq 427
cinq cents 427
cinq-épices chinois 139
cinquante 427
cintres 292
circonférence 428
circuit capteurs 357
circuit d'eau chaude 194
circuit d'eau froide 194
circuit d'évacuation 194
circuit de freinage 350, 357
circuit de photopiles 411
circuit de plomberie 194
circuit de ventilation 194
circuit électrique en parallèle 416
circuit imprimé 417
circuit intégré 417
circuit intégré en boîtier 417
circuit, course automobile 524
circulation sanguine 102
circulation sanguine, schéma 103
cirque 5
cirque glaciaire 30
cirro-cumulus 42
cirro-stratus 42
cirrus 42
cisaille à haies 234
cisaille à volaille 173
ciseau à bois 229
ciseaux 461, 531
ciseaux à cuticules 265
ciseaux à effiler 270
ciseaux à ongles 265
ciseaux de coiffeur 270
ciseaux de cuisine 173
ciseaux de pédicure 265
ciseaux de sûreté 265
ciseaux sculpteurs 270
citerne 364, 385
cithare 296

citron 134
citrouille 129
civière 460
clairon 307
clapet 196
claque 240, 263
claquette 291
clarinette 306
clarinette basse 295
clarinettes 295
classeur 339
classeur à soufflets 274
clavardage 335
clavicule 98
clavier 304, 310, 327, 330, 336
clavier accompagnement 296
clavier alphanumérique 327, 346, 442, 443
clavier chant 296
clavier d'identification personnelle 443
clavier de grand orgue 305
clavier de positif 305
clavier de récit 305
clavier numérique 423
claviers manuels 305
clayette 211
clé 306
clé à douille à cliquet 223
clé à fourches 223
clé à molette 223
clé à tuyau 216
clé coudée à tuyau 216
clé d'ut 298
clé de bocal 306
clé de bras 499
clé de contact 237
clé de fa 298
clé de mandrin 228
clé de sol 298
clé de voûte 284
clé en croix 356
clé mixte 223
clé polygonale 223
clé polygonale à cliquet 223
clé polygonale à têtes fendues 223
clé USB 333
clés 216, 223, 298, 311
client 317
climatiseur 361
climats arides 40
climats de montagne 40
climats du monde 40
climats polaires 40
climats tempérés chauds 40
climats tempérés froids 40
climats tropicaux 40
cliquet 221
clitoris 112
cloche 239
clocher 285, 446
clocheton 282, 284, 285
clochettes 309
cloison 58, 117, 457, 469, 528
cloison longitudinale 384
cloison transversale 384
clôture 122, 182
clôture du champ extérieur 475
clôture en lattis 230
clou 220
clou à maçonnerie 220
clou à tête homme 220
clou à tige spiralée 220
clou commun 220
clou coupé 220
clou de girofle 138
clous, exemples 220
cobra 77
coccinelle 69
coccyx 98
cochlée 116
cochon d'Inde 82
cockpit 520
code des produits 423
code temporel 291
coffre 203, 349, 369, 410, 411
coffre à bagages 361
coffre d'appareillage 376
coffre de rangement 364, 455

coffre-fort 443
coffret 318
coffret de branchement 198
coffret de sûreté 443
coiffe 53, 536
coiffeur 290
coiffeuse 195
coiffure 238, 268
coiffures d'homme 238
coiffures de femme 239
coiffures unisexes 239
coin 305, 498
coin de patinoire 506
coin-repas 164, 188
coing 133
col 29, 244, 245, 248, 262, 318
col de l'utérus 112
col du fémur 99
col italien 245
col pointes boutonnées 245
col roulé 250, 514
col tailleur 251
col transformable 248
col-de-cygne 191, 400
colibri 80
collant 257
collant fantaisie 260
collant sans pieds 263
collatéral 285
collatérale 110
colle 190
collecte sélective 49
collecteur d'appareil 194
collecteur d'échappement 350, 360
collecteur d'électrons 417
collecteur d'évacuation 194
collecteur de graisse 179
collecteur principal 194
collet 53, 101, 167, 193, 535
collet de l'axone 110
colley 86
collier 174, 511
collier coupe-feu 193
collier de perles, longueur matinée 264
collier de serrage 501
collier de serrage du casque 10
collier de soirée 264
collier-de-chien 264
colliers 264
colline 29
colline abyssale 33
collybie à pied velouté 123
Colombie 448
côlon ascendant 106
côlon descendant 106
côlon pelvien 106
côlon transverse 106
colonne 31, 279, 302, 313, 380
colonne corinthienne engagée 281
colonne d'alcool 424
colonne de collecte du papier 49
colonne de collecte du verre 49
colonne de direction 350
colonne de mercure 424
colonne de ventilation 194
colonne de ventilation principale 194
colonne dorique engagée 281
colonne ionique engagée 281
colonne montante d'eau chaude 194
colonne montante d'eau froide 194
colonne vertébrale 98, 109
colorant capillaire 267
columelle 73
coma 6
combattant 499
combinaison 247, 261, 513, 525
combinaison de course 508
combinaison de nuit 261
combinaison de protection 525
combinaison de saut à ski 513
combinaison de ski 510, 514
combinaison résistante au feu 524
combinaison-jupon 258
combinaison-pantalon 254
combinaisons au poker 468
combiné 258, 327
combiné 2 dans 1 268
combiné bucco-dentaire 272
combiné-culotte 258
combustible 408
combustible fossile 46, 48
comète 6
commande amovible 179
commande d'accélération 235
commande d'essuie-glace 354
commande de chauffage 354
commande de dossier 353
commande de température 211
commande de vitesse 176
commande de volume de la sonnerie 327
commande de volume du récepteur 327
commande du chariot 421
commande du rétroviseur 352
commande du zoom 320
commande mémoire 327
commandes de la bande vidéo 320
commandes de préréglage 319
commandes du magnétoscope 319
commandes du treuil 364
commerce électronique 335
commissure labiale 116
commode 203
communication par téléphone 327
communications 312
communications aériennes 317
communications individuelles 317
communications industrielles 317
communications maritimes 317
communications militaires 317
communications routières 317
commutateur alimentation/fonctions 320
commutateur d'alimentation 315
commutateur d'allumage 354, 368
commutateur marche/arrêt 314
Comores 452
compactage 49
compartiment 286
compartiment bagages 376
compartiment d'accessoires 209
compartiment de réservoirs d'eau 394
compartiment de sac 209
compartiment des voitures 386
compartiment moteur 362
compartiment voyageurs 376
compartiment-couchette 364
compétition de cyclisme sur route 522
complexe hydroélectrique 406
complexe sportif 431
compluvium 280
composition du sang 104
compresse stérilisée 461
compresseur du climatiseur 360
comprimé 467
compte-tours 355
compteur 194, 323
compteur d'électricité 198
compteur kilométrique 355
comptoir d'enregistrement 390
comptoir de renseignements 390, 442, 463
comptoir de vente de friandises 294
comptoir des fromages 121
comptoir des viandes libre-service 120
comptoir du bar 438
concentration des gaz à effet de serre 46
concentré de tomate 140
concessionnaire d'automobiles 433
conchiglie 146
concombre 128
concombre sans pépins 128
condensateur à film plastique 417
condensateur céramique 417
condensateurs électrolytiques 417
condensation 45, 414
condensation de la vapeur 408
condenseur 402, 421
condiments 140
conditionnement d'air 386
condor 80
conducteur d'alimentation 198
conducteur de mise à la terre 198
conducteur dérivé 416
conducteur neutre 198
conduction 415
conduit auditif 116
conduit auditif externe 100
conduit d'aération 278
conduit d'essence 351
conduit de chauffage 213
conduit de la glande 76
conduit de raccordement 192
conduit lactifère 113
conduite à la terre 404
conduite d'alimentation 194
conduite d'eau 214
conduite d'eau chaude 197
conduite d'eau froide 197
conduite d'eau potable 434
conduite de gaz 434
conduite forcée 406, 407
conduite principale 196
condyle externe 99
condyle interne 99
cône 65, 119, 318, 429
cône adventif 28
cône d'ombre 4, 5
cône de pénombre 4, 5
cône femelle 65
cône mâle 65
confessionnal 446
configuration des continents 14
configuration du littoral 35
confluent 32
congélateur 164, 211, 438
congélateur coffre 211
Congo 20, 451
conifère 65
conifères, exemples 65
conjonctive 119
connecteur USB 333
connexion 470
conque 115
conserves 121
consigne automatique 374
console 283, 302
console centrale 354
console d'accoudoir 200
console d'orgue 305
console de jeu 471
consommateurs primaires 45
consommateurs secondaires 45
consommateurs tertiaires 45
contact 470
contact de terre 198
contact électrique 314
contact négatif 410, 411
contact positif 410, 411
conteneur 383
conteneur à boîtes métalliques 49
conteneur à papier 49
conteneur à verre 49
conteneurs de collecte sélective 49
continent 5, 33
continental humide, à été chaud 40
continental humide, à été frais 40
continents, configuration 14
contre-fer 229
contre-flèche 397
contrebasse 301
contrebasses 295
contrebassons 295
contrefort 29, 262, 284
contremarche 191
contrepoids 8, 287, 345, 397, 400, 401
contrevent 186
contrôle 330
contrôle : sélection de groupe 330
contrôle de la stéréophonie 326
contrôle de la température du corps 10
contrôle de la vapeur 208
contrôle de sécurité 391
contrôle de tonalité des aigus 303, 322, 325
contrôle de tonalité des graves 303, 322, 325
contrôle des passeports 391
contrôle douanier 391
contrôle du champ sonore 322
contrôle du plateau 319, 323
contrôle du séquenceur 310
contrôle du volume 310
contrôles de l'équipement de survie 10
contrôles du lecteur de cassette 326
contrôles du lecteur de disque compact 326
contrôleur 374
contrôleur à vent de synthétiseur 311
contrôleur technique 509
convection 415
convertisseur catalytique 351
convertisseur de couple 212
convoyeur 402
coordonnées terrestres 21
copropriété 512
coq 81
coque 60, 157, 277, 361, 367, 520, 523
coque inférieure 511
coque supérieure 511, 527
coquelicot 56
coquillage bivalve 73
coquillage bivalve, anatomie 73
coquillage bivalve, morphologie 73
coquillage univalve 73
coquillage univalve, morphologie 73
coquille 72, 73, 79, 200, 486, 507
coquille Saint-Jacques 157
coquilleur à beurre 169
cor anglais 306
cor d'harmonie 307
corbeau 80, 192, 282
corbeille 293
corbeille à papier 341
corbeille à pollen 68
corbeille suspendue 230
corde 301, 302, 498, 535
corde à sauter 500
corde de couloir 517
corde de faux départ 516
corde de tension 297
corde de tirage 219
corde vocale 105
cordeau 225, 231
cordeau à tracer 225
cordée 55
cordes 297, 304
cordes d'accompagnement 296
cordes de mélodie 296
cordes de timbre 308
cordier 297, 301
Cordillère australienne 15
cordillère des Andes 17
cordon 208, 209, 217, 235, 237, 326
cordon coulissant 249
cordon d'alimentation 270, 271
cordon d'alimentation 177, 227, 229, 269, 322
cordon d'alimentation en courant continu 336
cordon d'alimentation pivotant 269
cordon d'alimentation secteur 336
cordon de combiné 327
cordon de dunes 36
cordon littoral 35
coriandre 142
corne antérieure 109
corne de feu 455
corne de guidage de l'attelage 376
corne postérieure 109
cornée 119, 419
cornemuse 296
cornet à dés 469
cornet à pistons 295, 307
cornet inférieur 117
cornet moyen 117
cornet supérieur 117
corniche 183, 185, 202, 279
cornichon 128
corolle 56
corona radiata 112
corps 118, 180, 228, 270, 305, 306, 312, 421, 425, 471, 536
corps calleux 109
corps caverneux 111
corps célestes 2
corps cellulaire 110
corps ciliaire 119
corps de garde 282
corps de l'ongle 114
corps de piston 307
corps de pompe 460
corps du fornix 109
corps humain 92
corps vertébral 110
corps vitré 119
corpuscule de Meissner 114
corpuscule de Pacini 114
corpuscule de Ruffini 114
correction d'exposition 314
cors anglais 295
cors d'harmonie 295
corsage-culotte 255
corsaire 254
corset 259
corymbe 57
cosse 60
Costa Rica 448
costume 290
côte 33, 152, 153, 536
côté 293
côte axiale 73
côté cour 293
Côte d'Ivoire 451
côte flottante (2) 98
côté jardin 293
côte spiralée 73
côtelette 153
côtes 98
côtes levées de dos 152
côtes, exemples 35
coton hydrophile 461
coton-tige 461
cotret 412
cottage 150
cotylédon 53
cou 76, 93, 94, 95, 111
cou-de-pied 92
couche 260
couche antireflet 410
couche arable 54
couche basale 114
couche claire 114
couche cornée 114
couche d'ozone 37
couche de cendres 28
couche de laves 28
couche de Malpighi 114
couche de surface 342
couche fluorescente 199
couche granuleuse 114
couche imperméable 403
couche-culotte 260
couches de déchets 47
coude 83, 86, 93, 95, 273
coudes 146
coudière 486, 527
coulant 273
coulée de boue 31
coulée de lave 28
couleur 468
couleurs, synthèse 418
couleuvre rayée 77
coulis de tomate 140
coulisse 246
coulisse d'accord 307
coulisse du deuxième piston 3
coulisse du premier piston 30
coulisse du troisième piston 3
coulisses 292
couloir 472, 490, 495, 516
couloir ascendant 278
couloir de sécurité 440
couloir descendant 278
coulomb 426
coulommiers 151
coup de patin 514
coupé 347
coupe à mousseux 165
coupe d'un bulbe 54
coupe d'un follicule : anis éto
coupe d'un grain de blé 61
coupe d'un observatoire astr
7
coupe d'un raisin 59
coupe d'un télescope 9
coupe d'une capsule : pavot

upe d'une centrale hydroélectrique
407
upe d'une fraise 59
upe d'une framboise 59
upe d'une gousse : pois 60
upe d'une lunette astronomique 8
upe d'une molaire 101
upe d'une noisette 60
upe d'une noix 60
upe d'une orange 58
upe d'une pêche 57
upe d'une pomme 58
pe d'une route 342
pe d'une rue 434
pe d'une silique : moutarde 60
pe de l'atmosphère terrestre 37
pe de la croûte terrestre 26
pe de la nacelle 413
pe sagittale 111, 112
pe transversale du tronc 63
pe-bordures 233
pe-circuit d'urgence 368
pe-cuticules 265
pe-fil 217
pe-ongles 265
pe-œuf 173
pe-papier 339
pelle 207
pelle d'étanchéité 459
peret 169
le 509
ole du mihrab 447
ole du porche 447
ole rotative 7
s 490
122, 282, 447
de récréation 445
ant de convection 415
ant électrique, mesure 426
ant, adaptateur 336
oure 538
e 128
e à cou droit 129
e à cou tors 129
e spaghetti 129
eron 129
ette 128
nne 4, 83, 101, 286, 308, 424,
1
nne d'orientation 400
nnement 191
er des lecteurs 313
er électronique 335
ie d'entraînement 212
ie de distribution 360
ie de tige 511
ie de transmission 383
ie de ventilateur 350, 360
d'eau 32, 48
automobile 524
er d'évacuateur 406
490
le service droit 491
le service gauche 491
éronier latéral 97
piste 508
e 282
us 144
ussier 175
arrière 502
n carré 204
n d'air 262
de rembourrage 498
de tête 502
et en mousse 458
157, 167, 176, 177, 180,
533
à beurre 168
à bifteck 168
à découper 169
à désosser 169
à dessert 168
à filets de sole 169
à fromage 168
à huîtres 169
à jambon 169
à pain 169
à pamplemousse 169
à poisson 168
couteau à zester 169
couteau d'office 169
couteau de chef 169
couteau de cuisine 169
couteau de table 168
couteau électrique 177
couteau suisse 531
couteaux de cuisine, exemples 169
couteaux, exemples 168
couture 477, 478
couture d'assemblage 243
couture médiane 245
couturier 96
couvercle 174, 177, 178, 179, 180,
181, 196, 198, 211, 212, 215,
225, 315, 454, 533
couvercle de batterie 359
couvercle de culasse 350, 360
couvercle de propreté 210
couvercle de réservoir 196
couvercle inférieur 417
couvercle supérieur 417
couvert 167
couverture 204
couvre-filtre 459
couvre-oreiller 204
couvre-prises 320
Cowper, glande 111
cœur 58, 71, 73, 104, 105, 154,
192, 468, 492
crabe 158
cracker de seigle 145
cracker scandinave 145
craie 503
crampon 263, 478
crampon de fermeture 277
crampons interchangeables 480
cran 244, 246, 422, 473, 536
cran de réglage 222, 511
crâne 92
crâne d'enfant 100
crâne, vue latérale 100
crapaud commun 75
cratère 5, 28
cravate 245
crawl 517
crayon 312, 409
crayon à sourcils 266
crayon blanchisseur d'ongles 265
crayon contour des lèvres 266
crayon en plomb 312
crédit photographique 313
crémaillère 178, 211, 473
crème 150
crème aigre 150
crème épaisse 150
crémier 166
crénelé 55
crépis 279
cresson alénois 127
cresson de fontaine 127
crête 29, 33, 406, 418
creux 33, 167, 418
creux barométrique 39
crevasse 30
crevette 158
cric 356
cricket 478
crinière 83
criquet mélodieux 69
cristallin 119, 419
cristallisation 414
cristaux liquides 424
critique gastronomique 313
Croatie 450
croche 299
crochet 70, 73, 186, 217, 225, 364,
397, 423, 460, 502, 509
crochet à venin 76
crochet de levage 403
crochet de petit doigt 307
crochet de pouce 307
crochet du plateau 422
crochet pétrisseur 176
crocodile 77
crocus 56
croisée 284
croisée du transept 285
croisillon 467
croissant 5, 144
croix d'autel 446
croix de Saint-André 187
crosne 124
crosse 52, 302, 466, 534
crosse de fougère 125
crosse de gardien de but 507
crosse de joueur 506
crottin de Chavignol 150
croupe 83
croupion 78
croûte basaltique 26
croûte continentale 26
croûte de cuir 246
croûte granitique 26
croûte océanique 26
croûte terrestre 26, 27
croûte terrestre, coupe 26
cruche 532
crucifix 446
crustacés 71, 158
Cuba 448
cube 429
cubes d'agneau 153
cubes de bœuf 152
cubes de veau 152
cubiculum 280
cubital antérieur 96, 97
cubital postérieur 97
cubitus 98
cuiller 167, 531, 538
cuiller à café 168
cuiller à dessert 168
cuiller à égoutter 173
cuiller à glace 173
cuiller à goûter 173
cuiller à soda 168
cuiller à soupe 168
cuiller à thé 168
cuiller de table 168
cuiller parisienne 173
cuilleron 167
cuillers doseuses 171
cuillers, exemples 168
cuisine 120, 162, 164, 188, 280,
439, 445
cuisinière à gaz 210
cuisinière électrique 210
cuissard 486, 522
cuissarde 241
cuissardes 538
cuisse 83, 86, 93, 95, 111, 112
cuit-vapeur 175
cuit-vapeur électrique 179
cuivres, famille 295
cul-de-sac de Douglas 112
cul-de-sac dural 109
cul-de-sac vésico-utérin 112
culasse 306
culbuteur 360
culée 284, 344
culot 199, 318, 359, 534
culot à baïonnette 199
culot à broches 199
culot à vis 199
culotte 259, 500, 506
culotte à ruchés 260
cumin 138
cumulo-nimbus 42
cumulus 42
cupule 60
curcuma 138
cure-ongles 265
curiosité 25
curleuse 515
curling 515
curry 138
curseur 422
curseur vers la droite 331
curseur vers la gauche 331
curseur vers le bas 331
curseur vers le haut 331
cuve 211, 212, 214
cuvette 196, 210, 302
cuvette ramasse-gouttes 181
cyan 418
cycle de l'eau 45
cycle des saisons 38
cyclisme 522
cyclisme sur route 522
cyclomoteur 369
cyclone 43
cyclone tropical 43
cylindre 429
cylindre de roue 357
cylindre de rubis 420
cylindre enregistreur 27
cylindre réflecteur 420
cymbale charleston 308
cymbale inférieure 308
cymbale supérieure 308
cymbale suspendue 308
cymbales 295, 309
cymbalette 309
cyme bipare 57
cyme unipare 57
cytopharynx 66
cytoplasme 50, 66, 112
cytoprocte 66
cytostome 66

D

dalle 230
dalmatien 86
Dame 468, 470
dames 469
dameuse 512
damier 470
Danemark 450
danois 86
Danube 18
date d'expiration 441
datte 132
dauphin 90
dauphin, morphologie 90
dé 469
dé à poker 468
dé doubleur 469
dé régulier 468
déambulateur 466
déambulatoire 285
débarbouillette 267
débardeur 250, 261, 263
débit de tabac 436
début 331
décagone régulier 429
décapeur thermique 219
décapeuse 400
décapsuleur 170, 531
décharge 431
déchets industriels 47
déchets nucléaires 48
déchiquetage 49
déclencheur 314
déclivité du terrain 182
décomposeurs 45
décor 291
décorateur 291
découpe 244
découpe princesse 258
découpes d'agneau 153
découpes de bœuf 152
découpes de porc 153
découpes de veau 152
défauts de la vision 419
défense 484
défenseur droit 506
défenseur gauche 506
défilement 331
déflecteur 236, 237, 364
déflecteur d'air chaud 192
déflecteur de chaleur 199
déflecteur de copeaux 227
déflecteur de fumée 192
défonceuse 229, 398
déforestation 47
dégagement d'air des citernes 385
dégagement du piston 216
dégrafeuse 341
degré 428
degré Celsius 426
Deimos 2
déjections animales 48
délégués techniques 509
delta 32, 35
deltoïde 96
démarreur manuel 237
démêloir 268
demeure seigneuriale 282
demi d'ouverture 482
demi de coin droit 484
demi de coin gauche 484
demi de mêlée 482
demi de sûreté droit 484
demi de sûreté gauche 484
demi offensif 485
demi-cercle 428, 488
demi-court de service en double 495
demi-court de service en simple 495
demi-lune 273
demi-manche 169
demi-membraneux 97
demi-pause 299
demi-soupir 299
demi-tendineux 97
demi-volée 490
dendrite 110
dénominations des cyclones tropicaux
43
dénoyauteur 173
dent 74, 76, 167, 226, 227, 235,
270, 398, 400, 503, 509
dent de défonceuse 398
dent de godet 399
dent de sagesse 101
denté 55
dentifrice 272
dents 101
denture humaine 101
dénude-fil 217
déodorant 267
dépanneuse 364
départ 469
départ des 400 m (course, haies,
relais) 473
départ des télécabines 512
départ des télésièges 512
départ du 10 000 m et du relais 4 x
400 m 473
départ du 100 m (course et haies)
472
départ du 110 m haies 472
départ du 1500 m 473
départ du 200 m 472
départ du 5000 m 472
départ du 800 m 473
déplacement 418
déplacement des électrons, sens 416,
417
déplacement diagonal 470
déplacement en équerre 470
déplacement horizontal 470
déplacement vertical 470
déplacements, échecs 470
déporteur 392
dépression 39
dérailleur 522
dérailleur arrière 370, 372
dérailleur avant 370, 372
derby 240
dérive 393, 395, 519, 520
dérive aérienne 383
dériveur 520, 521
derme 114
dernier croissant 5
dernier quartier 5
dés 468
descente 511
descente de gouttière 182
désert 36, 40, 44
désert d'Atacama 17
désert de Gobi 19
désert de pierres 36
désert de sable 36
désert du Kalahari 20
désert du Namib 20
désert du Sahara 20
déshabillé 256
desserte 202
dessous 292
destination 374
destructeur de documents 341
détecteur d'impact primaire 354
détecteur de fumée 454
détecteur de mouvement 286
détecteur de sécurité 354
détente 534
détroit 24
détroit de Bass 15
détroit de Béring 16
détroit de Cook 15

INDEX FRANÇAIS

détroit de Drake 15, 17
détroit de Gibraltar 18
détroit de Torres 15
deuxième but 474
deuxième espace 489
deuxième joueuse 515
deuxième ligne 482
deuxième molaire 101
deuxième prémolaire 101
deuxième radial externe 97
deuxième-but 474
devant 244, 245
devant d'autel 446
déverrouillage de l'objectif 314
déversement d'hydrocarbures 48
dévidoir 236
dévidoir de ruban adhésif 341
dévidoir pistolet 341
dévidoir sur roues 236
devise 441
diable 175, 396
diamètre 428
diaphragme 105
dièse 299
diesel-navire 405
différence de potentiel électrique, mesure 426
différentiel 351
diffuseur 290
diffusion d'information 335
dinde 155
dindon 81
diode 411
Dioné 3
directeur artistique 290
directeur de course 522
directeur de la photographie 291
direction de La Mecque 447
direction du vent 39
direction et force du vent 39
discontinuité de Gutenberg 26
discontinuité de Mohorovicic 26
disjoncteur 407
dispositif anti-bascule 467
dispositif antidébordement 214
dispositif de blocage 219
dispositif de fermeture 535
dispositif de poussée 312
dispositif de remorquage 364
dispositifs de contact 198
disposition des informations d'une station 39
disquaire 436
disque 6, 333, 357, 472, 501
disque abrasif 229
disque compact 326
disque de papier-diagramme 365
disque dur amovible 333
disque numérique polyvalent (DVD) 319
disques 177
disquette 333
distillation sous vide 405
distributeur d'essence 346
distributeur de billets 437, 442
distributeur de boissons 346, 463
distributeur de correspondances 379
distributeur de détergent 214
distributeur de glaçons 164, 346
distributeur de lames 271
distributeur de produit de rinçage 214
distributeur de trombones 341
distribution de la végétation 44
ditali 146
division 337, 427
division du noyau 415
division territoriale 23
divisions cartographiques 22
dix 427
Dix commandements 447
djembé 297
Djibouti 451
Dniepr 18
do 298
dodécagone régulier 429
doigt 75, 79, 82, 114, 243, 477
doigt de jupe 383
doigt externe 78
doigt interne 78
doigt lobé 79
doigt médian 78
doigt palmé 75, 79
doigt postérieur 78
doigt préhensile 91
doigtier 339
doline 31
dolique à œil noir 130
dolique asperge 130
dolique d'Égypte 130
doliques 130
dollar 440
domaine de premier niveau 334
domaine de second niveau 334
domaine skiable 512
Dominique 449
domino d'accouplement 305
dominos 468
donjon 282
dorade 159
dormant 186, 202
dormeuse de croissance 260
dormeuse-couverture 261
dorsale du Pacifique Est 34
dorsale médio-atlantique 34
dorsale médio-indienne 34
dorsale médio-océanique 33
dorsale Pacifique-Antarctique 34
dorsale Sud-Est-indienne 34
dorsale Sud-Ouest-indienne 34
dorsales océaniques 34
dos 78, 83, 86, 93, 95, 115, 167, 169, 226, 244
dos d'un gant 243
dos de la langue 118
dos du nez 117
dossard 473
dosseret 210, 212, 213
dossier 201, 205, 353, 369, 467, 523
dossier inclinable 460
dossier suspendu 340
dossière 76
double 468
double barre oblique 334
double bémol 299
double boutonnage 248
double croche 299
double dièse 299
double paire 468
double platine cassette 325
double toit 528, 529
double-blanc 468
double-six 468
doublement denté 55
doublure 240, 244, 245, 262, 274, 509
douche 189, 439, 464
douchette 195, 197
Douglas, cul-de-sac 112
douille 534
douille de lampe 199
douille de plastique 534
douilles, jeu 223
douve 282
dragonne 277, 320, 510, 514
drap 204
drap de bain 267
drap-housse 204
drapeau 482
drapeau amovible 504
drapeau de centre 480
drapeau de coin 481
drapeau de l'Union européenne 441
drapeaux 448
droit antérieur de la cuisse 96
droit interne 97
dromadaire 85
drumlin 29
drupéole 59
duffle-coat 249
dune 35
dune complexe 36
dune en croissant 36
dune parabolique 36
dunes longitudinales 36
dunes transversales 36
dunes, exemples 36
duo 300
duodénum 106
dure-mère 109, 110
durian 137
durite de radiateur 358
dyke 28
dynamo 370

E

eau 402
eau de fonte 30
eau de parfum 267
eau de toilette 267
eau dentifrice 272
eau des nuages 48
eau oxygénée 461
eaux usées 48
éboulement 31
ébrancheur 234
ébrasement 285
écaille 54, 74, 76, 79
écailles de cyprès 65
écailleur 531
écartement des électrodes 359
échalote 124
échancrure 301
échancrure de la conque 115
échangeur 431
échangeur en losange 342
échangeur en trèfle 342, 343
échangeur en trompette 342
échangeurs, exemples 342
échantillonneur 310
échappement 330
écharpe 187
échauguette 282
échecs 470
échecs, mouvements 470
échelle 184, 288, 361, 401, 404, 469, 533
échelle Celsius 424
échelle coulissante 219
échelle d'onglet 226
échelle de profondeur 227
échelle de tête 455
échelle des altitudes 37
échelle des températures 37
échelle Fahrenheit 424
échelle graduée 422, 423
échelles 219
échelon 219
échenilloir-élagueur 234
échinodermes 66
échiquier 470
éclair 41
éclairage 199, 269, 380
éclairage de sécurité 457
éclairage/clignotant 354
éclipse annulaire 4
éclipse de Lune 5
éclipse de Soleil 4
éclipse partielle 4, 5
éclipse totale 4, 5
éclipses de Lune, types 5
éclipses de Soleil, types 4
éclisse 301, 302
écluse 381
école 444
école de ski 512
économie 441
écorce 58, 63
écoulement souterrain 45
écoute de foc 520
écoute de grand-voile 520
écouteur 324
écouteurs 325, 326
écoutille 13
écoutille d'accès 12
écran 318, 326, 329, 336, 338, 346, 439, 442, 443, 471, 479
écran à cristaux liquides 315, 320, 326, 327
écran d'affichage 328
écran de contrôle 314
écran de l'ordinateur 10
écran de projection 294
écran de protection 474
écran protecteur 7
écran tactile 337
écrevisse 158
écritoire 275
écriture, instruments 312
écrou 222, 223
écrou à collet 197
écrou à oreilles 223
écrou borgne 223
écrou de blocage 536, 537
écrou de bonde 197
écrou de fixation 197
écrou de la lame 227
écrou de montage 535
écrou du porte-outil 229
écrou hexagonal 223, 359
écrous 223
écubier 383, 387
écueil 35
écume 33
écumoire 173
écureuil 82
écusson 73, 186, 477
édicule 378
édifice à bureaux 432, 435
édifice public 25
éditorial 313
édredon 204
éducation 444
effacement arrière : effacement 331
effacement de mémoire 337
effacement partiel 337
effacement total 337
effet de serre 46
effet de serre naturel 46
effigie 441
effluent 32
égal ou plus grand que 427
égal ou plus petit que 427
égale 427
égale à peu près 427
églefin 161
église 433, 446
égout 434
égout collecteur 434
Égypte 451
éjecteur de fouets 176
El Salvador 448
élan 85
élastique 204
électricien 291
électricité 198
électricité : outils 217
électrode centrale 359
électrode de masse 359
électron 414
électronique 417
élément chauffant 213, 214, 218
élément tubulaire 210
éléments d'architecture 286
éléments de la maison 185
éléphant 85
élevage intensif 46, 47
élévateur 400
élévateur pour fauteuils roulants 363
élévation 182
élévation de la tension 402, 408, 413
élève 444
élevon 13
émail 101
emballage 162
embase 473, 511
embase de plat de dos 200
emblème d'équipe 506
embouchure 307
embout 219, 221, 506, 536
embout auriculaire 460
embout buccal 467
embout de baleine 273
embout de caoutchouc 466
embout de protection 459
embout de vissage 228
embout isolant 269
embout Luer Lock 460
embrasse 466
embrayage 350
émerillon 535, 538
émetteur-récepteur radar 457
Émirats arabes unis 452
émission d'acide nitrique 48
émission d'acide sulfurique 48
émission d'oxyde d'azote 48
émission de dioxyde de soufre 48
émission de gaz polluants 47
émissole 158
emmanchure 247
emmarchement 191
emmenthal 151
empennage 393, 471, 495
empiècement 245, 249, 255
emplacement 182
emplacement de la statue 279
emporte-pièces 172
en équilibre 518
en-but 483
encadrement 192
enceinte acoustique 324, 325
enceinte ambiophonique 321
enceinte centrale 321
enceinte de confinement 408, 40
enceinte principale 321
enceintes d'extrêmes graves 321
encensoir 446
enclos 122
enclume 116
encoignure 203
encolure 83, 247
encolure en V 244, 250
encolure ras-de-cou 260
encre 312
encre à couleur changeante 441
endive 127
endocarde 104
endocarpe 57, 58
énergie calorifique 46
énergie éolienne 412, 413
énergie fossile 402
énergie géothermique 402
énergie nucléaire 408
énergie solaire 54, 410
énergie thermique 402
énergie, mesure 426
énergies 402
enfouissement 49
engrenage horaire 7
enjoliveur 349
ennéagone régulier 429
enregistrement 319, 323
enregistrement des bagages 374
enregistrement sismographique
enregistreur de DVD vidéo 319
enseignant 444
enseigne directionnelle 379
enseigne extérieure 378
ensemble du chevalet 303
ensemble oreillette/microphone
ensemble vide 427
entablement 185, 279
entier 55
entonnoir 72, 171, 177, 180
entrainement de la turbine par l
vapeur 408
entrainement du rotor de l'altern
408
entraineur 489, 498, 507
entraineur adjoint 489, 507
entraineurs 509
entre-nœud 53
entredent 167
entrée 343, 396
entrée d'air 395
entrée d'air du ventilateur 383
entrée de courant 199
entrée de garage 183
entrée de la pyramide 278
entrée des clients 438
entrée des marchandises 435
entrée des originaux 328
entrée du caloporteur 410
entrée du personnel 438, 445
entrée du public 278
entrée principale 188, 435, 4
entrées des acteurs 278
entrejambe 202, 247
entrejambe pressionné 260, 2
entreposage des produits cong
121
entrepôt 430
entrepôt frigorifique 381
entreprise 335
entreprise de distribution/ven
entretoise 219, 396, 412
enveloppe 477, 478, 505
enveloppe extérieure 7
enveloppe intérieure 7
enveloppe matelassée 339
environnement 44

INDEX FRANÇAIS

nvironnement naturel 504
olienne à axe horizontal 413
olienne à axe vertical 412
oliennes et production d'électricité 412
paisseur, mesure 425
pandage d'engrais 47
paule 83, 86, 92, 94, 492, 536
paulé-jeté 500
paulement 169, 223
aulière 486
peautre 143
eire 70
erlan 159
eron 308
i 57, 61
i, blé 61
i, maïs 61
i, millet 61
, orge 61
i, seigle 61
carpe 57, 58, 59
céa 65
centre 27
cerie fine 120
ces 138
ces à marinade 139
condyle 99
derme 114
didyme 111
glotte 105, 118
nard 127
ne de l'omoplate 99
ne nasale antérieure 100
ngle à bigoudi 268
ngle à cheveux 268
hyse 109
rochlée 99
cheur 169
nge à récurer 215
nge de mer 267
nge synthétique 266
nge végétale 267
uves, ski alpin 511
sette 538
teur 448
teur 17, 20, 21, 22, 43
rre 225
librage des haut-parleurs 322
noxe d'automne 38
noxe de printemps 38
pe au champ 479
pe médicale 499
pement 472
pement de survie 10
pement de survie, contrôles 10
pement divers 231
pement du tableau de bord 457
aut à 427
e 64

on 4
ée 451
eau 219
eaux 219
er 184, 188, 191, 283, 293,
4, 345, 378, 404, 412, 439,
3
er de la mezzanine 189
er mécanique 294, 378, 435
ers 283
got 72, 157
got, morphologie 72
in 241
in-sandale 241
e 330
e épidural 110
e insécable 330
eur de câbles 535
on 159
lle 242
e 449
au 261
e 405
e lourde 405
527
avant 401
se à salade 171
glace 348, 355
Est 23
est identique à 427
Est Nord-Est 23
Est Sud-Est 23
estomac 73, 103, 106
estomac cardiaque 71
estomac pylorique 71
Estonie 450
estrade 283, 444
estragon 142
estuaire 24, 35
esturgeon 158
étable 122
établi étau 224
établissement d'enseignement 335
établissement scolaire 433
étage 182, 189, 412
étai avant 520
étamine 56, 58
étang 504
étapes de maturation 62
État 23
État de la cité du Vatican 450
état présent du temps 39
états de la matière 414
États-Unis d'Amérique 448
étau 224
été 38
Éthiopie 451
étiquette 423
étiquettes autocollantes 340
étoile de David 447
étoile de freinage 537
étoile filante 37
étourneau 80
étranglement 424, 499
étrave 384, 520
être humain 92
étrésillon 187
étrier 116, 198, 357, 366
étui 265, 337, 531
étui à lentilles 272
étui à lunettes 275
étui à menottes 456
étui à munitions 456
étui à pistolet 456
étui de cuir 533
étui pour gants de latex 456
Eurasie 14
euro 440
Europe 2, 14, 18, 34, 449
Eutelsat 316
euthynterie 279
évacuateur 406
évaporation 45
évent 90, 312
évent de pignon 182
évier 164, 197
évier double 194
évier-broyeur 197
évolution de la pression 39
Ex-République yougoslave de Macédoine 450
ex-voto 446
examen psychiatrique 462
exemples d'algues 51
exemples d'amphibiens 75
exemples d'angles 428
exemples d'arachnides 70
exemples d'arbres feuillus 64
exemples d'avions 394
exemples d'échangeurs 342
exemples d'insectes 69
exemples d'oiseaux 80
exemples d'unités monétaires 440
exemples de bateaux et d'embarcations 382
exemples de becs 79
exemples de bicyclettes 373
exemples de branchement 197
exemples de camions 364
exemples de carrosseries 347
exemples de chaises 201
exemples de clous 220
exemples de conifères 65
exemples de corsages 255
exemples de côtes 35
exemples de couteaux 168
exemples de couteaux de cuisine 169
exemples de cuillers 168
exemples de dunes 36
exemples de fauteuils 200
exemples de fenêtres 287
exemples de feuilles 65
exemples de fleurs 56
exemples de fougères 52
exemples de fourchettes 168
exemples de groupes instrumentaux 300
exemples de jupes 253
exemples de lichens 50
exemples de lunettes 273
exemples de mammifères carnivores 88
exemples de mammifères lagomorphes 82
exemples de mammifères marins 90
exemples de mammifères ongulés 84
exemples de mammifères primates 91
exemples de mammifères rongeurs 82
exemples de mèches et de forets 228
exemples de motos 369
exemples de mousses 51
exemples de pantalons 254
exemples de pattes 79
exemples de plis 253
exemples de pneus 358
exemples de pointes 221
exemples de portes 286
exemples de prises 499
exemples de reptiles 77
exemples de robes 252
exemples de sacs de couchage 530
exemples de sauts 509
exemples de skis 510
exemples de tables 202
exemples de tentes 528
exemples de têtes 221
exemples de volcans 28
exemples de wagons 377
exosphère 37
expandeur 310
expédition du fret 391
extenseur 500
extenseur commun des doigts 97
extenseur commun des orteils 96
extérieur d'une maison 182
extincteur 454, 457
extrait de vanille 140
eye-liner liquide 266

F

fa 298
façade 285
face 91, 167, 493, 505
face antérieure 92, 94, 96
face postérieure 93, 95, 97
facteur rhésus négatif 426
facteur rhésus positif 426
factorielle 427
facule 4
faille 27
faîne 133
faisan 81, 154
faisceau bleu 318
faisceau d'électrons 318
faisceau laser 420
faisceau rouge 318
faisceau vert 318
faîtage 187
faîteau 283
faitout 175, 531
faits divers 313
falaise 5, 29, 35
falaise côtière 35
Fallope, trompe 112
famille des bois 295
famille des cuivres 295
famille du violon 295, 301
fanon 83
fard à joues en poudre 266
farine d'avoine 144
farine de blé complet 144
farine de maïs 144
farine et semoule 144
farine non blanchie 144
farine tout usage 144
fart 514
faucille 234
faucon 81
fausse côte (3) 99
fausse oronge 52
fausse poche 251
fausse-équerre 225
fauteuil 200, 293, 294, 444
fauteuil à bascule 200
fauteuil club 200
fauteuil de repos 464
fauteuil du réalisateur 291
fauteuil metteur en scène 200
fauteuil roulant 467
fauteuil Wassily 200
fauteuil-sac 201
fauteuils des acteurs 290
fauteuils, exemples 200
faux bourdon 68
Fédération de Russie 450
feijoa 137
femelle 426
femme 94
fémur 98
fenêtre 186, 189, 243, 361, 380, 519
fenêtre à guillotine 287
fenêtre à jalousies 287
fenêtre à l'anglaise 287
fenêtre à la française 287
fenêtre basculante 287
fenêtre coulissante 287
fenêtre de lecture 333
fenêtre de sous-sol 183
fenêtre en accordéon 287
fenêtre moustiquaire 528
fenêtre panoramique 435
fenêtre pivotante 287
fenêtres, exemples 287
fenil 122
fennec 88
fenouil 125
fente 178, 221, 274
fente de dépôt 442
fente de mise à jour du livret bancaire 442
fente de relevé d'opération 442
fente du lecteur de carte 346, 442, 443
fente latérale 244
fente médiane 244
fente pour carte PC 336
fentes branchiales 74
fentes d'aération 336
fenugrec 138
fer 229, 505
fer à friser 269
fer à souder 218
fer à vapeur 208
fer droit 505
ferme 122
fermeture à glissière 249, 261, 265, 277, 528
fermeture du soufflet 296
fermeture sous patte 261
fermeture Velcro® 260
fermoir 274, 275
ferret 240, 262, 273
ferrure 277
ferrure d'attelage 356
fertilisation des sols 47
fesse 93, 95, 111, 112
fettucine 146
feu antibrouillard 352, 364
feu anticollision 392
feu arrière 367, 368, 370
feu clignotant 352
feu clignotant arrière 367, 368
feu clignotant avant 366, 368
feu de circulation 434
feu de croisement 352
feu de freinage 352
feu de gabarit 364, 365
feu de navigation 383, 393
feu de plaque 352
feu de position 352, 376, 395
feu de recul 352
feu de route 352
feu de tête de mât 383
feu jaune 434
feu pour piétons 434
feu rouge 434
feu rouge arrière 352
feu vert 434
feuillage 63
feuille 51, 53, 54, 55, 61, 125
feuille d'acanthe 200
feuille de vigne 62, 126
feuille, bord 55
feuille, structure 55
feuilles composées 55
feuilles simples 55
feuilles, exemples 65
feuillet adhésif 338
feuillets 274
feuillets intercalaires 339
feutre d'étouffoir 304
feux arrière 352
feux avant 352
feux intermittents 362
fèves 130
fibre musculaire 110
fibre nerveuse 114
fibres 215
fiche 228, 326
fiche américaine 198
fiche d'alimentation 337
fiche européenne 198
fiche pour jack 324
fiche, adaptateur 198, 271
fichier 334
fichier rotatif 338
Fidji 453
figue 137
figue de Barbarie 137
fil 417
fil d'attache 70
fil de nylon 237
fil de sécurité 441
fil dentaire 272
filament 199
file d'attente 443
filet 56, 205, 221, 301, 302, 313, 487, 489, 491, 493, 495
filet de bœuf 152
filière 70
filigrane 441
filoir d'écoute 521
filtre 178, 184, 210
filtre à air 235, 350, 398
filtre à charpie 212, 213
filtre de polarisation 314
filum terminal 109
fin 331
finance 441
fines herbes 142
Finlande 450
fission de l'uranium 408
fission nucléaire 415
fixation 473, 513, 514
fixation à butée avant 514
fixation de sécurité 510, 511
fjords 35
flacon 267
flageolet 131
flamant 81
flamme 415
flanc 78, 83, 358
fléau 422
fléau arrière 422
fléau avant 422
flèche 285, 397, 399, 400, 469, 503
flèche de transept 284
flèche littorale 35
flèche télescopique 397, 455
fléchette 471
flétan 161
fleur 53, 56
fleur, structure 56
fleuriste 437
fleurs, exemples 56
fleuve 24, 25, 32
flexible 195, 197
flexible d'injection de boue 403
flexible de distribution 346
flip 509
floraison 62
flotteur 196, 394, 519, 538

flûte à champagne 165
flûte de Pan 297
flûte traversière 306
flûtes 295
foc 520
foie 103, 106, 154
foie gras 156
follicule 60, 114
follicule, coupe 60
fonctions système 310
fond 526
fond d'yeux 167
fond de l'océan 26
fond de l'océan 33
fond de protection 471
fond de robe 258
fond de teint liquide 266
fond de tour 405
fondation de pylône 344
fondation inférieure 342
fondation supérieure 342
fongicide 47
fontaine des ablutions 447
fontanelle antérieure 100
fontanelle mastoïdienne 100
fontanelle postérieure 100
fontanelle sphénoïdale 100
fonts baptismaux 446
football 480
football américain 484
football américain, protection 486
footballeur 480, 486
foramen apical 101
foramen cæcum 118
force du vent 39
force, mesure 426
forêt 29
forêt boréale 44
forêt de conifères 44
forêt de feuillus 44
foret de maçonnerie 228
foret hélicoïdal 228
forêt mixte 44
forêt tempérée 44
forêt tropicale 44
forêt tropicale humide 44
format du fichier 334
formation de jazz 300
formes géométriques 428
formes pharmaceutiques des médicaments 467
forte pluie 43
forum 335
fossé 342
fosse à plonger 184
fosse abyssale 33
fosse d'orchestre 292
fosse de Java 34
fosse de Porto Rico 34
fosse de sable 504
fosse des Aléoutiennes 34
fosse des Kouriles 34
fosse des Mariannes 34
fosse des Philippines 34
fosse des Ryukyu 34
fosse des Tonga-Kermadec 34
fosse du Japon 34
fosse Pérou-Chili 34
fosse septique 48
fosses nasales 117
fosses océaniques 34
fossette 76
fossette de l'anthélix 115
Fou 470
fouet 172, 176
fouet à fil 176
fouet en spirale 176
fouet quatre pales 176
fouets 176
fougère 52
fougère arborescente 52
fougère nid d'oiseau 52
fougère, structure 52
fouine 88
four 164, 210
four à micro-ondes 164, 178
four tubulaire 405
fourche 8, 371, 522, 525
fourche à bêcher 233
fourche à fleurs 232
fourche avant 522
fourche télescopique 369
fourche télescopique hydraulique 366
fourches 396
fourchette 167, 243, 531
fourchette à découper 169
fourchette à dessert 168
fourchette à fondue 168
fourchette à huîtres 168
fourchette à poisson 168
fourchette à salade 168
fourchette de table 168
fourchettes, exemples 168
fourgon-pompe 455
fourgonnette 347
fourmi 69
fournisseur de services Internet 335
fourreau 519
fourreau de la langue 76
fovéa 119
foyer 27, 419
foyer Cassegrain 7
foyer coudé 7
foyer des élèves 445
foyer primaire 7
foyer, accessoires 193
foyers 293
fraction 427
fraise 132
fraise, coupe 59
framboise 132
framboise, coupe 59
France 449
frappeur 475, 476
frein 501, 511, 522, 536
frein à disque 350, 357, 366, 525
frein à main 350
frein à tambour 357
frein arrière 370
frein avant 371
frein d'urgence 380
frein de chaîne 235
frein de talon 527
frein hydraulique à disque 522
freins 357
frelon 69
fréquence, mesure 426
fresque 280
frette 302, 303
frise 185, 202, 279, 293
frises 292
friteuse 178
fromage à la crème 150
fromages à pâte molle 151
fromages à pâte persillée 151
fromages à pâte pressée 151
fromages de chèvre 150
fromages frais 150
fronce 255
fronde 51, 52
front 78, 92
frontal 96, 98, 100
frontière 23
fronton 279
frottoir 218
fruit charnu 59
fruit charnu : agrume 58
fruit charnu à noyau 57
fruit charnu à pépins 58
fruit de la Passion 136
fruits 57, 120, 132
fruits à noyau 132
fruits à pépins 133
fruits secs 60, 133
fruits tropicaux 136
fumerolle 28
funicule 59, 60
furet de dégorgement 216
fuseau 254
fusée à propergol solide 12
fusée éclairante 457
fuselage 393
fusible 198, 411
fusil 169
fusil (canon lisse) 534
fusilli 146
fusion 414
fût 63, 207, 221, 308, 471, 534
futon 204

G

gâble 285
Gabon 451
gâchette 235, 332, 454
gâchette de sécurité 235
gaffe 454
Gai lon 127
gaine 55, 259, 417, 533
gaine d'air frais 345
gaine d'air vicié 345
gaine de myéline 110
gaine de Schwann 110
gaine-culotte 259
galaxie 6
galerie 285, 412
galerie de dérivation 406
galerie de liaison 345
galerie de visite 407
galerie marchande 435
galerie sèche 31
galet 332
galets tendeurs 372
galettes de riz 147
galon 238
galon d'ornement 260
galop 83
Gambie 451
gamme 298
ganache 83
ganglion cérébropleural 73
ganglion du tronc sympathique 109
ganglion spinal 109, 110
ganglion viscéral 73
ganse 531
gant 10, 477, 478, 498, 506, 508, 513, 514, 522, 525
gant à crispin 243
gant court 243
gant de conduite 243
gant de crin 267
gant de frappeur 476
gant de golf 505
gant de receveur 476
gant de ski 510
gant de softball 477
gant de toilette 267
gant en latex 460
gant long 243
gant saxe 243
gants 243
gants d'homme 243
gants de boxe 498
gants de femme 243
gants de gardien de but 480
gants de jardinage 232
Ganymède 2
garage 182, 345
garam masala 139
garant 240
garde de clé 306
garde de culasse 306
garde droit 485
garde gauche 485
garde-boue 370
garde-boue arrière 369
garde-boue avant 366
garde-corps 219, 344, 377
garde-fou 189
garde-manger 164, 188
garde-robe 189
gardien de but 481, 506, 507
gardien de guichet 479
gare 25, 375, 430, 432
gare de marchandises 375
gare de triage 430
gare de voyageurs 374, 375
gare maritime 381
gare routière 432
garniture 277
garniture de frein 357
garrot 83, 86
gaufrier-gril 178
gaz 403, 405, 414
gaz à effet de serre 46
gaz inerte 199
gazole 405
gazon 230, 492
geai 80
gélule 467
gencive 101, 116
générateur de vapeur 402
genou 83, 86, 92, 94
genouillère 476, 486, 500, 526, 527
géographie 14
géologie 26
géométrie 428
Géorgie 452
géothermie 402
gerboise 82
germe 61, 79
germes de soja 131
germination 53
geyser 28
Ghana 451
ghee 150
gibbeuse croissante 5
gibbeuse décroissante 5
gibbon 91
gibier 154
gicleur de lave-glace 348
gicleurs 408
gilet 244, 255
gilet de laine 250
gingembre 139
girafe 85
giron 191
girouette 413, 520
gisement de pétrole 403
givre 41
glace 45, 349, 352
glace de custode 349
glacier 30, 32, 44
glacier suspendu 30
glacière 532
glacis précontinental 33
gland 111
glande à venin 76
glande de Cowper 111
glande digestive 71, 73
glande lacrymale 119
glande mammaire 113
glande salivaire 118
glande sébacée 114
glande sudoripare apocrine 114
glande sudoripare eccrine 114
glande surrénale 107
glandes salivaires 106
glissement de terrain 31
glissière 214
glissière d'ajustement 324
glissière d'auvent 361
glissière de fixation 420
glissoir 240
globe 529
globe oculaire 75, 119
globe terrestre 444
globule blanc 104
globule rouge 104
glotte 76
glucose 54
gnocchi 146
go 470
godet 399
godet à poussière 208
godet de beurre 163
godet de lait/crème 163
godet rétro 399, 400
golf 504
golfe 24
golfe d'Aden 19, 20
golfe d'Alaska 16
golfe d'Oman 19
golfe de Botnie 18
golfe de Californie 16
golfe de Carpentarie 15
golfe de Guinée 20
golfe de Panama 17
golfe du Bengale 19
golfe du Mexique 16
golfe Persique 19
Golgi 50, 66
gombo 128
gomme 341
gonade 73
gond 185, 202
gondole 121
gonfleur 530
gonfleur-dégonfleur 530
gong 295, 309
gorge 31, 32, 78, 224, 538
gorgonzola 151
gorille 91
gorille, morphologie 91
gouffre 31
goujon 357
goujure 228
goulot de remplissage 351
goupille 454
gour 31
gourde 532
gourmand 62
gourmette 264
gourmette d'identité 264
gousse, coupe 60
gousset de latte 519, 520
goût 116
gouttelette lipidique 50
gouttes ophtalmiques lubrifiantes 2
gouttière 182, 207, 349
gouvernail 13, 384, 386, 412, 52
gouverne de direction 393
gouverne de profondeur 393
goyave 137
gradateur 198
gradins 278, 281
gradins mobiles 444
graduation 225, 424, 425, 460,
graduation de la règle 425
graduation du vernier 425
grain 61
grain d'amidon 50
grain de blé, coupe 61
graine 53, 57, 58, 59, 60
graine de soja 131
graines de pavot 139
grains de café torréfiés 148
grains de café verts 148
graisses 405
grand adducteur 97
Grand Canyon 16
grand complexus 97
Grand Désert de Sable 15
Grand Désert Victoria 15
grand dorsal 97
grand droit de l'abdomen 96
grand duc d'Amérique 81
grand fauchage extérieur 499
grand fauchage intérieur 499
grand fessier 97
grand oblique de l'abdomen 96,
grand palmaire 96
grand pectoral 96
grand rond 97
grand trochanter 99
grand-voile 520
Grande Baie australienne 15
grande échelle 455
grande galerie 278
grande lame 531
grande lèvre 112, 113
grande roussette 158
grande sauterelle verte 69
grande sus-alaire 78
grande ville 23
grandes lignes 375
Grands Lacs 16
grange 122
granulation 4
grappe 57
grappe de combustible 409
grappe de raisin 62
grappe, sarrasin 61
grasset 83
gratte-ongles 265
grattoir 219
graveur de disque compact 32
graveur de DVD 333
grébiche 274
Grèce 450
grelots 309
Grenade 449
grenade 136
grenier 182, 189

;renouille 75
renouille des bois 75
renouille léopard 75
renouille rousse 75
renouille, morphologie 75
renouillère 260
résil 41
riffe 71, 76, 82
iffe à fleurs 232
iffe porte-accessoires 314
il barbecue 179
il électrique 179
il pliant 533
illage de protection 217
ille 174, 210, 271, 279, 296, 318, 358, 407, 476
lle d'aération 214, 380
lle d'aspiration 270
lle d'éclairage 291
lle d'entrée d'air 367
lle d'extrémité 409
lle de chauffage 380
lle de départ 524
lle de sécurité 442
le de sortie d'air 270
le de ventilation 209
le des programmes de télévision 313
le métallique conductrice 410
le stabilisatrice 529
le-pain 178
enland 16
ndin 159
s intestin 106
s sel 141
seille à grappes 132
seille à maquereau 132
sse caisse 295, 308
te 31, 35
pe électropompe 357
pe frigorifique 365
pe turbo-alternateur 402, 407
pes instrumentaux, exemples 300
à flèche 381
à tour 397
sur ponton 381
sur porteur 397
s 397
petto 299
ère 151
emala 448
ard 89
e 69
ière 259
et 443, 479
et automatique bancaire 442, 43
et commercial 443
et de nuit 443
et de vente des billets 378
178, 226, 333
des températures 208
parallèle 227
-bande 341
-chaine 235, 372
-ligne 537
-papier 328
s de classement 340
n 237, 371, 501, 523, 534
n surélevé 522
arde 297
ant 519
eau 384
e 451
e équatoriale 451
e-Bissau 451
e acoustique 302
e basse 303
e électrique 303
berg, discontinuité 26
a 448
33
se 386, 444
stique 496
are 455

H

habilleur 290
habitacle 12, 525
habitation 122
hache 234, 454
hachette 533
hachoir 170
hackle 536
haie 183, 230
Haïti 448
halebas 520
hall 435, 439
hall d'entrée 188
hall public 390
halo 6
halte-garderie 437
haltère court 500
haltère long 500, 501
haltérophilie 500
hameçon 536, 538
hameçon monté 538
hameçon triple 538
hampe 538
hamster 82
hanche 93, 95
hanche ailée 499
hangar 122, 389
hangar de transit 381
hanneton 69
haptère 51
hareng 159
haricot adzuki 131
haricot d'Espagne 131
haricot de Lima 131
haricot jaune 131
haricot mungo 131
haricot mungo à grain noir 131
haricot noir 131
haricot pinto 131
haricot romain 131
haricot rouge 131
haricot vert 131
haricots 131
harissa 141
harmonica 296
harpe 302
harpes 295
hastée 55
hauban 370, 394, 412, 520, 528
hausse 301, 534
haut-de-forme 238
haut-parleur 294, 320, 326, 328, 336, 455
haut-parleur d'aigus 324
haut-parleur de graves 324
haut-parleur de médiums 324
hautbois 295, 306
hauteur de la vague 33
hauteur de marche 191
hébergement 512
hélice 384, 386, 387, 429
hélice arrière 384
hélice bipale 394
hélice d'étrave 384
hélice de propulsion 383
hélice tripale 394
hélicoptère 395
hélix 115
hémisphère 429
hémisphère austral 21
hémisphère boréal 21
hémisphère occidental 21
hémisphère oriental 21
hémisphères 21
hendécagone régulier 429
heptagone régulier 429
herbe longue 504
herbicide 47
herbivores 45
héron 80
herse 292
hertz 426
hétérotrophes 45
hêtre 64
hexagone régulier 429
hijiki 123
hile du rein 107
Himalaya 19
hippopotame 85
hirondelle 80
hiver 38
hockey sur glace 506
hockeyeur 506
homard 71, 158
homard, anatomie 71
homard, morphologie 71
homme 92
Honduras 448
Hongrie 450
hôpital 433, 462
horloge programmatrice 178, 210
hors-bord 385
hôtel 432, 439, 512
hôtel de ville 432
hotte 164, 192, 210
houe 233
hoummos 140
houppette 266
houppier 63
housse à vêtements 277
housse d'oreiller 204
housse pour automobile 356
Hubble, télescope spatial 7, 37
hublot 178, 179, 210, 386, 392
hublot d'atterrissage 395
hublot d'observation 13
huile d'arachide 149
huile d'olive 149
huile de maïs 149
huile de sésame 149
huile de tournesol 149
huiles 149
huiles lubrifiantes 405
huitième de soupir 299
huître creuse du Pacifique 157
huître plate 157
huméro-stylo-radial 96
humérus 98
humeur aqueuse 119
hutte 288
hydravion à flotteurs 394
hydroélectricité 406
hydromètre 359
hydroptère 387
hydrosphère 44
hyène 88
hygiène dentaire 272
hyperliens 334
hypermétropie 419
hyphe 52
hypoderme 114
hypophyse 109
hysope 142

I

identification du compte 443
igloo 288
igname 124
iguane 77
île 24
île de sable 35
île de Terre-Neuve 16
île volcanique 33
iléon 106
îles Aléoutiennes 16
îles Falkland 17
îles Fidji 15
Îles Marshall 453
Îles Salomon 453
îlot 164, 343
îlot rocheux 35
immeuble résidentiel 433
immobilisation 499
imparipennée 55
impériale 363
imperméable 248
impluvium 280
impression de l'écran 331
imprimante à jet d'encre 333
incendie de forêt 47
incinération 49
incisive centrale 101
incisive latérale 101
incisives 101
inclinaison de la semelle 227
inclusion 427
Inde 453
Index 539
index 115, 423
index de composition automatique 327
Index français 539
indicateur de charge 271
indicateur de ligne 362, 363
indicateur de niveau 323
indicateur de niveau d'eau 179
indicateur de niveau de carburant 355
indicateur de position 287
indicateur de réglage 511
indicateur de température 355
indicateur de vitesse 355, 368, 501
Indonésie 19, 453
industrie 335
infiltration 45, 47
infini 427
infirmière 464
inflorescence, modes 57
influx nerveux 110
infrastructure 342
inhalateur doseur 467
initiales de la banque émettrice 441
injecteur 360
insectes 67
insectes, exemples 69
insertion 331
insigne 456
insigne d'identité 456
insigne de grade 456
instruments à clavier 304
instruments à cordes 301
instruments à percussion 295, 308
instruments à vent 306
instruments d'écriture 312
instruments de bord 355
instruments électroniques 310
instruments scientifiques 13
instruments traditionnels 296
intégrale 427
intégration de l'électricité au réseau de transport 413
Intelsat 317
intensité lumineuse, mesure 426
interligne 298
internaute 334
Internet 334
interosseux 96
interrupteur 177, 181, 198, 206, 208, 209, 211, 218, 219, 229, 269, 270, 271, 272, 329, 416
interrupteur à gâchette 227, 228, 229
interrupteur d'accord 323
interrupteur d'alimentation 311, 318, 321, 322, 323, 328
interrupteur d'alimentation 319
interrupteur d'éclairage 269
interrupteur de démarrage 213
interrupteur de fin de course 287
interrupteur de la porte 213
interrupteur du magnétoscope 319
interrupteur du téléviseur 319
interrupteur principal 198
interruption 331
intersection 427
intertitre 313
intervalles 298
interview 313
intestin 71, 73, 103
intestin grêle 106
inverseur de marche 221, 228
inverseur de signe 337
inverseur route-croisement 368
Io 2
Iran 452
Iraq 452
iris 119
Irlande 449
isba 288
ischion 99
Islande 18, 450
isobare 39
isolant 190, 214, 410
isolateur 359
isoloir 443
Israël 452
isthme 24
isthme de la trompe utérine 113
isthme de Panama 16
isthme du gosier 116
Italie 450
ivoire 101

J

jaboticaba 137
jachère 122
jack de sortie 303
jacquet 469
jaguar 89
Jamahiriya arabe libyenne 451
Jamaïque 448
jambage 192
jambe 83, 91, 93, 95, 247
jambe élastique 247
jambier antérieur 96
jambière 263, 476, 478
jambière de gardien de but 507
jambon cuit 156
jambon fumé 153
jan extérieur 469
jan intérieur 469
jante 366, 371
Japet 3
Japon 19, 453
jaque 136
jardin 280
jardin d'agrément 230
jardin potager 122, 182
jardin public 435
jardinage 216, 230
jarlsberg 151
jarret 83, 86, 152, 153
jarretelle 259
jaune 79, 418
javelot 472
jazz, formation 300
jean 254
jéjunum 106
jet d'eau 185, 186
jet dentaire 272
jets d'eau 518
jeu 492
jeu d'ustensiles 173
jeu de brides 459
jeu de dames 470
jeu de douilles 223
jeu de fléchettes 471
jeu de petits outils 232
jeux 468
jeux de plateau 469
jeux en ligne 335
jicama 124
joint 214, 312
joint à coulisse 222
joint d'étanchéité 197, 404
joint de bougie 359
joint de carter 360
joint magnétique 211
Joker 468
jonc 264
jonction positif/négatif 410
jonquille 56
Jordanie 452
joue 86, 94, 220, 536
joueur de basketball 488
joueur de cricket : batteur 478
joueurs 492
joueuse de tennis 492
joule 426
journal 313
judo 499
judogi 499
juge 498, 499
juge arbitre 516, 518
juge de but 506
juge de champ arrière 485
juge de classement 516
juge de départ 516
juge de faute de pied 491
juge de filet 491
juge de ligne 487, 490, 494, 496, 507
juge de ligne en chef 485
juge de ligne médiane 490
juge de mêlée 485
juge de nage 516
juge de service 490, 494
juge de touche 481, 483, 485
juges 496, 497, 509, 518
juges de virages 517
jugulaire 486

jujube 137
jumeau 96, 97
jumelles à prismes 420
jupe 251
jupe à empiècement 253
jupe à lés 253
jupe à volants étagés 253
jupe de masque 459
jupe de piston 360
jupe droite 253
jupe fourreau 253
jupe froncée 253
jupe portefeuille 253
jupe souple 383
jupe-culotte 253
jupes, exemples 253
jupette 492
Jupiter 2
jupon 258
justaucorps 263
justice 440

K

kaki 137
Kazakhstan 452
kelvin 426
Kenya 451
kérosène 405
ketchup 141
kettle 29
kilogramme 426
kilt 253
kimono 256
kiosque 346, 379
Kirghizistan 452
Kiribati 453
kiwi 136
knicker 254
kombu 123
kora 297
Koweït 452
Kuiper, ceinture 2
kumquat 134

L

la 298
laboratoire 7
laboratoire américain 11
laboratoire de pathologie 465
laboratoire européen 11
laboratoire japonais 11
laboratoire spatial 13
lac 5, 24, 29, 32
lac artificiel 32
lac Baïkal 19
lac d'origine glaciaire 32
lac d'origine tectonique 32
lac d'origine volcanique 32
lac en croissant 32
lac Eyre Nord 15
lac Ladoga 18
lac Malawi 20
lac salé 36
lac Tanganyika 20
lac Tchad 20
lac Titicaca 17
lac Victoria 20
laccolite 28
lacet 240, 262, 395, 477, 498, 509
lacet de serrage 275
lacs 32
lactaire délicieux 123
lagomorphes 82
lagon 35
lagune 35
lait 150
lait concentré 150
lait de chèvre 150
lait en poudre 150
lait homogénéisé 150
laiterie 122
laitue asperge 126
laitue de mer 123
laitue frisée 126
laitue iceberg 126
laitue pommée 126
laize 520
lama 84
lambourde 187
lame 167, 169, 177, 190, 198, 216, 219, 221, 226, 227, 235, 270, 271, 297, 309, 341, 355, 398, 401, 506, 509
lame à double tranchant 271
lame criblée de l'ethmoïde 117
lame de coupe 180
lame de danse sur glace 509
lame de scie circulaire 227
lame dentée 270
lame droite 270
lame isolée 217
lame porte-objet 421
lame pour programme libre 509
lame racleuse 400
lame-ressort 460
lamelle 52, 190
lampadaire 206
lampe 217, 320, 421
lampe à économie d'énergie 199, 411
lampe à halogène 199
lampe à incandescence 199
lampe à souder 218
lampe au néon 217
lampe d'architecte 206
lampe de bureau 206
lampe de bureau halogène 206
lampe de chevet 439, 464
lampe de lecture 457
lampe de sanctuaire 446
lampe de table 206
lampe liseuse 206
lampe-tempête 532
lampe-torche 456
lampes témoins 318, 355
lamproie 159
lance à eau 455
lance d'arrosage 236
lance-canon 455
lancéolée 55
lancer 475, 479
lancer disque 473
lancer du javelot 473
lancer du poids 472
lancer marteau 473
lanceur 474, 475, 479
langouste 158
langoustine 158
langue 106, 116, 117, 154
langue bifide 76
langue glaciaire 30
langue, dos 118
languette 240, 262, 305, 509, 511
lanière 286, 500
lanterne 230, 529
lanterne de pied 207
lanterne murale 207
lapiaz 31
lapin 82, 154
lard 149
larynx 105
lasagne 146
laser à rubis pulsé 420
latitude 8, 9, 22
latrines 280
latte 412, 519, 520
laurier 142
lavabo 194, 195, 439, 464
lavabo du chirurgien 465
lave-auto 346
lave-linge 194, 212
lave-vaisselle 164, 214
lèchefrite 174
lecteur CD/DVD 471
lecteur de carte 321
lecteur de carte mémoire 333
lecteur de cassette 326, 333
lecteur de CD/DVD-ROM 329, 336
lecteur de disque compact 323, 325, 326
lecteur de disque dur 333
lecteur de disque dur amovible 333
lecteur de disquette 310, 329
lecteur de disquette externe 333
lecteur optique 121
lecture 319, 323, 328
lecture aléatoire 323
légende 313
légumes 120, 124
légumes bulbes 124
légumes feuilles 126
légumes fleurs 127
légumes fruits 128
légumes racines 129
légumes tiges 125
légumes tubercules 124
légumier 166
légumineuses 130
lémurien 91
lentille biconcave 419
lentille biconvexe 419
lentille concave 419
lentille convexe 419
lentille cylindrique 419
lentille de champ 420
lentille jetable 272
lentille objectif 8, 420
lentille plan-concave 419
lentille plan-convexe 419
lentille rigide 272
lentille souple 272
lentilles 130, 419
lentilles convergentes 419
lentilles de contact 272
lentilles de redressement 420
lentilles divergentes 419
léopard 89
Lesotho 452
lessivage du sol 48
lest 397
Lettonie 450
leucoplaste 50
lève-fil 208
levier 197, 222, 265, 269, 534
levier coudé 399
levier d'embrayage 366, 368
levier de blocage 224
levier de clé 306
levier de déclenchement 196
levier de dégagement 222
levier de frein à main 354
levier de frein avant 368
levier de manœuvre du mât 396
levier de perçage 180
levier de réglage latéral 229
levier de serrage 224
levier de vibrato 303
levier de vitesse 354
levier de vitesses 350
levier du bloc 229
levier du piston 216
levier du protège-lame inférieur 227
levier plat 220
lèvre 83, 87, 228
lèvre inférieure 116, 305
lèvre supérieure 116, 305
lézard 77
liaison 299
liaison chimique 414
Liban 452
libellule 69
liber 63
libération d'énergie 415
Liberia 451
libero 481, 487
librairie 436
lice 282
lichen 50
lichen crustacé 50
lichen foliacé 50
lichen fruticuleux 50
lichen, structure 50
lichens, exemples 50
Liechtenstein 450
liège 514
lierne 284
lieu noir 161
lièvre 82, 154
ligament 73
ligament alvéolo-dentaire 101
ligament large de l'utérus 113
ligament suspenseur 119
ligne 298
ligne arrière 515
ligne bleue 507
ligne câblée 335
ligne centrale 493, 507
ligne continue 342
ligne d'arrivée 473
ligne d'attaque 487
ligne de balayage 515
ligne de ballon mort 482
ligne de but 482, 484, 506
ligne de cadre 502
ligne de centre 484, 515
ligne de côté 487
ligne de couloir 473
ligne de croissance 72, 73
ligne de départ 473, 524
ligne de distribution à basse tension 198
ligne de distribution à moyenne tension 198
ligne de double 490, 495
ligne de fond 484, 487, 489, 491, 493, 494, 517
ligne de force 416
ligne de jeu 471, 474, 515
ligne de lancer franc 489
ligne de mêlée 485
ligne de retrait 479
ligne de sécurité 379
ligne de service 491
ligne de service court 495
ligne de service long 494
ligne de simple 491, 495
ligne de surface de réparation 480
ligne de suture 73
ligne de touche 481, 483, 484, 488
ligne de visée 533
ligne dédiée 334
ligne des 10 m 482
ligne des 15 m 483
ligne des 22 m 482
ligne des 5 m 483
ligne des verges 484
ligne discontinue 342, 343
ligne isosiste 27
ligne latérale 74, 493, 515
ligne médiane 481, 483, 488, 494
ligne médiane de service 491
ligne méridienne 533
ligne neutre 416
ligne sous-marine 334
ligne supplémentaire 298
ligne téléphonique 334
limbe 52, 55
lime 134, 229, 265, 531
lime à ongles 265
limes-émeri 265
limite de retour 479
limite du batteur 479
limite du terrain 182
limiteur de surchauffe 213
limon à crémaillère 191
limon à la française 191
limousine 347
linéaire 55
lingerie 439
linteau 185, 187, 192, 285
lion 89
liquette 255
liquide 414, 415
liquide céphalo-rachidien 110
lis 56
lisse d'assise 187
listel 228
lit 204, 361, 530
lit à barreaux 205
lit à deux places 439
lit à une place 439
lit d'hôpital 464
lit de camp pliant 530
lit de l'ongle 114
lit pliant 205
litchi 137
literie 204
lithosphère 26, 44
litière 54
littoral, configuration 35
Lituanie 450
livèche 142
livre 440
livrée 479
loafer 242
lob 491
lobe 79, 115
lobé 55
lobe du nez 117
lobe inférieur 105
lobe latéral inférieur 62
lobe latéral supérieur 62
lobe moyen 105
lobe supérieur 105
lobe terminal 62
local d'entreposage du matériel 444
local d'entretien 439, 443, 444
local technique 345
locaux administratifs 374
locaux de l'équipage 382
locaux de service 447
locomotive diesel-électrique 377
loge 58, 293
loge d'artiste 293
loge privée 290
logement de cassette 323
logement de la carte mémoire 320
logement de la cassette 320, 321
logement droit 272
logement du plateau 323
logement gauche 272
logiciel de courrier électronique 33
lointain 292, 293
loisirs de plein air 528
long péronier latéral 96
long supinateur 97
longane 136
longeron 365, 392
longeron de chenille 398
longitude 22
longue piste 508
longueur d'onde 418
longueur de la vague 33
longueur, mesure 425, 426
loquet 178, 214
lorgnette 273
lorum 78
losange 429
lotte de mer 160
louche 173
loup 88
loupe 421, 531
loupe et microscopes 421
loutre de rivière 88
lucarne 182, 183
lucarne de la cage d'escalier 189
lucarne de la salle de bains 189
Luer Lock, embout 460
luette 116, 117
lumière 7, 8, 9, 305
lumière perpétuelle 447
lumière visible 418
lumières de but 507
luminaires 206
Lune 2, 4, 5
Lune, éclipse 5
Lune, phases 5
Lune, relief 5
lunette astronomique 8
lunette astronomique, coupe 8
lunette de visée 420, 534
lunettes 218, 273, 513, 522
lunettes de nage 516
lunettes de protection 458, 522
lunettes de sécurité 458
lunettes de ski 510
lunettes de soleil 273
lunettes, exemples 273
lunettes, parties 273
lunule 73, 114, 115
lupin 130
lustre 207
lutrin 446
lutz 509
Luxembourg 449
luzerne 130
lynx 88
lyre 297
lysosome 66

M

macaque 91
mâche 127
mâchicoulis 282
machine à affranchir 339
machine à espresso 181
machine à faire les pâtes 170
machinerie 342
machinerie lourde 398
machiniste 290
mâchoire 217, 224
mâchoire dentée 222
mâchoire droite 222
mâchoire fixe 223
mâchoire incurvée 222
mâchoire mobile 223
mâchoires 224, 535
Mackenzie 16
maçonnerie : outils 216
macronucleus 66
Madagascar 20, 452
magasin 432
magasin à rayons 437
magasin d'articles de sport 437
magasin d'électronique 436
magasin de bricolage 436
magasin de cadeaux 436
magasin de chaussures 437
magasin de décoration 437
magasin de jouets 436
magasin de lingerie 436
magasin de prêt-à-porter 436
magazine 313
agenta 418
agma 28, 33
agnésie 497
agnétisme 416
agnétoscope 321
ail 436
aille 493
aillet 220
ailloche 297, 308
ailloches 309
aillon-gouge 235
aillot 473, 483, 488, 522
aillot d'équipe 476, 486
aillot d'équipe 480
aillot de bain 263, 516
aillot de corps 247, 476, 500
ain 91, 93, 95, 115
ain courante 191, 287, 385, 467
ain pleine 468
ine coon 87
ïs 61, 143
ïs : épi 61
ïs fourrager 122
ison 182, 515
ison à étage 289
ison de plain-pied 289
ison en adobe 288
son jumelée 289
son romaine 280
son sur pilotis 288
son, ameublement 200
son, charpente 187
son, éléments 185
son, extérieur 182
son, principales pièces 188
son, structure 188
sons de ville 289
sons en rangée 289
sons traditionnelles 288
re d'hôtel 438
re-autel 446
re-cylindre 357
eur 115
scule : sélection du niveau 2 330
ire 98, 100
isie 453
nga 129
wi 452
lives 453
426
451
277
ette de toilette 277
mallette porte-documents 274
Malpighi, couche 114
Malte 450
mamelon 92, 94, 113
mammifères carnivores 86
mammifères carnivores, exemples 88
mammifères lagomorphes, exemples 82
mammifères marins 90
mammifères marins, exemples 90
mammifères ongulés 83
mammifères ongulés, exemples 84
mammifères primates 91
mammifères primates, exemples 91
mammifères rongeurs 82
Manche 18
manche 167, 215, 216, 217, 219, 220, 221, 223, 244, 271, 272, 273, 297, 301, 302, 303, 477, 478, 492, 493, 494, 503, 505, 506
manche à balai 332, 395
manche isolant 217
manche isolé 217
manche montée 245
manche raglan 248, 251, 261
manche rotatif 332
manches à balai 471
manches précédentes 492
manchette 313, 487
manchon 219, 276, 395, 501
manchon de câble 228
manchon du cordon 218, 229
manchon refroidisseur 420
manchot 80
mandarine 134
mandibule 67, 74, 78
mandoline 170, 297
mandrin 221, 228
mandrin autoserrant 228
manette 178
manette d'admission d'air 192
manette de chasse d'eau 196
manette de contact 207
manette de dérailleur 371, 372, 522
manette de glissement 353
manette de jeu 471
manette des gaz 332
manette du frein 523
manette vapeur 181
mangoustan 136
mangouste 88
mangue 137
manille 521
manioc 124
manivelle 170, 224, 236, 356, 365, 372, 537
manivelle d'enroulement 225
manivelle de lève-glace 352
manomètre 455, 461
manomètre d'accord 308
manœuvre de la pelleteuse 399
mante religieuse 69
manteau 72, 73, 192, 251
manteau inférieur 26
manteau supérieur 26
manteaux 248, 251
manucure 265
manuel de premiers soins 461
manutention 396
maquereau 159
maquillage 266
maquillage des lèvres 266
maquillage des yeux 266
maquilleuse 290
maquis 44
marbre 475
marchand de journaux 437
marche 191, 219
marche de départ 191
marche/arrêt/volume 326
marchepied 219, 364, 395, 523
marchepied arrière 455
marchepied escamotable 361
marchepied latéral 377
margarine 149
marge continentale 33
margose 128
marinière 255
maritime, transport 381
marmite 175
marmotte 82
Maroc 451
maroquinerie 436
marque centrale 490
marque d'aire de prise de contact 391
marque d'axe de piste 390
marque de distance constante 391
marque de point d'attente 390
marques d'identification 390
marques de circulation 389
marques de seuil de piste 391
marques latérales de piste 390
marqueur 312, 487, 488
marqueurs 499
marron 133
Mars 2, 3
marteau 116, 304, 472
marteau à panne ronde 220
marteau de charpentier 220
marteau de maçon 216
marteau de menuisier 220
martin-pêcheur 80
martinet 80
martre 88
mascara en pain 266
mascara liquide 266
masque 476, 478, 486, 507
masque bucco-nasal 459
masque complet 454
masque de sélection des couleurs 318
masque respiratoire 459
masse 27
masse, mesure 422, 426
masse-tige 403
masséter 96
massif 183
massif d'ancrage des câbles 344
massif de fleurs 230
massif de fondation 403
massif montagneux 24
mât 281, 321, 396, 519, 520
mât avant 385
mât de charge 385
mât de toit 529
mât radar 384
matelas 204, 205, 460, 530
matelas autogonflant 530
matelas mousse 530
matelas pneumatique 530
mâtereau 385
matériau de scellement 417
matériel de camping 531
matériel de lutte contre les incendies 454
matériel de secours 460
mathématiques 427
matière 414
matière inorganique 45
matières grasses 149
matraque télescopique 456
matrice de l'ongle 114
maturation, vigne 62
maturité 62
Maurice 452
Mauritanie 451
maxillaire 74, 117
maxillaire basculant 76
maxillaire inférieur 98, 100
maxillaire supérieur 78, 98, 100
mazout domestique 405
mazout léger 405
mazout lourd 405
méandre 32
méat de l'urètre 111
mécanique d'accordage 303
mécanique d'accordage 303
mécanisme d'octave 306
mécanisme d'ouverture de l'anse 537
mécanisme de débrayage du tambour 537
mécanisme de déplacement de la lame 401
mécanisme de propulsion 372
mèche 301
mèche à centre plat 228
mèche hélicoïdale 228
mèche hélicoïdale à âme centrale 228
mèche hélicoïdale à double torsade 228
médaillon 264
médecin 464, 498
médiator 297
médicaments, formes 467
méditerranéen 40
Meissner, corpuscule 114
Mélanésie 15
mélange au manganèse (cathode) 417
mélange d'épices cajun 139
mélange de zinc et d'électrolyte (anode) 417
mélange dépolarisant 417
mélange eau-vapeur 402
mélangeur 176
mélangeur à main 176
mélangeur à pâtisserie 172
mélangeur bain-douche 194
mélasse 149
mêlée : attaque 485
mêlée : défense 484
mêlée spontanée 483
mélèze 65
mélisse 142
melon 238
melon à cornes 136
melon brésilien 135
melon brodé 135
melon Casaba 135
melon d'hiver chinois 128
melon d'Ogen 135
melon miel 135
melons 135
membrane 324
membrane cellulaire 66
membrane coquillière 79
membrane cytoplasmique 50
membrane du tympan 116
membrane médiane 60
membrane nucléaire 50, 66
membrane pellucide 112
membrane plasmique 66
membrane squelettique 50
membrane vitelline 79
membre inférieur 103
membre supérieur 103
meneur de jeu 489
méninges 109
ménisque convergent 419
ménisque divergent 419
menora 447
menthe 142
menton 78, 94
mentonnière 301, 367, 522
menuiserie : instruments de traçage et de mesure 225
menuiserie : matériel divers 225
menuiserie : outils pour clouer 220
menuiserie : outils pour façonner 229
menuiserie : outils pour percer 228
menuiserie : outils pour scier 226
menuiserie : outils pour serrer 222
menuiserie : outils pour visser 221
mer 5, 24, 32
mer Adriatique 18
mer Baltique 18
mer Caspienne 14, 19
mer d'Aral 19
mer d'Irlande 18
mer d'Oman 19
mer de Barents 18
mer de Beaufort 16
mer de Béring 14
mer de Chine méridionale 14, 19
mer de Chine orientale 19
mer de Corail 15
mer de Norvège 18
mer de Tasman 15
mer de Weddell 15
mer des Antilles 14, 16
mer du Groenland 14
mer du Japon 19
mer du Nord 14, 18
mer Égée 18
mer Méditerranée 14, 18, 20
mer Noire 14, 18, 19
mer Rouge 14, 19, 20
Mercure 2, 3
merguez 156
méridien de Greenwich 22
méridien est 22
méridien ouest 22
méridienne 200
merlan 161
mesa 36
mésocarpe 57, 58, 59
mésopause 37
mésosphère 37
message précédent 328
message suivant 328
mesure à deux temps 298
mesure à quatre temps 298
mesure à trois temps 298
mesure de l'énergie 426
mesure de l'épaisseur 425
mesure de l'intensité lumineuse 426
mesure de la charge électrique 426
mesure de la différence de potentiel électrique 426
mesure de la force 426
mesure de la fréquence 426
mesure de la longueur 425, 426
mesure de la masse 422, 426
mesure de la pression 426
mesure de la puissance 426
mesure de la quantité de matière 426
mesure de la radioactivité 426
mesure de la résistance électrique 426
mesure de la température 424
mesure de la température Celsius 426
mesure de la température thermodynamique 426
mesure du courant électrique 426
mesure du temps 424
mesure, appareils 424
mesures 171, 298
météorologie 37
mètre 426
mètre à ruban 225
métro 435
meubles d'enfants 205
meubles de rangement 202
Mexique 448
mezzanine 378
mi 298
mi-bas 247, 257
mi-chaussette 247, 257
micro 303
micro de fréquences aiguës 303
micro de fréquences graves 303
micro de fréquences moyennes 303
micro-ondes 418
micro-ordinateur 329
microfilament 66
micromètre palmer 425
Micronésie 453
micronucleus 66
microphone 320, 327, 328, 332, 337, 456
microphones 457
microscope 421
microscope binoculaire 421
microtubule 66
miel 149
mihrab 447
milieu défensif 481
milieu offensif droit 481
milieu offensif gauche 481
mille 427
millésime 441
millet 61, 143
millet : épi 61
Mimas 3
minaret 447
minbar 447
minibus 363

minichaine stéréo 325
minislip 247
minute 428
minuterie 178, 179
minuteur 171, 501
Miranda 3
mire 533, 535
miroir 195, 277, 421, 439, 533
miroir à réflexion partielle 420
miroir à réflexion totale 420
miroir de courtoisie 354
miroir de lecture 10
miroir de traversée avant 362
miroir double pivotant 269
miroir latéral 269
miroir lumineux 269
miroir plan rétractable 7
miroir primaire 7
miroir primaire concave 7, 9
miroir secondaire 7, 9
mise en balles 49
mise en marche 328
Mississippi 16
mitaine 243, 507
mitigeur d'évier 197
mitochondrie 50, 66
mitre 167, 169, 193
mitron 183
mocassin 242
mode d'acquisition 314
mode d'emploi 346
mode d'enregistrement 320
mode d'exposition 314
mode de mise au point 314
mode magnétoscope 319
mode télévision 319
modem 334
modem-câble 335
modérateur 408
modes d'inflorescence 57
modification fine des variables 310
modification rapide des variables 310
modulateur de pression de freinage 357
modulation de la hauteur du son 310
modulation du timbre du son 310
module d'habitation américain 11
module de commande électronique 357
module de communication 316
module de photopiles 411
module de propulsion 316
module de service 316
module russe 11
moelle 63, 154
moelle épinière 109, 110
moelle épinière, structure 109
Mohorovicic, discontinuité 26
moineau 80
molaire, coupe 101
molaires 101
mole 426
molécule 414
molette 223
molette d'ajustage 425
molette d'entraînement 180
molette de mise au point 420
molette de réglage de la saillie 229
mollet 93, 95
mollusques 72, 157
Monaco 450
Mongolie 453
moniteurs de contrôle du réalisateur 290
monnaie et modes de paiement 441
monocoques 521
mont de Vénus 112
montagne 29
montagnes Rocheuses 16
montant 184, 187, 201, 219, 297, 466, 509
montant de bâti 202
montant de ferrage 185, 202
montant de la serrure 185
montant de rive 186
montant embrevé 186
montant latéral 349
montant mouton 186
montant rembourré 489
Monténégro 450
monticule 475
montre à affichage analogique 424
montre à affichage numérique 424
monts Oural 18
monts Transantarctiques 15
monture 215, 224, 226, 296
monture en fer à cheval 7
monture réglable 226
monument 25
moquette 190
moraillon 277
moraine de fond 30
moraine frontale 30
moraine latérale 30
moraine médiane 30
moraine terminale 30
mordant 299
morille 123
morphologie de l'abeille : ouvrière 68
morphologie de l'araignée 70
morphologie de l'escargot 72
morphologie de l'oiseau 78
morphologie de la grenouille 75
morphologie de la perche 74
morphologie de la pieuvre 72
morphologie de la tortue 76
morphologie du cheval 83
morphologie du chien 86
morphologie du coquillage bivalve 73
morphologie du coquillage univalve 73
morphologie du dauphin 90
morphologie du gorille 91
morphologie du homard 71
morphologie du papillon 67
morphologie du rat 82
morphologie du requin 74
morphologie du serpent venimeux : tête 76
mors 221, 228, 265
mors fixe 224
mors mobile 224
mort 426
mortadelle 156
mortier 170
morue de l'Atlantique 161
mosaïque 280
mosquée 447
moteur 212, 213, 214, 227, 229, 237, 366, 396, 401, 403
moteur à essence 351, 360
moteur de manœuvre 13
moteur diesel 398, 399, 400, 401
moteur diesel de propulsion 383
moteur diesel de sustentation 383
moteur électrique 235, 237, 358
moteur hors-bord 385
moteur principal 13
motif 260, 261
moto 366
moto : vue en plongée 368
moto de Grand Prix et pilote 525
moto de motocross et supercross 525
moto de tête 522
moto de tourisme 369
moto tout-terrain 369
moto-caméra 522
motocyclisme 525
motoneige 523
motrice 376, 380
mouche 69, 502
mouche artificielle 536
mouche centrale 502
mouche de ligne de cadre 502
mouche supérieure 502
mouche tsé-tsé 69
moufette 88
moufle 243
moufle fixe 403
moufle mobile 403
mouflon 84
mouilleur 339
moule 157
moule à charlotte 172
moule à fond amovible 172
moule à gâteau 172
moule à muffins 172
moule à pain 179
moule à quiche 172
moule à soufflé 172
moule à tarte 172
moulin à café 180
moulin à légumes 170
moulin à vent 412
moulin pivot 412
moulin tour 412
moulinet à mouche 536
moulinet à tambour fixe 537
moulinet à tambour tournant 537
moulure de pare-chocs 348
mousqueton 521, 538
mousqueton à ressort 521
mousse 51
mousse à raser 271
mousse d'Irlande 123
mousse, structure 51
mousseline 171
moustaches 87
moustique 69
moutarde à l'ancienne 140
moutarde allemande 140
moutarde américaine 140
moutarde anglaise 140
moutarde blanche 138
moutarde de Dijon 140
moutarde en poudre 140
moutarde noire 138
mouton 84
mouvement horizontal du sol 27
mouvement vertical du sol 27
mouvements de l'avion 395
mouvements de terrain 31
moyen adducteur 96
moyenne sus-alaire 78
moyenne tectrice primaire 78
moyeu 341, 371, 413, 467
moyeu rotor 395
Mozambique 452
mozzarella 150
Mt Everest 37
muguet 56
mule 242
mulet 84, 160
mulot 82
multicoques 521
multiplication 337, 427
munster 151
muqueuse olfactive 117
mur 184, 528
mur bajoyer 406
mur d'arrivée 516
mur de fondation 187
mur de l'œil 43
mur de la qibla 447
mur de nuages 43
mur de virage 517
mur fortifié 447
mur latéral 517
muraille 385
mûre 132
muscle adducteur antérieur 73
muscle adducteur postérieur 73
muscle arrecteur 114
muscle bulbo-caverneux 111
muscle droit inférieur 119
muscle droit supérieur 119
muscle papillaire 104
muscles 96
museau 74, 75, 86, 87
musée 433
musique 296
Myanmar 453
mycélium 52
mye 157
mygale du Mexique 70
myocarde 104
myopie 419
myrtille 132

N

n'égale pas 427
n'est pas identique à 427
nacelle 413
nacelle d'observation 7
nacelle, coupe 413
nage sur le dos 517
nageoire anale 74
nageoire caudale 71, 74, 90
nageoire dorsale 74, 90
nageoire pectorale 74, 90
nageoire pelvienne 74
nages, types 517
naissance 426
Namibie 452
naos 279
nappe phréatique 31, 48
narine 74, 75, 76, 78, 117
nasal 100
naseau 83
natation 516
nationalité 497
Nauru 453
navet 129
navette ferroviaire 390
navette spatiale 12, 37
navette spatiale au décollage 12
navigateur 334
navire de forage 382
navire porte-conteneurs 381, 382
nébulosité 39
nécrologie 313
nectarine 132
nef 285
nef centrale 447
nèfle du Japon 133
neige 41
neiges acides 48
neiges éternelles 29
Népal 453
néphridie 71
Neptune 2, 3
nerf 114
nerf circonflexe 108
nerf cochléaire 116
nerf crural 108
nerf cubital 108
nerf digital 108
nerf fémoro-cutané 108
nerf fessier 108
nerf grand abdomino-génital 108
nerf grand sciatique 108
nerf intercostal 108
nerf médian 108
nerf musculo-cutané 108
nerf obturateur 108
nerf olfactif 117
nerf optique 119
nerf petit abdomino-génital 108
nerf petit sciatique 108
nerf rachidien 109, 110
nerf radial 108
nerf saphène externe 108
nerf saphène interne 108
nerf sciatique poplité externe 108
nerf sciatique poplité interne 108
nerf tibial antérieur 108
nerf vestibulaire 116
nerfs crâniens 108
nervure 67, 401, 458
nervure d'aile 392
nervure d'emplanture 392
nervure médiane 51
nervure principale 55, 60
nervure secondaire 55
neurone moteur 110
neurone sensoriel 110
neurones 110
neutron 414
neutron incident 415
névé 30
newton 426
nez 82, 94, 229, 392, 526
nez basculant 394
nez du guide 235
nez, parties externes 117
nez-de-marche 191
Nicaragua 448
niche de sécurité 345
nid d'ange 260
Niger 20, 451
Nigeria 451
Nil 20
nimbo-stratus 42
niveau à bulle 225
niveau d'eau 181
niveau d'équilibre 33
niveau de la mer 26, 33, 37
niveau de la réception 439
niveleuse 401
noir 418
noire 299
Noirs 470
noisette 133
noisette, coupe 60
noix 133
noix de cajou 133
noix de coco 133
noix de cola 133
noix de ginkgo 133
noix de macadamia 133
noix de muscade 138
noix de pacane 133
noix du Brésil 133
noix, coupe 60
nom de domaine 334
nom de la monnaie 441
nom de la station 378
nom du gymnaste 497
nom du titulaire 441
nombril 92, 94
non parallèle 428
non-appartenance 427
Nord 23
Nord Est 23
Nord Nord-Est 23
Nord Nord-Ouest 23
Nord Ouest 23
nori 123
Norvège 450
notation algébrique 470
notation musicale 298
note 497
nouaison 62
nouilles asiatiques 147
nouilles aux œufs 147
nouilles de haricots mungo 147
nouilles de riz 147
nouilles soba 147
nouilles somen 147
nouilles udon 147
nouvelle Lune 5
Nouvelle-Calédonie 15
Nouvelle-Zélande 15, 453
noyau 4, 6, 50, 57, 66, 110, 112, 305, 414, 534
noyau externe 26
noyau fissile 415
noyau galactique 6
noyau interne 26
noyer 64
nœud 53, 416
nœud d'arrimage de l'orbiteur 11
nœud de Ranvier 110
nœud papillon 245
nœud plat 238
nu-pied 242
nuage 37, 41
nuage de cendres 28
nuage de Oort 2
nuage en entonnoir 43
nuages 42
nuages à développement vertical
nuages de basse altitude 42
nuages de haute altitude 42
nuages de moyenne altitude 42
nucléole 50, 66, 112
nuisette 256
numéro d'autoroute 25
numéro de carte 441, 443
numéro de chambre 439
numéro de la pompe 346
numéro de quai 374
numéro de route 25
numéro de série 441
numéro du joueur 486, 488, 50
numéroteur 338
nuque 78, 93, 95

O

oasis 32, 36
Obéron 3
objectif 314, 327, 332, 421
objectif grand-angulaire 314
objectif macro 314
objectif zoom 314, 320
objectif, accessoires 314
objectifs 314
objet 419
objets personnels 264, 271
observation astronomique 7
observatoire 7
observatoire astronomique 7
observatoire astronomique, coupe 7
obstacle d'eau 504
obstacle d'eau 504
obturateur de baie 329
occipital 97, 99, 100
océan 5, 24, 45
océan Arctique 14
océan Atlantique 14, 15, 18, 20
océan Indien 14, 15, 19, 20
océan Pacifique 14, 15, 19
océan, dorsale 33
Océanie 14, 15, 453
océanique 40
octaèdre régulier 429
octave 298
octogone régulier 429
oculaire 8, 9, 320, 420, 421, 459
oculaire coudé 8
odorat 116
eil 43, 70, 71, 72, 76, 90, 94, 119, 220
eil composé 67, 68
eil simple 67
eillet 56, 240, 263, 275, 509, 538
eillet d'attache 315
esophage 105, 106
euf 79
euf d'autruche 155
euf d'oie 155
euf de caille 155
euf de cane 155
euf de faisane 155
euf de poule 155
ufrier 211
ufs 155
fice 392
m 426
e 81, 155
gnon à mariner 124
gnon blanc 124
gnon jaune 124
gnon rouge 124
gnon vert 124
seau 78
eau aquatique 79
seau de proie 79
seau échassier 79
seau granivore 79
eau insectivore 79
eau percheur 79
eau, morphologie 78
eaux 78
eaux, exemples 80
api 84
crane 99
oduc 404
oduc sous-marin 404
oduc surélevé 404
e 128
an 452
belle 57
bilic 30
ble de fontaine 161
ore 424
ore à paupières 266
oplate 93, 95, 98, 99
e 418
e de choc 403
e sismique 27
es radio 418
e 78, 115
et 163, 340, 531
et à fenêtre 340
, nuage 2
ra 432
cule 74
cule thermoscellé 163
opisthodome 279
opticien 437
optique 418
orang-outan 91
orange 134
orange, coupe 58
orbiculaire des paupières 96
orbite lunaire 4, 5
orbite terrestre 4, 5
orbiteur 12, 13
orchestre 278
orchestre symphonique 295
orchidée 56
ordinateur 444
ordinateur de bord 354, 457
ordinateur de bureau 334
ordinateur de poche 337
ordinateur portable 336
ordinateur portable : vue arrière 336
ordinateur portable : vue avant 336
ordures ménagères 47, 48
oreille 92, 201
oreille externe 116
oreille interne 116
oreille moyenne 116
oreille, pavillon 115
oreille, structure 116
oreille-de-Judas 123
oreiller 204
oreillette droite 103, 104
oreillette gauche 103, 104
Orénoque 17
organes des sens 114
organes génitaux féminins 112
organes génitaux masculins 111
organisation gouvernementale 335
organiseur 338
organisme culturel 335
organisme de santé 335
organismes simples 66
orge 61, 143
orge : épi 61
orgue 305
orifice d'alimentation 455
orifice de remplissage 208
orifice du conduit auditif 115
orifice du pied 305
origan 142
ormeau 157
ornements 299
oronge vraie 123
orque 90
orteil 86, 92, 94
ortie 127
os alvéolaire 101
os iliaque 98
os maxillaire 101
os propre du nez 117
oseille 127
osselets 116
otarie 90
oued 36
Ouest 23
Ouest Nord-Ouest 23
Ouest Sud-Ouest 23
Ouganda 451
ouïe 115, 301
ouïe, protection 458
ouistiti 91
ouragan 43
ours 313
ours noir 89
ours polaire 89
outils pour arroser 236
outils pour couper 234
outils pour remuer la terre 233
outils pour scier 226
outils pour semer et planter 231
outils pour serrer 222
outils pour visser 221
outils, électricité 217
outils, plomberie 216
outils, soudage 218
ouverture 73, 538
ouvre-boîtes 170, 180, 531
ouvrière 68
ouvrière, abeille 68
Ouzbékistan 452
ovaire 56, 112, 113
ovoïde 55
ovule 56, 112

P

Pacini, corpuscule 114
pack 163
page précédente 331
page suivante 331
pagode 283
paiement électronique, terminal 443
paille 163
pain 144
pain azyme 145
pain blanc 145
pain chapati indien 145
pain complet 145
pain de campagne 145
pain de maïs américain 145
pain de mie 145
pain de seigle allemand 145
pain de seigle danois 145
pain de seigle noir 144
pain grec 144
pain irlandais 145
pain multicéréales 145
pain naan indien 145
pain noir russe 145
pain parisien 144
pain pita 145
pain tchallah juif 145
paire 468
pak-choï 126
Pakistan 452
palais de justice 432
palais des congrès 433
Palaos 453
pale 412, 413
pale de rotor 395
palet 507
paletot 248, 251
palette 493, 535, 538
palette à ailes 396
palier 189, 191
palissade 282
palmée 55
palmeraie 36
palmette 200
palmier 64
palmure 75, 79
palonnier 400
palourde 157
palpe 73
palpe labial 67
pampille 207
pamplemousse 134
pan 245, 248, 255
pan arrière 245
pan avant 245
panais 129
Panama 448
panama 238
pancetta 156
pancréas 106
panicule, avoine 61
panicule, sorgho 61
panier 178, 181, 211, 214, 477, 489, 538
panier à couverts 214
panier à friture 171
panier cuit-vapeur 175
panier de lavage 212
panne 218
panne ronde 220
panneau 185, 489
panneau de citerne 385
panneau de commande 328, 455
panneau de distribution 198
panneau de fonctions 328
panneau de garniture 352
panneau de protection latéral 467
panneau de refroidissement 13
panneau de séparation 277
panneau de vantail 202
panneau indicateur 374
panneau publicitaire 378
panneau solaire 7, 316
panneaux solaires 11
pansement adhésif 461
pantalon 246, 263, 476, 486, 499, 525
pantalon molleton 262
pantalon pattes d'éléphant 254
pantalons, exemples 254
pantographe 376
paon 81
papaye 137
papier aluminium 162
papier de verre 229
papier paraffiné 162
papier sulfurisé 162
papille 114, 119
papille caliciforme 118
papille filiforme 118
papille foliée 118
papille fongiforme 118
papille rénale 107
papillon 67, 517
papillon, morphologie 67
Papouasie-Nouvelle-Guinée 15, 453
paprika 139
paquebot 386
paquet 163
parachute 12
parachute de cabine 287
paraffines 405
parafoudre 407
Paraguay 448
parallèle 22, 428
parallélépipède 429
parallélogramme 429
paramécie 66
Paraná 17
parapet 282
parapharmacie et cosmétiques 121
parapluie 273
parasoleil 314
paratonnerre 183, 413
parc 25, 433
parc à charbon 402
parc à échelles 455
parc à vélos 445
parc de stationnement 390, 430, 445, 512
parc de stockage 404
parc de stockage terminal 404
parc des expositions 430
parc national 25
parcours 504
parcours pittoresque 25
pardessus 248
pare-brise 348, 364, 366, 369, 385, 392, 523
pare-chocs 209, 364, 369
pare-chocs arrière 523
pare-feu 193
pare-soleil 8, 354, 356, 361
paréo 253
parfumerie 436
pariétal 99, 100
paripennée 55
parka 249
parking 375, 381
parmesan 151
paroi avant 365
paroi latérale 365
parquet 190
parquet à bâtons rompus 190
parquet à coupe de pierre 190
parquet à coupe perdue 190
parquet Chantilly 190
parquet d'Arenberg 190
parquet en chevrons 190
parquet en vannerie 190
parquet mosaïque 190
parquet sur chape de ciment 190
parquet sur ossature de bois 190
parquet Versailles 190
parquets, arrangements 190
parterre 293
parties 200, 201, 204
parties d'un cercle 428
parties d'une bicyclette 370
parties d'une chaussure 240
parties des lunettes 273
parties externes du nez 117
parure 264
pas 83
pas alternatif 514
pas de patineur 514
pascal 426
passage à niveau 375
passage inférieur 344
passage pour piétons 434
passage souterrain 375
passage supérieur 343, 344
passant 245, 246, 248
passavant 385
passe à billes 406
passe-bras 251
passe-sangle 532
passerelle 282, 292, 375, 379
passerelle de navigation 382, 386, 387
passerelle télescopique 389
passoire 171, 177, 180
passoire fine 171
pastèque 135
pastille de combustible 409
Patagonie 17
patate 124
pâte de tamarin 140
pâte phyllo 145
patelle 157
patère 200
pâtes alimentaires 146
pâtes won-ton 147
patient 464
patin 395, 506
patin à roues alignées 527
patin acrobatique 527
patin antidérapant 219
patin clap 508
patin d'appui 409
patin d'espacement 409
patin de courte piste 508
patin de figure 509
patin de gardien de but 507
patin de hockey 527
patin de vitesse 527
patinage artistique 509
patinage de vitesse 508
patineur : courte piste 508
patineur : longue piste 508
patineur d'eau 69
patineuse 527
patinoire 506, 509, 512
patins de course 508
pâtisson 129
patte 76, 244, 246, 248, 274, 477
patte à boutons-pression 249
patte ambulatoire 67
patte anale 67
patte antérieure 67, 68, 75
patte autocollante 339
patte boutonnée 246
patte capucin 245
patte d'entrejambe 255
patte d'épaule 248
patte d'épaule 456
patte de boutonnage 245
patte de serrage 248
patte locomotrice 70
patte médiane 67, 68
patte polo 250
patte postérieure 67, 68, 75
patte ventouse 67
pattes thoraciques 71
pattes, exemples 79
pâturage 122
paturon 83
paume 115, 243, 477
paume d'un gant 243
paumelle 186
paupière 76
paupière inférieure 75, 87, 119
paupière interne 87
paupière supérieure 75, 87, 119
pause 299, 323, 331
pause/arrêt sur l'image 319
pavé alphabétique 338
pavé alphanumérique 330
pavé numérique 331, 338
pavé tactile 336
pavillon 82, 116, 305, 306, 307, 349, 432, 460, 504
pavillon de la trompe utérine 113
pavillon des skieurs 512
pavillon, oreille 115
pavot, graines 139

pays 23
Pays-Bas 449
paysage végétal selon l'altitude 44
pe-tsai 126
peau 57, 58, 59, 110, 114, 309
peau de batterie 297, 308
peau de chamois 265
peau de timbre 297, 308
pécari 84
pêche 132, 536
pêche à la mouche 536
pêche au lancer 537
pêche, coupe 57
pédale 302, 308, 370, 372, 501, 522
pédale automatique 522
pédale avec cale élargie 522
pédale crescendo 305
pédale d'accélérateur 354
pédale de chaussage 511
pédale de combinaisons 305
pédale de débrayage 354
pédale de déchaussage 511
pédale de frein 350, 354, 357
pédale de frein arrière 368
pédale de sourdine 304
pédale douce 304, 311
pédale forte 304, 311
pédales d'expression 305
pédalier 305
pédicelle 51, 59, 62
pédieux 96
pédipalpe 70
pédoncule 56, 57, 58, 59, 62
peigne à crêper 268
peigne à tige 268
peigne afro 268
peigne de coiffeur 268
peignes 268
peignoir 256
peinture d'entretien 219
pelage 82, 91
pèlerine 251
pélican 80
pelle 173, 193, 233
pelle à poussière 215
pelle hydraulique 400
pelle-pioche pliante 532
pelleteuse 399
pellicule plastique 162
peloton 522
peloton de tête 522
pelouse 183
peltée 55
pendants d'oreille 264
pendeloque 207
pendentif 264
penderie 189, 203, 439
pendule 444
pêne demi-tour 186
pêne dormant 186
péninsule 24
péninsule Antarctique 15
péninsule d'Arabie 19
péninsule des Balkans 18
péninsule du Yucatan 16
péninsule Ibérique 18
péninsule Scandinave 18
pénis 92
penne 146
pennée 55
pennon 520
pentagone régulier 429
pente difficile 512
pente expert 512
pente facile 512
pente intermédiaire 512
pépin 58, 59
pepino 137
pepperoni 156
perceuse électrique 228
perceuse-visseuse sans fil 228
perche 160
perche truitée 160
perchiste 291
percolateur 181
perdrix 80
perforation 240, 243, 263
perforatrice 340
pergola 230
péricarde 105
péricarpe 60
périphérique 431
périphériques d'entrée 330
périphériques de sortie 333
périphériques de stockage 333
péristome 66
péristyle 279, 280
péritoine 111, 112
péroné 98
Pérou 448
peroxysome 66
perpendiculaire 428
perron 183, 188
persan 87
persienne 186
persil 142
perte de chaleur 46
pèse-lettres 339
pèse-personne 423
peso 440
peson 423
pesticide 47, 48
pétale 56
pétiole 52, 55
petit bois 186
petit montant 185
petit palmaire 96
petit rond 97
petite lame 531
petite lèvre 112, 113
petite sus-alaire 78
petites annonces 313
petits outils, jeu 232
petits pois 130
pétoncle 157
pétrole 403
pétrole brut 405
pétrolier 381, 384
peuplier 64
phalange distale 114
phalange médiane 114
phare 348, 364, 366, 368, 377, 381, 523
phare central 376
phare d'atterrissage 395
pharmacie 436, 462, 465
pharynx 105, 106
phase de glisse 514
phase de poussée 514
phases de la Lune 5
Philippines 19, 453
Phobos 2
phoque 90
photographe 436
photographe de plateau 291
photographie 314
photographie à la une 313
photon 420
photopile 410, 411
photorécepteurs 119
photosphère 4
photosynthèse 54
physique : électricité 416
physique : magnétisme 416
physique : optique 418
pi 428
piano 295
piano droit 304
piano électronique 311
pic 29, 80
piccolo 295, 306
pichet 166, 180
pictogrammes 330
pie-mère 109
pièce : avers 441
pièce : revers 441
pièce de jonction 455
pièce intermédiaire 111
pièce terminale 111
pièces 470
pièces buccales 68
pied 52, 72, 73, 91, 92, 93, 94, 95, 125, 199, 202, 204, 205, 206, 231, 247, 260, 302, 305, 308, 421, 493, 536, 537
pied à coulisse à vernier 425
pied à perfusion 464
pied arrière 201
pied avant 201
pied cambré 200
pied de lit 204
pied de mât 519
pied de nivellement 212, 213, 214
pied télescopique 460
pied-mélangeur 176
piédroit 285
pieds, protection 459
piège à patte à mâchoires 535
pierre 218
pierre à affûter 169
pierre blanche 470
pierre de Coyolxauhqui 283
pierre de curling 515
pierre noire 470
pierre sacrificielle 283
piètement 201, 219
pieuvre 72, 157
pieuvre, morphologie 72
pigeon 81, 154
pignon 65, 133, 163, 182
pika 82
pilastre 191
pilastre corinthien 281
pile 344
pile alcaline manganèse-zinc 417
pile carbone-zinc 417
pile rechargeable 320
piles 416
piles sèches 417
pilier 27, 283, 284
pilier droit 482
pilier du voile 116
pilier gauche 482
pilon 170, 173
pilote 524
piment 128
piment de Cayenne 139
piment de la Jamaïque 138
piment Jalapeño 139
piment oiseau 139
piments broyés 139
piments séchés 139
pin parasol 65
pinacle 284
pince 71, 173, 193, 246, 269
pince à boucles de cheveux 268
pince à cheveux 268
pince à cuticules 265
pince à défriser 269
pince à échardes 461
pince à épiler 265
pince à escargots 173
pince à étiqueter 340
pince à joint coulissant 222
pince à long bec 217
pince à spaghettis 173
pince d'électricien 217
pince de mise en plis 268
pince de taille 248
pince multiprise 222
pince noire 356
pince rouge 356
pince universelle 217
pince-étau 222
pinceau 219, 312
pinceau à lèvres 266
pinceau à pâtisserie 172
pinceau éventail 266
pinceau pour fard à joues 266
pinceau pour poudre libre 266
pincement 199
pinces 222
pinnule 52
pinson 80
pintade 81, 154
pioche 233
Pion 470
pion 469
pique 468
pique-notes 341
piquet 479, 528, 529
piscine 184, 386
piscine de stockage du combustible irradié 409
piscine enterrée 184
piscine hors sol 184
pissenlit 127
pistache 133
piste 390, 472, 515, 524
piste d'avertissement 475
piste d'élan 473
piste de ski alpin 512
piste de ski de fond 512
pistes d'élan 496
pistil 56
pistolet 216, 456
pistolet à calfeutrer 216
pistolet à souder 218
pistolet arrosoir 236
pistolet d'arrosage 236
pistolet de départ 472
pistolet de distribution 346
piston 307, 357, 360, 460
piston à décorer 172
piton sous-marin 33
pivot 217, 270, 271, 412, 489, 518, 533
pivot d'attelage 365
plafond 193
plafond acoustique 293
plafond cathédrale 189
plafond de cabine 287
plafonnier 206
plage 35
plage arrière 386
plage avant 383, 387
plaine 24, 32
plaine abyssale 33
plaine d'inondation 32
plaine fluvio-glaciaire 30
plan 279, 285
plan à langer 205
plan de travail 164
plan du terrain 183
plan urbain 25
plan, élévation 182
planche 501
planche à découper 169
planche à roulettes 526
planche à voile 519
plancher 193, 369
plancher de cabine 287
plancher inférieur 396
plancher supérieur 396
planchette à arches 340
planchette à pince 340
planchiste 526
planètes 2
planètes externes 2
planètes internes 3
planisphère 14
plantaire grêle 97
plante 53
plante grimpante 230
plante, structure 53
plantoir 231
plantoir à bulbes 231
plaque 178, 269
plaque à pâtisserie 172
plaque absorbante 410
plaque africaine 27
plaque antarctique 27
plaque antifriction 511
plaque chauffante 181
plaque costale 76
plaque d'instructions 228
plaque de commutateur 198
plaque de couche 534
plaque de montage 199
plaque de protection 303, 525
plaque des Caraïbes 27
plaque des îles Cocos 27
plaque du lanceur 475
plaque eurasiatique 27
plaque indo-australienne 27
plaque marginale 76
plaque motrice 110
plaque Nazca 27
plaque négative 359
plaque nord-américaine 27
plaque pacifique 27
plaque philippine 27
plaque positive 359
plaque Scotia 27
plaque signalétique 228
plaque sud-américaine 27
plaque supra-caudale 76
plaque tournante 344
plaque vertébrale 76
plaque-numéro 525
plaques convergentes 27
plaques divergentes 27
plaques tectoniques 27
plaques transformantes 27
plaquette 104, 273, 357
plaqueur droit 484
plaqueur gauche 484
plasma 104
plasmodesme 50
plastron 76, 259, 476, 486
plat 478
plat à escargots 173
plat à poisson 166
plat de dos 200
plat ovale 166
plate-bande 230
plate-forme 219, 363, 423, 516, 52
plate-forme de 10 m 518
plate-forme de 3 m 518
plate-forme de 5 m 518
plate-forme de 7,5 m 518
plate-forme de production 404
plateau 24, 29, 54, 202, 205, 219, 224, 225, 277, 278, 422, 423, 470, 522
plateau A 372
plateau B 372
plateau continental 33
plateau de chargement 319
plateau de clavier 304
plateau de frein 357
plateau de jeu 469
plateau de ponçage 229
plateau de tournage 290
plateau pour accessoires 8
plateau tournant 176
platine 421, 527
platine cassette 323
plats à rôtir 174
pleine Lune 5
pleurote en forme d'huître 123
plèvre pariétale 105
plèvre viscérale 105
plexus brachial 108
plexus lombaire 108
plexus sacré 108
pli 246
pli creux 253
pli d'aisance 253
pli de la columelle 73
pli plat 246, 253
pli surpiqué 253
plie commune 161
plinthe 191
plis, exemples 253
plissé accordéon 253
plomb 538
plomberie 194
plomberie : outils 216
plomberie, circuit 194
plombs 534
plongeoir 518
plongeon 518
plot de départ 516
pluie 41
pluie verglaçante 41
pluies acides 47, 48
plume 27, 312
plume creuse de roseau 312
plume d'oie 312
plume métallique 312
plume métallique romaine 312
plus grand que 427
plus ou moins 427
plus petit que 427
Pluton 3
pneu 349, 358, 364, 371, 522,
pneu à crampons 358, 369, 525
pneu autoroutier 358
pneu d'hiver 358
pneu de performance 358
pneu toutes saisons 358
pneumatique de guidage 380
pneumatique porteur 380

pneus, exemples 358
poche 225, 502, 505
poche à douilles 172
poche à rabat 248
poche américaine 274
poche cavalière 246
poche centrale 502
poche extérieure 274, 276
poche frontale 275
poche gilet 244
poche inférieure 502
poche intérieure 277
poche intérieure isolante 260
poche passepoilée 250
poche plaquée 244, 249, 260
poche poitrine 245, 248
poche prise dans une couture 251
poche raglan 248, 251
poche repose-bras 249, 251
poche secrète 274
poche soufflet 255
poche supérieure 502
poche tiroir 244
poche-revolver 246
poche-ticket 244
pochette 244, 274
pochette d'homme 276
pochette d'information 339
pochette de classement 340
pocheuse 175
podium des épreuves 496
poêle à combustion lente 192
poêle à crêpes 175
poêle à frire 175, 531
poêlon 175, 179
poids 422, 423, 472, 500, 501
poignée 170, 176, 177, 178, 179, 180, 192, 204, 208, 209, 210, 211, 215, 219, 221, 225, 226, 227, 229, 235, 269, 270, 273, 274, 275, 276, 277, 301, 325, 326, 341, 349, 366, 369, 380, 466, 492, 494, 500, 505, 510, 514, 515, 534, 535, 536, 537
ignée antivibrations 235
ignée arrière 537
ignée auxiliaire 228
ignée d'appui 501
ignée de conduite 467
ignée de départ (dos) 516
ignée de frein 371, 467, 522
ignée de guidage 229
ignée de maintien 352
ignée de porte 185
ignée de sécurité 237
ignée des gaz 368
ignée du démarreur 235
ignée intérieure 352
ignée isolante 179
ignée montoir 361, 364, 455
ignée profilée 269
gnée rentrante 274
gnée-pistolet 218, 228
gnées à ressort 500
gnet 86, 93, 95, 115, 245
gnet de force 500
l 114, 272
ls absorbants 53
nçon 531
nt 468
nt d'alimentation 198
nt d'amure 519
nt d'articulation 400
nt d'attache 55
nt d'attache 70
nt d'écoute 519
nt d'encochage 535
nt d'information 437
nt d'orgue 299
t de handicap 470
t de mise au jeu 506
t de raccordement 198
t de réparation 480
t fixe 357
t indicateur de température 269
tage de l'épreuve en cours 497
te 35, 55, 125, 167, 169, 220, 21, 226, 227, 246, 247, 301, 12, 471, 473, 510, 534, 538
te avant 208
te carrée 221
pointe cruciforme 221
pointe d'attache 304
pointe de centrage 228
pointe de col 245
pointe de dent 398
pointe de diamant 202
pointe de ski 514
pointe plate 221
pointes, exemples 221
pointeur 533
points 492
poire 133
poire à jus 173
poire de gonflage 461
poireau 124
pois 60, 130
pois cassés 130
pois chiches 130
pois mange-tout 130
poisson cartilagineux 74
poisson osseux 74
poissonnerie 121
poissonnière 174
poissons 74
poissons cartilagineux 158
poissons osseux 159
poitrail 83
poitrine 78
poivre blanc 138
poivre moulu 139
poivre noir 138
poivre rose 138
poivre vert 138
poivrière 166
poivron jaune 128
poivron rouge 128
poivron vert 128
Polaroid® 315
pôle Nord 21, 416
pole position 524
pôle Sud 15, 21, 416
polissoir d'ongles 265
politique 448
polluants atmosphériques 47
polluants non biodégradables 47
pollution agricole 47
pollution automobile 47
pollution de l'air 47
pollution de l'eau 48
pollution domestique 47
pollution du sol 47
pollution industrielle 47
pollution par le pétrole 48
polo 250, 255, 492
polochon 204
Pologne 450
polojama 261
polygones 429
Polynésie 453
polypode commun 52
polytric commun 51
pomelo 134
pomme 133, 236
pomme d'Adam 92
pomme de douche 195
pomme de terre 124
pomme poire 137
pomme, coupe 58
pommeau 229, 477
pompe 184, 212, 214, 370, 529
pompe à boue 403
pompier 454
ponceuse excentrique 229
poncho 251
pont 25, 273, 420
pont à poutre 344
pont bain de soleil 387
pont basculant à double volée 345
pont basculant à simple volée 345
pont cantilever 344
pont de Varole 109
pont inférieur 404
pont levant 345
pont principal 385
pont roulant 407
pont supérieur 392, 404
pont suspendu à câble porteur 344
pont tournant 344
pont-l'évêque 151
pont-levis 282
pont-promenade 386
pontet 534
ponton 525
ponts fixes 344
ponts mobiles 344
popote 531
porc 84
porc haché 153
porc-épic 82
porche 183, 285, 447
porcherie 122
pore 50, 60
pore sudoripare 114
porque 385
Porro, prisme 420
port 431
port clavier 329
port Ethernet 336
port FireWire 336
port infrarouge 336, 337
port jeux/MIDI 329
port maritime 381
port modem interne 329, 336
port parallèle 329
port pour adaptateur de courant 336
port réseau 329
port série 329
port souris 329
port USB 329, 336
port vidéo 329, 336
portail 285
porte 178, 210, 211, 213, 287, 361, 381, 392, 423, 439, 447, 528, 529
porte à deux vantaux 362
porte à lanières 286
porte à tambour manuelle 286
porte accordéon 286
porte automatique 390
porte avant 383, 386
porte classique 286
porte coulissante 195, 286
porte coulissante automatique 286
porte coupe-feu 286
porte d'entrée 362, 363
porte de garage basculante 286
porte de garage sectionnelle 286
porte de l'élévateur 363
porte de la soute 13
porte étagère 211
porte extérieure 185
porte latérale 380
porte moustiquaire 361
porte pliante 286
porte-adresse 277
porte-bagages 277, 361, 369, 370
porte-bagages arrière 369
porte-bidon 371
porte-bûches 193
porte-cartes 274
porte-chéquier 275
porte-clés 275
porte-coupures 275
porte-documents à soufflet 274
porte-documents plat 275
porte-fenêtre 164, 188, 189
porte-fil dentaire 272
porte-filtre 181
porte-foyer 192
porte-jarretelles 259
porte-marteau 225
porte-matraque 456
porte-mine 312
porte-monnaie 275
porte-moulinet 536, 537
porte-outil 229
porte-parapluies 273
porte-passeport 275
porte-rouleau 195
porte-sac 505
porte-savon 195
porte-serviettes 195
porte-skis 356
porte-stylo 274
porte-tube 421
porte-vélos 356
portée 298
portefeuille 275
portefeuille chéquier 274
portes d'entrée 294
portes, exemples 286
portière 349, 352
portique 381, 397, 406, 407, 447
portique de chargement de conteneurs 381
portique de signalisation 375
ports pour carte mémoire 471
ports pour manette 471
Portugal 449
position carpée 518
position d'équilibre 418
position des joueurs 474, 481, 482, 489
position droite 518
position groupée 518
positions de départ, plongeon 518
poste d'aiguillage 375
poste d'observation 7
poste de communication 380
poste de l'agent de sécurité 463
poste de patrouille 512
poste de pilotage 392, 395
poste de police 433
poste de secours 345, 512
poste des infirmières (urgence ambulatoire) 463
poste des infirmières (urgence majeure) 462
poste téléphonique 327
postillon 469
pot 163
pot d'échappement 351, 367, 368
pot d'échappement 369
poteau 187, 487, 490, 495
poteau cornier 187
poteau de but 485
poteau de ligne de jeu 475
poteau du ring 498
potence 371, 421, 467
poterne 282
potiron 129
pou 69
poubelle 215
pouce 79, 115, 243, 477
pouce opposable 91
poudre 534
poudre libre 266
poudre pressée 266
poudrier 266
pouf 201
poulailler 122
poule 81
poulet 155
poulie 219, 360, 535
poulie de chariot 397
poulie de tension du régulateur 287
poumon droit 103, 105
poumon gauche 103, 105
poumons 105
poupe 386, 519
pour broyer et râper 170
pour couper 177
pour cuire 178
pour l'emploi du temps 338
pour la correspondance 338
pour la pâtisserie 172
pour le classement 339
pour mélanger et battre 176
pour mesurer 171
pour ouvrir 170
pour passer et égoutter 171
pour presser 177
pourcentage 337, 427
pourpier 127
pousse 53
pousse de bambou 125
poussoir 170, 177, 180, 460
poussoir d'arrêt 424
poussoir de mise en marche 424
poussoir de remise à zéro 424
poutre 187, 283, 288, 496
poutre cantilever 344
poutre continue 344
poutre d'équilibre 497
poutre de levage 364
poutre de queue 395
poutre suspendue 344
poutre-châssis 401
praire 157
prairie 24, 122
prairie tempérée 44
praticable pour exercices au sol 496
précipitation 45
précipitations 41
précipitations hivernales 41
prémaxillaire 74
premier arbitre 487
premier assistant-cadreur 290
premier but 474
premier croissant 5
premier espace 489
premier quartier 5
premier radial externe 97
premier-but 474
première joueuse 515
première ligne 482
première molaire 101
première prémolaire 101
premières feuilles 53
premiers violons 295
prémolaires 101
préposé au banc des pénalités 507
préposé au contrôle des billets 294
prépuce 111
près du ring 498
présentoir de brochures 442
présentoir réfrigéré 438
presqu'île de Corée 19
presqu'île de Kola 18
presqu'île du Kamtchatka 19
presse à pectoraux 501
presse-agrumes 170, 177
presse-ail 170
presse-café 181
pressing 437
pression à la taille 260
pression au niveau de la mer 39
pression barométrique 39
pression devant 261
pression, mesure 426
prétoire 440
prévention de la criminalité 456
prévention des incendies 454
prévision météorologique 38
principales pièces d'une maison 188
principaux organes des systèmes automobiles 350
printemps 38
prise audio 329
prise casque 310, 311, 322, 323, 326
prise chronométrée 210
prise classique 493
prise d'air 383, 523
prise d'air 362
prise d'air de refroidissement du moteur 525
prise d'air du moteur 362
prise d'alimentation 329
prise d'eau 407
prise d'entrée/sortie audio 337
prise d'oxygène 464
prise de charge 271
prise de courant 198, 217
prise de courant commutée 322
prise de courant européenne 198
prise de la sonde thermique 178
prise de télécommande 314, 315
prise électrique 361
prise porte-plume 493
prise pour écouteurs 329
prises d'entrée/de sortie audio/vidéo 322
prises vidéo et numérique 315
prises, exemples 499
prisme de Porro 420
prix à l'unité 423
prix à payer 423
procédé 503
producteur 291
production d'électricité par énergie éolienne 413
production d'électricité par énergie géothermique 402
production d'électricité par énergie nucléaire 408
production d'électricité par énergie thermique 402
production d'électricité par l'alternateur 408
production de chaleur 408
produits céréaliers 144
produits d'emballage 120
produits d'entretien 120

produits de fission (noyaux radioactifs) 415
produits de la raffinerie 405
produits de traiteur 121
produits laitiers 120, 150
produits pétrochimiques 405
produits pour animaux familiers 121
profil du sol 54
profondeur du foyer 27
programmateur 212, 213, 214
programmation des voix 310
programmes informatiques 457
projecteur 290, 294, 371, 376
projecteur orientable 455
projecteur sous-marin 184
projecteurs 293
projection conique 22
projection cylindrique 22
projection d'épaule par un côté 499
projection en cercle 499
projection horizontale 22
projection interrompue 22
projections cartographiques 22
pronaos 279
propagation 418
propulseur 10
propulseur d'étrave 387
propulseurs de commande d'orientation 12
prosciutto 156
prospection terrestre 403
prostate 111
protecteur d'avant-bras 486
protecteur d'embout 460
protecteur lombaire 486
protection d'usure 525
protection de l'ouïe 458
protection de la tête 458
protection des pieds 459
protection des voies respiratoires 459
protection des yeux 458
protège-cheville 476
protège-côtes 486
protège-cou 486
protège-coude 526
protège-dents 486, 498
protège-gorge 476
protège-hanche 486
protège-lame inférieur 227
protège-lame supérieur 227
protège-main 525
protège-matelas 204
protège-orteils 459, 476
protège-poignet 527
protège-tibia 480, 513
protège-tympan 458
protocole de communication 334
proton 414
protoneurone sensitif 110
protubérance 4
proue 387, 519
province 23
prune 132
pseudopode 66
pubis 92, 94
puce 69
puisard 194
puissance, mesure 426
puits 278
puits d'injection 402
puits de dérive 519
puits de production 402
puits sous-marin 404
pulls 254
pulpe 57, 58, 59, 101, 114
pulvérisateur 236, 402
puma 88
punaise rayée 69
punaises 341
pupille 87, 119
pupille verticale 76
pupitre 305, 311
pupitre du chef d'orchestre 295
pyjama 256
pylône 344, 375
pylône du moteur 393
pyramide 278, 429
Pyrénées 18
python 77

Q

Qatar 452
quad 369
quadrant 428
quadrilatère 429
quadruple croche 299
quai 375, 379, 381, 390, 430
quai d'embarquement 389
quai de chargement 435
quai de déchargement 437, 439
quai de gare 374
quantité de matière, mesure 426
quark d 414
quark u 414
quart de soupir 299
quart-arrière 485
quarte 298
quartier 5, 58, 240, 262
quartier des affaires 430, 432
quatuor 300
queue 57, 58, 59, 76, 82, 83, 86, 90, 111, 228, 393, 412, 526, 531
queue de billard 503
queue de l'hélix 115
queue de poussières 6
queue ionique 6
queusot 199
quillard 521
quinoa 143
quinte 298, 468
quinte royale 468
quintette 300

R

rabat 244, 275, 532
rabot 229
raccord à compression 197
raccord de robinet 236
raccord de signalisation 361
raccord de tuyau 236
races de chats 87
races de chiens 86
racine 54, 101
racine antérieure 110
racine carrée 337
racine carrée de 427
racine de l'hélix 115
racine de l'ongle 114
racine du nez 117
racine motrice 109, 110
racine pivotante 63
racine postérieure 110
racine principale 53
racine secondaire 53
racine sensitive 109, 110
racine traçante 63
racines adventives 52
raclette 151
raclette-gril 179
racloir 514
radar 382, 383, 386, 387
radar météorologique 38, 392
radiateur 350, 358
radiateurs 11
radicelle 53, 63
radicule 53
radio 326, 457
radio portable 325
radio-réveil 325
radioactivité, mesure 426
radiocassette laser 326
radis 129
radis noir 129
radis oriental 129
radius 98
raffinerie 404, 431
raglan 251
raie 158
raie des fesses 93, 95
raie sourcilière 78
raifort 129
rail d'éclairage 207
rail de glissement 353, 521
rail-guide de contrepoids 287
rail-guide de la cabine 287
rails de travelling 290
rainette 75
rainure 169, 510
raisin 62, 132
raisin, coupe 59
ralenti 319
rallonge 202, 209
ramasseur 490
rambarde 384, 526
ramboutan 137
rame 501
rame de métro 378, 380
rameau 53, 62, 63, 65
rameau communicant 110
ramequin 166
rameur 501
ramille 63
rampant 279
rampe 188, 189, 191, 279, 281, 293
rampe d'accès 344, 386
rampe d'éclairage 207
rampe de quai 381
rampe de signalisation 455, 457
rampe, planche à roulettes 526
ramure 63
rang 272
rangée 293
rangement pour les gants 464
râpe 170
râpe à fromage cylindrique 170
râpe à muscade 170
rappel de mémoire 337
raquette de badminton 494
raquette de tennis 492
raquette de tennis de table 493
ras-de-cou 250, 255, 264
ras-el-hanout 139
rasage 271
rasette 305
rasoir à double tranchant 271
rasoir à manche 271
rasoir effileur 269
rasoir électrique 271
rasoir jetable 271
rat 82
rat, morphologie 82
rate 103
râteau 233, 503
ratissoire 233
raton laveur 88
ravier 166
ravioli 146
rayon 70, 273, 371, 428
rayon épineux 74
rayon lumineux 419
rayon médullaire 63
rayon mou 74
rayonnement 415
rayonnement infrarouge 46, 418
rayonnement solaire 45, 46, 410, 411
rayonnement solaire absorbé 46
rayonnement solaire réfléchi 46
rayonnement ultraviolet 418
rayons gamma 418
rayons X 418
ré 298
réacteur 408
réacteur nucléaire 409
réaction en chaîne 415
réalisateur 291
rebobinage 319, 323
rebord 210
rebord de cuve 212
rebras 243
récamier 200
réceptacle 51, 56, 59
réceptacle à déchets 365
réceptacle de brosses 272
récepteur 327
récepteur de radio par satellite 326
récepteur de son 460
récepteur sensoriel 110
récepteurs du goût 118
réception 439
réception des messages 328
réception directe 316
réception du fret 391
receveur 474, 475, 476, 490, 495
receveur éloigné 485
recharge 312
réchaud 174
réchaud à deux feux 529
réchaud à un feu 529
réchauffement global 46
recherche 335
recherche des canaux 319
récif de la Grande Barrière 15
récipient 176
recourbe-cils 266
rectangle 429
rectangle des instructeurs 474
rectangulaire 530
rectrice 78
rectum 106, 111, 112
recyclage 49
redingote 251
réflecteur 217, 321, 365
réflecteurs solaires 316
réformeur catalytique 405
réfrigérateur 164, 211, 438
réfrigérateurs 438
refroidissement 405
refroidissement de la vapeur par l'eau 408
regard de visite 434
régie 293
région auriculaire 78
région malaire 78
région négative 410
région positive 410
registre des aigus 296
registre des basses 296
réglage 466
réglage de centrage 329
réglage de hausse 420
réglage de l'afficheur 327
réglage de l'angle 229
réglage de la balance 303
réglage de la hauteur 501
réglage de la luminosité 329
réglage de la pression 272
réglage de la pression d'oxygène 10
réglage de la résistance 501
réglage de la tension 537
réglage de la tonalité 303
réglage de niveau d'enregistrement 323
réglage de profondeur 229
réglage de tempo 311
réglage des températures 208
réglage du contraste 329
réglage du diaphragme 421
réglage du four 210
réglage du volume 303, 311, 319, 322, 325, 329
réglage du volume des communications 10
réglage en hauteur du condenseur 421
réglage horizontal 329
réglage latéral 420
réglage micrométrique (azimut) 8, 9
réglage micrométrique (latitude) 8, 9
réglage vertical 329
réglages 328
règle 425
règle graduée 425, 531
règne animal 66
règne végétal 50
régulateur de pression 174, 529
régulateur de vitesse 287, 354
rehausseur 205
rein 73, 103
rein droit 107
rein gauche 107
reine 68
reine, abeille 68
reins 83, 93, 95
rejet 63
rejet d'oxygène 54
rejets industriels 47, 48
relevé de transaction 443
relief lunaire 5
religion 446
reliure à anneaux plastiques 340
reliure à glissière 339
reliure à pince 339
reliure à ressort 339
reliure à vis 339
reliure spirale 340
rémige primaire 78
rémige secondaire 78
rémige tertiaire 78
remise 182, 230
remorque 380
remorqueur 384
rempart 5, 282
remplage 285
remplissage 404
renard 88
renfort de nuque 525
réniforme 55
renne 84
renseignements 512
renversé 518
repère de ligne de marche 533
repère de niveau d'eau 208
repère de touche 302, 303
repère de virage de dos 517
répertoire 334
répertoire téléphonique 327, 338
répéteur 317
répondeur numérique 328
repose-main 332
repose-pied 467
repose-pied du passager 367, 368
repose-pied du pilote 367, 368
repose-pieds 205
repose-poignets détachable 330
repousse-chair 265
reproduction de clés 437
reprographie 442
reptation 31
reptiles 76
République arabe syrienne 452
République centrafricaine 451
République de Corée 453
République de Moldova 450
République démocratique du Congo 451
République démocratique populaire lao 453
République dominicaine 449
République populaire démocratique de Corée 453
République tchèque 450
République-Unie de Tanzanie 451
répulsion 416
requin, morphologie 74
réseau d'oléoducs 404
réseau national 316
réseau nerveux 101
réseau privé 316
réseau téléphonique 317
réserve d'eau 272
réserves alimentaires 439
réservoir 13, 181, 406, 407, 454, 529
réservoir à carburant 364, 377, 39
réservoir à essence 351, 366, 369
réservoir à toit flottant 404
réservoir auxiliaire 365
réservoir d'alcool 424
réservoir d'arrosage 408
réservoir d'eau 181
réservoir d'essence 235
réservoir d'huile 235
réservoir de brut 405
réservoir de chasse d'eau 195
réservoir de liquide de frein 357
réservoir de mercure 424
réservoir externe 12
réservoir magmatique 28, 402
réservoir propane 361
réservoir tampon 404
résidente 464
résidus non recyclables 49
résistance électrique, mesure 426
résistance hydraulique 501
résistances 417
résonateur 324
ressort 27, 206, 222, 312, 535
ressort athlétique 500
ressort de rappel 357
ressort de soupape 360

ressort de suspension 212
ressort de tension 355, 500
ressort hélicoïdal 351
restaurant 386, 432, 435, 436, 438
restaurants-minute 437
résurgence 31
retable 446
réticule 420
réticulum endoplasmique 50, 66
rétine 119, 419
retour 331
retour de l'eau au générateur de vapeur 408
retourné 518
rétroviseur 354, 363, 364, 366, 368, 369, 523
rétroviseur extérieur 348, 362
rétroviseur grand-angle 362, 363
réunion 427
réverbère 434
revers 240, 244, 246
revers à cran aigu 244
revers cranté 248
revêtement 187, 493
revêtement de sécurité 10
revêtement synthétique 492
revêtement thermique 12
revêtements de sol textiles 190
ez-de-chaussée 182, 188
Rhéa 3
hino-pharynx 117
hinocéros 85
hizoïde 51
hizome 52
hodyménie palmé 123
hubarbe 125
as 35
bosome 50, 66
chelieu 240
cotta 150
deau de fer 292
deau de scène 292, 293
deau séparateur 464
doir 521
gatoni 146
lettes 156
naye 30
iceau 200
ig 498
154
et 169, 222
ière 24, 32
ière souterraine 31
61, 143, 147
: panicule 61
basmati 147
blanc 147
complet 147
étuvé 147
sauvage 143
ère 47
e 404
e bain-de-soleil 252
e chemisier 252
e de maison 252
e enveloppe 252
e fourreau 252
e princesse 252
e taille basse 252
e tee-shirt 261
e trapèze 252
e tunique 252
e-manteau 252
e-polo 252
erval, balance 422
s, exemples 252
net 195
net d'arrêt 196, 197
net d'arrêt général 194
net de réglage de débit 454
net de vidange 404
net flotteur à clapet 196
net relais 529
nets 210
t boulanger 179
t de cuisine 177
27
lle 230
roche mère 54
roches d'intrusion 26
roches ignées 26
roches métamorphiques 26
roches sédimentaires 26
rognons 154
Roi 468, 470
romaine 126
romano 151
romarin 142
rond pronateur 96
rond-point 25
ronde 299
rondelle 417, 510
rondelle à denture extérieure 222
rondelle à denture intérieure 222
rondelle à ressort 222
rondelle conique 196
rondelle plate 222
rondelles 222
rongeur 82
roquefort 151
roquette 127
rorqual 90
rosace 302
rose 56, 285
rose des vents 23
rosée 41
rosette 186
rossignol 80
rôti 152, 153
rôti de côtes 152
rotini 146
rotonde 435
rotor 412, 537
rotor anticouple 395
rotule 98, 224
roue 231, 364, 467, 522, 525, 527
roue avant 401
roue de secours 361
roue de support 523
roue dentée 523
roue folle 398
roue libre 372
roue pivotante 467
roues motrices 401
rouge 418
rouge à lèvres 266
rouge-gorge 80
Rouges 469
rouget barbet 159
rouleau 219, 268
rouleau à pâtisserie 172
rouleaux de la Torah 447
roulement à billes 413
roulette 205, 209, 277, 308, 526
roulette de commande 337
roulette de défilement 332
roulette de pâtissier 172
roulis 395
Roumanie 450
roupie 440
route 25, 343, 430
route d'accès 388
route secondaire 25
route, coupe 342
routeur 334
Royaume-Uni de Grande-Bretagne et d'Irlande du Nord 449
ruban 225
ruban blanc 493, 495
ruban de bouclage 457
ruban de Téflon 216
ruban de tissu adhésif 461
ruche 122
ruché 260
rue 25, 433, 435
rue commerçante 432
rue, coupe 434
ruelle 433
Ruffini, corpuscule 114
rugby 482
rugbyman 483
ruisseau 32
ruissellement 45
russule verdoyante 123
rutabaga 129
Rwanda 451

S

sablier 171
sablière 377
sablière double 187
sabot 83, 224, 365, 473
sabot de protection 398
sac 296
sac à bandoulière 276
sac à dos 532
sac à provisions 276
sac accordéon 276
sac besace 276
sac boîte 276
sac cartable 275
sac de congélation 162
sac de golf 505
sac de sable 498
sac fourre-tout 276
sac gonflable 354
sac marin 276
sac polochon 276
sac seau 275
sac-filet 162
sachet 162
sacoche 369, 372
sacristie 446
sacrum 98, 99
sacs à main 275
sacs à provisions 121
sacs de couchage, exemples 530
safran 138, 384
saharienne 255
saindoux 149
saint-bernard 86
Saint-Kitts-et-Nevis 449
Saint-Laurent 16
Saint-Marin 450
saint-pierre 161
Saint-Vincent-et-les Grenadines 449
Sainte-Lucie 449
saisons, cycle 38
saladier 166
salamandre 75
salami allemand 156
salami de Gênes 156
salchow 509
salière 166
salle 293
salle à manger 188, 386, 438, 439
salle d'anesthésie 464
salle d'arts plastiques 444
salle d'attente 463
salle d'attente des familles 462
salle d'attente du centre de prélèvements 465
salle d'attente principale 465
salle d'attente secondaire 465
salle d'embarquement 391
salle d'entreposage 438
salle d'examen 465
salle d'examen audiométrique 465
salle d'examen et de soins 463
salle d'examen gynécologique 463
salle d'habillage 290
salle d'informatique 444
salle d'opération 464, 465
salle d'ophtalmologie et d'oto-rhino-laryngologie 463
salle de bains 189, 195, 439, 464
salle de bal 387
salle de classe 444, 445
salle de classe pour élèves en difficultés d'apprentissage 444
salle de commande 406
salle de conférences 442
salle de contrôle des machines 384
salle de musique 444
salle de plâtre 463
salle de prélèvements 465
salle de préparation chirurgicale 464
salle de prière 447
salle de projection 294
salle de quilles 436
salle de rangement du matériel médical 465
salle de réanimation 462
salle de réception 447
salle de repos des infirmières 465
salle de réunion 439, 442, 445
salle de réveil 464
salle de sciences 444
salle de séjour 188
salle de soins 465
salle de spectacle 292, 432
salle de stérilisation 464, 465
salle de stockage du matériel souillé 462, 464
salle de stockage du matériel stérile 462
salle de triage 463
salle des cartes 382
salle des enseignants 445
salle des jurés 440
salle des machines 386, 406, 407
salle des pas perdus 374
salles d'entrevue 440
salomé 241
salon 188, 386
salon d'attente 439
salon de coiffure 436
salon des employés 443
salon du personnel 463
salopette 254
salopette à bretelles croisées 261
salopette à dos montant 260
salsifis 129
sambal oelek 141
Samoa 453
sandale 241
sandalette 242
Sandow® 528, 529
sandre 160
sang désoxygéné 104
sang oxygéné 104
sang, composition 104
sangle 353, 491, 501, 505
sangle d'amortissement 458
sangle de compression 532
sangle de fermeture 532
sangle de nuque 458
sangle élastique 277
sangle serre-vêtements 277
sanglier 84
santé 460
São Tomé-et-Príncipe 451
sapin 65
sapotille 137
sarcloir 233
sardine 159
sarment 62
sarrasin 61, 143
sarrasin : grappe 61
sarriette 142
sas 286
sas du laboratoire 13
sas pressurisé 345
satellite 316
satellite artificiel 37
satellite de télécommunications 335
satellite météorologique 38
satellites 2
satellites de télécommunications 316
Saturne 2, 3
sauce aux prunes 141
sauce hoisin 140
sauce soja 140
sauce Tabasco® 140
sauce Worcestershire 140
saucière 166
saucisse de Francfort 156
saucisse de Toulouse 156
saucisson kielbasa 156
sauge 142
saule pleureur 64
saumon de l'Atlantique 161
saumon du Pacifique 161
saupoudreuse 172
saut à la perche 472
saut à ski 513
saut en hauteur 473
saut en longueur 472
sauterelle 402
sauteur 513
sauteuse 175
sautoir 264
sautoir, longueur opéra 264
sauts, exemples 509
savane 40, 44
savon de toilette 267
saxhorn 307
saxophone 306
scaphandre spatial 10
scapulaire 78
scarole 126
scellement, matériau 417
scène 278, 292, 293
schéma de la circulation 103
schnauzer 86
Schwann, gaine 110
scie à chantourner 226
scie à guichet 226
scie à métaux 226
scie à onglet manuelle 226
scie circulaire 227
scie d'élagage 234
scie de camping 533
scie égoïne 226
scie sauteuse 227
science 414
scion 536
scissure oblique 105
sclérotique 119
scooter 369
scooter de mer 523
score doublé 471
score triplé 471
scorpion 70
scorsonère 129
scripte 291
scrotum 92, 111
sculptures 358
seau 215
seau isotherme 180
sébaste 161
sécateur 234
sèche-cheveux 270
sèche-linge électrique 213
second arbitre 487
second assistant-cadreur 290
seconde 298, 428
secondeur extérieur droit 484
secondeur extérieur gauche 484
secondeur intérieur 484
seconds violons 295
secrétaire 203
secrétariat 443, 445
secteur 428
secteur des civières 462
section articulée 363
section de conduit 193
sécurité 454
segment 357, 360
segment abdominal 67
seiche 157
seigle 61, 143
seigle : épi 61
sein 92, 94, 113
séisme 27
seizième de soupir 299
séjour 528
sel fin 141
sel marin 141
sélecteur d'entrée 322
sélecteur d'inclinaison de la lame 227
sélecteur de bandes 323
sélecteur de coupe 271
sélecteur de fonctions 314
sélecteur de hauteur 209
sélecteur de micro 303
sélecteur de mode 326
sélecteur de mode sonore 322
sélecteur de niveau d'eau 212
sélecteur de programme 310
sélecteur de régime 237
sélecteur de rythme 311
sélecteur de stations 325, 326
sélecteur de température 178, 212, 213, 270
sélecteur de vitesse 176, 177, 227, 270
sélecteur de vitesse de rotation 228
sélecteur de vitesses 367, 368, 369
sélecteur de voix 311
sélecteur quadridirectionnel 315
sélecteur télé/vidéo 319
sélecteurs de fonctions 327
sélection des canaux 319
selle 369, 370, 501, 523
selle biplace 367
selle conducteur 369
selle passager 369
sellette d'attelage 364

semelle 187, 208, 227, 229, 247, 509, 510, 511
semelle antidérapante 261
semelle d'usure 240, 263
semelle intercalaire 262
semelle pivotante 224
semence 220
semi-rectangulaire 530
semi-remorque frigorifique 365
semoir à main 231
semoule 144
Sénégal 20, 451
sens de déplacement des électrons 416, 417
sensibilité 314
sépale 56, 58, 59
séparateur 359, 384, 402, 417
séparateur électrolytique 417
séparateur liquide/gaz 359
séparation magnétique 49
séparation papier/carton 49
séparation-classeur 274
septième 298
septum interventriculaire 104
septum lucidum 109
séquence 468
séquenceur 310
sérac 30
Serbie 450
serfouette 233
seringue 460
seringue pour lavage de cavités 460
serpe 234
serpent 76, 469
serpent à sonnette 77
serpent corail 77
serpent venimeux, morphologie 76
serpentin 210
serpents et échelles 469
serre 79, 122
serre-joint 224, 226
serre-joint à tuyau 224
serre-livres 341
serre-poignet 492
serre-tête 324, 458, 459
serre-tête antibruit 458
serrure 185, 186, 202, 211, 275, 277, 349, 352
serrure à clé 274
serrure à combinaison 274
sertissage 534
serveur 334, 335, 491, 494
serveur d'accès 335
service 487, 490
service à fondue 174
service à la clientèle 443
service d'entretien 346
service de colis 374
services d'assurance 442
services de crédit 442
services financiers 442
services sociaux 465
serviette 274
serviette de toilette 267
servofrein 350, 357
seuil 185
seuil de l'évacuateur 406
sextuor 300
Seychelles 452
shampooing 267
shekel 440
shiitake 123
short 254, 261, 473, 480, 483, 488
short boxeur 263
short de boxe 498
si 298
siamois 87
siège 196, 200, 201, 205, 353, 467
siège coulissant 501
siège de sécurité pour enfant 356
siège de vélo pour enfant 372
siège double 380
siège du rabbin 447
siège simple 380
siège-baquet : vue de face 353
siège-baquet : vue de profil 353
sièges 201
Sierra Leone 451
sifflet 180
signal de voie 375
signature du titulaire 441
signature officielle 441
silique, coupe 60
sill 28
sillet 301, 302, 303
sillon 118
sillon antérieur 115
sillon médian 118
sillon naso-labial 117
sillon terminal 118
silo-couloir 122
silo-tour 122
silos 381
simulateur d'escalier 501
Singapour 453
sinus frontal 117
sinus latéral inférieur 62
sinus latéral supérieur 62
sinus pétiolaire 62
sinus sphénoïdal 117
siphon 194, 196, 197
sirop antitussif 467
sirop d'érable 149
sirop de maïs 149
sismogramme 27
sismographe horizontal 27
sismographe vertical 27
sismographes 27
sistre 309
site d'enfouissement 47
sixte 298
ski 510, 523
ski alpin 510
ski de descente/super-G 510
ski de fond 514
ski de grand slalom 510
ski de saut 513
ski de slalom 510
skieur alpin 510
skieur de fond 514
skimmer 184
skis, exemples 510
slalom géant 511
slalom spécial 511
slip 247, 259
slip de bain 263
Slovaquie 450
Slovénie 450
smash 491
smog 47
snooker 503
société 430
socle 27, 176, 179, 180, 192, 206, 332, 412, 422
socle fixe 224
socle rembourré 489
socle-chargeur 208
socque 242
socquette 257
softball 477
soie 167, 169, 216, 271, 536
soies 219
soigneur 489, 498
soins de la pelouse 237
soins du corps 267
soja, germes 131
soja, graine 131
sol 48, 298
sol naturel 342
solarium 385
sole 161
soléaire 96
Soleil 2, 4, 5, 38
Soleil, éclipse 4
Soleil, structure 4
solide 414, 415
solide amorphe 414
solidification 414
solin 193
solive 190
solive de plafond 187
solive de plancher 187
solive de rive 187
solstice d'été 38
solstice d'hiver 38
solution multifonctions 272
Somalie 451
sommaire 313
sommation 427
sommelier 438
sommet 29, 512
sommier 304
sommier tapissier 204
sonde spatiale 37
sonde thermique 178
sorbetière 180
sore 52
sorgho 61
sorgho : panicule 61
sortie 343
sortie d'air chaud 192
sortie de piste 391
sortie de piste à grande vitesse 388
sortie des billets 442
sortie des originaux 328
sortie des tickets 346
sortie du caloporteur 410
sortie S-Video 336
soubassement 202, 283
souche 63
soudage : outils 218
Soudan 451
soudure 218
soufflet 274, 276, 296
soupape 174
soupape d'admission 360
soupape d'échappement 360
soupape d'évacuation 307, 461
soupape de sûreté 408
soupape expiratoire 459
soupape inspiratoire 459
soupière 166
soupir 299
source 32
source alimentaire fondamentale 45
source de courant 416
sourcils 87
sourdine 307
souris à roulette 332
souris mécanique 332
souris optique 332
souris sans fil 332
sous-couche 190
sous-épineux 97
sous-fondation 342
sous-pied 254
sous-plancher 187, 190
sous-sol 54, 182, 281, 435
sous-titre 313
sous-vêtement 524
sous-vêtements 247, 258
soustraction 337, 427
soustraction en mémoire 337
soute 12, 393
soute à bagages 362, 383, 395
soutien-gorge 259
soutien-gorge balconnet 259
soutien-gorge corbeille 259
spadice 57
spaghetti 146
spaghettini 146
spatule 173, 510, 514
spatulée 55
spécialiste technique 509
spécifications techniques 358
spectre électromagnétique 418
spencer 254
spermatozoïde 111
sphaigne squarreuse 51
sphénoïde 100
sphère 429
sphincter anal 106
spicule 4
spirale 70, 221
spirale centrale 70
spiruline 123
splénius de la tête 97
spores 52
sports 468
sports à roulettes 526
sports aquatiques 516
sports d'hiver 515
sports de balle 474
sports de ballon 474
sports de combat 498
sports de force 500
sports de précision 502
sports de raquette 493
sports gymniques 496
sports motorisés 524
sports nautiques 516
spot 207
spot à pince 206
squelette 98
Sri Lanka 453
stabilisateur 393, 395, 397, 400, 455, 523
stabilisateur de roulis 386
stade 431, 472
stalactite 31
stalagmite 31
stands 524
station d'accueil 337
station de métro 378, 432
station de pompage 404
station de pompage intermédiaire 404
station de pompage principale 404
station de ski 512
station locale 316
station météorologique d'aéronef 38
station météorologique océanique 38
station météorologique sur bouée 38
station météorologique, disposition des informations 39
station spatiale internationale 11
station terrestre 38
station terrestre de télécommunications 335
station-relais 316
station-relais à micro-ondes 334
station-service 346, 433
stationnement 435, 504
statue 446
steeple 472
steppe 40
sterno-cléido-mastoïdien 96
sternum 98
stéthoscope 460
stigmate 56, 60, 67
stilton 151
stimulateur de gencives 272
stipule 55
stop 86
stoppeur 481
store à enroulement automatique 356
strato-cumulus 42
stratopause 37
stratosphère 37
stratus 42
structure 186, 342
structure antitonneau 525
structure d'un arbre 63
structure d'un champignon 52
structure d'un lichen 50
structure d'une algue 51
structure d'une feuille 55
structure d'une fleur 56
structure d'une fougère 52
structure d'une maison 188
structure d'une mousse 51
structure d'une plante 53
structure de l'oreille 116
structure de la biosphère 44
structure de la moelle épinière 109
structure de la Terre 26
structure du Soleil 4
structure en treillis 11
structure métallique 374
style 56, 57, 58, 59, 60, 424
stylet 312, 337
stylo-bille 312
stylo-plume 312
stylobate 279
subarctique 40
subduction 27
sublimation 414
substance blanche 109, 110
substance corticale 107
substance grise 109, 110
substance médullaire 107
substratum imperméable 402
subtropical humide 40
suceur à tapis et planchers 209
suceur plat 209
suceur triangulaire à tissus 209
sucre 149
sucre candi 149
sucre glace 149
sucre granulé 149
sucrier 166
Sud 23
Sud Est 23
Sud Ouest 23
Sud Sud-Est 23
Sud Sud-Ouest 23
Suède 450
Suisse 450
sumac 139
super-géant 511
supermarché 120, 433, 437
supplément en couleurs 313
supplément littéraire 313
support 174, 199, 269, 308, 493
support à bagages 523
support de fixation 9, 206
support de main 297
support de panneau 489
support de plaquette 273
support de pouce 306
supports d'enregistrement 319
suppression 328, 331
surf acrobatique 513
surf alpin 513
surf des neiges 513
surface d'affichage 341
surface de but 480
surface de coin 481
surface de combat 499
surface de cuisson 179, 210
surface de frappe 477
surface de jeu 493
surface de l'eau 518
surface de la glace 515
surface de la peau 114
surface de réparation 480
surface de sécurité 499
surface dure (ciment) 492
surface verticale 526
surfaces 428
surfaces de jeu 492
surfeur 513
surfusion 414
surimpression 314
Suriname 448
suroît 239
surpiqûre 240, 246, 260, 262
surtitre 313
survêtement 262
suspension 206, 380
suspension arrière 522
suspente 344
suture 60
suture coronale 100
suture lambdoïde 100
suture squameuse 100
Swaziland 452
sweat à capuche 262
sweat-shirt 262
symboles scientifiques usuels 426
symboles, cartes 468
symphyse pubienne 111, 112
synagogue 447
synapse 110
synthèse additive 418
synthèse des couleurs 418
synthèse soustractive 418
synthétiseur 310
système audio 354
système d'alimentation en essence 351
système d'échappement 351
système de climatisation 46
système de contrôle de la rampe de signalisation 457
système de direction 351
système de freinage 351
système de freinage antiblocage 3
système de jeux vidéo 471
système de lentilles 420
système de pointage fin 7
système de refroidissement 351
système de retenue à sacs gonflables 354
système de suspension 351
système de transmission 351
système de verrouillage 209
système électrique 351
système hydraulique 396
système international d'unités 42
système nerveux 108
système nerveux central 109
système nerveux périphérique 10
système racinaire 53, 62
système rotary 403
système routier 342
système solaire 2
systèmes automobiles 351

INDEX FRANÇAIS

T

T.G.V. 376
tabernacle 446
table 202, 493, 502
table à abattants 202
table à langer 205
table à rallonges 202
table d'harmonie 301, 302, 304
table d'opération 464
table de chevet 439, 464
table de communion 446
table de cuisson 164
table de lecture 447
table de lit 464
table de rotation 403
table de service 438
table de travail 210
table des greffiers 440
table des résultats 518
tableau 444
tableau d'affichage 496
tableau d'affichage 341, 444, 492, 499
tableau d'affichage des vols 391
tableau de bord 354, 366, 368
tableau de commande 178, 179, 210, 212, 213, 214
tableau de manœuvre 287
tableau de pointage 497
tableau des scores 471
tableau du souvenir 447
tableau horaire 374
tableau indicateur 472
tables gigognes 202
tables, exemples 202
tablette 192, 203, 219
:ablette de verre 211
:ablette porte-outil 219
:ablier 344, 369, 396, 498
:ablier-blouse 255
:ablinum 280
:abloïd 313
'abouret 164, 201, 498
abouret de bar 438
abouret-bar 201
abouret-escabeau 219
abulation à droite 330
abulation à gauche 330
ache 4
ache jaune 119
achymètre 368
adjikistan 452
agliatelle aux épinards 146
ahini 140
aie d'oreiller 204
aille 93, 95
aille-bordures 237
aille-crayon 341
aille-haies 235
ailleur 251
ajine 174
alkie-walkie 456
aloche 216
lon 93, 95, 169, 226, 229, 240, 247, 262, 273, 301, 302, 358, 477, 492, 494, 503, 506, 509, 510, 514, 536, 537
lon d'appui 176, 208
lonnette de dessus 240
lonneur 482
lonnière 511, 514
us 342
us continental 33
n-tam 308
narillo 136
narin 91
nbour 170, 213, 357, 425, 536, 537
nbour d'aisselle 297
nbour de basque 309
nbourin 239
nia 82
nis 171, 492, 494
nis à farine 172
nis vibrant 403
npon encreur 338
dem 255, 373
tangage 395
taon 69
tapis 190, 498, 499, 502
tapis de plancher 356
tapis de réception 496
tapis de sol cousu 528, 529
tapis de souris 332
tapis roulant 390
taquet 520, 521
taquet coinceur 521
taquet de verrouillage 333
taro 124
tarse 78
Tasmanie 15
tasse 531, 532
tasse à café 166
tasse à mesurer 171
tasse à thé 166
tassergal 160
Tchad 451
té 505
té de base 193
techniques 487
tectrice primaire 78
tectrice sous-caudale 78
tectrice sus-alaire 78
tectrice sus-caudale 78
teddy 258
tégument 61
tégument de la graine 57
télécabine 512
télécommande 319, 321
télécommunications par satellite 317
télécopieur 328
télédiffusion par satellite 316
télémanipulateur 11, 12
téléobjectif 314
téléphone 439
téléphone portable 327
téléphone public 294, 437, 438, 463
téléport 317
télescope 7, 9
télescope spatial Hubble 7, 37
télescope, coupe 9
télésiège 512
téléski biplace 512
téléviseur 439, 444
téléviseur à cristaux liquides 318
téléviseur à écran cathodique 318
téléviseur à plasma 318
téléviseur grand écran 321
télévision 318
telson 71
témoin 472
témoin d'alimentation 329
témoin d'ouverture de porte 355
témoin de bas niveau de carburant 355
témoin de ceinture de sécurité 355
témoin de charge 355
témoin de clignotants 355, 368
témoin de niveau d'huile 355
témoin de phare 368
témoin de position neutre 368
témoin de pression d'huile 368
témoin des feux de route 355
témoin du retardateur 314
témoin lumineux 454
tempe 92
température Celsius, mesure 426
température de l'air 39
température du point de rosée 39
température thermodynamique, mesure 426
température, mesure 424
temple aztèque 283
temple de Huitzilopochtli 283
temple de Tlaloc 283
temple grec 279
temple grec, plan 279
temporal 98, 100
temps, mesure 424
tendance barométrique 39
tendeur 528
tendeur de timbre 308
tennis 242, 490
tennis de table 493
tenon 273
tenseur du fascia lata 96
tensiomètre 461
tentacule 72
tentacule oculaire 72
tentacule tactile 72
tente canadienne 529
tente deux places 528
tente dôme 529
tente familiale 528
tente grange 528
tente igloo 529
tente individuelle 529
tente intérieure 528, 529
tente rectangulaire 528
tente-caravane 361
tentes, exemples 528
tenue d'exercice 261, 262
tenue d'intervention 454
termes familiers 57, 58, 59
termes techniques 57, 58, 59
terminaison nerveuse 114
terminal à céréales 381
terminal à conteneurs 381, 430
terminal de paiement électronique 121, 443
terminal de vrac 381
terminal numérique 321
terminal pétrolier 381
termite 69
terrain 474, 479, 480, 482, 487, 488, 494
terrain de football américain 484
terrain de golf 430
terrasse 182, 230, 391
terrasse extérieure 387
terrassement 342
Terre 2, 3, 4, 5, 14
terre battue 492
Terre de Baffin 16
Terre de Feu 17
Terre de la Reine-Maud 15
Terre de Wilkes 15
Terre Marie-Byrd 15
Terre, structure 26
terre-plein 434
terre-plein central 343
terrine 174
tertre de départ 504
testicule 111
testicules 71
tête 6, 67, 72, 78, 87, 93, 95, 103, 111, 220, 221, 223, 229, 271, 272, 301, 302, 303, 492, 494, 503, 505, 536
tête à sens unique 221
tête basculante 176
tête bombée 221
tête creuse 221
tête cruciforme 221
tête d'attelage 361, 377
tête d'injection 403
tête de coupe 341
tête de dormant 186
tête de frappe 220
tête de gondole 121
tête de l'humérus 99
tête de lecture/écriture 333
tête de lit 204, 205
tête de mât 519
tête de rotor 395
tête de scion 536
tête du fémur 99
tête du vérin de levage 396
tête en liège 495
tête flottante 271
tête plate 221
tête ronde 221
tête, oiseau 78
tête, protection 458
têtes, exemples 221
Téthys 3
têtière 186
Thaïlande 453
thalle 50, 51
thé 148
thé en sachet 148
thé noir 148
thé oolong 148
thé vert 148
théâtre 433
théâtre grec 278
théière 166
thermocontact 358
thermomètre 404, 424
thermomètre à mercure 461
thermomètre à mesure instantanée 171
thermomètre à sucre 171
thermomètre à viande 171
thermomètre de four 171
thermomètre médical 424
thermomètre numérique 461
thermomètres médicaux 461
thermopause 37
thermosphère 37
thermostat 178, 211
thermostat réglable 179
thon 160
thorax 67, 68, 92, 94
thym 142
tibia 78, 98
tierce 298
tierceron 284
tige 51, 53, 54, 125, 181, 220, 221, 272, 424, 509, 511, 514
tige carrée d'entraînement 403
tige de carbone (cathode) 417
tige de forage 403
tige de selle 370
tige du poil 114
tige filetée 223
tigre 89
tilleul 148
timbale 308
timbales 295
timbre caoutchouc 338
timbre dateur 338
timon 361
timonerie 384
Timor oriental 452
tipi 288
tique 70
tirant 308, 397
tirant de réglage 244
tirant des cordes 498
tire-bouchon 531
tire-bouchon à levier 170
tire-bouchon de sommelier 170
tire-joint 216
tire-racine 232
tire-veille 519
tiroir 164, 202, 203, 205, 210
tisanes 148
tisonnier 193
tissu adipeux 113, 114
tissu conjonctif 114
Titan 3
Titania 3
titre 313
titre du journal 313
titres et horaires des films 294
Togo 451
toile 273
toile d'araignée 70
toile de fond 292
toilettes femmes 294
toilettes hommes 294
toit 183, 193, 283, 361
toit cathédrale 189
toit de protection 396
toit flottant 404
toit imperméable 402
toit ouvrant 349
tomate 128
tomate en grappe 128
tomatille 128
tombolo 35
tondeuse 269, 271
tondeuse à moteur 237
tong 242
Tonga 453
topinambour 124
toque 239
torchon 215
tore 429
tornade 43
tornade marine 43
torrent 29
torsade 228
tortellini 146
tortilla 145
tortue 76
tortue, morphologie 76
totalisateur journalier 355
toucan 80
touche 296, 301, 303, 304, 487
touche alternative 330
touche appareil photo 327
touche d'affichage 326
touche d'affichage des réglages 315
touche d'annulation 333
touche d'appel 327
touche d'arrêt 319
touche d'arrêt du défilement 331
touche d'échappement 330
touche d'effacement 331
touche d'effacement 315
touche d'éjection 471
touche d'enregistrement 319
touche d'enregistrement 320
touche d'impression de l'écran/d'appel système 331
touche d'index/agrandissement 315
touche d'insertion 331
touche de composition automatique 328
touche de confirmation 443
touche de contrôle 330
touche de correction 328
touche de courriel 330
touche de décimale 337
touche de démarrage 330
touche de fin d'appel/interrupteur 327
touche de lecture 319
touche de menu 320, 326, 327
touche de mise au point 320
touche de modulation 322
touche de navigation 327
touche de pause/d'interruption 331
touche de pédalier 305
touche de préréglage 326
touche de présélection 322
touche de prise de vues nocturne 320
touche de répétition 323
touche de résultat 337
touche de retour 331
touche de rétroéclairage 320
touche de saut d'images 315
touche de sélection 326
touche de sélection d'entrée 322
touche de sélection des menus 315
touche de sélection du magnétophone 322
touche de sélection du mode FM 322
touche de suppression 331
touche de tabulation 330
touche de verrouillage des majuscules 330
touche de verrouillage numérique 331
touche de visualisation des images 315
touche début 331
touche écran large/code de données 320
touche fin 331
touche fixe 425
touche lecture/pause 326
touche majuscule 330
touche mémoire 322, 326
touche menu 326
touche mobile 425
touche numérique 337
touche page précédente 331
touche page suivante 331
touche photo 320
touche précédent/retour rapide 326
touche programmable 327
touche suivant/avance rapide 326
toucher 114
touches d'action 471
touches d'opérations 442, 443
touches de catégories 326

touches de déplacement du curseur 331
touches de fonction 330
touches de fonctions 423
touches de fonctions programmables 443
touches de sélection des enceintes 322
touches de sélection des stations 322
touches directionnelles 471
touches Internet 330
touches numériques 323, 326
toundra 40, 44
toupet 83
toupie 177
Tour 470
tour 284, 397, 412, 413
tour à bureaux 435
tour d'angle 282
tour d'émission 316
tour d'habitation 289
tour de contrôle 388
tour de coquille 72
tour de cou 245
tour de flanquement 282
tour de forage 382, 403, 404
tour de fractionnement 405
tour de guidage 345
tour de refroidissement 402
tour de spire 73
tour de tête 458
tour du plongeoir 518
tour embryonnaire 73
tourelle 214, 282, 400, 455
tourelle porte-objectif 421
tourillon 503
tournesol 56
tournevis 221, 531
tournevis à spirale 221
tournevis cruciforme 531
tournevis sans fil 221
tourniquet d'accès 378
tourniquet de sortie 378
trachée 105
traçoir 228
tracteur 399
tracteur à chenilles 398
tracteur routier 364
tracteur-remorqueur 400
tractus olfactif 117
tragus 115
train 374
train à grande vitesse 376
train d'atterrissage avant 392
train d'atterrissage principal 393
train de banlieue 375
traineau 236
trainée lumineuse 5
trait de mise au jeu 484
traitement chimique 405
traitement des données 38
tranchant 167, 169, 270
tranche 441
transactions financières 335
transbordeur 381, 386, 391
transept 285
transfert de la chaleur 415
transformateur 207, 407
transformateur principal 376
transformation de l'eau en vapeur 408
transmission 212
transmission de la chaleur à l'eau 408
transmission hertzienne 316
transmission par câble aérien 316
transmission par câble sous-marin 317
transmission par câble souterrain 317
transpalette manuelle 396
transpiration 45
transplantoir 232
transport 342
transport aérien 388
transport de l'électricité 408
transport de l'électricité à haute tension 402, 413
transport ferroviaire 374
transport maritime 381
transport routier 342, 381
transport vers les usagers 402, 413
trapèze 96, 97, 429
trappe 281, 292
travée centrale 344
travée latérale 344
travée levante 345
travers 153
traverse 202, 297, 466
traverse de chargement 385
traverse inférieure 185, 202
traverse intermédiaire 185
traverse médiane 201
traverse supérieure 185, 201, 202
traverse supérieure d'ouvrant 186
traversée de transformateur 406, 407
traversin 204
trèfle 285, 468
treillis 230, 324
trémie de chargement 364
tremplin 184, 496
tremplin de 1 m 518
tremplin de 3 m 518
trench 248
trépan 403
trépied 8, 308
trépointe 240
tréteau 202
treuil 287, 364
treuil d'amarrage 385
treuil de forage 403
treuil de levage 397
tri des métaux 49
tri du papier/carton 49
tri du plastique 49
tri du verre 49
tri manuel 49
tri optique 49
tri sélectif des déchets 49
triangle 295, 309, 429, 503
tribord 387
tribunal 440
tribune 313
triceps brachial 97
triclinium 280
tricots 250
tricycle d'enfant 373
trifoliée 55
trille 299
trimaran 521
tringle de pédale 304
tringle de tension 308
Trinité-et-Tobago 449
trio 300
tripes 154
triple croche 299
triple saut 472
triticale 143
Triton 3
triton 75
trois-portes 347
troisième but 474
troisième ligne 482
troisième-but 474
trombe marine 43
trombone 307
trombones 295, 341
trompe 67
trompe d'Eustache 116, 117
trompe de Fallope 112
trompe utérine, ampoule 113
trompes de Fallope 113
trompette 307
trompettes 295
tronc 52, 62, 63, 75, 93, 95
tronc cœliaque 103, 107
tronc, coupe transversale 63
tronçon rigide arrière 363
tronçon rigide avant 363
tronçonneuse 235
trop-plein 194, 195, 196
tropical humide 40
tropical humide et sec (savane) 40
tropique du Cancer 20, 21, 22
tropique du Capricorne 20, 21, 22
tropopause 37, 46
troposphère 37
trot 83
trotteur 241
trotteuse 424
trottoir 183, 434
trou 504
trou d'homme 404
trou de normale 5 504
trousse de dépannage 372
trousse de fartage 514
trousse de manucure 265
trousse de secours 457, 461
trousse de toilette 276
truelle de maçon 216
truelle de plâtrier 216
truffe 87, 123
truite 161
trumeau 285
tuba 295, 307
tube 8, 9, 163, 199, 269, 420, 461
tube à éclairs 420
tube capillaire 424
tube d'alimentation 197
tube d'alimentation en air 454
tube de circulation 410
tube de direction 371
tube de force 409
tube de Pitot 525
tube de poussée 312
tube de remplissage de la cuvette 196
tube de remplissage du réservoir 196
tube de résonance 309
tube de selle 370
tube droit 209
tube en Y 460
tube flexible 460
tube fluorescent 199
tube horizontal 370
tube oblique 371
tube porte-oculaire 8, 421
tube-image 318
tubulure d'admission 360
tuile 12, 279, 280, 283
tulipe 56, 181
tunique 54, 255
Tunisie 451
tunnel 378
tunnel de communication 13
tunnel routier 345
turban 239
turbine 402
turboréacteur 393
turbot 161
turion 125
Turkménistan 452
Turquie 452
tuteur 230, 231
Tuvalu 453
tuyau 224, 454
tuyau à anche 305
tuyau à bouche 305
tuyau arrière 351
tuyau d'arrosage 236
tuyau d'aspiration 455
tuyau d'échappement 350, 351, 398
tuyau d'évacuation 194, 197, 212
tuyau d'insufflation 296
tuyau de chute 194, 196
tuyau de refoulement 454
tuyau de vidange 212, 214
tuyau flexible 209
tuyau perforé 236
tuyère 12, 383, 395
tuyère à section variable 394
tympan 75, 279, 285
type de carburant 346
type de la masse d'air 39
type de nuage bas 39
type de nuage élevé 39
type de nuage moyen 39
types d'éclipses 4, 5
types de bâtons de golf 505
types de déplacements 470
types de nages 517
types de prises 493
types de voitures 376
typhon 43

U

Ukraine 450
Umbriel 3
un 427
une 313
unicellulaires 66
uniforme 456
unisson 298
unité astronomique 2, 3
unité d'extraction par solvant 405
unité de soins ambulatoires 465
unité de soins intensifs 464
unité mobile d'entretien télécommandée 11
unités monétaires, exemples 440
université 432
Uranus 2, 3
uretère 107
urètre 107, 112
urètre pénien 111
urgence ambulatoire 463
urgence majeure 462
urgences 462
uropode 71
Uruguay 448
usager domestique 335
usine 430
usine à asphalte 405
usine des lubrifiants 405
usine pétrochimique 405
ustensiles de campeur 531
ustensiles de cuisine 169
ustensiles divers 173
ustensiles, jeu 173
utérus 112, 113
utilisations d'Internet 335

V

vache 84
vacuole 50, 66
vacuole contractile 66
vacuole digestive 66
vacuole digestive en formation 66
vagin 112, 113
vague 33
vague déferlante 33
vaisseau capillaire 114
vaisseau sanguin 104, 114
vaisselle 166
Valet 468
valet 421
valeur 441
valeur des notes 299
valeur des segments 471
valeur des silences 299
valise fin de semaine 277
valise pullman 277
vallée 29, 32
valve 60, 73, 371
valvule aortique 104
valvule mitrale 104
valvule pulmonaire 104
valvule tricuspide 104
vanne 406, 407
vantail 202, 286
Vanuatu 453
vapeur 402, 415
vaporisateur 208, 236
vaporisateur de poivre 456
vaporisation 414
varan 77
Varole, pont 109
vaste externe du membre inférieur 96, 97
vaste interne du membre inférieur 96
vautour 80
veau 84
veau haché 152
végétation 44
végétation, distribution 44
véhicule de sauvetage 11
véhicule de secours 345
véhicule spatial autonome 10
véhicule tout-terrain 347
veine axillaire 102
veine basilique 102
veine cave inférieure 102, 103, 104, 107
veine cave supérieure 102, 103, 104
veine céphalique 102
veine fémorale 102
veine iliaque 103
veine iliaque commune 107
veine jugulaire externe 102
veine jugulaire interne 102
veine mésentérique supérieure 102
veine porte 103
veine pulmonaire 102
veine pulmonaire droite 104
veine pulmonaire gauche 104
veine rénale 102, 107
veine saphène interne 102
veine sous-clavière 102
veine sus-hépatique 103
veines 102
velarium 281
vélo cross 373
vélo d'exercice 501
vélo de course et cycliste 522
vélo de cross-country et cycliste 522
vélo de descente et cycliste 522
vélo de montagne 522
velours 190
Venezuela 448
vent 47, 48
vent dominant 43
ventilateur 213, 322, 350, 358, 360
ventilateur de sustentation 383
ventilateur du bloc d'alimentation 32
ventilateur du boîtier 329
ventouse 72, 75, 216
ventre 83, 92, 94
ventricule droit 103, 104
ventricule gauche 103, 104
Vénus 2, 3
véraison 62
verge 111
verger 122
verglas 41
vérificateur de circuit 217
vérificateur de prise de courant 217
vérificateur de tension 217
vérification de la profondeur de cham 314
vérin 364
vérin d'orientation de la lame 401
vérin de défonceuse 398
vérin de direction 400
vérin de dressage 397, 455
vérin de la flèche 399, 400
vérin de levage de la lame 398, 401
vérin du bras 399, 400
vérin du bras de levage 399
vérin du godet 399, 400
vérin du godet rétro 399
vérin hydraulique 361
vermicelles de riz 147
vernier 422, 425
vernis à ongles 265
verre 273
verre à bordeaux 165
verre à bourgogne 165
verre à cocktail 165
verre à cognac 165
verre à eau 165
verre à gin 165
verre à liqueur 165
verre à mesurer 171
verre à porto 165
verre à vin blanc 165
verre à vin d'Alsace 165
verre à whisky 165
verres 165
verrière 188, 374, 394, 435
verrou 30, 332
verrou d'onglet 226
verrouillage 208
verrouillage des majuscules 330
verrouillage numérique 331
versant 29
verseuse 181
vert 418, 504

vert d'entraînement 504
vertèbre cervicale (7) 99
vertèbre dorsale (12) 99
vertèbre lombaire 110
vertèbre lombaire (5) 99
verveine 148
vésicule biliaire 106
vésicule séminale 111
vessie 107, 111, 112
veste 251, 499
veste de pêche 538
veste droite 244
vestes 254
vestiaire 188, 443, 444
vestiaire des clients 438
vestiaire du personnel 438, 465
vestibule 116, 188, 280, 439, 440, 442
veston croisé 244
veston et veste 244
vêtements 238
vêtements d'enfant 261
vêtements d'exercice 263
vêtements d'homme 244
vêtements de femme 251
vêtements de nouveau-né 260
vêtements de nuit 256
vêtements, pêche 538
viande 152
vibrisse 82
ice-capitaine 515
ide-poches 352
ide-pomme 173
iet Nam 453
igie 388
igne 62
ilebrequin 360
illage 430, 512
ille 430
n 120
naigre balsamique 141
naigre de cidre 141
naigre de malt 141
naigre de riz 141
naigre de vin 141
olette 56
olon 301
violon, famille 295, 301
violoncelle 301
violoncelles 295
vipère 77
virole 219, 503
virole femelle 536, 537
virole mâle 536, 537
vis 221, 301
vis calante 423
vis de blocage 425
vis de blocage (azimut) 8, 9
vis de blocage (latitude) 8, 9
vis de réglage 222
vis de réglage de tension 341
vis de réglage du condenseur 421
vis de serrage 224
vis de tension 308
vis macrométrique 421
vis micrométrique 421, 425
vis sans fin 365
visage 92
viseur 315
viseur électronique 320
visière 238, 239, 367, 458, 506, 525
visière antisolaire 10
vision 419
vision normale 419
vision, défauts 419
vison 88
Vistule 18
vitrage 410
vitrail 285, 446
vitre 411
vitre de protection 506
vitre protectrice 318
vitrine 203
voie 378
voie d'accélération 343
voie de banlieue 375
voie de circulation 343, 388
voie de décélération 343
voie de dépassement 343
voie de service 375, 388
voie des stands 524
voie ferrée 374, 431, 432
voie ferrée bord à quai 381
Voie lactée 6
voie latérale 343
voie pour véhicules lents 343
voies de circulation 343
voies respiratoires, protection 459
voile 412, 519, 520, 536
voile du palais 116, 117
voilure delta 394
voiture 380
voiture classique 376
voiture de formule 1 525
voiture de formule 3000 524
voiture de formule Indy 524
voiture de police 457
voiture de rallye 524
voiture micro-compacte 347
voiture restaurant 376
voiture sport 347
voiture suiveuse 522
voiture-lit 376
voitures, types 376
voiturette de golf électrique 505
volaille 155
volant 204, 350, 354, 360, 385, 525
volant d'inertie 501
volant de manœuvre 455
volant de plumes 495
volant synthétique 495
volcan 26, 28
volcan effusif 28
volcan en éruption 28
volcan explosif 28
volcans, exemples 28
volée 191, 490
volet 13, 333
volet d'air 365
volet de bord de fuite 392
volet mobile 7
volet transparent 274
Volga 18
volleyball 487
vols, plongeon 518
volt 426
voltigeur de centre 474
voltigeur droit 474
voltigeur gauche 474
volume 328
volumes 429
volute 200, 301
volve 52
voussure 285
voûte 284
voûte du palais 116, 117
voûte en berceau 281
voyant cartouche d'impression 333
voyant chargement du papier 333
voyant d'alarme/de mise en charge 337
voyant d'alimentation 333
voyant de charge 271
voyant de mise en circuit 327
voyant de mise sous tension/détection du papier 443
voyant lumineux 178, 179, 180, 181, 208, 210, 214, 269
voyants 331
voyants d'entrée 322
voyants d'indication du mode sonore 322
vraquier 382
vrille 62
vue 119
vue antérieure 98
vue d'ensemble 186
vue de face 478
vue de profil 478
vue postérieure 99, 113
vulve 94, 113

W

w.-c. 188, 189, 194, 195, 196, 437, 438, 439, 440, 443, 445, 463, 464, 465
w.-c. femmes 439
w.-c. hommes 439
wagon 375
wagon à bestiaux 377
wagon de queue 377
wagon intermodal 377
wagon plat 377
wagon porte-automobiles 377
wagon porte-conteneurs 377
wagon réfrigérant 377
wagon-citerne 377
wagons, exemples 377
wakamé 123
wasabi 141
watt 426
webcaméra 332
wigwam 288
winch 521
wishbone 519
wok 174

X

xylophone 295, 309

Y

yacht à moteur 385
yack 85
yaourt 150
Yémen 452
yen 440
yeux, protection 458
yourte 288

Z

Zambie 452
zèbre 84
zeste 58, 60
Zimbabwe 452
zone commerciale 431
zone d'attaque 487
zone de basse pression 43
zone de but 484, 507
zone de chute 472
zone de convection 4
zone de danger 499
zone de défense 487
zone de garde protégée 515
zone de haute pression 43
zone de passage du témoin 472
zone de précipitation 39
zone de radiation 4
zone de retrait des bagages 390
zone industrielle 431
zone libre 487
zone neutre 484, 507
zone réservée 489
zone résidentielle 431
zones de service 495